Rick Steves

BEST OF

EUROPE

Contents

Introduction

Big Ben, the Eiffel Tower, and the Roman Colosseum. Yodeling in the Alps, biking down cobblestone paths, and taking a canal ride under the stars. Michelangelo's *David* and "Mad" King Ludwig's castles. Sunny Riviera beaches, medieval German towns, and Spanish streets teeming with people after dark. Europe offers a rich smorgasbord of cultures: pasta and tapas, strudel and scones, Dutch pancakes and Swiss fondue, Parisian crêpes and Tuscan grapes... Follow your tastes and sample a little of everything for an unforgettable trip.

To wrestle Europe down to a manageable size, this selective book features its top destinations—from powerhouse cities to sleepy towns and cliff-hanging villages.

To help you assemble your dream trip, I've included advice on what to see and do in each destination, plus how to connect destinations by car or train. Whether you have a week or a month for your trip, this book will show you the best that Europe has to offer.

England

London, a thriving metropolis, teems with world-class museums, monuments, churches, parks, palaces, markets, theaters, pubs, and double-decker buses.

Spain

Barcelona is the center of Catalan culture, with the Ramblas people zone, Gothic old town, sandy beaches, and works by native sons Gaudí, Picasso, and Miró.

Madrid is urban Spain at its best, boasting top-notch art treasures (Prado Museum, Picasso's *Guernica*) and an unsurpassed tapas scene.

France

Paris, the stylish world capital of food and culture, features the Eiffel Tower, grand boulevards, cutting-edge architecture, corner cafés, chic boutiques, and incomparable art at the Louvre and Orsay.

Provence is home to Arles (with Van Gogh sights and a Roman Arena), Avignon (with the famous bridge and brooding Palace of the Popes), the ancient Roman aqueduct of Pont du Gard, and the beautiful Côtes du Rhone wine road.

The French Riviera, a tempting stretch of sun-washed resorts, stars the elegant city of Nice, with its relaxed vibe, delicious seafood, and inviting beaches.

Italy

Rome is truly the Eternal City, studded with Roman remnants (Forum, Colosseum, Pantheon), floodlit-fountain squares, and the Vatican's Sistine Chapel.

Florence, the cradle of the Renaissance, offers the masterpiece-strewn Uffizi Gallery, Brunelleschi's dome-topped Duomo, Michelangelo's *David*, and Italy's best gelato.

The Cinque Terre consists of five idyllic Riviera hamlets along a rugged coastline, connected by hiking trails and dotted with vineyards and beaches.

Venice is a romantic island city, powerful in medieval times and famous for St. Mark's Basilica, the Grand Canal, and singing gondoliers.

Germany

Munich is a bustling city with a traffic-free center, excellent museums, Baroque palaces, stately churches, rowdy beer halls, and the beautiful English Garden.

Rothenburg, a medieval, half-timbered town encircled by a walkable wall, is the highlight of the Romantic Road route, linking time-passed towns in the lovely countryside.

The Rhine Valley stars a mighty river steeped in legend, lined with storybook villages and imposing castles.

Berlin has thought-provoking museums, gleaming architecture, and trendy night-life, plus evocative sections of the Wall that once divided the city and country.

Switzerland

The **Swiss Alps'** best chunk is the **Berner Oberland,** featuring sky-high mountains, cliff-hanging villages, thundering waterfalls, scenic hikes, soaring lifts, and cogwheel train rides.

The Netherlands

Amsterdam is a progressive world capital with magnificent museums, dreamy canals, Golden-Age architecture, and the eye-opening Red Light District. Nearby Haarlem is a cozy, small-town home base alternative to big-city Amsterdam.

TRAVEL SMART

Approach Europe like a veteran traveler, even if it's your first trip. Design your itinerary thoughtfully, get an idea of your trip costs, and follow the travel strategies to help you be the best possible tour guide for yourself and your companions.

Designing an Itinerary

Choose your top destinations. The cosmopolitan cities of London and Paris are a must for anyone. Historians revel in Rome and romantics linger in Venice. If castles spark your imagination, explore along the Rhine. Artists are drawn to Florence and foodies love France. Munich wins the award for the best oompah bands in beer halls. For a mix of art, tapas, and irrepressible nightlife, experience Barcelona and Madrid. Hikers make tracks to the Swiss Alps and the Cinque Terre. To feel the pulse of 21st-century Germany, head to Berlin. Amsterdam, featuring Rembrandt, Anne Frank, Van Gogh, and marijuana cafés, has something of interest for everyone. If medieval towns are your passion, walk the walls around Rothenburg. Beach baskers unroll their towels in the Cinque Terre, Barcelona, and the French Riviera. Photographers want to go everywhere.

Decide when to go. Peak season in much of Europe is June through September. For Spain and Italy, the best travel months are May, June, September, and October, which combine the convenience of peak season with pleasant weather (July and August can be sweltering along

the Mediterranean). During peak season, it's best to reserve rooms well in advance, particularly in big cities. Throughout Europe, spring and fall generally have decent weather and lighter crowds. Winter can be cold and dreary, though big cities stay lively year-round.

As a general rule any time of year, the climate north of the Alps is mild (like Seattle), while south of the Alps it's like Arizona. If you wilt in the hot sun, avoid the Mediterranean in summer. If you want blue skies in the Alps and Britain, travel during the height of summer. (For climate specifics, see Wunderground.com.)

Draft an itinerary. Figure out how

∩ *Rick Steves Audio Europe*

My free **Rick Steves Audio Europe app** makes it easy for you to download my **audio tours** of many of Europe's

top attractions. For this book, my audio tours cover major sights in London, Paris, Berlin, Munich, the Rhine, Rothenburg, Rome, Venice, Florence, and Amsterdam. Sights covered by my audio tours are marked with this symbol: ∩. The app also offers a far-reaching library of insightful **travel interviews** from my public radio show with experts from around the globe—including many of the places in this book.

The Rick Steves Audio Europe app and all of its content are free. You can download it via Apple's App Store, Google Play, or the Amazon Appstore. For more info, see Ricksteves.com/audioeurope.

many destinations you can comfortably fit in the time you have. Don't overdo it— few travelers wish they'd hurried more. Allow sufficient time per place. As a rough guideline, figure about three days for most major destinations and two days for smaller ones (take more time if you want to relax or explore). Any four or five of my recommended destinations (for example, London, Paris, the Rhine Valley, Swiss Alps, and Venice) would make a wonderful two-week trip. To moderate culture shock, start in London.

Connect the dots. Link your destinations into a logical route. Determine which cities in Europe you'll fly into and out of. Even if you're flying into a cheap flight hub like Frankfurt, you don't need to begin your trip there (most major airports have their own train station). For a gentler start to your trip, you could take a train to a nearby, smaller town for your first stop (such as a Rhine village).

Decide if you'll be traveling by car, public transportation, or a combination. Trains connect big cities easily and frequently. Budget flights link many destinations. If your dream trip features Madrid, Amsterdam, Rome, and Berlin, take planes instead of trains. Regardless of how you travel, allow at least a half-day to get between destinations.

Regions that are fun to explore by car (such as Provence) have options for non-drivers, such as bus tours, public transit, or taxis. A car is useless in cities (park it).

Balance intense and relaxed days. After a day of hectic sightseeing, plan for some downtime. Follow up the bigger cities with laid-back towns. Minimize one-night stands to maximize rooted-ness; it's worth taking a drive (or train ride) after dinner to get settled in a town for two nights. Staying in a home base (such as Arles, Munich, or Florence) and making day trips can be more time-efficient than changing locations and hotels.

Fine-tune your itinerary. If you have any must-see sights, make sure they'll be open when you visit. Check if any holidays or festivals will fall during your trip—these attract crowds and can close sights. For the latest, visit each country's national tourism website: VisitBritain.com, FranceGuide.com, Germany.travel.com, Italia.it, Holland.com, Spain.info.com, MySwitzerland.com.

For detailed suggestions on how to

Average Daily Expenses Per Person: $160

Cost	Category	Notes
$50	Meals	$15 for lunch, $5 for snacks, $30 for dinner with drinks
$75	Lodging	Based on two people splitting the cost of a $150 double room that includes breakfast (solo travelers pay about $100 per room)
$30	Sights and Entertainment	Figure $10-20 per major sight, $5-7 for minor ones, and $25-50 for splurges (tours, shows, cruises). Allow an average of $30 per day.
$5	City Transit	Buses or Metro
$160	Total	Allow about $200 for London, Paris, and the Swiss Alps.

spend your time, I've included day plans for destinations in the chapters that follow.

Give yourself some slack. Every trip— and every traveler—needs slack time (picnics, people-watching, and so on). Many travelers greatly underestimate this. You can't see it all, so pace yourself. Assume you will return.

Ready, set... You've designed the perfect itinerary for the trip of a lifetime.

Trip Costs per Person

Run a reality check on your dream trip. You'll have major transportation costs in addition to daily expenses.

Airfare: A basic round-trip flight from the US to Europe can cost about $1,000 to $2,000 total, depending on where you fly from and when (cheaper in winter). Save time in Europe by flying into one city and out of another (e.g., into London and out of Rome). Begin your search for transatlantic flights at Kayak.com.

Car Rental: Figure on paying about $250 per week, not including tolls, gas, parking, and insurance. Weekly rentals are cheapest if arranged from the US. Note that some cities—especially in Italy— restrict or prohibit driving in the center.

Italy and Spain require drivers to carry an International Driving Permit (sold for $20 at your local AAA office; AAA.com).

Public Transportation: Depending on your itinerary, it can be worthwhile to buy a rail pass to save money. For a Europe-wide trip, a Eurail pass is generally a good choice. Rail passes normally must be purchased outside of Europe; exceptions are German and Swiss passes, which can be purchased on site.

Keep in mind that many fast trains (such as the Eurostar linking London and Paris, France's TGV, Spain's AVE, and more) require seat assignments, and advance booking is strongly recommended.

To cover long distances, consider flying, because budget airlines can be cheaper

Before You Go

❏ **Make sure your passport is valid**. If it's due to expire within six months of your ticketed date of return, renew it. Allow up to six weeks to get or renew a passport (www.travel.state.gov).

❏ **Book rooms well in advance,** especially if your trip falls during peak season or any major holidays or festivals. For tips on making hotel reservations, see page 1063.

❏ **Make reservations** for major sights to avoid wasting time in lines. For example, you can reserve in advance for the Eiffel Tower in Paris, Florence's Uffizi Gallery, Barcelona's Sagrada Família, Amsterdam's Anne Frank House, and more (specifics are included in this book) . Some sights require advance reservations, such as the Borghese Gallery in Rome.

❏ **Arrange your transportation.** Rent a car, or get a rail pass, or order train tickets for longer trips to get advance-purchase discounts when possible. (Or you can wing it in Europe, but it may cost more.)

❏ **Consider travel insurance.** Compare the cost of the insurance to the cost of your potential loss. Check whether your existing insurance (health, homeowners, or renters) covers you and your possessions overseas. For tips, see Ricksteves.com/insurance.

❏ **Call your bank.** Alert your bank that you'll be using your debit and credit cards in Europe; also ask about transaction fees, and get the PIN number for your credit card (see page 1060). You won't need to bring along any European currency for your trip—instead, withdraw currency from cash machines in Europe. You'll get pounds in England, Swiss francs in Switzerland, and euros everywhere else.

❏ **Bringing your phone?** Consider an international plan to reduce the cost of calls, texts, and data (or rely on Wi-Fi). See page 1064 for different ways to stay connected in Europe.

❏ **Download apps** to your mobile device to use on the road, such as maps, transit schedules, and my free *Rick Steves Audio Europe* app (which has audio tours of many of Europe's major sights and interesting neighborhoods).

❏ **Watt's up?** Bring an electrical adapter (sold at travel stores in the US) to plug into Europe's outlets. For the Continent, a two-prong adapter will do; for England, it's three prongs. A universal adapter covers it all. You won't need a convertor because newer electronics—such as tablets, laptops, and battery chargers—are dual voltage and convert automatically to Europe's 220-volt system. Don't bring an old hair dryer or curler; buy a cheapie in Europe.

❏ **Pack light.** You'll walk with your luggage far more than you think (see packing list on page 1073).

❏ **Refer to the Practicalities chapter,** where you'll find everything you need to know to travel smoothly in Europe.

❏ **Get updates** to this book at Ricksteves.com/update.

than taking the train; check Skyscanner. com for intra-European flights.

If you have more time than money, look into long-distance buses, which connect countries cheaper and slower than trains; Eurolines is one of several international companies.

For more on rail travel, buses, and flights, see page 1067.

Budget Tips: It's easy to cut your daily costs to $100 per day, particularly outside of the big cities. Cultivate the art of picnicking, stay in hostels or basic hotels, and see only the sights you most want to see. Seek out free sights (people-watching counts). When you splurge, save it for an experience you'll always remember (such as a concert, gondola ride, or alpine lift). Minimize souvenir shopping—how will you get it all home? Focus instead on collecting lifelong memories.

Travel Strategies on the Road

Be your own tour guide. As you travel, get up-to-date info on sights, reserve tickets and tours, reconfirm hotels and travel arrangements, and check transit connections. Upon arrival in a new town, lay the groundwork for a smooth departure; confirm the train, bus, or road you'll take when you leave. You can find out the latest by checking with tourist-information offices (TIs) and your hoteliers, and doing research on your own by phone or online.

Splurge for knowledge. Your appreciation of a city or region and its history can increase dramatically if you join a walking tour in any big city or even hire a private guide. If you want to learn more about any aspect of Europe, you're in the right place with experts happy to teach you.

Take advantage of deals and discounts. You'll find deals throughout Europe (and mentioned in this book). City transit passes (for multiple rides or all-day use) lessen your cost per ride. To take the financial bite out of sightseeing, consider combo-tickets and sightseeing passes (such as the Paris Museum Pass) that cover multiple museums.

This book lists only the full adult price for sights. However, many sights offer discounts for youths (up to age 18), students (with proper identification cards, www. isic.org), families, and seniors (roughly age 65 and over, though this varies). Always ask—though some discounts are only available for citizens of the European Union.

Outsmart thieves. It's always smart to wear a money belt. Tuck it under your clothes, and keep your cash, credit cards, and passport secure inside it. Carry only a day's spending money in your front pocket. In case of loss or theft, see page 1058.

Be proactive to minimize the effects of potential loss: Keep your expensive gear to a minimum. Bring photocopies of important documents (passport and cards) to aid in replacement if they're lost or stolen. While traveling, back up your digital photos and files frequently.

Guard your time, energy, and trip. Taking a taxi can be a good value if it saves you a long wait for a cheap bus or an exhausting walk across town. To avoid long lines, take advantage of the crowd-beating tips in this book, such as visiting sights early or late, or reserving tickets in advance when possible. When problems arise (e.g., miscommunication, a confusing restaurant bill, or a noisy hotel room), keep things in perspective. You're on vacation...and you're in Europe!

Connect with the culture. Enjoy the friendliness of the European people. Ask questions—many locals are as interested in you as you are in them. Slow down, step out of your comfort zone, and be open to unexpected experiences. When an interesting opportunity pops up, say "Yes!"

Happy travels!

Rick Steves

Key to This Book

Updates

This book is updated regularly—but things change. For the latest, visit www. ricksteves.com/update.

Abbreviations and Times

I use the following symbols and abbreviations in this book:

Sights are rated:

▲▲▲ Don't miss

▲▲ Try hard to see

▲ Worthwhile if you can make it

No rating Worth knowing about

Tourist information offices are abbreviated as **TI,** and bathrooms are **WC**s. To categorize accommodations, I use a **Sleep Code** (described on page 1062).

Like Europe, this book uses the **24-hour clock.** It's the same through 12:00 noon, and then keeps going: 13:00, 14:00, and so on. For anything over 12, subtract 12 and add p.m. (14:00 is 2:00 p.m.).

When giving **opening times,** I include both peak season and off-season hours if they differ. So, if a museum is listed as "May-Oct daily 9:00-16:00," it should be open from 9 a.m. until 4 p.m. from the first day of May until the last day of October (but expect exceptions).

For **transit** or **tour departures,** I first list the frequency, then the duration. So, a train connection listed as "2/hour, 1.5 hours" departs twice each hour, and the journey lasts an hour and a half.

Map Legend

⅃ Viewpoint	ⓣ Taxi Stand	Tunnel	
↟ Entrance	🅣 Tram Stop	Pedestrian Zone	
⊖ Tourist Info	Ⓜ Metro Stop	------ Railway	
🆆🅲 Restroom	⊖ Tube	············· Ferry/Boat Route	
⬛ Castle	🆄 U-Bahn	⊢——⊣ Tram	
▪ Statue/Point of Interest	Ⓢ S-Bahn	Stairs	
⬚ Church	🆅 Vaporetto Stop	· · · · · Walk/Tour Route	
☪ Mosque	🅣 Traghetto Crossing	------ Trail	
✡ Synagogue	🅖 Gondola Station	O⊞⊞⊞O Funicular	
◎ Fountain	🅐 Alilaguna Stop	•—•—• Mtn. Lift	
▲ Mountain Peak	Ⓑ Bus Stop	•⊞⊞⊞• Mtn. Rail	
▧ Park	🅿 Parking	⎏ Cable Car	
⌒ Mtn. Pass	Ⓢ S-Tog Station		
✈ Airport	🅗 Harbor Bus	⚘ Gondola	
	⛵ Boat Stop		
	🚲 Bike Rental		

England

Hilly England occupies the lower two-thirds of the island of Great Britain (with Scotland in the north). England is the size of Louisiana (about 50,000 square miles), with a population of just over 56 million. England's ethnic diversity sets it apart from the rest of the United Kingdom: Nearly one in three citizens is not associated with the Christian faith. The cradle of the Industrial Revolution, today's Britain has little heavy industry—its economic drivers are banking, insurance, and business services, plus energy production and agriculture.

London is England's—and Great Britain's—cosmopolitan capital. For the tourist, London offers a little of everything associated with Britain: castles, cathedrals, royalty, theater, and tea.

CUISINE SCENE AT A GLANCE

British cooking embraces international influences and good-quality ingredients. It's easy to eat well here. Even in London, plenty of inexpensive choices are available.

Pub grub is the most atmospheric budget option. You'll usually get reasonably priced, hearty lunches and dinners under ancient timbers. Meals are usually served 12:00-14:00 and 18:00-20:00—with a break in the middle. There's generally no table service. Order at the bar, then take a seat. Either they'll bring the food when it's ready, or you'll pick it up at the bar. Pay at the bar (sometimes when you order, sometimes after you eat). Don't tip unless it's a place with full table service. If you're on a tight budget, it's OK to share a meal.

Classier restaurants have some affordable deals. Lunch is usually cheaper than dinner; a top-end, £25-for-dinner restaurant often serves the same quality two courses as lunch deals for about half the price. Many restaurants have early-bird or pre-theater specials of two or three courses, often for significant savings, if you eat before 18:30 or 19:00; these deals may be offered daily or only on weekdays.

Ethnic restaurants add spice to England's cuisine. At Indian restaurants, an easy way to taste a variety of dishes is to order a *thali*—a sampler plate, generally served on a metal tray, with small servings of various specialties. Many Chinese and Thai places serve £6 meals and offer even cheaper takeaway boxes. Middle Eastern stands sell gyro sandwiches, falafel, and *shwarmas* (grilled meat in pita bread).

Chain restaurants abound, serving a variety of good-value meals, from sandwiches and salads (Pret à Manger, Le Pain Quotidien) and burgers (Byron) to sushi (Yo!, Wasabi, and Itsu), Indian (Masala Zone), Thai (Thai Square, Busaba Eathai), and more (Wagamama, Côte Brasserie, Ask, Pizza Express, Eat, and Loch Fyne Fish).

At **tearooms,** popular choices are a "cream tea," which consists of tea and a scone or two, or the pricier "afternoon tea," which comes with pastries and finger foods such as small, crust-less sandwiches. Two people can order one afternoon tea and one cream tea and share the afternoon tea's goodies.

Tipping: At pubs and places where you order at the counter, you don't have to tip. At restaurants and fancy pubs with waitstaff, tip about 10-12.5 percent. Most restaurants in London now add a 12.5 percent "optional" tip onto the bill. Tip only what you think the service warrants (if it isn't already added to your bill), and be careful not to tip double.

Other Budget Options: Fish-and-chips are a British classic; a takeaway box of fish-and-chips costs about £4-7. Grocery stores have inviting delis with good takeout food and sometimes sit-down eating. Good bets are the Marks & Spencer department stores, M&S Simply Food, and Sainsbury's Local.

London

A longtime tourist destination, London seems perpetually at your service, with an impressive slate of sights and entertainment. Blow through this urban jungle on the open deck of a double-decker bus and take a pinch-me-I'm-here walk through the West End. Hear the chimes of Big Ben and ogle the crown jewels at the Tower of London. Cruise the Thames River and take a spin on the London Eye. Hobnob with poets' tombstones in Westminster Abbey and rummage through civilization's attic at the British Museum.

London is also more than its museums and landmarks, it's a living, breathing, thriving organism...a coral reef of humanity. The city has changed dramatically in recent years: Many visitors are surprised to find how diverse and cosmopolitan it is. Chinese takeouts outnumber fish-and-chips shops. Eastern Europeans pull pints in British pubs, and Italians express your espresso. Outlying suburbs are home to huge communities of Indians and Pakistanis. This city of eight million separate dreams is learning—sometimes fitfully—to live as a microcosm of its formerly vast empire.

LONDON IN 4 DAYS

Day 1: Get oriented by taking my Westminster Walk from Big Ben to Trafalgar Square (stop in Westminster Abbey and the Churchill War Rooms on the way). Grab lunch near Trafalgar Square (maybe at the café at St. Martin-in-the-Fields Church), then visit the nearby National Gallery or National Portrait Gallery.

On any evening: Have an early-bird dinner and take in a play in the West End or at Shakespeare's Globe. Choose from a concert, walking tour, or nighttime bus tour. Extend your sightseeing into the evening hours; some attractions stay open late (see page 31). Settle in at a pub, or do some shopping at any of London's elegant department stores (generally open until 21:00). Stroll any of the main squares, fine parks, or the Jubilee Walkway for people-watching. Ride the London Eye Ferris wheel for grand city views.

Day 2: Take a double-decker hop-on, hop-off sightseeing bus tour from Victoria Station, and hop off for the Changing of the Guard at Buckingham Palace. After lunch, tour the British Museum and/or the nearby British Library.

Day 3: At the Tower of London, see the crown jewels and take the Beefeater tour. Then grab a picnic, catch a boat at Tower Pier, and have lunch on the Thames while cruising to Blackfriars Pier.

Tour St. Paul's Cathedral and climb its dome for views, then walk across Millen-

London's Neighborhoods

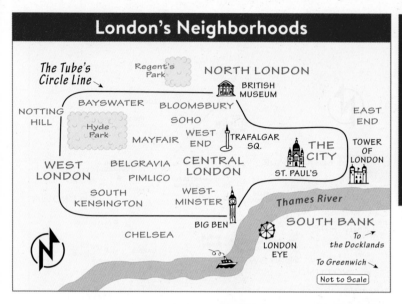

The Tube's Circle Line

Regent's Park

NORTH LONDON

BRITISH MUSEUM

BAYSWATER   BLOOMSBURY

NOTTING HILL

SOHO

Hyde Park

MAYFAIR   WEST END   TRAFALGAR SQ.

EAST END

THE CITY

TOWER OF LONDON

WEST LONDON   BELGRAVIA   CENTRAL LONDON

PIMLICO   ST. PAUL'S

SOUTH KENSINGTON   WEST-MINSTER

Thames River

BIG BEN

SOUTH BANK

CHELSEA

LONDON EYE

To the Docklands

To Greenwich

Not to Scale

nium Bridge to the South Bank to visit the Tate Modern, tour Shakespeare's Globe, or stroll the Jubilee Walkway.

Day 4: Take your pick of the Victoria and Albert Museum, Tate Britain, Imperial War Museum, or Houses of Parliament. Hit one of London's many lively open-air markets. Or cruise to Kew Gardens or Greenwich.

ORIENTATION

To make London more manageable, think of it as the old town in the city center without the modern, congested sprawl.

The Thames River (pronounced "tems") runs roughly west to east through the city, with most sights on the North Bank. Mentally, trim down your map to include only the area between the Tower of London (to the east), Hyde Park (west), Regent's Park (north), and the South Bank (south). This is roughly the area bordered by the Tube's Circle Line. This four-mile stretch between the Tower and Hyde Park (about a 1.5-hour walk), which looks like a milk bottle on its side, holds most of the sights mentioned in this chapter.

Central London contains **Westminster,** the location of Big Ben, Parliament, Westminster Abbey, Buckingham Palace, and Trafalgar Square, with its many major museums. It also includes the **West End,** the center of London's cultural life, where bustling Piccadilly Circus and Leicester Square host cinemas, tourist traps, and nighttime glitz. Soho and Covent Garden are thriving people zones with theaters, restaurants, pubs, and boutiques. And Regent and Oxford streets are the city's main shopping zones.

North London and its neighborhoods—including Bloomsbury, Fitzrovia, and Marylebone—contain such major sights as the British Museum and the overhyped Madame Tussauds Waxworks. Nearby, along busy Euston Road, is the British Library.

"The City," which is today's modern financial district, was a walled town in Roman times. Gleaming skyscrapers are interspersed with historical landmarks such as St. Paul's Cathedral and the Museum of London. The Tower of London and Tower Bridge lie at The City's eastern border.

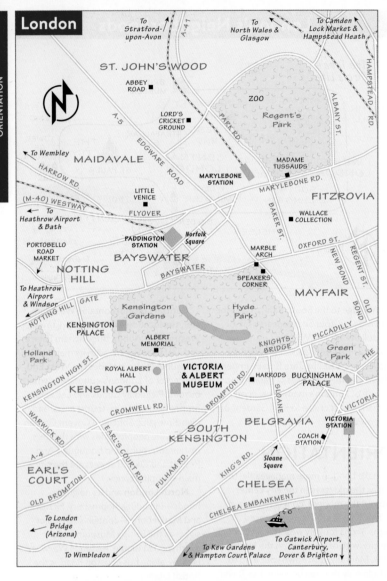

London

To Stratford-upon-Avon

To North Wales & Glasgow

To Camden Lock Market & Hampstead Heath

A-41

HAMPSTEAD RD.

ST. JOHN'S WOOD

ABBEY ROAD

ZOO

Regent's Park

ALBANY ST.

A-5

LORD'S CRICKET GROUND

PARK RD.

MADAME TUSSAUDS

To Wembley

MAIDAVALE

EDGWARE ROAD

MARYLEBONE STATION

MARYLEBONE RD.

FITZROVIA

HARROW RD.

LITTLE VENICE

BAKER ST.

WALLACE COLLECTION

(M-40) WESTWAY

FLYOVER

OXFORD ST.

REGENT ST.

To Heathrow Airport & Bath

PADDINGTON STATION

Norfolk Square

MARBLE ARCH

NEW BOND ST.

PORTOBELLO ROAD MARKET

BAYSWATER

BAYSWATER

SPEAKERS' CORNER

OLD BOND ST.

NOTTING HILL

MAYFAIR

To Heathrow Airport & Windsor

NOTTING HILL GATE

Kensington Gardens

Hyde Park

PICCADILLY

KENSINGTON PALACE

ALBERT MEMORIAL

KNIGHTS-BRIDGE

Green Park

THE MALL

Holland Park

KENSINGTON HIGH ST.

ROYAL ALBERT HALL

VICTORIA & ALBERT MUSEUM

HARRODS

BUCKINGHAM PALACE

KENSINGTON

CROMWELL RD.

BROMPTON RD.

SLOANE ST.

VICTORIA

WARWICK RD.

EARL'S COURT RD.

SOUTH KENSINGTON

BELGRAVIA

VICTORIA STATION

A-4

FULHAM RD.

COACH STATION

EARL'S COURT

KING'S RD.

Sloane Square

OLD BROMPTON

CHELSEA

To London Bridge (Arizona)

CHELSEA EMBANKMENT

To Gatwick Airport, Canterbury, Dover & Brighton

To Kew Gardens & Hampton Court Palace

To Wimbledon

The **East End** is the increasingly gentrified former stomping ground of Cockney ragamuffins and Jack the Ripper.

The **South Bank** of the Thames River offers major sights—Tate Modern, Shakespeare's Globe, and the London Eye—linked by a riverside walkway. Within this area, Southwark (SUTH-uck) stretches from the Tate Modern to London Bridge. Pedestrian bridges connect the South Bank with The City and Trafalgar Square.

West London contains neighborhoods such as Mayfair, Belgravia, Pimlico, Chelsea, South Kensington, and Notting Hill. It's home to London's wealthy and has many trendy shops and enticing restau-

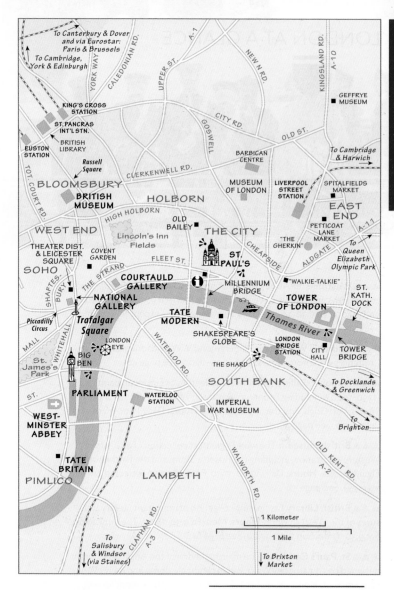

rants. Here you'll find the Victoria and Albert Museum, Tate Britain, and more museums, lively Victoria Station, and the vast green expanses of Hyde Park and Kensington Gardens.

Kew Gardens are outside the city center, southwest of London.

Rick's Tip: *Through an initiative called* **Legible London,** *the city has erected* **pedestrian-focused maps** *around town—especially handy when exiting* **Tube stations.** *In this sprawling city—where predictable grid-planned streets are relatively rare—it's smart to buy and use a good map.*

LONDON AT A GLANCE

▲▲▲**Westminster Abbey** Britain's finest church and the site of royal coronations and burials since 1066. **Hours:** Mon-Fri 9:30-16:30, Wed until 19:00, Sat 9:30-14:30, closed Sun to sightseers except for worship. See page 37.

▲▲▲**Churchill War Rooms** Underground WWII headquarters of Churchill's war effort. **Hours:** Daily 9:30-18:00. See page 46.

▲▲▲**National Gallery** Remarkable collection of European paintings (1250-1900), including Leonardo, Botticelli, Velázquez, Rembrandt, Turner, Van Gogh, and the Impressionists. **Hours:** Daily 10:00-18:00, Fri until 21:00. See page 48.

▲▲▲**British Museum** The world's greatest collection of artifacts of Western civilization, including the Rosetta Stone and the Parthenon's Elgin Marbles. **Hours:** Daily 10:00-17:30, Fri until 20:30 (selected galleries only). See page 57.

▲▲▲**British Library** Fascinating collection of important literary treasures of the Western world. **Hours:** Mon-Fri 9:30-18:00, Tue until 20:00, Sat 9:30-17:00, Sun 11:00-17:00. See page 61.

▲▲▲**St. Paul's Cathedral** The main cathedral of the Anglican Church, designed by Christopher Wren, with a climbable dome and daily evensong services. **Hours:** Mon-Sat 8:30-16:30, closed Sun except for worship. See page 64.

▲▲▲**Tower of London** Historic castle, palace, and prison housing the crown jewels and a witty band of Beefeaters. **Hours:** Tue-Sat 9:00-17:30, Sun-Mon 10:00-17:30; Nov-Feb closes one hour earlier. See page 70.

▲▲▲**Victoria and Albert Museum** The best collection of decorative arts anywhere. **Hours:** Daily 10:00-17:45, Fri until 22:00 (selected galleries only). See page 83.

▲▲**Houses of Parliament** Landmark famous for Big Ben and occupied by the Houses of Lords and Commons. **Hours:** When Parliament is in session, generally open Mon-Thu, closed Fri-Sun and most of Aug-Sept. Guided tours offered year-round on Sat and most weekdays during Aug-Sept. See page 41.

▲▲**Trafalgar Square** The heart of London, where Westminster, The City, and the West End meet. **Hours:** Always open. See page 46.

▲▲**National Portrait Gallery** A who's who of British history, featuring portraits of this nation's most important historical figures. **Hours:** Daily 10:00-18:00, Thu-Fri until 21:00, first and second floors open Mon at 11:00. See page 51.

▲▲**Covent Garden** Vibrant people-watching zone with shops, cafés, street musicians, and an iron-and-glass arcade that once hosted a produce market. **Hours:** Always open. See page 52.

▲▲**Changing of the Guard at Buckingham Palace** Hour-long spectacle at Britain's royal residence. **Hours:** Generally May-July daily at 11:30, Aug-April every other day. See page 54.

▲▲**London Eye** Enormous observation wheel, dominating—and offering commanding views over—London's skyline. **Hours:** Daily 10:00-20:30, later in July and Aug. See page 75.

▲▲**Imperial War Museum** Exhibits examining the military history of the bloody 20th century. **Hours:** Daily 10:00-18:00. See page 76.

▲▲**Tate Modern** Works by Monet, Matisse, Dalí, Picasso, and Warhol displayed in a converted powerhouse. **Hours:** Daily 10:00-18:00, Fri-Sat until 22:00. See page 78.

▲▲**Shakespeare's Globe** Timbered, thatched-roofed reconstruction of the Bard's original "wooden O." **Hours:** Theater complex, museum, and actor-led tours generally daily 9:00-17:30; in summer, theater tours usually run only in morning. Plays are also staged here. See page 79.

▲▲**Tate Britain** Collection of British paintings from the 16th century through modern times, including works by William Blake, the Pre-Raphaelites, and J. M. W. Turner. **Hours:** Daily 10:00-18:00. See page 80.

Tourist Information

It's hard to find unbiased sightseeing information in London. "Tourist Information" offices are advertised everywhere, but most are private agencies that sell tours and advance tickets for sights and the theater.

The **City of London Information Centre** next to St. Paul's Cathedral (just outside the church entrance) is the only publicly funded—and therefore impartial—TI. It sells Oyster cards, London Passes, and "Fast Track" sightseeing tickets. The TI gives out a free map of The City and sells several city-wide maps; ask if they have yet another free map with various coupons for discounts on sights (Mon-Sat 9:30-17:30, Sun 10:00-16:00; Tube: St. Paul's, tel. 020/7332-1456, www.visitthecity.co.uk).

Visit London, which serves the greater London area, doesn't have an office you can visit—but does have an information-packed website (www.visitlondon.com).

Sightseeing Passes and Advance Tickets

To skip the ticket-buying queues at certain sights, you can buy **Fast Track tickets** (sometimes called "priority pass" tickets) in advance—and they can be cheaper than tickets sold right at the sight. They're smart for the Tower of London, London Eye, and Madame Tussauds Waxworks, which get busy in high season. They're available through various sales outlets around London (including the City of London TI, souvenir stands, and faux-TIs scattered throughout touristy areas).

The **London Pass** covers many big sights and lets you skip some lines. It's expensive but potentially worth the investment for extremely busy sightseers (£52/1 day, multiday options available; sold at City of London TI, major train stations, and airports; www.londonpass.com).

Rick's Tip: *The Artful Dodger is alive and well in London.* **Beware of pickpockets,** *particularly on public transportation, among tourist crowds, and at street markets.*

Tours

🎧 To sightsee on your own, download my **free audio tours** for London's top sights and neighborhoods (see page 14 for details).

▲▲▲**HOP-ON, HOP-OFF BUS TOURS**
London is full of hop-on, hop-off bus companies, all competing for your tourist pound. To help narrow down your options, I've focused on the two companies I like the most: **Original** and **Big Bus.** Both offer essentially the same 2-to-3-hour, £32 tour of the city's sightseeing highlights, with nearly 30 stops on each route.

Rick's Tip: *For an efficient intro to London, catch an 8:30 departure of a* **hop-on, hop-off overview bus tour,** *riding 90 percent of the loop (which takes just over two hours, depending on traffic), and hopping off at Buckingham Palace in time to find a good spot to watch the* **Changing of the Guard** *ceremony at 11:30.*

Each company offers at least one route with live guides, and a second (sometimes slightly different route) that comes with recorded narration. Buses run daily about every 10-15 minutes in summer, every 10-20 minutes in winter. They start

Daily Reminder

SUNDAY: The Tower of London and British Museum are both especially crowded today. Speakers' Corner in Hyde Park rants from early afternoon until early evening. The Houses of Parliament are closed. Westminster Abbey and St. Paul's are open during the day for worship but closed to sightseers. With all these closures, this morning is a good time to take a bus tour. Most big stores open late (around 11:30) and close early (18:00). Street markets flourish at Camden Lock, Spitalfields (at its best today), Petticoat Lane, and Brick Lane, but the Portobello Road market is closed. Because of all the market action, it's a good day to visit the East End. Most theaters are dark today.

MONDAY: Virtually all sights are open. The Houses of Parliament may be open as late as 22:30.

TUESDAY: Virtually all sights are open. The British Library is open until 20:00, and the Houses of Parliament may be open as late as 22:00.

WEDNESDAY: Virtually all sights are open. The Houses of Parliament may be open as late as 22:00.

THURSDAY: All sights are open, plus evening hours at the National Portrait Gallery (until 21:00).

FRIDAY: All sights are open, except the Houses of Parliament. Sights open late include the British Museum (selected galleries until 20:30), National Gallery (until 21:00), National Portrait Gallery (until 21:00), Victoria and Albert Museum (selected galleries until 22:00), and Tate Modern (until 22:00).

SATURDAY: Most sights are open, except legal ones (skip The City). The Houses of Parliament are open only with a tour. Tate Modern is open until 22:00. The Tower of London is especially crowded today. Today's the day to hit the Portobello Road street market; the Camden Lock and Greenwich markets are also good.

at about 8:00 or 8:30 and run until early evening in summer or late afternoon in winter. The last full loop usually leaves Victoria Station at about 20:00 in summer, and at about 17:00 in winter.

Sunday morning—when the traffic is light and many museums are closed—is a fine time for a tour. Traffic is at its peak around lunch and during the evening rush hour (around 17:00).

Buy tickets online in advance, or on the day of your trip from drivers or at street kiosks (credit cards accepted at kiosks at major stops such as Victoria Station, ticket good for 24 hours, or 48 hours in winter).

Original: £32, £4 discount with this book, limit four discounts per book, they'll rip off the corner of this page—raise bloody hell if the staff or driver won't honor this discount; also online deals, info center at 17 Cockspur Street, tel. 020/8877-1722, www.theoriginaltour.com.

Big Bus: £32, discount available online, tel. 020/7808-6753, www.bigbustours.com.

NIGHT BUS TOURS

Various companies offer a lower-priced, after-hours sightseeing circuit (1-2 hours). The views at twilight are grand—though note that London just doesn't do flood-lighting as well as, say, Paris. **See London By Night** buses offer live guides and frequent evening departures—starting from 19:30—from Green Park (£18, next to Ritz Hotel, tel. 020/7183-4744, www. seelondonbynight.com). The pricier **Golden Tours** buses depart at 19:00 and 20:00 from the Golden Tours visitor center on Buckingham Palace Road (£27, tel. 020/7630-2028; www.goldentours.com). For a memorable and economical evening, munch a scenic picnic dinner on the top deck. (There are plenty of takeaway options near the departure points.)

Rick's Tip: *If you're taking a bus tour mainly to get oriented,* **save time and money by taking a night tour.**

▲▲ WALKING TOURS

Several times a day, top-notch local guides lead groups through specific slices of London's past. **London Walks** lists its daily schedule on their amusing website and in brochures available at hotels and in racks all over town. The two-hour walks are led year-round by professional guides (£10 cash only, private tours for groups-£140, tel. 020/7624-3978, tel. 020/7624-9255 for a recording of today's or tomorrow's walks and the Tube station they depart from, www.walks.com).

London Walks also offers day trips into the countryside (£18 plus £36-59 for transportation and admission costs, cash only: Stonehenge/Salisbury, Oxford/Cotswolds, Cambridge, Bath, and so on).

PRIVATE GUIDES AND DRIVERS

Rates for London's registered Blue Badge guides are standard (about £150-165 for four hours; £240 or more for nine hours). I know and like **Sean Kelleher** (tel. 020/8673-1624, mobile 07764-612-770, sean@seanlondonguide.com) and **Joel Reid,** who specializes in off-the-beaten-track London (mobile 07887-955-720, joelyreid@gmail.com). Also, **London Walks** has a huge selection of guides and can book one for your particular interest (£180/half-day).

Guides with cars or minivans offer regional tours for about £550/day,

depending on the itinerary. Consider **Janine Barton** (tel. 020/7402-4600, http://seeitinstyle.synthasite.com, jbsiis@aol.com) or cousins **Hugh Dickson** and **Mike Dickson** (Hugh's mobile 07771-602-069, hughdickson@hotmail.com; Mike's mobile 07769-905-811, michael.dickson5@btinternet.com).

▲▲ CRUISE BOAT TOURS

Several companies offer tourist cruises, most on slow-moving, open-top boats accompanied by entertaining commentary. Take a **short city-center cruise** by riding a boat 30 minutes from Westminster Pier to Tower Pier (particularly handy if you're interested in visiting the Tower of London anyway), or choose a **longer cruise** that includes a peek at the East End, riding from Westminster all the way to Greenwich.

Each company runs cruises daily, about twice hourly, from morning until dark; many reduce frequency off-season. Boats come and go from various docks in the city center (see sidebar). The most popular places to embark are Westminster Pier (at the base of Westminster Bridge across the street from Big Ben) and Waterloo Pier (at the London Eye, across the river on the South Bank).

A one-way trip within the city center costs about £10. A transit card (Oyster card or Travelcard) can earn you a discount on some cruises (see page 112).

Rick's Tip: *Zipping through London every 20-30 minutes, the* **Thames Clippers are designed for commuters.** *With no open deck and no commentary, they're* **not the best option for sightseeing.**

The three dominant companies are **City Cruises** (handy 45-minute cruise from Westminster Pier to Tower Pier; www.citycruises.com), **Thames River Services** (fewer stops, classic boats, friendlier and more old-fashioned feel; www.thamesriverservices.co.uk), and

Thames Boat Piers

While Westminster Pier is the most popular, it's not the only dock in town. Consider all the options (listed from west to east, as the Thames flows):

Millbank Pier (North Bank): At the Tate Britain Museum, used primarily by the Tate Boat service (express connection to Tate Modern at Bankside Pier).

Westminster Pier (North Bank): Near the base of Big Ben, offers round-trip sightseeing cruises and lots of departures in both directions (though Thames Clippers commuter boats don't stop here). Parliament and Westminster Abbey are nearby.

Waterloo Pier (a.k.a. London Eye Pier, South Bank): At the base of the London Eye, a good, less-crowded alternative to Westminster, with many of the same cruise options (Waterloo Station is nearby).

Embankment Pier (North Bank): Near Covent Garden, Trafalgar Square, and Cleopatra's Needle (the obelisk on the Thames). This pier is used mostly for lunch and dinner cruises.

Festival Pier (South Bank): Next to the Royal Festival Hall, just downstream from the London Eye.

Blackfriars Pier (North Bank): In The City, not far from St. Paul's.

Bankside Pier (South Bank): Directly in front of the Tate Modern and Shakespeare's Globe.

London Bridge Pier (South Bank): Close to London Bridge.

Tower Pier (North Bank): At the Tower of London, at the east edge of The City and near the East End.

St. Katharine's Pier (North Bank): Just downstream from the Tower of London.

Canary Wharf Pier (North Bank): At the Docklands.

Circular Cruise (full cruise takes about an hour, operated by Crown River Services, www.crownrivercruise.co.uk).

Cruising Downstream, to Greenwich: Both **City Cruises** and **Thames River Services** head from Westminster Pier to Greenwich. To maximize both efficiency and sightseeing, take a narrated cruise to Greenwich one way, and go the other way on the DLR (Docklands Light Railway).

Cruising Upstream, to Kew Gardens: Thames River Boats, operated by the Westminster Passenger Service Association, leave for Kew Gardens from Westminster Pier (£13 one-way, £20 round-trip, cash only, discounts with Travelcard, 2-4/

day depending on season, 1.5 hours, boats sail April-Oct, www.wpsa.co.uk).

Helpful Hints

Medical Help: Hospitals have 24-hour-a-day emergency care centers. St. Thomas' Hospital, immediately across the river from Big Ben, has a fine reputation.

Wi-Fi: Besides your hotel, many major museums, sights, and even entire neighborhoods offer free Wi-Fi. For easy access everywhere, sign up for a free account with **The Cloud,** a Wi-Fi service found in many convenient spots around London (www.thecloud.net/free-wifi, when you sign up, you'll have to enter a street address and postal code—use your hotel's, or the Queen's: Buckingham Palace, SW1A 1AA).

Useful Apps: Tube travelers may want to download Mapway's free **Tube Map London Underground** (www.mapway. com), which shows the easiest way to connect station A to station B. The **City-mapper** app for London covers every mode of public transit in the city. **City Maps 2Go** lets you download searchable offline maps; their London version is quite good. **Time Out** London's free app has reviews and listings for theater, museums, movies, and more (the "Make Your City Amazing" version is updated weekly).

Maps: Bensons *London Street Map,* sold at many newsstands and bookstores, is my favorite for efficient sightseeing and might be the best £3 you'll spend. I also like the *Handy London Map and Guide* version, which shows every little lane and all the sights, and comes with a transit map.

Baggage Storage: Train stations have replaced lockers with more secure left-luggage counters. Each bag must go through a scanner (just like at the airport). Expect long waits in the morning to check in (up to 45 minutes) and in the afternoon to pick up (most stations daily 7:00-23:00). You can also store bags at the airports (www.left-baggage.co.uk).

WESTMINSTER WALK

Just about every visitor to London strolls along the historic Whitehall road from Big Ben to Trafalgar Square. This walk gives you a whirlwind tour as well as a practical orientation to London. Most of the sights you'll see are described in more detail later. (🎧 You can download a free, extended audio version of this walk to your mobile device; see page 14.)

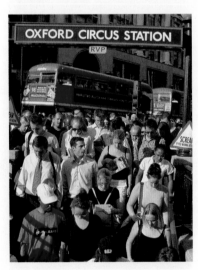

Rick's Tip: Cars drive on the left side of the road—*as confusing for foreign pedestrians as for foreign drivers. Always look right, look left, then look right again just to be sure.* **Jaywalking is treacherous** *when you're disoriented about which direction traffic is coming from.*

❷ Self-Guided Walk

Start halfway across ❶ **Westminster Bridge** for that "Wow, I'm really in London!" feeling. Get a close-up view of the **Houses of Parliament** and **Big Ben.** Downstream you'll see the **London Eye,** the city's giant Ferris wheel. Down the

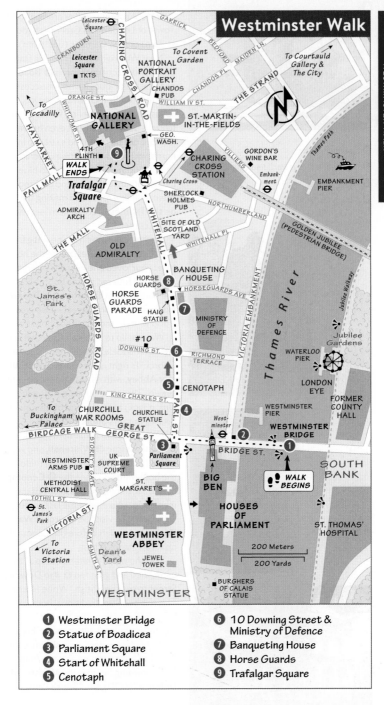

Westminster Walk

1. Westminster Bridge
2. Statue of Boadicea
3. Parliament Square
4. Start of Whitehall
5. Cenotaph
6. 10 Downing Street & Ministry of Defence
7. Banqueting House
8. Horse Guards
9. Trafalgar Square

A Boadicea statue

B Churchill statue in Parliament Square

C Horse Guards

D Banqueting House

stairs to Westminster Pier are boats to the Tower of London and Greenwich (downstream) or Kew Gardens (upstream).

Near Westminster Pier is a big statue of a lady on a chariot. This is ❷ **Boadicea,** the Celtic queen who unsuccessfully resisted Roman invaders in A.D. 60. Julius Caesar was the first Roman general to cross the Channel, but even he was weirded out by the island's strange inhabitants, who worshipped trees, sacrificed virgins, and went to war painted blue. Later, Romans subdued and civilized them, building roads and making this spot on the Thames—"Londinium"—a major urban center.

For fun, call home from near Big Ben at about three minutes before the hour to let your loved one hear the bell ring. You'll find four red phone booths lining the north side of ❸ **Parliament Square** along Great George Street—also great for a phone-box-and-Big-Ben photo op.

Wave hello to Winston Churchill and Nelson Mandela in Parliament Square. To Churchill's right is the historic **Westminster Abbey,** with its two stubby, elegant towers. The white building (flying the Union Jack) at the far end of the square houses Britain's **Supreme Court.**

Head north up Parliament Street, which turns into ❹ **Whitehall,** and walk toward Trafalgar Square. In the middle of the boulevard you'll see the ❺ **Cenotaph** memorial, reminding passersby of the many Brits who died in the last century's world wars. To visit the **Churchill War Rooms,** take a left before the Cenotaph, on King Charles Street.

Continuing on Whitehall, stop at the barricaded and guarded ❻ **#10 Downing Street** to see the British "White House." This has been the traditional home of the prime minister since the position was created in the early 18th century. Break the bobby's boredom and ask him a question. The huge building across Whitehall from Downing Street is the **Ministry of Defence** (MOD), the "British Pentagon."

Nearing Trafalgar Square, look for the **❼ Banqueting House** across the street. England's first Renaissance building (1619-1622) was designed by Inigo Jones, built by King James I, and decorated by his son Charles I. It's one of the few landmarks spared by the fire that devastated London in 1698. Today, you can enjoy its ceiling paintings by Peter Paul Rubens—and the exquisite hall itself (£6.60, daily 10:00-17:00, may close for government functions, www.hrp.org.uk).

Also take a look at the **❽ Horse Guards** behind the gated fence. For 200 years, soldiers in cavalry uniforms have guarded this arched entrance that leads to Buckingham Palace. These elite troops constitute the Queen's personal bodyguard. They change daily at 11:00 (10:00 on Sun), and a colorful dismounting ceremony takes place daily at 16:00.

❾ Trafalgar Square, London's central meeting point, bustles around the world's biggest Corinthian column, topped by Admiral Horatio Nelson (he's celebrated for defeating the once-invincible French Napoleonic navy, off the coast of Spain's Cape Trafalgar, in 1805). The stately domed building on the far side of the square is the **National Gallery,** filled with the national collection of European paintings. To the right is the 1722 **St. Martin-in-the-Fields Church.** Its steeple-over-the-entrance style is the inspiration behind many town churches in New England.

• *Our Westminster walk is over. But if you want to keep going, walk up Cockspur Street to Haymarket, then take a short left on Coventry Street to colorful Piccadilly Circus. Near here, you'll find a number of theaters and Leicester Square, with its half-price "TKTS" booth for plays (see page 88). Covent Garden, with street musicians and shops, is nearby.*

SIGHTS

Central London
Westminster

These sights are listed in roughly geographical order from Westminster Abbey to Trafalgar Square, and are linked in my self-guided Westminster Walk, earlier, and the ∩ free Westminster Walk audio tour (see page 14 for details).

▲▲▲WESTMINSTER ABBEY

The greatest church in the English-speaking world, Westminster Abbey is where the nation's royalty has been wedded, crowned, and buried since 1066. Indeed, the histories of Westminster Abbey and England are almost the same. A thousand years of English history—3,000 tombs, the remains of 29 kings and queens, and hundreds of memorials to poets, politicians, scientists, and warriors—lie within its stained-glass splendor and under its stone slabs.

Cost and Hours: £20, £40 family ticket (2 adults and 1 child), includes audioguide and entry to cloisters; Mon-Fri 9:30-16:30, Wed until 19:00 (main church only), Sat 9:30-14:30, last entry one hour before closing, closed Sun to sightseers but open for services; cloisters—daily 8:00-18:00; no photos allowed, café in cellar, Tube: Westminster or St. James's Park, tel. 020/7222-5152, www.westminster-abbey.org.

Trafalgar Square and St. Martin-in-the-Fields

Westminster Abbey Tour

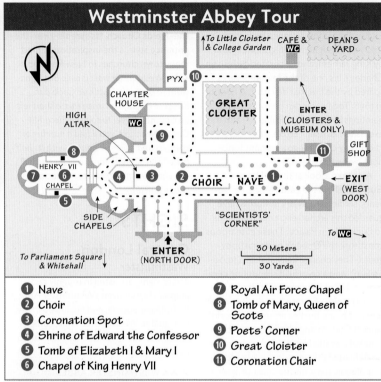

To Little Cloister
& College Garden

CAFÉ &
WC

DEAN'S
YARD

PYX

10

CHAPTER
HOUSE

GREAT
CLOISTER

ENTER
(CLOISTERS &
MUSEUM ONLY)

HIGH
ALTAR

WC

9

ENTER
(CLOISTERS &
MUSEUM ONLY)

GIFT
SHOP

8

HENRY VII

11

7 **6**

4 **3**

2 CHOIR NAVE

1

← EXIT
(WEST
DOOR)

CHAPEL

5

SIDE
CHAPELS

"SCIENTISTS'
CORNER"

To WC →

To Parliament Square
& Whitehall

ENTER
(NORTH DOOR)

30 Meters

30 Yards

1 Nave
2 Choir
3 Coronation Spot
4 Shrine of Edward the Confessor
5 Tomb of Elizabeth I & Mary I
6 Chapel of King Henry VII

7 Royal Air Force Chapel
8 Tomb of Mary, Queen of Scots
9 Poets' Corner
10 Great Cloister
11 Coronation Chair

The west facade of Westminster Abbey

Rick's Tip: Westminster Abbey *is most crowded at midmorning and all day Saturday and Monday.* **Visit early, during lunch, or late.** *Weekdays after 14:30—especially Wednesday—are less congested; come after that time and stay for the 17:00 evensong. From April through September, you can bypass the long line at the main entrance by* **booking advance tickets online** *at www. westminster-abbey.org.*

It's free to enter just the cloisters (through Dean's Yard, around the right side as you face the main entrance), but if it's too crowded inside, the marshal at the cloister entrance may not let you in.

Church Services and Music: Mon-Fri at 7:30 (prayer), 8:00 (communion), 12:30 (communion), 17:00 evensong (except on Wed, when the evening service is generally spoken—not sung); **Sat** at 8:00 (communion), 9:00 (prayer), 15:00 (evensong; May-Aug it's at 17:00); **Sun** services generally come with more music: at 8:00 (communion), 10:00 (sung Matins), 11:15 (sung Eucharist), 15:00 (evensong), and 18:30 (evening service). Services are free to anyone. Free **organ recitals** are usually held Sun at 17:45 (30 minutes).

Tours: The included **audioguide** is excellent. To add to the experience, you can take an entertaining **guided tour** from a verger—the church equivalent of a museum docent (£5, schedule posted both outside and inside entry, up to 6/day in summer, 2-4/day in winter, 1.5 hours).

❍ SELF-GUIDED TOUR

You'll have no choice but to follow the steady flow of tourists through the church, along the route laid out for the audioguide. My tour covers the Abbey's top stops.

• *Walk straight through the north transept. Follow the crowd to the right and enter the spacious...*

❶ Nave: The Abbey's 10-story nave is the tallest in England. With saints in stained glass, heroes in carved stone, and the bodies of England's greatest citizens under the floor stones, Westminster Abbey is the religious heart of England.

Find Edward the Confessor, the king who built the Abbey, in the stained-glass windows on the left side of the nave (as you face the altar). He's in the third bay from the end (marked *S: Edwardus rex...*), with his crown, scepter, and ring.

On the floor near the west entrance of the Abbey is the flower-lined Grave of the Unknown Warrior, an ordinary WWI soldier buried in soil from France with lettering made from melted-down weapons from that war. Contemplate the million-man army from the British Empire and all those who gave their lives. Their memory is so revered that when Kate Middleton walked up the aisle on her wedding day, by tradition she had to step around the tomb (and her wedding bouquet was later placed atop this tomb, also in accordance with tradition).

• *Walk up the nave toward the altar. This is the same route every future monarch walks before being crowned. Midway up the nave, you pass through the colorful enclosure known as the...*

❷ Choir: These elaborately carved wood and gilded seats are where monks once chanted their services in the "quire"—as it's known in British church-speak. Today, it's where the Abbey boys' choir sings the evensong. You're approaching the center of a cross-shaped church. The "high" (main) altar, which usually has a cross and candlesticks atop it, sits on the platform up the five stairs in front of you.

• *It's on this platform that the monarch is crowned.*

❸ **Coronation Spot:** The area immediately before the high altar is where every English coronation since 1066 has taken place. Royalty are also given funerals here. Princess Diana's coffin was carried to this spot for her funeral service in 1997. The "Queen Mum" (mother of Elizabeth II) had her funeral here in 2002. This is also where most of the last century's royal weddings have taken place, including the unions of Queen Elizabeth II and Prince Philip (1947), Prince Andrew and Sarah Ferguson (1986), and Prince William and Kate Middleton (2011).

• *Veer left and follow the crowd. Pause at the wooden staircase on your right.*

❹ **Shrine of Edward the Confessor:** Step back and peek over the dark coffin of Edward I to see the tippy-top of the green-and-gold wedding-cake tomb of King Edward the Confessor—the man who built Westminster Abbey.

God had told pious Edward to visit St. Peter's Basilica in Rome. But with the Normans planning conquest, it was too dangerous for him to leave England. Instead, he built this grand church and dedicated it to St. Peter. It was finished just in time to bury Edward and to crown his foreign successor, William the Conqueror, in 1066. After Edward's death, people prayed at his tomb and got good results, so Pope Alexander III canonized

him. This elevated central tomb—which lost some of its luster when Henry VIII melted down the gold coffin-case—is surrounded by the tombs of eight kings and queens.

• *At the top of the stone staircase, veer left into the private burial chapel of Queen Elizabeth I.*

❺ **Tomb of Queens Elizabeth I and Mary I:** Although only one effigy is on the tomb (Elizabeth's), there are actually two queens buried beneath it, both daughters of Henry VIII (by different mothers). Bloody Mary—meek, pious, sickly, and Catholic—enforced Catholicism during her short reign (1553-1558) by burning "heretics" at the stake.

Elizabeth—strong, clever, and Protestant—steered England on an Anglican course. She holds a royal orb symbolizing that she's queen of the whole globe. When 26-year-old Elizabeth was crowned in the Abbey, her right to rule was questioned (especially by her Catholic subjects) because she was considered the bastard seed of Henry VIII's unsanctioned marriage to Anne Boleyn. But Elizabeth's long reign (1559-1603) was one of the greatest in English history, a time when England ruled the seas and Shakespeare explored human emotions. When she died, thousands turned out for her funeral in the Abbey. Elizabeth's face on the tomb, modeled after her death mask, is considered an accurate take on this hook-nosed, imperious "Virgin Queen" (she never married).

• *Continue into the ornate, flag-draped room up a few more stairs, directly behind the main altar.*

❻ **Chapel of King Henry VII** (The Lady Chapel): The colorful banners overhead and the elaborate tracery in stone, wood, and glass give this room the festive air of a medieval tournament. The prestigious Knights of the Bath meet here, under the magnificent ceiling studded with gold pendants. The ceiling—of carved stone (1519)—is the finest English

Tomb of Elizabeth I (and Mary I)

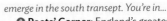

Perpendicular Gothic and fan vaulting you'll see (unless you're going to King's College Chapel in Cambridge). The ceiling was sculpted on the floor in pieces, then jigsaw-puzzled into place. It capped the Gothic period and signaled the vitality of the coming Renaissance.

• *Go to the far end of the chapel and stand at the banister in front of the modern set of stained-glass windows.*

❼ Royal Air Force Chapel: Saints in robes and halos mingle with pilots in parachutes and bomber jackets. This tribute to WWII flyers is for those who earned their angel wings in the Battle of Britain (July-Oct 1940). A bit of bomb damage has been preserved—look for the little glassed-over hole in the wall below the windows in the lower left-hand corner.

• *Exit the Chapel of Henry VII. Turn left into a side chapel with the tomb (the central one of three in the chapel).*

❽ Tomb of Mary, Queen of Scots: The beautiful, French-educated queen (1542-1587) was held under house arrest for 19 years by Queen Elizabeth I, who considered her a threat to her sovereignty. Elizabeth got wind of an assassination plot, suspected Mary was behind it, and had her first cousin (once removed) beheaded. When the childless Elizabeth died, Mary's son, James VI, King of Scots, also became King James I of England and Ireland. James buried his mum here (with her head sewn back on) in the Abbey's most sumptuous tomb.

• *Exit Mary's chapel. Continue on, until you emerge in the south transept. You're in...*

❾ Poets' Corner: England's greatest artistic contributions are in the written word. Here the masters of arguably the world's most complex and expressive language are remembered: Geoffrey Chaucer (*Canterbury Tales*), Lord Byron, Dylan Thomas, W. H. Auden, Lewis Carroll (*Alice's Adventures in Wonderland*), T. S. Eliot (*The Waste Land*), Alfred Tennyson, Robert Browning, and Charles Dickens. Many writers are honored with plaques and monuments; relatively few are actually buried here. Shakespeare is commemorated by a fine statue that stands near the end of the transept, overlooking the others.

• *Exit the church (temporarily) at the south door, which leads to the...*

❿ Great Cloister: The buildings that adjoin the church housed the monks. Cloistered courtyards gave them a place to meditate on God's creations. Monks had daily meetings in the **Chapter House,** which features fine architecture and stained glass, some faded but well-described medieval paintings and floor tiles, and—in the corridor—Britain's oldest door.

• *Go back into the church for the last stop.*

⓫ Coronation Chair: A gold-painted oak chair waits here under a regal canopy for the next coronation. For every English coronation since 1308 (except two), it's been moved to its spot before the high altar to receive the royal buttocks. The chair's legs rest on lions, England's symbol.

▲▲HOUSES OF PARLIAMENT (PALACE OF WESTMINSTER)

This Neo-Gothic icon of London, the site of the royal residence from 1042 to 1547, is now the meeting place of the legislative branch of government. Like the US Capitol in Washington, DC, the complex is open to visitors. You can view parliamentary sessions in either the bickering House of Commons or the sleepy House of Lords. Or you can simply wander on your own (through a few closely monitored

Poets' Corner

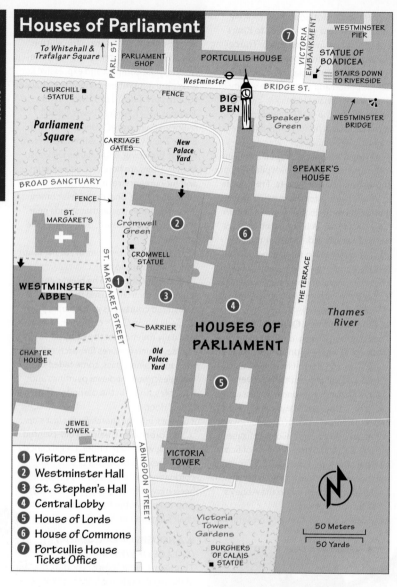

Houses of Parliament

To Whitehall & Trafalgar Square

PARL. ST.

PARLIAMENT SHOP

PORTCULLIS HOUSE

VICTORIA EMBANKMENT

WESTMINSTER PIER

STATUE OF BOADICEA

STAIRS DOWN TO RIVERSIDE

Westminster

BRIDGE ST.

CHURCHILL STATUE

FENCE

BIG BEN

Speaker's Green

WESTMINSTER BRIDGE

Parliament Square

CARRIAGE GATES

New Palace Yard

SPEAKER'S HOUSE

BROAD SANCTUARY

FENCE

ST. MARGARET'S

Cromwell Green

CROMWELL STATUE

WESTMINSTER ABBEY

ST. MARGARET STREET

BARRIER

HOUSES OF PARLIAMENT

THE TERRACE

Thames River

CHAPTER HOUSE

Old Palace Yard

JEWEL TOWER

ABINGDON STREET

VICTORIA TOWER

Victoria Tower Gardens

BURGHERS OF CALAIS STATUE

N

50 Meters

50 Yards

1 **Visitors Entrance**
2 **Westminster Hall**
3 **St. Stephen's Hall**
4 **Central Lobby**
5 **House of Lords**
6 **House of Commons**
7 **Portcullis House Ticket Office**

rooms) to appreciate the historic building itself.

The Palace of Westminster has been the center of political power in England for nearly a thousand years. In 1834, a horrendous fire gutted the Palace. It was rebuilt in a retro, Neo-Gothic style that recalled England's medieval Christian roots—pointed arches, stained-glass windows, spires, and saint-like statues. At the same time, Britain was also retooling its government. Democracy was on the rise, the queen became a constitutional monarch, and Parliament emerged as the nation's ruling body. The Palace of Westminster became a kind of cathedral of democracy.

Cost and Hours: Free when Parliament is in session; paid audioguide or guided tour required at other times (see "Tours," below); House of Commons—Oct-late July Mon 14:30-22:30, Tue-Wed 11:30-19:30, Thu 9:30-17:30; House of Lords—Oct-late July Mon-Tue 14:30-22:00, Wed 15:00-22:00, Thu 11:00-19:30; last entry depends on the debates; get the exact schedule at www.parliament.uk.

Tours: On Saturdays and when Parliament is recessed, the only way to enter is by taking a 1.5-hour behind-the-scenes tour—with either an audioguide (£18.50) or a live guide (£25.50). Tours depart every 10 to 15 minutes on a timed-ticket system (Saturdays 9:00-16:30 and most weekdays during recess—days and times vary, so confirm schedule at www.parliament.uk). To guarantee a time slot, book ahead online or by calling 020/7219-4114—same-day tickets are not always available (ticket office open Mon-Fri 10:00-16:00, Sat 9:00-16:30, closed Sun, located in Portcullis House, entrance on Victoria Embankment). To clear security, arrive at the visitor entrance on Cromwell Green 30 minutes before your tour time.

Rick's Tip: *For the* **public galleries** *in either House,* **lines are longest** *at the start of each session, particularly on Wednesdays. For the shortest wait, show up* **later in the afternoon** *(but don't push it, as things sometimes close down early).*

Choosing a House: If you visit only one of the bicameral legislative bodies in session, choose the House of Lords. Though less important politically, the Lords meet in a more ornate room, and the wait time is shorter (likely less than 30 minutes). The House of Commons is where major policy is made, but the room is sparse and wait times are longer (30-60 minutes or more).

❷ SELF-GUIDED TOUR

Enter midway along the west side of the building (across the street from Westminster Abbey), where a tourist ramp leads to the ❶ visitors entrance. Inside, you'll see all the public spaces described in this tour as you transit to the chamber you intend to visit.

• *First, take in the cavernous...*

❷ **Westminster Hall:** This vast hall—covering 16,000 square feet—survived the

The history of the Houses of Parliament spans more than 900 years.

Affording London's Sights

London is one of Europe's most expensive cities. But with its many free museums and affordable plays, you can still enjoy the city without pinching pennies (or pounds).

Free Museums: Free sights include the British Museum, British Library, National Gallery, National Portrait Gallery, Tate Britain, Tate Modern, Imperial War Museum, Victoria and Albert Museum, and the Museum of London. Some museums request a donation of a few pounds, but whether you contribute is up to you.

Free Churches: Smaller churches let worshippers (and tourists) in free, although they may ask for a donation. The big sightseeing churches—Westminster Abbey and St. Paul's—charge admission fees, but offer free evensong services nearly daily (though you can't stick around afterward to sightsee). Westminster Abbey also offers free organ recitals most Sundays.

Other Freebies: London has plenty of free performances, such as lunch concerts at St. Martin-in-the-Fields (see page 51). For other freebies, check out www.whatsfreeinlondon.co.uk. There's no charge to enjoy the pageantry of the Changing of the Guard, rants at Speakers' Corner in Hyde Park (on Sun afternoon), displays at Harrods, the people-watching scene at Covent Garden, and the colorful streets of the East End. It's free to view the legislature at work in the Houses of Parliament. And you can see a bit of the Tower of London by attending Sunday services in its chapel.

Good-Value Tours: The London Walks tours with professional guides (£10) are one of the best deals going. Hop-on, hop-off big-bus tours, while expensive (£32), provide a great overview and include free boat tours as well as city walks. (Or, for the price of a transit ticket, you could get similar views—though no narration—from the top of a double-decker public bus.)

Theater: Compared with Broadway's prices, London's theater is a bargain. Seek out the freestanding TKTS booth at Leicester Square to get discounts from 25 to 30 percent on good seats (see page 88). A £5 "groundling" ticket for a play at Shakespeare's Globe is the best theater deal in town (see page 90).

1834 fire, and is one of the oldest and most important buildings in England. England's legal system was invented in this hall, as this was the major court of the land for 700 years. King Charles I was tried and sentenced to death here. Guy Fawkes was condemned for plotting to blow up the Halls of Parliament in 1605.

• *Walking through the hall and up the stairs, you'll enter the busy world of today's government. You soon reach...*

❸ St. Stephen's Hall: This long, beau-

tifully lit room was the original House of Commons for three centuries (from 1550 until the fire of 1834). Members of Parliament (MPs) sat in church pews—the ruling party on one side of the hall, the opposition on the other.

• *Next, you reach the...*

❹ Central Lobby: This ornate, octagonal, high-vaulted room is often called the "heart of British government," because it sits midway between the House of Commons (to the left) and House of Lords (right). Video monitors list the schedule of meetings and events in this 1,100-room governmental hive. Admire the Palace's carved wood, chandeliers, statues, and floor tiles.

• *This lobby marks the end of the public space where you can wander freely. To see the House of Lords or House of Commons you must wait in line and check your belongings.*

❺ **House of Lords:** When you're called, you'll walk to the Lords Chamber by way of the long Peers' Corridor—referring to the House's 800 unelected members, called "Peers." Paintings on the corridor walls depict the antiauthoritarian spirit brewing under the reign of Charles I. When you reach the House of Lords Chamber, you'll watch the proceedings from the upper-level visitors gallery. Debate may occur among the few Lords who show up at any given time, but these days the Peers' role is largely advisory—they have no real power to pass laws on their own.

The Lords Chamber is impressive, with stained glass and intricately carved walls. At the far end is the gilded throne where the Queen sits once a year to give a speech to open Parliament. In front of the throne sits the woolsack—a cushion stuffed with wool. Here the Lord Speaker presides, with a ceremonial mace behind the backrest. To the Lord Speaker's right are the members of the ruling party (a.k.a. "government"), and to his left are the members of the opposition (the Labour Party). Unaffiliated Crossbenchers sit in between.

❻ **House of Commons:** The Commons Chamber is less grandiose than the Lords', but this is where the sausage is made. The House of Commons is as powerful as the Lords, prime minister, and Queen combined.

Of today's 650-plus MPs, only 450 can sit—the rest have to stand at the ends. As in the House of Lords, the ruling party sits on the right of the Speaker (in his canopied Speaker's Chair), and opposition sits on the left. Keep an eye out for two red lines on the floor, which cannot be crossed when debating the other side. (They're supposedly two sword-lengths apart, to prevent a literal clashing of swords.) The clerks sit at a central table that holds the ceremonial mace, a symbol of the power given to Parliament by the monarch, who is not allowed in the Commons Chamber.

When the prime minister visits, his ministers (or cabinet) join him on the front bench, while lesser MPs (the "backbenchers") sit behind. The prime minister defends his policies while the opposition grumbles and harrumphs in displeasure. It's not unusual for MPs to get out of line and be escorted out by the Serjeant at Arms.

Nearby: Across the street from the Parliament building's St. Stephen's Gate, the **Jewel Tower** is a rare remnant of the old Palace of Westminster, used by kings until Henry VIII. The crude stone tower (1365-1366) contains a fine exhibit on the medieval Westminster Palace and the tower (£4.70, April-Sept daily 10:00-18:00; Oct until 17:00; Nov-March

Big Ben

Sat-Sun 10:00-16:00, closed Mon-Fri; tel. 020/7222-2219). Next to the tower (and free) is a quiet courtyard with picnic-friendly benches.

Big Ben, the 315-foot-high clock tower at the north end of the Palace of Westminster, is named for its 13-ton bell, Ben. The light above the clock is lit when Parliament is in session. The face of the clock is huge—you can actually see the minute hand moving. For a good view of it, walk halfway over Westminster Bridge.

▲▲▲CHURCHILL WAR ROOMS

Take a fascinating walk through the underground headquarters of the British government's WWII fight against the Nazis. It has two parts: the war rooms themselves, and a top-notch museum dedicated to Winston Churchill, who steered the war from here. Pick up the excellent audioguide at the entry, and dive in. The museum's gift shop is great for anyone nostalgic for the 1940s.

Cost and Hours: £19, includes audioguide, advance tickets available online; daily 9:30-18:00, last entry one hour before closing; get rations at the Switch Room café; on King Charles Street, 200 yards off Whitehall, follow the signs, Tube: Westminster, tel. 020/7930-6961, www.iwm.org.uk/churchill.

Visiting the War Rooms and Museum: The 27 **War Rooms,** the heavily fortified nerve center of the British war effort, were used from 1939 to 1945. Churchill's room, the map room, and other rooms are just as they were in 1945. As you fol-

low the one-way route, the audioguide explains each room and offers first-person accounts of wartime happenings here. While the rooms are spartan, you'll see how British gentility survived even as the city was bombarded—posted signs informed those working underground what the weather was like outside, and a cheery notice reminded them to turn off the light switch to conserve electricity.

The **Churchill Museum,** which occupies a large hall amid the war rooms, dissects every aspect of the man behind the famous cigar, bowler hat, and V-for-victory sign. Artifacts, quotes, political cartoons, clear explanations, and interactive exhibits bring the colorful statesman to life. You'll get a taste of Winston's wit, irascibility, work ethic, and drinking habits. The exhibit shows Winston's warts as well: It questions whether his party-switching was just political opportunism, examines the basis for his opposition to Indian self-rule, and reveals him to be an intense taskmaster who worked 18-hour days and was brutal to his staffers (who deeply respected him nevertheless).

Many of the items on display—such as a European map divvied up in permanent marker, which Churchill brought home from the postwar Potsdam Conference—drive home the remarkable span of history this man influenced.

Rick's Tip: *Some sights automatically add a* **"voluntary donation" of about 10 percent** *to their admission fees (those are the prices I give), and some free museums request donations. All such contributions are completely optional.*

On Trafalgar Square

Trafalgar Square, London's central square (worth ▲▲), is at the intersection of Westminster, The City, and the West End. It's the climax of most marches and demonstrations and a thrilling place to simply hang out. At the top of the square

Churchill War Rooms

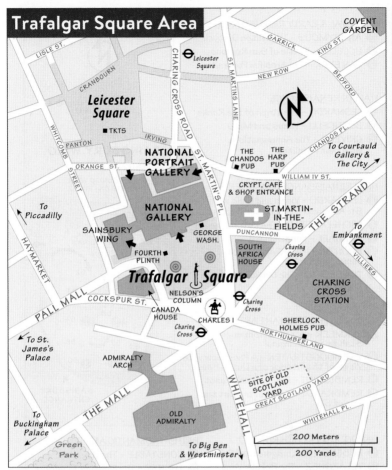

Trafalgar Square Area

COVENT
GARDEN

GARRICK

KING ST.

LISLE ST.

CRANBOURN

NEW ROW

BEDFORD

Leicester
Square

**Leicester
Square**

■ TKTS

IRVING

WHITCOMB STREET

PANTON

ORANGE ST.

**NATIONAL
PORTRAIT
GALLERY**

CHANDOS PL.

THE
CHANDOS
PUB

THE
HARP
PUB

To Courtauld
Gallery &
The City

WILLIAM IV ST.

CRYPT, CAFÉ
& SHOP ENTRANCE

To
Piccadilly

**NATIONAL
GALLERY**

ST.MARTIN-
IN-THE-
FIELDS

THE STRAND

SAINSBURY
WING

GEORGE
WASH.

DUNCANNON

To
Embankment

VILLIERS

HAYMARKET

FOURTH
PLINTH

SOUTH
AFRICA
HOUSE

Charing
Cross

CHARING
CROSS
STATION

Trafalgar ‖ *Square*

NELSON'S
COLUMN

Charing
Cross

PALL MALL

COCKSPUR ST.

CANADA
HOUSE

CHARLES I

Charing
Cross

SHERLOCK
HOLMES PUB

To St.
James's
Palace

Charing
Cross

NORTHUMBERLAND

ADMIRALTY
ARCH

SITE OF OLD
SCOTLAND
YARD

WHITEHALL

GREAT SCOTLAND YARD

To
Buckingham
Palace

THE MALL

OLD
ADMIRALTY

WHITEHALL PL.

Green
Park

To Big Ben
& Westminster

200 Meters

200 Yards

The massive National Gallery is one of the world's great art museums.

MEDIEVAL & EARLY RENAISSANCE
❶ ANONYMOUS – The Wilton Diptych
❷ UCCELLO – Battle of San Romano
❸ VAN EYCK – The Arnolfini Portrait

ITALIAN RENAISSANCE
❹ LEONARDO – The Virgin of the Rocks
❺ BOTTICELLI – Venus and Mars
❻ CRIVELLI – The Annunciation, with Saint Emidius

HIGH RENAISSANCE & MANNERISM
❼ LEONARDO – Virgin and Child with St. Anne and St. John the Baptist
❽ MICHELANGELO – The Entombment
❾ RAPHAEL – Pope Julius II
❿ BRONZINO – An Allegory with Venus and Cupid
⓫ TINTORETTO – The Origin of the Milky Way

NORTHERN PROTESTANT ART
⓬ VERMEER – A Young Woman Standing at a Virginal
⓭ VAN HOOGSTRATEN – A Peepshow with Views of the Interior of a Dutch House
⓮ REMBRANDT – Belshazzar's Feast
⓯ REMBRANDT – Self-Portrait at the Age of 63

BAROQUE & FRENCH ROCOCO
⓰ RUBENS – The Judgment of Paris
⓱ VELÁZQUEZ – The Rokeby Venus
⓲ VAN DYCK – Equestrian Portrait of Charles I
⓳ CARAVAGGIO –The Supper at Emmaus
⓴ BOUCHER – Pan and Syrinx

BRITISH ROMANTIC ART
㉑ CONSTABLE – The Hay Wain
㉒ TURNER – The Fighting Téméraire

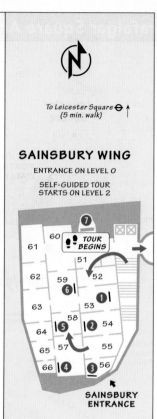

To Leicester Square (5 min. walk)

SAINSBURY WING
ENTRANCE ON LEVEL 0

SELF-GUIDED TOUR
STARTS ON LEVEL 2

TOUR BEGINS

SAINSBURY ENTRANCE

(north) sits the domed National Gallery with its grand staircase, and to the right, the steeple of St. Martin-in-the-Fields, built in 1722. In the center of the square, Lord Horatio Nelson stands atop a 185-foot-tall fluted granite column, gazing out toward Trafalgar, where he lost his life but defeated the French fleet. Part of this 1842 memorial is made from his victims' melt-ed-down cannons. He's surrounded by spraying fountains, giant lions, and hordes of people (Tube: Charing Cross).

▲▲▲NATIONAL GALLERY
Displaying an unsurpassed collection of European paintings from 1250 to 1900—including works by Leonardo, Botticelli, Velázquez, Rembrandt, Turner, Van Gogh, and the Impressionists—this is one of

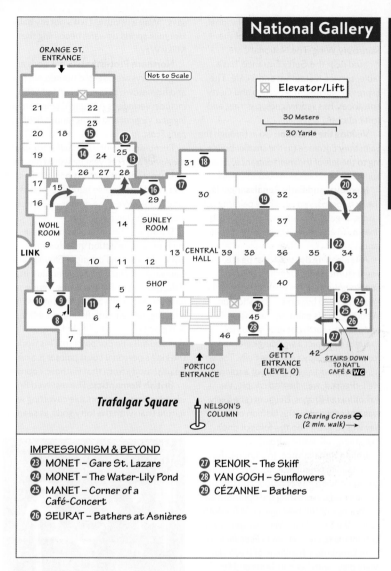

National Gallery

ORANGE ST.
ENTRANCE

Not to Scale

⊠ Elevator/Lift

30 Meters
30 Yards

21 22
23
20 18 **15**
19 **14** 24 25 **12**
13
26 27 28 31 **18**

17 15 **16** **17**
16 29 30 32 **20**
33

WOHL 14 SUNLEY
ROOM ROOM 37
9
LINK 13 CENTRAL 39 38 36 35 **22**
10 11 12 HALL 34
21
5 SHOP 40
10 **9** **11** **23** **24**
8 4 **29** **25** 41
8 6 45 **26**
7 46 **28**
27
42
STAIRS DOWN
TO NAT'L
PORTICO GETTY CAFÉ & **WC**
ENTRANCE ENTRANCE
(LEVEL 0)

Trafalgar Square NELSON'S
COLUMN
To Charing Cross ⊖
(2 min. walk)→

IMPRESSIONISM & BEYOND
23 MONET – Gare St. Lazare
24 MONET – The Water-Lily Pond
25 MANET – Corner of a
Café-Concert
26 SEURAT – Bathers at Asnières

27 RENOIR – The Skiff
28 VAN GOGH – Sunflowers
29 CÉZANNE – Bathers

Europe's great galleries.

Cost and Hours: Free, but £20 suggested donation, special exhibits extra, daily 10:00-18:00, Fri until 21:00, last entry to special exhibits 45 minutes before closing, on Trafalgar Square, Tube: Charing Cross or Leicester Square, tel. 020/7747-2885, www.nationalgallery.org.uk.

Tours: Free one-hour overview tours leave from the Sainsbury Wing information desk daily at 11:30 and 14:30, plus Fri at 19:00. The £4 audioguides are excellent—choose from the one-hour highlights tour, several theme tours, or a tour option that lets you dial up any painting in the museum. You can get a helpful £1 floor plan from the info desk.

Eating: Consider splitting afternoon

tea at the excellent-but-pricey National Dining Rooms, on the first floor of the Sainsbury Wing. The National Café, located near the Getty Entrance, has a table-service restaurant and a café. The Espresso Bar, near the Portico and Getty entrances, has sandwiches, pastries, and soft couches.

Visiting the Museum: Go in through the Sainsbury Entrance (in the smaller building to the left of the main entrance), and approach the collection chronologically.

Medieval and Early Renaissance: In the first rooms, you see shiny paintings of saints, angels, Madonnas, and crucifixions floating in an ethereal gold never-never land.

After leaving this gold-leaf peace, you'll stumble into Uccello's *Battle of San Romano* and Van Eyck's *The Arnolfini Portrait,* called by some "The Shotgun Wedding." This painting—a masterpiece of down-to-earth details—was once thought to depict a wedding ceremony forced by the lady's swelling belly. Today it's understood as a portrait of a solemn, well-dressed, well-heeled couple, the Arnolfinis of Bruges, Belgium (she likely was not pregnant—the fashion of the day was to gather up the folds of one's extremely full-skirted dress).

Italian Renaissance: In painting, the Renaissance meant realism. Artists rediscovered the beauty of nature and the human body, expressing the optimism and confidence of this new age. Look for Botticelli's *Venus and Mars,* Michelangelo's *The Entombment,* and Raphael's *Pope Julius II.*

In Leonardo's *The Virgin of the Rocks,* Mary plays with her son Jesus and little Johnny the Baptist (with cross, at left) while an androgynous angel looks on. Leonardo brings this holy scene right down to earth by setting it among rocks, stalactites, water, and flowering plants.

In *The Origin of the Milky Way,* by Venetian Renaissance painter Tintoretto, the god Jupiter places his illegitimate son, baby Hercules, at his wife's breast. Juno says, "Wait a minute. That's not my baby!" Her milk spurts upward, becoming the Milky Way.

Northern Protestant: Greek gods and Virgin Marys are out, and hometown folks and hometown places are in. Highlights include Vermeer's *A Young Woman Standing at a Virginal* and Rembrandt's *Belshazzar's Feast.*

Rembrandt painted his *Self-Portrait at the Age of 63* in the year he would die. He was bankrupt, his mistress had just passed away, and he had also buried several of his children. We see a disillusioned, wellworn, but proud old genius.

Baroque: The museum's outstanding Baroque collection includes Van Dyck's *Equestrian Portrait of Charles I* and Caravaggio's *The Supper at Emmaus.* In Velázquez's *The Rokeby Venus,* Venus lounges diagonally across the canvas, admiring herself, with flaring red, white, and gray fabrics to highlight her rosy white skin and inflame our passion. This work by the king's personal court painter is a rare Spanish nude from that Catholic country.

British Romantics: The reserved British were more comfortable cavorting with nature than with the lofty gods, as seen in

Van Eyck, The Arnolfini Portrait

Constable's *The Hay Wain* and Turner's *The Fighting Téméraire*. Turner's messy, colorful style influenced the Impressionists and gives us our first glimpse into the modern art world.

Impressionism: At the end of the 19th century, a new breed of artists burst out of the stuffy confines of the studio. They set up their canvases in farmers' fields or carried their notebooks into crowded cafés, dashing off quick sketches in order to catch a momentary...impression. Check out works such as Monet's *Gare St. Lazare* and *The Water-Lily Pond,* Renoir's *The Skiff,* Seurat's *Bathers at Asnières,* and Van Gogh's *Sunflowers.*

Cézanne's *Bathers* are arranged in strict triangles. Cézanne uses the Impressionist technique of building a figure with dabs of paint (though his "dabs" are often larger-sized "cube" shapes) to make solid, 3-D geometrical figures in the style of the Renaissance. In the process, he helped inspire a radical new style—Cubism—bringing art into the 20th century.

▲▲NATIONAL PORTRAIT GALLERY

While some might consider this as interesting as someone else's yearbook, a selective walk through this 500-year-long Who's Who of British history is quick and free, and puts faces on the history of England. The collection is well-described, not huge, and in historical sequence, from the 16th century to today's royal family. Highlights include Henry VIII and wives; portraits of the "Virgin Queen" Elizabeth I, Sir Francis Drake, and Sir Walter Raleigh; the only real-life portrait of William Shakespeare; Oliver Cromwell and Charles I with his head on; Queen Victoria and her era; and the present royal family, including the late Princess Diana and the current Duchess of Cambridge, Kate.

Cost and Hours: Free, but £5 suggested donation, special exhibits extra; daily 10:00-18:00, Thu-Fri until 21:00, first and second floors open Mon at 11:00, last entry to special exhibits one hour before closing; audioguide-£3, no photos, basement café and top-floor view restaurant; entry 100 yards off Trafalgar Square (around the corner from National Gallery, opposite Church of St. Martin-in-the-Fields), Tube: Charing Cross or Leicester Square, tel. 020/7306-0055, recorded info tel. 020/7312-2463, www.npg.org.uk.

▲ST. MARTIN-IN-THE-FIELDS

The church, built in the 1720s with a Gothic spire atop a Greek-type temple, is an oasis of peace on noisy Trafalgar Square. St. Martin cared for the poor. "In the fields" was where the first church stood on this spot in the 13th century, between Westminster and The City. Inside, you still see the church's compassion for the needy. The modern east window—with grillwork bent into the shape of a warped cross—was installed in 2008 to replace one damaged in World War II.

A freestanding glass pavilion to the left of the church serves as the entrance to its underground areas. There you'll find the concert ticket office, a gift shop, a brass-rubbing center, and the recommended support-the-church Café in the Crypt.

Cost and Hours: Free, but donations

Princess Diana's portrait at the National Portrait Gallery

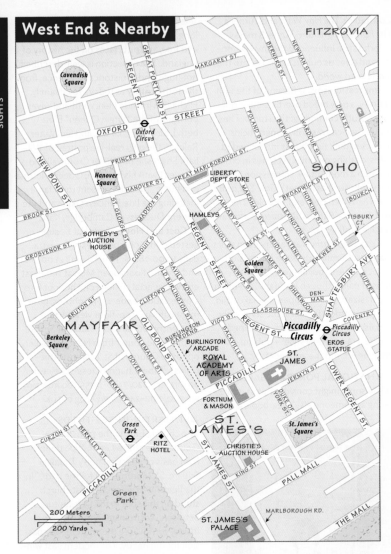

West End & Nearby

FITZROVIA

Cavendish
Square

OXFORD STREET

Oxford
Circus

PRINCES ST.

SOHO

Hanover
Square

HANOVER ST.

LIBERTY
DEP'T STORE

NEW BOND ST.

HAMLEYS

BROOK ST.

SOTHEBY'S
AUCTION
HOUSE

GROSVENOR ST.

CONDUIT ST.

Golden
Square

SHAFTESBURY AVE.

MAYFAIR

Berkeley
Square

OLD BOND ST.

BURLINGTON
GARDENS

VIGO ST.

Piccadilly
Circus

Piccadilly
Circus

EROS
STATUE

BURLINGTON
ARCADE

ROYAL
ACADEMY
OF ARTS

PICCADILLY

ST.
JAMES

FORTNUM
& MASON

LOWER REGENT ST.

Green
Park

ST.
JAMES'S

St. James's
Square

RITZ
HOTEL

CHRISTIE'S
AUCTION HOUSE

PALL MALL

PICCADILLY

Green
Park

200 Meters

200 Yards

MARLBOROUGH RD.

THE MALL

ST. JAMES'S
PALACE

welcome; hours vary but generally Mon-
Fri 8:30–13:00 & 14:00–18:00, Sat 9:30–
18:00, Sun 15:30–17:00; services listed
at entrance; Tube: Charing Cross, tel.
020/7766-1100, www.smitf.org.

Rick's Tip: St. Martin-in-the-Fields *is
famous for its* **concerts.** *Consider a free
lunchtime concert (£3.50 suggested donation; Mon, Tue, and Fri at 13:00), an evening*

*concert (£8-28, several weeknights at 19:30),
or* **Wednesday night jazz** *(£5.50-12,
Wed at 20:00). See www.smitf.org for the
schedule.*

The West End and Nearby
▲▲COVENT GARDEN
This large square teems with people
and street performers—jugglers, sword

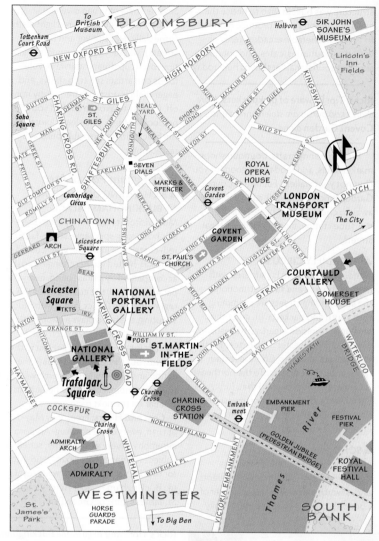

swallowers, and guitar players. London's buskers (including those in the Tube) are auditioned, licensed, and assigned times and places where they are allowed to perform.

The square's centerpiece is a covered marketplace. A market has been here since medieval times, when it was the "convent" garden owned by Westminster Abbey. Today's fine iron-and-glass

Covent Garden

structure was built in 1830 to house the stalls of London's chief produce market. In 1973, its venerable arcades were converted to boutiques, cafés, and antique shops. A tourist market thrives here today.

Rick's Tip: Beware of pickpockets. *More than 7,500 purses are stolen annually at* **Covent Garden** *alone.*

Browse trendy crafts, boutique shops, market stalls, and food that's good for you (but not your wallet). For better Covent Garden lunch deals, walk a block or two away to check out the places north of the Tube station, along Endell and Neal streets.

▲PICCADILLY CIRCUS

Although this square is slathered with neon billboards and tacky attractions, the surrounding streets are swimming with youth and packed with great shopping opportunities. Nearby Shaftesbury Avenue and Leicester Square teem with fun-seekers, theaters, Chinese restaurants, and street singers. To the northeast is Chinatown and, beyond that, funky Soho. And curling to the northwest from Piccadilly Circus is genteel Regent Street, lined with exclusive shops.

▲SOHO

North of Piccadilly, seedy Soho has become trendy—with many restaurants—and is worth a gawk. It's the epicenter of London's colorful youth scene, a funky

Sesame Street of urban diversity.

Soho is also London's red light district (especially near Brewer and Berwick streets), where "friendly models" wait in tiny rooms up dreary stairways, voluptuous con artists sell strip shows, and eager male tourists are frequently ripped off. It's easy to avoid trouble if you're not looking for it. The sleazy joints share the block with respectable pubs and restaurants.

Buckingham Palace Area
▲▲CHANGING OF THE GUARD AT BUCKINGHAM PALACE

Most visitors to London want to see this hour-long spectacle: stone-faced, red-coated (or, in winter, gray-coated), bearskin-hatted guards changing posts accompanied by a brass band. Everyone parades around, the guard passes the regimental flag (or "colour") with much shouting, the band plays a happy little concert, and then they march out. Most tourists just show up and get lost in the crowds, but those who anticipate the action and know where to perch will enjoy the event more. Follow the timeline in the sidebar on the next page.

Cost and Hours: Free, daily May-July at 11:30, every other day Aug-April, no ceremony in very wet weather; schedule subject to change—call 020/7766-7300 for the day's plan, or check www.royal.gov.uk; Buckingham Palace, Tube: Victoria, St. James's Park, or Green Park.

Rick's Tip: *Want to go inside* **Buckingham Palace?** *It's* **open to the public only in August and September,** *when the Queen is out of town (£22 for State Rooms; Aug-Sept daily from 9:15, last admission 17:15 in Aug and 16:15 in Sept; book timed-entry ticket in advance by phone, tel. 0303/123-7300, or online, www.royalcollection.org.uk).*

Sightseeing Strategies: The action takes place in stages over the course of

Piccadilly Circus

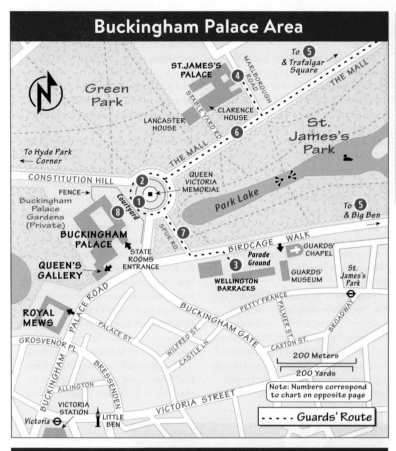

Buckingham Palace Area

Green
Park

To ⑤
& Trafalgar
Square

MARLBOROUGH ROAD

THE MALL

ST. JAMES'S
PALACE ④

LANCASTER
HOUSE

STABLE YARD RD.

CLARENCE
HOUSE ⑥

St.
James's
Park

To Hyde Park
← Corner

THE MALL

CONSTITUTION HILL

② QUEEN
VICTORIA
MEMORIAL

Park Lake

FENCE →

Buckingham
Palace
Gardens
(Private)

Courtyard

① ⑧

SPUR RD.

⑦

To ⑤
& Big Ben

BUCKINGHAM
PALACE

STATE
ROOMS
ENTRANCE

BIRDCAGE WALK

GUARDS'
CHAPEL ✚

QUEEN'S
GALLERY

③ Parade
Ground

WELLINGTON
BARRACKS

GUARDS'
MUSEUM

St.
James's
Park

ROYAL
MEWS

PALACE ROAD

PALACE ST.

BUCKINGHAM GATE

PETTY FRANCE

PALMER ST.

BROADWAY

GROSVENOR PL.

BRESSENDEN

WILFRED ST.

CASTLE LN.

CAXTON ST.

200 Meters

200 Yards

ALLINGTON

BUCKINGHAM

VICTORIA STREET

Note: Numbers correspond
to chart on opposite page

Victoria ⊖

VICTORIA
STATION

LITTLE
BEN

- - - - Guards' Route

Changing of the Guard Timeline

10:30	Arrive now for a spot front and center by the ① fence outside Buckingham Palace.
11:00-11:15	② Victoria Memorial gets crowded. "New Guard" gathers for inspection at ③ Wellington Barracks. "Old Guard" gathers at ④ St. James's Palace.
11:00 (10:00 Sun)	Changing of the Horse Guard at ⑤ Horse Guards Parade.
11:00-11:30	Tired St. James's Palace guards march down ⑥ the Mall toward Buckingham Palace. Replacement troops head from Wellington Barracks down ⑦ Spur Road to the palace. All guards gradually converge around the Victoria Memorial.
11:30-12:00	Changing of the Guard ceremony takes place inside ⑧ the palace courtyard.

an hour, at several different locations; see map on page 55. Here are a few options to consider:

Watch near the Palace: The main event is in the forecourt right in front of Buckingham Palace (between Buckingham Palace and the fence) from 11:30 to 12:00. Arrive no later than 10:30 to get a place front and center, next to the fence. Get right up front along the road or fence, or find some raised elevation to stand or sit on—a balustrade or a curb—so you can see over people's heads.

Watch near the Victoria Memorial: The high ground around the circular Victoria Memorial gives good (if more distant) views of the palace as well as the arriving and departing parades along The Mall and Spur Road. Come before 11:00 to get a place.

Watch near St. James's Palace: If you don't feel like jostling for a view, stroll down to St. James's Palace and wait near the corner for a great photo-op. At about 12:15, the parade marches up The Mall to the palace and performs a smaller changing ceremony—with almost no crowds.

Follow the Procession: You won't get the closest views, but you'll get something even better—the thrill of participating in the action. Start with the "Old Guard" mobilizing in the courtyard of St. James's Palace (11:00). Arrive early, and grab a spot just across the road (otherwise you'll be asked to move when the inspection begins). Just before they prepare to leave (at 11:13), march ahead of them down Marlborough Street to The Mall. Pause here to watch them parade past, band and all, on their way to the Palace, then cut through the park and head to the Wellington Barracks—where the "New Guard" is getting ready to leave for Buckingham (11:27). March along with full military band and fresh guards from the barracks to the Palace. At 11:30 the two guard groups meet in the courtyard, the band plays a few songs, and soldiers parade and finally exchange compliments before returning to Wellington Barracks and St. James's Palace (12:10). Use this time to snap a few photos of the guards before making your way across The Mall to Clarence House (on Stable Yard Road), where you'll see the "New Guard" pass one last time on their way to St. James's Palace. On their

The Changing of the Guard is all about pomp and ceremony.

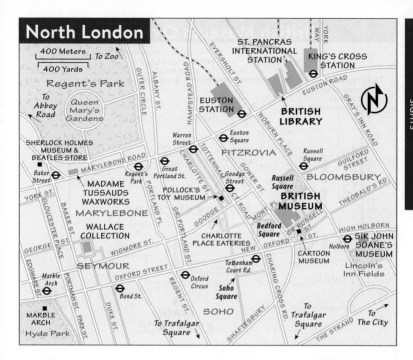

North London

400 Meters
400 Yards

To Zoo

To Abbey Road

Regent's Park

Queen Mary's Gardens

OUTER CIRCLE

ALBANY ST.

HAMPSTEAD ROAD

EVERSHOLT ST.

WAY

YORK WAY

ST. PANCRAS INTERNATIONAL STATION

KING'S CROSS STATION

EUSTON ROAD

GRAY'S INN ROAD

EUSTON STATION

BRITISH LIBRARY

WOBURN PLACE

SHERLOCK HOLMES MUSEUM & BEATLES STORE

MARYLEBONE ROAD

Warren Street

Euston Square

FITZROVIA

Russell Square

GUILFORD STREET

Baker Street

Regent's Park

Great Portland St.

CHARLOTTE ST.

TOTTENHAM CT. ROAD

GOWER ST.

Goodge Street

Russell Square

BLOOMSBURY

THEOBALD'S RD.

MADAME TUSSAUDS WAXWORKS

YORK ST.

GLOUCESTER PL.

BAKER ST.

PORTLAND PL.

POLLOCK'S TOY MUSEUM

Goodge Street

BRITISH MUSEUM

MARYLEBONE

WALLACE COLLECTION

GEORGE ST.

WIGMORE ST.

GT. PORTLAND ST.

CHARLOTTE PLACE EATERIES

NEW OXFORD ST.

Bedford Square

GT. RUSSELL ST.

HIGH HOLBORN

SIR JOHN SOANE'S MUSEUM

Holborn

Lincoln's Inn Fields

SEYMOUR

Marble Arch

OXFORD STREET

Tottenham Court Rd.

CHARING CROSS RD.

CARTOON MUSEUM

EDGWARE RD.

PORTMAN ST.

PARK ST.

DUKE ST.

REGENT ST.

BOND ST.

Oxford Circus

Bond St.

Soho Square

SOHO

SHAFTESBURY AV.

To Trafalgar Square

MARBLE ARCH

Hyde Park

To Trafalgar Square

To Trafalgar Square

To The City

THE STRAND

way, the final piece of ceremony takes place—one member of the "Old Guard" and one member of the first-relief "New Guard" change places here.

Join a Tour: Local tour companies such as **Fun London Tours** more or less follow the self-guided route above but add in history and facts about the guards, bands, and royal family to their already entertaining march (£15, tour starts at Piccadilly Circus at 10:00, must book online in advance, www.funlondontours.com).

North London

▲▲▲BRITISH MUSEUM

This is the greatest chronicle of civilization...anywhere. A visit here is like taking a long hike through *Encyclopedia Britannica* National Park. The vast British Museum is wrapped around its huge entrance hall—the Great Court—with the most popular sections filling the ground floor: Egyptian, Assyrian, and ancient Greek, with the famous frieze sculptures from

the Parthenon in Athens. The museum's stately Reading Room sometimes hosts special exhibits.

Cost and Hours: Free but £5 suggested donation, special exhibits usually extra; daily 10:00-17:30, Fri until 20:30 (selected galleries only), least crowded late on weekday afternoons; Great Russell Street, Tube: Tottenham Court Road, tel. 020/7323-8299, www.britishmuseum.org.

Tours: Free 30-minute **EyeOpener tours** are led by volunteers, who focus on select rooms (daily 11:00-15:45, generally

British Museum

LONDON
SIGHTS

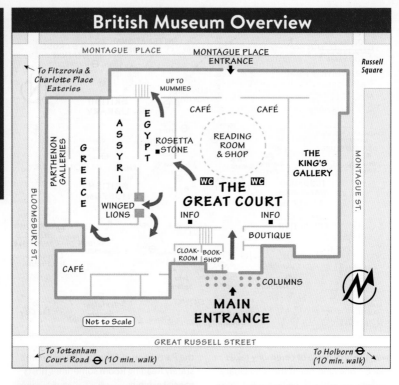

British Museum Overview

MONTAGUE PLACE

MONTAGUE PLACE
ENTRANCE

Russell
Square

← To Fitzrovia &
Charlotte Place
Eateries

UP TO
MUMMIES

CAFÉ   CAFÉ

EGYPT

ASSYRIA

ROSETTA
STONE

READING
ROOM
& SHOP

THE
KING'S
GALLERY

**PARTHENON
GALLERIES**

GREECE

WINGED
LIONS

WC **THE
GREAT COURT** WC

INFO   INFO

BOUTIQUE

MONTAGUE ST.

BLOOMSBURY ST.

CLOAK-
ROOM

BOOK-
SHOP

CAFÉ

COLUMNS

**MAIN
ENTRANCE**

Not to Scale

GREAT RUSSELL STREET

← To Tottenham
Court Road ⊖ (10 min. walk)

To Holborn ⊖ →
(10 min. walk)

A mummy case

every 15 minutes). Free 45-minute **gallery talks** on specific subjects are offered Tue-Sat at 13:15; a free 20-minute highlights tour is available on Friday evening. The £5 **multimedia guide** offers commentary on 200 objects, as well as several theme tours (must leave photo ID). There's also a fun children's multimedia guide. Or 🎧 download my free **audio tour**—see page 14.

⊙ SELF-GUIDED TOUR

From the Great Court, doorways lead to all wings. To the left are the exhibits on Egypt, Assyria, and Greece—the highlights of your visit.

EGYPT

Egypt was one of the world's first civilizations. The Egypt we think of—pyramids, pharaohs, and guys who walk funny—lasted from 3000 to 1000 B.C. with hardly any change in the government, religion, or arts. Imagine two millennia of Bush.

The first thing you'll see is the **Rosetta Stone.** When this black slab (dating from 196 B.C.) was unearthed in the Egyptian desert in 1799, it caused a sensation in Europe and led to a quantum leap in the study of ancient history. It contains a single inscription repeated in three languages. The bottom third is plain old Greek, while the middle is medieval Egyptian. By comparing the two known languages with the one they didn't know, translators figured out the hieroglyphics. Finally, Egyptian writing could be decoded.

Next, wander past the many **statues,** including a seven-ton Ramesses, with the traditional features of a pharaoh (goatee, cloth headdress, and cobra diadem on his forehead). When Moses told the king of Egypt "Let my people go!," this was the stony-faced look he got. You'll also see the Egyptian gods as animals—including Amun, king of the gods, as a ram, and Horus, the god of the living, as a falcon.

At the end of the hall, climb the stairs to **mummy** land (use the elevator if it's running). To mummify a body, you first disembowel it (but leave the heart inside), then pack the cavities with pitch, and dry it with natron, a natural form of sodium carbonate (and, I believe, the active ingredient in Twinkies). Then carefully bandage it head to toe with hundreds of yards of linen strips. Let it sit 2,000 years, and...*voilà!* The mummy was placed in a wooden coffin, which was put in a stone coffin, which was placed in a tomb. The result is that we now have Egyptian bodies that are as well preserved as Larry King. Many of the mummies here are from the time of the Roman occupation, when fine memorial portraits painted in wax became popular. X-ray photos in the display cases tell us more about these people. Don't miss the animal mummies. Cats were considered incarnations of the cat-headed goddess Bastet. Worshipped in life, preserved in death, and memorialized with statues, cats were given the adulation they've come to expect ever since.

ASSYRIA

The British Museum's valuable collection of Assyrian artifacts has become even more priceless since the recent destruction of ancient sites in the Middle East by ISIS terrorists. Long before Saddam Hussein, Iraq was home to other palace-building, iron-fisted rulers—the Assyrians, who conquered their southern neighbors and dominated the Middle East for 300 years (c. 900-600 B.C.). Their strength came from a superb army (chariots, mounted cavalry, and siege engines), a policy of terrorism against enemies, ethnic cleansing, and efficient administration (roads and express postal service).

Standing guard over the exhibit halls are two human-headed **winged lions** from an Assyrian palace (11th-8th century B.C.). With the strength of a lion, the wings of an eagle, the brain of a man, and the beard of ZZ Top, they protected the king from evil spirits and scared the heck out of foreign ambassadors and left-wing journalists. (What has five legs and flies? Take a close look. These winged quintupeds, which appear complete from both the front and the side, could guard both directions at once.)

Carved into the stone between the bearded lions' loins, you can see one of

Assyrian human-headed lions

civilization's most impressive achievements. This wedge-shaped **(cuneiform)** script is the world's first written language, invented 5,000 years ago by the Sumerians and passed down to their less-civilized descendants, the Assyrians.

The **Nimrud Gallery** is a mini version of the throne room and royal apartments of King Ashurnasirpal II's Northwest Palace at Nimrud (9th century B.C.). It's filled with royal propaganda reliefs, 30-ton marble bulls, and panels depicting wounded lions (lion-hunting was Assyria's sport of kings).

GREECE

During their civilization's Golden Age (500-430 B.C.), the ancient Greeks set the tone for all of Western civilization to follow. Democracy, theater, literature, mathematics, philosophy, science, gyros, art, and architecture, as we know them, were virtually all invented by a single generation of Greeks in a small town of maybe 80,000 citizens.

Your walk through Greek art history starts with pottery, usually painted red and black. The earliest featured geometric patterns (eighth century B.C.), then a painted black silhouette on the natural orange clay, then a red figure on a black background. Later, painted vases show a culture really into partying.

The highlight is the **Parthenon Sculptures,** taken from the temple dedicated to Athena—the crowning glory of an enormous urban-renewal plan during Greece's Golden Age. The sculptures are also called the Elgin Marbles for the shrewd British ambassador who had his men hammer, chisel, and saw them off the Parthenon in the early 1800s. Though the Greek government complains about losing its marbles, the Brits feel they rescued and preserved the sculptures. These much-wrangled-over bits of the Parthenon (from about 450 B.C.) are indeed impressive. The marble panels lining the walls of this large hall are part of the frieze that originally ran around the exterior of the Parthenon, under the eaves. The statues at either end of the hall once filled the Parthenon's triangular-shaped pediments and showed the birth of Athena. Decorative relief panels tell the story of the struggle between the forces of human civilization and barbarism.

THE REST OF THE MUSEUM

Venture upstairs to see artifacts from **Roman Britain** that surpass anything

Admiring the ancient Greek Parthenon sculptures at the British Museum

you'll see at Hadrian's Wall or elsewhere in the country. Also look for the Sutton Hoo Ship Burial artifacts from a seventh-century royal burial on the east coast of England (Room 41). A rare Michelangelo cartoon (preliminary sketch) is in Room 90 (level 4).

▲▲▲ BRITISH LIBRARY

Here, in just two rooms, are the literary treasures of Western civilization, from early Bibles, to Shakespeare's *Hamlet,* to Lewis Carroll's *Alice's Adventures in Wonderland,* to the Magna Carta. You'll see the Lindisfarne Gospels transcribed on an illuminated manuscript, Beatles lyrics scrawled on the back of a greeting card, and Leonardo da Vinci's genius sketched into his notebooks. The British Empire built its greatest monuments out of paper.

Cost and Hours: Free, but £5 suggested donation, fee for some special exhibits; Mon-Fri 9:30-18:00, Tue until 20:00, Sat 9:30-17:00, Sun 11:00-17:00; 96 Euston Road, Tube: King's Cross St. Pancras or Euston, tel. 019/3754-6060 or 020/7412-7676, www.bl.uk.

Tours: There are no guided tours or audioguides for the permanent collection, but you can 🎧 download my free British Library **audio tour** (see page 14). There are guided tours of the building itself—the archives and reading rooms. Touchscreens in the permanent collection let you page virtually through some of the rare books.

➲ SELF-GUIDED TOUR

Everything that matters for your visit is in the delightful Sir John Ritblat Gallery and an adjacent room. We'll concentrate on a handful of documents—literary and historical—that changed the course of history. Exhibits change often, and many of the museum's old, fragile manuscripts need to "rest" periodically in order to stay well preserved.

Start at the far side of the Ritblat Gallery and the display case of historic ❶ **maps** showing how humans' perspective of the world expanded over the centuries. Next, move into the area dedicated to ❷ **sacred texts and early Bibles** from several cultures. This section includes the oldest complete Bibles in existence. In the display cases called ❸ **Art of the Book,** you'll find illuminated Bibles from the early medieval period, including the Lindisfarne Gospels (A.D. 698). Look out

The British Library is filled with treasures ranging from the Magna Carta to Beatles song sheets.

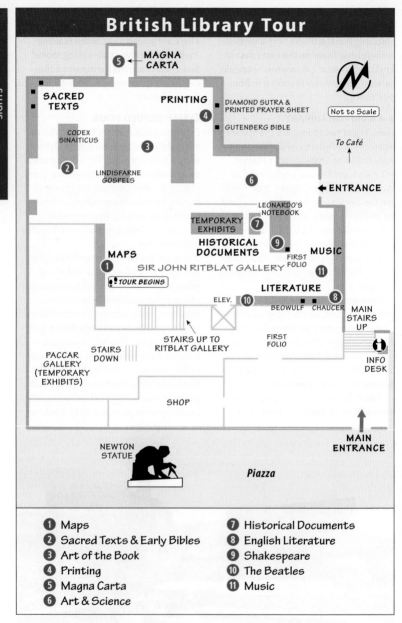

British Library Tour

MAGNA CARTA

SACRED TEXTS

PRINTING

DIAMOND SUTRA & PRINTED PRAYER SHEET

GUTENBERG BIBLE

Not to Scale

To Café

CODEX SINAITICUS

LINDISFARNE GOSPELS

ENTRANCE

LEONARDO'S NOTEBOOK

TEMPORARY EXHIBITS

HISTORICAL DOCUMENTS

MAPS

SIR JOHN RITBLAT GALLERY

FIRST FOLIO

MUSIC

TOUR BEGINS

LITERATURE

ELEV.

BEOWULF   CHAUCER

MAIN STAIRS UP

STAIRS UP TO RITBLAT GALLERY

STAIRS DOWN

FIRST FOLIO

INFO DESK

PACCAR GALLERY (TEMPORARY EXHIBITS)

SHOP

NEWTON STATUE

MAIN ENTRANCE

Piazza

① Maps
② Sacred Texts & Early Bibles
③ Art of the Book
④ Printing
⑤ Magna Carta
⑥ Art & Science
⑦ Historical Documents
⑧ English Literature
⑨ Shakespeare
⑩ The Beatles
⑪ Music

for some of the first-ever English translations of the Bible.

In the glass cases featuring early **printing,** you'll see the Diamond Sutra (c. 868), the world's earliest complete, printed book, and the Gutenberg Bible, the first book printed in Europe using movable type (c. 1455).

Through a nearby doorway is a small room that holds the ❺ **Magna Carta,** assuming it's not "resting." The basis for England's constitutional system of government, this "Great Charter" listing rules about mundane administrative issues was radical because of the simple fact that the king had agreed to abide by them as law.

Return to the main room to find display cases featuring ❻ **art and science.** Pages from Leonardo da Vinci's notebook show his powerful curiosity, his genius for invention, and his famous backward and inside-out handwriting. Nearby are many more ❼ **historical documents.** The displays change frequently, but you may see letters by Henry VIII, Queen Elizabeth I, Darwin, Freud, Gandhi, and others.

Next, trace the evolution of ❽ **English literature.** Check out the A.D. 1000 manuscript of *Beowulf,* the first English literary masterpiece, and *The Canterbury Tales* (c. 1410), Geoffrey Chaucer's bawdy collection of stories. The Literature wall is often a greatest-hits sampling of literature in English, from Brontë to Kipling to Woolf to Joyce to Dickens. The most famous of England's writers—❾ **Shakespeare**—generally gets his own display case. Look for the First Folio—one of the 750 copies of the first nearly complete collection of his plays, printed in 1623.

Now fast-forward a few centuries to ❿ **The Beatles.** Find photos of John Lennon, Paul McCartney, George Harrison, and Ringo Starr before and after their fame, as well as manuscripts of song lyrics written by Lennon and McCartney. In the ⓫ **music** section, there are manuscripts by Mozart, Beethoven, Schubert, and others (kind of an anticlimax after the Fab Four, I know). George Frideric Handel's famous oratorio, the *Messiah* (1741), is often on display and marks the end of our tour. Hallelujah.

Lewis Carroll's manuscript for Alice's Adventures in Wonderland

The only known manuscript of the epic saga Beowulf

▲MADAME TUSSAUDS WAXWORKS

This waxtravaganza is gimmicky, crass, crowded, and crazily expensive, but dang fun. The original Madame Tussaud did wax casts of heads lopped off during the French Revolution (such as Marie Antoinette's) and took her show on the road before ending up in London in 1835. Today, a visit is all about photo-ops with eerily realistic wax dummies—squeezing Leonardo DiCaprio's bum, singing with Lady Gaga, and partying with Brangelina. You can also tour a hokey haunted-house exhibit; learn how they created this waxy army; cruise through a kid-pleasing "Spirit of London" time trip; and visit with Marvel superheroes. A nine-minute "4-D" show features a 3-D movie heightened by wind, "back ticklers," and other special effects.

Rick's Tip: *To* skip Madame Tussauds' ticket-buying line *(which can be an hour or more), purchase a Fast Track ticket (from souvenir stands, tourist shops, or the TI) or consider getting the pricey* Priority Entrance *ticket and reserving a time slot at least a day in advance. If you* arrive after 15:00, *the crowds—which can mob popular exhibits—thin out a bit.*

Cost: £34, kids—£29.80 (free for kids under 5), family passes available online; up to 25 percent discount and shorter lines if you buy tickets on their website (also consider a combo-deal with the London Eye).

Hours: Mid-June-Aug and school

The Beatles at Madame Tussauds

holidays daily 8:30-19:30, Sept-mid-June Mon-Fri 9:30-17:30, Sat-Sun 9:00-18:00, these are last entry times—closing is roughly two hours later; Marylebone Road, Tube: Baker Street, tel. 0871-894-3000, www.madametussauds.com.

The City

When Londoners say "The City," they mean the one-square-mile business center in East London that 2,000 years ago was Roman Londinium. The outline of the Roman city walls can still be seen in the arc of roads from Blackfriars Bridge to Tower Bridge.

🎧 Download my free audio tour of The City, which peels back the many layers of history in this oldest part of London (see page 14).

▲▲▲ST. PAUL'S CATHEDRAL

There's been a church on this spot since 604. After the Great Fire of 1666 destroyed the old cathedral, Sir Christopher Wren replaced it with this Baroque masterpiece. Since World War II, St. Paul's has been Britain's symbol of resilience. Despite 57 nights of bombing, the Nazis failed to destroy the cathedral, thanks to volunteer fire watchmen who stayed on the dome.

Even now, as skyscrapers encroach, the 365-foot-high dome of St. Paul's rises majestically above the rooftops of the neighborhood. The tall dome is set on classical columns, capped with a lantern, topped by a six-foot ball, and iced with a cross. As the first Anglican cathedral built in London after the Reformation, it is Baroque: St. Peter's in Rome filtered through clear-eyed English reason. Though often the site of historic funerals (such as Queen Victoria's and Winston Churchill's), St. Paul's most famous recent ceremony was the wedding between Prince Charles and Lady Diana Spencer in 1981.

Cost and Hours: £18, £16 if purchased in advance online, includes church entry, dome climb, crypt, tour, and audioguide;

St. Paul's Cathedral

ENTER →

To
St. Paul's ⊖

To →
One New Change
Terrace View

5

11

10

6

DOME
3

1

2

NAVE

CHOIR **4**

HIGH
ALTAR

7

10

8

11

9

BISHOP'S
CHAIR

STAIRS

30 Meters

30 Yards

To
Millennium
Bridge ↓

N

1 Nave
2 Wellington Monument
3 Dome
4 Choir & High Altar
5 HUNT–The Light of the World
6 MOORE–Mother and Child

7 American Memorial
(Jesus Chapel)
8 John Donne Statue
9 Nelson & Cornwallis Monuments
10 Climb the Dome (2 entrances)
11 Crypt Entrance (2 entrances)

Majestic St. Paul's Cathedral is one of London's most iconic buildings.

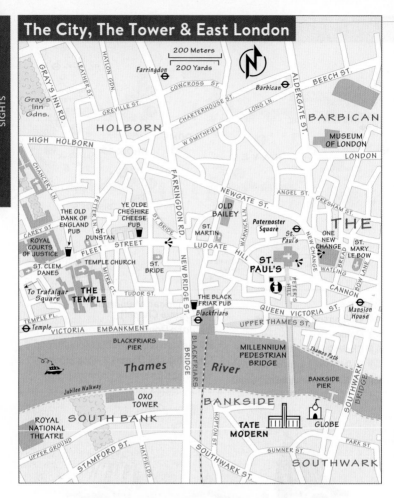

The City, The Tower & East London

Mon-Sat 8:30-16:30 (dome opens at 9:30), closed Sun except for worship; book ahead online to skip the line or you might be waiting 15-30 minutes at busy times; Tube: St. Paul's, recorded info tel. 020/7246-8348, reception tel. 020/7246-8350, www.stpauls.co.uk.

Church Services and Music: Check the website for worship times the day of your visit. Communion is generally Mon-Sat at 8:00 and 12:30. On Sunday, services are held at 8:00, 10:15 (Matins), 11:30 (sung Eucharist), 15:15 (evensong), and 18:00. The rest of the week, evensong is at 17:00 Tue-Sat (not Mon). On some Sundays, there's a free organ recital at 16:45.

Rick's Tip: *If you come to St. Paul's 20 minutes early for evensong worship (under the dome), you may be able to grab a big wooden stall in the choir, next to the singers.*

Tours: Along with the **audioguide**, admission includes a 1.5-hour guided **tour** (Mon-Sat at 10:00, 11:00, 13:00, and 14:00); reserve a place at the guiding desk when you arrive. Free 20-minute **introductory talks** are offered throughout the day. You

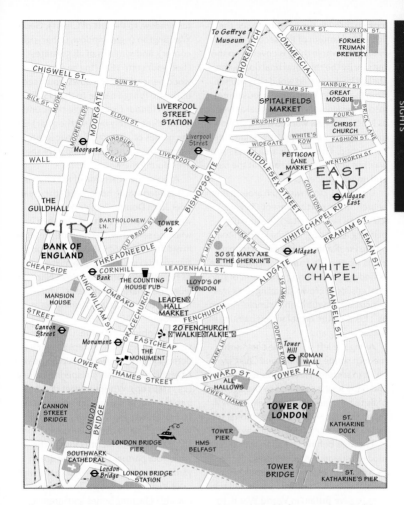

can also 🎧 download my free St. Paul's Cathedral **audio tour** (see page 14).

⊘ SELF-GUIDED TOUR

Enter, buy your ticket, pick up the free visitor's map, and stand at the far back of the ❶ **nave,** behind the font. At 515 feet long and 250 feet wide, this is Europe's fourth largest church, after cathedrals in Rome (St. Peter's), Sevilla, and Milan. The spaciousness is accentuated by the relative lack of decoration. The simple, cream-colored ceiling and the clear glass in the windows light everything evenly. Wren wanted a simple, open church with

nothing to hide. Unfortunately, only this entrance area keeps his original vision— the rest was encrusted with 19th-century Victorian ornamentation.

Ahead and on the left is the towering, black-and-white ❷ **Wellington Monument.** Wren would have been appalled, but his church has become so central to England's soul that many national heroes are buried here (in the basement crypt).

The ❸ **dome** you see from here, painted with scenes from the life of St. Paul, is only the innermost of three. From the painted interior of the first dome, look up through the opening to see the light-filled lantern of the second dome. Finally, the whole thing is covered on the outside by the third and final dome, the shell of lead-covered wood that you see from the street. Wren's ingenious three-in-one design was psychological as well as functional—he wanted a low, shallow inner dome so worshippers wouldn't feel diminished. The ❹ **choir** area blocks your way, but you can see the **altar** at the far end under a golden canopy.

Do a quick clockwise spin around the church. In the north transept (to your left as you face the altar), find the big painting, ❺ *The Light of the World* (1904), by the Pre-Raphaelite William Holman Hunt. Inspired by Hunt's own experience of finding Christ during a moment of spiritual crisis, the crowd-pleasing work was criticized as "syrupy" and "simple"—even as it became the most famous painting in Victorian England.

Along the left side of the choir is the modern statue ❻ *Mother and Child,* by modern sculptor Henry Moore. This Mary and Baby Jesus—inspired by the sight of British moms nursing babies in WWII bomb shelters—renders a traditional subject in an abstract, minimalist way.

The area behind the altar, with three modern stained-glass windows, is the ❼ **American Memorial Chapel**—honoring the Americans who sacrificed their lives to save Britain in World War II. In colored panes that arch around the big windows, spot the American eagle (center window, to the left of Christ), George Washington (right window, upper-right corner), and symbols of all 50 states (find your state seal). In the carved wood beneath the windows, you'll see birds and foliage native to the US. The Roll of Honour (a 500-page book under glass, immediately behind the altar) lists the names of 28,000 US servicemen and women based in Britain who gave their lives during the war.

Around the other side of the choir is a shrouded statue honoring ❽ the great poet **John Donne** ("never wonder for whom the bell tolls—it tolls for thee"), who also served as a passionate preacher in old St. Paul's (1621-1631). In the south transept are monuments to military greats ❾ **Horatio Nelson,** who fought Napoleon, and **Charles Cornwallis,** who was finished off by George Washington at Yorktown.

❿ **Climbing the Dome:** During your visit, you can climb 528 steps to reach the dome and great city views. Along the way, have some fun in the Whispering Gallery (257 steps up). Whisper sweet nothings into the wall, and your partner (and anyone else) standing far away can hear you. For best effects, try whispering (not talking) with your mouth close to the wall, while your partner stands a few dozen yards away with his or her ear to the wall.

⓫ **Visiting the Crypt:** The crypt is a world of historic bones and interesting cathedral models. Many legends are buried here—Horatio Nelson, the Duke

The cathedral's interior is dazzling.

The city views from St. Paul's dome are worth the climb.

London's Best Views

For some viewpoints, you need to pay admission. At the bars or restaurants, you'll need to buy a drink. The only truly free spots are One New Change Rooftop Terrace, 20 Fenchurch, and Primrose Hill.

London Eye: Ride the giant Ferris wheel for stunning London views. See page 75.

St. Paul's Dome: You'll earn a striking, unobstructed view by climbing hundreds of steps to the church's cupola. See page 64.

One New Change Rooftop Terrace: Get fine free views—nearly as good as those from St. Paul's Dome—from the rooftop terrace of the shopping mall just behind and east of the church.

Tate Modern: Take in a classic vista across the Thames from the restaurant/bar on the museum's sixth level. See page 78.

20 Fenchurch (a.k.a. "The Walkie-Talkie"): Get 360-degree views of London from the mostly enclosed Sky Garden, along with a garden, bar, restaurants, and lots of locals. It's free but you'll need to make reservations and bring a photo ID (Mon-Fri 10:00-18:00, Sat-Sun 11:00-21:00, 20 Fenchurch Street, Tube: Monument, www.skygarden.london).

National Portrait Gallery: A mod top-floor restaurant peers over Trafalgar Square and the Westminster neighborhood. See page 51.

Waterstones Bookstore: Its hip, low-key, top-floor café/bar has sweeping views of the London Eye, Big Ben, and the Houses of Parliament (www.5thview.co.uk).

OXO Tower: Perched high over the Thames River, the building's upscale restaurant/bar boasts views over London and St. Paul's, with al fresco dining in good weather (Barge House Street, Tube: Blackfriars or Southwark, tel. 020/7803-3888, www.harveynichols.com/restaurants/oxo-tower-london).

London Hilton, Park Lane: You'll spot Buckingham Palace, Hyde Park, and the London Eye from Galvin at Windows, its 28th-floor restaurant/bar (22 Park Lane, Tube: Hyde Park Corner, tel. 020/7208-4021, www.galvinatwindows.com).

The Shard: The observation decks that cap this 1,020-foot-tall skyscraper offer London's most commanding views, but at a high price (£25 if booked at least a day in advance, £30 for same-day reservations; daily 10:00-22:00, last entry slot at 21:00; Tube: London Bridge—use London Bridge exit and follow signs, tel. 0844-499-7111, www.theviewfromtheshard.com).

Primrose Hill: Get 360-degree views from this huge grassy expanse just north of Regent's Park (off Prince Albert Road, Tube: Chalk Farm or Camden Town, www.royalparks.org.uk/parks/the-regents-park).

of Wellington, and even Wren himself, whose tomb is marked by a simple black slab with no statue. Back up in the nave, on the floor directly under the dome, is Christopher Wren's name and epitaph (written in Latin): "Reader, if you seek his monument, look around you."

▲MUSEUM OF LONDON

This museum tells the fascinating story of London, taking you from its pre-Roman beginnings to the present and featuring distinguished citizens ranging from Neanderthals, to Romans, to Elizabethans, to Victorians, to Mods, to today. The displays are chronological, spacious, and informative. Scale models and costumes help you visualize everyday life in the city at different periods. In the last room, you'll see the museum's prized possession: the Lord Mayor's Coach, a golden carriage pulled by six white horses, looking as if it had pranced right out of the pages of *Cinderella*. There are enough whiz-bang multimedia displays (including for the Plague and the Great Fire) to spice up otherwise humdrum artifacts.

Cost and Hours: Free, daily 10:00-18:00, last admission an hour before closing, see the day's events board for special talks and tours, café, 150 London Wall at Aldersgate Street, Tube: Barbican or St. Paul's plus a five-minute walk, tel. 020/7001-9844, www.museumoflondon.org.uk.

THE MONUMENT

Wren's recently restored 202-foot-tall tribute to London's 1666 Great Fire is at the junction of Monument Street and Fish Street Hill. Climb the 311 steps inside the column for a monumental view of The City (£4, £10.50 combo-ticket with Tower Bridge, cash only, daily 9:30-18:00, until 17:30 Oct-March, Tube: Monument).

▲▲▲TOWER OF LONDON

The Tower has served as a castle in wartime, a king's residence in peacetime, and, most notoriously, as the prison and execution site of rebels. See the crown jewels, take a witty Beefeater tour, and ponder the executioner's block that dispensed with Anne Boleyn, Sir Thomas More, and troublesome heirs to the throne.

Cost and Hours: £15, family-£63, entry fee includes Beefeater tour (see later); Tue-Sat 9:00-17:30, Sun-Mon 10:00-17:30; Nov-Feb closes one hour earlier; skippable audioguide-£4; Tube: Tower Hill, tel. 0844-482-7788, www.hrp.org.uk.

Advance Tickets: To avoid the long ticket-buying lines at the Tower, buy your ticket at the Trader's Gate gift shop, located down the steps from the Tower Hill Tube stop (can be used any day). Tickets are also sold at various locations (such as travel agencies) throughout London. You can also try buying tickets, with credit card only, at the Tower Welcome Centre to the left of the normal ticket lines—though on busy days they may turn you away. It's easy to book online, but you must use your ticket within seven days from the date you select (www.hrp.org.uk, 10 percent discount).

Rick's Tip: *The* **Tower of London** *is most crowded in summer, on weekends (especially Sundays), and during school holidays. The line for the crown jewels can be just as long as the ticket line.* **Arrive before 10:00 and go straight for the jewels.** *Alternatively, arrive in the afternoon, tour the rest of the Tower first, and see the jewels an hour before closing time, when crowds die down.*

Tower of London

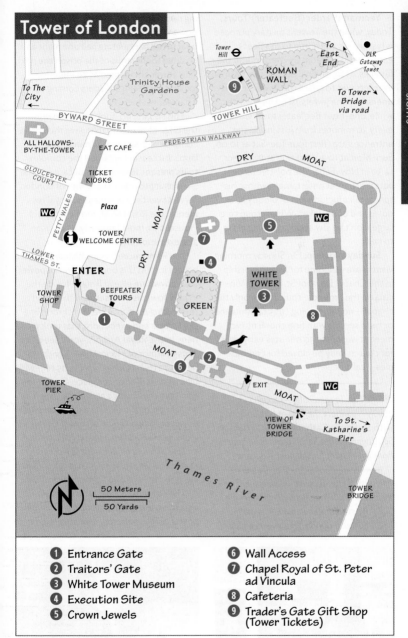

Tower of London

Map labels:

To The City ←
BYWARD STREET
Tower Hill
ROMAN WALL
Trinity House Gardens
To East End
DLR Gateway Tower
To Tower Bridge via road
TOWER HILL
PEDESTRIAN WALKWAY
ALL HALLOWS-BY-THE-TOWER
EAT CAFÉ
GLOUCESTER COURT
TICKET KIOSKS
WC
PETTY WALES
Plaza
DRY MOAT
TOWER WELCOME CENTRE
DRY MOAT
WC
WHITE TOWER
LOWER THAMES ST.
ENTER
TOWER SHOP
BEEFEATER TOURS
TOWER GREEN
EXIT
TOWER PIER
MOAT
MOAT
WC
VIEW OF TOWER BRIDGE
To St. Katharine's Pier
Thames River
50 Meters
50 Yards
TOWER BRIDGE

Legend:

1. Entrance Gate
2. Traitors' Gate
3. White Tower Museum
4. Execution Site
5. Crown Jewels
6. Wall Access
7. Chapel Royal of St. Peter ad Vincula
8. Cafeteria
9. Trader's Gate Gift Shop (Tower Tickets)

Yeoman Warder (Beefeater) Tours: Today, while the Tower's military purpose is history, it's still home to the Beefeaters—the 35 Yeoman Warders and their families. (The original duty of the Yeoman Warders was to guard the Tower, its prisoners, and the jewels.) The free, worthwhile, one-hour Beefeater tours leave every 30 minutes from just inside the entrance gate (first tour Tue-Sat at 10:00, Sun-Mon at 10:30, last one at 15:30—or 14:30 in Nov-Feb). The boisterous Beefeaters are great entertainers, whose historical talks include lots of bloody anecdotes and corny jokes. When groups are large, don't be shy about standing close to hear.

Sunday Worship: On Sunday morning, visitors are welcome for free to worship in the Chapel Royal of St. Peter ad Vincula on the grounds. You can see only the chapel—no sightseeing (9:15 communion or 11:00 service with fine choral music, meet at west gate 30 minutes early, dress for church, may be closed for ceremonies—call ahead).

Rick's Tip: To scenically—though circuitously—connect the **Tower of London with St. Paul's Cathedral,** detour through Southwark on the South Bank (and stop by Borough Market for the fun food scene).

Visiting the Tower: William the Conqueror, still getting used to his new title, built the stone "White Tower" (1077-1097) to keep Londoners in line, a gleaming reminder of the monarch's absolute power. You could be feasting on roast boar in the banqueting hall one night and chained to the walls of the prison the next. The Tower also served as an effective lookout for seeing invaders coming up the Thames.

This square, 90-foot-tall tower was the original structure that gave this castle complex of 20 towers its name. William's successors enlarged the complex to its present 18-acre size. Because of the security it provided, the Tower of London served over the centuries as a royal residence, the Royal Mint, the Royal Jewel House, and, most famously, as a prison and execution site.

You'll find more bloody history per square inch in this original tower of power than anywhere else in Britain. Inside the White Tower is a **museum** with exhibits re-creating medieval life and chronicling the torture and executions that took place here. In the Royal Armory, you'll see some suits of armor of Henry VIII—slender in his youth (c. 1515), heavyset by 1540—with his bigger-is-better codpiece. On the top floor, see the Tower's actual execution ax and chopping block. The **execution site,** however, in the middle of Tower Green, looks just like a lawn. Henry VIII axed a couple of his ex-wives here (divorced readers can insert their own joke), including Anne Boleyn and Catherine Howard.

The Tower's hard stone and glittering **crown jewels** represent the ultimate power of the monarch. The Sovereign's

A Beefeater on duty

Execution ax and block

Henry VIII (1491-1547)

The notorious king who single-handedly transformed England was a true Renaissance Man—six feet tall, handsome, charismatic, well-educated, and brilliant. When 17-year-old Henry, the second monarch of the House of Tudor, was crowned king, all of England rejoiced.

Henry left affairs of state in the hands of others and filled his days with sports, war, the arts—and women. In 1529, Henry's personal life changed the course of history. Henry wanted a divorce, partly because his wife had become too old to bear him a son, and partly because he'd fallen in love with Anne Boleyn. Henry begged the pope for an annulment, but the pope refused. Henry divorced his wife anyway and was excommunicated.

Henry's rejection of papal authority sparked the English Reformation. He forced monasteries to close, sold off some church land, and confiscated everything else for himself and the Crown. Within a decade, centuries-old monastic institutions were left gutted. Meanwhile, the church was reorganized into the Anglican Church of England, with Henry as its head. Though Henry himself adhered to basic Catholic doctrine, he discouraged the veneration of saints and relics, and commissioned an English translation of the Bible.

Henry famously had six wives. The issue was not his love life, but the politics of royal succession. To guarantee the Tudor family's dominance, he needed a male heir born by a recognized queen. Henry's first marriage, to Catherine of Aragon, bore Henry a daughter, but no sons. Next came Anne Boleyn, who also gave birth to a daughter. After a turbulent few years with Anne and several miscarriages, a frustrated Henry had her beheaded. His next wife, Jane Seymour, finally had a son (but Jane died soon after giving birth). A blind marriage with Anne of Cleves ended quickly when she proved to be politically useless. His next bride, Catherine Howard, cheated on him, so she was executed. Henry finally found comfort—but no children—in his later years with his final wife, Catherine Parr.

Henry's last years were marked by paranoia and sudden rages. His perceived enemies were charged with treason and beheaded. Once-wealthy England was depleted, thanks to Henry's expensive habits, which included making war on France, building and acquiring 50 palaces, and collecting fine tapestries and archery bows.

Still, Henry forged a legacy. He expanded the power of the monarchy while simultaneously strengthening Parliament—largely because it agreed with his policies. He annexed Wales and imposed English rule on Ireland (provoking centuries of resentment). He expanded the navy, paving the way for Britannia to rule the waves. And England would forever be a Protestant nation.

Scepter is encrusted with the world's larg-est cut diamond—the 530-carat Star of Africa. The Crown of the Queen Mother (Elizabeth II's famous mum, who died in 2002) has the 106-carat Koh-I-Noor diamond glittering on the front (considered unlucky for male rulers, it only adorns the crown of the king's wife). The Imperial State Crown is what the Queen wears for official functions such as the State Opening of Parliament. Among its 3,733 jewels are Queen Elizabeth I's former earrings (the hanging pearls, top center), a stunning 13th-century ruby look-alike in the center, and Edward the Confessor's ring (the blue sapphire on top, in the center of the Maltese cross of diamonds).

The Tower was defended by state-of-the-art **walls** and fortifications in the 13th century. Walking along them offers fine views of the famous Tower Bridge, with its twin towers and blue spans.

TOWER BRIDGE

The iconic Tower Bridge (often mistakenly called London Bridge) has been recently painted and restored. The hydraulically powered drawbridge was built in 1894 to accommodate the growing East End. While fully modern, its design has a retro Neo-Gothic look.

The drawbridge lifts to let ships pass a thousand times a year (best viewed from the Tower side of the Thames). For the bridge-lifting schedule, check the website or call.

You can tour the bridge at the **Tower Bridge Exhibition,** with a history display and a peek at the Victorian engine room that lifts the span. Included in your entrance is the chance to cross the bridge—138 feet above the road along a see-through glass walkway. The exhibit is overpriced, though the adrenaline rush and spectacular city views from the walkways might justify the cost.

Cost and Hours: £9, £10.50 combo-ticket with The Monument, daily 10:00-18:00 in summer, 9:30-17:30 in winter, enter at northwest tower, Tube: Tower Hill, tel. 020/7403-3761, www.towerbridge.org.uk.

On the South Bank

The South Bank of the Thames is a thriving arts and cultural center, tied together by the riverfront Jubilee Walkway. Most of these sights are in Southwark (SUTH-uck), the core of the tourist's South Bank. Southwark was for centuries the place

The Tower Bridge has spanned the Thames since 1894.

Londoners would go to let their hair down. A run-down warehouse district through the 20th century, it's now been gentrified with classy restaurants, office parks, pedestrian promenades, and major sights.

▲ JUBILEE WALKWAY

This riverside path is a popular, pub-crawling pedestrian promenade that stretches all along the South Bank, offering grand views of the Houses of Parliament and St. Paul's. On a sunny day, it's the place to see Londoners out strolling. The Walkway hugs the river except just east of London Bridge, where it cuts inland for a couple of blocks. It has been expanded into a 60-mile "Greenway" circling the city, including the 2012 Olympics site.

Rick's Tip: If you're visiting London in summer, visit the South Bank after hours. Take a trip around the London Eye at sunset (the wheel spins until late—last ascent at 20:30, later in July-Aug). Then cap your night with a stroll along the Jubilee Walkway.

▲▲ LONDON EYE

This giant Ferris wheel, towering above London opposite Big Ben, is one of the world's highest observational wheels. Riding it is a memorable experience, even though London doesn't have much of a skyline, and the price is borderline outrageous. Whether you ride or not, the wheel is a sight to behold.

The experience starts with an engaging, four-minute show combining a 3-D movie with wind and water effects. Then it's time to spin around the Eye, designed like a giant bicycle wheel. It's "green," running extremely efficiently and virtually silently. Twenty-five people ride in each of its 32 air-conditioned capsules (representing the boroughs of London) for the 30-minute rotation (you go around only once). From the top of this 443-foot-high wheel—the second-highest public viewpoint in the city—even Big Ben looks small.

Cost: £24.95, about 10 percent cheaper if bought online, family deal (online only). Combo-tickets save money if you plan on visiting Madame Tussauds. Buy tickets in advance at www.londoneye.com, by calling 0870-500-0600, or in person at the box office (in the corner of the County

The London Eye is one of the latest additions to London's skyline.

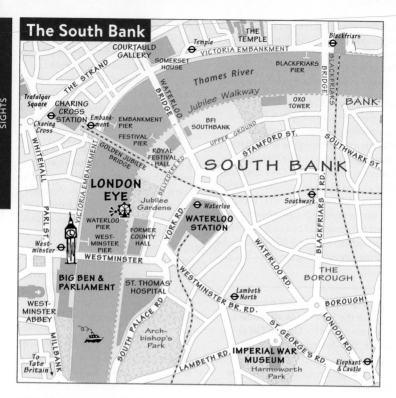

The South Bank

THE TEMPLE
Temple
VICTORIA EMBANKMENT
Blackfriars

COURTAULD
GALLERY
SOMERSET
HOUSE

BLACKFRIARS
PIER

Thames River

Jubilee Walkway

THE STRAND

WATERLOO BRIDGE

Trafalgar
Square
CHARING
CROSS
STATION
Embank-
ment
EMBANKMENT
PIER

Charing
Cross

Embankment

BFI
SOUTHBANK

OXO
TOWER

BLACKFRIARS BRIDGE

BANK

WHITEHALL

FESTIVAL
PIER

UPPER GROUND

STAMFORD ST.

VICTORIA EMBANKMENT

GOLDEN JUBILEE BRIDGE

ROYAL
FESTIVAL
HALL

SOUTH BANK

SOUTHWARK ST.

LONDON
EYE

Jubilee
Gardens

Waterloo

Southwark

BELVEDERE RD.

YORK RD.

PARL ST.

WATERLOO
PIER

WEST-
MINSTER
PIER

FORMER
COUNTY
HALL

WATERLOO
STATION

BLACKFRIARS RD.

West-
minster

WESTMINSTER

WATERLOO RD.

WESTMINSTER

BIG BEN &
PARLIAMENT

ST. THOMAS'
HOSPITAL

WESTMINSTER BR. RD.

Lambeth
North

THE
BOROUGH

BOROUGH

WEST-
MINSTER
ABBEY

SOUTH PALACE RD.

LONDON RD.

MILLBANK

Arch-
bishop's
Park

ST. GEORGE'S RD.

To
Tate
Britain

LAMBETH RD.

IMPERIAL WAR
MUSEUM

Harmsworth
Park

Elephant
& Castle

Hall building nearest the Eye).

Hours: Daily 10:00-20:30, until 21:30 or later in July and August, check the website for latest schedule, these are last-ascent times, closed Dec 25 and a few days in Jan for annual maintenance, Tube: Waterloo or Westminster. Thames boats come and go from Waterloo Pier at the foot of the wheel.

Rick's Tip: *The **London Eye** is busiest between 11:00 and 17:00, especially on weekends and every day in July and August.* **Call ahead or go online to book your ticket;** *then you can print it at home, or retrieve it from an onsite ticket machine (bring your confirmation code and payment card), or stand in the "Ticket Collection" line. Even with a reservation, you'll still have to wait to board the wheel (but it's not worth paying an extra £8 for a Fast Track ticket).*

By the Eye: The area next to the London Eye has developed a cotton-candy ambience of kitschy, kid-friendly attractions. There's a game arcade, an aquarium, and the Shrek's Adventure amusement ride.

▲▲IMPERIAL WAR MUSEUM

This impressive museum covers the wars of the last century—from World War I

Imperial War Museum

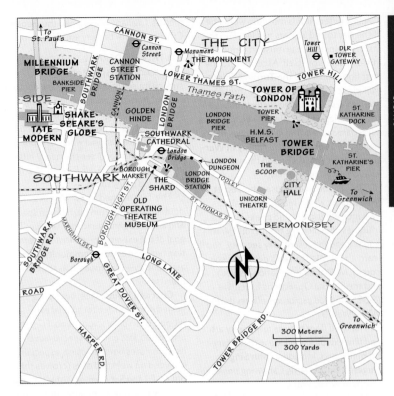

biplanes, to the rise of fascism, the Cold War, the Cuban Missile Crisis, the Troubles in Northern Ireland, the wars in Iraq and Afghanistan, and terrorism. Rather than glorify war, the museum encourages an understanding of the history of modern warfare and the wartime experience, including the effect it has on the everyday lives of people back home.

Highlights are the galleries devoted to World War I, World War II, the Secret War (espionage), and the Holocaust. War wonks love the place, as do history buffs who enjoy patiently reading displays. For the rest, there are enough interactive experiences and multimedia exhibits and submarines to keep it interesting.

The museum (which sits in an inviting park equipped with an equally inviting café) is housed in what had been the Royal Bethlam Hospital. Also known as "the Bedlam asylum," the place was so

wild that it gave the world a new word for chaos. Back in Victorian times, locals—without reality shows and YouTube—paid admission to visit the asylum on weekends for entertainment.

Cost and Hours: Free, £5 suggested donation, daily 10:00-18:00, special exhibits extra, various free audioguides may be available—ask at the info desk, Tube: Lambeth North or Elephant and Castle; buses #3, #12, and #159 come here from Westminster area; tel. 020/7416-5000, www.iwm.org.uk.

⊙ SELF-GUIDED TOUR

Start with the atrium to grasp the massive scale of warfare as you wander among and under notable battle machines, then head directly for the museum's recently renovated **WWI galleries.** Firsthand accounts connect the blunt reality of a brutal war with the contributions, heartache, and efforts of a nation.

How different this museum would be if the war to end all wars had lived up to its name. Instead, the museum, much like history, builds on itself. Ascending to the first floor, you'll find the **Turning Points** galleries progressing up to and through World War II, including sections explaining Blitzkrieg and its effects (see an actual Nazi parachute bomb like the ones that devastated London). The **Family in Wartime** exhibit shows London through the eyes of an ordinary family.

The second floor houses the **Secret War** exhibit, which features actual surveillance equipment and peeks into the intrigues of espionage from World Wars I and II through present-day security. You'll learn about MI5 (Britain's domestic spy corps), MI6 (their international spies), and the Special Operations Executive (SOE), who led espionage efforts during World War II.

The third floor houses temporary art and film exhibits speckled with military-themed works, including **John Singer** Sargent's *Gassed* (1919), showing besieged troops in World War I.

The fourth-floor section on the **Holocaust,** one of the best on the subject anywhere, tells the story with powerful videos, artifacts, and fine explanations.

Crowning the museum on the fifth floor is the Lord Ashcroft Gallery and the **Extraordinary Heroes** display. More than 250 stories celebrate Britain's highest military award for bravery with the world's largest collection of Victoria Cross medals. Civilians who earned the George Cross medal for bravery are also honored.

▲▲TATE MODERN

Dedicated in the spring of 2000, this striking museum opened the new century with art from the previous one. Filling a derelict old power station across the river from St. Paul's, its powerhouse collection highlights international works of modern art since 1900. You'll see the heavy hitters, including pieces by Dalí, Picasso, Warhol, Beuys, and many more.

The Tate opened a new wing in 2016, doubling the museum's exhibition space and adding a panoramic roof terrace. The goal of the expansion—to foster interaction between art and community in the 21st century—is as modern as the collection itself.

Cost and Hours: Free, but £4 suggested donation, fee for special exhibitions; open daily 10:00-18:00, Fri-Sat until 22:00, last entry to special exhibits 45 minutes before closing, especially crowded on weekend days (crowds thin out on Fri and Sat evenings); multimedia guide-£4.50, free 45-minute guided tours are offered about four times daily (ask for schedule at info desk), view restaurant on top floor, no photos beyond entrance hall; tel. 020/7887-8888, www.tate.org.uk.

Getting There: Cross the Millennium Bridge from St. Paul's; take the Tube to Southwark, London Bridge, St. Paul's, Mansion House, or Blackfriars and walk 10 to 15 minutes; or catch Thames Clippers' Tate Boat ferry from the Tate Britain

Imperial War Museum atrium

Tate Modern

for a 15-minute crossing (£7.50 one-way, discount with Travelcard or Oyster card, departs every 40 minutes when galleries are open, www.tate.org.uk/visit/tate-boat).

Visiting the Museum: Artworks in the permanent collection are arranged according to theme—such as "Poetry and Dream"—not chronologically or by artist. Paintings by Picasso, for example, are scattered throughout the building. Don't expect to see just the Old Masters of Modernism; the museum's collection is ever-growing with new contemporary works.

Temporary exhibits are cutting-edge. Each year, the vast main hall features a different monumental installation by a prominent artist.

▲MILLENNIUM BRIDGE

The pedestrian bridge links St. Paul's Cathedral and the Tate Modern across the Thames. This is London's first new bridge in a century, nicknamed the "blade of light" for its sleek minimalist design (370 yards long, 4 yards wide, stainless steel with teak planks). Its clever aerodynamic handrails deflect wind over the heads of pedestrians.

▲▲SHAKESPEARE'S GLOBE

This replica of the original Globe Theatre was built as it was in Shakespeare's time—half-timbered and thatched (in fact, with the first thatched roof constructed in London since they were outlawed after the Great Fire of 1666). The original Globe opened in 1599, with its debut play, Shakespeare's *Julius Caesar*. It accommodated 2,200 seated and another 1,000 standing. Today's Globe, allowing space for reasonable aisles, is slightly smaller, holding 800 seated and 600 groundlings. The working theater hosts authentic performances of Shakespeare's plays with actors in period costumes, modern interpretations of his works, and some works by other playwrights. For details on attending a play, see page 90.

The Globe complex has four parts: the Globe theater itself, the box office, a museum (called the Exhibition), and the Sam Wanamaker Playhouse (an indoor Jacobean theater around back). The Playhouse, which hosts performances through the winter, is horseshoe-shaped, intimate (seating fewer than 350), and sometimes uses authentic candle lighting for period performances. The repertoire focuses less on Shakespeare and more on the work of his contemporaries (Jonson, Marlow, Fletcher), as well as concerts.

Cost: £13.50 ticket (good all day) includes Exhibition, audioguide, and 40-minute tour of the Globe; when theater is in use, you can tour the Exhibition only for £6.

Hours: The complex is open daily 9:00-17:30; tours start every 30 minutes. During the Globe theater season (late April-mid-Oct), it's safest to arrive for a tour before noon (last tour Tue-Sat at 12:30, Sun at 11:30, Mon at 17:00). Located on the South Bank over the Millennium

Millennium Bridge

Shakespeare's Globe

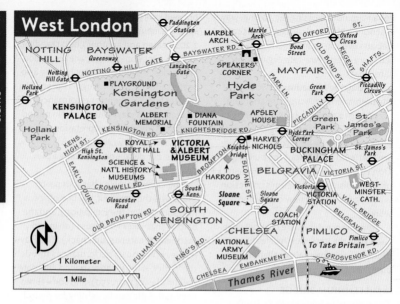

Bridge from St. Paul's, Tube: Mansion House or London Bridge plus a 10-minute walk; tel. 020/7902-1400, box office tel. 020/7401-9919, www.shakespearesglobe.com.

Visiting the Globe: You browse on your own in the **Exhibition** (with the included audioguide) through displays of Elizabethan-era costumes and makeup, music, script-printing, and special effects (the displays change). There are early folios and objects that were dug up on site. Videos and scale models help put Shakespearean theater within the context of the times. You'll also learn how they built the replica in modern times, using Elizabethan materials and techniques.

You must **tour the theater** at the time stamped on your ticket, but you can come back to the Exhibition museum afterward. A guide (usually an actor) leads you into the theater to see the stage and the various seating areas for the different classes of people. Learn how the new Globe is similar to the old Globe (open-air performances, standing-room by the stage, no curtain) and how it's different (female actors, lights for night performances, con-

crete floor). It's not a backstage tour, but the guides bring the Elizabethan period to life.

Eating: The Swan at the Globe café offers a restaurant (for lunch and dinner, reservations recommended, tel. 020/7928-9444), a drinks-and-plates bar, and a sandwich-and-coffee cart (daily 9:00-closing, depending on performance times).

West London
▲▲TATE BRITAIN

One of Europe's great art houses, Tate Britain specializes in British painting from the 16th century through modern times. This is people's art, with realistic paintings rooted in the people, landscape, and stories of the British Isles. The Tate shows off Hogarth's stage sets, Gainsborough's ladies, Blake's angels, Constable's clouds, Turner's tempests, the naturalistic realism of the Pre-Raphaelites, and the camera-eye portraits of Hockney and Freud.

Cost and Hours: Free but £4 suggested donation, admission fee for special exhibits; daily 10:00-18:00, last entry 45 minutes before closing; free tours generally daily (ask at the information desk or call ahead), or use the Tate's Wi-Fi to download their handy room-by-room app; café and restaurant, tel. 020/7887-8888, www.tate.org.uk.

Getting There: It's on the Thames River, south of Big Ben and north of Vauxhall Bridge. Tube to Pimlico, then walk seven minutes. Or hop on the Tate Boat museum ferry from Tate Modern (see page 112).

❍ SELF-GUIDED TOUR

Works from the early centuries are located in the west half of the building, 20th-century art is in the east half, and the works of J. M. W. Turner are in an adjacent wing (the Clore Gallery). Certain artists' work is placed in special rooms outside the chronological flow. Other rooms focus on a particular aspect of British art. The Tate's great strength is championing contemporary British art in special exhibitions—there are two exhibition spaces (one free, the other usually requiring separate admission).

• *From the main Millbank entrance, walk through the bright, white rotunda and down the long central hall. Near the far end, enter the rooms on the left, labeled* Walk Through British Art, *where you'll find the beginnings of British painting (as you enter each room, you'll see the year etched into the floor).*

1540s-1650s—Portraits Rule: Stuffy portraits of Lord and Lady Whoevertheyare try to turn crude country nobles into refined men and delicate women. Men in ruffled collars clutch symbols of power. Women in ruffled collars, puffy sleeves, and elaborately patterned dresses display their lily-white complexions, turning their pinkies out.

English country houses often had a long hall built specially to hang family portraits. You could stroll along and see your noble forebears looking down their noses at you.

1700s—Art Blossoms: With peace at home, a strong overseas economy, and a growing urban center in London,

England's artistic life began to bloom. As the English grew more sophisticated, so did their portraits. Painters branched out into other subjects, capturing slices of everyday life (find William Hogarth, with his unflinchingly honest portraits, and Thomas Gainsborough's elegant, educated women). The Royal Academy added a veneer of classical Greece to even the simplest subjects.

1800-1850—The Industrial Revolution: Many artists rebelled against "progress" and the modern world. They escaped the dirty cities to commune with nature (Constable and the Romantics), found a new spirituality in intense human emotions (dramatic scenes from history or literature)—or they left the modern world altogether.

William Blake, whose work hangs in a darkened room to protect his watercolors from deterioration, painted angels, not the dull material world. Blake turned his gaze inward, illustrating the glorious visions of the soul. In visions of the Christian heaven or Dante's hell, his figures have superhero musculature. The colors are almost translucent.

1837-1901—The Victorian Era: In the world's wealthiest nation, the prosperous middle class dictated taste in art. They admired paintings that were realistic, depicting slices of everyday life. Some paintings tug at the heartstrings, with scenes of parting couples, the grief of death, or the joy of families reuniting.

Victorian-era Lady of Shalott

Overdosed with the gushy sentimentality of their day, the Pre-Raphaelites were a band of artists—including Sir John Everett Millais, Dante Gabriel Rossetti, and William Holman Hunt—who dedicated themselves to creating less saccharine art. Like the Impressionists who followed them, they left stuffy studios to set up outdoors, painting trees, streams, and people. They captured nature with such a close-up clarity that it's downright unnatural.

British Impressionism: Realistic British art stood apart from the Modernist trends in France, but some influences drifted across the Channel. American-born John Singer Sargent studied with Parisian Impressionists, learning the thick, messy brushwork and play of light at twilight. James Tissot used Degas' snapshot technique to capture a crowded scene from an odd angle. And James McNeill Whistler (born in America, trained in Paris, lived in London) composed his paintings like music—see some of his paintings' titles.

The Turner Collection: Walking through J. M. W. Turner's life's work, you can trace his evolution from clear-eyed realism to hazy proto-Impressionism. You'll also see how Turner dabbled in different subjects: landscapes, seascapes, Roman ruins, snapshots of Venice, and so on.

The corner room of the Clore Gallery is dedicated to Turner's great rival and contemporary, John Constable, who painted the English landscape as it was—realistically, without idealizing it.

1900-1950—World Wars: As two world wars whittled down the powerful British Empire, it still remained a major cultural force. British art mirrored many of the trends pioneered in Paris: cubism like Picasso's, abstract art like Mondrian's, and so on.

Henry Moore's statues—mostly female, mostly reclining—catch the primitive power of carved stone. He captured the human body in a few simple curves, with minimal changes to the rock itself.

Britain survived the Blitz, World War II, and the loss of hundreds of thousands of men—but at war's end, the bottled-up horror came rushing out. Francis Bacon's deformed half-humans/half-animals express the existential human predicament of being caught in a world not of your making.

1950-2000—Modern World: No longer a world power, Britain in the Swinging '60s became a major exporter of pop culture. Look for works by David Hockney, Lucian Freud, Bridget Riley, and Gilbert and George.

▲HYDE PARK

London's "Central Park," originally Henry VIII's hunting grounds, has more than 600 acres of lush greenery, Santander Cycles rental stations, the huge man-made Serpentine Lake (with rental boats and a lakeside swimming pool), the royal Kensington Palace, and the ornate Neo-Gothic Albert Memorial across from the Royal Albert Hall. The western half of the park is known as Kensington Gardens. The park is huge—study a Tube map to choose the stop nearest to your destination (for more about the park, see www.royalparks.org.uk/parks/hyde-park).

On Sundays, from just after noon until early evening, **Speakers' Corner** offers soapbox oratory at its best. Characters climb their stepladders, wave their flags, pound emphatically on their sandwich boards, and share what they are convinced is their wisdom. Regulars have

Hyde Park

resident hecklers who know their lines and are always ready with a verbal jab or barb. "The grass roots of democracy" is actually a holdover from when the gallows stood here and the criminal was allowed to say just about anything he wanted to before he swung. Raise your voice and gather a crowd—it's easy to do (northeast corner of the park, Tube: Marble Arch).

The **Princess Diana Memorial Fountain** honors the "People's Princess," who once lived in nearby Kensington Palace. The low-key circular stream, great for cooling off your feet on a hot day, is in the south-central part of the park, near the Albert Memorial and Serpentine Gallery (Tube: Knightsbridge). A similarly named but different sight, the **Diana, Princess of Wales Memorial Playground,** in the park's northwest corner, is loads of fun for kids (Tube: Queensway).

KENSINGTON PALACE

For nearly 150 years (1689-1837), Kensington was the royal residence, before Buckingham Palace became the official home of the monarch. Sitting primly on its pleasant parkside grounds, the palace gives a glimpse into royal life, especially that of Queen Victoria, who was born and raised here.

After Queen Victoria moved the monarchy to Buckingham Palace, lesser royals bedded down at Kensington. Princess Diana lived here both during and after her marriage to Prince Charles (1981-1997). More recently, Will and Kate moved into a thoroughly renovated Apartment 1A

Kensington Palace

(the southern flank of the palace complex, with four stories and 20 rooms). And Prince Harry lives in their old digs, a "cottage" on the other side of the main building. However—as many disappointed visitors discover—none of these more recent apartments are open to the public.

The palace has three main exhibits. To see them chronologically, start with the **Queen's State Apartments** (with highly conceptual exhibits focusing on the later Stuart dynasty—William and Mary, and Mary's sister, Queen Anne). Then move on to the **King's State Apartments** (the grandest spaces, from Hanoverian times), and finish with the **Victoria Revealed** exhibit (telling the story, through quotes and artifacts, of Britain's longest-ruling monarch).

Cost and Hours: £18, daily 10:00-18:00, Nov-Feb until 17:00, last entry one hour before closing, booking online saves a few pounds; least crowded in mornings; friendly and knowledgeable "explainers" will answer questions for free; a long 10-minute stroll through Kensington Gardens from either High Street Kensington or Queensway Tube stations, tel. 0844-482-7788, www.hrp.org.uk.

Nearby: Garden enthusiasts enjoy popping into the secluded Sunken Garden, 50 yards from the exit. Consider afternoon tea at the nearby Orangery, built as a greenhouse for Queen Anne in 1704 (see page 96). On the south side of the palace are the golden gates that became famous in 1997 as the backdrop to the sea of flowers left here by Princess Diana's mourners.

▲▲▲VICTORIA AND ALBERT MUSEUM

You could spend days wandering "the V&A," which encompasses 2,000 years of decorative arts (ceramics, stained glass, fine furniture, clothing, jewelry, carpets, and more). There's much to see, including Raphael's tapestry cartoons, five of Leonardo da Vinci's notebooks, the huge

Islamic Ardabil Carpet (4,914 knots in every 10 square centimeters), a cast of Trajan's Column that depicts the emperor's conquests, and rock memorabilia, including the jumpsuit Mick Jagger wore for the Rolling Stones' 1972 world tour.

Cost and Hours: Free, but £5 suggested donation, extra for some special exhibits; daily 10:00-17:45, some galleries open Fri until 22:00; get the much-needed £1 museum map, free tours daily, on Cromwell Road in South Kensington, Tube: South Kensington, from the Tube station a long tunnel leads directly to museum, tel. 020/7942-2000, www.vam.ac.uk.

Rick's Tip: *The museum is huge and tricky to navigate. Spend £1 for the* **Greatest Treasures brochure** *available from the info desk. It describes—and tells you how to find—the museum's must-see objects.*

Visiting the Museum: In the Grand Entrance lobby, look up to see the colorful **chandelier/sculpture** by American artist Dale Chihuly. This elaborate piece epitomizes the spirit of the V&A's collection—beautiful manufactured objects that demonstrate technical skill and innovation, wedding the old with the new, and blurring the line between arts and crafts.

The V&A has arguably the best collection of **Italian Renaissance sculpture** outside Italy. One prime example is *Samson Slaying a Philistine,* by Giambologna (c. 1562), carved from a single block of marble. Its spiral-shaped pose is reminiscent of Michelangelo.

The museum's **Islamic art** reflects both religious influences and sophisticated secular culture. Notice floral patterns (twining vines, flowers, arabesques) and geometric designs (stars, diamonds). But the most common pattern is calligraphy—elaborate inscriptions in Arabic.

The **British Galleries** sweep through 400 years of British high-class living (1500-1900). Look for rare miniature portraits—a popular item of Queen Elizabeth I's day—including Hilliard's oft-reproduced *Young Man Among Roses* miniature. A room dedicated to Henry VIII has a portrait of him, his writing box, and a whole roomful of furniture, tapestries, jewelry, and dinnerware.

Greater London
▲▲KEW GARDENS

This fine riverside park and its palatial greenhouse are every botanist's favorite escape. Wander among 33,000 different types of plants, spread across 300 acres. For a quick visit, spend a fragrant hour wandering through three buildings: the Palm House, a humid Victorian world of iron, glass, and tropical plants built in 1844; a Waterlily House that Monet would swim for; and the Princess of Wales Conservatory, a modern greenhouse with many different climate zones. With extra time, check out the Xstrata Treetop Walkway, a 200-yard-long scenic steel walkway that puts you in the canopy 60 feet above the

Victoria and Albert Museum

Kew Gardens

ground. Young kids will love the Climbers and Creepers indoor/outdoor playground and little zip line, as well as a slow and easy ride on the hop-on, hop-off Kew Explorer tram (adults–£4.50, kids–£1.50 for narrated 40-minute ride, departs Victoria Gate, ask for schedule when you enter).

Cost and Hours: £16.50, June-Aug £11 after 16:00, kids 4-16 £3.50, free for kids under 4; April-Aug Mon-Fri 10:00-18:30, Sat-Sun until 19:30, closes earlier Sept-March—check schedule online, free one-hour walking tours daily at 11:00 and 13:30, tel. 020/8332-5000, www.kew.org.

Getting There: If taking the Tube, ride to Kew Gardens; from the Tube station, cross the footbridge over the tracks, which drops you in a community of plant-and-herb shops, a two-block walk from Victoria Gate (the main garden entrance). Another option is to take a boat, which runs April-Oct between Kew Gardens and Westminster Pier (see page 32).

Eating: For lunch or a snack, walk 10 minutes from the Palm House to the Orangery Cafeteria (Mon-Fri 10:00-17:30, Sat-Sun 10:00-18:30, until 15:15 in winter, closes early for events).

EXPERIENCES

Shopping

Most stores are open Monday through Saturday from roughly 9:00 or 10:00 until 17:00 or 18:00, with a late night on Wednesday or Thursday (usually until 19:00 or 20:00). Many close on Sundays. Large department stores stay open later during the week (until about 21:00 Mon-Sat) and are open shorter hours on Sundays.

Shopping Streets

London is famous for its shopping. The best and most convenient shopping streets are in the West End and West London (roughly between Soho and Hyde Park). You'll find midrange shops along **Oxford Street** (running east from Tube:

Marble Arch). Fancier shops line **Regent Street** (stretching south from Tube: Oxford Circus to Piccadilly Circus; funky Carnaby Street runs parallel a block east) and **Knightsbridge** (where you'll find Harrods and Harvey Nichols; Tube: Knightsbridge). Other streets are more specialized, such as **Charing Cross Road** for books, **Jermyn Street** for old-fashioned men's clothing (just south of Piccadilly Street), and **Floral Street** for fashion boutiques (connecting Leicester Square to Covent Garden).

Department Stores in West London

Harrods is London's most famous and touristy department store, with more than four acres of retail space covering seven floors (Mon-Sat 10:00-21:00, Sun 11:30-18:00, Brompton Road, Tube: Knightsbridge, tel. 020/7730-1234, www.harrods.com).

Harvey Nichols, once Princess Diana's favorite, remains the department store *du jour* (Mon-Sat 10:00-20:00, Sun 11:30-18:00, near Harrods, 109 Knightsbridge, Tube: Knightsbridge, tel. 020/7235-5000, www.harveynichols.com).

Rick's Tip: *The fifth floor at* **Harvey Nichols** *is a* **veritable food fest,** *with a gourmet grocery store, a fancy restaurant, a sushi bar, and a café. Get takeaway food for a* **picnic in the Hyde Park rose garden,** *two blocks away.*

Fortnum & Mason, the official department store of the Queen, embodies British upper-class taste, with a story-book atmosphere (Mon-Sat 10:00-21:00, Sun 11:30-18:00, 181 Piccadilly, Tube: Green Park, tel. 020/7734-8040, www. fortnumandmason.com). Elegant tea is served in its Diamond Jubilee Tea Salon (see page 96).

Liberty is a still-thriving 19th-century institution known for its artful displays and interior, constructed of two decommissioned battleships (Mon-Sat 10:00-20:00, Sun 12:00-18:00, Great Marlborough Street, Tube: Oxford Circus, tel. 020/7734-1234, www.liberty.co.uk).

Street Markets

Antiques buffs and people-watchers love London's street markets. The best, combining lively stalls and colorful neighborhoods with characteristic shops of their own, are Portobello Road and Camden Lock Market.

IN NOTTING HILL

Portobello Road stretches for several blocks through the funky-but-quaint Notting Hill neighborhood. Already-charming streets lined with pastel-painted houses and offbeat antique shops are enlivened on Fridays and Saturdays with 2,000 additional stalls (9:00-19:00), plus food, live music, and more (Tube: Notting Hill Gate, near recommended accommodations, tel. 020/7727-7684, www. portobelloroad.co.uk).

Rick's Tip: *Browse* **Portobello Road on Friday.** *Most stalls are open, but you can expect half the crowds of Saturday.*

IN CAMDEN TOWN

Camden Lock Market is a huge arts-and-crafts festival divided into three areas, each with its own vibe. The main market, set alongside the picturesque canal, sells boutique crafts and artisanal foods. The market on the opposite side of Chalk Farm Road has ethnic food stalls, punk crafts, and canalside seating. The Stables, a sprawling, incense-scented complex, is squeezed into tunnels under the old rail bridge just behind the main market (daily 10:00-18:00, busiest on weekends, tel. 020/3763-9999, www.camdenlockmarket. com).

IN THE EAST END

Spitalfields Market combines old brick buildings and sleek modern ones, all covered by a giant glass roof. The shops, stalls, and a rainbow of restaurants are open every day (Mon-Fri 10:00-17:00, Sat 11:00-17:00, Sun 9:00-17:00, Tube: Liverpool Street; from the Tube stop, take Bishopsgate East exit, turn left, walk to Brushfield Street, and turn right; www.spitalfields. co.uk).

Petticoat Lane Market, just a block from Spitalfields Market, sits on the otherwise dull Middlesex Street; adjoining Wentworth Street is grungier and more characteristic (Sun 9:00-14:00, sometimes later; smaller market Mon-Fri on Wentworth Street only; closed Sat; Middlesex Street and Wentworth Street, Tube: Liverpool Street).

The **Truman Markets,** housed in a former brewery on Brick Lane, are gritty and avant-garde, selling handmade clothes, home decor, and ethnic street food in the heart of the "Banglatown" Bangladeshi community. The markets are in full swing on Sundays (roughly 10:00-17:00), though you'll see some action on Saturdays (11:00-18:00). Surrounding shops and eateries are open all week (Tube: Liverpool Street or Aldgate East, tel. 020/7770-6028, www.bricklanemarket.com).

Brick Lane is lined with Sunday market stalls all the way up to Bethnal Green Road, about a 10-minute walk (leading north out of the Truman Markets). Continuing straight (north) about five more minutes takes you to Columbia Road, a colorful shopping street made even more so on Sunday by the **Columbia Road Flower Market** (Sun 8:00-15:00, closed Mon-Sat, http://columbiaroad.info). Halfway up Columbia Road, little Ezra Street has characteristic eateries, boutiques, and antiques vendors.

IN THE WEST END

The iron-and-glass **Covent Garden Market,** originally the garden of Westminster Abbey, is a mix of fun shops, eateries, and markets. Mondays are for antiques, while arts and crafts dominate the rest of the week. Produce stalls are open daily (10:30-18:00) and on Thursdays, a food market brightens up the square (Tube: Covent Garden, tel. 020/7395-1350, www.coventgardenlondonuk.com).

Jubilee Hall Market, on the south side of Covent Garden, features antiques on Mondays, a general market Tuesday through Friday, and arts and crafts on Saturdays and Sundays (Mon 5:00-17:00, Tue-Fri 10:30-19:00, Sat-Sun 10:00-18:00, tel. 020/7379-4242, www.jubileemarket.co.uk).

IN SOUTH LONDON

Borough Market has been serving Southwark for over 800 years. These days, there are as many people taking photos as buying fruit, cheese, and beautiful breads, but it's still a fun carnival atmosphere with fantastic stall foods. For maximum market and minimum crowds, join the locals on Thursdays (full market open Wed-Thu 10:00-17:00, Fri 10:00-18:00, Sat 8:00-17:00, closed Sun; surrounding food stalls open daily; south of London Bridge, where Southwark Street meets Borough High Street; Tube: London Bridge, tel. 020/7407-1002, www.boroughmarket.org.uk).

Theater (a.k.a. Theatre)

London's theater scene rivals Broadway's in quality and often beats it in price. Choose from 200 offerings—Shakespeare, musicals, comedies, thrillers, sex farces, cutting-edge fringe, revivals starring movie celebs, and more. London does it all well.

Rick's Tip: *For the best list of what's happening and a look at the* **latest London scene,** *check www.timeout.com/london.*

West End Shows

Nearly all big-name shows are hosted in the theaters of the West End, clustering

around Soho (especially along Shaftesbury Avenue) between Piccadilly and Covent Garden. With a centuries-old tradition of pleasing the masses, they present London theater at its grandest.

I prefer big, glitzy musicals over serious fare because London can deliver the multimedia spectacle I rarely get back home. If that's not to your taste, you might prefer revivals of classics or cutting-edge works by the hottest young playwrights. London is a magnet for movie stars who want to stretch their acting chops.

The free *Official London Theatre Guide*, updated weekly, is a handy tool (find it at hotels, box offices, the City of London TI, and online at www.officiallondontheatre. co.uk).

Most performances are nightly except Sunday, usually with two or three matinees a week. The few shows that run on Sundays are mostly family fare (*Matilda, The Lion King*, and so on). Tickets range from about £25 to £120. Matinees are generally cheaper and rarely sell out.

Rick's Tip: *Just like at home, London's* **theaters sell seats in a range of levels**— *but the Brits use different terms: stalls (ground floor), dress circle (first balcony), upper circle (second balcony), balcony (sky-high third balcony), and slips (cheap seats on the fringes). Discounted tickets are called "concessions" (abbreviated as "conc" or "s").*

TICKETS

Most shows have tickets available on short notice—likely at a discount. If your time in London is limited or you have your heart set on a particular show that's likely to sell out, you can buy peace of mind by booking your tickets from home. For floor plans of various theaters, see www. theatremonkey.com.

Advance Tickets: Buy your tickets directly from the theater, either through its website or by calling the box office. Often, a theater will reroute you to a third-party ticket vendor such as Ticketmaster. You'll pay with a credit card, and generally be charged a per-ticket booking fee (around £3). You can have your tickets emailed to you or pick them up before show time at the theater's Will Call window. Many third-party websites sell London theater tickets, but generally charge higher prices and fees.

Discount Tickets: The **TKTS Booth** at Leicester Square sells discounted tickets (25-30 percent off) for many shows, though they may not have the hottest shows in town. Buy in person at the kiosk. The best deals are same-day only (£3/ ticket service charge, open Mon-Sat 10:00-19:00, Sun 11:00-16:30).

Rick's Tip: *The* **real TKTS booth** *(with its prominent sign) is a freestanding kiosk at the south edge of Leicester Square. Several dishonest outfits advertise "official half-price tickets"—avoid these, where you'll actually pay much closer to full price.*

The list of shows and prices is posted outside the booth and on the constantly refreshed website www.tkts.co.uk. Come early in the day—the line starts forming even before the booth opens, but moves quickly. Have a second-choice show in mind, in case your first choice is sold out. If TKTS runs out of its ticket allotment for a certain show, it doesn't necessarily mean

Late-Night Sightseeing

Most sightseeing in London winds up by 18:00, but some attractions keep later hours. Keep in mind that sights typically stop admitting visitors well before their posted closing times.

Westminster Abbey (main church): Wed until 19:00

Houses of Parliament: House of Commons—Oct-late July Mon until 22:30, Tue-Wed until 19:30; House of Lords—Oct-late July Mon-Wed until 22:00, Thu until 19:30

London Eye: Last ascent daily at 20:30, at 21:30 or later July-Aug

Madame Tussauds: July-Aug daily until 19:30 (last entry time; stays open about 2 hours longer)

British Museum (some galleries): Fri until 20:30

British Library: Tue-Thu until 20:00

National Gallery: Fri until 21:00

National Portrait Gallery: Thu-Fri until 21:00

Tate Modern: Fri-Sat until 22:00

Victoria and Albert Museum (some galleries): Fri until 22:00

the show is sold out—you can still try the theater's box office.

Theater Box Office: Even if a show is "sold out," there's usually a way to get a seat. Many theaters offer various discounts or "concessions": same-day tickets, cheap returned tickets, standing-room, matinee, senior or student standby deals, and more. Start by checking the show's website, calling the box office, or simply dropping by (many theaters are right in the tourist zone).

Same-day tickets (called "day seats") are generally available only in person at the box office, starting at 10:00 (people start lining up well before then). These tickets (£20 or less) tend to be either in the nosebleed rows or have a restricted view (behind a pillar or extremely far to one side). For a helpful guide to "day seats," see www.theatremonkey.com/dayseatfinder.htm.

Another strategy is to show up at the box office shortly before show time (best on weekdays) and—before paying full price—ask about any cheaper options. Last-minute return tickets are often sold at great prices as curtain time approaches.

For more tips on getting cheap and last-minute tickets, visit www.london theatretickets.org and www.timeout.com/london/theatre.

Third-Party Agencies: Although booking through a middleman such as your hotel or a ticket agency is quick and easy, prices are greatly inflated. Ticket agencies and third-party websites are often just scalpers with an address. If you do buy from an agency, choose a member of the Society of Ticket Agents and Retailers (look for the STAR logo—short for "secure tickets from authorized retailers"). These legitimate resellers normally add a maximum 25 percent booking fee to tickets.

Scalpers (or "Touts"): As at any event, you'll find scalpers hawking tickets outside theaters. And, just like at home, those people may either be honest folk whose date just happened to cancel at the last minute...or they may be unscrupulous thieves selling forgeries. London has many of the latter.

Beyond the West End

Tickets for lesser-known shows tend to be cheaper (figure £15-30), in part because most of the smaller theaters are government-subsidized. Plays don't need a familiar title or famous actor to be a worthwhile experience—read up on the latest offerings online; Time Out's website is a great place to start.

Evensong

Evensong is an evening worship service that is typically sung rather than spoken. It follows the traditional Anglican service in the Book of Common Prayer, including prayers, scripture readings, canticles (sung responses), and hymns that are appropriate for the early evening—traditionally the end of the working day and before the evening meal. In major churches with resident choirs, a singing or chanting priest leads the service, and a choir—usually made up of both men and boys—sings the responses. The choir sings a cappella or is accompanied by an organ. Visitors are welcome and are given an order of service or a prayer book to help them follow along. (If you're not familiar with the order of service, watch the congregation to know when to stand, sit, and kneel.)

Impressive places for evensong in London include Westminster Abbey and St. Paul's. Evensong typically takes place in the small choir area, which is far more intimate than the main nave. It generally occurs daily between 17:00 and 18:00 (often two hours earlier on Sundays); check with individual churches for specifics. At smaller churches, evensong is sometimes spoken, not sung.

Evensong is not a performance—it's a worship service. If you enjoy worshipping in different churches, attending evensong can be a highlight. But if church services aren't your thing, consider an organ or choral concert, offered in most major churches. Look for posted schedules or ask at the information desk or gift shop.

MAJOR THEATERS

The **National Theatre** has a range of impressive options, often starring recognizable names. Deeply discounted tickets are commonly offered (looming on the South Bank by Waterloo Bridge, Tube: Waterloo, www.nationaltheatre.org.uk).

The **Barbican Centre** puts on high-quality, often experimental work (right by the Museum of London, just north of The City, Tube: Barbican, www.barbican.org.uk), as does the **Royal Court Theatre,** which has £10 tickets for its Monday shows (west of the West End in Sloane Square, Tube: Sloane Square, www.royalcourttheatre.com).

Menier Chocolate Factory in Southwark is gaining popularity for its impressive productions and intimate setting—a mix of plays, musicals, and even an occasional comedian (behind the Tate Modern at 56 Southwark Street, Tube: Southwark, www.menierchocolatefactory.com).

The **Royal Shakespeare Company** performs at various theaters around London and in Stratford-upon-Avon year-round. To get a schedule, contact the RSC (Royal Shakespeare Theatre, Stratford-upon-Avon, tel. 0844-800-1110, www.rsc.org.uk).

SHAKESPEARE'S GLOBE

To see Shakespeare in a replica of the theater for which he wrote his plays, attend a play at the Globe. In this round, thatch-roofed, open-air theater, the plays are performed much as Shakespeare intended—under the sky, with no amplification. I've never enjoyed Shakespeare as much as here, performed as it was meant to be in the "wooden O." If you can't attend a show, take a guided tour of the theater and museum by day (see page 79).

The play's the thing from late April through early October (usually Tue-Sat 14:00 and 19:30, Sun 13:00 and/or 18:30, tickets can be sold out months in advance). You'll pay £5 to stand and £17-43 to sit, usually on a backless bench. Because only a few rows and the pricier Gentlemen's Rooms have seats with backs, £1 cushions and £3 add-on backrests are a good investment. Dress for the weather.

The £5 "groundling" tickets—which are open to rain—are most fun. Scurry in early to stake out a spot on the stage's edge, where the most interaction with the actors occurs. You're a crude peasant. You can lean your elbows on the stage, munch a picnic dinner (yes, you can bring in food), or walk around.

The indoor Sam Wanamaker Playhouse allows Shakespearean-era plays and early-music concerts to be performed through the winter. Many of the productions in this intimate venue are one-offs and can be quite pricey.

For tickets, call or drop by the box office (Mon-Sat 10:00-18:00, Sun until 17:00, open one hour later on performance days, New Globe Walk entrance, tel. 020/7401-9919). You can also reserve online (www.shakespearesglobe.com, £2.50 booking fee). If tickets are sold out, don't despair; call around noon on the day of the performance to see if the box office expects any returned tickets. If so, show

up a little more than an hour before the show, when these tickets are sold (first-come, first-served).

The theater is on the South Bank, directly across the Thames over the Millennium Bridge from St. Paul's Cathedral (Tube: Mansion House or London Bridge).

EATING

Eating out has become an essential part of the London experience. The sheer variety of foods—from every corner of its former empire and beyond—is astonishing. But the thought of a £50 meal in Britain generally ruins my appetite, so my London dining is limited mostly to easygoing, moderately priced options. Pub grub and ethnic restaurants (especially Indian and Chinese) are good low-cost options. Chain restaurants are affordable and popular (see page 92 for a rundown). Picnicking is the fastest, cheapest way to go. Good grocery stores and sandwich shops, fine park benches, and polite pigeons abound.

Most London restaurants generally open daily no later than noon and close sometime between 22:00 and midnight.

Central London
Soho
Foodies skip the touristy zones near Piccadilly and Trafalgar Square and head to Soho. These restaurants are scattered throughout a chic, creative, and borderline-seedy zone that teems with hipsters, theatergoers, and London's gay community. Even if you plan to have dinner elsewhere, it's a treat just to wander around Soho.

A performance at Shakespeare's Globe

Rick's Tip: *While gentrification has mostly stripped this area of its former **"red light district"** vibe, a few pockets survive. Only fools fall for the "£5 drink and show" lure outside the strip clubs (especially on Great Windmill Street).*

ON AND NEAR WARDOUR STREET

Stroll up this street—particularly from Brewer Street northward—to take your pick from Thai, Indonesian, Vietnamese, Italian, French, and even...English.

Princi is a vast, bright, efficient deli/bakery with Milanese flair. Display cases offer a tempting array of pizza rustica, panini sandwiches, focaccia, a few pasta dishes, and desserts. Order your food at the counter, then find a space at a long shared table; or get it to go (£7-13 meals, daily 8:00-24:00, 135 Wardour Street, tel. 020/7478-8888).

Bi Bim Bap is a popular diner named for what it sells: Korean *bibimbap*, a steaming stone bowl of rice and thinly sliced veggies, topped with a fried egg. Other toppings—including chicken, beef strips, and mushrooms—are a few pounds extra (£7-10 meals, Mon-Sat 12:00-15:00 & 18:00-23:00, closed Sun, 11 Greek Street, second location near British Museum at 8 Charlotte Street, tel. 020/7287-3434).

Bocca di Lupo serves half and full portions of classic regional Italian food. Stylish but fun, it's a place where you're glad you made a reservation. The counter seating, on cushy stools with a view into the open kitchen, is particularly memorable, or you can take a table in the snug, casual back end (£12-20 dishes, daily 12:30-15:00 & 17:30-23:00, 12 Archer Street, tel. 020/7734-2223, www.boccadilupo.com).

Gelupo, Bocca di Lupo's sister *gelateria* across the street, has a wide array of ever-changing but delicious dessert favorites as well as espresso drinks (daily 11:00-23:00, 7 Archer Street, tel. 020/7287-5555).

Chain Restaurants: While I wouldn't waste a Soho meal on a **chain restaurant,** they're a convenient fallback—**Byron Hamburgers** (appealing industrial-mod branch at 97 Wardour Street, also near Golden Square at 16 Beak Street and at 1A St. Giles High Street), **Thai Square** (27 St. Anne's Court, also at 5 Princes Street on Hanover Square), **Wagamama** (42 Great Marlborough Street), **Masala Zone** (9 Marshall Street), **Yo! Sushi** (52 Poland Street), and **Côte** (124 Wardour Street and near Oxford Circus at 4 Great Portland Street).

ON LEXINGTON STREET

Andrew Edmunds Restaurant is a tiny, candlelit space with a loyal clientele—it's the closest I've found to Parisian quality in London. The extensive wine list, modern European cooking, and creative seasonal menu are worth the splurge (£12-20 main dishes, Mon-Sat 12:00-15:30 & 17:30-22:45, Sun 13:00-16:00 & 18:00-22:30, these are last-order times, come early or call ahead, request ground floor rather than basement, 46 Lexington Street, tel. 020/7437-5708, www.andrewedmunds.com).

Mildred's Vegetarian Restaurant, across from Andrew Edmunds, has an enjoyable menu and a pleasant interior filled with happy eaters (£8-11 meals, small takeaway menu, Mon-Sat 12:00-23:00, closed Sun, vegan options, 45 Lexington Street, tel. 020/7494-1634).

Near Trafalgar Square

St. Martin-in-the-Fields Café in the Crypt is just right for a tasty meal on a monk's budget—maybe even on a monk's tomb. Their enticing buffet line is kept stocked all day, serving breakfast, lunch, and dinner (£7-10 cafeteria plates, hearty traditional desserts). They also serve a restful cream tea (£6.50, daily 14:00-18:00). You'll find the café directly under the St. Martin-in-the-Fields Church, facing Trafalgar Square—enter through the glass pavilion next to the church (generally about 8:00-20:00 daily, Tube: Charing Cross, tel. 020/7766-1158 or 020/7766-1100). On Wednesday evenings you can dine to the music of a live jazz band at 20:00 (£5.50-12 tickets). While here, check out the concert schedule for the busy church upstairs (or visit www.smitf.org).

The Chandos Pub's Opera Room floats apart from the tacky tourism around Trafalgar Square. Look for it opposite the National Portrait Gallery (corner of William IV Street and St. Martin's Lane) and climb the stairs to the Opera Room. They serve sandwiches and traditional pub meals for under £10—meat pies and fish-and-chips are their specialty. The ground-floor pub offers snugs (private booths) and serious beer drinking; order upstairs and carry it down (kitchen open daily 11:30-21:00, Fri until 18:00, order and pay at the bar, 29 St. Martin's Lane, Tube: Leicester Square, tel. 020/7836-1401).

Convenient for sightseers, the **National Gallery** has three on-site eateries (page 48) and the **National Portrait Gallery** has two (page 51).

Near Piccadilly

The Wolseley is in the grand 1920s show-room of a long-defunct British car. Today, this old-time bistro bustles with formal waiters serving traditional Austrian and French dishes in an elegant setting fit for its location next to the Ritz. Although the food can be unexceptional, prices are reasonable considering the grand presentation and setting. It's popular for its fancy cream or afternoon tea. Reservations are a must (£13-30 main courses; cheaper "café menu" available; daily 7:00-24:00, 160 Piccadilly, tel. 020/7499-6996, www. thewolseley.com).

The Savini at the Criterion, a pala-tial dining hall, offers Italian cuisine in a dreamy Neo-Byzantine setting from the 1870s. It's a deal for the visual experience during lunch, especially if you order the £20-25 fixed-price meal (except on Sun, when you must order from the expensive à la carte menu). Anyone can drop in for coffee or a drink (daily 12:00-14:30 & 17:30-23:30, 224 Piccadilly, tel. 020/7930-0488, www.saviniatcriterion.co.uk).

Covent Garden

Joe Allen, tucked in a brick cellar a block away from the market, serves modern international and American cuisine with both style and hubbub. It's comfortably spacious and popular with the theater crowd (£11-30 main courses, specials at lunch and for early birds, open daily 12:00-24:00, piano music after 19:00, 13 Exeter Street, tel. 020/7836-0651).

Union Jacks, a venture of celebrity chef Jamie Oliver, uses traditional British ingredients to make inventive modern dishes. Wood-fired pizzas are topped not with cheese and tomatoes, but roast pig shoulder or oxtail and brisket (£12-14 piz-zas, £15 classic British dishes, daily 12:00-23:00, right inside Covent Garden market hall, tel. 020/3640-7086).

Near the British Museum

To avoid the tourist crush around the museum (and in Soho), Londoners head a few blocks west to the Fitzrovia area. Tiny Charlotte Place is lined with small eater-ies; nearby, much bigger Charlotte Street has several more options. This area is a short walk from the Goodge Street Tube station.

Salumeria Dino serves hearty sand-wiches, pasta, and coffee in an Italian deli so authentic you'll walk out singing "O Sole Mio" (£4-5 sandwiches, Mon-Fri 9:00-18:00, closed Sat-Sun, 15 Charlotte Place, tel. 020/7580-3938).

Lantana OUT, next door to Salume-ria Dino, is an Australian coffee shop that sells modern soups, sandwiches, and salads at their takeaway window (£3-8

Central London Eateries

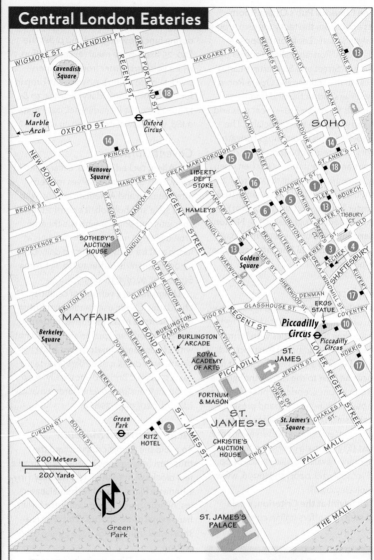

1. Princi Italian Deli
2. Bi Bim Bap
3. Bocca di Lupo
4. Gelupo Gelato
5. Andrew Edmunds Restaurant
6. Mildred's Vegetarian Rest.
7. St. Martin-in-the-Fields Café
8. The Chandos Pub
9. The Wolseley
10. The Savini at the Criterion
11. Joe Allen
12. Union Jacks
13. Byron (7)
14. Thai Square (5)
15. Wagamama (4)
16. Masala Zone (2)
17. Yo! Sushi (3)
18. Côte (4)

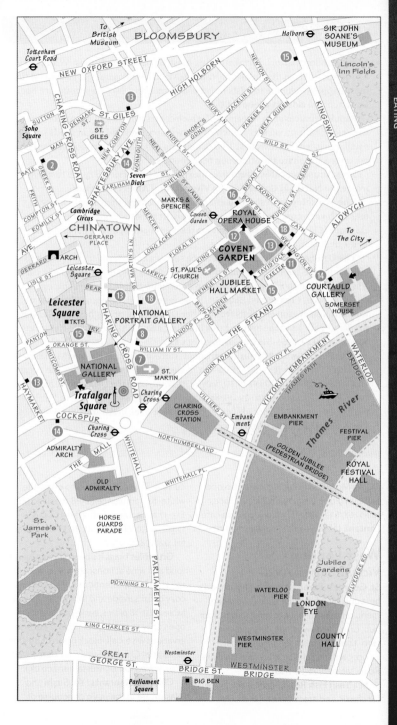

Taking Tea

Many London visitors partake in this most British of traditions. While some tearooms—such as the finicky Fortnum & Mason—still require a jacket and tie, most happily welcome tourists in jeans and sneakers. Most tearooms are open for lunch and close at about 17:00.

Popular choices are a "cream tea," which consists of tea and a scone or two, or the pricier "afternoon tea," which comes with pastries and finger foods such as small, crust-less sandwiches. Two people can order one afternoon tea and one cream tea and share the afternoon tea's goodies.

Many **museum cafés** offer a fine, inexpensive tea service. Try the restaurants inside the **National Gallery** or the **Victoria and Albert Museum.**

The Wolseley serves a good afternoon tea between their meal service. Split one with your companion and enjoy two light meals at a great price in classic elegance (£12 cream tea, £27 afternoon tea, £38 champagne tea, generally served 15:00-18:30 daily, see page 93).

The Orangery at Kensington Palace serves a £28 "Orangery tea" and a £34-38 champagne tea in its bright white hall. You can also order treats à la carte. The portions aren't huge, but who can argue with eating at a royal orangery or on the terrace? (Tea served 12:00-18:00, no reservations taken; a 10-minute walk through Kensington Gardens from either Queensway or High Street Kensington Tube stations to the orange brick building, about 100 yards from Kensington Palace; tel. 020/3166-6113, www.hrp.org.uk.)

The **Fortnum & Mason** department store offers tea at several different restaurants within its walls. Take tea in the Parlour (£24 including ice cream and scones; Mon-Sat 10:00-19:30, Sun 11:30-17:00) or in the Diamond Jubilee Tea Salon (£40-44, daily 12:00-19:00, Sun until 18:00, dress up—no shorts, "children must be behaved," 181 Piccadilly, reserve at least a week in advance, tel. 020/7734-8040, www.fortnumandmason.com).

meals, Mon-Fri 7:30-15:00, café also open Sat-Sun 9:00-17:00, 13 Charlotte Place, tel. 020/7637-3347). Pricier sit-down café **Lantana IN** serves £9-12 meals next door.

West London
Victoria Station Area

St. George's Tavern is the neighborhood's best pub for a full meal. Enjoy the same menu on the sidewalk, in the ground-floor pub, or in the downstairs dining room (£10-14 meals, food served daily 10:00-22:00, corner of Hugh Street and Belgrave Road, tel. 020/7630-1116).

Seafresh Fish Restaurant is the place for classic and creative fish-and-chips

cuisine. Take out or eat in to enjoy the white-fish ambience (£5-8 meals to go, £13-17 to sit, Mon-Sat 12:00-15:00 & 17:00-22:30, closed Sun, 80 Wilton Road, tel. 020/7828-0747).

Grumbles brags it's been serving "good food and wine at nonscary prices since 1964." This unpretentious little place has cozy booths inside and four nice sidewalk tables (£11-18 plates, early-bird specials, open daily 12:00-14:30 & 18:00-23:00, reservations wise, half-block north of Belgrave Road at 35 Churton Street, tel. 020/7834-0149, www.grumblesrestaurant.co.uk).

Chain Restaurants: Yo! Sushi and **Wasabi** are in the main concourse of

Victoria Station (another Wasabi is at 131 Victoria Street). You'll also find **Wagamama** (at Cardinal Place off Victoria Street) and an **Itsu** (163 Victoria Street). **Le Pain Quotidien** is a block east of the station (128 Wilton Road).

Groceries: A handy **M&S Simply Food** is inside Victoria Station (daily 7:00-24:00, near the front, by the bus terminus), along with a **Sainsbury's Local** (daily 6:00-23:00, at rear entrance, on Eccleston Street). A large **Sainsbury's Local** is a couple of blocks southeast of the station (Mon-Sat 7:00-23:00, Sun 11:00-17:00, on Wilton Road near Warwick Way).

Bayswater and Notting Hill

Geales has been serving Notting Hill-billies fish-and-chips since 1939. Today, the menu is varied, but the emphasis is still on fish. The crispy cod that put them on the map is still the best around (lunch—£10 two-course express menu; dinner—£4-11 starters and salads, £14-23 main dishes; daily 12:00-15:00 & 18:00-22:30, reservations smart, 2 Farmer Street, just south of Notting Hill Gate Tube stop, tel. 020/7727-7528, www.geales.com).

The Churchill Arms pub and **Thai Kitchen** (same location) are local hangouts, with good beer and a thriving old-English ambience in front, and hearty £9 Thai plates in an enclosed patio in the back. The place is festooned with Churchill memorabilia and chamber pots. Arrive by 18:00 or after 21:00 to avoid a line. During busy times, diners are limited to an hour at the table (food served daily 12:00-22:00, 119 Kensington Church Street, tel. 020/7727-4242 for the pub or tel. 020/7792-1296 for restaurant reservations, www.churchillarmskensington. co.uk).

Hereford Road, a cozy, mod eatery tucked away on Leinster Square, serves English cuisine with modern panache. Cozy two-person booths face the open kitchen up top; the main dining room is down below (£14-17 main dishes, reserva-

tions smart, daily 12:00-15:00 & 18:00-22:00, 3 Hereford Road, tel. 020/7727-1144, www.herefordroad.org).

The Prince Edward serves good grub in a comfy, family-friendly, upscale-pub setting and at its sidewalk tables (£10-15 meals, daily 10:30-23:00, 2 blocks north of Bayswater Road at the corner of Dawson Place and Hereford Road, 73 Prince's Square, tel. 020/7727-2221).

Chain Restaurants: Choices are **Byron Hamburgers** (103 Westbourne Grove), **Masala Zone** (75 Bishop's Bridge Road), **Yo! Sushi** (Whiteleys Shopping Centre), **Itsu** (100 Notting Hill Gate), and **Côte** (98 Westbourne Grove). To the south, past Kensington Palace, is **Wagamama** (26 Kensington High Street).

SLEEPING

I've focused my recommendations on good-value B&Bs that cluster near Victoria Station, and on a range of hotels found north of Kensington Gardens and near Paddington Station. Prices for London rooms often flex seasonally and/or with demand. Check online for specific rates and last-minute deals.

If you'd like to stay at a no-frills chain hotel with well-priced rooms, the following all have convenient London locations:

Sleep Code

Price Rankings for Double Rooms (Db)

$$$ Most rooms £125 or more
 $$ £75-125
  $ £75 or less

Abbreviations: Db=Double with bathroom. D=Double with bathroom down the hall

Notes: Room prices change; verify rates online or by email. For the best prices, book direct with the hotel.

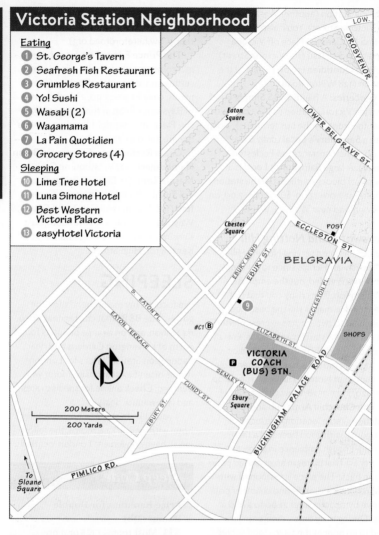

Victoria Station Neighborhood

Eating
1. St. George's Tavern
2. Seafresh Fish Restaurant
3. Grumbles Restaurant
4. Yo! Sushi
5. Wasabi (2)
6. Wagamama
7. La Pain Quotidien
8. Grocery Stores (4)

Sleeping
10. Lime Tree Hotel
11. Luna Simone Hotel
12. Best Western Victoria Palace
13. easyHotel Victoria

Premier Inn (King's Cross-St. Pancras, Euston, and Victoria; www.premierinn. com), **Travelodge** (King's Cross, Euston, and Covent Garden; www.travelodge. co.uk); and **Ibis** (Euston-St. Pancras; www.ibishotel.com).

EasyHotel, another no-frills chain, offers tiny, efficient but thin-walled rooms that feel popped out of a plastic mold. Rates can be very low (with doubles as cheap as £30 for early booking), but extras are pricey, such as TV use, Wi-Fi, bag storage, fresh towels, and daily cleaning. Book far ahead and skip the extras for the best price (Victoria, South Kensington, Earl's Court, and Paddington; www.easyhotel. com).

Also consider these accommodation discount sites: www.londontown. com, athomeinlondon.co.uk and www. londonbb.com (both list central B&Bs), and www.visitlondon.com.

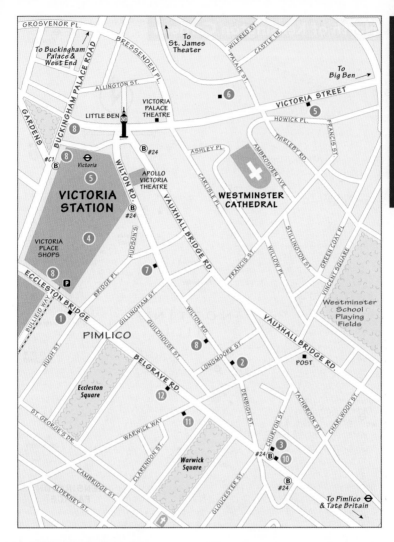

Near Victoria Station

The safe, surprisingly tidy streets behind Victoria Station teem with moderately priced B&Bs.

$$$ Lime Tree Hotel is a gem with 25 spacious, stylish, comfortable rooms, a helpful staff, and a fun-loving breakfast room. It's two blocks over from Victoria Station, in Belgravia (Db-£175, usually cheaper Jan-Feb, small lounge opens onto quiet garden, 135 Ebury Street, tel. 020/7730-8191, www.limetreehotel.co.uk, info@limetreehotel.co.uk).

$$ Luna Simone Hotel rents 36 fresh, spacious, remodeled rooms with modern bathrooms in Pimlico (Db-£115-140, family rooms, ask about Rick Steves discount, at 47 Belgrave Road near the corner of Charlwood Street, handy bus #24 stops out front, tel. 020/7834-5897, www.lunasimonehotel.com, stay@ lunasimonehotel.com).

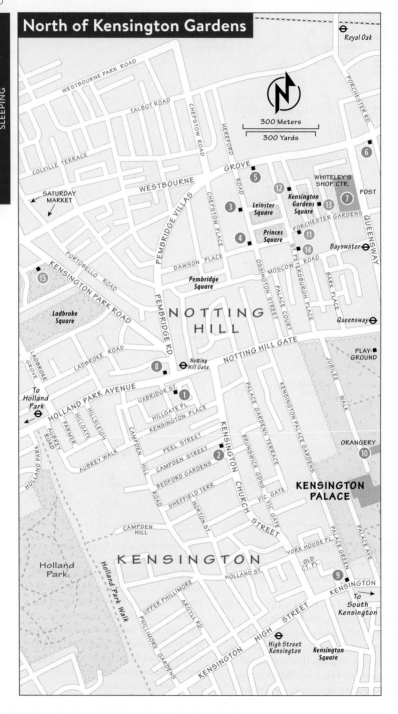

North of Kensington Gardens

300 Meters

300 Yards

Royal Oak

WESTBOURNE PARK ROAD

TALBOT ROAD

CHEPSTOW ROAD

HEREFORD ROAD

PORCHESTER RD

COLVILLE TERRACE

WESTBOURNE

GROVE

SATURDAY
MARKET

WHITELEY'S
SHOP. CTR.

POST

⑤

⑫

Kensington
Gardens
Square

⑬

⑦

⑥

PEMBRIDGE VILLAS

CHEPSTOW PLACE

Leinster
Square

③

Princes
Square

④

PORCHESTER GARDENS

⑪

QUEENSWAY

PORTOBELLO ROAD

DAWSON PLACE

ST. PETERSBURGH PLACE

⑭

Bayswater

KENSINGTON PARK ROAD

⑮

Pembridge
Square

OSSINGTON STREET

MOSCOW ROAD

PALACE COURT

BARK PLACE

Ladbroke
Square

PEMBRIDGE RD

NOTTING
HILL

Queensway

LADBROKE GROVE

LADBROKE ROAD

Notting
Hill Gate

NOTTING HILL GATE

PALACE GARDENS TERRACE

KENSINGTON PALACE GARDENS

JUBILEE WALK

PLAY-
GROUND

⑧

To
Holland
Park

HOLLAND PARK AVENUE

UXBRIDGE ST

①

FARMER

HILLGATE

HILLSLEIGH

HILLGATE PL.

KENSINGTON PLACE

AUBREY ROAD

AUBREY WALK

CAMPDEN HILL ROAD

PEEL STREET

CAMPDEN STREET

②

BEDFORD GARDENS

SHEFFIELD TERR.

HORTON ST.

KENSINGTON CHURCH STREET

BRUNSWICK GDNS.

VIC. VIC. GATE

ORANGERY

⑩

KENSINGTON
PALACE

HOLLAND PARK

CAMPDEN
HILL

KENSINGTON

Holland
Park

HOLLAND PARK WALK

UPPER PHILLIMORE

ARGYLL RD

PHILLIMORE GARDENS

HOLLAND ST.

YORK HOUSE PL.

OLD
CT. PL.

PALACE GREEN

PALACE AVE.

⑨

KENSINGTON

To
South
Kensington

KENSINGTON HIGH STREET

High Street
Kensington

Kensington
Square

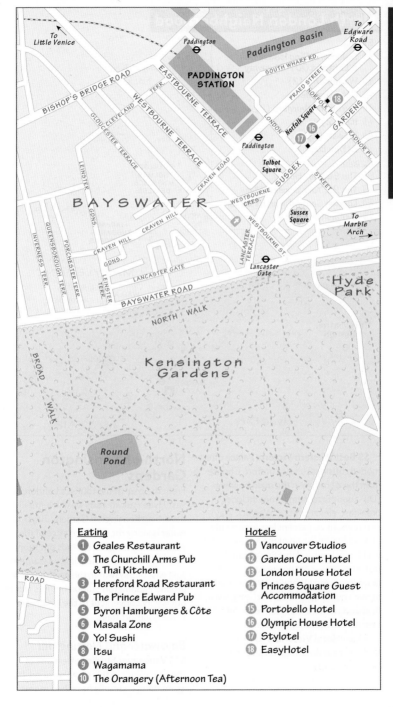

Eating

1. Geales Restaurant
2. The Churchill Arms Pub & Thai Kitchen
3. Hereford Road Restaurant
4. The Prince Edward Pub
5. Byron Hamburgers & Côte
6. Masala Zone
7. Yo! Sushi
8. Itsu
9. Wagamama
10. The Orangery (Afternoon Tea)

Hotels

11. Vancouver Studios
12. Garden Court Hotel
13. London House Hotel
14. Princes Square Guest Accommodation
15. Portobello Hotel
16. Olympic House Hotel
17. Stylotel
18. EasyHotel

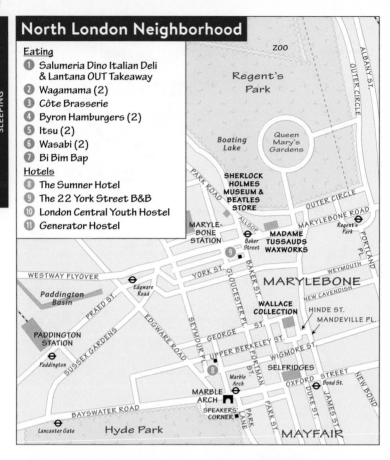

North London Neighborhood

Eating

1. Salumeria Dino Italian Deli & Lantana OUT Takeaway
2. Wagamama (2)
3. Côte Brasserie
4. Byron Hamburgers (2)
5. Itsu (2)
6. Wasabi (2)
7. Bi Bim Bap

Hotels

8. The Sumner Hotel
9. The 22 York Street B&B
10. London Central Youth Hostel
11. Generator Hostel

$$ Best Western Victoria Palace offers modern business-class comfort. Choose from the 43 rooms in the main building (Db-about £120, sometimes includes breakfast, elevator, at 60 Warwick Way), or pay about 20 percent less for a nearly identical room in one of the annexes, each a half-block away (Db-£85-90, breakfast-£12.50, air-con, no elevator, 17 Belgrave Road and 1 Warwick Way, reception at main building; tel. 020/7821-7113, www.bestwesternvictoriapalace.co.uk, info@bestwesternvictoriapalace.co.uk).

$ EasyHotel Victoria is part of the budget chain described on page 98 (36 Belgrave Road).

North of Kensington Gardens

From the core of the tourist's London, the vast Hyde Park spreads west, eventually becoming Kensington Gardens. Bayswater is along the northern edge of the park, and Notting Hill spreads out from the northwest tip of Kensington Gardens. Just east of Bayswater, the neighborhood around Paddington Station has less charm but is very convenient to the Heathrow Express airport train.

Bayswater and Notting Hill

$$$ Vancouver Studios offers one of the best values in this neighborhood. Its 45 modern, tastefully furnished rooms

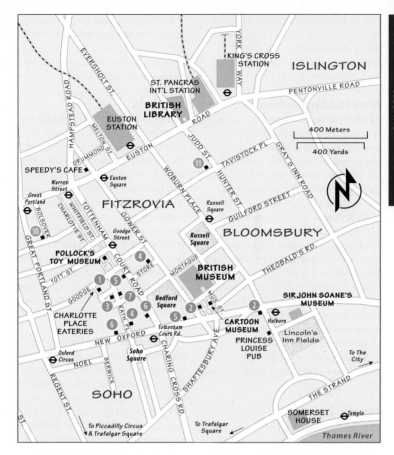

come with fully equipped kitchenettes (no breakfast). It has a welcoming lounge and its own tranquil garden patio out back, which is refreshing if you land a somewhat-smoky room (Db-£149, 30 Princes Square, tel. 020/7243-1270, www.vancouverstudios.co.uk, info@vancouverstudios.co.uk).

$$$ Garden Court Hotel is understated, with 40 simple, homey-but-tasteful rooms (Db-£129, family rooms, includes continental breakfast or pay £3.50 for English breakfast, elevator, 30 Kensington Gardens Square, tel. 020/7229-2553, www.gardencourthotel.co.uk, info@gardencourthotel.co.uk).

$$$ London House Hotel has 103 modern, cookie-cutter rooms on a tranquil, tidy park (generally Db-£105 weekdays and £130 on weekends, basement family rooms, continental breakfast-£7, elevator, 81 Kensington Gardens Square, tel. 020/7243-1810, www.londonhousehotels.com, reservations@londonhousehotels.com).

$$ Princes Square Guest Accommodation rents 50 crisp, businesslike rooms with pleasant, modern decor (generally Db-£100-160; elevator, 23 Princes Square, tel. 020/7229-9876, www.princessquarehotel.co.uk, info@princessquarehotel.co.uk).

$$$ Portobello Hotel is on a quiet residential street in the heart of Notting

Hill. Its 21 freshly refurbished rooms are funky yet elegant (Db-£175-315, elevator, 22 Stanley Gardens, tel. 020/7727-2777, www.portobellohotel.com, stay@portobellohotel.com, Hannah).

Near Paddington Station

$$ Olympic House Hotel has clean public spaces and 38 business-class rooms with predictable comfort (Db-£105, air-con in most rooms costs extra, elevator, pay Wi-Fi, 138 Sussex Gardens, tel. 020/7723-5935, www.olympichousehotel.co.uk, olympichousehotel@btinternet.com).

$$ Stylotel is stylish, modern, and aluminum-clad, with 39 tidy rooms. Rooms can be cramped, but the beds have space for luggage underneath (Db-£95, family rooms, elevator, pay Wi-Fi, 160 Sussex Gardens, tel. 020/7723-1026, www.stylotel.com, info@stylotel.com, well-run by Andreas). There are eight fancier, air-conditioned suites across the street (kitchenettes, no breakfast).

$ EasyHotel, part of the budget chain, has a branch at 10 Norfolk Place (see page 98).

North London

$$$ The Sumner Hotel rents 19 rooms in a 19th-century Georgian townhouse sporting large contemporary rooms. This swanky place packs in all the amenities and is conveniently located north of Hyde Park and near Oxford Street—it's close to Selfridges and a Marks & Spencer (Db-£193-£229, ask about Rick Steves rates, air-con, elevator, 54 Upper Berkeley Street, a block and a half off Edgware Road, Tube: Marble Arch, tel. 020/7723-2244, www.thesumner.com, reservations@thesumner.com).

$$$ The 22 York Street B&B offers a casual alternative in the city center, renting 10 traditional, hardwood, comfortable rooms, each named for a notable London landmark (Db-£150, inviting lounge; near Marylebone/Baker Street: from Baker Street Tube station, walk 2 blocks down Baker Street and take a right to 22 York Street—no sign, just look for #22; tel. 020/7224-2990, www.22yorkstreet.co.uk, mc@22yorkstreet.co.uk, energetically run by Liz and Michael Callis).

Hostels

$ London Central Youth Hostel is the flagship of London's hostels, with 300 beds and all the latest in security and comfortable efficiency. Families and travelers of any age will feel welcome in this wonderful facility. You'll pay the same price for any bed in a four- to eight-bed single-sex dorm—with or without private bathroom—so try to grab one with a bathroom (£18-34/bunk, twin D-£50-70, families welcome to book an entire room, members' kitchen, book long in advance, between Oxford Circus and Great Portland Street Tube stations at 104 Bolsover Street, tel. 0845-371-9154, www.yha.org.uk, londoncentral@yha.org.uk).

$ Generator Hostel is a brightly colored, hip hostel with a café, a DJ spinning the hits, and 870 beds in 220 rooms, including doubles. It's in a renovated building tucked behind a busy street halfway between Kings Cross and the British Museum (£18-34/bunk, twin Db-£70-120, breakfast-£5, 37 Tavistock Place, Tube: Russell Square, tel. 020/7388-7666, www.generatorhostels.com, london@generatorhostels.com).

TRANSPORTATION

Getting Around London

To travel smartly in a city this size, you must get comfortable with public transportation. London's excellent taxis, buses, and subway (Tube) system can take you anywhere you need to go—a blessing for travelers' precious vacation time, not to mention their feet. It's also the most expensive public transit in the world. While single-ride and paper tickets still exist, for most visitors the Oyster card is simply the only way to go—saving precious time and money.

For more information about public transit (bus and Tube), the best single source is the helpful *Hello London* brochure, which includes both a Tube map and a handy schematic map of the best bus routes (available free at TIs, museums, hotels, and at www.tfl.gov.uk). For specific directions on how to get from point A to point B on London's transit, detailed bus maps, updated prices, and general information, check www.tfl.gov.uk or call the automated info line at 0843-222-1234.

Public Transit Tickets and Passes

While the transit system has six zones, almost all tourist sights are within Zones 1 and 2, so those are the prices I've listed (for all the prices, see www.tfl.gov.uk/tickets).

INDIVIDUAL TICKETS

Individual paper tickets for the Tube are ridiculously expensive (£4.90 per Tube ride). Buy them at any Tube station, either at (often-crowded) ticket windows or at easy-to-use self-service machines. Tickets are valid only on the day of purchase. Unless you're taking only one Tube ride your entire visit, you'll save money (and time) by buying one of the following multiple-ride passes.

TRANSIT CARDS

Oyster Card: A pay-as-you-go transit card, the Oyster card allows you to ride the Tube, buses, Docklands Light Railway (DLR), and Overground (mostly sub-urban trains) for about half the rate of individual tickets. To use the card, simply touch it against the yellow card reader at the turnstile or entrance, the card reader flashes green, and the fare is automatically deducted. (You must also tap your card again to "touch out" as you exit.)

Buy the card at any Tube station ticket window, or look for nearby shops displaying the Oyster logo where you can purchase a card or add credit without the wait. You'll pay a £5 deposit up front, then load it with as much credit as you'll need. One ride in Zones 1 and 2 during peak time costs £2.90; off peak (after 9:30 on weekdays) is a little cheaper (£2.40 per ride). The system comes with an automatic price cap that guarantees you'll never pay more than £6.40 in one day for riding within Zones 1 and 2. If you think you'll take more than two rides in a day, £6.50 credit will cover you, but it's smart to add more if you expect to travel outside the city center. If you're staying five or more days, consider adding a 7-Day Travelcard to your Oyster card (details below).

Oyster cards are not shareable; each traveler will need his or her own. If your balance gets low, simply add credit—or "top up"—at a ticket window, machine, or shop. You can always see how much credit remains on your card by touching it to the pad at any ticket machine.

At the end of your trip, you can reclaim your deposit and unused balance (up to £10) by selecting "Pay as you go refund" on any ticket machine that gives change. This will deactivate your card. For balances of more than £10, you'll have to wait in line at a ticket window for your refund. If you don't deactivate your card, the credit never expires—you can use it again on your next trip.

Visitor Oyster cards, aimed specifically at tourists, function exactly the same as a regular Oyster card. But you must purchase it online in advance and have it delivered by mail before your trip, making it more expensive than a regular Oyster card.

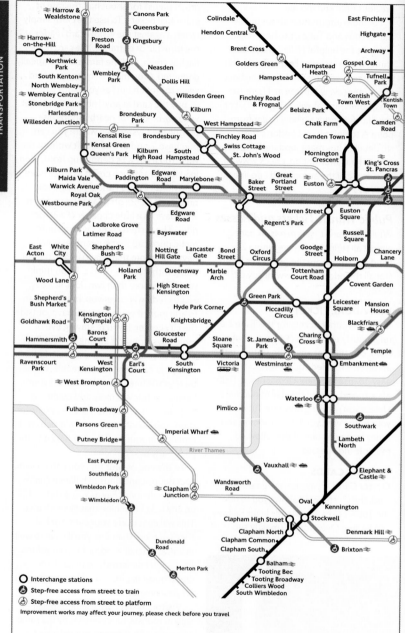

Interchange stations

Step-free access from street to train

Step-free access from street to platform

Improvement works may affect your journey, please check before you travel

MAYOR OF LONDON

Correct at time of going to print   Reg. user No. 16/2969/P   Version B 06.2016   © Transport for London

TRANSPORT FOR LONDON

EVERY JOURNEY MATTERS

UNDERGROUND

Travelcards: These paper tickets let you ride as many times as you want within a one- or a seven-day period for one fixed price, but are only a good deal in limited instances. Buy it at any Tube station ticket window or machine, then feed it into a turnstile (and retrieve it) to enter and exit the Tube. On a bus, just show it to the driver when you get on.

Your one-day options are the **Anytime Day Travelcard** (Zones 1-4, £12.10) or the **Off-Peak Day Travelcard** (Zones 1-6, covers one day of travel after 9:30 on weekdays, anytime on weekends, £12.10). However, an Oyster card with its daily cap is almost always a better deal.

The **7-Day Travelcard,** which comes in a paper version or can be added to an Oyster card, is the best option if you're staying five or more days and plan to use public transit a lot (£32.40 for Zones 1-2; £59.10 for Zones 1-6). For most travelers, the Zone 1-2 pass works best. (Heathrow Airport is in Zone 6, but you can pay a small supplement to cover the difference.)

The Bottom Line: Wondering which pass works best for your trip? On a short visit (three or fewer days), consider purchasing an Oyster card and adding £20-25 of credit (£6.50 daily cap times three days, plus extra for any rides outside Zones 1-2). If you'll be taking fewer rides, £15 will be enough (£2.90 per ride during peak time gets you 5 rides), and if not you can always top up. If you're in London for five days or longer, the 7-Day Travelcard will likely pay for itself.

DISCOUNTS AND DEALS

Families: A paying adult can take up to four kids (ages 10 and under) for free on the Tube, Docklands Light Railway (DLR), Overground, and buses. Explore other child and student discounts at www.tfl.gov.uk/tickets or ask a clerk at a Tube ticket window which deal is best.

River Cruises: A Travelcard gives you a 33 percent discount on most Thames cruises (see page 32). The Oyster card gives you roughly a 10 percent discount on Thames Clippers, including the Tate Boat museum ferry.

By Tube

London's subway system is called the Tube or Underground (but not "subway," which, in Britain, refers to a pedestrian underpass). The Tube is one of this planet's great people-movers and usually the fastest long-distance transport in town (runs Mon-Sat about 5:00-24:00, Sun about 7:00-23:00; Central, Jubilee, Northern, Piccadilly, and Victoria lines also run Fri-Sat 24 hours). Two other commuter rail lines are tied into the network and use the same tickets: the Docklands Light Railway (DLR) and the Overground.

Each line has a name (such as Circle, Northern, or Bakerloo) and two directions (indicated by the end-of-the-line stops). Find the line that will take you to your destination, and figure out roughly which direction (north, south, east, or west) you'll need to head to get there.

At the Tube station, there are two ways to pass through the turnstile. If using an Oyster card, touch it flat against the turnstile's yellow card reader, both when you enter and exit the station. With a paper ticket or Travelcard, you'll feed it into the turnstile, reclaim it, and hang on to it—you'll need it later.

Find your train by following signs to your line and the (general) direction it's

headed (such as Central Line: east). Since some tracks are shared by several lines, double-check before boarding a train—make sure your destination is one of the stops listed on the sign at the platform. Also, check the electronic signboards that announce which train is next, and make sure the destination (the end-of-the-line stop) is the direction you want. Some trains, particularly on the Circle and District lines, split off for other directions, but each train has its final destination marked above its windshield.

Trains run about every 3-10 minutes. For a rough idea of how long it takes to get from point A to point B by Tube, estimate five minutes per stop (which includes time to walk into and out of stations, and to change trains). So a destination six stops away will take you about 30 minutes.

When you leave the system, "touch out" with your Oyster card at the electronic reader on the turnstile, or feed your paper ticket into the turnstile (it will eat your now-expired ticket). With a Travelcard, it will spit out your still-valid card. When leaving a station, save walking time by choosing the best street exit—check the maps on the walls or ask any station personnel.

If you get confused, ask for advice from a local, a blue-vested staff person, or at the information window located before the turnstile entry. Online, get help from the "Plan a Journey" feature at www.tfl.gov.uk, which is accessible (via free Wi-Fi) on any mobile device within most Tube stations before you go underground.

TUBE ETIQUETTE

- When your train arrives, stand off to the side and let riders exit before you try to board.
- Avoid using the hinged seats near the doors of some trains when the car is jammed; they take up valuable standing space.
- If you're blocking the door when the train stops, step out of the car and off to the side, let others off, then get back on.
- On escalators, stand on the right and pass on the left. But note that in some passageways or stairways, you might be directed to walk on the left (the direction Brits go when behind the wheel).
- Discreet eating and drinking are fine (nothing smelly); drinking alcohol and smoking are not.

By Bus

If you figure out the bus system, you'll swing like Tarzan through the urban jungle of London (see sidebar for a list of handy routes). Get in the habit of hopping buses for quick little straight shots, even just to get to a Tube stop. However, during bump-and-grind rush hours (8:00-10:00 and 16:00-19:00), you'll usually go faster by Tube.

You can't buy single-trip tickets for buses, and you can't use cash to pay for your fare when boarding. Instead, you must have an Oyster card, a Travelcard, or a one-day Bus & Tram Pass (£5, can buy on day of travel only—not beforehand, available from ticket machine or window in any Tube station). If you're using your Oyster card, any bus ride in downtown London costs £1.50 (with a cap of £4.40 per day).

When you're waiting at a stop, as your bus approaches, it's wise to hold your arm out to let the driver know you want on. Hop on and confirm your destination with the driver (often friendly and helpful).

As you board, touch your Oyster card to the card reader, or show your paper Travelcard or Bus & Tram Pass to the driver (there's no need to show or tap your card when you hop off). On the older heritage "Routemaster" buses without card readers (used on the #15 route), you simply take a seat, and the conductor comes around to check cards and passes.

To alert the driver that you want to get off, press one of the red buttons (on the poles between the seats) before your stop.

Handy Bus Routes

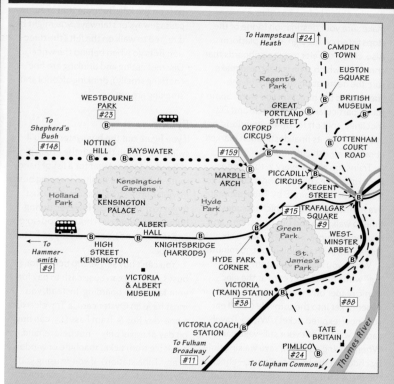

Ever since London instituted a congestion charge for cars, the bus system has gotten faster, easier, and cheaper. Tube-oriented travelers need to get over their tunnel vision, learn the bus system, and get around fast and easy. The best views are upstairs on a double-decker.

Here are some of the most useful routes:

Route #9: High Street Kensington to Knightsbridge (Harrods) to Hyde Park Corner to Trafalgar Square to Aldwych (Somerset House).

Route #11: Victoria Station to Westminster Abbey to Trafalgar Square to St. Paul's and Liverpool Street Station and the East End.

Route #15: Trafalgar Square to St. Paul's to Tower of London (sometimes with heritage "Routemaster" old-style double-decker buses).

Routes #23 and #159: Paddington Station (#159 begins at Marble Arch) to Oxford Circus to Piccadilly Circus to Trafalgar Square; from there, #23 heads east to St. Paul's and Liverpool Street Station, while #159 heads to Westminster and the Imperial War Museum. In addition, several buses (including #6, #13, and #139) also make the corridor run between Marble Arch, Oxford Circus, Piccadilly Circus, and Trafalgar Square.

Route #24: Pimlico to Victoria Station to Westminster Abbey to Trafalgar Square

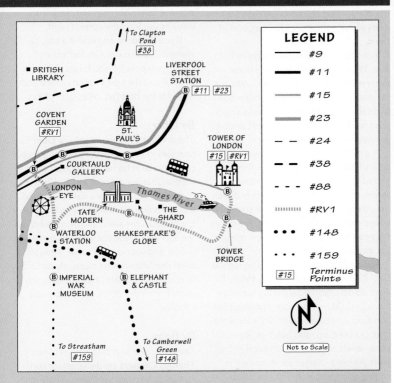

LEGEND

———	#9
▬▬▬	#11
———	#15
▬▬▬	#23
– –	#24
▬ ▬	#38
- - -	#88
‖‖‖‖‖‖	#RV1
● ● ●	#148
· · ·	#159
#15	Terminus Points

Not to Scale

to Euston Square, then all the way north to Camden Town (Camden Lock Market).

Route #38: Victoria Station to Hyde Park Corner to Piccadilly Circus to British Museum.

Route #88: Tate Britain to Westminster Abbey to Trafalgar Square to Piccadilly Circus to Oxford Circus to Great Portland Street Station (Regent's Park), then north to Camden Town.

Route #148: Westminster Abbey to Victoria Station to Notting Hill and Bayswater (by way of the east end of Hyde Park and Marble Arch).

Route #RV1 (a scenic South Bank joyride): Tower of London to Tower Bridge to Southwark Street (five-minute walk behind Tate Modern/Shakespeare's Globe) to London Eye/Waterloo Station, then over Waterloo Bridge to Aldwych and Covent Garden.

By Taxi

London is the best taxi town in Europe. Big, black, carefully regulated cabs are everywhere—there are about 25,000 of them.

I've never met a crabby cabbie in London. They love to talk, and they know every nook and cranny in town. I ride in a taxi each day just to get my London questions answered. Drivers must pass a rigorous test on "The Knowledge" of London geography to earn their license.

If a cab's top light is on, just wave it down. Drivers flash lights when they see you wave. They have a tight turning radius, so you can hail cabs going in either direction. If waving doesn't work, ask someone where you can find a taxi stand. Telephoning a cab will get you one in a few minutes, but it costs a little more.

Rates: Rides start at £2.40. The regular tariff #1 covers most of the day (Mon-Fri 6:00-20:00), tariff #2 is during "unsociable hours" (Mon-Fri 20:00-22:00 and Sat-Sun 6:00-22:00), and tariff #3 is for nighttime (22:00-6:00) and holidays. Rates go up about 20 percent with each higher tariff. All extra charges are explained in writing on the cab wall. Tip a cabbie by rounding up (maximum 10 percent).

Connecting downtown sights is quick and easy, and will cost you about £8-10 (for example, St. Paul's to the Tower of London, or between the two Tate museums). All cabs can carry five passengers, and some take six, for the same cost as a single traveler.

Don't worry about meter cheating. Licensed British cab meters come with a sealed computer chip and clock that ensures you'll get the correct tariff.

If you overdrink and ride in a taxi, be warned: Taxis charge £40 for "soiling" (a.k.a., pub puke). If you forget this book in a taxi, call the Lost Property office and hope for the best (tel. 0845-330-9882).

By Uber

The on-demand car hire service **Uber** operates in London with rates comparable to taxis. Like at home, you request a car via the Uber app on your mobile device (connected to Wi-Fi or a data plan), and the fare is automatically charged to your credit card. Cars aren't always marked, but the app will tell you the vehicle's make and model, and your driver's name. Keep in mind that Uber drivers often rely on GPS to route your trip, and may not have the same knowledge of the city as do many cabbies.

By Boat

The sleek, 220-seat catamarans used by **Thames Clippers** are designed for commuters rather than sightseers. Think of the boats as express buses on the river—they zip through London every 20-30 minutes, stopping at most of the major docks en route. They're fast: roughly 20 minutes from Embankment to Tower, 10 more minutes to Docklands, and 10 more minutes to Greenwich. However, the only outside access is on a crowded deck at the exhaust-choked back of the boat, where you're jostling for space to take photos. Any one-way ride costs £7.50, and a River Roamer all-day ticket costs £17.35 (discounts with Travelcard and Oyster card, www.thamesclippers.com).

Thames Clippers also offers two express trips. The **Tate Boat** ferry service, which directly connects the Tate Britain (Millbank Pier) and the Tate Modern (Bankside Pier), is made for art lovers (£7.50 one way, covered by River Roamer

day ticket; buy ticket at self-service machines before boarding or use Oyster Card; for frequency and times, see the Tate Britain and Tate Modern listings, earlier, or www.tate.org.uk/visit/tate-boat). The **O2 Express** runs only on nights when there are events at the O2 arena in Greenwich (departs from Waterloo Pier).

By Bike

London operates a citywide bike-rental program similar to ones in other major European cities, and new bike lanes are still cropping up around town.

Still, London isn't (yet) ideal for biking. Although the streets are relatively uncongested, the network of designated bike lanes is far from complete, and the city's many one-way streets (not to mention the need to bike on the "wrong" side) can make biking challenging.

Santander Cycles, intended for quick point-to-point trips, are fairly easy to rent. Approximately 700 bike-rental stations are scattered throughout the city (£2/day access fee; first 30 minutes free; £2 for every additional 30-minute period).

You can hire bikes as often as you like (which will start your free 30-minute period over again), as long as you wait five minutes between each use. Pick up a map of the docking stations at any major Underground station. The same map is also available online at www.tfl.gov.uk (click on "Santander Cycles") and in a free app (http://cyclehireapp.com).

By Car

If you have a car, stow it—you don't want to drive in London. A £10 **congestion charge** is levied on any private car entering the city center during peak hours (Mon-Fri 7:00-18:00, no charge Sat-Sun and holidays, fee payable at gas stations, convenience stores, and self-service machines at public parking lots, or online at www.cclondon.com). There are painfully stiff penalties for late payments.

Arriving and Departing
By Plane

London has six airports; I've focused my coverage on the two most widely used—Heathrow and Gatwick—with a few tips for using the others (Stansted, Luton, London City, and Southend).

HEATHROW AIRPORT

For Heathrow's airport, flight, and transfer information, call the switchboard at 0844-335-1801, or visit the helpful website at www.heathrowairport.com (airport code: LHR).

Heathrow's terminals are numbered T-1 through T-5. Each terminal is served by different airlines and alliances; for example, T-5 is exclusively for British Air and Iberia Air flights, while T-2 serves mostly Star Alliance flights, such as United and Lufthansa. Screens posted throughout the airport identify which terminal each airline uses; this information should also be printed on your ticket or boarding pass.

To navigate, read signs and ask questions. You can walk between T-2 and T-3. From this central hub (called "Heathrow Central"), T-4 and T-5 split off in opposite directions (and are not walkable). The easiest way to travel between the T-2/T-3 cluster and either T-4 or T-5 is by Heathrow Express train (free, departs every 15-20 minutes). You can also take a shuttle bus (free, serves all terminals), or the Tube (requires a ticket, serves all terminals).

If you're flying out of Heathrow, it's critical to confirm which terminal your flight will use—if it's T-4 or T-5, allow extra time. Taxi drivers generally know which terminal you'll need based on the airline, but bus drivers may not.

Services: Each terminal has an airport information desk (open long hours daily), car-rental agencies, exchange bureaus, ATMs, a pharmacy, a VAT refund desk, room-booking services, and baggage storage (daily 5:00-23:00, www.left-baggage.co.uk). Heathrow offers free Wi-Fi and

London's Airports

Luton •
✈ Luton
✈ Stansted

Not to Scale

#757

ST. PANCRAS
PADDINGTON
LIVERPOOL STREET
Southend
✈
Southend •

Reading
Windsor
#71 & #77i
Rail Air Link
Tube
VICTORIA
D.L.R.
✈

To Bath
Heathrow
VICTORIA COACH STN.
London City

Thames
London

Guildford

EUROSTAR

✈ **Gatwick**
Ashford

To Paris →

Rail
Eurostar Rail
Tube & D.L.R.
Bus

ALL BUSES ARE NATIONAL EXPRESS
UNLESS NOTED

↓ To Brighton

English Channel

pay Internet access points (in each terminal, check map for locations). You'll find a post office on the first floor of T-3 (departures area). Each terminal also has cheap eateries.

Heathrow's small **"TI"** (tourist info shop) is worth a visit if you're nearby and want to pick up a simple map or the *London Planner* visitors guide (long hours daily, 5-minute walk from T-3 in Tube station, follow signs to Underground; bypass queue for transit info to reach window for London questions).

Getting Between Heathrow and Downtown London: You have five basic options for traveling the 14 miles between Heathrow Airport and downtown London: Tube, bus, direct shuttle bus, express train (with connecting Tube or taxi), or taxi. The one that works best for you will depend on your arrival terminal, your

destination in central London, and your budget.

By Tube (Subway): The Tube takes you from any Heathrow terminal to downtown London in 50-60 minutes on the Piccadilly Line (6/hour, buy ticket at Tube station ticket window or self-service machine). If you plan to use the Tube for transport in London, it makes sense to buy a pay-as-you-go Oyster card or Travelcard at the airport's Tube station ticket window. (For details on these passes, see page 108) If your transit card covers only Zones 1-2, you'll need to pay a small supplement for the initial trip from Heathrow (Zone 6) to downtown.

If you're taking the Tube from downtown London *to* the airport, note that Piccadilly Line trains don't stop at every terminal. Trains either stop at T-4, then T-2/T-3 (also called Heathrow Central), in that order; or T-2/T-3, then T-5. When leaving central London on the Tube, allow extra time if going to T-4 or T-5, and check the reader board in the station before you board to make sure that the train goes to the right terminal.

By Bus: Most London-bound buses depart from the outdoor common area called the Central Bus Station, a five-minute walk from the T-2/T-3 complex. To connect between T-4 or T-5 and the Central Bus Station, ride the free Heathrow Express train or the shuttle buses.

National Express has regular service from Heathrow's Central Bus Station to Victoria Coach Station in downtown London, near several of my recommended hotels. While slow, the bus is affordable and convenient for those staying near Victoria Station (£6-9, 1-2/hour, less frequent from Victoria Station to Heathrow, 45-75 minutes depending on time of day, tel. 0871-781-8181, www.nationalexpress. com). A less-frequent National Express bus goes from T-5 directly to Victoria Coach Station.

By Shuttle Bus: Heathrow Shuttle is an economical shuttle-bus service that goes to/from your hotel and your terminal at Heathrow. You'll share a minivan with other travelers who are also being picked up or dropped off, so it's not much of a time-savings over taking the Tube (£20/person, progressive discounts for groups of two or more, 1 child under age 10 travels free with 2 adults, runs daily 4:00-18:00, book at least 24 hours in advance, tel. 020/309-2771, www.heathrowshuttle. com, info@heathrowshuttle.com). Another option is **Just Airports,** which offers a private car service between five London airports and the city center (from £32/car; see website for price quote, tel. 020/8900-1666, www.justairports.com).

By Train: Two different trains run between Heathrow Airport and London's Paddington Station. At Paddington Station, you're in the thick of the Tube system, with easy access to any of my rec-

ommended neighborhoods. The **Heathrow Connect** train is the slightly slower, much cheaper option, serving T-2/T-3 at a single station called Heathrow Central; use free transfers to get from either T-4 or T-5 to Heathrow Central (£10.20 one-way, £20.40 round-trip, 2/hour Mon-Sat, 1-2/hour Sun, 40 minutes, tel. 0345-604-1515, www.heathrowconnect.com).

The **Heathrow Express** train is fast and runs more frequently, but it's pricey (£22 one-way, £36 round-trip, £5 more if you buy your ticket on board, 4/hour; 15 minutes to downtown from Heathrow Central Station serving T-2/T-3, 21 minutes from T-5; for T-4 take free transfer to Heathrow Central; covered by BritRail pass, daily 5:10-23:48, tel. 0345-600-1515, www.heathrowexpress.co.uk).

By Taxi: Taxis from the airport cost £45-75 to west and central London (one hour). For four people traveling together, this can be a reasonable option. Hotels can often line up a cab back to the airport for about £50.

Getting to Bath: If you're going from the airport to Bath, the train via London will get you there fastest, and if you have a Britrail pass, your journey is covered (hourly, 2 hours). Otherwise, a train-and-bus combination via Reading is more affordable (allow 2.5 hours total). For details, see page 117.

GATWICK AIRPORT

More and more flights land at Gatwick Airport, which is halfway between London and the south coast (airport code: LGW, tel. 0844-892-0322, www.gatwickairport.com). Gatwick has two terminals, North and South, which are easily connected by a free two-minute monorail ride. Boarding passes say "Gatwick N" or "Gatwick S" to indicate your terminal. British Airways flights generally use Gatwick North. The Gatwick Express trains (described next) stop only at Gatwick South.

Getting Between Gatwick and Downtown London: Gatwick Express trains are the best way into London from this airport. They shuttle conveniently between Gatwick South and London's Victoria Station (£20 one-way, £35 round-trip, cheaper if purchased online, Oyster cards accepted, 4/hour, 30 minutes, runs 5:00-24:00 daily, a few trains as early as 3:30, tel. 0845-850-1530, www.gatwickexpress. com). If going from Victoria Station *to* the airport, note that Gatwick Express has its own ticket windows right by the platform (tracks 13 and 14).

A train also runs between Gatwick South and **St. Pancras International Station**—useful for travelers taking the Eurostar train (to Paris or Brussels) or staying in the St. Pancras/King's Cross neighborhood (£10.30, 6/hour, 60 minutes, www. thetrainline.com).

Even slower, but cheap and handy to the Victoria Station neighborhood, you can take the **bus.** National Express runs a bus from Gatwick direct to Victoria Station (£8, at least hourly, 1.5 hours, tel. 0871-781-8181, www.nationalexpress.com).

OTHER LONDON AIRPORTS

Stansted Airport: Airport code STN, tel. 0844-335-1803, www.stanstedairport. com. **Buses** run by National Express (£12, www.nationalexpress.com) and Terravision (£8-10, www.terravision.com)

connect the airport and London's Victoria Station neighborhood in about 1.5-2 hours. Or you can take the faster Stansted Express train (£19, www.stanstedexpress. com). Stansted is expensive by **cab;** figure £100-120 one-way from central London.

Luton Airport: Airport code LTN, tel. 01582/405-100, www.london-luton.co.uk. The fastest way into London is by **train** to St. Pancras International Station (£10-14, 25-45 minutes, www.eastmidlandstrains. co.uk); catch the shuttle bus from outside the airport terminal to the Luton Airport Parkway Station. The National Express **bus** A1 runs from Luton to Victoria Coach Station (£7-11, 1-1.5 hours, www.nationalexpress.com). The Green Line express **bus** #757 runs to Buckingham Palace Road, just south of Victoria Station, and stops en route near the Baker Street Tube station (£10, 1-1.5 hours, www. greenline.co.uk).

London City Airport: Airport code LCY, tel. 020/7646-0088, www. londoncityairport.com. Take the Docklands Light Railway (DLR) to the Bank Tube station, which is one stop east of St. Paul's on the Central Line (£5, covered by Oyster card, 20 minutes, www.tfl.gov. uk/dlr).

Southend Airport: Airport code SEN, tel. 01702/538-500, www.southendairport.com. Trains connect this airport to London's Liverpool Street Station (£16.80, 55 minutes, www.abelliogreateranglia.co.uk).

By Train

London, the country's major transportation hub, has a different train station for each region. There are nine main stations:

- **Euston:** Covers northwest England
- **St. Pancras International:** North and south England, plus the Eurostar to Paris or Brussels (for more on the Eurostar, see www.ricksteves.com/eurostar)
- **King's Cross:** Northeast England, including York
- **Liverpool Street:** East England
- **London Bridge:** South England
- **Waterloo:** South England
- **Victoria:** Canterbury, Oxford, and Bath, as well as Gatwick Airport
- **Paddington:** South and southwest England, including Heathrow Airport, Windsor, Bath, Oxford, and the Cotswolds

Marylebone: Southwest and central England, including Stratford-upon-Avon

Any train station has schedule information, can make reservations, and can sell tickets for any destination. Most stations offer a baggage-storage service; because of long security lines, it can take a while to check or pick up your bag (www.left-baggage.co.uk). For details on the services offered at each station, see www.nationalrail.co.uk/stations.

UK **train and bus info** is available at www.traveline.org.uk. For information on tickets and rail passes, see page 104.

TRAIN CONNECTIONS FROM LONDON

From Paddington Station to Points West: Windsor (Windsor & Eton Central Station, 2-3/hour, 35 minutes, easy change at Slough; you can also reach Windsor from Waterloo Station—2/hour, 50 minutes—but get off at Windsor & Eton Riverside Station), **Bath** (2/hour, 1.5 hours), **Oxford** (2/hour direct, 1 hour, more with transfer), **Moreton-in-Marsh** (hourly, 1.5 hours).

From King's Cross Station to Points North: York (hourly, 2 hours), **Durham** (hourly, 3 hours), **Cambridge** (2/hour, 45 minutes).

From Euston Station to Points North: Liverpool (at least hourly, 2-2.5 hours, more with transfer), **Keswick** (hourly, 4 hours, transfer to bus at Penrith).

From London's Other Stations to: Stratford-upon-Avon from Marylebone (1-2/hour with transfers, 2 hours), **Greenwich** from the Bank or Monument Tube stop on the DLR—Docklands Light Railway (6/hour, 20 minutes).

By Bus

Buses are slower but considerably cheaper than trains for reaching destinations around Britain and beyond. Most depart from **Victoria Coach Station,** which is one long block south of Victoria Station (Tube: Victoria). Inside the station, you'll find basic eateries, kiosks, and a helpful information desk.

Ideally you'll buy your tickets online (for tips on buying tickets and taking buses, see page 109). But if you must buy one at the station, try to arrive an hour before the bus departs, or drop by the day before. Ticketing machines are scattered around the station (separate machines for National Express/Eurolines and Megabus; you can buy either for today or for tomorrow); there's also a ticket counter near gate 21. For UK train and bus info, check www.traveline.org.uk.

National Express buses go to: **Bath** (nearly hourly, 3-3.5 hours), **Oxford** (2/hour, 2 hours), **Cambridge** (every 60-90 minutes, 2 hours), **Stratford-upon-Avon** (3/day, 3.5 hours), **Liverpool** (8/day direct, 5-6 hours, overnight available), **York** (4/day direct, 5.5 hours).

France

F rance is a place of gentle beauty. At 215,000 square miles (roughly 20 percent smaller than Texas), it is Western Europe's largest nation, with luxuriant forests, forever coastlines, and Europe's highest mountain ranges. You'll discover a dizzying array of artistic and architectural wonders—soaring cathedrals, chandeliered palaces, and museums filled with the cultural icons of the Western world.

Paris is the star of the show; Provence is small-town France at its best; and the French Riviera offers up beaches and an old-time elegance with a bit of glitz.

Wherever you visit in France, you'll enjoy *l'art de vivre*—the art of living. Experience the fine cuisine, velvety wines, and linger-long pastimes such as people-watching from sun-dappled cafés.

CUISINE SCENE AT A GLANCE

Know the terms for eating out: A menu is called *la carte* (which you use to order individual dishes *á la carte*). A *menu* is actually a multi-course, fixed-price meal. The daily special is a *plat du jour* (or just *plat*), a hearty, garnished hot plate for about €12-20. *Entrées* are appetizers. The main dish is the *plat principal*.

Cafés and brasseries are open long hours and serve food throughout the day. You're welcome to order just a salad, a sandwich, or a bowl of soup, even for dinner. It's also fine to split starters and desserts, though not main courses.

Check the price list first, which by law must be posted prominently (if you don't see one, go elsewhere). There are two sets of prices: You'll pay more for the same drink if you're seated at a table (*salle*) than if you're seated or standing at the bar or counter (*comptoir*).

Restaurants open for dinner around 19:00. Last seating is about 21:00 (22:00 in cities and Riviera towns). The table is yours for the night.

If a restaurant serves lunch, it generally begins at 12:00, with last orders taken at about 13:30. Lunches at restaurants are cheaper than dinners; to save money, make lunch your main meal.

If you're hungry when restaurants are closed (late afternoon), or if you want a light meal, head for a café, brasserie, deli, or *boulangerie*.

At restaurants, two people can split an *entrée* or a big salad and then each get a *plat principal*. It's considered inappropriate for two diners to share one main course.

Fixed-price *menus*, which include two or three courses, are generally a good value. With a three-course *menu* you'll choose a starter of soup, appetizer, or salad; select from several main courses with vegetables; and then finish up with a cheese course or dessert.

To order inexpensive wine with your meal, ask for table wine in a carafe (*pichet*; pee-shay), though finer restaurants usually offer wine only by the glass or bottle.

Tipping: A waiter will rarely bring you the bill unless you request it. At cafés and restaurants, a 12-15 percent service charge is always included in the price of what you order, but you won't see it listed on your bill. Most locals never tip. If you feel the service was exceptional, you could tip up to 5 percent extra in cash (credit-card receipts don't even have space to add a tip). But don't feel guilty if you don't leave a tip.

Budget Options: Try takeout delis, food stands, *crêperies*, and *boulangeries* (for sandwiches, quiches, and tiny pizzas). You can assemble a picnic at various small shops, a one-stop *supermarché*, or an open-air morning market.

Paris

Paris has been a beacon of culture for centuries. As a world capital of art, fashion, food, literature, and ideas, it stands as a symbol of all the fine things human civilization can achieve, with a splash of romance and *joie de vivre*.

Paris offers grand boulevards, chatty crêpe stands, chic boutiques, and world-class art galleries. Sip coffee at a sidewalk café near the Eiffel Tower, then step into an Impressionist painting in a tree-lined park. Rub shoulders with the gargoyles at Notre-Dame. Master the Louvre and Orsay museums. Explore the City of Light at night, when monuments are floodlit and Paris sparkles.

PARIS IN 3 DAYS

On your first day, follow my Historic Paris Walk, featuring Ile de la Cité, Notre-Dame, the Latin Quarter, and Sainte-Chapelle. In the afternoon, tour the Louvre. Late in the day, enjoy the Place du Trocadéro scene and a twilight ride up the Eiffel Tower.

On your second day, stroll the Champs-Elysées from the Arc de Triomphe (ascend for the view) to the Tuileries Garden, then tour the Orsay and Rodin museums.

On your third day, head to Versailles. Catch the RER suburban train by 8:00 to arrive early. Tour the palace's interior, then either visit the vast gardens, or return to Paris for more sightseeing.

On any evening: Take a nighttime tour by cruise boat, taxi, or bus. Or enjoy dinner on Ile St. Louis, then a floodlit walk by Notre-Dame. For a free skyline view, head to the rooftop of the neighboring Galeries Lafayette or Printemps department stores.

With extra time: Choose from Montmartre (Sacré-Cœur Basilica), the Army Museum and Napoleon's Tomb, the Marais neighborhood (Picasso Museum and Pompidou Center), or the Opéra Garnier (near the department stores).

ORIENTATION

Central Paris is circled by a ring road and split in half by the Seine River, which runs east-west. If you were floating downstream, the Right Bank (Rive Droite) would be on your right, and the Left Bank (Rive Gauche) on your left. The bull's-eye on your map is Notre-Dame, on an island in the middle of the Seine.

Twenty arrondissements (administrative districts) spiral out from the center, like an escargot shell. If your hotel's zip code is 75007, you know (from the last two digits) that it's in the 7th arrondissement. The city is peppered with Métro stops, and most Parisians locate addresses by the closest stop. So in Parisian jargon, the Eiffel Tower is on *la Rive Gauche* (the Left Bank) in the *7ème* (7th arrondissement), zip code 75007, Mo: Trocadéro (the nearest Métro stop).

The major sights cluster in convenient

Paris Neighborhoods

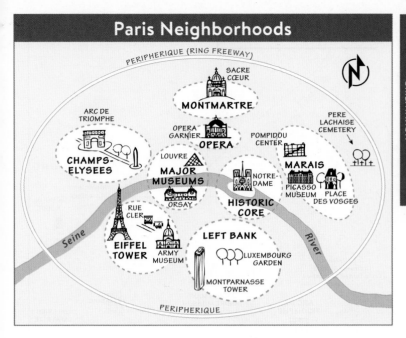

zones. Grouping your sightseeing, walks, dining, and shopping thoughtfully can save you lots of time and money.

Historic Core: This area centers on the Ile de la Cité ("Island of the City"), located in the middle of the Seine. On the Ile de la Cité, you'll find Paris' oldest sights, from Roman ruins to the medieval Notre-Dame and Sainte-Chapelle churches.

Major Museums Neighborhood: Located just west of the historic core, this is where you'll find the Louvre, Orsay, Orangerie, and Tuileries Garden.

Champs-Elysées: The greatest of the many grand, 19th-century boulevards on the Right Bank, the Champs-Elysées runs northwest from Place de la Concorde to the Arc de Triomphe.

Eiffel Tower Neighborhood: Dominated by the Eiffel Tower, this area also boasts the colorful Rue Cler, Army Museum and Napoleon's Tomb, and the Rodin Museum.

Opéra Neighborhood: Surrounding the Opéra Garnier, this area on the Right Bank is home to a series of grand boulevards and high-end shopping.

Left Bank: Anchored by the Luxembourg Garden, the Left Bank is the traditional neighborhood of Paris' intellectual, artistic, and café life.

Marais: Stretching eastward to Bastille along Rue de Rivoli/Rue St. Antoine, this neighborhood has lots of restaurants and hotels, shops, the delightful Place des Vosges, and artistic sights, such as the Pompidou Center and Picasso Museum.

Montmartre: This hill, topped by the bulbous white domes of Sacré-Cœur, hovers on the northern fringes of your Paris map.

Tourist Information

Paris' TIs can provide useful information but may have long lines (www.parisinfo. com). Most TIs sell Museum Passes and individual tickets to sights.

Paris has several TI locations, including **Pyramides** (daily May-Oct 9:00-19:00, Nov-April 10:00-19:00, 25 Rue des Pyramides—at Pyramides Métro stop), **Gare du Nord** (daily 8:00-18:00), **Gare de Lyon**

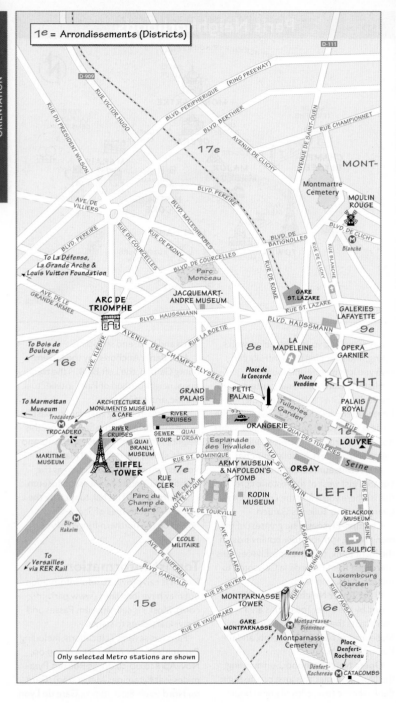

1e = Arrondissements (Districts)

Only selected Metro stations are shown

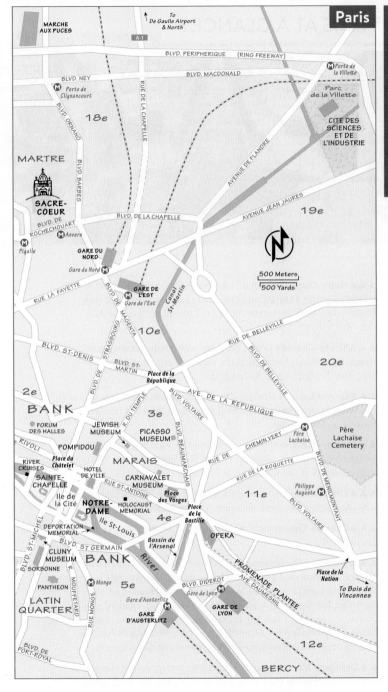

PARIS AT A GLANCE

▲▲▲**Notre-Dame Cathedral** Paris' most beloved church, with towers and gargoyles. **Hours:** Cathedral—daily 7:45-18:45, Sun until 19:15; Tower—daily April-Sept 10:00-18:30, Fri-Sat until 23:00 in July-Aug, Oct-March 10:00-17:30. See page 132.

▲▲▲**Sainte-Chapelle** Gothic cathedral with peerless stained glass. **Hours:** Daily March-Oct 9:30-18:00, Wed until 21:30 mid-May-mid-Sept, Nov-Feb 9:00-17:00. See page 140.

▲▲▲**Louvre** Europe's oldest and greatest museum, starring *Mona Lisa* and *Venus de Milo*. **Hours:** Wed-Mon 9:00-18:00, Wed and Fri until 21:45, closed Tue. See page 145.

▲▲▲**Orsay Museum** Nineteenth-century art, including Europe's greatest Impressionist collection. **Hours:** Tue-Sun 9:30-18:00, Thu until 21:45, closed Mon. See page 152.

▲▲▲**Eiffel Tower** Paris' soaring exclamation point. **Hours:** Daily mid-June-Aug 9:00-24:45, Sept-mid-June 9:30-23:45. See page 159.

▲▲▲**Champs-Elysées** Paris' grand boulevard. **Hours:** Always open. See page 166.

▲▲▲**Versailles** The ultimate royal palace (Château), with a Hall of Mirrors, vast gardens, a grand canal, plus a queen's playground (Trianon Palaces and Domaine de Marie-Antoinette). **Hours:** Château—April-Oct Tue-Sun 9:00-18:30, Nov-March until 17:30; Trianon/Domaine—April-Oct Tue-Sun 12:00-18:30, Nov-March until 17:30; Gardens—generally April-Oct daily 8:00-20:30, Nov-March Tue-Sun 8:00-18:00; entire complex closed Mon year-round. See page 209.

▲▲**Orangerie Museum** Monet's water lilies and modernist classics in a lovely setting. **Hours:** Wed-Mon 9:00-18:00, closed Tue. See page 158.

▲▲**Army Museum and Napoleon's Tomb** The emperor's imposing tomb, flanked by museums of France's wars. **Hours:** Daily 10:00-18:00, July-Aug until 19:00, Nov-March until 17:00; tomb plus WWI and WWII wings open Tue until 21:00 April-Sept; museum (except for tomb) closed first Mon of month Oct-June; Charles de Gaulle exhibit closed Mon year-round. See page 162.

▲▲**Rodin Museum** Works by the greatest sculptor since Michelangelo, with many statues in a peaceful garden. **Hours:** Tue-Sun 10:00-17:45, Wed until 20:45, closed Mon. See page 163.

▲▲**Cluny Museum** Medieval art with unicorn tapestries. **Hours:** Wed-Mon 9:15-17:45, closed Tue. See page 164.

▲▲**Arc de Triomphe** Triumphal arch marking start of Champs-Elysées. **Hours:** Always viewable; interior—daily April-Sept 10:00-23:00, Oct-March until 22:30. See page 168.

▲▲**Picasso Museum** World's largest collection of Picasso's works. **Hours:** Tue-Fri 11:30-18:00 (until 21:00 on third Fri of month), Sat-Sun 9:30-18:00, closed Mon. See page 171.

▲▲**Pompidou Center** Modern art in colorful building with city views. **Hours:** Wed-Mon 11:00-21:00, closed Tue. See page 176.

▲▲**Sacré-Cœur** White basilica atop Montmartre with spectacular views. **Hours:** Daily 6:00-22:30; dome climb—daily May-Sept 8:30-20:00, Oct-April 9:00-17:00. See page 178.

▲**Opéra Garnier** Grand belle époque theater with a modern ceiling by Chagall. **Hours:** Generally daily 10:00-16:30, mid-July-Aug until 18:00. See page 168.

▲**Père Lachaise Cemetery** Final home of Paris' illustrious dead. **Hours:** Mon-Fri 8:00-18:00, Sat 8:30-18:00, Sun 9:00-18:00, until 17:30 in winter. See page 177.

(Mon–Sat 8:00–18:00, closed Sun), **Gare de l'Est** (Mon–Sat 8:00–19:00, closed Sun), and two in **Montmartre** (both daily 10:00–18:00, 21 Place du Tertre—limited to Montmartre—and at the Anvers Métro stop). In summer, TI kiosks may pop up in the squares in front of Notre-Dame and Hôtel de Ville. Both city **airports** have handy TIs with long hours and short lines.

Event Listings: Several French-only but easy-to-decipher periodicals list the most up-to-date museum hours, art exhibits, concerts, festivals, plays, movies, and nightclubs. The best is the weekly *Pariscope* magazine; *L'Officiel des Spectacles* is similar (available at any newsstand). The *Paris Voice*, with snappy English-language reviews of concerts, plays, and current events, is available online only at www.parisvoice.com.

Sightseeing Pass

In Paris there are two classes of sight-seers—those with a **Paris Museum Pass,** and those who stand in line. The pass admits you to many of Paris' most popular sights, and it allows you to skip ticket-buying lines. You'll save time and money by getting this pass. Pertinent details about the pass are outlined here—for more info, visit www.parismuseumpass.com.

What the Pass Covers

Here's a list of key sights and their admission prices without the pass:

- Arc de Triomphe (€9.50)
- Army Museum (€9.50)
- Cluny Museum (€8)
- Conciergerie (€8.50)
- Louvre (€12)
- Notre-Dame Tower (€8.50)
- Orangerie Museum (€9)
- Orsay Museum (€11)
- Picasso Museum (€11)
- Pompidou Center (€14)
- Rodin Museum (€10)
- Sainte-Chapelle (€8.50)
- Versailles (€25)

Notable sights that are *not* covered by the pass include the Eiffel Tower, Opéra Garnier, Notre-Dame Treasury, and Sacré-Cœur's dome.

Buying the Pass

The pass pays for itself with four key admissions in two days (for example, the Louvre, Orsay, Sainte-Chapelle, and Versailles), and it lets you skip the ticket line at most sights (2 days–€42, 4 days–€56, 6 days–€69, no youth or senior discounts). It's sold at participating museums, monuments, and TIs (even at Paris' airports). Avoid buying the pass at a major museum (such as the Louvre), where the supply can be spotty and lines long. It's not worth the cost or hassle to buy the pass online.

Rick's Tip: Don't buy the Museum Pass for kids, *as most museums are free or discounted for those under age 18 (teenagers may need to show ID as proof of age). If parents have a Museum Pass, kids can usually skip the ticket lines as well. But a few places (Arc de Triomphe, Army Museum) require everyone—even passholders—to stand in line to collect free tickets for their children.*

Using the Pass

Plan carefully to make the most of your pass. Validate it only when you're ready to tackle the covered sights on consecutive days. Activating it is simple—just write the start date you want (and your name) on the pass. But first make sure the sights you want to visit will be open (many museums are closed Mon or Tue).

The pass provides the best value on days when sights close later, letting you extend your sightseeing day. Take advantage of late hours on selected evenings or times of year at the Arc de Triomphe, Pompidou Center, Notre-Dame Tower, Sainte-Chapelle, Louvre, Orsay, Rodin Museum, and Napoleon's Tomb. On days that you don't have pass coverage, plan to visit free sights and those not covered by the pass (see page 137 for a list of free sights).

To use your pass at sights, look for signs designating the entrance for reserved ticket holders. If it's not obvious, walk to the front of the ticket line, hold up your pass, and ask the ticket taker: "*Entrez, pass?*" (ahn-tray pahs). You'll either be allowed to enter at that point, or you'll be directed to a special entrance. For major sights, such as the Louvre and Orsay museums, I've identified passholder entrances on the maps in this book. Don't be shy—some places (the Orsay and the Arc de Triomphe, in particular) have long lines in which passholders wait needlessly. At a few sights with security lines (including the Louvre), passholders can skip to the front.

Avoiding Lines Without a Pass

If you don't purchase a Paris Museum Pass, or if a sight is not covered by the pass, there are other ways to avoid long waits in ticket-buying lines.

For some sights, you can reserve **timed-entry tickets** online. This is essential at the line-plagued Eiffel Tower, and it's a big advantage at the Picasso Museum.

You can buy **advance tickets** online for many other sights (including the Louvre, Orsay, Rodin Museum, and Monet's gardens at Giverny) as well as for activities and cultural events (Bateaux-Mouches cruises, Sainte-Chapelle concerts, and performances at the Opéra Garnier). Increasingly, other Paris sights are adding this timesaving service.

TIs, FNAC department stores, and travel-services companies sell individual *coupe-file* tickets (pronounced "koop feel") for some sights, which allow you to use the Museum Pass entrance (worth the trouble only for sights where lines are longest). TIs sell these tickets for no extra fee, but elsewhere you can expect a surcharge of 10-20 percent. FNAC stores are everywhere, even on the Champs-Elysées (ask your hotelier for the nearest one). Despite the surcharges and often-long lines to buy them, getting *coupe-file* tickets can still be a good idea.

Some sights, such as the Louvre, have **ticket-vending machines** that save time in line. These accept cash (usually no bills larger than €20) or chip-and-PIN cards

If you buy an advance ticket for the Eiffel Tower (or take the stairs), you can avoid this line.

Daily Reminder

SUNDAY: Many sights are free on the first Sunday of the month, including the Orsay, Rodin, Cluny, Pompidou, and Picasso museums. Several sights are free on the first Sunday, but only during winter, including the Louvre and Arc de Triomphe (both Oct-March) and all the sights at Versailles (Nov-March). These free days at popular sights attract hordes of visitors. Versailles is more crowded than usual on Sunday in any season, and the garden's fountains run (April-Oct).

Most of Paris' stores are closed on Sunday, but shoppers will find relief along the Champs-Elysées, at flea markets, and in the Marais neighborhood's lively Jewish Quarter, where many boutiques are open. Many recommended restaurants in the Rue Cler neighborhood are closed for dinner.

MONDAY: These sights are closed: Orsay, Rodin, Picasso, Victor Hugo's House at Place des Vosges, Deportation Memorial, and Versailles (but the gardens are open April-Oct). The Louvre is far more crowded because of these closings. From October through June, the Army Museum is closed the first Monday of the month, though Napoleon's Tomb remains open.

Market streets such as Rue Cler and Rue Mouffetard are dead today.

TUESDAY: Many sights are closed, including the Louvre, Orangerie, Cluny, and Pompidou museums. The Orsay and Versailles are crazy busy today. The fountains at Versailles run on Tuesdays from mid-May until late June; music (no fountains) fills the gardens April-mid-May and July-October. Napoleon's Tomb and the Army Museum's WWI and WWII wings are open until 21:00 (April-Sept).

WEDNESDAY: All sights are open, and some have late hours, including the Louvre (until 21:45, last entry 21:00), the Rodin (until 20:45), and Sainte-Chapelle (until 21:30 mid-May-mid-Sept).

THURSDAY: All sights are open. Some sights are open late, including the Orsay (until 21:45, last entry 21:00). Some department stores are open late.

FRIDAY: All sights are open. The Louvre is open until 21:45 (last entry 21:00) and Notre-Dame's tower is open until 23:00 (July-Aug). The Picasso Museum is open until 21:00 on the third Friday of every month.

SATURDAY: All sights are open. The fountains run at Versailles (April-Oct). Notre-Dame's tower is open until 23:00 (July-Aug).

(most American credit cards won't work). And at certain sights, including the Louvre and Orsay, **nearby shops** sell tickets, allowing you to avoid the main ticket lines (for details, see the Louvre and Orsay listings).

Tours

🎧 To sightsee on your own, download my **free audio tours** that illuminate some of Paris' top sights and neighborhoods, including the Historic Paris Walk, Louvre Museum, and Orsay Museum (see sidebar on page 14 for details).

Paris Walks offers a variety of thoughtful and entertaining two-hour walks, led by British and American guides (€12-20, generally 2/day, private tours available, family guides and Louvre tours are a specialty, tel. 01 48 09 21 40, www.paris-walks.

com). Reservations aren't necessary for most tours, but specialty tours—such as the Louvre, fashion, or chocolate tours—require advance reservations and pre-payment with credit card (deposits are nonrefundable).

Context Travel offers "intellectual by design" walking tours geared for serious learners. The tours are led by well-versed docents (historians, architects, and academics) and cover both museums and specific neighborhoods. It's best to book in advance—groups are limited to six participants and can fill up fast (€70-105/person, admission to sights extra, generally 3 hours, tel. 09 75 18 04 15, US tel. 800-691-6036, www.contexttravel.com). They also offer private tours and excursions outside Paris.

Bike About Tours offers easygoing tours with a focus on the eastern half of the city. Their four-hour tours run daily year-round at 10:00 (also at 15:00 May-Sept). You'll meet at the statue of Charlemagne in front of Notre-Dame, then walk nearby to get your bikes. Reserve online to guarantee a spot, or show up and take your chances (€30, ask about Rick Steves discount). Their private family tours of Paris include fun activities like scavenger hunts (€200 for 2 people, €25/person after that, complimentary boat-tour tickets—a €14 value).

For many, Paris merits hiring a Parisian as a personal guide. **Thierry Gauduchon** is a terrific guide and a gifted teacher (€230/half-day, €450/day, tel. 06 19 07 30 77, tgauduchon@gmail.com). **Sylvie Moreau** also leads good tours in Paris (€200 for 3 hours, €320 for 7 hours, tel. 01 74 30 27 46, mobile 06 87 02 80 67, sylvie.ja.moreau@gmail.com). **Elisabeth Van Hest** is another likable and very capable guide (€200/half-day, tel. 01 43 41 47 31, mobile 06 77 80 19 89, elisa.guide@gmail.com).

Helpful Hints

Theft Alert: Thieves thrive near famous monuments and on Métro and train lines that serve airports and high-profile tourist sights. Beware of pickpockets working busy lines (e.g., at ticket windows at train stations). Look out for groups of young girls who swarm around you (be very firm—even forceful—and walk away). Smartphones and tablets are thief magnets anytime, so be aware whenever you're using one or holding it up to take a picture.

It's smart to wear a money belt, put your wallet in your front pocket, loop your day bag over your shoulders, and keep a tight hold on your purse or shopping bag. When wearing a daypack, don't keep valuables in the outer pockets, and don't mark yourself as a tourist by wearing it on your front.

Muggings are rare, but they do occur. If you're out late, avoid the dark riverfront embankments and any place where the lighting is dim and pedestrian activity is minimal.

Tourist Scams: Be aware of the latest

Explore Paris by bike.

Learn from an expert guide.

tricks, such as the "found ring" scam (a con artist pretends to find a "pure gold" ring on the ground and offers to sell it to you) or the "friendship bracelet" scam (a vendor asks you to help with a demo, makes a bracelet on your arm that you can't easily remove, and then asks you to pay for it).

Distractions by a stranger—often a "salesman," someone asking you to sign a petition, or someone posing as a deaf person to show you a small note to read—can all be tricks that function as a smoke-screen for theft. As you try to wriggle away from the pushy stranger, an accomplice picks your pocket.

To all these scammers, simply say "no" firmly and step away purposefully. For reports from my readers on the latest scams, go to https://community.rick steves.com/travel-forum/tourist-scams.

Medical Help: There are a variety of English-speaking resources for medical help in Paris, including doctors who will visit your hotel. Try the **American Hospital** (tel. 01 46 41 25 25, www.american-hospital. org) or **SOS Médicins** (SOS Doctors, tel. 01 47 07 77 77, www.sosmedecins.fr).

Useful Apps: Gogo Paris is an intriguing app that reviews trendy places to eat, drink, relax, and sleep in Paris (www. gogocityguides.com/paris).

🎧 For free audio versions of some of the self-guided tours in this chapter, get the **Rick Steves Audio Europe** app (for details, see page 14).

Public WCs: Most public toilets are free. If it's a pay toilet, the price will be clearly indicated. If the toilet is free but there's an attendant, it's polite to leave a tip of €0.20-0.50. Bold travelers can walk into any sidewalk café like they own the place and find the toilet downstairs or in the back. Or do as the locals do—order a shot of espresso (un café) while standing at the café bar (then use the WC with a clear conscience). Keep tissues with you, as some WCs are poorly stocked.

Tobacco Stands (Tabacs): These little

kiosks—usually just a counter inside a café—sell public-transit tickets, cards for parking meters, postage stamps (though not all sell international postage), and...oh yeah, cigarettes. Just look for a red, elongated diamond-shaped *Tabac* sign.

HISTORIC PARIS WALK

Paris has been the cultural capital of Europe for centuries. We'll start where the city did—on the Ile de la Cité—and make a foray onto the Left Bank. Along the way, we'll step into some of the city's greatest sights, including Notre-Dame and Sainte-Chapelle.

Getting There: The closest Métro stops are Cité, Hôtel de Ville, and St. Michel, each a short walk away.

Length of This Walk: Allow four hours to do justice to this three-mile self-guided walk, beginning at Notre-Dame Cathedral and ending at Pont Neuf; just follow the dotted line on the "Historic Paris Walk" map.

Tours: 🎧 Download my free Historic Paris Walk audio tour.

➋ Self-Guided Walk

• Begin in front of Notre-Dame Cathedral, the physical and historic bull's-eye of your Paris map.

▲▲▲ Notre-Dame Cathedral

The church is dedicated to "Our Lady" (*Notre Dame*), Mary, the mother of Jesus. There she is, cradling God, right in the heart of the facade, surrounded by the halo of the rose window. Though the church is massive and imposing, it has always stood for the grace and compassion of Mary, the "mother of God."

Imagine the faith of the people who built this cathedral. They broke ground in 1163 with the hope that someday their great-great-great-great-great-great grandchildren might attend the dedication Mass, which finally took place two centuries later, in 1345. Look up the 200-foot-tall bell towers and imagine a tiny medieval community mustering the money and energy for construction. Master masons supervised, but the people did much of the grunt work themselves for free—hauling the huge stones from distant quarries, digging a 30-foot-deep trench to lay the foundation, and treading like rats on a wheel designed to lift the stones up, one by one. This kind of backbreaking, arduous manual labor created the real hunchbacks of Notre-Dame.

Rick's Tip: *In summer,* **sound-and-light displays** *about the history of Notre-Dame generally run twice a week (free, usually Thu and Sat at 21:00—check cathedral website or call).*

Cost and Hours: Cathedral—free, daily 7:45-18:45, Sun until 19:15; audioguide—€5, free English tours—normally Mon-Tue and Sat at 14:30, Wed-Thu at 14:00.

The cathedral hosts **Masses** several times daily. Call or check the website for a full schedule (tel. 01 42 34 56 10, www.notredamedeparis.fr).

Tower Climb: The entrance for Notre-Dame's tower climb is outside the cathedral, along the left side. You can hike to the top of the facade between the towers and then to the top of the south tower (400 steps total) for a gargoyle's-eye view of the cathedral, Seine, and city (€8.50, covered by Museum Pass but no bypass line for passholders; daily April-Sept 10:00-18:30, Fri-Sat until 23:00 in July-Aug, Oct-March 10:00-17:30, last entry 45 minutes before closing; to avoid the worst lines arrive before 10:00 or after 17:00—after 16:00 in winter; tel. 01 53 10 07 00, www.notre-dame-de-paris.monuments-nationaux.fr).

Rick's Tip: *If you're* **claustrophobic or acrophobic, skip climbing Notre-Dame's tower.** *It's a tight, crowded space—and once you start up, you're expected to finish.*

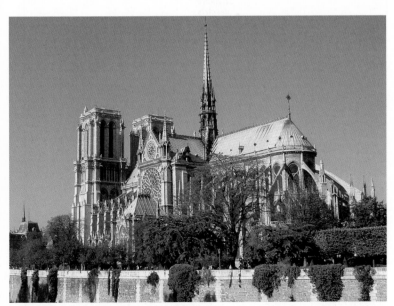

The best view of Notre-Dame is from the Left Bank.

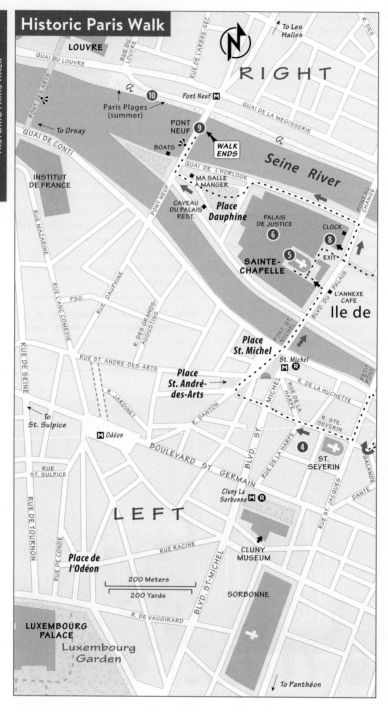

Historic Paris Walk

RIGHT

LOUVRE

QUAI DU LOUVRE

RUE DU LOUVRE

RUE DE L'ARBRE-SEC

R. DES

To Les Halles

N

Pont Neuf Ⓜ

10

Paris Plages (summer)

PONT NEUF

9

WALK ENDS

QUAI DE LA MÉGISSERIE

PONT DES ARTS

To Orsay

QUAI DE CONTI

BOATS

PONT NEUF

Seine River

PONT AU CHANGE

INSTITUT DE FRANCE

QUAI DE L'HORLOGE

MA SALLE À MANGER

CAVEAU DU PALAIS REST.

Place Dauphine

PALAIS DE JUSTICE

6

CLOCK

8

EXIT

RUE MAZARINE

SAINTE-CHAPELLE

5

RUE DAUPHINE

RUE DE L'ANC COMÉDIE

PSG.

RUE DES GRANDS AUGUSTINS

BLVD. DU PALAIS

L'ANNEXE CAFE

Île de

Place St. Michel

RUE DE SEINE

RUE ST. ANDRÉ-DES-ARTS

Place St. André-des-Arts

PONT ST. MICHEL

St. Michel Ⓜ Ⓡ

R. DE LA HUCHETTE

PETIT PONT

R. JARDINET

To St. Sulpice

Ⓜ Odéon

R. DANTON

BOULEVARD ST. GERMAIN

BLVD. ST. MICHEL

RUE DE LA HARPE

R. STE. SÉVERIN

4

GALANDE

RUE ST. SULPICE

RUE DE TOURNON

Cluny La Sorbonne Ⓜ Ⓡ

ST. SÉVERIN

DANTE

RUE ST. JACQUES

L E F T

RUE RACINE

RUE DE CONDE

Place de l'Odéon

CLUNY MUSEUM

200 Meters

200 Yards

BLVD. ST-MICHEL

SORBONNE

LUXEMBOURG PALACE

Luxembourg Garden

R. DE VAUGIRARD

To Panthéon

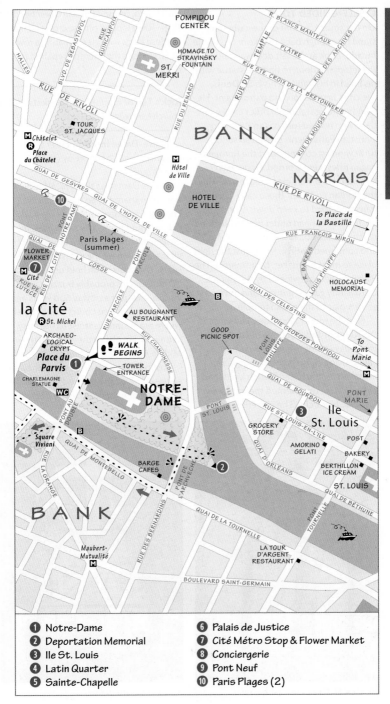

POMPIDOU
CENTER

R. BLANCS MANTEAUX

HALLES

BLVD DE SEBASTOPOL

RUE QUINCAMPOIX

HOMAGE TO
STRAVINSKY
FOUNTAIN

ST.
MERRI

RUE DU TEMPLE

PLÂTRE

RUE DES ARCHIVES

RUE STE. CROIX DE LA BRETONNERIE

RUE DE RIVOLI

RUE DU RENARD

BANK

RUE DE MOUSSY

TOUR
ST. JACQUES

M Châtelet
R Place
du Châtelet

M
Hôtel
de Ville

RUE DE RIVOLI

MARAIS

QUAI DE GESVRES

QUAI DE L'HOTEL DE VILLE

HOTEL
DE VILLE

To Place de
la Bastille

Pont Notre-Dame

QUAI DE LA CITE

Paris Plages
(summer)

RUE FRANÇOIS MIRON

FLOWER
MARKET

LA CORSE

PONT D'ARCOLE

R. BARRES

R. LOUIS PHILIPPE

Cité
RUE DE
LUTECE

la Cité

RUE DE LA CITE

QUAI DES CELESTINS

HOLOCAUST
MEMORIAL

R St. Michel

RUE D'ARCOLE

B

AU BOUGNANTE
RESTAURANT

VOIE GEORGES POMPIDOU

ARCHAEO-
LOGICAL
CRYPT

Place du
Parvis

RUE CHANOINESSE

GOOD
PICNIC SPOT

PONT LOUIS PHILIPPE

To
Pont
Marie

WALK
BEGINS

1

TOWER
ENTRANCE

QUAI DE BOURBON

M

CHARLEMAGNE
STATUE

WC

NOTRE-
DAME

PONT AU DOUBLE

PONT
ST. LOUIS

RUE ST. LOUIS-EN-L'ILE

3

PONT
MARIE

Ile
St. Louis

B

Square
Viviani

QUAI DE MONTEBELLO

GROCERY
STORE

POST

AMORINO
GELATI

BAKERY

RUE DE LA GRANGE

BARGE
CAFES

PONT DE L'ARCHEVÊCHÉ

2

QUAI D'ORLEANS

BERTHILLON
ICE CREAM

ST. LOUIS

QUAI DE BÉTHUNE

BANK

RUE DES BERNARDINS

QUAI DE LA TOURNELLE

PONT TOURNELLE

Maubert-
Mutualité
M

LA TOUR
D'ARGENT
RESTAURANT

BOULEVARD SAINT-GERMAIN

1 Notre-Dame
2 Deportation Memorial
3 Ile St. Louis
4 Latin Quarter
5 Sainte-Chapelle

6 Palais de Justice
7 Cité Métro Stop & Flower Market
8 Conciergerie
9 Pont Neuf
10 Paris Plages (2)

⊙ SELF-GUIDED TOUR

On the square in front of the cathedral, stand far enough back to take in the whole **facade.** Look at the left doorway, and to the left of the door, to find the statue with his head in his hands. This is **St. Denis,** the city's first bishop and patron saint. He stands among statues of other early Christians who helped turn pagan Paris into Christian Paris. Denis proved so successful at winning converts that the Romans' pagan priests got worried. Denis was beheaded as a warning to those forsaking the Roman gods. But those early Christians were hard to keep down. Denis got up, tucked his head under his arm, headed north, paused at a fountain to wash it off, and continued until he found just the right place to meet his maker: Montmartre. The Parisians were convinced by this miracle, Christianity gained ground, and a church soon replaced the pagan temple.

Find the row of 28 statues, known as the **Kings of Judah,** above the arches. In the days of the French Revolution (1789-1799), these biblical kings were mistaken for the hated French kings, and Notre-Dame represented the oppressive Catholic hierarchy. The citizens stormed the church, crying, "Off with their heads!" Plop—they lopped off the crowned heads of these kings with glee, creating a row of St. Denises that weren't repaired for decades.

Rick's Tip: Be careful—**pickpockets** attend church here religiously.

Notre-Dame Interior: Enter the church at the right doorway (the line moves quickly).

Notre-Dame has the typical basilica floor plan shared by so many Catholic churches: a long central nave lined with columns and flanked by side aisles. It's designed in the shape of a cross, with the altar placed where the crossbeam intersects. The church can hold up to 10,000 faithful, and it's probably buzzing with visitors now, just as it was 600 years ago. The quiet, deserted churches we see elsewhere are in stark contrast to the busy, center-of-life places they were in the Middle Ages.

Just past the altar is the choir, the area enclosed with carved-wood walls, where more intimate services can be held in

Headless St. Denis, Paris' patron saint

Pietà inside Notre-Dame

Affording Paris' Sights

Paris is an expensive city, with lots of pricey sights, but—fortunately—lots of free-bies, too. Smart travelers begin by buying and using the **Paris Museum Pass** (see page 128). Also consider these frugal sightseeing options.

Free (or Almost Free) Museums: Many of Paris' famous museums offer free entry on the first Sunday of the month year-round, including the Orsay, Rodin, Cluny, and Pompidou Center museums. Other sights are free on the first Sunday only in the off-season: the Louvre and Arc de Triomphe (both Oct-March) and Versailles (Nov-March). Expect big crowds on free days. You can usually visit the Orsay Museum for free right when the ticket booth stops selling tickets. For just €2, the Rodin Museum garden lets you enjoy many of his finest works in a lovely outdoor setting.

Other Freebies: There's no entry fee at Notre-Dame Cathedral, Père Lachaise Cemetery, Deportation Memorial, Paris *plages* (summers only), and Sacré-Cœur Basilica.

Reduced Prices: Several sights offer a discount if you enter later in the day, including the Orangerie and the Army Museum and Napoleon's Tomb. The Eiffel Tower costs less if you stick to the two lower levels—and even less if you use the stairs.

Free Concerts: Venues offering free or cheap (€6-8) concerts include the American Church, Army Museum, St. Sulpice Church, La Madeleine Church, and Notre-Dame Cathedral. For a listing of free concerts, check *Pariscope* magazine (under the "Musique" section) and look for events marked *entrée libre*.

Good-Value Tours: At about €16, Paris Walks' tours are a good value. The €13-14 Seine River cruises, best after dark, are also worthwhile. The scenic bus route #69, which costs only the price of a transit ticket, could be the best deal of all.

Pricey...but worth it? Certain big-ticket items—primarily the top of the Eiffel Tower, the Louvre, and Versailles—are expensive and crowded, but offer once-in-a-lifetime experiences. All together they amount to less than the cost of a ticket to Disneyland—only these are real.

---

this spacious building. Looking past the altar to the far end of the choir (under the cross), you'll see a fine **17th-century *pietà*,** flanked by two kneeling kings: Louis XIII (1601-1643, not so famous) and his son, Louis XIV (1638-1715, very famous, also known as the Sun King).

In the right transept, a statue of **Joan of Arc** (Jeanne d'Arc, 1412-1431), dressed in armor and praying, honors the French teenager who rallied her country's soldiers to try to drive English invaders from Paris.

Join the statue in gazing up to the blue-and-purple, **rose-shaped window** in the opposite transept—with teeny green Mary and baby Jesus in the center—the only one of the three rose windows still with its original medieval glass.

The back side of the choir walls feature scenes of the **resurrected Jesus** (c. 1350) appearing to his followers, starting with Mary Magdalene. Their starry robes still gleam, thanks to a 19th-century renovation. The niches below these carvings mark the tombs of centuries of archbishops.

Notre-Dame Side View: Back outside, alongside the church, you'll notice many of the elements are Gothic: pointed arches, lacy stone tracery of the windows, pinnacles, statues on rooftops, a lead roof, and a pointed steeple covered with the prickly "flames" (Flamboyant Gothic) of the Holy Spirit. Most distinctive of all are the **flying buttresses.** These 50-foot stone "beams" that stick out of the church were the key to the complex Gothic architecture. The pointed arches we saw inside cause the weight of the roof to push outward rather than downward. The "flying" buttresses support the roof by pushing back inward.

Picture Quasimodo (the fictional hunchback) limping around along the railed balcony at the base of the roof among the **gargoyles.** These grotesque beasts sticking out from pillars and buttresses represent souls caught between heaven and earth. They also function as rainspouts (from the same French root word as "gargle") when there are no evil spirits to battle.

The Neo-Gothic 300-foot **spire** is a product of the 1860 reconstruction of the dilapidated old church. Victor Hugo's book *The Hunchback of Notre-Dame* (1831) inspired a young architecture student named Eugène-Emmanuel Viollet-le-Duc to dedicate his career to a major renovation in Gothic style. Find Viollet-le-Duc at the base of the spire among the green apostles and evangelists (visible as you approach the back end of the church). The apostles look outward, blessing the city, while the architect (at top) looks up the spire, marveling at his fine work.

• *Behind Notre-Dame, cross the street and enter through the iron gate into the park at the tip of the island. Look for the stairs and head down to reach the...*

▲Deportation Memorial (Mémorial de la Déportation)

This memorial to the 200,000 French victims of the Nazi concentration camps (1940-1945) draws you into their experience. France was quickly overrun by Nazi Germany, and Paris spent the war years under Nazi occupation. Jews and dissidents were rounded up and deported—many never returned.

Cost and Hours: Free, Tue-Sun 10:00-19:00, Oct-March until 17:00, closed Mon year-round; at the east tip of Ile de la Cité, behind Notre-Dame and near Ile St. Louis (Mo: Cité); www.cheminsdememoire. gouv.fr.

Visiting the Memorial: As you descend the steps, the city around you disappears. Surrounded by walls, you have become a prisoner. Your only freedom is your view of the sky and the tiny glimpse of the river below. Enter the dark, single-file chamber up ahead. Inside, the circular plaque in the floor reads, "They went to the end of the earth and did not return."

The hallway stretching in front of you is lined with 200,000 lighted crystals, one

Deportation Memorial

Shakespeare and Company bookstore

for each French citizen who died. Flickering at the far end is the eternal flame of hope. The tomb of the unknown deportee lies at your feet. Above, the inscription reads, "Dedicated to the living memory of the 200,000 French deportees shrouded by the night and the fog, exterminated in the Nazi concentration camps." The side rooms are filled with triangles—reminiscent of the identification patches inmates were forced to wear—each bearing the name of a concentration camp. Above the exit as you leave is the message you'll find at many other Holocaust sites: "Forgive, but never forget."

• Back on street level, look across the river (north) to the island called...

Ile St. Louis

If Ile de la Cité is a tugboat laden with the history of Paris, it's towing this classy little residential dinghy, laden only with high-rent apartments, boutiques, characteristic restaurants, and famous ice cream shops.

Ile St. Louis was developed in the 17th century, much later than Ile de la Cité. What was a swampy mess is now harmonious Parisian architecture and one of the city's most exclusive neighborhoods. If you won't have time to return here later, consider taking a brief detour across the pedestrian bridge, Pont St. Louis. It connects the two islands, leading right to Rue St. Louis-en-l'Ile. This spine of the island is lined with appealing shops, reasonably priced restaurants, and a handy grocery. A short stroll takes you to the famous Berthillon ice cream parlor at #31, which is still family-owned. The ice cream is famous not just because it's good, but because it's made right here on the island. Gelato lovers can comparison-shop by also sampling the (mass-produced-but-who's-complaining) Amorino Gelati at 47 Rue St. Louis-en-l'Ile. This walk is about as peaceful and romantic as Paris gets. When you're finished exploring, loop back to the pedestrian bridge along the parklike quays (walk north to the river and turn left).

• From the Deportation Memorial, cross the bridge to the Left Bank. Turn right and walk along the river toward the front end of Notre-Dame. Stairs detour down to the riverbank if you need a place to picnic. This side view of the church from across the river is one of Europe's great sights and is best from river level. At times, you may find barges housing restaurants with great cathedral views docked here.

After passing the Pont au Double (the bridge leading to the facade of Notre-Dame), watch on your left for **Shakespeare and Company,** an atmospheric reincarnation of the original 1920s bookshop (open long hours daily, 37 Rue de la Bûcherie, Mo: St. Michel, tel. 01 43 25 40 93). Before returning to the island, walk a block behind Shakespeare and Company, and take a spin through the...

▲ The Latin Quarter

This area's touristy fame relates to its intriguing, artsy, bohemian character. This was perhaps Europe's leading university district in the Middle Ages, when Latin was the language of higher education. The neighborhood's main boulevards (St. Michel and St. Germain) are lined with cafés—once the haunts of great poets and philosophers, now the hangouts of tired tourists. Though still youthful

The Latin Quarter

and artsy, much of this touristy area is filled with cheap North African eateries. Exploring a few blocks up or downriver from here gives you a better chance of feeling the pulse of what survives of Paris' classic Left Bank. For colorful wandering and café-sitting, afternoons and evenings are best.

Walking along Rue St. Séverin, you can still see the shadow of the medieval sewer system. The street slopes into a central channel of bricks. In the days before plumbing and toilets, when people still went to the river or neighborhood wells for their water, flushing meant throwing it out the window. At certain times of day, maids on the fourth floor would holler, *"Garde de l'eau!"* ("Watch out for the water!") and heave it into the streets, where it would eventually wash down into the Seine.

Consider a visit to the **Cluny Museum** for its medieval art and unicorn tapestries (see page 164). The **Sorbonne**—the University of Paris' humanities department—is also nearby; visitors can ogle at the famous dome, but they are not allowed to enter the building (two blocks south of the river on Boulevard St. Michel).

Don't miss **Place St. Michel.** This square (facing Pont St. Michel) is the traditional core of the Left Bank's district of artists, poets, philosophers, winos, and *baba* cools (neo-hippies). In less commercial times, Place St. Michel was a gathering point for the city's malcontents and misfits. In 1830, 1848, and again in 1871, the citizens took the streets from the government troops, set up barricades Les Miz-style, and fought against royalist oppression. During World War II, the locals rose up against their Nazi oppressors (read the plaques under the dragons at the foot of the St. Michel fountain). Even today, whenever there's a student demonstration, it starts here.

• *From Place St. Michel, look across the river and find the prickly steeple of the Sainte-Chapelle church. Head toward it.*

Cross the river on Pont St. Michel and continue north along the Boulevard du Palais. On your left, you'll see the doorway to Sainte-Chapelle (usually with a line of people).

▲▲▲Sainte-Chapelle

This triumph of Gothic church architecture is a cathedral of glass like no other. It was speedily built between 1242 and 1248 for King Louis IX—the only French king who is now a saint—to house the supposed Crown of Thorns. Its architectural harmony is due to the fact that it was completed under the direction of one architect and in only six years—unheard of in Gothic times. In contrast, Notre-Dame took over 200 years.

Cost and Hours: €8.50, €13.50 combo-ticket with Conciergerie, covered by Museum Pass; daily March-Oct 9:30-18:00, Wed until 21:30 mid-May-mid-Sept, Nov-Feb 9:00-17:00; audio-guide-€4.50, 4 Boulevard du Palais, Mo: Cité, tel. 01 53 40 60 80, http://sainte-chapelle.monuments-nationaux.fr. For info on upcoming church concerts, see page 184.

Getting In: Expect long lines to get in (shortest wait first thing in the mornings and on weekends; longest on Tue and any day around 13:00-14:00). First comes the security line (all sharp objects and glass are confiscated). Once past security, you'll encounter the ticket-buying line—those with combo-tickets or Museum Passes can skip this queue.

Visiting the Church: Though the inside is beautiful, the exterior is basically functional. The muscular buttresses hold up the stone roof, so the walls are essentially there to display stained glass. The lacy spire is Neo-Gothic—added in the 19th century. Inside, the layout clearly shows an *ancien régime* approach to worship. The low-ceilinged basement was for staff and other common folks—worshipping under a sky filled with painted fleurs-de-lis, a symbol of the king. Royal Christians

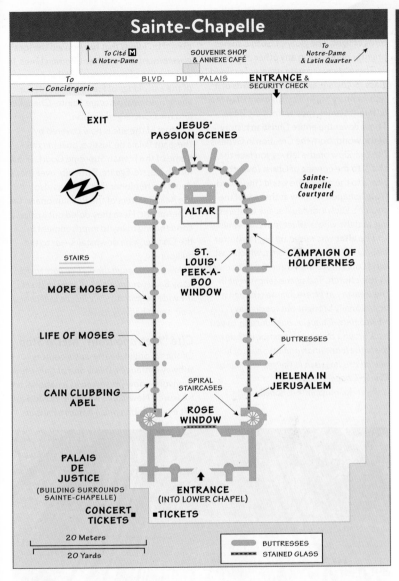

Sainte-Chapelle

To Cité Ⓜ
& Notre-Dame

SOUVENIR SHOP
& ANNEXE CAFÉ

To
Notre-Dame
& Latin Quarter

To
← Conciergerie

BLVD. DU PALAIS

ENTRANCE &
SECURITY CHECK

EXIT

JESUS'
PASSION SCENES

Sainte-
Chapelle
Courtyard

ALTAR

STAIRS

ST.
LOUIS'
PEEK-A-
BOO
WINDOW

CAMPAIGN OF
HOLOFERNES

MORE MOSES

LIFE OF MOSES

BUTTRESSES

CAIN CLUBBING
ABEL

SPIRAL
STAIRCASES

HELENA IN
JERUSALEM

ROSE
WINDOW

PALAIS
DE
JUSTICE
(BUILDING SURROUNDS
SAINTE-CHAPELLE)

ENTRANCE
(INTO LOWER CHAPEL)

CONCERT
TICKETS

■TICKETS

20 Meters

20 Yards

BUTTRESSES
STAINED GLASS

worshipped upstairs. The paint job, a 19th-century restoration, helps you imagine how grand this small, painted, jeweled chapel was. (Imagine Notre-Dame painted like this...) Each capital is playfully carved with a different plant's leaves.

Climb the spiral staircase to the Chapelle Haute. Fill the place with choral music, crank up the sunshine, face the top of the altar, and really believe that the Crown of Thorns is there, and this becomes one awesome space.

Fiat lux. "Let there be light." From the first page of the Bible, it's clear: Light is divine. Light shines through stained glass like God's grace shining down to earth.

Gothic architects used their new technology to turn dark stone buildings into lanterns of light. The glory of Gothic shines brighter here than in any other church.

There are 15 separate panels of **stained glass** (6,500 square feet—two thirds of it 13th-century original), with more than 1,100 different scenes, mostly from the Bible. These cover the entire Christian history of the world, from the Creation in Genesis (first window on the left, as you face the altar), to the coming of Christ (over the altar), to the end of the world (the round "rose"-shaped window at the rear of the church). Each individual scene is interesting, and the whole effect is overwhelming.

The **altar** was raised up high to better display the Crown of Thorns, which cost King Louis more than three times as much as this church. Today, the relic is kept in the treasury at Notre-Dame (though it's occasionally brought out for display).

• *Exit Sainte-Chapelle. Back outside, as you walk around the church exterior, look down to see the foundation and take note of how much Paris has risen in the 750 years since Sainte-Chapelle was built.*

Next door to Sainte-Chapelle is the...

Palais de Justice

Sainte-Chapelle sits within a huge complex of buildings that has housed the local government since ancient Roman times. It was the site of the original Gothic palace of the early kings of France. The only surviving medieval parts are Sainte-Chapelle and the Conciergerie prison.

Most of the site is now covered by the giant Palais de Justice, built in 1776, home of the French Supreme Court. The motto *Liberté, Egalité, Fraternité* over the doors is a reminder that this was also the headquarters of the Revolutionary government. Here they doled out justice, condemning many to imprisonment in the Conciergerie downstairs—or to the guillotine.

• *Now pass through the big iron gate to the noisy Boulevard du Palais. Cross the street to the wide, pedestrian-only Rue de Lutèce and walk about halfway down.*

Cité "Metropolitain" Métro Stop

Of the 141 original early-20th-century subway entrances, this is one of only a few survivors—now preserved as a national art treasure. (New York's Museum of Modern Art even exhibits one.) It marks Paris at

Sainte-Chapelle is a cathedral of stained glass like no other.

its peak in 1900—on the cutting edge of Modernism, but with an eye for beauty. The curvy, plantlike ironwork is a textbook example of Art Nouveau, the style that rebelled against the erector-set squareness of the Industrial Age. Other similar Métro stations in Paris are Abbesses and Porte Dauphine.

The flower and plant market on Place Louis Lépine is a pleasant detour. On Sundays this square flutters with a busy bird market.

• Pause here to admire the view.

Sainte-Chapelle is a pearl in an ugly architectural oyster. Double back to the Palais de Justice, turn right onto Boulevard du Palais, and enter the Conciergerie. It's free with the Museum Pass; passholders can sidestep the bottleneck created by the ticket-buying line.

▲Conciergerie

Though pretty barren inside, this former prison echoes with history. Positioned next to the courthouse, the Conciergerie was the gloomy prison famous as the last stop for 2,780 victims of the guillotine, including France's last *ancien régime* queen, Marie-Antoinette. Before then, kings had used the building to torture and execute failed assassins. (One of its towers along the river was called "The Babbler," named for the pain-induced sounds that leaked from it.) When the Revolution (1789) toppled the king, the building kept its same function, but without torture.

The progressive Revolutionaries proudly unveiled a modern and more humane way to execute people—the guillotine. The Conciergerie was the epicenter of the Reign of Terror—the year-long period of the Revolution (1793-94) during which Revolutionary fervor spiraled out of control and thousands were killed. It was here at the Conciergerie that "enemies of the Revolution" were imprisoned, tried, sentenced, and marched off to Place de la Concorde for decapitation.

Cost and Hours: €8.50, €13.50 combo-ticket with Sainte-Chapelle, covered by Museum Pass, daily 9:30-18:00, 2 Boulevard du Palais, Mo: Cité, tel. 01 53 40 60 80, http://conciergerie.monuments-nationaux.fr.

Visiting the Conciergerie: Pick up a free map and breeze through the one-way circuit. See the spacious, low-ceilinged Hall of Men-at-Arms (Room 1), originally a guards' dining room, with four big fireplaces (look up the chimneys). During the Reign of Terror, this large hall served as a holding tank for the poorest prisoners. Continue to the raised area at the far end of the room (Room 4, today's bookstore). In Revolutionary days, this was notorious as the walkway of the executioner, who was known affectionately as "Monsieur de Paris."

Upstairs is a memorial room with the names of the 2,780 citizens condemned to death by the guillotine, including ex-King Louis XVI, Charlotte Corday (who murdered the Revolutionary writer

Cité Métro entrance

Conciergerie prison

Jean-Paul Marat in his bathtub), and—oh, the irony—Maximilien de Robespierre, the head rabble-rouser of the Revolution, who himself sent so many to the guillotine.

Just past the courtyard is a re-creation of Marie-Antoinette's cell. On August 12, 1793, the queen was brought here to be tried for her supposed crimes against the people. Mannequins, period furniture, and the real cell wallpaper set the scene. In the glass display case, see her actual crucifix, rug, and small water pitcher. On October 16, 1793, the queen was awakened at 4:00 in the morning and led away. She walked the corridor, stepped onto the cart, and was slowly carried to Place de la Concorde, where she had a date with "Monsieur de Paris."

• *Back outside, turn left on Boulevard du Palais, then left again onto Quai de l'Horloge and walk along the river, past "The Babbler" tower.*

The bridge up ahead is the Pont Neuf, where we'll end this walk. At the first corner, veer left into a sleepy triangular square called **Place Dauphine.** *It's amazing to find such coziness in the heart of Paris. From the equestrian statue of Henry IV, turn right onto Pont Neuf. Pause at the little nook halfway across.*

Pont Neuf and the Seine

This "new bridge" is now Paris' oldest. Built during Henry IV's reign (about 1600), its arches span the widest part of the river. Unlike other bridges, this one never had houses or buildings growing on it. The turrets were originally for vendors and street entertainers. In the days of Henry IV, who promised his peasants "a chicken in every pot every Sunday," this would have been a lively scene. From the bridge, look downstream (west) to see the next bridge, the pedestrian-only Pont des Arts. Ahead on the Right Bank is the long Louvre museum. Beyond that, on the Left Bank, is the Orsay.

• *Our walk is finished. From here, you can tour the Seine by boat (the departure point for Seine River cruises offered by Vedettes du Pont Neuf is through the park at the end of the island—see page 179), continue to the Louvre, or (if it's summer) head to the...*

Pont Neuf crosses the widest part of the Seine.

▲Paris Plages (Paris Beaches)

The Riviera it's not, but this string of fanciful faux beaches—assembled in summer along a one-mile stretch of the Right Bank of the Seine—is a fun place to stroll, play, and people-watch on a sunny day. Each summer, the Paris city government closes the embankment's highway and trucks in potted palm trees, hammocks, lounge chairs, and 2,000 tons of sand to create colorful urban beaches. You'll also find "beach cafés," climbing walls, prefab pools, trampolines, *boules*, a library, beach volleyball, badminton, and Frisbee areas.

Cost and Hours: Free, mid-July-mid-Aug daily 8:00-24:00, on Right Bank of Seine, just north of Ile de la Cité, between Pont des Arts and Pont de Sully; for information, go to www.quefaire.paris.fr/parisplages.

SIGHTS

Major Museums Neighborhood

Paris' grandest park, the Tuileries Garden, was once the private property of kings and queens. Today it links the Louvre, Orangerie, and Orsay museums, all of which are within pleasant strolling distance of one another.

▲▲▲LOUVRE (MUSEE DU LOUVRE)

This is Europe's oldest, biggest, greatest, and second-most-crowded museum (after the Vatican). Housed in a U-shaped, 16th-century palace (accentuated by a 20th-century glass pyramid), it's home to the *Mona Lisa, Venus de Milo,* and hall after hall of Greek and Roman masterpieces, medieval jewels,

Major Museums Neighborhood

❶ Bus #69 eastbound
❷ Bus #69 westbound

Louvre Overview

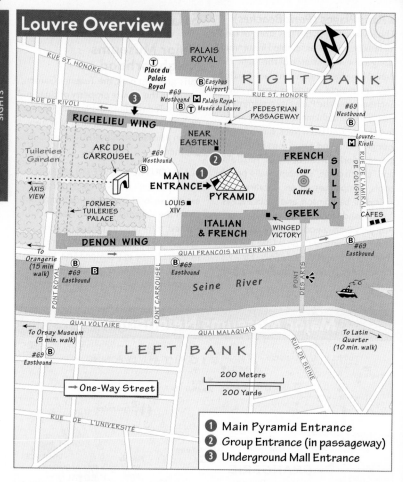

PALAIS ROYAL

RIGHT BANK

RUE ST. HONORE

Place du Palais Royal

Easybus (Airport)

RUE ST. HONORE

#69 Westbound

Palais Royal-Musée du Louvre

PEDESTRIAN PASSAGEWAY

#69 Westbound

RUE DE RIVOLI

RICHELIEU WING

Louvre-Rivoli

NEAR EASTERN

Tuileries Garden

ARC DU CARROUSEL

#69 Westbound

FRENCH

SULLY

RUE DE L'AMIRAL DE COLIGNY

MAIN ENTRANCE

Cour Carrée

AXIS VIEW

PYRAMID

FORMER TUILERIES PALACE

LOUIS XIV

GREEK

CAFES

ITALIAN & FRENCH

WINGED VICTORY

DENON WING

QUAI FRANCOIS MITTERRAND

#69 Eastbound

To Orangerie (15 min walk)

#69 Eastbound

#69 Eastbound

PONT ROYAL

PONT CARROUSEL

Seine River

PONT DES ARTS

QUAI VOLTAIRE

To Orsay Museum (5 min. walk)

QUAI MALAQUAIS

LEFT BANK

To Latin Quarter (10 min. walk)

#69 Eastbound

RUE DE SEINE

200 Meters

200 Yards

→ One-Way Street

RUE DE L'UNIVERSITE

1 Main Pyramid Entrance
2 Group Entrance (in passageway)
3 Underground Mall Entrance

Michelangelo statues, and paintings by the greatest artists from the Renaissance to the Romantics.

Under the Louvre's pyramid entrance

Touring the Louvre can be overwhelming, so be selective. Focus on the Denon wing, with Greek sculptures, Italian paintings (by Raphael and Leonardo), and—of course—French paintings (Neoclassical and Romantic), and the adjoining Sully wing, with Egyptian artifacts and more French paintings. For extra credit, tackle the Richelieu wing, displaying works from ancient Mesopotamia, as well as French, Dutch, and Northern art.

Expect Changes: The sprawling Louvre is constantly shuffling its deck. Rooms close, and pieces can be on loan or in restoration.

Cost and Hours: €12, €15 includes special exhibits, free on first Sun of month Oct-March, covered by Museum Pass, tickets good all day, reentry allowed; open Wed-Mon 9:00-18:00, Wed and Fri until 21:45 (except on holidays), closed Tue, galleries start shutting 30 minutes before closing, last entry 45 minutes before closing; videoguide-€5, several cafés, tel. 01 40 20 53 17, recorded info tel. 01 40 20 51 51, www.louvre.fr.

When to Go: Crowds are bad on Sun, Mon (the worst day), Wed, and in the morning (arrive 30 minutes before opening to secure a good place in line). Evening visits are quieter, and the glass pyramid glows after dark.

Buying Tickets: Self-serve ticket machines located under the pyramid may be faster to use than the ticket windows (machines accept euro bills, coins, and chip-and-PIN Visa cards). A shop in the underground mall sells tickets to the Louvre, Orsay, and Versailles, plus Museum Passes, for no extra charge (cash only). To find it from the Carrousel du Louvre entrance off Rue de Rivoli, turn right after the last escalator down onto Allée de France, and follow *Museum Pass* signs.

Rick's Tip: *Anyone can* **enter the Louvre from its less crowded underground entrance,** *accessed through the Carrousel du Louvre shopping mall. Enter the mall at 99 Rue de Rivoli (the door with the red awning) or directly from the Métro stop Palais Royal-Musée du Louvre (stepping off the train, take the exit to Musée du Louvre-Le Carrousel du Louvre).*

Getting There: It's at the Palais Royal-Musée du Louvre Métro stop. (The old Louvre Métro stop, called Louvre-Rivoli, is farther from the entrance.) Bus #69 also runs past the Louvre.

Getting In: There is no grander entry than through the main entrance at the **pyramid** in the central courtyard, but lines (for security reasons) can be long. Pass-holders should look for a queue that puts them near the head of the security line.

Tours: Ninety-minute English-

The Louvre and its pyramid glow at night.

language **guided tours** leave twice daily (except the first Sun of the month Oct-March) from the *Accueil des Groupes* area, under the pyramid (€12 plus admission, usually 11:15 and 14:00, tour tel. 01 40 20 52 63). **Videoguides** (€5) provide commentary on about 700 masterpieces.

🎧 Download my free Louvre Museum **audio tour.**

Baggage Check: The free *bagagerie* is under the pyramid, behind the Richelieu wing escalator (look for the *visiteurs individuels* sign).

❍ SELF-GUIDED TOUR

With more than 30,000 works of art, the Louvre is a full inventory of Western civilization. To cover it all in one visit is impossible. Let's focus on the Louvre's specialties—Greek sculpture, Italian painting, and French painting. If you don't find the artwork you're looking for, ask the nearest guard for its location.

• *We'll start in the Sully Wing, in Salle 16. To get there from the pyramid entrance, first enter the Denon Wing, ascend several flights of escalators, and follow the crowds—then get out your map or ask directions to the Venus de Milo.*

THE GREEKS

Venus de Milo (*Aphrodite,* late 2nd century B.C.): This goddess of love created

Venus de Milo

a sensation when she was discovered in 1820 on the Greek island of Melos. The Greeks pictured their gods in human form (meaning humans are godlike), telling us they had an optimistic view of the human race. *Venus'* well-proportioned body captures the balance and orderliness of the Greek universe. The twisting pose gives a balanced S-curve to her body (especially noticeable from the back view) that Golden Age Greeks and succeeding generations found beautiful. Most "Greek" statues are actually later Roman copies; this is a rare Greek original.

• *Now head to Salle 6, behind Venus de Milo.*

Parthenon Friezes (mid-5th century B.C.): These stone fragments once decorated the exterior of the greatest Athenian temple of the Greek Golden Age. The temple glorified the city's divine protector, Athena, and the superiority of the Athenians, who were feeling especially cocky, having just crushed their archrivals, the Persians. A model of the Parthenon shows where the panels might have hung.

• *About 50 yards away, find a grand staircase. Climb it to the first floor and the...*

Winged Victory of Samothrace (c. 190 B.C.): This woman with wings, poised on the prow of a ship, once stood on an island hilltop to commemorate a naval victory. Her clothes are windblown and sea-sprayed, clinging close enough to her body to win a wet T-shirt contest. Originally, her right arm was stretched high, celebrating the victory like a Super Bowl champion, waving a "we're number one" finger. This is the *Venus de Milo* gone Hellenistic, from the time after the culture of Athens was spread around the Mediterranean by Alexander the Great (c. 325 B.C.).

• *Facing Winged Victory, turn right (entering the Denon Wing), and proceed to the large Salle 3.*

THE MEDIEVAL WORLD, 1200-1500

Cimabue—*The Madonna and Child in Majesty Surrounded by Angels* (c. 1280): During the Age of Faith (1200s), almost every church in Europe had a painting like this one. Mary was a cult figure—even bigger than the late-20th-century Madonna—adored and prayed to by the faithful for bringing Baby Jesus into the world. These holy figures are laid flat on a gold background like cardboard cutouts, existing in a golden never-never land, as though the faithful couldn't imagine them as flesh-and-blood humans inhabiting our dark and sinful earth.

Giotto—*St. Francis of Assisi Receiving the Stigmata* (c. 1295-1300): Francis of Assisi (c. 1181-1226), a wandering Italian monk of renowned goodness, kneels on a rocky Italian hillside, pondering the pain of Christ's torture and execution. Suddenly, he looks up, startled, to see Christ himself, with six wings, hovering above. Christ shoots lasers from his wounds to the hands, feet, and side of the empathetic monk, marking him with the stigmata. Francis' humble love of man and nature inspired artists like Giotto to portray real human beings with real emotions, living in a physical world of beauty.

• *Room 3 spills into the long Grand Gallery. Find the following paintings in the Gallery, as you make your way to the Mona Lisa (midway down the gallery, in the adjoining Salle 6—just follow the signs and the people).*

ITALIAN RENAISSANCE, 1400-1600

Andrea Mantegna—*St. Sebastian* (c. 1480): Not the patron saint of acupuncture, St. Sebastian was a Christian martyr. Notice the *contrapposto* stance (all of his weight resting on one leg) and the Greek ruins scattered around him. His executioners look like ignorant medieval brutes bewildered by this enlightened Renaissance man. Italian artists were beginning to learn how to create human realism and earthly beauty on the canvas. Let the Renaissance begin.

Leonardo da Vinci—*The Virgin and Child with St. Anne* (c. 1510): Three generations—grandmother, mother, and child—are arranged in a pyramid, with Anne's face as the peak and the lamb as the lower right corner. It's as orderly as the

🅐 Winged Victory of Samothrace

🅑 *Giotto,* St. Francis Receiving the Stigmata

🅒 *Leonardo da Vinci,* Mona Lisa

- **A** *Raphael,* La Belle Jardinière
- **B** *Veronese,* The Marriage at Cana
- **C** *Ingres,* La Grande Odalisque
- **D** *Delacroix,* Liberty Leading the People

geometrically perfect universe created by the Renaissance god. There's a psychological kidney punch in this happy painting: Jesus, the picture of childish joy, is innocently playing with a lamb—the symbol of his inevitable sacrificial death.The Louvre has the greatest collection of Leonardos in the world—five of them. Look for the neighboring *Virgin of the Rocks* and *John the Baptist.*

Raphael—*La Belle Jardinière* (c. 1507): Raphael perfected the style Leonardo pioneered. This configuration of Madonna, Child, and John the Baptist is also a balanced pyramid with hazy grace and beauty. The interplay of gestures and gazes gives the masterpiece both intimacy and cohesiveness, while Raphael's blended brushstrokes varnish the work with an iridescent smoothness. With Raphael, the Greek ideal of beauty—reborn in the Renaissance—reached its peak.

Leonardo da Vinci—*Mona Lisa* (1503-1519): When Leonardo moved to France late in life, he packed light, bringing only a few paintings with him. One was a portrait of Lisa del Giocondo, the wife of a wealthy Florentine merchant. *Mona* may disappoint you. She's smaller than you'd expect, darker, engulfed in a huge room, and hidden behind a glaring pane of glass. The famous smile attracts you first, but try as you might, you can never quite see the corners of her mouth. The overall mood is one of balance and serenity, but there's also an element of mystery. Mona's smile and long-distance beauty are subtle and elusive, tempting but always just out of reach. Mona doesn't knock your socks off, but she winks at the patient viewer.

Paolo Veronese—*The Marriage at Cana* (1563): Venetian artists like Veronese painted the good life of rich, happy-go-lucky Venetian merchants. In a spacious setting of Renaissance architecture, colorful lords and ladies, decked out in their fanciest duds, feast on a great spread of food and drink. But believe it or not, this is a religious work showing the wedding celebration in which Jesus turned water into wine. With true Renaissance optimism, Venetians pictured Christ as a party animal, someone who loved the created world as much as they did.

• *Exit behind Mona into the Salle Denon (Room 76). Turn right for French Neo-classicism (Salle Daru, David and Ingres); then backtrack through the Salle Denon for French Romanticism (Room 77, Géricault and Delacroix).*

FRENCH PAINTING, 1780-1850

Jacques-Louis David—*The Coronation of Emperor Napoleon* (1806-1807): Napoleon holds aloft an imperial crown. This common-born son of immigrants is about to be crowned emperor of a "New Rome." He has just made his wife, Josephine, the empress, and she kneels at his feet. Seated behind Napoleon is the pope, who journeyed from Rome to place the imperial crown on his head. But Napoleon feels that no one is worthy of the task. At the last moment, he shrugs the pope aside... and crowns himself.

Jean-Auguste-Dominique Ingres—*La Grande Odalisque* (1814): Take *Venus de Milo*, turn her around, lay her down, and stick a hash pipe next to her, and you have the *Grande Odalisque*. Using clean, polished, sculptural lines, Ingres exaggerates the S-curve of a standing Greek nude. As in the *Venus de Milo*, rough folds of cloth set off her smooth skin. Ingres gave the face, too, a touch of *Venus'* idealized features, taking nature and improving on it. Ingres preserves Venus' backside for posterior—I mean, posterity.

Théodore Géricault—*The Raft of the Medusa* (1819): Clinging to a raft is a tangle of bodies and lunatics sprawled over each other. The scene writhes with agitated, ominous motion—the ripple of muscles, churning clouds, and choppy seas. The bodies rise up in a pyramid of hope, culminating in a flag wave. They signal frantically, trying to catch the attention of the tiny ship on the horizon, their last desperate hope...which did finally save them. Géricault uses rippling movement and powerful colors to catch us up in the excitement. (This painting was based on the actual sinking of the ship *Medusa* off the coast of Africa in 1816.)

Eugène Delacroix—*Liberty Leading the People* (1831): The year is 1830. Parisians take to the streets to fight royalist oppressors. Leading them on through the smoke and over the dead and dying is the figure of Liberty, a strong woman waving the French flag. Does this symbol of victory look familiar? It's the *Winged Victory*, wingless and topless. To stir our emotions, Delacroix uses only three major colors—the red, white, and blue of the French flag. France is the symbol of modern democracy, and this painting has long stirred its citizens' passion for liberty.

• *Exit the room at the far end, go downstairs, where you'll bump into...*

MORE ITALIAN RENAISSANCE

Michelangelo—*Slaves* (1513-1515): These two statues by the earth's greatest sculptor are a bridge between the ancient and

Michelangelo's Slave *sculptures*

modern worlds. Michelangelo, like his fellow Renaissance artists, learned from the Greeks. The perfect anatomy, twisting poses, and idealized faces appear as if they could have been created 2,000 years earlier.

The *Dying Slave* twists listlessly against his T-shirt-like bonds, revealing his smooth skin. This is probably the most sensual nude that Michelangelo, the master of the male body, ever created. The *Rebellious Slave* fights against his bondage. His shoulders rotate one way, his head and leg turn the other. He even seems to be trying to release himself from the rock he's made of. Michelangelo said that his purpose was to carve away the marble to reveal the figures God put inside. This slave shows the agony of that process and the ecstasy of the result.

• *But, of course, there's so much more. After a break (or on a second visit), consider a stroll through a few rooms of the Richelieu wing, which contain some of the Louvre's most ancient pieces.*

Rick's Tip: *Across from the Louvre (to the north) are the lovely courtyards of the stately* **Palais Royal** *(always open and free, entrance off Rue de Rivoli). Bring a picnic and create your own* **quiet break** *amid flowers and surrounded by a serene arcade.*

▲▲▲ORSAY MUSEUM (MUSÉE D'ORSAY)

The Musée d'Orsay houses French art of the 1800s and early 1900s, picking up where the Louvre's art collection leaves off. For us, that means Impressionism, the art of sun-dappled fields, bright colors, and crowded Parisian cafés. The Orsay houses the best general collection anywhere of works by Manet, Monet, Renoir, Degas, Van Gogh, Cézanne, and Gauguin.

Cost and Hours: €11, €8.50 Tue-Wed and Fri-Sun after 16:30 and Thu after 18:15, free on first Sun of month and often right when the ticket booth stops selling tickets (Tue-Wed and Fri-Sun at 17:00, Thu at 21:00; they won't let you in much after that), covered by Museum Pass, tickets valid all day, combo-ticket with Orangerie Museum (€16) or Rodin Museum (€15) valid four days. Museum open Tue-Sun 9:30-18:00, Thu until 21:45, closed Mon, last entry one hour before closing; cafés and a restaurant, tel. 01 40 49 48 14, www. musee-orsay.fr.

Avoiding Lines: You can skip long ticket-buying lines by using a Museum Pass or purchasing tickets online in advance, both of which entitle you to use a separate entrance. You can buy tickets and Museum Passes (no mark-up; tickets valid 3 months) at the newspaper kiosk just outside the Orsay entrance (along Rue de la Légion d'Honneur).

Rick's Tip: *If you're planning to* **get a combo-ticket for the Orsay Museum** *with either the Orangerie or the Rodin Museum, start at one of those museums instead, as they have shorter lines.*

Getting There: The museum, at 1 Rue de la Légion d'Honneur, sits above the RER-C stop called Musée d'Orsay; the nearest Métro stop is Solférino. Bus #69 also stops at the Orsay.

Getting In: As you face the entrance, passholders and ticket holders enter on the right (Entrance C). Ticket purchasers enter on the left (Entrance A). Security checks slow down all entrances.

Tours: Audioguides cost €5. English **guided tours** usually run daily at 11:30 (€6/1.5 hours, none on Sun, tours may also run at 14:30—inquire when you arrive).

🎧 Download my free Orsay Museum **audio tour.**

❍ SELF-GUIDED TOUR

This former train station, the Gare d'Orsay, barely escaped the wrecking ball in the 1970s, when the French realized it'd be a great place to house the enormous collections of 19th-century art scattered throughout the city.

The ground floor (level 0) houses early 19th-century art, mainly conservative art of the Academy and Salon, plus Realism. On the top floor is the core of the collection—the Impressionist rooms. If you're pressed for time, go directly there. The museum rotates its large collection often, so find the latest arrangement on your current Orsay map, and be ready to go with the flow.

CONSERVATIVE ART

In the Orsay's first few ground-floor rooms, you're surrounded by visions of idealized beauty—nude women in languid poses, Greek mythological figures, and anatomically perfect statues. This was the art adored by 19th-century French academics and the middle-class (bourgeois) public.

Jean-Auguste-Dominique Ingres' *The Source* (1856) is virtually a Greek statue on canvas. Like the Louvre's *Venus de Milo*, she's a balance of opposite motions. Alexandre **Cabanel** lays Ingres' *Source* on her back. His *Birth of Venus* (1863) is a perfect fantasy, an orgasm of beauty.

REALISM

The French Realists rejected idealized classicism and began painting what they saw in the world around them. For Honoré **Daumier,** that meant looking at the stuffy bourgeois establishment that controlled the Academy and the Salon. In the 36 bustlets of *Celebrities of the Happy Medium* (1835), Daumier, trained as a political cartoonist, exaggerates each subject's most distinct characteristic to capture with vicious precision the pomposity and self-righteousness of these self-appointed arbiters of taste.

Jean-François Millet's *The Gleaners* (1867) shows us three poor women who pick up the meager leftovers after a field has been harvested for the wealthy. Here he captures the innate dignity of these stocky, tanned women who bend their backs quietly in a large field for their small reward. This is "Realism" in two senses. It's painted "realistically," not prettified. And it's the "real" world—not the fantasy world of Greek myth, but the harsh life of the working poor.

For a Realist's take on the traditional Venus, find Edouard Manet's *Olympia* (1863). Compare this uncompromising

The Orsay Museum occupies an early-20th-century railway station.

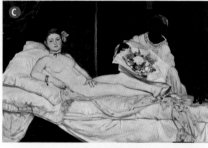

Ⓐ *Cabanel,*
Birth of Venus

Ⓑ *Millet,*
The Gleaners

Ⓒ *Manet,*
Olympia

Ⓓ *Toulouse-*
Lautrec, Jane
Avril Dancing

nude with Cabanel's idealized, pastel, Vaseline-on-the-lens beauty in the *Birth of Venus.* In *Olympia,* the sharp outlines and harsh, contrasting colors are new and shocking. Manet replaced soft-core porn with hard-core art.

Gustave Courbet's *The Painter's Studio* (1855) takes us backstage, showing us the gritty reality behind the creation of pretty pictures. We see Courbet himself in his studio, working diligently on a Realistic landscape, oblivious to the confusion around him. Milling around are ordinary citizens, not Greek heroes.

TOULOUSE-LAUTREC DETOUR

The Henri **Toulouse-Lautrec** paintings tucked away on the ground floor (Room 10) rightly belong with the Post-Impressionist works on level 2, but since you're already here, enjoy his paintings, which incarnate the artist's love of nightlife and show business. Every night, Toulouse-Lautrec put on his bowler hat and visited the Moulin Rouge to draw the crowds, the can-can dancers, and the backstage action. He worked quickly, creating sketches in paint that serve as snapshots of a golden era. In *Jane Avril Dancing* (1891), he depicts the slim, graceful, elegant, and melancholy dancer, who stood out above the rabble. Her legs keep dancing while her mind is far away.

IMPRESSIONISM

The Impressionist collection is scattered randomly through Rooms 29-36, on the top floor. Look for masterworks by these artists:

In Edouard Manet's *Luncheon on the Grass* (1863), you can see that a new revolutionary movement was starting to bud—Impressionism. Notice the background: the messy brushwork of trees and leaves, the play of light on the pond, and the light that filters through the trees onto the woman who stoops in the haze. Also note the strong contrast of colors (white skin, black clothes, green grass). Let the Impressionist revolution begin!

Orsay Museum—Ground Floor

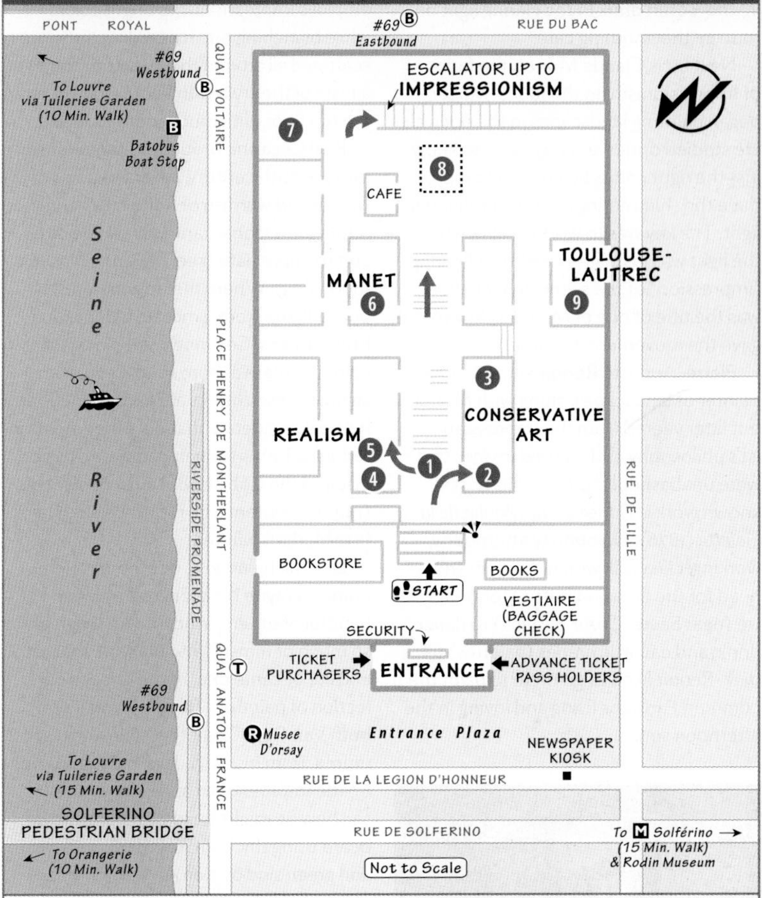

PONT ROYAL
#69 B Eastbound
RUE DU BAC

#69 Westbound B
To Louvre via Tuileries Garden (10 Min. Walk) B
Batobus Boat Stop

QUAI VOLTAIRE

ESCALATOR UP TO **IMPRESSIONISM**

❼

❽

CAFE

Seine River

PLACE HENRY DE MONTHERLANT

MANET ❻

TOULOUSE-LAUTREC ❾

RIVERSIDE PROMENADE

❸

REALISM ❺ ❶ ❷
❹

CONSERVATIVE ART

RUE DE LILLE

#69 Westbound B

QUAI ANATOLE FRANCE

BOOKSTORE

START

BOOKS

VESTIAIRE (BAGGAGE CHECK)

SECURITY
TICKET PURCHASERS T
ENTRANCE
ADVANCE TICKET PASS HOLDERS

To Louvre via Tuileries Garden (15 Min. Walk)

R Musee D'Orsay
Entrance Plaza
NEWSPAPER KIOSK

RUE DE LA LEGION D'HONNEUR

SOLFERINO PEDESTRIAN BRIDGE

RUE DE SOLFERINO

To M Solférino → (15 Min. Walk) & Rodin Museum

To Orangerie (10 Min. Walk)

Not to Scale

❶ Main Gallery Statues
❷ INGRES – The Source
❸ CABANEL – The Birth of Venus
❹ DAUMIER – Celebrities of the Happy Medium
❺ MILLET – The Gleaners
❻ MANET – Olympia
❼ COURBET – The Painter's Studio
❽ Opéra Exhibit
❾ TOULOUSE-LAUTREC – Jane Avril Dancing

Edgar **Degas** blends classical lines and Realist subjects with Impressionist color, spontaneity, and everyday scenes from urban Paris. He loved the unposed "snapshot" effect, catching his models off guard. Dance students, women at work, and café scenes are approached from odd angles that aren't always ideal but make the scenes seem more real. He gives us the backstage view of life. For instance, a dance rehearsal let Degas capture a behind-the-scenes look at bored, tired, restless dancers (*The Dance Class,* c. 1873-1875). In the painting *In a Café*

(1875-1876), a weary lady of the evening meets morning with a last, lonely, nail-in-the-coffin drink in the glaring light of a four-in-the-morning café.

Next up is Claude **Monet,** the father of Impressionism. In the 1860s, Monet began painting landscapes in the open air. He studied optics and pigments to know just the right colors he needed to reproduce the shimmering quality of reflected light. The key was to work quickly, when the light was just right, creating a fleeting "impression" of the scene. In fact, that was the title of one of Monet's canvases; it gave the movement its name.

Pierre-Auguste **Renoir** started out as a painter of landscapes, along with Monet, but later veered from the Impressionist's philosophy and painted images that were unabashedly "pretty." His best-known work is *Dance at the Moulin de la Galette* (1876). On Sunday afternoons, working-class folk would dress up and head for the fields on Butte Montmartre (near Sacré-Cœur Basilica) to dance, drink, and eat little crêpes (galettes) till dark. Renoir liked to go there to paint the common Parisians living and loving in the afternoon sun.

Degas, The Dance Class

POST-IMPRESSIONISM

Post-Impressionism—the style that employs Impressionism's bright colors while branching out in new directions—is scattered all around the museum. You'll get a taste of the style with Paul Cézanne, on the top floor, with much more on level 2.

Paul **Cézanne** brought Impressionism into the 20th century. After the color of Monet and warmth of Renoir, Cézanne's rather impersonal canvases can be difficult to appreciate (see *The Card Players,* 1890-1895). Where the Impressionists built a figure from a mosaic of individual brushstrokes, Cézanne used blocks of paint to create a more solid, geometrical shape. These chunks are like little "cubes." It's no coincidence that his experiments in reducing forms to their geometric basics inspired the Cubists. Because of his style (not the content), he is often called the first Modern painter.

Like Michelangelo, Beethoven, Rembrandt, Wayne Newton, and a select handful of others, Vincent **van Gogh** put so much of himself into his work that art and life became one. In the Orsay's collection of paintings (level 2), you'll see both Van Gogh's painting style and his life unfold, from his early days in Paris soaking up the Impressionist style (for example, see how he might build a bristling brown beard using thick strokes of red, yellow, and green side by side) to his richly creative but wildly unstable stint in the south of France (*Van Gogh's Room at Arles,* 1889). Don't miss his final self-portrait (1889), showing a man engulfed in a confused background of brushstrokes that swirl and rave. Perhaps his troubled eyes know that in only a few months he would take a pistol and put a bullet through his chest.

Nearby are the paintings of Paul **Gauguin,** who got the travel bug early and grew up wanting to be a sailor. Instead, he became a stockbroker. At the age of 35, he got fed up with it all, quit his job, abandoned his wife (her stern portrait bust may be nearby) and family, and took refuge in his art.

Gauguin traveled to the South Seas in search of the exotic, finally settling on Tahiti. Gauguin's best-known works capture an idyllic Tahitian landscape peopled by exotic women engaged in simple tasks and making music (*Arearea*, 1892). The style is intentionally "primitive," collapsing the three-dimensional landscape into a two-dimensional pattern of bright colors. Gauguin wanted to communicate to his "civilized" colleagues back home that he'd found the paradise he'd always envisioned.

🅐 *Renoir,* Dance at the Moulin de la Galette

🅑 *Cézanne,* The Card Players

🅒 *Van Gogh,* Van Gogh's Room at Arles

🅓 *Gauguin,* Arearea

FRENCH SCULPTURE

The open-air mezzanine of level 2 is lined with statues. Stroll the mezzanine, enjoying the work of great French sculptors, including Auguste **Rodin.**

Born of working-class roots and largely self-taught, Rodin combined classical solidity with Impressionist surfaces to become the greatest sculptor since Michelangelo. Like his statue *The Walking Man* (c. 1900), Rodin had one foot in the past, while the other stepped into the future. This muscular, forcefully striding man could be a symbol of Renaissance Man with his classical power. With no mouth or hands, he speaks with his body. But get close and look at the statue's surface. This rough, "unfinished" look reflects light in the same way the rough Impressionist brushwork does, making the statue come alive, never quite at rest in the viewer's eye. Rodin created this statue in a flash of inspiration. He took two unfinished statues—torso and legs—and plunked them together at the waist. You can still see the seam. Rodin's sculptures capture the groundbreaking spirit of much of the art in the Orsay Museum. With a stable base of 19th-century stone, he launched art into the 20th century.

▲▲ORANGERIE MUSEUM (MUSEE DE L'ORANGERIE)

This Impressionist museum is as lovely as a water lily. Step out of the tree-lined, sun-dappled Impressionist painting that is the Tuileries Garden and into the Orangerie (oh-rahn-zhuh-ree), a bijou of select works by Monet, Renoir, Matisse, Picasso, and others.

Cost and Hours: €9, €6.50 after 17:00, €16 combo-ticket with Orsay Museum, covered by Museum Pass; Wed-Mon 9:00-18:00, closed Tue; audioguide-€5, English guided tours usually Mon and Thu at 14:30 and Sat at 11:00, located in Tuileries Garden near Place de la Concorde, Mo: Concorde or scenic bus #24, tel. 01 44 77 80 07, www.musee-orangerie.fr.

Visiting the Museum: On the main floor you'll find the main attraction, Monet's *Water Lilies (Nymphéas)*, floating dreamily in oval rooms. These eight mammoth, curved panels immerse you in Monet's garden. We're looking at the pond in his garden at Giverny—dotted with water lilies, surrounded by foliage, and dappled by the reflections of the sky, clouds, and trees on the surface. But the true subject of these works is the play of reflected light off the surface of the pond.

Working at his home in Giverny, Monet built a special studio with skylights and wheeled easels to accommodate the canvases. For 12 years (1914-1926), Monet worked on these paintings obsessively. Monet completed all the planned canvases, but didn't live to see them installed here. In 1927, the year after his death, these rooms were completed and the canvases put in place. Some call this the first "art installation"—art displayed in a space specially designed for it in order to enhance the viewer's experience.

In the Orangerie's underground gallery are select works from the personal collection of Paris' trend-spotting art dealer of the 1920s, Paul Guillaume. These paintings—Impressionist, Fauvist, and Cubist—are a snapshot of what was hot in the world of art, circa 1920.

Monet's Water Lilies *at the Orangerie Museum*

Eiffel Tower & Nearby

Eiffel Tower and Nearby

▲▲▲EIFFEL TOWER
(LA TOUR EIFFEL)

It's crowded, expensive, and there are probably better views in Paris, but visiting this 1,000-foot-tall ornament is worth the trouble. Visitors to Paris may find the *Mona Lisa* to be less than expected, but the Eiffel Tower rarely disappoints, even in an era of skyscrapers. This is a once-in-a-lifetime, I've-been-there experience. Making the trip gives you membership in the exclusive society of the quarter of a billion other humans who have made the Eiffel Tower the most visited monument in the modern world.

Cost and Hours: €15.50 all the way to the top, €9 for just the two lower levels, €5 to climb the stairs to the first or second level, not covered by Museum Pass; daily mid-June-Aug 9:00-24:45, last ascent to top at 23:00 and to lower levels at 24:00 (elevator or stairs); Sept-mid-June 9:30-23:45, last ascent to top at 22:30 and to lower levels at 23:00 (elevator) or at 18:00 (stairs); cafés and great view restaurants, Mo: Bir-Hakeim or Trocadéro, RER: Champ de Mars-Tour Eiffel.

Reservations: You'd be crazy to show up without a reservation. At www.toureiffel.paris, you can book an entry date and time, and skip the initial entry line (the longest)—at no extra cost.

Time slots fill up months in advance (especially from April through September). Online ticket sales open up about three months before any given date (at 8:30 Paris time)—and can sell out for that day within hours. Reservations are nonrefundable. When you "Choose a ticket," make sure you select "Lift entrance ticket with access to the summit" to go all the way to the top. You must create an account, with a 10-digit mobile phone number as your log-in.

If no reservation slots are available, try buying a "Lift entrance ticket with access to 2nd floor" only—you can upgrade once inside. Or, try the website again about a week before your visit—last-minute spots occasionally open up.

When to Go: For the best of all worlds, arrive with enough light to see the views, then stay as it gets dark to see the lights. The views are grand whether you ascend or not. At the top of the hour, a five-minute display features thousands of sparkling lights (best viewed from Place du Trocadéro or the grassy park below).

Rick's Tip: **No reservation for the Eiffel Tower?** *Get in line 30 minutes before it opens. Going late is the next-best bet (after 19:00 May-Aug). You can bypass some (but not all) lines if you have a reservation at either of the tower's view restaurants (Le Jules Verne or 58 Tour Eiffel).*

Getting In: If you have a reservation, arrive at the tower 10 minutes before your entry time, and look for either of the two entrances marked *Visiteurs avec Reservation* (Visitors with Reservation),

The Eiffel Tower stands more than 1,000 feet tall.

where attendants scan your ticket and put you on the first available elevator. If you don't have a reservation, follow signs for *Individuels* or *Visiteurs sans Tickets* (avoid lines selling tickets only for *Groupes*). The stairs entrance (usually a shorter line) is at the south pillar (next to Le Jules Verne restaurant entrance). When you buy tickets on-site, all members of your party must be with you. To get reduced fares for kids, bring ID.

Security Check: Bags larger than 19" × 8" × 12" inches are not allowed, but there is no baggage check. All bags are subject to a security search. No knives, glass bottles, or cans are permitted.

Rick's Tip: *Tourists in crowded elevators are like fish in a barrel for* **pickpockets.** *Beware. Thieves plunder awestruck visitors gawking below the tower. A* **police station** *is at the Jules Verne pillar.*

Background: The first visitor to the Paris World's Fair in 1889 walked beneath the "arch" formed by the newly built Eiffel Tower and entered the fairgrounds. This event celebrated both the centennial of the French Revolution and France's position as a global superpower. Bridge builder Gustave Eiffel (1832-1923) won the contest to build the fair's centerpiece by beating out rival proposals such as a giant guillotine. The tower was nothing but a showpiece, with no functional purpose except to demonstrate to the world that France had the wealth, knowledge, and can-do spirit. The original plan was to dismantle the tower as quickly as it was built after the celebration ended, but it was kept by popular demand.

The tower, including its antenna, stands 1,063 feet tall, or slightly higher than the 77-story Chrysler Building in New York. Its four support pillars straddle an area of 3.5 acres. Despite the tower's 7,300 tons of metal and 60 tons of paint, it is so well-engineered that it weighs no

Open-Air Markets

Several traffic-free street markets overflow with flowers, bakeries, produce, fish vendors, and butchers, illustrating how most Parisians shopped before there were supermarkets. Shops are open daily except Sunday afternoons, Monday, and lunchtime throughout the week. You can shop for a picnic or grab a seat at a sidewalk café to watch the action.

Rue Cler—a wonderful place to sleep and dine as well as shop—is like a refined street market, serving an upscale neighborhood near the Eiffel Tower (Mo: Ecole Militaire).

Rue Montorgueil is a thriving and popular café-lined street. Ten blocks from the Louvre and five blocks from the Pompidou Center, Rue Montorgueil (mohn-tor-goo-ee) is just north of St. Eustache Church (Mo: Etienne Marcel).

Rue Mouffetard, on the Left Bank, is a happening market street by day and does double-duty as restaurant row at night. Hiding several blocks behind the Panthéon, it starts at Place Contrescarpe and ends below at St. Médard Church (Mo: Censier Daubenton). The upper stretch is touristic; the bottom stretch is purely Parisian.

more per square inch at its base than a linebacker on tiptoes.

VISITING THE TOWER

There are three observation platforms, at roughly 200, 400, and 900 feet. If you want to see the entire tower, from top to bottom, then see it...from top to bottom.

There isn't a single elevator straight to the top (*le sommet*). To get there, you'll first ride an elevator to the second level. (For the hardy, there are 360 stairs to the first level and another 360 to the second.) Once on the second level, immediately line up for the next elevator, to the top. Enjoy the views, then ride back down to the second level (which has the best views). When you're ready, head to the first level via the stairs (no line and can take as little as 5 minutes) or take the elevator down (ask if it will stop on the first level—some don't). Explore the shops and exhibits on the first level and have a snack. To leave, you can line up for the elevator, but it's quickest and most memorable to take the stairs back down to earth.

For a final look at the tower, stroll across the river to Place du Trocadéro or to the end of the Champ de Mars and look back for great views. However impressive it may be by day, the tower is an awesome thing to see at twilight, when it becomes filled with light, and virile Paris lies back and lets night be on top. When darkness fully envelops the city, the tower seems to climax with a spectacular light show at the top of each hour...for five minutes.

Near the Eiffel Tower

▲▲ARMY MUSEUM AND NAPOLEON'S TOMB (MUSEE DE L'ARMEE)

The Hôtel des Invalides—a former veterans' hospital topped by a golden dome—houses Napoleon's over-the-top-ornate tomb, as well as Europe's greatest military museum. Visiting the Army Museum's different sections, you can watch the art of war unfold from stone axes to Axis powers.

Cost and Hours: €9.50, €7.50 after 17:00, free for military personnel in uniform, free for kids but they must wait in line for ticket, covered by Museum Pass, special exhibits are extra; daily 10:00-18:00, July-Aug until 19:00, Nov-March until 17:00, tomb plus WWI and WWII wings open Tue until 21:00 April-Sept, museum (except for tomb) closed first Mon of month Oct-June, Charles de Gaulle exhibit closed Mon year-round; videoguide-€6, cafeteria, tel. 08 10 11 33 99, www.musee-armee.fr.

Getting There: The Hôtel des Invalides is at 129 Rue de Grenelle, a 10-minute walk from Rue Cler (Mo: La Tour Maubourg, Varenne, or Invalides). You can also take bus #69 (from the Marais and Rue Cler) or bus #87 (from Rue Cler and Luxembourg Garden area).

Visiting the Museum: At the center of the complex, Napoleon Bonaparte lies majestically dead inside several coffins under a grand dome—a goose-bumping pilgrimage for historians. The dome overhead glitters with 26 pounds of thinly

Hôtel des Invalides

pounded gold leaf.

Your visit continues through an impressive range of museums filled with medieval armor, cannons and muskets, Louis XIV-era uniforms and weapons, and Napoleon's horse—stuffed and mounted.

The best section is dedicated to the two World Wars. Walk chronologically through displays on the trench warfare of World War I, the victory parades, France's horrendous losses, and the humiliating Treaty of Versailles that led to World War II.

The WWII rooms use black-and-white photos, maps, videos, and artifacts to trace Hitler's rise, the Blitzkrieg that overran France, America's entry into the war, D-Day, the concentration camps, the atomic bomb, the war in the Pacific, and the eventual Allied victory. There's special insight into France's role (the French Resistance), and how it was Charles de Gaulle that actually won the war.

▲▲RODIN MUSEUM (MUSEE RODIN)

This user-friendly museum is filled with passionate works by the greatest sculptor since Michelangelo. You'll see *The Kiss*, *The Thinker*, *The Gates of Hell*, and many more.

Cost and Hours: €10 (special exhibits cost extra), free on first Sun of the month Oct-March, €4 for garden only (a good deal, as several important works are on display there), €15 combo-ticket with Orsay Museum, museum and garden covered by Museum Pass; Tue-Sun 10:00-17:45, Wed until 20:45, closed Mon; gardens close at 18:00, Oct-March at 17:00; audioguide-€6, mandatory baggage check, self-service café in garden, 79 Rue de Varenne, Mo: Varenne, tel. 01 44 18 61 10, www.musee-rodin.fr.

Visiting the Museum: Auguste Rodin (1840-1917) was a modern Michelangelo, sculpting human figures on an epic scale, revealing through their bodies his deepest thoughts and feelings. Like many of Michelangelo's unfinished works, Rodin's statues rise from the raw stone around them, driven by the life force. With missing limbs and scarred skin, these are prefab classics, making ugliness noble. Rodin's people are always moving restlessly. Even the famous *Thinker* is moving; while he's plopped down solidly, his mind is a million miles away.

Well-displayed in the mansion where the sculptor lived and worked, exhibits

Rodin's Burghers of Calais

Left Bank

LOUVRE

PONT DES ARTS

Seine River

RIGHT BANK

RUE DE RIVOLI

LEFT BANK

To Orsay Museum

To Rodin Museum

Rue du Bac

RUE DE VARENNE

RUE DE BABYLONE

BON MARCHE

Sèvres-Babylone

Vaneau

St. Placide

MONTPARNASSE TOWER

Montparnasse-Bienvenue

Major Bus Stop

LA COUPOLE CAFE

GARE MONTPARNASSE

Edgar Quinet

LE SELECT CAFE

Vavin

Rennes

Notre Dame des Champs

CAFES DEUX MAGOTS & LA FLORE

BOULEVARD

DELACROIX MUSEUM

St. Germain-des-Prés

ST. GERMAIN-DES-PRES

Mabillon

R. DU FOUR

ST. GERMAIN

ST. SULPICE

St. Sulpice

Y. COLOMBIER

SEVRES

SHOPPING AREA

ST. SULPICE

Odéon

THEATRE ODEON

LUXEMBOURG PALACE

POND

Luxembourg Garden

KIDS' PLAY AREA

R. AUGUSTE COMTE

RUE D'ASSAS

BLVD. DU MONTPARNASSE

Port-Royal

SAINTE-CHAPELLE

Cité

Île de la Cité

St. Michel

NOTRE-DAME

LATIN QUARTER

Cluny La Sorbonne

Maubert-Mutualité

CLUNY MUSEUM

R. DES ECOLES

SORBONNE

ST. ETIENNE DU MONT

Cardinal Lemoine

Luxembourg

PANTHEON

R. SOUFFLOT

RUE ST. JACQUES

BLVD. SAINT MICHEL

RUE D'ULM

RUE MOUFFETARD

Place Monge

Censier Daubenton

R. DE SEINE

BLVD. RASPAIL

RUE DE RENNES

RUE DU CHERCHE-MIDI

RUE DE VAUGIRARD

BLVD. ST. MICHEL

RUE DES ECOLES

MONGE

400 Meters

400 Yards

trace Rodin's artistic development, explain how his bronze statues were cast, and show some of the studies he created to work up to his masterpiece, the unfinished *Gates of Hell*. Learn about Rodin's tumultuous relationship with his apprentice and lover, Camille Claudel. Mull over what makes his sculptures some of the most evocative since the Renaissance. And stroll the beautiful gardens, packed with many of his greatest works (including *The Thinker*, *Balzac*, the *Burghers of Calais*, and the *Gates of Hell*) and ideal for artistic reflection.

Left Bank

Opposite Notre-Dame, on the left bank of the Seine, is the Latin Quarter. (For more about this neighborhood, see my Historic Paris Walk, earlier.)

▲▲CLUNY MUSEUM (MUSEE NATIONAL DU MOYEN AGE)

The Cluny is a treasure trove of Middle Ages (Moyen Age) art. Located on the site of a Roman bathhouse, it offers close-up looks at stained glass, Notre-Dame carvings, fine goldsmithing and jewelry, and rooms of tapestries. The highlights are several original stained-glass windows from Sainte-Chapelle and the exquisite series of six Lady and the Unicorn tapestries: A delicate, as-medieval-as-can-be noble lady introduces a delighted unicorn to the senses of taste, hearing, sight, smell, and touch.

Cost and Hours: €8, includes audioguide, free on first Sun of month, covered by Museum Pass; Wed-Mon 9:15-17:45, closed Tue, ticket office closes at 17:15; near corner of Boulevards St. Michel and

Grands Cafés Near St. Germain-des-Prés

On the Left Bank, where Boulevard St. Germain meets Rue Bonaparte, you'll find several Parisian cafés that seem like monuments to another time (all open daily, Mo: St. Germain-des-Prés; for locations, see map on page 182). Before visiting, review my tips on "Cafés and Brasseries" on page 119.

$$$ Les Deux Magots offers prime outdoor seating and a warm interior. Once a favorite of Ernest Hemingway (in *The Sun Also Rises*, Jake met Brett here) and Jean-Paul Sartre (he and Simone de Beauvoir met here), today the café is filled with international tourists (6 Place St. Germain des Prés).

$$$ Le Café de Flore, next door, feels more literary—wear your black turtleneck. Pablo Picasso was a regular (172 Boulevard St. Germain).

$ Café Bonaparte, just a block away, offers scenic outdoor seating and the same delightful view for a bit less (42 Rue Bonaparte).

$ Café le Procope, Paris' first and most famous (1686), was a café célèbre, drawing notables such as Voltaire, Rousseau, Honoré de Balzac, Emile Zola, Maximilien de Robespierre, Victor Hugo, and two Americans, Benjamin Franklin and Thomas Jefferson (13 Rue de l'Ancienne Comédie).

St. Germain at 6 Place Paul Painlevé; Mo: Cluny-La Sorbonne, St. Michel, or Odéon; tel. 01 53 73 78 16, www.musee-moyenage.fr.

ST. GERMAIN-DES-PRES

A church was first built on this site in A.D. 558. The church you see today was constructed in 1163 and is all that's left of a once sprawling and influential monastery. The colorful interior reminds us that medieval churches were originally painted in bright colors. The surrounding area hops at night with venerable cafés, fire-eaters, mimes, and scads of artists.

Cost and Hours: Free, daily 8:00-20:00, Mo: St. Germain-des-Prés.

▲LUXEMBOURG GARDEN (JARDIN DU LUXEMBOURG)

This lovely 60-acre garden is an Impressionist painting brought to life. Slip into a green chair pondside, enjoy the radiant flower beds, go jogging, play tennis or basketball, sail a toy sailboat, or take in a chess game or puppet show. Some of the park's prettiest (and quietest) sections lie around its perimeter.

Cost and Hours: Free, daily dawn until dusk, Mo: Odéon, RER: Luxembourg.

Cluny Museum's Lady and the Unicorn tapestry   *Luxembourg Garden*

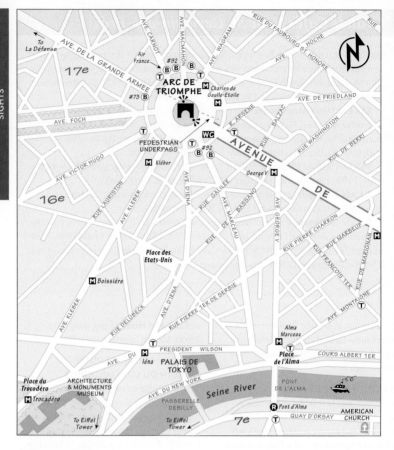

Champs-Elysées and Nearby

▲▲▲ CHAMPS-ELYSEES

This famous boulevard is Paris' backbone, with its greatest concentration of traffic. From the Arc de Triomphe down Avenue des Champs-Elysées, all of France seems to converge on Place de la Concorde, the city's largest square. And though the Champs-Elysées has become as international as it is Parisian, a walk down the two-mile boulevard is still a must.

In 1667, Louis XIV opened the first section of the street, and it soon became the place to cruise in your carriage. (It still is today.) By the 1920s, this boulevard was pure elegance—fancy residences, rich hotels, and cafés. Today it's home to big business, celebrity cafés, glitzy nightclubs, high-fashion shopping, and international people-watching. People gather here to

Looking down the Champs-Elysées from the Arc de Triomphe

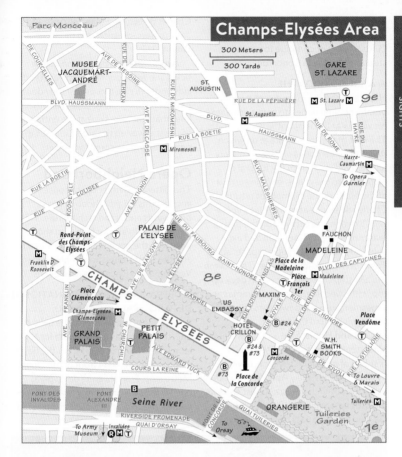

celebrate Bastille Day (July 14), World Cup triumphs, and the finale of the Tour de France.

⟩ SELF-GUIDED WALK

Start at the Arc de Triomphe (Mo: Charles de Gaulle-Etoile; if you're planning to tour the Arc, do it before starting this walk) and head downhill on the left-hand side. The arrival of McDonald's (at #140) was an unthinkable horror, but these days dining chez MacDo has become typically Parisian, and this branch is the most profitable McDonald's in the world.

Fancy car showrooms abound, including Peugeot (#136) and Mercedes-Benz (#118). The Lido (#116) is Paris' largest burlesque-type cabaret (and a multi-plex cinema). Across the boulevard is the flagship store of leather-bag makers Louis Vuitton (#101). Fouquet's café (#99) is a popular spot for French celebrities, especially movie stars—note the names in the sidewalk in front. Enter if you dare for an €8 espresso. Ladurée café (#75) is also classy but has a welcoming and affordable takeout bakery.

Continuing on, you pass international-brand stores, such as Sephora, Virgin, Disney, and the Gap. Car buffs should park themselves at the sleek café in the Renault store (#53, open until midnight). The car exhibits change regularly, but the great tables looking down onto the Champs-Elysées are permanent.

You can end your walk at the round Rond Point intersection (Mo: Franklin D. Roosevelt) or continue to obelisk-studded Place de la Concorde.

▲▲ARC DE TRIOMPHE

Napoleon had the magnificent Arc de Triomphe commissioned to commemorate his victory at the 1805 battle of Austerlitz. The foot of the arch is a stage on which the last two centuries of Parisian history have played out—from the funeral of Napoleon to the goose-stepping arrival of the Nazis to the triumphant return of Charles de Gaulle after the Allied liberation. Examine the carvings on the pillars, featuring a mighty Napoleon and excitable Lady Liberty. Pay your respects at the Tomb of the Unknown Soldier. Then climb the 284 steps to the observation deck up top, with sweeping skyline panoramas and a mesmerizing view down onto the traffic that swirls around the arch.

Cost and Hours: Free and always viewable; steps to rooftop—€9.50, free on first Sun of month Oct-March, covered by Museum Pass; daily April-Sept 10:00-23:00, Oct-March until 22:30, last entry 45 minutes before closing; Place Charles de Gaulle, use underpass to reach arch, Mo: Charles de Gaulle-Etoile, tel. 01 55 37 73 77, http://arc-de-triomphe.monuments-nationaux.fr.

Avoiding Lines: Bypass the *slooow* ticket line with your Museum Pass (your kids under 18 can, too, even if they don't have Museum Passes). Expect another line (that you can't skip) at the entrance to the stairway up the arch. Lines disappear after 17:00—come for sunset.

Opéra Neighborhood

The glittering Garnier opera house anchors this neighborhood of broad boulevards and grand architecture. This area is also nirvana for high-end shoppers, with the opulent Galeries Lafayette and the sumptuous shops that line Place Vendôme and Place de la Madeleine.

▲OPÉRA GARNIER (OPERA NATIONAL DE PARIS—PALAIS GARNIER)

A gleaming grand theater of the belle époque, the Palais Garnier was built for Napoleon III and finished in 1875. For the best exterior view, stand in front of the Opéra Métro stop. From Avenue de l'Opéra, once lined with Paris' most fashionable haunts, the facade suggests "all power to

Arc de Triomphe

the wealthy." And a shimmering Apollo, holding his lyre high above the building, seems to declare, "This is a temple of the highest arts."

But the elitism of this place prompted former President François Mitterrand to have an opera house built for the people in the 1980s, situated symbolically on Place de la Bastille, where the French Revolution started in 1789. The smaller Opéra Garnier is now home to ballet, some opera, and other performances.

You have two choices for seeing the interior: Take a guided or self-guided tour of the public areas, or buy tickets to a performance. If you opt to tour the building, note that the auditorium is sometimes off-limits due to performances and rehearsals (you'll get your best look at the auditorium on the fully guided tour).

Cost and Hours: €11, not covered by Museum Pass, generally daily 10:00-16:30, mid-July-Aug until 18:00, 8 Rue Scribe, Mo: Opéra, RER: Auber, www.visitepalaisgarnier.fr.

Tours: The €5 audioguide gives a good self-guided tour. Guided tours in English run at 11:30 and 14:30 July-Aug daily, Sept-Jun Wed and Sat-Sun—call to confirm schedule (€14.50, includes entry, 1.5 hours, tel. 01 40 01 17 89 or 08 25 05 44 05).

Visiting the Theater: You'll enter around the left side of the building (as you face the front), across from American Express on Rue Scribe. As you pass the bust of the architect, Monsieur Garnier, pay your respects and check out the bronze floor plan of the complex etched below. Notice how little space is given to seating.

Rick's Tip: *Across the street from the Opéra Garnier is the illustrious* **Café de la Paix** *(on Place de l'Opéra). It's been a meeting spot for the local glitterati for generations. If you can afford the coffee, this spot offers a delightful break.*

The building is huge—though the auditorium itself seats only 2,000. The building's massive foundations straddle an underground lake (inspiring the mysterious world of the *Phantom of the Opera*). The real show was before and after the performance, when the elite of Paris—out to see and be seen—strutted their elegant stuff in the extravagant lobbies. Think of the grand marble stairway as a theater. The upstairs foyer feels more like

Opéra Garnier

Baron Georges-Eugène Haussmann

The elegantly uniform streets that make Paris so Parisian are the work of Baron Haussmann (1809-1891), who oversaw the modernization of the city in the mid-19th century. He cleared out the cramped, higgledy-piggledy, unhygienic medieval cityscape and replaced it with broad, straight boulevards lined with stately buildings and linked by modern train stations.

The quintessential view of Haussmann's work is from the pedestrian island immediately in front of the Opéra Garnier. You're surrounded by Paris, circa 1870, when it was the capital of the world. Spin slowly and find the Louvre in one direction and Place Vendôme in another. Haussmann's uniform, cohesive buildings are all five stories tall, with angled, black slate roofs and formal facades. The balconies on the second and fifth floors match those of their neighbors, creating strong lines of perspective as the buildings stretch down the boulevard. Haussmann was so intent on putting the architecture at center stage that he insisted that no trees be planted along these streets.

Chagall ceiling at the Opéra Garnier

a ballroom at Versailles. As you wander the halls and gawk at the decor, imagine this place in its heyday, filled with beautiful people sharing gossip at the Salon du Glacier.

From the uppermost floor open to the public, visitors can peek from two boxes into the actual red-velvet performance hall. Admire Marc Chagall's colorful ceiling (1964), playfully dancing around the eight-ton chandelier. The box seats next to the stage are the most expensive in the house, with an obstructed view of the stage...but just right if you're here only to be seen. Snoop about to find the side library, information panels describing costume management, and a portrait gallery of famous ballerinas and guests.

Marais Neighborhood and Nearby

Naturally, when in Paris you want to see the big sights—but to experience the city, you also need to visit a vital neighborhood. The Marais fits the bill, with hip boutiques, busy cafés, trendy art galleries, narrow streets, leafy squares, Jewish bakeries, aristocratic châteaux, nightlife, and real Parisians. It's the perfect setting to appreciate the flair of this great city.

Place des Vosges and West
▲PLACE DES VOSGES

Henry IV (r. 1589-1610) built this centerpiece of the Marais in 1605 and called it "Place Royale." As he'd hoped, it turned the Marais into Paris' most exclusive neighborhood. Walk to the center, where Louis XIII, on horseback, gestures, "Look at this wonderful square my dad built." He's surrounded by locals enjoying their community park. You'll see children frolicking in the sandbox, lovers warming benches, and pigeons guarding their fountains while trees shade this escape from the glare of the big city.

Study the architecture: nine pavilions (houses) per side. The two highest—at the front and back—were for the king and queen (but were never used). Warm red brickwork—some real, some fake—is topped with sloped slate roofs, chimneys, and another quaint relic of a bygone era: TV antennas.

The insightful writer Victor Hugo lived at #6 from 1832 to 1848. (It's at the southeast corner of the square, marked by the French flag.) This was when he wrote much of his most important work, including his biggest hit, *Les Misérables*. Inside **Victor Hugo's House,** you'll wander through eight plush rooms, enjoy a fine view of the square, and find good WCs (€8, Tue-Sun 10:00-18:00, closed Mon, http://maisonsvictorhugo.paris.fr).

Sample the upscale art galleries ringing the square (the best ones are behind Louis). Consider a daring new piece for that blank wall at home. Or consider a pleasant break at one of the eateries on the square.

▲▲PICASSO MUSEUM (MUSEE PICASSO)

Whatever you think about Picasso the man, as an artist he was unmatched in the 20th century for his daring and productivity. The Picasso Museum has the world's largest collection of his work—some 400 paintings, sculptures, sketches, and ceramics—spread across this mansion in the Marais. A visit here walks you through the full range of this complex man's life and art.

Cost and Hours: €11, covered by Museum Pass, free on first Sun of month; open Tue-Fri 11:30-18:00 (until 21:00 on third Fri of month), Sat-Sun 9:30-18:00, closed Mon, last entry 45 minutes before closing; videoguide-€4, timed-entry tickets available via museum website; 5 Rue de Thorigny, Mo: St-Paul or Chemin Vert, tel. 01 42 71 25 21, www.musee-picasso.fr.

◆ SELF-GUIDED TOUR

The core of the museum is organized chronologically. Use this overview to trace Picasso's life and some of the themes in his work.

Early Years and Early Cubism (Floor 0): In 1900, Picasso set out from Barcelona to make his mark in Paris. The brash Spaniard quickly became a poor, homesick foreigner, absorbing the styles of many painters while searching for his own artist's voice. When his best friend committed suicide (*Death of Casagemas*, 1901), Picasso plunged into a "Blue Period," painting emaciated beggars,

Relaxing at the Place des Vosges

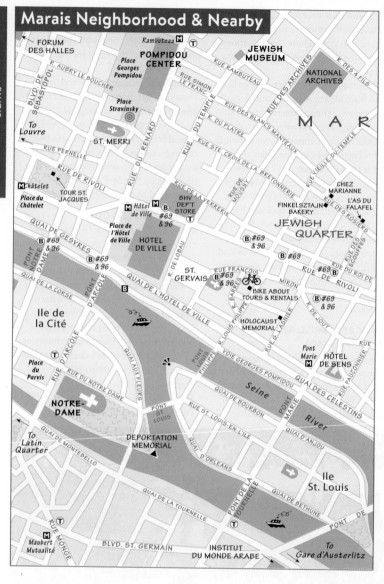

Marais Neighborhood & Nearby

FORUM DES HALLES

Rambuteau Ⓜ Ⓣ

POMPIDOU CENTER

JEWISH MUSEUM

R. DES 4 FILS

Place Georges Pompidou

NATIONAL ARCHIVES

RUE RAMBUTEAU

R. AUBRY LE BOUCHER

RUE SIMON LE FRANC

RUE DES ARCHIVES

BLVD. DE SEBASTOPOL

Place Stravinsky

RUE DES BLANCS MANTEAUX

RUE DU TEMPLE

M A R

ST. MERRI

R. DU PLATRE

RUE STE. CROIX DE LA BRETONNERIE

RUE VIEILLE-DU-TEMPLE

To Louvre

RUE DU RENARD

RUE PERNELLE

RUE DE RIVOLI

Ⓜ Châtelet

Place du Châtelet

TOUR ST. JACQUES

Hôtel de Ville Ⓜ Ⓑ

RUE DE LA VERRERIE

BHV DEP'T STORE

CHEZ MARIANNE

FINKELSZTAJN BAKERY

L'AS DU FALAFEL

RUE DE MOUSSY

JEWISH QUARTER

RUE DES ROSIERS

#69 & 96 Ⓣ

QUAI DE GESVRES

Place de l'Hôtel de Ville

HOTEL DE VILLE

Ⓑ #69 & 96

Ⓑ #69 & 96

R. DE LOBAU

Ⓑ #69 & 96

Ⓑ #69

RUE DES ÉCOUFFES

Pont Notre Dame

QUAI DE LA CORSE

QUAI DE L'HOTEL DE VILLE

ST. GERVAIS

RUE FRANÇOIS MIRON

Ⓑ #69

RUE DU ROI DE

Ⓑ #69 & 96

RUE DE RIVOLI

Ile de la Cité

PONT D'ARCOLE

Ⓑ

Ⓑ #69 & 96

BIKE ABOUT TOURS & RENTALS

R. DE JOUY

Ⓑ #69 & 96

RUE DE BARRES

R. DU JOUY

Ⓣ

Place du Parvis

RUE D'ARCOLE

RUE DU NOTRE DAME

QUAI AUX FLEURS

HOLOCAUST MEMORIAL

R. LOUIS PHILIPPE

R. G. LASNIER

RUE

RUE FAUCONNIER

Pont Marie Ⓜ

HÔTEL DE SENS

NOTRE-DAME

PONT LOUIS PHILIPPE

VOIE GEORGES POMPIDOU

QUAI DES CELESTINS

To Latin Quarter

QUAI DE MONTEBELLO

PONT ST. LOUIS

DÉPORTATION MEMORIAL

QUAI DE BOURBON

RUE ST. LOUIS-EN-L'ILE

Seine

PONT MARIE

River

QUAI D'ANJOU

Ile St. Louis

QUAI D'ORLEANS

QUAI DE BETHUNE

PONT DE

QUAI DE LA TOURNELLE

PONT DE LA TOURNELLE

Ⓣ

Ⓜ Maubert Mutualité

RUE MONGE

BLVD. ST. GERMAIN

INSTITUT DU MONDE ARABE

To Gare d'Austerlitz

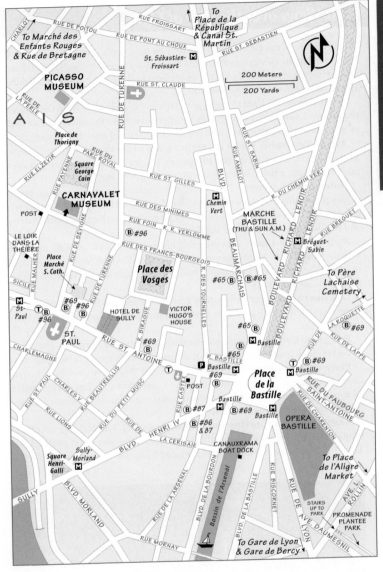

To
Place de la
République
& Canal St.
Martin

To Marché des
Enfants Rouges
& Rue de Bretagne

RUE DE POITOU

RUE FROISSART

RUE DE PONT AU CHOUX

RUE ST. SEBASTIEN

CHARLOT

St. Sébastien-
Froissart Ⓜ

200 Meters

200 Yards

PICASSO
MUSEUM

RUE ST. CLAUDE

RUE DE TURENNE

A I S

RUE DE
LA PERLE

Place de
Thorigny

RUE DU
PARC ROYAL

Square
George
Cain

RUE ST. GILLES

RUE ELZEVIR

RUE PAYENNE

CARNAVALET
MUSEUM

RUE DES MINIMES

Ⓜ
Chemin
Vert

MARCHE
BASTILLE
(THU & SUN A.M.)

RUE ST. SABIN

BLVD.

RUE AMELOT

R. DU CHEMIN VERT

RICHARD

LENOIR

BOULEVARD RICHARD LENOIR

RUE BRÉGUET

POST

RUE FOIN   R. R. VERLOMME

Ⓑ #96

RUE DES FRANCS-BOURGEOIS

BEAUMARCHAIS

Bréguet-
Sabin

LE LOIR
DANS LA
THÉIÈRE

RUE SÉVIGNÉ

RUE MALHER

Place
Marché
S. Cath.

Place des
Vosges

R. DES TOURNELLES

Ⓑ #65 Ⓑ #65

To Père
Lachaise
Cemetery

SICILE

Ⓜ
St-
Paul

Ⓣ Ⓑ
#96

Ⓑ #69 Ⓑ #96

HOTEL DE
SULLY

R. BIRAGUE

VICTOR
HUGO'S
HOUSE

#65 Ⓑ

LA ROQUETTE

Ⓑ #69

RUE DE TURENNE

ST.
PAUL

Ⓜ Bastille

RUE DE

RUE DE LAPPE

CHARLEMAGNE

RUE ST. ANTOINE

Ⓑ #69

R. BASTILLE

Ⓜ

#65

Ⓑ

Ⓣ Ⓑ #69

RUE ST. PAUL

CHARLES V

RUE BEAUTREILLIS

RUE DU PETIT MUSC

RUE CASTEX

Ⓟ Bastille
#69

POST Ⓑ

Place
de la
Bastille

Ⓜ Bastille

RUE DU FAUBOURG
SAINT-ANTOINE

RUE LIONS

Bastille
Ⓜ

Ⓑ #87

Ⓜ

Ⓑ #69

RUE DE CHARENTON

OPERA
BASTILLE

RUE DE
HENRI IV

Ⓑ #86
& 87

Bastille

To Place
de l'Aligre
Market

Square
Henri-
Galli
Ⓜ

Sully-
Morland
Ⓜ

BLVD.

LA CERISAIE

CANAUXRAMA
BOAT DOCK

RUE BISCORNET

RUE DE AVE. DAUMESNIL

AVE. L.
ROLLIN

SULLY

BLVD. MORLAND

RUE DE L'ARSENAL

BLVD. DE LA BOURDON

Bassin de l'Arsenal

BLVD. DE LA BASTILLE

RUE DE LYON

STAIRS
UP TO
PARK

PROMENADE
PLANTEE
PARK

RUE MORNAY

To Gare de Lyon
& Gare de Bercy

Best Views over the City of Light

The brilliance of the City of Light can only be fully appreciated by rising above it all. Many of the viewpoints I've listed are free or covered by the Museum Pass; otherwise, expect to pay €8-15. Views are best in the early morning or around sunset. Here are some prime locations:

Eiffel Tower: It's hard to find a grander view of Paris than from the tower's second level. Go around sunset and stay after dark to see the tower illuminated; or go in the early morning to avoid the midday haze and crowds (see page 159).

Arc de Triomphe: This is the perfect place to see the glamorous Champs-Elysées (if you can manage the 284 steps). It's great during the day, but even greater at night, when the boulevard glitters (see page 168).

Notre-Dame's Tower: This viewpoint couldn't be more central—but it requires climbing 400 steps and is usually crowded with long lines (arrive early or late). You'll get an unobstructed view of gargoyles, the river, the Latin Quarter, and the Ile de la Cité (see page 132).

Steps of Sacré-Cœur: Join the party on Paris' only hilltop. Walk uphill, or take the funicular or Montmartrobus, then hunker down on Sacré-Cœur's steps to enjoy the sunset. Stay in Montmartre for dinner, then see the view again after dark (free, see page 178).

Galeries Lafayette or Printemps: Take the escalator to the top floor of either department store (they sit side by side) for a stunning overlook of the old Opéra district (free).

Pompidou Center: Take the escalator up to admire the cityscape. There may be better views over Paris, but this is the best one from a museum (see page 176).

Place du Trocadéro: Start or end your Eiffel Tower visit at Place du Trocadéro for dramatic views of the tower, particularly at night. The square itself is a happening place, with street performers, souvenir vendors, skateboarders, and pickpockets. Gawk in moderation.

Arab World Institute (Institut du Monde Arabe): This building near Ile St. Louis has free views from its terrific roof terrace (Tue-Sun 10:00-18:00, closed Mon, 1 Rue des Fossés Saint-Bernard, Place Mohammed V, Mo: Jussieu, www.imarabe.org).

hard-eyed pimps, and himself, bundled up against the cold, with eyes all cried out (*Autoportrait*, 1901).

In 1904, Picasso got a steady girlfriend, and suddenly saw the world through rose-colored glasses (the Rose Period). With his next-door neighbor, Georges Braque, Picasso invented Cubism, a fragmented, "cube"-shaped style. He'd fracture a figure (such as the musician in *Man with a Mandolin*, 1911) into a barely recognizable jumble of facets. Picasso sketched reality from every angle, then pasted it all together, a composite of different views.

Cubist Experiments and *Guernica* (Floor 1): Modern art was being born. The first stage had been so-called Analytic Cubism: breaking the world down into small facets, to "analyze" the subject from every angle. Now it was time to "synthesize" it back together with the real world (Synthetic Cubism). Picasso created "constructions" that were essentially still-life paintings (a 2-D illusion) augmented with glued-on, real-life materials—wood, paper, rope, or chair caning (the real 3-D world). In a few short years, Picasso had turned painting in the direction it would go for the next 50 years.

Meanwhile, Europe was gearing up for war. From Paris, Picasso watched as his homeland of Spain erupted in a brutal civil war (1936-1939). Many canvases from this period are gray and gloomy. The most famous one—*Guernica* (1937)—captured the chaos of a Spanish village caught in an air raid (painted in Paris, but now hanging in Madrid). In 1940, Nazi tanks rolled into Paris. Picasso decided to stay for the duration and live under gray skies and gray uniforms.

The South of France and Last Years (Floor 2): At war's end, Picasso left Paris, finding fun in the sun in the south of France. Sixty-five-year-old Pablo Picasso was reborn, enjoying worldwide fame. Picasso's Riviera works set the tone for the rest of his life—sunny, light-hearted, childlike, experimenting in new media, and using motifs of the sea, Greek mythology (fauns, centaurs), and animals (birds, goats, and pregnant baboons). Picasso was fertile to the end, still painting with bright thick colors at age 91.

RUE DES ROSIERS: PARIS' JEWISH QUARTER

The intersection of Rue des Rosiers and Rue des Ecouffes marks the heart of the small neighborhood that Jews call the Pletzl ("little square"). Once the largest in Western Europe, Paris' Jewish Quarter is much smaller today but still colorful. Rue des Rosiers (named for the roses that once covered the city wall) has become the epicenter of Marais hipness and fashion. But it still features kosher (*cascher*) restaurants and fast-food places selling falafel, *shawarma, kefta,* and other Mediterranean dishes. Bakeries specialize in braided challah, bagels, and strudels. Delis offer gefilte fish, piroshkis, and blintzes.

Picasso Museum

The Jewish Quarter's Rue des Rosiers

Art galleries exhibit Jewish-themed works, and store windows post flyers for community events.

▲▲POMPIDOU CENTER (CENTRE POMPIDOU)

One of Europe's greatest collections of far-out modern art is housed in the Musée National d'Art Moderne, on the fourth and fifth floors of this colorful exoskeletal building. Created ahead of its time, the modern and contemporary art in this collection is still waiting for the world to catch up.

The Pompidou Center and the square that fronts it are lively, with lots of people, street theater, and activity inside and out—a perpetual street fair. Kids of any age enjoy the fun, colorful fountain (called *Homage to Stravinsky*) next to the Pompidou Center.

Cost and Hours: €14, free on first Sun of month, Museum Pass covers permanent collection and escalators to sixth-floor panoramic views (but not special exhibits); Wed-Mon 11:00-21:00, closed Tue, ticket counters close at 20:00, café and pricey view restaurant, Mo: Rambuteau or Hôtel de Ville, tel. 01 44 78 12 33, www.centrepompidou.fr.

🅐 *Pompidou Center*

🅑 *Otto Dix,* Portrait of Journalist Sylvia von Harden

🅒 *Joan Miró,* Le Catalan

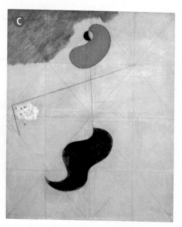

Visiting the Museum: Buy your ticket on the ground floor, then ride up the escalator (or run up the down escalator to get in the proper mood). When you see the view, your opinion of the Pompidou's exterior should improve a good 15 percent.

The Pompidou's "permanent" collection...isn't. It changes so often that a painting-by-painting tour is impossible. Generally, art from 1905 to 1980 is on the fifth floor, while the fourth floor contains more recent art. Use the museum's floor plans (posted on the wall) to find select artists. See the classics—Picasso, Matisse, Chagall, Braque, Dalí, Warhol—and leave time to browse the work of more recent artists.

As you tour, remember that most of the artists, including foreigners, spent their formative years in Paris. In the 1910s, funky Montmartre was the mecca of Modernism—the era of Picasso, Braque, and Matisse. In the 1920s the center shifted to the grand cafés of Montparnasse, where painters mingled with American expats such as Ernest Hemingway and Gertrude Stein. During World War II, it was Jean-Paul Sartre's Existentialist scene around St. Germain-des-Prés. After World War II, the global art focus moved to New York, but by the late 20th century, Paris had reemerged as a cultural touchstone for the world of Modern art.

Rick's Tip: *The sixth floor of the Pompidou has* **stunning views of the Paris cityscape.** *Your Pompidou ticket or Museum Pass gets you there, or you can buy the €3 View of Paris ticket (doesn't include museum entry).*

East of Place des Vosges
PROMENADE PLANTEE PARK (VIADUC DES ARTS)

This elevated viaduct, once used for train tracks, is now a two-mile-long, narrow garden walk and a pleasing place for a refreshing stroll or run. Botanists appreciate the well-maintained and varying vegetation.

Cost and Hours: Free, opens Mon-Fri at 8:00, Sat-Sun at 9:00, closes at sunset (17:30 in winter, 20:30 in summer). It runs from Place de la Bastille (Mo: Bastille) along Avenue Daumesnil to St. Mandé (Mo: Michel Bizot) or Porte Dorée, passing within a block of Gare de Lyon.

Getting There: To get to the park from Place de la Bastille (exit the Métro following *Sortie Rue de Lyon* signs), walk a looooong block down Rue de Lyon, hugging the Opéra on your left. Find the low-key entry and steps up the red-brick wall a block after the Opéra.

▲PERE LACHAISE CEMETERY (CIMETIERE DU PERE LACHAISE)

Lined with the tombstones of many of the city's most illustrious dead, this is your best one-stop look at Paris' fascinating, permanent residents.

Cost and Hours: Free, Mon-Fri 8:00-18:00, Sat 8:30-18:00, Sun 9:00-18:00, until 17:30 in winter; two blocks from Mo: Gambetta (do not go to Mo: Père Lachaise) and two blocks from bus #69's last stop; tel. 01 55 25 82 10, searchable map available at unofficial website: www.pere-lachaise.com.

Visiting the Cemetery: Enclosed by a massive wall and lined with 5,000 trees, the peaceful, car-free lanes and dirt paths of Père Lachaise cemetery encourage parklike meandering. Named for Father (*Père*) La Chaise, whose job was listening to Louis XIV's sins, the cemetery is relatively new, having opened in 1804 to accommodate Paris' expansion. Today, this city of the dead (pop. 70,000) still accepts new residents, but real estate prices are sky high (a 21-square-foot plot costs more than €11,000).

The 100-acre cemetery is big and confusing, with thousands of graves and tombs crammed every which way, and only a few pedestrian pathways to help you navigate. The maps available from street vendors can help guide your way. I recommend taking a one-way tour between two convenient Métro/bus stops (Gambetta and Père Lachaise),

Père Lachaise Cemetery

connecting a handful of graves from some of this necropolis' best-known residents, including Frédéric Chopin, Molière, Edith Piaf, Oscar Wilde, Gertrude Stein, Jim Morrison, Héloïse and Abélard, and more.

Rick's Tip: *To* **beat the crowds at Montmartre,** *come on a weekday or early on weekend mornings.*

Montmartre

Paris' highest hill, topped by Sacré-Cœur Basilica, is best known as the home of cabaret nightlife and bohemian artists. Struggling painters, poets, dreamers, and drunkards came here for cheap rent, untaxed booze, rustic landscapes, and the high-kicking cancan girls at the Moulin Rouge. These days, the hill is equal parts charm and kitsch—still vaguely village-like but mobbed with tourists and pickpockets on sunny weekends. Come for a bit of history, a getaway from Paris' noisy boulevards, and the view.

▲▲SACRE-CŒUR

You'll spot Sacré-Cœur, the Byzantine-looking white basilica atop Montmartre, from most viewpoints in Paris. Though only 130 years old, it's impressive and iconic, with a climbable dome.

Cost and Hours: Church—free, daily 6:00-22:30; dome—€6, not covered by Museum Pass, daily May-Sept 8:30-20:00, Oct-April 9:00-17:00; tel. 01 53 41 89 00, www.sacre-coeur-montmartre.com.

Getting There: For the location of the church, see the map on page 125. You can take the Métro to the Anvers stop (to avoid the stairs up to Sacré-Cœur, buy one more Métro ticket and ride up on the funicular). Alternatively, from Place Pigalle, you can take the "Montmartrobus," a city bus that drops you right by Sacré-Cœur (Funiculaire stop, costs one Métro ticket, 4/hour). A taxi from the Seine or the Bastille saves time and avoids sweat (about €15, €20 at night).

Visiting the Church: The Sacré-Cœur (Sacred Heart) Basilica's exterior, with its onion domes and bleached-bone pallor, looks ancient, but was finished only a century ago by Parisians humiliated by German invaders. Otto von Bismarck's Prussian army laid siege to Paris for more than four months in 1870. Things got so bad for residents that urban hunting for dinner (to cook up dogs, cats, and finally rats) became accepted behavior. Convinced they were being punished for the country's liberal sins, France's Catholics raised money to build the church as a "praise the Lord anyway" gesture.

The five-domed, Roman-Byzantine-looking basilica took 44 years to build (1875-1919). It stands on a foundation of 83 pillars sunk 130 feet deep, necessary because the ground beneath was honeycombed with gypsum mines. The exterior is laced with gypsum, which whitens with age.

Take a clockwise spin around the crowded interior to see impressive mosaics, a statue of St. Thérèse, a scale model of the church, and three stained-glass windows dedicated to Joan of Arc. Pause

Sacré-Cœur

near the Stations of the Cross mosaic to give St. Peter's bronze foot a rub. For an unobstructed panoramic view of Paris, climb 260 feet (300 steps) up the tight spiral stairs to the top of the dome.

EXPERIENCES

Seine Cruises

Several companies run boat cruises on the Seine. For the best experience, cruise at twilight or after dark. Another option is a longer dinner cruise, featuring multi-course meals and music (€100 and up, reservations required).

The companies listed below run daily one-hour sightseeing tours year-round (April-Oct 10:00-22:30, 2-3/hour; Nov-March shorter hours). On dinner cruises, proper dress is required—no denim, shorts, or sport shoes.

Bateaux-Mouches, the oldest boat company in Paris, departs from Pont de l'Alma's right bank and has the biggest open-top, double-decker boats (higher up means better views). The boats are often jammed and noisy (€13.50, kids 4-12-€5.50, RER: Pont de l'Alma, tel. 01 42 25 96 10, www.bateaux-mouches.fr). Dinner cruises include violin and piano music (jacket and tie required for men).

Bateaux Parisiens has smaller covered boats with handheld audioguides, fewer crowds, and only one deck. The boats leave from right in front of the Eiffel Tower (€14, kids 3-12-€5, tel. 01 76 64 14 45, www.bateauxparisiens.com). Dinner cruises feature a lively atmosphere with a singer, band, and dance floor.

Vedettes du Pont Neuf cruises start and end at Pont Neuf. The boats feature a live guide whose delivery (in English and French) is as stiff as a recorded narration—and as hard to understand, given the quality of their sound system (€14, ask about Rick Steves discount, tip requested, tel. 01 46 33 98 38, www.vedettesdupontneuf.com).

Shopping

Wandering among elegant boutiques provides a break from the heavy halls of the Louvre, and, if you approach it right, a little cultural enlightenment. Even if you don't intend to buy anything, do some window shopping, or as the French call it: *faire du lèche-vitrines* ("window licking").

Before you enter a Parisian store, remember the following points:

In small stores, always say, *"Bonjour, Madame* or *Mademoiselle* or *Monsieur"* when entering and *"Au revoir, Madame* or *Mademoiselle* or *Monsieur"* when leaving.

The customer is not always right. In fact, figure the clerk is doing you a favor by waiting on you.

Except in department stores, it's not normal for the customer to handle clothing. Ask first before you pick up an item: *"Je peux?"* (zhuh puh), meaning, "Can I?" Don't feel obliged to buy. If a shopkeeper offers assistance, just say, *"Je regarde, merci."*

Saturday afternoons are *très* busy and not for the faint of heart.

Stores are generally closed on Sunday. Exceptions include the Carrousel du Louvre (underground shopping mall at the Louvre with a Printemps department store) and some shops near Sèvres-Babylone, along the Champs-Elysées, and in the Marais (for eclectic, avant-garde boutiques in the Marais neighborhood, peruse the artsy shops between Place des Vosges and the Pompidou Center).

Department Stores (Les Grands Magasins)

Parisian department stores begin with their showy perfume sections, almost always central on the ground floor. Information desks are usually located at the main entrances near the perfume section (with floor plans in English). Stores generally have affordable restaurants (some with view terraces) and a good selection of fairly priced souvenirs and toys. Shop at **Galeries Lafayette** (Mo: Chaussée d'Antin–La Fayette, Havre–Caumartin, or Opéra), **Printemps** (next door to Galeries Lafayette), and **Bon Marché** (Mo: Sèvres-Babylone). Opening hours are customarily Monday through Saturday from 10:00 to 19:00, with some open later on Thursdays. All are jammed on Saturdays and closed on Sundays (except in December, and except for the Printemps store in the Carrousel du Louvre, which is open daily year-round).

Boutique Strolls

Two very different areas to lick some windows are Place de la Madeleine to Place de l'Opéra, and Sèvres-Babylone to St. Sulpice.

◑ LA MADELEINE TO L'OPERA

The ritzy streets connecting several high-priced squares—Place de la Madeleine, Place de la Concorde, Place Vendôme, and Place de l'Opéra—form a miracle mile of gourmet food shops, glittering jewelry stores, five-star hotels, exclusive clothing boutiques, and people who spend more on clothes in one day than I do all year.

Start at Place de la Madeleine (Mo: Madeleine). In the northeast corner at #24 is the black-and-white awning of **Fauchon.** Founded on this location in 1886, this bastion of over-the-top edibles became famous around the world, catering to the refined tastes of the rich and famous. **Hédiard** (#21, northwest corner of the square) is older than Fauchon, and

Sampling perfume

it's weathered the tourist mobs better. Wafting the aroma of tea and coffee, it showcases handsomely displayed produce and wines. Hédiard's small red containers—of mustards, jams, coffee, candies, and tea—make great souvenirs.

Step inside tiny **La Maison des Truffe** (#19) to get a whiff of the product—truffles, those prized edible mushrooms. Check out the tiny jars in the display case. The venerable **Mariage Frères** (#17) shop demonstrates how good tea can smell and how beautifully it can be displayed. **At Caviar Kaspia** (#16), you can add Iranian caviar, eel, and vodka to your truffle collection.

Continue along, past **Marquise de Sévígné chocolates** (#11) to the intersection with **Boulevard Malesherbes.** When the street officially opened in 1863, it ushered in the Golden Age of this neighborhood. Cross the three crosswalks traversing Boulevard Malesherbes. Straight ahead is **Patrick Roger Chocolates** (#3), famous for its chocolates, and even more so for M. Roger's huge, whimsical, 150-pound chocolate sculptures of animals and fanciful creatures.

Turn right down broad **Rue Royale.** There's Dior, Chanel, and Gucci. At Rue St. Honoré, turn left and cross Rue Royale, pausing in the middle for a great view both ways. Check out **Ladurée** (#16) for an out-of-this-world pastry break in the busy 19th-century tea salon or to just pick up some world-famous macarons. Continue east for three long blocks down **Rue St. Honoré.** The street is a parade of chic boutiques—L'Oréal cosmetics, Jimmy Choo shoes, Valentino...Looking for a €10,000 handbag? This is your spot.

Turn left on Rue de Castiglione to reach **Place Vendôme.** This octagonal square is *très* elegant—enclosed by symmetrical Mansart buildings around a 150-foot column. On the left side is the original Hôtel Ritz, opened in 1898. The square is also known for its upper-crust jewelry and designer stores—Van Cleef & Arpels, Dior,

La Madeleine to L'Opéra Walk

200 Meters
200 Yards

To Musée Jacquemart-André & Parc Monceau

BD. HAUSSMANN
RUE DE PROVENCE
PRINTEMPS
Havre Caumartin
GALERIES LAFAYETTE
RUE DE LA CHAUSSÉE
RUE LA FAYETTE
R. GLUCK
Chaussée d'Antin La Fayette
RUE DES MATHURINS
RUE AUBER
BD. D'ANJOU
RUE PASQUIER
R. CHAUVEAU LAGARDE
BD. MALESHERBES
RUE TRONCHET
RUE VIGNON
RUE GODOT DE MAUROY
OPERA GARNIER
FRAGONARD PERFUME MUSEUM
RUE SCRIBE
R. HALÉVY
CAFE DE LA PAIX
Place de l'Opéra
R. DE SURENE
Place de la Madeleine
LA MADELEINE
Madeleine
RUE DE SEZE
R. DES CAPUCINES
R. DES CAPUCINES
CAPUCINES
Opéra
RUE DU 4 SEPT
RUE D'ANJOU
BD. DES
RUE DANOU
Quatre Septembre
RUE ST. AUGUSTIN
RUE D'ANTIN
RUE BOISSY D'ANGLAS
RUE DE LA PAIX
RUE LE GRAND
AVE. DE L'OPÉRA
PASSAGE STE. ANNE
PASSAGE CHOISEUL
RUE ROYALE
RUE ST. FLORENTIN
R. DUPHOT
RUE CAMBON
HOTEL RITZ
Place Vendôme
RUE DES PETITS CHAMPS
HOTEL CRILLON
Concorde
RUE ST.
R. CASTIGLIONE
RUE ST. HONORE
RUE DU MARCHÉ
R. DE LA SOURDIÈRE
RUE ST. ROCH
Pyramides
RUE STE. ANNE
Place de la Concorde
JEU DE PAUME
RUE DE RIVOLI
RUE 29 JUILLET
RUE DES PYRAMIDES
Jardin des Tuileries

Chanel, Cartier, and others (if you have to ask how much...).

Leave Place Vendôme by continuing straight, up **Rue de la Paix**—strolling by still more jewelry, high-priced watches, and crystal—and enter **Place de l'Opéra**. Here you'll find the Opéra Garnier (described on page 168). If you're not shopped out yet, the Galeries Lafayette and Printemps department stores are located a block or two north, up Rue Halévy.

❍ SEVRES-BABYLONE TO ST. SULPICE

This Left Bank shopping stroll lets you sample smart clothing boutiques and clever window displays while enjoying one of Paris' more attractive neighborhoods. Start at the Sèvres-Babylone Métro stop (take the Métro or bus #87). You'll find

the **Bon Marché** (Mo: Sèvres-Babylone), Paris' oldest department store.

From the Bon Marché, follow Rue de Sèvres, where you'll find **La Maison du Chocolat** at #19. Their mouthwatering window display will draw you helplessly inside. The shop sells handmade chocolates in exquisitely wrapped boxes and delicious ice-cream cones in season.

Lick the chocolate off your fingers before entering **Hermès** (a few doors down, at #17), famous for pricey silk scarves. Don't let the doorman intimidate you: Everyone's welcome here. This store, opened in 2011, is housed in the original Art Deco swimming pool of Hôtel Lutetia, built in 1935.

Across the street sits the old-school **Au Sauvignon Café** (open daily, 10 Rue de Sèvres). It's well situated for watching

Sèvres-Babylone to St. Sulpice Walk

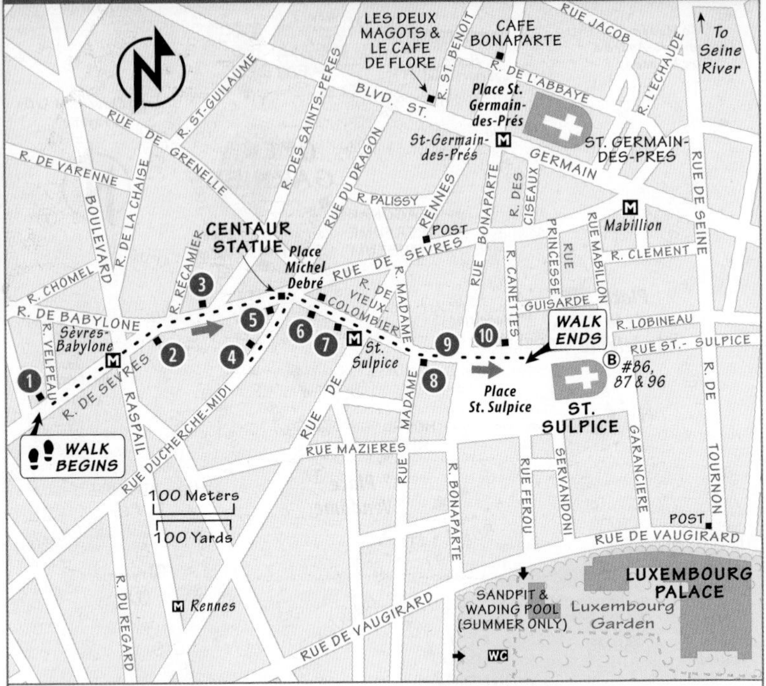

① Bon Marché

② La Maison du Chocolat & Hermès

③ Au Sauvignon Café

④ Poilâne

⑤ Comtesse du Barry

⑥ Théâtre du Vieux-Colombier & Longchamp

⑦ Victoire

⑧ Vilebrequin

⑨ Aubade & Hervé Chapelier

⑩ Café de la Mairie

smartly coiffed shoppers glide by. Continue a block farther down Rue de Sèvres to Place Michel Debré, a six-way intersection, where a *Centaur* statue stands guard. From here, boutique-lined streets fan out like spokes on a wheel.

Make a short detour up Rue du Cherche-Midi (follow the horse's fanny). This street offers an ever-changing but always chic selection of shoe, purse, and clothing stores. Find Paris' most celebrated bread—beautiful round loaves with designer crust—at the low-key **Poilâne** (#8). Return to the *Centaur* in

Place Michel Debré. Check out the **Comtesse du Barry** pâté store, which sells small gift packs. Then turn right and head down Rue du Vieux Colombier, passing the (#6) **Théâtre du Vieux-Colombier** (1913), one of three key venues for La Comédie Française, a historic state-run troupe. At **Longchamp** (#21), you can hunt for a stylish French handbag in any color, and **Victoire** offers items for the gentleman.

Cross busy Rue de Rennes and continue down Rue du Vieux Colombier. Here you'll find more specialty boutiques.

There's **Vilebrequin** (#5) for men's swimwear, **Aubade** (#4) for lingerie, and **Hervé Chapelier** (#1) for travel totes and handbags. Spill into Place St. Sulpice, with its big, twin-tower church. **Café de la Mairie** is a great spot to sip a *café crème*, admire the lovely square, and consider your next move.

Nightlife

Paris is brilliant after dark. Save energy to experience the City of Light lit. Whether it's a concert at Sainte-Chapelle, a cruise on the Seine, a walk in Montmartre, a hike up the Arc de Triomphe, or a late-night café, you'll see Paris at its best.

Jazz and Blues Clubs

With a lively mix of American, French, and international musicians, Paris has been an internationally acclaimed jazz capital since World War II. You'll pay €12-25 to enter a jazz club (may include one drink; if not, expect to pay €5-10 per drink; beer is cheapest). See *Pariscope* magazine under "Musique" for listings, or, even better, the *Paris Voice* website. You can also check each club's website (all have English versions), or drop by the clubs to check out the calendars posted on their front doors. Music starts after 21:00 in most clubs. Some offer dinner concerts from about 20:30 on. Here are several good bets:

Caveau de la Huchette fills an ancient Latin Quarter cellar with live jazz and frenzied dancing every night (admission about €13 on weekdays, €15 on weekends, €6-8 drinks, daily 21:30-2:30 in the morning or later, no reservations needed, buy tickets at the door, 5 Rue de la Huchette, Mo: St. Michel, tel. 01 43 26 65 05, www.caveaudelahuchette.fr).

Autour de Midi et Minuit is an Old World bistro that sits at the foot of Montmartre, above a *cave à jazz*. Eat upstairs if you like, then make your way down to the basement to find bubbling jam sessions Tuesday through Thursday and concerts on Friday and Saturday nights (no cover, €5 minimum drink order Tue-Thu; €18 cover Fri-Sat includes one drink; jam sessions at 21:30, concerts usually at 22:00; no music Sun-Mon; 11 Rue Lepic, Mo: Blanche or Abbesses, tel. 01 55 79 16 48, www.autourdemidi.fr).

For a spot teeming with late-night activity and jazz, go to the two-block-long **Rue des Lombards,** at Boulevard Sébastopol, midway between the river and the Pompidou Center (Mo: Châtelet). **Au Duc des Lombards** is one of the most popular and respected jazz clubs in Paris, with concerts nightly in a plush, 110-seat theater (admission €25-40, €50-80 with dinner, buy online and arrive early for best seats, cheap drinks, shows at 20:00 and 22:00, 42 Rue des Lombards, tel. 01 42 33 22 88, www.ducdeslombards.fr). **Le Sunside,** just a block away, offers two stages: "le Sunset" on the ground floor for contemporary world jazz; and "le Sunside" downstairs for more traditional and acoustic jazz (concerts range from free to €25, check their website; 60 Rue des Lombards, tel. 01 40 26 46 60, www.sunset-sunside.com).

Old-Time Parisian Cabaret

Au Lapin Agile, a historic little cabaret on Montmartre, tries its best to maintain the atmosphere of the heady days when bohemians would gather here to enjoy wine, song, and sexy jokes. Today, you'll mix in with a few locals and many tourists for a drink and as many as 10 different performers—mostly singers with a piano. Though tourists are welcome, there's no accommodation for English speakers (except on their website), so non-French speakers will be lost. The soirée covers traditional French standards, love ballads, sea chanteys, and more (€28, €8 drinks, Tue-Sun 21:00-2:00 in the morning, closed Mon, best to reserve ahead, 22 Rue des Saules, tel. 01 46 06 85 87, www.au-lapin-agile.com).

Classical Concerts

For classical music on any night, consult *Pariscope* magazine (check "Concerts Classiques" under "Musique" for listings), and look for posters at tourist-oriented churches. From March through November, these churches regularly host concerts: St. Sulpice, St. Germain-des-Prés, La Madeleine, St. Eustache, St. Julien-le-Pauvre, and Sainte-Chapelle.

At **Sainte-Chapelle,** enjoy the pleasure of hearing Mozart, Bach, or Vivaldi, surrounded by 800 years of stained glass. The acoustical quality is surprisingly good. There are usually two concerts per evening, at 19:00 and 20:30; specify which one you want when you buy or reserve your ticket. VIP tickets get you a seat in rows 3-10 (€40), Prestige tickets cover the next 15 rows (€30), and Normal tickets are the last 5 rows (€25). Seats are unassigned within each section, so arrive at least 30 minutes early to get through the security line and snare a good view. It's unheated—bring a sweater.

Book tickets at the box office, by phone, or online. Two different companies present concerts, but the schedule will tell you which one to contact for a particular performance. The small box office (with schedules and tickets) is to the left of the chapel entrance gate (8 Boulevard du Palais, Mo: Cité), or call 01 42 77 65 65 or 06 67 30 65 65 for schedules and reservations. You can leave your message in English—just speak clearly and spell your name. You can check schedules and buy your ticket at www.euromusicproductions.fr (ask about Rick Steves discount on Euromusic events—cash only at box office close to concert time).

Philharmonie de Paris, a dazzling, 2,400-seat concert hall situated in the Parc de la Villette complex, hosts world-class artists, from legends of rock and roll to string quartets to international opera stars (221 Avenue Jean-Jaurès, Mo: Porte de Pantin, tel. 01 44 84 44 84, www.philharmoniedeparis.fr).

You can also enjoy live classical **Concerts on the Seine** while cruising past Paris' iconic monuments (€30-40, summer months only, board at Vedettes du Pont Neuf, Square du Vert Galant, tel. 01 42 77 65 65, http://vedettesdupontneuf.com/concerts-en-seine). Also look for concerts in parks, such as the Luxembourg Garden, or even the Galeries Lafayette department store. Many are free *(entrée libre),* such as the Sunday atelier concert sponsored by the American Church (generally Sept-June at 17:00 but not every week and not in Dec, 65 Quai d'Orsay, Mo: Invalides, RER: Pont de l'Alma, tel. 01 40 62 05 00, www.acparis.org). The Army Museum offers inexpensive afternoon and evening classical music concerts year-round (for programs—in French only—see www.musee-armee.fr/programmation).

Paris churches host frequent concerts.

Extend your sightseeing into the night.

Night Walks

Go for one of these ▲▲▲ evening walks to best appreciate the City of Light. Break for ice cream, pause at a café, and enjoy the sidewalk entertainers as you participate in the post-dinner Parisian parade. Remember to exercise normal big-city caution when exploring Paris at night; avoid poorly lit areas and stick to main thoroughfares.

● TROCADERO AND EIFFEL TOWER

This stroll delivers one of Paris' most spectacular views at night. Take the Métro to the Trocadéro stop and join the party on Place du Trocadéro for a magnificent view of the glowing Eiffel Tower. It's a festival of hawkers, gawkers, drummers, and entertainers.

Walk down the stairs, passing the fountains and rollerbladers, then cross the river to the base of the tower, well worth the effort even if you don't go up. From the Eiffel Tower you can stroll through the Champ de Mars park past tourists and romantic couples, and take the Métro home (Ecole Militaire stop, across Avenue de la Motte-Picquet from far southeast corner of park). Or there's a handy RER stop (Champ de Mars-Tour Eiffel) two blocks west of the Eiffel Tower on the river.

● CHAMPS-ELYSEES AND THE ARC DE TRIOMPHE

The Avenue des Champs-Elysées glows after dark. Start at the Arc de Triomphe, then stroll down Paris' lively grand promenade. A right turn on Avenue George V leads to the Bateaux-Mouches river cruises. A movie on the Champs-Elysées is a fun experience (weekly listings in *Pariscope* under "Cinéma"), and a drink or snack at Renault's futuristic car café is a kick (at #53).

EATING

Entire books (and lives) are dedicated to eating in Paris. Though it lacks a style of its own (only French onion soup is truly Parisian; otherwise, there is no "Parisian cuisine" to speak of), it draws from the best of France.

My recommendations center on the same great neighborhoods as my hotel listings. Serious eaters looking for even more suggestions should consult the always appetizing www.parisbymouth.com, an eating-and-drinking guide.

To save piles of euros, go to a bakery for takeout, or stop at a café for lunch. Cafés and brasseries are happy to serve a *plat du jour* (garnished plate of the day, about €12-20) or a chef-like salad (about

Restaurant Price Code

$$$ **Higher Priced**—Most main
courses €25 or more

$$ **Moderately Priced**—Most
main courses €15-25

$ **Lower Priced**—Most main
courses €15 or less

€10-14) day or night. To save even more,
consider picnics (tasty takeout dishes
available at charcuteries).

Linger longer over dinner—restaurants expect you to enjoy a full meal.
Most restaurants I've listed have set-price
menus between €20 and €38. In most
cases, the few extra euros you pay are
well spent and open up a variety of better
choices. A service charge is included in the
prices (so little or no tipping is expected).

Rue Cler Area
Close to the Eiffel Tower
(Mo: Ecole Militaire)

$$ Le Florimond is fun for a special occasion. The setting is warm and welcoming.
Locals come for classic French cuisine
at fair prices. Friendly English-speaking
Laurent, whose playful ties change daily,
gracefully serves one small room of tables
and loves to give suggestions. The stuffed
cabbage and the *confit de canard* are particularly tasty, and the house wine is excellent (€37 *menu*, closed Sun and first and
third Sat of month, reservations encouraged, 19 Avenue de la Motte-Picquet, tel.
01 45 55 40 38, www.leflorimond.com).

$$ Bistrot Belhara, named for a legendary 35-foot wave and surfing spot off
the Basque coast, is a true French dining
experience. Watch as chef Thierry peers
from his kitchen window to ensure that
all is well. He bases his cuisine on what's
in season, but the foie gras and *riz au lait
de mémé*—his grandma's rice pudding—
are delicious any time of year. If you don't

know French, the charming Frédéric will
translate—and help you choose the perfect wine (€38 *menu*, closed Sun-Mon,
reservations smart, a block off Rue Cler at
23 Rue Duvivier, tel. 01 45 51 41 77, www.
bistrotbelhara.com).

$$ La Terrasse du 7ème is a sprawling, happening café with grand outdoor
seating and a living-room-like interior
with comfy love seats. Located on a corner, it overlooks a busy intersection with a
constant parade of people. Chairs are set
up facing the street, so a meal here is like
dinner theater—and the show is slice-of-
life Paris (€16-23 *plats,* good €13 *salade
niçoise* or Caesar salad, €8 French onion
soup, tasty foie gras, no fixed-price *menu,*
daily until at least 24:00, at Ecole Militaire
Métro stop, tel. 01 45 55 00 02).

Between Rue de Grenelle and the River
(Mo: Ecole Militaire)

$$$ L'Ami Jean offers authentic Basque
specialties in a snug-but-fun atmosphere
with red peppers and Basque stuff hanging from the ceiling. It's not cheap, but the
portions are hearty and delicious, and the
whole menu changes every two weeks.
Parisians detour long distances to savor
the gregarious chef's special cuisine and
convivial atmosphere. For dinner, arrive
by 19:30 or reserve ahead (€20 starters,
€35 plats, €78 eight-course dinner menu,
a more accessible lunch menu for €35,
closed Sun-Mon, 27 Rue Malar, Mo: La
Tour-Maubourg, tel. 01 47 05 86 89, www.
lamijean.fr).

$$$ La Fontaine de Mars, a longtime
favorite and neighborhood institution,
draws Parisians who want to be seen. It's
charmingly situated on a tiny, jumbled
square with tables jammed together for
the serious business of eating. Reserve in
advance for a table on the ground floor or
on the square, and enjoy the same meal
Barack Obama did. Street-level seats
come with the best ambience (€20-30
plats du jour, daily, superb foie gras, superb

Rue Cler Restaurants & Hotels

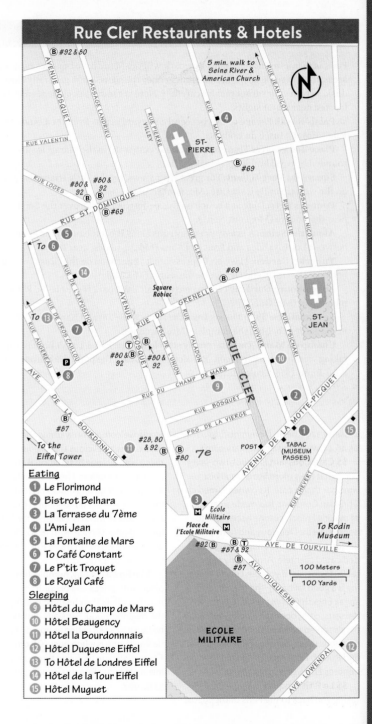

5 min. walk to
Seine River &
American Church

Eating
1 Le Florimond
2 Bistrot Belhara
3 La Terrasse du 7ème
4 L'Ami Jean
5 La Fontaine de Mars
6 To Café Constant
7 Le P'tit Troquet
8 Le Royal Café

Sleeping
9 Hôtel du Champ de Mars
10 Hôtel Beaugency
11 Hôtel la Bourdonnnais
12 Hôtel Duquesne Eiffel
13 To Hôtel de Londres Eiffel
14 Hôtel de la Tour Eiffel
15 Hôtel Muguet

Good Picnic Spots

Paris is picnic-friendly. Almost any park will do. Many have benches or grassy areas, though some lawns are off-limits—obey the signs. Parks generally close at dusk, so plan your sunset picnics carefully. Here are some especially scenic areas located near major sights:

Palais Royal: Escape to this peaceful courtyard across from the Louvre (Mo: Palais Royal-Musée du Louvre).

Place des Vosges: This exquisite grassy courtyard in the Marais is surrounded by royal buildings (Mo: Bastille).

Square du Vert-Galant: For great river views, try this little triangular park on the west tip of Ile de la Cité (Mo: Pont Neuf).

Pont des Arts: Dine at a bench on this pedestrian bridge over the Seine, near the Louvre (Mo: Pont Neuf).

Along the Seine: A grassy parkway runs along the left bank of the Seine between Les Invalides and Pont de l'Alma (Mo: Invalides, near Rue Cler).

Tuileries Garden: Have an Impressionist "Luncheon on the Grass" nestled between the Orsay and Orangerie museums (Mo: Tuileries).

Luxembourg Garden: This expansive Left Bank park is the classic Paris picnic spot (Mo: Odéon).

Les Invalides: Take a break from the Army Museum and Napoleon's Tomb in the gardens behind the complex (Mo: Varenne).

Champ de Mars: The long grassy strip below the Eiffel Tower has breathtaking views of this Paris icon. Eat along the sides of the park; the central lawn is off-limits (Mo: Ecole Militaire).

desserts, 129 Rue St. Dominique, tel. 01 47 05 46 44, www.fontainedemars.com).

$$ Café Constant is a cool, two-level place that feels more like a small bistro-wine bar than a café. Its owner, famed chef Christian Constant, has made a career of making French cuisine accessible to people like us. Delicious and fairly priced dishes are served in a snug setting to a dedicated clientele. Arrive early to get a table downstairs if you can (upstairs seating is a good fallback); the friendly staff speak English (€11 entrées, €16 plats, €7 desserts, daily, opens at 7:00 for breakfast, meals served nonstop 12:00-23:00, no reservations taken, corner of Rue Augereau and Rue St. Dominique, next to Hôtel de Londres Eiffel, tel. 01 47 53 73 34).

$$ Le P'tit Troquet is a petite eatery taking you back to the Paris of the 1920s.

Marie welcomes you warmly, and chef José cooks a delicious three-course €35 menu with a range of traditional choices prepared creatively. The homey charm and gourmet quality make this restaurant a favorite of connoisseurs (the same three-course menu is available for €25 at lunch, dinner service from 18:30, closed Sun, reservations smart, 28 Rue de l'Exposition, tel. 01 47 05 80 39).

$ Le Royal is a tiny, humble, time-warp place, with prices and decor from another era, that offers the cheapest meals in the neighborhood. Parisians dine here because "it's like eating at home." Gentle Guillaume is a fine host (€6 omelets, €9-12 plats, €14 for filling three-course menu, daily, 212 Rue de Grenelle, tel. 01 47 53 92 90).

In the Marais
On Romantic Place des Vosges
(Mo: Bastille or St-Paul)

$$ La Place Royale has a fine location on the square with good seating inside or out. Expect a warm welcome and patient waiters, as owner Arnaud prides himself on service. The cuisine is traditional, priced well, and served nonstop all day, and the exceptional wine list is reasonable (try the Sancerre white). The €42 *menu* comes with a kir, three courses, a half-bottle of wine per person, and coffee—plenty of food to allow you to savor the setting (€26-42 *menus*, €17 lunch special, daily, 2 bis Place des Vosges, tel. 01 42 78 58 16).

$$ Chez Janou, a Provençal bistro, tumbles out of its corner building and fills its broad sidewalk with happy eaters. Don't let the trendy and youthful crowd intimidate you: It's relaxed and charming, with helpful and calm service. The curbside tables are inviting, but I'd sit inside (with very tight seating) to immerse myself in the happy commotion. The style is French Mediterranean, with an emphasis on vegetables (€16-24 *plats du jour*, daily—book ahead or arrive when it opens, 2 blocks beyond Place des Vosges at 2 Rue Roger Verlomme, tel. 01 42 72 28 41, www.chezjanou.com). They're proud of their 81 varieties of *pastis* (licorice-flavored liqueur, €4.80 each, browse the list above the bar).

$$ Café des Musées is an unspoiled bistro serving traditional meaty dishes with little fanfare. They offer a great €17 lunch special. The place is just far enough away to be overlooked by tourists, but it's packed with locals, so arrive early or book ahead (€19-26 *plats*, daily, 49 Rue de Turenne, tel. 01 42 72 96 17, www.lecafedesmusees.fr).

Near the Place de la Bastille
(Mo: Bastille)

$$ Au Temps des Cerises serves wines by the glass and meals with a smile. The woody 1950s atmosphere has tight seating and wads of character. Come for a glass of wine at the small zinc bar and say *bonjour* to Ben (try their Viognier), or stay for a tasty dinner (€11 starters, €20 *plats*, good cheap wine, daily, at the corner of Rue du Petit Musc and Rue de la Cerisaie, tel. 01 42 72 08 63).

In the Heart of the Marais
(Mo: St-Paul)

$ Breizh (Brittany) Café is worth the walk. It's a simple Breton joint serving organic crêpes and small rolls made for dipping in rich sauces and salted butter. The crêpes are the best in Paris and run the gamut from traditional ham-cheese-and-egg to Asian fusion. They also serve oysters, have a fantastic list of sweet crêpes, and talk about cider like a sommelier would talk about wine. Try a sparkling cider, a Breton cola, or my favorite—*lait ribot*, a buttermilk-like drink (€7-13 dinner crêpes, serves nonstop from 11:30 to late, closed Mon-Tue, reservations recommended for lunch and dinner, 109 Rue du Vieille du Temple, tel. 01 42 72 13 77).

$$ Chez Marianne is a Jewish Quarter fixture that blends delicious Jewish cuisine with Parisian *élan* and wonderful atmosphere. Choose from several indoor zones with a cluttered wine shop/deli feeling, or sit outside. You'll select from two dozen *Zakouski* elements to assemble your €14-18 *plat*. For takeout, pay inside first and get a ticket before you order outside. Vegetarians will find great options (€12 falafel sandwich—half that if you order it to go, long hours daily, corner of Rue des Rosiers and Rue des Hospitalières-St-Gervais, tel. 01 42 72 18 86).

$$ Au Bourguignon du Marais is a handsome wine bar/bistro for Burgundy lovers, where excellent Burgundian wines blend with a good selection of well-designed dishes and efficient service. The *œufs en meurette* are mouthwatering, and the *bœuf bourguignon* could feed two (€11-14 starters, €20-30 *plats*, closed Sun-Mon, pleasing indoor and outdoor seating, 52 Rue François Miron, tel. 01 48 87 15 40).

On Ile St. Louis
(Mo: Pont Marie)

$$ L'Orangerie is an inviting eatery with soft lighting and comfortable seating where diners speak in hushed voices so that everyone can appreciate the delicious cuisine and tasteful setting. Patient owner Monika speaks fluent English, and her *gratin d'aubergines* is sinfully good (€27-35 *menus*, closed Mon, 28 Rue St. Louis-en-l'Ile, tel. 01 46 33 93 98).

$ Café Med, near the pedestrian bridge to Notre-Dame, is a tiny, cheery *crêperie* with good-value salads, crêpes, and €11 *plats* (€14 and €20 *menus*, daily, 77 Rue St. Louis-en-l'Ile, tel. 01 43 29 73 17). Two similar *crêperies* are just across the street.

On the Left Bank
Near the Odéon Theater
(Mo: Odéon or Cluny-La Sorbonne)

$$ La Méditerranée is all about seafood from the south served in a pastel and dressy setting...with similar clientele. The scene and the cuisine are sophisticated yet accessible, and the view of the Odéon is *formidable*. The sky-blue tablecloths and the lovingly presented dishes add to the romance (€29 two-course *menus*, €36 three-course *menus*, daily, reservations smart, facing the Odéon at 2 Place de l'Odéon, tel. 01 43 26 02 30, www.la-mediterranee.com).

$ L'Avant Comptoir, a stand-up-only hors d'oeuvres bar serving a delightful array of French-Basque tapas for €3-6 on a sleek zinc counter, was created to give people a sample of the cuisine from the *très* trendy Le Comptoir Restaurant next door, where the reservation wait time is four months. The menu is fun and accessible, it has a good list of wines by the glass, and crêpes are made fresh to go (daily 12:00-23:00, 9 Carrefour de l'Odéon, tel. 01 44 27 07 97).

$ Restaurant Polidor, a bare-bones neighborhood fixture since 1845, is much loved for its unpretentious quality cooking, fun old-Paris atmosphere, and fair value. Step inside to find noisy, happy diners sitting tightly at shared tables, savoring classic bourgeois *plats* from every corner of France (€12-17 *plats*, €25-35 three-course *menus*, daily 12:00-14:30 & 19:00-23:00, cash only, no reservations, 41 Rue Monsieur-le-Prince, tel. 01 43 26 95 34). Next door is the restaurant's wine shop, **Les Caves du Polidor,** where you can sip wine and nibble on cheese-and-meat plates (daily, wine and snacks served 18:00-20:00, opens earlier when weather or owner is feeling sunny).

Between the Panthéon and the Cluny Museum
(Mo: Cluny-La Sorbonne, RER: Luxembourg)

$$ At **Les Papilles** you just eat what's offered—and you won't complain. It's a foodie's dream come true—one *menu*, no choices, and no regrets. Choose your wine from the shelf or ask for advice from the burly, rugby-playing owner, then relax and let the food arrive. Book this place ahead (€35 four-course *menu*, €20 daily *marmite du marché*—a.k.a. market stew, bigger and cheaper selection at lunch, closed Sun-Mon, 30 Rue Gay Lussac, tel. 01 43 25 20 79, www.lespapillesparis.fr).

$$ Le Pré Verre, a block from the Cluny Museum, is a chic wine bistro—a refreshing alternative in a part of the Latin Quarter mostly known for low-quality, tourist-trapping eateries. Offering imaginative, modern cuisine at fair prices and a good wine list, the place is packed. The astonishing bargain lunch *menu* includes a starter, main course, glass of wine, and coffee for €15. The three-course dinner *menu* at €32 is worth every *centime* (closed Sun-Mon, 8 Rue Thénard, reservations necessary, tel. 01 43 54 59 47, www.lepreverre.com).

The Paris Food Scene

To dig deeper into the food scene in Paris, take a culinary tour, cooking class, or a wine-tasting class.

Food Tours

Rosa Jackson designs personalized **"Edible Paris"** itineraries based on your interests and three-hour "food-guru" tours (unguided from €125, guided from €300, tel. 06 81 67 41 22, www.edible-paris.com).

Paris by Mouth offers more casual and frequent small group tours, with a maximum of seven foodies per group. Tours are organized by location or flavor and led by local food writers (€95/3 hours, includes tastings, www.parisbymouth.com). Sit-down cheese and wine workshops include seven wines and 14 cheeses (€95/3 hours). Given that there are 350 different types of cheese in France, you may need to take this class more than once.

Cooking Classes

At **Les Secrets Gourmands de Noémie,** Noémie shares her culinary secrets in 2.5 hours of hands-on fun in the kitchen. Thursday classes, designed for English speakers, focus on sweets; classes on other days are in French, English, or both, depending on the participants, and tackle savory dishes with the possibility of a market tour (€75-105, 92 Rue Nollet, Mo: La Fourche, tel. 06 64 17 93 32, www.lessecretsgourmandsdenoemie.com).

Cook'n with Class gets rave reviews for its convivial cooking and wine and cheese classes with a maximum of six students; tasting courses offered as well (6 Rue Baudelique, Mo: Jules Joffrin or Simplon, tel. 06 31 73 62 77, www.cookn withclass.com).

La Cuisine Paris has a variety of classes in English, reasonable prices, and a beautiful space in central Paris (2- or 3-hour classes-€65-95, 80 Quai de l'Hôtel de Ville, tel. 01 40 51 78 18, www.lacuisineparis.com).

Susan Herrmann Loomis, an acclaimed chef and author, offers cooking courses in Paris or at her home in Normandy. Your travel buddy can skip the class but should come for the meal at a reduced "guest eater" price (www.onrue tatin.com).

If you're looking for a pricey demonstration course, you'll find it at **Le Cordon Bleu** (tel. 01 53 68 22 50, www.lcbparis.com) or **Ritz Escoffier Ecole de Gastronomie** (tel. 01 43 16 30 50, www.ritzparis.com).

Wine Tasting

Olivier Magny and his team of sommeliers teach fun wine-tasting classes at the **O Château** wine school/bar, in the 17th-century residence of Madame de Pompadour, King Louis XV's favorite mistress. Olivier's goal is to "take the snob out of wine." Learn the basics of wine regions, the techniques of tasting, and how to read a label (68 Rue Jean-Jacques Rousseau, Mo: Louvre-Rivoli or Etienne Marcel, tel. 01 44 73 97 80, www.o-chateau.com).

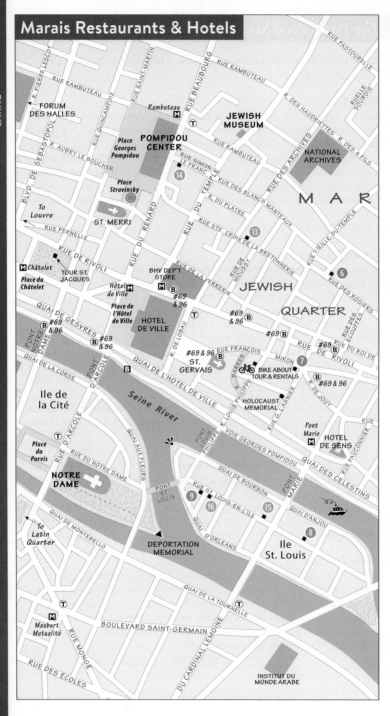

Marais Restaurants & Hotels

RUE PASTOURELLE

RUE PIERRE LESCOT

RUE RAMBUTEAU

R. PIERRE LESCOT

RUE SAINT-MARTIN

RUE BEAUBOURG

RUE RAMBUTEAU

R. DES HAUDRIETTES

RUELLE SOURDIS

R. DES 4 FILS

FORUM
DES HALLES

RUE QUINCAMPOIX

Rambuteau

JEWISH
MUSEUM

R. DES ARCHIVES

NATIONAL
ARCHIVES

BLVD. DE SÉBASTOPOL

R. AUBRY LE BOUCHER

Place
Georges
Pompidou

POMPIDOU
CENTER

RUE RAMBUTEAU

M A R

Place
Stravinsky

RUE SIMON
LE FRANC

14

RUE DES BLANCS MANTEAUX

RUE DU TEMPLE

To
Louvre

RUE PERNELLE

ST. MERRI

R. DU PLÂTRE

RUE STE-CROIX DE LA BRETONNERIE

RUE DE
MOUSSY

13

RUE VIEILLE-DU-TEMPLE

RUE DE RIVOLI

RUE DU RENARD

M Châtelet

TOUR ST.
JACQUES

BHV DEP'T
STORE

RUE DE LA VERRERIE

6

Place du
Châtelet

Hôtel
de Ville

M

#69
& 96

JEWISH

RUE DES ROSIERS

QUAI DE GESVRES

Place de
l'Hôtel
de Ville

T

#69
& 96

B

QUARTER

RUE DES
ÉCOUFFES

B #69
& 96

HOTEL
DE VILLE

B

#69
& 96

#69 B

#69 B

RUE DE RIVOLI

RUE DU ROI DE

B

#69

PONT NOTRE DAME

PONT D'ARCOLE

RUE DE LOBAU

QUAI DE LA CORSE

#69 & 96

RUE FRANÇOIS

MIRON

7

RUE DU ROI DE

B

#69 & 96

QUAI DE L'HÔTEL DE VILLE

ST.
GERVAIS

R. DES BARRES

RUE LOUIS PHILIPPE

BIKE ABOUT
TOUR & RENTALS

B

#69 & 96

R. DE JOUY

Ile de
la Cité

Seine River

HOLOCAUST
MEMORIAL

RUE G. CASNIER

Pont
Marie

RUE

HOTEL
DE SENS

Place
du
Parvis

T

RUE D'ARCOLE

RUE DU NOTRE DAME

QUAI AUX FLEURS

PONT
LOUIS
PHILIPPE

VOIE GEORGES POMPIDOU

M

QUAI DES CÉLESTINS

NOTRE
DAME

QUAI DE BOURBON

PONT
ST.
LOUIS

RUE ST-LOUIS-EN-L'ILE

9

16

15

QUAI D'ANJOU

PONT
MARIE

8

To
Latin
Quarter

QUAI DE MONTEBELLO

QUAI D'ORLÉANS

DEPORTATION
MEMORIAL

Ile
St. Louis

QUAI DE LA TOURNELLE

T

T

Maubert
Mutualité

M

BOULEVARD SAINT-GERMAIN

RUE MONGE

DU CARDINAL LEMOINE

RUE DES ÉCOLES

INSTITUT DU
MONDE ARABE

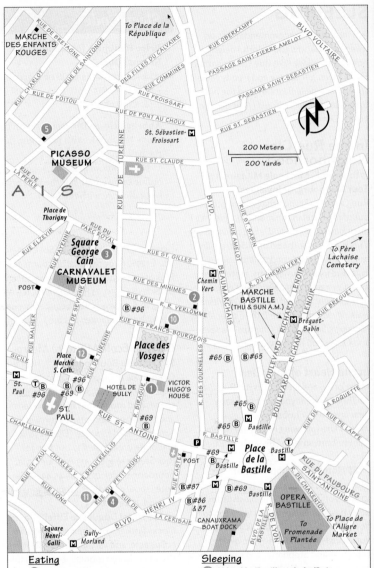

Eating
1 La Place Royale
2 Chez Janou
3 Café des Musées
4 Au Temps des Cerises
5 Breizh Café
6 Chez Marianne
7 Au Bourguignon du Marais
8 L'Orangerie
9 Café Med

Sleeping
10 Hôtel le Pavillon de la Reine
11 Hôtel St. Louis Marais
12 Hôtel Jeanne d'Arc
13 Hôtel de la Bretonnerie
14 Hôtel Beaubourg
15 Hôtel du Jeu de Paume
16 Hôtel Saint-Louis

SLEEPING

I've focused my recommendations on three safe, handy, and colorful neighborhoods: the village-like Rue Cler (near the Eiffel Tower); the artsy and trendy Marais (near Place de la Bastille); and the historic island of Ile St. Louis (next door to Notre-Dame).

In the Rue Cler Neighborhood

(7th arrond., Mo: Ecole Militaire, La Tour Maubourg, or Invalides)

Rue Cler is so French that when I step out of my hotel in the morning, I feel like I must have been a poodle in a previous life. This is a neighborhood of wide, tree-lined boulevards, stately apartment buildings, and lots of Americans. Hotels here are a fair value, considering the elegance of the neighborhood. And you're within walking distance of the Eiffel Tower, Army Museum, Seine River, Champs-Elysées, and Orsay and Rodin museums.

In the Heart of Rue Cler

Many of my readers stay in the Rue Cler neighborhood. If you want to disappear into Paris, choose a hotel elsewhere. The following hotels are within Camembert-smelling distance of Rue Cler.

$$ Hôtel du Champ de Mars*** is a top choice, brilliantly located barely 10 steps off Rue Cler. This plush little hotel has a small-town feel from top to bottom. The adorable rooms are snug but lovingly kept by hands-on owners Françoise and Stéphane, and single rooms can work as tiny doubles. It's popular, so book well ahead (Sb-€150, Db-€170, no air-con, 30 yards off Rue Cler at 7 Rue du Champ de Mars, tel. 01 45 51 52 30, www. hotelduchampdemars.com, reservation@ hotelduchampdemars.com).

$$ Hôtel Beaugency***, a fair value on a quieter street a short block off Rue Cler, has 30 smallish rooms and a lobby

that you can stretch out in (Sb-€109-193, Db-€129-213, occasional discounts for Rick Steves readers—ask when you book, breakfast-€9.50, 21 Rue Duvivier, tel. 01 47 05 01 63, www.hotel-beaugency.com, infos@hotel-beaugency.com).

Close to Ecole Militaire Métro

$$$ Hôtel la Bourdonnais****, near the Champs de Mars park, is upscale and tastefully designed, with comfy public spaces and rooms that blend modern and traditional accents. It's run well with American-style service (Db-€230-350, elaborate breakfast-€17 but free for Rick Steves readers, 113 Avenue de la Bourdonnais, tel. 01 47 05 45 42, www. hotellabourdonnais.fr, labourdonnais@ inwood-hotels.com).

$$$ Hôtel Duquesne Eiffel***, a few blocks farther from the action, is calm, hospitable, and very comfortable. It features handsome rooms (some with terrific Eiffel Tower views) and a welcoming lobby (Db-€249-300, Tb-€279-339, big, hot breakfast-€13 but free for Rick Steves readers, 23 Avenue Duquesne, tel. 01 44 42 09 09, www.hde.fr, contact@hde.fr).

Closer to Rue St. Dominique

$$$ Hôtel de Londres Eiffel*** is my closest listing to the Eiffel Tower and the Champ de Mars park. Here you get immaculate, warmly decorated rooms (several are connecting for families), snazzy public spaces, and a service-oriented staff. Some rooms are pretty small—request a bigger room. It's less convenient to the Métro (10-minute walk), but very handy to buses #69, #80, #87, and #92, and to RER-C: Pont de l'Alma (Sb-€185, small Db-€235, bigger Db-€260, Db with Eiffel Tower view-€380, Tb-€360, 1 Rue Augereau, tel. 01 45 51 63 02, www.hotel-paris-londres-eiffel.com, info@londres-eiffel.com, helpful Cédric and Arnaud).

$ **Hôtel de la Tour Eiffel**** is a solid two-star value on a quiet street near several of my favorite restaurants. The rooms are well-designed, well-kept, and comfortable, but they don't have air-conditioning and some have thin walls. The six sets of connecting rooms are ideal for families (snug Db-€115, bigger Db-€135-155, 17 Rue de l'Exposition, tel. 01 47 05 14 75, www.hotel-toureiffel.com, hte7@wanadoo.fr).

Near La Tour Maubourg Métro

$$$ **Hôtel Muguet***** has had a full face-lift. I thought the hotel was terrific before the renovation—it's still quiet, well-located, and well-run (Db-€150-235—more with view, Tb-€235-275, strict cancellation policy, 11 Rue Chevert, tel. 01 47 05 05 93, www.hotelparismuguet.com, muguet@wanadoo.fr).

In the Marais Neighborhood

Those interested in a more central, diverse, and lively urban locale should make the Marais their Parisian home. Running from the Pompidou Center east to the Bastille (a 15-minute walk), the Marais is jumbled, medieval Paris at its finest. Classy stone mansions sit alongside trendy bars, antique shops, and fashion-conscious boutiques. The streets are an intriguing parade of art-

ists, students, tourists, immigrants, and baguette-munching babies in strollers. The Marais is also known as a hub of the Parisian gay and lesbian scene. This area is *sans* doubt livelier and edgier than the Rue Cler area.

Near Place des Vosges
(3rd and 4th arrond., Mo: Bastille, St-Paul, or Sully-Morland)

$$$ **Hôtel le Pavillon de la Reine*****, 15 steps off the beautiful Place des Vosges, merits its stars with top service and comfort and exquisite attention to detail, from its melt-in-your-couch lobby to its luxurious rooms (Db-€350-1,000, buffet breakfast-€35, free access to spa and fitness room, free loaner bikes and parking, 28 Place des Vosges, tel. 01 40 29 19 19, www.pavillon-de-la-reine.com, contact@pavillon-de-la-reine.com).

$$ **Hôtel St. Louis Marais*****, an intimate and sharp little hotel, lies on a quiet street a few blocks from the river. The handsome rooms come with character, spacious bathrooms, and reasonable rates (Db-€175-230, Tb-€245, Qb-€265, buffet breakfast-€13, 1 Rue Charles V, Mo: Sully-Morland, tel. 01 48 87 87 04, www.saintlouismarais.com, marais@saintlouis-hotels.com).

$ **Hôtel Jeanne d'Arc****, a lovely small hotel with thoughtfully appointed rooms, is ideally located for (and very popular with) connoisseurs of the Marais. It's an exceptional value and worth booking way ahead. Corner rooms are wonderfully

Apartment Rentals

Intrepid travelers are accustomed to using Airbnb and VRBO when it comes to renting a vacation apartment. In Paris, you have many additional options among rental agencies; I've found the following to be the most reliable. Their websites are essential to understanding your choices. Read the rental conditions very carefully.

Paris Perfect has offices in Paris with English-speaking staff who seek the "perfect apartment" for their clients. Many units have Eiffel Tower views, and most have air-conditioning and washers and dryers (discount off regular rates for Rick Steves readers, US toll-free tel. 888-520-2087, www.parisperfect.com).

Adrian Leeds Group offers apartments owned by North Americans and is ideal for travelers looking for all the comforts, conveniences, and amenities of home (tel. 877-880-0265, ext. 701, www.adrianleeds.com).

Home Rental Service offers a big selection of apartments throughout Paris with no agency fees (120 Champs-Elysées, tel. 01 42 25 65 40, www.homerental. fr).

Haven in Paris offers exactly that—well-appointed, stylish havens for travelers looking for a temporary home. Also check out their fun blog, *Hip Paris* (tel. 617/395-4243, www.haveninparis.com).

Paris Home offers two little studios, both located on Rue Amélie in the heart of the Rue Cler area. Each has modern furnishings and laundry facilities. Friendly Slim, the owner, is the best part (no minimum stay, special rates for longer stays, free maid service, airport/train station transfers possible, mobile 06 19 03 17 55, www.parishome2000.com).

Cobblestone Paris Rentals is a small, North American-run outfit offering furnished rentals in central neighborhoods. Apartments come stocked with English-language DVDs about Paris, coffee, tea, cooking spices, basic bathroom amenities, and an English-speaking greeter who will give you the lay of the land (two free river cruises for Rick Steves readers who stay five nights or more, www. cobblestoneparis.com).

Paris for Rent, a San Francisco-based group, has been renting top-end apartments in Paris for more than a decade (US tel. 866-437-2623, www.parisforrent. com).

Cross-Pollinate is a reputable online booking agency representing B&Bs and apartments throughout Paris. Minimum stays vary from one to seven nights (US tel. 800-270-1190, France tel. 09 75 18 11 10, www.cross-pollinate.com).

bright in the City of Light but have twin beds only. Rooms on the street can be noisy until the bars close (Sb-€72-98, Db-€120, larger twin Db-€150, family rooms available, continental breakfast-€8, no air-con, 3 Rue de Jarente, Mo: St-Paul, tel. 01 48 87 62 11, www.hoteljeannedarc. com, information@hoteljeannedarc.com).

Near the Pompidou Center
(4th arrond., Mo: St-Paul, Hôtel de Ville, or Rambuteau)

$$ Hôtel de la Bretonnerie*, three blocks from Hôtel de Ville, makes a fine Marais home. It has a warm, welcoming lobby, helpful staff, and 29 well-appointed, good-value rooms with an antique, open-beam warmth (standard "classic" Db-€180, bigger "charming" Db-€220, Db suite-€250, Tb/Qb-€245, buffet breakfast-€10, no air-con, between Rue Vieille du Temple and Rue des Archives at 22 Rue Ste. Croix de la Bretonnerie, tel. 01 48 87 77 63, www.bretonnerie.com, hotel@bretonnerie.com).

$$ **Hôtel Beaubourg***** is a terrific three-star value on a small street in the shadow of the Pompidou Center. The lounge is inviting, and the 28 plush and traditional rooms are quiet and thoughtfully appointed (standard Db-€135-165, bigger twin or king-size Db-€145-175 and worth the extra cost, Db suite with private patio-€190-230, continental breakfast-€9.50, 11 Rue Simon Le Franc, Mo: Rambuteau, tel. 01 42 74 34 24, www.hotelbeaubourg.com, reservation@hotelbeaubourg.com).

On Ile St. Louis
(4th arrond., Mo: Pont Marie or Sully-Morland)

The peaceful, residential character of this river-wrapped island, with its brilliant location and homemade ice cream, has drawn Americans for decades. There are no budget deals here—all the hotels are three-star or more—though prices are fair considering the level of comfort and killer location.

$$$ **Hôtel du Jeu de Paume******, occupying a 17th-century tennis center, is among the most expensive hotels I list in Paris. When you enter its magnificent lobby, you'll understand why. Greet Scoop, *le chien*, then take a spin in the glass elevator for a half-timbered-treehouse experience. The 30 rooms are carefully designed and tasteful, though not particularly spacious (you're paying for the location and public areas). Most rooms face a small garden; all are pin-drop peaceful (Sb-€195-255, standard Db-€295-360, suite Db-€450-560, apartment for up to 6-€620-900, breakfast-€18, 54 Rue St. Louis-en-l'Ile, tel. 01 43 26 14 18, www.jeudepaumehotel.com, info@jeudepaumehotel.com).

$$ **Hôtel Saint-Louis***** blends character with modern comforts. The well-maintained rooms come with cool stone floors and exposed beams. Rates are reasonable...for the location (Db-€185-225, top-floor Db with micro-balcony-€255, Tb-€295, buffet breakfast-€13, 75 Rue St. Louis-en-l'Ile, tel. 01 46 34 04 80, www.hotelsaintlouis.com, isle@saintlouis-hotels.com).

TRANSPORTATION

Getting Around Paris

Paris is easy to navigate. Your basic choices are Métro (in-city subway), RER (suburban rapid transit tied into the Métro system), public bus, and taxi.

You can buy tickets and passes at Métro stations and at many *tabacs*. Staffed ticket windows in stations are being phased out, so expect some stations to have only machines and an information desk. Machines accept coins, small bills of €20 or less, and chip-and-PIN cards (no American magnetic-stripe or chip-and-signature cards).

Rick's Tip: Buy Métro tickets at a *tabac* shop to avoid long lines *at the Métro station, especially at the end of the month when crowds of locals are buying next month's pass. Just look for the distinctive red Tabac sign.*

Public-Transit Tickets: The Métro, RER, and buses all work on the same tickets. You can make as many transfers as you need on a single ticket when transferring between the Métro and RER system, but transfers between the Métro/RER and the bus system require an additional ticket. A **single ticket** costs €1.80. To save money, buy a *carnet* (kar-nay) of 10 tickets for €14.10. *Carnets* can be shared among travelers. Kids under four ride free.

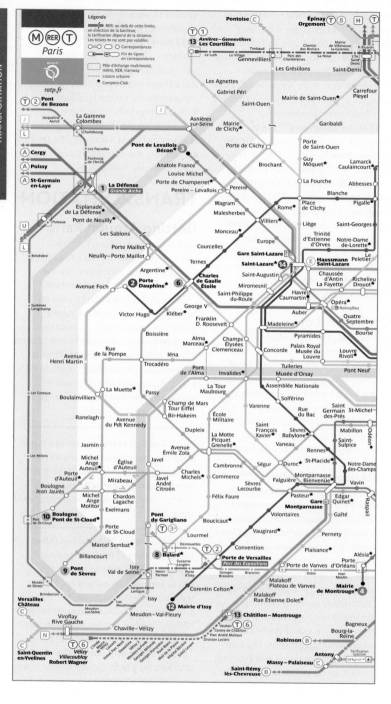

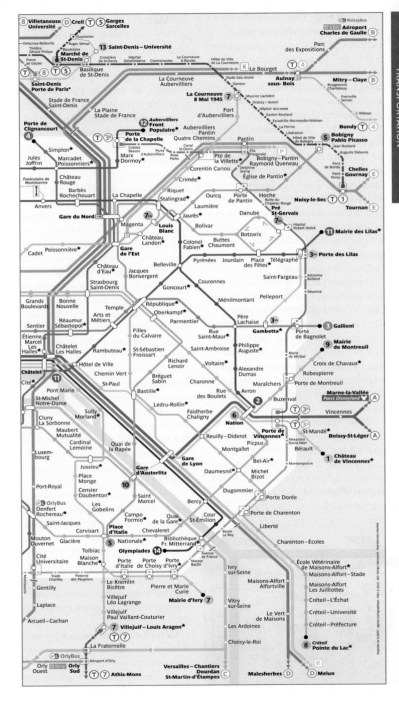

Passe Navigo: This chip-embedded card costs a one-time €5 fee (plus another €5 for the required photo; photo booths are in major Métro stations). The weekly unlimited pass (Navigo Semaine) costs €21.25 (plus the fees listed above) and covers all forms of transit from Monday to Sunday (expiring on Sunday, even if you buy it on, say, a Thursday). The pass is good for all zones in the Paris region, which means that you can travel anywhere within the city center, out to Versailles, and to Charles de Gaulle and Orly airports. To use the Navigo, touch the card to the purple pad, wait for the green validation light and the "ding," and you're on your way. You can buy your Passe Navigo at any Métro station in Paris (for more details, visit www.ratp.fr).

Navigo or *Carnet*? The Navigo covers a far greater area than *carnet* tickets, but cannot be shared, and is most worthwhile for visitors who use it for regional trips, stay a full week, and start their trip early in the week. Two 10-packs of *carnets*—enough for most travelers staying a week—cost €28.20, are shareable, don't expire, but are only valid in the center of Paris.

Other Passes: A handy one-day bus/Métro pass (called **Mobilis**) is available for €7. If you are under 26 and in Paris on a Saturday or Sunday, you can buy an unlimited daily transit pass called **Ticket Jeunes Week-end** for the unbeatable price of €3.85.

By Métro

In Paris, you're never more than a 10-minute walk from a Métro station. Europe's best subway system allows you to hop from sight to sight quickly and cheaply (runs Sun-Thu 5:30-24:30, Fri-Sat 5:30-2:00 in the morning, www.ratp.fr).

Using the Métro System: To get to your destination, determine the closest "Mo" stop and which line or lines will get you there. The lines are color-coded and numbered, and you can tell their direction by the end-of-the-line stops. For example, the La Défense/Château de Vincennes line, also known as line 1 (yellow), runs between La Défense, on its west end, and Vincennes on its east end. Once in the Métro station, you'll see the color-coded line numbers and/or blue-and-white signs directing you to the train going in your direction (e.g., *direction: La Défense*). Insert your ticket in the automatic turnstile, reclaim your ticket, pass through, and keep it until you exit the system (some stations require you to pass your ticket through a turnstile to exit). Be warned that fare inspectors regularly check for cheaters, accept absolutely no excuses, and have portable credit-card machines to fine you on the spot: Keep that ticket or pay a minimum fine of €45.

Transfers are free and can be made wherever lines cross, provided you do so within 1.5 hours.

When you reach your destination, look for the blue-and-white *sortie* signs pointing you to the exit. Before leaving the station, check the helpful *plan du quartier* (map of the neighborhood) to get your bearings.

After you finish the entire ride and exit onto the street, toss or tear your used ticket so you don't confuse it with unused tickets.

Métro Resources: Métro maps are free at Métro stations. Several good online tools can also help you navigate the public-transit system. The website Metro.paris provides an interactive map of Paris'

Métro ticket machines

Transit Basics

- The same tickets are good on the Métro, RER trains (within the city), and city buses.
- Save money by buying a *carnet* of 10 discounted tickets or a Passe Navigo.
- Beware of pickpockets, and don't buy tickets from men roaming the stations.
- Find your train by its end-of-the-line stop.
- Insert your ticket into the turnstile, retrieve it, and keep it until the end of your journey.
- Safeguard your belongings; avoid standing near the train doors with luggage.
- At a stop, if the door doesn't open automatically, either push a square button (green or black) or lift a metal latch.
- Transfers (*correspondances*) between the Métro and RER system are free (but not between Métro/RER and bus).
- Trash or tear used tickets after you complete your ride and leave the station (not before) to avoid confusing them with fresh ones.

sights and Métro lines (www.metro.paris). The free RATP mobile app (in English, download at www.ratp.fr) and the more user-friendly Kemtro app (www.kemtro.com) can estimate Métro travel times, help you locate the best station exit, and tell you when the next bus will arrive, among other things.

By RER

The RER (Réseau Express Régionale; air-ay-air) is the suburban arm of the Métro, serving outlying destinations such as Versailles and the airports. These routes are identified by the letters A, B, C, and so on.

Within the city center, the RER works like the Métro and can be speedier if it serves your destination directly, because it makes fewer stops. Métro tickets are good on the RER when traveling in the city center. You can transfer between the Métro and RER systems with the same ticket. But to travel outside the city (to Versailles or the airport, for example), you'll need a separate, more expensive ticket (unless you're using a Passe Navigo). Unlike the Métro, not every train stops at every station along the way; check the sign or screen over the platform to see if your destination is listed as a stop ("*toutes les gares*" means it makes all stops along the way), or confirm with a local before you board. For RER trains, you may need to insert your ticket in a turnstile to exit the system.

By City Bus

Paris' excellent bus system is worth figuring out (www.ratp.fr). Bus stops are everywhere, and every stop comes with all the information you need: a good city bus map, route maps showing exactly where each bus goes that uses the stop, a frequency chart and schedule, a *plan du quartier* map of the immediate neighborhood, and a *soirées* map explaining night service, if available. Bus-system maps are also available in any Métro station (and in the *Paris Pratique* map book sold at newsstands).

Using the Bus System: Buses use the same tickets and passes as the Métro and RER. One ticket buys you a bus ride anywhere in central Paris within the freeway ring road (*le périphérique*). Use your Métro ticket or buy one on board for €0.20 more, though note that tickets bought on board are *sans correspondance*, which means you can't use them to transfer to another bus.

Paris bus stops are getting a face-lift, and they are looking sharp; at some locations, you can charge your phone while you wait. Board your bus through the front door. Validate your ticket in the machine and reclaim it. With a Passe Navigo, scan it on the purple touchpad. Keep track of which stop is coming up next by following the on-board diagram or listening to recorded announcements. When you're ready to get off, push the red button to signal you want a stop, then exit through the central or rear door.

More Bus Tips: *Carnet* ticket holders—but not those buying individual tickets on the bus—can transfer from one bus to another on the same ticket (within 1.5 hours, revalidate ticket on next bus), but you can't do a round-trip or hop on and off on the same line. You can use the same ticket to transfer between buses and tramlines, but you can't transfer between the bus and Métro/RER systems.

By Taxi

Parisian taxis are reasonable, especially for couples and families. Fares and supplements (described in English on the rear windows) are straightforward and tightly regulated.

A taxi can fit three people comfortably. Cabbies are legally required to accept four passengers, though they don't always like it. Beyond three passengers, expect to pay €3 extra per person.

Rates: All Parisian taxis start with €2.60 on the meter and have a minimum charge of €7. A 20-minute ride (e.g., Bastille to the Eiffel Tower) costs about €20. Drivers charge higher rates at rush hour, at night, all day Sunday, for extra passengers, and to the airport. To tip, round up to the next euro (at least €0.50).

The A, B, or C lights on a taxi's rooftop sign correspond to hourly rates, which vary with the time of day and day of the week (for example, the A rate of €32.50/hour applies Mon-Sat 10:00-17:00). Tired travelers need not bother with these mostly subtle differences in fares—if you need a cab, take it.

Scenic Buses for Tourists

These scenic bus routes provide a great, cheap, and convenient introduction to the city.

Bus #69 runs east-west between the Eiffel Tower and Père Lachaise Cemetery by way of Rue Cler, Quai d'Orsay, the Louvre, and the Marais.

Bus #87 links the Marais and Rue Cler areas, but stays mostly on the Left Bank, connecting the Eiffel Tower, St. Sulpice Church, Luxembourg Garden, St. Germain-des-Prés, the Latin Quarter, the Bastille, and Gare de Lyon.

Bus #24 runs east-west along the Seine riverbank from Gare St. Lazare to Madeleine, Place de la Concorde, Orsay Museum, the Louvre, St. Michel, Notre-Dame, and Jardin des Plantes.

Bus #63 is another good east-west route, connecting Trocadéro (Eiffel Tower), Pont de l'Alma, Orsay Museum, St. Sulpice, Luxembourg Garden, Latin Quarter/Panthéon, and Gare de Lyon.

Bus #73 is one of Paris' most scenic lines, starting at the Orsay Museum and running westbound around Place de la Concorde, then up the Champs-Elysées, around the Arc de Triomphe, and down Avenue Charles de Gaulle to the La Défense business district.

How to Catch *un Taxi:* You can try waving down a taxi, but it's often easier to ask someone for the nearest taxi stand ("*Où est une station de taxi?*"; oo ay ewn stah-see-ohn duh tahk-see). Taxi stands are indicated by a circled "T" on good city maps and on many maps in this book. To order a taxi in English, call the reservation line for the G7 cab company (tel. 01 41 27 66 99), or ask your hotelier or waiter to call for you. When you summon a taxi by phone, a €4 surcharge is added to the fare (€7 if you schedule a timed pickup).

To download a taxi app, search for either "Taxi G7" or "Taxis Bleus" (the two major companies, both available in English).

If you need to catch a train or flight early in the morning, book a taxi the day before (especially for weekday departures). Some taxi companies require a €5 reservation fee by credit card for weekday morning rush-hour departures (7:00-10:00).

By Bike

Paris is surprisingly easy by bicycle. The city is flat, and riders have access to more than 370 miles of bike lanes and many of the priority lanes for buses and taxis (be careful on these). You can rent from a bike-rental shop or use the city-operated Vélib' bikes (details later). All bike-rental shops have good route suggestions. I biked along the river from Notre-Dame to the Eiffel Tower in 15 wonderfully scenic minutes. The riverside promenade between the Orsay Museum and Pont de l'Alma is magnificent for biking.

The TIs have a helpful "Paris à Vélo" map, which shows all the dedicated bike paths. Many other versions are available for sale at newsstand kiosks, some bookstores, and department stores.

Rental Bikes: **Bike About Tours** is your best bet for bike rental, with good information and kid-friendly solutions, such as baby seats, tandem attachments, and kid-sized bikes (bike rental—€15/day during office hours, €20/24 hours, includes lock and helmet; daily mid-Feb-Nov 9:00-17:00, closed Dec-mid-Feb; shop/café—called the Yellow Jersey Café—at 17 Rue du Pont Louis Philippe, Mo: Hôtel de Ville, tel. 06 18 80 84 92, www.bikeabouttours.com).

Vélib' Bikes: The city's Vélib' program (from *vélo* + *libre* = "bike freedom" or "free bike") gives residents and foreigners alike access to more than 20,000 bikes at nearly 1,500 stations scattered around the city. While the curbside stations only accept American Express or chip-and-PIN credit cards, any kind of credit card will work if you buy a subscription in advance online at http://en.velib.paris.fr. The subscription process is easy to follow; select the "Short-Term Subscription" to create a PIN, pay, and get an ID number. To pick up a bike, go to any bike rack, enter your ID number and PIN at the machine (all have English instructions), and away you go! Make sure to pick a bike in working order; if a bike has a problem, locals will

Bike tours are fun and informative.

turn the seat backward (€1.70/1 day, €8/7 days, tel. 01 30 79 79 30).

Arriving and Departing

Whether you're aiming to catch a train or plane, budget plenty of time to reach your departure point. Paris is a big, crowded city, and getting across town on time is a goal you'll share with millions of other harried people. Factor in traffic delays and walking time through huge stations and vast terminals.

By Plane

CHARLES DE GAULLE AIRPORT

Paris' main airport (airport code: CDG) has three terminals: T-1, T-2, and T-3. Most flights from the US use T-1 or T-2 (check your ticket). You can travel between terminals on the free CDGVAL automated shuttle train (departs every 5 minutes, 24/7, 30 minutes).

When leaving Paris, make sure you know which terminal you are departing from (if it's T-2, you'll also need to know which hall you're leaving from—they're labeled A through F). For flight info, visit www.adp.fr.

Car-rental offices, TIs, post offices, pharmacies, and ATMs are all well-signed. All terminals have shops, cafés, and bars. T-2 has a **train station,** with RER suburban trains into Paris (described later), as well as longer-distance trains to the rest of France (including high-speed TGV trains).

Getting between Charles de Gaulle and Paris: Buses, airport vans, commuter trains, and taxis link the airport's terminals with central Paris. Total travel time to your hotel should be around 1.5 hours by bus and Métro, one hour by train and Métro, or 50 minutes by taxi.

By RoissyBus: The RoissyBus drops you off on Rue Scribe at the Opéra Métro stop in central Paris (€11, runs 6:00-23:00, 4/hour until 20:45, 3/hour after that, 50 minutes, buy ticket on bus, tel. 3246, www.ratp.fr/en).

Rick's Tip: *When deciding how to get from Charles de Gaulle airport into Paris, keep in mind that* **using buses and taxis requires shorter walks than taking RER trains.** *Also remember that transfers to Métro lines often involve stairs.*

By Air France Bus: Several "Les Cars" Air France Bus routes drop off travelers at different points in and near the city (runs 5:45-23:00, at least 2/hour, tel. 08 92 35 08 20, www.lescarsairfrance.com). **Bus #2** goes to the Etoile stop near the Arc de Triomphe (€17, 45 minutes) and Porte Maillot (with connections to Beauvais Airport, described later). **Bus #4** runs to Gare de Lyon (€17.50, 45 minutes) and the Montparnasse Tower/train station (€17.50, 1 hour). **Bus #3** goes to Orly Airport (€21, 1 hour). You can book your tickets online or pay the driver.

From **Paris to the airport,** catch Air France buses at any of these locations: Etoile/Arc de Triomphe (on Avenue Carnot), Porte Maillot (on Boulevard Gouvion-St-Cyr), Gare Montparnasse (on Rue du Commandant René Mouchotte), or Gare de Lyon (look for *Navette-Aéroport* signs; the stop is on Rue Diderot).

By EasyBus Shuttle: The dirt-cheap EasyBus shuttle drops you off at Palais Royal, across from the Louvre. Catch the bus at terminal 2F, outside door 5. In Paris, catch the bus at 2 Place André Malraux, opposite La Comédie-Française (€2 if you book ahead online, otherwise €10—pay driver with cash or chip-and-PIN card, 2/hour, 45 minutes, www.easybus.co.uk).

By RER Train: Paris' suburban commuter **RER line B** is the fastest public-transit option for getting between the airport and the city center (€11, runs 5:00-24:00, 4/hour, about 35 minutes). It runs directly to well-located RER/Métro stations, including Gare du Nord, Châtelet-Les Halles, St. Michel, and Luxembourg. The RER is handy and cheap, but it can require walking with your luggage through big, crowded stations and may include stairs. For step-by-step instructions on taking the RER into Paris, see www.parisbytrain.com (under "CDG Airport to Paris RER Trains").

To **return to the airport by RER** from central Paris, allow plenty of time to get to your departure gate. Your Métro or bus ticket is not valid on the RER train to the airport (but a Passe Navigo is); buy the ticket from a clerk or the machines (coins only) at the RER-B station. When you catch your train, make sure the sign over the platform shows *Aéroport Roissy-Charles de Gaulle* as a stop served. (The line splits, so not every line B train serves the airport.) If you're not clear, ask another rider, "*Air-o-por sharl duh gaul?*"

By Shuttle Van: Shuttle vans work best for trips from your hotel to the airport, and can be a good value for single travelers and big families (about €32 for one person, €46 for two, €58 for three; have hotelier book at least a day in advance).

By Taxi or Uber: The 50-minute trip costs about €50-65. **Taxis** are less appealing on weekday mornings as traffic into Paris can be bad—in that case, the train is likely a better option. Don't take an unauthorized taxi from cabbies greeting you on arrival. Official taxi stands are well-signed.

For trips from Paris to the airport, have your hotel arrange it. Specify that you want a real taxi (*un taxi normal*), not a more expensive limo service. For weekday morning departures (7:00-10:00), reserve at least a day ahead (€7 reservation fee payable by credit card). For more on taxis

in Paris, see page 202.

Paris **Uber** also offers airport pickup or drop-off (€30-80, lower fares are for shared-ride UberPOP service, www.uber.com).

By Private Car Service: **Paris Webservices** will meet you inside the terminal and wait if you're late (€85 one-way for up to two people, about €165-195 round-trip for up to four people, tel. 01 45 56 91 67 or 09 52 06 02 59, www.pariswebservices.com).

Car Rental: Car-rental desks are well-signed from the arrival halls. Be prepared for a maze of ramps as you drive away from the lot—get directions from the rental clerks when you do the paperwork.

When **returning your car,** allow ample time to reach the drop-off lots. There are separate rental return lots depending on your T-2 departure hall—and imperfect signage can make the return lots especially confusing to navigate.

ORLY AIRPORT

This easy-to-navigate airport (airport code: ORY) feels small, but has all the services you'd expect at a major airport (www.adp.fr). Orly is good for rental-car pickup and drop-off, as it's closer to Paris and far easier to navigate than Charles de Gaulle Airport.

Orly has two terminals: Ouest (west) and Sud (south). You can connect the two terminals with the free Orlyval shuttle train (well signed) or with any of the shuttle buses that also travel into downtown Paris.

Getting between Orly and Paris: Shuttle buses (*navettes*), the RER, taxis, and airport vans connect Paris with either terminal.

By Bus: Bus bays are found in the Sud terminal outside exits L and G, and in the Ouest terminal outside exits C, D, and H.

"**Les Cars**" **Air France bus #1** runs to Gare Montparnasse, Invalides, and Etoile Métro stops. Upon request, drivers will also stop at the Porte d'Orléans Métro stop. Buses depart from Ouest arrival level exit B-C or Sud exit L: Look for signs to

navettes (€12.50 one-way, 4/hour, 40 min-utes to Invalides, buy ticket from driver or book online; see www.lescarsairfrance.com for details).

For the cheapest access to the Marais area, take **tramway line 7** from outside the Sud terminal (direction: Villejuif-Louis Aragon) to the Villejuif Métro station (€3.40—plus one Métro ticket, 4/hour, 35 minutes).

The next two bus options take you to the **RER suburban train's line B,** with access to the Luxembourg Garden area, Notre-Dame Cathedral, handy Métro line 1 at the Châtelet stop, Gare du Nord, and Charles de Gaulle Airport. The **Orlybus** goes directly to the Denfert-Rochereau Métro and RER-B stations (€7.50, 3/hour, 30 minutes). The **Orlyval shuttle train** takes you to the Antony RER station, where you can catch the RER-B (€11, 6/hour, 40 minutes, buy ticket before boarding). The Orlyval train leaves from the departure level at both terminals. Once at the RER-B station, take the train in direction Mitry-Claye or Aéroport Charles de Gaulle to reach central Paris stops.

For access to **RER line C,** take the bus marked *Pont de Rungis.* From the Pont de Rungis station, you can catch the RER-C to Gare d'Austerlitz, St. Michel/Notre-Dame, Musée d'Orsay, Invalides, and Pont de l'Alma (€7.50, 4/hour, 35 minutes).

By Taxi: Taxis are outside the Ouest terminal exit B, and to the far right as you leave the Sud terminal at exit M. Allow 30 minutes for a taxi ride into central Paris (about €30-40).

BEAUVAIS AIRPORT

Budget airlines such as Ryanair use this small airport, offering cheap airfares but leaving you 50 miles north of Paris. Still, this airport has direct buses to Paris and is handy for travelers heading to Normandy or Belgium (car rental available). The airport is basic, waiting areas are crowded, and services are sparse (airport code: BVA, airport tel. 08 92 68 20 66, www.aeroportbeauvais.com).

Getting Between Beauvais and Paris: You can take a bus (1.5 hours), train (at least 2 hours), or taxi (1.5 hours).

By Bus: Buses depart from the airport when they're full (about 20 minutes after flights arrive) and take 1.5 hours to reach Paris. Buy your ticket (€17 one-way, €16 online) at the little kiosk to the right as you exit the airport. Buses arrive at Porte Maillot on the west edge of Paris (on Métro line 1 and RER-C).

Buses heading to Beauvais Airport leave from Porte Maillot about 3.5 hours before scheduled flight departures. Catch the bus in the parking lot on Boulevard Pershing next to the Hyatt Regency. Arrive with enough time to purchase your bus ticket before boarding or buy online at http://tickets.aeroportbeauvais.com.

By Train: Trains connect Beauvais' city center and Paris' Gare du Nord (20/day, 1.5 hours). To reach Beauvais' train station, take the Beauvais *navette* shuttle bus (€5, 6/day, 30 minutes) or local bus #12 (12/day, 30 minutes).

By Taxi: Taxis run from Beauvais Airport to Beauvais' train station or city center (€15-20), or to central Paris (allow €150 and 1.5 hours).

By Train

Paris is Europe's rail hub, with six major stations and one minor one:
- Gare du Nord (northbound trains)
- Gare Montparnasse (west- and south-west-bound trains)
- Gare de Lyon (southeast-bound trains)
- Gare de l'Est (eastbound trains)
- Gare St. Lazare (northwest-bound trains)
- Gare d'Austerlitz (southwest-bound trains)
- Gare de Bercy (smaller station with non-TGV southbound trains)

The main train stations have free Wi-Fi, banks or currency exchanges, ATMs, train information desks, cafés, newsstands, and clever pickpockets (pay attention in ticket lines—keep your bag firmly gripped

Eurostar Routes

ENGLAND Amsterdam.

London

Ebbsfleet

Ashford

North Sea

NETH.

Calais-Fréthun

Lille-Europe

Brussels

BELG.

English Channel

FRANCE

Paris

Not to Scale

- - - - Eurostar
.... Channel Tunnel
.... Other Rail

GARE MONTPARNASSE

This big, modern station covers three floors, serves lower Normandy and Brittany, and has TGV service to the Loire Valley and southwestern France, as well as suburban service to Chartres.

From Gare Montparnasse to: Chartres (14/day, 1 hour), **Amboise** (8/day in 1.5 hours with change in St-Pierre-des-Corps, requires TGV reservation; non-TGV trains leave from Gare d'Austerlitz), **Pontorson/Mont St-Michel** (5/day, 5.5 hours, via Rennes or Caen), and **Sarlat** (4/day, 6-6.5 hours, change in Libourne or Bordeaux).

GARE DE LYON

This huge, bewildering station offers TGV and regular service to southeastern France, Italy, Switzerland, and other international destinations. **"Les Cars" Air France** buses to Gare Montparnasse (easy transfer to Orly Airport) and direct to Charles de Gaulle Airport stop outside the station's main entrance. They are signed *Navette-Aéroport*.

From Gare de Lyon to: Beaune (roughly hourly at rush hour but few midday, 2.5 hours, most require change in Dijon; direct trains from Paris' Bercy station take an hour longer), **Chamonix** (7/day, 5.5-7 hours, some change in Switzerland), **Avignon** (10/day direct, 2.5 hours to Avignon TGV Station, 5/day in 3.5 hours to Avignon Centre-Ville Station, more connections with change—3-4 hours), **Arles** (11/day, 2 direct TGVs—4 hours, 9 with change in Avignon—5 hours), **Nice** (hourly, 6 hours, may require change, 11.5-hour night train possible out of Gare d'Austerlitz), and **Carcassonne** (8/day, 7-8 hours, 1 change, night trains leave from Gare d'Austerlitz).

GARE DE L'EST

This two-floor station (with underground Métro) serves northeastern France and international destinations east of Paris.

From Gare de l'Est to: Colmar (12/day with TGV, 3.5 hours, change in

---

in front of you). You'll find TIs at Gare du Nord and Gare de Lyon. Because of security concerns, not all have baggage checks. Any train station has schedule information, can make reservations, and can sell tickets for any destination.

Each station offers two types of rail service: long distance to other cities, called **Grandes Lignes** (major lines); and suburban service to nearby areas, called **Banlieue, Transilien, or RER.** When arriving by Métro, follow signs for *Grandes Lignes-SNCF* to find the main tracks. Métro and RER trains, as well as buses and taxis, are well-marked at every station.

For clear communication at ticket/info windows, it helps to write down the ticket you want. For instance: "28/05 Paris-Nord→Lyon dep. 18:30." All stations have helpful information booths (*accueil*); the bigger stations have roving helpers, usually wearing red or blue vests.

GARE DU NORD

The granddaddy of Paris' train stations serves cities in northern France and international destinations north of Paris, including Copenhagen, Amsterdam, and London via the Eurostar (for more on the Eurostar, see www.ricksteves.com/eurostar).

From Gare du Nord to: Charles de Gaulle Airport (via RER-B, 4/hour, 35 minutes, track 41-44).

Strasbourg) and **Reims** Centre Station (12/day with TGV, 50 minutes).

GARE ST. LAZARE

This compact station serves upper Normandy, including Rouen and Giverny.

From Gare St. Lazare to: Giverny (train to Vernon, 8/day Mon-Sat, 6/day Sun, 45 minutes), **Honfleur** (13/day, 2-3.5 hours, via Lisieux, Deauville, or Le Havre, then bus), **Bayeux** (9/day, 2.5 hours, some change in Caen), and **Pontorson/Mont St-Michel** (2/day, 4-5.5 hours, via Caen; more trains from Gare Montparnasse).

GARE D'AUSTERLITZ

This small station currently provides non-TGV service to the Loire Valley, southwestern France, and Spain.

From Gare d'Austerlitz to: Versailles (via RER-C, 4/hour, 35 minutes), **Amboise** (3/day direct in 2 hours, 5/day with transfer in Blois or Les Aubrais-Orléans; faster TGV connection from Gare Montparnasse), **Sarlat** (1/day, 6.5 hours, requires change to bus in Souillac, 3 more/day via Gare Montparnasse), and **Carcassonne** (1 direct night train, 7.5 hours, plus a decent night train via Toulouse, better day trains from Gare de Lyon).

GARE DE BERCY

This smaller station mostly handles southbound non-TGV trains, but some TGV trains do stop here in peak season (Mo: Bercy).

By Bus

The main bus station, Gare Routière du Paris-Gallieni, is in the suburb of Bagnolet (28 Avenue du Général de Gaulle, Mo: Gallieni). Buses provide cheaper—if less comfortable and more time-consuming—transportation to major European cities. The bus is also the cheapest way to cross the English Channel; book at least two days in advance for the best fares. Eurolines' buses depart from here (tel. 08 92 89 90 91, www.eurolines.com). Look on their website for offices in central Paris.

Ouibus also offers cheap, Wi-Fi-equipped bus service with an English-speaking driver from Paris to London (6/day, 8.25 hours), Amsterdam (7/day, 6.5 hours), Cologne (3/day, 7.75 hours), and other cities, including many in France (toll tel. 08 92 68 00 68 inside France, www.ouibus.com).

By Car

A car is nothing but a headache in Paris: Park it and use public transportation. Street parking is generally free at night (19:00-9:00) and all day Sunday. To pay for streetside parking, you must go to a *tabac* and buy a parking card (*une carte de stationnement*), sold in €15 and €45 denominations (figure €2-3.60/hour in central Paris). Insert the card into the meter (chip-side in) and punch the desired amount of time, then take the receipt and display it in your windshield. Meters limit street parking to a maximum of two hours.

Underground garages are plentiful. You'll find them under Ecole Militaire, St. Sulpice Church, Les Invalides, the Bastille, and the Panthéon; all charge about €30-40/day (€60/3 days, €10/day more after that, for locations see www.vincipark. com). Some hotels offer parking for less—ask your hotelier.

For a longer stay, park for less at an airport (about €10/day) and take public transport or a taxi into the city. Orly is closer and easier for drivers to navigate than Charles de Gaulle.

NEAR PARIS

Day-trippers from Paris have it easy. Although there are many sights to choose from, one sight clearly stands crown and shoulders above the rest. Visit Versailles.

The palace at Versailles is fit for a king and queen. From its royally furnished residence to its grand canal, vast gardens, and rustic refuge, Versailles exemplifies the power of the *ancien régime,* and the excesses that led to its downfall. You'll come away with a sense of having seen the wheels of history turning. *Vive la France!*

Versailles

Every king's dream, Versailles (vehr-"sigh") was the residence of French monarchs and the cultural heartbeat of Europe for about 100 years—until the Revolution of 1789 changed all that.

Versailles offers three ▲▲▲ blockbuster sights: The main attraction is the palace itself, the **Château,** where you'll walk through dozens of lavish, chandeliered rooms once inhabited by the Sun King Louis XIV and his successors. Next come the expansive **Gardens,** a landscaped wonderland dotted with statues and fountains. The pastoral **Trianon Palaces and Domaine de Marie-Antoinette,** designed for frolicking blue bloods and featuring several small palaces, are perfect for getting away from the mobs at the Château.

Getting There

To reach Versailles, 10 miles west of Paris, take the **RER-C train** "Versailles Château Rive Gauche" (abbreviated "Versailles Chât" or "Versailles RG") from any of these Paris RER stops: Gare d'Austerlitz, St. Michel, Musée d'Orsay, Invalides, Pont de l'Alma, or Champ de Mars (€7.10 round-trip, 4/hour). You can also buy train tickets at any Métro ticket window in Paris (includes connection from that Métro stop to the RER).

To reach the Château from the Versailles train station, follow the flow: Turn

The Neptune fountain at Versailles

Versailles

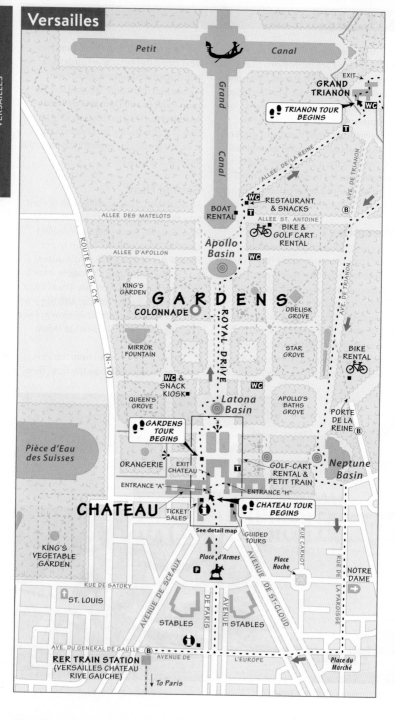

Petit **Grand** *Canal*

Grand Canal

EXIT

GRAND TRIANON

WC

🚶 *TRIANON TOUR BEGINS*

ALLÉE DE LA REINE

AVE. DE TRIANON

WC RESTAURANT & SNACKS

T

BOAT RENTAL

ALLÉE DES MATELOTS

ALLÉE ST. ANTOINE

🚴 BIKE & GOLF CART RENTAL

Apollo Basin

ALLÉE D'APOLLON

WC

AVE. DE TRIANON

KING'S GARDEN

G A R D E N S

COLONNADE

OBELISK GROVE

ROUTE DE ST. CYR

(N-10)

ROYAL DRIVE

MIRROR FOUNTAIN

STAR GROVE

BIKE RENTAL 🚴

WC & SNACK KIOSK

WC

QUEEN'S GROVE

Latona Basin

APOLLO'S BATHS GROVE

PORTE DE LA REINE **B**

Pièce d'Eau des Suisses

🚶 *GARDENS TOUR BEGINS*

Neptune Basin

ORANGERIE

EXIT CHATEAU

T

GOLF-CART RENTAL & PETIT TRAIN

ENTRANCE "A"

ENTRANCE "H"

CHATEAU

TICKET SALES

ℹ

🚶 *CHATEAU TOUR BEGINS*

See detail map

GUIDED TOURS

KING'S VEGETABLE GARDEN

Place d'Armes

Place Hoche

RUE CARNOT

RUE DE LA PAROISSE

NOTRE DAME

P

RUE DE SATORY

ST. LOUIS

AVENUE DE SCEAUX

AVENUE DE PARIS

DE PARIS

AVENUE

AVENUE DE ST-CLOUD

STABLES

STABLES

ℹ

AVE. DU GENERAL DE GAULLE **B**

RER TRAIN STATION (VERSAILLES CHATEAU RIVE GAUCHE)

AVENUE DE

L'EUROPE

Place du Marché

↓ *To Paris*

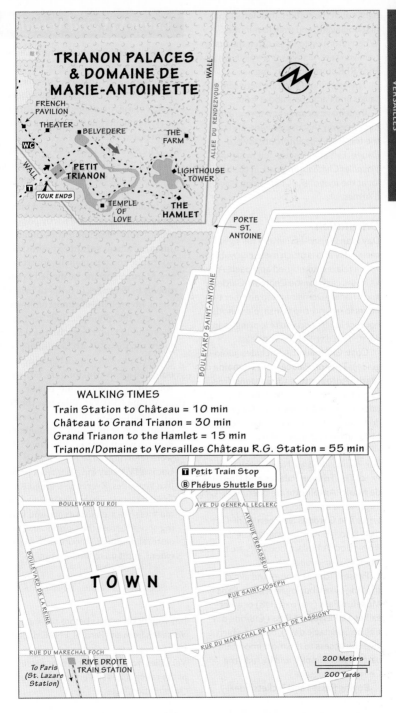

TRIANON PALACES & DOMAINE DE MARIE-ANTOINETTE

FRENCH PAVILION

THEATER

BELVEDERE

THE FARM

WC

PETIT TRIANON

LIGHTHOUSE TOWER

TOUR ENDS

TEMPLE OF LOVE

THE HAMLET

WALL

ALLÉE DU RENDEZVOUS

PORTE ST. ANTOINE

BOULEVARD SAINT-ANTOINE

WALKING TIMES

Train Station to Château = 10 min

Château to Grand Trianon = 30 min

Grand Trianon to the Hamlet = 15 min

Trianon/Domaine to Versailles Château R.G. Station = 55 min

T Petit Train Stop

B Phébus Shuttle Bus

BOULEVARD DU ROI

AVE. DU GENERAL LECLERC

AVENUE DE BASSEUX

BOULEVARD DE LA REINE

T O W N

RUE SAINT-JOSEPH

RUE DU MARÉCHAL DE LATTRE DE TASSIGNY

RUE DU MARECHAL FOCH

To Paris (St. Lazare Station)

RIVE DROITE TRAIN STATION

200 Meters

200 Yards

right out of the station, then left at the first boulevard, and walk 10 minutes. When returning to Paris, catch the first train you see: All trains serve all downtown Paris RER stops on the C line.

The 30-minute **taxi** ride between Versailles and Paris costs about €60.

If you have a **car,** get on the *périphérique* freeway that circles Paris, and take the toll-free A-13 autoroute toward Rouen. Exit at Versailles, follow signs to *Versailles Château*, and park in the big pay lot at the foot of the Château on Place d'Armes.

Orientation

Day Plan: Versailles merits a full sightseeing day and is much more enjoyable with a relaxed, unhurried approach. Allow 1.5 hours each for the Château, Gardens, and Trianon/Domaine. Add another two hours for round-trip transit, plus another hour for lunch, and you're looking at an eight-hour day—at the very least.

Cost: Château-€15 (includes audioguide); **Trianon Palaces and Domaine de Marie-Antoinette**-€10; **Gardens**-free, except on Spectacle days, when the fountains are on and admission is €9 (weekends April-Oct plus many Tue; see "Spectacles in the Gardens," later).

Hours: The **Château** is open April-Oct Tue-Sun 9:00-18:30, Nov-March until 17:30. The **Trianon Palaces and Domaine de Marie-Antoinette** are open April-Oct Tue-Sun 12:00-18:30, Nov-March until 17:30. The **Gardens** are open April-Oct daily 8:00-20:30; Nov-March Tue-Sun 8:00-18:00. All palace buildings are closed Monday year-round.

Passes: To save money and avoid the long ticket-buying line, buy a **Paris Museum Pass** (see page 128) or a **Versailles Le Passeport Pass** (€18/one day, €25 on Spectacle days), both of which give you access to the most important parts of the complex and include the Château audioguide.

Buying Passes and Tickets: Ideally, buy your ticket or pass before arriving at Versailles from any Paris TI, FNAC department store, or www.chateauversailles.fr. In Versailles, you can buy tickets or passes at the rarely crowded Versailles TI (see "Information," later).

Louis XIV and Versailles

Versailles is the architectural embodiment of a time when society was divided into rulers and the ruled. To some it's the pinnacle of civilization; to others, it's a sign of a civilization in decay. Either way, it remains one of Europe's most impressive sights.

The Sun King Louis XIV (r. 1643-1715) created Versailles, spending freely from the public treasury to turn his dad's hunting lodge into a palace fit for the gods (among whom he counted himself). His reasons were partly political—at Versailles, Louis consolidated his government's scattered ministries so that he could personally control policy. More important, he invited France's nobles to Versailles in order to control them. Living a life of almost enforced idleness, the "domesticated" aristocracy couldn't interfere with the way Louis ran things. With 18 million people united under one king, a booming economy, and a powerful military, France was Europe's number-one power.

Around 1700, Versailles was the cultural heartbeat of Europe, and French culture was at its zenith. Throughout Europe, when you said "the king," you were referring to the French king—Louis XIV. Every king wanted a palace like Versailles. Everyone learned French. French taste in clothes, hairstyles, table manners, theater, music, art, and kissing spread across the Continent. That cultural dominance continued, to some extent, right up to modern times.

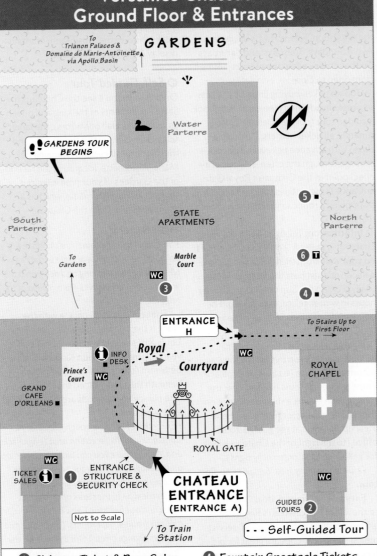

Versailles Château— Ground Floor & Entrances

GARDENS

To Trianon Palaces & Domaine de Marie-Antoinette via Apollo Basin

Water Parterre

GARDENS TOUR BEGINS

South Parterre

STATE APARTMENTS

North Parterre

To Gardens

Marble Court

WC

ENTRANCE H

To Stairs Up to First Floor

Royal Courtyard

INFO DESK

Prince's Court

WC

WC

ROYAL CHAPEL

GRAND CAFE D'ORLEANS

ROYAL GATE

ROYAL GATE

TICKET SALES

WC

ENTRANCE STRUCTURE & SECURITY CHECK

CHATEAU ENTRANCE (ENTRANCE A)

WC

GUIDED TOURS

Not to Scale

To Train Station

- - - Self-Guided Tour

1 Château Ticket & Pass Sales
2 Guided-Tour Reservations
3 Exit from State Apartments
4 Fountain Spectacle Tickets
5 Golf-Cart Rental
6 Petit Train (Tram)

Crowd-Beating Tips: Versailles is packed May-Sept 10:00-13:00, so come early or late. Consider seeing the Gardens during midmorning and the Château in the afternoon, when crowds die down. Avoid Sundays, Tuesdays, and Saturdays (in that order), when the place is jammed from open to close.

To skip ticket-buying lines, buy tickets or passes in advance (see earlier), or book a guided tour (covered below). Unfortunately, all ticket holders—including those with advance tickets and passes—must go through the often-slow security checkpoint at the Château's Royal Gate entrance (longest lines 10:00-12:00). Only by booking a tour can you skip the security line.

Information: Tel. 01 30 83 78 00, www.chateauversailles.fr. You'll pass the city TI on your walk from the RER Station to the palace—it's just past the Pullman Hôtel (daily 9:00-19:00, Sun until 18:00, shorter hours in winter, tel. 01 39 24 88 88). The on-site information office is to the left of the Château.

Tours: Taking the 1.5-hour English **guided tour** lets you bypass the long security check line (€22 includes palace entry; ignore the tours hawked near the train station). Book a tour in advance on the palace website, or reserve immediately upon arrival at the guided-tours office (to the right of the Château—look for yellow *Visites Conferences* signs).

🎧 Download my free Versailles **audio tour.**

Eating: The Grand Café d'Orléans, to the left of the Château's Royal Gate entrance, offers good-value self-service meals; the sandwiches are great for picnicking in the Gardens. In the Gardens, near the Latona Fountain and clustered at the Grand Canal, you'll find several cafés and snack stands with fair prices.

Spectacles in the Gardens: The fountains at Versailles come alive at selected times; check the website for current hours and prices. **Les Grandes Eaux Musicales** has 55 fountains gushing to classical music (April-Oct Sat-Sun, plus mid-May-June Tue). On some summer weekends, **Les Grandes Eaux Nocturnes** adds a fireworks show to the music-and-fountains display (mid-June-mid-Sept).

⊙ Self-Guided Tour

On this tour, you'll see the Château (the State Apartments of the king and queen as well as the Hall of Mirrors), the landscaped Gardens in the "backyard," and the Trianon Palaces and Domaine de Marie-Antoinette, located at the far end of the Gardens. If your time is limited, skip the Trianon/Domaine, which is a 30-minute hike from the Château.

THE CHATEAU

• *Stand in the huge courtyard and face the palace. The golden Royal Gate in the center—nearly 260 feet long and decorated with 100,000 gold leaves—is a replica of the original.*

The section of the palace with the clock is the original château, where little Louis XIV spent his happiest boyhood years. Naturally, the Sun King's private bedroom (the three arched windows beneath the clock) faced the rising sun. The palace and grounds are laid out on an east-west axis.

• *Enter the Château through Entrance A. Continue into the reception area (bag check and WCs), where you can pick up a free map and audioguide. Follow the crowds across the courtyard to Entrance H.*

On the way to the stairs up to the first floor (and our first stop), you'll pass through a dozen ground-floor rooms. (The route and displays change often.) Once you climb the stairs, you reach a palatial golden-brown room, with a doorway that overlooks the...

Royal Chapel: Dut-dutta-dah! Every morning at 10:00, the organist and musicians struck up the music, these big golden doors opened, and Louis XIV and his family stepped onto the balcony to attend Mass. While Louis looked down

Louis XIV attended Mass in Versailles' Royal Chapel.

on the golden altar, the lowly nobles on the ground floor knelt with their backs to the altar and looked up—worshipping Louis worshipping God.

• *Enter the next room, with a colorful painting on the ceiling.*

Hercules Drawing Room: Pleasure ruled. The main suppers, balls, and receptions were held in this room. Picture elegant partygoers in fine silks, wigs, rouge, lipstick, and fake moles (and that's just the men) as they danced to the strains of a string quartet.

• *From here on, it's a one-way tour—getting lost is not allowed.*

The King's Wing: The names of the rooms generally come from the paintings on the ceilings. For instance, the Venus room was the royal make-out space, where couples would cavort beneath the goddess of love, floating on the ceiling. In the **Diana Room,** Louis and his men played pool on a table that stood in the center of the room, while ladies sat surrounding them on Persian-carpet cushions, and music wafted in from next door.

Also known as the Guard Room (as it was the room for Louis' Swiss bodyguards), the red **Mars Room** is decorated with a military flair. The **Mercury Room** may have served as Louis' official (not actual) bedroom, where the Sun King would ritually rise each morning to warm his subjects.

The **Apollo Room** was the grand throne room. Louis held court from a 10-foot-tall, silver-and-gold, canopied throne on a raised platform placed in the center of the room. Even when the king was away, passing courtiers had to bow to the empty throne.

The final room of the King's Wing is the **War Room,** depicting Louis' victories—in marble, gilding, stucco, and paint.

• *Next you'll visit the magnificent...*

Hall of Mirrors: No one had ever seen anything like this hall when it was opened. Mirrors were still a great luxury at the time, and the number and size of these monsters were astounding. The hall is nearly 250 feet long. There are 17 arched mirrors, matched by 17 windows letting in that breathtaking view of the Gardens.

In another age altogether, this is where Germany and the Allies signed the Treaty of Versailles, ending World War I (and, some say, starting World War II).

• *Next up: the queen's half of the palace.*

The vast painted ceiling of the Hercules Drawing Room

A *Hall of Mirrors*

B *A royal bedchamber*

C *Louis XIV, the Sun King*

D *Domaine de Marie-Antoinette*

Getting Around the Gardens

On Foot: It's a 45-minute walk from the palace and down the Grand Canal to the far end of Domaine de Marie-Antoinette. Allow more time for stops.

By Bike: You can bike through the gardens, but not inside the grounds of the Trianon/Domaine (about €7/hour or €16/half-day).

By *Petit Train*: The slow-moving tram leaves from behind the Château (north side) and makes a one-way loop, stopping at the Petit and Grand Trianons (entry points to Domaine de Marie-Antoinette), and then the Grand Canal before returning to the Château (€7.50, round-trip only, free under age 11, 4/hour, runs 10:00-18:00, 11:00-17:00 in winter). You can hop on or off the train at stops.

By Golf Cart: A cart makes for a fun drive, though it's not allowed off its circuit or in the Trianon/Domaine. Late fees are steep. To go out to the Hamlet, sightsee quickly, and return within your allotted hour, you'll need to rent a cart at the Grand Canal and put the pedal to the metal (€32/hour, €8/15 minutes after that, 4-person limit per cart, rent down by canal or just behind Château, near *petit train* stop).

By Shuttle Bus: Phébus runs an hourly TRI line shuttle bus between the Versailles Château Rive Gauche train station and the Trianon/Domaine (but doesn't stop at the Château). It works well for the end of your Versailles visit, if you want to go directly from the Trianon/Domaine to the train station (€2 or one Métro ticket, mid-April-Oct only, check schedule for "Ligne TRI" at www.phebus.tm.fr or at small Phébus office across from Versailles Château Rive Gauche train station, near McDonald's).

The Queen's Wing: The King's Wing was mostly ceremonial and used as a series of reception rooms; the Queen's Wing is more intimate.

The **Queen's Bedchamber** was where the queen rendezvoused with her husband. Two queens died here, and this is where 19 princes were born. Louis XIV made a point of sleeping with the queen as often as possible, regardless of whose tiara he tickled earlier in the evening. This room looks just like it did in the days of the last queen, Marie-Antoinette, who substantially redecorated the entire wing. That's her bust over the fireplace, and the double eagle of her native Austria in the corners.

THE GARDENS

Louis XIV was a divine-right ruler. One way he proved it was by controlling nature like a god. These lavish grounds—elaborately planned, pruned, and decorated—showed everyone that Louis was in total command. Louis loved his gardens and, until his last days, presided over their care. He personally led VIPs through them and threw his biggest parties here.

Rick's Tip: *It's fun pedaling around the greatest royal park in all of Europe. A bike-rental station is by the Grand Canal, with kid-size bikes and tandems available.*

TRIANON PALACES AND DOMAINE DE MARIE-ANTOINETTE

Versailles began as an escape from the pressures of kingship. But in a short time, the Château had become as busy as Paris ever was. Louis XIV needed an escape from his escape and built a smaller palace out in the boonies. Delicate, pink, and set amid gardens, the **Grand Trianon** was the perfect summer getaway. Nearby is the fantasy world of palaces, ponds, pavilions, and pleasure gardens called the **Domaine de Marie-Antoinette.**

Provence

This magnificent region is shaped like a giant wedge of quiche. From its sunburned crust, fanning out along the Mediterranean coast, it stretches north along the Rhône Valley. The splendid recipe *provençale* mixes pastel hills, appealing cities, bountiful vineyards, and sweet, hilltop villages.

The Romans were here in force and left many ruins—some of the best anywhere. Over the centuries, they were followed by seven popes, who resided in a formidable palace in Avignon, and artist Vincent van Gogh, whose work celebrates Provence's sunflowers and starry nights.

A tour of Provence villages is best on your own by car. Public transit is good between cities and decent to some towns, but marginal at best to the smaller towns. For those traveling *sans* car, a variety of minivan tours can help fill in the gaps.

PROVENCE IN 2 DAYS

Make Arles or Avignon your sightseeing base—particularly if you have no car. While Francophiles usually pick urban Avignon, Italophiles prefer smaller Arles.

You'll want one day for sightseeing in Arles and Les Baux. Spend most of the day in Arles—try to time your arrival for Wednesday or Saturday, to enjoy the market. Then visit Les Baux in the late afternoon or early evening. On the second day, allow a half-day for Avignon and a half-day for Pont du Gard.

With another day, measure the pulse of rural Provence and spend at least one night in a smaller town, such as Vaison-la-Romaine. Exploring the Côtes du Rhône wine country takes about a half-day, but you may want to linger.

Provence

To Lyon & Burgundy
Ardèche
Grignan
Valréas
To Chamonix & Alps
Ardèches Gorges
Bollène
Nyons
Buis-les-Baronnies
St. Cécile
Vaison-la-Romaine
Rasteau
Sablet
Séguret
Dentelles de Montmirail
Orange
Gigondas
Suzette
Malaucène
Vacqueyras
Beaumes de Venise
Mont Ventoux
Gard
Uzès
Châteauneuf-du-Pape
CÔTES DU RHÔNE
To Gorges du Tarn
PONT DU GARD
Remoulins
Avignon
Isle-sur-la-Sorgue
Joucas
Roussillon
Nîmes
Durance
Gordes
Oppède
Apt
Beaucaire
Tarascon
Cavaillon
Les Baux
St-Rémy
LUBERON
Fontvieille
Alpilles
Lourmarin
Arles
Pertuis
Aigues-Mortes
CAMARGUE
Petit Rhône
Rhône
Saintes-Maries-de-la-Mer
Aix-en-Provence
To Gorges du Verdon
Palette
Martigues
To Nice & Côte d'Azur
Marseille
Aubagne
FRANCE
Paris
Mediterranean Sea
Les Calanques
Cassis
20 Kilometers
100 Miles
20 Miles

PROVENCE AT A GLANCE

Arles

▲▲**Roman Arena** A big amphitheater, once used by gladiators, that hosts summer "bullgames" and occasional bullfights. **Hours:** Daily May-Sept 9:00-19:00, shorter hours off-season. See page 232.

▲▲**St. Trophime Church** Church with exquisite Romanesque entrance. **Hours:** Daily 9:00-12:00 & 14:00-18:30, until 17:00 Oct-March. See page 236.

▲▲**Ancient History Museum** Filled with models and sculptures, taking you back to Arles' Roman days. **Hours:** Wed-Mon 10:00-18:00, closed Tue. See page 240.

▲**Fondation Van Gogh** Small gallery with works by major contemporary artists paying homage to Van Gogh. **Hours:** Generally daily 11:00-19:00, likely closed Mon off-season. See page 238.

Avignon

▲▲**Palace of the Popes** Fourteenth-century Gothic palace built by the popes who made Avignon their home. **Hours:** Daily March-Oct 9:00-19:00, July-Aug until 20:00, Nov-Feb 9:30-17:45. See page 254.

▲**St. Bénezet Bridge** The "Pont d'Avignon" of nursery-rhyme fame, once connecting the pope's territory to France. **Hours:** Daily March-Oct 9:00-19:00, July-Aug until 20:00, Nov-Feb 9:30-17:45. See page 253.

▲**Jardin du Rochers des Doms** View park overlooking the Rhône River Valley and Avignon's famous broken bridge. **Hours:** Daily from 7:30 until dark. See page 253.

Nearby

▲▲▲**Pont du Gard** Part bridge and part aqueduct, a huge stone structure heralding the greatness of Rome. **Hours:** Aqueduct—daily until 24:00; museum—daily May-Sept 9:00-19:00, until 20:00 July-Aug, until 17:00 Oct-April, closed two weeks in Jan. See page 259.

▲▲▲**Les Baux** Rock-top village sitting in the shadow of its ruined medieval citadel. **Hours:** Village always open; castle—daily Easter-June and Sept 9:00-19:15, July-Aug 9:00-20:15, March and Oct 9:30-18:30, Nov-Feb 10:00-17:00. See page 263.

▲▲▲**Côtes du Rhône Wine Road** A drive through picturesque villages and vineyards, unfurling along a scenic wine-tasting route. See page 268.

▲**Vaison-la-Romaine** History-rich town atop a 2,000-year-old Roman site. See page 264.

ARLES

In Roman times, Arles (pronounced "arl") was an important port city. With the first bridge over the Rhône River, it was a key stop on the Roman road from Italy to Spain, the Via Domitia. After reigning as the seat of an important archbishop and a trading center for centuries, the city became a sleepy backwater of little importance in the 1700s. Vincent van Gogh settled here in the late 1800s, but left only a chunk of his ear (now long gone). American bombers destroyed much of Arles in World War II as the townsfolk hid out in its underground Roman galleries. But today Arles thrives again, with its evocative Roman ruins, an eclectic assortment of museums, made-for-ice-cream pedestrian zones, and squares that play hide-and-seek with visitors.

Roman Arena

Workaday Arles is not a wealthy city and, compared to its neighbor Avignon, it feels unpolished and even a little dirty. But to me, that's part of its charm.

Orientation

Though the town is built along the Rhône, it largely ignores the river. Landmarks hide in Arles' medieval tangle of narrow, winding streets. Hotels have good, free city maps, and helpful street-corner signs point you toward sights and hotels.

Tourist Information: The TI is on the ring road Boulevard des Lices, at Esplanade Charles de Gaulle (April-Sept daily 9:00-18:45; Oct-March Mon-Sat 9:00-16:45, Sun 10:00-13:00; tel. 04 90 18 41 20, www.arlestourisme.com).

Sightseeing Pass: A good-value €11 combo-ticket—the **Liberty Passport** (Le Passeport Liberté)—covers any four monuments and the Ancient History Museum (but not the Fondation Van Gogh gallery). Buy the pass at the TI or any included sight. While only the Ancient History Museum is essential, the pass makes the city fun to explore, as you can pop into any sight, even for just a couple of minutes.

Rick's Tip: In Arles, the **ancient monuments**—*Roman Arena, Classical Theater, Cryptoporticos, and St. Trophime Cloisters—* **all have the same hours** *(daily May-Sept 9:00-19:00, April and Oct 9:00-18:00, Nov-March 10:00-17:00).*

Baggage Storage and Bike Rental: Hôtel Régence will store your bags for a small fee (daily, closed in winter, 5 Rue Marius Jouveau). They also rent bikes (reserve ahead for electric bikes, one-way rentals within Provence possible).

Car Rental: Avis is at the train station (tel. 04 90 96 82 42). Downtown you'll find **Europcar** (61 Avenue de Stalingrad, tel. 04 90 93 23 24) and **Hertz** (10 Boulevard Emile Combes, nearer Place Voltaire, tel. 04 90 96 75 23).

Local Guide: Charming **Agnes Barrier** offers tours covering Van Gogh and Roman history (€130/3 hours, mobile 06 11 23 03 73, agnes.barrier@hotmail.fr).

Minivan Excursions: Provence Reservation runs day tours to nearby sights (such as Pont du Gard) from Arles, Avignon, and other cities. While the tours provide introductory commentary, there's no guiding at the actual sights. They use eight-seat, air-conditioned minivans (about €60-80/half-day, €100-120/day). Ask about their cheaper big-bus excursions, or consider hiring a van and driver for your private use (plan on €220/half-day, €490/day, tel. 04 90 14 70 00, www.provence-reservation.com).

Arles City Walk

The joy of Arles is how its compact core mixes ancient sights, Van Gogh memories, and a raw and real contemporary scene that can be delightfully covered on foot. All the dimensions of the city come together in this self-guided walk. While workable in the evening, taking this walk during business hours allows you to pop into the sights and shops that give the city its unique character.

Much of the walk focuses on the story of Van Gogh in Arles. We'll also visit ancient sites, including the Roman Arena, Classical Theater, Cryptoporticos, and the cloisters at St. Trophime Church (all covered by the Liberty Passport), along with some of Arles' most characteristic streets and squares.

At the Café Van Gogh

Arles

<u>Arles Walk</u>
1. The Yellow House (Easel)
2. Starry Night over the Rhône (Easel)
3. Rue de la Cavalerie
4. Old Town
5. Arena (Easel) & Roman Arena
6. Alpilles Mountains View
7. Jardin d'Eté (Easel)
8. Classical Theater
9. Republic Square
10. Cryptoporticos
11. St. Trophime Church
12. Rue de la République
13. Espace Van Gogh (Easel)
14. Fondation Van Gogh
15. Rue du Docteur Fanton
16. Forum Square (Place du Forum) & Café at Night (Easel)

RUE GEORGES GUYNEMER

RUE DES CAPUCINS

RUE ROBESPIERRE

RUE DE LA VERRIERE

RUE CAMARGUE

TRINQUETAILLE

QUAI ST. PIERRE

Rhône

TRINQUETAILLE BRIDGE

PROMENADE

QUAI MARX DORMOY

R. DE LA TOUR DU FABRE

R. DR. FANTON

R. TRUCHET

Ⓑ Envia Bus Stops

Ⓑ

14

15

LIBERTE

RUE A. FRANCE

R. JOUVENE

Ⓑ

QUAI DE LA ROQUETTE

ARLATEN FOLK MUSEUM
(REOPENS IN 2018)

Place Paul Doumier

R. DES PORCELETS

RUE DE LA REPUBLIQUE

RUE GAMBETTA

12

Ⓑ

RUE CROIX ROUGE

RUE DE LA ROQUETTE

RUE DE CHARTROUSE

RUE JEAN GRANAUD

13

ESPACE VAN GOGH

R. FRED. WILSON

To Ancient History Museum

LA ROQUETTE

RUE MOLIERE

Place Genive

RUE RAILLON

RUE FLEURY PRUDHON

RUE MOLIERE

To Nîmes via A-84

BLVD. G CLEMENCEAU

Ⓑ

RUE PARMENTIER

To Ancient History Museum

Ⓑ

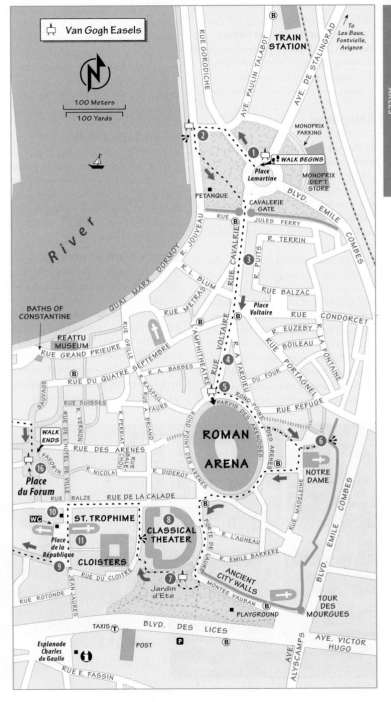

Van Gogh Easels

N

100 Meters
100 Yards

TRAIN
STATION

To
Les Baux,
Fontvielle,
Avignon

RUE GORODICHE

AVE. PAULIN TALABOT

AVE. DE STALINGRAD

MONOPRIX
PARKING

1 WALK BEGINS

*Place
Lamartine*

MONOPRIX
DEP'T
STORE

BLVD. EMILE COMBES

2

PETANQUE

CAVALERIE
GATE

RUE

RUE CAVALERIE

JULES FERRY

R. TERRIN

3 R. PUITS

RUE BALZAC

RUE CONDORCET

*Place
Voltaire*

RUE

R. EUZEBY

R. BOILEAU

LA FONTAINE

RUE VOLTAIRE

R. A. TARDIEU

DU FOUR

RUE PORTAGNEL

River

QUAI MARX DORMOY

R. JOUVEAU

R. L. BLUM

RUE METRAS

L'AMPHITHEATRE

BATHS OF
CONSTANTINE

REATTU
MUSEUM

RUE GRAND PRIEURE

RUE DU QUATRE SEPTEMBRE

R. A. BARBES

RUE GRILLE

4

5

ROND-POINT

PARVIS DES ARENES

RUE REFUGE

SAUVAGE

RUE SUISSES

RUE DE VERNON

R. RASPAIL

R. A. BRIAND

R. PERRIAT

R. FAURE

ROND-POINT DES ARENES

ROMAN

ARENA

RUE DES ARENES

R. ARDALE CHOU

RUE MADELEINE

6

NOTRE
DAME

BLVD. EMILE COMBES

WALK
ENDS

16

*Place
du Forum*

FAVORIN RUE

RUE DE L'HOTEL DE VILLE

R. NICOLAS

R. DIDEROT

RUE

BALZE

RUE DE LA CALADE

WC **10**

11

ST. TROPHIME

8

CLASSICAL
THEATER

R. L'AGNEAU

*Place
de la
République*

CLOISTERS

PORTE DE LAURE

R. EMILE BARRERE

ANCIENT
CITY WALLS

9

RUE JEAN JAURES

RUE DU CLOITRE

7

*Jardin
d'Ete*

MONTEE VAUBAN

TOUR
DES
MOURGUES

RUE ROTONDE

PLAYGROUND

AVE. ALYSCAMPS

TAXIS T

BLVD. DES LICES

AVE. VICTOR
HUGO

*Esplanade
Charles
de Gaulle*

POST

P

RUE E. FASSIN

Rick's Tip: *Before following my self-guided Arles walk,* **visit the Ancient History Museum** *for a helpful overview. Because it's located at the edge of town, drivers should try to stop on their way into Arles.*

Background

The life and artistic times of Dutch artist **Vincent van Gogh** form a big part of Arles' draw, and the city does a fine job of highlighting its Van Gogh connection: Throughout town, about a dozen steel-and-concrete "easels," with photos of the final paintings and the actual view of that painting's subject, provide then-and-now comparisons.

In the dead of winter in 1888, 35-year-old Van Gogh left big-city Paris for Provence, hoping to jump-start his floundering career and social life. He was as inspired as he was lonely. Coming from the gray skies and flat lands of the north, Vincent was bowled over by everything Provençal—the sun, bright colors, rugged landscape, and down-to-earth people. For the next two years he painted furiously, cranking out a masterpiece every few days.

Only a few of the 200-plus paintings that Van Gogh did in the south can be found today in the city that so moved him (you can see a few at the Fondation Van Gogh gallery, which we'll visit on this stroll). But here you can walk the same streets he knew and see the places he painted.

⊙Self-Guided Walk

• *Start at the north gate of the city, just outside the medieval wall in Place Lamartine (100 yards in front of the medieval gate, with the big Monoprix store across the street to the right, just beyond the roundabout). A four-foot-tall metal panel (or "easel") shows Van Gogh's painting.*

❶ THE YELLOW HOUSE EASEL

Vincent arrived in Arles on February 20, 1888, to a foot of snow. He rented a small house on the north side of Place Lamartine. The house was destroyed in 1944 by an errant bridge-seeking bomb, but the four-story building behind it—where you see the brasserie—still stands (find it in the painting). The house had four rooms, including a small studio and the cramped trapezoid-shaped bedroom made

Van Gogh "easels" throughout Arles pair the artist's paintings with actual views.

The Rules of Boules

The game of *boules*—also called *pétanque*—is the horseshoes of France. Invented here in the early 1900s, it's a social yet serious sport, and endlessly entertaining to watch— even more so if you understand the rules.

The game is played with heavy metal balls and a small wooden target ball called a *cochonnet* (piglet). Whoever gets his *boule* closest to the *cochonnet* is awarded points. Teams commonly have specialist players: a *pointeur* and a *tireur*. The pointeur's goal is to lob his balls as close to the target as he can. The tireur's job is to blast away opponents' *boules*.

In teams of two, each player gets three *boules*. The starting team traces a small circle in the dirt (in which players must stand when launching their *boules*), and tosses the *cochonnet* about 30 feet to establish the target. The *boule* must be thrown under-hand, and can be rolled, launched sky-high, or rocketed at its target. The first *pointeur* shoots, then the oppos-ing *pointeur* shoots until his *boule* gets closer. Once the second team lands a *boule* nearer the *cochonnet*, the first team goes again. If the other team's *boule* is near the *cochonnet*, the *tireur* will likely attempt to knock it away.

Once all *boules* have been launched, the tally is taken. The team with a *boule* closest to the *cochon-net* wins the round, and they receive a point for each *boule* closer to the target than their opponents' near-est *boule*. The first team to get to 13 points wins. A regulation *boules* field is 10 feet by 43 feet, but the game is played everywhere—just scratch a throwing circle in the sand, toss the *cochonnet*, and you're off.

famous in paintings. It was painted yel-low inside and out, and Vincent named it…"The Yellow House." In the distance, the painting shows the same bridges you see today.

• *Walk directly to the river. You'll pass a monument in honor of two WWII American pilots killed in action during the liberation of Arles, a post celebrating Arles' many sister cities (left), and a big concrete high school (right).*

At the river, find the easel in the wall where ramps lead down.

❷ STARRY NIGHT OVER THE RHONE EASEL

One night, Vincent set up shop along the river and painted the stars boiling above the city skyline. Vincent looked to the night sky for the divine and was the first to paint outside after dark, adapting his straw hat to hold candles (which must have blown the minds of locals back then). The lone couple in the painting pops up again and again in his work. (This painting is not the *Starry Night* you're thinking of—that one was painted later in another town.)

To his sister Wilhelmina, Vincent wrote, "At present I absolutely want to paint a starry sky. It often seems to me that night is still more richly colored than the day; having hues of the most intense violets, blues, and greens. If only you pay atten-tion to it, you will see that certain stars are lemon yellow, others pink or a green, blue, and forget-me-not brilliance." Vin-cent painted this scene on his last night in Arles.

• *With your back to the river, angle right through the small park of sycamore trees. Continue into town through the park (past a WC) and through the stumpy 14th-century stone towers where the city gates once stood.*

❸ RUE DE LA CAVALERIE

Van Gogh walked into town the same way. Arles' 19th-century red light district was just east of Rue de la Cavalerie, and the far-from-home Dutchman spent many lonely nights in its bars and brothels. The street still has a certain edgy local color. Belly up to the bar in the down-and-dirty café at Hôtel de Paris for a taste. It's a friendly watering hole with fun paintings of football and bull fighting.

• *Continuing uphill, you'll come to an ornately decorated fountain from 1887: two columns with a mosaic celebrating the high culture of Provence (she's the winged woman who obviously loves music and reading).*

Stay left and keep walking uphill to Place Voltaire, a center of this working-class neighborhood (you'll see the local Communist Party headquarters across on the left).

❹ OLD TOWN

You've left the bombed-out part of town and entered the old town, with buildings predating World War II. The stony white arches of the ancient Roman Arena ahead mark your destination. As you hike up Rue Voltaire, notice the shutters, which contribute to Arles' character. The old town is strictly preserved: These traditional shutters come in a variety of styles but cannot be changed.

• *Keep straight up Rue Voltaire, climb to the Roman Arena, and find the Arena easel at the top of the stairs, to the right.*

❺ ARENA EASEL

All summer long, fueled by sun and alcohol, Vincent painted the town. He loved the bullfights in the arena and sketched the colorful surge of the crowds, spending more time studying the people than watching the bullfights (notice how the bull is barely visible). Vincent had little interest in Arles' antiquity—it was people and nature that fascinated him.

• *Now, let's visit the actual...*

ROMAN ARENA (AMPHITHEATRE)

This well-preserved arena is worth ▲▲ and is still in use today. Nearly 2,000 years ago, gladiators fought wild animals here to the delight of 20,000 screaming fans. Now local daredevils still fight wild animals here—"bullgame" posters around the arena advertise upcoming spectacles (see page 242).

Cost and Hours: €8 combo-ticket with Classical Theater, covered by Liberty Passport; open daily May-Sept 9:00-19:00, April and Oct 9:00-18:00, Nov-March 10:00-17:00, Rond-point des Arènes, tel. 04 90 49 36 86, www.arenes-arles.com.

Visiting the Arena: After passing the ticket kiosk, find the helpful English infor-

Arles' old town

Inside the Roman Arena

mation display that describes the arena's history and renovation, then take a seat in the upper deck. In Roman times, games were free (sponsored by city bigwigs), and fans were seated by social class. More than 30 rows of stone bleachers extended all the way to the top of those vacant arches that circle the arena. All arches were numbered to help distracted fans find their seats. The many passageways you'll see (called vomitoires) allowed for rapid dispersal after the games—fights would break out among frenzied fans if they couldn't leave quickly. During medieval times and until the early 1800s, the arches were bricked up and the stadium became a fortified town—with 200 humble homes crammed within its circular defenses. Parts of three of the medieval towers survive (the one above the ticket booth is open and rewards those who climb it with terrific views).

• *Leaving the arena, walk clockwise around its perimeter, marveling at the ancient stonework. A quarter of the way around, go up the cute stepped lane (Rue Renan, next to Volubilis Restaurant). Take three steps and turn around to study the arena.*

The big stones are Roman. Notice the little medieval stones—more like rubble—filling two upper-level archways. These serve as a reminder of how the arena encircled a jumble of makeshift houses through the Middle Ages. You can even see rooflines and beam holes where the Roman structure provided a solid foundation to lean on.

• *Hike up the pretty lane and continue past the stark and stony church to the highest point in Arles. Take in the view.*

❻ ALPILLES MOUNTAINS VIEW

This view pretty much matches what Vincent, an avid walker, would have seen. Imagine him hauling his easel into those fields under intense sun, leaning against a ferocious wind, struggling to keep his hat on.

Vincent carried his easel as far as the medieval Abbey of Montmajour, that bulky structure three miles straight ahead on the hill. The St. Paul Hospital, where he was eventually treated in St-Rémy, is on the other side of the Alpilles mountains, several miles beyond Montmajour.

• *Continue circling the Roman Arena. At the high point, turn left and walk out Rue de Porte de Laure. (You'll pass the Classical Theater on your right, which we'll see later.) After a couple of blocks, just after the street turns left, go right, down the curved staircase into the park. At bottom of the stairs take the second right (through the gate and into the park) and find the...*

❼ JARDIN D'ETE EASEL

Vincent spent many a sunny day painting the leafy Jardin d'Eté. In another letter to his sister, Vincent wrote, "I don't know whether you can understand that one may make a poem by arranging colors... In a similar manner, the bizarre lines, purposely selected and multiplied, meandering all through the picture may not present a literal image of the garden, but they may present it to our minds as if in a dream."

• *Hike uphill through the park toward the three-story surviving tower of the ancient Roman Theater. At the tower, follow the white metal fence to the left along "the garden of stone"—a collection of ancient carved bits of a once grand Roman theater. Go up four steps and around to the right for a fine view of the...*

The well-preserved arena

How About Them Romans?

Many scholars claim the best-preserved ancient Roman buildings are not in Italy, but in France. These ancient stones will compose an important part of your sight-seeing agenda.

Classical Rome endured from about 500 B.C. through A.D. 500—spending about 500 years growing, 200 years peaking, and 300 years declining. Julius Caesar conquered Gaul—which included Provence—during the Gallic Wars (58-51 B.C.), then crossed the Rubicon River in 49 B.C. to incite civil war within the Roman Republic. He erected a temple to Jupiter on the future site of Paris' Notre-Dame Cathedral.

The concept of one-man rule lived on with his grandnephew, Octavian (whom he had also adopted as his son). Octavian took the title "Augustus" and became the first in a line of emperors who would control Rome for the next 500 years. Rome morphed from a Republic into an Empire: a collection of many diverse territories ruled by a single man. At its peak (c. A.D. 117), the Roman Empire had 54 million people; "Rome" didn't just refer to the city, but to all of Western civilization.

Provence, with its strategic location, benefited greatly from Rome's global economy and grew to become an important part of its worldwide empire. After Julius Caesar conquered Gaul, Emperor Augustus Romanized it, building and renovating cities in the image of Rome.

When it came to construction, the Romans' magic building ingredient was concrete. Easier to work than stone, and longer-lasting than wood, concrete served as flooring, roofing, filler, glue, and support. Builders would start with a foundation of brick, then fill it in with poured concrete. They would then cover important structures, such as basilicas, in sheets of expensive marble (held on with nails), or decorate floors and walls with mosaics.

Most cities had a theater, baths, and aqueducts; the most important cities had sports arenas. A typical Roman city (such as Arles) was a garrison town, laid out on a grid plan with two main roads: one running north-south (the *cardus*), the other east-west (the *decumanus*). Approaching the city on your chariot, you'd pass by the cemetery, which was located outside town for hygienic reasons. You'd enter the main gate and speed past warehouses and apartment houses to the town square (forum). Facing the square were the most important temples, dedicated to the patron gods of the city. Nearby, you'd find bathhouses; like today's fitness clubs, these served the almost sacred dedication to personal vigor. Also close by were businesses that catered to the citizens' needs: the marketplace, bakeries, banks, and brothels. Aqueducts brought fresh water for drinking, filling the baths, and delighting the citizens with bubbling fountains.

Some cities in Provence were more urban 2,000 years ago than they are today. For instance, Roman Arles had a population of 100,000—double today's size.

❽ CLASSICAL THEATER (THEATRE ANTIQUE)

This elegant, three-level, first-century B.C. Roman theater once seated 10,000. There was no hillside to provide structural support, so the builders created 27 buttress arches, which radiate out behind the seats. From the outside, it looked much like the adjacent arena.

Cost and Hours: €8 combo-ticket with Roman Arena, covered by Liberty Passport, same hours as Arena.

Visiting the Theater: Start with the 10-minute video outside, which provides helpful background and images that make it easier to put the scattered stones back in place. A large information panel nearby on the grass adds more context.

Walk into the theater and pull up a stone seat in a center aisle. Imagine that for 500 years, ancient Romans gathered here for entertainment. The original structure was much higher, with 33 rows of seats covering three levels to accommodate demand. During the Middle Ages, the old theater became a convenient town quarry—much of St. Trophime Church was built from theater rubble.

Precious little of the original theater survives—though it still is used for events, with seating for 2,000 spectators.

• *From the theater, walk downhill on Rue de la Calade. Take the first left into a big square.*

❾ REPUBLIC SQUARE (PLACE DE LA REPUBLIQUE)

This square was called "Place Royale"— until the French Revolution. The obelisk was once the centerpiece of Arles' Roman Circus. The lions at its base are the symbol of the city, whose slogan is (roughly) "the gentle lion." Observe the age-old scene: tourists, peasants, shoppers, pilgrims, children, and street musicians. The City Hall (Hôtel de Ville) has a French Baroque facade, built in the same generation as Versailles. Where there's a City Hall, there's always a free WC (if you win the Revolution, you can pee for free at the mayor's home). Notice the flags: The yellow-and-red of Provence is the same as the yellow-and-red of Catalunya, the region's linguistic cousin in Spain.

• *Today's City Hall sits upon an ancient city center. Inside you'll find the entrance to an ancient cryptoportico (foundation).*

Classical Theater

⑩ CRYPTOPORTICOS (CRYPTOPORTIQUES)

This dark, drippy underworld of Roman arches was constructed to support the upper half of Forum Square. Two thousand years ago, most of this gallery of arches was at or above street level; modern Arles has buried about 20 feet of its history over the millennia. Through the tiny windows high up you would have seen the sandals of Romans on their way to the forum. Other than dark arches and broken bits of forum littering the dirt floor, there's not much down here beyond ancient memories (€3.50, covered by Liberty Passport, same hours as Arena).

• The highlight of Place de la République is St. Trophime Church. Enjoy its exquisitely carved facade.

⑪ ST. TROPHIME CHURCH

Named after a third-century bishop of Arles, this church, worth ▲▲, sports the finest Romanesque main entrance I've seen anywhere. The Romanesque and Gothic interior—with tapestries, relics, and a rare painting from the French Revolution when this was a "Temple of Reason"—is worth a visit.

Cost and Hours: Free, daily 9:00-12:00 & 14:00-18:30, until 17:00 Oct-March.

Exterior: Like a Roman triumphal arch, the church **facade** trumpets the promise of Judgment Day. The tympanum (the semicircular area above the door) is filled with Christian symbolism. Christ sits in majesty, surrounded by symbols of the four evangelists: Matthew (the winged man), Mark (the winged lion), Luke (the ox), and John (the eagle). The 12 apostles are lined up below Jesus. It's Judgment Day...some are saved and others aren't. Notice the condemned (on the right)—a chain gang doing a sad bunny-hop over the fires of hell. For them, the tune trumpeted by the three angels above Christ is not a happy one. Below the chain gang, St. Stephen is being stoned to death, with his soul leaving through his mouth and instantly being welcomed by angels. Study the exquisite detail. In an illiterate medieval world, this was colorfully painted, like a neon billboard over the town square. It's full of meaning, and a medieval pilgrim understood it all.

Interior: Just inside the door on the right, a chart locates the interior highlights and helps explain the carvings you just

St. Trophime Church

saw on the tympanum. The tall 12th-century Romanesque nave is decorated by a set of tapestries (typical in the Middle Ages) showing scenes from the life of Mary (17th century, from the French town of Aubusson). Circle the church counterclockwise.

Step into the brightly lit **Chapel of Baptism** to view a statue of St. John Paul II under the window. Facing the window, look to the right wall where you'll see a faded painting from 1789. The French Revolution secularized the country and made churches "Temples of Reason." The painting of a triangle with a sunburst is the only example of church decor I've seen from this age.

Amble around the ambulatory toward the **Gothic apse.** Choose which chapel you need or want: If you have the plague or cholera, visit the chapel devoted to St. Roch—notice the testimonial plaques of gratitude on the wall. Some spaces are still available...if you hurry.

Two-thirds of the way around, find the **relic chapel** behind the ornate wrought iron gate, with its fine golden boxes that hold long-venerated bones of obscure saints. These relics generated lots of money for the church from pilgrims through the ages. Pop in a coin to share some light. The next chapel houses the skull of St. Anthony of the Desert.

Several chapels down, look for the early-Christian **sarcophagi** from Roman Arles (dated about A.D. 300). One sarcophagus shows Moses and the Israelites crossing the Red Sea. You'll see Christians wearing togas and praying like evangelicals do today—hands raised. The heads were likely lopped off during the French Revolution.

This church is a stop on the ancient pilgrimage route to Santiago de Compostela in northwest Spain. For 800 years pilgrims on their way to Santiago have paused here...and they still do today. Notice the modern-day pilgrimages advertised on the far right near the church's entry.

• *To reach the adjacent peaceful cloister, leave the church, turn left, then left again through a courtyard.*

ST. TROPHIME CLOISTERS

Worth seeing if you have the Liberty Passport (otherwise €4, same hours as Arena), the cloisters' many small columns were scavenged from the ancient Roman theater. Enjoy the sculpted capitals, the rounded Romanesque arches (12th century), and the pointed Gothic ones (14th century). The pretty vaulted hall exhibits 17th-century tapestries showing scenes from the First Crusade to the Holy Land. There's an instructive video at the base of the stairs. On the second floor, you'll walk along an angled rooftop designed to catch rainwater—notice the slanted gutter that channeled the water into a cistern and the heavy roof slabs covering the tapestry hall below.

• *From Place de la République, exit on the far corner (opposite the church and kitty-corner from where you entered) to stroll a delightful pedestrian street.*

⑫ RUE DE LA REPUBLIQUE

Rue da la République is Arles' primary shopping street. Walk downhill, enjoying the scene and popping into shops that catch your interest.

At the start is **Soulier Bakery.** Inside, you'll be tempted by *fougasse* (bread studded with herbs, olives, and bacon bits), *sablés Provençal* (cookies made with honey and almonds), *tarte lavande* (a sweet almond lavender tart), and big crispy meringues. A few doors down is **Restaurant L'Atelier** (with two prized Michelin stars), **L'Occitane en Provence** (local perfumes), **Puyricard Chocolate** (with enticing €1 treats and *calisson*, a sweet/bitter almond delight), as well as local design and antique shops. The fragile spiral columns on the right (just before the tourist-pleasing Lavender Boutique on the corner) show what 400 years of weather can do to decorative stonework.

• *Take the first left onto Rue Président*

*Wilson. Just after the butcher shop, turn right to find **Hôtel Dieu,** a hospital made famous by one of its patients: Vincent van Gogh.*

⑬ ESPACE VAN GOGH EASEL

In December 1888, shortly after his famous ear-cutting incident (see *Café at Night* easel, described later), Vincent was admitted into the local hospital—today's Espace Van Gogh cultural center (free, only the courtyard is open to the public). It surrounds a flowery courtyard that the artist loved and painted when he was being treated for blood loss, hallucinations, and severe depression that left him bedridden for a month. The citizens of Arles circulated a petition demanding that the mad Dutchman be kept under medical supervision. Félix Rey, Vincent's kind doctor, worked out a compromise: The artist could leave during the day so that he could continue painting, but he had to sleep at the hospital at night. Look through the postcards sold in the courtyard and find a painting of Vincent's ward showing nuns attending to patients in a gray hall (*Ward of Arles Hospital*).

• *Return to Rue de la République. Take a left and continue two blocks downhill. Take the second right up Rue Tour de Fabre and follow signs to Fondation Van Gogh. After a few steps, you'll pass **La Main Qui Pense** (The Hand That Thinks), a pottery workshop. A couple blocks farther, at the no right turn sign, turn right onto Rue du Docteur Fanton. On your immediate right is the...*

⑭ FONDATION VAN GOGH

This art foundation, worth ▲, delivers a refreshing stop for modern-art lovers and Van Gogh fans, with two temporary exhibits per year in which contemporary artists pay homage to Vincent through thought-provoking interpretations of his works. You'll also see at least one original work by Van Gogh (painted during his time in the region).

Cost and Hours: €9, daily 11:00-19:00 except closed between exhibits and likely Mon off-season—check website for current hours, audioguide-€3, Hôtel Leautaud de Donines, 35 Rue du Docteur Fanton, tel. 04 90 49 94 04, www.fondation-vincentvangogh-arles.org.

• *Continue down Rue du Docteur Fanton toward the river.*

⑮ RUE DU DOCTEUR FANTON

A string of recommended restaurants is on the left. On the right is **Crèche Municipale.** Open workdays, this is a free government-funded daycare where parents can drop off their infants up to two years old. The notion: No worker should face financial hardship in order to receive quality childcare. At the next corner is the recommended **Soleileis,** Arles' top ice cream shop.

At the strawberry-and-vanilla ice cream cone, turn right and step into **Bar El Paseo** at 4 Rue des Thermes. The main museum-like room is absolutely full of bull—including the mounted heads of three big ones who died in the local arena and a big black-and-white photo of Arles'

Fondation Van Gogh *A café on Forum Square*

arena packed to capacity. Senora Leal—whose family is famous for its bullfighters—has wallpapered the place with photos and bullfighting memorabilia, and serves good Spanish Rioja wine and sangria.

• *A few steps farther is...*

🔟 FORUM SQUARE (PLACE DU FORUM)

Named for the Roman forum that once stood here, Forum Square, worth ▲, was the political and religious center of Roman Arles. Still lively, this café-crammed square is a local watering hole and popular for a *pastis* (anise-based aperitif). The bistros on the square can put together a passable salad or *plat du jour*—and when you sprinkle on the ambience, that's €14 well spent.

At the corner of Grand Hôtel Nord-Pinus, a plaque shows how the Romans built a foundation of galleries to level the main square and to compensate for Arles' slope down to the river. The two columns are all that survive from the upper story of the entry to the forum. Steps leading to the entrance are buried—the Roman street level was about 20 feet below you.

The statue on the square is of **Frédéric Mistral** (1830-1914). This popular poet, who wrote in the local dialect rather than in French, was a champion of Provençal culture. After receiving the Nobel Prize in Literature in 1904, Mistral used his prize money to preserve and display the folk identity of Provence. He founded a regional folk museum at a time when France was rapidly centralizing and regions like Provence were losing their unique identities. (The fierce, local mistral wind—literally "master"—has nothing to do with his name.)

• *Nearby, facing the brightly painted yellow café, find your final Van Gogh easel.*

CAFE AT NIGHT EASEL

In October 1888, lonely Vincent—who dreamed of making Arles a magnet for fellow artists—persuaded his friend Paul Gauguin to come south. He decorated Gauguin's room with several humble canvases of sunflowers (now some of the world's priciest paintings). Their plan was for Gauguin to be the "dean" of a new art school in Arles, and Vincent its instructor-in-chief. At first, the two got along well. They spent days side by side, rendering the same subject in their distinct styles. At night, they hit the bars and brothels. Van Gogh's well-known *Café at Night* captures the glow of an absinthe buzz at Café la Nuit on Place du Forum.

After two months together, the two artists clashed over art and personality differences (Vincent was a slob around the house, whereas Gauguin was meticulous). The night of December 23, they were drinking absinthe at the café when Vincent suddenly went ballistic. He threw his glass at Gauguin. Gauguin left. Walking through Place Victor Hugo, Gauguin heard footsteps behind him and turned to see Vincent coming at him, brandishing a razor. Gauguin quickly fled town. The local paper reported what happened next: "At 11:30 p.m., Vincent van Gogh, painter from Holland, appeared at the brothel at no. 1, asked for Rachel, and gave her his cut-off earlobe, saying, 'Treasure this precious object.' Then he vanished." He woke up the next morning at home with his head wrapped in a bloody towel and his earlobe missing. Was Vincent emulating a successful matador, whose prize is cutting off the bull's ear?

The **bright-yellow café**—called Café la Nuit—was the subject of one of Vincent van Gogh's most famous works in Arles. Although his painting showed the café in a brilliant yellow from the glow of gas lamps, the facade was bare limestone, just like the other cafés on this square. The café is now a tourist trap painted by its current owners to match Van Gogh's version...and to cash in on the Vincent-crazed hordes who pay too much to eat or drink here.

In spring 1889, the bipolar genius (a modern diagnosis) checked himself into the St. Paul Monastery and Hospital in St-Rémy-de-Provence. He spent a year there, thriving in the care of nurturing doctors and nuns. Painting was part of his therapy, so they gave him a studio to work in, and he produced more than 100 paintings. Alcohol-free and institutionalized, he did some of his wildest work. With thick, swirling brushstrokes and surreal colors, he made his placid surroundings throb with restless energy.

Eventually, Vincent's torment became unbearable. In the spring of 1890, he left Provence to be cared for by a sympathetic doctor in Auvers-sur-Oise, just north of Paris. On July 27, he wandered into a field and shot himself. He died two days later.
• *With this walk, you have seen the best of Arles. It's time to enjoy a drink on the Place du Forum and savor the essence of Provence.*

On the Outskirts
▲▲ANCIENT HISTORY MUSEUM (MUSEE DE L'ARLES ET DE LA PROVENCE ANTIQUES)
The Ancient History Museum provides valuable background on Arles' Roman history. Begin your town visit here before delving into the city's sights (drivers should stop on the way into town).

Located on the site of the Roman chariot racecourse (the arc of which is built into the parking lot), this air-conditioned, all-on-one-floor museum is just west of central Arles along the river. Models and original sculptures re-create the Roman city, making workaday life and culture easier to imagine.

Cost and Hours: €8, covered by Liberty Passport; open Wed-Mon 10:00-18:00, closed Tue; Presqu'île du Cirque Romain, tel. 04 13 31 51 03, www.arles-antique.cg13.fr.

Getting There: Drivers entering the city will see signs for the museum. If you're coming from the city center, take the free **Envia minibus** (stops at the train station and along Rue du 4 Septembre, then along the river—see map on page 228; 2/hour Mon-Sat, none Sun). If you're walking from the city center (allow 20 minutes), turn left at the river and take the scruffy riverside path under two bridges to the big, modern blue building. Approach-

Model of Arles' Classical Theater

ing the museum, you'll pass the verdant Hortus Garden—designed to recall the Roman circus and chariot racecourse that were located here. A **taxi** ride costs €11.

Visiting the Museum: The permanent collection is housed in a large hall flooded with natural light. You'll tour it counterclockwise: models of the ancient city and its major landmarks, a Roman boat (with a fine video in a tiny theater at the end of the hall), statues, mosaics, and sarcophagi. Read what English you can find, but—as much of the exhibit is in French only—here's a rundown on what you'll see.

A wall **map** of the region during the Roman era greets visitors and shows the geographic importance of Arles: Three important Roman trade routes—vias Domitia, Grippa, and Aurelia—all converged on or near Arles.

After a small exhibit on pre-Roman Arles you'll come to fascinating **models** of the Roman city and the impressive Roman structures in (and near) Arles. These breathe life into the buildings as they looked 2,000 years ago. Start with the model of Roman Arles and ponder the city's splendor over 2,000 years ago when Arles' population was double that of today. Find the forum—still the center of town today, though only two columns survive (the smaller section of the forum is where today's Place du Forum is built).

At the museum's center stands the original **statue** of Julius Caesar that once graced Arles' ancient theater stage wall. From there find individual models of the major buildings shown in the city model: the elaborately elegant forum; the floating wooden bridge that gave Arles a strategic advantage (over the widest, and therefore slowest, part of the river); the theater (with its magnificent stage wall); the arena (with its movable stadium cover to shelter spectators from sun or rain); and the hydraulic mill of Barbegal (with its 16 waterwheels powered by water cascading down a hillside).

Don't miss the large model of the **chariot racecourse.** Part of the original racecourse was just outside the windows, and though long gone, it likely resembled Rome's Circus Maximus.

A wing (to the right) is dedicated to the museum's newest and most exciting exhibit: a **Gallo-Roman vessel** and much of its cargo. This almost-100-foot-long Roman barge was hauled out of the Rhône in 2010, along with some 280 amphorae and 3,000 ceramic artifacts. It was typical of flat-bottomed barges used to shuttle goods between Arles and ports along the Mediterranean (vessels were manually towed upriver).

Continuing your counterclockwise circle of the museum, you'll see displays of pottery, jewelry, metal, and glass artifacts, as well as well-crafted mosaic floors that illustrate how Roman Arles was a city of art and culture. The many **statues** are all original, except for the greatest—the *Venus of Arles,* which Louis XIV took a liking to and had moved to Versailles.

Experiences
▲▲MARKETS
Provençal market days offer France's most colorful and tantalizing outdoor shopping. On Wednesday and Saturday mornings, Arles' ring road erupts into an open-air festival of fish, flowers, produce...and everything Provençal. The main event is on Saturday, with vendors jamming the ring road from Boulevard Emile Combes to the east, along Boulevard des Lices

Wednesday and Saturday are market days in Arles.

near the TI (the heart of the market), and continuing down Boulevard Georges Clemenceau to the west. Wednesday's market runs only along Boulevard Emile Combes, between Place Lamartine and Avenue Victor Hugo; the segment nearest Place Lamartine is all about food, and the upper half features clothing, tablecloths, purses, and so on. On the first Wednesday of the month, a flea market doubles the size of the usual Wednesday market along Boulevard des Lices near the main TI. Both markets are open until about 12:30.

▲▲BULLGAMES (COURSES CAMARGUAISES)

The nonviolent *courses camarguaises* (bullgames) held in Arles are more sporting than bloody bullfights (though traditional Spanish-style bullfights still take place on occasion). Spectators occupy the same seats that fans have used for nearly 2,000 years. The bulls of Arles (who, locals insist, "die of old age") are promoted in posters even more boldly than their human foes. In the bullgame, a ribbon (*cocarde*) is laced between the bull's horns. The *razeteur,* with a special hook, has 15 minutes to snare the ribbon. Local businessmen encourage a *razeteur*

(dressed in white, with a red cummerbund) by shouting out how much money they'll pay for the *cocarde.* If the bull pulls a good stunt, the band plays the famous "Toreador" song from *Carmen.* The following day, newspapers report on the games, including how many *Carmens* the bull earned.

Three classes of bullgames—determined by the experience of the *razeteurs*—are advertised in posters: The *course de protection* is for rookies. The *trophée de l'Avenir* comes with more experience. And the *trophée des As* features top professionals. During Easter (*Féria du Pâques*) and the fall rice-harvest festival (*Féria du Riz*), the arena hosts traditional Spanish bullfights (look for *corrida*) with outfits, swords, spikes, and the whole gory shebang. (Nearby villages also stage *courses camarguaises* in small wooden bullrings nearly every weekend; TIs have the latest schedule.)

Cost and Hours: Arles' bullgame tickets usually run €7-20; bullfights are pricier (€36-100). Schedules for bullgames vary (usually July-Aug on Wed and Fri)—ask at the TI or check online at www.arenes-arles.com.

Bulls are not harmed in Provençal-style "bullgames."

Provence's Cuisine Scene

The extravagant use of garlic, olive oil, herbs, and tomatoes makes Provence's cuisine France's liveliest. To sample it, order anything *à la provençale*. Among the area's specialties are **ratatouille** (a mixture of vegetables in a thick, herb-flavored tomato sauce), **aioli** (a rich, garlicky mayonnaise spread over vegetables, potatoes, fish, or whatever), **tapenade** (a paste of pureed olives, capers, anchovies, herbs, and sometimes tuna), *soupe au pistou* (thin yet flavorful vegetable soup with a sauce of basil, garlic, and cheese), and *soupe à l'ail* (garlic soup, called *aigo bouido* in the local dialect). Look for *riz de Camargue* (reddish, chewy, nutty-tasting rice) and *taureau* (bull's meat). The native goat cheeses are **Banon de Banon** or **Banon à la Feuille** (wrapped in chestnut leaves) and spicy **Picodon**. Don't miss the region's prized **Cavaillon melons** (cantaloupes) or its delicious cherries and apricots, which are often turned into jams and candied fruits.

Wines of Provence: Provence produces some of France's great wines at relatively reasonable prices. Look for wines from **Gigondas, Rasteau, Cairanne, Beaumes-de-Venise, Vacqueyras,** and **Châteauneuf-du-Pape.** For the cheapest but still tasty wines, look for labels showing **Côtes du Rhône Villages** or **Côtes de Provence.** If you like rosé, you'll be in heaven. **Rosés from Tavel** are considered among the best in Provence. For reds, splurge for Châteauneuf-du-Pape or Gigondas, and for a fine aperitif wine or a dessert wine, try the **Muscat** from **Beaumes-de-Venise.**

Eating

You can dine well in Arles on a modest budget (most of my listings have *menus* for under €25). Sunday is a quiet night for restaurants, though eateries on Place du Forum are open. For groceries, consider the big, Monoprix supermarket/department store on Place Lamartine (closed Sun).

Rick's Tip: *Cafés on the Place du Forum deliver great atmosphere and fair prices, but mediocre food.* **Avoid the garish yellow tourist trap Café la Nuit.** *For serious cuisine, wander away from the square.*

On Rue du Docteur Fanton

Les Filles du 16 is a warm, affordable place to enjoy a fresh salad (€11), or a fine two- or three-course dinner (€21-27). The choices are limited, so check the selection before sitting down. The *taureau* (bull's meat) in a tasty sauce is a good choice (closed Sat-Sun, 16 Rue du Docteur Fanton, tel. 04 90 93 77 36).

Le Plaza buzzes with happy diners and is run by a young couple (Stéphane cooks while Graziela serves). It features delicious Provençal cuisine at good prices (€23 *menus*, closed Wed Oct-March, 28 Rue du Docteur Fanton, tel. 04 90 96 33 15).

Le Galoubet is a popular local spot,

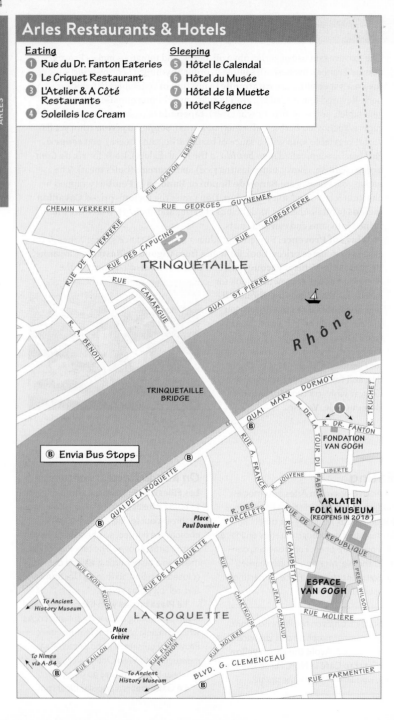

Arles Restaurants & Hotels

Eating
1. Rue du Dr. Fanton Eateries
2. Le Criquet Restaurant
3. L'Atelier & A Côté Restaurants
4. Soleileis Ice Cream

Sleeping
5. Hôtel le Calendal
6. Hôtel du Musée
7. Hôtel de la Muette
8. Hôtel Régence

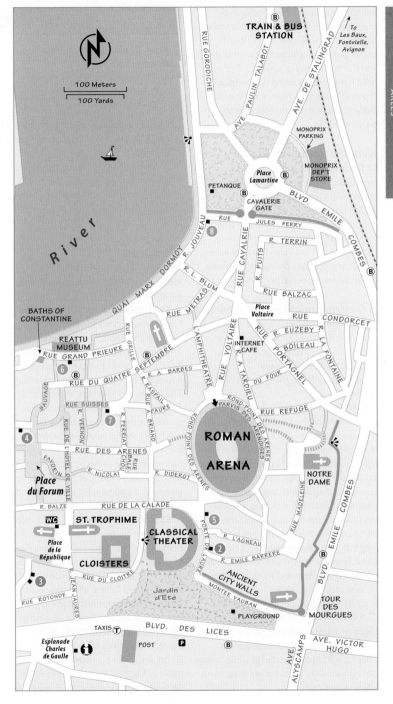

blending a warm interior, traditional French cuisine, and service with a smile, thanks to owner Frank. It's the most expensive of the places I list on this street and the least flexible, serving a €32 *menu* only. If it's cold, a roaring fire keeps you toasty (closed Sun-Mon, great fries and desserts, 18 Rue du Docteur Fanton, tel. 04 90 93 18 11).

Near the Roman Arena

Le Criquet, a sweet little eatery two blocks above the arena, serves Provençal classics with joy at good prices. If you're really hungry, try the €25 *bourride*—a creamy fish soup thickened with aioli and garlic and stuffed with mussels, clams, calamari, and more (good €24-28 *menus*, indoor and outdoor dining, 21 Rue Porte de Laure, tel. 04 90 96 80 51).

A Gastronomic Dining Experience

One of France's most recognized chefs, Jean-Luc Rabanel, runs two different places 50 yards from Place de la République (at 7 Rue des Carmes). They sit side by side, both offering indoor and terrace seating.

L'Atelier, a destination restaurant with two Michelin stars, attracts people from great distances to happily pay €125 for dinner and €65 for lunch. There is no menu, just a parade of delicious taste sensations served in artsy dishes. Don't plan on a quick dinner, and don't come for a traditional setting: Everything is enthusiastically contemporary. You'll probably see or hear the famous chef with his long salt-and-pepper hair and a deep voice. Friendly servers will hold your hand through this palate-widening experience (closed Mon-Tue, book ahead, tel. 04 90 91 07 69, www.rabanel.com).

A Côté, next door, offers a wine bar/bistro ambience and the chef's top-quality cuisine for much less money. There is a limited selection of wines by the glass (open daily, tel. 04 90 47 61 13, www.bistro-acote.com).

Sleeping

Hotels are a great value here. Many are air-conditioned, though few have elevators.

$$$ Hôtel le Calendal* is a thoughtfully managed place ideally located between the Roman Arena and Classical Theater. The hotel opens to the street with airy lounges and a lovely palm-shaded courtyard, providing an enjoyable refuge. The rooms sport Provençal decor and come in random shapes and sizes (standard Db-€119, larger or balcony Db-€139-159, family rooms available, breakfast buffet-€12, air-con, reserve ahead for parking-€8/day, café/sandwich bar open daily, just above arena at 5 Rue Porte de Laure, tel. 04 90 96 11 89, www.lecalendal.com, contact@lecalendal.com).

$$ Hôtel du Musée is a quiet, affordable manor-home hideaway tucked deep in Arles (if driving, ask for access code to street barrier so you can drop off your bags). This delightful place comes with 28 wood-floored rooms, a flowery courtyard, and comfortable lounges. Light-hearted Claude and English-speaking Laurence are good hosts (Sb-€65, Db-€70-90, family rooms available, buffet breakfast-€8.50, no elevator, garage parking-€10/day, follow signs to *Réattu Museum* to 11 Rue du Grand Prieuré, tel.

04 90 93 88 88, www.hoteldumusee.com, contact@hoteldumusee.com).

$$ Hôtel de la Muette**, run by Brigitte and Alain, is located in a quiet corner of Arles. Rooms come with stone walls, tiled floors, and pebble showers (Db-€81, family rooms available, direct booking discount for Rick Steves readers, buffet breakfast-€9, no elevator, private garage-€10/day, 15 Rue des Suisses, tel. 04 90 96 15 39, www.hotel-muette.com, hotel.muette@wanadoo.fr).

Rick's Tip: *An international photo event* **jams hotels in Arles the second weekend of July,** *while the twice-yearly Féria* **draws crowds over Easter and in mid-September.**

$ Hôtel Régence**, a top budget deal, has a riverfront location, comfortable Provençal rooms, safe parking, and a location near the train station. Gentle Valérie and Eric speak English (Db-€60-75, family rooms available, choose river-view or quieter courtyard rooms, good buffet breakfast-€6, no elevator but only two floors, garage parking-€7/day; from Place Lamartine, turn right after passing between towers to reach 5 Rue Marius Jouveau; tel. 04 90 96 39 85, www.hotel-regence.com, contact@hotel-regence.com).

Transportation
Getting Around Arles

In this flat city, everything's within **walking** distance. Only the Ancient History Museum requires a healthy walk (20 minutes). The elevated riverside promenade provides Rhône views and a direct route to the Ancient History Museum (to the southwest) and the train station (to the northeast). Keep your head up for *Starry Night* memories, but eyes down for doggie droppings.

Arles' **taxis** charge a set fee of about €11, but nothing except the Ancient History Museum is worth a taxi ride. To call a cab, dial 04 90 96 52 76 or 04 90 96 90 03.

The free **Envia minibus** circles the town, useful for access to the train station, hotels, and the Ancient History Museum (2/hour, Mon-Sat 7:00-19:00, none Sun).

Arriving and Departing

Compare train and bus schedules: For some nearby destinations the bus may be the better choice, and it's usually cheaper.

BY TRAIN

The train station is on the river, a 10-minute walk from the town center. There's no baggage storage at the station, but you can walk 10 minutes to stow it at Hôtel Régence (see "Orientation," earlier).

To reach the town center or Ancient History Museum from the train station, wait for the free **Envia minibus** at the glass shelter facing away from the station (cross the street and veer left, 2/hour Mon-Sat 7:00-19:00, none Sun). The bus makes a counterclockwise loop around Arles, stopping near most of my recommended hotels (see map on page 244 for stops). **Taxis** usually wait in front of the station.

Train Connections from Arles to: Paris (11/day, 2 direct TGVs—4 hours, 9 more with transfer in Avignon—5 hours), **Avignon Centre-Ville** (roughly hourly, 20 minutes; 5-minute shuttle train from Avignon Centre-Ville connects to Avignon TGV Station), **Carcassonne** (4/day direct, 2.5 hours, more with transfer in Narbonne, direct trains may require reservations), **Beaune** (10/day, 5 hours), **Nice** (11/day, 4 hours, most require transfer in Marseille).

BY BUS

Arles' bus station is next to its train station. All buses to regional destinations depart from here and most cost only €1.50. Get schedules at the TI or from the bus company (tel. 08 10 00 13 26, www.lepilote.com).

Bus Connections from Arles Train Station to Avignon TGV Station: The direct SNCF bus is easier than the train

(€9, 9/day, 1 hour, included with rail pass).

Bus Connections from Arles to Les Baux: Bus #57 connects Arles to Les Baux (6/day daily July-Aug, Sat-Sun only in May-June and Sept, none Oct-April; 35 minutes to Les Baux, then runs to Avignon).

BY CAR

For most hotels, first follow signs to *Centre-Ville*, then *Gare SNCF* (train station). You'll come to a big roundabout (Place Lamartine) with a Monoprix department store to the right. You can park along the city wall (except on Tue night when tow trucks clear things out for the Wed market); the hotels I list are no more than a 15-minute walk from here. Fearless drivers can plunge into the narrow streets between the two stumpy towers via Rue de la Calade, and follow signs to their hotel. Theft is a problem—leave nothing in your car, and trust your hotelier's advice on where to park.

Most hotels have metered parking nearby (free Mon-Sat 12:00-14:00 & 19:00-9:00, and all day Sun; some meters limited to 2.5 hours). If you can't find a space near your hotel, Parking des Lices (Arles' only parking garage), near the TI on Boulevard des Lices, is a good fallback.

AVIGNON

Famous for its nursery rhyme, medieval bridge, and brooding Palace of the Popes, contemporary Avignon (ah-veen-yohn) bustles and prospers behind its mighty walls. For nearly 100 years (1309-1403) Avignon was the capital of Christendom, home to seven popes. (And, for a difficult period after that—during the Great Schism when there were two competing popes—Avignon was "the other Rome.") During this time, it grew from a quiet village into a thriving city.

Today, with its large student population and fashionable shops, Avignon is an intriguing blend of medieval history, youthful energy, and urban sophistica-

tion. Street performers entertain the international throngs who fill Avignon's ubiquitous cafés and trendy boutiques. And each July the city goes crazy during its huge theater festival (with about 2,000 performances, big crowds, higher prices, and hotels booked up long in advance). Clean, lively, and popular with tourists, Avignon is more impressive for its outdoor ambience than for its museums and monuments.

Orientation

Cours Jean Jaurès, which turns into Rue de la République, runs straight from the Centre-Ville train station to Place de l'Horloge and the Palace of the Popes, splitting Avignon in two. The larger eastern half is where the action is. Climb to the Jardin du Rochers des Doms for the town's best view, tour the pope's immense palace, lose yourself in Avignon's back streets, and find a shady square to call home.

Tourist Information: The TI is helpful, with lots of information about the city and the region (April-Oct Mon-Sat 9:00-18:00, Sun 10:00-17:00, daily until 19:00 in July, shorter hours off-season; between the train station and the old town at 41 Cours Jean Jaurès, tel. 04 32 74 32 74, www.avignon-tourisme.com).

Sightseeing Pass: At the TI, pick up the free **Avignon Passion Pass** (for up to 5 family members). Get it stamped at your first sight to receive discounts at the others. The pass comes with the Avignon "Passion" map and guide, which includes several good (but tricky-to-follow) walking tours. The TI also has bike maps for good rides in the area, including the Ile de la Barthelasse.

Bike Rental: Rent pedal and electric bikes and scooters near the train station at **Provence Bike** (April-Oct 9:00-18:30, 7 Avenue St. Ruf, tel. 04 90 27 92 61, www.provence-bike.com). You'll enjoy riding on the Ile de la Barthelasse (the TI has bike maps).

Car Rental: The TGV Station has counters for all the big companies; only Avis is at the Centre-Ville Station.

Local Guides: Imagine Tours focuses on cultural excursions adapted to your interests. Guides will meet you at your hotel or the departure point of your choice (€190/half-day, €315/day, prices for up to 4 people starting from near Avignon or Arles, mobile 06 89 22 19 87, www. imagine-tours.net, imagine.tours@gmail. com). The **Avignon Gourmet Walking Tour** is a wonderful experience if you like to eat; charming Aurelie meets small groups daily (except Sun and Mon) at the TI at 9:15 for a well-designed three-hour, eight-stop walk. Book in advance on her website (€55/person, 2-8 people per group, tel. 06 35 32 08 96, www. avignongourmetours.com).

Tourist Train: The little train leaves regularly from in front of the Palace of the Popes and offers a decent overview of the city, including the Jardin du Rochers des Doms and St. Bénezet Bridge (€7, 2/hour, 40 minutes, English commentary, mid-March-mid-Oct daily 10:00-18:00, July-Aug until 19:00).

Minivan Excursions: Provence Reser- vation offers day tours by minivan or bus to nearby sights (such as lavender fields) from Avignon, Arles, and more. Tours from Avignon run year-round and cover a great variety of destinations; tours from other cities run April through September only and are more limited in scope. You'll get comfortable transportation but not guiding; you're on your own at the sights (about €60-80/half-day, €100-120/day for minivan tours, less for their big-bus tours, tel. 04 90 14 70 00, www.provence-reservation.com).

◉ Avignon Walk

This self-guided walk, worth ▲▲, offers a fine overview of the city and its major sights.

• *Start your tour where the Romans did, on Place de l'Horloge, in front of City Hall (Hôtel de Ville).*

PLACE DE L'HORLOGE

In ancient Roman times this was the forum, and in medieval times it was the market square. The square is named for the clock tower (now hiding behind the more recently built City Hall), which, in its day, was a humanist statement. In medieval France, the only bells in town rang

Place de l'Horloge

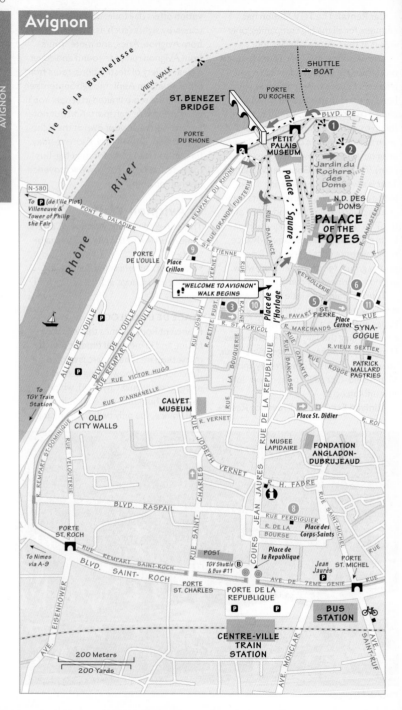

Avignon

Ile de la Barthelasse

VIEW WALK

Rhône River

SHUTTLE BOAT

PORTE DU ROCHER

ST. BENEZET BRIDGE

BLVD. DE LA

PORTE DU RHONE

PETIT PALAIS MUSEUM

Jardin du Rochers des Doms

N.D. DES DOMS

PALACE OF THE POPES

Palace Square

R. REMPART DU RHONE

R. GRANDE FUSTERIE

RUE BALANCE

N-580

To P (de l'Ile Plot) Villeneuve & Tower of Philip the Fair

PONT E. DALADIER

PORTE DE L'OULLE

R. ST. ETIENNE

R. VERNET

Place Crillon

9

PEYROLLERIE

"WELCOME TO AVIGNON" WALK BEGINS

Place de l'Horloge

6

RUE BANASTERIE

R. PETITE FUST

R. RACINE

3

10

5

ST. PIERRE

Place Carnot

R. FAVART

11

RUE

SYNA-GOGUE

ALLEE DE L'OULLE

BLVD. DE L'OULLE

RUE REMPART DE L'OULLE

RUE JOSEPH

R. ST. AGRICOL

R. LA BOUQUERIE

R. MARCHANDS

RUE GALANTE

R. VIEUX SEXTIER

PATRICK MALLARD PASTRIES

P

RUE VICTOR HUGO

RUE D'ANNANELLE

CALVET MUSEUM

RUE VERNET

RUE BANCASSE

R.VIEUX SEXTIER

Place St. Didier

R. ROI

To TGV Train Station

OLD CITY WALLS

RUE DE LA REPUBLIQUE

MUSEE LAPIDAIRE

FONDATION ANGLADON-DUBRUJEAUD

R. REMPART ST-DOMINIQUE

RUE VELOUTERIE

RUE JOSEPH VERNET

R. H. FABRE

RUE SAINT-MICHEL

BLVD. RASPAIL

RUE SAINT-CHARLES

COURS JEAN JAURES

RUE PERDIGUIER

8

PORTE ST. ROCH

To Nimes via A-9

RUE REMPART SAINT-ROCH

BLVD. SAINT-ROCH

R. DE LA BOURSE

Place des Corps-Saints

POST

TGV Shuttle B & Bus #11

Place de la Republique

Jean Jaurès

PORTE ST. MICHEL

PORTE ST. CHARLES

PORTE DE LA REPUBLIQUE

AVE. DE 7EME GENIE

BUS STATION

AVE. EISENHOWER

P

P

CENTRE-VILLE TRAIN STATION

AVE. MONCLAR

AVE. SAINT-RUF

200 Meters

200 Yards

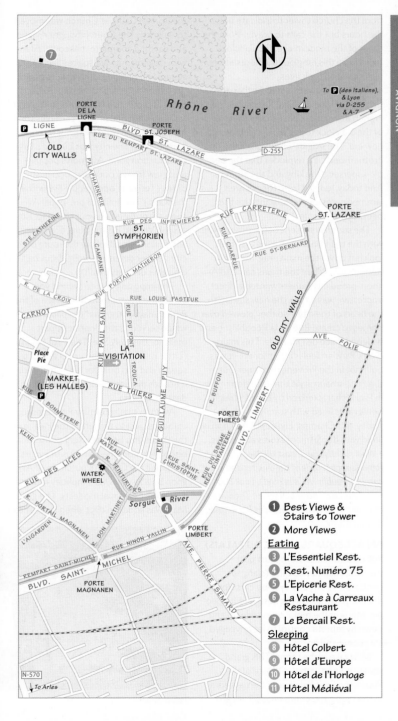

7

PORTE DE LA LIGNE

P LIGNE

OLD CITY WALLS

Rhône River

To **P** *(des Italiens),*
& Lyon
via D-255
& A-7

BLVD. ST. JOSEPH

PORTE ST. JOSEPH

RUE DU REMPART ST. LAZARE

ST. LAZARE

D-255

R. PALAPHARNERIE

PORTE ST. LAZARE

STE. CATHERINE

RUE DES INFIRMIERES

RUE CARRETERIE

ST. SYMPHORIEN

RUE CHARRUE

RUE ST-BERNARD

R. CAMPANE

RUE PORTAIL MATHERON

R. DE LA CROIX

RUE LOUIS PASTEUR

CARNOT

RUE DU PONT TROUCA

RUE PAUL SAYN

OLD CITY WALLS

AVE. FOLIE

Place Pie

LA VISITATION

MARKET (LES HALLES)

P

RUE THIERS

R. BUFFON

RUE GUILLAUME PUY

RUE BONNETERIE

R. BONNETERIE

PORTE THIERS

BLVD. LIMBERT

RENE

RUE DES LICES

RUE RATEAU

RUE VEINTURIERS

RUE SAINT-CHRISTOPHE

RUE DU 5ÈME REG. D'INFANTERIE

WATER-WHEEL

R. BON MARTINET

Sorgue ■ *River*

4

PORTE LIMBERT

R. PORTAIL MAGNANEN

L'AIGARDEN

RUE NINON-VALLIN

MICHEL

AVE. PIERRE SEMARD

REMPART SAINT-MICHEL

BLVD. SAINT-MICHEL

PORTE MAGNANEN

N-570

↓ To Arles

1 Best Views & Stairs to Tower

2 More Views

Eating

3 L'Essentiel Rest.

4 Rest. Numéro 75

5 L'Epicerie Rest.

6 La Vache à Carreaux Restaurant

7 Le Bercail Rest.

Sleeping

8 Hôtel Colbert

9 Hôtel d'Europe

10 Hôtel de l'Horloge

11 Hôtel Médiéval

from the church tower to indicate not the hours but the calls to prayer. With the dawn of the modern age, secular clock towers like this rang out the hours as people organized their lives.

Taking humanism a step further, the City Hall (Hôtel de Ville), built after the French Revolution, obstructed the view of the old clock tower while celebrating a new era. The slogan "liberty, equality, and brotherhood" is a reminder that the people supersede the king and the church. And today, judging from the square's jammed cafés and restaurants, it's the people who do rule.

The square's present popularity arrived with the trains in 1854. Facing City Hall, look left down the main drag, Rue de la République. When the trains came to Avignon, proud city fathers wanted a direct, impressive way to link the new station to the heart of the city—so they plowed over homes to create Rue de la République and widened Place de l'Horloge. This main drag's Parisian feel is intentional—it was built not in the Provençal manner, but in the Haussmann style that is so dominant in Paris (characterized by broad, straight boulevards lined with stately buildings). Today, this Champs-Elysées of Avignon is lined with department stores and banks.

• *Walk slightly uphill past the Neo-Renaissance facade of the theater and the carousel (public WCs behind). Look back to see the late Gothic bell tower. Then veer right at the Hôtel des Palais des Papes and continue into...*

PALACE SQUARE (PLACE DU PALAIS)

Pull up a concrete stump just past the café. Nicknamed *bites* (slang for penis), these effectively keep cars from double-parking in areas designed for people. Many of the metal ones slide up and down by remote control to let privileged cars come and go.

Now take in the scene. This grand square is lined with the Palace of the Popes, the Petit Palais, and the cathedral. In the 1300s, the entire headquarters of

the Roman Catholic Church was moved to Avignon. The Church bought Avignon and gave it a complete makeover. Along with clearing out vast spaces like this square and building a three-acre palace, the Church erected more than three miles of protective wall (with 39 towers), "appropriate" housing for cardinals (read: mansions), and residences for its entire bureaucracy. The city was Europe's largest construction zone. Avignon's population grew from 6,000 to 25,000 in short order. (Today, 13,000 people live within the walls.) The limits of pre-papal Avignon are outlined on your city map: Rues Joseph Vernet, Henri Fabre, des Lices, and Philonarde all follow the route of the city's earlier defensive wall (about half the diameter of today's wall).

The imposing facade behind you, across the square from the Palace of the Popes' main entry, was "the papal mint," which served as the finance department for the Holy See. The Petit Palais (Little Palace) seals the uphill end of the square and was built for a cardinal; today it houses medieval paintings (museum described next).

Avignon's 12th-century Romanesque cathedral, just to the left of the Palace of the Popes, has been the seat of the local bishop for more than a thousand years. Predating the Church's purchase of Avignon by 200 years, its simplicity reflects Avignon's pre-papal modesty. The gilded Mary was added in 1854 when the Vatican

Palace Square

established the doctrine of her Immaculate Conception (born without the stain of original sin).

• *You can visit the massive **Palace of the Popes** (described on page 254) now, but it's better to visit it at the end of this walk.*

Now is a good time to take in the...

PETIT PALAIS MUSEUM (MUSEE DU PETIT PALAIS)

This former cardinal's palace now displays the Church's collection of mostly art. The information is only in French, but a visit here before going to the Palace of the Popes helps furnish and populate that otherwise barren building. You'll see bits of statues and tombs—an inventory of the destruction of exquisite Church art wrought by the French Revolution (which tackled established French society with Taliban-esque fervor). Then come many rooms filled with religious Italian paintings, organized in chronological order from early Gothic to late Renaissance.

Cost and Hours: €6, Wed-Mon 10:00-13:00 & 14:00-18:00, closed Tue, at north end of Palace Square, tel. 04 90 86 44 58, www.petit-palais.org.

• *From Palace Square, head up to the cathedral (enjoy the viewpoint overlooking the square), and zig-zag up the ramps to the top of a rocky hill where Avignon was first settled. Atop the hill is an inviting café and pond in a park—our next stop. At the far side is a viewpoint high above the river from where you can see Avignon's beloved broken bridge.*

Petit Palais Museum

▲ JARDIN DU ROCHERS DES DOMS

Enjoy the view from this bluff. On a clear day, the tallest peak you see, with its white limestone cap, is Mont Ventoux ("Windy Mountain"). Below and just to the right, you'll spot free passenger ferries shuttling across the river to Ile de la Barthelasse, an island nature-preserve where Avignon can breathe. Tucked amid the trees on the island side of the river is a fun, recommended restaurant, Le Bercail, a local favorite. To the left in the distance is the TGV rail bridge.

The Rhône River marked the border of Vatican territory in medieval times. Fort St. André (across the river on the hill) was across the border, in the kingdom of France. The fort was built in 1360, shortly after the pope moved to Avignon, to counter the papal incursion into this part of Europe. Avignon's famous bridge was a key border crossing, with towers on either end—one was French, and the other was the pope's. The French one, across the river, is the Tower of Philip the Fair.

• *Take the walkway down to the left and find the stairs (closed at dusk) leading down to the tower. You'll catch glimpses of the...*

RAMPARTS

The only bit of the rampart you can walk on is accessed from St. Bénezet Bridge (pay to enter—see next). Just after the papacy took control of Avignon, the walls were extended to take in the convents and monasteries that had been outside the city. What you see today was partially restored in the 19th century.

• *When you leave the tower on street level, exit the walls, then turn left along the wall to the old bridge. Pass under the bridge to find its entrance shortly after.*

▲ ST. BENEZET BRIDGE (PONT ST. BENEZET)

This bridge, whose construction and location were inspired by a shepherd's religious vision, is the "Pont d'Avignon" of nursery-rhyme fame. The ditty (which you've probably been humming all day) dates back to the 15th century: *Sur le Pont d'Avignon, on y danse, on y danse, sur le Pont d'Avignon, on y danse tous en rond* ("On the bridge of Avignon, we will dance, we will dance, on the bridge of Avignon, we will dance all in a circle").

And the bridge was a big deal even outside of its kiddie-tune fame. Built between 1171 and 1185, it was strategic—one of only three bridges crossing the mighty Rhône in the Middle Ages, important to pilgrims, merchants, and armies. It was damaged several times by floods and subsequently rebuilt. In 1668 most of it was knocked out for the last time by a disastrous icy flood. The townsfolk decided not to rebuild this time, and for more than a century, Avignon had no bridge across the Rhône. While only 4 arches survive today, the original bridge was huge: Imagine a 22-arch, 3,000-foot-long bridge extending from Vatican territory across the island to the lonely Tower of Philip the Fair, which marked the beginning of France (see displays of the bridge's original length).

Cost and Hours: €5, includes audio-guide, €13.50 combo-ticket includes Palace of the Popes, daily March-Oct 9:00-19:00, July-Aug until 20:00, Nov-Feb 9:30-17:45, last entry one hour before closing; tel. 04 90 27 51 16.

• *To get to the Palace of the Popes from here, leave via the riverfront exit, turn left, then turn left again back into the walls. Walk to the end of the short street, then turn right following signs to Palais des Papes. Next, look for brown signs leading left under the passageway, then stay the course up the narrow steps to Palace Square.*

▲▲PALACE OF THE POPES (PALAIS DES PAPES)

In 1309 a French pope was elected (Pope Clément V). His Holiness decided that dangerous Italy was no place for a pope, so he moved the whole operation to Avignon for a secure rule under a supportive French king. The Catholic Church literally bought Avignon (then a two-bit town), and popes resided here until 1403. Meanwhile, Italians demanded a Roman pope,

St. Bénezet Bridge

so from 1378 on, there were twin popes—one in Rome and one in Avignon—causing a schism in the Catholic Church that wasn't fully resolved until 1417.

Cost and Hours: €11, €13.50 combo-ticket includes St. Bénezet Bridge, daily March-Oct 9:00-19:00, July-Aug until 20:00, Nov-Feb 9:30-17:45, last entry one hour before closing; thorough and essential audioguide-€2; tel. 04 90 27 50 00, www.palais-des-papes.com.

Visiting the Palace: You'll follow a one-way route. A big room near the start functions as "the museum," with artifacts (such as cool 14th-century arrowheads) and a good intro video.

The palace was built stark and strong, before the popes knew how long they'd be staying (and before the affluence and fanciness of the Renaissance and Baroque ages). This was the most fortified palace of the time (remember, the pope left Rome to be more secure). With 10-foot-thick walls, it was a symbol of power. There are huge ceremonial rooms (rarely used) and more intimate living quarters. The bedroom comes with the original wall paintings, a decorated wooden ceiling,

and fine tiled floor. And there's one big "chapel" (twice the size of the adjacent cathedral) that, while simple, is majestic in its pure French Gothic lines.

This largest surviving Gothic palace in Europe was built to accommodate 500 people as the administrative center of the Holy See and home of the pope. Seven popes ruled from here, making this the center of Christianity for nearly 100 years. The last pope checked out in 1403, but the Church owned Avignon until the French Revolution in 1791. During this interim period, the palace still housed Church authorities. Avignon residents, many of whom had come from Rome, spoke Italian for a century after the pope left, making the town a cultural oddity within France.

The palace is pretty empty today—nothing portable survived both the pope's return to Rome and the French Revolution. You can climb the tower (Tour de la Gâche) for grand views. The artillery room is now a gift shop, channeling all visitors on a full tour of knickknacks for sale.
• *You'll exit at the rear of the palace. To return to Palace Square, make two rights after exiting the palace.*

Palace of the Popes

Experiences
Ile de la Barthelasse Saunter

A free shuttle boat, the *Navette Fluviale*, plies back and forth across the Rhône River to Ile de la Barthelasse. This peaceful island offers grassy walks, bike rides, and the recommended riverside restaurant Le Bercail. For great views, walk the riverside path to Daladier Bridge, and then cross back over the bridge into town.

Cost and Hours: Free; 3 boats/hour depart from near St. Bénezet Bridge, daily April-June and Sept 10:00-12:30 & 14:00-18:00, July-Aug 11:00-21:00; Oct-March weekends and Wed afternoons only.

Rick's Tip: *If you stay on the island for dinner, check the schedule to make sure you* **don't miss the last return boat.**

Eating

Avignon offers a good range of restaurants and settings, from lively squares to atmospheric streets. Skip the overpriced, underwhelming restaurants on Place de l'Horloge and find a more intimate location for your dinner. At the finer places, reservations are generally smart (especially on weekends).

Fine Dining

L'Essentiel is where locals go for a fine meal. The setting is classy-contemporary inside, the back terrace is romantic, the wine list is extensive, the cuisine is classic French, and gentle owner Dominique makes timid diners feel at ease (€31-45 *menus,* closed Sun-Mon, inside and outdoor seating, 2 Rue Petite Fusterie, tel. 04 90 85 87 12, www.restaurantlessentiel. com).

Restaurant Numéro 75 is worth the walk. It fills the Pernod mansion (of *pastis* liquor fame) with a romantic, chandeliered, Old World dining hall that extends to a leafy, gravelly courtyard. They serve delightful lunch salads, fish is a forte, and

the French cuisine is beautifully presented (€32 lunch *menu,* dinner *menus:* €29 two-course and €37 three-course, closed Sun, 75 Rue Guillaume Puy, tel. 04 90 27 16 00, www.numero75.com).

Dining on a Moderate Budget

L'Epicerie sits alone under green awnings on the romantic Place St-Pierre and is ideal for dinner outside (or in the small but cozy interior). The cuisine is as delicious as the setting (€10 starters, €24 *plats,* daily, 10 Place St-Pierre, tel. 04 90 82 74 22).

La Vache à Carreaux venerates cheese and wine while offering a range of choices from its big chalkboard. It's a young, lively place, with colorful decor, easygoing service (thanks to owner Jean-Charles), and a reasonable wine list (€12 starters, €12-16 *plats,* €5 wines by the glass, daily, just off atmospheric Place des Châtaignes at 14 Rue de la Peyrolerie, tel. 04 90 80 09 05).

Across the Rhône

Le Bercail offers a fun opportunity to get out of town (barely) and take in *le fresh air* with a terrific riverfront view of Avignon, all while enjoying big portions of Provençal cooking (*menus* from €28, daily April-Oct, serves late, reservations recommended, tel. 04 90 82 20 22). Take the free shuttle boat (located near St. Bénezet Bridge) to the Ile de la Barthelasse, turn right, and

walk five minutes. As the boat usually stops running at about 18:00 (except in July-Aug, when it runs until 21:00), you can either taxi back or walk 25 minutes along the pleasant riverside path and over Daladier Bridge.

Sleeping

Hotel values are better in Arles, though I've found some pretty good deals in Avignon. Drivers should ask about parking discounts through hotels.

Rick's Tip: *During the* July theater festival, *rooms are few in Avignon—you must book long ahead and pay inflated prices.* It's better to stay in Arles.

Near Centre-Ville Station

$$ Hôtel Colbert** is on a quiet lane, with a dozen spacious rooms gathered on four floors around a skinny spiral staircase (no elevator). Patrice decorates each room with a colorful (occasionally erotic) flair. There are warm public spaces and a sweet little patio (Sb-€74, small Db-€82, bigger Db-€100, some tight bathrooms, rooms off the patio can be musty, closed Nov-mid-March, 7 Rue Agricol Perdiguier, tel. 04 90 86 20 20, www.lecolbert-hotel.com, contact@avignon-hotel-colbert.com).

Near Place de l'Horloge

$$$ Hôtel d'Europe*****, with Avignon's most prestigious address, lets peasants sleep royally—but only if they land one of the 13 reasonable "classique" rooms. Enter through a shady courtyard, linger in the lounges, and savor every comfort. The hotel is located on the handsome Place Crillon, near the river (standard "classique" Db-€230, large Db-€390-590, view suites-€1,100, breakfast-€22, garage parking-€20/day, near Daladier Bridge at 12 Place Crillon, tel. 04 90 14 76 76, www.heurope.com, reservations@heurope.com).

$$$ Hôtel de l'Horloge**** is as central as it gets—on Place de l'Horloge. It offers 66 unimaginative but comfortable rooms at fair rates, some with terraces and views of the city and the Palace of the Popes (standard Db-€140-170, bigger Db with terrace-€180-225, elaborate €18 buffet breakfast/brunch, 1 Rue Félicien David, tel. 04 90 16 42 00, www.hotel-avignon-horloge.com, hotel.horloge@hotels-ocre-azur.com).

$$ Hôtel Médiéval**, burrowed deep a few blocks from the Church of St. Pierre, was built as a cardinal's home. This stone mansion's grand staircase leads to 35 comfortable, pastel rooms (Sb-€65, Db-€75-102, family rooms available, no elevator, 5 blocks east of Place de l'Horloge, behind Church of St. Pierre at 15 Rue Petite Saunerie, tel. 04 90 86 11 06, www.hotelmedieval.com, hotel.medieval@wanadoo.fr, run by helpful Régis).

Transportation
Getting Around Avignon

Avignon's walled city is compact, and all the major sights can be visited on foot. The streets are cobbled, so wear comfortable shoes.

Arriving and Departing
BY TRAIN

Avignon has two train stations: Centre-Ville and TGV. While most TGV trains serve only the TGV Station, some also stop at Centre-Ville— check your ticket and verify your station in advance.

Centre-Ville Station (*Gare Avignon Centre-Ville*): This station gets all non-TGV trains and a few TGV trains. To reach the town center, cross the busy street in front of the station and walk through the city walls onto Cours Jean Jaurès (the TI is three blocks down).

Train Connections from Centre-Ville Station to: Arles (roughly hourly, 20 minutes, less frequent in the afternoon), Carcassonne (8/day, 7 with transfer in Narbonne or Nîmes, 3 hours).

TGV Station (*Gare TGV*): On the outskirts of town, this station has a summer-only TI (short hours), but no baggage storage. Car rental, buses, and taxis are outside the north exit (*sortie nord*). To reach the city center, take the **shuttle train** from platform A or B to Centre-Ville Station (€1.60, 2/hour, 5 minutes, buy ticket from machine on platform or at desk in main hall). A **taxi** ride between the TGV station and downtown Avignon costs about €15.

If you're connecting from the TGV Station to other points, you'll find **buses** to Arles' Centre-Ville train station at the second bus shelter (€9, 9/day, 1 hour, included with rail pass, schedule posted on shelter and available at info booths inside station). If you're **driving** a rental car directly to Arles or Les Baux, leave the station following signs to *Avignon Sud*, then *La Rocade*. You'll soon see exits to Arles (best for Les Baux, too).

Train Connections from TGV Station to: Nice (10/day, most by TGV, 4 hours, many require transfer in Marseille), Paris' Gare de Lyon (10/day direct, 2.5 hours; more connections with transfer, 3-4 hours), Paris' **Charles de Gaulle airport** (7/day, 3.25 hours).

BY BUS

The efficient bus station (*gare routière*) is 100 yards to the right as you leave the Centre-Ville train station, beyond and below Hôtel Ibis (info desk open Mon-Fri 8:00-19:30, Sat 10:00-12:30 & 13:30-18:00, closed Sun, tel. 04 90 82 07 35). Nearly all buses leave from this station (a few leave from the ring road outside the station—ask, buy tickets on bus, small bills only).

Service is reduced or nonexistent on Sundays and holidays. Make sure to verify your destination with the driver.

Bus Connections from Avignon to: Pont du Gard (3/day, 50 minutes, departs from bus station), **Arles** (9/day, 1 hour, leaves from TGV Station), **Vaison-la-Romaine** and **Séguret** (3-6/day during the school year—*période scolaire*, 3/day otherwise; 1/day from TGV Station; 1.5 hours, all buses pass through Orange—faster to take train to Orange, and transfer to bus there; express bus runs to Vaison-la-Romaine from Avignon, 1/day, 1 hour).

BY CAR

Drivers entering Avignon follow *Centre-Ville* and *Gare SNCF* (train station) signs. You'll find central pay lots in the garage next to the Centre-Ville train station and at the Parking Jean Jaurès under the ramparts across from the station (enter the old city through the Porte St-Michel gate). Hotels have advice for overnight parking, and some offer parking deals.

Two free parking lots have complimentary shuttle buses to the center except on Sunday (follow *P Gratuit* signs): **Parking de l'Île Piot** is across Daladier Bridge (Pont Daladier) on Ile de la Barthelasse, with shuttles to Place Crillon; **Parking des Italiens** is along the river east of the Palace of the Popes, with shuttles to Place Carnot (allow 30 minutes to walk from either to the center). Street parking is free in the *bleu* zones 12:00-14:00 and 19:00-9:00. (Hint: If you put €2 in the meter anytime between 19:00 and 9:00, you're good until 14:00.)

No matter where you park, leave nothing of value in your car.

NEAR ARLES AND AVIGNON

It's a short hop from Arles or Avignon to splendid scenery, Roman sights, warm stone villages, and world-class wine. See the great Roman Pont du Gard aqueduct; explore the ghost town that is ancient Les Baux; and spend time in pleasant Vaison-la-Romaine, a handy hub for the sunny Côtes du Rhône wine road.

Pont du Gard

Throughout the ancient world, aqueducts were like flags of stone that heralded the greatness of Rome. A visit to ▲▲▲ Pont du Gard still works to proclaim the wonders of that age. This impressively preserved Roman aqueduct was built in about 19 B.C., and while most of it is on or below the ground, at Pont du Gard it spans a canyon on a massive bridge over the Gardon River—one of the most remarkable surviving Roman ruins anywhere. The 30-mile aqueduct supported a small canal that, by dropping one inch for every 350 feet, supplied nine million gallons of water per day (about 100 gallons per second) to Nîmes—one of ancient Europe's largest cities. Allow about four or five hours for visiting Pont du Gard (including transportation time from Avignon).

Cost and Hours: €18/car (regardless of number of passengers), otherwise €7/ person; aqueduct—daily until 24:00; museum—daily May-Sept 9:00-19:00,

Pont du Gard

TRAIL ALONG CANAL

Wow!

PONT DU GARD

To Canal Ruins

CANAL TUNNEL

N

Gardon River

Garrigue Natural Area

P Rive Droite DON'T PARK HERE

To Remoulins & Nîmes

B To/From Avignon & Nîmes (Summer Only)

P Rive Gauche PARK HERE

MUSEUM COMPLEX
CINEMA, LUDO (KIDS' SPACE), INFO, SHOP, WC & RESTAURANT

To Avignon & Nîmes

B

D-981

To Uzès

D-981

B From Avignon & Nîmes

ROUNDABOUT

To Remoulins, Nîmes, Avignon, Arles & A-9 Freeway

Not to scale:
Roundabout to Museum is a 10-minute walk
Museum to Pont du Gard is a 5-minute walk

until 20:00 July-Aug, until 17:00 Oct-April, closed two weeks in Jan.

After Hours: The aqueduct is illuminated on summer evenings, and after the museum closes, you'll pay only €10 per carload to enter.

Getting There: The aqueduct is a 30-minute **drive** due west of Avignon (via N-100), and 45 minutes northwest of Arles (via Tarascon on D-6113). It's also reachable from Avignon by **bus** (3/day, 50 minutes), **taxi** (about €60), or **minivan tour** (Provence Reservation, also runs tours from Arles; see page 227).

Information: Tel. 04 66 37 59 99, www.pontdugard.fr.

Tours: In July and August, six tours a day go through the water channel at the top of the aqueduct (€4, check times posted at the museum and entry, no reservations are taken—limited to 33 people).

Canoe Rental: Floating under Pont du Gard by canoe is an unforgettable experience. **Collias Canoes** will pick you up at Pont du Gard (or elsewhere, if pre-arranged) and shuttle you to the town of Collias. You'll float down the river to the nearby town of Remoulins, where they'll pick you up and take you back to Pont du Gard (€21/person, €12/child under 12, usually 2 hours, though you can take as long as you like, reserve the day before in July-Aug, tel. 04 66 22 85 54).

Rick's Tip: *Pont du Gard is perhaps best enjoyed on your back and in the water—* **bring a swimsuit and flip-flops** *for the rocks. The best Pont du Gard viewpoints are up steep hills with uneven footing—***bring good shoes, too.**

Visiting the Aqueduct: There are two riversides to Pont du Gard—the Left Bank (Rive Gauche) and Right Bank (Rive Droite). Park on the Rive Gauche, where you'll find the ticket booth and TI. You'll see the aqueduct in two parts: first the

Pont du Gard

fine ▲ museum complex, then the actual river gorge spanned by the ancient bridge.

In the state-of-the-art **museum** (well-presented in English), you'll enter to the sound of water and understand the critical role fresh water played in the Roman "art of living." You'll see copies of lead pipes, faucets, and siphons; walk through a mock rock quarry; and learn how they moved those huge rocks into place and how those massive arches were made. A wooden model shows how Roman engineers determined the proper slope. While actual artifacts from the aqueduct are few, the exhibit shows the immensity of the undertaking as well as the payoff. Imagine the jubilation when this extravagant supply of water finally tumbled into Nîmes.

A park-like path leads to the **aqueduct.** Until a few years ago, this was an actual road—adjacent to the aqueduct—that had spanned the river since 1743. Before you cross the bridge, walk to the riverside viewpoint: Pass under the bridge and aqueduct and hike about 300 feet along the riverbank to the concrete steps leading down to a grand view of the world's second-highest standing Roman structure.

Ninety percent of the aqueduct is on or under the ground, but a few river canyons like this required bridges—and this was the biggest bridge in the whole 30-mile-long aqueduct. The arches are twice the width of standard aqueducts, and the main arch is the largest the Romans ever built—80 feet across (the width of the river). The bridge is about 160 feet high and was originally about 1,200 feet long.

A stone lid hides a four-foot-wide, six-foot-tall chamber lined with waterproof mortar that carried the stream for more than 400 years. For 150 years, this system provided Nîmes with good drinking water.

Hike over the bridge for a closer look and the best views. Steps lead up a high trail (marked *view point/panorama*) to a superb vista (go right at the top;

best views are soon after the trail starts descending).

Les Baux

Tucked between Arles and Avignon, the hilltop town of Les Baux crowns the rugged Alpilles mountains. Many of the ancient walls of its striking castle still stand, a testament to the proud past of this village—now more a museum than a living town.

Orientation

Les Baux is actually two visits in one: castle ruins perched on an almost lunar landscape, and a medieval town below.

Day Plan: It's mobbed with tourists most of the day, but Les Baux rewards those who arrive by 9:00 or after 17:30. Savor the castle, then tour—or blitz—the lower streets on your way out. The lower town's polished-stone gauntlet of boutiques is a Provençal dream come true for shoppers.

---

*Rick's Tip: From Arles you can **ride a rental bike to Les Baux** (25 miles round-trip). It's a darn steep climb going into Les Baux, so consider busing up there (regional buses have bike racks) and gliding back.*

Getting There: Les Baux is a 20-minute **drive** from Arles: Follow signs for *Avignon*, then *Les Baux*. From Arles, Cartreize **bus #57** runs to Les Baux (daily July-Aug, Sat-Sun only in May-June and Sept, no service Oct-April, 6/day, 35 min-

A demonstration at Les Baux

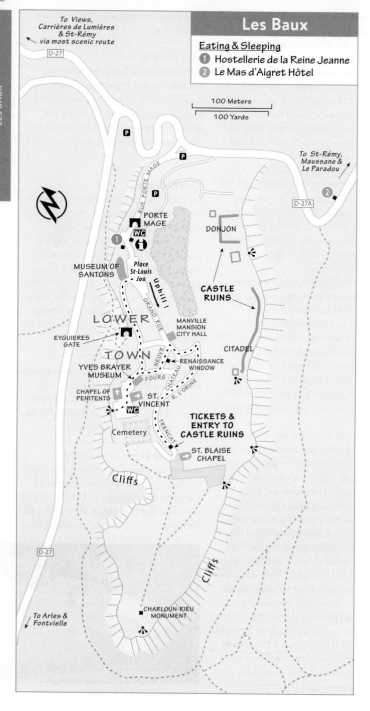

Les Baux

Eating & Sleeping

1 Hostellerie de la Reine Jeanne
2 Le Mas d'Aigret Hôtel

100 Meters
100 Yards

To Views,
Carrières de Lumières
& St-Rémy
via most scenic route

D-27

To St-Rémy,
Maussane &
Le Paradou

D-27A

RUE PORTE MAGE

PORTE
MAGE

WC

MUSEUM OF
SANTONS

Place
St-Louis-
Jou

Uphill!

GRAND RUE

DONJON

CASTLE
RUINS

LOWER

MANVILLE
MANSION
CITY HALL

EYGUIERES
GATE

TOWN

NEUVE

YVES BRAYER
MUSEUM

FOURS

RENAISSANCE
WINDOW

CHATEAU

R. L'ORME

CITADEL

CHAPEL OF
PENITENTS

ST.
VINCENT

WC

TRENCAT

Cemetery

TICKETS &
ENTRY TO
CASTLE RUINS

ST. BLAISE
CHAPEL

Cliffs

D-27

Cliffs

To Arles &
Fontvielle

CHARLOUN-RIEU
MONUMENT

utes, www.lepilote.com). The best option for many is a **minivan tour** from Arles or Avignon; consider Provence Reservation tours (see page 227).

Arrival in Les Baux: Drivers will find pay lots near the entrance to the village. Or park for free at the Carrières de Lumières (described later) and walk along the road to Les Baux. The cobbled street into town and up the main drag leads directly to the castle—just keep going uphill (10-minute walk).

Tourist Information: The TI is immediately on the left as you enter the village (daily April-Oct, closed Sun off-season).

Sights
▲▲▲THE CASTLE RUINS (CHATEAU DES BAUX)
The sun-bleached ruins of the stone fortress of Les Baux are carved into, out of, and on top of a rock 650 feet above the valley floor. Here you can imagine the struggles of a strong community of people who lived a rough-and-tumble life—more interested in top-notch fortifications than dramatic views.

In the 11th century, Les Baux was a powerhouse in southern France, controlling about 80 towns. The lords of Baux fought the counts of Barcelona for control of Provence...and eventually lost. Later, Les Baux struggled with the French kings, who destroyed the fortress in 1483 and again in 1632. The once-powerful town of 4,000 was forever crushed.

Cost and Hours: €8, €10 if there's entertainment (see next), €15 combo-ticket with Carrières de Lumières (described later), includes excellent audioguide, daily Easter-June and Sept 9:00-19:15, July-Aug 9:00-20:15, March and Oct 9:30-18:30, Nov-Feb 10:00-17:00, tel. 04 90 54 55 56, www.chateau-baux-provence.com.

Rick's Tip: **Château des Baux** *closes at the end of the day, but once you're inside, you can* **stay as long as you like.** *You're welcome to bring a picnic (no food sold inside) and live out your medieval fantasies, all night long.*

View from the Château des Baux

Entertainment: Every day from April through September, the castle presents medieval pageantry, tournaments, demonstrations, and jousting matches. Pick up a schedule as you enter (or check online).

Visiting the Castle: As you walk on the windblown spur (*baux* in French), you'll pass kid-thrilling medieval siege weaponry (go ahead, try the battering ram). Good displays help reconstruct the place. Imagine 4,000 people living up here. Notice the water-catchment system (a slanted field that caught rainwater and drained it into cisterns—necessary during a siege) and find the reservoir cut into the rock below the castle's highest point. Look for post holes throughout the stone walls that reveal where beams once supported floors. For the most sensational views, climb to the blustery top of the citadel. Hang on. The mistral wind just might blow you away.

▲LOWER TOWN

After your castle visit, you can shop and eat your way back through the lower town. Or, escape some of the crowds by dropping in at these minor but worthwhile

Castle ruins at Les Baux

sights as you descend. The 15th-century **City Hall** offers art exhibits under its cool vaults; the enjoyable Musée Yves Brayer lets you peruse three floors of Van Gogh-like Expressionist paintings; the 12th-century Romanesque **St. Vincent Church** was built short and wide to fit the terrain; and the free and fun **Museum of Santons** displays a collection of *santons* ("little saints"), popular folk figurines that decorate local Christmas mangers.

▲CARRIERES DE LUMIERES (QUARRIES OF LIGHT)

A 10-minute walk from Les Baux, this colossal quarry-cave with immense vertical walls offers a mesmerizing sound-and-slide experience. The show lasts 40 minutes and runs continuously. Dress warmly, as the cave is cool.

Cost and Hours: €11, €16 combo-ticket with Les Baux castle ruins, daily April-Sept 9:30-19:30, March and Oct-Dec 10:00-18:00, closed Jan-Feb, tel. 04 90 54 47 37, www.carrieres-lumieres.com.

Eating and Sleeping

In the **lower town**, you'll find quiet view cafés such as **Hostellerie de la Reine Jeanne****, which also offers $ good-value rooms (just inside the town gate, www.la-reinejeanne.com). A plusher overnight option is **$$$ Le Mas d'Aigret*****, a 10-minute walk east of Les Baux on D-27 (www.masdaigret.com).

Vaison-la-Romaine

With quick access to vineyards and villages, this lively little town of 6,000 (rated ▲) sits north of Avignon and makes a good base for exploring the Côtes du Rhône wine region. You get two villages for the price of one: The "modern" lower city has Roman ruins and a bustling main square—café-lined Place Montfort. The car-free medieval hill town looms above, with meandering cobbled lanes and a ruined castle with a fine view.

Le Mistral

Provence lives with its vicious mistral winds, which blow 30 to 60 miles per hour, about 100 days of the year. The mistral clears people off the streets and turns lively cities into ghost towns. You'll likely spend a few hours or days taking refuge.

When the mistral blows, you can't escape. Author Peter Mayle said it could blow the ears off a donkey (I'd include the tail). According to the natives, it ruins crops, shutters, and roofs (look for stones holding tiles in place on many homes). They'll also tell you that this pernicious wind has driven many people crazy (including young Vincent van Gogh).

The mistral starts above the Alps and Massif Central mountains, then gathers steam as it heads south, funneling through the Rhône Valley before exhausting itself when it hits the Mediterranean. And though this wind rattles shutters everywhere in the Riviera and Provence, it's strongest over the Rhône Valley...so Avignon, Arles, and the Côtes du Rhône villages bear its brunt. While wiping the dust from your eyes, remember the good news: The mistral brings clear skies.

Orientation

The city is split in two by the Ouvèze River. The town's Roman Bridge connects the lower town (Ville-Basse) with the hill-capping upper town (Ville-Haute).

Getting There: Bus service connects Avignon and Vaison-la-Romaine, usually via Orange (3-6/day, 1.5 hour; 1 express bus/day, 1 hour). Vaison-la-Romaine is about a 40-minute **drive** from Avignon.

Arrival in Vaison-la-Romaine: If you're riding the bus, tell the driver you want to go to the *Office de Tourisme*. From the bus stop, walk five minutes down Avenue Général de Gaulle to reach the TI. Drivers should follow signs to *Centre-Ville*, then *Office de Tourisme*; parking is free across from the TI and at most places in town.

Tourist Information: The superb TI is in the lower city, between the two Roman ruin sites, at Place du Chanoine Sautel (daily but closed Sun off-season, tel. 04 90 36 02 11, www.vaison-ventoux-tourisme.com).

Private Guide: For historic town walks, try **Anna-Marie Melard** (tel. 04 90 36 50 48) or **Janet Henderson** (www.provencehistorytours.com).

Cooking Classes: Charming Barbara Schuerenberg offers reasonably priced cooking classes from her view home (€80, cash only, includes lunch, www.cuisinedeprovence.com).

Sights

ROMAN RUINS

Ancient Vaison-la-Romaine had a treaty that gave it a preferred "federated" relationship with Rome. This, along with a healthy farming economy (olives and vineyards), made it a prosperous place, as a close look at its sprawling ruins demonstrates.

Cost and Hours: €8; daily April-May 9:30-18:00, June-Sept until 18:30, shorter hours off-season, closed Jan-Feb; videoguide-€3 or download free app, tel. 04 90 36 50 48, www.vaison-la-romaine.com.

Visiting the Ruins: Vaison-la-Romaine's Roman ruins are split by a modern road into two sites: Puymin and La Villasse. Each is well-presented, thanks to the videoguide and information panels, offering a good look at life during the Roman Empire. What you can see is only a small fraction of the ancient town's extent—most is still buried under today's city.

Visit **Puymin** first. Nearest the entry are the scant but impressive ruins of a sprawling mansion. Find the faint remains of a colorful frescoed wall. Climb the hill

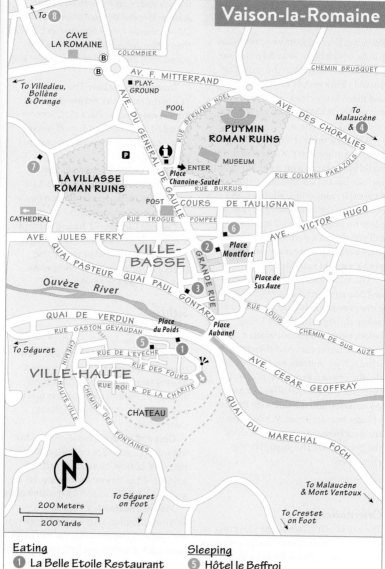

Vaison-la-Romaine

To ⑧

CAVE
LA ROMAINE
COLOMBIER
B
AV. F. MITTERRAND
CHEMIN BRUSQUET
B
To Villedieu,
Bollène
& Orange
PLAY-
GROUND

POOL

AVE. DU GENERAL DE GAULLE

RUE BERNARD NOEL

PUYMIN
ROMAN RUINS

MUSEUM

AVE. DES CHORALIES

To
Malaucène
& ④

P

⑦

LA VILLASSE
ROMAN RUINS

ENTER
Place
Chanoine-Sautel

RUE BURRUS

RUE COLONEL PARAZOLS

POST
COURS DE TAULIGNAN
RUE TROGUE POMPEE
CATHEDRAL

AVE. JULES FERRY

VILLE-
BASSE

⑥

② Place
Montfort

AVE. VICTOR HUGO

QUAI PASTEUR QUAI PAUL GONTARD

GRANDE RUE

Place de
Sus Auze

Ouvèze River

③

RUE LOUIS

QUAI DE VERDUN
RUE GASTON GEVAUDAN

Place
du Poids

Place
Aubanel

CHEMIN DE SUS AUZE

To Séguret

⑤

①

AVE. CESAR GEOFFRAY

CHEMIN HAUTE VILLE

RUE DE L'EVECHE
RUE DES FOURS

VILLE-HAUTE

RUE ROI R. DE LA CHARITE

CHATEAU

CHEMIN DES FONTAINES

QUAI DU MARECHAL FOCH

N

200 Meters
200 Yards

To Séguret
on Foot

To Malaucène
& Mont Ventoux

To Crestet
on Foot

Eating

① La Belle Etoile Restaurant
② O'Natur'elles Restaurant
③ Le Brin d'Olivier Restaurant
④ To Auberge d'Anaïs

Sleeping

⑤ Hôtel le Beffroi
⑥ Hôtel Burrhus
⑦ Les Tilleuls d'Elisée
⑧ To L'Ecole Buissonnière Chambres

to the good little **museum** (pick up your videoguide here). Be sure to see the **3-D film** that takes you inside the home of a wealthy Vaison resident and explores daily life some 2,000 years ago. Behind the museum is a still well-used, 6,000-seat theater, with just enough seats for the whole town (of yesterday and today).

Back across the modern road in **La Villasse,** you'll explore a "street of shops" and the foundations of more houses. You'll also see a few wells, used before Vaison's two aqueducts were built.

LOWER TOWN (VILLE-BASSE)

Vaison-la-Romaine's modern town centers on café-friendly Place Montfort. A 10-minute walk below Place Montfort, the stout **Notre-Dame de Nazareth Cathedral** is a good example of Provençal Romanesque dating from the 11th century, with an evocative cloister and fine stone carvings (free, daily, closed Oct-March). The pedestrian-only Grand Rue is a lively shopping street leading to the small river gorge and the **Roman Bridge,** a sturdy, no-nonsense vault cut by the Romans into the canyon rock 2,000 years ago.

UPPER TOWN (VILLE-HAUTE)

Although there's nothing of particular importance to see in the fortified medieval old town atop the hill, the cobbled lanes and enchanting fountains make you want to break out a sketchpad. Vaison-la-Romaine was ruled by a prince-bishop starting in the fourth century. He came under attack by the Count of Toulouse in the 12th century. Anticipating a struggle, the prince-bishop abandoned the lower town and built a castle on this rocky outcrop (about 1195). Over time, the townspeople followed, vacating the lower town and building their homes at the base of the château behind the upper town's fortified wall.

To reach the upper town, hike up from the Roman Bridge through the medieval gate, under the lone tower crowned by an 18th-century wrought-iron bell cage. The château is closed, but a steep, uneven trail to its base rewards hikers with a sweeping view.

Vaison-la-Romaine's ancient theater

▲HIKING AND BIKING

The hills above Vaison-la-Romaine are picture-perfect for hikers and bikers. The TI has good information on your options, and can direct you to bike-rental shops. For destinations, consider the quiet hill town of Crestet, cute little Séguret, or delightful Villedieu.

Eating

La Belle Etoile is where locals go for fresh, good-value meals (closed Thu, 5 Rue du Pont Romain). **O'Natur'elles** is ideal for vegetarians; the all-organic dishes can be served with or without meat (reservations smart, closed Tue eve, tel. 04 90 65 81 67). Romantic **Le Brin d'Olivier** has soft lighting and good food (closed Wed except July-Aug, 4 Rue du Ventoux). With a car, drive 10 minutes east from town to **Auberge d'Anaïs** for a true Provençal experience—ask for a table *sur la terrasse* (closed Sun eve and Mon, on the road to St-Marcellin, tel. 04 90 36 20 06).

Sleeping

In the upper town, try the cozy **$$$ Hôtel le Beffroi***** (www.le-beffroi.com); in the lower town, two good choices are **$$ Hôtel Burrhus**** (1 Place Montfort,

www.burrhus.com) and **$$ Les Tilleuls d'Elisée** (1 Avenue Jules Mazen, www.vaisonchambres.info). Drivers will enjoy a stay at **$$ L'Ecole Buissonnière Chambres,** a restored farmhouse 10 minutes north of town (cash only, between Villedieu and Buisson on D-75, www.buissonniere-provence.com).

Rick's Tip: *Sleep in Vaison-la-Romaine on Monday night, and you'll wake to an amazing* **Tuesday market,** *one of France's best. But be* **careful where you park:** *Avoid anyplace signed Stationnement Interdit le Mardi (parking forbidden on Tuesday), or you won't find your car where you left it.*

Côtes du Rhône Wine Road

To experience the best of the Côtes du Rhône vineyards and villages, take this half-day ▲▲▲ loop around the rugged Dentelles de Montmirail mountain peaks (figure about 40 miles total; see map on facing page). You'll experience the finest this region has to offer: natural beauty, glowing limestone villages, inviting wineries, and rolling hills of vineyards.

Start just south of Vaison-la-Romaine in little **Séguret.** This town is best for a visit early or late, when it's quieter. Explore the village (ideal for a morning coffee break), then drive up and up to the **Domaine de Mourchon** winery. From here, return to Vaison-la-Romaine and follow signs toward *Carpentras/ Malaucène*, pass through Crestet, then follow signs leading up to *Le Village* (D-76).

After ambling the quiet village of **Crestet,** follow signs to *Malaucène* and turn right on D-90 (direction: Suzette) just before the gas station. The D-90 route is the scenic highlight of this loop, which follows the back side of the Dentelles de Montmirail past mountain views, remote villages, and beautifully situated wineries (**Domaine de Coyeux** is best).

Côtes du Rhône Driving Tour

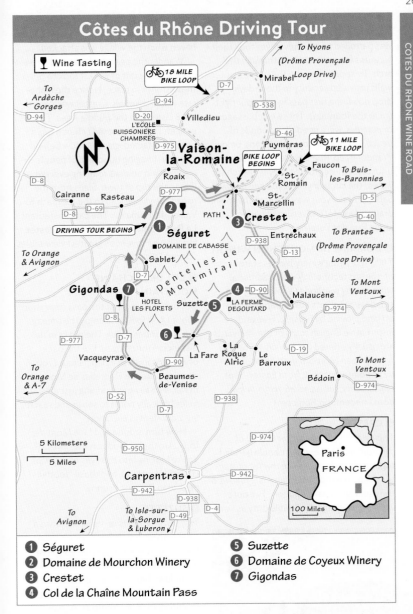

| Wine Tasting |

🚲 **18 MILE BIKE LOOP**

🚲 **11 MILE BIKE LOOP**

To Nyons
(Drôme Provençale
Loop Drive)

Mirabel

To Ardèche Gorges

D-94

D-7

D-94

D-538

D-20

Villedieu

L'ECOLE BUISSONIÈRE CHAMBRES

D-975

Vaison-la-Romaine

D-46

Puyméras

BIKE LOOP BEGINS

St-Romain

Faucon

To Buis-les-Baronnies

Roaix

D-977

St-Marcellin

D-5

D-8

Cairanne

Rasteau

PATH

❸ Crestet

D-40

D-8

D-69

DRIVING TOUR BEGINS

❶ **Séguret**

Entrechaux

To Brantes
(Drôme Provençale
Loop Drive)

■DOMAINE DE CABASSE

D-938

D-13

Sablet

D e n t e l l e s   d e
M o n t m i r a i l

To Orange & Avignon

D-7

Gigondas ❼

❹ D-90

Malaucène

To Mont Ventoux

HOTEL LES FLORETS

Suzette ❺

■LA FERME DEGOUTARD

D-974

D-8

❻ |

D-977

D-7

La Fare

La Roque Alric

Le Barroux

D-19

To Mont Ventoux

Vacqueyras

D-90

Beaumes-de-Venise

Bédoin

D-974

To Orange & A-7

D-52

D-938

D-7

D-974

5 Kilometers

D-950

Carpentras

D-942

Paris

FRANCE

5 Miles

D-942

D-938

D-4

To Avignon

To Isle-sur-la-Sorgue & Luberon

D-49

100 Miles

❶ Séguret
❷ Domaine de Mourchon Winery
❸ Crestet
❹ Col de la Chaîne Mountain Pass
❺ Suzette
❻ Domaine de Coyeux Winery
❼ Gigondas

Take your time for this drive: You'll pass trailheads, scenic pullouts, and good picnic spots. Consider lunch along the way.

D-90 ends in Beaumes de Venise. Follow signs back toward *Vaison-la-Romaine* to **Gigondas** and explore this village.

⊙ *Self-Guided Tour*
❶ SEGURET

Séguret's name comes from the Latin word *securitas* (meaning "security"). The bulky entry arch came with a massive gate, which drilled in the message of the village's name. In the Middle Ages, Séguret was patrolled 24/7—they never took their *securitas* for granted. Walk through the arch. To appreciate how the homes' outer walls provided security in those days, drop down the first passage on your right (near the fountain). These exit passages, or *poternes*, were needed in periods of peace to allow the town to expand below. Wander deep. Rue Calade leads up to the unusual 12th-century St. Denis church for views (the circular village you see below is Sablet). Make your way down to the main drag and a café, and return to parking along Rue des Poternes.

❷ DOMAINE DE MOURCHON WINERY

This high-flying winery blends state-of-the-art technology with traditional winemaking methods (a shiny ring of stainless-steel vats holds grapes grown on land plowed by horses). Free and informative English tours of the vineyards are usually offered (wines–€8-33/bottle; winery open Mon-Sat 9:00-18:00, Sun by appointment only; from Easter-Sept, call to verify; tel. 04 90 46 70 30, www. domainedemourchon.com).

❸ CRESTET

This village—founded after the fall of the Roman Empire, when people banded together in high places like this for protection from marauding barbarians—followed the usual hill-town evolution. The outer walls of the village did double duty as ram-

parts and house walls. The castle above (from about A.D. 850) provided a final safe haven when the village was attacked.

Wander the peaceful lanes and appreciate the amount of work it took to put these stones in place. Notice the elaborate water channels. Crestet was served by 18 cisterns in the Middle Ages. The peaceful (usually closed) church has a beautiful stained-glass window behind the altar. Imagine hundreds of people living here and animals roaming everywhere. Get to the top of town. Signs from the top of the village lead to the footpath to Vaison-la-Romaine. The café-restaurant **Le Panoramic,** at the top of old **Crestet,** must have Provence's greatest view tables (closed Dec-March).

❹ COL DE LA CHAINE MOUNTAIN PASS

Get out of your car at the pass (elevation: about 1,500 feet) and enjoy the breezy views. Wander about. The peaks in the distance—thrusting up like the back of a stegosaurus or a bad haircut (you decide)—are the Dentelles de Montmirail, a small range running just nine miles basically north to south and reaching 2,400 feet in elevation.

Now turn around and face Mont Ventoux. Are there clouds on the horizon? You're looking into the eyes of the Alps (behind Ventoux), and those "foothills" help keep Provence sunny.

❺ SUZETTE

Tiny Suzette floats on its hilltop, with a small 12th-century chapel, one café, a handful of residents, and the gaggle of houses where they live. Park in Suzette's lot, below, then find the big orientation board above the lot. Look out to the broad shoulders of Mont Ventoux. At 6,000 feet, it always seems to have some clouds hanging around. If it's clear, the top looks like it's snow-covered; if you drive up there, you'll see it's actually white stone.

The village of Séguret

❻ DOMAINE DE COYEUX WINERY

A private road winds up and up to this impossibly beautiful setting, with the best views of the Dentelles I've found. Olive trees frame the final approach, and *Le Caveau* signs lead to a modern tasting room (you may need to ring the buzzer). This stop is for serious wine lovers—skip it if you only want a quick taste or are not interested in buying (wines–€8-16/bottle; winery generally open daily 10:00-12:00 & 14:00-18:00, except closed Sun off-season and no midday closure July-Aug; tel. 04 90 12 42 42, http://domainedecoyeux.com/en, some English spoken).

❼ GIGONDAS

This town produces some of the region's best reds and is ideally situated for hiking, mountain biking, and driving into the mountains. The **TI** has lists of wineries, rental bikes, and tips for good hikes or drives (Mon-Sat 10:00-12:30 & 14:00-18:00, closed Sun, Place du Portail, tel. 04 90 65 85 46, www.gigondas-dm.fr). Take a short walk through the village lanes above the TI—the church is an easy destination with good views over the heart of the Côtes du Rhône vineyards.

You'll find several good tasting opportunities on the main square; **Le Caveau de Gigondas** is the best (daily 10:00-12:00 & 14:00-18:30, near TI, www.caveaudugigondas.com). The restaurant at **Hôtel les Florets,** serving classic French cuisine with Provençal accents, is well worth it—particularly if you dine on the magnificent terrace (closed Wed, service can be slow).

Ⓐ *Wine tasting in the Côtes du Rhône*
Ⓑ *Vineyards of Domaine de Coyeux*
Ⓒ *Côtes du Rhône vineyards*
Ⓓ *Café in Suzette*

The French Riviera

A hundred years ago, celebrities from London to Moscow flocked to the French Riviera to socialize, gamble, and escape the dreary weather at home. Today, budget vacationers and heat-seeking Europeans fill belle époque resorts at France's most sought-after fun-in-the-sun destination.

Some of the Continent's most stunning scenery and intriguing museums lie along this strip of land—as do millions of sun-worshipping tourists. The Riviera's gateway is urban Nice, with world-class museums, a splendid beachfront promenade, a seductive old town, the best selection of hotels in all price ranges, and good nightlife options.

This sunny sliver of land is well served by public transportation, making day trips by train or bus almost effortless. If you drive here, expect traffic—although you'll be rewarded with sensational views on the coastal routes. If you head east from Nice, you'll find little Villefranche-sur-Mer staring across the bay at exclusive Cap Ferrat. Farther along, Monaco offers a royal welcome and a fairytale past. To the west, Antibes has a thriving port and silky sand beaches. Wherever you choose to spend your days, evenings everywhere on the Riviera are radiant—made for a promenade and outdoor dining.

THE FRENCH RIVIERA IN 2 DAYS

My favorite home bases are Nice, Villefranche-sur-Mer, and Antibes. Nice, with convenient train and bus connections to most regional sights, is the most practical base for train travelers. Villefranche-sur-Mer is the romantic's choice, with a peaceful setting and small-town warmth, while midsize Antibes has the best beaches and works best for drivers.

Allow a full day for Nice: Spend your morning sifting through the old city (called Vieux Nice; take my Old Nice Walk) and ascend the elevator up Castle Hill for fine views. Devote the afternoon to the museums (Chagall is best, closed Tue) and strolling the Promenade des Anglais, taking my self-guided walk (best before or after dinner, but anytime is fine).

Save most of your second day for Monaco (tour Monaco-Ville, have lunch, and drop by the famous Monte Carlo casino), then consider a late afternoon or dinner in Villefranche-sur-Mer. With more time, explore Antibes' fine Picasso Museum and sandy old town. Or stop by lush Cap Ferrat, filled with mansions, gardens, and beaches.

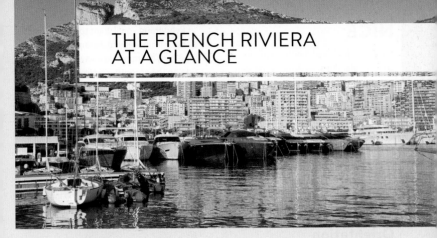

THE FRENCH RIVIERA AT A GLANCE

Nice

▲▲▲**Promenade des Anglais Walk** Nice's sun-struck seafront promenade. **Hours:** Always open. See page 278

▲▲▲**Chagall Museum** The world's largest collection of Marc Chagall's work, popular even with people who don't like modern art. **Hours:** May-Oct Wed-Mon 10:00-18:00, Nov-April until 17:00, closed Tue year-round. See page 286.

▲▲**Old Nice Walk** Exploring the enjoyable old city, with its charming French-Italian cultural blend. **Hours:** Always open. See page 283.

▲**Matisse Museum** Modest collection of Henri Matisse's paintings, sketches, and paper cutouts. **Hours:** Wed-Mon 10:00-18:00, closed Tue. See page 288.

▲**Russian Cathedral** Finest Orthodox church outside Russia. **Hours:** Mon 13:30-17:00, Tue-Sun 10:00-17:00. See page 289.

▲**Castle Hill** Site of an ancient fort boasting great views. **Hours:** Park closes at 20:00 in summer, earlier off-season. See page 289.

Nearby

▲▲▲**Villefranche-sur-Mer** Romantic Italianate beach town with a serene setting, yacht-filled harbor, and small-town ambience. See page 301.

▲▲▲**Monaco** Tiny independent municipality known for its classy casino and Grand Prix car race. See page 307.

▲▲**Cap Ferrat** Exclusive, woodsy peninsula with a family-friendly beach and tourable Rothschild mansion. See page 305.

▲▲**Antibes** Laid-back beach town with a medieval center, worthwhile Picasso Museum (closed Mon), sandy beaches, and view-strewn hikes. See page 313.

NICE

Nice (sounds like "niece"), with its spectacular Alps-to-Mediterranean surroundings, is the big-city highlight of the Riviera. Its traffic-free old town mixes Italian and French flavors to create a spicy Mediterranean dressing, while its big squares, broad seaside walkways, and long beaches invite lounging and people-watching. Nice may be nice, but it's hot and jammed in July and August—reserve ahead and get a room with air-conditioning.

Orientation

The main points of interest lie between the beach and the train tracks (about 15 blocks apart). The city revolves around its grand Place Masséna, where pedestrian-friendly Avenue Jean Médecin meets Vieux (Old) Nice and the Albert I parkway (with quick access to the beaches). It's a 20-minute walk (or about €12 by taxi) from the train station to the beach, and a 20-minute stroll along the promenade from the fancy Hôtel Negresco to the heart of Vieux Nice.

Everything you'll want to see in Nice is either within walking distance, or a short bike, bus, or tram ride away. A 10-minute ride on the smooth-as-silk tram through the center of the city connects the train station, Place Masséna, Vieux Nice, and the port (from nearby Place Garibaldi).

Tourist Information: Nice has several helpful TIs (tel. 08 92 70 74 07, www. nicetourisme.com), including branches at the **airport** (daily 9:00-18:00, April-Sept until 20:00), the **train station** (summer, daily 8:00-20:00, rest of year Mon-Sat 9:00-19:00, Sun 10:00-17:00), at 5 **Promenade des Anglais** (daily 9:00-18:00, July-Aug until 20:00), and on the north side of **Place Masséna** (May-mid-Sept only, daily 10:00-17:00). Ask for day-trip information, including details on boat excursions, and train and bus schedules.

Theft Alert: Nice has its share of pickpockets (especially at the train station, on the tram, and trolling the beach). Stick to main streets in Vieux Nice after dark.

SNCF Boutique: A French rail ticket office is a half-block west of Avenue Jean Médecin at 2 Rue de la Liberté (Mon-Fri 10:00-17:50, closed Sat-Sun).

Nice's historic Hôtel Negresco overlooks the Promenade des Anglais.

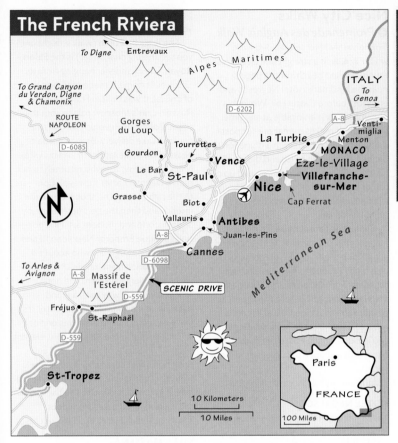

The French Riviera

To Digne • Entrevaux

Alpes Maritimes

ITALY
To Genoa

To Grand Canyon
du Verdon, Digne
& Chamonix

D-6202

A-8

ROUTE
NAPOLEON

D-6085

Venti-
miglia

Gorges
du Loup

La Turbie

Menton

MONACO

Tourrettes

Gourdon

Vence

Eze-le-Village

Le Bar

St-Paul

Villefranche-
sur-Mer

Nice

Grasse

Cap Ferrat

Biot

Vallauris

Antibes

Juan-les-Pins

A-8

D-6098

Cannes

Mediterranean Sea

To Arles &
Avignon

A-8

Massif de
l'Estérel

D-559

SCENIC DRIVE

Fréjus

St-Raphaël

D-559

St-Tropez

10 Kilometers

10 Miles

Paris

FRANCE

100 Miles

Renting a Bike (and Other Wheels): **Holiday Bikes** has multiple locations, including one across from the train station, and they have electric bikes (www.loca-bike.fr). **Roller Station** is well-situated near the sea and rents bikes, rollerblades, skateboards, and Razor-style scooters (bikes-€5/hour, €10/half-day, €15/day, leave ID as deposit, open daily, next to yellow awnings of Pailin's Asian restaurant at 49 Quai des Etats-Unis, tel. 04 93 62 99 05).

Private Guide: Consider **Pascale Rucker,** an art-loving guide who teaches with the joy and wonder of a flower child (€160/half-day, €260/day, tel. 06 16 24 29 52, pascalerucker@gmail.com).

Minivan Tours: These two energetic and delightful women have comfortable minibuses and enjoy taking couples and small groups anywhere in the region: **Sylvie Di Cristo** (€600/day, €350/half-day for up to 8 people, mobile 06 09 88 83 83, www.frenchrivieraguides.net, dicristosylvie@gmail.com) and **Ingrid Schmucker** (€490/day for 4 people or €550/day for 5-7 people, €180/half-day or €285/day if you don't need transportation, tel. 06 14 83 03 33, www.kultours.fr, info@kultours.fr). The TI and most hotels have information on more economic shared minivan excursions from Nice (roughly €50-70/person per half-day, €80-120/person per day).

Nice City Walks

◐ Promenade des Anglais Walk

This leisurely, level self-guided walk, worth ▲▲▲, is a straight line along this much-strolled beachfront. It begins near the landmark Hôtel Negresco and ends just before Castle Hill. While this one-mile walk is enjoyable at any time, the first half makes a great pre- or post-dinner stroll (perhaps with a dinner on the beach). If you plan to extend this stroll to Castle Hill, try to time it so you end up on top of the hill at sunset. Allow one hour at a promenade pace to reach the elevator up to Castle Hill.

Biking the Promenade: To rev up the pace of your promenade, rent a bike and glide along the coast in either or both directions (about 30 minutes each way; for rental info, see page 277). The path to the **west** stops just before the airport at perhaps the most scenic *boules* courts in France. If you take the path heading **east,** you'll round Castle Hill to the harbor of Nice, with a chance to survey some fancy yachts.

• *Start your walk at the pink-domed...*

HOTEL NEGRESCO

Nice's finest hotel is also a historic monument, offering up the city's most expensive beds and a museum-like interior. While the hotel is off-limits to nonguests, the doorman explained to me that shoppers and drinkers are "guests" as much as people actually sleeping there. So if you say you're going in for a drink (at their

Biking the promenade

pricey Le Bar du Negresco) or to shop, you may be allowed in.

The huge ballroom (walk straight until you see the big chandelier) is the **Salon Royal.** The chandelier hanging from its Eiffel-built dome is made of 16,000 pieces of crystal. It was built in France for the Russian czar's Moscow palace...but thanks to the Bolshevik Revolution in 1917, he couldn't take delivery. Bronze portrait busts of Czar Alexander III and his wife, Maria Feodorovna—who returned to her native Denmark after the revolution—are to the right, facing the shops. Circle the interior and then the perimeter to enjoy both historic and modern art. Fine portraits include Emperor Napoleon III and wife, Empress Eugénie (who acquired Nice for France from Italy in 1860), and Jeanne Augier (who owns the hotel).

If you wonder why such a grand hotel has such an understated entry, it's because today's front door was originally the back door. In the 19th century, elegant people stayed out of the sun, and any posh hotel that cared about its clientele would design its entry on the shady north side. If you walk around to the back you'll see a grand but unused front door.

• *Across the street from Hôtel Negresco is...*

VILLA MASSENA

When Nice became part of France, France invested heavily in what it expected to be the country's new high society retreat—an elite resort akin to Russia's Sochi on the Black Sea. The government built this fine palace for the military hero of the Napoleonic age, Jean-Andre Masséna and his family. Take a moment to stroll around the lovely garden (free, daily 10:00-18:00).

• *From Villa Masséna, head for the beach and begin your Promenade des Anglais stroll. But first, grab a blue chair and gaze out to the...*

BAY OF ANGELS (BAIE DES ANGES)

Face the water. The body of Nice's patron saint, Réparate, was supposedly escorted into this bay by angels in the fourth century. To your right is where you might have been escorted into France—Nice's airport, built on a massive landfill. The tip of land beyond the runway is Cap d'Antibes. Until 1860, Antibes and Nice were in different countries—Antibes was French, but Nice was a protectorate of the Italian kingdom of Savoy-Piedmont, a.k.a. the Kingdom of Sardinia. During that period, the Var River—just west of Nice—was the geographic border between these two peoples. In 1850 the people here spoke Italian and ate pasta. As Italy was uniting, the region was given a choice: Join the new country of Italy or join France (which was enjoying prosperous times under the rule of Napoleon III). The vast majority voted in 1860 to go French...and *voilà!* (In reality, the Italian king needed France's support in helping Italian regions controlled by Austria break away to join the emerging union of Italian states. Italy's price for France's support against Austria: Nice.)

The lower green hill to your left is Castle Hill. Farther left lie Villefranche-sur-Mer and Cap Ferrat (marked by the tower at land's end, and home to lots of millionaires), then Monaco (which you can't see, with more millionaires), then Italy. Behind you are the foothills of the Alps, which trap threatening clouds, ensuring that the Côte d'Azur enjoys sunshine more than 300 days each year.

• *With the sea on your right, begin strolling.*

THE PROMENADE

Nearby sit two fine belle époque establishments: the West End and Westminster hotels, both boasting English names to help those original guests feel at home (the West End is now part of the Best Western group...to help American guests feel at home). These hotels symbolize Nice's arrival as a tourist mecca in the 19th century, when the combination of leisure time and a stable economy allowed visitors to find the sun even in winter.

As you walk, be careful to avoid the green bike lane. You'll pass a number of separate rocky beaches. You can go local and rent gear—about €15 for a *chaise longue* (long chair) and a *transat* (mattress), €5 for an umbrella, and €4 for a towel. You'll also pass several beach restaurants. Some of these eateries serve breakfast, all serve lunch, some do dinner, and a few have beachy bars...tailor-made for a break from this walk. (Plage Beau

The Bay of Angels epitomizes the beauty of the French Riviera.

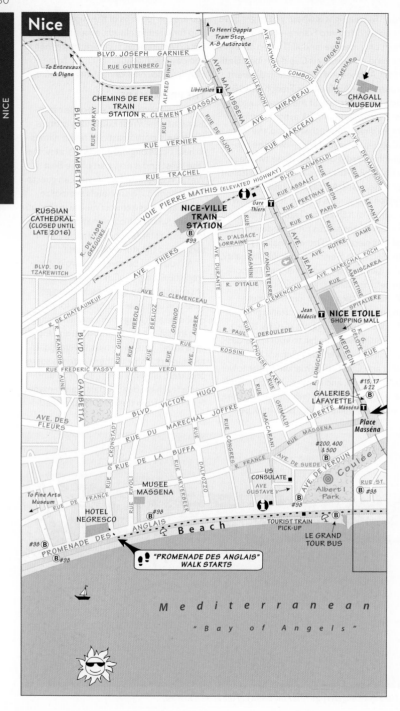

Nice

To Henri Sappia
Tram Stop,
A-8 Autoroute

BLVD. JOSEPH GARNIER
RUE GUTENBERG
To Entrevaux
& Digne
Libération T

CHEMINS DE FER
TRAIN
STATION   R. CLEMENT ROASSAL
RUE DE DIJON
RUE VERNIER
RUE TRACHEL

BLVD. GAMBETTA
RUE DABRAY
RUE DE L'ABBE GREGOIRE

VOIE PIERRE MATHIS (ELEVATED HIGHWAY)
NICE-VILLE
TRAIN
STATION
B #99

RUSSIAN
CATHEDRAL
(CLOSED UNTIL
LATE 2016)

BLVD. DU
TZAREWITCH

AVE. THIERS
AVE. DURANTE
R. D'ALSACE-LORRAINE
PAGANINI
R. D'ITALIE
R. D'ANGLETERRE

Gare
Thiers T

AVE. MALAUSSENA
ALFRED BINET
AVE. VILLERMONT
AVE. MIRABEAU
AVE. MARCEAU
AVE. RAYMOND
COMBOU
AVE. GEORGES V
AVE. D. MENARD

CHAGALL
MUSEUM

RUE MARCEAU
AVE. DESAMBROIS
RUE DE LEPANTE
BLVD. RAIMBALDI
RUE ASSALIT
RUE PERTINAX
RUE DE PARIS
AVE. NOTRE-DAME
AVE. MARECHAL FOCH
BISCARRA
RUE LAMARTINE
SPITALIERE

RUE MIRON
RUE JEAN
MEDECIN

Jean
Médecin T NICE ETOILE
SHOPPING MALL

R. DE CHATEAUNEUF
R. FRANCOIS
BLVD. GAMBETTA
RUE GIUGLIA
RUE HEROLD
RUE BERLIOZ
RUE GOUNOD
RUE AUBER
ROSSINI
R. PAUL ALPHONSE DEROULEDE
AVE. G. CLEMENCEAU

AVE. G. CLEMENCEAU

AVE. DES
FLEURS

RUE FREDERIC PASSY   RUE VERDI
AUNE

RUE DE CRONSTADT
BLVD. VICTOR HUGO
RUE DU MARECHAL JOFFRE
RUE DE LA BUFFA
RUE MEYERBEER
DALPOZZO
RUE DE FRANCE

RUE KARR
RUE GRIMALDI
RUE MACCARANI
AVE. DE SUEDE
R. FRANCE

RUE MASSENA
AVE. MASSENA
LIBERTE
GALERIES
LAFAYETTE
Masséna T

#15, 17
& 22
B

Place
Masséna

#200, 400
& 500

MUSEE
MASSENA

HOTEL
NEGRESCO

To Fine Arts
Museum

RUE RIVOLI
B #98

US
CONSULATE
AVE
GUSTAVE
B
#98

AVE. DE VERDUN
Coulée
Albert I
Park

RUE ST.
B #98

TOURIST TRAIN
PICK-UP
LE GRAND
TOUR BUS
B

PROMENADE DES   ANGLAIS   B e a c h
B #98
#98 B

"PROMENADE DES
ANGLAIS"
WALK STARTS

M e d i t e r r a n e a n

" B a y   o f   A n g e l s "

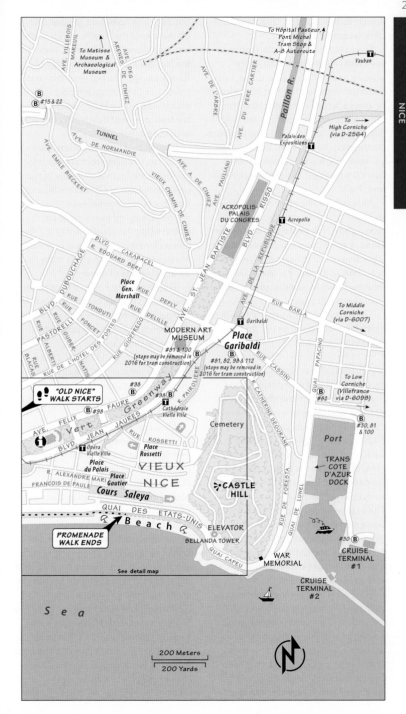

To Matisse
Museum &
Archaeological
Museum

To Hôpital Pasteur,
Pont Michel
Tram Stop &
A-8 Autoroute

Vauban

(B) (B) #15 & 22

Paillon R.

To
High Corniche
(via D-2564)

TUNNEL

AVE. DE NORMANDIE

VIEUX CHEMIN DE CIMIEZ

AVE. ÉMILE BIECKERT

Palais des
Expositions

ACROPOLIS-
PALAIS
DU CONGRÈS

Acropolis

BLVD. CARABACEL

R. ÉDOUARD BÉRI

Place Gen.
Marshall

BLVD. DUBOUCHAGE

RUE TONDUTI

RUE DELILLE

RUE DEFLY

BLVD. PASTORELLI

RUE GIOFFREDO

RUE DE L'HOTEL DES POSTES

To Middle
Corniche
(via D-6007)

RUE BARLA

Garibaldi

MODERN ART
MUSEUM

#81 & 100
(stops may be removed in
2016 for tram construction)

Place
Garibaldi

(B) (B) #81, 82, 98 & 112
(stops may be removed in
2016 for tram construction)

RUE CASSINI

To Low
Corniche
(Villefranche
via D-6098)

(B) #82

"OLD NICE"
WALK STARTS

#98

#98

Greenway

AVE. FÉLIX FAURE

(B) #98

Cathédrale
Vieille Ville

Cemetery

(B) #30, 81
& 100

BLVD. JEAN JAURÈS

RUE ROSSETTI

Opéra
Vieille Ville

Place
Rossetti

VIEUX

Port

Place
du Palais

R. ALEXANDRE MARI

Place
Gautier

NICE

TRANS
COTE
D'AZUR
DOCK

FRANÇOIS DE PAULE

Cours Saleya

QUAI DES ÉTATS-UNIS

CASTLE
HILL

PROMENADE
WALK ENDS

Beach

ELEVATOR

BELLANDA TOWER

QUAI CAPEU

WAR
MEMORIAL

CRUISE
TERMINAL
#1

#30 (B)

See detail map

CRUISE
TERMINAL
#2

S e a

200 Meters

200 Yards

N

Rivage, farther along on Quai des Etats-Unis, is cool for a drink.)

Even a hundred years ago, there was sufficient tourism in Nice to justify building its first casino (a leisure activity imported from Venice). Part of an elegant casino, La Jetée Promenade stood on those white-covered pilings (with flags flapping) just offshore, until the Germans destroyed it during World War II. When La Jetée was thriving, it took gamblers two full days to get to the Riviera by train from Paris.

Although La Jetée Promenade is gone, you can still see the striking 1927 Art Nouveau facade of the **Palais de la Méditerranée,** a grand casino, hotel, and theater. It became one of the grandest casinos in Europe, and today it is one of France's most exclusive hotels, though the casino feels cheap and cheesy.

The unappealing Casino Ruhl (with the most detested facade on the strip) disfigures the next block. Anyone can drop in for some one-armed-bandit fun, but to play the tables at night, you'll need to dress up and bring your passport.

Albert I Park is named for the Belgian king who enjoyed wintering here—these were his private gardens. While the English came first, the Belgians and Russians were also big fans of 19th-century Nice. That tall statue at the edge of the park commemorates the 100-year anniversary of Nice's union with France. The happy statue features two beloved women embracing the idea of union (Marianne, the symbol of the Republic of France, and Catherine Ségurane, a 16th-century heroine who helped Nice against Saracen pirates).

The park is a long, winding greenbelt called the Promenade du Paillon. The Paillon River flows under the park on its way to the sea. This is the historical divide between Old Nice and the new town. Continue along, past the vintage belle époque carousel. You're now on Quai des Etats-Unis ("Quay of the United

States"). This name was given as a tip-of-the-cap to the Americans for finally entering World War I in 1917. Check out the laid-back couches at the Plage Beau Rivage lounge. The big, blue chair statue celebrates the inviting symbol of this venerable walk and kicks off what I consider the best stretch of beach—quieter and with less traffic.

The tall, rusted **steel girders** reaching for the sky were erected in 2010 to celebrate the 150th anniversary of Nice's union with France. (The seven beams represent the seven valleys of the Nice region.) Designed by the same artist who created the popular Arc of the Riviera sculpture in the parkway near Place Masséna, this "art" infuriates many locals as an ugly waste of money.

The elegant back side of Nice's opera house faces the sea. In front of it, a tiny bronze Statue of Liberty reminds all that this stretch of seafront promenade is named for the USA.

The long, low building lining the walk on the left once served the city's fishermen. Behind its gates bustles the Cours Saleya Market—long the heart and soul of Old Nice.

Ahead, on the right, find the three-foot-tall white **metal winch.** It's a reminder that before tourism, hardworking fishing boats lined the beach rather than vacationing tourists. The boats were hauled in through the surf by winches like this and tied to the iron rings on either side.

• *Your walk is over. From here you have several great options: Continue 10 minutes along the coast to the* ***port,*** *around the foot of Castle Hill (fine views of the entire promenade and a monumental war memorial carved into the hillside); hike or ride the free elevator up to* ***Castle Hill*** *(see page 289); head into the* ***old town*** *(you can follow my "Old Nice Walk," next); or grab a blue chair or piece of* ***beach*** *and just be on vacation— Riviera style.*

Rick's Tip: *To make life tolerable on the rocks, swimmers should buy a pair of the cheap plastic* **beach shoes** *sold at many shops.* **Go Sport** *at #13 on Place Masséna is a good bet (open daily).*

Old Nice Walk

This self-guided walk through Nice's old town, from Place Masséna to Place Rossetti, gives you a helpful introduction to the city's bicultural heritage and its most interesting neighborhoods. Allow about an hour at a leisurely pace for this level walk, rated ▲▲. It's best done in the morning (while the outdoor market thrives), and preferably not on a Sunday, when things are quiet. This ramble is also a joy at night, when fountains glow and pedestrians control the streets.

• *Start where Avenue Jean Médecin hits the people-friendly Place Masséna—the successful result of a long, expensive city upgrade and the new center of Nice.*

PLACE MASSENA

The grand Place Masséna is Nice's drawing room, where old meets new, and where the tramway bends between Vieux (Old) Nice and the train station. The square's black-and-white pavement feels like an elegant outdoor ballroom, with the sleek tram waltzing across its dance floor. While once congested with cars, the square today is frequented only by these trams, which swoosh silently by every couple of minutes. The men on pedestals sitting high above are modern-art additions that arrived with the tram. For a mood-altering experience, return after dark and watch the illuminated figures float yoga-like above. Place Masséna is at its sophisticated best after the sun goes down.

This vast square dates from 1848 and pays tribute to Jean-André Masséna, a French military leader during the Revolutionary and Napoleonic wars. Not just another pretty face in a long lineup of French military heroes, he's considered among the greatest commanders in history—anywhere, anytime. Napoleon called him "the greatest name of my military Empire."

Standing in the center of the square, face the sea and start a clockwise spin tour: The towering **modern swoosh sculpture** in the park is meant to represent the arc of the bay. To the right stretches modern Nice, born with the arrival of tourism in the 1800s. **Avenue Jean Médecin,** Nice's main street, cuts from here through the new town to the train station. In the distance you can see the tracks, the freeway, and the Alps beyond that. Once crammed with cars, buses, and delivery vehicles, Avenue Jean Médecin was turned into a walking and cycling nirvana in 2007. Businesses flourish in the welcoming environment of generous sidewalks and no traffic.

Appreciate the city's Italian heritage—it feels as much like Venice as Paris. The portico flanking Avenue Jean Médecin is Italian, not French. The rich colors of the buildings reflect the taste of previous Italian rulers.

Turn to your right and look east to see the **Promenade du Paillon,** a green parkway that stretches from the sea to Place Masséna. Notice the fountain—its surprise geysers delight children by day and its fine lighting enhances romance at night. Beyond the fountain stands a

Promenade du Paillon

bronze statue of the square's namesake, Masséna. And the hills beyond that separate Nice from Villefranche-sur-Mer.

Turn farther to the right to see the old town, with its jumbled facades below Castle Hill. The **statue of Apollo** holds a beach towel as if to say, "It's beer o'clock, let's go."

• *Walk past Apollo with the beach towel into the old town. After a block down Rue de l'Opéra, turn left onto Rue St. François de Paule (or you can detour right one block to the* **Molinard** *perfume shop at #20, which has a free one-room museum and offers create-your-own-perfume sessions for a price; see www.molinard.com).*

RUE ST. FRANÇOIS DE PAULE

This colorful street leads into the heart of Vieux Nice. On the left is Hôtel de Ville (City Hall). Peer into the **Alziari olive oil shop** (at #14 on the right). Dating from 1868, the shop produces top-quality stone-ground olive oil. The proud and charming owner, Gilles Piot, claims that stone wheels create less acidity, since metal grinding builds up heat (see photo in back over the door). Locals fill their own containers from the huge vats.

La Couqueto (at #8) is a colorful shop filled with Provençal handicrafts, including lovely folk characters (*santons*).

Across the street is Nice's grand **opera house.** Imagine this opulent jewel back in the 19th century. With all the fancy big-city folks wintering here, this rough-edged town needed some high-class entertainment. And Victorians needed an alternative to those "devilish" gambling houses. (Queen Victoria, so disgusted at casinos, would actually close the drapes on her train window when passing Monte Carlo.) The four statues on top represent theater, dance, music, and party poopers.

On the left (at #7), **Pâtisserie Auer's** grand old storefront tempts you with chocolates and candied fruits. It's changed little over the centuries. The writing on the window says, "Since 1820 from father to son." The gold royal shields on the back wall remind shoppers that Queen Victoria indulged her sweet tooth here.

• *Continue on, sifting your way through a cluttered block of tacky souvenir shops to the big market square.*

COURS SALEYA

Named for its broad exposure to the sun (*soleil*), Cours Saleya is a commotion of color, sights, smells, and people. It's been Nice's main market square since the Middle Ages (flower market all day Tue-Sun, produce market Tue-Sun until 13:00, antiques on Mon). While you're greeted by the ugly mouth of an underground parking lot, much of this square itself was a parking lot until 1980, when the mayor of Nice had this solution dug.

The first section is devoted to the Riviera's largest flower market. In operation since the 19th century, this market offers

Cours Saleya Market

A movable art gallery

plants and flowers that grow effortlessly and ubiquitously in this climate, including these favorites: carnations, roses, and jasmine. Locals know the season by what's on sale (mimosas in February, violets in March, and so on). Until the recent rise in imported flowers, this region supplied all of France with flowers. Still, fresh flowers are cheap here, the best value in this notoriously expensive city. The Riviera's three big industries are tourism, flowers, and perfume (made from these flowers… take a whiff).

Rick's Tip: The **Cours Saleya** produce and flower market is replaced by antique stalls **on Mondays.**

The boisterous produce section trumpets the season with mushrooms, strawberries, white asparagus, zucchini flowers, and more—whatever's fresh gets top billing.

The market opens up at Place Pierre Gautier. It's also called Plassa dou Gouvernou—you'll see bilingual street signs here that include the old Niçois language, an Italian dialect. This is where farmers set up stalls to sell their produce and herbs directly.

Look up to the **hill** that dominates to the east. In the Middle Ages, a massive castle stood there with soldiers at the ready. Over time, the city grew down to where you are now. With the river guarding one side and the sea the other, this mountain fortress seemed strong—until Louis XIV leveled it in 1706. Nice's medieval seawall ran along the line of two-story buildings where you're standing.

Now, look across Place Pierre Gautier to the large "palace." The **Ducal Palace** was where the kings of Sardinia, the city's Italian rulers until 1860, resided when in Nice. (For centuries, Nice was under the rule of the Italian capital of Torino.) Today, the palace is the police headquarters. The land upon which the Cours Saleya sits was once the duke's gardens and didn't

become a market until Nice's union with France.

• *Continue down Cours Saleya. The fine golden building that seals the end of the square is where Henri Matisse spent 17 years. I imagine he was inspired by his view. The* **Café les Ponchettes** *is perfectly positioned for you to enjoy the view, too, if you want a coffee break. At the café, turn onto…*

RUE DE LA POISSONNERIE

Look up at the first floor of the first building on your right. **Adam and Eve** are squaring off, each holding a zucchini-like gourd. This scene represents the annual rapprochement in Nice to make up for the sin of too much fun during Carnival (Mardi Gras, the pre-Lenten festival). Residents of Nice have partied hard during Carnival for more than 700 years.

Next, check out the small **Baroque church** (Notre-Dame de l'Annonciation) dedicated to St. Rita, the patron saint of desperate causes and desperate people. She holds a special place in locals' hearts, making this the most popular church in Nice. Drop in for a peek at the dazzling Baroque interior. Inside, the first chapel on the right is dedicated to St. Erasmus, protector of mariners.

• *Turn right on the next street, where you'll pass Vieux Nice's most happening bar (**Distilleries Ideales**). Pause at the next corner and simply study the classic Old Nice scene. Now turn left on Rue Droite and enter an area that feels like Little Naples.*

RUE DROITE

In the Middle Ages, this straight, skinny street provided the most direct route from river to sea within the old walled town. Pass the recommended restaurant L'Acchiardo. Notice stepped lanes leading uphill to the castle. Stop at **Espuno's bakery** (at Place du Jésus) and say "*Bonjour,* what's cooking?" to Natalie from England and her husband Fabrice, who's from here. Notice the firewood stacked behind the oven. Try the house specialty, *tourte aux blettes*—a tart stuffed with

Swiss chard, apples, pine nuts, and raisins.

Pop into the Jesuit **Eglise St-Jacques** for an explosion of Baroque exuberance hidden behind that plain facade.

The balconies of the large mansion on the left mark the **Palais Lascaris** (c. 1647), home of one of Nice's most prestigious families. Today it is a museum with an impressive collection of antique musical instruments—harps, guitars, violins, and violas—along with elaborate tapestries and a few well-furnished rooms. The palace has four levels: The ground floor was used for storage, the first floor was devoted to reception rooms (and musical events), the owners lived a floor above that, and the servants lived at the top. Look up and make faces back at the guys under the balconies.

• *Turn left on the Rue de la Loge, then left again on Rue Benoît Bunico.*

In the 18th century, Rue Benoît served as a **ghetto** for Nice's Jews. At sunset, gates would seal the street at either end, locking people in until daylight. To identify Jews as non-Christians, the men were forced to wear yellow stars and the women wore yellow scarves. The white columns across from #19 mark what was the synagogue until 1848, when revolution ended the notion of ghettos in France.

• *Around the corner and downhill on Rue Benoît Bunico find...*

PLACE ROSSETTI

The most Italian of Nice's piazzas, Place Rossetti comes alive after dark—in part because of the **Fenocchio gelato shop,** popular for its many innovative flavors.

Check out the **Cathedral of St. Réparate**—an unassuming building for a big-city cathedral. It was relocated here in the 1500s, when Castle Hill was temporarily converted to military use. The name comes from Nice's patron saint, a teenage virgin named Réparate, whose martyred body floated to Nice in the fourth century accompanied by angels.

• *This is the end of our walk. From here you can hike up* **Castle Hill** *(from Place Rossetti, take Rue Rossetti uphill; see page 289). Or you can have ice cream and browse the colorful lanes of Old Nice. Or you can grab Apollo and hit the beach.*

Sights

Some of Nice's top attractions—the Promenade des Anglais, the beach, and the old town—are covered in my self-guided walks. But Nice offers other worthwhile sights as well.

The Chagall and Matisse museums are a long walk northeast of the city center. If you want to visit both, combine them in one trip, because they're in the same direction and served by the same bus line (#15 Mon-Sat, #22 Sun). From Place Masséna, the Chagall Museum is a 10-minute bus ride, and the Matisse Museum is a few stops beyond that.

▲▲▲CHAGALL MUSEUM (MUSEE NATIONAL MARC CHAGALL)

Even if you don't get modern art, this museum—with the world's largest collection of Marc Chagall's work in captivity—

Eglise St-Jacques

Place Rossetti

is a delight. After World War II, Chagall returned from the United States to settle in Vence, not far from Nice. Between 1954 and 1967 he painted a cycle of 17 large murals designed for, and donated to, this museum. These paintings, inspired by the biblical books of Genesis, Exodus, and the Song of Songs, make up the "nave," or core, of what Chagall called the "House of Brotherhood."

Rick's Tip: *Both the* **Chagall** *and* **Matisse museums** *are* **closed on Tuesdays.**

Cost and Hours: €8, €1-2 more with special exhibits, includes audioguide, May-Oct Wed-Mon 10:00-18:00, Nov-April until 17:00, closed Tue year-round, Avenue Docteur Ménard, tel. 04 93 53 87 20, http://en.musees-nationaux-alpesmaritimes.fr. An idyllic café awaits in the corner of the garden.

Getting There: Taxis to and from the city center cost €12. Buses connect the museum with downtown Nice and the train station. From downtown, catch bus #15 (6/hour, 10 minutes) from the east end of the Galeries Lafayette department store, near the Masséna tram stop, on Rue Sacha Guitry; on Sunday catch #22 from the same stop. Exit the bus at the stop called Musée Chagall on Boulevard de Cimiez.

Visiting the Museum: This small museum consists of six rooms: two rooms (the main hall and Song of Songs room) with the 17 murals, two rooms for special exhibits, an auditorium with stained-glass windows, and a mosaic-lined pond.

In the **main hall** you'll find the core of the collection (Genesis and Exodus scenes). Each painting is a lighter-than-air collage of images that draws from Chagall's Russian folk-village youth, his Jewish heritage, biblical themes, and his feeling that he existed somewhere between heaven and earth. He believed that the Bible was a synonym for nature, and that color and biblical themes were key for understanding God's love for his creation. Chagall's brilliant blues and reds celebrate nature, as do his spiritual and folk themes. Notice the focus on couples. To Chagall, humans loving each other mirrored God's love of creation.

The adjacent **octagonal room** houses five paintings inspired by the Old Testament Song of Songs. Chagall was one of the few "serious" 20th-century artists to portray unabashed love. Where the Bible uses the metaphor of earthly, physical, sexual love to describe God's love for humans, Chagall uses unearthly colors and a mystical ambience to celebrate human love. These red-toned canvases are hard to interpret on a literal level, but they capture the rosy spirit of a man in love with life.

The **auditorium** is worth a peaceful moment to enjoy three Chagall stained-glass windows depicting the seven days of creation. This is also where you'll find a wonderful film (52 minutes) on Chagall, which plays at the top of each hour.

Chagall Museum

Chagall, Song of Songs IV

The Riviera's Art Scene

The list of artists who have painted the Riviera reads like a *Who's Who* of 20th-century art. Henri Matisse, Marc Chagall, Georges Braque, Raoul Dufy, Fernand Léger, and Pablo Picasso all lived and worked here—and raved about the region's wonderful light. Their simple, semiabstract, and—most important—colorful works reflect the pleasurable atmosphere of the Riviera. You'll experience the same landscapes they painted in this bright, sun-drenched region, punctuated with views of the "azure sea." Try to imagine the Riviera with a fraction of the people and development you see today.

The Riviera's collection of museums allows art lovers to appreciate these masters' works while immersed in the same sun and culture that inspired them. The designs of many of the museums blend artworks with surrounding views, gardens, and fountains, thus highlighting that modern art is not only stimulating, but sometimes simply beautiful.

Leaving the Museum: From here, you can return to downtown Nice or the train-station area, or go to the Matisse Museum. For the bus back to downtown Nice, turn right out of the museum, then make another right down Boulevard de Cimiez, and ride bus #15 or #22 heading downhill. To continue on to the Matisse Museum, catch #15 or #22 using the uphill stop located across the street. To walk to the train-station area from the museum takes about 20 minutes.

▲MATISSE MUSEUM (MUSEE MATISSE)

This small and neglected little museum, which fills an old mansion in a park surrounded by scant Roman ruins, contains a sampling of works from the various periods of Henri Matisse's artistic career. The museum offers an introduction to the artist's many styles and materials, both shaped by Mediterranean light and by fellow Côte d'Azur artists Picasso and Renoir.

Matisse, the master of leaving things out, could suggest a woman's body with a single curvy line—letting the viewer's mind fill in the rest. Ignoring traditional 3-D perspective, he expressed his passion for life through simplified but recognizable scenes in which dark outlines and saturated, bright blocks of color create an overall decorative pattern. As you tour the museum, look for Matisse's favorite motifs—including fruit, flowers, wallpaper, and sunny rooms—often with a window opening onto a sparkling landscape.

Matisse "cutout" painting

Another favorite subject is the *odalisque* (harem concubine), usually shown sprawled in a seductive pose and with a simplified, masklike face. You'll also see a few souvenirs from his foreign travels, which influenced much of his work.

Cost and Hours: €10, Wed-Mon 10:00-18:00, closed Tue, 164 Avenue des Arènes de Cimiez, tel. 04 93 81 08 08, www.musee-matisse-nice.org.

Getting There: Take a cab (€15 from Promenade des Anglais). Alternately, hop bus #15 Mon-Sat or #22 on Sun (6/hour, 15 minutes, board from east end of Galeries Lafayette department store, near Masséna tram stop, on Rue Sacha Guitry—see map on page 281). Get off at the Arènes-Matisse bus stop (look for the crumbling Roman arena), then walk 50 yards into the park to find the pink villa.

Leaving the Museum: Turn left from the museum into the park, exiting at the Archaeological Museum. The bus stop across the street is for bus #20, which heads to the port. For buses #15 and #22 (frequent service to downtown and the Chagall Museum), turn right, passing the stop above, walk to the small roundabout, and find the shelter (facing downhill).

▲**RUSSIAN CATHEDRAL (CATHEDRALE RUSSE)**

Nice's Russian Orthodox church—claimed by some to be the finest outside Russia—is worth a visit.

Five hundred rich Russian families wintered in Nice in the late 19th century, and they needed a worthy Orthodox house of worship. Czar Nicholas I's widow provided the land and Czar Nicholas II gave this church to the Russian community in 1912. (A few years later, Russian comrades who *didn't* winter on the Riviera assassinated him.) Here in the land of olives and anchovies, these proud onion domes seem odd. But, I imagine, so did those old Russians.

Pick up an English info sheet on your way in. The one-room interior is filled with icons and candles, and traditional Russian music adds to the ambience. The park around the church makes a fine setting for picnics.

Cost and Hours: Free; Mon 13:30-17:00, Tue-Sun 10:00-17:00; services Sat at 17:00, Sun at 10:00; no tourist visits during services, no shorts allowed, 17 Boulevard du Tzarewitch, tel. 04 93 96 88 02, www.sobor.fr.

▲**CASTLE HILL (COLLINE DU CHATEAU)**

This hill—in an otherwise flat city center—offers sensational views over Nice, the port (to the east, created for trade and military use in the 15th century), the foothills of the Alps, and the Mediterranean. The views are best early, at sunset, or whenever the weather's clear.

Nice was founded on this hill. Its residents were crammed onto the hilltop until the 12th century, as it was too risky to live in the flatlands below. Today you'll find a playground, a café, and a cemetery—but no castle—on Castle Hill.

Russian Cathedral

Cost and Hours: Park is free and closes at 20:00 in summer, earlier off-season.

Getting There: You can get to the top by foot or by elevator (free, daily 10:00-19:00, until 20:00 in summer, next to beachfront Hôtel Suisse).

See the Promenade des Anglais Walk on page 278 for a pleasant stroll that ends near Castle Hill.

Leaving Castle Hill: After enjoying the views and hilltop fun, you can walk via the cemetery directly down into Vieux Nice (just follow the signs), descend to the beach (via the elevator or a stepped lane next to it), or hike down the back side to Nice's port (departure point for boat trips and buses to Monaco and Villefranche-sur-Mer).

Experiences
Mediterranean Cruise

To see Nice from the water, hop aboard a one-hour ▲ **Trans Côte d'Azur cruise.** You'll travel on a comfortable yacht-size vessel to Cap Ferrat and past Villefranche-sur-Mer, then return to Nice with a final lap along Promenade des Anglais.

Guides play Robin Leach (in French and English), pointing out mansions owned by famous people, including Elton John, Sean Connery, and Microsoft co-founder Paul Allen (€18; April-Oct Tue-Sun 2/day, usually at 11:00 and 15:00, no boats Mon or in off-season; verify schedule, arrive 30 minutes early to get best seats; boats leave from Nice's port—

The view from Castle Hill is worth the climb.

Bassin des Amiraux, tel. 04 92 98 71 30, www.trans-cote-azur.com).

Nightlife

While you should choose your neighborhoods with caution, the city is a delight after dark. Promenade des Anglais, Cours Saleya, the old town, and Rue Masséna are all safe and worth an evening walk. Nice's bars play host to a happening late-night scene, filled with jazz, rock, and trolling singles.

Most activity focuses on Vieux Nice. Rue de la Préfecture and Place du Palais are ground zero for bar life, though Place Rossetti and Rue Droite are also good targets. **Distilleries Ideales** is a good place to start or end your evening, with a lively international crowd, a *Pirates of the Caribbean* interior, and a *Cheers* vibe (15 beers on tap, happy hour 18:00-21:00, where Rue de la Poissonnerie and Rue Barillerie meet). **Wayne's Bar** is a happening spot for the younger, English-speaking backpacker crowd (15 Rue Préfecture). Along the Promenade des Anglais, the plush bar at **Hôtel Negresco** is fancy-cigar old English.

Eating

For the most energy and variety, I'd eat in Vieux Nice. If Vieux Nice is too far, I've listed good places handier to your hotel. Promenade des Anglais is ideal for picnic dinners on warm, languid evenings or a meal at a beachside restaurant. For a more romantic (and expensive) meal, head for nearby Villefranche-sur-Mer (see page 301). Avoid the fun-to-peruse but terribly touristy eateries lining Rue Masséna.

In Vieux Nice

Le Safari is a fair option for Niçois cuisine and outdoor dining on Cours Saleya. The place, convivial and rustic with a mix of modern art inside, is packed with locals and tourists, and staffed with hurried waiters (€18-30 *plats,* open daily, 1 Cours Saleya, tel. 04 93 80 18 44,

The Riviera's Cuisine Scene

While many of the same dishes served in Provence are available throughout the Riviera, there are differences, especially if you look for anything Italian or from the sea. When dining on the Riviera, I expect views and ambience more than top-quality cuisine.

La salade niçoise is where most Riviera meals start. A true specialty from Nice, the classic version is a base of green salad with boiled potatoes, tomatoes, anchovies, olives, hard-boiled eggs, and lots of tuna. This is my go-to salad for a tasty, healthy, and fast lunch. I like to spend a couple of extra euros and eat it in an elegant, atmospheric place with a view.

For lunch on the go, look for a **pan bagnat** (like a *salade niçoise* stuffed into a hollowed-out soft roll). Other tasty bread treats include *pissaladière* (bread dough topped with onions, olives, and anchovies), *fougasse* (a spindly, lace-like bread sometimes flavored with nuts, herbs, olives, or ham), and **socca** (a thin chickpea crêpe, seasoned with pepper and olive oil and often served in a paper cone by street vendors).

Bouillabaisse is the Riviera's most famous dish; you'll find it in any seafront village or city. It's a spicy fish stew based on recipes handed down from sailors in Marseille. This dish often requires a minimum order of two and can cost up to €40-60 per person.

Those on a budget can enjoy other seafood soups and stews. Far less pricey than bouillabaisse and worth trying is the local **soupe de poisson** (fish soup). It's a creamy soup flavored like bouillabaisse, with anise and orange, and served with croutons and *rouille* sauce (but has no chunks of fish).

The Riviera specializes in all sorts of fish and shellfish. Options include **fruits de mer,** or platters of seafood (including tiny shellfish, from which you get the edible part only by sucking really hard), herb-infused mussels, stuffed sardines, squid (slowly simmered with tomatoes and herbs), and tuna *(thon)*. The popular **loup flambé au fenouil** is grilled sea bass, flavored with fennel and torched with *pastis* prior to serving.

Do as everyone else does, and drink **wines** from Provence. **Bandol** (red) and **Cassis** (white) are popular and from a region nearly on the Riviera. The only wines made in the Riviera are **Bellet** rosé and white, the latter often found in fish-shaped bottles.

www.restaurantsafari.fr).

L'Acchiardo is a homey eatery that mixes loyal clientele with hungry tourists. As soon as you sit down you know this is a treat. The simple, hearty Niçois cuisine is served by Monsieur Acchiardo and his good-looking sons. The small plaque under the menu outside says the restaurant has been run by father and son since 1927 (€9 starters, €16 *plats,* €7 desserts,

closed Sat-Sun, indoor seating only, 38 Rue Droite, tel. 04 93 85 51 16).

Bistrot D'Antoine has street appeal. It's a warm, popular, vine-draped option whose menu emphasizes Niçois cuisine and good grilled selections. The food is delicious and the prices are reasonable. Call a day ahead to reserve a table—the upstairs room is quieter (€10 starters, €17 *plats,* €7 desserts, closed Sun-Mon, 27

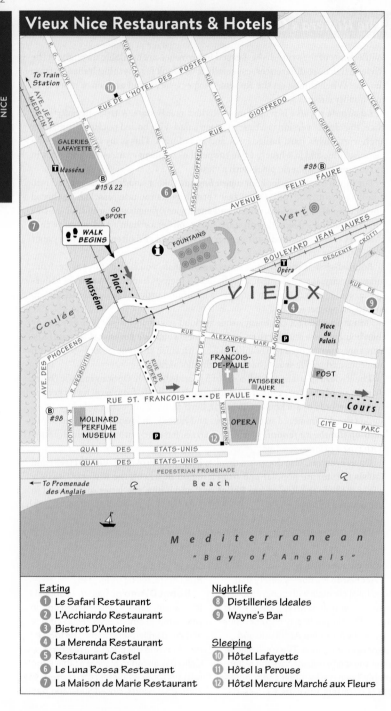

Vieux Nice Restaurants & Hotels

To Train Station

AVE. JEAN MEDECIN

R. G. DELOYE

RUE BLACAS

RUE DE L'HOTEL DES POSTES

RUE ALBERTI

RUE DU LYCEE

GIOFFREDO

RUE GUBERNATIS

R. S. GUITRY

GALERIES LAFAYETTE

T Masséna

RUE CHAUVAIN

PASSAGE GIOFFREDO

RUE

GIOFFREDO

B #15 & 22

#98 **B**

FELIX FAURE

6

AVENUE

Vert ◎

GO SPORT

7

WALK BEGINS

FOUNTAINS

BOULEVARD JEAN JAURES

DESCENTE CROTTI

R.

Place

T Opéra

V I E U X

RUE DE

Masséna

4

RUE DE

Coulée

RAOUL BOSIO

Place du Palais

9

AVE. DES PHOCEENS

R. DESBOUTIN

RUE

ALEXANDRE MARI

P

RUE DE L'OPERA

R. L'HOTEL DE VILLE

ST. FRANCOIS-DE-PAULE

PATISSERIE AUER

POST

RUE ST. FRANCOIS - - - DE PAULE

Cours

B #98

R. VANLOO

MOLINARD PERFUME MUSEUM

P

RUE ROBBINS

OPERA

CITE DU PARC

QUAI DES ETATS-UNIS

12

QUAI DES ETATS-UNIS

PEDESTRIAN PROMENADE

To Promenade des Anglais

Beach

⚓

M e d i t e r r a n e a n

" B a y   o f   A n g e l s "

Eating
1 Le Safari Restaurant
2 L'Acchiardo Restaurant
3 Bistrot D'Antoine
4 La Merenda Restaurant
5 Restaurant Castel
6 Le Luna Rossa Restaurant
7 La Maison de Marie Restaurant

Nightlife
8 Distilleries Ideales
9 Wayne's Bar

Sleeping
10 Hôtel Lafayette
11 Hôtel la Perouse
12 Hôtel Mercure Marché aux Fleurs

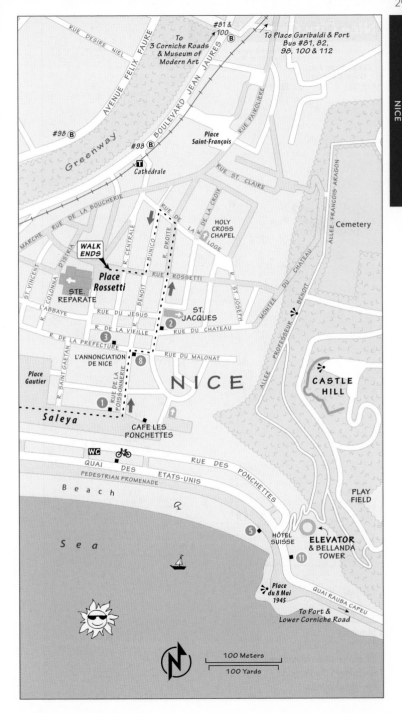

RUE DESIRE NIEL

AVENUE FELIX FAURE

BOULEVARD JEAN JAURES

#81 &
100 B

To
3 Corniche Roads
& Museum of
Modern Art

To Place Garibaldi & Port
Bus #81, 82,
98, 100 & 112

#98 B

Greenway

#98 B

Place
Saint-François

RUE FAROLIERE

Cathédrale

RUE ST. CLAIRE

RUE DE LA BOUCHERIE

MARCHE

DISTRIA

ST. VINCENT

COLONNA

RUE DE LA CROIX

RUE DE LA LOGE

HOLY
CROSS
CHAPEL

R. CENTRALE

BUNICO

R. DROITE

WALK
ENDS

Place
Rossetti

STE.
REPARATE

L'ABBAYE

R. BENOIT

RUE ROSSETTI

R. ST-JOSEPH

RUE DU JESUS

ST.
JACQUES
2

R. DE LA VIEILLE

R. DE LA PREFECTURE
3

RUE DU CHATEAU

MONTEE DU CHATEAU

ALLEE FRANCOIS ARAGON

Cemetery

R. SAINT GAETAN

L'ANNONCIATION
DE NICE

8

RUE DU MALONAT

N I C E

ALLEE PROFESSEUR BENOIT

CASTLE
HILL

Place
Gautier

RUE DE LA POISSONNERIE

1

Saleya

CAFE LES
PONCHETTES

WC

QUAI   DES

PEDESTRIAN PROMENADE

RUE DES PONCHETTES

ETATS-UNIS

B e a c h

PLAY
FIELD

S e a

5

HÔTEL
SUISSE

ELEVATOR
& BELLANDA
TOWER

11

QUAI RAUBA CAPEU

Place
du 8 Mai
1945

To Port &
Lower Corniche Road

100 Meters

100 Yards

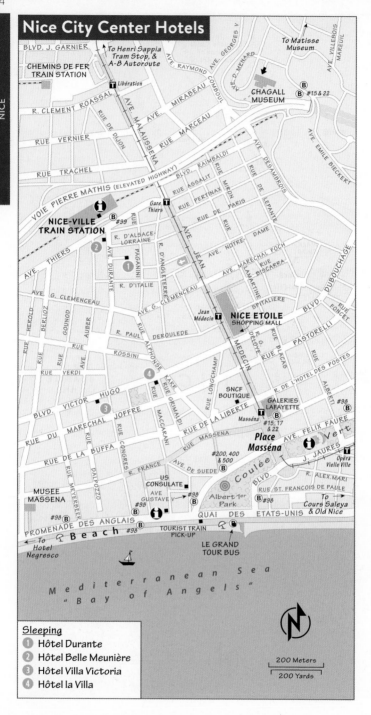

Nice City Center Hotels

Sleeping
1. Hôtel Durante
2. Hôtel Belle Meunière
3. Hôtel Villa Victoria
4. Hôtel la Villa

Rue de la Préfecture, tel. 04 93 85 29 57).

La Merenda is a shoebox where you'll sit on small stools and dine on simple, home-style dishes in a communal environment. The menu changes with the season, but the hardworking owner, Dominique, does not. This place fills fast, so arrive early, or better yet, drop by during the day to reserve—they have two seatings at 19:00 and 21:00 (€10 starters, €14 *plats,* €6 desserts, closed Sat-Sun, cash only, 4 Rue Raoul Bosio, no telephone, www.lamerenda.net).

On the Beach
Restaurant Castel is a fine eat-on-the-beach option, thanks to its location at the very east end of Nice, under Castle Hill. The city vanishes as you step down to the beach. The food is creative and nicely presented, and the tables feel classy, even at the edge of the sand. Arrive for the sunset and you'll have an unforgettable meal (€19 salads and pastas, €20-25 daily plates, open for dinner mid-May-Aug, lunch April-Sept, 8 Quai des Etats-Unis, tel. 04 93 85 22 66, www.castelplage.com). Sunbathers

can rent beach chairs and have drinks and meals served literally on the beach (lounge chairs €16/half-day, €19/day).

In the City Center
For a more contemporary slice of France, try one of these spots around the Nice Etoile shopping mall.

Rick's Tip: *Nice's* **dinner scene converges on Cours Saleya,** *which is entertaining enough in itself to make the generally mediocre food a good deal. It's a fun spot to compare tans and mussels—and worth wandering through even if you eat elsewhere.*

Le Luna Rossa is a small neighborhood eatery serving delicious French-Italian dishes. Owner Christine welcomes diners with attentive service and reasonable prices. Dine inside (classy tables) or outside on a sidewalk terrace (€10 starters, €14-27 *plats,* closed Sun-Mon, just north of parkway at 3 Rue Chauvin, tel. 04 93 85 55 66).

La Maison de Marie is a surprisingly high-quality refuge off Nice's touristy

Pick an outdoor table in Nice and try the socca *(thin chickpea crêpe).*

restaurant row—Rue Masséna. The interior tables are as appealing as those in the courtyard, but expect some smokers outside. The €24 *menu* is a good value (€12-18 starters, €20-30 *plats*, open daily, 5 Rue Masséna, tel. 04 93 82 15 93).

Sleeping

Don't look for charm in Nice. I prefer to stay in the new town—a 10-minute walk from the old town—for modern, clean, and air-conditioned rooms. For parking, ask your hotelier, or see page 300.

In the City Center

The train station area offers Nice's cheapest sleeps, but the neighborhood can feel seedy after dark. The cheapest places are older, well-worn, and come with some street noise. Places closer to Boulevard Victor Hugo are more expensive and in a more comfortable area.

Rick's Tip: *The Riviera is famous for staging major* **events.** *Stay away unless you're actually participating, as you'll only experience room shortages, higher prices, and traffic jams. The three biggies are the* **Nice Carnival** *(Feb-March, www.nicecarnaval. com),* **Cannes Film Festival** *(mid-May, www.festival-cannes.com), and* **Grand Prix of Monaco** *(late May, www.acm.mc). To accommodate the busy schedules of the rich and famous (and really mess up a lot of normal people), the film festival and car race often overlap.*

$$ Hôtel Durante*** feels Mediterranean—a happy, orange building with rooms wrapped around a flowery courtyard. All but two of its quiet rooms overlook the well-maintained patio. The rooms are good enough (mostly modern decor), the price is right enough, and the parking is free—book well ahead (Sb-€85-115, Db-€100-130, Tb-€155-185, Qb-€190-220, breakfast-€10, 16 Avenue Durante, tel. 04 93 88 84 40, www.hotel-

Sleep Code

Price Rankings for Double Rooms (Db)

$$$ Most rooms €200 or more
 $$ €100-200
  $ €100 or less

Abbreviations: Db=Double with bathroom. D=Double with bathroom down the hall

Notes: Room prices change; verify rates online or by email. For the best prices, book directly with the hotel.

durante.com, info@hotel-durante.com).

$$ Hôtel Lafayette***, located a block behind the Galeries Lafayette department store, is a modest, homey place with 17 mostly spacious and good-value rooms (some with thin walls, some traffic noise, all one floor up from the street). It's family-run by Kiril and George (standard Db-€105-130, spacious Db-€120-150, Tb-€130-180, preferential direct booking rates for Rick Steves readers, breakfast-€12, no elevator, 32 Rue de l'Hôtel des Postes—see map on page 292, tel. 04 93 85 17 84, www.hotellafayettenice.com, info@hotellafayettenice.com).

$ Hôtel Belle Meunière*, in an old mansion built for Napoleon III's mistress, attracts budget-minded travelers of all ages with cheap beds and private rooms a block below the train station. Creaky but well-kept, the place has adequate rooms, thin mattresses, and charismatic Mademoiselle Marie-Pierre presiding with her perfect English (bunk in 4-bed dorm-€28 with private bath, less with shared bath; Db-€60-86, Tb-€86-100, Qb-€118-135, breakfast-€6 or free if you book direct, no air-con, no elevator, laundry service, limited parking-€9/day, 21 Avenue Durante, tel. 04 93 88 66 15, www.bellemeuniere.com, hotel.belle.meuniere@cegetel.net).

In or near Vieux Nice

These Vieux Nice hotels are either on the sea or within an easy walk of it. For locations, see the map on page 292.

$$$ Hôtel la Perouse** , built into the rock of Castle Hill at the east end of the bay, is a fine splurge. This refuge-hotel is top-to-bottom flawless in every detail—from its elegant rooms (satin curtains, velour headboards) and attentive staff to its rooftop terrace with Jacuzzi, sleek pool, and lovely garden restaurant (€40 *menus*). Sleep here to be spoiled and escape the big city (garden-view Db-€300-400, seaview Db-€420-580, good family options and Web deals, 11 Quai Rauba Capeu, tel. 04 93 62 34 63, www.hotel-la-perouse.com, lp@hotel-la-perouse.com).

$$ Hôtel Mercure Marché aux Fleurs** is ideally situated near the sea and Cours Saleya. Rooms are tastefully designed and prices can be reasonable— check their website for deals (standard Db-€180, superior Db-€225-260 and worth the extra euros, smaller seaview room-€50 extra, 91 Quai des Etats-Unis, tel. 04 93 85 74 19, www.hotelmercure. com, h0962@accor.com).

Near the Promenade des Anglais

These hotels are close to the beach (and mostly far from Vieux Nice).

$$$ Hôtel Villa Victoria** is managed by cheery Marlena, who welcomes travelers into this spotless, classy old building that has an open, attractive lobby overlooking a sprawling garden-courtyard. Rooms are comfortable and well-kept, with space to stretch out (streetside Db-€170-200, gardenside Db-€175-225, Tb-€190-240, suites-€210, breakfast-€15, parking-€18/day, 33 Boulevard Victor Hugo, tel. 04 93 88 39 60, www. villa-victoria.com, contact@villa-victoria. com).

$$ Hôtel la Villa* is a well-run hotel with 47 rooms, contemporary decor in its light-filled public spaces, and a small front terrace (standard Db-€100-160, larger Db-€200, good breakfast-€12, 19 bis Boulevard Victor Hugo, tel. 04 93 87 15 00, www.hotels-la-villa.com, contact@hotel-villa-nice-centre.com).

Transportation
Getting Around Nice
BY PUBLIC TRANSPORTATION

Although you can walk to most attractions, smart travelers make good use of the buses and tram.

Tickets: Both buses and trams are covered by the same €1.50 single-ride ticket, or you can pay €10 for a 10-ride ticket that can be shared (each use good for 74 minutes in one direction, including transfers between bus and tram). The €5 all-day pass is valid on city buses and trams, as well as buses to some nearby destinations (including Villefranche-sur-Mer and Cap Ferrat, but not buses to the airport). You must validate your ticket on every bus or tram trip. Buy single tickets from the bus driver or from the ticket machines on tram platforms (coins only—press the button twice at the end to get your ticket). Passes and 10-ride tickets are also available from machines at tram stops. Info: www. lignesdazur.com.

Buses: The bus is handy for reaching the Chagall and Matisse museums (for specifics, see museum listings under "Sights"), and the Russian Cathedral. Route diagrams inside the buses identify each stop. For more on riding buses in Nice and throughout the Riviera, see page 299.

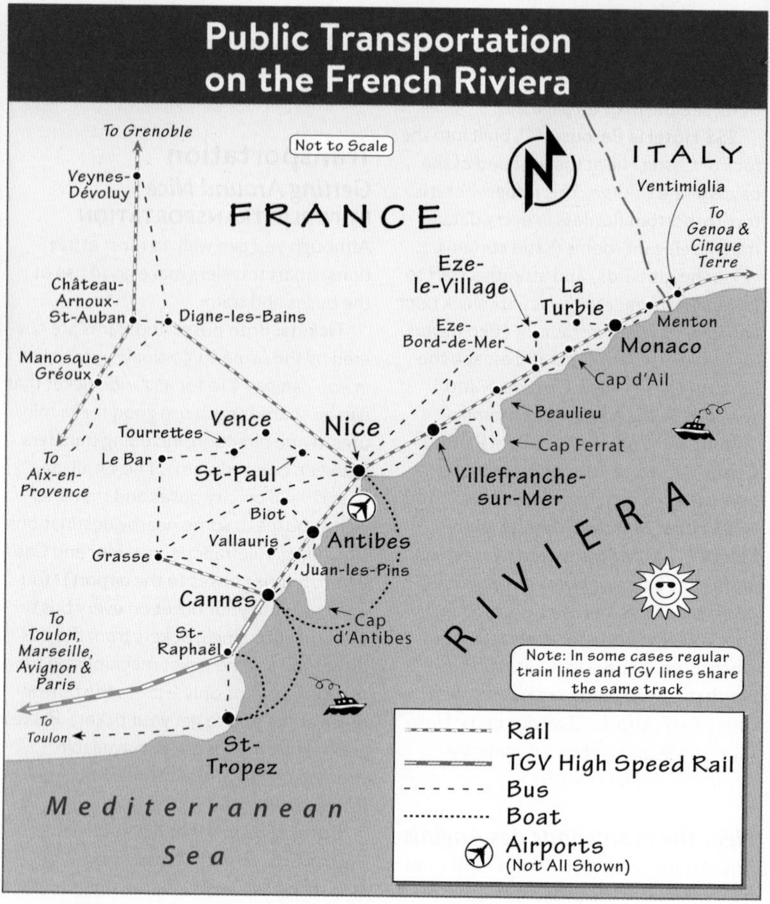

Public Transportation on the French Riviera

Not to Scale

Map labels: To Grenoble, Veynes-Dévoluy, Château-Arnoux-St-Auban, Digne-les-Bains, Manosque-Gréoux, To Aix-en-Provence, Tourrettes, Le Bar, Vence, St-Paul, Nice, Biot, Vallauris, Grasse, Antibes, Juan-les-Pins, Cannes, To Toulon, Marseille, Avignon & Paris, St-Raphaël, Cap d'Antibes, To Toulon, St-Tropez, FRANCE, ITALY, Ventimiglia, To Genoa & Cinque Terre, Eze-le-Village, La Turbie, Eze-Bord-de-Mer, Menton, Monaco, Cap d'Ail, Beaulieu, Cap Ferrat, Villefranche-sur-Mer, RIVIERA, Mediterranean Sea

Note: In some cases regular train lines and TGV lines share the same track

- Rail
- TGV High Speed Rail
- Bus
- Boat
- Airports (Not All Shown)

Trams: Nice has a single modern and efficient L-shaped tram line. Trams run every few minutes along Avenue Jean Médecin and Boulevard Jean Jaurès, and connect the main train station with Place Masséna and Old Nice (Opéra stop), the port (Place Garibaldi stop), and buses east along the coast (Vauban stop). Boarding the tram in the direction of Hôpital Pasteur takes you toward the beach and Vieux Nice (direction: Henri Sappia goes the other way). Tram info: http://tramway.nice.fr.

BY TAXI

While pricey, cabs can be useful for getting to Nice's less-central sights. Cabbies normally pick up only at taxi stands (tête de station), or you can call 04 93 13 78 78.

Getting Around the Riviera from Nice

Nice is perfectly situated for exploring the Riviera. Trains and buses do a good job of linking towns along the coast, with bonus views along many routes. Have coins handy. Ticket machines don't take US credit cards or euro bills; smaller train stations may be unstaffed; and bus drivers can't make change for large bills.

BY BUS

Buses are an amazing deal in the Riviera, whether you're riding just within Nice or to Villefranche-sur-Mer, Cap Ferrat, Monaco, or Antibes. The €1.50 single-ride ticket allows transfers between the buses of the Lignes d'Azur (the region's main bus company, www.lignesdazur.com) and the TAM (Transports Alpes-Maritimes); if you board a TAM bus and need a transfer, ask for *un ticket correspondance*. The €5 all-day ticket good on Nice's city buses and tramway also covers buses serving Villefranche and Cap Ferrat. The maps throughout this chapter indicate the locations of the handiest bus stops.

Rick's Tip: *I follow this general rule of thumb when riding a Nice-area bus with an* **all-day bus pass:** *If the bus number has one or two digits, it's covered with the pass; with three digits, it's not.*

Bus Connections Heading East to: **Villefranche-sur-Mer** (#100, 3-4/hour, 20 minutes; or #81, 2-3/hour, 20 minutes), **St-Jean-Cap-Ferrat** (#81, 2-3/hour, 30 minutes), **Monaco** (#100, 3-4/hour, 45 minutes). Due to work on the tram system, eastbound buses may stop only at the port (Le Port stop) when you visit. Ask at the TI if a closer bus stop is now available.

Bus Connections Heading West to: **Antibes** (#200, 4/hour Mon-Sat, 2/hour Sun, 1.5 hours). Use the Albert I/Verdun stop on Avenue de Verdun, a 10-minute walk along the parkway west of Place Masséna.

BY TRAIN

Speedy trains link the Riviera's beach-front destinations. The train is a bit more expensive than the bus (Nice to Monaco by train is about €4), but there's no quicker way to move about the Riviera (http://en.voyages-sncf.com). Never board a train without a ticket or valid pass—fare inspectors accept no excuses. The minimum fine is €70. See "Arriving and Departing" below for specific trip information.

BY CAR

This is France's most challenging region to drive in. Beautifully distracting vistas (natural and human), loads of Sunday-driver tourists, and every hour being lush-hour in the summer make for a dangerous combination. Parking can be exasperating. Bring lots of coins and patience.

Rick's Tip: *The Riviera is awash with* **scenic roads.** *To sample one of its most beautiful and thrilling drives, take the coastal* **Middle Corniche road** *from Nice to Monaco. You'll find breathtaking views over the Mediterranean and several scenic pullouts.*

BY BOAT

Trans Côte d'Azur offers boat service from Nice to Monaco seasonally (reservations required, tel. 04 92 98 71 30, www.trans-cote-azur.com). They also run one-hour round-trip cruises along the coast to Cap Ferrat (see page 305).

Arriving and Departing
BY TRAIN

All trains stop at Nice's main station, called Nice-Ville (you don't want the suburban Nice Riquier Station). The TI is straight out the main doors. Nice's single tram line zips you to the center in a few minutes (exit left as you leave the station, departs every few minutes, direction: Hôpital Pasteur). To walk to the beach, Promenade des Anglais, or many of my recommended hotels, cross Avenue Thiers in front of the station, go down the steps by Hôtel Interlaken, and continue down Avenue Durante.

Train Connections from Nice to: **Antibes** (2/hour, 20 minutes), **Villefranche-sur-Mer** (2/hour, 10 minutes), **Monaco** (2/hour, 20 minutes), **Arles** (11/day, 4 hours, most require transfer in Marseille or Avignon), **Avignon** (10/day, most by TGV, 4 hours, many require transfer in Marseille), Paris' Gare de Lyon (hourly, 6 hours, may require change; 11-hour night train goes to Paris' Gare d'Austerlitz), **Chamonix** (4/day, 10 hours, many change in St-Gervais and Lyon), **Beaune** (7/day, 7 hours, 1-2 transfers). Most long-distance train connections to other French cities require a change in Marseille.

BY CAR

To reach the city center on the autoroute from the west, take the first Nice exit (for the airport—called *Côte d'Azur, Central*) and follow signs for *Nice Centre* and *Promenade des Anglais*. Hoteliers know where to park (allow €18-30/day; some hotels offer deals but space is limited—book ahead). The parking garage at the Nice Etoile shopping center on Avenue Jean Médecin is near many recommended hotels (ticket booth on third floor, about €26/day, 18:00-8:00). Other centrally located garages have similar rates. All on-street parking is metered (9:00-18:00), but usually free on Sunday.

You can avoid driving in the center—and park for free during the day (no overnight parking)—by ditching your car at a parking lot at a remote tram or bus stop. Look for blue-on-white *Parcazur* signs (find locations at www.lignesdazur.com), and ride the bus or tram into town (must buy round-trip tram or bus ticket and keep it with you because you'll need it later to exit the parking lot; for details on riding the tram, see "Getting Around Nice," earlier). As lots are unguarded, don't leave anything in your car.

BY PLANE

Nice's easy-to-navigate airport (Aéroport de Nice Côte d'Azur, airport code: NCE) is literally on the Mediterranean, with landfill runways a 30-minute drive west of the city center. The two terminals are connected by shuttle buses (*navettes*). Both terminals have TIs, banks, ATMs, and buses to Nice (tel. 04 89 88 98 28, www.nice.aeroport.fr).

A **taxi into the city center** is expensive considering the short distance (figure €35

to Nice hotels, €60 to Villefranche-sur-Mer, €70 to Antibes, small fee for bags). Nice's airport taxis are notorious for overcharging. Before riding, confirm that your fare into town is roughly €35 (or €40 at night or on Sun). Don't pay much more. It's always a good idea to ask for a receipt (*reçu*).

Airport shuttles work better for trips from your hotel to the airport, since they offer a fixed price (figure €30 for one person, and only a little more for additional people). Your hotel can arrange this. Try **Nice Airport Shuttle** (1-2 people-€32, additional person-€14, mobile 06 60 33 20 54, www.nice-airport-shuttle.com) or **Med-Tour** (tel. 04 93 82 92 58, mobile 06 73 82 04 10, www.med-tour.com).

Two **bus lines** connect the airport with the city center. **Bus #99** (airport express) runs to Nice's main train station (€6, 2/hour, 8:00-21:00, 30 minutes, drops you within a 10-minute walk of many recommended hotels). To take this bus *to* the airport, catch it right in front of the train station (departs on the half-hour). **Bus #98** runs along Promenade des Anglais and along the edge of Vieux Nice (€6, 3/hour, from the airport 6:00-23:00, to the airport until 21:00, 30 minutes).

For all buses, buy tickets from the driver. To reach the bus-information office and stops at Terminal 1, turn left after passing customs and exit the doors at the far end. Buses serving Terminal 2 stop across the street from the airport exit (info kiosk and ticket sales to the right as you exit).

Getting from the Airport to Nearby Destinations: To reach **Villefranche-sur-Mer,** take bus #98 (described above) to Place Garibaldi; from there, use the same ticket to transfer to bus #81 or #100 (you may need to walk to the port to catch eastbound buses in 2016, due to work on the tram system). To get to **Antibes,** take bus #250 from either terminal (about 2/hour, 40 minutes, €10). Express bus #110 runs from the airport directly to **Monaco** (2/hour, 50 minutes, €20).

NEAR NICE

Day-trip possibilities from Nice are easy and exciting. Villefranche-sur-Mer has a serene setting and small-town warmth. Woodsy Cap Ferrat boasts belle époque mansions and a family-friendly beach. Glitzy little Monaco offers a fancy casino and royal flair. Antibes has sandy beaches, a Picasso museum, and good walking trails. Quick and easy public transportation gets you where you want to go (see "Getting Around the Riviera from Nice" on page 298 for details).

Villefranche-sur-Mer

Villefranche-sur-Mer, just east of Nice, is a romantic's top Riviera choice. Come here for an upscale Mediterranean atmosphere, narrow cobbled streets tumbling into a mellow waterfront, and fancy yachts bobbing in the harbor. Pebbly beaches and a handful of interesting sights keep visitors just busy enough.

Orientation

Tiny and easy-to-cover, Villefranche-sur-Mer snuggles around its harbor.

Day Plan: My self-guided walk laces together everything of importance in town. Your biggest decision will be choosing between a beachfront dinner or an ice-cream-licking village stroll.

Getting There: From Nice, **trains** run to Villefranche twice an hour (10 minutes); **bus #81** or **#100** will also get you there (2-4/hour, 20 minutes). From Nice's port, **drivers** should follow signs for *Menton, Monaco,* and *Basse Corniche.*

Arrival in Villefranche: The train station is just above the beach, a short stroll from the old town. Bus riders can get off at the Octroi stop and walk downhill past the TI to town. Drivers will find pay lots just below the TI or on the water (at Parking Wilson).

Rick's Tip: Skip the useless white tourist train, *which goes nowhere interesting.*

Tourist Information: The main TI is off the road that runs between Nice and Monaco, located in a park—Jardin François Binon—below the Nice/Monaco

The beautiful deep-water bay at Villefranche-sur-Mer attracts every kind of boat.

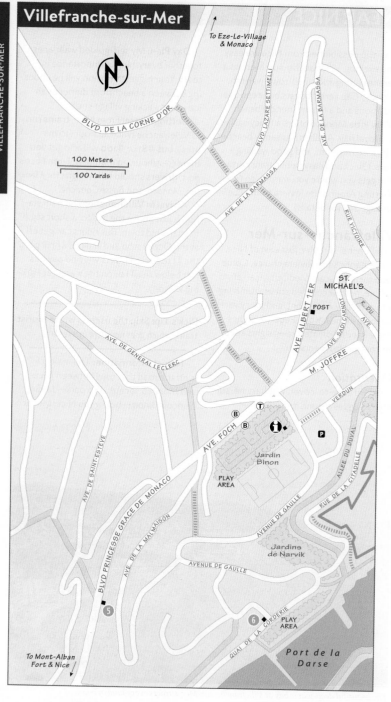

Villefranche-sur-Mer

To Eze-Le-Village & Monaco

BLVD. DE LA CORNE D'OR

BLVD. LAZARE SETTIMELLI

AVE. DE LA BARMASSA

RUE VICTOIRE

100 Meters
100 Yards

AVE. DE LA BARMASSA

ST. MICHAEL'S

AVE. ALBERT 1ER

POST

R. DU

AVE.

AVE. SADI CARNOT

AVE. DE GENERAL LECLERC

M. JOFFRE

VERDUN

T

B

B

P

AVE. DE SAINT-ESTEVE

AVE. FOCH

Jardin Binon

PLAY AREA

ALLEE DU DUVAL

RUE DE LA CITADELLE

BLVD PRINCESSE GRACE DE. MONACO

AVE. DE LA MALMAISON

AVENUE DE GAULLE

Jardins de Narvik

AVENUE DE GAULLE

5

6

PLAY AREA

QUAI DE LA CORDERIE

To Mont-Alban Fort & Nice

Port de la Darse

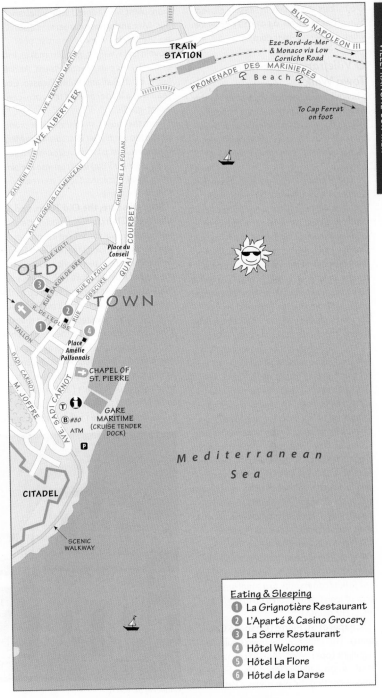

BLVD. NAPOLEON III

To
Eze-Bord-de-Mer
& Monaco via Low
Corniche Road

**TRAIN
STATION**

PROMENADE DES MARINIERES

Beach

To Cap Ferrat
on foot

AVE. FERNAND MARTIN

AVE. ALBERT 1ER

GALLIENI

AVE. GEORGES CLEMENCEAU

CHEMIN DE LA FOUAN

QUAI COURBET

RUE VOLTI

RUE BARON DE BRES

RUE DU POILU

RUE OBSCURE

*Place du
Conseil*

OLD

TOWN

❸

❷

❶

❹

R. DE L'EGLISE

*Place
Amélie
Pollonnais*

CHAPEL OF
ST. PIERRE

VALLON

SADI CARNOT

M. JOFFRE

AVE. SADI CARNOT

Ⓣ

Ⓑ #80

ATM

Ⓟ

GARE
MARITIME
(CRUISE TENDER
DOCK)

*M e d i t e r r a n e a n
S e a*

CITADEL

SCENIC
WALKWAY

Eating & Sleeping

❶ La Grignotière Restaurant
❷ L'Aparté & Casino Grocery
❸ La Serre Restaurant
❹ Hôtel Welcome
❺ Hôtel La Flore
❻ Hôtel de la Darse

Octroi bus stop (daily in season, closed Sun off-season, tel. 04 93 01 73 68, www.villefranche-sur-mer.com).

◯ *Villefranche-sur-Mer Town Walk*

This quick self-guided stroll starts at the waterfront and finishes at the citadel.

• *Go to the end of the little pier directly in front of Hôtel Welcome, where we'll start with a spin tour (spin to the right) to get oriented.*

The Harbor: At 2,000 feet, this is the deepest natural harbor on the Riviera and was the region's most important port until Nice built its own in the 18th century. Look out to sea. Cap Ferrat, the hill across the bay, is a landscaped paradise where the 1 percent of the 1 percent compete for the best view. Geologically, Cap Ferrat is the southern tip of the Alps. The range emerges from the sea here and arcs all across Europe, over 700 miles, to Vienna. The Rothschild's pink mansion, Villa Ephrussi (slightly left of center, hugging the top) is the most worthwhile sight to visit on the Cap (see page 305).

Up on the hill, the 16th-century citadel is marked by flags. The yellow fisherman's chapel (with the little-toe bell tower) has an interior painted by the writer/artist Jean Cocteau. Hôtel Welcome offers the balconies of dreams. Up the lane is the baroque facade of St. Michael's Church. The promenade, lined by fancy fish restaurants, leads to the town beach. Fifty yards above the beach stands the train station and above that, supported by arches, is the Low Corniche road, which leads to Monaco.

• *Walk left 30 yards past the last couple of boats surviving from the town's once important fishing community to a small bronze bust of Jean Cocteau. Step up to the little chapel he painted.*

Chapel of St. Pierre (Chapelle Cocteau): This chapel is the town's cultural highlight (open Wed-Mon 10:00-12:00 & 15:00-19:00, usually closed Tue). Cocteau, who decorated the place, was a Parisian

transplant who adored little Villefranche-sur-Mer and whose career was distinguished by his work as an artist, poet, novelist, playwright, and filmmaker. Influenced by his pals Marcel Proust, André Gide, Edith Piaf, and Pablo Picasso, Cocteau was a leader among the 20th-century avant-garde.

• *From the chapel, stroll the harbor promenade 100 yards past Restaurant La Mère Germaine. Just past the restaurant, a lane (signed Vieille Ville) leads up into the old town. Walk a few steps until you reach a long tunnel-like street.*

Rue Obscure, the Old Town, and St. Michael's Church: Here, under these 13th-century vaults, you're in another age. Before the long stepped lane (which we'll climb later), turn right and walk to the end of Rue Obscure (which means "dark street"). At the end, wind up to the sunlight past a tiny fountain at Place du Conseil, and a few steps beyond that to a viewpoint overlooking the beach. Then stroll back past the fountain and gently downhill. At Place des Deux Canons, turn right and climb the stepped lanes, and then take your first left (at a restaurant) to St. Michael's Church, facing a delightful square (Place de l'Eglise) with a single

Chapel of St. Pierre

magnolia tree. The church features an 18th-century organ, a particularly engaging crucifix at the high altar, and a fine statue of a recumbent Christ—carved, they say, from a fig tree by a galley slave in the 1600s.

• *Leaving St. Michael's, go downhill halfway to the water, where you hit the main commercial street. Go right on Rue du Poilu to Place de la République. Head through the square and angle left, up the hill to the...*

Citadel: The town's mammoth castle, with walls sloping thickly at the base, was built in the 1500s, the so-called "Age of Black Powder." With the advent of gunpowder, stout cannonball-deflecting walls became a necessity for any effective fortification.

• *That concludes our introductory walk.*

Experiences
BOAT RIDES *(PROMENADES EN MER)*
To view this beautiful coastline from the sea, take a quick sightseeing cruise (€12 for one-hour trip around Cap Ferrat, €20 for two-hour cruise as far as Monaco, departures from harbor across from Hôtel Welcome, June-Sept Wed and Sat, also Thu in July-Aug, no trips Oct-May, reservations a must, tel. 04 93 76 65 65, www.amv-sirenes.com).

HIKE TO MONT-ALBAN FORT
This fort, with a remarkable setting on the high ridge that separates Nice and Villefranche-sur-Mer, is a good destination for hikers (also accessible by car; info at TI). From the TI, walk on the main road toward

Nice about 200 yards past Hôtel Versailles. Look for wooden trail signs labeled *Escalier de Verre* and climb about 45 minutes as the trail makes long switchbacks through the woods up to the ridge. Find your way to Mont-Alban Fort (interior closed to tourists) and its view terrace.

MARKETS
A fun bric-a-brac market enlivens Villefranche-sur-Mer on Sundays (on Place Amélie Pollonnais by Hôtel Welcome, and in Jardin François Binon by the TI). On Saturday and Wednesday mornings, a small food market sets up in Jardin François Binon.

Eating and Sleeping
La Grignotière serves generous and tasty *plats* (closed Wed off-season, 3 Rue du Poilu). **L'Aparté** is where locals go for fresh cuisine and a special experience (closed Mon, 1 Rue Obscure). **La Serre** serves well-priced dinners (open evenings only, 16 Rue de May). Picnickers can raid the handy **Casino grocery** (closed Sun afternoon and all day Wed, 12 Rue du Poilu).

Overnighters will find seaview rooms at **$$$ Hôtel Welcome****** (3 Quai Amiral Courbet, www.welcomehotel.com; **$$ Hôtel La Flore***** (5 Boulevard Princesse Grace de Monaco, www.hotel-la-flore.fr), and **$ Hôtel de la Darse**** (32 Avenue du Général de Gaulle, www.hoteldeladarse.com).

Cap Ferrat
Exclusive Cap Ferrat is a peaceful eddy off the busy Nice-Monaco route. If you owned a house here, some of the richest people on the planet would be your neighbors. Take a leisurely tour of the Villa Ephrussi de Rothschild mansion and gardens, then enjoy the late afternoon on the beach at Plage de Passable.

Getting There: Take **Bus #81** (direction: *Le Port/Cap Ferrat*); for the Villa Ephrussi or the beach, get off at the Passable stop (the return bus is direction:

Waterfront tables line Villefranche's harbor.

Nice). **Warning:** Late-afternoon buses back to Villefranche-sur-Mer or Nice can be jammed (worse on weekends), potentially leaving passengers stranded at stops for long periods.

Cap Ferrat is quick by **car** (take the Low Corniche) or **taxi** (allow €25 one-way from Villefranche-sur-Mer, €50 from Nice).

Tourist Information: The main TI is near the Villa Ephrussi (Mon-Fri 9:00-16:00, closed Sat-Sun, 59 Avenue Denis Séméria, bus #81 stops here). A smaller TI is in the sleepy village of St-Jean-Cap-Ferrat (closed Sun, 5 Avenue Denis Séméria, tel. 04 93 76 08 90, office-tourisme@saintjeancapferrat.fr).

---

*Rick's Tip: Cap Ferrat is perfect for a walk; you'll find **well-maintained, mostly level foot trails** covering most of its length. The TIs in Villefranche-sur-Mer and on the Cap have maps with walking paths marked.*

Sights

▲VILLA EPHRUSSI DE ROTHSCHILD

In what seems like the ultimate in Riviera extravagance, Venice, Versailles, and the Côte d'Azur come together in the pastel-pink Villa Ephrussi. Rising above Cap Ferrat, this 1905 mansion has views west to Villefranche-sur-Mer and east to Beaulieu-sur-Mer.

Cost and Hours: Palace and gardens-€13, includes audioguide; mid-Feb-

Villa Ephrussi de Rothschild

Oct daily 10:00-18:00, July-Aug until 19:00, shorter hours off-season; tel. 04 93 01 33 09, www.villa-ephrussi.com.

Visiting the Villa: Pick up the audio-guide and garden map as you enter, then start with the well-furnished belle époque **interior.** Upstairs, an 18-minute film covers the life of rich and eccentric Beatrice, Baroness de Rothschild, the French banking heiress who built and furnished the place. Don't miss the view over the gardens from the terrace.

As you stroll through the rooms, you'll pass royal furnishings and personal possessions, including the baroness's porcelain collection and her bathroom case for cruises. An appropriately classy **garden-tearoom** serves drinks and lunches with a view (12:00-17:30).

Behind the mansion are literally ship-shape gardens, inspired by Beatrice's many ocean-liner trips. The seven lush gardens are re-created from locations all over the world. Highlights include the Jardin Exotique's wild cactus, the rose garden at the far end, and the view back to the house from the "Temple of Love" gazebo.

PLAGE DE PASSABLE

Located below the Villa Ephrussi is a pebbly little beach with great views, popular with families. One half is public (free, with snack bar, shower, and WC), and the other is run by a small restaurant (€22 includes changing locker, lounge chair, and shower; they have 260 "beds," but still reserve ahead in summer or on weekends as this is a prime spot, tel. 04 93 76 06 17). If you were ever to do the French Riviera rent-a-beach ritual, this would be the place.

Getting There: Bus #81 stops just above the beach (Passable stop). Drivers can park curbside or in a pay lot near the beach.

Eating: Plage de Passable is a great place for dinner. Arrive before sunset, then watch as darkness descends and lights flicker over Villefranche-sur-Mer's heavenly setting. **Restaurant de la Plage**

de Passable is your chance to dine on the beach with romance and class while enjoying terrific views and the sounds of children still at play (€12-16 starters, €18-30 *plats*, open daily late May-early Sept, always make a reservation, tel. 04 93 76 06 17, www.plage-de-passable.com).

Monaco

The minuscule principality of Monaco (less than a square mile) is a special place—it's home to one of the world's most famous auto races and one of its fanciest casinos. The glamorous 1956 marriage of the American actress Grace Kelly to Prince Rainier added to Monaco's mystique. Don't look for anything too deep in this glittering little land of luxury; the majority of its 36,000 residents have relocated here mainly to avoid paying income tax. Yet despite high prices, wall-to-wall daytime tourists, and a Disney-esque atmosphere, Monaco is a Riviera must for many a traveler.

Orientation

All of Monaco's major sights except the casino are in Monaco-Ville, packed within a few cheerfully tidy blocks. The famous casino is in the Monte Carlo neighborhood.

Day Plan: The surgical-strike plan is to start with my self-guided walk in Monaco-Ville, and then finish by gambling away whatever you have left in the Monte Carlo Casino.

Getting There: Ride **bus #100** (3-4/hour) from Nice (45 minutes) or Villefranche-sur-Mer (20 minutes). Trains run twice an hour (20 minutes from Nice, 10 minutes from Villefranche). Monaco's traffic isn't worth the fight for drivers—leave the car behind and ride the train or bus into town.

Arrival in Monaco: Bus riders wanting to start with the self-guided walk should disembark at the *Place d'Armes* stop at the base of Monaco-Ville; casino-goers should wait for the *Monte Carlo-Casino* stop.

From the train station, for Monaco-Ville, take the exit marked *Sortie Fontvieille/Le Rocher*, which leads through a long tunnel to Place d'Armes. For the casino, follow *Sortie Port* and *Accès Port* signs until you pop out at the port. From here, it's a 20-minute walk to the casino (up Avenue d'Ostende to your left), or a short trip via bus (#1 or #2, find stops across the busy street).

Getting Around Monaco: City buses #1 and #2 link all areas with frequent service (single ticket-€2, 6 tickets-€10, day pass-€5, pay driver or buy from curbside machines). You can split a six-ride ticket with your travel partners.

Tourist Information: The main TI is at the top of the park above the casino (Mon-Sat 9:00-19:00, Sun 11:00-13:00, 2 Boulevard des Moulins, tel. 00-377/92 16 61 16 or 00-377/92 16 61 66, www.visitmonaco.com). Another TI is at the train station (Tue-Sat 9:00-18:00, also open Sun-Mon in July-Aug, closed 12:00-14:00 off-season).

Rick's Tip: *If you want an official memento of your Monaco visit, you can get your* **passport stamped** *at the main TI.*

◑ Monaco-Ville Walk

This self-guided walk connects many of the main sights with a tight little loop, starting from the palace square, Monaco-Ville's sightseeing center.
• *If you're walking up from the Place d'Armes stop for bus #100, a well-marked lane leads directly to the palace.*

PALACE SQUARE (PLACE DU PALAIS)

This square is the best place to get oriented to Monaco. Facing the palace, go to the right and look out over the city (er... principality). This rock gave birth to the little pastel Hong Kong look-alike in 1215, and it's managed to remain an independent country for most of its 800 years. Looking beyond the glitzy port, notice the

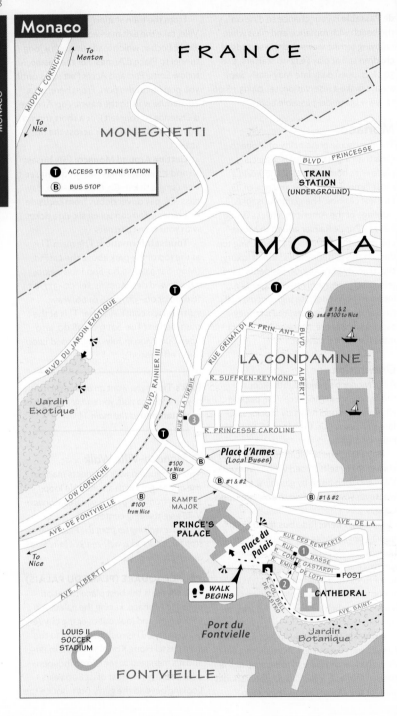

Monaco

FRANCE

To Menton

MIDDLE CORNICHE

To Nice

MONEGHETTI

BLVD. PRINCESSE

T ACCESS TO TRAIN STATION

B BUS STOP

TRAIN STATION (UNDERGROUND)

M O N A

T

T

B #1 & 2 and #100 to Nice

BLVD. DU JARDIN EXOTIQUE

RUE GRIMALDI

R. PRIN. ANT.

BLVD. ALBERT I

LA CONDAMINE

Jardin Exotique

BLVD. RAINIER III

RUE DE LA TURBIE

R. SUFFREN-REYMOND

3

T

R. PRINCESSE CAROLINE

B **Place d'Armes** (Local Buses)

#100 to Nice **B**

B #1 & #2

B #1 & #2

LOW CORNICHE

B #100 from Nice

RAMPE MAJOR

AVE. DE FONTVIEILLE

To Nice

AVE. ALBERT II

PRINCE'S PALACE

Place du Palais

AVE. DE LA

RUE DES REMPARTS

RUE BASSE

R. COMTE GASTARDI

1

R. EMILE DE LOTH

R. COL. BEL. DE CASTRO

2

■ POST

✝ CATHEDRAL

👣 WALK BEGINS

AVE. SAINT.

LOUIS II SOCCER STADIUM

Port du Fontvieille

Jardin Botanique

FONTVIEILLE

BEAUSOLIEL

To
Villa
Sauber &
Menton

BLVD. DES MOULINS

BLVD. LARVOTTO

Ⓑ
#112 to
Eze-le-Village

Ⓑ #100 from Nice &
#11 to La Turbie

Casino
Gardens

AVE. SPEL

Ⓑ #1 & 2
and #100 to Nice

Ⓑ #1 & 2

AMERICAN-
STYLE
CASINO

CHARLOTTE

AVE. DE LA COSTA

*Place du
Casino*

CASINO

MONTE CARLO

C O

AVE. D'OSTENDE

PALAIS DES
CONGRES &
Ⓟ "Le Casino"

SHUTTLE
BOAT

Port
LOTSA
YACHTS!

CRUISE
TENDER
DOCK

MONACO-
VILLE

FORT
ANTOINE

AVE. QUARANTINE

PORTE NEUVE

*Place de la
Visitation*
Ⓟ

RUE EMILE DE LOTH

*Mediterranean
Sea*

Ⓑ #1 & #2

Petit Train
Stop

MARTIN

Ⓟ "Le Palais"

AQUARIUM

WALK
ENDS

300 Meters

300 Yards

Eating & Sleeping
❶ Boulangerie
❷ U Cavagnetu Rest.
❸ Hôtel de France

faded green roof above and to the right: It belongs to the casino that put Monaco on the map in the 1800s.

The modern buildings just past the casino mark the eastern limit of Monaco. The famous Grand Prix runs along the port and then up the ramp to the casino (at top speeds of 180 mph). Italy is so close, you can almost smell the pesto. Just beyond the casino is France again (which flanks Monaco on both sides)—you could walk one-way from France to France, passing through Monaco in about 60 minutes.

The odd statue of a woman with a fishing net is dedicated to the glorious reign of **Prince Albert I** (1889-1922). The son of Charles III (who built the casino), Albert I was a true Renaissance man. He had a Jacques Cousteau-like fascination with the sea (and built Monaco's famous aquarium) and was a determined pacifist who made many attempts to dissuade Germany's Kaiser Wilhelm II from becoming involved in World War I.

• *As you head toward the palace, you'll find a statue of a monk grasping a sword nearby.*

Meet **François Grimaldi,** a renegade Italian dressed as a monk, who captured Monaco in 1297 and began the dynasty that still rules the principality. The current ruler, Prince Albert, is his great-great-great...grandson, which gives Monaco's royal family the distinction of being the longest-lasting dynasty in Europe.

• *Now walk to the...*

PRINCE'S PALACE (PALAIS PRINCIER)

A medieval castle sat where the palace is today. Its strategic setting has had a lot to do with Monaco's ability to resist attackers. Today, Prince Albert and his wife live in the palace, while poor Princesses Stephanie and Caroline live down the street. The palace guards protect the prince 24/7 and still stage a **Changing of the Guard** ceremony with all the pageantry of an important nation (daily at 11:55, fun to watch but jam-packed, arrive by 11:30). Audioguide tours take you through part of the prince's lavish palace in 30 minutes. The rooms are well-furnished and impressive, but interesting only if you haven't seen a château lately (€8, includes audioguide, €19 combo-ticket also covers Oceanographic Museum and Aquarium; April-Oct daily 10:00-18:00, closed Nov-March, www.palais.mc).

• *Head to the west end of the palace square. Below the cannonballs is the district known as...*

FONTVIEILLE

Monaco's newest, reclaimed-from-the-sea area has seen much of Monaco's post-WWII growth (notice the lushly planted building tops). Prince Rainier continued—some say, was obsessed with—Monaco's economic growth, creating landfills (and topping them with apartments such as in Fontvieille), flashy ports, more beaches, a big sports stadium marked by tall arches, and a rail station.

• *With your back to the palace, leave the square through the arch at the far right (Rue Colonel Bellando de Castro) and find the...*

Monaco's classy port

Palace Square

CATHEDRAL OF MONACO (CATHEDRALE DE MONACO)

The somber but beautifully lit cathedral, rebuilt in 1878, shows that Monaco cared for more than just its new casino. It's where centuries of Grimaldis are buried, and where Princess Grace and Prince Rainier were married. Inside, circle slowly behind the altar (counterclockwise). The second tomb is that of Albert I, who did much to put Monaco on the world stage. The second-to-last tomb—inscribed *"Gratia Patricia, MCMLXXXII"*—is where Princess Grace was buried in 1982. Prince Rainier's tomb lies next to Princess Grace's (daily 8:30-19:15).

• *As you leave the cathedral, find the 1956 wedding photo of Princess Grace and Prince Rainier, then dip into the immaculately maintained* **Jardin Botanique,** *with more fine views. In the gardens, turn left. Eventually you'll find the impressive building housing the...*

Rick's Tip: *If you're into* **stamps,** *drop by the* **post office,** *where postcard writers with panache can see—or buy—impressive Monegasque stamps (closed Sun, on Place de la Mairie, a few blocks from the Oceanographic Museum and Aquarium).*

OCEANOGRAPHIC MUSEUM AND AQUARIUM (MUSEE OCEANOGRAPHIQUE)

Prince Albert I built this cliff-hanging aquarium in 1910 as a monument to his enthusiasm for things from the sea. The aquarium, which Jacques Cousteau captained for 32 years, has 2,000 different specimens, representing 250 species. You'll find Mediterranean fish and colorful tropical species. Rotating exhibits occupy the entry floor. Upstairs, the fancy Albert I Hall houses a museum that's filled with ship models, whale skeletons, and oceanographic instruments. Take the elevator to the rooftop terrace view café (€14, €19 combo-ticket includes Prince's Palace;

🅐 *Changing of the guard*
🅑 *Cathedral of Monaco*
🅒 *Fontvieille harbor*
🅓 *Oceanographic Museum*

daily April-Sept 10:00-19:00, July-Aug until 19:30, Oct-March until 18:00, www. oceano.mc).

• *Our walk is over. The red-brick steps across from the aquarium lead up to stops for buses #1 and #2, both of which run to the casino and the train station.*

Rick's Tip: *For a* **cheap and scenic loop ride** *through Monaco, ride bus #2 from one end to the other and back (25 minutes each way). You need two tickets (€2 each) and have to get off the bus at the last stop and then get on again.*

Experiences
▲ MONTE CARLO CASINO (CASINO DE MONTE-CARLO)

Monte Carlo, which means "Charles' Hill" in Spanish, is named for the prince who presided over Monaco's 19th-century makeover. In the mid-1800s, olive groves stood here. Then, with the construction of a casino and spas, and easy road and train access, one of Europe's poorest countries was on the Grand Tour map—*the* place for the vacationing aristocracy to play. Today, Monaco has the world's highest per-capita income.

The Monte Carlo casino is intended to make you feel comfortable while losing your retirement nest egg. Charles Garnier designed the place (with an opera house inside) in 1878, in part to thank the prince for his financial help in completing Paris' Opéra Garnier (which the architect also designed).

The **first rooms** (Salle Renaissance, Salon de l'Europe, and Salle des Amériques) have European and English roulette, blackjack, craps, and slot machines. The more glamorous **private game rooms** (Salons Touzet, Salle Medecin, and Terrasse Salle Blanche) have those same games, plus Trente et Quarante, Ultimate Texas Hold 'Em poker, and Punto Banco—a version of baccarat.

Cost and Hours: Hours and entry fees are shuffled regularly. Plan on €10 to enter at any hour, whether you gamble or not. Public areas are open daily 9:00-12:30 (no gambling). Guided tours may be available, or take an English brochure and tour on your own. From 14:00 to very late the gaming rooms are open to appropriately attired humans over 18 (bring your passport as proof, www.montecarlocasinos.com).

Lush gardens lead to Monte Carlo Casino.

Dress Code: Before 14:00, shorts are allowed in the atrium area, though you'll need decent attire to go any farther. After 14:00, shorts are off-limits everywhere, and tennis shoes are not permitted. Men should wear a jacket and slacks, and women should dress up a bit as well.

Take the Money and Run: The stop for buses returning to Nice and Villefranche-sur-Mer and for local buses #1 and #2 is on Avenue de la Costa, at the top of the park above the casino (at the small shopping mall). To reach the train station from the casino, take bus #1 or #2 from this stop, or walk about 15 minutes down Avenue d'Ostende toward the port, and follow signs to *Gare SNCF*.

Eating and Sleeping

In Monaco-Ville, you'll find massive *pan bagnat*, quiche, and sandwiches at the yellow-bannered **Boulangerie,** a block off Place du Palais (8 Rue Basse). At **U Cavagnetu,** just a block from Albert's palace, you'll dine cheaply on specialties from Monaco (14 Rue Comte Félix Gastaldi).

Centrally located and comfortable, **$$ Hôtel de France**** is reasonably priced—for Monaco (6 Rue de la Turbie, www.monte-carlo.mc/france).

Antibes

Rising above the blue Mediterranean south and west of Nice, Antibes is charming in a sandy-sophisticated way. Besides offering wide, pleasant beaches, it's the launching point for several scenic hikes along the rocky coast.

Orientation

Day Plan: Visitors can browse Europe's biggest yacht harbor, snooze on a sandy beach, loiter through the charming old town, and hike along a sea-swept trail. The town's cultural claim to fame, the Picasso Museum, shows off its appealing collection in a fine old building.

Getting There: Trains and buses run from Nice to Antibes, but the train is the better choice—it's faster and won't get you stuck in traffic (2/hour, 20 minutes).

Arrival in Antibes: To walk from the train station to the port, the old town, and

Antibes' Plage de la Gravette

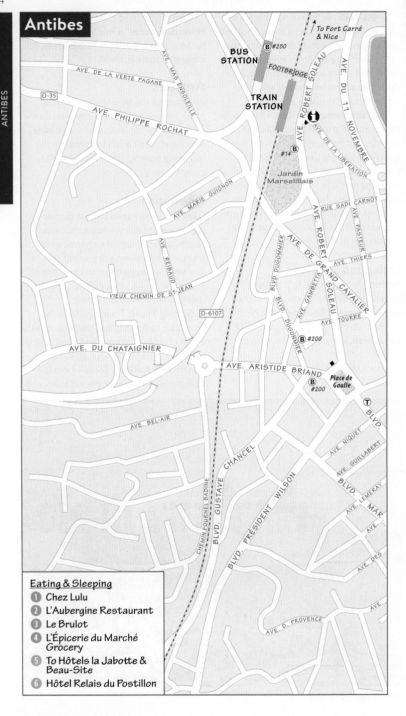

Antibes

BUS STATION

TRAIN STATION

To Fort Carré & Nice

FOOTBRIDGE

(B) #250

AVE. DE LA VERTE PAGANE

AVE. MAS ENSOLEILLE

D-35

AVE. PHILIPPE ROCHAT

AVE. ROBERT SOLEAU

AVE. DU 11 NOVEMBRE

AVE. DE LA LIBERATION

#14 (B)

Jardin Marselillais

RUE SADI CARNOT

AVE. MARIE GUIGNON

AVE. PASTEUR

AVE. ROBERT DE GRAND CAVALIER

AVE. REBAUD

BLVD. DUGOMMIER

AVE. THIERS

VIEUX CHEMIN DE ST-JEAN

AVE. GAMBETTA

AVE. TOURRE

D-6107

BLVD. DUGOMMIER

(B) #200

AVE. DU CHATAIGNIER

AVE. ARISTIDE BRIAND

Place de Gaulle

(B) #200

(T)

BLVD.

AVE. BEL-AIR

AVE. NIQUET

AVE. GUILLABERT

BLVD.

BLVD. GUSTAVE CHANCEL

CHEMIN FOURNEL BADINE

BLVD. PRESIDENT WILSON

AVE. LEMERAY

MAR.

AVE.

AVE. DES

AVE. D. PROVENCE

AVE.

Eating & Sleeping

1. Chez Lulu
2. L'Aubergine Restaurant
3. Le Brulot
4. L'Épicerie du Marché Grocery
5. To Hôtels la Jabotte & Beau-Site
6. Hôtel Relais du Postillon

Port Vauban

"QUAI DES MILLIARDAIRES"

BASTION ST. JAUME

Vieux Port

QUAI H. RAMBAUD

AVE. DE VERDUN

Best Parking P

ARCH

MEDIEVAL WALL

AVE. MISTRAL

BLVD. D'AGUILLON

BLVD. D'AGUILLON

RUE D'ANDREOSSY

RUE THURET

AVE. MIRABEAU

R. AUBERNON

Plage de la Gravette

OLD

RUE ROSTAN

RUE LACAN

R. PALMIERS

ANTIBES BOOKS

MARKET HALL

CHURCH OF THE IMMACULATE CONCEPTION

AV. DOUMER

POST

R. DE LA RÉPUBLIQUE

Tourist Train

Place Nationale

① ③

R. SADE

②

PICASSO MUSEUM
CHATEAU GRIMALDI

R. VAUBAN

⑥

Place des Martyrs de la Résistance

RUE VIAL

RUE J. CLOSE

RUE GUILLAUMONT

COURS MASSENA

RUE BATEAU

#2 & #14
Ⓑ

RUE DE FERSEN

④

TOURAQUE

DE GRASSE

BUS STATION

R. G. VANDENBERG

RUE REVENNES

TOWN

ALBERT I

AVE. MARECHAL REILLE

PROM. AMIRAL

Place du Sanfranier

RUE CASTELET

GAZAN

FRERES ROUSTAN

FOCH

MAIZIERE

MEDIEVAL WALL

BOURGEOIS

BARQUIER

HISTORY & ARCHAEOLOGY MUSEUM

Mediterranean Sea

BLVD. G. ALBERT I

BLVD. M. LECLERC

Place Albert I

PLAY TOYS

Plage de l'Ilette

To Plage Ponteil, Plage Salis, Cap D'Antibes & ⑤

Pointe de l'Ilette

100 Meters

100 Yards

the Picasso Museum (15 minutes), cross the street in front of the station, skirting left of the café, and follow Avenue de la Libération downhill as it bends left. At the end of the street, head right along the port. Day-trippers arriving by car should follow signs to *Centre-Ville*, then *Port Vauban*.

Tourist Information: The TI is a few blocks from the train station at 42 Avenue Robert Soleau (open daily, tel. 04 22 10 60 10, www.antibesjuanlespins.com).

Rick's Tip: *Antibes'* **market hall,** *on Cours Masséna, bustling under a 19th-century canopy, changes throughout the day: flowers and produce until 13:30 (daily but closed Mon Sept-May), handicrafts most afternoons (Thu-Sun), and outdoor dining in the evenings.*

Sights

▲▲PICASSO MUSEUM (MUSEE PICASSO)

Sitting serenely where the old town meets the sea, this compact three-floor museum offers a manageable collection of Picasso's paintings, sketches, and ceramics. Picasso lived in this castle (the former Château Grimaldi) for several months in 1946, when he cranked out an amazing amount of art. Most of the paintings you'll see here are from this short but prolific stretch of his long career. The resulting collection (donated by Picasso) put

Terrace at the Picasso Museum

Antibes on the tourist map.

Cost and Hours: €6; mid-June-mid-Sept Tue-Sun 10:00-18:00, July-Aug Wed and Fri until 20:00, mid-Sept-mid-June Tue-Sun 10:00-12:00 & 14:00-18:00, closed Mon year-round; tel. 04 92 90 54 20, www.antibes-juanlespins.com.

▲BEACHES (*PLAGES*)

Good beaches stretch from the south end of Antibes toward Cap d'Antibes. They're busy but manageable in summer and on weekends, with cheap snack stands and good views of the old town. The closest beach is at the port (Plage de la Gravette) and seems calm in any season.

Rick's Tip: *Locals* **don't swim in July and August,** *as the warming sea brings swarms of* **stinging jellyfish.** *Ask before you dip.*

Hikes

The two hikes below are easy to combine by bus, bike, or car. For bus schedules, ask at the TI or consult www.envibus.fr.

▲▲CHAPELLE ET PHARE DE LA GAROUPE HIKE

The exceptional territorial views—best in the morning—from this lighthouse viewpoint more than merit the 20-minute uphill climb from Plage de la Salis. An orientation table explains that you can see from Nice to Cannes and up to the Alps.

Getting There: Take Envibus bus #2 or #14 to the Plage de la Salis stop and find the trail a block ahead (a few blocks after Maupassant Apartments; where the road curves left, follow signs and the rough, cobbled Chemin du Calvaire up to the lighthouse tower). By car or bike, follow signs for *Cap d'Antibes*, then look for *Chapelle et Phare de la Garoupe* signs.

▲▲CAP D'ANTIBES LOOP HIKE (SENTIER TOURISTIQUE DE TIREPOIL)

Cap d'Antibes is filled with exclusive villas and mansions. Roads are just lanes, bounded on both sides by the high and greedy walls of some of the most expensive real estate in France. But all the money in the world can't buy you the beach in France, so a thin strip of rocky coastline forms a two-mile long, park-like zone with an extremely scenic, mostly paved but often rocky trail (Sentier Touristique de Tirepoil).

At a fast clip you can walk the entire circle in just over an hour. Don't do the hike without the tourist map (available at hotels or the TI). While you can do it in either direction (or in partial segments), I prefer a counterclockwise loop.

___

Rick's Tip: *You can tour star-shaped* **Fort Carré,** *on the headland overlooking the harbor, but there's little to see inside. It's only worth a visit for* **fantastic views** *over Antibes.*

___

Getting There: Ride Envibus bus #2 from Antibes for about 15 minutes to the La Fontaine stop at Rond-Point A. Meiland (next to Hôtel Beau-Site). By car or bike, follow signs to *Cap d'Antibes,* then to *Plage de la Garoupe,* and park there. The trail begins at the far-right end of Plage de la Garoupe.

Eating and Sleeping

Chez Lulu is a fun family dining adventure (arrive early, opens at 19:00, closed Sun-Mon, 5 Rue Frédéric Isnard). Intimate **L'Aubergine** delivers fine cuisine at fair prices (opens at 18:30, closed Wed, 7 Rue Sade). **Le Brulot** is known for its meats cooked on an open fire (closed Sun, 2 Rue Frédéric Isnard). Romantics on a shoestring can drop by the handy **L'Épicerie du Marché** and assemble a picnic dinner to enjoy on the beach or ramparts (3 Cours Masséna).

$$$ Hôtel la Jabotte** is a cozy boutique hotel (13 Avenue Max Maurey, www.jabotte.com). The comfortable **$$ Hôtel Beau-Site***** is a good-value option, a 10-minute drive from town (141 Boulevard Kennedy, www.hotelbeausite.net). **$ Hôtel Relais du Postillon**** has cute rooms at good rates (8 Rue Championnet, www.relaisdupostillon.com).

Cap d'Antibes' seaside walk

Spain

S pain (*España*) is in Europe, but not *of* Europe—it has a unique identity and history, thanks largely to the Pyrenees Mountains that physically isolate it from the rest of the continent. Spain's seclusion contributed to the creation of distinctive customs: bullfights, flamenco dancing, and a national obsession with ham.

Spain, with 47 million people (mostly Roman Catholic), is a little bigger than California. It's been ruled by Roman emperors, Muslim sultans, hard-core Christians, conquistadors, French dandies, and a Fascist dictator; all left their mark on Spain's art, architecture, and culture.

Your two best stops in Spain are trend-setting Barcelona and lively Madrid. Nursing a glass of wine at a sidewalk table on any square gets you a front-row seat to Spain's urban scene, the best show in town.

CUISINE SCENE AT A GLANCE

Spanish cuisine is hearty, and meals are served in big, inexpensive portions. You can eat well in restaurants for about €15-20—or even more cheaply with more variety if you graze on tapas in bars.

The Spanish eating schedule—lunch from 13:00 to 16:00, and dinner after 21:00—frustrates many visitors. Lunch, eaten around 14:00, is the major meal of the day for most Spaniards. Because many people work until 19:30, dinner is usually served at about 21:00 or 22:00.

Here's how a hungry tourist can get an earlier dinner: Hit the bars to build a light meal out of appetizers. At **tapas bars**, you can eat well any time of day. Tapas are small portions of seafood, salads, meat-filled pastries, and on and on, typically costing about €2-3 apiece.

In the bar, locate the price list (often posted in fine type on a wall somewhere) to know the menu options and price tiers. Eating and drinking at a bar is usually cheapest if you sit or stand at the counter (*barra*). You may pay a little more to eat sitting at a table (*mesa* or *salón*) and still more for an outdoor table (*terraza*). Traditionally, tapas are served at the bar. It's bad form to order food at the bar, then take it to a table.

When you're ready to order, be assertive or you'll never be served. *Por favor* (please) grabs the guy's attention. You can often just point to what you want in the display case, and get your food. Don't worry about paying until you're ready to leave (he's keeping track of your tab).

Many bars push larger portions called *raciones* (dinner plate-sized). Ask for the smaller tapas portions or a *media-ración* (listed as ½ *ración* on a menu)—though some bars simply don't serve anything smaller than a *ración*.

Most **restaurants** (like bars) serve their dishes as *raciones* and *media-raciones*. Enjoy this as an opportunity to explore the regional cuisine. Two people can fill up on four *media-raciones*.

For a budget meal in a restaurant, try a *plato combinado* (combination plate), which usually includes portions of one or two main dishes, a vegetable, and bread. Another option is the *menú del día* (menu of the day, also known as *menú turístico*), a substantial three- to four-course meal that usually comes with a carafe of house wine.

Tipping: Most sit-down restaurants include a service charge in the bill (*servicio incluido*). If you like to tip for good service, round up to about 5 percent. If service is not included (*servicio no incluido*), tip up to 10 percent.

Budget Options: Fast-food sandwich shops such as Pans & Company serve fresh sandwiches and salads. Many bakeries sell sandwiches and *empanadas* (pastry turnovers filled with seasoned meat and veggies). For a hearty snack any time of day, drop by a bar for a *tortilla española*—a potato omelet cooked fresh every morning and sold in wedges. Pizza shops offer slices to go. The popular El Corte Inglés department stores have a cafeteria and supermarket.

Barcelona

Barcelona may be Spain's second city, but it's undoubtedly the first city of the proud and distinct region of Catalunya. Catalan flags wave side by side with Spanish flags, and locals—while fluent in both languages—insist on speaking Catalan first. Joining hands to dance the patriotic *sardana* is a tradition that's going strong. This lively culture is on an unstoppable roll in Spain's most cosmopolitan corner.

The city itself is a work of art. Catalan architects, including Antoni Gaudí, Lluís Domènech i Montaner, and Josep Puig i Cadafalch, forged the Modernista style and remade the city's skyline into a curvy fantasy—culminating in Gaudí's over-the-top Sagrada Família, a church still under construction. Pablo Picasso lived here as a teenager, right as he was on the verge of reinventing painting; his legacy is today's Picasso Museum.

Barcelona bubbles with life—in the narrow alleys of the Barri Gòtic, along the pedestrian boulevard called the Ramblas, in the funky bohemian quarter of El Born, along the bustling beach promenade, and throughout the chic Eixample. The cafés are filled by day, and people crowd the streets at night, popping into tapas bars for a drink and a perfectly composed bite of seafood.

If you surrender to any city's charms, let it be Barcelona.

BARCELONA IN 3 DAYS

Day 1: In the cool of the morning, follow my Barri Gòtic Walk, exploring the winding lanes, unique boutiques, and historic cathedral.

Then take my Ramblas Ramble, strolling down the grand pedestrian boulevard—a festival of people-watching, street performers, and pickpockets. On the Ramblas, duck into La Boqueria Market for fresh produce and unforgettable taste treats. In the afternoon, head to the trendy El Born district to tour the Picasso Museum or Palace of Catalan Music, or both.

On any evening: Have a tapa-hopping dinner in El Born, the Barri Gòtic, or the Eixample. Take in some music (flamenco, guitar, concerts). Zip up to the hilltop of Montjuïc for the sunset, then down to the Magic Fountains (illuminated on weekends). Or stroll the long, inviting beach promenade.

Day 2: Tour the city's fanciful Modernista architecture, championed by Antoni Gaudí. Marvel at the buildings on the

Barcelona Neighborhood Overview

GRÀCIA

Park Güell

EIXAMPLE

LA
■ PEDRERA

SAGRADA
■ FAMÍLIA

PASSEIG DE GRÀCIA

CASA
BATLLÓ

Citadel
Park

Plaça de
Catalunya

EL
BORN

CITY

■ PICASSO
MUSEUM

VIA LAIETANA

■ CATHEDRAL

OLD

BARRI
GÒTIC

LAS RAMBLAS

SANTS
STATION ■

EL
RAVAL

BARCELONETA

Plaça
d'Espanya ●

■ FUNDACIÓ
JOAN MIRÓ

Port
Vell

Not to Scale

MONTJUÏC

← To Airport

CRUISE
PORT

Mediterranean Sea

Block of Discord and the street's master-piece, La Pedrera. Tour Gaudí's soaring church, the Sagrada Família. Then head to Park Güell, with its colorful mosaics, fountains, and stunning city views.

Day 3: Tour the museums on Montjuïc: The Catalan Art Museum displays top medieval sculptures (reservation required), while Fundació Joan Miró features the hometown artist's whimsical work. The hilltop castle ramparts offers sweeping views. You could head back downtown (for museums, shopping, exploring) or take the slow, scenic cable-car from Montjuïc to the port. For a pleasant evening, stroll the beach along Barceloneta, collect another sunset, and find your favorite *chiringuito* (beach bar).

Rick's Tip: *Located in the far northeast corner of Spain,* **Barcelona makes a good first or last stop for your trip.** *With the high-speed AVE train, Barcelona is three hours away from Madrid—faster and simpler than flying. If you want to rent a car, start your trip in Barcelona, take the train or fly to Madrid, and see Madrid and Toledo, all before picking up your car—cleverly saving on several days of rental fees.*

ORIENTATION

A large square, **Plaça de Catalunya** at the center of Barcelona, divides the older and newer parts of town. Below Plaça de Catalunya is the Old City, with the Ramblas boulevard running down to the harbor.

The **Old City (Ciutat Vella)** is the compact core of Barcelona—ideal for strolling, shopping, and people-watching. It's a labyrinth of narrow streets, once confined by medieval walls. The lively pedestrian drag called the **Ramblas** goes through the heart of the Old City from Plaça de Catalunya to the harbor. The Old City is divided into thirds by the Ramblas and another major thoroughfare (running roughly parallel to the Ramblas), **Via Laietana.** Between the Ramblas and Via Laietana is the characteristic **Barri Gòtic** (BAH-ree GOH-teek, Gothic Quarter), with the cathedral as its navel. Locals call it "El Gòtic" for short. To the east of Via Laietana is the **El Born** district (a.k.a. "La Ribera"), a shopping, dining, and nightlife mecca centered on the Picasso Museum and the Church of Santa Maria del Mar. To the west of the Ramblas is the **Raval** (rah-VAHL), with a modern-art museum and a university. The Raval is of least interest to tourists (some parts of it are dodgy and should be avoided).

The old harbor, **Port Vell,** gleams with landmark monuments and new developments. A pedestrian bridge links the Ramblas with the modern Maremagnum entertainment complex. On the peninsula across the quaint sailboat harbor is **Barceloneta,** a traditional fishing neighborhood with gritty charm and good seafood restaurants. Beyond Barceloneta, a gorgeous man-made **beach** several miles long leads to the commercial and convention district called the **Fòrum.**

Above the Old City, beyond the bustling hub of Plaça de Catalunya, is the elegant **Eixample** (eye-SHAM-plah) district, its grid plan softened by cutoff corners. Much of Barcelona's Modernista architecture is here—especially along the swanky **Passeig de Gràcia,** an area called **Quadrat d'Or** ("Golden Quarter"). To the east is the **Sagrada Família;** to the north is the **Gràcia** district and Antoni Gaudí's **Park Güell.**

The large hill overlooking the city to the southwest is **Montjuïc** (mohn-jew-EEK), home to some excellent museums (Catalan Art, Joan Miró).

Tourist Information

Barcelona's **TI** has several branches (central tel. 932-853-834, www.barcelona turisme.cat). The primary one is beneath the main square, **Plaça de Catalunya** (daily 8:30-20:30, entrance across from El Corte Inglés department store—look for red sign and take stairs down, tel. 932-853-832); this TI offers a **Picasso walk** (€22, includes museum admission; Tue-Sat at 15:00; 2 hours including museum visit)**,** as well as walks for **gourmets** (€22, Mon-Fri at 10:30, 2 hours) and fans of **Modernisme** (€16; April-Oct Mon, Wed, and Fri at 18:00; Nov-March Wed and Fri at 15:30; 2 hours). Inside the TI is also the privately run **Ruta del Modernisme** desk, which gives out a route map showing all 116 Modernista buildings and offers a sightseeing discount package (€12), with a great guidebook and discounts on many Modernista sights—worthwhile if going beyond the biggies I cover (www.ruta delmodernisme.com).

The TI on **Plaça de Sant Jaume,** just south of the cathedral in the City Hall, offers great guided **Barri Gòtic walks** (€16, daily at 9:30, 2 hours, groups limited to 35, buy your ticket 15 minutes early at the TI desk—not from the guide, in summer stop by the office a day ahead to reserve, Mon-Fri 8:30-20:30, Sat 9:00-19:00, Sun 9:00-14:00, Ciutat 2, tel. 932-853-832, www.barcelonaturisme.cat).

Other convenient branches include a kiosk near the top of the **Ramblas** (#115); near the **cathedral** in the Catalan College of Architects building; inside the base of the **Columbus Monument** at the harbor; at the **airport** (Terminals 1 and 2B); and at the **Sants Train Station.** Smaller kiosks are on **Plaça d'Espanya,** in the park across from the **Sagrada Família** entrance, and on **Plaça de Catalunya.**

At any TI, pick up the free city map (although the free El Corte Inglés map provided by most hotels is better), the small Metro map, the monthly *Barcelona Planning.com* guidebook (with tips

Daily Reminder

SUNDAY: Most sights are open, but the Boqueria and Santa Caterina markets are closed. Some sights close early today, including the Fundació Joan Miró (closes at 14:30), along with the Catalan Art Museum (closes at 15:00). Informal performances of the *sardana* national dance take place in front of the cathedral at noon (none in Aug). Some museums are free at certain times: Catalan Art Museum and Palau Güell (free on first Sun of month), and the Picasso Museum. The Magic Fountains come alive on summer evenings (May-Sept).

MONDAY: Many sights are closed, including the Picasso Museum, Catalan Art Museum, Palau Güell, Casa Lleó Morera, and Fundació Joan Miró. Most major Modernista sights are open today, including the Sagrada Família, La Pedrera, Park Güell, Casa Batlló, and Casa Amatller.

TUESDAY/WEDNESDAY: All major sights are open.

THURSDAY: All major sights are open. Fundació Joan Miró is open until 21:00 and the Picasso Museum is open until 21:30 year-round, and the Magic Fountains spout on summer evenings (May-Sept).

FRIDAY: All major sights are open. The Magic Fountains light up Montjuïc year-round.

SATURDAY: All major sights are open. Barcelonans occasionally dance the *sardana* on Saturdays at 18:00 in front of the cathedral, and in summer you're likely to see traditional folk activities there at 19:30. The Magic Fountains dance all year. The Catalan Art Museum is free after 15:00.

LATE-HOURS SIGHTSEEING: Sights with **year-round** evening hours (19:30 or later) include La Boqueria Market, Cathedral of Barcelona, Casa Batlló, and Church of Santa Maria del Mar.

Sights offering later hours only in **peak season** (roughly April-Sept) include the Sagrada Família, La Pedrera, Palau Güell, Park Güell, Fundació Joan Miró, Catalan Art Museum, and Gaudí House Museum.

on sightseeing, shopping, events, and restaurants), and the quarterly *See Barcelona* guide (with practical information on museums and a neighborhood-by-neighborhood sightseeing rundown). The monthly *Time Out BCN Guide* offers a concise but thorough day-by-day list of events. The monthly *Barcelona Metropolitan* magazine has timely, substantial coverage of local topics and events. All are free.

The **Regional Catalunya TI** can help with travel and sightseeing tips for the entire region and even Madrid (Mon-Sat 10:00-19:00, Sun 10:00-14:00, in Palau Robert building near the intersection of Passeig de Gràcia and Diagonal at Passeig de Gràcia 107, tel. 932-388-091, www.catalunya.com).

Advance Tickets and Sightseeing Passes

To save time, it's smart to **buy tickets in advance online,** especially for the Picasso Museum, Sagrada Família, La Pedrera, and Park Güell's Monumental Zone (advance tickets also available for Casa Batlló and Palau Güell, but less necessary).

Advance tickets are required to tour Casa Lleó Morera (either online or you can buy in Barcelona) and the Palace of Catalan Music.

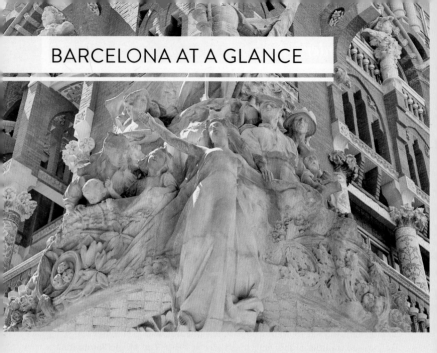

BARCELONA AT A GLANCE

▲▲▲**The Ramblas** Barcelona's colorful, gritty, tourist-filled pedestrian thoroughfare. **Hours:** Always open. See page 351.

▲▲▲**Picasso Museum** Extensive collection offering insight into the brilliant Spanish artist's early years. **Hours:** Tue-Sun 9:00-19:00, Thu until 21:30, closed Mon. See page 356.

▲▲▲**Sagrada Família** Gaudí's remarkable, unfinished church—a masterpiece in progress. **Hours:** Daily April-Sept 9:00-20:00, Oct-March 9:00-18:00. See page 371.

▲▲**Palace of Catalan Music** Best Modernista interior in Barcelona. **Hours:** 50-minute English tours daily every hour 10:00-15:00, plus frequent concerts. See page 363.

▲▲**La Pedrera (Casa Milà)** Barcelona's quintessential Modernista building and Gaudí creation. **Hours:** Daily March-Oct 9:00-20:00, Nov-Feb 9:00-18:30. See page 369.

▲▲**Park Güell** Colorful Gaudí-designed park overlooking the city. **Hours:** Daily April-Oct 8:00-20:00 (May-Aug until 21:30), Nov-March 8:30-18:15. See page 379.

▲▲**Catalan Art Museum** World-class showcase of this region's art, including a substantial Romanesque collection. **Hours:** May-Sept Tue-Sat 10:00-20:00 (Oct-April until 18:00), Sun 10:00-15:00, closed Mon. See page 381.

▲**La Boqueria Market** Colorful but touristy produce market, just off the Ramblas. **Hours:** Mon-Sat 8:00-20:00, best mornings after 9:00, closed Sun. See page 351.

▲**Palau Güell** Exquisitely curvy Gaudí interior and fantasy rooftop. **Hours:** Tue-Sun 10:00-20:00, Nov-March until 17:30, closed Mon. See page 351.

▲**Cathedral of Barcelona** Colossal Gothic cathedral ringed by distinctive chapels. **Hours:** Generally open to visitors Mon-Fri 8:00-19:30, Sat-Sun 8:00-20:00. See page 354.

▲*Sardana* **Dances** Patriotic dance in which proud Catalans join hands in a circle, often held outdoors. **Hours:** Every Sun at 12:00, sometimes also Sat at 18:00, no dances in Aug. See page 356.

▲**Santa Caterina Market** Fine market hall built on the site of an old monastery and updated with a wavy Gaudí-inspired roof. **Hours:** Mon-Sat 7:30-15:30, Thu-Fri until 20:30, closed Sun. See page 364.

▲**Church of Santa Maria del Mar** Catalan Gothic church in El Born, built by wealthy medieval shippers. **Hours:** Generally open to visitors daily 9:00-20:30. See page 364.

▲**Casa Batlló** Gaudí-designed home topped with fanciful dragon-inspired roof. **Hours:** Daily 9:00-21:00. See page 365.

▲**Casa Lleó Morera** One of the best-preserved Modernista interiors in the city. **Hours:** Tour times vary, open Tue-Sun, closed Mon. See page 365.

▲**Fundació Joan Miró** World's best collection of works by Catalan modern artist Joan Miró and his contemporaries. **Hours:** Tue-Sat 10:00-20:00 (Nov-March until 18:00), Thu until 21:00, Sun until 14:30, closed Mon year-round. See page 384.

▲**Magic Fountains** Lively fountain spectacle. **Hours:** May-Sept Thu-Sun 21:00-23:00, Oct-April Fri-Sat 19:00-20:30. See page 385.

▲**Barcelona's Beaches** Fun-filled, man-made beach reaching from the harbor to the Fòrum. **Hours:** Always open. See page 385.

"You're Not in Spain, You're in Catalunya!"

You may see this popular nationalistic refrain on T-shirts or stickers around town. Catalunya is *not* the land of bullfighting and flamenco that many visitors envision when they think of Spain (visit Madrid or Sevilla for those).

Catalunya, with Barcelona as its capital, has its own language, history, and culture. Its eight million people have a proud, independent spirit. Historically, Catalunya ("Cataluña" in Spanish, sometimes spelled "Catalonia" in English) has often been at odds with the central Spanish government in Madrid. The Catalan language and culture were discouraged or even outlawed at various times in history, as Catalunya often chose the wrong side in wars and rebellions against the kings in Madrid. In the Spanish Civil War (1936-1939), Catalunya was one of the last pockets of democratic resistance against the military coup of fascist dictator Francisco Franco, who punished the region with four decades of repression. During that time, the Catalan flag was banned—but locals vented their national spirit by flying their football team's flag instead.

Reminders of royal and Franco-era suppression live on in Barcelona's landmarks. Citadel Park (Parc de la Ciutadella) was originally a much-despised military citadel, constructed in the 18th century to keep locals in line. The Castle of Montjuïc has been the site of numerous political executions, including hundreds during the Franco era. Today, many Catalans favor breaking away from Spain, but the central government has vowed to block any referendum on independence.

To see Catalan culture, look for the *sardana* dance or an exhibition of *castellers* (both described on page 355). The main symbol of Catalunya is the dragon, which was slain by St. George ("Jordi" in Catalan)—the region's patron saint. You'll find dragons all over Barcelona, along with the Catalan flag—called the Senyera—with four horizontal red stripes on a gold field.

After the end of the Franco era in the mid-1970s, the Catalan language made a huge comeback. Schools are now required by law to conduct classes in Catalan; most children learn Catalan first and Spanish second. While all Barcelonans still speak Spanish, nearly all understand Catalan, three-quarters speak Catalan, and half can write it.

Consider getting the **Articket BCN pass** if you plan to visit the Picasso Museum, Catalan Art Museum, and Fundació Joan Miró. The pass saves you money and lets you skip the ticket lines (especially helpful at the Picasso Museum). It covers admission to six museums and their temporary exhibits. Just show your Articket BCN (to the ticket taker, at the info desk, or at a special Articket window), and you'll get your entry ticket (€30, valid for three months; sold at participating museums and the TIs at Plaça de Catalunya, Plaça de Sant Jaume, and Sants Station; www.articket bcn.org).

Skip the Barcelona Card and the Barcelona Card Express, which cover public transportation and include free admission to mostly minor sights, with only small discounts on some major sights (Barcelona Card—€45/3 days, €55/4 days, €60/5 days; Barcelona Card Express—€20/2 days; sold at TIs and El Corte Inglés

Here are the essential Catalan phrases:

English	Catalan	Pronounced
Hello	*Hola*	OH-lah
Please	*Si us plau*	see oos plow
Thank you	*Gracies*	GRAH-see-es
Goodbye	*Adéu*	ah-DAY-oo
Long live Catalunya!	*¡Visca Catalunya!*	BEE-skah kah-tah-LOON-yah

When finding your way, these words and place names will come in handy:

exit	*sortida*	sor-TEE-dah
square	*plaça*	PLAS-sah
street	*carrer*	kah-REHR
boulevard	*passeig*	PAH-sage
avenue	*avinguda*	ah-veen-GOO-dah

Here's how to pronounce the city's major landmarks:

Plaça de Catalunya	PLAS-sah duh kah-tah-LOON-yah
Eixample	eye-SHAM-plah
Passeig de Gràcia	PAH-sage duh grass-EE-ah
Catedral	KAH-tah-dral
Barri Gòtic	BAH-ree GOH-teek
Montjuïc	mohn-jew-EEK

department stores, www.barcelona turisme.com).

Tours

The handy **hop-on, hop-off Tourist Bus** (Bus Turístic), which departs from Plaça de Catalunya, offers three multistop circuits in double-decker buses, all with headphone commentary. The two-hour blue route covers north Barcelona (most Gaudí sights, departs from El Corte Inglés). The two-hour red route covers south Barcelona (Barri Gòtic and Montjuïc, departs from the west—Ramblas—side of the square). A short 40-minute green route covers the beaches in summer (1 day-€27, 2 days-€38; buy on bus, from TI, or online; offers small discounts on major sights; daily 9:00-20:00 in summer, off-season until 19:00, buses run every 10-25 minutes, www.barcelonabusturistic.cat).

Reliable **Runner Bean Tours** offer 2.5-hour walks covering the Old City and Gaudí, as well as night tours, family walks,

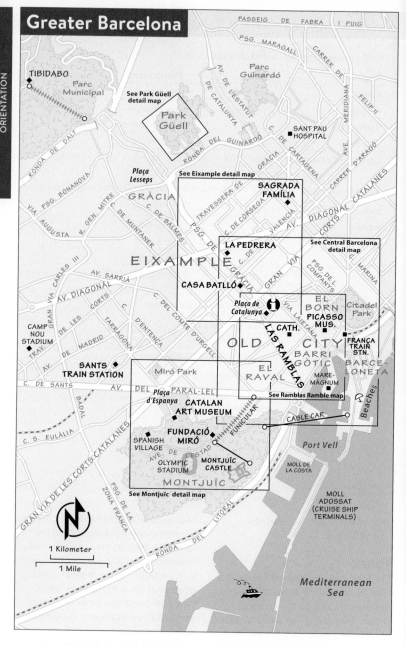

Greater Barcelona

PASSEIG DE FABRA I PUIG

PSG. MARAGALL

CARRER DE MERIDIANA

TIBIDABO

Parc Municipal

Parc Guinardó

AV. DE L'ESTATUT DE CATALUNYA

See Park Güell detail map

Park Güell

RONDA DE DALT

SANT PAU HOSPITAL

C. DE CARTAGENA

RONDA DEL GUINARDÓ

AVE. FELIP II

Plaça Lesseps

GRÀCIA

See Eixample detail map

SAGRADA FAMÍLIA

VIA AUGUSTA

PSG. BONANOVA

R. GEN. MITRE

C. DE BALMES

C. DE MUNTANER

TRAVESSERA DE GRACIA

C. DE CORSEGA

VALÈNCIA

PSG. DE GRÀCIA

DIAGONAL

CORTS CATALANES

CARRER D'ARAGÓ

EIXAMPLE

LA PEDRERA

C. DE

See Central Barcelona detail map

Cl. MARINA

GRAN VIA CARLES III

AV. SARRIÀ

AV. DIAGONAL

DE LES CORTS

C. DEL COMTE D'URGELL

CASA BATLLÓ

GRAN VIA

PSG. DE L. COMPANYS

EL BORN

Citadel Park

Plaça de Catalunya

CAMP NOU STADIUM

C. D'ENTENÇA

TARRAGONA

AV. DE MADRID

PICASSO MUS.

OLD CITY

CATH.

LAS RAMBLAS

VIA LAIETANA

BARRI GÒTIC

FRANÇA TRAIN STN.

BARCE-LONETA

SANTS TRAIN STATION

Miró Park

EL RAVAL

MARE-MAGNUM

C. DE SANTS

BADAL

AV.

DEL

PARAL-LEL

Plaça d'Espanya

CATALAN ART MUSEUM

MARE-MAGNUM

See Ramblas Ramble map

Beaches

C. S. EULÀLIA

GRAN VIA DE LES CORTS CATALANES

SPANISH VILLAGE

AV. DE L'ESTADI

FUNDACIÓ MIRÓ

FUNICULAR

CABLE CAR

Port Vell

PSG. DE LA ZONA FRANCA

OLYMPIC STADIUM

MONTJUÏC CASTLE

MONTJUÏC

MOLL DE LA COSTA

See Montjuïc detail map

MOLL ADOSSAT (CRUISE SHIP TERMINALS)

N

1 Kilometer

1 Mile

RONDA DEL LITORAL

Mediterranean Sea

and more (tours depart from Plaça Reial daily at 11:00 year-round, plus daily at 16:30 in April-mid-Oct, mobile 636-108-776, www.runnerbeantours.com). **Discover Walks** offers similar tours—the Gaudí Tour (daily at 10:30) and Ramblas & Barri Gòtic (15:00 Tue, Thu, and Sat), each costing €19—along with pricier tours (www.discoverwalks.com, tel. 931-816-810).

Food tours, lasting about three hours, make several informative, fun stops for tastings in a characteristic neighborhood. Consider **The Barcelona Taste** (€80/person, Tue-Sat, run by US expats, www.thebarcelonataste.com) or **Food Lovers Company** (€90/person Mon-Sat, www.foodloverscompany.com). **Cook & Taste** offers daily cooking classes (€65/person, www.cookandtaste.com).

The **Barcelona Guide Bureau** is a co-op with about 20 local guides. Tour options include day trips outside the city to Montserrat and Figures (customized tours-€102/person for 2, €53/person for 4, Via Laietana 54, tel. 932-682-422, www.barcelonaguidebureau.com).

Helpful Hints

Theft and Safety: You're more likely to be pickpocketed here—especially on the Ramblas—than about anywhere else in Europe. Most crime is nonviolent, but muggings do occur. Leave valuables in your hotel and wear a money belt.

Street scams are easy to avoid if you recognize them. Most common is the too-friendly local who tries to engage you in conversation by asking for the time or whether you speak English. If a friendly man acts drunk and wants to dance, he's a pickpocket. Beware of thieves posing as lost tourists who ask for your help. Don't fall for street-gambling shell games. Beware of groups of women aggressively selling carnations, people offering to clean off a stain from your shirt, and so on.

Some areas feel seedy and can be unsafe after dark. Avoid the southern part of the Barri Gòtic (basically the two or three blocks directly south and east of Plaça Reial—though the strip near the Carrer de la Mercè tapas bars is better). Don't venture too deep into the Raval (just west of the Ramblas).

Internet Access: The free city network, Barcelona Wi-Fi, has hundreds of hotspots around town; look for the blue diamond-shaped sign with a big "W" (see www.bcn.cat/barcelonawifi).

Baggage Storage: Locker Barcelona is located near Hotel Denit. Pay for the day and access your locker as many times as you want. You can also leave bags overnight (€3.50-11 depending on locker size, daily 9:00-21:00, Carrer Estruc 36, tel. 933-028-796, www.lockerbarcelona.com).

BARCELONA WALKS

My two self-guided walks will help you explore the old town—down the main boulevard ("The Ramblas Ramble") and through the cathedral neighborhood ("Barri Gòtic Walk").

The Ramblas Ramble

For more than a century, this walk down Barcelona's pedestrian-only boulevard has drawn locals and visitors alike for the best people-watching in town. Raft the river of Barcelonan life, passing a grand opera house, elegant cafés, flower stands, artists, street mimes, con men, prostitutes, people charging more for a shoeshine than what you paid for the shoes.

The Ramblas is a one-hour, level stroll that goes from Plaça de Catalunya to the waterfront, with an easy return by the Metro. The word "Ramblas" is plural; the street is actually a succession of five separately named segments. But street signs and addresses treat it as a single long street—"La Rambla," singular.

Be alert for pickpockets. Assume any commotion is a distraction by a team of thieves. Don't be intimidated...be smart. Wear your money belt.

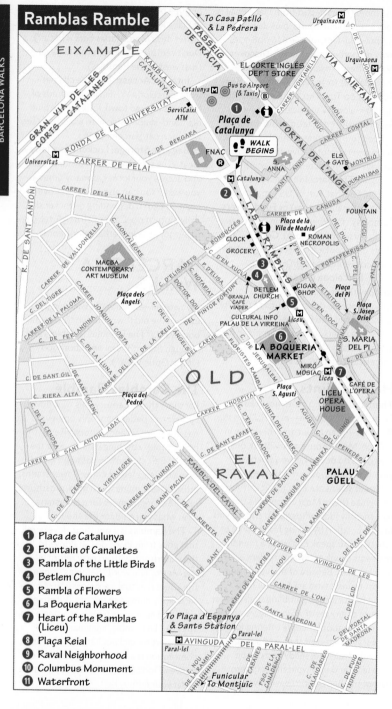

Ramblas Ramble

EIXAMPLE

To Casa Batlló
& La Pedrera

Urquinaona

PASSEIG DE GRÀCIA

RAMBLA DE CATALUNYA

GRAN VIA DE LES CORTS CATALANES

RONDA DE LA UNIVERSITAT

C. DE BERGARA

ServiCaixi ATM

Catalunya

EL CORTE INGLÉS DEP'T STORE

Bus to Airport (& Taxis)

Plaça de Catalunya

WALK BEGINS

FNAC

Universitat

CARRER DE PELAI

CARRER DELS TALLERS

Catalunya

S. ANNA

C. SANTA ANNA

ELS 4 GATS

MONTSIÓ

DURANIBAS

CARRER DE LA CANUDA

FOUNTAIN

VIA LAIETANA

Urquinaona

PORTAL DE L'ÀNGEL

C. DE SANT ANTONI

R. DE SANT ANTONI

C. DE VALLDONZELLA

MACBA CONTEMPORARY ART MUSEUM

Plaça dels Àngels

CARRER DEL TIGRE

CARRER DE LA PALOMA

CARRER DE FERLANDINA

CARRER JOAQUIM COSTA

C. DE LA LLUNA

C. DE SANT GIL

C. RIERA ALTA

Plaça del Pedró

CARRER DE SANT VICENÇ

C. DEL PEU DE LA CREU

C. DELS ÀNGELS

C. DEL CARME

C. D'ELISABETS

P. D'ELISA

C. NOTARIAT

DOCTOR DOU

DEL PINTOR FORTUNY

C. D'EN XUCLÀ

BONSUCCÉS

CLOCK

GROCERY

GRANJA CAFÉ VIADER

CULTURAL INFO PALAU DE LA VIRREINA

BETLEM CHURCH

Plaça de la Vila de Madrid

ROMAN NECROPOLIS

C. D'EN BOT

DE LA PORTAFERRISSA

CIGAR SHOP

D'EN ROCA

C. DEL DUC

Plaça del Pi

Plaça S. Josep Oriol

S. MARIA DEL PI

C. DE LA

CARDENAL

Liceu

LA BOQUERIA MARKET

C. FLORISTES RAMBLA

C. DE JERUSALEM

MIRÓ MOSAIC

Plaça S. Agustí

Liceu

LICEU OPERA HOUSE

CAFÉ DE L'OPERA

PALAU GÜELL

OLD

CARRER L'HOSPITAL

C. JUNTA DEL COMERÇ

C. AGUSTÍ DURAN

C. DEL PENEDÈS

C. DE L'AURORA

RAMBLA DEL RAVAL

C. DE SANT PACIÀ

C. DE LA RIERETA

CARRER DE SANT PAU

C. DE ST. OLEGUER

CARRER MÀRQUES DE BARBERÀ

C. DE L'ARC DEL

AVINGUDA DE LES

CARRER DE L'OM

C. DEL CID

C. DEL PORTAL DE SANTA MADRONA

EL RAVAL

C. VISTALEGRE

C. DE LA CERA

C. DE LA CENDRA

CARRER DE SANT ANTONI ABAT

C. DE SANT RAFAEL

C. D'EN ROBADOR

C. DE SANT PAU

C. NOU DE LA RAMBLA

SANTA MADRONA

To Plaça d'Espanya
& Sants Station

Paral·lel

AVINGUDA DEL PARAL·LEL

Funicular
To Montjuïc

C. DE LES TÀPIES

C. DE LES CABANES

DE LA CANADENCA

C. DEL PALAUDÀRIES

C. DE PUIG I XORIGUER

1 Plaça de Catalunya
2 Fountain of Canaletes
3 Rambla of the Little Birds
4 Betlem Church
5 Rambla of Flowers
6 La Boqueria Market
7 Heart of the Ramblas (Liceu)
8 Plaça Reial
9 Raval Neighborhood
10 Columbus Monument
11 Waterfront

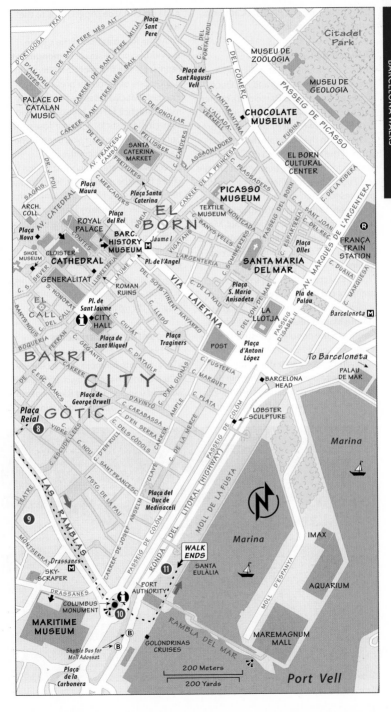

Citadel Park

MUSEU DE ZOOLOGIA

MUSEU DE GEOLOGIA

PASSEIG DE PICASSO

Plaça Sant Pere

C. D. DEL PORTAL NOU

C. DEL COMERÇ

C. DE FONOLLAR

C. TANTARANTANA

C. L'ALIADA VERMELL

Plaça de Sant Augustí Vell

CHOCOLATE MUSEUM

C. FUSINA

EL BORN CULTURAL CENTER

PALACE OF CATALAN MUSIC

C. DE SANT PERE MÉS ALT

C. DE SANT PERE MITJA

C. DE SANT PERE MÉS BAIX

D'ORTIGOSA TRAF.

D'AMADEU VIVES

CARRER SANT PERE

DE LES

CARRER

C. PELLISSER

C. CADERS

C. ASSAONADORS

AV. FRANCESC CAMBÓ

SANTA CATERINA MARKET

PREIXURES

C. DE LA PRINCESA

CARRER DE LA RIBERA

SAGRIS

DR. J. POU

ARCH. COLL.

AV. CATEDRAL

Plaça Maura

C. MERCADERS

BORIA

Plaça Santa Caterina

PICASSO MUSEUM

TEXTILE MUSEUM

C. FLASSADERS

PASSEIG DEL BORN

C. A. SANT JOAN

C. DEL REC

C. DE L'ESPARTERIA

R

Plaça Nova

ROYAL PALACE

Plaça del Rei

BARC. HISTORY MUSEUM

EL BORN

BANYS VELLS

C. ESPARTERIA

Jaume I

C. DE L'ARGENTERA

FRANÇA TRAIN STATION

SHOE MUSEUM

CLOISTER

CATHEDRAL

SEVER

C. DELS COMTES

M

Pl. de l'Angel

VIGATANS

L'ARGENTERIA

SANTA MARIA DEL MAR

C. DEL REC

Plaça Olles

C. DUANA

Barceloneta M

GENERALITAT

C. S. HONORAT

C. DEL CALL

JAUME I

LLIBRETERIA

ROMAN RUINS

DEL

SOTS-TINENT NAVARRO

VIA LAIETANA

Plaça S. Maria Anisadeta

LA LLOTJA

Pla de Palau

PASSEIG D'ISABEL II

AV. MARQUES D'ARGENTERA

EL CALL

BANYS NOUS

Pl. de Sant Jaume

CITY HALL

C. CIUTAT

C. LLEDÓ

C. DE LA NAU

POST

Plaça d'Antoni López

To Barceloneta

BOQUERIA

FERRAN

C. GEGANTS

Plaça de Sant Miquel

C. D'ATAÜLF

Plaça Traginers

C. FUSTERIA

C. MARQUET

BARCELONA HEAD

PALAU DE MAR

BARRI

C. ESC. BLANCS

CITY

GÒTIC

Plaça de George Orwell

C. D'EN GIGNÀS

C. PLATA

LOBSTER SCULPTURE

Marina

Plaça Reial

8

C. VIDRELLERS

C. CECUDELLERS

C. NOU DE

C. D'EN SERRA

D'AVINYÓ

C. CARABASSA

AMPLE

C. DE LA MERCÈ

PASSEIG DE COLÓM

DE JOSEP ANSELM

C. DELS CODOLS

C. SANT FRANCESC

PSTG. DE LA PAU

Plaça del Duc de Medinaceli

RONDA DEL LITORAL (HIGHWAY)

MOLL DE LA FUSTA

IMAX

Marina

AQUARIUM

LAS RAMBLAS

MONTSERRAT

9

TEATRE

Drassanes

SKY-SCRAPER

M

DRASSANES

MARITIME MUSEUM

Shuttle Bus for Moll Adossat

Plaça de la Carbonera

COLUMBUS MONUMENT

i

10

PORT AUTHORITY

B

B

GOLONDRINAS CRUISES

WALK ENDS

11

SANTA EULÀLIA

RAMBLA DEL MAR

MOLL D'ESPANYA

MAREMAGNUM MALL

Port Vell

N

200 Meters

200 Yards

• *Start your ramble on Plaça de Catalunya, at the top of the Ramblas.*

❶ Plaça de Catalunya

Dotted with fountains, statues, and pigeons, and ringed by grand Art Deco buildings, this plaza is Barcelona's center. The square's straight lines are a reaction to the curves of Modernisme (which predominates in the Eixample district, just north of the square). Plaça de Catalunya is the hub for the Metro, bus, airport shuttle, and Tourist Bus. It's where Barcelona congregates to watch soccer matches on the big screen, to demonstrate, to celebrate, and to enjoy concerts and festivals. More than half of the eight million Catalans live in greater Barcelona; this is their Times Square.

The 12-acre square links the narrow streets of old Barcelona with the broad boulevards of the newer city. Four great thoroughfares radiate from here. The Ramblas is the popular pedestrian promenade. Passeig de Gràcia has fashionable shops and cafés (and traffic). Rambla de Catalunya is equally fashionable but cozier and more pedestrian-friendly. Shopper-friendly and traffic-free Avin-

guda del Portal de l'Angel leads to the Barri Gòtic.

At the Ramblas end of the square, the odd, inverted-staircase **monument** represents the shape of Catalunya and honors one of its former presidents, Francesc Macià i Llussà, who declared independence for the breakaway region in 1931. (It didn't stick.) Sculptor Josep Maria Subirachs, whose work you'll see at the Sagrada Família, designed it.

Venerable Café Zürich, just across the street from the monument, is a popular rendezvous spot. Homesick Americans might prefer the nearby Hard Rock Café. The giant El Corte Inglés department store (on the northeast side) has just about anything you might need.

• *Cross the street and head down the Ramblas. To get oriented, pause 20 yards down, at the ornate lamppost with a fountain as its base (on the right, near #129).*

❷ Fountain of Canaletes

The black-and-gold fountain has been a local favorite for more than a century. When Barcelona tore down its medieval wall and transformed the Ramblas into an elegant promenade, this fountain was one

Plaça de Catalunya

of its early attractions. Legend says that a drink from the fountain ensures that you'll come back to Barcelona one day. Watch tourists struggle with the awkwardly high water pressure. It's still a popular rendez-vous spot.

Get your bearings for our upcoming stroll. You'll see the following features here and all along the way:

The wavy **tile work** of the pavers underfoot represents the stream that once flowed here. *Rambla* means "stream" in Arabic. Look up to see the city's char-acteristic shallow **balconies.** The **plane trees** lining the boulevard are known for their hardiness in urban settings. These deciduous trees let in maximum sun in the winter and provide maximum shade in the summer.

Nearby, notice the **chairs** fixed to the sidewalk at jaunty angles. At one time, you'd pay to rent a chair for the view of passersby. Enjoy these chairs—you'll find virtually no public benches or other seat-ing farther down the Ramblas, only cafés that serve beer and sangria in just one expensive size: *gigante.*

• *Continue strolling.*

All along the Ramblas are **24-hour newsstands.** Among their souvenirs, you'll see soccer paraphernalia, especially the scarlet-and-blue of FC Barcelona (known as "Barça"). The team is owned by its more than 170,000 "members"—fans who buy season tickets, which come with a share of ownership. Their motto, "More than a club" *(Mes que un club)*, suggests that Barça represents not only athletic prowess but the Catalan cultural identity. This comes to a head during a match nicknamed "El Clásico," in which they face their bitter rivals, Real Madrid (whom many fans view as stand-ins for Castilian cultural chauvinism).

Walk 100 yards farther to #115 and the venerable **Royal Academy of Sci-ence and Arts building** (now home to a theater). Look up: The clock high on the facade marks official Barcelona time—synchronize. The **TI** kiosk right on the Ramblas is a handy stop for any questions. The **Carrefour** supermarket just behind it (at #113) has cheap groceries (daily 10:00-22:00).

• *You're now standing at the...*

Subirachs' sculpture on Plaça de Catalunya

❸ Rambla of the Little Birds

Traditionally, kids brought their parents here to buy pets, especially on Sundays. Today, only one of the traditional pet kiosks survives—there's not a bird in sight. You'll find bird-related pet supplies and recorded chirping.

• At #122 (the big, modern Citadines Hotel on the left, just behind the pet kiosk), take a 100-yard detour through a passageway marked Passatge de la Ramblas to a restored...

Roman Necropolis: Look down and imagine a 2,000-year-old tomb-lined road. Outside the walls of Roman cities, tombs typically lined the roads leading into town. Emperor Augustus spent time in modern-day Spain conquering new land, so the Romans incorporated Hispania into the empire's infrastructure. This road, Via Augusta, led into the Roman port of Barcino (today's highway to France still follows the route laid out by this Roman thoroughfare).

• Return to the Ramblas and continue 100 yards or so to the next street, Carrer de la Portaferrissa (across from the big church). Turn left a few steps and look right to see the **decorative tile** over a fountain still in use by locals. The scene shows the original city wall with the gate that once stood here. Now cross the boulevard to the front of the big church.

❹ Betlem Church

This church is dedicated to Bethlehem, and for centuries locals have flocked here at Christmastime to see Nativity scenes.

The church's sloping roofline, ball-topped pinnacles, corkscrew columns, and scrolls above the entrance all identify it as 17th-century Baroque. The Baroque style is unusual in Barcelona because it missed out on several centuries of architectural development. Barcelona enjoyed two heydays: during the medieval period (before the Renaissance) and during the turn of the 20th century (after Baroque). In between those periods, from about 1500 until 1850, the city's importance dropped—first, New World discoveries shifted lucrative trade to ports on the Atlantic, and then the Spanish crown kept unruly Catalunya on a short leash.

For a sweet treat, head around to the narrow lane on the far side of the church (running parallel to the Ramblas) to **Café Granja Viader,** which has specialized in baked and dairy delights since 1870. Step inside to see Viader family photos and early posters advertising Cacaolat—the local chocolate milk Barcelonans love. (For other sugary treats nearby, follow "A Short, Sweet Walk" on page 390.)

• Continue down the boulevard, through the stretch called the...

Canaletes fountain

Rambla of Flowers

❺ Rambla of Flowers

This colorful block is lined with flower stands. Besides admiring the blossoms on display, gardeners covet the seeds sold here for varieties of radishes, greens, peppers, and beans seldom seen in the US—including the iconic green Padrón pepper. (If you buy seeds, you're obligated to declare them at US customs when returning home.) On the left, at #100, **Gimeno** sells cigars. Step inside and appreciate the dying art of cigar boxes.

If you want to buy advance required tickets for Casa Lleó Morera, stop by the cultural center at Palau de la Virreina at Ramblas 99, on your right (tickets aren't sold at the actual sight).

• *Continue to the Metro stop marked by the red M. At #91 (on the right) is the arcaded entrance to Barcelona's covered market, La Boqueria. If this main entry is choked with visitors (as it often is), you can skirt around to a side entrance, one block in either direction (look for the round arches that mark passages into the market colonnade).*

❻ La Boqueria Market

This lively market hall is an explosion of chicken legs, bags of live snails, stiff fish, delicious oranges, odd odors, and sleeping dogs. The best day for a visit is Saturday, when the market is thriving. It's closed on Sundays, and locals avoid it on Mondays, when it's open but (they believe) vendors are selling items that aren't necessarily fresh—especially seafood, since fishermen stay home on Sundays.

While tourists are drawn to the area around the main entry (below the colorful stained-glass sign), locals know that the stalls up front pay the highest rent—and therefore inflate their prices and cater to out-of-towners. For example, the juice bars along the main drag charge more than those a couple of aisles to the right.

Stop by the **Pinotxo Bar**—just inside the market, under the sign, and snap a photo of animated Juan giving a thumbs-up for your camera. Juan and his family are busy feeding shoppers. The stools nearby are a fine perch for enjoying both coffee and people-watching.

The market and lanes nearby are busy with tempting little eateries (see page 389). Drop by a café for an *espresso con leche* or *tortilla española* (potato omelet). Once you get past the initial gauntlet, do some exploring.

The produce stands show off seasonal fruits and vegetables. The fishmonger stalls could double as a marine biology lab. Fish is sold whole—local shoppers like to look their dinner in the eye to be sure it's fresh. At meat stands, full legs of *jamón* (ham)—some costing upwards of €200—tempt the Spaniards who so love this local delicacy. You'll see many types of *chorizo* (red spicy sausage). *Huevos del toro* are bull testicles—surprisingly inexpensive... and oh so good.

• *Head back out to the street and continue down the Ramblas.*

You're skirting the western boundary of the old Barri Gòtic. As you walk, glance to the left through a modern cutaway arch for a glimpse of the medieval church tower of **Santa Maria del Pi,** a popular venue for guitar concerts. This also marks Plaça del Pi and a great shopping street, Carrer Petritxol, which runs parallel to the Ramblas.

At the corner directly opposite the modern archway, find the **Escribà** bakery, with its fine Modernista facade and interior (look for the *Antigua Casa Figueras* sign over the doorway). Notice the mosaics of twining plants, the stained-glass peacock, and woodwork. In the sidewalk in front of the door, a plaque dates the building to 1902.

• *After another block, you reach the Liceu Metro station, marking the...*

❼ Heart of the Ramblas

At the Liceu Metro station's elevators, the Ramblas widens into a small, lively square (Plaça de la Boqueria). Liceu marks the midpoint of the Ramblas, halfway

A *Chinese dragon ornament*

B *Joan Miró's mosaic*

C *Plaça Reial*

D *La Boqueria Market*

E *Columbus monument*

F *Palau Güell*

between Plaça de Catalunya and the waterfront.

Underfoot in the center of the Ramblas, find the red-white-yellow-and-blue **mosaic** by homegrown abstract artist Joan Miró. The mosaic's black arrow represents an anchor, a reminder of the city's attachment to the sea. Miró's colorful designs are found all over the city, from murals to mobiles to the La Caixa bank logo. The best place in Barcelona to see his work is in the Fundació Joan Miró.

The surrounding buildings have playful ornamentation typical of the city. The **Chinese dragon** holding a lantern (at #82) decorates a former umbrella shop (notice the umbrella mosaics high up). The dragon is a symbol of Catalan pride for its connection to local patron saint, dragon-slayer St. George (Jordi).

Hungry? Swing around the back of the umbrella shop to **Taverna Basca Irati** (a block up Carrer del Cardenal Casanyes), one of many user-friendly tapas bars in town. Instead of ordering, just grab or point to what looks good on the display platters, then pay per piece.

Back on the Ramblas, a few steps down (on the right) is the **Liceu Opera House** (Gran Teatre del Liceu), which hosts world-class opera, dance, and theater (box office around the right side, open Mon-Fri 13:30-20:00). Opposite the opera house is Café de l'Opera (#74), an elegant stop for an expensive beverage. This bustling café, with Modernista decor and a historic atmosphere, has been open since 1929, even during the Spanish Civil War.

• *We've seen the best stretch of the Ramblas; to cut this walk short, you could catch the Metro back to Plaça de Catalunya. Otherwise, let's continue to the port. The wide, straight street that crosses the Ramblas in another 30 yards (Carrer de Ferran) leads left to Plaça de Sant Jaume, the government center.*

Head down the Ramblas another 50 yards (to #46), and turn left down an arcaded lane (Carrer de Colom) to the square called...

❽ *Plaça Reial*

Dotted with palm trees, surrounded by an arcade, and ringed by yellow buildings with white Neoclassical trim, this elegant square has a colonial ambience. It comes complete with old-fashioned taverns, modern bars with patio seating, and a Sunday coin-and-stamp market (10:00-14:00). Completing the picture are Gaudí's first public works—the two colorful helmeted lampposts. The square is a lively hangout by day or night (though the small streets stretching toward the water from the square can be sketchy). To just relax over a drink, the Ocaña cocktail bar is a good bet.

• *Head back out to the Ramblas.*

Across the boulevard, a half-block detour down Carrer Nou de la Rambla brings you to **Palau Güell** (on the left, at #3), the first of Antoni Gaudí's Modernista buildings, built 1886-1890. The two parabolic-arch doorways and elaborate wrought-iron work signal his emerging nonlinear style. Palau Güell offers an informative look at a Gaudí interior (see page 351).

• *Proceed along the Ramblas.*

❾ *Raval Neighborhood*

The neighborhood on the right-hand side of this stretch of the Ramblas is El Raval. In the last century, this was a rough neighborhood, frequented by sailors, prostitutes, and poor immigrants. Today, it's becoming gentrified, but the back streets can be edgy.

Along this part of the Ramblas, you'll often see surreal **human statues.** These performers—with creative and elaborate costumes—must audition and register with the city government; only 15 can work along the Ramblas at any one time. To enliven your Ramblas ramble, stroll with a pocketful of small change. As you wander downhill, drop coins into their cans (the money often kicks the statues into entertaining gear). But remember, wherever people stop to gawk, pickpockets are at work.

You're also likely to see some old-fashioned **shell games** in this part of town. Stand back and observe these nervous no-necks at work. They swish around their little boxes, making sure to show you the pea. Their shills play and win. Then, in hopes of making easy money, fools lose big time.

Near the bottom of the Ramblas, take note of the Drassanes Metro stop, which can take you back to Plaça de Catalunya when you're ready. The skyscraper to the right of the Ramblas is the Edificio Colón. Built in 1970, the 28-story structure was Barcelona's first high-rise. Near the skyscraper is the Maritime Museum, housed in what were the city's giant medieval shipyards.

• *Up ahead is the...*

⑩ Columbus Monument

The 200-foot **column** honors Christopher Columbus, who came to Barcelona in 1493 after journeying to America. It was erected for the 1888 Universal Exposition, an international fair that helped vault a surging Barcelona onto the world stage.

It's ironic that Barcelona celebrates Columbus; his discoveries started 300 years of decline for the city, as Europe began to face West (the Atlantic and the New World) rather than East (the Mediterranean and the Orient). Within a few decades of Columbus, Barcelona had become a depressed backwater, and it didn't rebound until events like the 1888 Expo cemented its comeback.

A tiny elevator ascends to the top of the monument, lifting visitors to an observation area for fine panoramas over the city (€4.50, daily 8:30-20:30, last entry 30 minutes before closing, entrance/ticket desk in TI inside the base of the monument).

• *Scoot across the busy traffic circle to survey the...*

⑪ Waterfront

Stand on the boardwalk (between the modern bridge and the kiosks selling harbor cruises), and survey Barcelona's bustling maritime zone. Although the city is one of Europe's top 10 ports, with many busy industrial harbors and several cruise terminals, this low-impact stretch of sea-

Modernista port authority building and the Old Port

front is clean, fresh, and people-friendly.

As you face the water, the frilly yellow building to your left is the fanciful Modernista-style port-authority building. The wooden pedestrian **bridge** jutting straight out into the harbor is a modern extension of the Ramblas. Called La Rambla de Mar ("Rambla of the Sea"), the bridge swings out to allow boat traffic into the marina; when closed, the footpath leads to an entertainment and shopping complex. Just to your right are the *golondrinas*—**harbor cruise boats,** (€7.20-15, daily on the hour 11:30-19:00, more in summer, fewer in winter, tel. 934-423-106, www.lasgolondrinas.com), which can be fun if you love to be out on the water (though the views from the harbor aren't great).

• *Turn left and walk 100 yards along the promenade between the port authority and the harbor.*

This delightful promenade is part of Barcelona's Old Port (Port Vell). The port's pleasant sailboat marina is completely enclosed by a modern complex with the Maremagnum shopping mall, an IMAX cinema, and a huge aquarium. Along the promenade is a moored historic schooner, the *Santa Eulália* (part of the Maritime Museum; €3 for entry without museum visit, Tue-Sun 10:00-20:30 except Sat when it opens at 14:00, Nov-March until 17:30, closed Mon). On a sunny day, it's fun to walk the length of the promenade to the iconic *Barcelona Head* sculpture (by American artist Roy Lichtenstein, not quite visible from here), which puts you right at the edge of El Born.

From here, you can also pick out some of Barcelona's more distant charms. The triangular spit of land across the harbor is **Barceloneta.** This densely populated community was custom-built to house fishermen and sailors whose traditional neighborhood in El Born was razed so Philip V could build a military citadel there in the 18th century. Today's Barceloneta is popular for its easy access to a gorgeous stretch of sandy beaches (on the other side of the Barceloneta peninsula).

Looking back toward the Columbus Monument, you'll see in the distance the majestic, 570-foot bluff of **Montjuïc,** a parklike setting dotted with sights and museums (see page 380; to get there, ride the Metro from Drassanes one stop to the Paral-lel stop, then take the funicular up).

• *Your ramble is over. If it's a nice day, consider strolling the promenade and looping back around on La Rambla del Mar. Or maybe dip into El Born. If you're truly on vacation, walk through Barceloneta to the beach.*

To get to other points in town, your best bet is to backtrack to the Drassanes Metro stop, at the bottom of the Ramblas. Alternatively, you can catch buses #14 or #59 from along the top of the promenade back to Plaça de Catalunya.

Barri Gòtic Walk

The Barri Gòtic (Gothic Quarter) is a bustling world of shops, bars, and nightlife packed into narrow, winding lanes and undiscovered courtyards. This is Barcelona's birthplace—where the ancient Romans built a city, where medieval Christians built their cathedral, where Jews gathered together, and where Barcelonans lived within a ring of protective walls until the 1850s, when the city expanded.

Today "El Gòtic" is a grab bag of grand squares, Art Nouveau storefronts, Thursday flea markets, antique and junk shops, and street musicians. In the center of it all is the cathedral, surrounded by other legacy sights from the city's 2,000-year history. Use this walk to get the lay of the land, then explore the shopping streets nearby.

• *Start on Barcelona's grand main square,* **Plaça de Catalunya.** *From the northeast corner (between the giant El Corte Inglés department store and the Banco de España), head down the broad pedestrian boulevard called...*

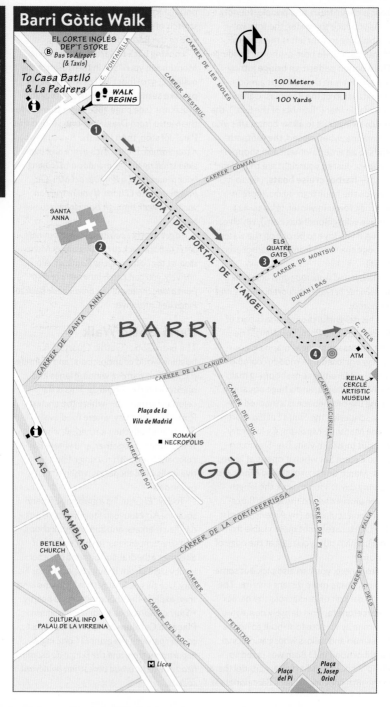

Barri Gòtic Walk

EL CORTE INGLÉS
DEP'T STORE
B *Bus to Airport
(& Taxis)*

To Casa Batlló
& La Pedrera

**WALK
BEGINS**

1

N

100 Meters
100 Yards

CARRER DE LES MOLES

C. FONTANELLA

CARRER D'ESTRUC

CARRER COMTAL

SANTA
ANNA

AVINGUDA DEL PORTAL DE L'ANGEL

2

ELS
QUATRE
GATS

3

CARRER DE MONTSIÓ

DURAN I BAS

CARRER DE SANTA ANNA

B A R R I

4

C. DELS

ATM

REIAL
CERCLE
ARTISTIC
MUSEUM

CARRER DE LA CANUDA

CARRER DEL DUC

Plaça de la
Vila de Madrid

ROMAN
■ NECROPOLIS

CARRER D'EN BOT

CARRER CUCURULLA

G Ò T I C

LAS

RAMBLAS

BETLEM
CHURCH

CARRER DE LA PORTAFERRISSA

CARRER DEL PI

CARRER DE LA PALLA

C. DELS

CULTURAL INFO
PALAU DE LA VIRREINA

CARRER D'EN ROCA

CARRER

PETRITXOL

M Liceu

Plaça
del Pi

Plaça
S. Josep
Oriol

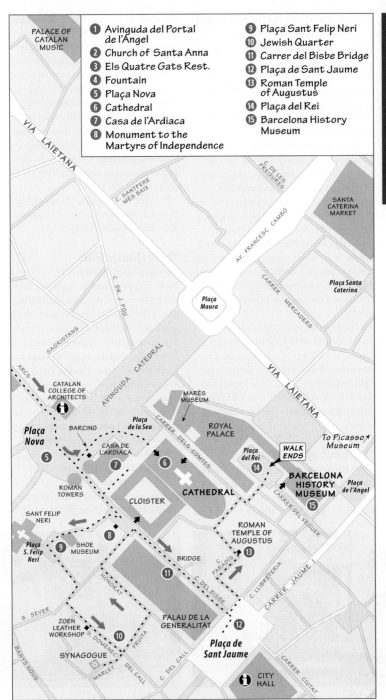

1. Avinguda del Portal de l'Angel
2. Church of Santa Anna
3. Els Quatre Gats Rest.
4. Fountain
5. Plaça Nova
6. Cathedral
7. Casa de l'Ardiaca
8. Monument to the Martyrs of Independence
9. Plaça Sant Felip Neri
10. Jewish Quarter
11. Carrer del Bisbe Bridge
12. Plaça de Sant Jaume
13. Roman Temple of Augustus
14. Plaça del Rei
15. Barcelona History Museum

❶ Avinguda del Portal de l'Angel

For much of Barcelona's history, this was a major city gate. A medieval wall enclosed the city, and there was an entrance here—the "Gate of the Angel" that gives the street its name. It was thought that the angel statue atop the gate kept the city safe from plagues and bid voyagers safe journey as they left the city.

Today, the pedestrians-only street is choked with shoppers cruising through some of the most expensive retail space in town. It's globalized and sanitized, with high-end Spanish and international chains, but a handful of local businesses survive. At the first corner (at #21), a green sign marks **Planelles Donat**—long appreciated for ice cream, sweet *turró* (or *turrón* in Spanish, almond candy), refreshing *orxata* (or *horchata,* almond-flavored drink), and *granissat* (or *granizado,* ice slush).

• A block farther down, pause at Carrer de Santa Anna to admire the Art Nouveau awning at another El Corte Inglés department store. Take a half-block detour to the right on Carrer de Santa Anna to the doorway at #29 (on the right), which leads into to the pleasant, flower-fragrant courtyard of the...

❷ Church of Santa Anna

This 12th-century gem, which used to be part of a convent, has a fine cloister—an arcaded walkway around a leafy courtyard (viewable to the left of the church). Climb the modern stairs for views of the bell tower. Inside, you'll see a bare Romanesque interior and Greek-cross floor plan, topped with an octagonal wooden roof. The door at the far end of the nave leads to the cloister (€2, church generally open Mon-Fri 11:00-19:00, closed Sat-Sun).

As you head back to the main drag, you'll pass—a few doors down—a **condom shop** on your left. It advertises (to men with ample self-esteem): *Para los pequeños placeres de la vida* ("For the little pleasures in life").

• Backtrack to Avinguda Portal de l'Angel. At Carrer de Montsió (on the left), opposite the Zara store, side-trip a half-block to...

❸ Els Quatre Gats

This restaurant (at #3) is a historic monument, tourist attraction, nightspot, and eatery. It's famous as the bohemian hangout where Picasso nursed drinks with friends and had his first one-man show (in 1900). The building itself, by prominent architect Josep Puig i Cadafalch, is Neo-Gothic Modernisme, inspired by the Paris bohemian intellectual scene. While you can have a snack, meal, or drink here, if you just want to admire the menu cover art—originally painted by Picasso—and take a look around, ask *"Solo mirar, por favor?"*

• Return to and continue down Avinguda del Portal de l'Angel. In a square on the left is a rack of **city loaner bikes,** part of the popular and successful "Bicing" program designed to reduce car traffic (available only

Architectural details enliven the shopping street.

Fountain with tilework

to Barcelona residents). You'll soon reach a fork in the road and a building with a...

❹ *Fountain*

The blue-and-yellow tilework, a circa-1918 addition to this even older fountain, depicts ladies carrying jugs of water. In the 17th century, this was the last watering stop for horses before leaving town. As recently as 1940, about 10 percent of Barcelonans got their water from fountains like this.

• *You may feel the pull of wonderful little shops down the street to the right. But take the left fork, down Carrer dels Arcs.*

Pause after a few steps at the yellow La Caixa ATM (on the right, under the terrace). Touch the screen to see various languages pop up—in addition to English, French, and German, you'll see the **four languages of Spain** and their flags: Català (Catalan; thin red-and-gold stripes), Galego (Galicia, in northwest Spain; white with a diagonal blue slash), Castellano (Español or Spanish; broad red, yellow, and red bands), and Euskara (Basque; red, green, and white). Fiercely proud of its own customs and language, Catalunya is in solidarity with other small ethnic groups.

Just past the ATM, you'll pass the **Reial Cercle Artistic Museum,** a private collection of Dalí's work sculptures that's fun for fans of Surrealism. Don't miss the smaller rooms with additional artworks that are behind the red curtains inside (€10, daily 10:00-22:00).

• *Enter the large square called...*

❺ *Plaça Nova*

Two bold Roman towers flank the main street. These once guarded the entrance gate of the ancient Roman city of Barcino. The big stones that make up the base of the reconstructed towers are actually Roman. Near the base of the left tower, modern bronze letters spell out "BAR-CINO." The city's name may have come from Barca, one of Hannibal's generals,

who is said to have passed through during Hannibal's roundabout invasion of Italy. At Barcino's peak, the Roman wall (see the section stretching to the left of the towers) was 25 feet high and a mile around, with 74 towers. It enclosed a population of 4,000.

One of the towers has a bit of reconstructed **Roman aqueduct** (notice the stream bed on top). In ancient times, bridges of stone carried fresh water from the distant hillsides into the walled city.

Opposite the towers is the modern **Catalan College of Architects** building (Collegi d'Arquitectes de Barcelona, TI inside), which is, ironically for a city with so much great architecture, quite ugly. The frieze was designed by Picasso (1962) in his distinctive simplified style, showing Catalan traditions: shipping, music, the *sardana* dance, bullfighting, and branch-waving kings and children celebrating a festival. Picasso spent his formative years (1895-1904, ages 14-23) here in the old town. He frequented brothels a few blocks from here on Carrer d'Avinyó ("Avignon")—which inspired his influential Cubist painting *Les Demoiselles d'Avignon.*

Picasso frieze on the Catalan College building

• *Immediately to the left as you face the Picasso frieze,* **Carrer de la Palla** *is an inviting shopping street (and the starting point of my "Barri Gòtic Shopping Stroll"; see page 386). But let's head left through Plaça Nova and take in the mighty façade of the...*

❻ Cathedral of Barcelona

While this location has been a center of Christian worship since the fourth century, what you see today dates mainly from the 14th century, with a 19th-century Neo-Gothic façade. The façade is a virtual catalog of Gothic motifs: a pointed arch over the entrance, robed statues, tracery in windows, gargoyles, and bell towers with winged angels. This Gothic variation is called French Flamboyant (meaning "flame-like"), and the roofline sports the prickly spires meant to give the impression of a church flickering with spiritual fires. The area in front of the cathedral is where Barcelonans dance the *sardana* (see page 355).

The cathedral's interior—with its vast size, peaceful cloister, and many ornate chapels—is worth a visit (see page 354). If you interrupt this tour and visit the cathedral now, you'll exit from the cloister a block down Carrer del Bisbe. From there you can circle back to the right to visit stop #7—or skip #7 and step directly into stop #8.

• *As you stand in the square facing the cathedral, look far to your left to see the multicolored, wavy canopy marking the roofline of the* **Santa Caterina Market.** *The busy street between here and the market—called Via Laietana—is the boundary between the Barri Gòtic and the funkier, edgier* **El Born** *neighborhood.*

For now, return to the Roman towers. Pass between the towers to head up Carrer del Bisbe, and take an immediate left, up the ramp to the entrance of...

❼ Casa de l'Ardiaca

It's free to enter this mansion, formerly the archdeacon's residence and now the city archives. The elaborate doorway is Renaissance. Enter a small courtyard with a fountain, then step inside the lobby (often featuring free temporary exhibits). Go through the archway at the left end of the lobby and look down into the stairwell at the back side of the ancient Roman wall. Back in the courtyard, climb the balcony for views of the cathedral steeple, gargoyles, and the small Romanesque chapel (on the right)—the only surviving 13th-century bit of the cathedral.

• *Return to Carrer del Bisbe and turn left. After a few steps, you reach a small square with a bronze statue ensemble.*

❽ Monument to the Martyrs of Independence

Five Barcelona patriots—including two priests—calmly receive their last rites before being strangled for resisting Napoleon's occupation of Spain in the early 19th century. They'd been outraged by French atrocities in Madrid (depicted in Goya's famous *Third of May* painting in Madrid's Prado Museum). According to the plaque marking their mortal remains, these martyrs gave their lives in 1809 *"por Dios, por la Patria, y por el Rey"*—for God, country, and king.

The plaza offers interesting views of the cathedral's towers. Opposite the square is the "back door" entrance to the cathedral (through the cloister; relatively uncrowded and open sporadically).

• *Exit the square down tiny Carrer de Montjuïc del Bisbe (to the right as you face the martyrs). This leads to the cute...*

❾ Plaça Sant Felip Neri

This square serves as the playground of an elementary school and is often bursting with energetic kids speaking Catalan (just a generation ago, this would have been illegal). The Church of Sant Felip Neri, which Gaudí attended, is still pockmarked with bomb damage from the Spanish Civil War. As a stronghold of democratic, anti-Franco forces, Barcelona saw a lot

Cathedral of Barcelona

A Roman towers on Plaça Nova

B Carrer del Bisbe Bridge

C Church of Sant Felip Neri

D Monument to the Martyrs of Independence

E Architectural detail, Casa de l'Ardiaca

of fighting. A plaque on the wall (left of church door) honors the 42 killed—mostly children—in a 1938 aerial bombardment.

The buildings that ring the square were paid for and decorated by the guilds that once powered the local economy. On the corner where you entered the square is the former home of the coppersmiths' and shoemakers' guilds; look up to find a carved relief in the shape of a lion, representing St. Mark, the patron saint of shoemakers. Also fronting the square is the fun **Sabater Hermanos** artisanal soap shop.

• *Exit the square down Carrer de Sant Felip Neri. At the T-intersection, turn right onto Carrer de Sant Sever, then immediately left on Carrer de Sant Domènec del Call (look for the blue El Call sign). You've entered the...*

⑩ Jewish Quarter (El Call)

In Catalan, a Jewish quarter goes by the name El Call—literally "narrow passage," for the tight lanes where medieval Jews were forced to live, under the watchful eye of the nearby cathedral. At the peak of Barcelona's El Call, some 4,000 Jews were crammed into just a few alleys in this neighborhood.

Walk down Carrer de Sant Domènec del Call, passing the **Zoen leather workshop and showroom,** where everything is made on the spot (on the right, at #15). Pass though the charming little square (a gap in the dense tangle of medieval buildings cleared by another civil war bomb) where you will find a rust-colored sign displaying a map of the Jewish Quarter. Take the next lane to the right (Carrer de Marlet). On the right (#5) is the low-profile entrance to what was likely Barcelona's **Old Main Synagogue** during the Middle Ages (Antigua Sinagoga Mayor, €2.50 admission includes a little tour by the attendant if you ask, open Mon-Fri 10:30-18:00, Sat-Sun 10:30-15:00, shorter hours off-season, tel. 931-170-790, www.calldebarcelona.org).

• *At the synagogue, start back the way you came, continuing straight as the street becomes Carrer de la Fruita. At the T-intersection, turn left, then right, to find your way back to the Martyrs Statue. From here, turn right down Carrer del Bisbe to the...*

⑪ Carrer del Bisbe Bridge

This structure connects the Catalan government building (on the right) with the Catalan president's ceremonial residence (on the left). Though the bridge looks medieval, it was constructed in the 1920s by Catalan architect Joan Rubió, who also carved the ornamentation on the buildings.

The delicate facade a few steps farther down on the right marks the 15th-century entry to the government palace.

• *Continue along Carrer del Bisbe to...*

⑫ Plaça de Sant Jaume

This stately central square of the Barri Gòtic takes its name from the Church of St. James (in Catalan: Jaume, JOW-mah) that once stood here.

Set at the intersection of ancient Barcino's main thoroughfares, this square was once a Roman forum. In that sense, it's been the seat of city government for 2,000 years. Today it's home to the two top governmental buildings in Catalunya: Palau de la Generalitat and, across from it, the Barcelona City Hall.

For more than six centuries, the **Palau de la Generalitat** (to your immediate right as you enter the square) has housed the offices of the autonomous government of Catalunya. It flies the Catalan flag next to the obligatory Spanish one. Above the doorway is Catalunya's patron saint—St. George (Jordi), slaying the dragon. From these balconies, the nation's leaders (and soccer heroes) greet the people on momentous days. The square is often the site of demonstrations, from a single aggrieved citizen with a megaphone to riotous thousands.

Look left and right down the main streets branching off the square; they're lined with ironwork streetlamps and balconies draped with plants. Carrer de Ferran, which leads to the Ramblas, is classic Barcelona.

• *Facing the Generalitat, exit the square going up the second street to the right of the building, on tiny Carrer del Paradís. Follow this street as it turns right. When it swings left, pause at #10, the entrance to the...*

⓭ Roman Temple of Augustus

You're standing at the summit of Mont Tàber, the Barri Gòtic's highest spot. A plaque on the wall reads: "Mont Tàber, 16.9 meters" (elevation 55 feet). A millstone inlaid in the pavement at the doorstep of #10 also marks the spot. Here the ancient Romans founded the town of Barcino around 15 B.C. They built a *castrum* (fort) on the hilltop, protecting the harbor.

Go inside for a peek at the last vestiges of the imposing **Roman Temple of Augustus** (free, daily 10:00-19:00 except Mon until 14:00, good English info on-site, Carrer del Paradís 10, tel. 933-152-311). All that's left now are four columns and some fragments of the transept and its plinth. The huge columns are as old as Barcelona itself, dating from the late first century B.C. They were part of a temple dedicated to the Emperor Augustus, who was worshipped as a god. These Corinthian columns were the back corner of a 120-foot-long temple that extended from here to Barcino's forum.

• *Continue down Carrer del Paridís one block. When you bump into the back end of the cathedral, take a right, and go downhill a block (down Carrer de la Pietat/Baixada de Santa Clara) until you emerge into a square called...*

⓮ Plaça del Rei

The buildings enclosing this square exemplify Barcelona's medieval past. The central section (topped by a five-story addition) was the core of the **Royal Palace** (Palau Reial Major). A vast hall on its ground floor once served as the throne room and reception room. From the 13th to the 15th century, the Royal Palace housed Barcelona's counts as well as the resident kings of Aragon. In 1493, a triumphant Christopher Columbus, accompanied by six New World natives and several gold statues, entered the Royal Palace. King Ferdinand and Queen Isabel welcomed him home, honoring him with the title "Admiral of the Oceans." To the right is the palace's church, the 14th-century **Chapel of Saint Agatha,** which sits atop the foundations of a Roman wall.

• *From the square, go downhill onto Carrer del Veguer, where you'll find the entrance to the...*

⓯ Barcelona History Museum

This museum primarily contains objects from archaeological digs around Barcelona. But the real highlight is underground, where you can examine excavated Roman ruins (€7, free all day first Sun of month and other Sun from 15:00; open Tue-Sat 10:00-19:00, Sun 10:00-20:00, closed

Roman Temple of Augustus

Mon; ticket includes English audioguide). For a peek at the Roman streets, look through the low windows lining the street.
• *Your walk is over. Get your bearings by backtracking to either Plaça de Sant Jaume or the cathedral. The Jaume I Metro stop is two blocks away (leave the square on Carrer del Veguer and turn left). Or simply wander and enjoy Barcelona at its Gothic best.*

SIGHTS

On or near the Ramblas
▲▲▲THE RAMBLAS
Rife with people-watching opportunities, Barcelona's most famous boulevard meanders through the heart of the Old City, from Plaça de Catalunya, past the core of the Barri Gòtic, to the harborfront Columbus Monument. Boasting a generous pedestrian strip down the middle, the Ramblas features vibrant flower vendors, costumed "human statues," and La Boqueria Market. For a self-guided walk, see page 337.

▲LA BOQUERIA MARKET
Housed in a cool glass-and-steel structure, La Boqueria features a wide variety of edibles that are priced at a premium. Its handy location in the heart of the Old City makes it well worth a visit. For more on the market, see page 351. For a less touristy market, consider Santa Caterina in El Born (page 364).

Cost and Hours: Free, Mon-Sat 8:00-20:00, best on mornings after 9:00, closed Sun, Rambla 91, tel. 933-192-584, www.boqueria.info.

▲PALAU GÜELL
This early mansion by Antoni Gaudí (completed in 1890) shows the architect taking his first tentative steps toward what would become his trademark curvy style. Dark and masculine, with its castle-like rooms, Palau Güell (pronounced "gway") was custom-built to house the Güell clan and gives an insight into Gaudí's artistic genius. Despite the eye-catching roof (visible from the street), I'd skip touring the interior of Palau Güell if you plan to see the more interesting La Pedrera (see page 369).

Cost and Hours: €12, free first Sun of the month, open Tue-Sun 10:00-20:00, Nov-March until 17:30, closed Mon, last entry one hour before closing, includes audioguide, a half-block off the Ramblas at Carrer Nou de la Rambla 3, Metro: Liceu or Drassanes, tel. 934-725-775, www.palauguell.cat.

Tickets: As with any Gaudí sight, you may encounter lines. Each ticket has an entry time, so at busy times you may have to wait to enter. It's best to buy advance tickets for a set day and time of your choice, either on-site or online (though the predominantly Catalan website is tricky).

Visiting the House: The parabolic-arch **entryways** are the first clue that this is not a typical townhouse. For inspiration, Gaudí hung a chain to create a U-shape, then flipped it upside down. The wrought-iron doors were cleverly designed so that those inside could see out, and light from the outside could get in—but not vice versa.

Once inside, an engaging 24-stop audioguide, included with your admission, fills in the details. The Neo-Gothic **cellar,** with its mushroom pillars, was used as a stable—notice the big carriage doors in the back and the rings on some of the posts used to tie up the horses.

A grand staircase leads to the **living space.** The intricacy of Gaudí's design work evokes the complex patterns that decorate great Moorish palaces. Step onto the terrace out back to take a look at the elaborate (and unmistakably organic-looking) bay window.

The tall, atrium-like **central hall** fills several floors under a parabolic dome. Behind the gilded doors is a personal chapel, which made it easy to convert the hall from a secular space to a religious one.

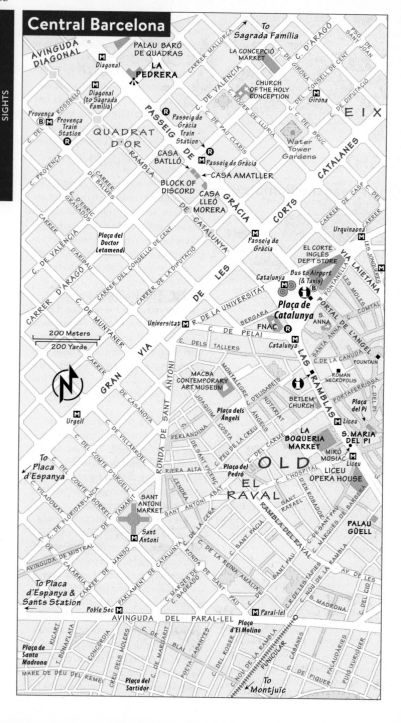

Central Barcelona

To Sagrada Família

AVINGUDA DIAGONAL

PALAU BARÓ DE QUADRAS

LA CONCEPCIÓ MARKET

C. D'ARAGÓ

Diagonal

LA PEDRERA

C. DE MALLORCA

CHURCH OF THE HOLY CONCEPTION

Diagonal (to Sagrada Família)

C. DE VALÈNCIA

Girona

Provença

Provença Train Station

C. DEL

PASSEIG

Passeig de Gràcia Train Station

C. DE PAU CLARIS

C. DE ROGER DE LLÚRIA

C. DEL CONSELL DE CENT

C. DE DIPUTACIÓ

EIX

QUADRAT D'OR

DE

Passeig de Gràcia

CASA BATLLÓ

Passeig de Gràcia

CASA AMATLLER

C. DE PROVENÇA

C. DE BALMES

C. D'ENRIC GRANADOS

C. DE VALÈNCIA

CARRER

GRÀCIA

BLOCK OF DISCORD

CASA LLEÓ MORERA

Water Tower Gardens

CATALANES

Plaça del Doctor Letamendi

DE CATALUNYA

CORTS

CARRER DE CASP

C. DE MUNTANER

C. D'ARIBAU

C. DE VALÈNCIA

CARRER DEL CONSELLO DE CENT

CARRER DE LA DIPUTACIÓ

DE LES

Passeig de Gràcia

EL CORTE INGLÉS DEP'T STORE

Urquinaona

VIA LAIETANA

LES JONQUERES

Bus to Airport (& Taxis)

FONTANELLA

LES MOLES

COMTAL

200 Meters
200 Yards

VIA

GRAN

CARRER

DE CASANOVA

C. DE VILLAROEL

C. DEL COMTE D'URGELL

DE LA UNIVERSITAT

Catalunya

Plaça de Catalunya

Universitat

Bergara

R. DE LA UNIVERSITAT

C. DE PELAI

FNAC

Catalunya

PORTAL DE L'ÀNGEL

S. ANNA

SANTA ANNA

C. DE LA CANUDA

FOUNTAIN

DE SANT ANTONI

C. DELS TALLERS

MONTALEGRE

D'ELISABETS

NOTARIAT

LAS

ROMAN NECROPOLIS

PORTAFERRISSA

C. DE LA CANUDA

Urgell

MACBA CONTEMPORARY ART MUSEUM

Plaça dels Àngels

JOAQUIM COSTA

DE SANT VICENÇ

FERLANDINA

RIERA ALTA

RONDA DE SANT ANTONI

C. DELS ÀNGELS

PEU DE LA CREU

C. DEL CARME

L'HOSPITAL

BETLEM CHURCH

Plaça del Pi

RAMBLAS

LA BOQUERIA MARKET

S. MARIA DEL PI

MIRÓ MOSIAC

Liceu

LICEU OPERA HOUSE

To Plaça d'Espanya

RIERA ALTA

CENDRA

Plaça del Pedró

OLD

EL RAVAL

C. D'EN ROBADOR

SANT RAFAEL

RAMBLA DEL RAVAL

C. DE BARBERA

PALAU GÜELL

SANT ANTONI MARKET

C. DE FLORIDABLANCA

C. DE BORRELL

Sant Antoni

SANT ANTONI ABAT

C. DE LA CERA

C. DE SANT PAU

C. DE SANT PAU

C. DEL MARQUÈS DE BARBERA

To Plaça d'Espanya & Sants Station

C. DE VILADOMAT

C. DE CALABRIA

CARRER DE MANSO

PARLAMENT DE CATALUNYA

RONDA DE SANT PAU

C. MARGES DE SANT

C. DE LA REINA AMALIA

SANT PAU

C. DE SANT PAU

C. DE SANT OLEGUER

C. NOU DE LA RAMBLA

AV. DE LES

C. DEL CID

Poble Sec

AVINGUDA DEL PARAL·LEL

Plaça d'El Molino

Paral·lel

Plaça de Santa Madrona

RICART

J. BONAPLATA

CONCÒRDIA

CREU DELS MOLERS

C. DE MARGARIT

BLAI

POETA CABANYES

C. DEL ROSER

C. NOU DE LA RAMBLA

FUNICULAR

CABANES

PALAUDÀRIES

PUIG I XURIGUER

MARE DE DÉU DEL REMEI

Plaça del Sartidor

To Montjuïc

C. DE PIQUER

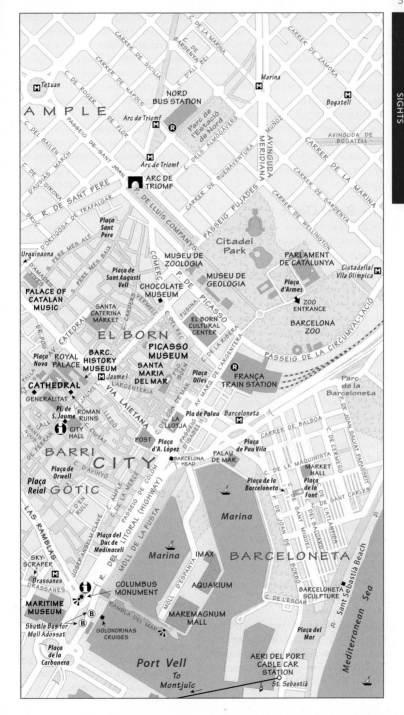

Upstairs are the Güells' his-and-hers bedrooms, along with a **film** telling the story of the two men behind this building: Gaudí and his patron, Eusebi Güell. At a time when most wealthy urbanites were moving to the Eixample, Güell decided to stay in the Old City.

The most dramatic space is the **rooftop.** Gaudí slathered the 20 chimneys and ventilation towers with bits of stained glass, ceramic tile, and marble to create a forest of giant upside-down ice-cream cones.

The Barri Gòtic

For an interesting route from Plaça de Catalunya to the cathedral neighborhood, see page 341.

▲CATHEDRAL OF BARCELONA

The city's 14th-century, Gothic-style cathedral (with a Neo-Gothic facade) has played a significant role in Barcelona's history—but as far as grand cathedrals go, this one is relatively unexciting. Still, it's worth a visit to see its richly decorated chapels, finely carved choir, tomb of St. Eulàlia, and restful cloister with gurgling fountains and resident geese.

Cost and Hours: Generally open to visitors Mon-Fri 8:00-19:30, Sat-Sun 8:00-20:00. Free to enter Mon-Sat before 12:45, Sun before 13:45, and daily after 17:15, but during free times you must pay to enter the cathedral's three minor sights (museum-€2, terrace-€3, choir-€3). The church is officially "closed" for a few hours each afternoon (Mon-Sat 13:00-17:00, Sun 14:00-17:00), but you can get in to see the interior sights by paying €7. Tel. 933-151-554, www.catedralbcn.org.

Dress Code: The dress code is strictly enforced; don't wear tank tops, shorts, or skirts above the knee.

Getting There: The huge, can't-miss-it cathedral is in the center of the Barri Gòtic on Plaça de la Seu (Metro: Jaume I).

Getting In: The front door is open most of the time. While it can be crowded, the line generally moves fast. Sometimes you can also enter directly into the cloister (through the door facing the Martyrs Statue on the small square along Carrer del Bisbe) or through the side door (facing Carrer dels Comtes).

Services: A tiny, semiprivate WC is in the center of the cloister.

Visiting the Cathedral: This has been Barcelona's holiest spot for 2,000 years, since the Romans built their Temple of Jupiter here. In A.D. 343, the pagan temple was replaced with a Christian cathedral, and in the 11th century, by a Romanesque-style church. The current Gothic structure was started in 1298 and finished in 1450, during the medieval glory days of the Catalan nation. The facade was humble, so in the 19th century the proud local bourgeoisie (enjoying a second Golden Age) renovated it in a more ornate, Neo-Gothic style. Construction was capped in 1913 with the central spire, 230 feet tall.

Inside, the nave is ringed with 28 **chapels.** These serve as interior buttresses supporting the roof (which is why the exterior walls are smooth, without the normal Gothic buttresses outside).

In the middle of the nave, the 15th-century choir (coro) features ornately carved stalls. During the standing parts of the Mass, the chairs were folded up, but VIPs still had those little wooden ledges to lean on. Each was creatively carved and—since you couldn't sit on sacred things—the artists were free to enjoy some secular and naughty fun here.

Look behind the high altar (beneath the crucifix) to find the bishop's chair, or cathedra. To the left of the altar is the organ and the elevator up to the terrace.

The steps beneath the altar lead to the **crypt,** featuring the marble-and-alabaster sarcophagus (1327-1339) containing the remains of St. Eulàlia. The cathedral is dedicated to the 13-year-old Eulàlia, daughter of a prominent Barcelona family, who was martyred by the Romans for her faith in A.D. 304. Legends say she was

Circle Dances in Squares and Castles in the Air

From group circle dancing to human towers, Catalans have interesting, unique traditions. A memorable Barcelona experience is watching (or participating in) the patriotic **sardana** dances. Locals of all ages seem to spontaneously appear. For some it's a highly symbolic, politically charged action representing Catalan unity—but for most it's just a fun chance to kick up their heels. Participants gather in circles after putting their things in the center. All are welcome, even tourists cursed with two left feet. The dances are held in the square in front of the cathedral on Sundays at noon (and occasionally on Saturdays at 18:00).

Holding hands, dancers raise their arms—slow-motion, *Zorba the Greek*-style—as they hop and sway gracefully to the music. The band (*cobla*) consists of a long flute, tenor and soprano oboes, strange-looking brass instruments, and a tiny bongo-like drum (*tambori*). During 36 years of Franco's dictatorship, the *sardana* was forbidden.

Another Catalan tradition is the **castell,** a tower erected solely of people. *Castells* pop up on special occasions, such as the Festa Major de Gràcia in mid-August and La Mercè festival in late September. Towers can be up to 10 humans high. Imagine balancing 50 or 60 feet in the air, with nothing but a pile of flesh and bone between you and the ground. The base is formed by burly supports called *baixos;* above them are the *manilles* ("handles"), which help haul up the people to the top. The *castell* is capped with a human steeple—usually a child—who extends four fingers into the air, representing the four red stripes of the Catalan flag. A scrum of spotters (called *pinyas*) cluster around the base in case anyone falls. *Castelleres* are judged both on how quickly they erect their human towers and how fast they can take them down. Besides during festivals, you can usually see this spectacle in front of the cathedral on spring and summer Saturdays at 19:30 (as part of the Festa Catalana).

One thing that these two traditions have in common is their communal nature. Perhaps it's no coincidence, as Catalunya is known for its community spirit, team building, and socialistic bent.

subjected to 13 tortures.

Exit through the right transept and into the circa-1450 **cloister**—the arcaded walkway surrounding a lush courtyard. It's a tropical atmosphere of palm, orange, and magnolia trees; a fish pond; trickling fountains; and squawking geese. As you wander the cloister (clockwise), check out the coats of arms as well as the tombs in the pavement. These were rich merchants who paid to be buried as close to the altar as possible. Notice the symbols of their trades: scissors, shoes, bakers, and so on. The resident geese have been here for at least 500 years. There are always 13, in memory of Eulàlia's 13 years and 13 torments.

The little museum (at the far end of the cloister) has the six-foot-tall, 14th-century Great Monstrance, a ceremonial display case for the communion wafer that's paraded through the streets during the Corpus Christi festival in June. The next room, the Sala Capitular, has several altarpieces, including a *pietá* (a.k.a. *Desplà*) by Bartolomé Bermejo (1490).

▲*SARDANA* DANCES

If you're in town on a weekend, you can see the *sardana*, a patriotic dance in which Barcelonans link hands and dance in a circle (see sidebar).

Cost and Hours: Free, Sun at 12:00, sometimes also Sat at 18:00, no dances in Aug, event lasts 1-2 hours, in the square in front of the cathedral.

El Born

Despite being home to the top-notch Picasso Museum, El Born (also known as "La Ribera") feels wonderfully local, with a higher ratio of Barcelonans to tourists than most other city-center zones. Narrow lanes sprout from the neighborhood's main artery, Passeig del Born—the perfect springboard for exploring artsy boutiques, inviting cafés and restaurants, funky shops, and rollicking nightlife. For tips on shopping streets in El Born, see page 386. The most convenient Metro stop is Jaume I.

▲▲▲PICASSO MUSEUM (MUSEU PICASSO)

Pablo Picasso may have made his career in Paris, but the years he spent in Barcelona—from age 14 through 23—were among the most formative of his life. Here, young Pablo mastered the realistic painting style of his artistic forebears—and also first felt the freedom that would allow him to leave all that behind and explore his creative, experimental urges. When he left Barcelona, Picasso went to Paris...and revolutionized art forever.

The pieces in this museum capture the moment just before this bold young thinker changed the world. While you won't find Picasso's famous later Cubist works here, you will enjoy a representative sweep of his early years, from the careful crafting of art-school pieces to the gloomy hues of his Blue Period and the revitalized cheer of his Rose Period. You'll also see works from his twilight years, including dozens of wild improvisations inspired by Diego Velázquez's seminal *Las Meninas*, as well as works that reflect the exuberance of an old man playing like a child on the French Riviera. It's the top collection of Picassos in his native country, and the best anywhere of his early years.

Rick's Tip: *To avoid wasting time in ticket-buying lines, buy* **advance tickets** *for the* **Picasso Museum.**

Cost and Hours: €11-14 for timed-entry ticket, cost depends on temporary exhibits and time of year, free all day first Sun of month and other Sun from 15:00; open Tue-Sun 9:00-19:00, Thu until 21:30, closed Mon; audioguide-€5, tel. 932-563-000, www.museupicasso.bcn.cat.

Crowd Control: There's almost always a line, sometimes with waits of more than an hour. During peak season, it's possi-

Picasso Museum—First Floor

(Not to Scale)

Map legend	
1 Portraits & Art-School Work	10 Rooftops of Barcelona
2 First Communion	11 Portrait of Bernadetta Bianco
3 Science and Charity	12 Woman with Mantilla
4 Velázquez Copy	13 Gored Horse
5 Horta de San Joan	14 Synthetic Cubism
6 Cancan Dancer	15 Las Meninas Studies
7 Still Life	16 Ceramics
8 The Waiting (Margot)	17 French Riviera
9 Motherhood	18 Portraits of Jacqueline (2)

ble that tickets, which include an entry time, may sell out altogether. It's best to buy tickets online in advance, or get an **Articket BCN** (see page 325), which lets you go straight to the special Articket window near the main entrance (you'll be allowed in at the next timed-entry slot).

Advance tickets are sold via the museum website (no additional booking fee) and guarantee an entry time with no wait. Note that the ticketing part of the website can be temperamental; if you can't get it to work, try it on another device (such as your mobile phone).

Pablo Picasso (1881-1973)

Pablo Picasso was the most famous and—OK, I'll say it—greatest artist of the 20th century. He became the master of many styles (Cubism, Surrealism, Expressionism) and many media (painting, sculpture, prints, ceramics, and assemblages). Still, anything he touched looked unmistakably like "a Picasso."

Born in Málaga, Spain, Picasso was the son of an art teacher. At a young age, he quickly advanced beyond his teachers. Picasso's teenage works are stunningly realistic and capture the inner complexities of the people he painted. As a youth in Barcelona, he fell in with a bohemian crowd that mixed wine, women, and art.

In 1904, Picasso moved to the City of Light to paint. When his best friend, Spanish artist Carlos Casagemas, committed suicide, Picasso plunged into a **Blue Period** (1901-1904)—the dominant color in these paintings matches their melancholy mood and subject matter (such as emaciated beggars, and hard-eyed pimps).

In 1904, Picasso got a steady girlfriend (Fernande Olivier) and suddenly saw the world through rose-colored glasses—his **Rose Period.** Picasso played with the "building blocks" of line and color to find new ways to reconstruct the real world on canvas. At his studio in Montmartre, Picasso and his neighbor Georges Braque worked together, in poverty so dire they often didn't know where their next bottle of wine was coming from.

Then, at the age of 25, Picasso reinvented painting. Fascinated by the primitive power of African and Iberian tribal masks, he sketched human faces with simple outlines and almond eyes. He sketched nudes from every angle, then experimented with showing several different views on the same canvas. Nine months and a hundred paintings later, Picasso gave birth to a monstrous can-

Picasso's Portrait of Bernadetta Bianco, *a Rose Period work*

To buy **same-day tickets,** go as early as possible. Upon arrival, check the screen near the ticket office for the day's available entry times (and how many spaces are open for each). Depending upon availability, you can either buy tickets for immediate entry, or purchase tickets to return later that day. You can also buy same-day tickets online, up to two hours before you want to go. Off-season, you can probably just line up for tickets and get right in.

Note that the museum's busiest times are mornings before 13:00, all day Tuesday, and during the free entry times on Sundays.

Getting There: It's at Carrer de Montcada 15; the ticket office is at #21. From the Jaume I Metro stop, it's a quick five-minute walk. Just head down Carrer

vas of five nude, fragmented prostitutes with mask-like faces—*Les Demoiselles d'Avignon* (1907).

This bold new style was called **Cubism.** With Cubism, Picasso shattered the Old World and put it back together in a new way. The subjects are somewhat recognizable (with the help of the titles), but they're built with geometric shards ("cubes")—like viewing the world through a kaleidoscope of brown and gray.

In 1918, Picasso traveled to Rome and entered a **Classical Period** (the 1920s) of more realistic, full-bodied women and children, inspired by the three-dimensional sturdiness of ancient statues. While he flirted with abstraction, throughout his life, Picasso always kept a grip on "reality." His favorite subject was people. The anatomy might be jumbled, but it's all there.

Though he lived in France and Italy, Picasso remained a Spaniard at heart, incorporating Spanish motifs into his work. Unrepentantly macho, he loved bullfights, seeing them as a metaphor for the timeless human interaction between the genders. To Picasso, the horse symbolizes the feminine, and the bull, the masculine. Spanish imagery—bulls, screaming horses, a Madonna—appears in Picasso's most famous work, *Guernica* (1937, on display in Madrid). The monumental canvas of a bombed village summed up the pain of Spain's brutal Civil War (1936-1939) and foreshadowed World War II.

At war's end, Picasso left Paris behind, finding fun in the sun in the **south of France** (1948-1954). Sixty-five-year-old Picasso was reborn, enjoying worldwide fame and the love of a beautiful 23-year-old painter named Françoise Gilot. Bursting with creativity, Picasso cranked out more than one painting a day. His Riviera works set the tone for the rest of his life—sunny, lighthearted, and uncomplicated, using motifs of the sea, Greek myths, and animals. His simple sketch of a dove holding an olive branch became an international symbol of peace.

Picasso also made collages, built "statues" out of wood, wire, ceramics, and papier-mâché, and turned everyday household objects into statues (like his famous bull's head made of a bicycle seat with handlebar horns). **Multimedia** works like these have become so standard today that we forget how revolutionary they were when Picasso invented them. His last works have the playfulness of someone much younger. It's said of Picasso, "When he was a child, he painted like a man. When he was old, he painted like a child."

de la Princesa (across the busy Via Laietana from the Barri Gòtic), turning right on Carrer de Montcada.

Services: The ground floor, which is free to enter, has a required bag check, as well as a handy array of other services (bookshop, WC, and cafeteria). For places to eat near the museum, see page 394.

⊙ SELF-GUIDED TOUR

The Picasso Museum's collection of nearly 300 paintings is presented more or less chronologically. With the help of thoughtful English descriptions (and guards who don't let you stray), it's easy to follow the evolution of Picasso's work. This tour is arranged by the stages of his life and art. If you don't see a specific piece, it may be out for restoration, on tour, or "sleeping," as the museum guards say. The rooms might be rearranged every so often, but the themes and chronology of the museum remain constant.

• *Begin in Rooms 1 and 2.*

BOY WONDER

Pablo's earliest art (in the first room) is realistic and earnest. Childish pencil drawings from about 1890 quickly advance through a series of technically skilled **art-school works** (copies of plaster feet and arms), to oil paintings of impressive technique. Even at a young age, his **portraits** of grizzled peasants demonstrate surprising psychological insight. Because his father—himself a curator and artist—kept everything his son ever did, Picasso has the best-documented youth of any great painter.

• *In Room 2, you'll find more paintings relating to Pablo's...*

DEVELOPING TALENT

During a summer trip to Málaga in 1896, Picasso dabbles in a series of fresh, Impressionistic-style landscapes (rare in Spain at the time). As a 15-year-old, Pablo dutifully enters art-school competitions. His first big work, **First Communion,** features a prescribed religious subject, but Picasso makes it an excuse to paint his family. His sister Lola is the model for the communicant (notice her exquisitely painted veil), and the features of the man beside her belong to Picasso's father.

Picasso's relatives star in a number of portraits from this time. Find the **portrait of his mother** if it's on view (these portraits are among the works that are frequently rotated). The teenage Pablo is working on the fine details and gradients of white in her blouse and the expression in her cameo-like face. Notice the signature: Pablo Ruiz Picasso. Spaniards keep both parents' surnames, with the father's first, followed by the mother's.

• *Continue into Room 3.*

EARLY SUCCESS

Science and Charity (1897), which won second prize at a fine-arts exhibition, got Picasso the chance to study in Madrid. Now Picasso conveys real feeling. The doctor (modeled on Pablo's father) represents science. The nun represents charity and religion. From her hopeless face and lifeless hand, it seems that Picasso believes nothing will save this woman from death.

Picasso travels to Madrid for further study. He hangs out in the Prado Museum and learns by copying the masters. An example of his mimicry is at the end of this room. Notice young Picasso's nearly perfect copy of a **portrait of Philip IV** by an earlier Spanish master, Diego Velázquez.

• *Head to Room 4.*

BARCELONA FREEDOM

Art Nouveau is all the rage in Barcelona when Picasso returns there in 1900. He falls in with the bohemian crowd, who congregate daily at Els Quatre Gats ("The Four Cats," a popular restaurant to this day). Picasso even created the **menu cover** for this favorite hangout (it's sometimes on view here in Room 4). He paints **portraits** of his new friends, including one of Jaume Sabartés (who later became his personal assistant and donated the works to establish this museum). Still a teenager, Pablo puts on his first one-man show at Els Quatre Gats in 1900.

• *Continue through Room 5. The next few pieces are displayed in Rooms 6 and 7.*

PARIS

In 1900 Picasso makes his first trip to Paris, where he befriends poets, artists, and prostitutes. He paints **cancan dancers** like Toulouse-Lautrec, **still lifes** like Paul Cézanne, brightly colored Fauvist works like Henri Matisse, and Impressionist **landscapes** like Claude Monet. In **The Waiting (Margot),** the subject—with her bold outline and strong gaze—pops out from the vivid, mosaic-like background. It is Cézanne's technique of "building" a

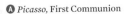

Ⓐ *Picasso*, First Communion

Ⓑ *Picasso*, Science and Charity

Ⓒ *Picasso's menu design for Els Quatre Gats*

Ⓓ *Picasso*, La Mujer del Mechón

Ⓔ *Picasso*, Woman with Mantilla

Ⓕ *Picasso*, Las Meninas

figure with "cubes" of paint that will later inspire Picasso to invent Cubism.

• *Turn right into the hall, then—farther along—right again, to find Rooms 8 and 9.*

BLUE PERIOD

Picasso travels to Paris several times (settling there permanently in 1904). The suicide of his best friend, his own poverty, and the influence of new ideas linking color and mood lead Picasso to abandon jewel-bright color for his Blue Period (1901-1904). He cranks out stacks of blue art just to stay housed and fed. With blue backgrounds and depressing subjects, this period was revolutionary in art history. The artist is painting not what he sees, but what he feels.

Back home in Barcelona, Picasso paints his hometown at night from **rooftops** (in the main part of Room 8). The painting is still blue, but here we see proto-Cubism... five years before the first real Cubist painting.

• *In the left section of Room 8, we get a hint of Picasso's...*

ROSE PERIOD

Picasso is finally lifted out of his funk after meeting a new lady, Fernande Olivier, and moves into his happier Rose Period (1904-1907). For a fine example, see the portrait of a woman wearing a classic Spanish mantilla, **Portrait of Bernadetta Bianco.** Its soft pink and reddish tones are the colors of flesh and sensuality. (This is the only actual Rose Period painting in the museum, but don't be surprised if it is on loan.)

BARCELONA

Picasso spent six months back in Barcelona in 1917 (his girlfriend, a Russian ballet dancer, had a gig in town). The paintings in these rooms demonstrate the artist's irrepressible versatility: He's already developed Cubism (with his friend Georges Braque), but he also continues to play with other styles. In **Woman with Mantilla** (Room 9), we see a little Post-Impressionistic Pointillism in a

portrait as elegant as a classical statue. Nearby, **Gored Horse** has all the anguish and power of his iconic *Guernica* (painted years later).

CUBISM

Pablo's role in the invention of the revolutionary Cubist style is well-known—at least I hope so, since this museum has no true Cubist paintings. A Cubist work gives not only the basics of a subject—it shows every aspect of it simultaneously. The technique of "building" a subject with "cubes" of paint simmered in Picasso's artistic stew for years. In this museum, you'll see some so-called **Synthetic Cubist paintings** (Room 10)—a later variation that flattens the various angles, as opposed to the purer, original "Analytical Cubist" paintings, in which you can simultaneously see several 3-D facets of the subject.

• *Remember that this museum focuses on Picasso's early years. As a result, it has little from the most famous and prolific "middle" part of his career—basically, from Picasso's adoption of Cubism to his sunset years on the French Riviera. Skip ahead more than 30 years and into Rooms 12-14 (at the end of the main hallway, on the right).*

PICASSO AND VELÁZQUEZ

A series of Picasso's works relate to what many consider the greatest painting by anyone, ever: Diego Velázquez's *Las Meninas* (the 17th-century original is displayed in Madrid's Prado Museum). Heralded as the first completely realistic painting, *Las Meninas* became an obsession for Picasso centuries later.

Picasso, who had great respect for Velázquez, painted more than **40 interpretations** of this piece. Picasso seems to enjoy a relationship of equals with Velázquez. Like artistic soul mates, the two Spanish geniuses spar and tease. Picasso deconstructs Velázquez and then injects light, color, and perspective as he improvises on the earlier masterpiece. See the fun Picasso had playing paddleball with Velázquez's tour de force—filtering Velázquez's realism through the kaleidoscope of Cubism.

• *Head back down the hall and turn right, through the* **ceramics** *area (Room 16), to find a flock of carefree white birds in Room 15. Enjoy the palace decoration as it looked before the building became a museum.*

THE FRENCH RIVIERA (LAST YEARS)

Picasso spends the last 36 years of his life living simply in the south of France. He said many times that "Paintings are like windows open to the world." We see his sunny Riviera world: With simple black outlines and Crayola colors, Picasso paints sun-splashed nature, peaceful doves, and the joys of the beach. He dabbles in the timeless art of ceramics, shaping bowls and vases into fun animals decorated with simple, childlike designs. He's enjoying life with his second (and much younger) wife, Jacqueline Roque, whose portraits hang nearby.

Picasso died with brush in hand. Sadly, since he vowed never to set foot in a fascist, Franco-ruled Spain, the artist never returned to his homeland...and never saw this museum (his death came in 1973—two years before Franco's). Picasso continued exploring and loving life through his art to the end.

▲▲PALACE OF CATALAN MUSIC (PALAU DE LA MÚSICA CATALANA)

This concert hall, built in just three years and finished in 1908, features an unexceptional exterior but boasts my favorite Modernista interior in town (by Lluís Domènech i Montaner). Its inviting arches lead you into the 2,138-seat hall, which is accessible only with a tour (or by attending a concert). A kaleidoscopic skylight features a choir singing around the sun, while playful carvings and mosaics celebrate music and Catalan culture. If you're interested in Modernisme, taking this tour is one of the best in town—and helps balance the local fixation on Gaudí as "Mr. Modernisme."

Cost and Hours: €18, 50-minute tours in English run daily every hour 10:00-15:00, tour times may change based on performance schedule, about 6 blocks northeast of cathedral, Carrer Palau de la Música 4, Metro: Urquinaona, tel. 902-442-882, www.palaumusica.cat.

Tour Reservations: You must buy your ticket in advance to get a spot on an English guided tour (tickets available up

Palace of Catalan Music

to 4 months in advance—purchase yours at least 2 days before, though they're sometimes available the same day or day before—especially Oct-March). You can buy the ticket in person at the concert hall box office (open daily 9:30-15:30, less than a 10-minute walk from the cathedral or Picasso Museum); by phone with your credit card (for no extra charge, tel. 902-475-485); or online at the concert hall website (€1 fee).

Concerts: Another way to see the hall is by attending a concert (300 per year, €20-50 tickets, box office tel. 902-442-882, see website for details and online purchases).

▲SANTA CATERINA MARKET

This eye-catching market hall's colorful, rippling roof covers a delightful shopping zone that caters more to locals than tourists. Come for the outlandish architecture, but stay for a chance to shop for a picnic without the tourist logjam of La Boqueria Market on the Ramblas. Besides fresh produce, it has many inviting eateries.

Cost and Hours: Free, Mon-Sat 7:30-15:30, Thu-Fri until 20:30, closed Sun, Avinguda de Francesc Cambó 16, www.mercatsantacaterina.cat.

▲CHURCH OF SANTA MARIA DEL MAR

This "Cathedral of the Sea" was built entirely with local funds and labor, in the heart of the El Born quarter (home to wealthy merchants). Proudly independent, the church features a purely Catalan Gothic interior that was forcibly uncluttered of its Baroque decor by civil war belligerents.

Cost and Hours: Free admission daily 9:00-13:00 & 17:00-20:30, also open 13:00-17:00 with €5 ticket; €8 guided rooftop tours in summer; English tours on the hour Mon-Fri 12:00-16:00, Sat-Sun 11:00-16:00, in summer tours run until 19:00; Plaça Santa Maria, Metro: Jaume I, tel. 933-102-390.

Visiting the Church: On the big front doors, notice the figures of workers who donated their time and sweat to build the church. The stone for the church was quarried at Montjuïc and carried across town on the backs of porters.

Step inside. The church features a purely Catalan Gothic interior. During the Spanish Civil War (1936-1939), Catalan patriots fighting Franco burned the ornate Baroque decoration (carbon still blackens the ceiling), leaving behind this unadorned Gothic. The colorful windows come with modern themes. The tree-like columns inspired Gaudí's work on Sagrada Família. Befitting a church "of the sea," sailors traditionally left models of ships at the altar to win Mary's protection—one remains today.

The Eixample

For many visitors, Modernista architecture is Barcelona's main draw. And at the heart of the Modernista movement was the Eixample, a carefully planned "new town," just beyond the Old City, with wide sidewalks, hardy shade trees, and a rigid

Church of Santa Maria del Mar

grid plan cropped at the corners to create space and lightness at each intersection. Conveniently, all of this new construction provided a generation of Modernista architects with a blank canvas for creating boldly experimental designs.

Block of Discord

At the center of the Eixample is the Block of Discord, where three colorful Modernista facades compete for your attention: Casa Batlló, Casa Amatller, and Casa Lleó Morera (all three are on Passeig de Gràcia—near the Metro stop of the same name—between Carrer del Consell de Cent and Carrer d'Aragó). All were built by well-known Modernista architects at the end of the 19th century. Because the mansions look as though they are trying to outdo each other in creative twists, locals nicknamed the noisy block the "Block of Discord." By the way, if you're tempted to snap photos from the middle of the street, be careful—Gaudí died after being struck by a streetcar.

▲CASA BATLLÓ

While the highlight of this Gaudí-designed residence is its roof, the interior is also interesting—and much more over-the-top than La Pedrera's. Paid for with textile industry money, the house features a funky mushroom-shaped fireplace nook on the main floor, a blue-and-white-ceramic-slathered atrium, and an attic (with parabolic arches). There's barely a straight line in the house. You can also get a close-up look at the dragon-inspired rooftop. Because preservation of the place is privately funded, the entrance fee is steep—but it includes a good (if long-winded) audioguide.

Cost and Hours: €21.50, daily 9:00-21:00, may close early for special events—closings posted in advance at entrance, €3 videoguide shows rooms as they may have been, Passeig de Gràcia 43, tel. 932-160-306, www.casabatllo.cat. Purchase a ticket online to avoid lines, which are especially fierce in the morning. Your eticket isn't a timed reservation (it's good any time within 3 months of purchase), but it will let you skip to the front of the queue.

CASA AMATLLER

The middle residence of the Block of Discord, Casa Amatller was designed by Josep Puig i Cadafalch in the late 19th century for the Amatller chocolate-making family. It is viewable via guided tour, allowing you to see the modernist interior design, including many original pieces.

Rick's Tip: *If you don't want to pay for a ticket, you can step inside* **Casa Amatller's foyer (free during opening hours)** *to see the Modernist stained-glass door and ceiling, and an elaborate staircase.*

Cost and Hours: €15 for guided tour, daily 11:00-18:00, English tours at 11:00 and 15:00, advance tickets available online, Passeig de Gràcia 41, tel. 934-617-460, www.amatller.org.

▲CASA LLEÓ MORERA

This house, designed by Lluís Domènech i Montaner and finished in 1906, has one of the finest Modernista interiors in town. Access is by guided tour only, which begins with the history of the Lleó Morera family and a look at the paella-like mix of styles on the building's exterior. Inside, you'll marvel at finely crafted mosaics, ceramic work, wooden ceilings and doors, stone sculptures, and stained glass—all of which paint a picture of the life of a Catalan bourgeoisie family in the early 20th century.

Cost and Hours: €15 for 70-minute English tour, €12 for express 45-minute tour (in a mix of English, Spanish, and Catalan); open Tue-Sun, closed Mon; tour times change, so check website for the latest; there is no on-site box office—you must reserve and purchase your ticket online at www.casalleomorera.com, or in person at the cultural center

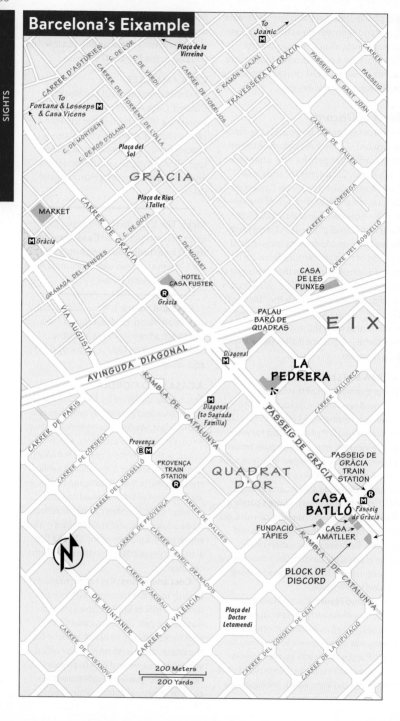

Barcelona's Eixample

To Joanic

Plaça de la Virreina

CARRER D'ASTÚRIES
C. DE L'OR
C. DE VERDI
CARRER DEL TORRENT DE L'OLLA
CARRER DE TORRIJOS
C. RAMÓN Y CAJAL
TRAVESSERA DE GRÀCIA
PASSEIG DE SANT JOAN
CARRER
PASSEIG

To Fontana & Lesseps & Casa Vicens

C. DE MONTSENY
C. DE ROS D'OLANO
CARRER DE BAILÈN

Plaça del Sol

GRÀCIA

MARKET

CARRER DE GRÀCIA

Plaça de Rius i Tallet

C. DE GOYA
C. DE MOZART

CARRER DE CÒRSEGA
CARRER DEL ROSSELLÓ

Gràcia

GRANADA DEL PENEDÈS

HOTEL CASA FUSTER

CASA DE LES PUNXES

VIA AUGUSTA

Gràcia

PALAU BARÓ DE QUADRAS

EIX

Diagonal

LA PEDRERA

AVINGUDA DIAGONAL

RAMBLA DE CATALUNYA

PASSEIG DE GRÀCIA

CARRER MALLORCA

CARRER DE PARÍS

Diagonal (to Sagrada Família)

CARRER DE CÒRSEGA

Provença

PROVENÇA TRAIN STATION

QUADRAT D'OR

PASSEIG DE GRÀCIA TRAIN STATION

CARRER DEL ROSSELLÓ

CARRER DE PROVENÇA

CARRER DE BALMES

CASA BATLLÓ

Passeig de Gràcia

FUNDACIÓ TÀPIES

CASA AMATLLER

CARRER D'ENRIC GRANADOS

RAMBLA DE CATALUNYA

N

BLOCK OF DISCORD

C. DE MUNTANER

C. DE ARIBAU

CARRER DE VALÈNCIA

Plaça del Doctor Letamendi

CARRER DE CASANOVA

CARRER DEL CONSELL DE CENT

CARRER DE LA DIPUTACIÓ

200 Meters
200 Yards

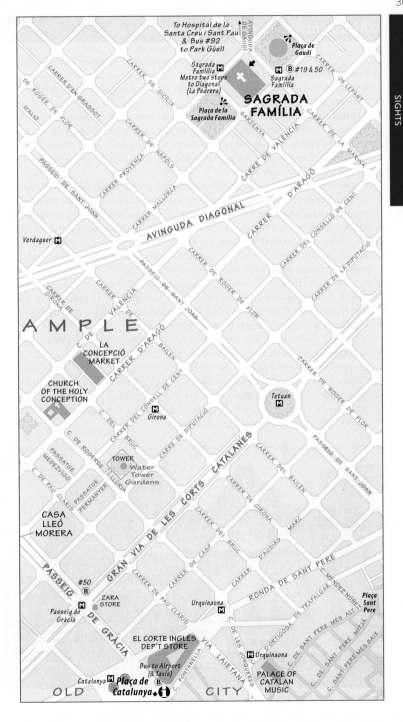

To Hospital de la
Santa Creu i Sant Pau
& Bus #92
to Park Güell

Plaça de
Gaudí

Sagrada
Família
Metro two stops
to Diagonal
(La Pedrera)

Sagrada
Família

Ⓑ #19 & 50

CARRER DE SICÍLIA

CARRER D'EN GRASSOT

DE ROGER DE FLOR

D'ALIÓ

AVINGUDA DE GAUDÍ

Plaça de la
Sagrada Família

SAGRADA
FAMÍLIA

CARRER DE LEPANT

CARRER DE NÀPOLS

CARRER PROVENÇA

CARRER MALLORCA

SARDENYA

CARRER DE VALÈNCIA

CARRER DE LA MARINA

PASSEIG DE SANT JOAN

CARRER DE ARAGÓ

CARRER DEL CONSELLO DE CENT

AVINGUDA DIAGONAL

CARRER

PASSEIG DE SANT JOAN

CARRER DE ROGER DE FLOR

Verdaguer Ⓜ

CARRER DEL CONSELLO DE CENT

CARRER DE LA DIPUTACIÓ

CARRER DE GIRONA

CARRER DE VALÈNCIA

A M P L E

C. DE VALÈNCIA

CARRER D'ARAGÓ

BAILEN

LA
CONCEPCIÓ
MARKET

CARRER DE ROGER DE FLOR

CHURCH
OF THE HOLY
CONCEPTION

C. DEL CONSELL DE CENT

Girona Ⓜ

Tetuan
Ⓜ

C. DE DIPUTACIÓ

CARRER DEL BAILEN

PASSATGE
MEDEZVIGO

C. DE ROGER DE LLÚRIA

C. DE BRUC

CARRER DE DIPUTACIÓ

CARRER DEL BRUC

CARRER DE GIRONA

PASSEIG DE SANT JOAN

TOWER
Water
Tower
Gardens

PASSATGE
PERMANYER

C. DE PAU CLARIS

CASA
LLEÓ
MORERA

GRAN VIA DE LES CORTS CATALANES

CARRER DE GASP

MARC

CARRER D'AUSIAS

CARRER DEL BRUC

PASSEIG

#50
Ⓑ

ZARA
STORE

CARRER DE PAU CLARIS

Urquinaona Ⓜ

RONDA DE SANT PERE

C. MÉNDEZ NÚÑEZ

Plaça
Sant
Pere

Passeig de
Gràcia

DE GRÀCIA

EL CORTE INGLÉS
DEP'T STORE

VIA LAIETANA

PORTIGOSA DE TRAFALGAR

C. DE SANT PERE MÉS ALT

C. DE SANT PERE MÉS BAIX

C. DE LES JONQUERES

Urquinaona Ⓜ

C. DE SANT PERE MITJÀ

Bus to Airport
(& Taxis)

Catalunya Ⓜ Plaça de
Catalunya ◆ ⓘ

Ⓑ

C. FONTANELLA

PALACE OF
CATALAN
MUSIC

OLD

CITY

Modernisme and the Renaixença

Modernisme is Barcelona's unique contribution to the European Art Nouveau movement. Meaning "a taste for what is modern"—things like streetcars, electric lights, and big-wheeled bicycles—this free-flowing organic style lasted from 1888 to 1906.

The starting point for the style was a kind of Neo-Gothic, clearly inspired by medieval castles, towers, and symbols—logically, since architects wanted to recall Barcelona's glory days of the 1400s. From the Neo-Gothic look, Antoni Gaudí branched off on his own, adding the color and curves we most associate with Barcelona's Modernisme look.

The aim was to create objects that were both practical and decorative. Modernista architects experimented with new construction techniques, especially concrete, which they could use to make a hard stone building that curved and rippled like a wave. Then they sprinkled it with brightly colored glass and tile. The structure was fully modern, but the decoration was a clip-art collage of nature images, exotic Moorish or Chinese themes, and fanciful Gothic crosses and knights to celebrate Catalunya's medieval glory days.

It's ironic to think that Modernisme was a response to the Industrial Age—and that all those organic shapes were only made possible thanks to Eiffel Tower-like iron frames. The Eixample's fanciful facades and colorful, leafy ornamentation were built at the same time as the first skyscrapers.

Fueling Modernisme was the Catalan cultural revival called the Renaixença. As Europe was waking up to the modern age, downtrodden peoples across Europe—from the Basques to the Irish to the Hungarians to the Finns—were throwing off the cultural domination of other nations and celebrating what made their own cultures unique. Here in Catalunya, the Renaixença encouraged everyday people to get excited about all things Catalan: their language, patriotic dances, art—and their surprising architecture.

Casa Amatller, with stepped roofline, and Casa Batlló, to the right

Palau de la Virreina (Ramblas 99, tel. 933-161-000, www.lavirreina.bcn.cat). The house itself is at Passeig de Gràcia 35, tel. 936-762-733.

▲▲LA PEDRERA (CASA MILÀ)

One of Gaudí's trademark works, this house—built between 1906 and 1912—is an icon of Modernisme. The wealthy industrialist Pere Milà i Camps commissioned it, and while some still call it Casa Milà, most call it La Pedrera (The Quarry) because of its jagged, rocky facade. While it's fun to ogle from the outside, it's also worth going inside, as it's arguably the purest Gaudí interior in town—executed at the height of his abilities (unlike his earlier Palau Güell)—and still contains original furnishings. While Casa Batlló has a Gaudí facade and rooftop, these were appended to an existing building; La Pedrera, on the other hand, was built from the ground up according to Gaudí's plans. Besides entry to the interior, a ticket also gets you access to the delightful rooftop, with its forest of colorful tiled chimneys.

Cost and Hours: €20.50, daily March-Oct 9:00-20:00, Nov-Feb 9:00-18:30, last entry 30 minutes before closing, good audioguide-€4, at the corner of Passeig de Gràcia and Provença (visitor entrance at Provença 261), Metro: Diagonal, info tel. 902-400-973, www.lapedrera.com.

Crowd Control: As lines can be long (up to a 1.5-hour wait to get in), it's best to reserve ahead at www.lapedrera.com (tickets come with an assigned entry time). If you come without a ticket, the best time to arrive is right when it opens.

Rick's Tip: For a **peek at La Pedrera** *without paying for a ticket, find the door directly on the corner, which offers* **free entrance to the main atrium.** *Upstairs on the first floor are temporary exhibits (generally free, daily 10:00-20:00, closed between exhibitions).*

Nighttime Visits: The building hosts after-hour visits dubbed "The Secret Pedrera." On this pricey visit, you'll get a guided tour of the building with the lights

La Pedrera rooftop

Modernista Masters

Here's a summary of the major players who took part in the architectual revolution of Modernisme:

Antoni Gaudí (1852-1926), Barcelona's most famous Modernista artist, was descended from four generations of metalworkers—a lineage of which he was quite proud. He incorporated ironwork into his architecture and came up with novel approaches to architectural structure and space. His work strongly influenced his younger Catalan contemporary, Salvador Dalí. While Dalí was creating unlikely and shocking juxtapositions of photorealistic images, Gaudí did the same in architecture—using the spine of a reptile for a bannister or a turtle shell design on windows. His best work in Barcelona includes his great unfinished church, the Sagrada Família; several mansions in the town center,

including La Pedrera, Casa Batlló, and Palau Güell; and Park Güell, his ambitious and never-completed housing development.

Lluís Domènech i Montaner (1850-1923), a professor and politician, was responsible for some major civic buildings, including his masterwork, the Palace of Catalan Music (see page 363). He also designed Casa Lleó Morera on the Block of Discord. Although Gaudí is more famous, Domènech i Montaner's work is perhaps more purely representative of the Modernista style.

Josep Puig i Cadafalch (1867-1956) was a city planner who oversaw the opening up of Via Laietana through the middle of the Old City. He was instrumental in the redevelopment of Montjuïc for the 1929 World Expo. He designed Casa Amatller (see page 365). Perhaps most important, Puig i Cadafalch designed the building housing Els Quatre Gats (see page 344), a bar that became a cradle for the Modernista movement.

All architects worked with a team of people who, while not famous, made real contributions. For example, Gaudí's colleague **Josep Maria Jujol** (1879-1949) is primarily responsible for the broken-tile mosaic decorations (called *trencadís*) on Park Güell's benches and Casa Milà's chimneys—which became Gaudí's trademark.

Though not an artist, businessman **Eusebi Güell** (1846-1918) used his nearly $90 billion fortune to bankroll Gaudí and other Modernista masters. Güell's name still adorns two of Gaudí's most important works: Palau Güell (see page 351) and Park Güell (see page 379).

turned down low and a glass of *cava* (€30; English tour offered daily March-Oct at 21:15, but check changeable schedule and offerings online).

Concerts: On summer weekends, La Pedrera has an evening rooftop concert series, "Summer Nights at La Pedrera," featuring live jazz. In addition to the music, it gives you the chance to see the rooftop illuminated (€27, late June-early Sept Thu-Sat at 22:30, book advance tickets online or by phone, tel. 902-101-212, www.lapedrera.com).

Visiting the House: A visit covers three sections—the apartment, the attic, and the rooftop. Enter and head upstairs to the apartment. If it's near closing time, continue up to see the attic and rooftop first, to make sure you have enough time to enjoy Gaudí's works and the views (note that the roof may close when it rains).

The typical bourgeois **apartment** is decorated as it might have been when the building was first occupied by middle-class urbanites (a 7-minute video explains Barcelona society at the time). Notice Gaudí's clever use of the atrium to maximize daylight in all of the apartments.

The **attic** houses a sprawling multimedia exhibit tracing the history of the architect's career, with models, photos, and videos of his work. It's all displayed under distinctive parabola-shaped arches.

From the attic, a stairway leads to the undulating, jaw-dropping **rooftop,** where 30 chimneys and ventilation towers play volleyball with the clouds.

Back at the **ground level** of La Pedrera, poke into the dreamily painted original entrance courtyard.

▲▲▲SAGRADA FAMÍLIA (HOLY FAMILY CHURCH)

Antoni Gaudí's grand masterpiece sits unfinished in a residential Eixample neighborhood 1.5 miles north of Plaça de Catalunya. An icon of the city, the Sagrada Família boasts bold, wildly creative, unmistakably organic architecture and decor inside and out—from its melting Glory Facade to its skull-like Passion Facade to its rainforest-esque interior. Begun under Gaudí's careful watch in 1883, the project saw some setbacks in the mid-20th century, but lately the progress has been remarkable. The city has set a goal of finishing by 2026, the centennial of Gaudí's death. For now, visitors get a close-up view of the dramatic exterior flourishes, the chance to walk through the otherworldly interior, and access to a fine museum detailing the design and engineering behind this one-of-a-kind architectural marvel.

The main challenges for this massive undertaking today are to ensure that construction can withstand the vibrations caused by the speedy AVE trains rumbling underfoot, to construct the tallest church spire ever built, and to find a way to buy out the people who own the condos in front of the planned Glory Facade so that Gaudí's vision of a grand esplanade approaching the church can be realized.

Rick's Tip: *To avoid wasting time in ticket-buying lines, buy* **advance tickets** *for the* **Sagrada Família.**

Cost and Hours: Church-€15, tower elevators-€4.50 each, €18.50 combo-ticket includes church (no towers) and Gaudí House Museum at Park Güell (see page 379); daily April-Sept 9:00-20:00, Oct-March 9:00-18:00.

Advance Tickets: Reserve entry times and buy tickets in advance for both the church and the tower elevators (this is the best way to synch up the timing of your church visit and elevator ride). The easiest option is to book at www.sagrada familia.cat and print tickets at home.

Crowd Control: Waits can be up to 45 minutes at peak times—and occasionally stretch much longer (most crowded in the morning). To minimize waiting, arrive right at 9:00 (when the church opens) or after

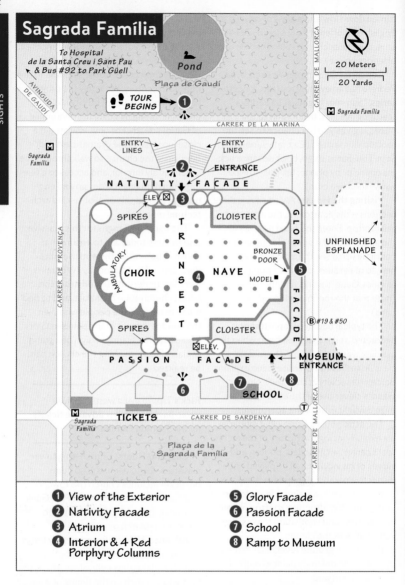

Sagrada Família

To Hospital de la Santa Creu i Sant Pau & Bus #92 to Park Güell

AVINGUDA DE GAUDÍ

Pond

Plaça de Gaudí

TOUR BEGINS ➊

CARRER DE MALLORCA

20 Meters
20 Yards

Ⓜ Sagrada Família

CARRER DE LA MARINA

Ⓜ Sagrada Família

ENTRY LINES — ENTRY LINES

ENTRANCE

➋

N A T I V I T Y   F A C A D E

ELEV. ⊠ ➌

SPIRES

CLOISTER

CARRER DE PROVENÇA

T R A N S E P T

AMBULATORY

CHOIR

➍ NAVE

BRONZE DOOR

MODEL ■

G L O R Y   F A C A D E

➎

UNFINISHED ESPLANADE

Ⓑ #19 & #50

SPIRES

CLOISTER

⊠ELEV.

P A S S I O N   F A C A D E

MUSEUM ENTRANCE

➑

➏

➐ SCHOOL

Ⓣ

Ⓜ Sagrada Família

TICKETS

CARRER DE SARDENYA

CARRER DE MALLORCA

Plaça de la Sagrada Família

➊ View of the Exterior
➋ Nativity Facade
➌ Atrium
➍ Interior & 4 Red Porphyry Columns

➎ Glory Facade
➏ Passion Facade
➐ School
➑ Ramp to Museum

16:00. To skip the line, buy advance tickets, take a tour, or hire a private guide.

Getting There: The church address is Carrer de Mallorca 401. The Sagrada Família Metro stop puts you right on its doorstep.

Getting In: The ticket windows are on the west side of the church, at the Passion Facade (from the Metro, exit toward Plaça de la Sagrada Família). If you already have tickets, head straight for the Nativity Facade (in front of Plaça de Gaudí), where you'll find entry lines for individuals. Show your ticket to the guard, who will direct you to the right line.

Information: Good English information is posted throughout. Tel. 932-073-031, www.sagradafamilia.cat.

Tours: The 50-minute **English tours** (€4.50) run daily at 11:00, 12:00, 13:00, and 15:00 (no 12:00 tour Mon-Fri in Nov-April; choose tour time when you buy ticket). Or rent the good 1.5-hour **audioguide** (€4.50).

Tower Elevators: Two different elevators take you (for a fee) partway up the towers for a great view of the city and a gargoyle's-eye perspective of the loopy church. Reserve an elevator time when you buy your church ticket.

The easier option is the **Passion Facade elevator,** which takes you 215 feet up and down. You can climb higher, but expect the spiral stairs to be tight, hot, and congested.

The **Nativity Facade elevator** is more exciting and demanding. You'll get the opportunity to cross the dizzying bridge between the towers, but you'll need to take the stairs all the way down.

❯ SELF-GUIDED TOUR

• *Start outside the Nativity Facade (where the entry lines for individuals are located), on the eastern side of the church. Before heading to the entrance, take in the...*

❶ View of the Exterior: Stand and imagine how grand this church will be when completed. The four 330-foot spires topped with crosses are just a fraction of this mega-church. When finished, the church will have 18 spires. Four will stand at each of the three entrances. Rising above those will be four taller towers, dedicated to the four Evangelists. A tower dedicated to Mary will rise still higher—400 feet. And in the center of the complex will stand the grand 560-foot Jesus tower, topped with a cross that will shine like a spiritual lighthouse, visible even from out at sea.

The Nativity Facade, where tourists enter today, is only a side entrance to the church. The grand main entrance will be around to the left. That means that the nine-story apartment building will eventually have to be torn down to accommodate it. The three facades—Nativity, Passion, and Glory—will chronicle Christ's life from birth to death to resurrection. Inside and out, a goal of the church is to bring the lessons of the Bible to the world. Despite his boldly modern architectural vision, Gaudí was fundamentally traditional and deeply religious. He designed

Sagrada Família

Sagrada Família nave

the Sagrada Família to be a bastion of solid Christian values in the midst of what was a humble workers' colony in a fast-changing city.

When Gaudí died, only one section (on the Nativity Facade) had been completed. The rest of the church has been inspired by Gaudí's long-range vision but designed and executed by others. This artistic freedom was amplified in 1936, when civil war shelling burned many of Gaudí's blueprints. Supporters of the ongoing work insist that Gaudí, who enjoyed saying, "My client [God] is not in a hurry," knew he wouldn't live to complete the church and recognized that later architects and artists would rely on their own muses for inspiration.

• *Now approach the...*

❷ Nativity Facade: This is the only part of the church essentially finished in Gaudí's lifetime. The four spires decorated with his unmistakably nonlinear sculpture mark this facade as part of his original design. Mixing Gothic-style symbolism, images from nature, and Modernista asymmetry, the Nativity Facade is the best example of Gaudí's original

Nativity Facade detail

vision, and it established the template for future architects who would work on the building.

The theme of this facade, which faces the rising sun, is Christ's birth. A statue above the doorway shows Mary, Joseph, and Baby Jesus in the manger, while curious cows peek in. It's the Holy Family—or "Sagrada Família"—to whom this church is dedicated. Flanking the doorway are the three Magi and adoring shepherds. Other statues show Jesus as a young carpenter and angels playing musical instruments. Higher up on the facade, in the arched niche, Jesus crowns Mary triumphantly.

The four **spires** are dedicated to apostles, and they repeatedly bear the word "Sanctus," or holy. Their colorful ceramic caps symbolize the miters (formal hats) of bishops. The shorter spires (to the left) symbolize the Eucharist (communion), alternating between a chalice with grapes and a communion host with wheat.

• *Enter the church. As you pass through the* **❸ atrium,** *look right to see one of the* **elevators** *up to the towers. For now, continue into the...*

❹ Interior: Typical of even the most traditional Catalan and Spanish churches, the floor plan is in the shape of a Latin cross, 300 feet long and 200 feet wide. Ultimately, the church will encompass 48,000 square feet, accommodating 8,000 worshippers. The nave's roof is 150 feet high. The crisscross arches of the ceiling (the vaults) show off Gaudí's distinctive engineering. The church's roof and flooring were only completed in 2010—just in time for Pope Benedict XVI to arrive and consecrate the church.

Part of Gaudí's religious vision was a love for nature. He said, "Nothing is invented; it's written in nature." Like the trunks of trees, these **columns** (56 in all) blossom with life, complete with branches, leaves, and knot-like capitals. The columns are a variety of colors—brown clay, gray granite, dark-gray basalt. The taller columns are 72 feet tall; the shorter ones are exactly half that.

Little **windows** let light filter in like the canopy of a rainforest, giving both privacy and an intimate connection with God. The clear glass is temporary and will gradually be replaced by stained glass. High up at the back half of the church, the U-shaped **choir**—suspended above the nave—can seat 1,000. The singers will eventually be backed by four organs (there's one now).

Work your way up the grand nave, walking through this forest of massive columns. At the center of the church stand four **red porphyry columns,** each marked with an Evangelist's symbol and name in Catalan: angel (Mateu), lion (Marc), bull (Luc), and eagle (Joan).

Stroll behind the altar through the **ambulatory** to reach a small chapel set aside for prayer and meditation. Look through windows down at the **crypt** (which holds the tomb of Gaudí). Peering down into that surprisingly traditional space, imagine how the church was started as a fairly conventional, 19th-century Neo-Gothic building until Gaudí was given the responsibility to finish it.

• *Head to the far end of the church, to what will eventually be the main entrance. Just inside the door, find the* **bronze model** *of the floor plan for the completed church. Facing the doors, look high up to see Subirachs' statue of one of Barcelona's patron saints,* **George (Jordi).** *While you can't see it, imagine that outside these doors will someday be the...*

❺ Glory Facade: Study the life-size image of the **bronze door,** emblazoned with the Lord's Prayer in Catalan, surrounded by "Give us this day our daily bread" in 50 languages. If you were able to walk through the actual door, you'd be face-to-face with...drab, doomed apartment blocks. In the 1950s, the mayor of Barcelona, figuring this day would never really come, sold the land destined for the church project. Now the city must buy back these buildings in order to complete

Gaudí's vision: that of a grand esplanade leading to this main entry. Four towers will rise. The facade's sculpture will represent how the soul passes through death, faces the Last Judgment, avoids the pitfalls of hell, and finds its way to eternal glory with God. Gaudí purposely left the facade's design open for later architects—stay tuned.

• *Head back up the nave, and exit through the left transept. Before passing through the doors, look down at the fine porphyry floor with scenes of Jesus' entry into Jerusalem. To the left, notice the second* **elevator** *up to the towers. Once outside, back up to take in the...*

❻ Passion Facade: Judge for yourself how well Gaudí's original vision has been carried out by later artists. The Passion Facade's four spires were designed by Gaudí and completed (quite faithfully) in 1976. But the lower part was only inspired by Gaudí's designs. The stark sculptures were interpreted freely (and controversially) by Josep Maria Subirachs (1927-2014), who completed the work in 2005.

Subirachs tells the story of Christ's torture and execution. The various scenes—Last Supper, betrayal, whipping, and so on—zigzag up from bottom to top, culminating in Christ's crucifixion over the doorway. The style is severe and unadorned, quite different from Gaudí's signature playfulness. But the bone-like archways are closely based on Gaudí's original designs. And Gaudí had made it clear that this facade should be grim and terrifying.

• *Now head into the small building outside the Passion Facade. This is the...*

❼ School: Gaudí erected this school for the children of the workers building the church. Today it includes exhibits about the design and engineering of the church, along with a classroom and a replica of Gaudí's desk as it was the day he died.

• *Back outside, head down the ramp, where you'll find WCs and the entrance to the...*

Sagrada Família Passion Facade

❽ Museum: Housed in what will someday be the church's crypt, the museum displays Gaudí's original models and drawings, and chronicles the progress of construction over the last 130-plus years.

Upon entering, you'll see **photos** (including one of the master himself) and a **timeline** illustrating how construction work has progressed from Gaudí's day to now. Before turning into the main hall, find **three different visions** for this church.

As you wander, notice how the **plaster models,** used for the church's construction, don't always match the finished product—these are ideas, not blueprints. The Passion Facade model shows Gaudí's original vision, with which Subirachs tinkered freely (see "Passion Facade," earlier). The models also make clear the influence of nature. The columns seem light, with branches springing forth and capitals that look like palm trees.

Turn right up the main hallway, walking under a huge **model of the nave,** and past some original **sculptures** from the different facades (on the left). Farther along, a small hallway on the left leads to some original Gaudí architectural **sketches** in a dimly lit room and a worthwhile 20-minute **movie** (continuously shown in Catalan with English subtitles).

From the end of this hall, you have another opportunity to look down into the crypt and at **Gaudí's tomb.** Gaudí lived on the site for more than a decade and is buried in the Neo-Gothic 19th-century crypt (also viewable from the apse). There's a move afoot to make Gaudí a saint. Gaudí prayer cards provide words of devotion to his beatification. Perhaps someday his tomb will be a place of pilgrimage.

On the right, you can peek into a busy **workshop** still used for making the same kind of plaster models Gaudí used to envision the final product in three dimensions.

• *Our tour is over. From here, you could...*

Visit Park Güell: *The park is nearly two (uphill) miles to the northwest. The easiest way to get there is to spring for a taxi (around €10-12). Or you could reach the park by taking the Metro to the Joanic stop, then hopping on bus #116 (described next, under the "Park Güell" listing).*

Return to Central Barcelona: *You can either hop on the Metro or take one of two handy buses (both stop on Carrer de Mallorca, directly in front of the Glory Facade). Bus #19 takes you back to the* **Old City** *in 15 minutes, stopping near the cathedral and in the El Born district. Bus #50 goes from the Sagrada Família to the heart of the* **Eixample** *(corner of Gran Via de les Corts Catalanes and Passeig de Gràcia), then continues on to Plaça Espanya, where you can get off for* **Montjuïc.**

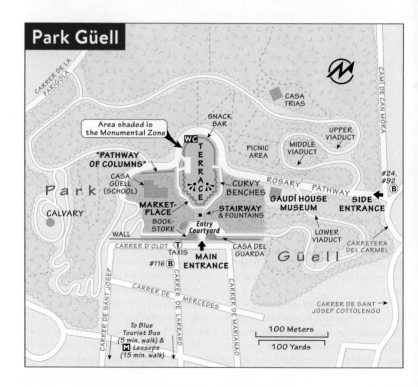

Beyond the Eixample
▲▲PARK GÜELL

Tucked in the foothills at the edge of Barcelona, this fanciful park—designed by Antoni Gaudí as part of an upscale housing development for early-20th-century urbanites—combines playful whimsy, inviting spaces, and a terrace offering sweeping views over the rooftops of the city.

When the entire park was free to enter, it became so popular that it was nearly trampled by tourists, obscuring the very sights they'd come to see. To control crowds, the part of the park with the most popular sights was declared the Monumental Zone, which requires an admission fee and a timed entry to visit. This fairly compact zone contains a pair of gingerbread-style houses, a grand staircase monitored by a colorful dragon, a forest of columns supporting a spectacular view terrace, and an undulating balcony slathered in tile shards.

The park also contains the Gaudí House Museum, Calvary viewpoint, picnic area, and a pleasant network of nature trails. Except for the Monumental Zone

and museum, the rest of the park is free.

No matter where you visit—inside the zone or out—what you're sure to see is Barcelonans and tourists alike enjoying a day at the park.

Cost and Hours: Monumental Zone—€8 at the gate or €7 online, smart to reserve timed-entry tickets in advance, daily April-Oct 8:00-20:00 (May-Aug until 21:30), Nov-March 8:30-18:15, www.parkguell.cat; Gaudí House Museum—€5.50, €18.50 combo-ticket also includes Sagrada Família (church but no towers), daily April-Sept 10:00-20:00, Oct-March 10:00-18:00, www.casamuseu gaudi.org.

Getting There: Park Güell is about 2.5 miles from Plaça de Catalunya, beyond the Gràcia neighborhood in Barcelona's foothills. If asking for directions, be aware that Catalans pronounce it "Park Gway" (sounds like "parkway").

From downtown, a **taxi** will drop you off at the main entrance for about €12. From Plaça de Catalunya, the blue Tourist Bus stops about two blocks downhill from the main entrance, and **public bus** #24 travels from Plaça de Catalunya to the park's side entrance. Or you can ride

Park Güell's entry stairway

the Metro to Joanic, exit toward Carrer de l'Escorial, and find the bus stop in front of #20, where you can catch bus #116 to the park's main entrance. For instructions on linking the Sagrada Família to Park Güell, check page 83 .

Visiting the Park: This tour assumes you're arriving at the front/main entrance.

Entering the park, you walk through a palm-frond **gate** and pass Gaudí's gas lamps (1900-1914), both made of wrought iron. His dad was a blacksmith, and he always enjoyed this medium.

Two Hansel-and-Gretel gingerbread lodges flank the entrance, signaling to visitors that this park is a magical space. One of the buildings houses a good bookshop; the other is home to the skippable **La Casa del Guarda,** a branch of the Barcelona History Museum (MUHBA). The Gaudí House Museum, described later, is more interesting to me.

Climb the grand **stairway,** past the famous ceramic dragon fountain. At the top, dip into the "Hall of 100 Columns," designed to house a produce market for the neighborhood's 60 mansions. The fun columns—each different, made from concrete and rebar, topped with colorful ceramic, and studded with broken bottles and bric-a-brac—add to the market's vitality.

As you continue up (on the left-hand staircase), look left, down the playful **"pathway of columns"** that supports a long arcade. Gaudí drew his inspiration from nature, and this arcade is like a surfer's perfect tube.

Once up top on the **terrace,** sit on a colorful bench—designed to fit your body ergonomically—and enjoy one of Barcelona's best views. Look for the Sagrada Família church in the distance.

As a community development, Park Güell ultimately failed, but it was an idea a hundred years ahead of its time. Back then, high-society ladies didn't want to live so far from the cultural action. Today, the surrounding neighborhoods are some of the wealthiest in town, and a gated community here would be a big hit.

Gaudí House Museum: This pink house with a steeple, standing in the middle of the park (near the side entrance), was Gaudí's home for 20 years (though he didn't design the actual house). It was originally built as a model home to attract prospective residents. His humble artifacts are mostly gone, but the house is now a museum with some quirky Gaudí furniture. Though small, it offers a good taste of what could have been if the envisioned housing development had prospered.

Montjuïc

Montjuïc (mohn-jew-EEK), overlooking Barcelona's hazy port, has always been a show-off. Ages ago, it was capped by an impressive castle. When the Spanish enforced their rule in the 18th century, they built the imposing fortress that you'll see the shell of today. Montjuïc was also prominent during the last century. In 1929, it hosted an international fair, from which many of today's sights originated. And in 1992, the Summer Olympics directed the world's attention to this pincushion of attractions once again.

For art lovers, the most worthwhile sights are the Fundació Joan Miró and Catalan Art Museum. The hilltop castle isn't worth entering, but offers great city views from its ramparts. It serves as a park, jogging destination, and host to a popular summer open-air cinema.

For evening fun, you could drop by the Magic Fountains, and any time of day, you can escalate up to the top of Las Arenas Mall for a view of Montjuïc.

Getting to Montjuïc: You have several choices. The simplest is to take a **taxi** directly to your destination (about €8 from downtown). If you want to visit only the Catalan Art Museum, you can just take the **Metro** to Plaça d'Espanya and ride the escalators up the hill (with some stairs as well).

Buses also take you up to Montjuïc. From Plaça de Catalunya, **bus #55** rides as far as Montjuïc's cable-car station/funicular. If you want to get higher (to the castle), ride the Metro to Plaça d'Espanya, then make the easy transfer to **bus #150** to ride all the way up the hill—then you can do the rest of your Montjuïc sightseeing going downhill. Alternatively, the red Tourist Bus will get you to the Montjuïc sights.

Another option is by **funicular** (covered by Metro ticket, runs every 10 minutes 9:00-22:00). To reach it, take the Metro to the Paral-lel stop, then follow signs for *Parc Montjuïc* and the little funicular icon—you can enter the funicular without using another ticket. From the top of the funicular, turn left and walk gently downhill 4 minutes to the Miró museum or 12 minutes to the Catalan Art Museum. If you're heading all the way up to the castle, you can catch a bus or cable car from the top of the funicular.

For a scenic (if slow) approach to Montjuïc, you could ride the fun, circa-1929 Aeri del Port **cable car** (*telefèric*) from the tip of the Barceloneta peninsula (across the harbor, near the beach) to the Miramar viewpoint park in Montjuïc.

Since the cable car is expensive, loads slowly, and goes between two relatively remote parts of town, it's only worthwhile for its sweeping views or if you'd like to cap off your Montjuïc day with some beach time near Barceloneta (€11 one-way, €16.50 round-trip, 3/hour, daily 11:00-17:30, June-Sept until 20:00, closed in high wind, tel. 934-414-820, www.teleferico debarcelona.com).

Getting Around Montjuïc: Up top, it's easy and fun to walk between the sights—especially downhill. You can also connect the sights using the red Tourist Bus or one of the public buses: Bus #150 does a loop around the hilltop and is the only bus that goes to the castle; on the way up, it stops at or passes the Catalan Art Museum, Fundació Joan Miró, the lower castle cable-car station/top of the funicular, and finally, the castle. On the downhill run, it loops by Miramar, the cable-car station for Barceloneta. Bus #55 connects only the funicular/cable-car stations, Fundació Joan Miró, and the Catalan Art Museum.

▲▲CATALAN ART MUSEUM (MUSEU NACIONAL D'ART DE CATALUNYA)

This wonderful museum showcases Catalan art from the 10th century through

Montjuïc's Magic Fountains

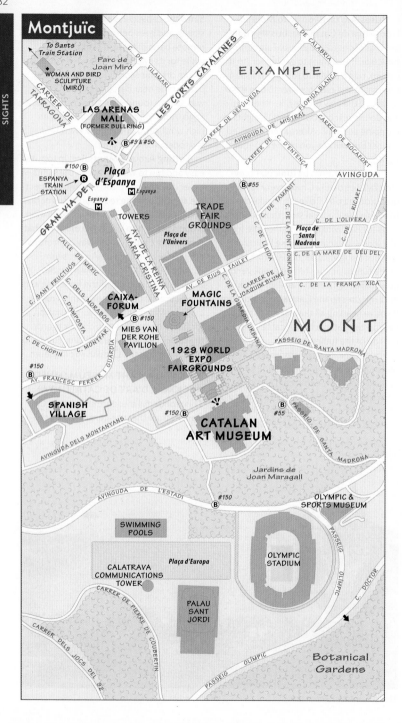

Montjuïc

To Sants
Train Station

Parc de
Joan Miró

WOMAN AND BIRD
SCULPTURE
(MIRÓ)

LAS ARENAS
MALL
(FORMER BULLRING)

B #9 & #50

C. DE VILAMARI

C. DE

LES CORTS CATALANES

EIXAMPLE

C. DE CALABRIA

CARRER DE SEPÚLVEDA

FLORIDA BLANCA

AVINGUDA DE MISTRAL

CARRER DE C. D'ENTENÇA

CARRER DE ROCAFORT

CARRER DE TARRAGONA

#150 B

ESPANYA
TRAIN
STATION

R

Plaça
d'Espanya

M Espanya

Espanya

M

TOWERS

B #55

AVINGUDA

GRAN VIA DE

CALLE DE MEXIC

C. SANT FRUCTUÓS

C. DELS MORABOS

C. D'AMPOSTA

AV. DE LA REINA MARIA CRISTINA

TRADE
FAIR
GROUNDS

Plaça de
l'Univers

C. DE TAMARIT

C. DE LLEIDA

C. DE LA FONT HONRADA

Plaça de
Santa
Madrona

C. DE L'OLIVERA

C. DE RICART

C. DE LA MARE DE DÉU DEL

CAIXA-
FORUM

B #150

MIES VAN
DER ROHE
PAVILION

MAGIC
FOUNTAINS

AV. DE RIUS I TAULET

C. DE LA GUARDIA URBANA

CARRER DE
JOAQUIM BLUME

C. DE LA FRANÇA XICA

C. DE CHOPIN

C. MONTFAR

1929 WORLD
EXPO
FAIRGROUNDS

MONT

PASSEIG DE SANTA MADRONA

#150
AV. FRANCESC FERRER I GUARDIA

SPANISH
VILLAGE

AVINGUDA DELS MONTANYANS

#150 B

CATALAN
ART MUSEUM

B #55

PASSEIG DE SANTA MADRONA

Jardins de
Joan Maragall

AVINGUDA DE L'ESTADI

#150 B

OLYMPIC &
SPORTS MUSEUM

SWIMMING
POOLS

CALATRAVA
COMMUNICATIONS
TOWER

Plaça d'Europa

PALAU
SANT
JORDI

OLYMPIC
STADIUM

PASSEIG OLIMPIC

C. DOCTOR

CARRER DE PIERRE DE COUBERTIN

CARRER DELS JOCS DEL 92

PASSEIG OLIMPIC

Botanical
Gardens

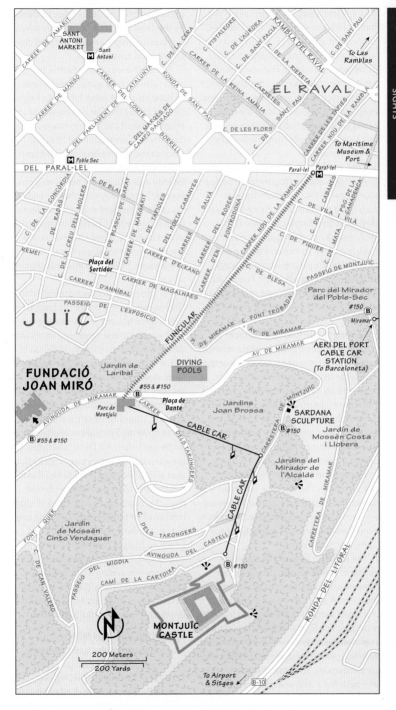

SANT ANTONI MARKET

Sant Antoni

CARRER DE TAMARIT

CARRER DE MANSO

CARRER DEL CATALUNYA

CARRER DEL PARLAMENT DE COMTE

C. DEL MARQÈS DE CAMPO SAGRADO

BORRELL

Poble Sec

C. DE LA CERA

C. DE VISTALEGRE

C. DE L'AURORA

RAMBLA DEL RAVAL

C. DE SANT PAU

C. DE SANT PACIA

CARRER DE LA REINA AMALIA

C. CARRETES

RONDA DE SANT PAU

EL RAVAL

To Las Ramblas

C. DE LES FLORS

C. DE LES TAPIES

CARRER NOU DE LA RAMBLA

To Maritime Museum & Port

C. DE SANT PAU

DEL PARAL-LEL

Paral-lel

Paral-lel

C. DE LA CONCORDIA

C. DE BLAI

C. DE RADAS

C. DE BLASCO DE GARAY

C. DE TAPIOLES

C. DE MARGARIT

C. DEL POETA CABANYES

CARRER DE SALVA

CARRER DEL ROSER

FONTRODONA

CARRER NOU DE LA RAMBLA

C. DE PIQUER

C. DE VILA I VILA

C. DE CABANES

PSG DE LA CANADENCA

C. DE LA CREU DELS MOLERS

REMEI

Plaça del Sortidor

CARRER D'EN

CARRER D'ELKANO

CARRER DE MAGALHÃES

C. DE BLESA

C. DE MATA

PASSEIG DE MONTJUIC

CARRER D'ANNIBAL

PASSEIG DE L'EXPOSICIÓ

JUÏC

FUNICULAR

C. FONT TROBADA

P. DE MIRAMAR

AV. DE MIRAMAR

Parc del Mirador del Poble-Sec

#150

Miramar

AV. DE MIRAMAR

AERI DEL PORT CABLE CAR STATION
(To Barceloneta)

FUNDACIÓ JOAN MIRÓ

Jardin de Laribal

DIVING POOLS

AVINGUDA DE MIRAMAR

#55 & #150

Parc de Montjuïc

Plaça de Dante

CARRER

Jardins Joan Brossa

CARRETERA DE MONTJUIC

SARDANA SCULPTURE

#150

Jardin de Mossèn Costa i Llobera

#55 & #150

CABLE CAR

DELS TARONGERS

Jardins del Mirador de l'Alcalde

CABLE CAR

CARRETERA DE MIRAMAR

Jardin de Mossèn Cinto Verdaguer

FONT I QUER

C. DELS TARONGERS

AVINGUDA DEL CASTELL

#150

PASSEIG DEL MIGDIA

CAMÍ DE LA CARTOIXA

C. DE CAN VALERO

N

200 Meters

200 Yards

MONTJUÏC CASTLE

RONDA DEL LITORAL

To Airport & Sitges

B-10

the mid-20th century. Often called "the Prado of Romanesque art" (and "MNAC" for short), it also holds Europe's best collection of Romanesque frescoes. Art aficionados are sure to find something in this diverse collection to tickle their fancy. It's all housed in the grand Palau Nacional, an emblematic building from the 1929 World Expo, with magnificent views over Barcelona, especially from the building's rooftop terrace.

Cost and Hours: €12, includes temporary exhibits and rooftop terrace, rooftop access only-€3.50, museum free Sat from 15:00 and first Sun of month; open May-Sept Tue-Sat 10:00-20:00 (Oct-April until 18:00), Sun 10:00-15:00, closed Mon, last entry 30 minutes before closing; audioguide-€3.10; in massive National Palace building above Magic Fountains, near Plaça d'Espanya—take escalators up; tel. 936-220-376, www.museunacional. cat.

Getting to the Rooftop Terrace: To reach the terrace from the main entrance, walk past the bathrooms to the left and show your ticket to get on the elevator. You'll ride up nearly to the viewpoint, and from there hike up a couple of flights of stairs to the terrace. To take an elevator the whole way, go to the far end of the museum, through the huge dome room, to the far right corner.

Visiting the Museum: As you enter, pick up a map. The left wing is Romanesque, and the right wing is Gothic, exquisite Renaissance, and Baroque. Upstairs is more Baroque, plus modern art, photography, coins, and more.

The MNAC's rare, world-class collection of **Romanesque** (Romànic) art came mostly from remote Catalan village churches. A series of videos shows the process of extracting the frescoes from the churches. The Romanesque wing features a remarkable array of 11th- to 13th-century frescoes, painted wooden altar fronts, and ornate statuary. This classic Romanesque art—with flat 2-D scenes, each saint holding his symbol, and Jesus (easy to identify by the cross in his halo)—is impressively displayed on replicas of the original church ceilings and apses.

Across the way, in the Gothic wing, are vivid 14th-century wood-panel paintings of Bible stories. A roomful of paintings (Room 26) by the Catalan master Jaume Huguet (1412-1492) deserves a look, particularly his *Consecration of St. Agustí Vell.* Also on the ground floor is a selection of **Renaissance** works covering Spain's Golden Age (Zurbarán, heavy religious scenes, Spanish royals with their endearing underbites) and examples of Romanticism (dewy-eyed Catalan landscapes). In addition, you'll find minor works by major—if not necessarily Catalan—names (Velázquez, El Greco, Tintoretto, Rubens, and so on).

For a break, go to the right from the Gothic exit to glide under the huge **dome,** which once housed an ice-skating rink. This was the prime ceremony room and dance hall for the 1929 World Expo.

From the big ballroom, you can ride the glass elevator upstairs to the **Modern Art** section, which takes you on an enjoyable walk from the late 1800s to about 1950, offering a big chronological clockwise circle covering Symbolism, Modernisme, fin de siècle fun, Art Deco, and more. Find the early 20th-century paintings by Catalan artists Santiago Rusiñol and Ramon Casas, both of whom had a profound impact on a young Picasso (and, through him, on all of modern art). Crossing over to the "Modern 2" section, you'll find furniture (pieces that complement the empty spaces you likely saw in Gaudí's buildings—including a Gaudí wooden sofa), Impressionism, the shimmering landscapes of Joaquim Mir, and several distinctly Picasso portraits of women.

▲FUNDACIÓ JOAN MIRÓ

This museum has the best collection anywhere of work by Catalan artist Joan Miró (ZHOO-ahn mee-ROH, 1893-1983). Born in Barcelona, Miró divided his time between Paris and Catalunya (including Barcelona and his favorite village, Mont-roig del Camp). This building—designed in 1975 by Josep Lluís Sert, a friend of Miró and a student of Le Corbusier—was purpose-built to show off Miró's art.

The museum displays an always-changing, loosely chronological over-view of Miró's work (as well as generally excellent temporary exhibits of 20th- and 21st-century artists). Consider renting the wonderful audioguide, well worth the extra charge.

If you don't like abstract art, you'll leave here scratching your head. But those who love this place are not faking it...they under-stand the genius of Miró and the fun of abstraction. Children probably understand it the best. Eavesdrop on what they say about the art; you may learn something.

Cost and Hours: €11; Tue-Sat 10:00-20:00 (Nov-March until 18:00), Thu until 21:00, Sun until 14:30, closed Mon year-round; great audioguide-€5, 200 yards from top of funicular, Parc de Montjuïc, tel. 934-439-470, www.fundaciomiro-bcn.org. The museum has a restaurant, café, and bookshop (all accessible without museum ticket).

▲MAGIC FOUNTAINS

These fountains, near the base of Mont-juïc, make an artistic, colorful, and coor-dinated splash some summer evenings, accompanied by music (free 20-min-ute shows start on the half-hour; almost always May-Sept Thu-Sun 21:00-23:00,

no shows Mon-Wed; Oct-April Fri-Sat 19:00-20:30, no shows Sun-Thu, near Plaça d'Espanya).

LAS ARENAS MALL

This mall, on Plaça d'Espanya, was built inside a former bullring. It hosts the usual shops and a food-court basement. Worth ascending, the rooftop terrace offers fine views of Montjuïc (daily 10:00-22:00, small fee for exterior elevator to terrace, but interior escalators are free).

The Beaches and Nearby

▲BARCELONA'S BEACHES

Barcelona has created a summer tour-ist trade by building a huge stretch of beaches east of the town center. The overall scene is great for sunbathing and for an evening paseo before dinner. A bustling night scene keeps the harborfront busy until the wee hours.

This artificial peninsula, once the home of working-class sailors, is like a resort today—complete with lounge chairs, volleyball, showers, WCs, bike paths, and inviting beach bars called *chirin-guitos*. Each beach segment has its own vibe: Sant Sebastià (closest, popular with older beachgoers and families), Barcelo-neta (with many seafood restaurants), Nova Icària (pleasant family beach), and Mar Bella (attracts a younger crowd, clothing-optional). As you wander the promenade, you'll see Frank Gehry's striking "fish" sculpture shining brightly in the sun.

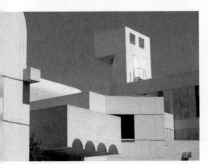

Fundació Joan Miró

Nova Icària beach

Getting There: The Barceloneta Metro stop leaves you blocks from the sand. To get to the beaches without a hike, take the bus. From the Ramblas, bus #59 will get you as far as Barceloneta Park; bus #D20 leaves from the Columbus Monument and follows a similar route. Bus #V15 runs from Plaça de Catalunya to the tip of Barceloneta (near the W Hotel).

---

*Rick's Tip: Biking is a joy in Citadel Park and along the beachfront. To rent a bike on the beach, try **Biciclot** (€5/hour, €10/3 hours, €17/24 hours, daily in summer 10:00-20:00, shorter hours off-season, Passeig Maritime 33, tel. 932-219-778, www.biking inbarcelona.net).*

CITADEL PARK (PARC DE LA CIUTADELLA)

In 1888, Barcelona's biggest, greenest park, originally the site of a much-hated military citadel, was transformed for a Universal Exhibition (world's fair). The stately Triumphal Arch at the top of the park, celebrating the removal of the citadel, was built as the main entrance. Inside you'll find wide pathways, plenty of trees and grass, a zoo, and museums of geology and zoology. Barcelona, one of Europe's most densely populated cities, suffers from a lack of real green space. This park is a haven and is especially enjoyable on weekends, when it teems with happy families. Enjoy the ornamental fountain that the young Antoni Gaudí helped design, and consider a jaunt in a rental rowboat on the lake in the center of the park. Check out the tropical Umbracle greenhouse and the Hivernacle winter garden, which has a pleasant café-bar (Mon-Sat 10:00-14:00 & 17:00-20:30, Sun 10:30-14:00, shorter hours off-season).

Cost and Hours: Park—free, daily 10:00 until dusk, north of França train station, Metro: Arc de Triomf, Barceloneta, or Ciutadella-Vila Olímpica.

EXPERIENCES

Shopping

The streets of the Barri Gòtic and El Born are bursting with characteristic hole-in-the-wall shops, while the Eixample is the upscale "uptown" shopping district. Near Plaça de Catalunya, Avinguda Portal de l'Angel has a staggering array of department and chain stores.

Souvenir Items: In this artistic city, consider picking up art prints, posters, and books. Museum gift shops (Picasso Museum, La Pedrera, and more) offer a bonanza of classy souvenirs. Home-decor shops have Euro-style housewares unavailable back home. Decorative tile and pottery (popularized by Modernist architects) and Modernista jewelry are easy to pack. Foodies might bring back olive oil, wine, spices (such as saffron or sea salts), cheese, or the local nougat treat, torró. An *espadenya*—or *espadrille* in Spanish—is the trendy canvas-and-rope shoe that originated as humble Catalan peasant footwear. For a souvenir of Catalan culture, consider a Catalan flag, a dragon of St. Jordi, or a jersey or scarf from the wildly popular Barça soccer team.

Barri Gòtic Shopping Stroll

This route, from the cathedral to the Ramblas, takes you through interesting streets lined with little shops. Avoid the midafternoon siesta and Sundays, when many shops are closed.

Face the cathedral, turn 90 degrees right, and exit Plaça Nova (just to the left of the Bilbao Berria "BB" restaurant) on the tight lane called Carrer de la Palla. This street has a half-dozen antique shops crammed with mothballed treasures. Mixed in are a few art galleries, offbeat shops, and a motorcycle museum. When you reach the fork in the road (where the inviting Caelum café is), you have a choice. If you go left, explore Carrer dels Banys Nous, another great shopping street (with Artesania Catalunya, a city-run market space featuring handmade items from Catalan artisans).

To carry on toward the Ramblas, take the right fork. You'll pass by the Oro Líquido shop ("Liquid Gold," high-quality olive oils) and soon reach the Church of Santa Maria del Pi, ringed by a charming, café-lined square, Plaça de Sant Josep Oriol. Skirt around the right side of the church to find Plaça del Pi, a delightful square, with Josep Roca, a genteel gentleman's shop. Head up the narrow street, Carrer Petritxol, immediately left of the Josep Roca shop. The street is a fun combination of art galleries, jewelry shops, and simple places for hot chocolate and churros (check out Granja La Pallaresa, just after #11).

You'll dead-end onto Carrer de la Portaferrissa, with its international teen clothing stores. From here, head one block left to reach the Ramblas.

El Born

Although the main streets—Carrer de la Princesa, the perpendicular Carrer de Montcada, and the diagonal Carrer de l'Argenteria—are disappointing for shoppers, if you lose yourself in the smaller back lanes between those arteries, you'll discover a world of artsy, funky little boutiques. Stroll along Carrer dels Flassaders (behind the Picasso Museum), Carrer dels Banys Vells (between Montcada and l'Argenteria), and Carrer del Rec (just south of Passeig del Born)—and all of the little lanes crossing each of these streets.

Plaça de Catalunya and Avinguda Portal de l'Angel

Barcelona natives do most of their shopping at big department stores. You'll find the highest concentration of stores on Avinguda del Portal de l'Angel, which leads south from Plaça de Catalunya to the cathedral.

Plaça de Catalunya hosts the gigantic **El Corte Inglés,** the Spanish answer to one-stop shopping, with clothing, electronics, a travel agency, events box office, a basement supermarket, and a ninth-floor view café (Mon-Sat 10:00-22:00, closed Sun). Across the square is **FNAC**—a French department store that sells electronics, music, books, and tickets for major concerts and events (Mon-Sat

Open-air market in the Barri Gòtic

10:00-22:00, closed Sun).

Along Avinguda Portal de l'Angel, you'll see popular clothing chains such as **Zara,** the Barcelona-based **Mango, Desigual** (with boldly colorful designs), the teen-oriented French chain **Pimkie,** and the more sophisticated **Podivm** and **Blanco.**

The Eixample

This ritzy "uptown" district is home to some of the city's top-end shops. From Plaça de Catalunya, head north up Passeig de Gràcia, which starts out with lower-end international stores (like Zara) and ends up with top-end brands at the top (Gucci, Luis Vuitton, Escada, Chanel). Detour one block west to Rambla de Catalunya for more local (but still expensive) options for fashion, jewelry, perfume, home decor, and more.

Nightlife

For evening entertainment, Barcelonans stroll the streets, greet neighbors, pop into a bar for drinks and tapas, nurse a cocktail on a floodlit square, or enjoy a late meal. Dinnertime is around 22:00, and even families with children can be out well after midnight. If you're near Montjuïc, take in the hilltop view, Magic Fountains, or both.

Neighborhoods for Tapas and Drinks

These neighborhoods party late, but they're also lively for tapas and drinks in the early evening.

El Born: Passeig del Born, a broad park-like strip stretching from the Church of Santa Maria del Mar, is lined with inviting bars and nightspots. Wander the side streets for more options. Miramelindo (Passeig del Born 15) is a favorite for mojitos. La Vinya del Senyor is mellower, for tapas and wine on the square in front of Santa Maria del Mar.

Plaça Reial (in the Barri Gòtic): A block off the Ramblas, this palm-tree-graced square bustles with trendy eateries

charging inflated prices for pleasant out-door tables—perfect for nursing a drink. Try the Ocaña Bar (€5-14 tapas, reasonable drinks, at #13).

Carrer de la Mercè: This Barri Gòtic street near the harbor is lined with salty tapas bars, with a few trendy ones mixed in.

Barceloneta: The broad beach is dotted with *chiringuitos*—shacks selling drinks and snacks, creating a fun, lively scene on a balmy summer evening.

Performing Arts

Barcelona always has a vast array of cultural events. Pick up the TI's free monthly English-language magazine, *In BCN Culture & Leisure.* Another good source of info is the Palau de la Virreina ticket office (daily 10:00-20:30, Ramblas 99, tel. 933-161-000, www.lavirreina.bcn.cat).

You can buy tickets directly from the venue's website, from box offices at El Corte Inglés or the FNAC store (both on Plaça de Catalunya), from Palau de Verreina, or at www.ticketmaster.es or www.telentrada.com.

The **Palace of Catalan Music,** with one of the finest Modernista interiors in town, offers everything from symphonic to Catalan folk songs to chamber music to flamenco (Palau de la Música Catalana, €20-50 tickets, purchase online or in person, box office open daily 9:30-21:00, Carrer Palau de la Música 4, Metro: Urquinaona, box office tel. 902-442-882).

The **Liceu Opera House** right in the heart of the Ramblas, is a sumptuous venue for opera, dance, and concerts (Gran Teatre del Liceu, tickets from €10, buy tickets online up to 1.5 hours before the show or in person, Ramblas 51, box office just around the corner at Carrer Sant Pau 1, Metro: Liceu, box office tel. 934-859-913, www.liceubarcelona.cat).

"Masters of Guitar" concerts are offered nearly nightly at 21:00 in the Barri Gòtic's **Church of Santa Maria del Pi** (€23 at the door, €4 less if you buy at least 3 hours ahead—look for ticket sellers in front of church and scattered throughout town, Plaça del Pi 7, or sometimes in Sant Jaume Church at Carrer de Ferran 28, tel. 647-514-513, www.maestrosdelaguitarra. com).

Though flamenco music is not typical of Barcelona (it's from Andalucía), **Tarantos** offers entertaining concerts nightly (€10, at 20:30, 21:30, and 22:30; Plaça Reial 17, tel. 933-191-789, www.masimas.com/ en/tarantos). **La Pedrera** hosts "Summer Nights at La Pedrera" jazz concerts on its fanciful floodlit rooftop, weekends from June to September (book ahead at tel. 902-101-212 or www.lapedrera.com).

EATING

Barcelona, the capital of Catalan cuisine, offers a tremendous variety of colorful places to eat, ranging from workaday eateries to homey Catalan bistros (cans) to crowded tapas bars to avant-garde restaurants. Many eateries serve both stand-up tapas and sit-down meals, often starring seafood.

Basque-style tapas places are popular and user-friendly. Just scan the enticing buffets of bite-size tapas, grab what looks good, order a drink, and save your toothpicks (they'll count them up to tally your bill). I've listed my favorite tapas bars (Taverna Basca Irati, Xaloc, and Sagardi Euskal Taberna), though there are many others (look for basca or euskal; both mean "Basque").

Budget Meals: Sandwich shops are everywhere, serving made-to-order bocadillos. Choose between bright (mass-produced) chains such as **Bocatta** and **Pans & Company,** or colorful holes-in-the-wall. **Mucci's Pizza** has good, fresh, €2 pizza slices and empanadas (just off the Ramblas, at Bonsuccés 10 and Tallers 75), and **Wok to Walk** has takeaway noodle and rice dishes (€6-9, near the main door of the Boqueria Market). Kebab places are another standby for quick and tasty €3-4 meals. For a fast, affordable lunch with a view, the ninth-floor cafeteria at **El Corte Inglés department store** on Plaça de Catalunya can't be beat. Picnickers can buy groceries at the basement supermarket in El Corte Inglés, or at **La Boqueria Market** on the Ramblas.

The fun Pinotxo Bar at La Boqueria Market

Near the Ramblas

Do not eat or drink at the tourist traps on the Ramblas. Within a few steps of the Ramblas, you'll find handy lunch places, an inviting market hall, and some good vegetarian options.

Taverna Basca Irati serves hot and cold Basque *pintxos* for €2 each. These small open-faced sandwiches are like sushi on bread. Muscle in through the hungry local crowd, get an empty plate from the waiter, and then help yourself. Every few minutes, waiters circulate with platters of new, still-warm munchies. Grab munchies as they pass by...it's addictive (you'll be charged by the number of toothpicks left on your plate). For drink options, look for the printed menu on the wall in the back. Wash down your food with €3 glasses of Rioja (full-bodied red wine), Txakolí (sprightly Basque white wine), or *sidra* (apple wine) poured from on high to add oxygen and bring out the flavor (daily 11:00-24:00, a block off the Ramblas, behind arcade at Carrer del Cardenal Casanyes 17, Metro: Liceu, tel. 933-023-084).

Family-run since 1870, **Café Granja Viader** boasts about being the first dairy business to bottle and distribute milk in Spain. This quaint time capsule—specializing in baked and dairy treats, toasted sandwiches, and light meals—is ideal for a traditional breakfast. Or indulge your sweet tooth: Try a glass of *orxata* (or *horchata*—chufa-nut milk, summer only), *llet mallorquina* (Majorca-style milk with cinnamon, lemon, and sugar), *crema catalana* (crème brûlée, their specialty), or *suis* ("Swiss"—hot chocolate with a snowcap of whipped cream). *Mel i mató* is fresh cheese with honey...very Catalan (Mon-Sat 9:00-13:00 & 17:00-21:00, closed Sun, a block off the Ramblas behind Betlem Church at Xuclà 4, Metro: Liceu, tel. 933-183-486).

Biocenter, a soup-and-salad restaurant popular with local vegetarians, takes its cooking seriously (€8-10 weekday

A Short, Sweet Walk

Here's a dessert walk in three stops—all within a three-minute walk of one another just off the Ramblas (Metro: Liceu). Start at the corner of Carrer de la Portaferrissa midway down the Ramblas. For the best atmosphere, begin your walk at about 18:00.

Torró: Walk down Carrer de la Portaferrissa to #8 (on the right). **Casa Colomina,** founded in 1908, specializes in homemade *torró* (*turrón* in Spanish)—nougat made with almond, honey, and sugar (€2.20 wrapped chunks on counter, daily 10:00-20:30). In summer, try the refreshing *orxata* drink (*horchata* in Spanish).

Churros con Chocolate: Continue down Carrer de la Portaferrissa, taking a right at Carrer Petritxol to #11 to the fun-loving **Granja La Pallaresa,** where you can dip greasy *churros* into cups of hot chocolate pudding for €4.50 (daily 9:00-13:00 & 16:00-21:00).

Chocolate: Continue down Carrer Petritxol to the square, Plaça del Pi, hook left through the two-part square, then left up Carrer del Pi to the corner of Carrer de la Portaferrissa. Founded in 1827, **Fargas,** a traditional chocolate shop, sells even little morsels by weight, so don't be shy (Mon-Sat 9:30-20:30, closed Sun).

lunch specials include soup or salad and plate of the day, €15 dinner specials, otherwise €7-9 salads and €12-13 main dishes, Mon-Sat 13:00-23:00, Sun 13:00-16:00, 2 blocks off the Ramblas at Carrer del Pintor Fortuny 25, Metro: Liceu, tel. 933-014-583).

Try eating at **La Boqueria Market** at least once. It's ringed by colorful, good-value eateries and several good bars—many with enticing seafood options. Lots of stalls sell fun takeaway food—especially fruit salads and fresh-squeezed juices—ideal for **picnics** (Mon-Sat 8:00-20:00). Just to the right as you enter the market, **Pinotxo Bar** is a fun, if touristy, spot for coffee, breakfast (spinach *tortillas*), or tapas. Fun-loving Juan and his family are La Boqueria fixtures. Be careful—this place can get expensive (Mercat de la Boqueria 466, tel. 933-171-731, www.pinotxobar.com). **Kiosko Universal** is popular for its great prices on wonderful fish dishes. As you enter the market from the Ramblas, it's all the way to the left. It's always packed, but less crowded before 12:30. If you see people waiting, go to the cashier to put your name on a list (€8-12 *platos del día* with different fresh-fish options, €8 mixed veggies, €10 mushroom stir-fries, tel. 933-178-286).

In the Barri Gòtic

In the atmospheric Gothic Quarter, you can choose between sit-down meals at restaurants or a string of tapas bars.

Restaurants

If you want to eat outdoors on a convivial, mellow square, **Café de l'Academia** is the place. They serve refined market-fresh Catalan cuisine. The candlelit, air-conditioned interior is rustic yet elegant, with soft jazz, flowers, and modern art. Reservations are smart (€10-15 first courses, €13-20 second courses, fixed-price lunch for €11.50 at the bar or €15 at a table, Mon-Fri 13:00-15:30 & 20:00-23:00, closed Sat-Sun, near the City Hall square, off Carrer de Jaume I, up Carrer de la Dagueria at Carrer dels Lledó 1, Metro: Jaume I, tel. 933-198-253).

Els Quatre Gats was once the haunt of the Modernista greats—including a teen-aged Picasso, who first publicly displayed his art here, and architect Josep Puig i Cadafalch, who designed the building. Inspired by Paris' famous Le Chat Noir café/cabaret, Els Quatre Gats ("The Four Cats") celebrated all that was modern

at the turn of the 20th century. You can snack or drink at the bar, or go into the back for a sit-down meal (€18 three-course lunch special Mon-Fri 13:00-16:00, €12-28 plates, daily 10:00-24:00, just steps off Avinguda del Portal de l'Angel at Carrer de Montsió 3, Metro: Catalunya, tel. 933-024-140).

Xaloc offers nicely presented gourmet tapas in a woody, modern, and spacious dining room, with fun energy, good service, and reasonable prices. The walls are covered with *Ibérica* hamhocks and wine bottles. They focus on homestyle Catalan classics and serve only one top-quality ham. A gazpacho, plank of ham, *pa amb tomàquet*, and nice glass of wine make a terrific light meal (€3-8 tapas, €6-14 main dishes, open daily, drinks and cold tapas 11:00-23:00, kitchen open 13:00-17:00 & 19:00-23:00, a block toward the cathedral from Plaça de Sant Josep Oriol at Carrer de la Palla 13, Metro: Catalunya, tel. 933-011-990).

Bar del Pi is a simple, hardworking bar serving good salads, sandwiches, and tapas. It has just a handful of tables on the most inviting little square in the Barri Gòtic (daily 9:00-23:00 except closed Tue in winter, Plaça de Sant Josep Oriol 1, Metro: Liceu, tel. 933-022-123).

Restaurant Agut, around since 1924, features a comfortable, wood-paneled dining room that's modern and sophisticated, but still retains a slight bohemian air. The pictures lining the walls are by Catalan artists who are said to have exchanged their canvases for a meal. The menu includes tasty traditional Catalan food (€14 three-course weekday lunch special, €10-15 starters, €13-29 main dishes, Tue-Sat 13:30-16:00 & 20:30-23:30, Sun 13:30-16:00, closed Mon, just up from Carrer de la Mercè and the harbor at Carrer d'En Gignàs 16, Metro: Jaume I, tel. 933-151-709).

La Crema Canela, a few steps above Plaça Reial, feels cozier than the restaurants on that atmospheric square, which

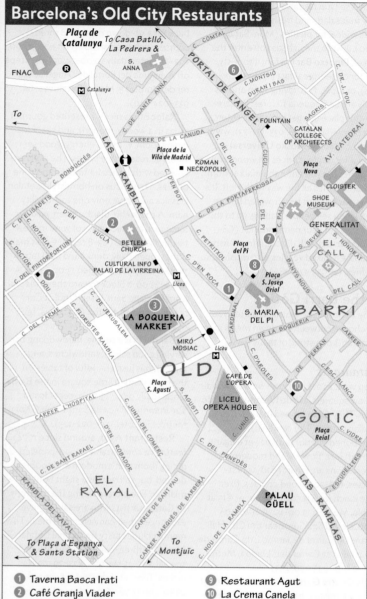

Barcelona's Old City Restaurants

1. Taverna Basca Irati
2. Café Granja Viader
3. La Boqueria Market Eateries
4. Biocenter Veggie Restaurant
5. Café de l'Academia
6. Els Quatre Gats
7. Xaloc
8. Bar del Pi
9. Restaurant Agut
10. La Crema Canela
11. Carrer de la Mercè Tapas
12. Sagardi Euskal Taberna
13. El Xampanyet
14. Bar del Pla
15. Mercat Princesa Food Circus

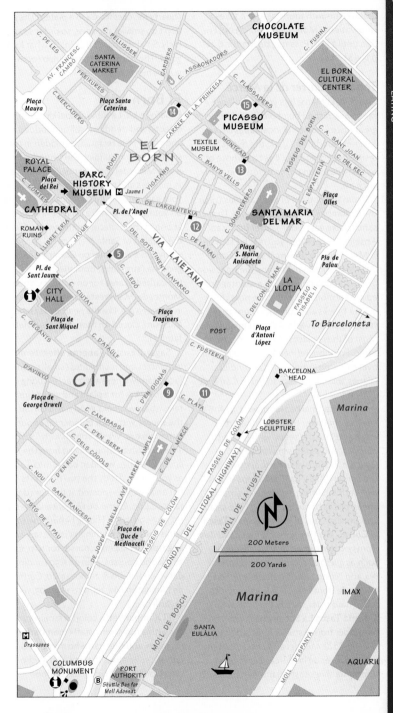

are overrun with tourists. And it takes reservations (Mon-Thu 13:00-23:00, Fri-Sun until 23:30, Passatge de Madoz 6, tel. 933-182-744).

Tapas on Carrer de la Mercè

Carrer de la Mercè lets you experience a rare, unvarnished bit of old Barcelona with great *tascas*—colorful local tapas bars. The neighborhood's dark, the regulars are rough-edged, and you'll get a glimpse of a crusty Barcelona from before the affluence hit.

From the bottom of the Ramblas (near the Columbus Monument, Metro: Drassanes), hike east along Carrer de Josep Anselm Clavé. When you reach Plaça de la Mercè, follow the small street (Carrer de la Mercè) that runs along the right side of the square's church. For a montage of edible memories, wander the next three or four blocks and consider these spots, stopping wherever looks most inviting. Most of these places close down around 23:00. For more refined bar-hopping, skip over to Carrer Ample and Carrer d'En Gignàs, inland streets parallel to Carrer de la Mercè.

Bar Celta (marked *la pulpería*, at #16) has less character than the others, but eases you into the scene with fried fish, octopus, and *patatas bravas*, all with Galician Ribeiro wine. Farther down at the corner (#28), **La Plata** keeps things wonderfully simple, serving extremely cheap plates of sardines (€3), little salads, and small glasses of keg wine (€1). **Tasca el Corral** (#17) serves mountain favorites from northern Spain by the half-*ración*, such as *queso de cabrales*, chorizo *al diablo*, and *cecina* (cured meat, like *jamón* but made from beef)—drink them with *sidra* (hard cider sold by the bottle-€6). **Sidrería Tasca La Socarrena** (#21) offers hard cider from Asturias in €6.50 bottles with *queso de cabrales* and chorizo. At the end of Carrer de la Mercè, **Cervecería Vendimia** slings tasty clams and mussels

(hearty *raciones* for €4-6 a plate). They don't do smaller portions, so order sparingly. Sit at the bar and point to what looks good. The house specialty, *pulpo* (octopus) is more expensive.

El Born

El Born (a.k.a. La Ribera) sparkles with eclectic and trendy as well as subdued and classy little restaurants hidden in the small lanes surrounding the Church of Santa Maria del Mar. Wander around for 15 minutes and pick the place that tickles your gastronomic fancy. Consider starting off your evening with a glass of fine wine at one of the *enotecas* on the square facing the Church of Santa Maria del Mar. Most of my picks are either on Carrer de l'Argenteria (stretching from the church to the cathedral area) or on or near Carrer de Montcada. Many restaurants and shops in this area are, like the nearby Picasso Museum, closed on Mondays. Use Metro: Jaume I.

Sagardi Euskal Taberna offers tempting *pintxos* and *montaditos* (small open-faced sandwiches) at €2 each—along its huge bar. Ask for a plate and graze (just take whatever looks good). You can sit on the square with your plunder for about 20 percent extra. Wash it down with Txakolí, a Basque white wine poured from the spout of a huge wooden barrel into a glass as you watch. Study the two price lists—bar and terrace—posted at the bar (daily 12:00-24:00, Carrer de l'Argenteria 62-64, tel. 933-199-993). Hiding behind the tapas bar is the mod and minimalist restaurant, **Sagardi** (€11-24 first courses for two, €20-28 second courses, plan on €50 for dinner; daily 13:00-16:00 & 20:00-24:00, Carrer de l'Argenteria 62, tel. 933-199-993, www.sagardi.com).

El Xampanyet, a colorful family-run bar with a fun-loving staff (Juan Carlos, his mom, and the man who may be his father), specializes in tapas and anchovies. Don't be put off by the seafood

Catalan Cuisine

Like its culture and language, Catalan food is a fusion of styles and influences. Cod, hake, tuna, squid, and anchovies appear on many menus, and you'll see Catalan favorites such as *fideuà,* a thin, flavor-infused noodle served with seafood—a kind of Catalan paella—and *arròs negre,* black rice cooked in squid ink. *Pa amb tomàquet* is the classic Catalan way to eat your bread—toasted white bread with olive oil, tomato, and a pinch of salt. It's often served with tapas and used to make sandwiches. As everywhere in Spain, Catalan cooks love garlic and olive oil—many dishes are soaked in both.

Catalan cuisine can be heavy for Americans more accustomed to salads, fruits, and grains. A few perfectly good vegetarian and lighter options exist, but you'll have to seek them out. The secret to getting your veggies at restaurants is to order two courses, because the first course generally has a green option. Resist the cheese-and-ham appetizers and instead choose first-course menu items such as creamed vegetable soup, *parrillada de verduras* (sautéed vegetables), or *ensalada mixta.* (Spaniards rarely eat only a salad, so salads tend to be small and simple—just iceberg lettuce, tomatoes, and maybe olives and tuna.)

While the famous cured *jamón* (ham) is not as typically Catalan as it is Spanish, you'll still find lots of it in Catalunya. Another popular Spanish dish is the empanada—a pastry turnover filled with seasoned meat and vegetables. The cheapest meal is a simple *bocadillo de jamón* (ham sandwich on a baguette), sold virtually everywhere.

from a tin: Catalans like it this way. A *sortido* (assorted plate) of *carne* (meat) or *pescado* (fish) with *pa amb tomàquet* makes for a fun meal. It's filled with tourists during the day, but is a local favorite after dark. The scene is great, but it can be tough without Spanish skills. Plan on spending €25 for a meal with wine (same price at bar or table, Tue-Sat 12:00-15:30 & 19:00-23:00, Sun 12:00-16:00, closed Mon, a half-block beyond the Picasso Museum at Carrer de Montcada 22, tel. 933-197-003).

Local favorite **Bar del Pla** is near the Picasso Museum but far enough away from the tourist crowds. Overlooking a tiny crossroads next to Barcelona's oldest church, this brightly lit, classic diner serves traditional Catalan dishes, *raciones,* and tapas. Crispy beef with foie gras (€6) is a highlight. The local IPA on tap is a change of pace from regular Spanish beer. Prices are the same at the bar or at a table, but eating at the bar puts you in the middle of a great scene (€6-15 tapas, Mon-Sat 12:00-23:00, closed Sun; with your back to the Picasso Museum, head right two blocks past Carrer de la Princesa to Carrer de Montcada 2; tel. 932-683-003, www. bardelpla.cat).

Corporate venture **Mercat Princesa Food Circus** fills an old palace with a hive of trendy new bars and eateries sharing a central zone of tables. The energy is great, as is the variety: oysters, sushi, paella, and pizza. It's fun to simply explore, but at busy times, expect to wait in successive slow-moving lines (daily 12:30-24:00, behind the Picasso Museum, Carrer dels Flassaders 21, tel. 932-681-518, www.mercatprincesa.com).

In the Eixample

The people-packed boulevards of the Eixample are lined with appetizing eateries featuring breezy outdoor seating. For the best variety, walk down Rambla de Catalunya.

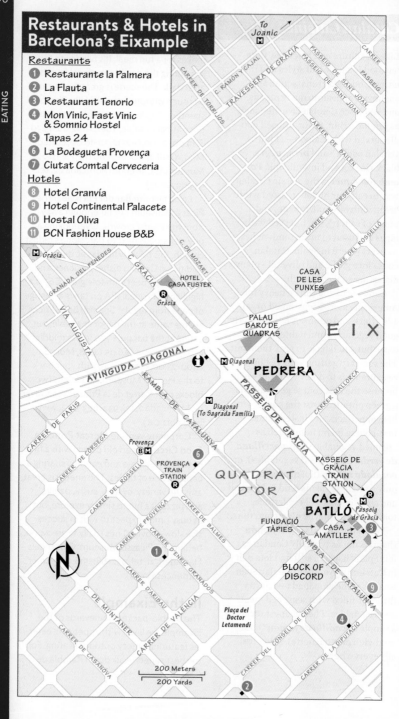

Restaurants & Hotels in Barcelona's Eixample

Restaurants
1. Restaurante la Palmera
2. La Flauta
3. Restaurant Tenorio
4. Mon Vinic, Fast Vinic & Somnio Hostel
5. Tapas 24
6. La Bodegueta Provença
7. Ciutat Comtal Cerveceria

Hotels
8. Hotel Granvía
9. Hotel Continental Palacete
10. Hostal Oliva
11. BCN Fashion House B&B

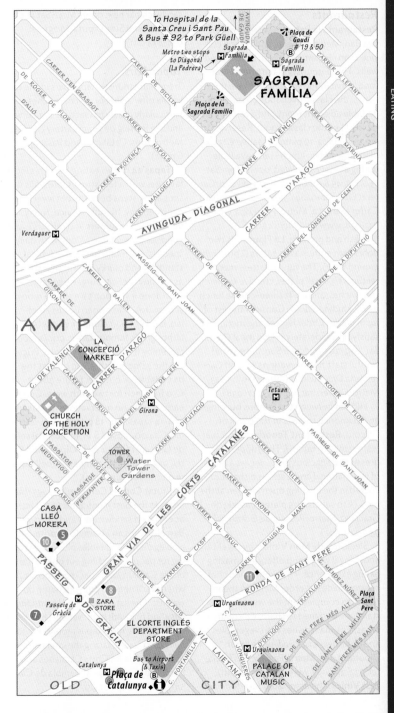

To Hospital de la
Santa Creu i Sant Pau
& Bus # 92 to Park Güell

Metro two stops
to Diagonal
(La Pedrera)

AVINGUDA DE GAUDÍ

Plaça de
Gaudí

19 & 50

Sagrada
Família

Sagrada
Família

SAGRADA
FAMÍLIA

Plaça de la
Sagrada Família

CARRER DE L'IFANT

CARRER D'EN GRASSOT

CARRER DE SICILIA

CARRER DE MALLORCA

CARRER DE NÀPOLS

CARRER PROVENÇA

CARRER DE VALÈNCIA

CARRER DE LA MARINA

DE ROGER DE FLOR

DALIÓ

Verdaguer

AVINGUDA DIAGONAL

CARRER D'ARAGÓ

CARRER DEL CONSELL DE CENT

PASSEIG DE SANT JOAN

CARRER DE BAILEN

CARRER DE ROGER DE FLOR

CARRER DE GIRONA

CARRER DE LA DIPUTACIÓ

A M P L E

LA
CONCEPCIÓ
MARKET

C. DE VALÈNCIA

CARRER D'ARAGÓ

CARRER DEL BRUC

CARRER DEL CONSELL DE CENT

Girona

CARRER DE DIPUTACIÓ

Tetuan

CARRER DE ROGER DE FLOR

PASSEIG DE SANT JOAN

CHURCH
OF THE HOLY
CONCEPTION

PASSATGE
MEDEZVIGO

C. DE PAU CLARIS

PASSATGE PERMANYER DE LLÚRIA

PASSATGE DE ROGER DE LLÚRIA

TOWER
Water
Tower
Gardens

GRAN VIA DE LES CORTS CATALANES

CARRER DEL BRUC

CARRER DE CASP

CARRER DE GIRONA

CARRER DEL BAILEN

CARRER D'AUSIÀS MARC

CASA
LLEÓ
MORERA

10

5

8

ZARA
STORE

PASSEIG DE GRÀCIA

CARRER DE PAU CLARIS

11

RONDA DE SANT PERE

C. MÉNDEZ NÚÑEZ

Plaça
Sant
Pere

7

Passeig de
Gràcia

Urquinaona

CARRER DE TRAFALGAR

EL CORTE INGLÉS
DEPARTMENT
STORE

VIA LAIETANA

Urquinaona

C. DE SANT PERE MÉS ALT

C. DE SANT PERE MÉS BAIX

Catalunya

Plaça de
Catalunya

Bus to Airport
(& Taxis)

C. FONTANELLA

VIA LES JONQUERES

D'ORTIGOSA

PALACE OF
CATALAN
MUSIC

OLD

CITY

Restaurants

Restaurante la Palmera serves a mix of Catalan, Mediterranean, and French cuisine in an elegant room with bottle-lined walls. This untouristy place offers great food, service, and value. They have three zones: the classic main room, a more forgettable adjacent room, and a few outdoor tables. I like the classic room. Reservations are smart (€12-19 plates, creative €23 six-plate *degustation* lunch—also available during dinner Mon-Wed, open Mon-Sat 13:00-15:45 & 20:00-23:15, closed Sun, Carrer d'Enric Granados 57, at the corner with Carrer Mallorca, Metro: Provença, tel. 934-532-338, www.lapalmera.cat).

Fresh and modern, **La Flauta** fills two floors with enthusiastic eaters (I prefer the ground floor). The fun, no-stress menu features €5 small plates, creative €5 *flauta* sandwiches, and a €13 three-course lunch deal including a drink. Consider the list of *tapas del día*. Order high on the menu for a satisfying, moderately priced meal (Mon-Sat 7:00-24:00, closed Sun, upbeat and helpful staff, no reservations, just off Carrer de la Diputació at Carrer d'Aribau 23, Metro: Universitat, tel. 933-237-038).

Hidden between the famous buildings and clamoring tourists in the Block of Discord, **Restaurant Tenorio** is an actual restaurant (no tapas!). This modern, dressy, and spacious place serves a mix of international and Catalan dishes, concocted in the bustling open kitchen at the back (€10 salads, €15 plates, Passeig de Gràcia 37, Metro: Passeig de Gràcia, tel. 932-720-592).

Sleek, trendy **Mon Vinic** is evangelical about local wines and offers an amazing eating experience. Their renowned chef creates made-to-order Mediterranean dishes to complement the wine (€12-18 starters—designed to share, €8 creative tapas, €25 main dishes with vegetables and potatoes, €20 fixed-price lunch, Diputació 249, Metro: Passeig de Gràcia, tel. 932-726-187, www.monvinic.com). **Fast Vinic** is the associated fast-food and sandwich bar next door (Mon-Sat 12:00-24:00, closed Sun, Diputació 251, tel. 934-873-241).

Tapas Bars

Trendy and touristic tapas bars in the Eixample offer a cheery welcome. These are particularly handy to Plaça de Catalunya and the Passeig de Gràcia artery (closest Metro stops: Catalunya and Passeig de Gràcia).

Tapas 24 makes eating fun. This local favorite, with a few street tables, fills a spot a few steps below street level with happy energy, friendly service, funky decor (white counters and mirrors), and good yet pricey tapas. Along with daily specials, the menu has all the typical standbys and quirky inventions (such as the tiny McFoie burger—order it well-done if you don't want it to moo on your plate). The owner, Carles Abellan, is one of Barcelona's hot chefs; although his famous fare is pricey, you can enjoy it without going broke. Prices are the same whether you dine at the bar, a table, or outside. Figure about €50 for lunch for two with wine. Come early or wait; no reservations are taken (€4-14 tapas, €12-18 plates, Mon-Sat 9:00-24:00, closed Sun, just off Passeig de Gràcia at Carrer de la Diputació 269, tel. 934-880-977, www.carlesabellan.es/restaurantes-tapas-24).

Ciutat Comtal Cerveceria brags that it serves the best *montaditos* (€2-4 little open-faced sandwiches) and beers in Barcelona. It's an Eixample favorite, with an elegant bar and tables plus good seating for people-watching out on the Rambla de Catalunya. It's packed 21:00-23:00, when you'll need to put your name on a wait list. The list of tapas and *montaditos* is easy and fun, with great variety (including daily specials, most tapas around €4-10, daily 8:00-24:00, facing the intersection of Gran Via de les Corts Catalanes and Rambla de Catalunya at Rambla de Catalunya 18, tel. 933-181-997).

SLEEPING

Although Barcelona is Spain's most expensive city, it still has reasonably priced rooms. Book well in advance. Cheap places are more crowded in summer. Business-class hotels fill up in winter and offer discounts in summer (and on weekends)—when you can often get modern comfort in a centrally located business hotel for about the same price (€100) as you'll pay for ramshackle charm.

Near Plaça de Catalunya

These hotels are on big streets within two blocks of Barcelona's exuberant central square, where the Old City meets the Eixample. Expect shiny reception areas, modern bedrooms, and air-conditioning. As business-class hotels, they have hard-to-pin-down prices that fluctuate with demand. I've listed the average rate you'll pay. Most of these are located between two Metro stops: Catalunya and Universitat; if arriving by Aerobus, note that the bus stops at both places. For hotels on busy Carrer Pelai, request a quieter room in back.

$$$ Hotel Catalonia Plaça Catalunya has four stars, an elegant old entryway with a modern reception area, splashy public

spaces, slick marble and hardwood floors, 140 comfortable but simple rooms, and a garden courtyard with a pool a world away from the big-city noise (Db-€200 but can swing much higher or lower with demand, extra bed-€38, breakfast-€19, air-con, elevator, a half-block off Plaça de Catalunya at Carrer de Bergara 11, Metro: Catalunya, tel. 933-015-151, www.hoteles-catalonia.com, catalunya@hoteles-catalonia.es).

$$ Hotel Denit is a small, stylish, 36-room hotel on a pedestrian street two blocks off Plaça de Catalunya. It's chic, minimalist, and fun: Guidebook tips decorate the halls, and the rooms are sized like T-shirts ("small" Sb-€79-109, "medium" Db-€99-119, "large" Db-€119-144, "XL" Db-€149-164, more on Fri-Sat, includes breakfast when you book directly with the hotel, air-con, elevator, Carrer d'Estruc 24, Metro: Catalunya, tel. 935-454-000, www.denit.com, info@denit.com).

$$ Hotel Inglaterra has 60 rooms, a more traditional style, a rooftop terrace, and mini swimming pool (Sb-€119, Db-€139, higher rates Fri-Sat, €20-40 more for bigger "deluxe" rooms, breakfast €15, air-con, elevator, Carrer de Pelai 14, Metro: Universitat, tel. 935-051-100, www.hotel-inglaterra.com, reservas@hotel-inglaterra.com).

$$ Hotel Reding, on a quiet street a 10-minute walk west of the Ramblas and Plaça de Catalunya action, is slick and sleek, renting 44 mod rooms at a reasonable price (Db-€130, €15-30 more for deluxe rooms, extra bed-€33, €15 breakfast, prices go up during trade fairs, air-con, elevator, Carrer de Gravina 5, Metro: Universitat, tel. 934-121-097, www.hotelreding.com, recepcion@hotelreding.com).

$$ Hotel Lleó (YAH-oh) is well-run, with 92 big, bright, and comfortable rooms; a great breakfast room; a generous lounge; and a small rooftop pool (Db-€140 but varies with demand, extra bed-about €30, breakfast-€13, air-con, elevator, Carrer de Pelai 22, midway between

Sleep Code

Price Rankings for Double Rooms (Db)

$$$ Most rooms €150 or more
$$ €100-150
$ €100 or less

Abbreviations: Db=Double with bathroom. D=Double with bathroom down the hall

   Notes: Hotels charge a mandatory 10 percent IVA room tax. Room prices change; verify rates online or by email. For the best prices, book directly with the hotel.

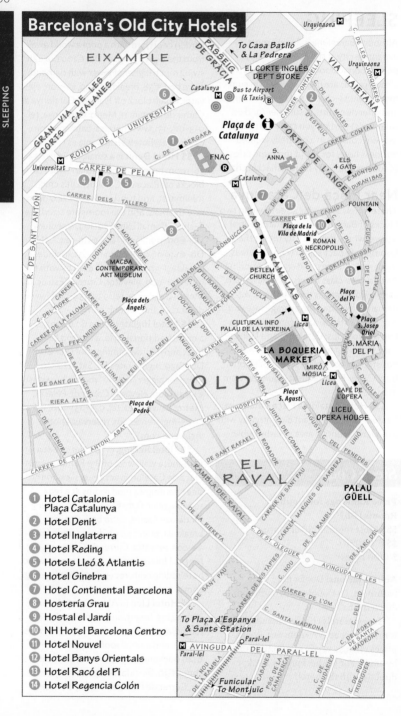

Barcelona's Old City Hotels

1 Hotel Catalonia Plaça Catalunya
2 Hotel Denit
3 Hotel Inglaterra
4 Hotel Reding
5 Hotels Lleó & Atlantis
6 Hotel Ginebra
7 Hotel Continental Barcelona
8 Hostería Grau
9 Hostal el Jardí
10 NH Hotel Barcelona Centro
11 Hotel Nouvel
12 Hotel Banys Orientals
13 Hotel Racó del Pi
14 Hotel Regencia Colón

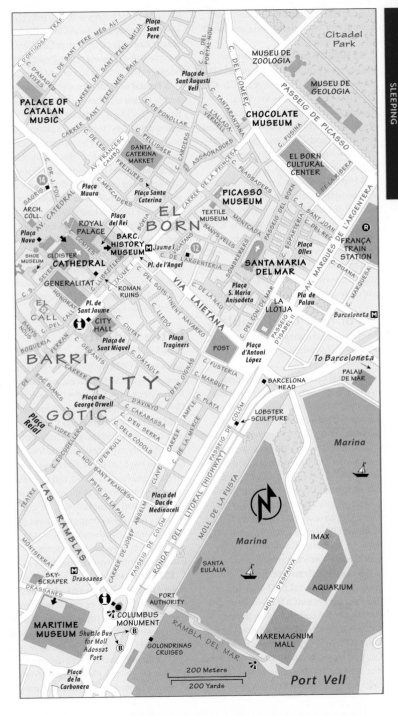

C. D'ORTIGOSA TRAF.

C. DE SANT PERE MÉS ALT

C. D'AMADEU VIVES

C. DE SANT PERE MÉS BAIX

CARRER SANT PERE MÉS BAIX

Plaça Sant Pere

C. D. DEL PORTAL-NOU

C. DEL COMERÇ

Citadel Park

MUSEU DE ZOOLOGIA

MUSEU DE GEOLOGIA

PASSEIG DE PICASSO

Plaça de Sant Augustí Vell

C. TANTARANTANA

C. L'ALLADA VERMELL

PALACE OF CATALAN MUSIC

C. DE FONOLLAR

CHOCOLATE MUSEUM

C. FUSINA

CARRER SANT PERE MÉS BAIX

C. DE LES

C. DE FRANCESC CAMBO

C. PELLISSER

C. CADERS

C. ASSAONADORS

AV. FRANCESC CAMBO

SANTA CATERINA MARKET

FREIXURES

EL BORN CULTURAL CENTER

C. DE LA RIBERA

C. DR.J. POU

SAGRIS.

Plaça Maura

C. MERCADERS

Plaça Santa Caterina

C. DE LA PRINCESA

C. FLASSADERS

PICASSO MUSEUM

PASSEIG DEL BORN

C. DE SANT JOAN

C. SANT ANTONI

A. DEL REC

C. DE L'ARGENTERA

ARCH. COLL.

AV. CATEDRAL

Plaça del Rei

BORIA

EL BORN

C. CARDERS

MONTCADA

TEXTILE MUSEUM

C. ESPARTERIA

Plaça Olles

FRANÇA TRAIN STATION

Plaça Nova

ROYAL PALACE

BARC. HISTORY MUSEUM

C. COMTES

Jaume I

BANYS VELLS

SOMBRERERS

C. DE MAR

SANTA MARIA DEL MAR

AV. MARQUES

C. DUANA

C. MARQUESA

SHOE MUSEUM

CLOISTER

CATHEDRAL

C. LLIBRETERIA

C. DE L'ARGENTERIA

Pl. de l'Angel

VIA LAIETANA

Plaça S. Maria Anisadeta

LA LLOTJA

Pla de Palau

Barceloneta

GENERALITAT

C. SEVERI

C. S. HONORAT

ROMAN RUINS

C. DEL SOTS-TINENT NAVARRO

C. DE LA NAU

PASSEIG D'ISABEL II

EL CALL

BANYS NOUS

Pl. de Sant Jaume

JAUME I

C. CIUTAT

C. LLEDO

POST

Plaça d'Antoni López

To Barceloneta

PALAU DE MAR

CITY HALL

BOQUERIA

FERRAN

C. GEGANTS

Plaça de Sant Miquel

C. DATAÜF

Plaça Traginers

C. FUSTERIA

BARCELONA HEAD

BARRI

C. ESC. BLANCS

CARRER

CITY

D'AVINYÓ

C. D'EN GIGNAS

C. MARQUET

LOBSTER SCULPTURE

Marina

GÒTIC

Plaça de George Orwell

C. CARABASSA

C. D'EN SERRA

C. DELS CODOLS

AMPLE

C. PLATA

PASSEIG DE COLOM

Plaça Reial

C. VIDRE

C. ESCUDELLERS

C. D'EN RULL

C. NOU SANT FRANCESC

CLAVE

C. DE LA MERCE

RONDA DEL LITORAL (HIGHWAY)

MOLL DE LA FUSTA

Marina

IMAX

TEATRE

LAS RAMBLAS

MÒNTSERRAT

PSTG. DE LA PAU

Plaça del Duc de Medinaceli

CARRER DE JOSEP ANSELM

PASSEIG DE COLOM

SANTA EULÀLIA

MOLL D'ESPANYA

AQUARIUM

SKY-SCRAPER

Drassanes

DRASSANES

PORT AUTHORITY

N

COLUMBUS MONUMENT

RAMBLA DEL MAR

MAREMAGNUM MALL

MARITIME MUSEUM

Shuttle Bus for Moll Adossat Port

B

B

GOLONDRINAS CRUISES

Plaça de la Carbonera

200 Meters

200 Yards

Port Vell

Metros: Universitat and Catalunya, tel. 933-181-312, www.hotel-lleo.com, info@hotel-lleo.com).

$$ Hotel Atlantis is solid, with 50 big, nondescript, modern rooms and fair prices for the location (Sb-€80, Db-€120, Tb-€150, check website for deals, includes breakfast, air-con, elevator, Carrer de Pelai 20, midway between Metros: Universitat and Catalunya, tel. 933-189-012, www.hotelatlantis-bcn.com, inf@hotelatlantis-bcn.com).

$ Hotel Ginebra is a modern, fresh version of the old-school *pension* in a classic, well-located building at the corner of Plaça Catalunya (Sb-€50-120, Db-€70-150, Tb-€80-180, Qb-€90-240, breakfast-€8, laundry, air-con, elevator, Rambla de Catalunya 1, Metro: Catalunya, tel. 932-502-017, www.barcelonahotelginebra.com, info@barcelonahotelginebra.com).

On or near the Ramblas

These places are generally family-run, with ad-lib furnishings, more character, and lower prices.

$$ Hotel Continental Barcelona, in a building overlooking the top of the Ramblas, has 40 comfortable but faded rooms that come with clashing carpets and wallpaper. Choose between your own little Ramblas-view balcony or a quieter back room. The free breakfast and all-day snack-and-drink bar are a plus (Sb-€110, Db-€130, twin Db-€140, Db with Ramblas balcony-€150, extra bed-€40/adult or €20/child, air-con, elevator, quiet terrace, Ramblas 138, Metro: Catalunya, tel. 933-012-570, www.hotelcontinental.com, barcelona@hotelcontinental.com).

$$ Hostería Grau is homey, family-run, and eco-conscious (LEED-certified). It has 24 cheery rooms a few blocks off the Ramblas in the colorful university district—but double-glazed windows keep it quiet (Db-€115-135, €20 more for superior Db, €50 more for family room, 5 percent discount for booking directly, breakfast extra, strict cancellation policy, air-con,

elevator, some rooms with balcony, 200 yards up Carrer dels Tallers from the Ramblas at Ramelleres 27, Metro: Catalunya, tel. 933-018-135, www.hostalgrau.com, bookgreen@hostalgrau.com, Monica).

$ Hostal el Jardí offers 40 tight, plain, comfy rooms on a breezy square in the Barri Gòtic. Many of the rooms come with petite balconies (for an extra charge) and enjoy an almost Parisian ambience. Book well in advance, as this family-run place has an avid following (small interior Db-€75, nicer interior Db-€90, outer Db with balcony or twin with window-€95, large outer Db with balcony or square-view terrace-€110, no charge for extra bed, breakfast-€6, air-con, elevator, some stairs, halfway between Ramblas and cathedral at Plaça Sant Josep Oriol 1, Metro: Liceu, tel. 933-015-900, www.eljardi-barcelona.com, reservations@eljardi-barcelona.com).

In the Old City

These accommodations are buried in Barcelona's Old City, mostly in the Barri Gòtic. The Catalunya, Liceu, and Jaume I Metro stops flank this tight tangle of lanes; I've noted which stops are best for each.

$$$ NH Hotel Barcelona Centro, with 156 rooms and tasteful chain-hotel predictability, is professional yet friendly, buried in the Barri Gòtic just three blocks off the Ramblas (Db-€160, but rates fluctuate with demand, €25 more for bigger superior rooms, breakfast-€15, air-con, elevator, pay guest computer, Carrer del Duc 15, Metro: Catalunya or Liceu, tel. 932-703-410, www.nh-hotels.com, barcelonacentro@nh-hotels.com).

$$$ Hotel Nouvel, in an elegant, Victorian-style building on a handy pedestrian street, offers more character than the others, boasting royal lounges and 78 comfy rooms (Sb-€75-100, Db-€110-165, online deals can be far cheaper, extra bed-€35, includes breakfast, €20 deposit for TV remote, air-con, elevator, pay Wi-Fi, Carrer de Santa Anna 20, Metro: Catalunya, tel. 933-018-274, www.hotelnouvel.com, info@hotelnouvel.com).

$$ Hotel Banys Orientals, a modern, boutique place, has refreshingly straightforward prices. Its 43 restful rooms are located in El Born on a pedestrianized street between the cathedral and Church of Santa Maria del Mar (Sb-€96, Db-€116, breakfast-€14, air-con, Carrer de l'Argenteria 37, 50 yards from Metro: Jaume I, tel. 932-688-460, www.hotelbanysorientals.com, reservas@hotelbanysorientals.com). They also run the adjacent, recommended El Senyor Parellada restaurant.

$$ Hotel Racó del Pi, part of the H10 hotel chain, is a quality, professional place with generous public spaces and 37 modern, bright, quiet rooms. It's located on a wonderful pedestrian street immersed in the Barri Gòtic (Db-often around €130-145, can be as low as €80, cheaper for booking "nonrefundable" online, breakfast-€16, air-con, around the corner from Plaça del Pi at Carrer del Pi 7, 3-minute walk from Metro: Liceu, tel. 933-426-190, www.h10hotels.com, h10.raco.delpi@h10.es).

$$ Hotel Regencia Colón, in a handy location one block in front of the cathedral, offers 50 slightly older but solid, classy, and well-priced rooms (Db-€120-155 but fluctuates with demand, extra bed-€37, breakfast-€13, air-con, elevator, Carrer dels Sagristans 13, Metro: Jaume I, tel. 933-189-858, www.hotelregenciacolon.com, info@hotelregenciacolon.com).

In the Eixample

For an uptown neighborhood, sleep in the Eixample, a 10-minute walk from the Ramblas action. Most of these places use the Passeig de Gràcia or Catalunya Metro stops. Because these stations are so huge—especially Passeig de Gràcia, which sprawls underground for a few blocks—study the maps posted in the station to establish which exit you want before surfacing.

$$ Hotel Granvía, filling a palatial, brightly renovated 1870s mansion, offers a large, peaceful sun patio, several comfortable common areas, and 58 spacious modern rooms (Sb-€75-185, Db-€90-180, superior Db-€105-225, family room-€150-260, breakfast €14, air-con, elevator, Gran Via de les Corts Catalanes 642, Metro: Passeig de Gràcia, tel. 933-181-900, www.hotelgranvia.com, hgranvia@nnhotels.com).

$$ Hotel Continental Palacete, with 22 small rooms, fills a 100-year-old chandeliered mansion. With flowery wallpaper and ornately gilded stucco, it's more gaudy than Gaudí, but it's also friendly, quiet, and well-located. Guests have unlimited access to the outdoor terrace and the fruit, veggie, and drink buffet (Sb-€114, Db-€153, €35-45 more for bigger and brighter view rooms, extra bed-€55/adult or €40/child, includes breakfast, air-con, 2 blocks northwest of Plaça de Catalunya at corner of Rambla de Catalunya and Carrer de la Diputació, Rambla de Catalunya 30, Metro: Passeig de Gràcia, tel. 934-457-657, www.hotelcontinental.com, palacete@hotelcontinental.com).

$ Hostal Oliva, family-run with care, has 15 spartan but bright and high-ceilinged rooms and no breakfast or public spaces. It's on the fourth floor of a classic old Eixample building in a perfect location, just a couple of blocks above Plaça de Catalunya (S-€41, Sb-€55, D-€71, Db-€95, elevator, corner of Passeig de Gràcia and Carrer de la Diputació, Passeig de Gràcia 32, Metro: Passeig de Gràcia, tel. 934-880-162, www.hostaloliva.com, hostaloliva@lasguias.com).

$ BCN Fashion House B&B has 10 basic rooms, a peaceful lounge, and a leafy backyard terrace on the first floor of a nondescript old building (S-€36-56, D-€56-83, bigger "veranda" D-€73-93, Db-€90-125, 2-night minimum, includes breakfast, between Carrer d'Ausiàs Marc and Ronda de Sant Pere at Carrer del Bruc 13, just steps from Metro: Urquinaona, mobile 637-904-044, www.bcnfashionhouse.com, info@bcnfashionhouse.com).

Hostels

$ Somnio Hostel, an innovative smaller place, has nine simple, clean rooms (S-€49-75, D-€57-84, Db-€65-99, air-con, self-service laundry, Carrer de la Diputació 251, second floor, Metro: Passeig de Gràcia, tel. 932-725-308, www. somniohostels.com, info@somniohostels. com). They have a second location that's five blocks farther out.

TRANSPORTATION

Getting Around Barcelona

Barcelona's Metro and bus system is run by **TMB**—Transports Metropolitans de Barcelona. Ask for TMB's excellent Metro/bus map at the TI, larger stations, or the TMB information counter in the Sants Train Station. Metro maps are often included on tourist maps as well (tel. 902-075-027, www.tmb.cat).

By Metro

The city's Metro, among Europe's best, connects just about every place you'll visit. A **single-ride ticket** (*bitllet senzill*) costs €2.15. The **T10 Card** is a great deal—€9.95 gives you 10 rides (cutting the per-ride cost more than in half). The card is shareable, even by companions traveling with you the entire ride (insert the card in the machine once per passenger). The back of your T10 Card will show how many trips were taken, with the time and date of each ride. One "ride" covers you for 1.25 hours of unlimited use on all Metro and local bus lines, as well as local rides on the RENFE and Rodalies de Catalunya train lines (including rides to the airport and train station) and the suburban FGC trains. Transfers made within your 1.25-hour limit are not counted as a new ride, but you still must revalidate your T10 Card whenever you transfer.

Multiday **"Hola BCN!" passes** are also available. Machines at the Metro entrance have English instructions and sell all types of tickets (€14/2 days, €20.50/3 days, €26.50/4 days, €32/5 days; most machines accept credit/debit cards as well as cash).

Enter the Metro by inserting your ticket into the turnstile (with the arrow pointing in), then reclaim it. Follow signs for your line and direction. On board, most trains have handy lighted displays that indicate upcoming stops. Because the lines cross one another multiple times, there can be several ways to make any one journey. (Keep a general map with you—especially if you're transferring.) Hang onto your ticket until you have exited the subway. You don't need the ticket to exit, but inspectors occasionally ask to see it. When riding the Metro, watch your valuables.

Barcelona has several color-coded lines. Most useful for tourists and pickpockets is the **L3 (green)** line, with handy city-center stops:

Sants Estació—Main train station

Espanya—Plaça d'Espanya, with access to the lower part of Montjuïc and trains to Montserrat

Paral-lel—Funicular to the top of Montjuïc

Drassanes—Bottom of the Ramblas, near Maritime Museum and Maremagnum mall

Liceu—Middle of the Ramblas, near the heart of the Barri Gòtic and cathedral

Plaça de Catalunya—Top of the Ramblas and main square with TI, airport bus, and lots of transportation connections

Passeig de Gràcia—Classy Eixample street at the Block of Discord; also connection to L2 (purple) line to Sagrada Família and L4 (yellow) line (described below)

Diagonal—Gaudí's La Pedrera

The **L4 (yellow)** line, which crosses the L3 (green) line at Passeig de Gràcia, is also useful. Helpful stops include **Joanic** (bus #116 to Park Güell), **Jaume I** (between the Barri Gòtic/cathedral and El Born/Picasso Museum), and **Barceloneta** (at the south end of El Born, near the harbor action).

By Bus

Given the excellent Metro service, it's unlikely you'll spend much time on buses. Buses are useful for reaching Park Güell, connecting the sights on Montjuïc, and getting to the beach (also €2.15, covered by T10 Card, insert ticket in machine behind driver).

Also consider using the hop-on, hop-off Bus Turístic for transportation; it's far pricier than public transit, but it stops at the main sights (see page 329).

By Taxi

Barcelona is one of Europe's best taxi towns. Taxis are plentiful and honest. The light on top shows which tariff they're charging; a **green light** on the roof indicates that a taxi is available. **Cab rates** are reasonable (€2.10 drop charge, about €1/ kilometer, these "Tarif 2" rates are in effect 8:00-20:00, pay higher "Tarif 1" rates off-hours, €2.10 surcharge to/from train station, €3.10 surcharge for airport or cruise port, other fees posted in window). Figure €10 from Ramblas to Sants Station.

Arriving and Departing
By Plane

Most international flights arrive at **El Prat de Llobregat Airport,** eight miles southwest of town. Some budget airlines, including Ryanair, fly into **Girona-Costa Brava Airport,** 60 miles north of Barcelona near Girona.

EL PRAT DE LLOBREGAT AIRPORT

Barcelona's **El Prat de Llobregat Airport** is eight miles southwest of town (airport code: BCN, info tel. 913-211-000, www. aena-aeropuertos.es). Its two large terminals are linked by shuttle buses. **Terminal 1** serves Air France, Air Europa, American, British Airways, Delta, Iberia, Lufthansa, United, US Airways, Vueling, and others. EasyJet and minor airlines use the older **Terminal 2,** which is divided into sections A, B, and C.

Terminal 1 and the bigger sections of

Terminal 2 (A and B) each have a post office, a pharmacy, a left-luggage office, plenty of good cafeterias in the gate areas, and ATMs—use the bank-affiliated ATMs in the arrivals hall.

Getting Downtown: To reach central Barcelona cheaply and quickly, take the bus or train (about 30 minutes on either).

The **Aerobus** (#A1 and #A2, corresponding with Terminals 1 and 2) stops immediately outside the arrivals lobby of both terminals (and in each section of Terminal 2). In about 30 minutes, it takes you downtown, where it makes several stops, including Plaça d'Espanya and Plaça de Catalunya—near many of my recommended hotels (departs every 5 minutes, from airport 6:00-1:00 in the morning, from downtown 5:30-24:15, €5.90 one-way, €10.20 round-trip, buy ticket from machine or from driver, tel. 934-156-020, www.aerobusbcn.com).

The **RENFE train** (on the "R2 Sud" Rodalies line) leaves from Terminal 2 and involves more walking. Head down the long orange-roofed overpass between sections A and B to reach the station (2/ hour at about :08 and :38 past the hour, 20 minutes to Sants Station, 25 minutes to Passeig de Gràcia Station—near Plaça de Catalunya and many recommended hotels, 30 minutes to França Station; €4.10 or covered by T10 Card). If you are arriving or departing from Terminal 1, you will have to use the airport shuttle bus to connect with the train station, so leave extra time.

A **taxi** between the airport and downtown costs about €35 (including €3.10 airport supplement). For good service, you can round up to the next euro on the fare—but keep in mind that the Spanish don't tip cabbies.

GIRONA-COSTA BRAVA AIRPORT

Some budget airlines, including Ryanair, use **Girona-Costa Brava Airport,** located 60 miles north of Barcelona near Girona (airport code: GRO, tel. 972-186-600, www.aena-aeropuertos.es). Ryanair runs

Barcelona's Public Transportation

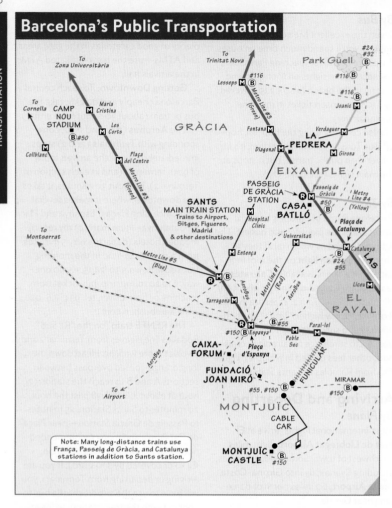

Note: Many long-distance trains use França, Passeig de Gràcia, and Catalunya stations in addition to Sants station.

a **bus,** operated by Sagalés, to the Barcelona Nord bus station (€16, departs airport about 20-25 minutes after each arriving flight, 1.5 hours, tel. 902-361-550, www. sagales.com). You can also take a Sagalés bus (hourly, 25 minutes, €2.75) or a taxi (€25) to the town of Girona, then catch a train to Barcelona (at least hourly, 1.5 hours, €15-20). A taxi between the Girona airport and Barcelona costs at least €120.

By Train

Virtually all trains arrive at Barcelona's Sants Train Station, west of the Old City. AVE trains from Madrid go only to Sants Station. But many trains also pass through other stations en route, such as França Station (between the El Born and Barceloneta neighborhoods), or the downtown Passeig de Gràcia or Plaça de Catalunya stations (which are also Metro stops—and close to most of my recommended hotels). Ask the conductor where your train stops and get off at the station most convenient to your hotel.

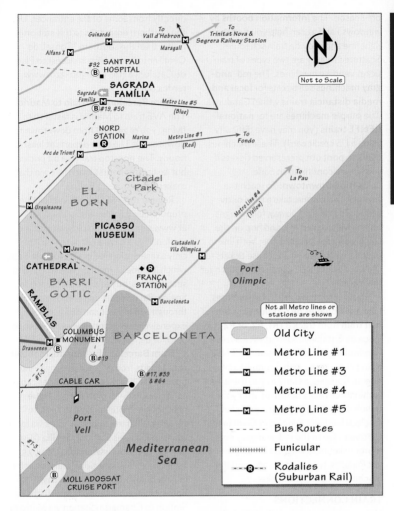

To
Vall d'Hebron
To
Trinitat Nova &
Segrera Railway Station

Guinardó

Maragall

Alfans X Ⓜ

#92 Ⓑ SANT PAU
HOSPITAL

SAGRADA
FAMÍLIA

Sagrada
Família
Ⓑ #19, #50

Metro Line #5
(Blue)

NORD
STATION
■Ⓡ

Marina Ⓜ

Metro Line #1
(Red)

To
Fondo

Arc de Triomf Ⓜ

Citadel
Park

EL
BORN

To
La Pau

Ⓜ Urquinaona

Metro Line #4
(Yellow)

PICASSO
MUSEUM

Ⓜ Jaume I

Ciutadella /
Vila Olimpica Ⓜ

CATHEDRAL

Port
Olimpic

BARRI
GÒTIC

Ⓡ
FRANÇA
STATION

RAMBLAS

Ⓜ Barceloneta

Not all Metro lines or
stations are shown

COLUMBUS
MONUMENT

BARCELONETA

Drassenes Ⓜ Ⓑ

Ⓑ #19

Ⓑ #17, #39
& #64

CABLE CAR ●

Port
Vell

Mediterranean
Sea

#T-3

Ⓑ MOLL ADOSSAT
CRUISE PORT

	Old City
—Ⓜ—	Metro Line #1
—Ⓜ—	Metro Line #3
—Ⓜ—	Metro Line #4
—Ⓜ—	Metro Line #5
- - - - -	Bus Routes
┅┅┅┅┅	Funicular
--Ⓡ--	Rodalies (Suburban Rail)

Not to Scale

SANTS TRAIN STATION

Barcelona's main **Sants Train Station** is vast and sprawling, but manageable. In the large lobby area under the upper tracks, you'll find a TI, ATMs, handy shops and eateries, car-rental kiosks, and, in the side concourse, a classy, quiet Sala Club lounge for travelers with first-class reservations (TV, free drinks, coffee bar). Sants is the only Barcelona station with **luggage storage** (big bag–€5.20/day, requires security check, daily 5:30-23:00, follow signs to *consigna*, at far end of hallway

from tracks 13-14).

In the vast main hall is a long wall of ticket windows. Figure out which one you need before you wait in line. Generally, **windows 1-7** (on the left) are for **local commuter** and **media distancia trains,** such as to Sitges. **Windows 8-21** handle advance tickets for **long-distance *(larga distancia)* trains** beyond Catalunya. **Windows 22-26** offer **general information**. **Windows 27-31** sell tickets for **long-distance trains** leaving today. These window assignments can shift during the off-season. The **information booths** by windows 1 and 21 can help you find the right line and provide train schedules. Scattered nearby are two types of train-ticket vending machines. The **red-and-gray machines** sell tickets for **local and media distancia trains** within Catalunya. The **purple machines** are for **national RENFE trains** (you may have difficulty using a US credit card). These machines can also print out prereserved tickets if you have a confirmation code.

Getting Downtown: To reach the center of Barcelona, take a train or the Metro. To ride the subway, follow signs for the **Metro (red M),** and hop on the **L3 (green)** or **L5 (blue)** line; both link to useful points in town. Purchase tickets for the Metro at touch-screen machines near the tracks.

To zip downtown in just five minutes, take any **Rodalies de Catalunya suburban train** from **track 8 (R1, R3, or R4)** to Plaça de Catalunya (departs at least every 10 minutes). Your long-distance RENFE train ticket comes with a complimentary ride on Rodalies, as long as you use it within three hours before or after your travels. Look for a code on your ticket labeled *Combinat Rodalies* or *Combinado Cercanías.* Go to the red-and-gray commuter ticket machines, touch *Combinat Rodalies,* type in your code, and the machine will print your ticket.

TRAIN CONNECTIONS

Unless otherwise noted, all of the following trains depart from Sants Station; however, remember that some trains also stop at other stations more convenient to the downtown tourist zone: França Station, Passeig de Gràcia, or Plaça de Catalunya. If your train stops at these stations, you can board there, saving yourself the trip to Sants.

If departing from the downtown Passeig de Gràcia Station, where three Metro lines converge with the rail line, you might find the underground tunnels confusing. You can't access the RENFE station

directly from some of the entrances. Use the northern entrances to this station—rather than the southern "Consell de Cent" entrance, which is closest to Plaça de Catalunya (tel. 902-320-320, www.renfe.com).

From Barcelona by Train to Madrid: The AVE train to Madrid is faster than flying (you're zipping from downtown to downtown). The train departs at least hourly. The nonstop train is a bit pricier but faster (2.5 hours) than the train that makes a few stops (3 hours).

Regular reserved AVE tickets can be prepurchased (often with a discount) at www.renfe.com and picked up at the station. If you have a rail pass, you'll pay only a reservation fee of €23 for first class, which includes a meal on weekdays (€10 second class, buy at any train station in Spain). Passholders can't reserve online through RENFE but can make a more expensive reservation at www.raileurope.com for delivery before leaving the US.

From Barcelona by Train to: Montserrat (departs from Plaça d'Espanya—*not* from Sants, hourly, 1 hour, includes cable car or rack train to monastery); **Figueres** (hourly, 1 hour via AVE or Alvia to Figueres-Vilafant; hourly, 2 hours via local trains to Figueres Station); **Sevilla** (8-9/day, 5.5-6.5 hours); **Granada** (1/day, 7.5 hours via AVE and regional train, transfer in Antequera); **Salamanca** (8/day, 6-7.5 hours, change in Madrid from Atocha Station to Chamartín Station via Metro or *cercanías* train; also 1/day with a change in Valladolid, 8.5 hours); **San Sebastián** (2/day, 5.5-6 hours).

By Bus

Most buses depart from the Nord bus station at Metro: Arc de Triomf, but confirm when researching schedules (www.barcelonanord.com). Destinations served by Alsa buses (tel. 902-422-242, www.alsa.es) include **Madrid** and **Madrid's Barajas Airport** (nearly hourly, 8 hours), and **Salamanca** (2/day, 11 hours). Sarfa buses (tel. 902-302-025, www.sarfa.com) serve many **coastal resorts,** including **Cadaqués** (2-3/day, 3 hours).

The Mon-Bus leaves from the university and Plaça d'Espanya in downtown Barcelona to **Sitges** (4/day, 1 hour, www.monbus.cat). One bus departs daily for the **Montserrat** monastery, leaving from Carrer de Viriat near Sants Station.

By Car

You won't need a car in Barcelona because the taxis and public transportation are so good. Parking fees are outrageously expensive (the lot behind La Boqueria Market charges upwards of €25/day). If you want to rent a car, remember that it's smart to do it after you visit Madrid and Toledo.

Madrid

Madrid is upbeat and vibrant. You'll feel it the moment you set foot in the city. Even the living-statue street performers have a twinkle in their eyes.

Like its people, the city is relatively young. In medieval times, it was just another village, wedged between the powerful kingdoms of Castile and Aragon. When newlyweds Ferdinand and Isabel united those kingdoms in 1469, Madrid—at the center of Spain—became the focal point of a budding nation. By 1561, Spain ruled the world's most powerful empire, and Madrid was transformed into a European capital. By 1900, Madrid had 500,000 people.

Today, the hub of Spain—with a population of 3.3 million—is working to make itself more livable with urban improvements such as pedestrianized streets, parks, and commuter lines. Fortunately, the historic core is still intact and easy to navigate.

So dive into the city's grandeur as well as its intimate charms. Feel the vibe in Puerta del Sol, the pulsing heart of Spain itself. The lavish Royal Palace, with its gilded rooms and frescoed ceilings, rivals Versailles. The Prado has Europe's top collection of paintings, and nearby hangs Picasso's chilling masterpiece, *Guernica*. Retiro Park invites you to take a shady siesta. Save time for Madrid's elegant shops and pedestrian zones. After dark, take to the streets for an evening paseo that can continue past midnight. Lively Madrid has enough street-singing, bar-hopping, and people-watching for everyone.

MADRID IN 2 DAYS

Day 1: Take a brisk 20-minute walk along the pedestrianized Calle de las Huertas, from Puerta del Sol to the Prado. Spend the morning at the Prado (reserve in advance). Enjoy an afternoon siesta—or rent a rowboat—in nearby Retiro Park. Then tackle modern art at the Reina Sofía museum (closed Tue), which displays Picasso's *Guernica*.

On any evening: Have a progressive tapas dinner at a series of characteristic bars. Join the evening paseo; my favorite time is right before sunset, when beautifully lit people fill the city. Take in a flamenco or zarzuela performance.

Day 2: Follow my self-guided walk—a loop from Puerta del Sol—and break it up midway to tour the Royal Palace. Linger in Madrid's grand public spaces: Puerta del Sol, Plaza Mayor, and Gran Vía (take my self-guided walk). With extra time, try a walking or food-tasting tour, visit more museums, or do some shopping.

Rick's Tip: *If you're heading from Madrid to Barcelona, take the speedy* **AVE train** *(takes just 2.5 to 3 hours). Reserve ahead; see page 480 for details. You could leave Madrid after breakfast and have lunch in Barcelona.*

ORIENTATION

Puerta del Sol marks the center of Madrid. No major sight is more than a 20-minute walk or a €7 taxi ride from this central square. Get out your map and frame off Madrid's historic core: To the west of Puerta del Sol is the Royal Palace. To the east, you'll find the Prado Museum, along with the Reina Sofía museum. North of Puerta del Sol is Gran Vía, a broad east-west boulevard bubbling with shops and cinemas. Between Gran Vía and Puerta del Sol is a bustling pedestrian shopping zone. And southwest of Puerta del Sol is Plaza Mayor, the center of a 17th-century, slow-down-and-smell-the-cobblestones district.

This entire historic core around Puerta del Sol—Gran Vía, Plaza Mayor, the Prado, and the Royal Palace—is easily covered on foot. A wonderful chain of pedestrian streets crosses the city east to west, from the Prado to Plaza Mayor (along Calle de las Huertas) and from Puerta del Sol to the Royal Palace (on Calle del Arenal). Stretching north from Gran Vía, Calle de Fuencarral is a trendy shopping and strolling pedestrian street.

Tourist Information

Madrid's city-run TIs share a website, a central phone number, and hours (generally daily 9:30-20:30, tel. 914-544-410, www.esmadrid.com). The best and most central city TI is on **Plaza Mayor.** Others are at **Plaza de Colón** (in the under-

ground passage accessed from Paseo de la Castellana and Calle de Goya), **Palacio de Cibeles** (closed Mon, inside, up the stairs and to the right), **Plaza de Cibeles** (at Paseo del Prado), **Paseo del Arte** (on Plaza Sánchez Bustillo, near the Reina Sofía museum), and at the **airport** (Terminals 2 and 4). In summer, the city sends mobile TIs to major sites around town.

Madrid also has regional TIs, privately run by Turismo Madrid (and therefore profit-motivated), with branches near the **Prado Museum** (daily 8:00-15:00, on Duque de Medinaceli, across from Palace Hotel), at **Chamartín train station** (Mon-Sat 8:00-15:00, Sun 9:00-14:00, near track 20), at the **Atocha train station** (daily 8:00-20:00, AVE arrivals side), and at the **airport** (Mon-Sat 9:00-20:00, Sun 9:00-14:00, Terminals 1 and 4, www.turismo madrid.es).

Pick up and use the free, well-designed *Public Transport* map, which includes detailed transportation routes throughout the city center.

At most TIs, you can get the *Es Madrid* English-language monthly, which lists events around town.

For arts and culture listings, pick up the Spanish-language weekly entertainment guide **Guía del Ocio,** which lists daily live music (*"Conciertos"*), museum exhibits, and restaurants (€1, sold at newsstands, sometimes free at TI or hotels, www. guiadelocio.com).

Rick's Tip: *You'll find* **one-stop shopping** *at the department store* **El Corte Inglés,** *which takes up several buildings in the pedestrian zone a block off Puerta del Sol (Mon-Sat 10:00-22:00, Sun 11:00-21:00, Preciados 3). The main (tallest) building gives out free city maps, hosts two* **travel agencies** *(both sell* **train tickets***), and has a top-floor* **cafeteria** *and a basement* **supermarket.** *The other branch has an electronics department for help with* **mobile devices** *and a top-floor* **box office.**

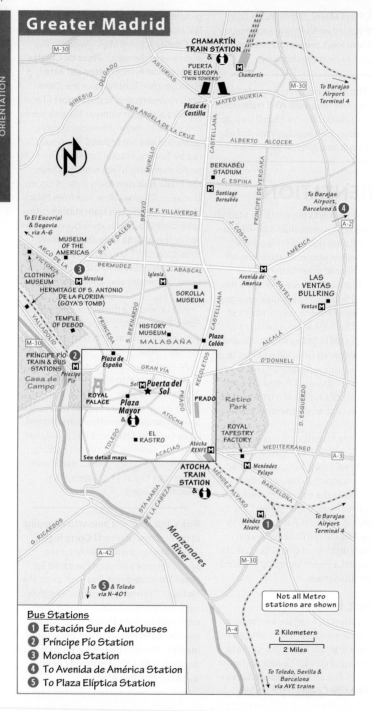

Greater Madrid

CHAMARTÍN
TRAIN STATION
&
Chamartín

PUERTA
DE EUROPA
"TWIN TOWERS"

M-30

M-30

To Barajas
Airport
Terminal 4

Plaza de
Castilla

ASTURIAS

DELGADO

SINESIO

SOR ANGELA DE LA CRUZ

MURILLO

MATEO INURRIA

CASTELLANA

ALBERTO ALCOCER

BERNABÉU
STADIUM

C. ESPINA

Santiago
Bernabéu

PRÍNCIPE DE VERGARA

To Barajas
Airport,
Barcelona &

A-2

To El Escorial
& Segovia
via A-6

MUSEUM
OF THE
AMERICAS

BRAVO

R.F. VILLAVERDE

S.F. DE SALES

BERMÚDEZ

J. COSTA

AMÉRICA

F. SILVELA

Avenida de
América

LAS
VENTAS
BULLRING

Ventas

ARCO DE LA

VICTORIA

CLOTHING
MUSEUM

Moncloa

Iglesia

J. ABASCAL

SOROLLA
MUSEUM

CASTELLANA

ALCALÁ

HERMITAGE OF S. ANTONIO
DE LA FLORIDA
(GOYA'S TOMB)

PRINCESA

S. BERNARDO

HISTORY
MUSEUM

MALASAÑA

Plaza
Colón

RECOLETOS

O'DONNELL

TEMPLE
OF DEBOD

VALLADOLID

M-30

PRÍNCIPE PÍO
TRAIN & BUS
STATIONS

Casa de
Campo

Príncipe
Pío

Plaza de
España

GRAN VÍA

Sol

Puerta del
Sol

PRADO

PRADO

Retiro
Park

D. ESQUERDO

ROYAL
PALACE

Plaza
Mayor
&

TOLEDO

EL
RASTRO

ATOCHA

Atocha
RENFE

ACACIAS

ROYAL
TAPESTRY
FACTORY

MEDITERRÁNEO

A-3

Menéndez
Pelayo

See detail maps

ATOCHA
TRAIN
STATION
&

STA MARÍA
DE LA CABEZA

MÉNDEZ ÁLVARO

BARCELONA

To Barajas
Airport
Terminal 4

Manzanares
River

Méndez
Álvaro

G. RICARDOS

A-42

M-30

To 5 & Toledo
via N-401

A-4

Not all Metro
stations are shown

Bus Stations

1 Estación Sur de Autobuses
2 Príncipe Pío Station
3 Moncloa Station
4 To Avenida de América Station
5 To Plaza Elíptica Station

2 Kilometers

2 Miles

To Toledo, Sevilla &
Barcelona
via AVE trains

Daily Reminder

SUNDAY: The Prado Museum and Centro de Arte Reina Sofía close earlier than normal today (19:00), as does the National Archaeological Museum (15:00). The flea market at El Rastro is held today (9:00-15:00). Midday, Retiro Park erupts into a carnival-like atmosphere. Bullfights take place on some Sundays (March through mid-Oct). Some flamenco places are closed today.

MONDAY: The National Archaeological Museum is closed today, and the Thyssen-Bornemisza Museum has shorter hours (12:00-16:00).

TUESDAY: The Reina Sofía is closed today.

WEDNESDAY/THURSDAY/FRIDAY: All major sights are open.

SATURDAY: All major sights are open. Midday, enjoy the scene at Retiro Park.

LATE-HOURS SIGHTSEEING: Sights with evening hours (20:30 or later) include the Reina Sofía (Mon and Wed-Sat until 21:00) and the Thyssen-Bornemisza Museum (exhibits only, Sat until 21:00 in summer).

FREE SIGHTSEEING: The Prado is free every evening from 18:00 (17:00 on Sun), the Reina Sofía has free evening hours Mon and Wed-Sat from 19:00 (15:00 on Sun), and the Thyssen-Bornemisza is free on Mon. The National Archaeological Museum is free all day Sun and on Sat afternoon (Sat from 14:00).

Sightseeing Passes

Very energetic travelers can save a little money and some valuable sightseeing time by buying the **Madrid Card.** It covers more than 50 sights—including the Royal Palace, Prado, Thyssen-Bornemisza, and Centro de Arte Reina Sofía—and lets you skip lines, a definite plus in high season, especially at the palace and the Prado. Additionally, the pass covers all the Essential Madrid tours and it's good for a 10 percent discount at El Corte Inglés. The three-day card for €67 is the best deal (other options include €47/24 hours and €60/48 hours, online discounts available, www.madridcard.com). You can pay extra to add the hop-on, hop-off bus tour (saves a maximum of €2) or public transport (only worthwhile if you ride multiple times a day).

If you want to visit the Prado, Thyssen-Bornemisza, and Centro de Arte Reina Sofía during day-time hours, you can save a few euros by buying the **Paseo del Arte combo-ticket,** though keep in mind that the Prado and Reina Sofía are free in the evenings, and the Thyssen is free on Mondays (€25.60, sold at each museum, good for a year, allows you to skip lines).

Tours

Essential Madrid offers interesting tours in English that depart from the Plaza Mayor TI; book at least a few hours in advance (€17, 20 percent discount for booking three different tours, 2 hours, 902-221-424, www.esmadrid.com).

Madrid Tours & Tastings bring together Spanish history, food, and wine (walking tours €15/person, tapas tours from €75/person, wine tastings from €65/person, mobile 620-883-900, www.madridtandt.com, nmurrell@madridtandt.com).

Frederico and Cristina specialize in family tours. They also offer museum tours and excursions to nearby towns (prices per group: €155/2 hours, €195/4 hours, €235/6 hours, tel. 913-102-974, mobile 649-936-222, www.spainfred.com, info@spainfred.com).

MADRID AT A GLANCE

▲▲▲**Royal Palace** Spain's sumptuous, lavishly furnished national palace. **Hours:** Daily April-Sept 10:00-20:00, Oct-March 10:00-18:00. See page 433.

▲▲▲**Prado Museum** One of the world's great museums, loaded with masterpieces by Diego Velázquez, Francisco de Goya, El Greco, Hieronymus Bosch, Albrecht Dürer, and more. **Hours:** Mon-Sat 10:00-20:00, Sun 10:00-19:00. See page 443.

▲▲▲**Centro de Arte Reina Sofía** Modern-art museum featuring Picasso's epic masterpiece *Guernica*. **Hours:** Mon and Wed-Sat 10:00-21:00, Sun 10:00-19:00, closed Tue. See page 457.

▲▲▲**Paseo** Evening stroll among the Madrileños. **Hours:** Sundown until the wee hours. See page 463.

▲▲**Puerta del Sol** Madrid's lively central square. **Hours:** Always bustling. See page 420.

▲▲**Thyssen-Bornemisza Museum** A great complement to the Prado, with lesser-known yet still impressive works and an especially good Impressionist collection. **Hours:** Mon 12:00-16:00, Tue-Sun 10:00-19:00, Sat until 21:00 in summer (exhibits only). See page 456.

▲▲**National Archaeological Museum** Traces the history of Iberia through artifacts. **Hours:** Tue-Sat 9:30-20:00, Sun 9:30-15:00, closed Mon. See page 462.

▲▲**Bullfights** Spain's controversial pastime. **Hours:** Scattered Sundays and holidays March-mid-Oct, plus almost daily in May-early June. See page 465.

▲▲**Flamenco** Captivating music and dance performances, at various venues throughout the city. **Hours:** Shows every night, some places closed on Sun. See page 464.

▲**Plaza Mayor** Historic cobbled square. **Hours:** Always open. See page 424.

▲**Retiro Park** Festive green escape from the city, with rental rowboats and great people-watching. **Hours:** Closes at dusk. See page 461.

▲**Royal Botanical Garden** A relaxing museum of plants from around the world. **Hours:** Daily 10:00-21:00, shorter hours off-season. See page 462.

▲**El Rastro** Europe's biggest flea market, filled with bargains and pickpockets. **Hours:** Sun 9:00-15:00, best before 11:00. See page 462.

▲**Zarzuela** Madrid's delightful light opera. **Hours:** Evenings. See page 465.

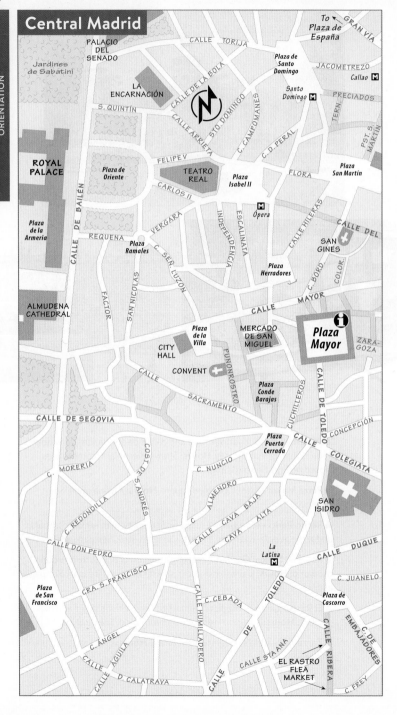

Central Madrid

GRAN VÍA

Jardines de Sabatini

PALACIO DEL SENADO

CALLE TORIJA

Plaza de Santo Domingo

JACOMETREZO

Callao

LA ENCARNACIÓN

CALLE DE LA BOLA

Santo Domingo

PRECIADOS

STO. DOMINGO

S. QUINTÍN

CALLE ARRIETA

C. CAMPOMANES

C. D. PERAL

PST. S. MARTÍN

ROYAL PALACE

FELIPE V

Plaza de Oriente

TEATRO REAL

Plaza Isabel II

FLORA

Plaza San Martín

CALLE DE BAILÉN

CARLOS II

Ópera

CALLE DEL

Plaza de la Armería

VERGARA

REQUENA

Plaza Ramales

C. SEÑ. LUZÓN

INDEPENDENCIA

ESCALINATA

CALLE HILERAS

SAN GINES

SAN NICOLAS

FACTOR

Plaza Herradores

C. BORD.

COLOR

ALMUDENA CATHEDRAL

CALLE MAYOR

Plaza de la Villa

MERCADO DE SAN MIGUEL

Plaza Mayor

ZARAGOZA

CITY HALL

PUÑONROSTRO

CONVENT

CALLE

SACRAMENTO

Plaza Conde Barajas

CUCHILLEROS

CALLE DE TOLEDO

CALLE DE SEGOVIA

Plaza Puerta Cerrada

CONCEPCIÓN

CALLE

COLEGIATA

C. MORERIA

COSTA DE S. ANDRÉS

C. NUNCIO

SAN ISIDRO

C. REDONDILLA

C. ALMENDRO

CALLE CAVA BAJA

C. CAVA ALTA

CALLE DON PEDRO

La Latina

CALLE DUQUE

C. JUANELO

Plaza de San Francisco

CRA. S. FRANCISCO

CALLE HUMILLADERO

C. CEBADA

TOLEDO

Plaza de Cascorro

C. DE EMBAJADORES

C. ANGEL

DE

CALLE RIBERA

CALLE AGUILA

CALLE D. CALATRAVA

CALLE STA ANA

CALLE

EL RASTRO FLEA MARKET

C. FREY

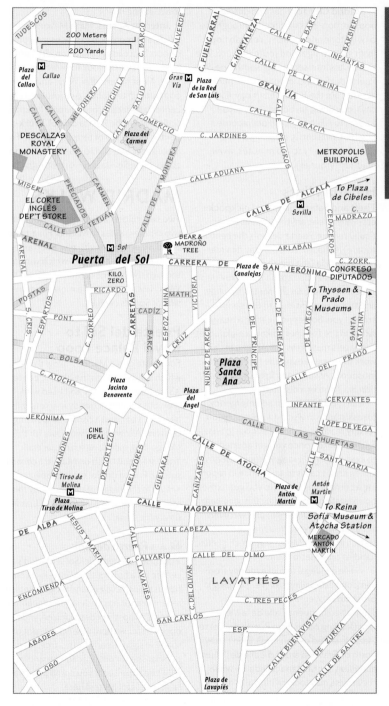

Madrid City Tour has two different hop-on, hop-off bus circuits through the city: historic and modern. You can hop from sight to sight and route to route. The two routes intersect at the south side of Puerta del Sol and in front of Starbucks across from the Prado (€21/1 day, €25/2 days, buy ticket on board; daily 9:30-22:00, Nov-Feb 10:00-18:00; recorded English narration, 15 stops, 1.5 hours, departures every 10-20 minutes, www.madridcitytour.es).

Helpful Hints

Theft and Safety: Beware of **pickpockets**—anywhere, anytime. Areas of particular risk are Puerta del Sol (the central square), El Rastro (the Sunday flea market), Gran Vía (the paseo zone: Plaza del Callao to Plaza de España), any crowded street, anywhere on the Metro, bus #27, and the airport. Be alert to the people around you: Someone wearing a heavy jacket in the summer is likely a pickpocket. Teenagers may dress like Americans and work the areas around the three big art museums. Assume any fight or commotion is a scam or a distraction.

Call the **SATE line** in an **emergency,** or for assistance in visiting a police station for any reason (24-hour tel. 902-102-112, English spoken once you get connected to a person). Help ranges from canceling stolen credit cards to assistance in reporting a crime. They can help you get to the police station (at Calle Leganitos 19 near Plaza de Santo Domingo) and will even act as an interpreter. You may see a police station in the Sol Metro station; this office handles only Metro theft.

While it's illegal to make money from someone else selling sex (i.e., pimping), **prostitutes** over 18 can solicit legally. They often frequent Calle de la Montera (leading north from Puerta del Sol to Plaza de la Red de San Luis). Don't stray north of Gran Vía around Calle de la Luna and Plaza Santa María Soledad—while the streets may look inviting, this area is a meat-eating flower.

Internet Access: Plaza Mayor has free Wi-Fi, and more public spaces may offer it soon. You can get online on all Madrid buses and trains—look for *Wi-Fi gratis* signs. Most hotels offer Wi-Fi and a guest computer in the lobby. Any *locutorio* call center is generally the cheapest Internet option. Near the Puerta del Sol, **Workcenter** has plenty of terminals (Mon-Fri 8:00-21:00, Sat-Sun 10:00-14:30 & 17:00-20:30, Calle Sevilla 4, tel. 913-601-395).

MADRID WALKS

Two self-guided walks provide a look at two different sides of Madrid. For a taste of old Madrid, start with my "Puerta del Sol to Royal Palace Loop," which winds through the historic center. My "Gran Vía Walk" lets you glimpse a more modern side of Spain's capital.

Puerta del Sol to Royal Palace Loop

For a taste of old Madrid, follow this loop, which winds through the historic center. It's pedestrian-friendly and filled with spacious squares, a trendy market, bulls' heads in a bar, and a cookie-dispensing convent. Allow about two hours for this self-guided, mile-long triangular walk. You'll start and finish on Madrid's central square, Puerta del Sol (Metro: Sol).

• *Head to the middle of the square, by the equestrian statue of King Charles III, and survey the scene.*

❶ ▲▲*Puerta del Sol*

The bustling Puerta del Sol is Madrid's center. It's a hub for the Metro, local *cercanías* trains, revelers, and pickpockets. In recent years it has undergone a facelift to become a mostly pedestrianized, wide-open space...without a bench or spot of shade in sight. Nearly traffic-free, it's a popular site for political demonstrations. Don't be surprised if you come across a large, peaceful protest here.

The equestrian statue in the middle of the square honors **King Charles III** (1716-1788) whose enlightened urban policies earned him the affectionate nickname "the best mayor of Madrid." He decorated the city squares with beautiful fountains, got those meddlesome Jesuits out of city government, established the public school system, mandated underground sewers, opened his private Retiro Park to the general public, built the Prado, made the Royal Palace the wonder of Europe, and generally cleaned up Madrid.

Head to the slightly uphill end of the square and find the **statue of a bear** pawing a tree—a symbol of Madrid since medieval times. Bears used to live in the royal hunting grounds outside the city. And the *madroño* trees produce a berry that makes the traditional *madroño* liqueur. Near the statue, locate the Metro entrance and the glass-fish entrance to the *cercanías* trains.

Charles III faces a red-and-white building with a bell tower. This was Madrid's first post office, founded by Charles III in the 1760s. Today it's the **county governor's office** (Residencia de la Comunidad de Madrid), home to the president who governs greater Madrid. The building is notorious for having once been dictator Francisco Franco's police headquarters. An amazing number of those detained and interrogated by the Franco police "escaped" by jumping out its windows to their deaths. Notice the hats of the civil guardsmen at the entry. It's said the hats have square backs, cleverly designed so that the men can lean against the wall while enjoying a cigarette. On the opposite side of the square, look up to see the famous Tío Pepe sign, a neon advertisement from the 1950s for sherry wine.

Crowds fill the square on New Year's Eve as the rest of Spain watches the Times Square-style action on TV. The bell atop the governor's office chimes 12 times, while Madrileños eat one grape for each ring to bring good luck through each of the next 12 months.

• *Cross the square, walking to the governor's office.*

Puerta del Sol

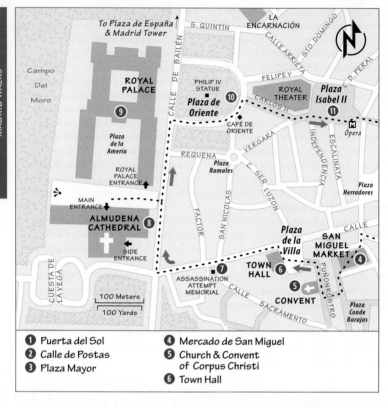

1 Puerta del Sol
2 Calle de Postas
3 Plaza Mayor
4 Mercado de San Miguel
5 Church & Convent of Corpus Christi
6 Town Hall

Look at the curb directly in front of the entrance to the governor's office. The marker is **"kilometer zero,"** the symbolic center of Spain (with its six main highways indicated). Standing on the zero marker with your back to the governor's office, get oriented visually: At twelve o'clock (straight ahead), notice how the pedestrian commercial zone (with the huge El Corte Inglés department store) is thriving. At two o'clock starts the seedier Calle de la Montera, a street with shady characters and prostitutes that leads to trendy, pedestrianized Calle de Fuencarral. At three o'clock is the biggest Apple store in Europe; the Prado is about a mile farther to your right. At 10 o'clock, you'll see the pedestrianized Calle del Arenal Street (which leads to the Royal Palace) dumping into this square...just where you will

end this walk.

On either side of the entrance to the governor's office are **two plaques** tied to important dates, expressing thanks from the regional government to its citizens for assisting in times of dire need. To the left of the entry, a plaque on the wall honors those who helped during the terrorist bombings of March 11, 2004 (we have our 9/11—Spain commemorates its 3/11). A similar plaque on the right marks the spot where the war against Napoleon started in 1808. When Napoleon invaded Spain and tried to appoint his brother (rather than the Spanish heir) as king of Spain, an angry crowd gathered outside this building. The French soldiers attacked and simply massacred the mob. Painter Francisco de Goya, who worked just up the street, observed the event and cap-

Puerta del Sol to Royal Palace Loop

7 Assassination Attempt
   Memorial
8 Almudena Cathedral
9 Royal Palace
10 Plaza de Oriente
11 Plaza de Isabel II
12 Calle del Arenal

tured the tragedy in his paintings *Second of May, 1808* and *Third of May, 1808,* now in the Prado.

On the corner of Puerta del Sol and Calle Mayor (downhill end of Puerta del Sol, across from McDonald's) is the busy *confitería* **La Mallorquina,** *"fundada en 1.894"* (daily 9:00-21:00, closed mid-July-Aug). Go inside for a tempting peek at racks with goodies hot out of the oven. Enjoy observing the churning energy at the bar lined with Madrileños popping in for a fast coffee and a sweet treat. The shop is famous for its cream-filled *Napolitana* pastry (€1.20). Or sample Madrid's answer to doughnuts, *rosquillas* (*tontas* means "silly"—plain, and *listas* means "all dressed up and ready to go"—with icing, about €1 each). The room upstairs is more genteel, with nice views of the square.

From inside the shop, look back toward the entrance and notice the tile above the door with the 18th-century view of Puerta del Sol. Compare this with today's view out the door. This was before the square was widened, when a church stood at its top end.

Puerta del Sol ("Gate of the Sun") is named for a long-gone gate with the rising sun carved onto it, which once stood at the eastern edge of the old city. From here, we begin our walk through the historic town that dates back to medieval times.
• *Head west on busy Calle Mayor, just past McDonald's, and veer left up the pedestrian alley called...*

❷ Calle de Postas
The street sign shows the post coach heading for that famous first post office.

Medieval street signs posted on the lower corners of buildings included pictures so the illiterate (and monolingual tourists) could "read" them. Fifty yards up the street on the left, at Calle San Cristóbal, is Pans & Company, a popular Catalan sandwich chain offering lots of healthy choices. While Spaniards consider American fast food unhealthy—both culturally and physically—they love it. McDonald's and Burger King are thriving in Spain.

• *Continue up Calle de Postas, and take a slight right on Calle de la Sal through the arcade, where you emerge into...*

❸ ▲Plaza Mayor

In medieval times, this was the city's main square; today it's a vast, cobbled, traffic-free chunk of 17th-century Spain. The equestrian statue (wearing a ruffled collar) honors Philip III, who (in 1619) transformed the medieval marketplace into a Baroque plaza. The square is 140 yards long and 102 yards wide, enclosed by three-story buildings with symmetrical windows, balconies, slate roofs, and steepled towers. Each side of the square is uniform, as if a grand palace were turned inside-out. This distinct look, pioneered by architect Juan de Herrera (who finished El Escorial), is found all over Madrid.

This site served as the city's 17th-century open-air theater. Upon this stage, much Spanish history has been played out: bullfights, fires, royal pageantry, and events of the gruesome Inquisition. Worn-down reliefs on the seatbacks under the lampposts tell the story. During the Inquisition, many were tried here—suspected heretics, Protestants, Jews, tour guides without a local license, and Muslims whose "conversion" to Christianity was dubious. The guilty were paraded around the square before their executions, wearing billboards listing their many sins. Bleachers were built for bigger audiences, while the wealthy rented balconies. The heretics were burned, and later, criminals were slowly strangled as they held a crucifix, hearing the reassuring words of a priest as the life was squeezed out of them with a garrote.

The square's buildings are mainly private apartments. Want one? Costs run from €400,000 for a tiny attic studio to €2 million and up for a 2,500-square-foot flat. The square is painted a democratic shade of burgundy—the result of a citywide vote. Three different colors were painted as samples on the walls of this square, and the city voted for its favorite. Since the end of decades of dictatorship in 1975, there's been a passion for voting here.

A stamp-and-coin market bustles at Plaza Mayor on Sundays (10:00-14:00). The Casa Yustas shop at #30 (in the northeast corner) has been making hats here since 1894.

The building to Philip's left, on the north side beneath the twin towers, was once home to the baker's guild and now houses the TI. It's air-conditioned and offers daily walking tours with **Essential Madrid** (€17, 20 percent discount for booking three different tours, 2 hours, www.esmadrid.com). Consider reserving a spot now.

Day or night, Plaza Mayor is a colorful place to enjoy an affordable cup of coffee or overpriced food. Throughout Spain, lesser *plazas mayores* provide peaceful pools in the whitewater river of Spanish life.

For some interesting, if gruesome, bullfighting lore, drop by **La Torre del Oro Bar Andalú** (north side of the square at #26, a few doors to the left of the TI). With *Andalú* (Andalusian) ambience and an entertaining staff, this bar is a good place to end your Plaza Mayor visit. (Beware: They may push expensive tapas on tourists.) The price list posted outside the door makes your costs perfectly clear: "*barra*" indicates the price at the bar; "*terraza*" is the price at an outdoor table. Step inside, stand at the bar, and order a drink—a *caña* (small draft beer) shouldn't cost more than €2. At the outdoor tables, only larger size *cañas dobles* are available (for €4.50).

The interior is a temple to bullfighting, festooned with gory decor. Notice the breathtaking action captured in the many photographs. Look under the stuffed head of Barbero the bull. At eye level you'll see a *puntilla,* the knife used to put poor Barbero out of his misery at the arena. Just to the left of Barbero is a photo of longtime dictator Franco with the famous bullfighter Manuel Benítez Pérez—better known as El Cordobés, the Elvis of bullfighters and a working-class hero. At the top of the stairs to the WC, find the photo of El Cordobés and Robert Kennedy—looking like brothers. To the left of them (and elsewhere in the bar) is a shot of Che Guevara enjoying a bullfight. At the end of the bar, in a glass case, is the "suit of lights" that El Cordobés wore in an ill-fated 1967 fight in which the bull gored him. El Cordobés survived; the bull didn't. In the same case is the photo of a matador (not El Cordobés) hooked by a bull's horn.

Consider taking a break at one the sidewalk tables of any café/bar terrace facing Madrid's grandest square. Nearby Cafetería Margerit occupies the sunniest corner of the square and is a good place to enjoy a coffee with the view. The scene is easily worth the extra euro you'll pay for the drink.

• *Leave Plaza Mayor on Calle de Ciudad Rodrigo (at the northwest corner of the square), passing a series of solid turn-of-the-20th-century storefronts and sandwich joints, such as Casa Rúa, famous for its cheap bocadillos de calamares—fried squid rings on a roll. Emerging from the arcade, turn left and head downhill toward the covered market hall.*

❹ Mercado de San Miguel

To wash down those *calamares* in a more refined setting, pop into this trendy market hall (daily 10:00-24:00). The historic iron-and-glass structure from 1916 stands on the site of an even earlier marketplace. Renovated in the 21st century, it now hosts some 30 high-end vendors of fresh produce, gourmet foods, wines by the glass, tapas, and full meals. Locals and tourists alike pause here for its food, natural-light ambience, and social scene.

Alongside the market, look down the street called Cava de San Miguel. If you like singing and sangria, come back after 22:00 on a Friday or Saturday night and visit one of the **mesones** that line the street. These cave-like bars, stretching far back from the street, get packed with Madrileños out on dates who—emboldened by sangria and the setting—are prone to suddenly breaking out in song. It's a lowbrow, electric-keyboard, karaoke-type ambience.

• *After you walk through the market and exit, continue west a few steps, then turn left, heading downhill on Calle del Conde de Miranda. At the first corner, turn right and cross the small plaza to the brick church in the far corner.*

Plaza Mayor

Mercado de San Miguel

❺ Church and Convent of Corpus Christi

The proud coats of arms over the main entry announce the rich family that built this Hieronymite church and convent in 1607. In 17th-century Spain, the most prestigious thing a noble family could do was build and maintain a convent. To harvest all the goodwill created in your community, you'd want your family's insignia right there for all to see. (You can see the donating couple, like a 17th-century Bill and Melinda Gates, kneeling before the communion wafer in the central panel over the entrance.) Inside is a quiet oasis with a Last Supper altarpiece.

Now for a unique shopping experience—buying goodies from cloistered nuns. A half-block to the right from the church entrance is its associated convent—it's the big brown door on the left, at Calle del Codo 3 (Mon-Sat 9:30-13:00 & 16:00-18:30, closed Sun). The sign reads: *Venta de Dulces* (Sweets for Sale). Buzz the *monjas* button, then wait patiently for the sister to respond over the intercom. Say *"dulces"* (DOOL-thays), and she'll let you in. When the lock buzzes, push open the door and follow the sign to the *torno,* the lazy Susan that lets the sisters sell their baked goods without being seen. Scan the menu, announce your choice to the sequestered sister (she may tell you she has only one or two of the options available), place your money on the *torno,* and your goodies (and change) will appear. *Galletas* (shortbread cookies) are the least expensive item (a *medio-kilo* costs about €9). Or try the *pastas de almendra* (almond cookies).

• *Continue uphill on Calle del Codo (where those in need of bits of armor shopped—see the street sign) and turn left, heading toward the Plaza de la Villa (pictured here). Before entering the square, notice an* **old door** *to the left of the* **Real Sociedad Económica** *sign, made of wood lined with metal. This is considered the oldest door in town on Madrid's oldest building—inhabited since 1480. It's set in a Moorish keyhole arch. Look up at what was a prison tower. Now continue into the square called Plaza de la Villa, dominated by Madrid's...*

❻ Town Hall

The impressive structure features Madrid's distinctive architectural style—symmetrical square towers, topped with steeples

Church and Convent of Corpus Christi

Town Hall

and a slate roof. The building still functions as Madrid's ceremonial Town Hall, though the city council and hands-on duties have moved elsewhere. Over the doorway, the three coats of arms sport many symbols of Madrid's rulers: Habsburg crowns, castles of Castile, and the city symbol—the berry-eating bear (the shield on the left). This square was the ruling center of medieval Madrid, a tiny remnant of the 14th-century town. Even before then, when Madrid was an Arab-Moorish community, this was the only square in town.

Imagine how Philip II took this city by surprise in 1561 when he decided to move the capital of Europe's largest empire (even bigger than ancient Rome at the time) from Toledo to humble Madrid. To better administer their empire, the Habsburgs went on a building spree. But because their empire was drained of its riches by prolonged religious wars, they built Madrid with cheap brick instead of elegant granite.

The statue in the garden is of Philip II's admiral, Don Alvaro de Bazán—mastermind of the Christian victory over the Turkish Ottomans at the naval battle of Lepanto in 1571. This pivotal battle, fought off the coast of Greece, slowed the Ottoman threat to Christian Europe. However, mere months after Bazán's death in 1588, his "invincible" Spanish Armada was destroyed by England...and Spain's empire began its slow fade.

• *From here, walk along busy Calle Mayor, which leads downhill toward the Royal Palace. A few blocks down Calle Mayor, on a tiny square, you'll find the...*

❼ Assassination Attempt Memorial

This statue memorializes a 1906 assassination attempt. The target was Spain's King Alfonso XIII and his bride, Victoria Eugenie, as they paraded by on their wedding day. While the crowd was throwing flowers, an anarchist (what terrorists used to be called) threw a bouquet lashed to a bomb from a balcony at #84 (across the street). He missed the royal newlyweds, but killed 23 people. Gory photos of the event hang inside the Casa Ciriaco restaurant, which now occupies #84 (photos to the right of the entrance). The king and queen went on to live to a ripe old age, producing many great-grandchildren, including the current king, Felipe VI.

Almudena Cathedral

• *Continue down Calle Mayor one more block to a busy street, Calle de Bailén. Take in the big, domed...*

❽ Almudena Cathedral (Catedral de la Almudena)

Madrid's massive, gray-and-white cathedral (110 yards long and 80 yards high) opened in 1993, 100 years after workers started building it. This is the side entrance for tourists (€1 donation requested). The main entrance (selling €6 museum-and-cupola tickets) is a block north, facing the Royal Palace. If you go inside, you'll see a refreshingly modern and colorful ceiling, a glittering 5,000-pipe organ, and a grand 15th-century painted altarpiece—striking in the otherwise Neo-Gothic interior. The highlight is the 12th-century coffin (empty, painted leather on wood, in a chapel behind the altar) of Madrid's patron saint, Isidro. A humble farmer, the exceptionally devout Isidro was said to have been helped by angels who did the plowing for him while he prayed. Forty years after he died, this coffin was opened, and his body was found to have been miraculously preserved. This convinced the pope to canonize Isidro as the patron saint of Madrid and of farmers, with May 15 as his feast day.

Turn right on Calle de Bailén to reach the main entrance. The doors feature reliefs of the cathedral's 1993 consecration, including one with Pope John Paul II and former king and queen Juan Carlos I and his wife Sofía.

• *From the cathedral's front steps, face the imposing...*

❾ Royal Palace

Since the ninth century, this spot has been Madrid's center of power: from Moorish castle to Christian fortress to Renaissance palace to the current structure, built in the 18th century. With its expansive courtyard surrounded by imposing Baroque architecture, it represents the wealth of Spain before its decline. Its 2,800 rooms, totaling nearly 1.5 million square feet, make it Europe's largest palace.

• *You could visit the palace now, using my self-guided tour (page 435). To follow the rest of this walk back to Puerta del Sol, continue one long block north up Calle de Bailén (walking alongside the palace) to where the street opens up into...*

Plaza de Oriente

⓾ *Plaza de Oriente*

As its name suggests, this square faces east. The grand yet people-friendly plaza is typical of today's Europe, where energetic governments are converting car-congested wastelands into public spaces. A recent mayor of Madrid earned the nickname "The Mole" for all the digging he did. Where's the traffic? Under your feet.

Notice the quiet. You're surrounded by more than three million people, yet you can hear the birds, bells, and fountain. The park is decorated with statues of Visigothic kings who ruled from the third to seventh century. Romans allowed them to administer their province of Hispania on the condition that they'd provide food and weapons to the empire. The Visigoths inherited real power after Rome fell, but lost it to invading Moors in 711. The fine bronze equestrian statue honors King Philip IV; he faces Madrid's opera house, the 1,700-seat **Royal Theater** (Teatro Real). To your left, in the distance, the once-impressive **Madrid Tower** skyscraper (460 feet tall, built of concrete in 1957) marks Plaza de España (and the end of my "Gran Vía Walk").

• *Walk along the Royal Theater, on the right side, to the...*

⓫ *Plaza de Isabel II*

This square is marked by a statue of Isabel II, who ruled Spain in the 19th century. Although she's immortalized here, Isabel had a rocky reign, marked by uprisings and political intrigue. A revolution in 1868 forced her to abdicate, and she lived out her life in exile.

Evidence of Moorish walls turn up in this neighborhood and elsewhere in Madrid. Check out the tactile model in this square: The position of the old Moorish fortress and walls is outlined, with the modern city faintly depicted underneath. Notice also the grooved sidewalk you're standing on—designed for the white canes of people who can't see.

• *From here, follow Calle del Arenal, walking gradually uphill. You're heading straight to Puerta del Sol.*

Calle del Arenal

⑫ *Calle del Arenal*

As depicted on the tiled street signs, this was the "street of sand"—where sand was stockpiled during construction. Each cross street is named for a medieval craft that, historically, was plied along that lane (for example, "Calle de Bordadores" means "Street of the Embroiderers"). Wander slowly uphill. As you stroll, imagine this street as a traffic inferno—which it was until the city pedestrianized it a decade ago. Notice also how orderly the side streets are. Where a mess of cars once lodged chaotically on the sidewalks, bollards (*bolardos*) now keep vehicles off the walkways.

The brick **St. Ginés Church** (on the right) means temptation to most locals. From the uphill corner of the church, look to the end of the lane where—like a high-calorie red-light zone—a neon sign spells out *Chocolatería San Ginés*...every local's favorite place for hot chocolate and *churros* (always open). The charming bookshop clinging like a barnacle to the wall of the church has been selling books on this spot since 1650.

Next door is the **Joy Eslava disco,** a former theater famous for operettas in the Gilbert-and-Sullivan days and now a popular club. In Spain, when you're 18 you can do it all (buy tobacco, drink, drive, serve in the military). This place is an alcohol-free disco for the younger kids until midnight, when it becomes a thriving adult space, with the theater floor and balconies all teeming with clubbers. Their slogan: "Go big or go home."

Next, **Soccer Shop** (at #11) carries team regalia, postcards of today's stars, official mouth guards, etc., for soccer fans. Many Europeans come to Madrid primarily to see its 80,000-seat Bernabéu soccer stadium. The Starbucks on the next corner (opposite) is popular with young locals for its inviting ambience and American-style muffins, though the coffee is too tame for many Spaniards.

Kitty-corner from there is **Ferpal** (at #7), an old-school deli with an inviting bar and easy takeout options. Wallpapered with ham hocks, it's famous for selling the finest Spanish cheeses, hams, and other tasty treats. Spanish saffron costs half what you'd pay for it back in the US. While they sell quality sandwiches, cheap and ready-made, it's fun to buy some bread and—after a little tasting—choose a ham or cheese for a memorable picnic or snack. If you're lucky, you may get to taste a tiny bit of Spain's best ham (Ibérico de Bellota). Close your eyes and let the taste fly you to a land of happy acorn-fed pigs.

Across the street, in a little mall (at #8), a lovable mouse cherished by Spanish children is celebrated with a six-inch-tall bronze statue in the lobby. Upstairs is the fanciful **Casita Museo de Ratón Pérez** (€3, daily 11:00-14:00 & 17:00-20:00, Spanish only) with a fun window display. A steady stream of adoring children and their parents pour through here to learn about the wondrous mouse who is Spain's tooth fairy.

On the other side of the street is **Pronovias** (#3, opposite Burger King), a famous Spanish wedding-dress shop that attracts brides-to-be from across Europe. Computer terminals inside let young women virtual-shop for the dress of their dreams.

• *You're just a few steps from where you started this walk, at Puerta del Sol. Back in the square, you're met by a statue popularly known as La Mariblanca. This mythological Spanish Venus—with Madrid's coat of arms at her feet—stands tall amid all the modernity, as if protecting the people of this great city.*

Gran Vía Walk

This walk lets you glimpse a more modern side of Spain's capital.

Built primarily between 1900 and the 1950s, the Gran Vía is Spain's version of Fifth Avenue, affording a fun view of early-20th-century architecture and a chance to be on the street with workaday

Madrileños. I've broken this self-guided walk into five sections, each of which was the ultimate in its day.

• *Start at the skyscraper at Calle de Alcalá #42 (Metro: Banco de España).*

❶ Circulo de Bellas Artes

This 1920s skyscraper has a venerable café on its ground floor (free entry) and the best rooftop view around. Ride the elevator to the seventh-floor roof terrace (€4, daily 11:00-14:00 & 17:00-21:00), and stand under a black, Art Deco statue of Minerva, perhaps put here to associate Madrid with this mythological protector of culture and high thinking. Walk the perimeter of the rooftop from the far left for a clockwise tour.

Looking to the left, you'll see the gold-fringed dome of the landmark Metropolis building (inspired by Hotel Negresco in Nice), once the headquarters of an insurance company. It stands at the start of the Gran Vía and its cancan of proud facades

Circulo de Bellas Artes

celebrating the good times in pre-civil war Spain. On the horizon, the Guadarrama Mountains hide Segovia. Farther to the right, in the distance, skyscrapers mark the city's north gate, Puerta de Europa (with its striking slanted twin towers). The big traffic circle and fountain below are part of Plaza de Cibeles, with its ornate and bombastic cultural center and observation deck (Palacio de Cibeles). Behind that is the vast Retiro Park. Farther to the right, the big low-slung building surrounded by green is the Prado Museum. And, finally, at the far right (and hard to see) is the old town.

• *Descend the elevator and cross the busy boulevard immediately in front of Circulo de Belles Artes to reach the start of Gran Vía.*

❷ 1910s Gran Vía

This first stretch, from the Banco de España Metro stop to the Gran Vía Metro stop, was built in the 1910s. While the people-watching and window-shopping can be enthralling, be sure to look up and enjoy the beautiful facades, too.

❸ 1920s Gran Vía

The second stretch, from the Gran Vía Metro stop to the Callao Metro stop, starts where two recently pedestrianized streets meet. To the right, Calle de Fuencarral is the trendiest pedestrian zone in town, with famous brand-name shops and a young vibe (the 14-story 1920s Telefónica skyscraper at the corner was one of the city's first). To the left, Calle de la Montera is notorious for its prostitutes. The action pulses from the McDonald's down a block or so. Some find it an eye-opening detour.

❹ 1930s Gran Vía

The final stretch, from the Callao Metro stop to Plaza de España, is considered the "American Gran Vía," built in the 1930s to emulate the buildings of Chicago and New York City. You'll even see the Nebraska Cafeteria restaurant—a

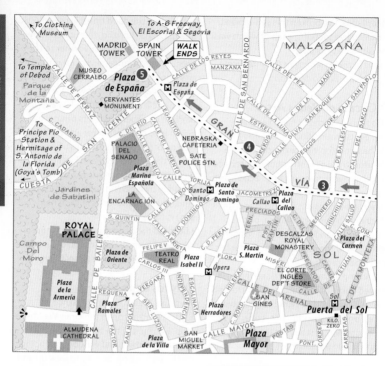

reminder that American food was trendy long before the advent of fast-food chains. This section is the Spanish version of Broadway, with all the big theaters and plays.

➎ Plaza de España

End your walk at Plaza de España (with a Metro station of the same name). Once the Rockefeller Plaza of Madrid, these days it's pretty tired. While statues of the

Gran Vía

Gran Vía Walk

1. Círculo de Bellas Artes
2. 1910s Gran Vía (Banco de España to Gran Vía Metro)
3. 1920s Gran Vía (Gran Vía to Callao Metro)
4. 1930s Gran Vía (Callao to Plaza de España Metro)
5. Plaza de España

epic Spanish characters Don Quixote and Sancho Panza (part of a Cervantes monument) are ignored in the park, two Franco-era buildings do their best to scrape the sky above. Franco wanted to show he could keep up with America, so he had the Spain Tower (shorter) and Madrid Tower (taller) built in the 1950s. But they succeed in reminding people more of Moscow than the USA.

Plaza de España

SIGHTS

▲▲▲ROYAL PALACE (PALACIO REAL)

This is Europe's third-greatest palace, after Versailles and Vienna's Schönbrunn. It has arguably the most sumptuous original interior, packed with tourists and royal antiques.

The palace is the product of many kings over several centuries. Philip II (1527-1598) made a wooden fortress on this site his governing center when he established Madrid as Spain's capital. When that palace burned down, the current structure was built by King Philip V (1683-1746). Philip V wanted to make it his own private Versailles, to match his French upbringing; as the grandson of Louis XIV, he was born in Versailles—and ordered his tapas in French. His son, Charles III (whose statue graces Puerta del Sol), added interior decor in the Italian style, since he'd spent his formative years in Italy. These civilized Bourbon kings were trying to raise Spain to the cultural level of the rest of Europe. They hired foreign artists to oversee construction and established Spanish porcelain and tapestry factories to copy works done in Paris or Brussels. Over the years, the palace was expanded and enriched, as each Spanish king tried to outdo his predecessor.

Today's palace is ridiculously supersized—with 2,800 rooms, tons of luxurious tapestries, a king's ransom of chandeliers, frescoes by Tiepolo, priceless porcelain, and bronze decor covered in gold leaf. While these days the royal family lives in a mansion a few miles away, this place still functions as the ceremonial palace, used for formal state receptions, royal weddings, and tourists' daydreams.

Cost and Hours: €11; open daily April-Sept 10:00-20:00, Oct-March 10:00-18:00, last entry one hour before closing; from Puerta del Sol, walk 15 minutes down pedestrianized Calle del Arenal (Metro: Ópera); palace can close for royal functions—confirm in advance.

Crowd Control: The palace is most crowded on Wednesdays and Thursdays, when it's free for locals. On any day, arrive early or go late to avoid lines and crowds.

Madrid Card holders get to skip the line: Enter around the right side at the group entry point, a block down, along Calle de Bailén.

Information: Short English descriptions posted in each room complement what I describe in my tour. The museum guidebook demonstrates a passion for meaningless data. Tel. 914-548-800, www.patrimonionacional.es.

Tours: You can wander on your own or join a €4 **guided tour.** Check the time of the next English-language tour and decide as you buy your ticket; the tours are dry, depart sporadically, and aren't worth a long wait. The excellent €4 **audioguide** is much more interesting.

Services: Free lockers and a WC are just past the ticket booth. Upstairs you'll find a more serious bookstore with good books on Spanish history.

Photography: Not allowed.

Eating: Though the palace has a refreshing air-conditioned cafeteria upstairs (with a salad bar), I prefer to walk a few minutes and find a place near the Royal Theater or on Calle del Arenal. Another great option is **Café de Oriente,** boasting fin-de-siècle elegance immediately across the park from the Royal

Royal Palace

Palace. Its lunch special is good and reasonable—three courses for €15 (Mon-Fri 13:00-16:00)—but the restaurant and terrace menus are pricey (Plaza de Oriente 2, tel. 915-413-974, www.cafedeoriente.es).

● SELF-GUIDED TOUR

You'll follow a simple one-way circuit on a single floor covering more than 20 rooms.

• Buy your ticket, pass through the bookstore, stand in the middle of the vast open-air courtyard, and face the palace entrance.

Palace Exterior: The palace sports the French-Italian Baroque architecture so popular in the 18th century—heavy columns, classical-looking statues, a balustrade roofline, and false-front entrance. The entire building is made of gray-and-white local stone (very little wood) to prevent the kind of fire that leveled the previous castle. Imagine the place in its heyday, with a courtyard full of soldiers on parade, or a lantern-lit scene of horse carriages arriving for a ball.

• Enter the palace and show your ticket.

Palace Lobby: In the old days, horse-drawn carriages would drop you off here. Today, stretch limos do the same thing for gala events. (If you're taking a guided palace tour, this is where you wait to begin.) The modern black bust in the corner is of Juan Carlos I, a "people's king," who is credited with bringing democracy to Spain after 36 years under dictator Franco. (Juan Carlos passed the throne to his son in 2014.)

Grand Stairs: Gazing up the imposing staircase, you can see that Spain's kings wanted to make a big first impression. Whenever high-end dignitaries arrive, fancy carpets are rolled down the stairs (notice the little metal bar-holding hooks). Begin your ascent, up steps that are intentionally shallow, making your climb slow and regal. Overhead, the white-and-blue ceiling fresco gradually opens up to your view. It shows the Spanish king, sitting on clouds, surrounded by female Virtues.

At the first landing, the burgundy coat of arms represents Felipe VI, Spain's current king and the son of Juan Carlos. J. C. knew Spain was ripe for democracy after Francisco Franco's dictatorial regime. Rather than become "Juan the Brief" (as some were nicknaming him), he returned real power to the parliament. You'll see his (figure) head on the back of the Spanish €1 and €2 coins.

Continue up to the top of the stairs. Before entering the first room, look to the right of the door to find a white marble bust of J. C.'s great-great-g-g-g-great-grandfather Philip V, who began the Bourbon dynasty in Spain in 1700 and had this palace built.

Guard Room: The palace guards used to hang out in this relatively simple room. Notice the two fake doors, added to give the room symmetry. The old clocks—still in working order—are part of a collection of hundreds amassed as a hobby by Spain's royal family. Throughout the palace, the themes chosen for the ceiling frescoes relate to the function of the room they decorate. In this room, the ceiling fresco is the first we'll see in a series by the great Venetian painter Giambattista Tiepolo. It depicts the legendary hero Aeneas (in red, with the narrow face of Charles III) standing in the clouds of heaven, gazing up at his mother Venus (with the face of Charles' own mother).

Notice the carpets in this room. Although much of what you see in the palace dates from the 18th century, the carpet on the left (folded over to show the stitching) is new, from 1991. It was produced by Madrid's royal tapestry factory, the same works that made the older original carpet. This new carpet was woven the traditional way—by hand. At the fine inlaid stone table in this room, the king signed the treaty finalizing Spain's entry into the European Union.

Hall of Columns: Originally a ballroom and dining room, today this space is used for formal ceremonies and intimate concerts. This is where Spain formally joined the European Union in 1985

Spain's Royal Families: From Habsburg to Bourbon

Spain as we know it was born when four long-established medieval kingdoms were joined by the 1469 marriage of Isabel, ruler of Castile and León, and Ferdinand, ruler of Aragon and Navarre. The "Catholic Monarchs" (Reyes Católicos) wasted no time in driving the Islamic Moors out of Spain (the Reconquista). By 1492, Isabel and Ferdinand conquered a fifth kingdom, Granada, establishing more or less the same borders that Spain has today.

This was an age when foreign policy was conducted, in part, by marrying royal children into other royal families. Among the dynastic marriages of their children, Isabel and Ferdinand arranged for their third child, Juana "the Mad," to marry the crown prince of Austria, Philip "the Fair." This was a huge coup for the Spanish royal family. A member of the Habsburg dynasty, Philip was heir to the Holy Roman Empire, which then encompassed much of today's Austria, Czech Republic, Hungary, Transylvania, the Low Countries, southern Italy, and more. And when Juana's brothers died, making her ruler of the kingdoms of Spain, it paved the way for her son, Charles, to inherit the kingdoms of his four grandparents—creating a vast realm and making him the most powerful man in Europe. He ruled as Charles I (king of Spain, from 1516) and Charles V (Holy Roman emperor, from 1519).

He was followed by Philip II, Philip III, Philip IV, and finally Charles II. Over this period, Spain rested on its laurels, eventually squandering much of its wealth and losing some of its holdings. Arguably the most inbred of an already very inbred dynasty (his parents were uncle and niece), Charles II was weak, sickly, and unable to have children, ending the 200-year Habsburg dynasty in Spain with his death in 1700.

Charles II willed the Spanish crown to the Bourbons of France, and his grand-nephew Philip of Anjou, whose granddaddy was the "Sun King" Louis XIV of

(the fancy table used to be in here) and honored its national soccer team after their 2010 World Cup victory. The tapestries (like most you'll see in the palace) are 17th-century Belgian, from designs by Raphael.

The central theme in the ceiling fresco (by Jaquinto, following Tiepolo's style) is Apollo driving the chariot of the sun, while Bacchus enjoys wine, women, and song with a convivial gang. This is a reminder that the mark of a good king is to drive the chariot of state as smartly as Apollo, while providing an environment where the people can enjoy life to the fullest.

• *The next several rooms were the living quarters of King Charles III (r. 1759-1788). First comes his* **lounge** *(with red walls), where the king would enjoy the company of a similarly great ruler—the Roman emperor Trajan—depicted "triumphing" on the ceiling. The heroics of Trajan, one of two Roman emperors born in Spain, naturally made the king feel good. Next, you enter the blue-walled...*

Antechamber: This was Charles III's dining room. The four paintings—all originals by Francisco de Goya—are of Charles III's son and successor, King Charles IV (looking a bit like a dim-witted George Washington), and his wife, María Luisa (who wore the pants in the palace). María

France, took the throne. But the rest of Europe feared allowing the already powerful Louis XIV to add Spain (and its vast New World holdings) to his empire. Austria, the Germanic States, Holland, and England backed a different choice (Archduke Charles of Austria). So began the War of Spanish Succession (1700-1714), involving all of Europe. The French eventually prevailed, but with the signing of the Treaty of Utrecht (1713), Philip had to give up any claim to the throne of France. This let him keep the Spanish crown but ensured that his heirs—the future Spanish Bourbon dynasty—couldn't become too powerful by merging with the French Bourbons.

In 1714, the French-speaking Philip became the first king of the Bourbon dynasty in Spain (with the name Philip V). He breathed new life into the monarchy, which had grown ineffectual and corrupt. When the wooden Habsburg royal palace burned on Christmas Eve of 1734, Philip (who was born at Versailles) built a spectacular late-Baroque-style palace as a bold symbol of his new dynasty. This is the palace that wows visitors to Madrid today. Construction was finished in 1764, and Philip V's son Charles III was the palace's first occupant. You'll see Charles III's decorations if you visit the palace's interior.

The Bourbon palace remained the home of Spain's kings from 1764 until 1931, when democratic elections led to the Second Spanish Republic and forced King Alfonso XIII into exile. After Francisco Franco took power in 1939, he sidelined the royals by making himself ruler-for-life. But later he handpicked as his successor Alfonso XIII's grandson, the Bourbon Prince Juan Carlos, whom Franco believed would continue his hard-line policies. When Franco died in 1975, Juan Carlos surprised everyone by voluntarily turning the real power back over to Spain's parliament. Juan Carlos abdicated the throne in 2014. Today, his son Felipe VI is a figurehead Bourbon king and Spain is a constitutional monarchy.

Luisa was famously hands-on, tough, and businesslike, while Charles IV was pretty wimpy as far as kings go. To meet the demand for his work, Goya made replicas of these portraits, which you'll see in the Prado.

The 12-foot-tall clock—showing Cronus, god of time, in porcelain, bronze, and mahogany—sits on a music box. Reminding us of how time flies, Cronus is shown both as a child and as an old man. The palace's clocks are wound—and reset—once a week (they grow progressively less accurate as the week goes on). The gilded decor you see throughout the palace is bronze with gold leaf. Velázquez's famous painting,

Las Meninas (which you'll marvel at in the Prado), originally hung in this room.

Gasparini Room: (Gasp!) The entire room is designed, top to bottom, as a single gold-green-pink ensemble: from the frescoed ceiling, to the painted stucco figures, silk-embroidered walls, chandelier, furniture, and multicolored marble floor. Each marble was quarried in, and therefore represents, a different region of Spain. Birds overhead spread their wings, vines sprout, and fruit bulges from the surface. With curlicues everywhere (including their reflection in the mirrors), the room dazzles the eye and mind. It's a triumph of the Rococo style, with

Ⓐ *Grand Stairs*

Ⓑ *Armory*

Ⓒ *Gasparini Room*

Ⓓ *Gala Dining Hall*

Ⓔ *Porcelain Room*

Ⓕ *Stradivarius Room*

Ⓖ *Throne Room*

exotic motifs such as the Chinese people sculpted into the corners of the ceiling. (These figures, like many in the palace, were formed from stucco, or wet plaster.) The fabric gracing the walls was recently restored. Sixty people spent three years replacing the rotten silk fabric and then embroidering back on the silver, silk, and gold threads.

Note the micro-mosaic table—a typical royal or aristocratic souvenir from any visit to Rome in the mid-1800s. The chandelier, the biggest in the palace, is mesmerizing, especially with its glittering canopy of crystal reflecting in the wall mirrors.

The room was the king's dressing room. For a divine monarch, dressing was a public affair. The court bigwigs would assemble here as the king, standing on a platform—notice the height of the mirrors—would pull on his leotards and toy with his wig.

• *In the next room, the silk wallpaper is from modern times—the intertwined "J. C. S." indicates the former monarchs Juan Carlos I and Sofía. Pass through the silk room to reach...*

Charles III Bedroom: Charles III died here in his bed in 1788. His grandson, Ferdinand VII, redid the room to honor the great man. The room's blue color scheme recalls the blue-clad monks of Charles' religious order. A portrait of Charles (in blue) hangs on the wall. The ceiling fresco shows Charles establishing his order, with its various (female) Virtues. At the base of the ceiling (near the harp player) find the baby in his mother's arms—that would be Ferdy himself, the long-sought male heir, preparing to continue Charles' dynasty.

The chandelier is in the shape of the fleur-de-lis (the symbol of the Bourbon family) capped with a Spanish crown. As you exit the room, notice the thick walls between rooms. These hid service corridors for servants, who scurried about mostly unseen.

Porcelain Room: This tiny but lavish room is paneled with green-white-gold porcelain garlands, vines, babies, and mythological figures. The entire ensemble was disassembled for safety during the civil war. (Find the little screws in the greenery that hides the seams between panels.) Notice the clock in the center with Atlas supporting the world on his shoulders.

Yellow Lounge: This was a study for Charles III. The properly cut crystal of the chandelier shows all the colors of the rainbow. Stand under it, look up, and sway slowly to see the colors glitter. This is not a particularly precious room, but its decor pops because the lights are generally left on. Imagine the entire palace as brilliant as this when fully lit. As you leave the room, look back at the chandelier to notice its design of a temple with a fountain inside.

• *Next comes the...*

Gala Dining Hall: Up to 12 times a year, the king entertains as many as 144 guests at this bowling lane-size table, which can be extended to the length of the room. The parquet floor was the preferred dancing surface when balls were held in this fabulous room. Note the vases from China, the tapestries, and the ceiling fresco depicting Christopher Columbus kneeling before Ferdinand and Isabel, presenting exotic souvenirs and his new friends. Imagine this hall in action when a foreign dignitary dines here. The king and queen preside from the center of the room. Find their chairs (slightly higher than the rest). The tables are set with fine crystal and cutlery (which we'll see a couple of rooms later). And the whole place glitters as the 15 chandeliers (and their 900 bulbs) are fired up. (The royal kitchens, where the gala dinners were prepared, may be open for viewing; ask the staff where to enter.)

• *Pass through the next room of coins and medals, known as the **Cinema Room** because the royal family once enjoyed Sunday afternoons at the movies here. The royal* string ensemble played here to entertain during formal dinners. From here, move into the...

Silver Room: Some of this 19th-century silver tableware—knives and forks, bowls, salt and pepper shakers, and the big tureen—is used in the Gala Dining Hall on special occasions. If you look carefully, you can see quirky royal necessities, including a baby's silver rattle and fancy candle snuffers.

• Head straight ahead to the...

Crockery and Crystal Rooms: Philip V's collection of china is the oldest and rarest of the various pieces on display; it came from China before that country was opened to the West. Since Chinese crockery was in such demand, any self-respecting European royal family had to have its own porcelain works (such as France's Sèvres or Germany's Meissen) to produce high-quality knockoffs (and cutesy Hummel-like figurines). The porcelain technique itself was kept a royal secret. As you leave, check out Isabel II's excellent 19th-century crystal ware.

• Exit to the hallway and notice the interior courtyard you've been circling one room at a time.

Courtyard: You can see how the royal family lived in the spacious middle floor while staff was upstairs. The kitchens, garage, and storerooms were on the ground level. The new king, Felipe VI, married a commoner (for love) and celebrated their wedding party in this courtyard, which was decorated as if another palace room. Spain's royals take their roles and responsibilities seriously—making a point to be approachable and empathizing with their subjects—and are very popular.

• Between statues of two of the giants of Spanish royal history (Isabel and Ferdinand), you'll enter the...

Royal Chapel: This chapel is used for private concerts and funerals. The royal coffin sits here before making the sad trip to El Escorial to join the rest of Spain's past royalty. The glass case contains the

Tiepolo's Frescoes

In 1762, King Charles III invited Europe's most celebrated palace painter, Giambattista Tiepolo (1696-1770), to decorate three rooms in the newly built palace. Sixty-six-year-old Tiepolo made the trip from Italy with his two well-known sons as assistants. They spent four years atop scaffolding decorating in the fresco technique, troweling plaster on the ceiling and quickly painting it before it dried.

Tiepolo's translucent ceilings seem to open up to a cloud-filled heaven, where Spanish royals cavort with Greek gods and pudgy cherubs. Tiepolo used every trick to "fool the eye" (trompe l'oeil), creating dizzying skyscapes of figures tumbling at every angle. He mixes 2-D painting with 3-D stucco figures that spill over the picture frame. His colorful, curvaceous ceilings blend seamlessly with the flamboyant furniture of the room below. Tiepolo's Royal Palace frescoes are often cited as the final flowering of Baroque and Rococo art.

entire body of St. Felix, given to the Spanish king by the pope in the 19th century. Note the "crying room" in the back for royal babies. While the royals rarely worship here (they prefer the cathedral adjacent to the palace), the thrones are here just in case.

• Pass through the **Queen's Boudoir**—where royal ladies hung out—and into the...

Stradivarius Room: Of all the instruments made by Antonius Stradivarius (1644-1737), only 300 survive. This is the world's best collection and the only matching quartet set: two violins, a viola, and a cello. Charles III, a cultured man, fiddled around with these. Today, a single Stradivarius instrument might sell for $15 million.

• Continue into the room at the far left.

Crown and Scepter Room: The stunning crown and scepter of the last Habsburg king, Carlos II, are displayed in a glass case in the middle. Look for the 2014 proclamations of Juan Carlos' abdication of the crown and Felipe VI's acceptance as king of Spain. Notice which writing implement each man chose to sign with: Juan Carlos' traditional classic pen and Felipe VI's modern one.

• *Walk back through the Stradivarius Room and into the courtyard hallway. Continue your visit through the Antechamber, where ambassadors would wait to present themselves, and the Small Official Chambers, where officials are received by royalty and have their photos taken. Walk through two rooms, decorated in blue and red with tapestries and paintings, to the grand finale, the...*

Throne Room: This room, where the Spanish monarchs preside, is one of the palace's most glorious. And it holds many of the oldest and most precious things in the palace: silver-and-crystal chandeliers (from Venice's Murano Island), elaborate lions, and black bronze statues from the fortress that stood here before the 1734 fire. The 12 mirrors, impressively

Tiepolo ceiling fresco in the Throne Room

large in their day, each represent a different month.

The throne stands under a gilded canopy, on a raised platform, guarded by four lions (symbols of power found throughout the palace). The coat of arms above the throne shows the complexity of the Bourbon empire across Europe—which, in the 18th century, included Tirol, Sicily, Burgundy, the Netherlands, and more. Though the room was decorated under Charles III (late 18th century), the throne itself is modern. In Spain, a new throne is built for each king or queen, complete with a gilded portrait on the back.

Today, this room is where the king's guests salute him before they move on to dinner. He receives them relatively informally...standing at floor level, rather than seated up on the throne.

The ceiling fresco (1764) is the last great work by Tiepolo (see sidebar on page 440), who died in Madrid in 1770. His vast painting (88 × 32 feet) celebrates the vast Spanish empire—upon which the sun also never set. The Greek gods look down from the clouds, overseeing Spain's empire, whose territories are represented by the people ringing the edges of the ceiling. Find the Native American (hint: follow the rainbow to the macho red-caped conquistador who motions to someone he has conquered). From the near end of the room (where tourists stand), look up to admire Tiepolo's skill at making a pillar seem to shoot straight up into the sky. The pillar's pedestal has an inscription celebrating Tiepolo's boss, Charles III ("Carole Magna"). Notice how the painting spills over the gilded wood frame, where 3-D statues recline alongside 2-D painted figures. All of the throne room's decorations—the fresco, gold garlands, mythological statues, wall medallions—unite in a multimedia extravaganza.

• *Exit the palace down the same grand stairway you climbed at the start. Cross the big courtyard, heading to the far-right corner to the...*

Armory: Here you'll find weapons and armor belonging to many great Spanish historical figures. While some of it was actually for fighting, the great royal pastimes included hunting and tournaments, and armor was largely for sport or ceremony. Much of this armor dates from Habsburg times, before this palace was built. Circle the big room clockwise.

In the three glass cases on the left, you'll see the oldest pieces in the collection. In the central case (case III), the shield, sword, belt, and dagger belonged to Boabdil, the last Moorish king, who surrendered Granada in 1492. In case IV, the armor and swords belonged to Ferdinand, the husband of Isabel, and Boabdil's contemporary.

The center of the room is filled with knights in armor on horseback—mostly suited up for tournament play. Many of the pieces belonged to the two great kings who ruled Spain at its 16th-century peak, Charles I and his son Philip II.

The long wall on the left displays the personal armor wardrobe of Charles I (a.k.a. the Holy Roman emperor Charles V). At the far end, you'll meet Charles on horseback. The mannequin of the king wears the same armor and assumes the same pose as in Titian's famous painting of him (in the Prado).

The opposite wall showcases the armor and weapons of Philip II, the king who helped Spain start its long slide downward, impoverishing the country with his wars against the Protestants. Anticipating that debt collectors would ransack his estate after his death, he specifically protected his impressive collection of armor by founding this armory.

Downstairs is more armor, mostly from the 17th century. The pint-size armor wasn't for children to fight in. It's training armor for noble youngsters, who as adults would be expected to ride, fight, and play gracefully in these clunky getups. Before you leave, notice the life-saving breastplates dimpled with bullet dents (to the right of exit door).

• *Climb the steps from the armory exit to the viewpoint.*

View of the Gardens: Looking down from this high bluff, it's clear why rulers have built on this strategically located spot since the ninth century. The vast palace backyard, once the king's hunting ground, is now a city park, dotted with fountains.

• *Walk to the center of the huge square and face the palace. Notice how the palace of the king faces the palace of the bishop (the cathedral). Whew. After all those rooms, frescoes, chandeliers, knickknacks, kings, and history, consider a final stop in the palace's upstairs café for a well-deserved rest.*

Madrid's Museum Neighborhood

Three great museums, all within a 10-minute walk of one another, cluster in east Madrid. The Prado is Europe's top collection of paintings. The Thyssen-Bornemisza sweeps through European art from old masters to moderns. And the Centro de Arte Reina Sofía has a choice selection of modern art, starring Picasso's famous *Guernica.*

Rick's Tip: *To really save money,* **visit when the sights are free:** *every evening for the Prado, every evening but Tuesday (when it's closed) for the Reina Sofía, and Mondays for the Thyssen-Bornemisza.*

Remember that the **Paseo del Arte** combo-ticket (€25.60, sold at the museums, allows line-skipping) is cheaper than paying admission.

▲▲▲PRADO MUSEUM (MUSEO NACIONAL DEL PRADO)

With more than 3,000 canvases, including entire rooms of masterpieces by superstar painters, the Prado (PRAH-doh) is my vote for the greatest collection anywhere of paintings by the European masters. The Prado is *the* place to enjoy the great Spanish painter Francisco de Goya, and

it's also the home of Diego Velázquez's *Las Meninas,* considered by many to be the world's finest painting, period. In addition to Spanish works, you'll find paintings by Italian and Flemish masters, including Hieronymus Bosch's fantastical *Garden of Earthly Delights* altarpiece.

Cost: €14, additional (obligatory) fee for occasional temporary exhibits, free Mon-Sat 18:00-20:00 and Sun 17:00-19:00, under age 18 always free.

Hours: Mon-Sat 10:00-20:00, Sun 10:00-19:00, last entry 30 minutes before closing.

Crowd Control and Avoiding Lines: It's generally less crowded at lunchtime (13:00-16:00), when there are fewer groups, and on weekdays. It can be busy on free evenings and weekends.

Ticket-buying lines can be long. Here are your time-saving options:

1. Use the ticket machines at the Goya entrance (credit cards only).

2. Book an entry time in advance online (www.museodelprado.es, print out ticket) or by phone (tel. 902-107-077, get a reference number). Same-day advance purchase is possible if space is available.

3. Buy a Paseo del Arte combo-ticket

Prado Museum

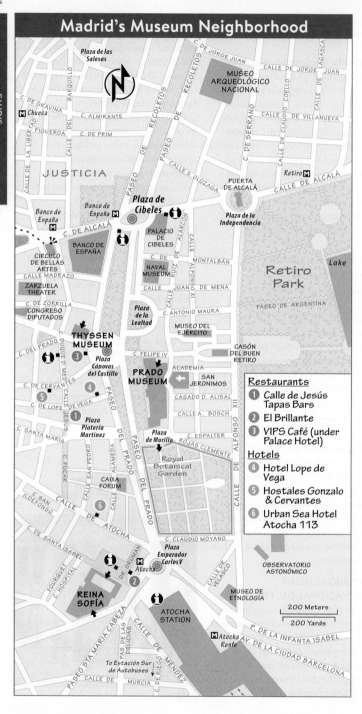

Madrid's Museum Neighborhood

Restaurants

1 Calle de Jesús Tapas Bars

2 El Brillante

3 VIPS Café (under Palace Hotel)

Hotels

4 Hotel Lope de Vega

5 Hostales Gonzalo & Cervantes

6 Urban Sea Hotel Atocha 113

200 Meters
200 Yards

(described earlier) at the less-crowded Thyssen-Bornemisza or Reina Sofía museums.

4. Get a Madrid Card beforehand (see page 415).

Getting There: It's at the Paseo del Prado. The nearest Metro stops are Banco de España (line 2) and Atocha (line 1), each a five-minute walk from the museum. It's a 15-minute walk from Puerta del Sol.

Getting In: While there are several entrances, you must buy tickets at the Goya (north) entrance. (Even at free-entry times, you need to pick up a gratis ticket at the Goya ticket window.) Once you have your ticket, you can enter at the Goya, Jerónimos, or Velázquez entrance. Those who book in advance or have a Madrid Card can pick up their tickets at the adjacent Jerónimos entrance, skipping the main line. The Murillo entrance is generally reserved for student groups. Your bags will be scanned as you enter.

Information: Tel. 913-302-800, www.museodelprado.es.

Tours: The €3.50 audioguide is a helpful supplement to my self-guided tour. Given the ever-changing locations of paintings (making my tour tough to follow), the audioguide is a good investment, allowing you to wander and dial up commentary on 250 masterpieces.

Services: The Jerónimos entrance has an information desk, bag check, audioguides, bookshop, WCs, and café. Larger bags must be checked. No drinks, food, backpacks, or large umbrellas are allowed inside.

Photography: Not allowed.

Eating: The self-service cafeteria and restaurant are open daily (€9 main dishes, €6 salads and sandwiches, Mon-Sat 10:00-19:30, Sun 10:00-18:30, hot dishes served only 12:30-16:00). A block west of the Prado, you'll find **VIPS**, a bright, popular chain restaurant, handy for a cheap and filling salad, engulfed in a shop selling books and candy (daily 9:00-24:00, across boulevard from north end of Prado at Plaza de Canova del Castillo, under Palace Hotel). Next door is Spain's first Starbucks, opened in 2001. A strip of wonderful tapas bars is just a few blocks west of the museum, lining Calle de Jesús (see page 467). If you want to take a break outside the museum for lunch, you can reenter the museum on the same ticket as long as you get it stamped at a desk marked "*Educación*," near the Jerónimos entrance.

➲ SELF-GUIDED TOUR

Centuries of powerful kings (and lots of New World gold) funded the Prado, the greatest painting museum in the world. You'll see first-class Italian Renaissance art (especially Titian), Northern art (Bosch, Rubens, Dürer), and Spanish art (El Greco, Velázquez, Goya). This huge museum is not laid out chronologically, so this tour will not be chronological. Instead, we'll hit the highlights with a minimum of walking. Paintings are moved around frequently—if you can't find a particular one, ask a guard.

• *Pick up a museum map as you enter. Once inside, make your way to the main gallery on the ground floor. Plans are in the works to renumber the rooms. Compare the map in this book with the museum's printed map. Even if the room numbers are different, the paintings should be in the same physical locations. Follow your map and signs to Sala 49. Look for the following paintings in Room 49 and the adjoining galleries.*

ITALIAN RENAISSANCE

During its Golden Age (the 1500s), Spain may have been Europe's richest country, but Italy was still the most cultured. Spain's kings loved how Italian Renaissance artists captured a three-dimensional world on a two-dimensional canvas, bringing Bible scenes to life and celebrating real people and their emotions.

Raphael (1483-1520) was the undisputed master of realism. When he

painted *Portrait of a Cardinal* (*El Cardenal,* c. 1510), he showed the sly Vatican functionary with a day's growth of beard and an air of superiority, locking eyes with the viewer. The cardinal's slightly turned torso is as big as a statue. Nearby are Raphael's *Holy Family* and other paintings.

Fra Angelico's *The Annunciation* (*La Anunciación,* c. 1426) is in nearby Room 56b. It's half medieval piety, half Renaissance realism. In the crude Garden of Eden scene (on the left), a scrawny, sinful First Couple hovers unrealistically above the foliage, awaiting eviction. The angel's Annunciation to Mary (right side) is more Renaissance, both with its upbeat message (that Jesus will be born to redeem sinners like Adam and Eve) and in the budding photorealism, set beneath 3-D arches. (Still, aren't the receding bars of the porch's ceiling a bit off? Painting three dimensions wasn't that easy.)

Also in Room 56b, the tiny *Dormition of the Virgin* (*El Transito de la Virgen*), by **Andrea Mantegna** (c. 1431-1506), shows his mastery of Renaissance perspective. The apostles crowd into the room to mourn the last moments of the Virgin Mary's life. The receding floor tiles and open window in the back create the subconscious effect of Mary's soul finding its way out into the serene distance.

• *Find examples of Northern European art, including Dürer, in Room 55b.*

NORTHERN ART

Albrecht Dürer's *Self-Portrait* (*Autorretrato*), from 1498, is possibly the first time an artist depicted himself. The artist, age 26, is German, but he's all dolled up in a fancy Italian hat and permed hair. He'd recently returned from Italy and wanted to impress his countrymen with his sophistication. Dürer (1471-1528) wasn't simply vain. He'd grown accustomed, as an artist in Renaissance Italy, to being treated like a prince. Note Dürer's signature, the pyramid-shaped "A. D." (D inside the A), on the windowsill.

Dürer's 1507 panel paintings of Adam

A *Raphael,* Portrait of a Cardinal
B *Fra Angelico,* The Annunciation
C *Mantegna,* Dormition of the Virgin

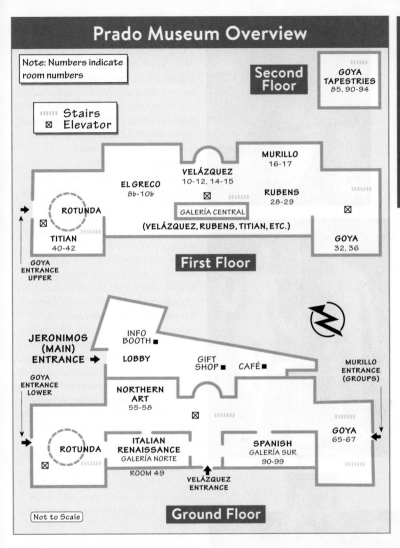

Prado Museum Overview

Note: Numbers indicate room numbers

⸽⸽⸽⸽⸽ Stairs
⊠ Elevator

Second Floor

GOYA TAPESTRIES
85, 90-94

First Floor

MURILLO
16-17

VELÁZQUEZ
10-12, 14-15

EL GRECO
8b-10b

RUBENS
28-29

ROTUNDA

GALERÍA CENTRAL
(VELÁZQUEZ, RUBENS, TITIAN, ETC.)

TITIAN
40-42

GOYA
32, 36

GOYA ENTRANCE UPPER

Ground Floor

JERONIMOS (MAIN) ENTRANCE →

INFO BOOTH ■

LOBBY

GIFT SHOP ■   CAFÉ ■

MURILLO ENTRANCE (GROUPS)

GOYA ENTRANCE LOWER

NORTHERN ART
55-58

ROTUNDA

ITALIAN RENAISSANCE
GALERÍA NORTE
ROOM 49

SPANISH
GALERÍA SUR
90-99

GOYA
65-67

VELÁZQUEZ ENTRANCE

Not to Scale

and Eve are the first full-size nudes in Northern European art. Like Greek statues, they pose in their separate niches, with three-dimensional, anatomically correct bodies. This was a bold humanist proclamation that the body is good, man is good, and the things of the world are good.

• Backtrack through Room 56b, and go through Rooms 57b and 57 to Room 58.

Descent from the Cross (El Descendimiento) by **Rogier van der Weyden** (c. 1399-1464) is a masterpiece. The Flemish painter reveals the psychological drama of this biblical event by placing the characters of real people in a contemporary (1435) scene. The Flemish were masters of detail, as you can see in the cloth, jewels, faces, and even tears. These effects are all enhanced by the artist's choice of oil paint, a relatively new and vibrant medium especially suited to conveying

Ⓐ *Dürer*, Self-Portrait
Ⓑ *Dürer*, Adam and Eve
Ⓒ *Van der Weyden*, Descent from the Cross

textural realism and intense color. The creative composition suggests that, in losing her son, Mary suffered along with Jesus, which is conveyed by showing their bodies in the same position. Note the realism, especially in the mournful faces, and the gorgeous arc of Mary Magdalene's pose (far right). As the Netherlands was then a part of the Spanish empire, this painting ended up in Madrid.

• *Continue to Room 56a.*

Hieronymus Bosch (c. 1450-1516), in his cryptic triptych *The Garden of Earthly Delights* (*El Jardín de las Delicias*, c. 1505), relates the message that the pleasures of life are fleeting, and we'd better avoid them or we'll wind up in hell.

This is a triptych—a three-paneled altarpiece, with a central image and two hinged outer panels. When the panels are closed, another image is revealed on their back side. All four images work together to teach a religious message. First notice the back side of this otherwise colorful work. It's a black-and-white scene depicting Creation on Day Three—before God added animals and humans to the mix. So, imagine the altarpiece closed. All is mellow. Then open it up, bring on the people, and splash into the colorful *Garden of Earthly Delights*.

On the left is Paradise, showing naked Adam and Eve before original sin. Everything is in its place, with animals behaving virtuously. Innocent Adam and Eve get married, with God himself performing the ceremony.

The central panel is a riot of hedonistic men and women on a perpetual spring break. Men on horseback ride round and round, searching for but never reaching the elusive Fountain of Youth. Others frolic in earth's "Garden," oblivious to where they came from (left) and where they may end up (exit...right).

Now, go to Hell (right panel). It's a burning Dante's Inferno-inspired wasteland where genetic-mutant demons torture sinners. Everyone gets their just

Bosch, The Garden of Earthly Delights

desserts, like the glutton who is eaten and re-eaten eternally, the musician strung up on his own harp, and the gamblers with their table forever overturned. In the center, hell is literally frozen over. A creature with a broken eggshell body hosting a tavern, tree-trunk legs, and a hat featuring a bagpipe (symbolic of hedonism) stares out—it's the face of Bosch himself.

If you like this Bosch, you'll enjoy the others in this gallery. The table in the center features his *Seven Deadly Sins (Los Pecados Capitales,* late 15th century). Each of the four corners has a theme: death, judgment, paradise, and hell. The fascinating wheel, with Christ in the center, names the sins in Latin (lust, envy, gluttony, and so on), and illustrates each

with a vivid scene that works as a slice of 15th-century Dutch life.

Another triptych, *The Hay Wain (El Carro de Heno,* c. 1516), hangs nearby. Like *The Garden of Earthly Delights,* it teaches morality in what must have been an effective and frightening way back when Bosch painted it.

Nearby, **Pieter Bruegel** the Elder's (c. 1525-1569) work chronicles the 16th century's violent Catholic-Protestant wars in *The Triumph of Death (El Triunfo de la Muerte).* The painting is one big, chaotic battle, featuring skeletons attacking helpless mortals. Bruegel's message is simple and morbid: No one can escape death.

• *But you can escape this room. Continue through the next few galleries (55a and 55) and into the red lobby. Find the elevators on the right, and go up to level 1. Exiting the elevator, turn left into Room 11. This is one of several rooms with work by Velázquez, but Las Meninas is around the corner to the right in the large, lozenge-shaped Room 12.*

SPANISH MASTERS
Diego Velázquez (vel-LAHTH-keth, 1599-1660) was the photojournalist of court painters, capturing the Spanish king and his court in formal portraits that take on aspects of a candid snapshot. Room

Bruegel, The Triumph of Death

12 is filled with the portraits Velázquez was called on to produce. Kings and princes prance like Roman emperors. Get up close and notice that his remarkably detailed costumes are nothing but a few messy splotches of paint—the proto-Impressionism Velázquez helped pioneer.

The room's renowned centerpiece is Velázquez's *Las Meninas*, c. 1656. It's a peek at nannies caring for Princess Margarita and, at the same time, a behind-the-scenes look at Velázquez at work. One hot summer day in 1656, Velázquez (at left, with paintbrush and Dalí moustache) stands at his easel and stares out at the people he's painting—the king and queen. They would have been standing about where we are, and we see only their reflection in the mirror at the back of the room. Their daughter (blonde hair, in center) watches her parents being painted, joined by her servants (*meninas*), dwarves, and the family dog. At that very moment, a man happens to pass by the doorway at back and pauses to look in. Why's he there? Probably just to give the painting more depth.

This frozen moment is lit by the window on the right, splitting the room into bright and shaded planes that recede into the distance. The main characters look right at us, making us part of the scene, seemingly able to walk around, behind, and among the characters. Notice the exquisitely painted mastiff.

If you stand in the center of the room, the 3-D effect is most striking. This is art come to life.

• *Facing this painting, leave to the left and go back into Room 11.*

Look around this gallery and see how Velázquez enjoyed capturing light—and capturing the moment. *The Feast of Bacchus* (*Los Borrachos*, c. 1628) is a cell-phone snapshot in a blue-collar bar, with a coupl of peasants mugging for a photo-op with a Greek god—Bacchus, the god of wine. This was an early work, before Velázquez got his court-painter gig. A personal homage to the hardworking farmers enjoying the fruit of their labor, it shows how Velázquez had a heart for real people and believed they deserved portraits, too. Notice the almost-sacramental presence of the ultrarealistic bowl of wine in the center, as Bacchus, with the honest gut, crowns a fellow hedonist.

• *Backtrack through the big gallery with Las Meninas to Room 14.*

Velázquez's boss, King Philip IV, had an affair, got caught, and repented by commissioning the *Crucified Christ* (*Cristo Crucificado*, c. 1632). Christ hangs his head, humbly accepting his punishment. Philip would have been left to stare at the slowly dripping blood, contemplating how long Christ had to suffer to atone for Philip's sins. This is an interesting death scene. There's no anguish, no tension, no torture. Light seems to emanate from Jesus as if nothing else matters. The crown of thorns and the cloth wrapped around his waist are particularly vivid. Above it all, a sign reads in three languages: "Jesus of Nazareth, King of the Jews."

• *The nearby rooms (16 and 17) are filled with Murillo paintings. Look for a couple of his immaculately conceived virgins.*

Velázquez, Las Meninas

Bartolomé Murillo (1618-1682) put a human face on the abstract Catholic doctrine that Mary was conceived and born free of original sin. Murillo painted several versions of the *Immaculate Conception,* of which the Prado has five that sometimes rotate. *The Immaculate Conception of Los Venerables* (*La Inmaculada Concepción de los Venerables,* c. 1678) hangs in Room 16, and another version is in Room 17. Murillo's "immaculate" virgin floats in a cloud of Ivory Soap cleanliness, radiating youth and wholesome goodness. She wears the usual colors of the Virgin Mary—white for purity and blue for divinity. Sweet and escapist, Murillo's work was a hit, and must have been comforting to the wretched people of post-plague Sevilla (his hometown was hit hard in 1647-1652).

• *Return to the main gallery (Rooms 28 and 29) for lots of fleshy excitement, courtesy of Peter Paul Rubens.*

NORTHERN BAROQUE

A native of Flanders, **Peter Paul Rubens** (1577-1640) painted Baroque-style art meant to play on the emotions, titillate the senses, and carry you away. His paintings surge with Baroque energy and ripple with waves of figures. Surveying his big, boisterous canvases, you'll notice his trademarks: sex, violence, action, emotion, bright colors, and ample bodies, with the wind machine set on full. Gods are melodramatic, and nymphs flee half-human predators. Rubens painted the most beautiful women of his day—well-fed, no tan lines, and very sexy.

Rubens' *The Three Graces* (*Las Tres Gracias,* c. 1630-1635) celebrates cellulite. The ample, glowing bodies intertwine as the women exchange meaningful glances. The Grace at the left is Rubens' young second wife, Hélène Fourment, who shows up regularly in his paintings.

• *From the main gallery with the Rubens, look to the near end of the hall, where Goya's royal portraits hang. We'll end up there. But first, head the other way to Titian and El Greco. Titians line the main gallery, and the El Grecos are in Rooms 8b, 9b, and 10b.*

SPANISH MYSTIC

El Greco (1541-1614) was born in Greece (his name is Spanish for "The Greek"), trained in Venice, then settled in Toledo—60 miles from Madrid. His paintings are like Byzantine icons drenched in Venetian color and fused in the fires of Spanish mysticism. The El Greco paintings displayed here rotate, but they all glow with his unique style.

Murillo, The Immaculate Conception of Los Venerables

Rubens, The Three Graces

In *Christ Carrying the Cross (Cristo Abrazado a la Cruz*, c. 1602), Jesus accepts his fate, trudging toward death with blood running down his neck. He hugs the cross and directs his gaze along the cross-bar. His upturned eyes (sparkling with a streak of white paint) lock onto his next stop—heaven.

The Adoration of the Shepherds (La Adoración de los Pastores, c. 1614), originally painted for El Greco's own burial chapel in Toledo, has the artist's typical two-tiered composition—heaven above, earth below. The long, skinny shepherds are stretched unnaturally in between, flickering like flames toward heaven.

The Nobleman with His Hand on His Chest (El Caballero de la Mano al Pecho, c. 1580) shows an elegant and somewhat arrogant man whose hand has the middle fingers touching—El Greco's trademark way of expressing elegance (or was it the 16th-century symbol for "Live long and prosper"?). The signature is on the right in faint Greek letters—"Doménikos Theotokópoulos," El Greco's real name.

• *Return to the main gallery. Spot several Titian paintings in Rooms 25-26, and meander through the Italian wing, including Venetian portraits in Rooms 40-44 (this collection may have moved into the main gallery—Rooms 24-27—by the time you visit). Continue down the main gallery to the center, under the dome (and opposite Las Meninas), where Charles I sits royally on horseback.*

VENETIAN PAINTER TO THE COURT

Spain's Golden Age kings Charles I (a.k.a. Charles V) and Philip II were both staunch Catholics, but that didn't stop them from amassing this sometimes surprisingly racy collection. Both kings sat for portraits by the Venetian master **Titian** (c. 1485-1576).

In *The Emperor Charles V at Mühlberg (Carlos V en la Batalla de Mühlberg*, 1548), the king rears on his horse, raises his lance, and rides out to crush an army of Lutherans. Charles, having inherited many kingdoms and baronies through his family connections, was the world's most powerful man in the 1500s. (You can see the suit of armor depicted in the painting in the Royal Palace.)

In contrast (just to the left), Charles I's son, *Philip II (Felipe II*, c. 1550-1551), looks pale, suspicious, and lonely—a scholarly and complex figure. He built the austere, monastic palace at El Escorial, but also indulged himself with Titian's bevy of Renaissance Playmates—a sampling of

El Greco, Christ Carrying the Cross

El Greco, The Nobleman with His Hand on His Chest

Titian, The Emperor Charles V at Mühlberg

which is here in the Prado.

These are the faces of the Counter-Reformation. While father and son ruled differently, both had underbites, a product of royal inbreeding (which Titian painted... but very delicately).

• *Now walk to the far end of the main gallery and enter the round Room 32, where you'll see royal portraits by Goya. The museum's exciting Goya collection is on three levels at this end of the building: classic Goya (royal portraits and La Maja), on this floor; early cartoons, upstairs; and his dark and political work, downstairs.*

PAINTER OF KINGS AND DEMONS

Follow the complex **Francisco de Goya** (1746-1828) through the stages of his life—from dutiful court painter, to political rebel and scandal maker, to the disillusioned genius of his "black paintings."

In the group portrait *The Family of Charles IV* (*La Familia de Carlos IV,* 1800), the royals are all decked out in their Sunday best. Goya himself stands at his easel to the far left, painting the court (a tribute to Velázquez in *Las Meninas*) and revealing the shallowness beneath the fancy trappings. Charles, with his ridiculous hairpiece and goofy smile, was a vacuous, henpecked husband. His toothless yet domineering queen upstages him, arrogantly stretching her swanlike neck. The other adults, with their bland faces, are bug-eyed with stupidity.

• *Exit to the right across a small hallway and enter Room 36, where you'll find Goya's most scandalous work.*

Rumors flew that Goya was fooling around with the vivacious Duchess of Alba, who may have been the model for two similar paintings, **Nude Maja** (*La Maja Desnuda,* c. 1800) and **Clothed Maja** (*La Maja Vestida,* c. 1808). A *maja* was a trendy, working-class girl. Whether she's a duchess or a *maja,* Goya painted a naked lady—an actual person rather than some mythic Venus. And that was enough to risk incurring the wrath of the Inquisition. In a Titian-esque pose, the nude stretches to display her charms, her pale body with realistic pubic hair highlighted by cool green sheets. (Notice the artist's skillful rendering of the transparent fabric on the pillow.) According to a believable legend, the two paintings were displayed in a double frame, with the *Clothed Maja* sliding over the front to hide the *Nude Maja* from Inquisitive minds.

• *Find the nearby staircase and elevator, and head up to level 2 to Rooms 85 and 90-94 for more Goya.*

These rooms display Goya's **designs for tapestries** (known as "cartoons") for nobles' palaces. As you stroll around, the scenes make it clear that, while revolution was brewing in America and France, Spain's lords and ladies were playing, blissfully ignorant of the changing times. Dressed in their "Goya-style" attire, they're picnicking, dancing, flying kites, playing paddleball and Blind Man's Bluff, or just relaxing in the sun—as in the well-known *The Parasol* (*El Quitasol,* Room 85).

• *For more Goya, take the stairs or elevator down to level 0. Room 66 leads into Goya's final paintings, with a darker edge. But first go to Room 65, which takes you to powerful military scenes.*

Ⓐ *Goya,* The Family of Charles IV

Ⓑ *Goya,* Nude Maja

Ⓒ *Goya,* Second of May, 1808

Ⓓ *Goya,* Third of May, 1808

Goya became a political liberal, a champion of democracy. He was crushed when France's hero of the French Revolution, Napoleon, morphed into a tyrant and invaded Spain. In the **Second of May, 1808** (*El 2 de Mayo de 1808*, 1814), Madrid's citizens rise up to protest the occupation in Puerta del Sol, and the French send in their dreaded Egyptian mercenaries. They plow through the dense tangle of Madrileños, who have nowhere to run. The next day, the **Third of May, 1808** (*El 3 de Mayo de 1808*, 1814), the French rounded up ringleaders and executed them. The colorless firing squad—a faceless machine of death—mows them down, and they fall in bloody, tangled heaps. Goya throws a harsh prison-yard floodlight on the main victim, who spreads his arms Christ-like to ask, "Why?"

Politically, Goya was split—he was a Spaniard, but he knew France was leading Europe into the modern age. His art, while political, has no Spanish or French flags. It's a universal comment on the horror of war. Many consider Goya the last classical and first modern painter...the first painter with a social conscience.

• About-face to the "black paintings" in Room 67.

Depressed and deaf from syphilis, Goya retired to his small home and smeared its walls with his "**black paintings**"—dark in color and in mood. During this period in his life, Goya would paint his nightmares...literally. The style is considered Romantic—emphasizing emotion over beauty—but it foreshadows 20th-century Surrealism with its bizarre imagery, expressionistic and thick brushstrokes, and cynical outlook.

Stepping into Room 67, you are surrounded by art from Goya's dark period. These paintings are the actual murals from the walls of his house, transferred onto canvas. Imagine this in your living room. Goya painted what he felt with a radical technique unburdened by reality—a century before his time.

Dark forces convened continually in

Goya's dining room, where *The Great He-Goat* (*El Aquelarre/El Gran Cabrón*, c. 1820-1823) hung. The witches, who look like skeletons, swirl in a frenzy around a dark, Satanic goat in monk's clothing who presides over the obscene rituals. The black goat represents the Devil and stokes the frenzy of his wild-eyed subjects. Amid this adoration and lust, a noble lady (far right) folds her hands primly in her lap ("I thought this was a Tupperware party!"). Or, perhaps it's a pep rally for her execution, maybe inspired by the chaos that accompanied Plaza Mayor executions. Nobody knows for sure.

In *Fight to the Death with Clubs* (*Duelo a Garrotazos*, c. 1820-1823), two giants stand face-to-face, buried up to their knees, and flail at each other with clubs. It's a standoff between superpowers in the never-ending cycle of war—a vision of a tough time when people on the streets would kill for a piece of bread.

In *Saturn* (*Saturno*, c. 1820-1823), the king of the Roman gods—fearful that his progeny would overthrow him—eats one of his offspring. Saturn, also known as Cronus (Time), may symbolize how time devours us all. Either way, the painting brings new meaning to the term "child's portion."

The Drowning Dog (*Perro Semihundido*, c. 1820-1823) is, according to some, the hinge between classical art and modern art. The dog, so full of feeling and sadness, is being swallowed by quicksand...much as, to Goya, the modern age was overtaking a more classical era. And look closely at the dog. It also can be seen as a turning point for Goya. Perhaps he's bottomed out—he's been overwhelmed by depression, but his spirit has survived.

• *Head back to Room 66, and look on the right.*

🅐 *Goya*, The Great He-Goat

🅑 *Goya*, Fight to the Death with Clubs

🅒 *Goya*, Saturn

The last painting we have by Goya is *The Milkmaid of Bordeaux* (*La Lechera de Burdeos,* c. 1827). Somehow, Goya pulled out of his depression and moved to France, where he lived until his death at 82. While painting as an old man, color returned to his palette. His social commentary, his passion for painting what he felt (more than what he was hired to do), and, as you see here, the freedom of his brushstrokes explain why many consider Francesco de Goya to be the first modern artist.

• *There's lots more to the Prado, but there's also lots more to Madrid. The choice is yours.*

▲▲THYSSEN-BORNEMISZA MUSEUM

Locals call the stunning Museo del Arte Thyssen-Bornemisza simply the Thyssen (TEE-sun). It displays the impressive collection that Baron Thyssen (a wealthy German married to a former Miss Spain) sold to Spain for $350 million. The museum offers a unique chance to enjoy the sweep of all of art history—including a good sampling of the "isms" of the 20th century—in one collection. It's basically minor works by major artists and major works by minor artists. (Major works by major artists are in the Prado.) But art lovers appreciate how the good baron's art complements the Prado's collection by filling in where the Prado is weak—such as Impressionism, which is the Thyssen's forte.

Cost and Hours: €10, extra charge for special exhibits, free for kids under age 12, free on Mon; open Mon 12:00-16:00, Tue-Sun 10:00-19:00, Sat until 21:00 in summer (exhibits only), last entry 45 minutes before closing; audioguide-€4; kitty-corner from the Prado at Paseo del Prado 8 in Palacio de Villahermosa, Metro: Banco de España; tel. 902-760-511, www.museothyssen.org.

Services: The museum has free baggage storage (bags must fit through a small X-ray machine), a cafeteria and restaurant, and a shop/bookstore.

Visiting the Museum: After purchasing your ticket, continue down the wide main hall past larger-than-life paintings of former monarchs Juan Carlos I and Sofía, and then paintings of the baron (who died in 2002) and his art-collecting baroness, Carmen. At the info desk, pick up a museum map. Each of the three floors is divided into two separate areas: the permanent collection (numbered

Thyssen-Bornemisza Museum

rooms) and additions from the baroness since the 1980s (lettered rooms). Ascend to the top floor and work your way down, taking a delightful walk through art history. Visit the rooms on each floor in numerical order, from Primitive Italian (Room 1) to Surrealism and Pop Art (Room 45-47).

Rick's Tip: *If you're tired and want to* **get from the Thyssen to the Reina Sofía,** *hail a cab at the gate to zip straight there, or take bus #27.*

▲▲▲CENTRO DE ARTE REINA SOFÍA

Home to Picasso's *Guernica,* the Reina Sofía is one of Europe's most enjoyable modern art museums. Its exceptional collection of 20th-century art is housed in what was Madrid's first public hospital. The focus is on 20th-century Spanish artists—Picasso, Dalí, Miró, Gris, and Tàpies—but you'll also find plenty of works by Kandinsky, Braque, and many other giants of modern art.

The curator, who has a passion for cinema, has paired paintings with films from the same decade, which play continuously in nearby rooms. This provides a fascinating insight into the social context that inspired the art of Spain's tumultuous 20th century. Those with an appetite for modern and contemporary art can spend several delightful hours in this museum.

Cost: €8 (includes most temporary exhibits), €3 if you're under 18 or over 65, free Mon and Wed-Sat 19:00-21:00, Sun 15:00-19:00 (free times are often crowded, and you must pick up a ticket).

Hours: Mon and Wed-Sat 10:00-21:00, Sun 10:00-19:00 (fourth floor not accessible Sun after 15:00), closed Tue.

Getting There: It's a block from the Atocha Metro stop, on Plaza Sánchez Bustillo (at Calle de Santa Isabel 52). In the Metro station, follow signs for the Reina Sofía exit. Emerging from the Metro, walk straight ahead a half-block and look for an opening between the group of buildings. You'll see the tall, exterior glass elevators that flank the museum's main entrance.

A second entrance in the newer section of the building sometimes has shorter lines, especially during the museum's free hours. Facing the glass elevators, walk left around the old building to the large gates of the red-and-black Nouvel Building.

Information: Tel. 917-741-000, www.museoreinasofia.es.

Tours: The hardworking audioguide is €4.

Services: Bag storage is free. The *librería* just outside the Nouvel wing has a larger selection of Picasso and Surrealist reproductions than the main gift shop at the entrance.

Photography: Photos are not allowed in the room containing *Guernica* or in the surrounding rooms. Otherwise, photos without flash are OK.

Eating: The museum's café (a long block around the left from the main entrance) is a standout for its tasty cuisine. The square immediately in front of the museum is ringed by fine places for a simple meal or drink. My favorite is **El**

Centro de Arte Reina Sofía

Brillante, a classic dive offering pricey tapas and baguette sandwiches, but everyone comes for the fried squid sandwiches (evidenced by the older *señoras* with mouthfuls of *calamares*). Sit at the simple bar or at an outdoor table (long hours daily, two entrances—one on Plaza Sánchez Bustillo, the other at Plaza del Emperador Carlos V 8, tel. 915-286-966). Also nearby is my favorite strip of tapas bars, on Calle de Jesús (see page 467).

● SELF-GUIDED TOUR

Pick up a free map and use the good information sheets to supplement this tour.

The permanent collection is divided into three groups: art from 1900 to 1945 (second floor), art from 1945 to 1968 (fourth floor), and art from 1962 to 1982 (adjoining Nouvel wing, which also has space for bigger installations). Temporary exhibits are on the first and third floors.

While the collection is roughly chronological, it's displayed thematically. The second-floor grand hallway leads around a courtyard connecting a series of rooms, each clearly labeled with a theme. For a good first visit, ride the fancy glass elevator to level 2 and tour that floor clockwise (Goya, Surrealism, Cubism, Picasso's *Guernica*), and then finish with post-WWII art on level 4.

• *Begin in Room 201, with examples of...*

PROTO-MODERN GOYA

The wonderful curator insightfully begins your look at modern art with Goya engravings. That's because Goya is a proto-modernist—the first painter with a social conscience, the first to show inner feelings, and the first to deal with social reality. He painted because he had something to say, not just to get a paycheck.

• *Browse through the next rooms, whose underlying theme is the conflict between tradition (the powerful Church) and progress (social modernization). Find your way to Room 205 and...*

SURREALISM AND SALVADOR DALÍ

In 1914 a generation marched enthusiastically into combat, believing the Great War would be the "war to end all wars." Many artists embraced this fight, volunteered to serve, and died for the cause. But when it was over, it was clear: World War I brought no lasting change. Frustrated, many survivors turned their backs on society.

In the postwar years, a class of artists abandoned the outer world and looked inside (with inspiration from Freud). They painted mindscapes rather than landscapes. They had learned that reality is deeper than what you first "see." These were the Surrealists. To "see" their art, you need to vary your position: your physical perspective and your mental perspective. See it happy, sad, before coffee, after coffee.

In the Dalí room, you'll see the artist's distinct, Surrealist, melting-object style. Dalí places familiar items in a stark landscape, creating an eerie effect. Figures

Dalí, The Invisible Man

morph into misplaced faces and body parts. Background and foreground play mind games—is it an animal (seen one way) or a man's face? A waterfall or a pair of legs? It's a wide shot...no, it's a close-up. Look long at paintings like Dalí's *Endless Enigma* (1938) and *The Invisible Man* (c. 1933); they take different viewers to different places.

The Great Masturbator (1929) is psychologically exhausting, depicting in its Surrealism a lonely, highly sexual genius in love with his muse, Gala (while she was still married to a French poet). This is the first famous Surrealist painting.

During this productive period, Dalí was working on the classic Surrealist film *Un Chien Andalou* (**The Andalusian Dog,** 1928) with his collaborator Luis Buñuel (the film plays in Room 203). Both men were members of the Generation of '27, a group of nonconformist Spanish bohemians whose creative interests had a huge influence on art and literature in their era.
• *Skirt back around the courtyard to find Room 210 and...*

CUBISM

Cubism was born in the first decade of the 20th century. You could make a good case that the changes in society in the year 1900 were more profound than those we lived through in 2000. Trains and cars brought speed to life. Electricity brought light. Einstein introduced us to abstract ideas. Photography captured reality. And art broke away. At the turn of the century there were two ways to express art: line (Picasso) and color (Matisse)—but it was still in two dimensions. With Cubism, three dimensions are shown in two. Imagine walking around a statue to take in all the angles, and then attempting to put it on a 2-D plane. With Cubism, everyone sees things differently. To appreciate it, take your time and free your imagination.

Room 210 shows the birth of Cubism—a movement in which Spaniards were at the forefront (with works by Picasso, Braque, Léger, and Gris). To literally see a 2-D picture plane leap to life, watch the Lumière brothers' early film *Partie d'Écarté* (c. 1898).
• *In Room 206, you come to what is likely the reason for your visit...*

PICASSO'S *GUERNICA*

Perhaps the single most impressive piece of art in Spain is Pablo Picasso's *Guernica* (1937). The monumental canvas—one of Europe's must-see sights—is not only a piece of art but a piece of history, capturing the horror of modern war in a modern style.

While it's become a timeless classic representing all war, it was born in response to a specific conflict—the civil war (1936-1939), which pitted the democratically elected Second Republican government against the fascist general Francisco Franco. Franco won and ended up ruling Spain with an iron fist for the next 36 years. At the time Franco cemented his power, *Guernica* was touring internationally as part of a fund-raiser for the Republican cause. With Spain's political situation deteriorating and World War II looming, Picasso in 1939 named New York's Museum of Modern Art as the depository for the work. It was only after Franco's death, in 1975, that *Guernica* ended its decades of exile. In 1981 the painting finally arrived in Spain (where it had never before been), and it now stands as Spain's national piece of art.

Guernica—The Bombing: On April 26, 1937, Guernica—a Basque market town in northern Spain and an important Republican center—was the target of the world's first saturation-bombing raid on civilians. Franco gave permission to his fascist confederate Hitler to use the town as a guinea pig to try out Germany's new air force. The raid leveled the town, causing destruction that was unheard of at the time (though by 1944 it would be commonplace).

News of the bombing reached Picasso in Paris, where coincidentally he was just beginning work on a painting commission awarded by the Republican government. Picasso scrapped his earlier plans and immediately set to work sketching scenes of the destruction as he imagined it. In a matter of weeks he put these bomb-shattered shards together into a large mural (286 square feet). For the first time, the world could see the destructive force of the rising fascist movement—a prelude to World War II.

Guernica—The Painting: The bombs are falling, shattering the quiet village. A woman looks up at the sky (far right), horses scream (center), and a man falls from a horse and dies, while a wounded woman drags herself through the streets. She tries to escape, but her leg is too thick, dragging her down, like trying to run from something in a nightmare. On the left, a bull—a symbol of Spain—ponders it all, watching over a mother and her dead baby...a modern *pietà*. A woman in the center sticks her head out to see what's going on. The whole scene is lit from above by the stark light of a bare bulb. Picasso's painting threw a light on the brutality of Hitler and Franco, and suddenly the whole world was watching.

Picasso's abstract, Cubist style reinforces the message. It's as if he'd picked up the shattered shards and pasted them onto a canvas. The black-and-white tones are as gritty as the black-and-white newspaper photos that reported the bombing. The drab colors create a depressing, almost nauseating mood.

Picasso chose images with universal symbolism, making the work a commentary on all wars. Picasso himself said that the central horse, with the spear in its back, symbolizes humanity succumbing to brute force. The fallen rider's arm is severed and his sword is broken, more symbols of defeat. The bull, normally a proud symbol of strength and independence, is impotent and frightened. Between the bull and the horse, the faint dove of peace can do nothing but cry.

The bombing of Guernica—like the entire civil war—was an exercise in brutality. As one side captured a town, it might systematically round up every man, old and young—including priests—line them up, and shoot them in revenge for atrocities by the other side.

Thousands of people attended the Paris exhibition, and *Guernica* caused an immediate sensation. They could see the horror of modern war technology, the vain struggle of the Spanish Republicans, and the cold indifference of the fascist war machine. Picasso vowed never to return to Spain while Franco ruled (the dictator outlived him).

With each passing year, the canvas seemed more and more prophetic—honoring not just those who died in Guernica, but also in Spain's bitter civil war (estimates range from 200,000 to 500,000) and the 55 million worldwide who perished

Picasso, Guernica

in World War II. Picasso put a human face on what we call "collateral damage."

• *After seeing* Guernica, *view the additional exhibits that put the painting in its social context.*

OTHER PICASSO EXHIBITS

On the back wall on the *Guernica* room is a line of **photos** showing the evolution of the painting, from Picasso's first concept to the final mural. The photos were taken in his Paris studio by Dora Maar, Picasso's mistress-du-jour (and whose portrait by Picasso hangs nearby). Notice how his work evolved from the defiant fist in early versions to a broken sword with a flower.

The room behind *Guernica* contains **studies** Picasso did for the painting. These studies are filled with motifs that turn up in the final canvas—iron-nail tears, weeping women, and screaming horses. Picasso returned to these iconic images in his work for the rest of his life. He believed that everyone struggles internally with aspects of the horse and bull: rationality vs. brutality. The Minotaur—half-man and half-bull—powerfully captures Picasso's poet/rapist vision of man. Having lived through World War I, the Spanish Civil War, and World War II, his outlook is understandable.

In the far end of this hall, you'll also find a **model of the Spanish Pavilion** at the 1937 Paris exposition where *Guernica* was first displayed (look inside to see Picasso's work). Because of this painting, the pavilion became a vessel for propaganda and a fund-raising tool against Franco.

Near the Spanish Pavilion are posters and political cartoons that are pro-communist and anti-Franco. Made the same year as *Guernica* and the year after, these touch on timeless themes related to rich elites, industrialists, agricultural reform, and the military industrial complex versus the common man, as well as promoting autonomy for Catalunya and the Basque Country.

• *Head up to level 4, where the permanent collection continues.*

POST-WWII ART

After World War II, the center of the art world moved from Paris to New York City. The organizing theme in this part of the museum is "Art in a Divided World." On this floor especially, you'll want to take full advantage of the English info sheets in each room and the narration provided by your audioguide.

You'll see Kandinsky as a bridge into abstract art and the Abstract Expressionism of Jackson Pollock and company. Room 419 is particularly interesting, with late works by Picasso and Miró (from the 1960s and 1970s). On this floor, you can see photographs and watch films documenting Spain's slow recovery from its devastating civil war.

• *End your visit in the...*

NOUVEL WING

The newest wing of the museum features art from the 1960s through the 1980s, with a thematic focus on the complexity of modern times. While these galleries have fewer household names, the pieces displayed demonstrate the many aesthetic directions of more recent modern art.

Near the Prado

▲RETIRO PARK

Once the private domain of royalty, the majestic Parque del Buen Retiro has been a favorite of Madrid's commoners since Charles III decided to share it with his subjects in the late 18th century. Siesta in this 300-acre green-and-breezy escape from the city. At midday on Saturday and Sunday, the area around the lake becomes a street carnival, with jugglers, puppeteers, and lots of local color. These peaceful gardens offer great picnicking and people-watching (closes at dusk). From the Retiro Metro stop, walk to the big lake (El Estanque), where you can rent a rowboat. Past the lake, a grand boulevard of statues leads to the Prado.

▲ROYAL BOTANICAL GARDEN

After your Prado visit, you can take a lush and fragrant break in the sculpted Real Jardín Botánico. Wander among trees from around the world, originally gathered by the enlightened King Charles III. This garden was established when the Prado's building housed the natural science museum. A flier in English explains that this is actually more than a park—it's a museum of plants.

Cost and Hours: €3, daily 10:00-21:00, shorter hours off-season, last entry 30 minutes before closing, entrance is opposite the Prado's Murillo/south entry, Plaza de Murillo 2, tel. 914-203-017.

▲▲NATIONAL ARCHAEOLOGICAL MUSEUM

The Museo Arqueológico Nacional (MAN) takes you on a chronological walk through the story of Iberia. With a well-curated, rich collection of artifacts and tasteful multimedia displays, the museum shows off the wonders of each age: Celtic pre-Roman, Roman, a fine and rare Visigothic section, Moorish, Romanesque, and beyond. A highlight is the Lady of Elche (Room 13), a prehistoric Iberian female bust and a symbol of Spanish archaeology. You may also find underwhelming replica artwork from northern Spain's Altamira Caves (big on bison), giving you a faded peek at the skill of the cave artists who created the originals 14,000 years ago.

Cost and Hours: €3, free on Sat 14:00-20:00 and all day Sun; open Tue-Sat 9:30-20:00, Sun 9:30-15:00, closed Mon; €2 multimedia guide (also available as mobile app—MAN Museo Arqueológico Nacional); 20-minute walk north of the Prado at Calle Serrano 13, Metro: Serrano or Colón, tel. 915-777-912, www.man.es.

EXPERIENCES

Shopping

Madrileños have a passion for shopping. It's a social event, often incorporated into their afternoon paseo, which eventually turns into drinks and dinner. Most shoppers focus on the colorful pedestrian area between and around Gran Vía and Puerta del Sol. The fanciest big-name shops (Gucci, Prada, etc.) tempt strollers along Calle Serrano, northwest of Retiro Park. For trendier chain shops and local fashion, head to pedestrian Calle Fuencarral, Calle Augusto Figueroa, and the streets surrounding Plaza Chueca (north of Gran Vía, Metro: Chueca).

The giant El Corte Inglés, a block off Puerta del Sol, is a handy place to pick up just about anything you need (Mon-Sat 10:00-22:00, Sun 11:00-21:00).

▲EL RASTRO FLEA MARKET

Europe's biggest flea market is a field day for shoppers, people-watchers, and pickpockets. It's best before 11:00, though bargain shoppers like to go around 14:00, when vendors are more willing to strike

Retiro Park

National Archaeological Museum

end-of-day deals. Thousands of stalls titillate more than a million browsers with mostly new junk. Locals have lamented the tackiness of El Rastro—on the main drag, you'll find cheap underwear and bootleg CDs, but no real treasures (Sun only, 9:00-15:00, Metro: Tirso de Molina).

Rick's Tip: *El Rastro offers a fascinating chance to see gangs of young* **thieves** *overwhelming and ripping off naive tourists with no police anywhere in sight. Seriously:* **Don't even bring a wallet.** *The pickpocket action is brutal, and tourists are targeted.*

For an interesting market day (Sun only), start at Plaza Mayor, where Europe's biggest stamp and coin market thrives. Enjoy this genteel delight as you watch old-timers paging lovingly through one another's albums, looking for win-win trades. When you're done, head south or take the Metro to Tirso de Molina for El Rastro. Walk downhill, wandering off on the side streets to browse antiques, old furniture, and garage-sale-style sellers who often simply throw everything out on a sheet.

A typical Madrileño's Sunday could involve a meander through the Rastro streets with several stops for *cañas* (small beers) at the gritty bars along the way.

Nightlife

Those into clubbing may have to wait until after midnight for the most popular places to even open, much less start hopping. Spain has a reputation for partying late into the night—not stopping until offices open in the morning. (Spaniards, often awake into the wee hours of the morning, have a special word for this time of day: *la madrugada.*) If you're out early in the morning, it's actually hard to tell who is finishing their day and who's just starting it. Even if you're not an after-midnight party animal, make a point to be out with the happy masses, luxuriating in the cool evening air between 22:00 and midnight. The scene is unforgettable.

▲▲▲PASEO

Just walking the streets seems to be the way the Madrileños spend their evenings. Even past midnight on a hot summer night, entire families with little kids are strolling, licking ice cream, enjoying small beers and tapas in a series of bars, and greeting their neighbors. Good areas to wander include along Gran Vía (from about Plaza de Callao to Plaza de España;

El Rastro flea market

you could try my "Gran Vía Walk"); from Puerta del Sol to Plaza Mayor and down Calle del Arenal until you hit Plaza de Isabel II; the pedestrianized Calle de las Huertas from Plaza Mayor to the Prado; and, to window shop with the young and trendy, from Gran Vía up Calle de Fuencarral (keep going until you hit traffic).

▲▲FLAMENCO

Although Sevilla is the capital of flamenco, Madrid has a few easy and affordable options. And on summer evenings, Madrid puts on live flamenco events in the Royal Palace gardens (ask TI for details). Among the listings below, Casa Patas is grumpy, while Carboneras is friendlier—but Casa Patas has better-quality artists and a riveting seriousness. Considering that prices are comparable, Casa Patas is the better value. And regardless of what your hotel receptionist may want to sell you, flamenco places other than the ones I recommend are filled with tourists and pushy waiters.

Taberna Casa Patas attracts big-name flamenco artists. You'll quickly understand why this intimate venue (30 tables, 120 seats) is named "House of Feet."

Since this is for locals as well as tour groups, the flamenco is contemporary and may be jazzier than your notion—it depends on who's performing (€36 includes cover and first drink, Mon-Thu at 22:30, Fri-Sat at 21:00 and 24:00, closed Sun, 1.25-1.5 hours, reservations smart, no flash cameras, Cañizares 10, tel. 913-690-496, www.casapatas.com). Its restaurant is a logical spot for dinner before the show (€30 dinners, Mon-Sat from 20:00). Or, since it's three blocks south of the tapas bars on Plaza Santa Ana, this could be your pre- or post-tapas-crawl entertainment.

Las Carboneras, more downscale, is an easygoing, folksy little place a few steps from Plaza Mayor with a nightly hour-long flamenco show. Dinner is served one hour before showtime (€36 includes entry and a drink, €69 gets you a table up front with dinner and unlimited cheap drinks if you reserve ahead, daily at 20:30, also Mon-Thu at 22:30 and Fri-Sat at 23:00, reservations recommended, Plaza del Conde de Miranda 1, tel. 915-428-677, www.tablao lascarboneras.com).

Las Tablas Flamenco offers a less expensive nightly show respecting the

Madrid offers plenty of intimate flamenco venues.

traditional art of flamenco. You'll sit in a plain room with a mix of tourists and cool, young Madrileños in a modern, nondescript office block just over the freeway from Plaza de España (€27 with drink, reasonable drink prices, shows daily at 20:00 and 22:00, 1.25 hours, corner of Calle de Ferraz and Cuesta de San Vicente at Plaza de España 9, tel. 915-420-520, www.lastablasmadrid.com).

▲ZARZUELA

For a delightful look at Spanish light opera that even English speakers can enjoy, try zarzuela. Guitar-strumming Napoleons in red capes; buxom women with masks, fans, and castanets; Spanish-speaking pharaohs; melodramatic spotlights; and aficionados clapping and singing along from the cheap seats, where the acoustics are best—this is zarzuela...the people's opera. Originating in Madrid, zarzuela is known for its satiric humor and surprisingly good music. Performances occur evenings at Teatro de la Zarzuela, which alternates between zarzuela, ballet, and opera throughout the year. The TI's monthly guide has a special zarzuela section.

Getting Tickets: Prices range from €16-40, 50 percent off for Wed shows and anytime for those over 65, Teatro de la Zarzuela box office open Mon-Fri 12:00-18:00 and Sat-Sun 15:00-18:00 for advance tickets or until show time for same-day tickets, near the Prado at Jovellanos 4, Metro: Sevilla or Banco de España, tel. 915-245-400, http://teatrodelazarzuela.mcu.es. To purchase tickets online, go to www.entradasinaem.es and click on "*Espacios*" ("Spaces") to find Teatro de la Zarzuela; you will receive an email with your tickets, which you need to print before you arrive at the theater.

▲▲BULLFIGHTS

Madrid's Plaza de Toros hosts Spain's top bullfights on some Sundays and holidays from March through mid-October, and nearly every day during the San Isidro festival (May-early June—but often sold out long in advance). Fights start between 17:00 and 21:00 (early in spring and fall, late in summer). The bullring is at the Ventas Metro stop (a 25-minute Metro ride from Puerta del Sol, tel. 913-562-200, www.las-ventas.com).

Madrid hosts Spain's top bullfights.

Getting Tickets: Bullfight tickets range from €5 to €150. There are no bad seats at Plaza de Toros; paying more gets you in the shade and/or closer to the gore. (The action often intentionally occurs in the shade to reward the expensive-ticket holders.) To be close to the bullring, choose areas 8, 9, or 10; for shade: 1, 2, 9, or 10; for shade/sun: 3 or 8; for the sun and cheapest seats: 4, 5, 6, or 7. Note these key words: *corrida*—a real fight with professionals; *novillada*—rookie matadors, younger bulls, and cheaper tickets.

Getting tickets through your hotel or a booking office is convenient, but they add 20 percent or more and don't sell the cheap seats. There are two booking offices; call both before you buy: at Plaza del Carmen 1 (Mon-Sat 9:00-13:00 & 16:30-19:00, Sun 9:30-14:00, tel. 915-319-131, or buy online at www.bullfight ticketsmadrid.com), run by José and his English-speaking son, also José, who also sells soccer tickets; and at Calle Victoria 3 (Mon-Fri 10:00-14:00 & 17:00-19:00, Sat-Sun 10:00-13:00, tel. 915-211-213).

To save money, you can stand in the ticket line at the bullring. Except for important bullfights—or during the San Isidro festival—there are generally plenty of seats available. About a thousand tickets are held back to be sold in the five days leading up to and on the day of a fight. Scalpers hang out before the popular fights at the Calle Victoria booking office.

Beware: Those buying scalped tickets are breaking the law and can lose the ticket with no recourse.

For a dose of the experience, you can buy a cheap ticket and just stay to see a couple of bullfights. Each fight takes about 20 minutes, and the event consists of six bulls over two hours.

EATING

In Spain, only Barcelona rivals Madrid for taste-bud thrills. Note that many restaurants close in August.

For maximum fun, go mobile for dinner: Do the *tapeo*, going from one bar to the next, munching, drinking, and socializing. Rather than tapas plates, most of Madrid's bars offer bigger plates called *raciones* for around €6 (vegetables) to €15 (fish). The action begins late, around 21:00. But for beginners, an earlier start, with less commotion, can be easier.

In Madrid, any proper bar gives a free tapa to anyone ordering a drink. If you don't get one, ask, "Tapa?" After you get it, then order additional food as you like.

Two streets are particularly rewarding for a bar-crawl meal: **Calle de Jesús** (near the Prado) and **Calle Cava Baja** (fancier and energetic, with more bars). For a good, authentic Madrid dinner experience, survey the options and then choose your favorites. For a sit-down meal, pick one with tables in the back. Another good area for a tapas crawl (though a bit pricier) is **Plaza Santa Ana,** with inviting, trendy bars spilling out onto the square.

Budget Eats: Enjoy a quick bite on **Plaza Mayor,** where locals get take-out food from a nearby bar and plant themselves somewhere on the atmospheric square to eat. Tasty squid sandwiches, called *bocadillos de calamares*, are popular (€2.80 at Casa Rúa, at the square's northwest corner, a few steps up Calle Ciudad Rodrigo).

For cheap sandwiches and salads, look for **Rodilla** and **Pans & Company** on nearly every square (daily 9:00-23:00). Picnickers like **El Corte Inglés** for its supermarket (on lower level, Mon-Sat 10:00-22:00, Sun 11:00-21:00). You could gather a picnic at the produce stands in the touristy **Mercado de San Miguel,** which also has a food circus of eateries (daily 10:00-24:00, one block east of Plaza Mayor); it's fun to browse, hang out at the bars, or take a break at one of the market's tables.

If you like dunkable **churros con chocolate** for breakfast or anytime, try these places near Puerta del Sol: the classy **Chocolatería San Ginés** (open 24 hours, Pasadizo de San Ginés 5) and the modern **Chocolaterías Valor** (daily 8:00-22:30, Postigo de San Martín 7).

Tapas on Calle de Jesús

For locations, see map on page 444.

Cervecería Cervantes serves hearty *raciones,* specializes in octopus, and has both a fine bar and good restaurant seating (intersection of Plaza de Jesús and Calle de Cervantes, tel. 914-296-093).

Taberna de la Daniela Medinaceli has a lovely dining area. It's popular for its specialty *cocido madrileño,* a rich chickpea-based soup (Plaza de Jesús 7, tel. 913-896-238).

La Dolores, with a rustic little dining area, has been a hit since 1908 and is still extremely popular. Its canapés (€2.50 little sandwiches) are listed on the wall (Plaza de Jesús 4, tel. 914-292-243).

Cervezas La Fabrica packs in seafood lovers at the bar; there's a quieter back room with tables. Prices are the same in both spots (Calle de Jesús 2, tel. 913-690-671).

Cervecería Los Gatos is a kaleidoscope of Spanish culture, with chandeliers swinging above wine barrels in the bar area and characteristic tables below (Calle de Jesús 2, tel. 914-293-067).

La Anchoíta takes its name from its top-notch *anchoas* (cured anchovies) and *boquerones* (uncured anchovies). When these tasty little tidbits share a slice of bread, it's a *"matrimonio."* The three taps serve beer, "sin" (nonalcoholic) beer, and *vermut* (vermouth) from a tap shaped like a shrimp. If drinking white wine, get it in a frozen glass—ask for *"copa fría"* (Calle de Jesús 4, tel. 913-601-674).

Cervecería El Diario dates from 1879, yet today feels formulaic. It's known for *calamares* (intersection of Calle de las Huertas and Calle de Jesús, tel. 914-292-800).

Choosing tapas

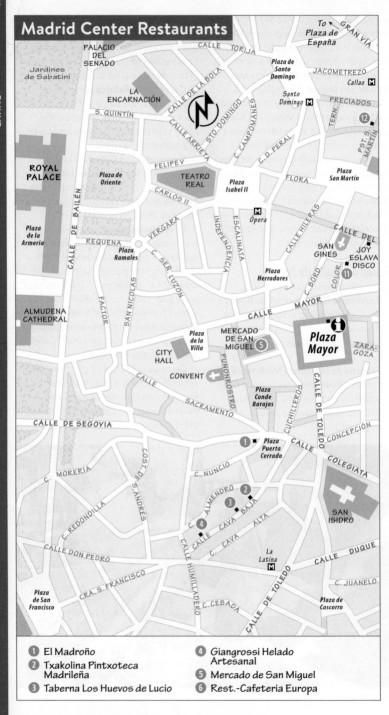

Madrid Center Restaurants

1. El Madroño
2. Txakolina Pintxoteca Madrileña
3. Taberna Los Huevos de Lucio
4. Giangrossi Helado Artesanal
5. Mercado de San Miguel
6. Rest.-Cafeteria Europa

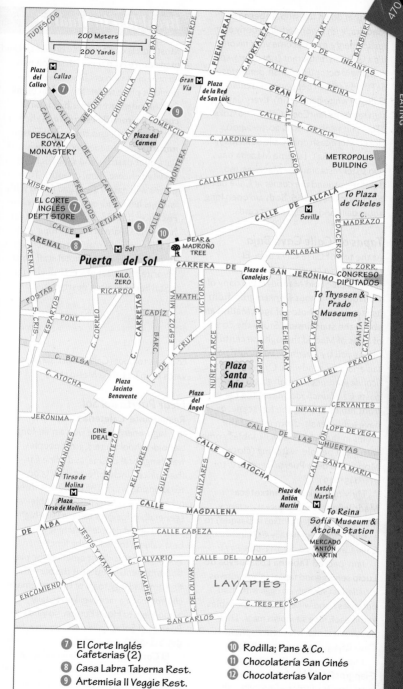

TUDESCOS

200 Meters

200 Yards

Plaza del Callao

Callao ⑦

C. VALVERDE

C. BARCO

C. FUENCARRAL

C. HORTALEZA

CALLE C. S. BART.

BARBIERI

CALLE DE INFANTAS

Gran Vía

Plaza de la Red de San Luis

GRAN VÍA

CALLE DE LA REINA

CALLE

MESONERO

CHINCHILLA

CALLE DEL CARMEN

CALLE SALUD

COMERCIO

⑨

Plaza del Carmen

DESCALZAS ROYAL MONASTERY

C. JARDINES

C. GRACIA

C. PELIGROS

METROPOLIS BUILDING

MISERI.

PRECIADOS

CALLE DE LA MONTERA

CALLE ADUANA

To Plaza de Cibeles

EL CORTE INGLÉS DEP'T STORE ⑦

CALLE DE TETUAN

⑥

CALLE DE ALCALÁ

Sevilla

C. MADRAZO

CEDACEROS

ARENAL ⑧

Sol ⑩

BEAR & MADROÑO TREE

ARLABÁN

C. ZORR.

Puerta del Sol

KILO. ZERO

CARRERA DE SAN JERÓNIMO

Plaza de Canalejas

CONGRESO DIPUTADOS

POSTAS

RICARDO

S. CRIS.

ESPARTOS

PONT.

C. CORREO

C. CARRETAS

CADIZ

MATH.

C. ESPOZ Y MINA

VICTORIA

To Thyssen & Prado Museums

SANTA CATALINA

C. BOLSA

C. DE LA CRUZ

NUÑEZ DE ARCE

C. DEL PRINCIPE

C. DE ECHEGARAY

C. DE LA VEGA

DEL

PRADO

C. ATOCHA

Plaza Jacinto Benavente

Plaza del Ángel

Plaza Santa Ana

CALLE DEL

INFANTE

CERVANTES

JERÓNIMA

BARC.

LOPE DE VEGA

CALLE DE LAS HUERTAS

SANTA MARIA

CINE IDEAL

ROMANONES

DR. CORTEZO

RELATORES

GUEVARA

CAÑIZARES

CALLE DE ATOCHA

LEON

Tirso de Molina

Plaza Tirso de Molina

CALLE

Antón Martín

Plaza de Antón Martín

CALLE MAGDALENA

To Reina Sofía Museum & Atocha Station

DE ALBA

JESUS Y MARIA

C. CALVARIO

CALLE CABEZA

CALLE DEL OLMO

MERCADO ANTÓN MARTÍN

ENCOMIENDA

C. LAVAPIÉS

C. DE OLIVAR

LAVAPIÉS

C. TRES PECES

SAN CARLOS

---

⑦ El Corte Inglés Cafeterias (2)

⑧ Casa Labra Taberna Rest.

⑨ Artemisia II Veggie Rest.

⑩ Rodilla; Pans & Co.

⑪ Chocolatería San Ginés

⑫ Chocolaterías Valor

Farther down the strip, **Taberna Maceira,** with a wonderfully woody and rustic energy, may become your favorite. It's a Galician restaurant (not a bar), specializing in octopus, codfish, *pimientos de Padrón* (green peppers), and *caldo Gallego* (white bean soup). Every day, the sign reads, *no hay Coca-Cola*—"no Coke" (Tue-Sun 13:00-16:00 & 20:30-24:00, closed Mon, cash only, Calle de Jesús 7, tel. 914-291-584). Taberna Maceira has two sister restaurants—Maceiras and Belesar—around the corner at Calle de las Huertas 64 and 66. Both are open long hours daily and accept credit cards.

Tapas on Calle Cava Baja

At the top of Calle Cava Baja, **El Madroño** is a cowboy bar that preserves a bit of old Madrid. A tile copy of Velázquez's famous *Drinkers* grins from its facade and photos of 1902 Madrid are above the stairs inside. Study the coats of arms of Madrid through the centuries as you try a *vermut* (vermouth) on tap and a €4 sandwich. Or ask to try the *licor de madroño;* a small glass (*chupito*) costs €2. Munch *raciones* at the bar or front tables to be in the fun scene, or have a quieter sit-down meal at the tables in the back. Sidewalk tables come with great people-watching (closed Mon, Plaza de la Puerta Cerrada 7, tel. 913-645-629).

Thriving **Txakolina Pintxoteca Madrileña** serves Basque-style fancy sandwiches (called *pintxos* in Basque) to a young crowd (generally €3/sandwich, Calle Cava Baja 26, tel. 913-664-877).

Jam-packed **Taberna Los Huevos de Lucio** serves good tapas, salads, *huevos estrellados* (scrambled eggs with fried potatoes), and wine. Head to the tables in the back for a sit-down meal. Their basement is much less atmospheric (Calle Cava Baja 30, tel. 913-662-984).

End your *tapeo* with ice cream at **Giangrossi Helado Artesanal**—it has great flavors (ask for a free taste) and cocktails to boot (Calle Cava Baja 40, 50 yards from La Latina Metro stop).

Breakfast in Madrid

Most hotels don't include breakfast (and many don't even serve it), so you may be out on the streets first thing looking for a place to eat. My typical breakfast, found at any corner bar, is *café con leche, tortilla española* (a slice of potato omelet), and *zumo de naranja natural* (fresh-squeezed orange juice). Bars offer pastries and sandwiches, too (toasted cheese, ham, or both). Touristy places will have a *desayuno* menu with various ham-and-eggs deals. Try *churros* once; if you're not in the mood for heavy chocolate in the morning, go local and dip your *churros* in a *café con leche.* Get advice from your hotel staff for their favorite breakfast place. If all else fails, a Starbucks is often nearby (just like home).

Near Puerta del Sol

Restaurante-Cafeteria Europa is a fun, high-energy scene with a mile-long bar, old-school waiters, great people-watching, local cuisine, and a fine €11 fixed-price lunch (offered daily 13:00-16:00, inside only). The menu lists three price levels: bar (inexpensive), table (generally pricey), or terrace (sky-high but with good people-watching). Your best value is to stick to the lunch menu if you're sitting inside, or order off the plastic *barra* menu if you sit at the bar—the €3 ham-and-egg toast or the homemade *churros* make a nice breakfast (daily 7:00-24:00, next to Hotel Europa, 50 yards off Puerta del Sol at Calle del Carmen 4, tel. 915-212-900).

El Corte Inglés' top-floor cafeterias (in two of its buildings) are fresh, modern, and popular, though not particularly cheap.

The better one is near Plaza del Callao: Its snazzy Gourmet Experience houses a specialty grocery mart and 10 different mini-restaurants with cuisines ranging from Mexican to Chinese. The lunch hour is busy, though it's worth the wait for its great views of Gran Vía and Plaza de España. Take a seat at any of the indoor tables, or out on the open terrace (Mon-Sat 10:00-24:00, Sun 11:00-24:00). The other cafeteria has shorter hours (just off Puerta del Sol at the intersection of Calle de Preciados and Calle de Tetuán).

Casa Labra Taberna Restaurante is famous as the birthplace of the Spanish Socialist Party in 1879...and as a spot for great cod. Packed with Madrileños, it manages to be both dainty and rustic. It's a wonderful scene with three distinct sections: the stand-up bar (cheapest, with two lines: one for munchies, the other for drinks), a peaceful little sit-down area in back (a little more expensive but still cheap; €6 salads), and a fancy restaurant (€20 fixed-price lunch). Their tasty little €1.40 *tajada de bacalao* cod dishes put them on the map. The waiters are fun to joke around with (daily 11:00-15:30 & 18:00-23:00, a block off Puerta del Sol at Calle Tetuán 12, tel. 915-310-081).

Artemisia II, a hit with vegetarians and vegans, serves good, healthy food without the typical hippie ambience that comes with most veggie places (great €12 three-course fixed-price lunch Mon-Fri only, open daily 13:30-16:00 & 21:00-24:00, north of Puerta del Sol at Tres Cruces 4, a few steps off Plaza del Carmen, tel. 915-218-721).

SLEEPING

Madrid has plenty of centrally located budget hotels and *pensiones.* Most of the accommodations I've listed are within a few minutes' walk of Puerta del Sol.

You should be able to find a sleepable double for €60, a good double for €90, and a modern, air-conditioned double

with all the comforts for €120. Prices vary throughout the year at bigger hotels, but remain about the same for the smaller hotels and *hostales.* Anticipate full hotels only during May (for the San Isidro festival, celebrating Madrid's patron saint with bullfights and zarzuelas—especially around his feast day on May 15) and September (when conventions can clog the city). During the hot months of July and August, prices can be soft—ask for a discount.

To avoid street noise, request the highest floor possible. Rooms with twin beds are generally larger than rooms with double beds for the same price. You may find good deals by emailing several hotels (including business-class hotels) to ask for their best price.

Hotels are still allowed to designate up to 10 percent of their rooms for smokers.

Mid-Range and Fancier Places

These mostly business-class hotels are good values. Their formal prices may be inflated, but most offer weekend and summer discounts when it's slow. Drivers pay about €24 a day for parking.

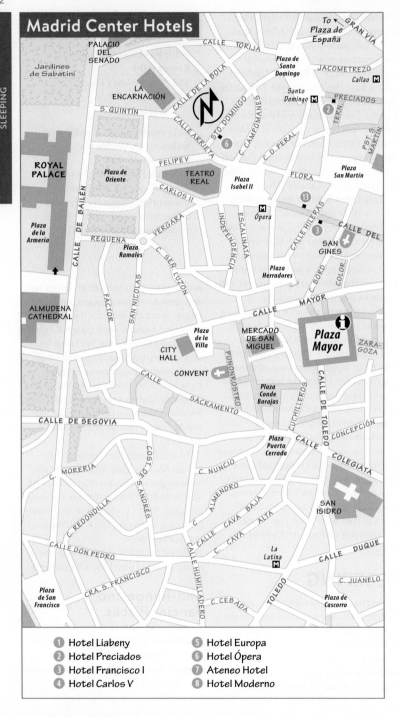

Madrid Center Hotels

1. Hotel Liabeny
2. Hotel Preciados
3. Hotel Francisco I
4. Hotel Carlos V
5. Hotel Europa
6. Hotel Ópera
7. Ateneo Hotel
8. Hotel Moderno

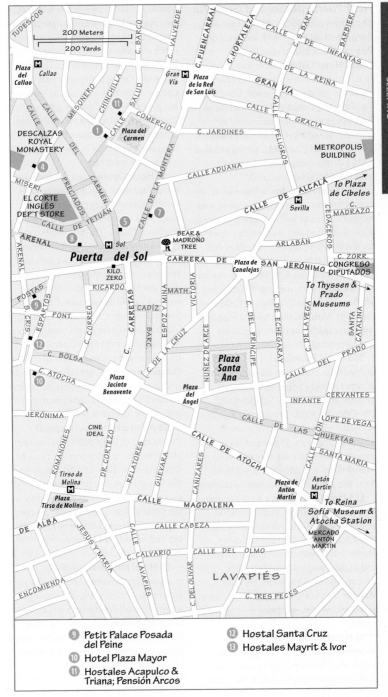

Plaza del Callao · Callao M

200 Meters
200 Yards

TUDESCOS

C. BARCO

C. VALVERDE

C. FUENCARRAL

C. HORTALEZA

C. S. BART

BARBIERI

CALLE · DE · INFANTAS

CALLE DE LA REINA

Gran M
Vía
Plaza de la Red de San Luis

GRAN VÍA

MESONERO

CHINCHILLA

CALLE SALUD

COMERCIO

⑪

①

CALLE

Plaza del Carmen

C. JARDINES

CALLE C. GRACIA

C. PELIGROS

DESCALZAS ROYAL MONASTERY

CALLE DEL

CARMEN

PRECIADOS

C. JARDINES

METROPOLIS BUILDING

④

MISERI.

EL CORTE INGLÉS DEP'T STORE

CALLE DE TETUÁN

CALLE DE LA MONTERA

CALLE ADUANA

CALLE DE ALCALÁ

To Plaza de Cibeles

Sevilla M

CEDACEROS

C. MADRAZO

⑤

⑦

ARLABÁN

C. ZORR.

ARENAL

⑧

M Sol

BEAR & MADROÑO TREE

🐻

Puerta del Sol

CARRERA DE SAN JERÓNIMO

Plaza de Canalejas

CONGRESO DIPUTADOS

KILO. ZERO

RICARDO

POSTAS

⑨

S. CRIS.

ESPARTOS

PONT.

C. CORREO

CADIZ

CARRETAS

BARC.

MATH.

ESPOZ Y MINA

VICTORIA

C. DE LA CRUZ

NÚÑEZ DE ARCE

C. DEL PRÍNCIPE

C. DE ECHEGARAY

C. DE LA VEGA

SANTA CATALINA

To Thyssen & Prado Museums

⑫

C. BOLSA

⑩

C. ATOCHA

Plaza Jacinto Benavente

Plaza del Ángel

Plaza Santa Ana

CALLE DEL PRADO

JERÓNIMA

CINE IDEAL

ROMANONES

DR. CORTEZO

RELATORES

GUEVARA

CAÑIZARES

CALLE DE ATOCHA

INFANTE

CALLE DE LAS LEÓN

CERVANTES

LOPE DE VEGA

HUERTAS

SANTA MARIA

Tirso de Molina
M

Plaza Tirso de Molina

CALLE

MAGDALENA

Plaza de Antón Martín

Antón Martín
M

To Reina Sofía Museum & Atocha Station

DE ALBA

JESUS Y MARIA

C. CALVARIO

C. LAVAPIES

CALLE CABEZA

CALLE DEL OLMO

C. DEL OLIVAR

MERCADO ANTÓN MARTÍN

ENCOMIENDA

LAVAPIÉS

C. TRES PECES

⑨ Petit Palace Posada del Peine

⑩ Hotel Plaza Mayor

⑪ Hostales Acapulco & Triana; Pensión Arcos

⑫ Hostal Santa Cruz

⑬ Hostales Mayrit & Ivor

Near Puerta del Sol and Gran Vía

These hotels are located in and around the pedestrian zone north and west of Puerta del Sol. Use Metro: Sol.

$$$ Hotel Liabeny rents 220 plush, spacious, business-class rooms offering all the comforts (Sb-€108, Db-€127, Tb-€165, 10 percent cheaper mid-July-Aug, prices vary widely according to demand, breakfast-€16, air-con, elevator, sauna, gym, off Plaza del Carmen at Salud 3, tel. 915-319-000, www.liabeny.es, reservas@hotelliabeny.com).

$$$ Hotel Preciados, a four-star business hotel, has 100 welcoming, sleek, and modern rooms as well as elegant lounges. It's well-located and reasonably priced for the luxury it provides (Db-€125-160, prices often soft, check Web specials in advance, breakfast-€18, free mini-bar, air-con, elevator, gym, parking-€21/day, just off Plaza de Santo Domingo at Calle Preciados 37, Metro: Callao, tel. 914-544-400, www.preciadoshotel.com, preciados hotel@preciadoshotel.com).

$$$ Hotel Francisco I is a big, quiet, and well-run place with 60 rooms, nicely situated midway between the Royal Theater and Puerta del Sol (Sb-€115, Db-€160, Tb-€200, breakfast-€8, prices fluctuate—book a month or more in advance to save 30-35 percent, air-con, showers only—no tubs, elevator, Calle del Arenal 15, tel. 915-480-204, www.hotel francisco.com, info@hotelfrancisco.com).

$$$ Hotel Carlos V is a Best Western with 67 high-ceilinged and somewhat worn-out rooms and a pleasant lounge (Sb-€80-120, standard Db-€100-173, Tb-€115-200, rates depend on demand and season, elegant breakfast-€10, air-con, nonsmoking floors, elevator, Maestro Victoria 5, tel. 915-314-100, www. hotelcarlosv.com, recepcion@hotelcarlos v.com).

$$ Hotel Europa, with sleek marble, red carpet runners along the halls, happy Muzak charm, and an attentive staff, is a tremendous value. It rents 100 squeaky-clean rooms, many with balconies overlooking the pedestrian zone or an inner courtyard. The hotel has an honest ethos and offers a straight price (Sb-€79, Db-€99, Db with view-€119, Tb-€142, Qb-€168, Quint/b-€190, sometimes cheaper with Web specials, air-con, elevator, gym, Calle del Carmen 4, tel. 915-212-900, www.hoteleuropa.eu, info@hotel europa.eu). The Europa cafeteria-restaurant next door is lively and convivial—fun for breakfast.

$$ Hotel Ópera, a serious and contemporary hotel with 79 classy rooms, is located just off Plaza Isabel II, a four-block walk from Puerta del Sol toward the Royal Palace (Db-€85-110 but prices spike wildly with demand, mentioning this book may get you a discount, includes breakfast, air-con, elevator, sauna and gym, ask for a higher floor—there are nine—to avoid street noise, Cuesta de Santo Domingo 2, Metro: Ópera, tel. 915-412-800, www.hotelopera.com, reservas@hotelopera.com). Hotel Ópera's cafeteria is deservedly popular. Consider their **"singing dinners"**—great operetta music with a delightful dinner—offered nightly (around €60, reservations smart, call 915-426-382 or reserve at hotel).

$$ Ateneo Hotel, just steps off Puerta del Sol, lacks public spaces and character, but its 38 rooms are close to business-class (Db-€75-90, occasionally less or more, can be as high as €115, 5 percent discount if you book directly with the hotel with this year's book, air-con, elevator, Calle de la Montera 22, tel. 915-212-012, www.hotel-ateneo.com, info@hotel-ateneo.com).

$$ Hotel Moderno, renting 97 rooms in a quiet, professional, and friendly atmosphere, has a comfy first-floor lounge and is just steps off Puerta del Sol (Db-€74-129, extra person-€25, breakfast-€11, air-con, Calle del Arenal 2, tel. 915-310-900, www.hotel-moderno.com, info@hotel-moderno.com).

Near Plaza Mayor

Both of these are a block off Plaza Mayor.

$$$ Petit Palace Posada del Peine is part of a big, modern chain, but fills its well-located old building with fresh, efficient character. Behind the ornate Old World facade is a comfortable and modern business-class hotel with 67 rooms (Db-€80-160 depending on demand, breakfast-€10, air-con, free use of iPads, Calle Postas 17, tel. 915-238-151, www.petitpalace. com, posadadelpeine@petitpalace.com).

$$ Hotel Plaza Mayor, with 41 solidly outfitted rooms, is tastefully decorated and beautifully situated (Sb-€40-90, Db-€50-100, superior Db-€60-120, Tb-€80-140, breakfast-€8, air-con, elevator, Calle de Atocha 2, tel. 913-600-606, www.h-plazamayor.com, info@h-plaza mayor.com).

Near the Prado

$$ Hotel Lope de Vega is a good business-class hotel near the Prado. With 59 rooms, it feels cozy and friendly (Sb-€97, Db-€69-117, extra person-€20, rates vary wildly based on demand, cheaper July-Aug, one child under 12 sleeps free, air-con, elevator, limited parking-€25/day—request ahead, Calle Lope de Vega 49, tel. 913-600-011, www.accor.com, H9618@ accor.com).

Cheap Sleeps

Near Plaza del Carmen

These three are all in the same building at Calle de la Salud 13, north of Puerta del Sol. The building overlooks Plaza del Carmen—a little square with a sleepy, almost Parisian ambience.

$ Hostal Acapulco rents 16 bright rooms with air-conditioning and all the big hotel gear. The neighborhood is quiet so a room with a balcony is worthwhile (Sb-€49-54, Db-€59-64, Tb-€77-80, elevator, fourth floor, reasonable laundry service, overnight luggage storage, limited parking available—ask when you reserve, tel. 915-311-945, www.hostalacapulco.com, hostal_acapulco@yahoo.es).

$ Hostal Triana, also a good deal, is bigger—with 40 rooms—and offers a little less charm for a little less money (Sb-€38, Db-€53, Tb-€69, rooms facing the square have air-con and cost €3 extra, other rooms have fans, elevator and some stairs, first floor, tel. 915-326-812, www.hostal triana.com, triana@hostaltriana.com).

$ Pensión Arcos is tiny and old-fashioned—it's been in the Hernández family since 1936. You can reserve by phone (in Spanish), and must pay in cash. It has five clean, quiet rooms, an elevator, a tiny roof terrace, and a nice little lounge. For cheap beds in a great locale, it's unbeatable (D-€36, Db-€40, air-con, closed Aug, fifth floor, tel. 915-324-994).

Near Puerta del Sol

$ Hostal Santa Cruz, simple and well-located (but with a smoky office), has 16 rooms at a good price (Sb-€40, Db-€55, Tb-€70, air-con, elevator, Plaza de Santa Cruz 6, second floor, tel. 915-222-441, www.hostalsantacruz.com, info@hostal santacruz.com).

$ Hostal Mayrit and **Hostal Ivor** rent 28 rooms with thoughtful touches on a pedestrianized street (Sb-€40-55, Db-€55-65, air-con, elevator, near Metro: Ópera at Calle del Arenal 24, reception on third floor, tel. 915-480-403, www.hostal ivor.com, reservas@hostalivor.com).

Near the Prado

Two fine budget *hostales* are at Cervantes 34 (Metro: Antón Martín—but not handy to Metro). Both are homey, with inviting lounge areas; neither serves breakfast.

$ Hostal Gonzalo has 15 spotless, comfortable rooms on the third floor and is well-run by friendly and helpful Javier. Reserve in advance (Sb-€45, Db-€60, Tb-€75, air-con, elevator, tel. 914-292-714, www.hostalgonzalo.com, hostal@hostal gonzalo.com). Downstairs, the nearly as polished **$ Hostal Cervantes** also has 15 rooms (Sb-€35-40, Db-€45-50, Tb-€55-60, cheaper when slow and for longer stays, some rooms with air-con, tel. 914-298-365, www.hostal-cervantes.com, correo@hostal-cervantes.com).

$ Urban Sea Hotel Atocha 113 is a basic but contemporary option, nicely located between the Prado and the Reina Sofía, near Atocha Station (Sb-€40-45, Db-€50-75, rates vary on demand, includes self-service snacks, small rooftop terrace, Calle de Atocha 113, tel. 913-692-895, www.urbanseahotels.com, recepcion atocha@blueseahotels.es).

TRANSPORTATION

Getting Around Madrid
By Metro

Madrid's Metro is simple, cheap, and speedy (www.metromadrid.es). It costs €1.50 for a ride within zone A, which covers most of the city, but not trains out to the airport. The 10-ride, €12.20 Metrobus ticket can be shared by several travelers and works on both the Metro and buses. Buy tickets in the Metro (from easy-to-use machines or ticket booths), at newspaper stands, or at Estanco tobacco shops. Insert your ticket in the turnstile, then retrieve it and pass through. The Metro runs 6:00-1:30 in the morning. At all times, be alert to thieves, who thrive in crowded stations.

Study your Metro map. The lines are color-coded and numbered; use end-of-the-line station names to choose your direction of travel. Once in the Metro station, signs direct you to the train line and direction (e.g., Linea 1, *Valdecarros*). To transfer, follow signs in the station leading to connecting lines. Once you reach your final stop, look for the green *salida* signs pointing to the exits. Use the helpful neighborhood maps to choose the right *salida* and save yourself lots of walking.

By Bus

City buses, though not as easy as the Metro, can be useful. Find bus maps at the TI or info booth on Puerta del Sol; poster-size maps are usually posted at bus stops (€1.50 tickets sold on bus, €12.20 for a 10-ride Metrobus ticket, buses run 6:00-24:00, less frequent *Buho* buses run all night, www.emtmadrid.es).

By Taxi

Madrid's 15,000 taxis are reasonably priced and easy to hail. A green light on the roof indicates that a taxi is available. Foursomes travel as cheaply by taxi as by Metro. For example, a ride from the Royal Palace to the Prado costs about €6. After the drop charge (about €3, higher on weekends and late at night), the per-kilometer rate depends on the time: *Tarifa 1* (€1.05/kilometer) is charged Monday-Friday 6:00-21:00; *Tarifa 2* (€1.20/kilometer) is valid after 21:00 and on Saturdays, Sundays, and holidays. If your cabbie uses anything other than *Tarifa 1* on weekdays (shown as an isolated "1" on the meter), you're being cheated. Rates can be higher if you go outside Madrid. There is a flat rate of €30 between the city center and any of the airport terminals. Other legitimate charges include the €3 supplement for leaving any train or bus station, €20 per hour for waiting, and a few extra euros if you call to have the taxi come to you. Make sure the meter is turned on as soon as you get into the cab so the driver can't tack anything onto the official rate. If the driver starts adding up "extras," look for the sticker detailing all legitimate surcharges (which should be on the passenger window).

Arriving and Departing
By Plane
BARAJAS AIRPORT

Ten miles east of downtown, Madrid's modern airport has four terminals. Terminals 1, 2, and 3 are connected by long

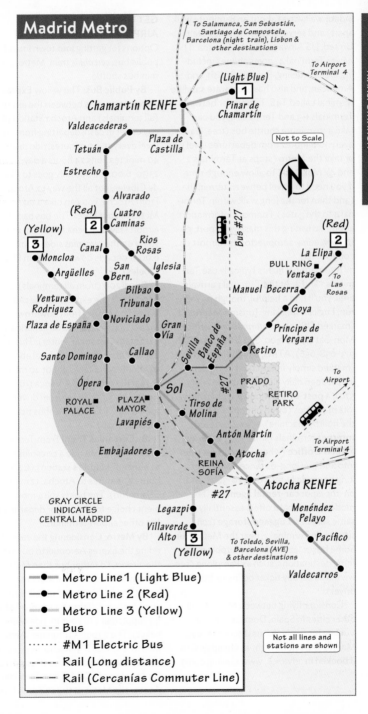

indoor walkways (about an 8-minute walk apart) and serve airlines including Delta, United, US Airways, and Air Canada. The newer Terminal 4 serves airlines including Iberia, Vueling, Ryanair, British, and American, and also has a separate satellite terminal called T4S. To transfer between Terminals 1-3 and Terminal 4, you can take a 10-minute shuttle bus (free, leaves every 10 minutes from departures level), or take the Metro (stops at Terminals 2 and 4). Make sure to allow enough time if you need to travel between terminals (and then for the long walk within Terminal 4 to the gates). For more information about navigating this massive airport, go to www.aena-aeropuertos.es (airport code: MAD).

International flights typically use Terminals 1 and 4. At the Terminal 1 arrivals area, you'll find a helpful, though privately run, English-speaking Turismo Madrid **TI** (marked *Oficina de Información Turística*, Mon-Sat 8:00-20:00, Sun 9:00-14:00, tel. 913-058-656), **ATMs**, a **flight info office** (marked simply *Information* in airport lobby, open daily 24 hours, tel. 902-353-570), a **post-office** window, a pharmacy, lots of phones (buy a phone card from the nearby machine), a few scattered **Internet** terminals (small fee), **eateries**, a **RENFE office** (where you can get train info and buy long-distance train tickets, long hours daily, tel. 902-320-320), and on-the-spot **car-rental agencies.** The modern Terminal 4 offers essentially the same services. **Luggage storage** (*consigna*) is in Terminal 2, near the Metro exit. Some buses leave from the airport to far-flung destinations, such as Pamplona (see www.alsa.es; buy ticket online or from the driver).

Consider flying between Madrid and other cities in Spain. Domestic airline Vueling is popular for its discounts (e.g., Madrid-Barcelona flight as cheap as €30 if booked in advance, www.vueling.com).

GETTING BETWEEN THE AIRPORT AND DOWNTOWN

Options for getting into town include public bus, *cercanías* train, Metro, taxi, and minibus shuttle.

By Public Bus: The yellow **Exprés Aeropuerto** runs between the airport (all terminals) and Atocha Station (€5, pay driver in cash, departing from arrivals level every 15-20 minutes, ride takes about 40 minutes, runs 24 hours a day; from 23:30-6:00, the bus only goes to Plaza de Cibeles, not all the way to Atocha). From Atocha, you can take a taxi or the Metro to your hotel. The bus back to the airport leaves Atocha from near the taxi stand on the *cercanías* side (from 23:30-6:00, it departs downtown from Plaza de Cibeles).

Bus #200 (from all terminals) is less handy than the express bus because it leaves you farther from downtown (at the Metro stop at Avenida de América, northeast of the historical center). This bus departs from the arrivals level about every 10 minutes and takes about 20 minutes to reach Avenida de América (runs 6:00-24:00, buy €1.50 ticket from driver; or get a shareable 10-ride Metrobus ticket at a tobacco shop).

By Cercanías Train: From Terminal 4, passengers can ride a *cercanías* train to either of Madrid's stations (€2.60, 2/hour, 25 minutes to Atocha, 12 minutes to Chamartín). The bus is still a more convenient choice for arriving or departing from the other airport terminals.

By Metro: Considering the ease of riding the Exprés Aeropuerto bus in from the airport, I'd rather bus than Metro. The subway involves two transfers to reach the city; it's not difficult, but usually involves climbing some stairs (€4.50-6; or add a €3 supplement to your 10-ride Metrobus ticket). The airport's futuristic "Aeropuerto T-1, T-2, T-3" Metro stop (notice the ATMs, subway info booth, and huge lighted map of Madrid) is in Terminal 2. Access the Metro at the check-in level; to reach the Metro from Terminal 1's arrivals level, stand with your back to the baggage claim, then go to your far right, up the stairs, and follow red-and-blue Metro diamond signs to the station (8-minute walk). The Terminal 4 stop is the end of the line. To get to Puerta del Sol, take line 8 for 12 minutes to Nuevos Ministerios, then continue on line 10 to Tribunal, then line 1 to Puerta del Sol (30 minutes more total); or exit at Nuevos Ministerios and take a €5 taxi or bus #150 straight to Puerta del Sol.

By Taxi: With cheap and easy alternatives available, there's not much reason to take a taxi unless you have lots of luggage or just want to go straight to your hotel. If you do take a taxi between the airport and downtown, the flat rate is €30. There is no charge for luggage. Plan on getting stalled in traffic.

By Minibus Shuttle: The AeroCity shuttle bus provides door-to-door transport in a seven-seat minibus with up to three hotel stops en route. It's promoted by hotels, but if you want door-to-door service, simply taking a taxi generally offers a better value.

By Train

Madrid's two train stations, Chamartín and Atocha, are both on Metro lines with easy access to downtown Madrid. Both stations offer long-distance trains (*largo recorridos*) as well as smaller local trains (*regionales* and *cercanías*) to nearby destinations. Chamartín handles most international trains. Atocha generally covers southern Spain, as well as the AVE trains to and from Barcelona, Córdoba, Sevilla, and Toledo.

Buying Tickets: You can buy tickets at the stations, at travel agencies, or—not as easily—online (www.renfe.es). While travel agencies add a small fee, they can be worthwhile, especially during the high season or holidays, when the station's ticket counters have long lines. Convenient travel agencies include the El Corte

Inglés department store at Atocha (Mon-Fri 8:00-22:00, Sat-Sun 10:00-18:00, on ground floor of AVE side at the far end) and the El Corte Inglés a block off Puerta del Sol (Mon-Sat 10:00-22:00, Sun 11:00-21:00, Preciados 3, tel. 913-798-000).

Traveling Between Chamartín and Atocha Stations: You can take the Metro (line 1, 30-40 minutes, €1.50), but the *cercanías* trains are faster (6/hour, 13 minutes, €1.65)—and free with a rail pass or any regular train ticket to Madrid. Show it at ticket window in the middle of the turnstiles. Lines C3 and C4 are the most convenient; leave Atocha on track 6 or leave Chamartín from tracks 1, 3, 8, or 9—check the *Salidas Inmediatas* board to confirm.

CHAMARTÍN STATION

The TI is near track 20. The information, tickets, and customer-service office is at track 11. If you have a first-class rail pass and first-class seat or sleeper reservations, you can relax in the Sala VIP Club (between tracks 13 and 14, cooler of free drinks). Luggage storage (*consigna*) is across the street, opposite track 17. The station's Metro stop is also called Chamartín (not "Pinar de Chamartín").

ATOCHA STATION

The station is split in two: an AVE side (mostly long-distance trains) and a *cercanías* side (mostly local trains to the suburbs and the Metro for connecting into downtown). These two parts are connected by a corridor of shops. Each side of the station has separate schedules and customer-service offices. The TI, which is on the AVE arrivals side, offers tourist info, but no train info (Mon-Sat 8:00-20:00, Sun 9:00-14:00, tel. 915-284-630). To get to Atocha, use the "Atocha RENFE" Metro stop (not "Atocha").

Ticket Offices: The *cercanías* side has two offices—a small one for local trains and a big one for major trains (such as AVE). The AVE side sells tickets for AVE and other long-distance trains (two lines: "Tickets in Advance" or "Selling Out

Today"/"Departures Today"). A ticket counter will sometimes open up to sell tickets for trains departing soon—if you need to make a last-minute purchase, look for your destination and departure time, and get in line at that counter. If the line at one office is long, check the other offices. To secure your place in line, grab a number from a machine, usually located in the middle of the office by a sign with an image of a ticket. Ticket machines outside and around the office require a chip-and-PIN credit card.

AVE Side: Located in the towering old-station building, this half of the station boasts a lush, tropical garden filling its grand hall. It has the AVE trains, other fast trains (Grandes Líneas), a pharmacy (daily 8:00-22:00, facing garden), and Samarkanda—with both an affordable cafeteria (daily 13:00-20:00) and a pricey restaurant (daily from 21:00, tel. 915-309-746). Luggage storage (*consigna*, daily 6:00-22:20) is below Samarkanda. In the departure lounge on the upper floor, TV monitors announce track numbers. (A few trains, such as those for Toledo, depart from the lower floor.) For info, try the *Información* counter (daily 6:30-22:30), next to Centro Servicios AVE (which handles only AVE changes and problems). The *Atención al Cliente* office deals with problems on Grandes Líneas (daily 6:30-23:30). Also on the AVE side is the Club AVE/Sala VIP, a lounge reserved for AVE business-class travelers and for first-class ticket-holders or Eurailers with a first-class reservation (upstairs, past the security check on right; free drinks, newspapers, showers, and info service).

Cercanías Side: This is where you'll find the local *cercanías* trains, *regionales* trains, some eastbound faster trains, and the "Atocha RENFE" Metro stop. The *Atención al Cliente* office in the *cercanías* section has information only on trains to destinations near Madrid. During busy times, some AVE trains will pull in on this side—clearly marked signs lead you to the Metro, taxi stand, or back to the AVE side.

Terrorism Memorial: The terrorist bombings of March 11, 2004, took place in Atocha. Security is understandably tight here. A compelling memorial is in the *cercanías* part of the station near the Atocha RENFE Metro stop. Walk inside and under the cylinder to see thousands of condolence messages in many languages. The 36-foot-tall cylindrical glass memorial towers are visible from outside the station (daily 11:00-14:00 & 17:00-19:00).

AVE TRAINS

Spain's bullet train opens up some good itinerary options. You can get from Madrid's Atocha Station to **Barcelona** in about three hours, with trains running at least hourly. The AVE train is generally faster and easier than flying, but not necessarily cheaper. Basic second-class tickets are about €110-130 one-way for most departures; first-class tickets are €180. Advance purchase discounts (40-60 days ahead) are available through the national rail company (RENFE), but sell out quickly. Save by not traveling on holidays.

The AVE is also handy for visiting **Sevilla** (and, on the way, **Córdoba**). The basic Madrid-Sevilla second-class AVE fare is €75, depending upon departure time; first-class AVE costs €130 and comes with a meal. Consider this exciting day trip: 7:00-depart Madrid, 8:45-12:40-in Córdoba, 13:30-20:45-in Sevilla, 23:15-back in Madrid.

Other AVE destinations include **Toledo, Segovia,** and **Valencia.** Prices vary with times, class, date of purchase—RENFE discounts unsold AVE tickets as departure dates near. Eurail Pass holders pay a seat reservation fee (for example, Madrid to Sevilla is €13 second-class, but only at RENFE ticket windows—discount not available at ticket machines). Reserve each AVE segment ahead (tel. 902-320-320 for Atocha AVE info). For the latest, pick up the AVE brochure at the station, or check www.renfe.com.

TRAIN CONNECTIONS

Below I've listed both non-AVE and (where available) AVE trains to help you compare your options. General train info: tel. 902-320-320; international journeys: tel. 902-243-402; www.renfe.com.

From Madrid by Train to: Toledo (AVE or cheaper Avant: nearly hourly, 30 minutes, from Atocha); **El Escorial** (2/hour, but bus is better); **Segovia** (AVE: 8-10/day, 30 minutes plus 20-minute shuttle bus into Segovia center, from Chamartín, take train going toward Valladolid; slower *cercanías* trains: 9/day, 2 hours, from both Chamartín and Atocha); **Salamanca** (7/day, 3 hours, from Chamartín); **Santiago de Compostela** (4/day, 5.5-8.5 hours, most transfer in Ourense, includes night train, from Chamartín); **Barcelona** (AVE: at least hourly, 2.5-3 hours from Atocha); **San Sebastián** (4/day, 5.5-7.5 hours, from Chamartín); **Bilbao** (2-3/day, 5-6.5 hours, some transfer in Zaragoza, from Chamartín); **Pamplona** (3/day direct, 3 hours, more with transfer in Zaragoza, from Atocha); **Granada** (2/day on Altaria, 4.5 hours; also 2/day with transfer to AVE in Málaga, 4 hours); **Sevilla** (AVE: hourly, 2.5 hours, departures from 16:00-19:00 can sell out far in advance, from Atocha); **Córdoba** (AVE: 2-3/hour, 2 hours; Altaria trains: 4/day, 2 hours; all from Atocha); **Málaga** (AVE: 9/day, 2.5-3 hours, from Atocha).

By Bus

Madrid has several major bus stations with good Metro connections. Multiple bus companies use these stations, including Alsa (tel. 902-422-242, www.alsa.es), Avanza and Auto-Res (tel. 902-020-052, www.avanzabus.com), and La Sepulvedana (tel. 901-119-699, www.lasepulvedana.es). If you take a taxi from any bus station, you'll be charged a legitimate €3 supplement (not levied for trips to the station).

Plaza Elíptica Station: Alsa buses to Toledo leave from here (2/hour, 1-1.5 hours, *directo* faster than *ruta,* Metro: Plaza Elíptica).

Estación Sur de Autobuses (South Station): Served by Alsa, Socibus, and Avanza; buses go to **Ávila** (9/day, 6/day on weekends, 1.5 hours, Avanza), **Salamanca** (hourly express, 2.5-3 hours, Avanza), **León** (10/day, 3.5-4.5 hours, Alsa), **Santiago de Compostela** (5/day, 8-11 hours, includes 1 night bus, Alsa), **Granada** (nearly hourly, 5-6 hours, Alsa), and **Lisbon** (2/day, 9 hours, Avanza). The station sits squarely on top of the Méndez Álvaro Metro stop (has TI, tel. 914-684-200, www.estacionautobusesmadrid.com).

Príncipe Pío Station: Príncipe Pío, in a trendy mall, is a bus hub for local lines including Segovia (2/hour from platforms 6 or 7, 1.5 hours, runs from around 6:30-21:30, service starts later on Sat-Sun). From the Príncipe Pío Metro stop, follow signs to *terminal de autobuses* or follow pictures of a bus. Buy a ticket from the Sepulvedana window (platform 4). Reservations are rarely necessary.

By Car

Avoid driving in Madrid. If you're planning to rent a car, do it when you depart the city.

Renting a Car: It's cheapest to make car-rental arrangements before you leave home. In Madrid, consider **Europcar** (central reservations tel. 902-105-030, San Leonardo 8 office tel. 915-418-892, Atocha Station tel. 902-105-055, Chamartín Station tel. 912-035-070, airport tel. 902-105-055), **Hertz** (central reservations tel. 902-402-405, Plaza de España 18 tel. 915-425-805, Chamartín Station tel. 917-330-400, airport tel. 913-228-331), **Avis** (central reservations tel. 933-443-700, Gran Vía 60 tel. 915-484-204, airport tel. 902-200-162), and **Enterprise Atesa** (central reservations tel. 902-100-101). Ask about free delivery to your hotel. At the airport, most rental cars are returned at Terminal 1.

Italy

Stretching 850 miles long and 150 miles wide, art-drenched Italy is the cradle of European civilization. Visitors here come face to face with some of the world's most iconic images: Michelangelo's *David* in Florence, Rome's ancient Colosseum, Venice's gondolas, and the colorful, coastal villages of the Cinque Terre—Italy's Riviera.

Italy's 61 million inhabitants are more social and communal than most other Europeans. Because they're so outgoing and their language is so fun, Italians are a pleasure to communicate with. This boot-shaped country has all the elements that make travel to Europe forever fresh and rewarding: visible history, enthusiastic locals, and plenty of pasta.

CUISINE SCENE AT A GLANCE

For Italians, lunch (between 13:00 and 15:00) is the largest meal of the day, and dinner is light and late (around 20:00-21:30). Most **restaurants** close between lunch and dinner; good restaurants don't reopen for dinner before 19:00. To bridge the gap, people drop into a bar in the late afternoon for a snack.

A full Italian meal consists of several courses—an appetizer (*antipasto*), a first course (*primo piatto*), and a second course (*secondo piatto*)—but no one is obliged to order all that food. To save money and avoid getting stuffed, order any two courses. For example, a couple could order and share two *antipasti* and two *primi*.

At restaurants with self-serve buffets, you can choose various cooked appetizers from a salad-type bar. Generally buffets are not all-you-can-eat; take a one-time moderate serving (watch locals and imitate).

Understand prices before ordering. Seafood and steak may be sold by weight, either priced by the kilo (1,000 grams, or just over two pounds) or by the *etto* (100 grams, about a quarter-pound). The abbreviation *s.q.* (*secondo quantità*) means an item is priced "according to quantity" (such as the size of a fish). Fish is usually served whole, with the head and tail. As for steak, restaurants may require a minimum order of four or five *etti* (which diners can share). Some special dishes come in big quantities for two people (shown as "X2" on the menu), though the price listed generally indicates the cost per person.

You can save money by getting a fixed-price, multicourse meal, such as a basic *menù turistico* or often tastier *menù del giorno* (menu of the day). While fixed-price meals are convenient, galloping gourmets prefer to order à la carte.

Cover and Tipping: Before you sit down, look at a menu to see the extra charges that are often tacked on: *coperto* and *servizio*. The *coperto* (or *pane e coperto*) is a cover charge, added onto your bill as a flat fee (€1-3.50 per person; the amount should be clearly noted on the menu). The *servizio* (service charge) of about 10 percent pays for the waitstaff. Usually the words *servizio incluso* are written on the menu or bill, which means the listed prices already include the fee. You don't need to tip further (many Italians don't), but if you want to tip more for good service, you could include €1-2 for each person in your party.

A few restaurants tack on a 10 percent *servizio* charge to your bill; in this case, the menu will read: *servizio 10%*.

Budget Options: Take advantage of bars—inexpensive cafés that quickly serve up sandwiches, mini-pizzas, salads, and more. Bars have a two- or three-tiered pricing system. If you order, say, a sandwich, it's cheapest if you eat it while standing at the bar, more if you sit at an indoor table, and the most at an outdoor table.

Self-serve cafeterias are easy. Pizzerias are affordable, and takeout shops sell pizza by the slice or by weight. Or assemble a delicious picnic at a grocery or a deli (*rosticceria*).

Rome

Rome is magnificent and brutal at the same time. It's a showcase of Western civilization, with truly ancient sights and a modern vibrance. But with the wrong attitude, you'll be frustrated by the kind of chaos that only an Italian can understand. On my last visit, a cabbie struggling with the traffic said, *"Roma chaos."* I responded, *"Bella chaos."* He agreed.

Over 2,000 years ago the word "Rome" meant civilization itself. Today, Rome is Italy's political capital, the capital of Catholicism, and the center of its ancient empire, littered with evocative remains. As you peel through its fascinating and jumbled layers, you'll find Rome's buildings, cats, laundry, traffic, and 2.7 million people endlessly entertaining.

Despite Rome's rough edges, you'll fall in love with it...if you pace yourself, if you're well-organized, if you protect yourself and your valuables with extra caution, if your hotel provides a comfortable refuge, and if you embrace the siesta. Rome is much easier to love if you can avoid the midsummer heat.

ROME IN 3 DAYS

Rome wasn't built in a day, and you can't hope to see it all in three. Pace yourself; never regret a siesta. If you miss something, add it to your list of excuses to return.

Remember to check the Daily Reminder before you head out (see page 491).

Day 1: The Colosseum is the best place to begin your tour of ancient Rome. Then continue to the Arch of Constantine, Roman Forum, Trajan's Column, and Pantheon. Have dinner on the atmospheric Campo de' Fiori. Then take this book's Heart of Rome Walk to the Trevi Fountain and Spanish Steps.

Day 2: See St. Peter's Basilica and climb its dome, then tour the Vatican Museums, featuring the divine Sistine Chapel (closed Sun, except first Sun of month; smart to reserve a museum entry time in advance).

With any remaining stamina, choose among these sights (or save for tomorrow afternoon): the Church of San Giovanni in Laterano (Holy Stairs), St. Peter-in-Chains (Michelangelo's *Moses*), and Capuchin Crypt (bone chapel).

Evening options: Do as the Romans do—join the Dolce Vita Stroll along the Via del Corso. Explore the Monti neighborhood; linger over dinner, or stop by an *enoteca* (wine bar) for a drink. Enjoy a classical concert or jazz.

Day 3: See the Borghese Gallery

Rome's Neighborhoods

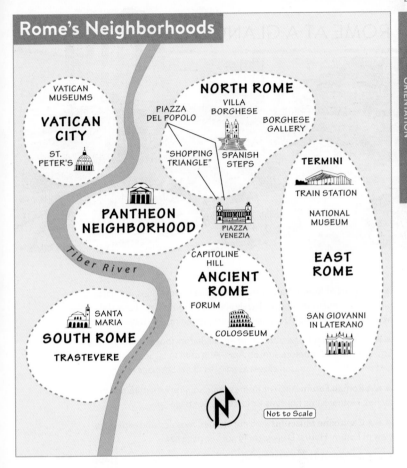

VATICAN
MUSEUMS

**VATICAN
CITY**

ST.
PETER'S

NORTH ROME

VILLA
BORGHESE

PIAZZA
DEL POPOLO

BORGHESE
GALLERY

"SHOPPING
TRIANGLE"

SPANISH
STEPS

TERMINI

TRAIN STATION

NATIONAL
MUSEUM

**PANTHEON
NEIGHBORHOOD**

PIAZZA
VENEZIA

Tiber River

CAPITOLINE
HILL

**ANCIENT
ROME**

FORUM

COLOSSEUM

**EAST
ROME**

SAN GIOVANNI
IN LATERANO

SANTA
MARIA

SOUTH ROME

TRASTEVERE

N

Not to Scale

(reservations required, closed Mon; stroll through the park afterwards) and the Capitoline Museums. Zip up to the top of the Victor Emmanuel Monument for a grand view of the Eternal City.

Rick's Tip: *The* **siesta is the key to survival** *in summertime Rome. Lie down and contemplate the extraordinary power of gravity in the Eternal City. Drink lots of cold, refreshing water from Rome's many drinking fountains.*

ORIENTATION

Sprawling Rome actually feels manageable once you get to know it. The old core, with most of the tourist sights, sits in a diamond formed by Termini train station (in the east), the Vatican (west), Villa Borghese Gardens (north), and the Colosseum (south). The Tiber River runs through the diamond from north to south. In the center of the diamond sits Piazza Venezia, a busy square and traffic hub. It takes about an hour to walk from Termini Station to the Vatican. Think of Rome as a series of neighborhoods, huddling around major landmarks.

ROME AT A GLANCE

▲▲▲**Heart of Rome Walk** A stroll lacing the narrow lanes, intimate piazzas, fanciful fountains, and lively scenes of Rome's most colorful neighborhood. **Hours:** Any time, but best in evening. See page 495.

▲▲▲**Colosseum** Huge stadium where gladiators fought. **Hours:** Daily 8:30 until one hour before sunset: April-Aug until 19:15, Sept until 19:00, Oct until 18:30, off-season closes as early as 16:30. See page 506.

▲▲▲**Roman Forum** Ancient Rome's main square, with ruins and grand arches. **Hours:** Same hours as Colosseum. See page 511.

▲▲▲**Capitoline Museums** Ancient statues, mosaics, and expansive view of Forum. **Hours:** Daily 9:30-19:30. See page 521.

▲▲▲**Pantheon** The defining domed temple—2,000 years old. **Hours:** Mon-Sat 8:30-19:30, Sun 9:00-18:00, holidays 9:00-13:00, closed for Mass Sat at 17:00 and Sun at 10:30. See page 525.

▲▲▲**St. Peter's Basilica** Most impressive church on earth, with Michelangelo's *Pietà* and dome. **Hours:** Church—daily April-Sept 7:00-19:00, Oct-March 7:00-18:30, often closed Wed mornings; dome—daily April-Sept 8:00-18:00, Oct-March 8:00-17:00. See page 527.

▲▲▲**Vatican Museums** Four miles of the finest art of Western civilization, culminating in Michelangelo's glorious Sistine Chapel. **Hours:** Mon-Sat 9:00-18:00. Closed on religious holidays and Sun, except last Sun of the month (open 9:00-14:00). May be open some Fri nights by online reservation only. See page 535.

▲▲▲**Borghese Gallery** Bernini sculptures and paintings by Caravaggio, Raphael, and Titian in a Baroque palazzo. Reservations mandatory. **Hours:** Tue-Sun 9:00-19:00, closed Mon. See page 541.

▲▲▲**National Museum of Rome** Greatest collection of Roman sculpture anywhere. **Hours:** Tue-Sun 9:00-19:45, closed Mon. See page 544.

▲▲**Dolce Vita Stroll** Evening *passeggiata*, where Romans strut their stuff. **Hours:** Roughly Mon-Sat 17:00-19:00 and Sun afternoons. See page 503.

▲▲**Trajan's Column** Tall ancient Roman column with narrative relief. **Hours:** Column always viewable. See page 523.

▲▲**Museo dell'Ara Pacis** Shrine marking the beginning of Rome's Golden Age. **Hours:** Daily 9:30-19:30. See page 543.

▲▲**Church of San Giovanni in Laterano** Grandiose and historic "home church of the popes," with one-of-a-kind Holy Stairs across the street. **Hours:** Church—daily 7:00-18:30; Holy Stairs—generally same hours but closed for lunch. See page 545.

▲**Arch of Constantine** Honors the emperor who legalized Christianity. **Hours:** Always viewable. See page 510.

▲**Monti Neighborhood** Lively fun-to-explore neighborhood with trendy eateries, workaday shops, and inviting lanes. **Hours:** Always open. See page 523.

▲**Palatine Hill** Ruins of emperors' palaces, Circus Maximus view, and museum. **Hours:** Same hours as Colosseum. See page 519.

▲**Piazza del Campidoglio** Square atop Capitoline Hill, designed by Michelangelo, with a museum, grand stairway, and Forum overlooks. **Hours:** Always open. See page 519.

▲**Spanish Steps** Popular hangout by day and night, particularly atmospheric when floodlit at night. **Hours:** Always open. See page 543.

▲**Victor Emmanuel Monument** Gigantic edifice celebrating Italian unity, with Rome from the Sky elevator ride up to 360-degree city view. **Hours:** Monument—daily 9:30-18:30; elevator—Mon-Thu 9:30-18:30, Fri-Sun 9:30-19:30. See page 522.

▲**St. Peter-in-Chains Church** with Michelangelo's *Moses.* **Hours:** Daily 8:00-12:20 & 15:00-19:00, until 18:00 in winter. See page 524.

▲**Trevi Fountain** Baroque hot spot into which tourists throw coins to ensure a return trip to Rome. **Hours:** Always flowing. See page 527.

Ancient Rome: In ancient times, this was home to the grandest buildings of a city of a million people. Today, the best of the classical sights stand in a line from the Colosseum to the Forum to the Pantheon. Just north of this area, between Via Nazionale and Via Cavour, is the atmospheric and trendy Monti district.

Pantheon Neighborhood: The Pantheon anchors the neighborhood I like to call the "Heart of Rome." It stretches eastward from the Tiber River through Campo de' Fiori and Piazza Navona, past the Pantheon to the Trevi Fountain.

Vatican City: Located west of the Tiber, it's a compact world of its own, with two great sights: St. Peter's Basilica and the Vatican Museums.

North Rome: With the Spanish Steps, Villa Borghese Gardens, and trendy shopping streets (Via Veneto and the "shopping triangle"—the area along Via del Corso and between the Spanish Steps, Piazza Venezia, and Piazza del Popolo), this is a more modern, classy area.

East Rome: This includes the area around Termini Station and Piazza della Repubblica, with many public-transportation connections.

South Rome: South of Vatican City is Trastevere, the colorful, wrong-side-of-the-river neighborhood that provides a look at village Rome. It's the city at its crustiest—and perhaps most "Roman."

Tourist Information

Rome has two main tourist information offices and several TI kiosks. The TI offices are at the airport (daily 8:00-19:30, Terminal 3) and Termini train station (daily 8:00-19:30, 100 yards down track 24). Kiosks (generally open daily 9:30-19:00) are near the Roman Forum (on Piazza del Tempio della Pace), on Via Nazionale (at Palazzo delle Esposizioni), between the Trevi Fountain and Pantheon (at the corner of Via del Corso and Via Minghetti), and near Piazza Navona (at Piazza delle Cinque Lune). Additionally, an information center is directly across from the Forum entrance, on Via dei Fori Imperiali. The TI's website is www.turismo roma.it, but most practical information is found at www.060608.it. That's also the number for Rome's **call center**—the best source of up-to-date tourist information, with English speakers on staff (answered daily 9:00-21:00, just dial 06-0608, and press 2 for English).

Two English-oriented **websites** provide insight into events and daily life in the city: www.inromenow.com (light tourist info on lots of topics); www.wantedinrome.com (events and accommodations).

Advance Tickets and Sightseeing Passes

Roma Pass: Rome offers several sightseeing passes. The Roma Pass is the clear winner (www.romapass.it). Two versions are available: three-day and 48-hour.

The **three-day Roma Pass** costs €36,

Spiral staircase at the Vatican Museums

Backstreet Rome

Daily Reminder

SUNDAY: The Vatican Museums are closed, except for last Sunday of the month, when they're free and even more crowded. These sights are free to all on the *first* Sunday of the month, and no reservations are available: Colosseum, Roman Forum, Palatine Hill, Borghese Gallery, and the National Museum of Rome.

MONDAY: Many sights are closed, including the National Museum of Rome, Borghese Gallery, and Ostia Antica. Major sights that are open include the Colosseum, Forum, Vatican Museums, Capitoline Museum, and Ara Pacis, among others. Churches are open as usual.

TUESDAY: All sights are open in Rome. This isn't a good day for a side trip to Naples because its Archaeological Museum is closed.

WEDNESDAY: St. Peter's Basilica is typically closed in the morning for a papal audience.

THURSDAY/FRIDAY/SATURDAY: All recommended sights are open.

includes free admission to your first two sights, a discount on many others, and unlimited use of public transit (buses, trams, and Metro). Using the pass at the Colosseum/Roman Forum/Palatine Hill (considered a single sight) gives you access to a special entrance that bypasses long ticket lines. Other sights covered (or discounted) include: Borghese Gallery (reservations required), Capitoline Museums, Ara Pacis, and Trajan's Market. The pass also covers the National Museum of Rome. The pass does not cover the Vatican Museums (which contain the Sistine Chapel).

If you'll be using public transit and visiting any two of the major sights in a three-day period, get the full pass. They are sold at participating sights, TIs, and many tobacco shops and newsstands all over town (look for a *Roma Pass* sign; all should charge the same price). Try to buy it at a less crowded TI or sight (even if you don't intend to visit that sight). There's no advantage in ordering a pass online—you still have to pick it up in Rome.

Validate your Roma Pass by writing your name and validation date on the card. Then insert it directly into the turn-

stile at your first two (free) sights. At other sights, show it at the ticket office to get about 30 percent off.

Rick's Tip: *To get the most out of your* **Roma Pass, visit the two most expensive sights first**—*for example, the Colosseum/ Roman Forum/Palatine Hill (€12) and the National Museum of Rome (€10).*

To use the included transit pass, write your name and birthdate on the pass and validate it on your first bus or Metro ride by passing it over a sensor at a turnstile or validation machine (look for a yellow circle). Now you can take unlimited rides within Rome's city limits (until midnight of the third day). Once the pass is validated you can hop on any bus without showing it, but you'll need to swipe it to get through Metro turnstiles.

The **48-hour Roma Pass** costs €28 and includes free entry to one sight, small discounts on additional ones, and unlimited use of public transit (for 48 hours after validation).

Children under age 18 get into covered sights for free, and they can skip the lines

Rome

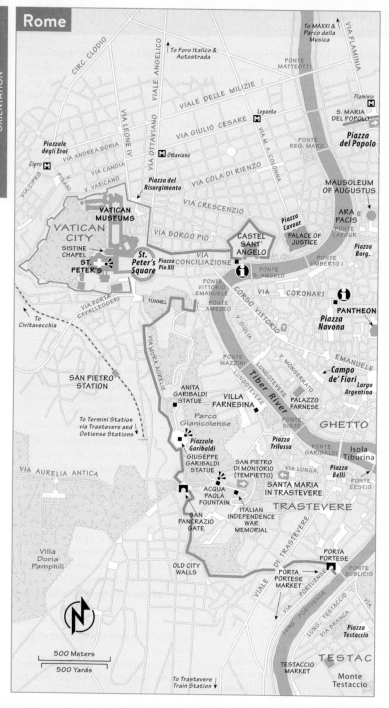

CIRC. CLODIO

↑ To Foro Italico & Autostrada

PONTE MATTEOTTI

VIA FLAMINIA

VIALE ANGELICO

VIALE DELLE MILIZIE

To MAXXI & Parco della Musica →

Flaminio Ⓜ

VIA GIULIO CESARE

Lepanto Ⓜ

S. MARIA DEL POPOLO

Piazza del Popolo

VIA A. COLONNA

PONTE REG. MARG.

Piazzale degli Eroi

VIA ANDREA DORIA

Cipro Ⓜ

VIA CIPRO

PISANI

VIA CANDIA

V. VATICANO

Ottaviano Ⓜ Ottaviano

VIA OTTAVIANO

VIA LEONE IV

Piazza del Risorgimento

VIA COLA DI RIENZO

MAUSOLEUM OF AUGUSTUS

ARA PACIS

VIA CRESCENZIO

Piazza Cavour

PONTE CAVOUR

Piazza Borg.

VATICAN MUSEUMS

VATICAN CITY

VIA BORGO PIO

PALACE OF JUSTICE

CASTEL SANT' ANGELO

SISTINE CHAPEL

ST. PETER'S

St. Peter's Square

Piazza Pio XII

VIA CONCILIAZIONE

PONTE S. ANGELO

PONTE UMBERTO I

VIA PORTA CAVALLEGGERI

TUNNEL

PONTE VITTORIO EMANUELE

PONTE AMEDEO

CORSO VITTORIO

VIA CORONARI

PANTHEON

Piazza Navona

↖ To Civitavecchia

SAN PIETRO STATION

VIA MURA AURELIE

ANITA GARIBALDI STATUE

V. GIULIA

VILLA FARNESINA

PONTE MAZZINI

LUNGOTEVERE

V. MONSERRATO

PALAZZO FARNESE

EMANUELE

Campo de' Fiori

Largo Argentina

To Termini Station via Trastevere and Ostiense Stations ↓

Parco Gianicolense

Tiber River

PONTE SISTO

GHETTO

Piazzale Garibaldi

GIUSEPPE GARIBALDI STATUE

SAN PIETRO DI MONTORIO (TEMPIETTO)

Piazza Trilussa

PONTE GARIBALDI

Isola Tiburina

VIA AURELIA ANTICA

ACQUA PAOLA FOUNTAIN

SANTA MARIA IN TRASTEVERE

VIA LUNGA

Piazza Belli

PONTE CESTIO

Villa Doria Pamphili

SAN PANCRAZIO GATE

ITALIAN INDEPENDENCE WAR MEMORIAL

TRASTEVERE

OLD CITY WALLS

VIALE DI TRASTEVERE

PORTA PORTESE

PONTE SUBLICIO

PORTA PORTESE MARKET

VIA PORTUENSE

VIA

Piazza Testaccio

LUNG. TESTACCIO

VIA BRANCA

500 Meters

500 Yards

TESTACCIO MARKET

TESTAC

Monte Testaccio

↓ To Trastevere Train Station

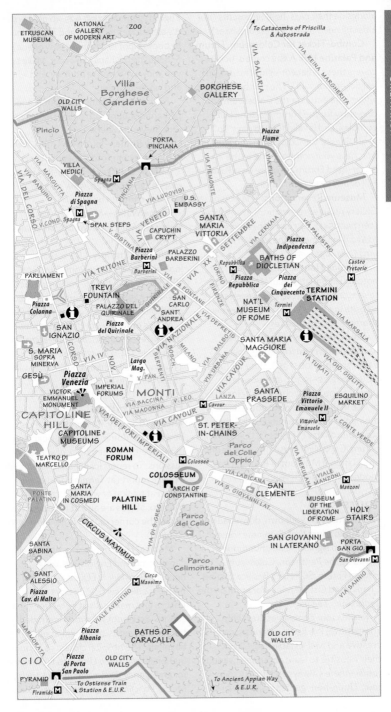

alongside their pass-holding parents (but kids still need transit tickets or passes).

Combo-Ticket for Colosseum, Forum, and Palatine Hill: A €12 combo-ticket covers these adjacent sights (no individual tickets are sold). The combo-ticket allows one entry for the Colosseum and one entry for the Forum/Palatine Hill complex, and is valid for two days. To avoid lines at the Colosseum and Forum, purchase your combo-ticket at the lesser-used Forum entrance near Palatine Hill or buy it online in advance.

Museum Reservations: The Borghese Gallery requires reservations in advance (see page 541). You can also reserve online to avoid long lines at the Vatican Museums (see page 535).

Opening Hours: Rome's sights have notoriously variable hours from season to season. It's smart to check each sight's website in advance. On holidays, expect shorter hours or closures.

Churches: Many churches, which have divine art and free entry, open early (around 7:00-7:30), close for lunch (roughly 12:00-15:30), and close late (about 19:00). Visit churches before 9:00 or late in the day; if you're not resting during the siesta, see major sights that stay open all day (St. Peter's, Colosseum, Forum, Capitoline Museums, Pantheon, and National Museum of Rome). Dress modestly for church visits.

Tours

🎧 To sightsee on your own, download my **free audio tours** that illuminate some of Rome's top sights and neighborhoods, including the Pantheon, Colosseum, Roman Forum, St. Peter's Basilica, Sistine Chapel, and Ostia Antica (for more on the audio tours, see page 14).

Rome's tour companies are highly competitive; I've listed several that are creative and well-established. Check their websites to learn about their various tours—there's always an introductory tour. Three-hour guided walks (always in

English) generally cost €25-30 per person. It's sometimes required, and always smart, to book a spot in advance (easy online). Scheduling mishaps can occur. Make sure you know what you're booking, and when and where to meet.

Each of these companies offers a 10 percent discount with online bookings for Rick Steves travelers:

Enjoy Rome—Tel. 06-445-1843, www.enjoyrome.com, info@enjoyrome.com.

Europe Odyssey—Tel. 06-8854-2416, mobile 328-912-3720, www.europeodyssey.com, run by Rahul.

Rome Walks—Mobile 347-795-5175, www.romewalks.com, info@romewalks.com, run by Annie.

Through Eternity—For discount look for "Group Tours Rome" and enter "RICKSTEVES"; tel. 06-700-9336, mobile 347-336-5298, www.througheternity.com, office@througheternity.com, run by Rob.

Walks of Italy—For discount enter "10ricksteves"; US tel. 888/683-8670, Italian mobile 334-974-4274, tel. 06-9558-3331, www.walksofitaly.com, info@walksofitaly.com, run by Jason.

Helpful Hints

Theft and Safety: Pickpocketing must be a sport in Rome. Stay alert, wear your money belt, and keep track of your possessions. To report lost or stolen items, file a police report (at Termini Station, with *polizia* at track 11 or with Carabinieri at track 20; offices are also at Piazza Venezia and at the corner of Via Nazionale and Via Genova).

Medical Help: Embassies and hotels can recommend English-speaking doctors. Consider MEDline, a 24-hour home-medical service; doctors speak English and make calls at hotels for €150 (tel. 06-808-0995). Anyone is entitled to free emergency treatment at public hospitals. The hospital closest to Termini Station is Policlinico Umberto 1 (entrance for emergency treatment on Via Lancisi, Metro: Policlinico, translators available).

Readers report that the staff at Santa Susanna Church, home of the American Catholic Church in Rome, offer useful advice and medical referrals.

Emergency Numbers: Police—tel. 113. Ambulance—tel. 118.

Beggars: Throughout Rome, you'll encounter downtrodden people asking for money. Many are actually able-bodied foreigners preying on people's sympathy. You may see them at churches trying to collect money, sometimes for opening church doors. But they are not affiliated, and are lining their own pockets. Know that social services are available to them, so give at your own discretion.

Traffic Safety: Use extreme caution when crossing streets. Some streets have pedestrian-crossing signals (red means stop—or jaywalk carefully; green means go...also carefully; and yellow means go... extremely carefully, as cars may be whipping around the corner). Just as often, multilane streets have crosswalks with no signals at all. And even when there are traffic lights, they are provisional: Scooters don't need to stop at red lights, and even cars exercise what drivers call the "logical option" of not stopping if they see no oncoming traffic. As noisy, gasoline-powered scooters are replaced by electric ones, the streets get quieter (hooray) but more dangerous for pedestrians.

Follow locals like a shadow when you cross a street. Find a gap in the traffic and walk with confidence while making eye contact with approaching drivers—they won't hit you if they can tell where you intend to go.

Internet Access: Most hotels have Wi-Fi, but if yours doesn't, your hotelier can point you to the nearest Internet café.

Free Water: Carry a **water bottle** and refill it at Rome's many public drinking spouts.

WCs: Public restrooms are scarce. Use them when you can at museums, restaurants, and bars.

Travel Agencies: You can get train tickets and rail-pass-related reservations and supplements at travel agencies (at little or no additional cost), avoiding a trip to a train station. Your hotelier will know of an agency nearby.

ROME WALKS

These two self-guided walks give you a moving picture of this ancient yet modern city.

⊙ Heart of Rome Walk

Rated ▲▲▲, this walk through Rome's most colorful neighborhood takes you through squares lively with locals, small lanes sporting shops or chunks of Roman ruins, and playful fountains that are people-magnets. During the day, this walk shows off the Campo de' Fiori market and trendy fashion boutiques as it meanders past major monuments such as the Pantheon and the Spanish Steps.

But the sunset brings unexpected magic. A stroll in the cool of the evening offers the romance of the Eternal City at its best. Sit so close to a bubbling fountain that traffic noise evaporates. Jostle with kids to see the gelato flavors. Watch lovers straddling more than the bench. And marvel at the ramshackle elegance that softens this brutal city. These are the flavors of Rome, best enjoyed after dark.

This walk is equally pleasant in reverse order. You could ride the Metro to the Spanish Steps and finish at Campo de' Fiori, near my recommended restaurants.

• *Start this walk at Campo de' Fiori, my favorite outdoor dining room (see page 496). It's a few blocks west of Largo Argentina, a major transportation hub. Buses #40, #64, and #492 stop at Largo Argentina and along Corso Vittorio Emanuele II (a long block northwest of Campo de' Fiori). A taxi from Termini Station costs about €8.*

❶ CAMPO DE' FIORI

This picturesque, bohemian piazza hosts a fruit and vegetable **market** in the morning, cafés in the evening, and pub-crawlers at night. In ancient times, the "Field of Flowers" was an open meadow. Later, Christian pilgrims passed through on their way to the Vatican, and a thriving market developed.

The square is watched over by a brooding statue of **Giordano Bruno,** an intellectual heretic who was burned on this spot in 1600. The pedestal shows scenes from Bruno's trial and execution, and reads, "And the flames rose up." When this statue honoring a heretic was erected in 1889, the Vatican protested, but they were overruled by angry Campo locals. The neighborhood is still known for its free spirit and anti-authoritarian demonstrations.

Campo de' Fiori is the product of centuries of unplanned urban development. At the east end of the square (behind Bruno), ramshackle apartments are built right into the outer wall of ancient Rome's mammoth Theater of Pompey. Julius Caesar was assassinated in the Theater, where the Senate was renting space.

The square is surrounded by fun eateries, and is great for people-watching. Bruno faces the bustling **Forno** (in a corner of the square), where takeout *pizza bianca* ("white pizza," without red sauce) is sold hot out of the oven. On weekend nights, when the Campo is packed with beer-drinking kids, the medieval square is transformed into a vast street party.

• *If Bruno did a hop, step, and jump forward, then turned left, in a block he'd reach...*

❷ PIAZZA FARNESE

While Campo de' Fiori feels free and easy, the 16th-century Renaissance Piazza Farnese, named for the family whose palace dominates it, stresses order. The nouveau riche Farnese family hired Michelangelo to design the top part of their palace's facade—which today houses the French embassy. The twin Roman tubs in the fountains decorating the square date from the third century and are from the Baths of Caracalla. They ended up here because Pope Paul III, who was a Farnese, ordered the excavation of the baths, and the family had first dibs on the choicest finds.

• *Walk back to Campo de' Fiori, cross the square, and continue a couple of blocks down...*

Campo de' Fiori

❸ VIA DEI BAULLARI AND CORSO VITTORIO EMANUELE II

With a crush of cheap cafés, bars, and restaurants, the center of medieval Rome is now a playground for tourists, students, and suburban locals. High rents are driving families out and changing the character of this district. That's why the Campo de' Fiori market increasingly sells more gifty edibles than basic fruits and vegetables with each passing year.

• *After a couple of blocks, you reach busy Corso Vittorio Emanuele II. In Rome, any road big enough to have city buses like this is post-unification: constructed after 1870. Look left and right down the street—the facades are mostly 19th century Neo-Renaissance, built after this main thoroughfare sliced through the city. Traffic in much of central Rome is limited to city buses, taxis, motorbikes, "dark cars" (limos and town cars of VIPs), delivery vans, residents, and disabled people with permits (a.k.a. friends of politicians). This is one of the rare streets where anything goes.*

Cross Corso Vittorio Emanuele II, and enter a square with a statue of Marco Minghetti, an early Italian prime minister. Angle left at the statue, walking along the left side of the Museum of Rome, down Via di San Pantaleo. A block down, at the corner, you'll find a beat-up old statue.

❹ PASQUINO

A third-century B.C. statue that was discovered near here, Pasquino is one of Rome's "talking statues." For 500 years, this statue has served as a kind of community billboard, allowing people to complain anonymously when it might be dangerous to speak up. To this day, you'll see old Pasquino strewn with political posters, strike announcements, and grumbling graffiti. The statue looks literally worn down by centuries of complaining about bad government.

• *Wrap around Pasquino and head up Via di Pasquino to...*

❺ PIAZZA NAVONA

This square retains the oblong shape of the athletic grounds built here around A.D. 80 by the emperor Domitian. Today's square, while following its ancient foundation, is from the late Renaissance.

Three Baroque fountains decorate the piazza. The first fountain, at the southern end, features a Moor wrestling with a dolphin. In the fountain at the northern end,

Piazza Navona with Bernini's Four Rivers fountain

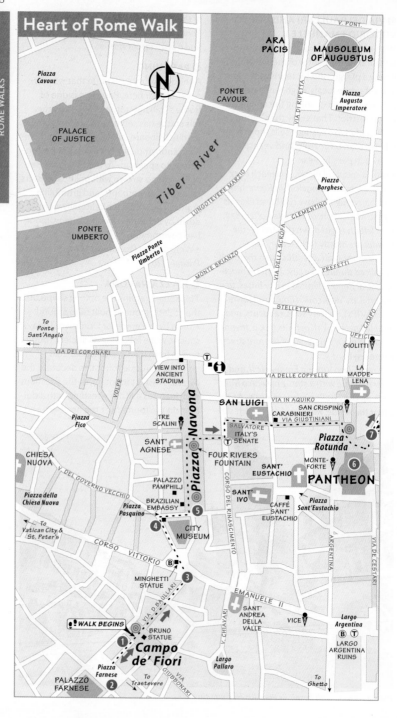

Heart of Rome Walk

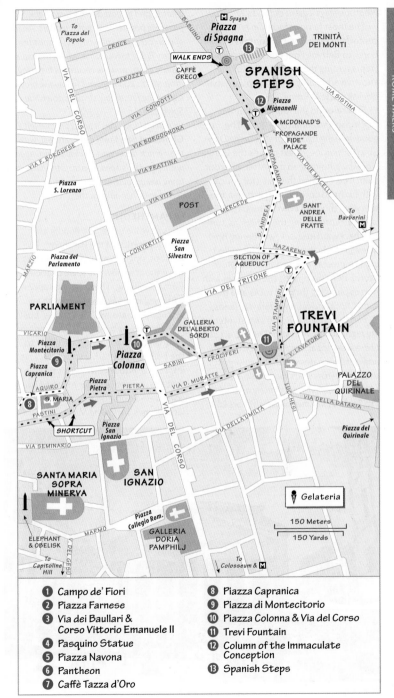

1 Campo de' Fiori	**8** Piazza Capranica
2 Piazza Farnese	**9** Piazza di Montecitorio
3 Via dei Baullari & Corso Vittorio Emanuele II	**10** Piazza Colonna & Via del Corso
4 Pasquino Statue	**11** Trevi Fountain
5 Piazza Navona	**12** Column of the Immaculate Conception
6 Pantheon	
7 Caffè Tazza d'Oro	**13** Spanish Steps

Neptune slays a giant octopus.

The most famous fountain is in the center: the **Four Rivers Fountain** by Gian Lorenzo Bernini. Four burly river gods (representing the four quarters of the known world) support an Egyptian-style obelisk made in Rome.

Stroll around the fountain counter-clockwise and admire the gods: The good-looking figure represents the Danube (for Europe). Next comes the Ganges (for Asia), holding an oar. After an exotic palm tree, you find the Nile (for Africa) with his head covered, since its headwaters were then unknown. Uruguay's Rio de la Plata, representing the Americas, tumbles backward in shock, wondering how he even made the top four. The spilled coins represent the wealth of the New World. Bernini enlivens the fountain with horses plunging through rocks and the exotic flora and fauna of faraway lands.

Piazza Navona is Rome's most interesting night scene, with street music, artists, fire-eaters, local Casanovas, ice cream, and outdoor cafés worth the splurge for their front-row seats for people-watching.
• *Leave Piazza Navona directly across from* **Tre Scalini** *(famous for its rich chocolate*

gelato), and go east down Corsia Agonale, past rose peddlers and palm readers. Ahead of you (across the busy street) stands the stately Palazzo Madama, where the Italian Senate meets and the security is high. Jog left around this building, and follow the brown sign to the Pantheon, straight down Via del Salvatore.

After a block, you'll pass (on your left) the **Church of San Luigi dei Francesi,** *with its très French decor and precious Caravaggio paintings. If it's open, pop in. Otherwise, continue along, following the crowd, as everyone seems to be heading for the...*

⑥ PANTHEON

Sit for a while under the floodlit and moonlit portico of the Pantheon. The 40-foot, single-piece granite columns of the entrance show the scale of ancient Roman building. The columns support a triangular Greek-style roof with an inscription that says "M. Agrippa" built it. In fact, it was built *(fecit)* by Emperor Hadrian (A.D. 120), who gave credit to the builder of an earlier structure. This impressive entranceway gives no clue that the greatest wonder of the building is inside—a domed room that inspired later domes, including Michelangelo's

Pantheon

St. Peter's and Brunelleschi's Duomo in Florence.

• With your back to the Pantheon, veer to the right, uphill toward the yellow sign on Via Orfani that reads Casa del Caffè—you've reached the...

❼ CAFFÈ TAZZA D'ORO

This is one of Rome's top coffee shops, dating back to the days when this area was licensed to roast coffee beans. Locals come here for *granita di caffè con panna* (coffee and crushed ice with whipped cream).

*• From here, our walk continues past some interesting landmarks to the Trevi Fountain. But if you'd like to get to the fountain directly, take a **shortcut** by bearing right at the coffee shop onto Via de' Pastini, which leads through Piazza di Pietra, then across busy Via del Corso, where it becomes the pedestrianized Via delle Muratte and heads straight for the fountain.*

If you'd rather stick with me for the slightly longer version, bear left at the coffee shop and continue up Via degli Orfani to the next square...

❽ PIAZZA CAPRANICA

This square is home to the big, plain Florentine-Renaissance-style Palazzo Capranica (directly opposite as you enter the square). The six-story building to the left was once an apartment building for 17th-century Rome's middle class. Like so many of Rome's churches, Santa Maria in Aquiro, the church on the square, is older than the facade it was given during the Baroque period. Notice the little circular shrine on the street corner (between the palace and the apartment building).

• Leave the piazza to the right of the palace, heading down Via in Aquiro. The street jogs to the left and into a square.

❾ PIAZZA DI MONTECITORIO

The square is marked by a sixth-century B.C. **Egyptian obelisk,** taken as a trophy by Augustus after his victory in Egypt over Mark Antony and Cleopatra. The obelisk

was originally set up as a sundial. Follow the zodiac markings to the well-guarded front door of Italy's **parliament building.**

• One block to your right is Piazza Colonna, where we're heading next—unless you like gelato. A one-block detour to the left (past Albergo Nazionale) brings you to Rome's most famous gelateria, Giolitti, reasonable for takeout or elegant and splurge-worthy for a sit among classy locals (open daily until past midnight, Via Uffici del Vicario 40).

❿ PIAZZA COLONNA AND VIA DEL CORSO

The centerpiece of **Piazza Colonna** is a huge second-century column. Its relief depicts the victories of Emperor Marcus Aurelius over the barbarians. Marcus once capped the column, but he was replaced by Paul, one of Rome's patron saints.

Beyond Piazza Colonna runs noisy **Via del Corso,** Rome's main north-south boulevard. It's named for the riderless horse races that took place here during Carnevale. In 1854, the Via became one of Rome's first gas-lit streets and hosted the classiest boutiques. Nowadays the northern part of Via del Corso is closed to traffic, and for a few hours every evening it becomes a wonderful parade of Romans out for a stroll (see the next walk, "Dolce Vita Stroll"). Before crossing the street, look left (to the obelisk marking Piazza del Popolo—the ancient north gate of the city) and right (to the Victor Emmanuel Monument).

*• Cross Via del Corso to enter a big palatial building with columns, the **Galleria Alberto Sordi** shopping mall. To the left are convenient toilets and ahead is Feltrinelli, the biggest Italian bookstore chain.*

Go to the right and exit out the back (if you're here after 21:00, when the mall is closed, circle around the right side of the Galleria on Via dei Sabini). Once out the back, the tourist kitsch builds as you head up Via de Crociferi to the roar of the water, lights, and people at the...

⑪ TREVI FOUNTAIN

This watery avalanche celebrates the abundance of pure water, which has been brought into the city since the days of ancient aqueducts. Oceanus rides across the waves in his chariot, pulled by horses and horn-blowing tritons, as he commands the flow of water. The illustrious Bernini sketched out the first designs. Nicola Salvi continued the project (c. 1740), using the palace behind the fountain as a theatrical backdrop.

The magic of the square is enhanced by the fact that no vehicular streets directly approach it. You can hear the excitement as you draw near, and then—*bam!*—you're there. The scene is always lively, with lucky Romeos clutching dates while unlucky ones clutch beers. Romantics toss a coin over their shoulder, thinking it will give them a wish and assure their return to Rome. It sounds silly, but every year I go through this tourist ritual...and it actually seems to work.

• *Facing the Trevi Fountain, walk along its right side up Via della Stamperia. Cross busy Via del Tritone. Continue 100 yards up Via del Nazareno. At the T-intersection ahead,*

Trevi Fountain

veer right on Via Sant'Andrea delle Fratte. The security is protecting the headquarters of Italy's Democratic Party (on the right).

The street becomes Via di Propaganda, and at the far end (on the right), it's dominated by a palace that housed the 17th-century Propagande Fide, where missionaries learned how to evangelize. Here the street opens up into a long piazza. You're approaching the Spanish Steps. But first, pause at the...

⑫ COLUMN OF THE IMMACULATE CONCEPTION

This ancient column is dedicated to the Immaculate Conception of Mary. For Mary to be a worthy and pure vessel for Jesus, the Catholic Church decided she needed to be "immaculately conceived"—born without sin. Pope Pius IX and the Vatican finally settled the long theological debate in 1854 by formally establishing the dogma of Mary's Immaculate Conception. Three years later, officials erected this column honoring Mary. Every year on December 8, the feast day of the Immaculate Conception, this spot is the scene of a special celebration. The pope attends, the fire department places flowers on Mary's statue, and the Christmas season begins.

To Mary's immediate left stands the Spanish embassy to the Vatican. Rome has double the embassies of a normal capital because here countries need two: one to Italy and one to the Vatican. And because of this embassy, the square and its famous steps are called "Spanish."

• *Just 100 yards past Mary, you reach the...*

⑬ SPANISH STEPS

Piazza di Spagna, with the popular Spanish Steps, has been the hangout of many Romantics over the years (Keats, Wagner, Openshaw, Goethe, and others). The British poet John Keats pondered his mortality, then died of tuberculosis at age 25 in the orange building on the right side of the steps. Fellow Romantic Lord Byron lived across the square at #66.

The 138 steps lead sharply up from Piazza di Spagna, forming a butterfly shape as they fan out around a central terrace. The design culminates in an obelisk framed between two Baroque church towers.

The **Sinking Boat Fountain** at the foot of the steps, built by Bernini or his father, Pietro, is powered by an aqueduct (like all of Rome's fountains).

The main sight here is not the steps but the people who gather around them. By day, shoppers swarm the high-fashion boutiques at the base of the steps, along Via Condotti. At night, the area is alive with people enjoying—and creating—the ambience of Rome's piazzas.

• *Our walk is finished. If you'd like to reach the top of the steps sweat-free, take the free elevator just inside the Spagna Metro stop (to the left, as you face the steps; elevator closes at 21:00). A pay WC is underground in the piazza near the Metro entrance, by the middle palm tree (10:00-19:30). A huge McDonald's (with a WC) is a block to the right of the steps. When you're ready to leave, zip home on the Metro or grab a taxi at either end of the piazza.*

➲ Dolce Vita Stroll

This chic evening stroll, rated ▲▲, moves from Piazza del Popolo (Metro: Flaminio) down a traffic-free section of Via del Corso, and up Via Condotti to the Spanish Steps. You'll see people-watchers, flirts on the prowl, and shoppers browsing Rome's most fashionable stores (some are open roughly 16:00-19:30, after the siesta).

Although it's busy at any hour, crowds really come out from 17:00 to 19:00 (Fri and Sat are best), except on Sunday, when the stroll begins earlier in the afternoon. Leave before 18:00 if you plan to visit the Ara Pacis (Altar of Peace), which closes at 19:30 (last entry at 18:30). If you get hungry, see page 551 for a couple of restaurant listings.

To reach **Piazza del Popolo,** take Metro line A to Flaminio and walk south to the square. The car-free piazza is marked by an obelisk that was brought to

Piazza del Popolo

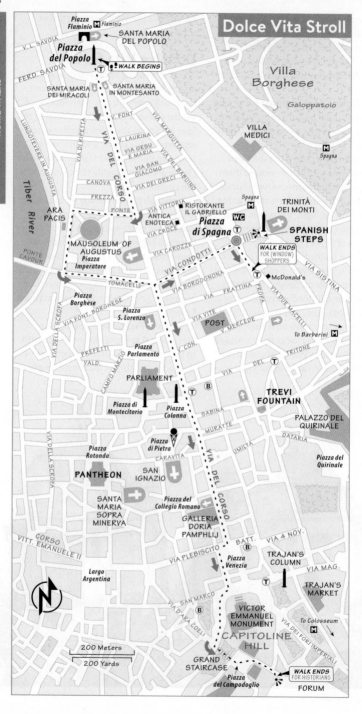

Rome by Augustus after he conquered Egypt. It used to stand in the Circus Maximus.

If you're starting your stroll early enough, visit the Baroque church of **Santa Maria del Popolo,** next to the gate in the old wall on the north side of the square (Mon-Sat until 19:00, Sun until 19:30); look for Raphael's Chigi Chapel (second on left as you face main altar) and two paintings by Caravaggio (in Cerasi Chapel, left of altar).

From Piazza del Popolo, browse your way down **Via del Corso.** With the proliferation of shopping malls, many chain stores lining Via del Corso are losing customers and facing hard times. Still, this remains a fine place to feel the pulse of Rome at twilight.

Historians should turn right down **Via Pontefici** to see the massive, round-brick **Mausoleum of Augustus,** topped with overgrown cypress trees. This neglected sight, honoring Rome's first emperor, is slated for restoration and redevelopment. Beyond it, next to the river, is Augustus' **Ara Pacis,** enclosed within a protective glass-walled museum (see page 543). From the mausoleum, walk down Via Tomacelli to return to Via del Corso and the 21st century.

From Via del Corso, window shoppers should take a left down **Via Condotti** to join the parade to the **Spanish Steps,** passing big-name boutiques. The streets that parallel Via Condotti to the south (Borgognona and Frattina) are also filled with high-end shops. A few streets to the north hides the narrow Via Margutta, where Gregory Peck's *Roman Holiday* character lived (at #51). Today it's filled with pricey artisan and antique shops.

Historians should ignore Via Condotti and forget the Spanish Steps. Stay on Via del Corso and walk a half-mile down to the **Victor Emmanuel Monument.** Climb Michelangelo's stairway to his glorious square atop Capitoline Hill, floodlit at night. The mayor's palace is straight ahead. Stand on the balcony (to the right of the palace) overlooking the Forum. Enjoy one of the finest views in the city as the horizon reddens and cats prowl the unclaimed rubble of ancient Rome.

Spanish Steps

SIGHTS

I've clustered Rome's sights into walkable neighborhoods, some close together.

When you see a 🎧 in a listing, it means the sight is covered on a free audio tour (via my Rick Steves Audio Europe app—see page 14).

The best website for current opening hours is www.060608.it.

Rick's Tip: *Make it a point to* **visit sights in a logical order.** *Needless backtracking wastes precious time and energy.*

Ancient Rome

The core of ancient Rome, where the grandest monuments were built, is between the Colosseum and Capitoline Hill. You can tour these sights in one great day: Start at the Colosseum, then it's a few minutes' walk to the Forum, then Capitoline Hill. From there, it's another 15-minute walk to the Pantheon. As a pleasant conclusion to your busy day, walk back south along the broad, parklike Via dei Fori Imperiali.

Ancient Core

▲▲▲COLOSSEUM (COLOSSEO)

This 2,000-year-old stadium is one of Europe's most recognizable landmarks—and a classic example of Roman engineering. Whether you're playing gladiator or simply marveling at the ancient design and construction, the Colosseum gets a unanimous thumbs-up.

Cost and Hours: €12 combo-ticket includes Roman Forum and Palatine Hill, free and crowded first Sun of the month, open daily 8:30 until one hour before sunset: April-Aug until 19:15, Sept until 19:00, Oct until 18:30, off-season closes as early as 16:30, last entry one hour before closing, audioguide-€5.50, Metro: Colosseo, tel. 06-3996-7700, www.archeoroma. beniculturali.it/en.

Avoiding Lines: Crowds are thinner and lines shorter in the afternoon (especially after 15:00 in summer).

You'll save time if you...

1. Buy your combo-ticket (or Roma Pass) at a less-crowded place. Try the Forum/Palatine Hill entrance facing the Colosseum. If that's also crowded, try the entrance 150 yards away, on Via di San Gregorio (facing the Forum, with Col-

Colosseum

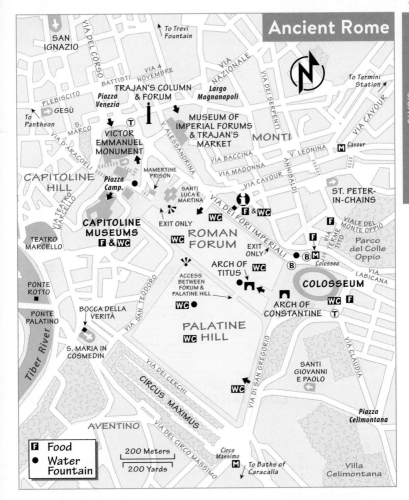

Ancient Rome

Legend:
- **F** Food
- ● Water Fountain

200 Meters
200 Yards

osseum at your back, go left down the street). You can also buy a Roma Pass at the green kiosk in front of the Colosseo Metro station, the information center on Via dei Fori Imperiali (across from the entrance to the Forum), or other sights around town. It costs the same no matter where you buy it.

2. Buy and print a combo-ticket online at www.coopculture.it (€2 booking fee). The "free tickets" you'll see listed are valid only for EU citizens with ID.

3. Pay for an official guided tour or rent an audioguide or videoguide. Tell the guard at the ticket-holders entrance that you want a tour or audioguide, and they'll direct you to the right desk, bypassing the ticket lines. The extra cost might be worth it just to skip the line.

4. Hire a private guide. Guides linger outside the Colosseum, offering tours that allow you to bypass the line. Be aware that these private guides may try to mislead you into thinking the Colosseum lines are longer than they really are.

Getting There: The Colosseo Metro stop on line B is just across the street from the monument. Buses #51, #85, #87, #118,

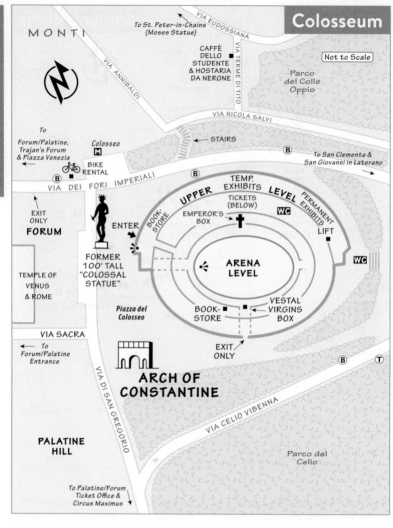

Colosseum

Not to Scale

MONTI

VIA EUDOSSIANA

To St. Peter-in-Chains
(Moses Statue)

CAFFÈ DELLO
STUDENTE
& HOSTARIA
DA NERONE

VIA ANNIBALDI

VIA TERME DI TITO

Parco
del Colle
Oppio

VIA NICOLA SALVI

STAIRS

To
Forum/Palatine,
Trajan's Forum
& Piazza Venezia

Colosseo
M

BIKE
RENTAL

B

To San Clemente &
San Giovanni in Laterano

VIA DEI FORI IMPERIALI

B

TEMP.
EXHIBITS

UPPER LEVEL

TICKETS
(BELOW)

PERMANENT EXHIBITS

EXIT
ONLY

FORUM

ENTER

BOOK-STORE

EMPEROR'S
BOX

WC

LIFT

FORMER
100' TALL
"COLOSSAL
STATUE"

ARENA
LEVEL

WC

TEMPLE OF
VENUS
& ROME

Piazza del
Colosseo

BOOK-STORE

VESTAL
VIRGINS
BOX

VIA SACRA

EXIT
ONLY

B

T

To
Forum/Palatine
Entrance

ARCH OF
CONSTANTINE

VIA CELIO VIBENNA

VIA DI SAN GREGORIO

PALATINE
HILL

Parco del
Celio

To Palatine/Forum
Ticket Office &
Circus Maximus

#186, and #810 stop along Via dei Fori Imperiali near the Colosseum entrance, one of the Forum/Palatine Hill entrances, and Piazza Venezia.

Getting In: Follow the signs to get in the right line. The entrance is divided into two queues: The longer line is for those who need to buy a ticket. The shorter line is for ticket holders (combo-ticket, online ticket, or Roma Pass) and those requesting a tour or audioguide (go to the front of the line to talk to the guard). There's a separate entrance for groups.

Tours: A fact-filled **audioguide** is available just past the turnstiles (€5.50/2 hours). A handheld **videoguide** senses where you are in the site and plays related clips (€6).

🎧 Download my free Colosseum **audio tour.**

Official guided tours in English depart nearly hourly between 10:00 and 17:00, and last 45-60 minutes (€5 plus Colosseum ticket, purchase inside the

Colosseum near the ticket booth marked *Visite didattiche*).

A 1.5-hour **"Colosseum, Underground and Third Ring" tour** takes you through areas that are off-limits to regular visitors, including the top floor and underground passageways, but isn't essential. If you want to sign up, it's smart to reserve by phone or online a day or more in advance (no same-day reservations). The tour is operated by CoopCulture (€9 plus Colosseum ticket, tel. 06-3996-7700, answered Mon-Fri 9:00-18:00, Sat 9:00-14:00, www. coopculture.it).

Private guides stand outside the Colosseum looking for business (€25-30/2-hour tour of the Colosseum, Forum, and Palatine Hill). Make sure that your tour will start right away and covers all three sights: the Colosseum, Forum, and Palatine Hill.

Services: A WC is inside the Colosseum.

Background: Built when the Roman Empire was at its peak in A.D. 80, the Colosseum represents Rome at its grandest. Known as the Flavian Amphitheater, it was an arena for gladiator contests and public spectacles. When killing became a spectator sport, the Romans wanted to share the fun with as many people as possible, so they stuck two semicircular theaters together to create a freestanding amphitheater. Towering 150 feet high, it could accommodate 50,000 roaring fans (100,000 thumbs). The outside (where slender cypress trees stand today) was decorated with a 100-foot-tall bronze statue of Nero that gleamed in the sunlight. In a later age, the colossal structure was nicknamed a "coloss-eum."

Rick's Tip: *Beware of the* **greedy, modern-day gladiators,** *who intimidate gullible tourists into paying too much money (€4-5) for a photo op. Also, look out for* **pickpockets.**

Exterior: The Romans were great engineers, not artists; the building is more functional than beautiful. (Ancient Romans visiting the US today might send home postcards of our greatest works of art—freeways.) While the essential structure is Roman, the four-story facade is decorated with mostly Greek columns—Tuscan columns on the ground level, Ionic on the second story, Corinthian on the

Colosseum interior

next level, and at the top, half-columns with a mix of all three. Copies of Greek statues once stood in the arches of the middle two stories, adding sophistication to this arena of death.

Only a third of the original Colosseum remains. Earthquakes destroyed some of it, but most was carted off to build other buildings during the Middle Ages and Renaissance.

Interior: The games took place in the oval-shaped arena, 280 feet long by 165 feet wide. When you look down into the arena, you're seeing the underground passages beneath the playing surface (which can only be visited on a private tour). The arena was originally covered with a wooden floor, then sprinkled with sand (*arena* in Latin). The bit of reconstructed floor gives you a sense of the original arena level and the subterranean warren where animals and prisoners were held. The spectators ringed the playing area in bleacher seats that slanted up from the arena floor. Around you are the big brick masses that supported the tiers of seats.

The games began with a few warm-up acts—dogs bloodying themselves attacking porcupines, female gladiators fighting each other, or a one-legged man battling a dwarf. Then came the main event—the gladiators.

"Hail, Caesar! (*Ave, Caesar!*) We who are about to die salute you!" The gladiators would enter the arena from the west end, parade around to the sound of trumpets, acknowledge the Vestal Virgins (on the south side), then stop at the emperor's box (marked today by the cross that stands at the "50-yard line" on the north side—although no one knows for sure where it was). They would then raise their weapons, shout, and salute—and begin fighting. The fights pitted men against men, men against beasts, and beasts against beasts. Picture 50,000 screaming people around you (did gladiators get stage fright?), and imagine that they want to see you die.

▲ARCH OF CONSTANTINE

This well-preserved arch, which stands between the Colosseum and the Forum, commemorates a military coup and, more important, the acceptance of Christianity by the Roman Empire. The ambitious Emperor Constantine (who had a vision that he'd win under the sign of the cross) defeated his rival Maxentius in A.D. 312

Arch of Constantine

to become sole emperor of the Roman Empire. He legalized Christianity soon after. The arch is free and always open.

🎧 It's covered in my free Colosseum audio tour.

▲▲▲ROMAN FORUM (FORO ROMANO)

This is ancient Rome's birthplace and civic center, and the common ground between Rome's famous seven hills. As just about anything important that happened in ancient Rome happened here, it's arguably the most important piece of real estate in Western civilization. While only fragments of that glorious past remain, you'll find plenty to ignite your imagination amid the half-broken columns and arches.

Cost: €12 combo-ticket covers both the Roman Forum/Palatine Hill and the Colosseum (valid two consecutive days, but each sight can only be entered once); also covered by the Roma Pass. The Forum is free (and extremely crowded) the first Sunday of the month.

Hours: The Roman Forum, Palatine Hill, and Colosseum are open daily 8:30 until one hour before sunset: April-Aug until 19:15, Sept until 19:00, Oct until 18:30, Nov-mid-Feb until 16:30, mid-Feb-mid-March until 17:00, mid-March-late March until 17:30; last entry one hour before closing.

Avoiding Lines: Buy your combo-ticket (or Roma Pass) at a less-crowded place or get a combo-ticket online; for specifics, see page 490. Or visit later in the day when crowds diminish.

Getting There: The closest Metro stop is Colosseo. Buses #51, #85, #87, #118, #186, and #810 stop along Via dei Fori Imperiali near the Colosseum, the Forum, and Piazza Venezia.

Getting In: The Forum and Palatine Hill share three entrances. The handiest (but often most crowded) is directly across from the **Colosseum.** This entrance puts you right by the Arch of Titus, where our tour begins. The **Palatine Hill** ticket office

(on Via di San Gregorio) is often less crowded. After buying your ticket, reach the Arch of Titus by taking the path to the right; the path to the left goes uphill to the Palatine Hill ruins. A third entrance is along **Via dei Fori Imperiali,** about halfway between the Colosseum and Piazza Venezia, near the intersection with Via Cavour (and through a low-profile building set well back from the street). To reach the Arch of Titus from here, walk down the ramp and turn left.

Information: The free info center, located across from the Via dei Fori Imperiali entrance, has a TI (which sells the Roma Pass), bookshop, small café, and WCs (daily 9:30-19:00). Vendors outside sell a variety of colorful books with plastic overlays that restore the ruins (official price in bookstore for larger version with DVD is €20 and for smaller version is €10—don't pay more than these prices). Info office tel. 06-3996-7700, http://archeoroma.beniculturali.it/en.

Tours: An **audioguide** helps decipher the rubble (€5/2 hours, €7 version includes Palatine Hill and lasts 3 hours, must leave ID), but you have to return it to where you rented it—meaning you may not be able to exit directly to Capitoline Hill or the Colosseum, for example. Official **guided tours** in English might be available (inquire at ticket office).

🎧 Download my free Roman Forum **audio tour.**

Length of This Walk: Allow 1.5 hours. If you have less time, end the walk at the Arch of Septimius Severus. And don't miss the Basilica of Constantine hiding behind the trees.

Services: WCs are at the ticket entrances at Palatine Hill and at Via dei Fori Imperiali. Within the Forum itself, there's one near the Arch of Titus (in the "Soprintendenza" office), and another in the middle, near #6 on the map. Others are atop Palatine Hill.

Plan Ahead: The ancient paving at the Forum is uneven; wear sturdy shoes.

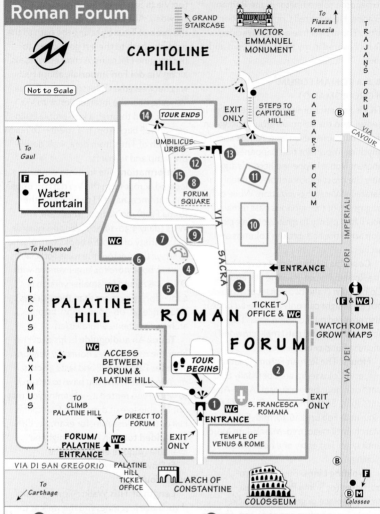

Roman Forum

GRAND STAIRCASE

VICTOR EMMANUEL MONUMENT

To Piazza Venezia

TRAJAN'S FORUM

CAPITOLINE HILL

Not to Scale

To Gaul

14 TOUR ENDS

EXIT ONLY

STEPS TO CAPITOLINE HILL

CAESAR'S FORUM

B

VIA CAVOUR

UMBILICUS URBIS

13

12

15

8 FORUM SQUARE

11

F Food
• Water Fountain

To Hollywood

WC

7

9

10

VIA SACRA

FORI IMPERIALI

6

4

5

3

← ENTRANCE

CIRCUS MAXIMUS

PALATINE HILL

WC •

ROMAN

FORUM

TICKET OFFICE & WC

(**F** & WC)

"WATCH ROME GROW" MAPS

VIA DEI

WC

ACCESS BETWEEN FORUM & PALATINE HILL

TOUR BEGINS

2

EXIT ONLY

S. FRANCESCA ROMANA

TO CLIMB PALATINE HILL

DIRECT TO FORUM

1

WC

ENTRANCE

FORUM/ PALATINE ENTRANCE

WC

EXIT ONLY

TEMPLE OF VENUS & ROME

VIA DI SAN GREGORIO

PALATINE HILL TICKET OFFICE

ARCH OF CONSTANTINE

B

F

To Carthage

COLOSSEUM

B M Colosseo

1 Arch of Titus	**8** The Forum's Main Square
2 Basilica of Constantine	**9** Temple of Julius Caesar
3 Temple of Antoninus Pius & Faustina	**10** Basilica Aemilia
4 Temple of Vesta	**11** The Curia
5 House of the Vestal Virgins	**12** Rostrum
6 Caligula's Palace	**13** Arch of Septimius Severus
7 Temple of Castor & Pollux	**14** Temple of Saturn
	15 Column of Phocas

I carry a water bottle and refill it at the Forum's public drinking fountains.

Improvise: Because of ongoing restoration, paths through the Forum are often rerouted. Use this tour as a starting point, but be prepared for a few detours and backtracking.

◗ SELF-GUIDED TOUR

• *Start at the Arch of Titus (Arco di Tito). It's the white triumphal arch that rises above the rubble on the east end of the Forum (closest to the Colosseum). Stand at the viewpoint alongside the arch and gaze over the valley known as the Forum.*

Viewing the Ruins: Try to see the Forum with "period eyes." We imagine the structures in ancient Rome as mostly white, but ornate buildings and monuments were originally more colorful. Through the ages, builders scavenged stone from the Forum; the colored marble was cannibalized first. The white stone is generally what was left. Statues were vividly painted, but the organic paint rotted away as they lay buried for centuries. Lettering was inset bronze and eyes were inset ivory. Even seemingly intact structures, like the Arch of Titus, have been reassembled. The columns are half smooth and half fluted. The fluted halves are original; the smooth parts are reconstructions.

❶ Arch of Titus (Arco di Tito): The Arch of Titus commemorated the Roman victory over the province of Judaea (Israel) in A.D. 70. The Romans had a reputation as benevolent conquerors who tolerated local customs and rulers. All they required was allegiance to the empire, shown by worshipping the emperor as a god. No problem for most conquered people, who already had half a dozen gods on their prayer lists anyway. But Israelites believed in only one god, and it wasn't the emperor. Israel revolted. After a short but bitter war, the Romans defeated the rebels, took Jerusalem, destroyed their temple (leaving only a fragment of one wall's foundation—today's revered "Wailing Wall"), and brought home 50,000 Jewish slaves...who were forced to build the Colosseum (and this arch).

Roman propaganda decorates the inside of the arch. A relief shows the emperor Titus in a chariot being crowned by the goddess Victory. The other side shows booty from the sacking of the

Roman Forum

Rome's Rise and Fall (500 B.C.–A.D. 500)

Ancient Rome lasted for 1,000 years, from about 500 B.C. to A.D. 500. During that time, Rome expanded from a small tribe of barbarians to a vast empire, then dwindled slowly to city size again. For the first 500 years, when Rome's armies made her ruler of the Italian peninsula and beyond, Rome was a republic governed by elected senators. Over the next 500 years, a time of world conquest and eventual decline, Rome was an empire ruled by a military-backed dictator.

Julius Caesar bridged the gap between republic and empire. This ambitious, charismatic general and politician, popular because of his military victories, suspended the Roman constitution and assumed dictatorial powers in about 50 B.C. A few years later, he was assassinated by a conspiracy of senators. His adopted son, Augustus, succeeded him, and soon "Caesar" was not just a name but a title.

Emperor Augustus ushered in the Pax Romana, or Roman peace (A.D. 1-200), a time when Rome reached its peak, controlling an empire that stretched from England to Egypt, from Turkey to Morocco.

Then Rome fell into 300 years of gradual decay. Its fall had many causes, among them the barbarians who pecked away at Rome's borders. Christians blamed the fall on moral decay. Pagans blamed it on Christians. Socialists blamed it on a shallow economy based on the spoils of war. (Republicans blamed it on Democrats.) Whatever the reasons, the far-flung empire could no longer keep its grip on conquered lands. Barbarian tribes from Germany and Asia attacked the Italian peninsula, looting Rome itself in A.D. 410. In 476, when the last emperor checked out and switched off the lights, Europe plunged into centuries of ignorance and poverty—the Dark Ages.

But Rome lived on in the Catholic Church. Christianity was the state religion of Rome's last generations. Emperors became popes (both called themselves "Pontifex Maximus"), senators became bishops, orators became priests, and basilicas became churches. The glory of Rome remains eternal.

temple in Jerusalem. Carved after Titus' death, the relief at the top of the ceiling shows him riding an eagle to heaven, where he'll become one of the gods.

• *Walk down Via Sacra into the Forum. The original basalt stones under your feet were walked on by Caesar Augustus 2,000 years ago. After about 50 yards, turn right and follow a path uphill to the three huge arches of the...*

❷ **Basilica of Constantine (Basilica Maxentius):** These arches represent only one-third of the original Basilica of Constantine, a mammoth hall of justice. There was a similar set along the Via Sacra side (only a few brick piers remain). Between

them ran the central hall, spanned by a roof 130 feet high—about 55 feet higher than the side arches you see. (The stub of brick you see sticking up began an arch that once spanned the central hall.) The hall itself was as long as a football field, lavishly furnished with inlaid marble, a bronze ceiling, and statues. At the far (west) end was an enormous marble statue of Emperor Constantine on a throne. Pieces of this statue, including a hand the size of a man, are on display in Rome's Capitoline Museums.

• *Now stroll deeper into the Forum, downhill along Via Sacra, through the trees. Pass by Tempio di Romolo, with its original bronze door. Just past that, 10 columns stand in front of a much newer church. The colonnade was part of the...*

❸ Temple of Antoninus Pius and Faustina: This temple honors Emperor Antoninus Pius (A.D. 138-161) and his deified wife, Faustina. The 50-foot-tall Corinthian (leafy) columns were awe-inspiring to out-of-towners who grew up in thatched huts. Although the temple has been inhabited by a church, you can still see the basic layout—a staircase led to a shaded porch (the columns), which admitted you to the main building (now a church), where the statue of the god sat. Originally, these columns supported a triangular pediment decorated with sculptures.

Picture these columns supporting brightly painted statues in the pediment, with the whole building capped by a bronze roof. Today's gray rubble is a faded black-and-white photograph of a 3-D Technicolor era.

• With your back to the colonnade, walk straight ahead—jogging a bit to the right to stay on the path—and head for the three short columns, all that's left of the...

❹ Temple of Vesta: This was perhaps Rome's most sacred spot. Rome considered itself one big family, and this temple represented a circular hut, like the kind that Rome's first families lived in. Inside, a fire burned, just as in a Roman home. As long as the sacred flame burned, Rome would stand. The flame was tended by priestesses known as Vestal Virgins.

• Just to the left and up the stairs is a big, enclosed field with two rectangular brick pools (just below the hill). This was the courtyard of the...

❺ House of the Vestal Virgins: The Vestal Virgins lived in a two-story building surrounding a long central courtyard with two pools at one end. This place was the model—both architecturally and sexually—for medieval convents and monasteries.

Chosen from noble families before they reached the age of 10, the six Vestal Virgins served a 30-year term. Honored and revered, the Vestals even had their own box opposite the emperor in the Colosseum. The statues that line the courtyard honor dutiful Vestals.

A Vestal took a vow of chastity. If she served her term faithfully—abstaining for 30 years—she was given a huge dowry and allowed to marry. But if they found any Virgin who wasn't, she was strapped to a funeral car, paraded through the streets of the Forum, taken to a crypt...and buried alive. Many suffered the latter fate.

• Looming just beyond this field is Palatine Hill—the corner of which may have been...

❻ Caligula's Palace (Palace of Tiberius): Emperor Caligula (ruled A.D. 37-41) had a huge palace on Palatine Hill overlooking the Forum. It actually sprawled down the hill into the Forum (some supporting arches remain in the hillside). Caligula tortured enemies, stole senators' wives, and parked his chariot in handicap spaces. He was not a nice person. But Rome's luxury-loving emperors only added to the glory of the Forum, with each one trying to make his mark on history.

• Continue downhill, passing the three short columns of the Temple of Vesta, and head for the three taller columns just beyond it.

❼ Temple of Castor and Pollux: These three columns are all that remain of a prestigious temple—one of the city's oldest, built in the fifth century B.C. It

Temple of Antoninus Pius

commemorated the Roman victory over the Tarquin, the notorious, oppressive Etruscan king. After the battle, the legendary twin brothers Castor and Pollux watered their horses here, at the Sacred Spring of Juturna (which was recently excavated nearby). As a symbol of Rome's self-governing republic, the temple was often used as a meeting place of senators; its front steps served as a podium for free speech.

• *You're now standing at the corner of a flat, grassy area.*

❽ Forum's Main Square: The original Forum, or main square, was this flat patch about the size of a football field, stretching to the foot of Capitoline Hill. Surrounding it were temples, law courts, government buildings, and triumphal arches.

Rome was born here. According to legend, twin brothers Romulus and Remus were orphaned in infancy and raised by a she-wolf on top of Palatine Hill. Growing up, they found it hard to get dates. So they and their cohorts attacked the nearby Sabine tribe and kidnapped their women.

Temple of Castor and Pollux

After they made peace, this marshy valley became the meeting place and then the trading center for the scattered tribes on the surrounding hillsides.

The square was the busiest—and often the seediest—section of town. Besides the senators, politicians, and currency exchangers, there were souvenir hawkers, pickpockets, fortune-tellers, gamblers, slave marketers, drunks, hookers, lawyers, and tour guides.

Ancient Rome's population exceeded one million, more than any city until London and Paris in the 19th century. All those Roman masses lived in tiny apartments as we would live in tents at a campsite, basically just to sleep. The Forum—today's piazza—is where they did their living. To this day, urban Italians spend a major part of their time outside, in the streets and squares.

The Forum is now rubble, but imagine it in its prime: brilliant marble buildings with 40-foot-high columns and shining metal roofs; rows of statues painted in realistic colors; processional chariots rattling down Via Sacra. Mentally replace tourists in T-shirts with tribunes in togas. Imagine people buzzing around you while an orator gives a rabble-rousing speech. If you still only see a pile of rocks, at least tell yourself, "Julius Caesar once leaned against these rocks."

• *At the near (east) end of the main square (the Colosseum is to the east) are the foundations of a temple now capped with a peaked wood-and-metal roof.*

❾ Temple of Julius Caesar (Tempio del Divo Giulio, or Ara di Cesare): On March 15, in 44 B.C., Julius Caesar was stabbed 23 times by political conspirators. After his assassination, Caesar's body was cremated on this spot (under the metal roof). Afterward, this temple was built to honor him. Peek behind the wall into the small apse area, where a mound of dirt usually has fresh flowers—given to remember the man who personified the greatness of Rome.

Caesar (100-44 B.C.) changed Rome—and the Forum—dramatically. He cleared out many of the wooden market stalls and began to ring the square with even grander buildings. Caesar's house was located behind the temple, near that clump of trees. He walked by here on the day he was assassinated ("Beware the Ides of March!" warned a street-corner Etruscan preacher).

Though he was popular with the masses, not everyone liked Caesar's urban design or his politics. When he assumed dictatorial powers, he was ambushed and stabbed to death by a conspiracy of senators, including his adopted son, Brutus ("Et tu, Brute?").

The funeral was held here, facing the main square. Mark Antony stood up to say (in Shakespeare's words), "Friends, Romans, countrymen, lend me your ears. I come to bury Caesar, not to praise him." When Caesar's body was burned, his adoring fans threw anything at hand on the fire, requiring the fire department to come put it out. Later, Emperor Augustus dedicated this temple in his name, making Caesar the first Roman to become a god.

• *Continue past the Temple of Julius Caesar, to the open area between the columns of the Temple of Antoninus Pius and Faustina (which we passed earlier) and the boxy brick building (the Curia). You can view these ruins of the Basilica Aemilia from a ramp next to the Temple of Antoninus Pius and Faustina, or find the entrance near the Curia.*

⓿ Basilica Aemilia: A basilica was a covered public forum, often serving as a hall of justice. In a society that was as legal-minded as America is today, you needed a lot of lawyers—and a big place to put them. Citizens came here to work out inheritances, file building permits, and sue each other.

It was a long, rectangular building. The row of stubby columns forms one long, central hall flanked by two side aisles. Medieval Christians required a larger meeting hall for their worship services than Roman temples provided, so they used the spacious Roman basilica as the model for their churches. Cathedrals from France to Spain to England, from Romanesque to Gothic to Renaissance, all have this same basic floor plan.

• *Now head for the big, well-preserved brick building (just beyond the basilica ruins) with the triangular roof—the Curia. (Ongoing archaeological work may restrict access to the Curia, as well as the Arch of Septimius Severus—described later—and the exit to Capitoline Hill.)*

⓫ Curia (Senate House): The Curia was the most important political building in the Forum. While the present building dates from A.D. 283, this was the site of Rome's official center of government since the birth of the republic. Three hundred senators, elected by the citizens of Rome, met here to debate and create the laws of the land. Their wooden seats once circled the building in three tiers; the Senate president's podium sat at the far end. The marble floor is from ancient times. Listen to the echoes in this vast room—the acoustics are great.

Rome prided itself on being a republic. Early in the city's history, its people threw out the king and established rule by elected representatives. Each Roman citizen was free to speak his mind and have a say in public policy. Even when emperors became the supreme authority, the Senate was a power to be reckoned with. The Curia building is well preserved, having been used as a church since early Christian times. In the 1930s, it was restored and opened to the public as a historic site. (Although Julius Caesar was assassinated in "the Senate," it wasn't here—the Senate was temporarily meeting across town.)

• *Go back down the Senate steps and find the 10-foot-high wall just to the left of the big arch, marked...*

⓬ Rostrum: Nowhere was Roman freedom more apparent than at this "Speaker's Corner." The Rostrum was a raised platform, 10 feet high and 80 feet long, decorated with statues, columns, and the prows of ships.

On a stage like this, Rome's orators, great and small, tried to draw a crowd and sway public opinion. Mark Antony rose to offer Caesar the laurel-leaf crown of kingship, which Caesar publicly refused—while privately becoming a dictator. Men such as Cicero railed against the corruption and decadence that came with the city's new-found wealth. In later years, daring citizens even spoke out against the emperors, reminding them that Rome was once free.

In front of the Rostrum are trees bearing fruits that were sacred to the ancient Romans: olives (provided food, light, and preservatives), figs (tasty), and wine grapes (made a popular export product).

• *The big arch to the right of the Rostrum is the...*

⓭ Arch of Septimius Severus: In imperial times, the Rostrum's voices of democracy would have been dwarfed by images of the empire, such as the huge six-story-high Arch of Septimius Severus (A.D. 203). The reliefs commemorate the African-born emperor's battles in Mesopotamia. Near ground level, see soldiers marching captured barbarians back to Rome for the victory parade.

• *Pass underneath the Arch of Septimius Severus and turn left. If the path is blocked, backtrack toward the Temple of Julius Caesar and around the square. On the slope of Capitoline Hill are the eight remaining columns of the...*

⓮ Temple of Saturn: These columns framed the entrance to the Forum's oldest temple (497 B.C.). Inside was a humble wooden statue of the god Saturn. But the statue's pedestal held the gold bars, coins, and jewels of Rome's state treasury, the booty collected by conquering generals.

Even older than the Temple of Saturn is the Umbilicus Urbis, which stands nearby (next to the Arch of Septimius Severus). A humble brick ruin marks this historic "Navel of the City." The spot was considered the center of the cosmos, and all distances in the empire were measured from here.

• *Standing at the Temple of Saturn, one of the Forum's first buildings, look east at the lone, tall...*

⓯ Column of Phocas: The Forum's last monument (A.D. 608) was a gift from the powerful Byzantine Empire to a fallen empire—Rome. Given to commemorate the pagan Pantheon's becoming a Christian church, it's like a symbolic last nail in ancient Rome's coffin. After Rome's 1,000-year reign, the city was looted by Vandals, the population of a million-plus shrank to about 10,000, and the once-grand Forum was abandoned, slowly covered by centuries of silt and dirt. In the 1700s, English historian Edward Gibbon overlooked this spot from Capitoline Hill, pondered the decline and fall of the Roman Empire, and thought, "Hmm, that's a catchy title..."

• *Your tour is over. From the Forum, you have several options:*

Arch of Septimius Severus

Temple of Saturn

1. Your closest exit is by the Arch of Septimius Severus. From here, you can walk out to Via dei Fori Imperiali, near Trajan's Column. Or you can climb 50 steps up to Capitoline Hill.

2. You can exit through the Forum's Via dei Fori Imperiali entrance.

3. An exit next to the Basilica of Constantine leads to Piazza del Colosseo, near the Colosseo Metro stop.

4. To exit near the Colosseum, return to the Arch of Titus. At the Arch, turn right, then (after walking uphill a few steps) turn left into the tunnel marked uscita/exit.

5. You could visit Palatine Hill. From the Arch of Titus, climb to the top of the hill.

▲PALATINE HILL (MONTE PALATINO)

The hill overlooking the Forum is jam-packed with history—"the huts of Romulus," the huge Imperial Palace, a view of the Circus Maximus—but there's only the barest skeleton of rubble left to tell the story.

We get our word "palace" from this hill, where the emperors chose to live. It was once so filled with palaces that later emperors had to build out. (Looking up at it from the Forum, you see the substructure that supported these long-gone palaces.) The Palatine Museum contains statues and frescoes that help you imagine the luxury of the imperial Palatine. From the pleasant garden, you'll get an overview of the Forum. On the far side, unless excavations are blocking the viewpoint, look down into an emperor's private stadium and then beyond at the grassy Circus Maximus, once a chariot course.

While many tourists consider Palatine Hill extra credit after the Forum, it offers insight into the greatness of Rome. If you're visiting the Colosseum or Forum, you've already got a ticket.

Cost and Hours: €12 combo-ticket includes Roman Forum and Colosseum—see page 494, free and crowded first Sun of the month, open same hours as Forum and Colosseum, audioguide-€5, Metro: Colosseo, tel. 06-3996-7700, www.archeoroma.beniculturali.it/en.

Getting In: The closest Metro stop is Colosseo. The handiest entrance to the Forum/Palatine Hill complex is at the Forum's Arch of Titus (near the Colosseum and Colosseo Metro stop). Next best is the one on Via di San Gregorio, which is 150 yards from the Colosseum and possibly less crowded. Once inside, just climb the hill.

Be sure to combine your visit with the Roman Forum; if you leave the complex, your ticket doesn't cover re-entry.

Services: WCs are at the ticket office when you enter, at the museum in the center of the site, and hiding among the orange trees in the Farnese Gardens.

Capitoline Hill

Of Rome's famous seven hills, this is the smallest, tallest, and most famous—home of the ancient Temple of Jupiter and the center of city government for 2,500 years. There are several ways to get to the top of Capitoline Hill. If you're coming from the north (from Piazza Venezia), take Michelangelo's impressive stairway to the right of the big, white Victor Emmanuel Monument. Coming from the southeast (the Forum), take the steep staircase near the Arch of Septimius Severus. From near Trajan's Forum along Via dei Fori Imperiali, take the winding road. All three converge at the top, in the square called Campidoglio (kahm-pee-DOHL-yoh).

▲PIAZZA DEL CAMPIDOGLIO

This square atop the hill, once the religious and political center of ancient Rome, is still the home of the city's government. In the 1530s, the pope called on Michelangelo to reestablish this square as a grand center. Michelangelo placed the ancient equestrian statue of Marcus Aurelius as its focal point. (The original statue is now in the adjacent museum.) The twin buildings on either side are

Capitoline Hill & Piazza Venezia

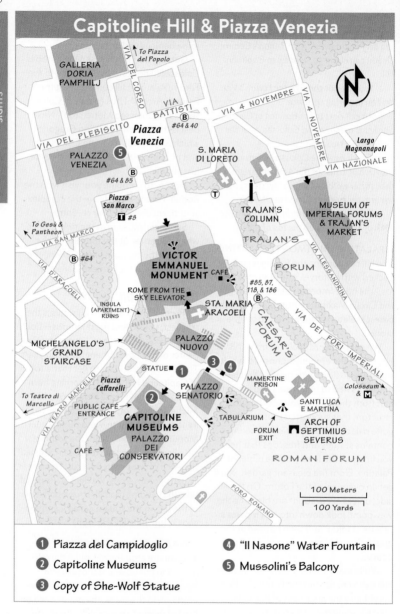

GALLERIA DORIA PAMPHILJ

To Piazza del Popolo

VIA DEL CORSO

VIA BATTISTI

B #64 & 40

VIA 4 NOVEMBRE

VIA 4 NOVEMBRE

VIA DEL PLEBISCITO

Piazza Venezia

S. MARIA DI LORETO

Largo Magnanapoli

PALAZZO VENEZIA **5**

B #64 & 85

VIA NAZIONALE

Piazza San Marco #8

To Gesù & Pantheon

VIA SAN MARCO

TRAJAN'S COLUMN

MUSEUM OF IMPERIAL FORUMS & TRAJAN'S MARKET

TRAJAN'S

VIA D'ARACOELI

B #64

VICTOR EMMANUEL MONUMENT CAFÉ

FORUM

VIA ALESSANDRINA

#85, 87, 118, & 186 B

ROME FROM THE SKY ELEVATOR

INSULA (APARTMENT) RUINS

STA. MARIA ARACOELI

CAESAR'S FORUM

VIA DEI FORI IMPERIALI

MICHELANGELO'S GRAND STAIRCASE

PALAZZO NUOVO

STATUE **1**

3 **4**

MAMERTINE PRISON

To Colosseum & M

Piazza Caffarelli

VIA TEATRO MARCELLO

2

PALAZZO SENATORIO

SANTI LUCA E MARTINA

To Teatro di Marcello

PUBLIC CAFÉ ENTRANCE

CAPITOLINE MUSEUMS

TABULARIUM

FORUM EXIT

ARCH OF SEPTIMIUS SEVERUS

CAFÉ

PALAZZO DEI CONSERVATORI

ROMAN FORUM

FORO ROMANO

100 Meters

100 Yards

1 Piazza del Campidoglio

2 Capitoline Museums

3 Copy of She-Wolf Statue

4 "Il Nasone" Water Fountain

5 Mussolini's Balcony

the Capitoline Museums. Behind the replica of the statue is the mayor's palace (Palazzo Senatorio).

Michelangelo intended that people approach the square from his grand stairway off Piazza Venezia. From the top of the stairway, you see the new Renaissance face of Rome, with its back to the Forum. Michelangelo gave the buildings the "giant order"—huge pilasters make the existing two-story buildings feel one-storied and more harmonious with the new square.

The statues atop these buildings welcome you and then draw you in.

The terraces just downhill from the square (past either side of the mayor's palace) offer grand views of the Forum. To the left of the mayor's palace is a copy of the famous she-wolf statue on a column. Farther down is *il nasone* ("the big nose"), a refreshing water fountain. Block the spout with your fingers, and water spurts up for drinking. Romans joke that a cheap Roman boy takes his date out for a drink at *il nasone*.

There are two sights atop Capitoline Hill that you can't access from the square; instead you'd need to enter them from street level. One is the Victor Emmanuel Monument (described later) with its superb city view from its Rome from the Sky elevator, and the other is the Santa Maria in Aracoeli Church (accessed by a looong stairway from street level, on the right side of the Victor Emmanuel Monument as you face it). The church stands on the site where Emperor Augustus said he had a premonition of the coming of Mary and Christ standing on an "altar in the sky" *(ara coeli)*.

▲▲▲CAPITOLINE MUSEUMS

Some of ancient Rome's most famous statues and art are housed in the two palaces (Palazzo dei Conservatori and Palazzo Nuovo) that flank the equestrian statue in the Campidoglio. They're connected by an underground passage that leads to the Tabularium, an ancient building with panoramic views of the Roman Forum.

Cost and Hours: €15, €9.50 if no special exhibitions, daily 9:30-19:30, last entry one hour before closing, audioguide-€5, tel. 06-0608, www.museicapitolini.org.

Visiting the Museums: You'll enter at Palazzo dei Conservatori (on your right as you face the equestrian statue), then walk through a passageway underneath the square—stopping for a look at the Tabularium—to Palazzo Nuovo (on your left), where you'll exit.

With lavish rooms and several great statues, the worthwhile **Palazzo dei Conservatori** was founded in 1471 when a pope gave ancient statues to the citizens of Rome. Many of the museum's statues have become recognizable cultural icons, including the 13th-century *Capitoline She-Wolf* (the statues of Romulus and Remus

Piazza del Campidoglio

were added in the Renaissance). Don't miss the *Boy Extracting a Thorn* and the *Commodus as Hercules.* Behind Commodus is a statue of his dad, Marcus Aurelius, on a horse. The greatest surviving equestrian statue of antiquity, it was the original centerpiece of the square (where a copy stands today). Christians in the Dark Ages thought that the statue's hand was raised in blessing, which probably led to their misidentifying him as Constantine, the first Christian emperor. While most pagan statues were destroyed by Christians, "Constantine" was spared.

The museum's second-floor café, **Caffè Capitolino,** has a patio offering city views—lovely at sunset (public entrance for those without a museum ticket off Piazzale Caffarelli and through door #4).

The **Tabularium,** built in the first century B.C., once held the archives of ancient Rome. Its name comes from "tablet," on which Romans wrote their laws. You won't see any tablets, but you will see a stunning head-on view of the Forum from the windows. **Palazzo Nuovo** houses two must-see statues: the *Dying Gaul* and the *Capitoline Venus* (both on the first floor up).

Piazza Venezia

This vast square, dominated by the Victor Emmanuel Monument, is the focal point of modern Rome. With your back to the monument (you'll get the best views from the terrace by the guards and eternal flame), look down Via del Corso, the city's axis, surrounded by Rome's classiest shopping district. In the 1930s, fascist dictator Benito Mussolini whipped up Italy's nationalistic fervor from a balcony above the square (it's the less-grand building on the left) and created the boulevard Via dei Fori Imperiali (to your right, capped by Trajan's Column) to open up views of the Colosseum in the distance.

With your back still to the monument, circle around the left side. At the back end of the monument, look down into the ditch on your left to see the ruins of an ancient apartment building from the first century A.D.; part of it was transformed into a tiny church (faded frescoes and bell tower). Rome was built in layers—almost everywhere you go, there's an earlier version beneath your feet.

▲VICTOR EMMANUEL MONUMENT

This oversize monument to Italy's first king, built to celebrate the 50th anniversary of the country's initial unification in 1861, was part of Italy's attempt to create a national identity. The over-the-top monument is 200 feet high and 500 feet wide. The 43-foot-long statue of the king on his high horse is one of the biggest equestrian statues in the world. The king's moustache forms an arc five feet long. A person could sit within the horse's hoof. At the base of this statue, Italy's Tomb of the Unknown Soldier is watched over by the goddess Roma (with the gold mosaic background).

Cost and Hours: Monument—free, daily 9:30-18:30, a few WCs scattered throughout, tel. 06-6920-2049. **Rome from the Sky elevator**—€7, Mon-Thu 9:30-18:30, Fri-Sun 9:30-19:30, ticket office closes 45 minutes earlier, WC at entrance, tel. 06-679-3598; follow *ascensori panoramici* signs inside the Victor Emmanuel Monument or take the shortcut from Capitoline Hill (no elevator access from street level).

Visiting the Monument: The "Vittoriano" (as locals call it) is open and free

Victor Emmanuel Monument

to the public. You can simply climb the front stairs, or go inside from one of several entrances: midway up the monument through doorways flanking the central statue, on either side at street level, and at the base of the colonnade (two-thirds of the way up, near the shortcut from Capitoline Hill). The little-visited **Museum of the Risorgimento** fills several floors with displays on the movement and war that led to the unification of Italy (€5 to enter museum, temporary exhibits around €10, tel. 06-322-5380, www.risorgimento.it).

Climb the stairs to the midway point for a decent view, keep climbing to the base of the colonnade for a better view, or, for the best view, ride the **Rome from the Sky** (Roma dal Cielo) **elevator,** which zips you from the top of the stair climb (at the back of the monument) to the rooftop for a 360-degree view of Rome that is even better than from the top of St. Peter's dome. Once on top, you stand on a terrace between the monument's two chariots. Look north up Via del Corso to Piazza del Popolo, west to the dome of St. Peter's Basilica, and south to the Roman Forum and Colosseum. Panoramic diagrams describe the skyline, with powerful binoculars available for zooming in. It's best in late afternoon, when it's beginning to cool off and Rome glows.

▲▲TRAJAN'S COLUMN

This 140-foot column is decorated with a spiral relief of 2,500 figures trumpeting the emperor's exploits. It has stood for centuries as a symbol of a cosmopolitan civilization. At one point, the ashes of Trajan and his wife were held in the base, and the sun glinted off a polished bronze statue of Trajan at the top. (Today, it's been replaced with St. Peter.) Built as a stack of 17 marble doughnuts, the column is hollow (note the small window slots) with a spiral staircase inside, leading up to the balcony.

The **relief** unfolds like a scroll, telling the story of Rome's last and greatest foreign conquest, Trajan's defeat of Dacia

(modern-day Romania). Originally, the entire story was painted in bright colors. If you were to unwind the scroll, it would stretch over two football fields.

North of Via dei Fori Imperiali
▲MONTI NEIGHBORHOOD: VILLAGE ROME

This quintessentially Roman district called Monti is one of the oldest corners of Rome...and newly trendy. Tucked behind Via dei Fori Imperiali, and squeezed between Via Nazionale and Via Cavour, this hilly tangle of lanes shows why Romans see their hometown not as a sprawling metropolis, but as a collection of villages. Neighbors hang out on the square and chat. Funky boutiques share narrow streets with hole-in-the-wall hardware shops and grocery shops; and wisteria-strewn cobbled lanes beckon photographers.

Whether you're coming from Piazza Venezia or the Roman Forum, cross Via dei Fori Imperiali and angle up Via Cavour two blocks to Via dei Serpenti. Turn left, and in one block, you hit Monti's main

Trajan's Column

square, **Piazza della Madonna dei Monti.** (The Cavour Metro stop also gets you steps away.) To get oriented, face uphill, with the big fountain to your right.

From this hub, interesting streets branch off in every direction. I recommend strolling one long street with three names: **Via della Madonna dei Monti,** which leads to the central Piazza Madonna dei Monti, before continuing uphill as **Via Leonina** and then **Via Urbana.** Monti is an ideal place for a quick lunch or early dinner (see page 551).

▲ST. PETER-IN-CHAINS CHURCH (SAN PIETRO IN VINCOLI)

Built in the fifth century to house the chains that held St. Peter, this church is most famous for its Michelangelo statue of Moses, intended for the tomb of Pope Julius II (which was never built). Note that this church is not the famous St. Peter's Basilica, which is in Vatican City.

After viewing the much-venerated chains under the high altar, focus on mighty Moses. Pope Julius II commissioned Michelangelo to build a massive tomb, with 48 huge statues, topped with a grand statue of the egomaniacal pope himself. The pope had planned for his tomb to be in the center of St. Peter's Basilica. When Julius died, the work had barely started; no one had the money or necessary commitment to finish the project.

In 1542, remnants of the project were brought to St. Peter-in-Chains and pieced together by Michelangelo's assistants. Some of the best statues ended up elsewhere (*Prisoners* is in Florence and the *Slaves* is in the Louvre). *Moses* and the *Slaves* are the only statues Michelangelo personally completed for the project.

The statue of Moses is powerful. As he holds the Ten Commandments, his eyes show a man determined to win salvation for the people of Israel. Why the horns? Centuries ago, the Hebrew word for "rays" was mistranslated as "horns." Flanking *Moses* are the Old Testament sister-wives of Jacob, Leah (to our right) and Rachel, both begun by Michelangelo but probably finished by pupils.

Cost and Hours: Free, daily April-Sept 8:00-12:20 & 15:00-19:00, until 18:00 in winter, modest dress required; the church is a 10-minute uphill walk from the Colosseum, or a shorter, simpler walk (but with more uphill steps) from the Cavour Metro stop; tel. 06-9784-4950.

Michelangelo, Moses

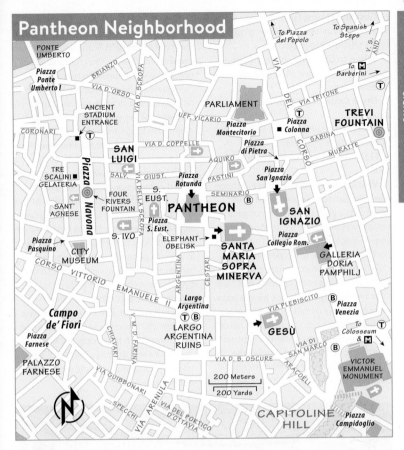

Pantheon Neighborhood

Pantheon Neighborhood

The Pantheon area, despite its ancient sites and historic churches, has an urban-village feel. Exploring this neighborhood is especially good in the evening, when the restaurants bustle and the streets teem with pedestrians. Gather with the locals in squares marked by bubbling fountains.

Getting There: The Pantheon neighborhood is a 15-minute walk from Capitoline Hill. Taxis and buses stop at a chaotic square called Largo Argentina, a few blocks south of the Pantheon—from here you can walk north on either Via dei Cestari or Via di Torre Argentina to the Pantheon. Buses #40 and #64 run frequently between the Termini train station and Vatican City (#492 serves the same areas via a different route). Buses #85 and #87 connect to the Colosseum (stop: Corso/Minghetti). The *elettrico* minibus #116 runs between Campo de' Fiori and Piazza Barberini via the Pantheon.

▲▲▲PANTHEON

Built two millennia ago, this influential domed temple is perhaps the most influential building in art history, serving as the model for the Florence cathedral dome, which launched the Renaissance, and for Michelangelo's dome of St. Peter's, which capped it off. Its preserved interior offers the greatest look at the splendor of Rome.

Cost and Hours: Free, Mon-Sat 8:30-19:30, Sun 9:00-18:00, holidays 9:00-13:00, tel. 06-6830-0230.

When to Go: Don't go midday, when it's packed. To have it all to yourself, visit when it opens.

Dress Code: No skimpy shorts or bare shoulders.

Tours: The Pantheon has a €5 audio-guide that lasts 25 minutes.

🎧 Download my free Pantheon audio tour.

Visiting the Pantheon: The Pantheon was a Roman temple dedicated to all (*pan*) of the gods (*theos*). The original temple was built in 27 B.C. by Augustus' son-in-law, Marcus Agrippa. The inscription below the triangular **pediment** proclaims in Latin, "Marcus Agrippa, son of Lucio, three times consul made this." But after two fires, the structure we see today was completely rebuilt by the emperor Hadrian around A.D. 120. After the fall of Rome, the Pantheon became a Christian church (from "all the gods" to "all the martyrs"), which saved it from architectural plunder and ensured its upkeep through the Dark Ages.

The **portico** is Greek in style, a visual reminder of the debt Roman culture owed to the Greeks. You cross this Greek space to enter a purely Roman space, the rotunda. The columns are huge and unadorned, made from 40-foot-high single pieces of red-gray granite. They were quarried in Egypt, then shipped down the Nile and across the Mediterranean to Rome.

The **dome,** which was the largest made until the Renaissance, is set on a circular base. The mathematical perfection of this design is a testament to Roman engineering. The dome is as high as it is wide—142 feet from floor to rooftop and from side to side. To picture it, imagine a basketball wedged inside a wastebasket so that it just touches bottom. It is made from concrete that gets lighter and thinner as it reaches the top. The base of the dome is 23 feet thick and made from heavy concrete mixed with travertine, while near the top, it's less than five feet thick and made with a lighter volcanic rock (pumice) mixed in.

Inside the Pantheon

At the top, the **oculus,** or eye-in-the-sky, is the building's only light source. It's completely open and almost 30 feet across. The 1,800-year-old floor—with 80 percent of its original stones surviving—has holes in it and slants toward the edges to let the rainwater drain. Though some of the floor's marble has been replaced, the design—alternating circles and squares—is original.

While its ancient statuary is long gone, the interior holds decorative statues and the tombs of famous people from more recent centuries. The artist **Raphael** lies to the left of the main altar. Facing each other across the base of the dome are the tombs of modern Italy's first two kings.

▲TREVI FOUNTAIN

The bubbly Baroque fountain is a minor sight to art scholars...but a major nighttime gathering spot for teens on the make and tourists tossing coins. For more on the fountain, see page 502.

Vatican City

Vatican City, the world's smallest country, contains St. Peter's Basilica (with Michelangelo's exquisite *Pietà*) and the Vatican Museums (with the Sistine Chapel). The entrances to St. Peter's and the Vatican Museums are a 15-minute walk apart (follow the outside of the Vatican wall, which links the two sights). The nearest Metro stop—Ottaviano—still involves a 10-minute walk to either sight.

▲▲▲ST. PETER'S BASILICA (BASILICA SAN PIETRO)

This is the richest and grandest church on earth. To call it vast is like calling Einstein smart. Plaques on the floor show you where other, smaller churches would end if they were placed inside. The ornamental cherubs would dwarf a large man. Birds roost inside, and thousands of people wander about, heads craned heavenward. Bernini's altar work and twisting, towering canopy are brilliant. Don't miss Michelangelo's *Pietà* (behind bulletproof glass) to the right of the entrance. The huge square in front of the church is marked by an obelisk and bordered by Bernini's colonnade.

Cost: Free entry to basilica and crypt. Dome climb—€5 if you take the stairs

St. Peter's Square and Basilica

Hello from Vatican City

The Vatican is the religious capital of 1.2 billion Roman Catholics. If you're not a Catholic, become one for your visit. The pope is both the religious and secular leader of Vatican City. For centuries, the Vatican was the capital of the Papal States, and locals referred to the pontiff as "King Pope." Because of the Vatican's territorial ambitions, it didn't always have good relations with Italy. Even though modern Italy was created in 1870, the Holy See didn't recognize it as a country until 1929.

The tiny independent country of Vatican City is contained entirely within Rome. The Vatican has its own postal system, armed guards, a helipad, mini train station, and radio station (KPOP). Like every European country, Vatican City has its own versions of the euro coin (with a portrait of the pope). You're unlikely to find one in your pocket, though, as they're snatched up by collectors before falling into circulation.

Post Offices: The Vatican postal service is famous for its stamps, which you can get from offices on St. Peter's Square (one next to the TI, another between the columns just before the security checkpoint), in the Vatican Museums (closed Sun), or from a "post bus" that's often parked on St. Peter's Square (open Sun). To get a Vatican postmark, mail your cards from postboxes at the Vatican itself (although the stamps are good throughout Rome).

all the way up, or €7 to ride an elevator part way (to the roof), then climb to the top of the dome (cash only). Treasury Museum—€7 (€3 audioguide).

Hours: The **church** is open daily April-Sept 7:00-19:00, Oct-March 7:00-18:30. It closes on Wednesday mornings during papal audiences, until roughly 13:00. The **dome** (cupola) is open to climbers daily from 8:00; if you're climbing the stairs all the way up, the last entry time is 17:00 (16:00 Oct-March); if you're riding the elevator, you can enter until 18:00 (17:00 Oct-March). The **Treasury Museum** is open daily April-Sept 8:00-18:50, Oct-March 8:00-17:50. The **crypt** (grotte) is open daily 9:00-16:00.

Avoiding Lines: To avoid the worst crowds, visit before 10:00. Going after 16:00 works, too, but the crypt will be closed, and the area around the altar is often roped off to prepare for Mass. There's no surefire way to avoid the long security lines; the checkpoint is typ-

ically on the right (north) side of the huge square in front of the church, but is sometimes closer to the church or tucked under the south colonnade.

St. Peter's is often accessible directly from the Sistine Chapel inside the Vatican Museums—a great time-saving trick, but unfortunately not a reliable one (for details, see page 536).

Dress Code: No shorts, above-the-knee skirts, or bare shoulders (this applies to men, women, and children). Attendants enforce this dress code, even in hot weather. Carry a cover-up, if necessary.

Getting There: Take the Metro to Ottaviano, then walk 10 minutes south on Via Ottaviano. The #40 express bus drops off at Piazza Pio, next to Castel Sant'Angelo (Hadrian's Tomb)—a 10-minute walk from St. Peter's. The more crowded bus #64 stops just outside St. Peter's Square to the south (get off the bus after it crosses the Tiber, at the first stop past the tunnel; backtrack toward the tunnel and turn left when you see the rows of columns; the return bus stop is adjacent to the tunnel). Bus #492 heads through the center of town, stopping at Largo Argentina, and gets you near Piazza Risorgimento (get off when you see the Vatican walls). Be alert for pickpockets on all public transit. A taxi from Termini train station to St. Peter's costs about €12.

Information: The Vatican TI on the left (south) side of the square is excellent (Mon-Sat 8:30-18:15, closed Sun, tel. 06-6988-1662). For the Vatican, see www.vaticanstate.va.

Church Services: Mass is said daily, generally in Italian, usually in one of these three places: in the south (left) transept, the Blessed Sacrament Chapel (on the right side of the nave), or the apse. Typical schedule: Mon-Sat at 8:30, 10:00, 11:00, 12:00, and 17:00 (in Latin, in the apse); and on Sun and holidays at 9:00, 10:30 (in Latin), 11:30, 12:15, 13:00, 16:00, 17:00 (vespers), and 17:45.

Tours: The Vatican TI conducts free 1.5-hour **tours of St. Peter's** (depart from TI Mon-Fri at 14:15, confirm schedule at TI). **Audioguides** can be rented near the checkroom (€5 plus ID, for church only, daily 9:00-17:00).

🎧 Download my free St. Peter's Basilica **audio tour.**

To see St. Peter's original grave, you can take a *Scavi* (excavations) tour into the **Necropolis** under the basilica (€13, 1.5 hours, ages 15 and older only, no photos). Book at least two months in advance by phone (tel. 06-6988-5318), email (scavi@fsp.va), or fax (06-6987-3017), following the detailed instructions at www.vatican.va (search for "Excavations Office"); no response means they're booked.

Dome Climb: You can take the elevator (€7) or stairs (€5) to the roof (231 steps), then climb another 323 steps to the top of the dome. The entry to the elevator is just outside the north side of the basilica—look for signs to the *cupola*.

Length of This Tour: Allow one hour,

plus another hour if you climb the dome (or a half-hour to the roof). With less time, you could stroll the nave, glance up at the dome, down at St. Peter's resting place, and adore the *Pietà* on your way out.

Vatican Museums Tickets: Although it's best to make advance reservations, there's often a table selling priority-entry tickets to the Vatican Museums (with the Sistine Chapel) just inside the entrance of St. Peter's. You pay the regular €16 admission plus a €9 service fee. It's more than what you'd pay online, but you get an entry time and no wait, generally for the same day (see page 535 for other Vatican Museums ticketing options).

Baggage Check: The free bag check (mandatory for bags larger than a purse or daypack) is outside the basilica (to the right as you face the entrance), just inside the security checkpoint.

Services: WCs are to the right and left on St. Peter's Square (next to the Vatican post offices, with another near the baggage storage down the steps on the right side of the entrance) and on the roof.

⊘ SELF-GUIDED TOUR

To sample the basilica's highlights, follow these points:

❶ **The atrium** is itself bigger than most churches. The huge white columns on the portico date from the first church (fourth century). Five famous bronze doors lead into the church. The central door, made from the melted-down bronze of the original door of Old St. Peter's, was the first Renaissance work in Rome (c. 1450). It's only opened on special occasions. The far-right entrance is the **Holy Door,** opened only during Holy Years (and Jubilee years, designated by the pope). On Christmas Eve every 25 years, the pope knocks three times with a silver hammer and the door opens, welcoming pilgrims to pass through.

❷ On the floor near the central doorway is a round slab of porphyry stone in the maroon color of ancient Roman

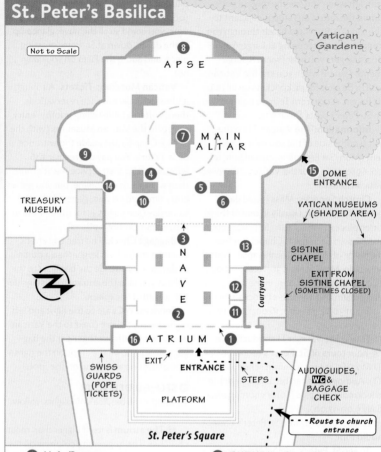

St. Peter's Basilica

Not to Scale

Vatican Gardens

APSE

MAIN ALTAR

DOME ENTRANCE

TREASURY MUSEUM

VATICAN MUSEUMS (SHADED AREA)

SISTINE CHAPEL

EXIT FROM SISTINE CHAPEL (SOMETIMES CLOSED)

N A V E

Courtyard

ATRIUM

EXIT   ENTRANCE

STEPS

AUDIOGUIDES, **WC** & BAGGAGE CHECK

SWISS GUARDS (POPE TICKETS)

PLATFORM

- - - Route to church entrance

St. Peter's Square

1. Holy Door
2. Charlemagne's Coronation Site
3. Extent of Original "Greek Cross" Plan
4. St. Andrew Statue; View of Dome; Crypt Entrance
5. St. Peter Statue (with Kissable Toe)
6. Pope John XXIII
7. Main Altar (under Bernini's Canopy & over Peter's Tomb)
8. BERNINI – Dove Window & Throne of St. Peter
9. St. Peter's Crucifixion Site
10. RAPHAEL – Mosaic Copy of The Transfiguration
11. MICHELANGELO – Pietà
12. Tomb of St. Pope John Paul II
13. Blessed Sacrament Chapel
14. Treasury Museum
15. Dome Entrance
16. Vatican Museums Tickets

officialdom. This is the spot where in A.D. 800 the king of the Franks, **Charlemagne,** was crowned Holy Roman Emperor. Look down the main hall—the golden window at the far end is two football fields away. The dove in the window has the wingspan of a 747 (OK, not quite, but it *is* big). The church covers six acres. The babies at the base of the pillars along the main hall are adult-size. The lettering in the gold band along the top of the pillars is seven feet high. The church has a capacity of 60,000 standing worshippers (or 1,200 tour groups).

❸ Michelangelo was 71 years old when he took over the church project. He intended to put the dome over Donato Bramante's original **Greek-Cross** floor plan, with four equal arms. In the Renaissance, this symmetrical arrangement symbolized perfection—the orderliness of the created world and the goodness of man (created in God's image). But the Church, struggling against Protestants and its own corruption, opted for a plan designed to impress the world with its grandeur—the Latin cross of the Crucifixion, with its nave extended to accommodate the grand religious spectacles of the Baroque period.

❹ Park yourself in front of the **statue of St. Andrew** to the left of the altar, the guy holding an X-shaped cross. (The **crypt entrance,** described later, is usually here.) Like Andrew, gaze up into the dome and gasp. The dome soars higher than a football field on end, 448 feet from the floor of the cathedral to the top of the lantern. It glows with light from its windows, the blue and gold mosaics creating a cool, solemn atmosphere. In this majestic vision of heaven (not painted by Michelangelo), we see (above the windows) Jesus, Mary, and a ring of saints, rings of more angels above them, and, way up in the ozone, God the Father (a blur of blue and red, unless you have binoculars).

❺ Back in the nave sits a bronze **statue of Peter** under a canopy. This is one of a handful of pieces of art that were in the earlier church. In one hand he holds keys, the symbol of the authority given him by Christ, while with the other hand he blesses us. His big right **toe** has been worn smooth by the lips of pilgrims and foot fetishists. Stand in line to kiss it, or, to avoid foot-and-mouth disease, touch your hand to your lips, then rub the toe. This is an act of reverence with no legend attached.

The nave of St. Peter's Basilica

❻ Circle to the right around the statue of Peter to find the lighted glass niche with the red-robed body of **Pope John XXIII,** whose papacy lasted from 1958 to 1963. He is best known for initiating the landmark Vatican II Council (1962-1965), bringing the Church into the modern age. In 2000, during the beatification process (a stop on the way to sainthood), Church authorities checked his body, and it was surprisingly fresh. So they moved it upstairs, put it behind glass, and now older Catholics who remember him fondly enjoy another stop on their St. Peter's visit. Pope John was canonized in 2014.

❼ Sitting over St. Peter's tomb, the **main altar** (the white marble slab with cross and candlesticks) is used only when the pope himself says Mass. He sometimes conducts the Sunday morning service when he's in town. The tiny altar would be lost in this enormous church if it weren't for Gian Lorenzo Bernini's seven-story **bronze canopy,** which "extends" the altar upward and reduces the perceived distance between floor and ceiling. The corkscrew columns echo the marble ones that surrounded the altar in Old St. Peter's.

❽ Bernini's **dove window** shines above the smaller front altar used for everyday services. The Holy Spirit, in the form of a six-foot-high dove, pours sunlight onto the faithful through the alabaster windows, turning into artificial rays of gold and reflecting off swirling gold clouds, angels, and winged babies. During a service, real sunlight passes through real clouds of incense, mingling with Bernini's sculpture. Beneath the dove is the centerpiece of this structure, the **Throne of St. Peter,** an oak chair built in medieval times for a king. Subsequently, it was encrusted with tradition and encased in bronze by Bernini as a symbol of papal authority.

❾ According to tradition, this is the exact spot of **Peter's crucifixion** 1,900 years ago. During the reign of Emperor Nero, he was arrested and brought to Nero's Circus so all of Rome could witness his execution. When the authorities told Peter he was to be crucified just like his Lord, Peter said, "I'm not worthy" and insisted they nail him on the cross upside down.

❿ Around the corner (heading back toward the central nave), pause at the mosaic copy of Raphael's epic painting of

Michelangelo, Pietà

The Transfiguration. The original is now in the Pinacoteca of the Vatican Museums. This and all the other "paintings" in the church are actually mosaic copies made from thousands of colored chips the size of a fingernail. Because smoke and humidity would damage real paintings, since about 1600 church officials have replaced the paintings with mosaics produced by the Vatican Mosaic Studio.

⓫ Michelangelo was 24 years old when he completed this **pietà**—a representation of Mary with the body of Christ taken from the cross. It was his first major commission, for Holy Year 1500. Michelangelo, with his total mastery of the real world, captures the sadness of the moment. Mary cradles her crucified son in her lap. Christ's lifeless right arm drooping down lets us know how heavy this corpse is. Mary looks at her dead son with tenderness; her left hand turns upward, asking, "How could they do this to you?"

⓬ **John Paul II** (1920-2005) was one of the most beloved popes of recent times. During his papacy (1978-2005), he was the face of the Catholic Church. The first non-Italian pope in four centuries, he oversaw the fall of communism in his native Poland, survived an assassination attempt, and stoically endured Parkinson's disease. When he died in 2005, hundreds of thousands lined up outside, waiting up to 24 hours to pay their respects. He was sainted in April 2014, just nine years after his death. St. John Paul II lies beneath a painting of the steadfast St. Sebastian, his favorite saint.

⓭ Step through the metalwork gates into the **Blessed Sacrament Chapel,** an oasis of peace reserved for prayer and meditation. It's next to St. John Paul II's tomb, on the right-hand side of the church, about midway to the altar.

⓮ The skippable **Treasury Museum,** located on the left side of the nave near the altar, contains the room-size tomb of Sixtus IV by Antonio Pollaiuolo, a big pair of Roman pincers used to torture Christians, an original corkscrew column from Old St. Peter's, and assorted jewels, papal robes, and golden reliquaries.

• *When you're finished viewing the church's interior, go down to the foundations of Old St. Peter's, to the* **crypt** *(grotte or tombe) containing tombs of popes and memorial chapels. Save the crypt for last because it exits outside the basilica.*

The **crypt entrance** is usually beside the ❹ statue of St. Andrew, to the left of the main altar. Stairs lead you down to the floor level of the previous church, where you'll pass the sepulcher of Peter. This lighted niche with an icon is not Peter's actual tomb, but part of a shrine that stands atop Peter's tomb. Next are the tombs of past popes. Finally, you can see a few column fragments from Old St. Peter's (a.k.a. "Basilica Costantiniana"). Continue your one-way visit until it spills you out, usually near the checkroom.

⓯ For one of the best views of Rome, go up to the **dome.** The entrance is along the right (north) side of the church, but the line begins to form out front, at the church's right door (as you face the

The view from atop St. Peter's

Seeing the Pope

Your best chances for a sighting are on Sunday or Wednesday. Most Sundays (though not always, especially in July or August), the pope gives a **blessing** at noon from the papal balcony (to the right as you face the basilica) on St. Peter's Square. You don't need a ticket—just show up. On most Wednesdays, the pope holds a **general audience** at 10:00, giving a short sermon from a platform on the square. (In winter, it's sometimes held indoors at the Paolo VI Auditorium, next to St. Peter's Basilica, though Pope Francis prefers the square, even in cold weather.) Whenever the pope appears on the square, the basilica closes and crowds are substantial—so avoid these times if you just want to sightsee.

General Audience Tickets: For the Wednesday audience, you need a free ticket to get a seat. You have several options:

• Reserve tickets a month or two in advance by sending a fax request (access the form at www.vatican.va, under "Prefecture of the Papal Household"—this path also shows his schedule) or by calling 06-6988-3114. Pick up the tickets at St. Peter's Square before the audience (available Tue 15:00-19:00 and Wed 7:00-9:00; usually under Bernini's colonnade, to the left of the church).

• You can book tickets online through Santa Susanna, the American Catholic Church in Rome (free, but donations appreciated). Pick up your reserved tickets or check for last-minute availability at the church the Tuesday before the audience between 16:30 and 18:15—some stay for the 18:00 English Mass (Via XX Settembre 15, Metro: Repubblica, tel. 06-4201-4554, www.santasusanna.org).

• Starting the Monday before the audience, Swiss Guards hand out tickets from their station near the basilica exit. There's no need to go through security—just march up, ask nicely, and say "danke." While this is perhaps the easiest way, it's best to reserve in advance.

Without a Ticket: If you just want to see the pope, get a photo, and don't mind standing, show up for the Wednesday audience at least by 9:30, and take your place in the standing section in the back half of the square.

General Audience Tips: Dress appropriately (shoulders covered, no short shorts or tank tops; long pants or knee-length skirts are safest) and clear security (no big bags; lines move more quickly on the side of the square farthest from the Metro stop). To get a seat, get there a couple of hours early; there are far fewer seats than ticketholders. The service gets under way around 9:30 when the names of attending pilgrim groups are announced. Shortly thereafter, the Popemobile appears, winding through the adoring crowd (the best views are near the cloth-covered wooden fences that line the Popemobile route). Around 10:00, the Pope's multilingual message begins and lasts for about an hour (you can leave at any time).

church). Look for *cupola* signs. There are two levels: the rooftop of the church and the top of the dome. Climb (for €5) or take an elevator (€7) to the first level, on the church roof just above the facade. From the roof, you can also go inside the gallery ringing the interior of the dome and look down inside the church. To get to the top of the dome, you'll take a staircase that winds between the outer shell and the inner one. It's a sweaty, crowded, claustrophobic 15-minute, 323-step climb, but the view from the summit is great, the fresh air even better. Admire the arms of Bernini's colonnade encircling St. Peter's Square. Find the Victor Emmanuel Monument and the Pantheon. The large rectangular building to the left of the obelisk is the Vatican Museums complex, stuffed with art. And down in the square are tiny pilgrims buzzing like electrons around the nucleus of Catholicism.

Rick's Tip: *If you're* claustrophobic *or* acrophobic, skip climbing the dome.

▲▲▲VATICAN MUSEUMS (MUSEI VATICANI)

The four miles of displays in this immense museum complex culminate in the Raphael Rooms and Michelangelo's glorious Sistine Chapel. This is one of Europe's top three or four houses of art. It can be exhausting, so plan your visit carefully, focusing on a few themes. Allow two hours for a quick visit, three or four hours for enough time to enjoy it.

Cost and Hours: €16, €4 online reservation fee, Mon-Sat 9:00-18:00, last entry at 16:00 (though the official closing time is 18:00, the staff starts ushering you out at 17:30), closed on religious holidays and Sun except last Sun of the month (when it's free, more crowded, and open 9:00-14:00, last entry at 12:30); may be open Fri nights May-July and Sept-Oct 19:00-23:00 (last entry at 21:30) by online reservation only—check the website. Hours are subject to constant change.

The museum closes frequently for holidays, including: Jan 1 (New Year's), Jan 6 (Epiphany), Feb 11 (Vatican City established), March 19 (St. Joseph's Day), Easter Sunday and Monday, May 1 (Labor Day), June 29 (Sts. Peter and Paul), Aug 15 (Assumption of the Virgin), Nov 1 (All Saints' Day), Dec 8 (Immaculate Conception), and Dec 25 and 26 (Christmas). Before you visit, check the current hours, holiday closures, and calendar at http://mv.vatican.va. Info tel. 06-6988-4676 or 06-6988-3145.

Reservations: Expect waits of up to two hours to buy tickets. Bypass the long ticket lines by reserving an entry time at http://mv.vatican.va for €20 (€16 ticket plus €4 booking fee). Choose your day and time, then check your email for your confirmation and print out the voucher. At the Vatican Museums, bypass the ticket-buying line and queue up at the "Visitor Entrance with Online Reservations" line (to the right). Show your voucher to the guard and go in. Once inside the museum, present your voucher at a ticket window (*cassa*), either in the lobby or upstairs, and they'll issue your ticket.

When to Go: The museum is generally hot and crowded, except in winter. The worst days are Saturdays, the last Sunday of the month (when it's free), Mondays, rainy days, and any day before or after a holiday closure. Mornings are most crowded. It's best to visit on a weekday after 14:00—the later the better. Another good time is during the papal audience on Wednesday morning, when many tourists are at St. Peter's Square (the only drawback is that St. Peter's Basilica is closed until roughly 13:00, as is the exit to it from the Sistine Chapel—described later, under "Exit Strategies").

Avoiding Lines: Booking a **guided tour** (see "Tours," later) gets you right in—just show the guard your voucher. You can often buy **same-day, skip-the-line tickets** (for the same €20 online price) through the TI in St. Peter's Square (to the left, as you face the basilica). Also, the Opera Romana Pellegrinaggi (a.k.a., Roma Cristiana), a Vatican-affiliated tour company, sells same-day tickets for €27.50 (entrances almost hourly, office in front of St. Peter's Square, Piazza Pio XII 9, tel. 06-6980-6380, www.operaromana pellegrinaggi.org). If you're going to St. Peter's Basilica first, you can buy priority-entry Vatican Museums tickets just inside the entrance (€25 includes admission plus service fee). Hawkers peddling skip-the-line access swarm the Vatican area, offering tours with guides of varying quality. It's smarter to plan in advance, but if all else fails, this will get you in.

Dress Code: Modest dress is required (no shorts, above-knee skirts, or bare shoulders).

Getting There: The Ottaviano Metro stop is a 10-minute walk from the entrance. Bus #49 from Piazza Cavour/Castel Sant'Angelo stops at Piazza Risorgimento and continues right to the entrance. Bus #492 heads from the city center past Piazza Risorgimento and the Vatican walls, and also stops on Via Leone IV. Bus #64 stops on the other side of St. Peter's Square, a 15- to 20-minute walk (facing the church from the obelisk, take a right through the colonnade and follow the Vatican Wall). A few other handy buses (see page 563) can get you close enough to snag a taxi for the final stretch. Or take a taxi from the city center—they are reasonable (hop in and say, "moo-ZAY-ee vah-tee-KAH-nee").

Getting In: Make sure you get in the right entry line. Generally, individuals without tickets line up against the Vatican City wall (to the left of the entrance as you face it), and reservation holders (both individuals and groups) enter on the right. All visitors must pass through a metal detector (no pocket knives allowed).

Tours: A €7 **audioguide** is available at the top of the spiral ramp/escalator. A security ID is not required to rent an

audioguide, and you can drop it off either where you rented it or after leaving the Sistine Chapel if taking the shortcut to St. Peter's (described later, under "Exit Strategies"). Confirm the drop-off location when renting.

🎧 Download my free Sistine Chapel **audio tour.**

The Vatican offers **guided tours** in English that are easy to book on their website (€32, includes admission). As with individual ticket reservations, present your confirmation voucher to a guard to the right of the entrance; then, once inside, go to the Guided Tours desk (in the lobby, up a few stairs).

For a list of **private tour** companies and guides, see page 494.

Length of This Tour: Until you expire, the museum closes, or 2.5 hours pass, whichever comes first. If you're short on time, see the octagonal courtyard (*Laocoön*), then follow the crowd flow directly to the Sistine Chapel, sightseeing along the way. From the Sistine Chapel, head straight to St. Peter's (see "Exit Strategies," next).

Exit Strategies: The museum has two exits. The **main exit** is near the entrance. Use this one if you're asked to return an audioguide there or if you plan on following this self-guided tour exactly as laid out, visiting the Pinacoteca at the end.

The other exit is a handy (but sometimes closed) **shortcut** that leads from the Sistine Chapel directly to St. Peter's Basilica (spilling out alongside the church). The shortcut saves you a 30-minute walk backtracking to the basilica's main entrance and lets you avoid the long security line there. Officially, this exit is for Vatican guides and their groups only. However, it's often open to anyone (depending on how crowded the chapel is and how the guards feel). It's worth a shot (try blending in with a group that's leaving), but be prepared for the possibility that you won't get through.

Baggage Check: The museum's

Vatican Museums Overview

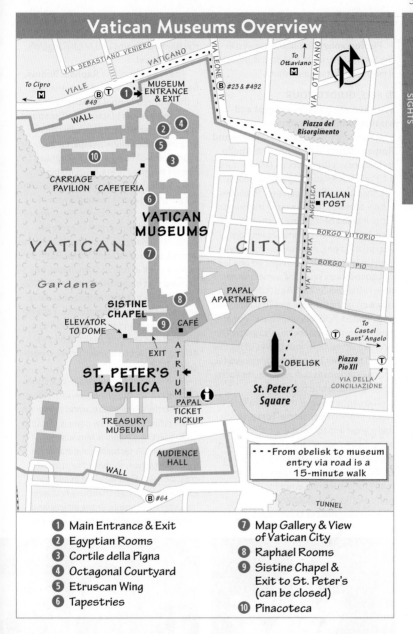

1. Main Entrance & Exit
2. Egyptian Rooms
3. Cortile della Pigna
4. Octagonal Courtyard
5. Etruscan Wing
6. Tapestries
7. Map Gallery & View of Vatican City
8. Raphael Rooms
9. Sistine Chapel & Exit to St. Peter's (can be closed)
10. Pinacoteca

"checkroom" (to the right after security) takes only bigger bags, not day bags.

Photography: No photos allowed in the Sistine Chapel, but photos without flash are permitted elsewhere.

◐ SELF-GUIDED TOUR

Start, as civilization did, in **Egypt and Mesopotamia.** Decorating the museum's courtyard are some of the best **Greek and Roman statues** in captivity. The **Apollo Belvedere** is a Roman copy (4th century B.C.) of a Hellenistic original that followed the style of the Greek sculptor Praxiteles. It fully captures the beauty of the human form. Instead of standing at attention, face-forward with his arms at his sides (Egyptian-style), Apollo is on the move, coming to rest with his weight on one leg.

Laocoön was sculpted some four centuries after the Golden Age (5th-4th century B.C.), after the scales of "balance" had been tipped. *Apollo* is serene and graceful, while *Laocoön* is emotional and gritty. The figures (carved from four blocks of marble pieced together seamlessly) are powerful, with twisted poses that accentuate each rippling muscle and bulging vein.

The centerpiece of the next hall is the 2,000-year-old **Belvedere Torso,** which had a great impact on the art of Michelangelo. Finishing off the classical statuary are two fine fourth-century porphyry sarcophagi. These royal purple tombs were made for the Roman emperor Constantine's mother and daughter.

After long halls of tapestries, old maps, broken penises, and fig leaves, you'll come to what most people are looking for: the Raphael Rooms and Michelangelo's Sistine Chapel.

The highlight of the **Raphael Rooms,** frescoed by Raphael and his assistants, is the restored **School of Athens.** It is remarkable for its blatant pre-Christian classical orientation, especially considering it originally wallpapered the apartments of Pope Julius II. Raphael honors the great pre-Christian thinkers—Aristotle, Plato, and company—who are portrayed as the leading artists of Raphael's day. Leonardo da Vinci, whom Raphael worshipped, is in the role of Plato. Michelangelo, brooding in the foreground, was added later. When Raphael snuck a peek at the Sistine Chapel, he decided that his arch-competitor was so good that he put their differences aside and included him in this tribute. Today's St. Peter's was under construction as Raphael was working. In the *School of Athens,* he gives us a sneak preview of the unfinished church.

Next is the brilliantly restored **Sistine Chapel.** This is the pope's personal chapel and also the place where, upon the death of the ruling pope, a new pope is elected.

The Sistine Chapel is famous for Michelangelo's pictorial culmination of the Renaissance, showing the story of creation, with God weaving in and out of each scene through that busy first week. It's a stirring example of the artistic and theological maturity of the 33-year-old

Laocoön

Raphael, School of Athens

Sistine Chapel

Michelangelo, who spent four years on this work.

The ceiling shows the history of the world before the birth of Jesus. We see God creating the world, creating man and woman, destroying the earth by flood, and so on. God himself, in his purple robe, actually appears in the first five scenes. Along the sides (where the ceiling starts to curve), we see the Old Testament prophets and pagan Greek prophetesses who foretold the coming of Christ. Dividing these scenes and figures are fake niches (a painted 3-D illusion) decorated with nude figures with symbolic meaning.

In the central panel of the **Creation of Adam,** God and man take center stage in this Renaissance version of creation. Adam, newly formed in the image of God, lounges dreamily in perfect naked innocence. God, with his entourage, swoops in with a swirl of activity (which—with a little imagination—looks like a cross-section of a human brain...quite a strong humanist statement). Their reaching hands are the center of this work. Adam's is passive; God's is forceful, his finger twitching upward with energy. Here is the very moment of creation, as God passes the spark of life to man, the crowning work of his creation.

This is the spirit of the Renaissance. God is not reaching down to puny man from way on high. They are on an equal plane, divided only by the diagonal bit of sky. God's billowing robe and the patch of green that holds Adam balance each other. They are like the yin and yang symbols finally coming together—uniting, complementing each other, creating wholeness. God and man work together in the divine process of creation.

When the ceiling was finished and revealed to the public, it blew 'em away. It both caps the Renaissance and turns it in a new direction. The style is more dramatic and emotional than the balanced Renaissance works before it. This is a personal work—the Gospel according to Michelangelo—but its themes and subject matter are universal. Many art scholars contend that the Sistine ceiling is the single greatest work of art by any one human being.

Later, after the Reformation wars had begun and after the Catholic army of Spain had sacked the Vatican, the reeling Church began to fight back. As part of its Counter-Reformation, a much older Michelangelo was commissioned to paint the **Last Judgment** (behind the altar).

It's Judgment Day, and Christ—the powerful figure in the center, raising his arm to spank the wicked—has come to find out who's naughty and who's nice. Beneath him, a band of angels blows its trumpets Dizzy Gillespie-style: a wake-up call to the sleeping dead. The dead at lower left leave their graves and prepare to be judged. The righteous, on Christ's right hand (the left side of the picture), are carried up to heaven. The wicked on the other side are hurled into hell. Charon, from the underworld of Greek mythology, waits below to ferry the souls of the damned to hell.

When *The Last Judgment* was unveiled to the public in 1541, it caused a sensation. The pope dropped to his knees and cried, "Lord, charge me not with my sins when thou shalt come on the Day of Judgment."

And it changed the course of art. The complex composition, with more than 300 figures swirling around the figure of Christ, went far beyond traditional Renaissance balance. The twisted figures shown from every imaginable angle challenged other painters to try and top this master of 3-D illusion. The sheer terror and drama of the scene was a striking contrast to the placid optimism of, say, Raphael's *School of Athens*. Michelangelo had Baroque-en all the rules of the Renaissance, signaling a new era of art.

If you take the long march back, you'll find, along with the Pinacoteca, a cafeteria (long lines, uninspired food), the underrated early-Christian art section, and the exit via the souvenir shop.

Rick's Tip: *A handy (but sometimes closed)* **shortcut leads from the Sistine Chapel directly to St. Peter's Basilica,** *saving a 30-minute walk backtracking to the basilica's main entrance and avoiding the security line there. Exit through the corner door labeled "for authorized guides and tour groups only." Try blending in, or pretend that your group has left you behind.*

North Rome

▲▲▲BORGHESE GALLERY (GALLERIA BORGHESE)

This plush museum, filling a cardinal's mansion in Rome's semiscruffy three-square-mile "Central Park," offers one of Europe's most sumptuous art experiences. Enjoy a collection of world-class Baroque sculpture, including Bernini's *David* and his excited statue of Apollo chasing Daphne, as well as paintings by Caravaggio, Raphael, Titian, and Rubens. The museum's mandatory reservation system keeps crowds to a manageable size.

Cost and Hours: €13, price includes €2 reservation fee, free and crowded first Sun of the month, Tue-Sun 9:00-19:00, closed Mon. Reservations are mandatory. The 1.5-hour audioguide (€5) is excellent.

Reservations: Required reservations are easy to get. Book online at user-friendly www.galleriaborghese.it. When the site asks what "Dispatch Type" you want, choose "Pick-up at the venue box office." You can also reserve by phone (tel. 06-32810, press 2 for English); call during Italian office hours: Mon-Fri 9:00-18:00, Sat 9:00-13:00 (office closed Sat in Aug and Sun year-round).

Entry times are 9:00, 11:00, 13:00, 15:00, and 17:00; you'll get exactly two hours for your visit. Reserve at least several days in advance for a weekday visit, and at least a week ahead for weekends.

After you reserve a day and time, you'll get a claim number. Arrive at the gallery 30 minutes before your appointed time to pick up your ticket in the lobby on the lower level. Check your bags (free and mandatory), then peruse the gift shop or relax in the garden until your designated entry time. Arriving late can mean forfeiting your reservation.

You can use a Roma Pass for entry, but you're still required to make a reservation (by phone only—not online; specify that you have the Roma Pass).

Getting There: The museum is set idyllically but inconveniently in the vast Villa Borghese Gardens. Bus #910 goes from Termini train station (and Piazza Repubblica) to the Via Pinciana stop, 100 yards from the museum. By Metro, from the Barberini Metro stop, walk 10 minutes up Via Veneto, enter the park, and turn right, following signs another 10 minutes to the Borghese Gallery.

Tours: Guided English tours are offered at 9:10 and 11:10 (€6.50). You can't book a tour when you make your museum reservation—sign up as soon as you arrive. The superb 1.5-hour audioguide tour (€5) covers more than my description.

Planning Your Time: Two hours is all you get...and you'll want every minute. Budget most of your time for the more interesting ground floor, but set aside 30 minutes for the paintings of the Pinacoteca upstairs (highlights are marked by the audioguide icons).

Services: Baggage check is free, mandatory, and strictly enforced.

Photography: Allowed without flash.

Visiting the Museum: It's hard to believe that a family of cardinals and popes would display so many works with secular and sensual—even erotic—themes. But the Borgheses felt that all forms of human expression, including pagan myths and physical passion, glorified God.

The essence of the collection is the connection of the Renaissance with

Borghese Gallery—Ground Floor

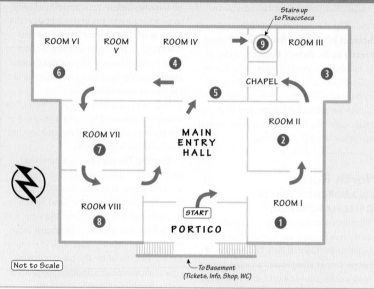

Stairs up to Pinacoteca

ROOM VI ❻	ROOM V	ROOM IV ❹	❾	ROOM III ❸

CHAPEL

MAIN ENTRY HALL

ROOM VII ❼

ROOM II ❷

ROOM VIII ❽

START

PORTICO

ROOM I ❶

UNKNOWN – Diana the Hunter; other marbles ❺

Not to Scale

To Basement (Tickets, Info, Shop, WC)

❶ CANOVA – Pauline Borghese as Venus
❷ BERNINI – David
❸ BERNINI – Apollo and Daphne
❹ BERNINI – The Rape of Proserpina
❺ UNKNOWN – Diana the Hunter; other marbles
❻ BERNINI – Aeneas and Anchises
❼ "Theater of the Universe"
❽ CARAVAGGIO – Various
❾ Stairs up to Pinacoteca

the classical world. As you enter, notice the second-century Roman reliefs with Michelangelo-designed panels above either end of the portico. The villa was built in the early 17th century by art collector Cardinal Scipione Borghese, who wanted to prove that the glories of ancient Rome were matched by the Renaissance.

In the main entry hall, high up on the wall, is a thrilling first-century Greek sculpture of a horse falling. The Renaissance-era rider was added by Pietro Bernini, father of the famous Gian Lorenzo Bernini.

Each room seems to feature a Baroque masterpiece. In Room I is **Pauline Bor-**

ghese as Venus, for which Napoleon's sister went the full monty for the sculptor Antonio Canova, scandalizing Europe. ("How could you have done such a thing?!" she was asked. She replied, "The room wasn't cold.") With the famous nose of her conqueror brother, she strikes the pose of Venus as conqueror of men's hearts. Her relaxed afterglow say she's already had her man.

In Room II, Gian Lorenzo Bernini's **David** twists around to put a big rock in his sling. He purses his lips, knits his brow, and winds his body like a spring as his eyes lock onto the target: Goliath, who's somewhere behind us, putting us right in the line of fire. Compared with Michelangelo's *David,* this is unvarnished realism—an unbalanced pose, bulging veins, unflattering face, and armpit hair. Michelangelo's *David* thinks, whereas Bernini's acts. Bernini slays the pretty-boy *David*s of the Renaissance and prepares to invent Baroque.

In Room III, Bernini's **Apollo and Daphne** is the perfect Baroque subject. Apollo—made stupid by Cupid's arrow of love—chases after Daphne, who has been turned off by the "arrow of disgust." Just as he's about to catch her, she calls to her father to save her. Magically, she transforms into a tree. Frustrated Apollo will end up with a handful of leaves.

In Room IV, Bernini's **The Rape of Proserpina** proves that even at the age of 24 the sculptor was the master of marble.

In Room VI, Bernini's **Aeneas and Anchises** reveals the then 20-year-old sculptor's astonishing aptitude for portraying human flesh.

Bernini, Apollo and Daphne

In Room VIII is a fabulous collection of paintings by **Caravaggio,** who brought Christian saints down to earth with gritty realism.

Upstairs, in the Pinacoteca (Painting Gallery), are busts and paintings by Bernini, as well as works by Raphael, Titian, Correggio, and Domenichino.

CAPUCHIN CRYPT

If you want to see artistically arranged bones, this is the place. The crypt is below the Church of Santa Maria della Immacolata Concezione on the tree-lined Via Veneto, just up from Piazza Barberini. The bones of about 4,000 friars who died in the 1700s are in the basement, all lined up in a series of six crypts to instruct wide-eyed visitors of the inevitability of mortality. Its macabre motto (in the first chapel) is: "What you are now, we used to be."

Cost and Hours: €8, daily 9:00-19:00, modest dress required, no photos but postcards are sold, Via Veneto 27, Metro: Barberini, tel. 06-8880-3695.

▲SPANISH STEPS

The wide, curving staircase, culminating with an obelisk between two Baroque church towers, is one of Rome's iconic sights. Beyond that, it's a people-gathering place. By day, the area hosts shoppers looking for high-end fashions; on balmy evenings, it attracts young and old alike. For more about the steps, see page 502.

▲▲MUSEO DELL'ARA PACIS (MUSEUM OF THE ALTAR OF PEACE)

On January 30, 9 B.C., soon-to-be-emperor Augustus led a procession of priests up the steps and into this newly built "Altar of Peace." They sacrificed an animal on the altar and poured an offering of wine, thanking the gods for helping Augustus pacify barbarians abroad and rivals at home. This marked the dawn of the Pax Romana (c. A.D. 1-200), a Golden Age of good living, stability, dominance, and peace (*pax*). The Ara Pacis (AH-rah PAH-chees) hosted annual sacrifices by the emperor until the area was flooded by the Tiber River. For an idea of how high the water could get, find the measure (*idrometro*) scaling the right side of the church closest to the entrance. Buried under silt, it was abandoned and forgotten until the 16th century, when various parts were discovered and excavated. Mussolini had the altar's scattered parts reconstructed in a building here in 1938. Today, the Altar of Peace stands in a striking pavilion designed by American architect Richard Meier (opened 2006). It's about the only entirely new structure permitted in the old center of Rome since Mussolini's day.

Cost and Hours: €14, €8.50 when no special exhibits, daily 9:30-19:30, last entry one hour before closing, good audio-guide-€4; a long block west of Via del Corso on Via di Ara Pacis, on the east bank of the Tiber near Ponte Cavour, Metro: Spagna plus a 10-minute walk down Via dei Condotti; tel. 06-0608, www.arapacis.it.

Visiting the Museum: Start with the model in the museum's lobby. The Altar of Peace was originally located east of here, along today's Via del Corso. The model shows where it stood in relation to the Mausoleum of Augustus (now next door) and the Pantheon. Approach the Ara Pacis and look through the doorway to see the raised altar. This simple structure has just the basics of a Roman temple: an altar for sacrifices surrounded by cubicle walls that enclose a consecrated space. Climb the 10 steps and go inside. From here, the priest would climb the 8 altar steps to make sacrifices. The walls of the enclosure are decorated with the offerings to the gods: animals, garlands of fruit, and ceremonial platters. The reliefs on the north and south sides depict the parade of dignitaries who consecrated the altar, while the reliefs on the west side (near the altar's back door) celebrate peace (goddess Roma as a conquering Amazon, right side) and prosperity (fertility goddess surrounded by children, plants, and animals, left side).

East Rome

▲▲▲NATIONAL MUSEUM OF ROME

The National Museum's main branch houses the greatest collection of ancient Roman art anywhere, including busts of emperors and a Roman copy of the Greek *Discus Thrower*.

Cost and Hours: €10 combo-ticket

Ara Pacis

covers three other branches—all skip-pable, free and crowded first Sun of the month, Tue–Sun 9:00–19:45, closed Mon, last entry 45 minutes before closing, audioguide-€5, about 100 yards from train station, Metro: Repubblica or Termini, tel. 06-3996-7700, www.archeoroma.beni culturali.it/en.

Getting There: The museum is in Pala-zzo Massimo, situated between Piazza della Repubblica (Metro: Repubblica) and Termini Station (Metro: Termini). It's a few minutes' walk from either Metro stop. As you leave Termini, it's the sand-stone-brick building on your left. Enter at the far end, at Largo di Villa Peretti.

Visiting the Museum: The museum is rectangular, with rooms and hallways built around a central courtyard. The ground-floor displays follow Rome's history as it changes from a republic to a dictatorial empire. The first-floor exhibits take Rome from its peak through its slow decline. The second floor houses rare frescoes and fine mosaics, and the basement presents coins and everyday objects.

On the first floor, along with statues and busts showing such emperors as Trajan and Hadrian, you'll see the best-preserved Roman copy of the Greek *Discus Thrower*. Statues of athletes like this commonly stood in the baths, where Romans cultivated healthy bodies, minds, and social skills, hoping to lead well-rounded lives. Other statues on this floor originally stood in the pleasure gardens of the Roman rich—surrounded by greenery

with the splashing sound of fountains, all painted in bright, lifelike colors. Though created by Romans, the themes are mostly Greek, with godlike humans and human-looking gods.

The second floor contains frescoes and mosaics that once decorated the walls and floors of Roman villas. They feature everyday people, animals, flowery patterns, and geometrical designs. The Villa Farnesina frescoes—in black, red, yellow, and blue—are mostly architec-tural designs, with fake columns, friezes, and garlands. The Villa di Livia frescoes, owned by the wily wife of Augustus, immerse you in a leafy green garden full of birds and fruit trees, symbolizing the gods.

Finally, descend into the basement to see fine gold jewelry, an eight-year-old girl's mummy, and vault doors leading into the best coin collection in Europe, with fancy magnifying glasses maneuvering you through cases of coins from ancient Rome to modern times.

▲▲CHURCH OF SAN GIOVANNI IN LATERANO

Built by Constantine, the first Christian emperor, this was Rome's most import-ant church through medieval times. A building alongside the church houses the **Holy Stairs** (Scala Santa) said to have been walked up by Jesus, which today are ascended by pilgrims on their knees. You can join them.

Cost and Hours: Church and Holy Stairs—free, cloister—€5, chapel at Holy Stairs—€3.50 (€8 combo-ticket covers

Boxer at Rest *at the National Museum of Rome*

Pilgrims climbing the Holy Stairs

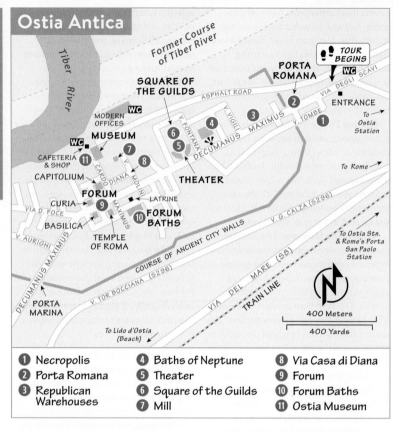

Ostia Antica

- Former Course of Tiber River
- Tiber River
- SQUARE OF THE GUILDS
- ASPHALT ROAD
- PORTA ROMANA
- TOUR BEGINS
- WC
- VIA DEGLI SCAVI
- ENTRANCE
- To Ostia Station
- MODERN OFFICES
- WC
- MUSEUM
- V. FONTANA
- V. VIGILI
- DECUMANUS MAXIMUS
- V. TOMBE
- To Rome →
- WC
- CAFETERIA & SHOP
- CARDO DIANA
- V. DEI MOLINI
- THEATER
- CAPITOLIUM
- FORUM
- CURIA
- LATRINE
- CARDO MAXIMUS
- FORUM BATHS
- V. G. CALZA (S296)
- To Ostia Stn. & Rome's Porta San Paolo Station
- VIA D. FOCE
- BASILICA
- TEMPLE OF ROMA
- COURSE OF ANCIENT CITY WALLS
- V. AURIGHI
- DECUMANUS MAXIMUS
- V. TOR BOCCIANA (S296)
- VIA DEL MARE (S8)
- TRAIN LINE
- PORTA MARINA
- To Lido d'Ostia (Beach) ↙
- N
- 400 Meters
- 400 Yards

① Necropolis
② Porta Romana
③ Republican Warehouses
④ Baths of Neptune
⑤ Theater
⑥ Square of the Guilds
⑦ Mill
⑧ Via Casa di Diana
⑨ Forum
⑩ Forum Baths
⑪ Ostia Museum

both); church open daily 7:00-18:30, audioguide available; Holy Stairs open Mon-Sat 6:00-13:00 & 15:00-19:00, Sun 7:00-12:30 & 15:30-19:00, Oct-March closes daily at 18:30. The church is on Piazza di San Giovanni in Laterano (east of the Colosseum and south of Termini train station, Metro: San Giovanni, or bus #85 or #87). Tel. 06-6988-6409, www.scalasantaroma.it.

Near Rome: Ostia Antica

For an exciting day trip, pop down to the Roman port of Ostia, which is similar to Pompeii but a lot closer and, in some ways, more interesting. Because Ostia was a working port town, it offers a more complete and gritty look at Roman life than wealthier Pompeii. Wandering around today, you'll see warehouses, apartment flats, mansions, shopping arcades, and baths that served a once-thriving port of 60,000 people. With over 70 peaceful acres to explore and relatively few crowds, it's a welcome break from the bustle of Rome. Buy a map, then explore the town, including the 2,000-year-old theater. Finish with its fine little museum.

Cost and Hours: €8 for the site and museum, €10 with special exhibits, April-Aug Tue-Sun 8:30-19:15, Sept until 19:00, Oct until 18:30, Nov-mid-Feb 8:30-16:30, mid-Feb-March until 17:00, late March until 17:30, closed Mon year-round, last entry one hour before closing. The museum sometimes closes from 13:30 to 14:30 for lunch.

Getting There: Getting from Rome to Ostia Antica is a 45-minute combination Metro/train ride (costs only one Metro ticket each way): Take Metro line B to the Piramide stop, which is part of the Roma Porta San Paolo train station. Exiting the Metro, follow signs to *Lido*—go up the escalator, turn left, and go down the steps into the Roma-Lido train station. All trains depart for the Lido, leave every 15 minutes, and stop at Ostia Antica. Hop on the next train, ride for about 30 minutes (no need to stamp your Metro ticket again, but keep it handy in case it's checked), and get off at Ostia Antica. Leaving the train station, walk over the blue skybridge, then head straight down Via della Stazione di Ostia Antica, continuing straight (through a small parking lot) to the large parking lot for the site (entrance on your left).

Information: A map of the site with suggested itineraries is available for €2 from the ticket office. Tel. 06-5635-0215. Helpful websites include www.ostiaantica. beniculturali.it and www.ostia-antica.org.

Tours: Although you'll see audioguide markers throughout the site, there may not be audioguides for rent. However, you can 🎧 download my free Ostia Antica audio tour.

EXPERIENCES

Nightlife

The best after-dark activity is to grab a gelato and stroll the medieval lanes that connect the romantic, floodlit squares and fountains. Head for Piazza Navona, the Pantheon, Campo de' Fiori, Trevi Fountain, and the Spanish Steps; these marvelous sights are linked together in my self-guided "Heart of Rome" walk (page 495). Another great evening activity is my "Dolce Vita Stroll" along Via del Corso (page 503).

A fun neighborhood to explore at night is **Monti,** which is more like a lively village. Hang out at the fountain on Piazza della Madonna dei Monti, which becomes the hottest scene around. Stop at the shop on the uphill side of the square, which sells cheap bottles of wine with plastic glasses, beer, fruit, and munchies. Or head to an actual bar, like **Fafiuché** (Via della Madonna dei Monti 28) or **Enoteca Cavour 313** (Via Cavour 313).

Ostia Antica Theater

Performances

Get a copy of the entertainment guide *Evento* (free at TIs and many hotels) and check the listings of concerts, operas, dance, and films. For the most up-to-date events calendar, check these English-language websites: www.inromenow.com, www.wantedinrome.com, and www.rome. angloinfo.com.

The **Teatro dell'Opera** has an active schedule of opera and classical concerts. You'll see locals in all their finery, so pull your fanciest outfit from your backpack (Via Firenze 72, tel. 06-4816-0255, www. operaroma.it).

The Episcopal **Church of St. Paul's Within the Walls** offers musical events from orchestral concerts (usually Tue and Fri) to full operatic performances, usually on Saturdays (€20-30, performances at 20:30, tickets usually available on day of show, arrive 30-45 minutes early for a good seat, lasts 1.5-2.5 hours, corner of Via Nazionale at Via Napoli 58, tel. 06-482-6296, www.musicaemusicasrl.com and www.operaelirica.com). On Sunday evenings at 18:30, the church occasionally hosts hour-long candlelit *Luminaria* concerts (€10-20, buy tickets at the church on Sun, www.stpaulsrome.it).

The venerable **Alexanderplatz** hosts **jazz performances** most evenings (Sun-Thu concerts at 21:45, Fri-Sat at 22:30, closed in summer, Via Ostia 9, Metro: Ottaviano, tel. 06-3972-1867, www. alexanderplatzjazzclub.com).

EATING

Romans take great pleasure in dining well, treating it as a lengthy social occasion. Embrace this passion over a multicourse meal at an outdoor table, watching a parade of passersby while you sip wine with loved ones.

Rome's fabled nightspots (most notably Piazza Navona, near the Pantheon, and Campo de' Fiori) are lined with the outdoor tables of touristy restaurants with enticing menus and formal-vested waiters. The atmosphere is romantic, but you'll likely be surrounded by tourists, killing the ambience and leaving you with a forgettable and overpriced meal. Restaurants in these areas are notorious for surprise charges, forgettable food, microwaved ravioli, and bad service. If you're set on dining on a famous piazza, circle the square, observing both the food and the people eating it. Pizza is probably your best value and least risky bet. I enjoy the view by savoring just a drink or dessert on a famous square, but I dine with locals on nearby low-rent streets, where the proprietor needs to serve a good-value meal to stay in business.

I'm impressed by how small the price difference can be between a mediocre Roman restaurant and a fine one. You can pay about 20 percent more for double the quality. If I had $100 for three meals in Rome, I'd spend $50 for one and $25 each for the other two, rather than $33 on all three. For splurge meals, I'd consider Gabriello and Fortunato, in that order (details listed later).

Budget Eating: For a light budget meal, consider an *aperitivo* buffet offered by many bars. They serve complimentary, tasty appetizers to anyone buying a drink (at an inflated price), who then gets to eat "for free." Drinks generally cost around

Roman Cuisine

Simple, fresh, seasonal ingredients dominate Roman cuisine. It's robust, strongly flavored, and unpretentious—much like the people who've created it. Roman cooking didn't come out of emperors' or popes' kitchens, but from the *cucina povera*—the home cooking of the common people. That could explain why Romans have a fondness for meats known as the *quinto quarto* ("fifth quarter"), such as tripe *(trippa)*, tail, brain, and pigs' feet.

Appetizers (*Antipasti*): Popular choices are *prosciutto e melone* (thin slices of ham wrapped around cantaloupe), *bruschetta* (toasted bread topped with chopped tomatoes), and *antipasto misto* (a plate of marinated or grilled vegetables, cheeses, cured meats, or seafood). *Fritti* are fried snacks that have been either battered or breaded, such as stuffed olives, potato croquettes, rice balls, and stuffed squash blossoms.

First Courses (*Primi*): A pasta dish born in Rome is *spaghetti alla carbonara*, with eggs, pancetta (Italian bacon), cheese, and pepper. Another traditional pasta is *bucatini all'amatriciana*, with tomato sauce, onions, pancetta, and cheese. *Gnocchi alla romana* are small, flattened dumplings baked with butter and cheese. If you like spaghetti with clams, try *spaghetti alle vongole veraci*.

Second Courses (*Secondi*): A very Roman dish is *saltimbocca alla romana* (thinly sliced, lightly fried veal layered with prosciutto). *Filetti di baccalà* is fried salt cod, like fish-and-chips minus the chips. Other choices are baby lamb chops *(abbacchio alla scottadito)*, stewed baby eels *(anguillette in umid)*, and braised oxtails *(coda alla vaccinara)*. *Trippa alla romana* is braised tripe with onions and carrots.

Desserts (*Dolci*): Dessert can be a seasonal fruit, such as strawberries, peaches, or even cheese. *Bignè* are cream puff-like pastries filled with *zabaione* (egg yolks, sugar, and Marsala wine). *Tartufo* is a rich dark-chocolate gelato ball with a cherry inside, sometimes served *con panna* (with whipped cream). When you're out and about on a hot day, try a *grattachecca* (flavored, sweetened shaved ice) from a vendor's stand.

Local Wines (*Vini*): Frascati, probably the best-known wine of the region, is an inexpensive dry white. Others are Castelli Romani, Marino, Colli Albani, and Velletri. Torre Ercolana is a medium-bodied red; the merlot is the region's best-quality red, aged at least five years.

€8-12, and the food's out anywhere from about 18:00 to 21:00. Some places limit you to one plate; others allow refills.

For the cheapest meal, assemble a picnic and dine with Rome as your backdrop. Buy ingredients for your picnic at one of Rome's open-air produce markets (mornings only), an *alimentari* (corner grocery store), a *rosticcerie* (cheap food to go), or a *supermercato,* such as Conad, Despar, or Co-op. You'll find handy late-night supermarkets near the Pantheon (on Via Giustiniani), Spanish Steps (Via Vittoria), Trevi Fountain (Via del Bufalo), and Campo de' Fiori (Via di Monte della Farina). Rome discourages people from picnicking or drinking at historic monuments (such as on the Spanish Steps) in the old center. Violators can be fined, though it rarely happens. You'll be okay if you eat *with* a view rather than *on* the view.

Pantheon Neighborhood

I've listed restaurants in this central area based on which landmark they're closest to: Piazza Navona, the Trevi Fountain, or the Pantheon.

Near Piazza Navona

The joints lining venerable Piazza Navona are classic tourist eateries. For better values, head several blocks west of the square. These squares and streets, such as Piazza del Fico and Via del Corallo, host a thriving jungle of inviting eateries.

Ristorante del Fico is a sprawling, rustic-chic place—a huge Italian saloon filled with young locals. It has both a fun energy and a traditional Italian menu (€7 pizzas, €13-15 *secondi,* nightly from 19:30, 3 blocks west of Piazza Navona at Via della Pace 34, tel. 06-688-91373). Its **Bar del Fico** around the corner on Piazza del Fico has a similar local vibe—plus an antipasto buffet (buffet free with any drink, 19:00-21:00, www.bardelfico.com).

Ristorante Pizzeria "da Francesco," bustling and authentic, has a 50-year-old tradition, great indoor seating, and a few

tables on the quiet street (€9-11 pizzas and pastas, €13-20 *secondi,* daily 12:00-15:30 & 19:00-24:00, next to Bar del Fico at Piazza del Fico 29, tel. 06-686-4009).

Vivi Bistrot, known as the Museum of Rome café, is a good value at the south end of Piazza Navona, with two delightful window tables overlooking the square. Enjoy light meals any time or a €10 drink and antipasto buffet deal nightly after 19:00 (closed Mon, Piazza Navona 2, tel. 06-683-3779).

L'Insalata Ricca, specializing in healthy €6-9 salads alongside pastas and main courses, is handy and central (daily 12:00-24:00). They have a branch on Piazza Pasquino (tel. 06-6830-7881) and a more spacious location a few blocks away, on a bigger square next to busy Corso Vittorio Emanuele (between Piazza Navona and Campo de' Fiori at Largo dei Chiavari 85, tel. 06-6880-3656).

Near the Trevi Fountain

The streets surrounding the Trevi Fountain are littered with mediocre restaurants catering to tourists—try one of these instead.

Hostaria Romana is a busy bistro with a hustling, fun-loving gang of waiters. The upstairs is a glassed-in terrace, while the cellar has noisy walls graffitied by happy eaters. Try the traditional *saltimbocca alla romana* (veal) or the pasta dish, *bucatini all'amatriciana* (€11 pastas, €15 *secondi,* Mon-Sat 12:30-15:00 & 19:15-23:00, closed Sun and Aug, reservations smart, a block past the entrance to the big tunnel near the Trevi Fountain, corner of Via Rasella and Via del Boccaccio, tel. 06-474-5284, www.hostariaromana.it).

L'Antica Birreria Peroni serves hearty mugs of Peroni beer and lots of beerhall food and Italian classics (€7 pastas, €4-12 *secondi,* Mon-Sat 12:00-24:00, closed Sun, midway between Trevi Fountain and Capitoline Hill, a block off Via del Corso at Via di San Marcello 19, tel. 06-679-5310).

Close to the Pantheon

Eating on the square facing the Pantheon is a temptation worth considering, but a block or two away, you'll get fewer views and better value.

Ristorante da Fortunato is an Italian classic, with fresh flowers on the tables and white-coated waiters serving good meat and fish to dignitaries and tourists with good taste. On the walls, everyone from Muammar Gaddafi and Prince Charles to Bill Clinton are pictured with Signore Fortunato, who started this restaurant in 1975. It's a reliable and surprisingly reasonable choice—reserve ahead (plan on €50 per person, daily 12:30-23:30, a block in front of the Pantheon at Via del Pantheon 55, tel. 06-679-2788, www.ristorantefortunato.it).

Enoteca Corsi is a wine shop that grew into a thriving lunch spot, serving traditional cuisine to an appreciative crowd of office workers. Kids do their homework at the family table in back. Enjoy pastas, main dishes, and fine wine at a third of the price of most restaurants—buy from their shop and pay a corking fee (€9 pastas, €13 *secondi*, Mon-Sat 12:00-15:30, closed Sun, no reservations, a block toward the Pantheon from Gesù Church at Via del Gesù 87, tel. 06-679-0821).

Ristorante la Campana is an authentic slice of old Rome, claiming a history dating to 1518. It still serves appreciative locals typical Roman dishes and daily specials, plus a good self-service *antipasti* buffet (€10-12 pastas, €11-18 *secondi*, Tue-Sun 12:30-15:00 & 19:30-23:00, closed Mon, inside seating only, reserve for dinner, just off Via della Scrofa and Piazza Nicosia at Vicolo della Campana 18, tel. 06-687-5273, www.ristorantelacampana.com).

Osteria delle Coppelle serves traditional dishes to a local crowd. It has a rustic interior, jumbled exterior seating, and a fun selection of €3 *cicchetti* (€7 pizza, €9 pastas, €12 *secondi*, 12:30-16:00 & 19:00-late, Piazza delle Coppelle 54, tel. 06-4550-2826).

Miscellanea is run by much-loved Mikki, who's on a mission to keep foreign students well-fed with inexpensive, hearty food (€4 sandwiches, €7 salads, €7-8 pastas, €10-15 *secondi*, daily 11:00-24:00, indoor/outdoor seating, facing the rear of the Pantheon at Via della Palombella 34, tel. 06-6813-5318).

North Rome
Near the Spanish Steps and Ara Pacis

These restaurants are located near the route of the "Dolce Vita Stroll" (see map on page 503).

Ristorante il Gabriello is inviting and small—modern under medieval arches—serving creative Roman cuisine using farm-fresh, organic products. Trust your waiter and say, "Bring it on." The atmosphere is fun and convivial (€11-18 pastas, €14-20 *secondi*, dinner only, Mon-Sat 19:00-23:00, closed Sun, reservations smart, air-con, dress respectfully—no shorts, 3 blocks from Spanish Steps at Via Vittoria 51, tel. 06-6994-0810, www.ilgabriello.it).

Antica Enoteca is an upbeat, atmospheric 200-plus-year-old *enoteca*. For a light lunch, enjoy a glass of their best wine at the bar (€6-10, listed on a big blackboard) and split a €14 *antipasti* plate of veggies, *salumi*, and cheese (€6-12 salads, €10-14 pastas, €12-18 *secondi*, daily 12:00-24:00, reserve for outdoor seating, Via della Croce 76, tel. 06-679-0896).

Ancient Rome
Near the Colosseum and Forum

Within a block of the Colosseum and Forum, eateries cater to weary sightseers, offering neither memorable food nor good value. To get your money's worth, head to the Monti neighborhood. From the Forum, head up Via Cavour and then left on Via dei Serpenti; the action centers on Piazza della Madonna dei Monti and nearby lanes.

Restaurants & Hotels in the Pantheon Neighborhood

Tiber River

Piazza Nicosia

Piazza Cardelli

PREFETTI

Piazza delle Coppelle

UFF

LUNGOTEVERE MARZIO

VIA DELLA SCROFA

CAMPANA

To Ponte Sant'Angelo

VIA DEI CORONARI

ANCIENT STADIUM ENTRANCE

VIA D. COPPELLE

SAN LUIGI

POZZO D. CORN.

Piazza Fico

VIA DELLA PACE

V. DI TOR MILLINA

PHARMACY

SALVATORE

VIA GIUSTINIANI

VIA DEL CORALLO

V. DELLA VETRINA

V. DI SANT AGNESE

Piazza Navona

CRESCENZI

Piazza Rotonda

CHIESA NUOVA

SANT' AGNESE

FOUR RIVERS FOUNTAIN

PANTHEON

VIA DI PARIONE

VIA GOV. VECCHIO

Piazza della Chiesa Nuova

SODA

Piazza S. Eustachio

Piazza Pasquino

CITY MUSEUM

VIA DELLA SCROFA

CORSO VITTORIO

VIA DEL PELLEGRINO

VIA DEI CAPPELLARI

CANCELLERIA

VIA DEL BAULLARI

BOVARI

EMANUELE II

Largo Argentina

SANT' ANDREA DELLA VALLE

ARGENTINA

VIA MONSERRATO

BRUNO STATUE

Campo de' Fiori

Largo Pallaro

CHIAVARI

LARGO ARGENTINA RUINS

Piazza Farnese

PALAZZO FARNESE

VIA GIUBBONARI

Largo Arenula

FLORIDA

VIA GIULIA

CAPO DE FERRO

VIA SPECCHI

Tiber River

To Trastevere

Piazza Cairoli

GHETTO

Restaurants

1. Ristorante del Fico
2. Bar del Fico
3. Rist. Pizzeria "da Francesco"
4. Vivi Bistrot
5. L'Insalata Ricca
6. To Hostaria Romana
7. L'Antica Birreria Peroni
8. Ristorante da Fortunato
9. Enoteca Corsi
10. Ristorante la Campana
11. Osteria delle Coppelle
12. Miscellanea

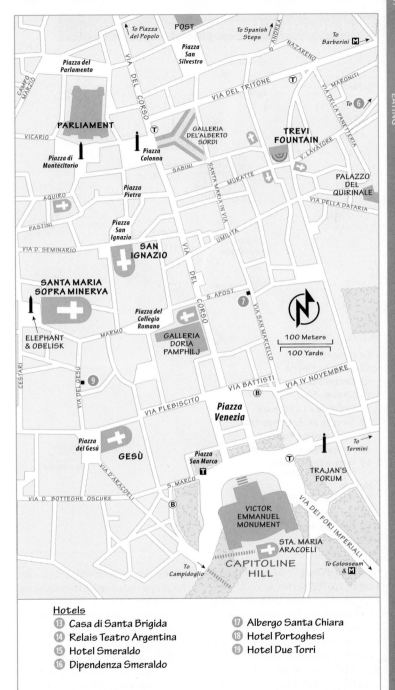

Hotels

13 Casa di Santa Brigida
14 Relais Teatro Argentina
15 Hotel Smeraldo
16 Dipendenza Smeraldo
17 Albergo Santa Chiara
18 Hotel Portoghesi
19 Hotel Due Torri

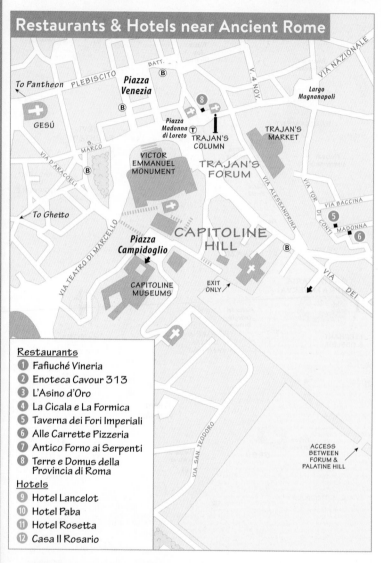

Restaurants & Hotels near Ancient Rome

Restaurants

1. Fafiuché Vineria
2. Enoteca Cavour 313
3. L'Asino d'Oro
4. La Cicala e La Formica
5. Taverna dei Fori Imperiali
6. Alle Carrette Pizzeria
7. Antico Forno ai Serpenti
8. Terre e Domus della Provincia di Roma

Hotels

9. Hotel Lancelot
10. Hotel Paba
11. Hotel Rosetta
12. Casa Il Rosario

L'Asino d'Oro ("The Golden Donkey"), a top choice for foodies, serves Umbrian cuisine with a creative twist—mingling savory and sweet. The modern space is filled with savvy diners (€11-13 pastas, €14-17 main dishes, Tue-Sat 19:30-23:00, closed Sun-Mon, reserve ahead, Via del Boschetto 73, tel. 06-4891-3832).

La Cicala e La Formica has its own nook on Via Leonina, with a terrace good for people-watching and a lively, homey interior. Weekday lunch specials are good values (€10 pastas, €10 *secondi,* daily 12:00-15:30 & 19:00-23:00, Via Leonina 17, tel. 06-481-7490).

Taverna dei Fori Imperiali serves typical Roman cuisine in a snug interior that bustles with energy (€9 *antipasti,* €9-12

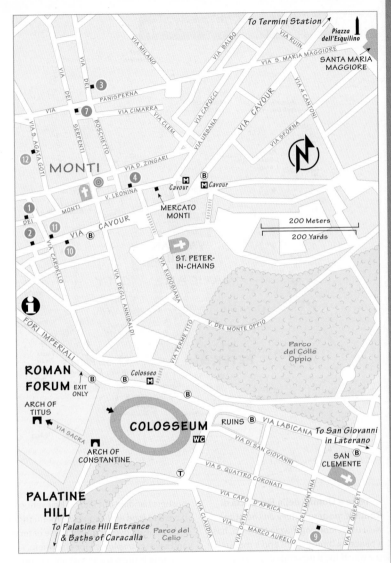

pastas, €12-16 *secondi,* Wed-Mon 12:30-15:00 & 19:30-23:00, closed Tue, reserve for dinner, Via della Madonna dei Monti 9, tel. 06-679-8643).

Alle Carrette Pizzeria, simple and rustic, serves the best pizza in Monti (€8 pizzas, daily 19:00-24:00, Vicolo delle Carrette 14, across from Taverna dei Fori Imperiali, tel. 06-679-2770).

Antico Forno ai Serpenti ("Old Bakery on Serpenti Street") feels anything but old. This hip bakery serves good bread and pastries to enjoy at one of their few tables or to go. At noon they put out a small buffet of pastas and vegetables for €10, which includes a drink (daily 8:00-20:00, Via dei Serpenti 122, tel. 06-4542-7920).

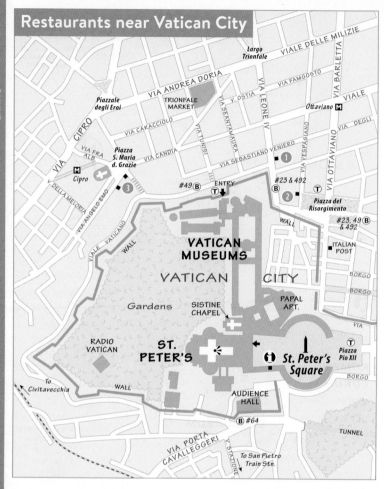

Restaurants near Vatican City

Terre e Domus della Provincia di Roma, a modern eatery on the otherwise unwelcoming Piazza Venezia, has a peaceful dining room and a menu that shows off local ingredients and cuisine (€12 pastas, €12-15 *secondi*, daily 12:00-23:30, Foro Traiano 82, immediately below Trajan's Column, tel. 06-6994-0273).

Near Vatican City

Eateries near the Vatican cater to exhausted tourists. Avoid the restaurant pushers handing out fliers: Their venues have bad food and expensive menu tricks. Tide yourself over at any of these eateries and save your splurges for elsewhere.

These listings are all fast and cheap, a stone's throw from the Vatican wall, near Piazza Risorgimento: **Hostaria dei Bastioni** has noisy streetside seating and a quiet interior (€8-10 pastas, €8-13 *secondi,* Mon-Sat 12:00-15:30 & 18:30-23:00, closed Sun, at corner of Vatican wall at Via Leone IV 29, tel. 06-3972-3034); **L'Insalata Ricca** serves hearty salads

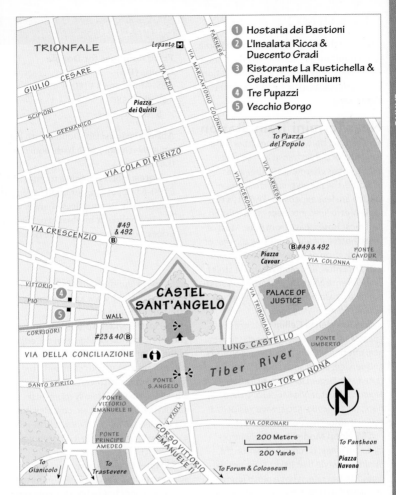

① Hostaria dei Bastioni
② L'Insalata Ricca & Duecento Gradi
③ Ristorante La Rustichella & Gelateria Millennium
④ Tre Pupazzi
⑤ Vecchio Borgo

and pastas (€7-12 meals, daily 12:00-23:30, across from Vatican walls at Piazza Risorgimento 5, tel. 06-3973-0387); and **Duecento Gradi** is a good bet for fresh and creative €5-8 sandwiches (daily 11:00-24:00, Piazza Risorgimento 3, tel. 06-3975-4239).

Ristorante La Rustichella serves tasty wood-fired pizzas (€6-9) and the usual pastas (€7-10) in addition to an excellent *antipasti* buffet (€8 for a single plate) in a no-frills setting (daily 12:00-15:00 & 19:00-24:00, closed for lunch Mon, opposite

church at end of Via Candia, Via Angelo Emo 1, tel. 06-3972-0649). Consider the fun and fruity **Gelateria Millennium** next door.

The pedestrians-only Borgo Pio—a block from Piazza San Pietro near St. Peter's Basilica—has restaurants worth a look. Consider **Tre Pupazzi** (Mon-Sat 12:00-15:00 & 19:00-23:00, closed Sun, at the corner of Via Tre Pupazzi and Borgo Pio) or **Vecchio Borgo,** across the street (Mon-Sat 9:00-21:00, closed Sun, Borgo Pio 27a).

SLEEPING

Choosing the right neighborhood in Rome is as important as choosing the right hotel. All of my recommended accommodations are in safe, pleasant areas convenient to sightseeing.

Near Termini Train Station

The Termini train station neighborhood is handy for public transit and services. While not as charming as other areas of Rome, the hotels near Termini train station are less expensive. The city's two main Metro lines intersect at the station, and most buses leave from here. Most of these hotels are a 10-minute walk west of the station, on or near Via Firenze, a safe, handy, central, and relatively quiet street. The Defense Ministry is nearby, so you've got heavily armed guards watching over you all night.

$$$ Residenza Cellini feels like the guest wing of a gorgeous Neoclassical palace, offering 11 rooms, four-star comforts and service, and a small, breezy terrace (Db-€195, larger Db-€215, extra bed-€25, air-con, elevator, Via Modena 5, third floor, tel. 06-4782-5204, www.residenza cellini.it, info@residenzacellini.it).

$$$ Hotel Modigliani, a delightful 23-room place, is run in a clean, bright, minimalist style that its artist namesake would appreciate. It has a plush lounge and a garden (Db-€202, air-con, elevator; northwest of Via Firenze—from Tritone Fountain on Piazza Barberini, go 2 blocks up Via della Purificazione to #42; tel. 06-4281-5226, www.hotelmodigliani.com, info@hotelmodigliani.com).

$$$ IQ Hotel, facing the Opera House, lacks charm, but compensates with modern amenities. Its 88 rooms are fresh and spacious, the roof garden has foosball and a play area, and vending machines dispense bottles of wine (Db-€100-230, varies with room size and season—likely €200 in peak season, extra bed-€40, breakfast-€10, air-con, elevator, cheap

self-service laundry, gym, Via Firenze 8, tel. 06-488-0465, www.iqhotelroma.it, info@iqhotelroma.it).

$$ Hotel Raffaello offers 41 rooms in a grand 19th-century building on the edge of the Monti district. This formal hotel comes with a courteous staff and a breakfast room fit for aristocrats (Sb-€100, Db-€180, Tb-€228, family rooms, ask about Rick Steves rate, air-con, elevator, Via Urbana 3, Metro: Cavour, tel. 06-488-4342, www.hotelraffaello.it, info@hotel-raffaello.it).

$$ Hotel Oceania is a peaceful slice of air-conditioned heaven. This comfortable 24-room manor house has tastefully decorated rooms and lots of thoughtful extra touches (Sb-€135, Db-€168, Tb-€198, Qb-€220, deep discounts in summer and winter, family suite, elevator, videos in TV lounge, Via Firenze 38, third floor, tel. 06-482-4696, www.hoteloceania.it, info@hoteloceania.it).

$$ Hotel Aberdeen combines quality and friendliness, with 37 cozy rooms (Sb-€102, Db-€170, Tb-€180, Qb-€200, air-con, Via Firenze 48, tel. 06-482-3920, www.hotelaberdeen.it, info@hotelaberdeen.it).

Sleep Code

Price Rankings for Double Rooms (Db)

$$$ Most rooms €180 or more
$$ €125-180
$ €125 or less

Abbreviations: Db=Double with bathroom. D=Double with bathroom down the hall

Notes: Hotels charge a room tax of €1.50-6 per person, per night, often payable in cash. Room prices change; verify rates online or by email. For the best prices, book directly with the hotel.

$$ Hotel Opera Roma boasts 15 spacious, modern, and well-appointed rooms (Db-€150, Tb-€165, 5 percent discount if you pay cash, air-con, elevator, Via Firenze 11, tel. 06-487-1787, www.hotel operaroma.com, info@hoteloperaroma. com, Reza, Litu, and Federica).

$$ Hotel Selene Roma spreads its 40 stylish rooms out on a few floors of an elegant palazzo (Db-€160, Tb-€190, email directly to get the Rick Steves rate, plus an additional discount if you pay cash, air-con, elevator, family rooms, Via del Viminale 8, tel. 06-474-4781, www. hotelseleneroma.it, reception@hotel seleneroma.it).

$$ Hotel Sonya offers 40 small, well-equipped if small rooms, a hearty breakfast, and decent prices (Sb-€90, Db-€150, Tb-€165, Qb-€185, Quint/b-€200, air-con, elevator, faces the Opera House at Via Viminale 58, Metro: Repubblica or Termini, tel. 06-481-9911, www.hotel sonya.it, info@hotelsonya.it, Francesca and Ivan).

$$ Hotel Italia Roma is located safely on a quiet street next to the Ministry of the Interior, with 35 modest but comfortable rooms. The four "residenza" rooms upstairs on the third floor are newer and about €10 more expensive. They also have eight similar annex rooms across the street for the same price as the main hotel (Sb-€90, Db-€130, Tb-€160, Qb-€190, book directly via email for the best rates, air-con, elevator, Via Venezia 18, just off Via Nazionale, tel. 06-482-8355, www.hotel italiaroma.it, info@hotelitaliaroma.it).

$ Hotel Nardizzi Americana has a small rooftop terrace and 40 standard rooms spread throughout the building (Sb-€95, Db-€125, Tb-€155, Qb-€175; email to get the best rates, additional discount if you pay cash, air-con, tiny elevator, reception on fourth floor, Via Firenze 38, tel. 06-488-0035, www.hotelnardizzi. it, info@hotelnardizzi.it; friendly Stefano, Fabrizio, Mario, and Giancarlo).

Near Ancient Rome

Stretching from the Colosseum to Piazza Venezia, this area is central. Sightseers are a short walk from the Colosseum, Roman Forum, and Trajan's Column—and all of these listings (except Hotel Lancelot) are close to or in the charming Monti district, with good restaurants and shopping. While buses are your best bet here, I list a Metro stop if it's convenient.

$$$ Hotel Lancelot is a 60-room hotel with the ambience of a comfortable B&B. Located in a pleasant, residential neighborhood, it's quiet and safe, with a shady courtyard, restaurant, bar, and communal sixth-floor terrace (Sb-€128, Db-€196, Tb-€226, Qb-€266, €20 extra for Colosseum view, air-con, elevator, wheelchair-accessible, parking-€10/day, 10-minute walk behind Colosseum near San Clemente Church at Via Capo d'Africa 47, tel. 06-7045-0615, www.lancelot hotel.com, info@lancelothotel.com).

$$ Hotel Paba is a cozy throwback, with seven fresh, chocolate-box-tidy rooms. It's just two blocks from the Forum. Although it overlooks busy Via Cavour, it's quiet enough (Db-€135, extra bed-€40, big beds, breakfast served in room, air-con, elevator, Via Cavour 266, second floor, Metro: Cavour, tel. 06-4782-4902, www.hotelpaba.com, info@hotel paba.com).

$ Hotel Rosetta, a homey and family-run *pensione*, rents 15 simple rooms. There's no lounge and no breakfast, but its great location makes it a fine budget option (Sb-€75, Db-€110, Tb-€130, air-con, up one flight of stairs, Via Cavour 295, tel. 06-4782-3069, www.rosettahotel. com, info@rosettahotel.com).

$ Casa Il Rosario is a tranquil, well-run Dominican convent renting 40 rooms with monastic simplicity in a steep but pleasant corner of the Monti neighborhood (S-€42, Sb-€56, Db-€94, Tb-€120, single beds only but can be pushed together, reserve several months in advance, some rooms with air-con

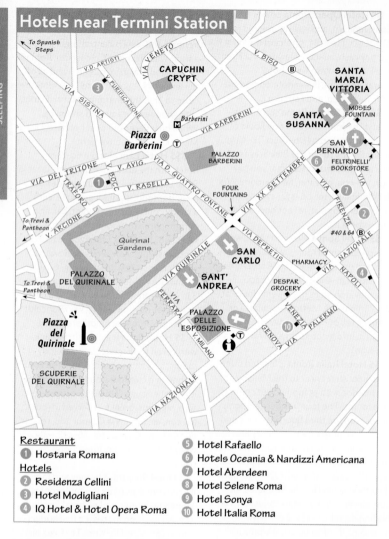

Hotels near Termini Station

Restaurant
1. Hostaria Romana

Hotels
2. Residenza Cellini
3. Hotel Modigliani
4. IQ Hotel & Hotel Opera Roma
5. Hotel Rafaello
6. Hotels Oceania & Nardizzi Americana
7. Hotel Aberdeen
8. Hotel Selene Roma
9. Hotel Sonya
10. Hotel Italia Roma

and others with fans, elevator, small garden and rooftop terrace, 23:00 curfew, near bottom of Via Nazionale at Via Sant'Agata dei Goti 10, bus #40 or #170 from Termini, tel. 06-679-2346, www. casailrosarioroma.it, irodopre@tin.it).

Pantheon Neighborhood

The most romantic ambience is in neighborhoods near the Pantheon. Winding, narrow lanes are filled with foot traffic

and lined with boutique shops and tiny trattorias... Rome at its best. Buses and taxis are the only practical way to connect with other destinations. The atmosphere doesn't come cheap, but this is where you want to be—especially at night.

This neighborhood has two main transportation hubs: Piazza delle Cinque Lune (just north of Piazza Navona) has a TI, a taxi stand, and (just around the corner) handy buses #81 and #87; Largo Argen-

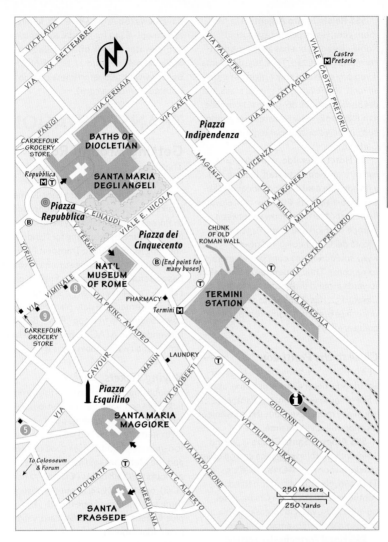

tina has buses to almost everywhere and a taxi stand.

Near Campo de' Fiori

You'll pay a premium (and endure a little extra night noise), but these places are set deep in the tangled back streets near idyllic Campo de' Fiori.

$$$ Casa di Santa Brigida overlooks the elegant Piazza Farnese. With soft-spoken sisters gliding down polished hallways and pearly gates instead of doors, this lavish 20-room convent will make you feel you've entered paradise. If you don't need a double bed, it's worth the splurge just for its ample public spaces and lovely roof terrace (Sb-€120, twin Db-€200, book well in advance, air-con, elevator, tasty €25 dinners, roof garden, plush library, Monserrato 54, tel. 06-6889-2596, www.brigidine.org, piazzafarnese@brigidine.org).

$$$ Relais Teatro Argentina, a six-room gem, is steeped in tasteful old-Rome elegance, but has all the modern comforts (Db-€220, Tb-€265, discounts if you pay cash and stay 3 nights or more, air-con, no elevator, 3 flights of stairs, Via del Sudario 35, tel. 06-9893-1617, mobile 331-198-4708, www.relaisteatroargentina.com, info@relaisteatroargentina.com, Carlotta).

$$ Hotel Smeraldo, with 50 rooms run by a no-nonsense staff, is clean and a reasonable deal in a good location (Sb-€110, Db-€140, Tb-€170, air-con, elevator, flowery roof terrace, midway between Campo de' Fiori and Largo Argentina at Vicolo dei Chiodaroli 9, tel. 06-687-5929, www.smeraldoroma.com, info@smeraldoroma.com). Their **Dipendenza Smeraldo,** 10 yards around the corner at Via dei Chiavari 32, has 16 similar rooms (same price, free breakfast, same reception and contact info).

Close to the Pantheon

These places are buried in the pedestrian-friendly heart of ancient Rome, about a five-minute walk from the Pantheon. You'll pay more here—but the convenient location will save you time.

$$$ Albergo Santa Chiara is big and solid, with marbled elegance and 99 quiet, spacious rooms (Sb-€138, Db-€215, Tb-€260, elevator, air-con, behind Pantheon at Via di Santa Chiara 21, tel. 06-687-2979, www.albergosantachiara.com, info@albergosantachiara.com).

$$$ Hotel Portoghesi is a classic hotel with 27 peaceful, colorful rooms and a delightful roof terrace (Sb-€160, Db-€200, Tb-€260, Qb suite-€300, €30 extra for bigger deluxe room, breakfast on roof, air-con, elevator, Via dei Portoghesi 1, tel. 06-686-4231, www.hotelportoghesiroma.it, info@hotelportoghesiroma.it).

$$$ Hotel Due Torri, on a tiny quiet street, feels professional yet homey, with generous public spaces and 26 rooms—the ones on upper floors are smaller but have views (Sb-€125, Db-€200, family apartment-€240 for 3 and €265 for 4, air-con, elevator, a block off Via della Scrofa at Vicolo del Leonetto 23, tel. 06-6880-6956, www.hotelduetorriroma.com, info@hotelduetorriroma.com).

TRANSPORTATION

Getting Around Rome

The cheap, efficient public transportation system consists primarily of buses, a few trams, and two Metro lines. Rome Walks has produced an orientation video to Rome's transportation system; find it on YouTube by searching for "Understanding Rome's Public Transport." For information, visit www.atac.roma.it, which has a useful route planner in English, or call 06-57003. If you have a smartphone and an international data plan, consider downloading the free app "Roma Bus" by Movenda. The ATAC mobile website has similar info (www.muovi.roma.it).

Buying Tickets

All public transportation uses the same ticket (€1.50), valid for one Metro ride—including transfers underground—plus unlimited city buses and trams during a 100-minute period. Passes good on buses and the Metro are sold in increments of 24 hours (€7), 48 hours (€12.50), 72 hours (€18), one week (€24, about the cost of three taxi rides), and one month (€35, plus €3 for the rechargeable card, valid for a calendar month).

Metro stations rarely have human ticket sellers and the machines are unreliable (it helps to insert your smallest coin first). You can purchase tickets and passes at some newsstands, tobacco shops (*tabacchi*, marked by a black-and-white *T* sign), and major Metro stations and bus stops—but not on board.

Validate your ticket (arrow-side first) at the Metro turnstile or in the machine when you board the bus. It'll return with your expiration time printed on it. At a Metro turnstile, use a transit pass or Roma Pass just like a ticket; on buses and trams, validate your pass only the first time you use it.

Rick's Tip: **Stock up on Metro tickets early** (or buy a Roma Pass) to avoid wasting time searching for an open tobacco shop that sells tickets.

By Metro

The Roman subway system ("Metro") is simple, with two clean, cheap, fast lines—A and B—that intersect at Termini Station. The Metro runs from 5:30 to 23:30 (Fri-Sat until 1:30 in the morning). The C line serves Rome's suburbs and is of little use to tourists.

Rick's Tip: **Beware of pickpockets** when boarding, while on board, and when leaving buses and subways. To experience less crowding and commotion—and less risk—**wait for the end cars** of a subway rather than boarding the middle cars.

The following stops are helpful:

Termini (intersection of lines A and B): Termini Station, shuttle train to airport, National Museum of Rome, and recommended hotels

Repubblica (line A): Via Nazionale and recommended hotels

Barberini (line A): Capuchin Crypt and Trevi Fountain

Spagna (line A): Spanish Steps, classy shopping area, and Borghese Gallery

Flaminio (line A): Piazza del Popolo—the start of my "Dolce Vita Stroll" down Via del Corso, and easy buses to Borghese Gallery

Ottaviano (line A): St. Peter's Basilica, Vatican Museums, and recommended hotels

Tiburtina (line B): Tiburtina train and bus station (direction: Rebibbia; trains going in the direction of Conca d'Oro/

Jonio do not stop at Tiburtina)

Colosseo (line B): Colosseum, Roman Forum, and recommended hotels

San Giovanni (line B): Church of San Giovanni in Laterano

Piramide (line B): Trains to Ostia Antica

By Bus

The Metro is handy, but it won't get you everywhere—take the bus (or tram). Bus routes are clearly listed at the stops. TIs usually don't have bus maps, but with some knowledge of major stops, you won't necessarily need one.

Regular bus lines start running about 5:30, and during the day run every 10-15 minutes or so. After 23:30 (and sometimes earlier) and on Sundays, buses are less frequent. Night buses are marked with an *N* and an owl symbol on the bus-stop signs. The exact frequency of various bus routes is difficult to predict (and not printed at bus stops). At major stops, an electronic board shows the number of minutes until the next buses arrive.

These are the major bus routes:

Bus #64: Links Termini Station with the Vatican, stopping at Piazza della Repubblica (sights), Via Nazionale (recommended hotels), Piazza Venezia (near Forum), Largo Argentina (near Pantheon and Campo de' Fiori), St. Peter's Basilica (get off just past the tunnel), and San Pietro Station.

Bus #40: This express bus mostly follows the #64 route but has fewer

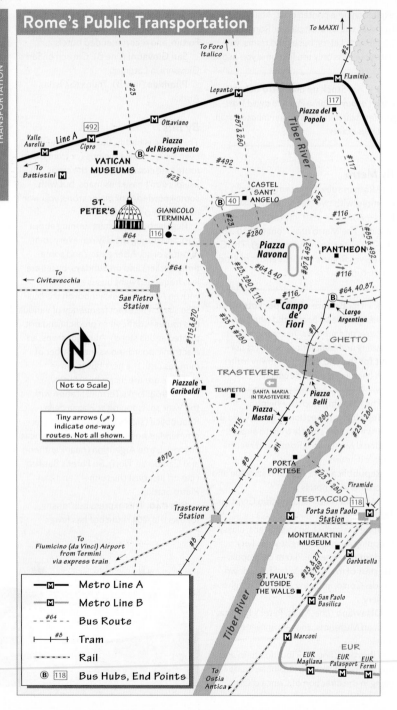

Rome's Public Transportation

To MAXXI

#2

Flaminio

To Foro
Italico

Lepanto

117

Piazza del
Popolo

#117

Tiber River

Ottaviano

492

Line A

Valle
Aurelia

Cipro

To
Battistini

VATICAN
MUSEUMS

Piazza
del Risorgimento

#492

#23

CASTEL
SANT'
ANGELO

#87 & 280

#87

#116

#85 & 492

ST.
PETER'S

GIANICOLO
TERMINAL

#64

116

#25

#280

Piazza
Navona

#87 & 492

PANTHEON

#116

To
Civitavecchia

#64

San Pietro
Station

#23, 280 & 116

#64 & 40

#116

Campo
de'
Fiori

#64, 40, 87,

Largo
Argentina

GHETTO

#115 & 870

#23 & 280

#8

N

Not to Scale

Tiny arrows (↗)
indicate one-way
routes. Not all shown.

TRASTEVERE

SANTA MARIA
IN TRASTEVERE

Piazzale
Garibaldi

TEMPIETTO

Piazza
Mastai

Piazza
Belli

#23 & 280

#23 & 280

#115

#23 & 280

#870

#8

#8

PORTA
PORTESE

Piramide

#23 & 280

TESTACCIO

118

Trastevere
Station

#8

To
Fiumicino (da Vinci) Airport
from Termini
via express train

Porta San Paolo
Station

MONTEMARTINI
MUSEUM

Garbatella

ST. PAUL'S
OUTSIDE
THE WALLS

#25 & 271
& 769

San Paolo
Basilica

Tiber River

Marconi

EUR

EUR
Magliana

EUR
Palasport

EUR
Fermi

To
Ostia
Antica

─M─	**Metro Line A**
─M─	**Metro Line B**
--- #64	**Bus Route**
⊢—#8—⊢	**Tram**
------	**Rail**
Ⓑ 118	**Bus Hubs, End Points**

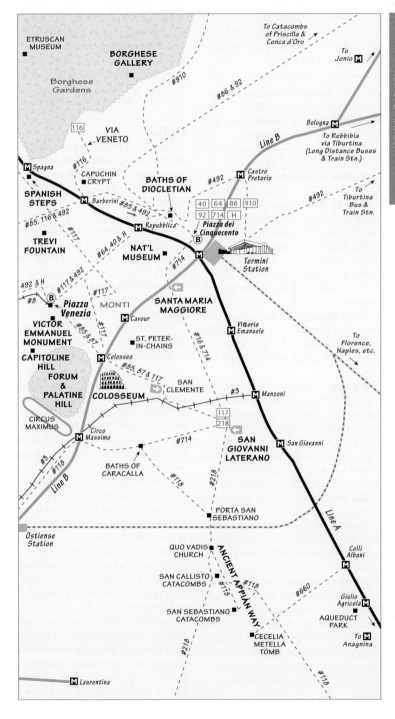

stops and fewer crowds. It ends near Castel Sant'Angelo (Hadrian's Tomb, a 10-minute walk from St. Peter's) on the Vatican side of the river.

Rick's Tip: Buses #64 and #40 are popular with tourists and pickpockets. If one bus is packed, there's likely a second one on its tail with fewer crowds and thieves.

Other useful routes include:

Bus #16: Termini Station, Santa Maria Maggiore, and San Giovanni in Laterano.

Bus #49: Piazza Cavour/Castel Sant'Angelo, Piazza Risorgimento (Vatican), and Vatican Museums.

Bus #62: Largo Argentina to near St. Peter's Square and Castel Sant'Angelo.

Bus #81: San Giovanni in Laterano, Largo Argentina, and Piazza Risorgimento (Vatican).

Buses #85 and #87: Piazza Navona (#87 only), Pantheon, Via del Corso (#85 only), Piazza Venezia, Forum, Colosseum, San Clemente, and San Giovanni in Laterano.

Bus #492: Travels east-west across the city, connecting Tiburtina (train and bus stations), Largo Santa Susanna (near Piazza della Repubblica), Piazza Barberini, Piazza Venezia, Largo Argentina (near Pantheon and Campo de' Fiori), Piazza Cavour (Castel Sant'Angelo), and Piazza Risorgimento (St. Peter's Basilica and Vatican).

Bus #714: Termini Station, Santa Maria Maggiore, and San Giovanni in Laterano.

Tram #3: This handy tram zips from the Colosseum to the Etruscan Museum in one direction, and to Trastevere in the other.

Elettrico Minibuses: Two elettrico minibuses wind through the narrow streets of old neighborhoods. Elettrico #117 connects San Giovanni in Laterano, Colosseo, Via dei Serpenti, Trevi Fountain, Piazza di Spagna, and Piazza del Popolo—and vice versa. Where Via del Corso hits Piazza del Popolo, a #117 is usually parked and

ready to go. Elettrico #116 (which may be discontinued) runs through the medieval core of Rome: Ponte Vittorio Emanuele II (near Castel Sant'Angelo, on the Vatican side of Rome) to Campo de' Fiori, near the Pantheon and Piazza Navona, Piazza Barberini, and the Villa Borghese Gardens.

By Taxi

Taxis in Rome are reasonable and useful for efficient sightseeing. Taxis start at €3, then charge about €1.50 per kilometer (surcharges: €1.50 on Sun, €3.50 for nighttime hours of 22:00-7:00, one regular suitcase or bag rides free, tip by rounding up—€1 or so). Sample fares: Termini area to Vatican-€11; Termini area to Colosseum-€7; Termini area to the Borghese Gallery-€8 (or look up your route at www.worldtaximeter.com). Three or four companions with more money than time should taxi almost everywhere.

You can wave a taxi down, but an available one (with the sign on top illuminated) can be tough to find, especially at night. Find the nearest taxi stand (many are marked on this book's maps) or ask a passerby or a clerk in a shop, "Dov'è una fermata dei taxi?" (doh-VEH OO-nah fehr-MAH-tah DEH-ee TAHK-see). Easiest of all, have your hotelier or restaurateur call a taxi for you. The meter starts when the call is received. To call a cab on your own, dial 06-3570, 06-4994, or 06-6645, or use the official city taxi line, 06-0609; they'll ask for an Italian phone number (give them your mobile number or your hotel's).

Beware of corrupt taxis, including rip-off "express taxis" at the train station or airport. Only use official Rome taxis. They're white, with a taxi sign on the roof and a maroon logo on the door that reads Roma Capitale. When you get in, make sure the meter (tassametro) is turned on. If the meter isn't on, get out and hail another cab. Check that the meter is reset to the basic drop charge (should be around €3, or around €5 if you phoned for the taxi). Some meters show both the fare and the time elapsed during the ride, and some tourists—mistaking the time for the fare—pay more than the fair meter rate. Also, keep an eye on the fare on the meter as you near your destination; some cabbies turn the meter off instantly when they stop and tell you a higher price.

By law, every cab must display a multilingual official price chart—usually on the back of the seat in front of you. If the fare doesn't seem right, point to the chart and ask the cabbie to explain it.

Rick's Tip: *A* **common cabbie scam** *is to take your €20 note, drop it, and pick up a €5 note (similar color), claiming that's what you gave him. Pay in small bills; if you only have a large bill, show it to the cabbie as you state its face value.*

Arriving and Departing
Termini Train Station

Termini, Rome's main train station, is a buffet of tourist services. Along track 24, about 100 yards down, you'll find the **TI** (daily 8:00-19:30) and **car rental** desks. The **baggage storage** (deposito bagagli) is downstairs, hiding down the long corridor past the bathrooms, under track 24 and the TI. A snack bar and a good self-service **cafeteria** are perched above the ticket windows, accessible from the side closest to track 24 (daily 11:00-22:30). Elsewhere in the station are **ATMs and late-hours banks.**

Termini is a major transit hub. Local **Metro lines A and B** intersect downstairs at Termini Metro station. **Buses** leave from the square directly in front of the station. Hop-on, hop-off buses and those going to the airport leave from the north side of the station. The **Leonardo Express train** to Fiumicino Airport runs from track 23 or 24. **Taxis** queue in front and outside exits on both the north and south sides; if there's a long taxi line in front, try a side exit instead.

Rick's Tip: **Shady characters** *linger around the station, especially* **near ticket machines.** *Some offer help for a "tip"; others have official-looking business cards.* **Avoid anybody selling anything** *unless they're in a legitimate shop at the station. There are no official porters;* **carry your own bags.**

The banks of Trenitalia's user-friendly ticket machines (marked *Biglietto Veloce/ Fast Ticket*) are handy, but cover Italian destinations only. They take euros and credit cards, display schedules, issue tickets, and even make reservations for rail pass holders (found under the "Global Pass" ticket type).

TRAIN CONNECTIONS FROM TERMINI STATION

The customer service and ticket windows in the station's main hall (out in the big atrium, beyond the head of the tracks) can be jammed with travelers—take a number and wait. Handy red info kiosks are located near the head of the tracks. Ticket machines can also be helpful for checking schedules. Most trains departing from Termini are operated by Italy's state rail company, Trenitalia, though a few Italo trains also use the station (for more on the privately run Italo, see page 568 and www.italotreno.it). Unless otherwise specified, the following connections are for Trenitalia.

Rick's Tip: *Minimize your time in a train station—if you're not near a station,* **it's quicker to get tickets and train info from travel agencies or online.**

From Rome by Train to: Venice (roughly hourly, 3.5 hours, overnight possible), **Florence** (2-3/hour, 1.5 hours, some stop at Orvieto en route), **Siena** (1-2/hour, 1 change, 3-4 hours), **Orvieto** (roughly hourly, 1-1.5 hours), **Assisi** (nearly hourly, 2-3.5 hours, 5 direct, most others change in Foligno), **Pisa** (2/hour, 3-4 hours, many change in Florence), **Milan** (2-3/hour, 3-3.5 hours), **Milan's Malpensa Airport** (hourly, 5 hours, change in Milan), **Naples** (Trenitalia: 2-4/hour, 1 hour on Frecciarossa, otherwise 2 hours; Italo: 8/day, 1 hour).

Tiburtina Train and Bus Station

The smaller Tiburtina station (which also has a bus station) is located in the city's northeast corner. Tiburtina has high-speed rail, including some Frecce trains and the private Italo service. A separate "Casa Italo" area has dedicated service counters, red ticket machines, and a small waiting area (in the upper part of the station, across from track 23). The station also has slower trains and some night trains (from Milan and Venice).

Tiburtina is known as a hub for bus service all across Italy (including a night bus to Fiumicino Airport). **Buses** depart from the piazza in front of the station. Ticket offices are located in the piazza and around the corner on Circonvallazione Nomentana (just beyond the elevated freeway).

Tiburtina is on **Metro line B,** with easy connections to Termini (a straight shot, four stops away) and the entire Metro system (when going to Tiburtina, Metro line B splits—you want a train signed *Rebibbia*). Or take **bus #492** from Tiburtina to various city-center stops (such as Piazza Barberini, Piazza Venezia, and Piazza Navona) and the Vatican neighborhood (as you emerge from the station, the bus stop is to the left).

TRAIN AND BUS CONNECTIONS FROM TRIBUTINA STATION
From Rome by Train to: Florence (2-4/hour, 1.5 hours), **Milan** (hourly, 3-3.5 hours, overnight possible), **Venice** (almost hourly, 3.5 hours, overnight possible), **Assisi** (nearly hourly, 2-3.5 hours, 5 direct, most others change in Foligno), **Naples** (Trenitalia: almost hourly, 1.5 hours; Italo: at least hourly, 1-1.5 hours).

From Rome by Bus to: Assisi (2/day,

3 hours—the train makes more sense), **Siena** (9/day, 3 hours), **Sorrento** (1-2/day, 4 hours; this is a cheap and easy way to go straight to Sorrento, buy tickets at Ticket Bus at Tiburtina, other travel agencies, or on board for a €3 surcharge; tel. 080-579-0111).

By Plane

Rome has two airports: Fiumicino and the smaller Ciampino.

FIUMICINO AIRPORT

Rome's major airport, **Fiumicino** is manageable (a.k.a. Leonardo da Vinci, airport code: FCO, www.adr.it). Terminals T1, T2, and T3 are all under one roof—walkable end to end in 20 minutes. T5 is a separate building requiring a short shuttle trip. (T4 is still being built.) The T1-2-3 complex has a TI (daily 8:00-19:30, in T3), ATMs, banks, luggage storage, shops, and bars. For airport info, call 06-65951. To inquire about flights, call 06-6595-3640.

To get from the airport to downtown, take the direct **Leonardo Express train** to **Termini train station** (30 minutes for €14). Trains run twice hourly in both directions from roughly 6:00 to 23:00. From the airport's arrival gate, follow signs to the train icon or *Stazione/Railway Station*. Buy your ticket from a machine, the Biglietteria office, or a newsstand near the platform; then validate it in a green or yellow machine near the track. Board the train going to the central "Roma Termini" station, not "Roma Orte" or others.

Trains from Termini train station to the airport depart at about :05 and :35 past each hour, usually from track 23 or 24. Check the departure boards for "Fiumicino Aeroporto" and confirm with an official on the platform that the train is indeed going to the airport (€14, buy ticket from any tobacco shop or a newsstand in the station, or at the self-service machines, Termini-Fiumicino trains run 5:35-22:35). Direct flights to the US usually depart from T5.

Allow lots of time going to and from the airport; there's a fair amount of transportation involved. Flying to the US involves an extra level of security—plan on getting to the airport even earlier than normal (2.5 hours ahead of your flight).

Buses, including Terravision (www.terravision.eu), SIT (www.sitbusshuttle.com), and also T.A.M (www.tambus.it), connect Fiumicino and Termini train station, departing roughly every 40 minutes. While cheaper than the train (about €5 one-way), buses take twice as long (about an hour). The Terravision bus also stops near the Vatican. At the airport, the companies' desks line up in T3, near the entrance to the train station.

Airport Shuttle vans can be economical for one or two people. It's cheaper to go from the airport to downtown (around €10-15). To get from your hotel to the airport, consider Rome Airport Shuttle (€25/1 person, extra people-€6 each, by reservation only, tel. 06-4201-4507, www.airportshuttle.it).

Your hotelier can arrange a taxi or private car service to the airport at any hour. A **taxi** between Fiumicino and downtown Rome takes 45 minutes in normal traffic and costs €48. (Add a tip for good service.) Cabbies not based in Rome or Fiumicino are allowed to charge €70. It's best to use a white Rome city cab (with a roof-top taxi sign and a maroon *Roma Capitale* logo on the door); the airport fare should be posted on the door. Confirm the price before you get in. If your Roman cabbie tries to overcharge you, state the correct price and say, *"È la legge"* (ay lah LEJ-jay; which means, "It's the law"), and they should back off.

CIAMPINO AIRPORT

Rome's smaller airport (tel. 06-6595-9515) handles charter flights and some budget airlines (including most Ryanair flights).

Various **bus** companies—including Cotral, Terravision, and SIT—will take you to Rome's Termini train station (about €5 and 2/hour for each company, 45 minutes). Cotral also runs a quicker route (25 minutes) from the airport to the Anagnina Metro stop, where you can connect by Metro to the stop nearest your hotel (departs every 40 minutes).

The fixed price for any official **taxi** (with the maroon *"Roma Capitale"* logo on the door) is €30 to downtown (within the old city walls, including most of my recommended hotels).

Rick's Tip: *A car is a worthless headache in Rome. To save money and a pile of stress,* **park in the hill town of Orvieto** *at the huge, easy, and relatively safe lot behind the train station (follow P signs from autostrada) and catch the train to Rome (roughly hourly, 1-1.5 hours). Or, if Rome is the first stop of your trip,* **enjoy the city car-free,** *then take the train to Orvieto and rent a car there.*

By Car

I don't advise driving into or within Rome, but if you need to, here's how: Rome's ring road, the Grande Raccordo Anulare, encircles the city, with spokes that lead into the center. Entering from the north, leave the autostrada at the Settebagni exit. Following Via Salaria and black-and-white *Centro* signs, work your way doggedly into the Roman thick of things. This will take you along the Villa Borghese Gardens and dump you right on Via Veneto in downtown Rome. Avoid rush hour and drive defensively: Roman cars stay in their lanes like rocks in an avalanche.

Park your car in a safe place during your stay. Get advice from your hotelier, use Villa Borghese's handy underground garage (€24/day, Metro: Spagna), or park at Tiburtina Station (€1/hour, www.atac.roma.it) and take a 10-minute ride on Metro line B into the center.

Florence

Florence is the birthplace of the Renaissance and the modern world. It's geographically small but culturally rich—containing more artistic masterpieces per square mile than anyplace else. In a single day, you can look Michelangelo's *David* in the eyes, fall under the seductive sway of Botticelli's *Birth of Venus,* and climb the modern world's first dome, which still dominates the skyline.

A cosmopolitan vibe courses through the city's narrow lanes. You'll encounter children licking gelato, students riding Vespas, supermodels wearing Gucci fashions, and artisans sipping Chianti—Florence has long been perfecting the art of civilized living.

FLORENCE IN 2 DAYS

Compact Florence is packed with sights, but crowds and long lines can ruin your day's agenda. To maximize your time, either reserve the top two sights—Accademia (Michelangelo's *David*) and Uffizi Gallery (Renaissance paintings), or get a pricey Firenze Card that allows you to skip the lines. Avoid both sights on Monday when they're closed, and on the first Sunday of the month, when they're free but impossibly crowded. Some sights such as the Bargello close early and on Sundays or Mondays.

Day 1: In the cool of the morning, take my Renaissance Walk. Afterwards, depending on your interests, choose among Florence's many sights: the Bargello (best statues), Medici Chapels (Michelangelo statues), Santa Maria Novella (Masaccio's 3-D painting), Palazzo Vecchio (Medici palace), Santa Croce Church (famous tombs), Galileo Science Museum, Pitti Palace (art), and Brancacci Chapel (more Masaccio). For lunch, grab a quick bite between sights; you have many options, including Mercato Centrale's upscale, upstairs food hall.

Around 16:30 when crowds die down, see the Uffizi Gallery's unforgettable paintings.

On any evening: Linger over dinner. Take a stroll, gelato in hand. Or take a taxi or bus to Piazzale Michelangelo for spectacular city views, and walk back into town for dinner. You can sightsee late at some sights, attend a concert at a church, or drop by a wine bar.

Day 2: See the Accademia (*David*) and visit the nearby Museum of San Marco (Fra Angelico's art). Then hit the street markets, wander, or do more museum-going. Stroll to the river and cross the historic bridge, Ponte Vecchio, to the Oltrarno neighborhood for dinner.

ORIENTATION

Florence (pop. 380,000) can be intense. Prepare for scorching summer heat, crowded lanes and sidewalks, slick pickpockets, few WCs, steep prices, and long lines. The best of the city lies on the north bank of the Arno River. The main sights cluster around the dome of the cathedral (Duomo). Everything is within a 20-minute walk of the train station, cathedral, or Ponte Vecchio (Old Bridge). The less famous but more characteristic Oltrarno area (south bank) is just over the bridge. Here's a neighborhood-by-neighborhood rundown:

Historic Core: The Duomo—with its iconic, towering dome—is the visual and geographical center of Florence; all other sights radiate out from here. The Duomo sits at the northeast corner of the oblong, grid-planned old town. At the southeast corner is Piazza della Signoria—marked by the tower of the Palazzo Vecchio (city hall) and adjacent Uffizi Gallery, with the Galileo Science Museum tucked just behind it. These two main landmarks— the Duomo and Piazza della Signoria—are connected by the wide, pedestrianized, heavily tourist-trod Via de' Calzaiuoli, which bisects the old Roman town. To the west is a glitzy shopping zone (on the streets near Piazza della Repubblica), and to the east is a characteristic web of narrow lanes. This central axis—Via de' Calzaiuoli—is the spine for Florentine sightseeing and the route of my self-guided Renaissance Walk.

Rick's Tip: Don't drive into the city center. Don't even try it. Florence's traffic-reduction system is confusing even to locals. If you don't have a permit, you'll get a €100 traffic ticket in the mail. The no-go zone is confusing; several streets are classified ZTL ("limited traffic zone") at only certain times of day.

North of the Duomo: Via Cavour runs north from the Duomo through a non-descript urban zone to the **Accademia,** with Michelangelo's *David,* and nearby, the Museum of San Marco. The western part clusters around the **Basilica of San Lorenzo,** with its Medici Chapels, and (a block north) Mercato Centrale, with the vendor stalls of San Lorenzo Market. The streets surrounding Mercato Centrale (especially the pedestrianized Via Faenza) teem with midrange and budget hotels, and trattorias catering to out-of-towners. This touristy area is convenient, but insulated from authentic Florence.

West of the Duomo: Northwest of the historic core, things get more urban and dreary. This area, dominated by the **train station** and **Church of Santa Maria Novella,** specializes in inexpensive hotels and characteristic eateries. Closer to the river (especially around Palazzo Strozzi) is a posh shopping zone; more affordable shops line Via del Parione and Borgo Ognissanti.

East of the Duomo: Tourists make the 10-minute trek from Piazza della Signoria east to **Piazza Santa Croce,** facing the landmark Santa Croce Church. Along the way—effectively across the street from the old town—is the Bargello, filling a former police station with some of Florence's best sculptures.

South of the River: The neighborhood called the **Oltrarno neighborhood** (literally the "other side of the Arno River") opens up just across Ponte Vecchio from the main tourist zone. In the middle of the Oltrarno is the giant Pitti Palace and surrounding gardens (Boboli and Bardini). To the west of the palace is the lavishly frescoed Brancacci Chapel (inside the Church of Santa Maria del Carmine). To the east of the palace is Piazzale Michelangelo, perched high upon the hill, with Florence's most popular viewpoint. Wandering through the Oltrarno, you may catch glimpses of a time before tourism— artisans still have workshops here, and open their doors to passing visitors.

FLORENCE AT A GLANCE

▲▲▲**Duomo Museum** Underrated cathedral museum with sculptures. **Hours:** Daily 10:00-19:00. See page 594.

▲▲▲**Accademia** Michelangelo's *David* and powerful (unfinished) *Prisoners*. Reserve ahead or get a Firenze Card. **Hours:** Tue-Sun 8:15-18:50, closed Mon. See page 595.

▲▲▲**Uffizi Gallery** Greatest collection of Italian paintings anywhere. Reserve well in advance or get a Firenze Card. **Hours:** Tue-Sun 8:15-18:35, closed Mon. See page 597.

▲▲▲**Bargello** Underappreciated sculpture museum with Michelangelo, Donatello, and Medici treasures. **Hours:** Tue-Sat 8:15-17:00, until 13:50 if no special exhibits; also open second and fourth Mon and first, third, and fifth Sun of each month. See page 601.

▲▲**Duomo** Gothic cathedral with colorful facade and the first dome built since ancient Roman times. **Hours:** Mon-Fri 10:00-17:00, Thu until 16:00 May and Oct, until 16:30 Nov-April; Sat 10:00-16:45, Sun 13:30-16:45. See page 590.

▲▲**Museum of San Marco** Best collection anywhere of artwork by the early Renaissance master Fra Angelico. **Hours:** Tue-Fri 8:15-13:50, Sat 8:15-16:50; also open 8:15-13:50 on first, third, and fifth Mon and 8:15-16:50 on second and fourth Sun of each month. See page 596.

▲▲**Medici Chapels** Tombs of Florence's great ruling family, designed and carved by Michelangelo. **Hours:** April-Oct Tue-Sat 8:15-16:50, Nov-March Tue-Sat 8:15-13:50; also open second and fourth Mon and first, third, and fifth Sun of each month. See page 596.

▲▲**Palazzo Vecchio** Fortified palace, once the home of the Medici family, wallpapered with history. **Hours:** Museum open April-Sept Fri-

Wed 9:00-24:00, Thu 9:00-14:00; Oct-March Fri-Wed 9:00-19:00, Thu 9:00-14:00; tower keeps similar but shorter hours. See page 600.

▲▲**Galileo Science Museum** Fascinating old clocks, telescopes, maps, and three of Galileo's fingers. **Hours:** Wed-Mon 9:30-18:00, Tue 9:30-13:00. See page 600.

▲▲**Santa Croce Church** Precious art, tombs of famous Florentines, and Brunelleschi's Pazzi Chapel in 14th-century church. **Hours:** Mon-Sat 9:30-17:30, Sun 14:00-17:30. See page 601.

▲▲**Church of Santa Maria Novella** Thirteenth-century Dominican church with Masaccio's famous 3-D painting. **Hours:** Mon-Thu 9:00-17:30, Fri 11:00-17:30, Sat 9:00-17:00, Sun 12:00-17:00 July-Sept (from 13:00 Oct-June). See page 602.

▲▲**Pitti Palace** Several museums in lavish palace plus sprawling Boboli and Bardini Gardens. **Hours:** Palatine Gallery, Royal Apartments, and Gallery of Modern Art—Tue-Sun 8:15-18:50, closed Mon; Boboli and Bardini Gardens, Costume Gallery, Argenti/Silverworks Museum, and Porcelain Museum—daily June-Aug 8:15-19:30, April-May and Sept-Oct 8:15-18:30, March 8:15-17:30, Nov-Feb 8:15-16:30, closed first and last Mon of each month. See page 603.

▲▲**Brancacci Chapel** Works of Masaccio, early Renaissance master who reinvented perspective. **Hours:** Mon and Wed-Sat 10:00-17:00, Sun 13:00-17:00, closed Tue. Reservations required, though often available on the spot. See page 605.

▲**Mercato Centrale** Bustling covered market with picnic fare on the ground floor and an upscale foodie court upstairs. **Hours:** Produce—Mon-Fri 7:00-14:00, Sat 7:00-17:00, closed Sun; food court—daily 10:00-24:00. See page 596.

▲**Ponte Vecchio** Famous bridge lined with gold and silver shops. **Hours:** Bridge always open. See page 589.

▲**Climbing the Duomo's Dome** Grand view into the cathedral, close-up of dome architecture, and, after 463 steps, a glorious city vista. **Hours:** Mon-Fri 8:30-19:00, Sat 8:30-17:40, Sun 13:00-16:40. See page 591.

▲**Campanile** Bell tower with views similar to Duomo's, 50 fewer steps, and shorter lines. **Hours:** Daily 8:30-19:30. See page 591.

▲**Baptistery** Bronze doors fit to be the gates of paradise. **Hours:** Doors always viewable; interior open Mon-Sat 11:15-19:00 except first Sat of each month 8:30-14:00, Sun 8:30-14:00. See page 591.

▲**Piazzale Michelangelo** Hilltop square with stunning view of Duomo and Florence. **Hours:** Always open. See page 606.

Tourist Information

The city TI has three branches. The crowded main branch is across the square from the **train station** (Mon-Sat 9:00-19:00, Sun 9:00-14:00; with your back to tracks, exit the station—it's 100 yards away, near the corner of the church at Piazza della Stazione 4; tel. 055-212-245, www.firenzeturismo.it). Upstairs from this branch, drop by the easy-to-miss "Experience Florence" visitors center, with big touch screens to help you virtually explore the city and plan an itinerary, and a well-produced 3-D movie about the city, offering evocative slices of Florentine life and lingering images of the big landmarks (free, 13 minutes, English subtitles).

The smaller branch is centrally located at **Piazza del Duomo,** at the west corner of Via de' Calzaiuoli (Mon-Sat 9:00-19:00, Sun 9:00-14:00, inside the loggia, tel. 055-288-496). They also have a branch at the **airport.**

A separate TI, which covers both the city and the greater province of Florence, can be less crowded and more helpful. It's a couple of blocks **north of the Duomo** (Mon-Fri 9:00-13:00, closed Sat-Sun, at Via Cavour 1 red, tel. 055-290-832).

At any TI, you'll find free, handy resources in English: the **Firenze Info** booklet, **The Places of Interest,** the monthly **Florence & Tuscany News,** and the **Florence Newspaper** (www.the florencenewspaper.com).

Sightseeing Pass and Advance Reservations
Firenze Card

The **Firenze Card** is pricey (€72) but convenient. This three-day sightseeing pass gives you admission to many of Florence's sights, including the Uffizi Gallery and Accademia. Just as important, it lets you skip the ticket-buying lines without needing to make reservations.

Simply go to the entrance at a covered sight (look for the Firenze Card logo), show the card, and you'll be let in. At some sights, you must first present your card at the ticket booth or info desk to get a physical ticket before proceeding to the entrance.

Cost and Coverage: The Firenze Card costs €72 and is valid for 72 hours from when you validate it at your first museum (e.g., Tue at 15:00 until Fri at 15:00). Validate your card only when you're ready to tackle the covered sights on three consecutive days. Make sure the sights you want to visit will be open (some sights are closed Sun or Mon; for details, see the "Daily Reminder" on page 578).

The Firenze Card covers the regular admission price as well as any special-exhibit surcharges, and is good for one visit per sight.

To make the card pay for itself, you'd need to see all of these sights within three days—an ambitious plan: the Uffizi, Accademia, Bargello, Palazzo Vecchio, Medici Chapels, Museum of San Marco, Duomo sights, and Pitti Palace's Palatine Gallery and Royal Apartments. But the real value of the card is that you can spend more time sightseeing rather than waiting in ticket-buying lines.

The card covers every sight I listed except for Pitti Palace's Bardini Gardens. For a complete list of included sights, see www.firenzecard.it. Don't confuse this card with the lesser Firenze PASSport.

You can **buy the Firenze Card** at either of two TIs (the one across from the train station or at Via Cavour 1 red—a couple of blocks north of the Duomo) or at several participating sights: the Uffizi Gallery's door #2 (enter to the left of the ticket-buying line), the back entrance of the Church of Santa Maria Novella, the Bargello, Palazzo Vecchio, and the Brancacci Chapel. Lines are shortest at the Via Cavour TI (credit cards only) and Church of Santa Maria Novella (facing the train station, at Piazza della Stazione 4); if you're doing the Uffizi first, door #2 is relatively quick. Don't bother buying the card online, as you have to go to one of these desks to swap the voucher for the actual pass. The Firenze Card is not shareable, and there are no family or senior discounts.

Children under 18 are allowed free into any state museum in Italy, and into any municipal museum in Florence. However, at the Uffizi and Accademia, if they want to skip the lines with their Firenze Card-holding parents, children still must (technically) pay the €4 "reservation fee" (which can be paid on the spot—no need to reserve ahead). Enforcement of this policy varies.

Advance Reservations

If you only want to see the Accademia and Uffizi, you can skip the Firenze Card and instead make **reservations** for these two top sights, ideally as soon as you know when you'll be in town. From April through October and on weekends year-round, the sights can be crowded even late in the day (from Nov through March, reservations aren't as critical—you can usually enter without significant lines after 16:00). Reservations are not possible on the first Sunday of the month, when the museums are free and very busy.

You can also make reservations for several other Florence sights—including the Bargello, Medici Chapels, and Pitti Palace—though they're unnecessary. The Brancacci Chapel officially requires a reservation, but it's usually possible to get one on the spot.

There are several ways to make reservations for the **Accademia** and **Uffizi:**

Online: Book and pay for your Accademia or Uffizi visit via the city's official site. You'll receive an order confirmation email, which is followed shortly by a voucher email. Bring your voucher to the ticket desk to swap for an actual ticket (€4/ticket reservation fee, www.firenze musei.it—click on "B-ticket").

Pricey middleman sites—such as www. uffizi.com and www.tickitaly.com—are generally reliable and more user-friendly than the official site, but their booking fees run about €10 per ticket. (If ordering from these broker sites, don't confuse Florence's Accademia with Venice's gallery of the same name.)

By Phone: From a US phone, dial 011-39-055-294-883, or from an Italian phone call 055-294-883. When you get through, an English-speaking operator talks you through the process within a few minutes, and you'll end up with an entry time and a confirmation number. Present your confirmation number at the museum and pay for your ticket. You pay only for the tickets you pick up; for example, if you reserved two tickets, but only you can go, you'll pay for just one ticket (€4/ticket reservation fee; booking office open Mon-Fri 8:30-18:30, Sat 8:30-12:30, closed Sun).

Through Your Hotel: Some hoteliers will make museum reservations (for a

You can avoid waiting in line...

...if you make advance reservations.

Daily Reminder

SUNDAY: The Duomo's dome opens late (13:00-16:40), and the Baptistery's interior closes early, at 14:00. The ground-floor market stalls in Mercato Centrale are closed, but the popular foodie restaurants upstairs are open.

A few sights are open only in the afternoon: Duomo (13:30-16:45), Santa Croce Church (14:00-17:30), Brancacci Chapel (13:00-17:00), and Church of Santa Maria Novella (12:00-17:00, from 13:00 Oct-June).

The Bargello and the Medici Chapels close on the second and fourth Sundays of the month. The Museum of San Marco is closed on the first, third, and fifth Sundays.

The following sights are free and crowded on the first Sunday of the month (when reservations aren't available): Uffizi, Accademia, Pitti Palace, Bargello, Medici Chapels, and Museum of San Marco.

MONDAY: The biggies are closed, including the Accademia (*David*) and Uffizi Gallery, as well as Pitti Palace's Palatine Gallery, Royal Apartments, and Gallery of Modern Art.

The Museum of San Marco closes on the second and fourth Mondays. Pitti Palace's Boboli and Bardini Gardens, Costume Gallery, Argenti/Silverworks Museum, and Porcelain Museum close on the first and last Mondays of the month. The Bargello and Medici Chapels are closed on the first, third, and fifth Mondays. San Lorenzo Market is closed Mondays in winter.

Target these sights on Mondays: the Duomo and its dome, Campanile, Baptistery, Brancacci Chapel, Mercato Centrale, Galileo Science Museum, and churches (including Santa Croce and Santa Maria Novella).

TUESDAY: The Brancacci Chapel is closed. The Galileo Science Museum closes early (13:00).

small fee) for guests who request this service when they book their room.

Private Tour: Various tour companies—including the ones listed on the next page—offer tours that include a reserved museum admission.

Last-Minute Strategies: If you arrive without a reservation, call the reservation number (tel. 055-294-883); ask your hotelier for help; or head to a booking window, either at Orsanmichele Church (daily 9:00-16:00, closed Sun off-season, along Via de' Calzaiuoli) or at My Accademia Libreria bookstore across from the Accademia's exit (Tue-Sun 8:15-17:30, closed Mon, Via Ricasoli 105 red). It's also possible to ask at the Uffizi's ticket office if they have any short-notice reserva-

tions available (use door #2 and skirt to the left of the long ticket-buying line). Any of these options will cost you the €4 reservation fee. Because both museums are closed on Mondays, the hardest day to snare last-minute, same-day reservations is Tuesday. If you've exhausted these options without success, remember you can buy a Firenze Card or take a private tour to see the sights.

The Duomo Combo-Ticket

While the Duomo itself is free to enter, several related sights are all covered by a single €15 **combo-ticket:** the Baptistery, dome climb, Campanile, and Duomo Museum. Only get this combo-ticket if you don't have a Firenze Card (which

WEDNESDAY: All sights are open.

THURSDAY: All sights are open, though these close early: Palazzo Vecchio (14:00) and off-season, the Duomo (16:00 May and Oct, 16:30 Nov-April).

FRIDAY: All sights are open.

SATURDAY: All sights are open, but the Duomo's dome closes earlier than usual, at 17:40.

EARLY-CLOSING WARNING: Some of Florence's sights close surprisingly early most days, as early as 13:50 for the following sights—the Bargello (unless it's hosting a special exhibit, when it closes at 17:00), Medici Chapels (early closure off-season only), and the Museum of San Marco (on weekdays only). Mercato Centrale's ground floor closes at 14:00 (except in winter, when it stays open until 17:00 on Sat).

LATE-HOURS RELIEF: The Accademia and Pitti Palace's Palatine Gallery, Royal Apartments, and Gallery of Modern Art are open until 18:50 (and the Uffizi until 18:35) daily except Monday.

Several sights are open until 19:00 on certain days: the Duomo's dome (Mon-Fri), the Baptistery (Mon-Sat, except first Sat of month until 14:00), and the Lorenzo Market (daily, but closed Mon in winter).

These sights are open until 19:30: Campanile (daily), and in summer, Pitti Palace's Boboli and Bardini Gardens (daily except some Mon, June-Aug only). Mercato Nuovo (for shoppers) is open long hours daily.

In summer (April-Sept), the best late-hours sightseeing is at Palazzo Vecchio, which stays open until 24:00 (except on Thu, when it closes at 14:00); off-season, it's open until 19:00 (Fri-Wed).

covers the same sights). See page 590 for details.

Tours

🎧 To sightsee on your own, download free audio tours via my free **Rick Steves Audio Europe** app (see page 14 for details).

Tour companies offer city tours as well as excursions in Tuscany (such as Siena, San Gimignano, Pisa, and the Chianti region for wine-tasting); see their websites for details. Several offer Accademia and Uffizi tours, gaining you easy access to these popular sights. (And they often run cooking classes, too.)

Florencetown runs tours on foot or by bike. Their "Walk and Talk Florence" introductory tour includes the Oltrarno neighborhood (€19, 2.5 hours). My readers get a 10 percent discount, with an extra 10 percent off for second tours (if booking online, enter code "RICKSTEVES"; Via de Lamberti 1, facing Orsanmichele Church, tel. 055-281-103, www.florencetown.com).

Artviva offers a variety of tours (18 people maximum), including these popular overviews: "Original Florence" town walk (€29, 3 hours) and "Florence in One Glorious Day" (€99, 6 hours, adds Uffizi and Accademia tours). They offer a 10 percent discount at www.artviva.com/ricksteves (username "ricksteves," password "reader"; Via de' Sassetti 1, second floor, near Piazza della Repubblica, tel. 055-264-5033, www.artviva.com).

Good private guides for walking tours

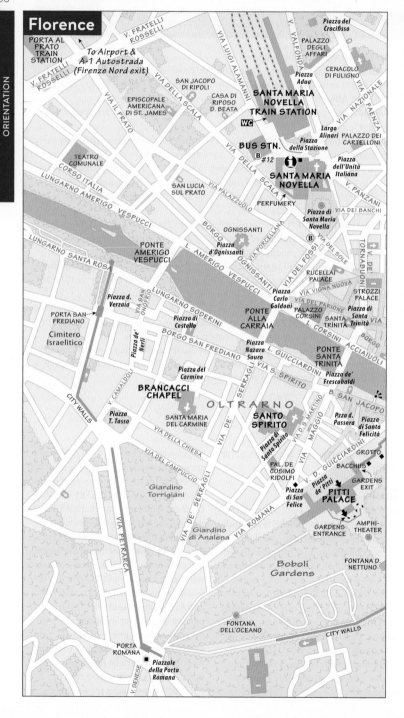

Florence

PORTA AL PRATO TRAIN STATION

To Airport & A-1 Autostrada (Firenze Nord exit)

V. FRATELLI ROSSELLI

V. LUIGI ALAMANNI

V. VALFONDA

Piazza del Crocifisso

PALAZZO DEGLI AFFARI

CENACOLO DI FULIGNO

VIA NAZIONALE

VIA FAENZA

SAN JACOPO DI RIPOLI

VIA DELLA SCALA

EPISCOPALE AMERICANA DI ST. JAMES

CASA DI RIPOSO D. BEATA

Piazza Adua

SANTA MARIA NOVELLA TRAIN STATION

WC

Largo Alinari

PALAZZO DEI CARTELLONI

VIA IL PRATO

BUS STN.

#12

Piazza della Stazione

SANTA MARIA NOVELLA

Piazza dell'Unità Italiana

V. PANZANI

TEATRO COMUNALE

CORSO ITALIA

VIA DELLA SCALA

VIA PALAZZUOLO

SAN LUCIA SUL PRATO

PERFUMERY

Piazza di Santa Maria Novella

VIA DEI BANCHI

LUNGARNO AMERIGO VESPUCCI

OGNISSANTI

Piazza d'Ognissanti

VIA DEL SOLE

(B)

V. DEI TORNABUONI

LUNGARNO SANTA ROSA

PONTE AMERIGO VESPUCCI

L. AMERIGO VESPUCCI

BORGO OGNISSANTI

VIA PORCELLANA

VIA DEL FOSSI

RUCELLAI PALACE

VIA VIGNA NUOVA

STROZZI PALACE

Piazza d. Verzaia

LUNGARNO SODERINI

VIA DEL PARIONE

Piazza Carlo Goldoni

PONTE ALLA CARRAIA

PALAZZO CORSINI

L. CORSINI

Piazza di Santa Trinità

SANTA TRINITÀ

VIA

PORTA SAN FREDIANO

VIA SAN ONOFRIO

Piazza di Cestello

BORGO SAN FREDIANO

Piazza Nazaro Sauro

L. GUICCIARDINI

PONTE SANTA TRINITÀ

BORGO ACCIAIUOLI

Cimitero Israelitico

Piazza de' Nerli

VIA S. SPIRITO

Piazza de' Frescobaldi

CITY WALLS

V. CAMALDOLI

Piazza del Carmine

BRANCACCI CHAPEL

VIA DE' SERRAGLI

O L T R A R N O

VIA DI S. MARTINO

B. SAN JACOPO

Piazza T. Tasso

SANTA MARIA DEL CARMINE

SANTO SPIRITO

VIA D. S. MAGGIO

Pzza d. Passera

Piazza di Santa Felicità

VIA DELLA CHIESA

Piazza di Santa Spirito

V. D. GUICCIARDINI

GROTTO

BACCHUS

VIA DEL CAMPUCCIO

PAL. DE COSIMO RIDOLFI

GARDENS EXIT

Giardino Torrigiani

VIA ROMANA

Piazza di San Felice

Piazza de' Pitti

PITTI PALACE

VIA DE SERRAGLI

Giardino di Analena

GARDENS ENTRANCE

AMPHI-THEATER

VIA PETRARCA

Boboli Gardens

FONTANA D. NETTUNO

V. SENESE

FONTANA DELL'OCEANO

CITY WALLS

PORTA ROMANA

Piazzale della Porta Romana

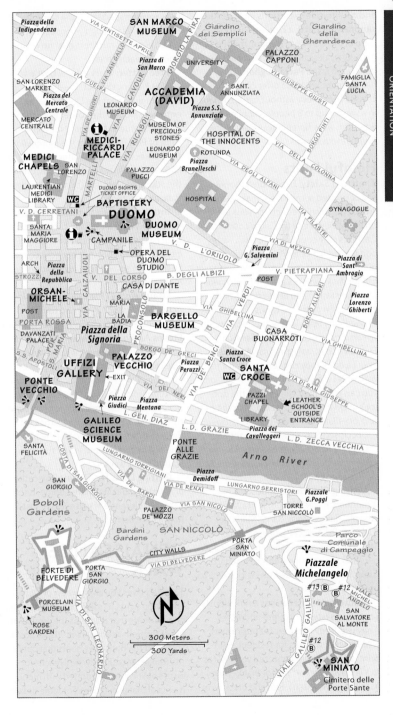

Piazza della Indipendenza
SAN MARCO MUSEUM
VIA VENTISETTE APRILE
GIORGIO LA PIRA
Giardino dei Semplici
Giardino della Gherardesca

PALAZZO CAPPONI
VIA GIUSEPPE GIUSTI
Piazza di San Marco
UNIVERSITY
SANT. ANNUNZIATA
FAMIGLIA SANTA LUCIA

SAN LORENZO MARKET
VIA GUELFA
VIA SAN GALLO
CAVOUR
ACCADEMIA (DAVID)
Piazza S.S. Annunziata

Piazza del Mercato Centrale
LEONARDO MUSEUM
MUSEUM OF PRECIOUS STONES
HOSPITAL OF THE INNOCENTS

MERCATO CENTRALE
VIA DEI GINORI
VIA RICASOLI
LEONARDO MUSEUM
ROTUNDA
BORGO PINTI

MEDICI-RICCARDI PALACE
Piazza Brunelleschi
VIA DELLA COLONNA

MEDICI CHAPELS
SAN LORENZO
MARTELLI
PALAZZO PUCCI
VIA DEGLI ALFANI

LAURENTIAN MEDICI LIBRARY
DUOMO SIGHTS TICKET OFFICE
HOSPITAL
SYNAGOGUE

WC
V. D. CERRETANI
BAPTISTERY
DUOMO
VIA PILASTRI

SANTA MARIA MAGGIORE
CAMPANILE
DUOMO MUSEUM
VIA DI MEZZO

ARCH
STROZZI
Piazza della Repubblica
VIA CALZAIUOLI
V. D. L'ORIUOLO
Piazza G. Salvemini
Piazza di Sant' Ambrogio

OPERA DEL DUOMO STUDIO
B. DEGLI ALBIZI
V. PIETRAPIANA
POST

ORSAN-MICHELE
V. DEL CORSO
CASA DI DANTE
Piazza Lorenzo Ghiberti

POST
PORTA ROSSA
S. MARIA
VIA GHIBELLINA
VIA VERDI
BORGO ALLEGRI

DAVANZATI PALACE
LA BADIA
PROCONSOLO
BARGELLO MUSEUM
CASA BUONARROTI

Piazza della Signoria
VIA GHIBELLINA

S.S. APOSTOLI
POR S. MARIA
BORGO DE' GRECI
Piazza Santa Croce

PALAZZO VECCHIO
Piazza Peruzzi
SANTA CROCE

UFFIZI GALLERY
EXIT
VIA DE' BENCI
VIA DI SAN GIUSEPPE
WC

PONTE VECCHIO
VIA DE' NERI
PAZZI CHAPEL
LEATHER SCHOOL'S OUTSIDE ENTRANCE

Piazza Giudici
Piazza Mentana
LIBRARY

GALILEO SCIENCE MUSEUM
L. GEN. DIAZ
L.D. GRAZIE
Piazza dei Cavalleggeri
L.D. ZECCA VECCHIA

PONTE ALLE GRAZIE
Arno River

SANTA FELICITÀ
LUNGARNO TORRIGIANI
VIA DE' BARDI
Piazza Demidoff
LUNGARNO SERRISTORI

COSTA DI SAN GIORGIO
VIA DE' RENAI
Piazzale G. Poggi

SAN GIORGIO
PALAZZO DE' MOZZI
VIA SAN NICOLO
TORRE SAN NICCOLÒ

Boboli Gardens
Bardini Gardens
SAN NICCOLÒ
Parco Comunale di Campeggio

CITY WALLS
PORTA SAN MINIATO

VIA DI SAN LEONARDO
VIA DI BELVEDERE
Piazzale Michelangelo

FORTE DI BELVEDERE
PORTA SAN GIORGIO
#13 B #12
VIALE MICHELANGELO

PORCELAIN MUSEUM
SAN SALVATORE AL MONTE

ROSE GARDEN
VIALE GALILEO GALILEI
#12

300 Meters
300 Yards
SAN MINIATO
Cimitero delle Porte Sante

and countryside excursions include **Alessandra Marchetti,** a Florentine who has lived in the US (€60-75/hour, mobile 347-386-9839, alessandramarchettitours@gmail.com), and **Paola Migliorini** and her partners, who also offer cooking classes (€60/hour without car, €70/hour in a van for up to 8 people, mobile 347-657-2611, www.florencetour.com, info@florencetour.com).

Helpful Hints

Theft and Safety: Easy tourist money has corrupted some locals, making them greedy and dishonest; check your bill carefully. Beware of the "slow count": Cashiers may count change back with odd pauses in hopes you'll gather up the money early and say *"Grazie."* Keep an eye out for slick pickpockets, especially near the train station and at major sights. Some thieves even dress like tourists to fool you.

Medical Help: To reach a doctor who speaks English, call **Medical Service Firenze** at 055-475-411 (answered 24 hours a day); they can send a doctor to your hotel within an hour of your call, or you can go to their clinic when the doctor's in (Mon-Fri 11:00-12:00, 13:00-15:00 & 17:00-18:00, Sat 11:00-12:00 & 13:00-15:00, closed Sun, no appointment necessary, Via Roma 4, between the Duomo and Piazza della Repubblica, www.medicalservice.firenze.it).

Visiting Churches: Modest dress is required at the Duomo, Santa Maria Novella, Santa Croce, Santa Maria del Carmine/Brancacci Chapel, and the Medici Chapels. Be respectful of worshippers and the paintings; don't use a flash. Churches usually close from 12:00 or 12:30 until 15:00 or 16:00.

Addresses: Florence has a ridiculously confusing system for street addresses. They use "red" numbers for businesses and "black" numbers for residences; in print, addresses are indicated with "r" (as in Via Cavour 2r) or "n" (for black—*nero,* as in Via Cavour 25n). Red and black numbers are interspersed on the same street; each set goes in roughly consecutive order, but their numbers bear no connection with each other.

Free Water: Carry a water bottle to refill at Florence's twist-the-handle public fountains (near the Duomo dome entrance, around the corner from the "Piglet" statue at Mercato Nuovo, or in front of Pitti Palace). Try the *fontanello* (dispenser of free cold water, *frizzante* or *naturale*) on Piazza della Signoria, behind the statue of Neptune (on the left side of Palazzo Vecchio).

Internet Access: Virtually all hotels have free **Wi-Fi** and many cafés will share their password if you buy something. The city's free Wi-Fi hotspot network covers all the main squares (no registration, good for two hours).

Useful App: ∩ For free audio versions of my Renaissance Walk and tours of the Uffizi and Accademia Gallery, get the **Rick Steves Audio Europe** app (see page 14).

WCs: Public restrooms are scarce. Use them when you can, in any café or museum. Pay WCs are typically €1. Handy locations include one at the Baptistery ticket office (near the Duomo); just down the street from Piazza Santa Croce (at Borgo Santa Croce 29 red); up near Piazzale Michelangelo; and inside the train station (near track 5).

Getting Lost: The Duomo, the cathedral with the distinctive red dome, is the center of Florence. If you ever get lost, home's the dome.

RENAISSANCE WALK

This walk gives you an overview of Florence's top sights. We'll start with the soaring church dome that stands as the proud symbol of the Renaissance spirit. Just opposite, you'll find the Baptistery doors that opened the Renaissance. Finally, we'll reach Florence's political center, dotted with monuments of that proud time. For more details on many of the sights on this walk, see the individual listings later in this chapter.

Length of This Walk: Allow two hours if you add visits to the interiors of the Baptistery and Orsanmichele Church (but not the other sights mentioned). With limited time, view the Baptistery and Orsanmichele Church from the outside.

Tours: 🎧 Download my free Renaissance Walk audio tour.

➲ Self-Guided Walk

• *Stand in front of the Duomo as you get your historical bearings.*

Florentine Renaissance

During the Dark Ages, it was obvious to the people of Italy—sitting on the rubble of the Roman Empire—that there had to be a brighter age on the horizon. The long-awaited rebirth, or Renaissance, began in Florence for good reasons: It

The Renaissance lives on in Florence.

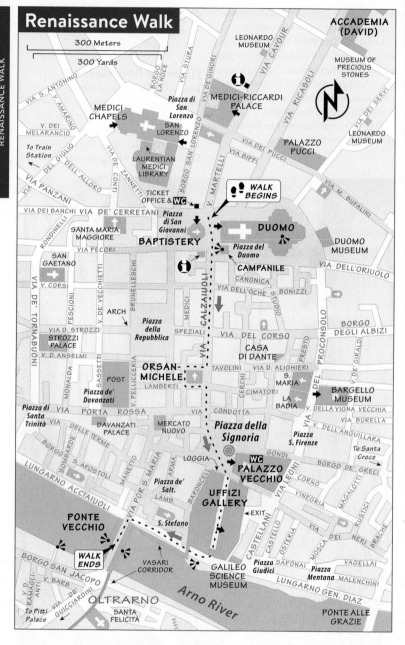

Renaissance Walk

ACCADEMIA (DAVID)

300 Meters
300 Yards

LEONARDO MUSEUM

VIA S. STURA
VIA DEGINORI
VIA CAVOUR

MUSEUM OF PRECIOUS STONES

MEDICI-RICCARDI PALACE

VIA RICASOLI
VIA DEI SERVI

BORGO LA NOCE
VIA DELLA

V. DEI MELARANCIO
VIA S. ANTONINO
V. AMARINO

MEDICI CHAPELS

Piazza di San Lorenzo

SAN LORENZO

LEONARDO MUSEUM

To Train Station

DEL GIGLIO
DELL' ALLORO
VIA DE' ZANNETTI
VIA DE' CONTI

LAURENTIAN MEDICI LIBRARY

BORGO SAN LORENZO

PALAZZO PUCCI

VIA DEI PUCCI
VIA BIFFI

VIA PANZANI

TICKET OFFICE & WC

WALK BEGINS

VIA M. BUFALINI

VIA DEI BANCHI   VIA DE' CERRETANI

Piazza di San Giovanni

VIA MARTELLI

DUOMO

V. DE' VECCHIETTI

RONDINELLI

SANTA MARIA MAGGIORE

BAPTISTERY

Piazza del Duomo

DUOMO MUSEUM

SAN GAETANO

VIA PECORI

CAMPANILE

VIA DELL'ORIUOLO

V. CORSI

BRUNELLESCHI

CANONICA

VIA DELL'OCHE   STUDIO   BONIZZI

VIA DE' TORNABUONI

PESCIONI

ARCH

Piazza della Repubblica

MEDICI

VIA CALZAIUOLI

SPEZIALI

PRESTO

BORGO DEGLI ALBIZI

VIA D. STROZZI

STROZZI PALACE

VIA   DEL   CORSO

CASA DI DANTE

V. D. ANSELMI

MONALDA

SASSETTI

ORSAN-MICHELE

TAVOLINI   VIA D. ALIGHIERI

CERCHI

S. MARIA LA BADIA

V. DE' GIRALDI

BARGELLO MUSEUM

V. DEL PROCONSOLO

POST

LAMBERTI

CIMATORI

Piazza di Santa Trinità

VIA   PORTA   ROSSA

Piazza de' Davanzati

VIA

CONDOTTA

V. DELLA VIGNA VECCHIA
VIA BURELLA

DAVANZATI PALACE

DELLE TERME

MERCATO NUOVO

Piazza della Signoria

Piazza S. Firenze

V. DELL'ANGUILLARA

BORGO S. APOSTOLI

VIA POR S. MARIA

LOGGIA

WC

PALAZZO VECCHIO

GONDI

BORGO DE' GRECI

To Santa Croce

LUNGARNO ACCIAIUOLI

MANETTO

Piazza de' Salt.

BARONCELLI

CORNO

VINEGRIA

MAGALOTTI

RUSTICI

PONTE VECCHIO

LAMB.

UFFIZI GALLERY

EXIT

CASTELLANI

OSTERIA

VIA   DEI   NERI

MOSCA

BRACHE

WALK ENDS

S. Stefano

VASARI CORRIDOR

GALILEO SCIENCE MUSEUM

Piazza Giudici

SAPONAI

Piazza Mentana

VAGELLAI

MALENCHINI

BORGO SAN JACOPO

V. D. RAMAGLI-ANTI

V. BARB.

VIA DE' GUICCIARDINI

OLTRARNO

Arno River

LUNGARNO GEN. DIAZ

PONTE ALLE GRAZIE

To Pitti Palace

SANTA FELICITA

N

was wealthy because of its cloth industry, trade, and banking, notably the powerful Medici, the rich banking family who ruled Renaissance Florence. Locals were powered by a fierce city-state pride—they'd pee into the Arno with gusto, knowing rival city-state Pisa was downstream. And Florence was fertile with more than its share of artistic genius; imagine guys like Michelangelo and Leonardo attending the same high school.

The cultural explosion called the Renaissance—the "rebirth" of Greek and Roman culture that swept across Europe—started around 1400 and lasted about 150 years. In politics, the Renaissance meant democracy; in science, a renewed interest in exploring nature. Renaissance art was a return to the realism and balance of Greek and Roman sculpture. In architecture, domes and round arches replaced Gothic spires and pointed arches. The Duomo kicked off the architectural Renaissance in Florence.

• *The dome of the Duomo is best viewed just to the right of the facade, from the corner of the pedestrian-only Via de' Calzaiuoli. Stand near the kiosk.*

The Duomo and Its Dome

The dome of Florence's cathedral—visible from all over the city—inspired Florentines to do great things. (Most recently, it inspired the city to make the area around the cathedral traffic-free.) The big church itself (called the Duomo) is Gothic, built in the Middle Ages by architects who left it unfinished.

Think of the confidence of the age: The Duomo was built with a big hole in its roof, just waiting for a grand dome to cover it. They could envision it—but the technology needed to create such a dome had yet to be invented. *No problema.* In the 1400s, the architect Filippo Brunelleschi was called on to finish the job. Brunelleschi capped the church Roman-style—with a tall, self-supporting dome as grand as the ancient Pantheon's

(which he had studied).

He used a dome within a dome. First, he built the grand white skeletal ribs, which you can see, then filled them in with interlocking bricks in a herringbone pattern. The dome grew upward like an igloo, supporting itself as it proceeded from the base. When the ribs reached the top, Brunelleschi arched them in and fixed them in place with the cupola at the top. His dome, built in only 14 years, was the largest since Rome's Pantheon.

Brunelleschi's dome was the wonder of the age, the model for many domes to follow, from St. Peter's to the US Capitol. Michelangelo, setting out to construct the dome of St. Peter's, drew inspiration from the dome of Florence. He said, "I'll make its sister...bigger, but not more beautiful."

The church's facade looks old, but was completed in 1870 (about 600 years after the building began) to celebrate Italian unity, here in the city that for a few years served as the young country's capital.

Its Neo-Gothic "retro" look captures the feel of the original medieval facade, with green, white, and pink marble sheets that cover the brick construction; pointed Gothic arches; and three horizontal stories decorated with mosaics and statues. Still, the facade is generally ridiculed (some call it "the cathedral in pajamas").

The cavernous interior feels bare after being cleaned out during the Neoclassical age and by the terrible flood of 1966. (For more about climbing the dome and the Duomo interior, see page 591.)

Campanile (Giotto's Tower)

The bell tower (to the right of the cathedral's front) offers an easier, less crowded, and faster climb than the Duomo's dome, though the unobstructed views from the Duomo are better. Giotto, like any artistic genius, wore several hats. He's considered the father of modern painting, as well as being the architect of this 270-foot-tall bell tower for the Duomo, built two centuries before the age of Michelangelo. (For details on climbing the tower, see page 591.)

• *The Baptistery is the octagonal building in front of the church. If you decide to go inside, get a ticket at the office across the piazza (Firenze Card holders also need to get a ticket at the ticket office). If you just want to look at the exterior doors, there's no charge.*

Baptistery and Ghiberti's Bronze Doors

The Baptistery's bronze doors bring us out of the Middle Ages and into the Renaissance. (These are copies; the originals are in the Duomo Museum.) Lorenzo Ghiberti beat out heavyweights such as Brunelleschi to design the **north doors,** which show scenes from the Old Testament. (The original entries of Brunelleschi and Ghiberti are in the Bargello.) About the time Ghiberti completed the first set of doors, the Baptistery needed another set of doors for the entrance that faces the church. Ghiberti's bronze panels for the **east doors** added a new dimension to art: depth. Here we see how the Renais-

sance masters merged art and science. Realism was in, and Renaissance artists used math, illusion, and dissection to create it. Ghiberti spent 27 years (1425-1452) working on these panels. That's him in the center of the door frame, atop the second row of panels—the head on the left with the shiny male-pattern baldness.

The Baptistery **interior** features a fine example of pre-Renaissance mosaic art (1200s-1300s) in the Byzantine style (more on page 591).

• *Head south toward the river, taking the main pedestrian drag...*

Via de' Calzaiuoli

This street, Via de' Calzaiuoli (kahlts-ay-WOH-lee), has always been the main axis of the city; it was part of the ancient Roman grid plan that became Florence. In medieval times, this street connected the religious center (where we are now) with the political center (where we're heading), a five-minute walk away. In recent years this historic core has been transformed into a pleasant place to stroll, window-shop, lick your gelato cone, and won-

The Campanile

Ghiberti's bronze doors

der why American cities can't be more pedestrian-friendly.

Two blocks down from the Baptistery, look right on Via degli Speziali to see a triumphal arch that marks **Piazza della Repubblica.** The arch celebrates the unification of Italy in 1870 and stands as a reminder that, in ancient Roman times, this piazza was the city center. (Today the square hosts a carousel and the Rinascente department store, with a rooftop, view-terrace café.)

• *A block farther, at the intersection with Via Orsanmichele, is the...*

Orsanmichele Church

Originally, this was an open loggia (covered porch) with a huge grain warehouse upstairs. The arches of the loggia were artfully filled in (14th century), and the building gained a new purpose—as a church. The 14 niches in the exterior walls feature replicas of the remarkable-in-their-day statues paid for by the city's rising middle class of merchants and their 21 guilds. The interior has a glorious Gothic tabernacle (1359) and a painted wooden panel that depicts *Madonna delle Grazie* (1346).

Head up Via Orsanmichele (to the right of the church) and circle the church exterior counterclockwise to enjoy the statues. In the third niche is **Nanni di Banco's Quattro Santi Coronati** (c. 1415-1417). These four early Christians were sculptors martyred by Roman emperor Diocletian because they refused to sculpt pagan gods. They seem to be contemplat-

ing the consequences of the fatal decision they're about to make. While Banco's saints are deep in the church's niche, the next statue, just to the right, feels ready to step out. **Donatello's St. George** is alert, perched on the edge of his niche, scanning the horizon for dragons. He's anxious, but he's also self-assured. Comparing this Renaissance-style *St. George* to *Quattro Santi Coronati,* you can psychoanalyze the heady changes underway. This is humanism. (This statue is a copy of the c. 1417 original, which is now in the Bargello.)

Continue counterclockwise around the church (bypassing the entrance), all the way to the opposite side. The first niche you come to features **Donatello's St. Mark** (1411-1413). The evangelist cradles his gospel in his strong, veined hand and gazes out, resting his weight on the right leg while bending the left. Though subtle, St. Mark's twisting *contrapposto* pose was the first seen since antiquity. Eighty years after young Donatello carved this statue, a teenage Michelangelo Buonarroti stood here and marveled at it.

The church hosts evening **concerts;** tickets are sold on the day of the concert from the door facing Via de' Calzaiuoli; you can also book tickets here for the Uffizi and Accademia (ticket window open daily 9:00-16:00, closed Sun off-season).

• *Continue down Via de' Calzaiuoli 50 more yards, to the huge and historic square.*

Donatello, St. George

Donatello, St. Mark

Piazza della Signoria

What a view! The main civic center of Florence is dominated by Palazzo Vecchio, the Uffizi Gallery, and the marble greatness of old Florence littering the cobbles. Piazza della Signoria still vibrates with the echoes of the city's past—executions, riots, and celebrations. There's even Roman history: Look for the **chart** showing the ancient city (on a freestanding display to your right as you enter the square, in front of Chanel). Today, it's a tourist's world with pigeons, selfie sticks, horse buggies, and tired tourists. For a sugar jolt, stop in at the **Rivoire** café to enjoy its fine desserts, pudding-thick hot chocolate, and the best view seats in town.

Before you towers **Palazzo Vecchio,** the palatial Town Hall of the Medici—a fortress designed to contain riches and survive the many riots that went with local politics. The windows are just beyond the reach of angry stones, and the tower was a handy lookout post. Justice was doled out sternly on this square. Until 1873, Michelangelo's **David** stood where you see the replica today. The original was damaged in a 1527 riot (when a bench thrown from a palace window knocked its left arm off),

but it remained here for several centuries, vulnerable to erosion and pollution, before being moved indoors for protection.

Step past the fake *David* through the front door into Palazzo Vecchio's courtyard (free). This palace was Florence's symbol of civic power. You're surrounded by art for art's sake—a cherub frivolously marks the courtyard's center, and ornate stuccoes and frescoes decorate the walls and columns. Such luxury represented a big change 500 years ago. (For more on the palazzo and climbing its tower, see page 600.)

• *Back outside, check out the statue-filled...*

Loggia dei Lanzi

The loggia, a.k.a. **Loggia della Signoria,** was once a forum for public debate, perfect for a city that prided itself on its democratic traditions. But later, when the Medici figured that good art was more desirable than free speech, it was turned into an outdoor sculpture gallery. Notice the squirming Florentine themes—conquest, domination, rape, and decapitation. The statues lining the back are Roman originals brought back to Florence by a Medici when his villa in Rome was

Piazza della Signoria

sold. Two statues in the front deserve a closer look: Giambologna's **The Rape of the Sabine Women** (c. 1583)—with its pulse-quickening rhythm of muscles— is from the restless Mannerist period, which followed the stately and confident Renaissance; Benvenuto **Cellini's Perseus** (1545-1553), the loggia's most noteworthy piece, shows the Greek hero who decapitated the snake-headed Medusa.

• *Cross the square to the big* **fountain of Neptune** *by Bartolomeo Ammanati that Florentines (including Michelangelo) consider a huge waste of marble. The guy on the horse, to the left, is Cosimo I, one of the post-Renaissance Medici. Find the round bronze plaque on the ground 10 steps in front of the fountain.*

Savonarola Plaque

The Medici family was briefly thrown from power by an austere monk named Savonarola, who made Florence a constitutional republic. He organized huge rallies lit by bonfires here on the square where he preached. While children sang hymns, the devout brought their rich "vanities" (such as paintings, musical instruments, and playing cards) and threw them into the flames. Encouraged by the pope, the Florentines fought back and arrested Savonarola. For two days, they tortured him, trying unsuccessfully to persuade him to see their side of things. Finally, on the very spot where Savonarola's followers had built bonfires of vanities, the monk was burned. The bronze plaque, engraved in Italian (*"Qui dove..."*), reads, "Here, Girolamo Savonarola and his Dominican brothers were hanged and burned" in the year "MCCCCXCVIII" (1498). Soon after, the Medici returned to power. The Renaissance picked up where it left off.

Thirsty? A free water dispenser (*frizzante* or *naturale*) is behind the Neptune statue.

• *Stay cool, we have 200 yards to go. Follow the gaze of the fake David into the courtyard of the two-tone horseshoe-shaped building.*

Uffizi Courtyard

The top floor of this building, known as the *uffizi* (offices) during Medici days, is filled with the greatest collection of Florentine painting anywhere. It's one of Europe's top art galleries (described on page 597). The courtyard, filled with souvenir stalls and hustling young artists, is watched over by 19th-century statues of the great figures of the Renaissance: artists (Michelangelo, Giotto, Donatello, and Leonardo), philosophers (Niccolò Machiavelli), scientists (Galileo), writers (Dante), poets (Petrarch), cartographers (Amerigo Vespucci), and the great patron of so much Renaissance thinking, Lorenzo "the Magnificent" de' Medici. His support of Leonardo, Botticelli, and teenage Michelangelo helped Florence become Europe's most enlightened city.

After hours, talented street musicians take advantage of the space's superior acoustics.

• *Exiting at the far end of the courtyard, pause at the Arno River, overlooking...*

Ponte Vecchio

Ponte Vecchio (Old Bridge), rated ▲, has spanned this narrowest part of the Arno since Roman times. While Rome "fell," Florence never really did, remaining a bustling trade center along the river.

• *Hike to the center of the bridge.*

A fine bust of the great goldsmith Cellini graces the central point of the bridge. This statue is a reminder that, in the

Ponte Vecchio

1500s, the Medici booted out the bridge's butchers and tanners and installed the gold- and silversmiths who still tempt visitors to this day.

During World War II, the Nazi occupiers were ordered to blow up Ponte Vecchio. An art-loving German consul intervened and saved the bridge. The buildings at either end were destroyed, leaving the bridge impassable but intact. Look up to notice the protected and elevated passageway (called the Vasari Corridor) that led the Medici from Palazzo Vecchio through the Uffizi, across Ponte Vecchio, and up to Pitti Palace, four blocks beyond the bridge.

• *Now that you've had a full meal of high culture, finish it off with a dessert of the world's finest gelato. Enjoy.*

SIGHTS

When you see a 🎧 in a listing, it means the sight is covered in an audio tour via my free **Rick Steves Audio Europe** app (see page 14).

The Duomo and Nearby Sights

A single **combo-ticket** covers all the paid Duomo sights. The main ticket office faces the Baptistery entrance (at #7 on the square) and has a staffed counter (credit cards or cash) as well as ticket machines (credit cards only, requires PIN); there's another office at the Duomo Museum. You can buy cash-only tickets at the Campanile. **Advance tickets** are available online (www.museumflorence.com).

The Firenze Card also covers all the Duomo sights; pass holders must stop at the main ticket office to obtain a combo-ticket.

▲▲DUOMO

Florence's Gothic cathedral has the third-longest nave in Christendom. The church's noisy Neo-Gothic facade (from 1870) is covered with pink, green, and white Tuscan marble. The cathedral's claim to artistic fame is Brunelleschi's magnificent dome—the first Renaissance dome and the model for domes to follow. While viewing it from the outside is well worth ▲▲ and described earlier, on my Renaissance walk, the massive but empty-feeling interior is lucky to rate ▲—it doesn't justify the massive crowds that line up to get inside. Much of the church's great art is stored in the Duomo Museum behind the church.

Cost and Hours: Free; Mon-Fri 10:00-17:00, Thu until 16:00 May and Oct, until 16:30 Nov-April; Sat 10:00-16:45, Sun 13:30-16:45; opening times sometimes change due to religious functions, audioguide-€5, modest dress code enforced, tel. 055-230-2885, www.operaduomo.firenze.it.

Tours: Themed tours (€30 each) cover the Duomo (daily at 10:30), Baptistery mosaics (Mon, Wed, and Fri at 16:30), and the still-active workshop where Michelangelo carved *David* (Mon, Wed, and Fri at

The Duomo and Brunelleschi's dome

12:00). To reserve, call 055-282-226, email info@operaduomo.firenze.it, or go to the ticket office next to the Baptistery.

🎧 The Duomo is covered on my free Renaissance Walk audio tour.

Rick's Tip: *The* **Duomo sights** *don't take reservations, but you can* **skip the dome-climb line with a Firenze Card**. *(However, you can't use the card to bypass the line at the Campanile or the Duomo.)*

▲CLIMBING THE DUOMO'S DOME

For a grand view into the cathedral from the base of the dome, a peek at some of the tools used in the dome's construction, a chance to see Brunelleschi's "dome-within-a-dome" construction, a glorious Florence view from the top, and the equivalent of 463 plunges on a Stair-Master, climb the dome. The claustrophobic one-way route takes you up narrow staircases and walkways to the top of the dome.

Rick's Tip: *If you're* **claustrophobic** *or* **acrophobic, skip climbing the dome.** *Once you start up the narrow staircase, there's no turning back until you reach the top. The slow climb to the top can feel like torture.*

As you're waiting in line, spend a few minutes studying the precious Donatello sculpture above the side entrance door, called the Porta della Mandorla ("Door of the Almond"): Madonna and Bambino are carried by angels in an almond-shaped frame, above delicately carved barrel leaf and *Annunciation* mosaics by Nanni di Banco. Even the side door of this cathedral boasts priceless works by masters.

Cost and Hours: €15 combo-ticket covers all Duomo sights, covered by Firenze Card, Mon-Fri 8:30-19:00, Sat 8:30-17:40, Sun 13:00-16:40, last entry 40 minutes before closing, crowds may subside at lunchtime (13:00-14:30) or near the end of the day, enter from outside church on north side.

🎧 The dome is covered on my free Renaissance Walk audio tour.

▲CAMPANILE

The 270-foot bell tower has 50-some fewer steps than the Duomo's dome (but that's still 414 steps—no elevator); offers a faster, relatively less-crowded climb (with typically shorter lines); and has a view of that magnificent dome to boot. On the way up, there are several intermediate levels where you can catch your breath and enjoy ever-higher views. The stairs narrow as you go up, creating a mosh-pit bottleneck near the top—but the views are worth the hassle. While the various viewpoints are enclosed by cage-like bars, the gaps are big enough to let you snap great photos. Still, acrophobes and claustrophobes should beware!

Cost and Hours: €15 ticket covers all Duomo sights, covered by Firenze Card, daily 8:30-19:30, last entry 40 minutes before closing.

🎧 The Campanile is covered on my free Renaissance Walk audio tour.

▲BAPTISTERY

This is the octagonal building next to the Duomo. Check out the gleaming copies of Lorenzo Ghiberti's bronze doors facing the Duomo's facade (the originals are in the Duomo Museum); Michelangelo said these doors were fit to be the gates of paradise. Making a breakthrough in perspective, Ghiberti used mathematical laws to

Last Judgment mosaic in the Baptistery

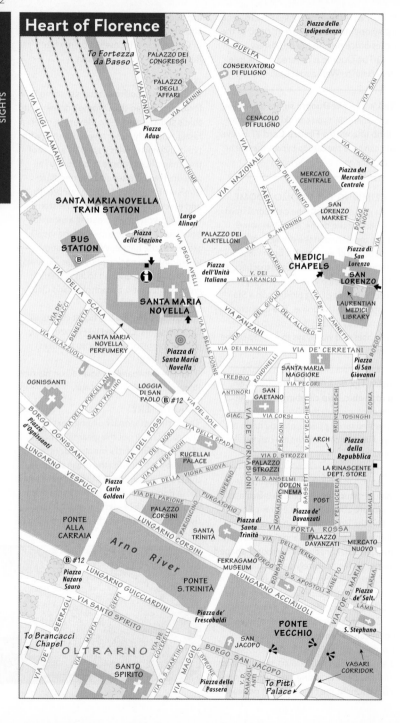

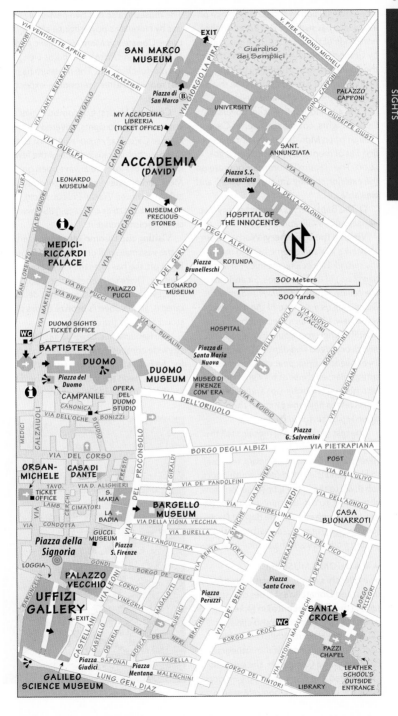

create the illusion of receding distance on a basically flat surface. The doors on the north side of the building were designed by Ghiberti when he was young; he'd won the honor and opportunity by beating Brunelleschi in a competition (the rivals' original entries are in the Bargello).

Cost and Hours: €15 ticket covers all Duomo sights, covered by Firenze Card, interior open Mon-Sat 11:15-19:00 except first Sat of month 8:30-14:00, Sun 8:30-14:00. The (facsimile) bronze doors are on the exterior, so they are always "open" and viewable.

🎧 The Baptistery is covered on my free Renaissance Walk audio tour.

Visiting the Baptistery: Workers from St. Mark's in Venice came here to make the remarkable ceiling mosaics (of Venetian glass) in the late 1200s. Sit and savor the ceiling, where it's always Judgment Day, giving us a glimpse of the medieval worldview. Life was a preparation for the afterlife, when you would be judged and saved, or judged and damned—with no in-between. Christ, peaceful and reassuring, blessed those at his right hand with heaven (thumbs-up) and sent those on his left to hell (the ultimate thumbs-down) to be tortured by demons.

The rest of the ceiling mosaics tell the history of the world, from Adam and Eve (over the north/entrance doors, top row) to Noah and the Flood (over south doors, top row), to the life of Christ (second row, all around), to the life, ministry, and eventual beheading of John the Baptist (bottom row, all around)—all bathed in the golden glow of pre-Renaissance heaven.

▲▲▲ DUOMO MUSEUM

Brunelleschi's dome, Ghiberti's bronze doors, and Donatello's statues define the 1400s (the Quattrocento) in Florence, when the city blossomed and classical arts were reborn. While copies now decorate the exteriors of the cathedral, Baptistery, and Campanile, the originals are restored and displayed safely indoors, filling the underrated Duomo Museum.

The museum also has two powerful statues by Florence's powerhouse sculptors—Donatello's *Mary Magdalene* and Michelangelo's *Pietà*), and holds Donatello's playful choir loft. The museum has just reopened after a remodel—expect changes.

Cost and Hours: €15 combo-ticket covers all Duomo sights, covered by Firenze Card. Daily 9:00-19:00, last entry one hour before closing, one of the few museums in Florence always open on Mon, audioguide-€5, guided tours available in summer, Via del Proconsolo 9, tel. 055-282-226 or 055-230-7885, www.operaduomo.firenze.it.

Visiting the Duomo Museum: Start in the vast main hall on the ground floor. Right off, the hall puts the collection in context. There's a model of the Duomo's medieval facade, the statues that decorated it, and Ghiberti's **bronze doors** that stood opposite the church.

The Renaissance began in 1401 with a citywide competition to build new doors for the Baptistery. Lorenzo Ghiberti (c. 1378-1455) won the job and built the doors for the north side of the building. Every-

Michelangelo, Pietà

one loved them, so he was then hired to make another set of doors—these panels—for the east entrance, facing the Duomo. These bronze "Gates of Paradise" (1425-1452) revolutionized the way Renaissance people saw the world around them.

Also on the ground floor are rooms dedicated to the museum's most famous statues. Donatello's **Mary Magdalene** (*Maddalena*, c. 1455), carved from white poplar and originally painted with realistic colors, is less a Renaissance work of beauty than a medieval object of intense devotion. The aging Michelangelo designed his own tomb, with this **Pietà** (1547-1555) as the centerpiece. Three mourners tend the broken body of the crucified Christ. We see Mary, his mother; Mary Magdalene (on the left); and Nicodemus, the converted Pharisee, whose face is that of Michelangelo himself. The polished body of Christ stands out from the unfinished background. Michelangelo (as Nicodemus), who spent a lifetime bringing statues to life by "freeing" them from the stone, looks down at what could be his final creation, the once-perfect body of Renaissance Man that is now twisted, disfigured, and dead. The figures seem to interact with each other, their sketchy faces changing emotions from grief to melancholy to acceptance.

The first floor displays two marble **choir lofts** (*cantorie;* by Lucca della Robbia and Donatello) that once sat above the sacristy doors of the Duomo, and **Brunelleschi's model** of the dome.

North of the Duomo
▲▲▲ACCADEMIA
This museum houses Michelangelo's *David,* the consummate Renaissance statue of the buff, biblical shepherd boy ready to take on the giant. When you look into the eyes of this magnificent sculpture, you're looking into the eyes of Renaissance Man.

Rick's Tip: *On the first Sunday of the month, all state museums are free.* **Free admission makes the Accademia impossibly crowded.** *Avoid visiting on that day.*

Cost and Hours: €12.50 (or €8 if there's no special exhibit), additional €4 for reservation, free and crowded on first Sun of the month, covered by Firenze Card; Tue-Sun 8:15-18:50, closed Mon; audioguide-€6, Via Ricasoli 60, reservation tel. 055-294-883, www.polomuseale. firenze.it. To bypass long lines in peak season, get the Firenze Card (see page 576) or make reservations (see page 577).

🎧 Download my free Accademia audio tour.

Visiting the Accademia: In 1501, Michelangelo Buonarroti, a 26-year-old Florentine, was commissioned to carve a large-scale work. The figure comes from a Bible story. The Israelites are surrounded by barbarian warriors, who are led by a brutish giant named Goliath. When the giant challenges the Israelites to send out someone to fight him, a young shepherd boy steps forward. Armed only with a sling, David defeats the giant. This 17-foot-tall symbol of divine victory over evil represents a new century and a whole new Renaissance outlook.

Originally, *David* was meant to stand on the roofline of the Duomo, but was placed more prominently at the entrance of Palazzo Vecchio (where a copy stands today). In the 19th century, *David* was moved

Michelangelo, David

indoors for his own protection; he stands under a Renaissance-style dome designed just for him.

Nearby are some of the master's other works, including his powerful (unfinished) *Prisoners, St. Matthew,* and a *Pietà* (possibly by one of his disciples). Michelangelo Buonarroti believed that the sculptor was a tool of God, responsible only for chipping away at the stone until the intended sculpture emerged.

▲▲MUSEUM OF SAN MARCO (MUSEO DI SAN MARCO)

Located one block north of the Accademia, this 15th-century monastery houses the greatest collection of frescoes and paintings by Renaissance master Fra Angelico. Upstairs are 43 cells decorated by Fra Angelico and his assistants. Trained in the medieval style, he adopted Renaissance techniques to produce works that blended Christian symbols with realism. Don't miss the cell of Savonarola, the charismatic monk who threw out the Medici, and sponsored "bonfires of the vanities."

Cost and Hours: €4, free and crowded on first Sun of the month, covered by Firenze Card, Tue-Fri 8:15-13:50, Sat 8:15-16:50; also open 8:15-13:50 on first, third, and fifth Mon and 8:15-16:50 on second and fourth Sun of each month; on Piazza San Marco, tel. 055-238-8608, www.polomuseale.firenze.it.

▲▲MEDICI CHAPELS

The burial site of the ruling Medici family in the Basilica of San Lorenzo includes the dusky crypt; the big, domed Chapel of Princes; and the magnificent New Sacristy, featuring architecture, tombs, and statues almost entirely by Michelangelo. The Medici made their money in textiles and banking, and patronized a dream team of Renaissance artists that put Florence on the cultural map. Michelangelo, who spent his teen years living with the Medici, was commissioned to create the family's final tribute.

Cost and Hours: €8 (or €6 if no special exhibits), free and crowded on first Sun of the month, covered by Firenze Card; April-Oct Tue-Sat 8:15-16:50, Nov-March Tue-Sat 8:15-13:50; also open second and fourth Mon and first, third, and fifth Sun of each month; audioguide-€6, modest dress required, tel. 055-238-8602, www.polomuseale.firenze.it.

▲MERCATO CENTRALE

Florence's giant iron-and-glass-covered central market is a wonderland of picturesque produce. While the San Lorenzo Market that fills the surrounding streets is only a step up from a flea market, Mercato Centrale retains its Florentine elegance.

Downstairs, you'll see parts of the cow (and bull) you'd never dream of eating (no, that's not a turkey neck), enjoy generous free samples, watch pasta being made, and have your pick of plenty of

Michelangelo sculptures in the Medici Chapels

Mercato Centrale

fun eateries sloshing out cheap and tasty pasta to locals (Mon-Fri 7:00-14:00, Sat 7:00-17:00, closed Sun).

Upstairs, the meticulously restored glass roof and steel rafters soar over a sleek and modern food court, serving up a bounty of Tuscan cuisine (daily 10:00-24:00). This is clearly Florence's bid to have an upscale foodie market to call its own.

On and near Piazza della Signoria

▲▲▲UFFIZI GALLERY

This greatest collection of Italian paintings anywhere features works by Giotto, Leonardo, Raphael, Caravaggio, Titian, and Michelangelo, and a room-ful of Botticellis, including the *Birth of Venus*. Start with Giotto's early stabs at Renaissance-style realism, then move on through the 3-D experimentation of the early 1400s to the real thing rendered by the likes of Botticelli and Leonardo. Finish off with Michelangelo and Titian. Because only 600 visitors are allowed inside the building at any one time, there's generally a very long wait. The good news: no Louvre-style mob scenes inside. The museum is nowhere near as big as it is great. Few tourists spend more than two hours inside.

Rick's Tip: The Uffizi is terribly crowded when it's free, *on the first Sunday of the month. Don't visit on that day.*

Cost and Hours: €12.50 (or €8 if there's no special exhibit), extra €4 for reservation, free and crowded on first Sun of the month, covered by Firenze Card, Tue-Sun 8:15-18:35, closed Mon, audio-guide-€6, reservation tel. 055-294-883, www.uffizi.firenze.it. To avoid the long ticket lines, get a Firenze Card (see page 576) or make reservations (see page 577).

🎧 Download my free Uffizi Gallery audio tour.

Getting In: There are several entrances; which one you use depends on whether you have a Firenze Card, a reservation, or neither.

Firenze Card holders enter at door #1 (labeled *Reservation Entrance*), close to Palazzo Vecchio. Get in the line for individuals, not groups.

People **buying a ticket on the spot** line up with everyone else at door #2, marked *Main Entrance*. (The wait can be hours long—an estimated wait time is posted.)

To **buy a Firenze Card,** or to see if there are any same-day reservations available (€4 extra), enter door #2 to the left of the same-day ticket-buying line (marked *Booking Service and Today*). Don't get into the long ticket-buying line. The left side of the doorway is kept open for same-day reservation buyers.

If you've **already made a reservation** and need to pick up your ticket, go to door #3 (labeled *Reservation Ticket Office,* across the courtyard from doors #1 and #2, closer to the river). Tickets are available for pickup 10 minutes before your appointed time. If you booked online and have already prepaid, you'll exchange your voucher for a ticket. If you booked by phone, give them your confirmation number and pay for the ticket. Then walk briskly past the ticket-buying line to door #1. Get in the correct queue—one is for groups, one for individuals.

Expect long waits even if you have a reservation or Firenze Card in hand. There may be a queue to pick up your reservation at door #3, another 30-minute wait to enter at door #1, and a slow shuffle through security.

Visiting the Uffizi: The Uffizi is U-shaped, running around the courtyard. The east wing contains Florentine paintings from medieval to Renaissance times. At the south end, you pass through a short hallway filled with sculpture. The west wing has later Florentine art (especially Michelangelo) and a café terrace facing the Duomo. Many more rooms of art are downstairs, showing how the Florentine

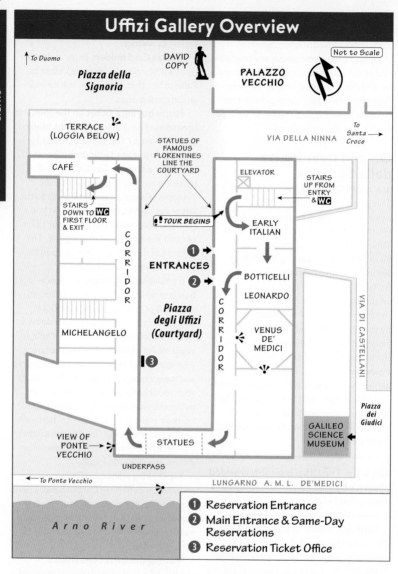

Uffizi Gallery Overview

To Duomo

DAVID COPY

Piazza della Signoria

Not to Scale

PALAZZO VECCHIO

TERRACE (LOGGIA BELOW)

VIA DELLA NINNA

To Santa Croce

CAFÉ

STATUES OF FAMOUS FLORENTINES LINE THE COURTYARD

ELEVATOR

STAIRS UP FROM ENTRY & **WC**

STAIRS DOWN TO **WC** FIRST FLOOR & EXIT

TOUR BEGINS

EARLY ITALIAN

CORRIDOR

1 ENTRANCES

2

BOTTICELLI

LEONARDO

CORRIDOR

Piazza degli Uffizi (Courtyard)

VENUS DE' MEDICI

MICHELANGELO

3

VIA DI CASTELLANI

Piazza dei Giudici

VIEW OF PONTE VECCHIO

STATUES

GALILEO SCIENCE MUSEUM

UNDERPASS

To Ponte Vecchio

LUNGARNO A. M. L. DE'MEDICI

Arno River

1 Reservation Entrance
2 Main Entrance & Same-Day Reservations
3 Reservation Ticket Office

Renaissance spread to Rome (Raphael) and Venice (Titian), and inspired the Baroque (Caravaggio).

Medieval (1200-1400): Paintings by **Duccio, Cimabue,** and **Giotto** show the baby steps being made from the flat Byzantine style toward realism. In his *Madonna and Child with Angels,* Giotto created a "stage" and peopled it with real beings. The triumph here is Mary herself—big and monumental, like a Roman statue. Beneath her robe, she has knees and breasts that stick out at us. This three-dimensionality was revolutionary, a taste of the Renaissance a century before it began.

Early Renaissance (mid-1400s): Paolo Uccello's *Battle of San Romano* is an early study in perspective with a few obvious flubs. Piero della Francesca's *Federico da Montefeltro and Battista Sforza* heralds the era of humanism and the new centrality of ordinary people in art. Fra Filippo Lippi's radiant Madonnas are light years away from the generic Marys of the medieval era.

Renaissance (1450-1500): The Botticelli room is filled with masterpieces and classical fleshiness (the famous *Birth of Venus* and *Spring*), plus two minor works by Leonardo da Vinci. (If this room is under renovation, the paintings are in Room 41.) Here is the Renaissance in its first bloom. This is a return to the pagan world of classical Greece, where things of the flesh are not sinful. Madonna is out; Venus is in.

Classical Sculpture: The foundation of the Renaissance was classical sculpture. Sculptors, painters, and poets turned for inspiration to ancient Greek and Roman works as the epitome of balance, 3-D perspective, human anatomy, and beauty.

In the Tribune Room, the highlight is the *Venus de' Medici,* a Roman copy of the lost original of the great Greek sculptor Praxiteles' *Aphrodite.* Balanced, harmonious, and serene, this statue was considered the epitome of beauty and sexuality in Renaissance Florence.

The **sculpture hall** has 2,000-year-old copies of 2,500-year-old Greek originals... and the best view in Florence of the Arno River and Ponte Vecchio through the window, dreamy at sunset.

High Renaissance (1500-1550): Don't miss Michelangelo's *Holy Family,* the only surviving completed easel painting by the greatest sculptor in history (in the Michelangelo Room).

After a break to enjoy Duomo views from the café terrace, head downstairs to find Raphael's *Madonna of the Goldfinch,* with Mary and the Baby Jesus brought down from heaven into the real world (Room 66), and Titian's voluptuous *Venus of Urbino* (Room 83).

More Art on the Lower Floor: On your way out, you'll see temporary exhibitions and works by foreign painters. It's worth pausing in Room 90 for works by Caravaggio.

Nearby: The statue-filled Uffizi courtyard and Loggia dei Lanzi are covered in the Renaissance Walk on page 582 and in my 🎧 free Renaissance Walk audio tour.

Titian, Venus of Urbino

▲▲PALAZZO VECCHIO

This fortress with the 300-foot spire dominates Florence's main square. In Renaissance times, it was the Town Hall, where citizens pioneered the once-radical notion of self-rule. Its official name—Palazzo della Signoria—refers to the elected members of the city council. In 1540, the tyrant Cosimo I made the building his personal palace, redecorating the interior in lavish style. Today the building functions once again as the Town Hall.

Entry to the ground-floor courtyard is free, so even if you don't go upstairs to the museum, you can step inside and feel the essence of the Medici. Paying customers can see Cosimo's lavish royal apartments, decorated with paintings and statues by Michelangelo and Donatello. The highlight is the 13,000-square-foot Grand Hall (Salone dei Cinquecento), lined with frescoes and statues.

Cost and Hours: Courtyard-free to enter, museum-€10, tower climb-€10 (418 steps), museum plus tower-€14, museum and tower covered by Firenze Card (first pick up ticket at ground-floor info desk before entering museum). Museum is open April-Sept Fri-Wed 9:00-24:00, Thu 9:00-14:00; Oct-March Fri-Wed 9:00-19:00, Thu 9:00-14:00; tower has similar but shorter hours (last entry to either is one hour before closing); videoguide-€5, English tours available, Piazza della Signoria, tel. 055-276-8224, http://museicivici fiorentini.comune.fi.it.

▲▲GALILEO SCIENCE MUSEUM

When we think of the Renaissance, we think of visual arts: painting, mosaics, architecture, and sculpture. But when the visual arts declined in the 1600s (abused and co-opted by political powers), music and science flourished. Florence hosted many scientific breakthroughs, as you'll see in this collection of clocks, telescopes, maps, and ingenious gadgets. Trace the technical innovations as modern science emerges from 1000 to 1900. Exhibits include various tools for gauging the world, from a compass and thermometer to Galileo's telescopes. Some of the most talked about bottles in Florence are the ones here that contain Galileo's fingers. The museum is friendly, comfortably cool,

Palazzo Vecchio

Celestial globe at Galileo Science Museum

never crowded, and just a block east of the Uffizi on the Arno River.

Cost and Hours: €9, €22 family ticket, covered by Firenze Card, Wed-Mon 9:30-18:00, Tue 9:30-13:00, guided tours available, Piazza dei Giudici 1, tel. 055-265-311, www.museogalileo.it.

East of Piazza della Signoria

▲▲▲BARGELLO

The Renaissance began with sculpture—the great Florentine painters were "sculptors with brushes." You can see the birth of this revolution of 3-D in the Bargello (bar-JEL-oh), which boasts the best collection of Florentine sculpture. Housed in a former police station, this small, uncrowded museum is a pleasure to visit.

Highlights include Donatello's influential, painfully beautiful *David* (the first male nude to be sculpted in a thousand years), multiple works by Michelangelo, and rooms of Medici treasures. Moody Donatello, who embraced realism with his lifelike statues, set the personal and artistic style for many Renaissance artists to follow. The best pieces are in the ground-floor room at the foot of the outdoor staircase (with fine works by Michelangelo, Cellini, and Giambologna) and in the "Donatello room" directly above (including his two different *David*s, plus Ghiberti and Brunelleschi's revolutionary dueling door panels and yet another *David* by Verrocchio).

Cost and Hours: €7 (or €4 if no special exhibits), cash only, free and crowded on first Sun of the month, covered by Firenze Card, Tue-Sat 8:15-17:00—or until 13:50 if no special exhibits; also open these times on the second and fourth Mon and the first, third, and fifth Sun of each month; reservations possible but unnecessary, audioguide-€6 (€10/2 people), Via del Proconsolo 4, tel. 055-238-8606, www.polomuseale.firenze.it.

▲▲SANTA CROCE CHURCH

This 14th-century Franciscan church, decorated with centuries of precious art, holds the tombs of great Florentines. The loud 19th-century Victorian Gothic facade faces a huge square ringed with tempting shops and littered with footsore tourists. Escape into the church and admire its sheer height and spaciousness.

Cost and Hours: €6, covered by Firenze Card, Mon-Sat 9:30-17:30, Sun 14:00-17:30, multimedia guide-€6 (€8/2 people), modest dress required, 10-minute walk east of Palazzo Vecchio along Borgo de' Greci, tel. 055-246-6105, www.santacroceopera.it. The **leather school,** at the back of the church, is free and sells church tickets—handy when the church has a long line (daily 10:00-18:00, closed Sun Nov-March, has own entry behind church, plus an entry within church, www.scuoladelcuoio.com).

Visiting the Church: On the left wall (as you face the altar) is the tomb of **Galileo Galilei** (1564-1642), the Pisan who lived his last years under house arrest near Florence. His crime? Defying the Church

Donatello, David

Santa Croce Church

by saying that the earth revolved around the sun. His heretical remains were only allowed in the church long after his death.

Directly opposite (on the right wall) is the tomb of **Michelangelo Buonarroti** (1475-1564). Santa Croce was Michelangelo's childhood church, as he grew up a block west of here. Farther up the nave is the tomb of **Niccolò Machiavelli** (1469-1527), a champion of democratic Florence and author of *The Prince,* a how-to manual on hardball politics—which later Medici rulers found instructive.

The first chapel to the right of the main altar features the famous *Death of St. Francis* fresco by Giotto. With simple but eloquent gestures, Francis' brothers bid him a sad farewell. In the hallway near the bookstore, notice the photos of the devastating flood of 1966. Beyond that is the leather school (free entry).

Exit between the Rossini and Machiavelli tombs into the delightful cloister (peaceful open-air courtyard). On the left, enter Brunelleschi's Pazzi Chapel, which captures the Renaissance in miniature.

Near the Train Station
▲▲CHURCH OF SANTA MARIA NOVELLA

This 13th-century Dominican church is rich in art. Along with crucifixes by Giotto and Brunelleschi, it contains every textbook's example of the early Renaissance mastery of perspective: *The Trinity* by Masaccio. The exquisite chapels trace art in Florence from medieval times to early Baroque. The outside of the church features a dash of Romanesque (horizontal stripes), Gothic (pointed arches), Renaissance (geometric shapes), and Baroque (scrolls). Step in and look down the 330-foot nave for a 14th-century optical illusion.

Next to the church are the cloisters and the **museum,** located in the old Dominican convent of Santa Maria Novella. Its highlight is the breathtaking Spanish Chapel, with walls covered by a series of frescoes by Andrea di Bonaiuto.

Cost and Hours: Church and museum-€5, covered by Firenze Card, Mon-Thu 9:00-17:30, Fri 11:00-17:30, Sat 9:00-17:00, Sun 12:00-17:00 July-Sept

(Sun from 13:00 Oct-June), last entry 45 minutes before closing, audioguide-€5, modest dress required, main entrance on Piazza Santa Maria Novella, Firenze Card holders must enter behind the church at Piazza della Stazione 4, tel. 055-219-257, www.chiesasantamarianovella.it.

South of the Arno River

▲▲PITTI PALACE

Pitti Palace, several blocks southwest of Ponte Vecchio, offers many reasons for a visit: the palace itself, with its imposing exterior and lavish interior; the second-best collection of paintings in town; the statue-dotted Boboli Gardens; and a host of secondary museums. Focus on the highlights: the painting collection in the Palatine Gallery, plus the sumptuous rooms of the Royal Apartments. The paintings pick up where the Uffizi leaves off, at the High Renaissance. Lovers of Raphael's Madonnas and Titian's portraits will find some of the world's best here. If it's a nice day, take a stroll in the inviting Boboli Gardens, a rare patch of green space within old Florence.

You can't buy a ticket for the Palatine Gallery alone; to see it you'll need to buy ticket #1, which includes the Palatine Gallery, Royal Apartments, and Gallery of Modern Art. Ticket #2 covers the Boboli and Bardini Gardens, Costume Gallery, Argenti/Silverworks Museum, and Porcelain Museum. Behind door #3 is a combo-ticket covering the whole shebang.

Cost and Hours: Ticket #1—€13 (€8.50 if no special exhibits), Tue-Sun 8:15-18:50, closed Mon, last entry 45 minutes before closing. Ticket #2—€10 (€7 if no special exhibits), daily June-Aug 8:15-19:30, April-May and Sept-Oct 8:15-18:30, March 8:15-17:30, Nov-Feb 8:15-16:30, closed first and last Mon of each month, last entry one hour before closing. Ticket #3—€11.50, valid 3 days, not available during special exhibitions. The place is free and crowded on the first Sun of the month, and everything is covered by the Firenze Card (except the Bardini Gardens—an additional €6 for cardholders). The €8 audioguide (€13/2 people) explains the sprawling palace. Tel. 055-238-8614, www.polomuseale.firenze.it.

Pitti Palace

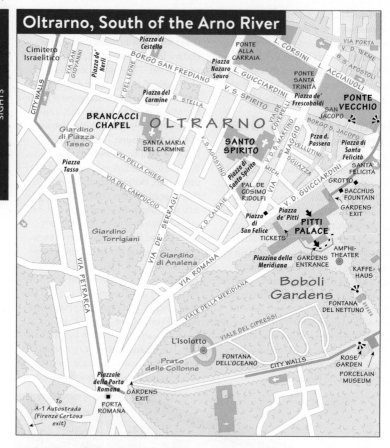

Oltrarno, South of the Arno River

Cimitero Israelitico · CITY WALLS · VIA SAN GIOVANNI · Piazza de' Nerli · V. DELL'EONE · Piazza di Cestello · BORGO SAN FREDIANO · Piazza Nazaro Sauro · PONTE ALLA CARRAIA · L. CORSINI · L. GUICCIARDINI · VIA PORTA · V. D. TERME · B. S. APOSTOLI · PONTE SANTA TRINITA · Piazza de' Frescobaldi · SAN JACOPO · PONTE VECCHIO

BRANCACCI CHAPEL · Piazza del Carmine · B. STELLA · V. S. SPIRITO · VIA DE COVERELLI · BORGO S. JACOPO

Giardino di Piazza Tasso · OLTRARNO · SANTA MARIA DEL CARMINE · V. S. AGOSTINO · SANTO SPIRITO · V. DE' MARTINO · V. D. S. MARTINO · VELLUTINI · Pza d. Passera · Piazza di Santa Felicità · SANTA FELICITÀ

Piazza Tasso · VIA DELLA CHIESA · Piazza di Santo Spirito · MICH. · SGUAZZA · VIA MAGGIO · V. D. GUICCIARDINI · GROTTO · BACCHUS FOUNTAIN

VIA DEL CAMPUCCIO · PAL. DE COSIMO RIDOLFI · GARDENS EXIT

Giardino Torrigiani · VIA DE' SERRAGLI · V. D. CALDAIE · Piazza di San Felice · Piazza de' Pitti · PITTI PALACE · TICKETS

Giardino di Analena · VIA ROMANA · Piazzina della Meridiana · GARDENS ENTRANCE · AMPHI-THEATER · KAFFE-HAUS

VIA PETRARCA · VIALE DELLA MERIDIANA · Boboli Gardens · FONTANA DEL NETTUNO

L'Isolotto · VIALE DEI CIPRESSI · Prato delle Collonne · FONTANA DELL'OCEANO · CITY WALLS · ROSE GARDEN · PORCELAIN MUSEUM

Piazzale della Porta Romana · GARDENS EXIT · PORTA ROMANA · To A-1 Autostrada (Firenze Certosa exit)

Visiting Pitti Palace: In the **Palatine Gallery** you'll walk through one palatial room after another, walls sagging with masterpieces by 16th- and 17th-century masters, including Rubens, Titian, and Rembrandt. The Pitti's Raphael collection is the second-biggest anywhere—the Vatican beats it by one. Each room has some descriptions in English, though the paintings themselves have limited English labels.

The collection is all on one floor. To see the highlights, walk straight down the spine through a dozen or so rooms. Before you exit, consider a visit to the Royal Apartments. These 14 rooms (of which only a few are open at any one time) are where the Pitti's rulers lived in the 18th

and 19th centuries. Each room features a different color and time period. Here, you get a real feel for the splendor of the dukes' world.

The rest of Pitti Palace is skippable, unless the various sights match your interests: the **Gallery of Modern Art** (second floor; Romantic, Neoclassical, and Impressionist works by 19th- and 20th-century Tuscan painters), **Argenti/Silverworks Museum** (ground and mezzanine floors; Medici treasures from jeweled crucifixes to gilded ostrich eggs), **Costume Gallery, Porcelain Museum,** and **Boboli and Bardini gardens** (behind the palace; enter from Pitti Palace courtyard—be prepared to climb uphill).

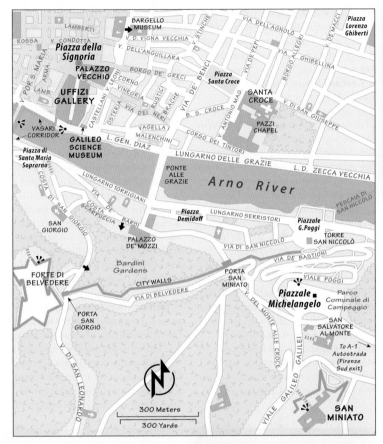

▲▲ BRANCACCI CHAPEL

For the best look at works by Masaccio (one of the early Renaissance pioneers of perspective in painting), see his restored frescoes here. Instead of medieval religious symbols, Masaccio's paintings feature simple, strong human figures with facial expressions that reflect their emotions. The accompanying works of Masolino and Filippino Lippi provide illuminating contrasts.

Your ticket includes a 20-minute film (English subtitles) on the chapel, the frescoes, and Renaissance Florence; find it in the room next to the bookstore. (If the film's not showing, consider the €2 videoguide.) The film's computer anima-

Masaccio, Expulsion from the Garden of Eden

tion brings the paintings to 3-D life, while narration describes the events depicted in the panels. The film takes liberties with the art, but it's the best way to see the frescoes close up.

Cost and Hours: €6, cash only, covered by Firenze Card; free and easy reservations required if you don't have a Firenze Card (see next); Mon and Wed-Sat 10:00-17:00, Sun 13:00-17:00, closed Tue, last entry 45 minutes before closing; free 20-minute film, videoguide-€2, knees and shoulders must be covered; in Church of Santa Maria del Carmine, on Piazza del Carmine in Oltrarno neighborhood; reservations tel. 055-276-8224 or 055-276-8558, ticket desk tel. 055-284-361, http://museicivicifiorentini.comune.fi.it.

Reservations: Although reservations are required, on weekdays and any day off-season, it's often possible to walk right in, especially if you come before 15:30. To reserve in advance, call the chapel a day ahead (tel. 055-276-8224 or 055-276-8558, English spoken, call center open Mon-Sat 9:30-13:00 & 14:00-17:00, Sun 9:30-12:30). You can also try reserving via email (info.museoragazzi@comune.fi.it).

▲PIAZZALE MICHELANGELO

Overlooking the city from across the river (look for the huge bronze statue of *David*), this square has a superb view of Florence and the stunning dome of the Duomo. It's worth the 30-minute hike, short drive, or bus ride.

The best cityscape photos are taken from the street immediately below the overlook (go around to the right and down a few steps). Nearby is an an inviting café (open seasonally) with great views. Off the west side of the piazza is a hidden terrace, excellent for a retreat from the mobs. After dark, the square is packed with school kids licking ice cream and each other. About 200 yards beyond is the stark, beautiful, crowd-free, Romanesque San Miniato Church. A WC is located just off the road, halfway between the two sights.

Getting There (and Back): It makes sense to take a taxi or ride the bus up and then enjoy the easy downhill walk back into town. Bus #12 takes you up (departs from train station, near Piazza di Santa Maria Novella, and just over the Ponte alla Carraia bridge on Oltrarno side of river; takes 20-30 minutes, longer in bad traffic).

The view from Piazzale Michelangelo

The hike down is quick and enjoyable (or take bus #13 back down). Find the steps between the two bars on the San Miniato Church side of the parking lot (Via San Salvatore al Monte). At the first landing (marked #3), peek into the rose garden (Giardino delle Rose). After a few minutes, you'll walk through the old wall (Porta San Miniato) and emerge in the funky little neighborhood of San Niccolò in the Oltrarno.

EXPERIENCES

Shopping

One of Europe's best shopping towns, Florence has been known for its sense of style since the Medici days. Smaller stores are generally open about 9:00-13:00 and 15:30-19:30, usually closed on Sunday, often closed on Monday (or at least Monday morning), and sometimes closed for a couple of weeks around August 15. Bigger stores have similar hours, without the afternoon break.

Busy street scenes and markets abound. The vast open-air **San Lorenzo**

Market sprawls in the streets ringing Mercato Centrale, between the Duomo and the train station (daily 9:00-19:00, closed Mon in winter). Originally a silk and straw market, **Mercato Nuovo** still functions as a rustic yet touristy market at the intersection of Via Calimala and Via Porta Rossa. It's where you'll find *Il Porcellino* (a statue of a wild boar nicknamed "The Piglet"), which people rub and give coins to ensure their return to Florence. Other shopping areas can be found near Santa Croce and on Ponte Vecchio. At stalls or shops, prices are soft—don't be shy about bargaining, especially at San Lorenzo.

Leather jackets and handbags, perfume and cosmetics, edible goodies, and stationery are popular souvenirs. For authentic, locally produced wares, look for shops displaying the **Esercizi Storici Fiorentini** ("Historical Florentine Ventures") seal, with a picture of Palazzo Vecchio's tower. You may pay a premium, but you can be assured of quality (for a list of shops, see www.esercizistorici.it).

The area between the Arno River and the cathedral is busy with fashion boutiques; browse along **Via della**

San Lorenzo Market

Florence is the place to buy leather.

Vigna Nuova (runs west from Via de' Tornabuoni) and **Via degli Strozzi** (runs east from Via de' Tornabuoni to Piazza della Repubblica). A tempting string of streets—**Borgo Santi Apostoli, Via del Parione,** and **Borgo Ognissanti**—runs parallel to the river one block inland, from near the Uffizi westward.

Across the river in the Oltrarno, known for its artisanal workshops, a short walk past the tourist crowds takes you to some less-discovered zones: near Pitti Palace, and the main street parallel to the river (**Borgo San Jacopo** to **Via di Santo Spirito**). Pick up the brochure "A Tour of Artisan Workshops" from the TI or at participating shops.

Nightlife

For me, nighttime is for dining, catching a concert, strolling through the old town with a gelato, or hitting one of the many pubs. Get the latest on nightlife from *The Florentine* magazine (free from TI, www. theflorentine.net) or *Firenze Spettacolo* (sold at newsstands, www.firenzespetta colo.it), or check www.firenzeturismo.it.

Strolling After Dark: Join the parade of locals on their evening *passegiata,* strolling from the Duomo to the Arno on Via de' Calzaiuoli, enjoying cafés, gelato shops, great people-watching, and street performers. Pop into a wine bar *(enoteca)* to sample regional wines by the glass or a plate of meats and cheeses. (Psst. Near the Duomo, find La Congrega Lounge Bar—a tiny retreat on a tiny lane just off the main pedestrian drag, at Via Tosinghi 3/4 red.) End at the Arno, to stand atop Ponte Vecchio and watch the sun set, the moon rise, and lovers kiss.

Lively squares include Piazzale Michelangelo's marvelous viewpoint, Piazza della Repubblica (with a carousel and street musicians), Piazza Santa Croce (with popular, youthful Moyo bar nearby, at Via de' Benci 23 red), and Piazza di Santo Spirito (with trendy Volume and Pop Café on this Oltrarno square).

Live Music: Orsanmichele Church hosts chamber music under its Gothic arches (tickets sold on day of concert from door facing Via de' Calzaiuoli). **Santo Stefano Church,** near Ponte Vecchio, hosts concerts nearly nightly at 21:15 (on Piazza San Stefano, tel. 055-289-367, www.notearmoniche.com).

The recommended **Golden View**

Ponte Vecchio after dark

Open Bar, a river-view restaurant near Ponte Vecchio, has live jazz several nights a week at 21:00 (see page 612). The Box Office sells tickets for rock concerts and more (Via delle Vecchie Carceri 1, tel. 055-210-804, www.boxofficetoscana.it).

Sightseeing: Some sights stay open later, such as Palazzo Vecchio, allowing you to extend your sightseeing into the evening (see "Daily Reminder" on page 578).

Movies: Find English-language films at **Odeon Cinema** (near Piazza della Repubblica on Piazza Strozzi, tel. 055-214-068, www.odeonfirenze.com).

EATING

Restaurants in Florence like to serve what's fresh. Seasonal ingredients are featured in the *piatti del giorno* (specials of the day) section on menus. Foodies should consider purchasing Elizabeth Minchilli's excellent app, Eat Florence (www.elizabethminchilliinrome.com).

Budget Eating: To save money and time, you can keep lunches fast and simple by eating at pizzerias, self-service cafeterias, or the countless sandwich shops and stands (though you may want to avoid the *trippa* carts selling tripe sandwiches—a prized local specialty).

Picnicking is easy. You can picnic your way through Mercato Centrale. You'll also find good *supermercati* throughout the city. I like the classy Sapori & Dintorni markets (run by Conad), which has branches near the Duomo (Borgo San

Lorenzo 15 red) and just over Ponte Vecchio in the Oltrarno (Via de Bardi 45). Despar is another handy grocery chain (there's one around the corner from the Duomo Museum at Via dell'Oriuolo 66).

Mercato Centrale and Nearby
In Mercato Centrale

The Mercato Centrale (Central Market) is a foodie wonderland.

Ground Floor: The market zone, with lots of raw ingredients and a few humble food counters, is open only through lunchtime (Mon-Fri 7:00-14:00, Sat 7:00-17:00, closed Sun). Buy a picnic of fresh mozzarella cheese, olives, fruit, and crunchy bread to munch on the steps of the nearby Basilica of San Lorenzo. The fancy deli, **Perini,** is famous for its quality (pricey) products and enticing display. For a sit-down meal, head for **Nerbone in the Market.** Join the shoppers and workers who crowd the bar to grab their €4-7 plates, and then find a stool at the cramped shared tables nearby (lunch menu served Mon-Sat 12:00-14:00, sandwiches available from 8:00 until the bread runs out, closed Sun, cash only, on the side closest to the Basilica of San Lorenzo, mobile 339-648-0251). Its less-famous sisters, nearby, have better seating and fewer crowds.

Upstairs: Under a gleaming glass roof, a dozen upscale food counters let you browse for your perfect meal. Each is labeled with the type of food and proprietor—a *Who's Who* of Florentine chefs. Grab what you want—pizza, pasta, fish, meat, *salumi, lampredotto,* wine—and pull up a stool at one of the tables between the stalls. Higher up, there are restaurants with designated seating and table service: a casual pizzeria on one side, and a more formal place on the other. These eateries are open longer than the traditional, downstairs places—for lunch, dinner, and on Sunday, too (daily 10:00-24:00, www.mercatocentrale.it).

Gelato

The best ice cream in Italy—maybe the world—is in Florence. But beware of scams at touristy joints that turn a simple request for a cone into a €10 rip-off. Survey the options and specify the size you want—for example, *un cono da tre euro* (a €3 cone).

All of these places, a cut above, are open daily for long hours:

Near the Accademia: Gelateria Carabè is famous for *granite* (Italian ices made with fresh fruit). Try a *cremolata*: a *granita* with a dollop of gelato (Via Ricasoli 60 red; from the Accademia, it's a block toward the Duomo).

Between the Duomo and Ponte Vecchio: Grom, near the Duomo, touts its organic ingredients (Via delle Oche 24 red). Creative **Perchè No!** is near Orsanmichele Church, just off busy Via de' Calzaiuoli (Via dei Tavolini 19). Mod **Carapina,** near Ponte Vecchio, has unusual flavors and seasonal ingredients (Via Lambertesca 18 red).

Near the Church of Santa Croce: Gelateria de' Neri has a wide array of enticing flavors (Via dei Neri 9 red).

In the Oltrarno: Tiny **Il Gelato di Filo** boasts some of Florence's best gelato (Via San Miniato 5 red). **Gelateria della Passera** is classy and popular (Via Toscanella 15, between Pitti Palace and the Brancacci Chapel).

Near Mercato Centrale

If you can't find what you want in the market itself, consider one of these alternatives on the surrounding streets. These eateries skew to an especially touristy clientele.

Trattoria Mario, serving hearty lunches since 1953, has a simple formula: no-frills, bustling service, old-fashioned good value, and shared tables. It's *cucina casalinga*—home cooking *con brio*. Their best dishes (*ribollita,* bean soup, *amatriciana*) often sell out, so go early (€5-6 pastas, €8 *secondi,* Mon-Sat 12:00-15:30, closed Sun and Aug, no reservations, cash only, Via Rosina 2, tel. 055-218-550).

Pepò, colorful and charming, offers a short menu of Florentine classics, such as *melanzane parmigiana* (eggplant parmesan) and *pollo alla cacciatora* (chicken cacciatore). It's an easy neighborhood fallback where you won't feel like you've settled for second-best (€9-10 pastas, €11-14 *secondi,* daily 12:00-14:30 & 19:00-22:30, Via Rosina 4 red, tel. 055-283-259).

Trattoria Gozzi Sergio is a classic neighborhood lunch place, serving basic Florentine since 1915—long before the tourist crush (€6 pastas, €10 *secondi,* Mon-Sat 12:00-15:00, closed Sun, reservations smart, Piazza di San Lorenzo 8, tel. 055-281-941).

Near the Duomo

Enoteca Coquinarius—hip and welcoming—has a slow food ethic and great €15 salads and €10 pastas (open daily, a couple blocks south of the Duomo at Via delle Oche 11 red, tel. 055-230-2153).

Miso di Riso Vegetarian Bistro serves nothing with eyeballs. You'll find organic, seasonal, and vegan dishes—especially great salads—and an inviting garden courtyard (€10 lunch plates, €13 dinner plates, Tue-Sun 10:00-23:00, closed Mon, Borgo degli Albizi 54 red, tel. 055-265-4094).

Fast Meals

Self-Service Ristorante Leonardo is a quick, no-frills, inexpensive, air-conditioned cafeteria. The food, with lots of veggies, is better than many table-service eateries in this part of town. It's just a block from the Duomo, southwest of the Baptistery (€5 *primi,* €6-7 main courses, daily 11:45-14:45 & 18:45-21:45, upstairs at Via Pecori 11, tel. 055-284-446).

Paszkowski, a grand café on Piazza della Repubblica, serves quick, inexpensive lunches. Order a salad, €6 plate of pasta, or cooked veggies (or half-and-half for €7), pay the cashier, and find a seat upstairs. Better yet, eat at one of the tables on the square—you can sit on the right side of the terrace for no extra charge. Full-table service prices are much higher (daily 7:00-24:00, lunch served 12:00-15:00, Piazza della Repubblica 35 red—northwest corner, tel. 055-210-236).

EATaly is part of a growing chain of foodie mini-malls that are popping up in big Italian cities (as well as in New York City, thanks to part-owner Mario Batali). This slick, modern space just a half-block from the Duomo includes an espresso counter; a soft-serve gelato counter and tempting pastry shop; a high-end grocery store; and, in back, a cluster of food counters serving €9-12 pastas and pizzas and €10-16 *secondi.* It's a handy place to assemble a gourmet picnic or stock up on edible souvenirs (daily 9:00-22:30, restaurants open 12:00-15:30 and from 19:00, Via de' Martelli 22 red, tel. 055-015-3601).

Near Piazza della Signoria

Piazza della Signoria, the scenic square facing Palazzo Vecchio, is ringed by beautifully situated yet touristy eateries serving overpriced and probably microwaved food. You'll find better values off the square.

Dining

Colorful **Osteria Vini e Vecchi Sapori** serves a fun, accessible menu of delicious €8-10 pastas and €9-15 *secondi* (Mon-Sat 12:30-14:30 & 19:30-22:30, closed Sun, reserve for dinner; a half-block north of Palazzo Vecchio at Via dei Magazzini 3 red; facing the bronze equestrian statue in Piazza della Signoria, go behind its tail into the corner and to your left; tel. 055-293-045).

Frescobaldi Ristorante and Wine Bar, the showcase of Italy's aristocratic wine family, is a good choice for a formal dinner. Candlelight reflects off glasses of wine, and high-vaulted ceilings complement the sophisticated dishes. Make a reservation and dress up. The same seasonal menu is available in their cozy wine bar and at a few outside tables, with a lighter wine-bar menu at lunch (€11-15 appetizers and pastas, €19-26 *secondi,* daily 12:00-14:30

& 19:00-22:30, air-con, a half-block north of Palazzo Vecchio at Via dei Magazzini 2 red, tel. 055-284-724, www.deifrescobaldi. it).

Cheap, Simple Fare

Cantinetta dei Verrazzano, a long-established bakery/café/wine bar, serves delightful sandwich plates in an old-time setting. Their *selezione Verrazzano* is a fine plate of four little crostini (€7.50). The *tagliere di focacce,* a sampler plate of mini-focaccia sandwiches, is also fun (€16 for big plate for two). Add a €6 glass of Chianti to make a fine, light meal. They also have benches and tiny tables for eating at takeout prices (Mon-Sat 8:00-21:00, Sun 10:00-16:30, just off Via de' Calzaiuoli, across from Orsanmichele Church at Via dei Tavolini 18, tel. 055-268-590).

I Fratellini, a little hole-in-the-wall place, has served sandwiches and a wonderful selection of wine at great prices since 1875. Join the local crowd to order, then sit on a nearby curb to eat, placing your glass on the wall rack before you leave. It's worth ordering the most expensive wine they're selling by the glass (€3 sandwiches, daily 9:00-19:30 or until the bread runs out, 20 yards in front of Orsanmichele Church on Via dei Cimatori, tel. 055-239-6096).

Café with a View

Head to **Caffè La Terrazza** if you're willing to pay extra to enjoy a drink surrounded by Florentine splendor. Perched on the rooftop of La Rinascente department store overlooking Piazza della Repubblica, you're paying for one of the best views of the Duomo, which looms gloriously on the horizon (€6 coffee drinks).

The Oltrarno

Dining in the Oltrarno, south of the Arno River, offers a more authentic experience. While it's just a few minutes' walk from Ponte Vecchio, it sees far fewer tourists.

Cooking Classes

At cooking classes, you'll typically spend a couple of hours cooking, then sit down to a hard-earned meal. The options listed below represent only a few of your many choices. As this is a fast-changing scene, it's worth doing some homework online and booking well ahead.

In Tavola is a dedicated cooking school in the Oltrarno, featuring Italian, English-speaking chefs who quickly demonstrate each step before setting you loose. You'll work in a kitchen, then eat in the cozy wine cellar (€53-73/person, between Pitti Palace and Brancacci Chapel at Via dei Velluti 18 red, tel. 055-217-672, www.intavola.org, info@intavola.org, Fabrizio).

Both **Artviva** and **Florencetown** (listed under "Tours" on page 579) offer cooking classes and a 10 percent discount to my readers (Artviva: €53-68/person; Florencetown: €85/person for 5-hour class that includes shopping for the food you'll cook; €49/person for 3-hour pizza- and gelato-making class).

Dining or Drinking with a Ponte Vecchio View

Signorvino is a wine shop with an *enoteca* (simple wine-bar restaurant) that has a terrace literally over the river with Ponte Vecchio views. It's a fun-loving place with no pretense yet a passion for quality Italian ingredients. They serve €10 regional dishes, plates of tasty meats and cheeses, and fine wines by the glass. You can also choose a bottle from their fairly-priced selection and drink it at the table. Call to reserve (daily 12:00-23:00, Via dei Bardi 46 red, tel. 055-286-258, www.signorvino. com).

Golden View Open Bar, a noisy and touristy bistro, is good for a salad, pizza, or pasta with wine and a fine view of Ponte Vecchio. Its white, minimalist interior is a stark contrast to atmospheric old Florence. Their impressive wine bar serves a buffet of appetizers free with your €10 drink from 19:00 to 21:30 (jazz usually Mon, Fri, and Sat nights at 21:00). Make a reservation for a window table. They have three seating areas (with the same menu and prices): a riverside pizza place, a classier restaurant, and a jazzy lounge (€10 pizzas, €11-16 pastas, big €13 salads, €20-30 *secondi,* daily 11:30-24:00, 50 yards east of Ponte Vecchio at Via dei Bardi 58, tel. 055-214-502, www.goldenviewopen bar.com).

On or near Piazza di Santo Spirito

Piazza di Santo Spirito is a thriving neighborhood square with a collection of lively eateries and bars. Several bars offer *aperitivo* buffets with their drinks during happy hour. Late in the evening the area becomes a clubbing scene.

Gusta Osteria, just around the corner from the piazza, serves predictable Tuscan fare at fun, cozy indoor seating or at outdoor tables (€10-12 *secondi,* open long hours Tue-Sun, closed Mon, Via de' Michelozzi 13, tel. 055-289-033). Its cheaper sister restaurant, **Gustapanino,** is a sandwich bar directly on the square.

At **Trattoria Casalinga,** an inexpensive standby, Florentines enjoy the tripe and tongue while tourists opt for easier to swallow Tuscan favorites (€7 pastas,

€9-11 *secondi,* Mon-Sat 12:00-14:30 & 19:00-22:00, after 20:00 reserve or wait, closed Sun and Aug, just off Piazza di Santo Spirito, near the church at Via de' Michelozzi 9 red, tel. 055-218-624, www. trattorialacasalinga.it, Andrea and Paolo).

Dining Well

These are my favorite restaurants in the Oltrarno. Make reservations for dinner or come early.

Il Santo Bevitore Ristorante, lit like a Rembrandt painting, serves creative Tuscan cuisine. They're enthusiastic about matching local produce with the right wine and have a good wine list by the glass or bottle (€9-12 pastas, €8-12 meat-and-cheese *taglieri,* €10-18 *secondi,* daily 12:30-14:30 & 19:30-22:30, closed Sun for lunch, three tables on sidewalk, Via di Santo Spirito 64 red, tel. 055-211-264, www.il santobevitore.com). Next door, sister wine bar **Enoteca Il Santino Gastronomia** is a cozy hangout for foodies (daily 12:30-23:00, no reservations, Via di Santo Spirito 60 red, tel. 055-230-2820).

Popular **Trattoria 4 Leoni** creates the quintessential Oltrarno dinner scene, serving Tuscan food with an innovative twist. Enjoy the energy and characteristic seating, both inside and outside on the colorful square. Wines by the glass are pricey, but the house wine is good (€10-14 *primi,* €12-15 *secondi,* daily 12:00-24:00, on Piazza della Passera, midway between Ponte Vecchio and Piazza di Santo Spirito, tel. 055-218-562, www.4leoni.com).

Olio & Convivium, a top-end catering company, showcases their artful, slow-food cooking in three intimate rooms surrounded by fine *prosciutti,* cheeses, and wine shelves. Well-dressed foodies will appreciate the clubby atmosphere (€14-18 pastas, €14-25 *gastronomia* plates, €20-22 *secondi,* €18 lunches with wine, €40 and €45 tasting menus, Tue-Sun 12:00-14:30 & 19:00-22:30, closed Mon, Via di Santo Spirito 4, tel. 055-265-8198, Tommaso).

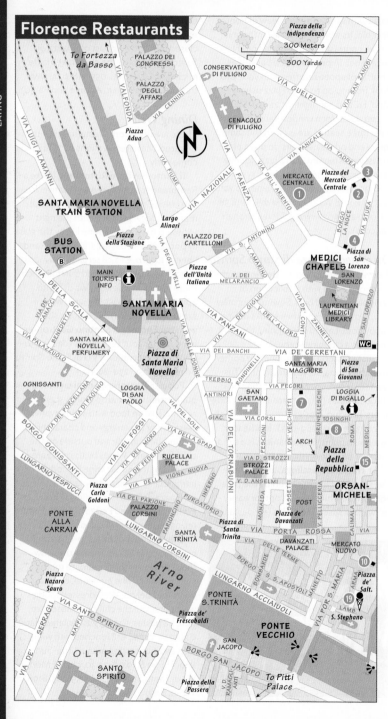

Florence Restaurants

300 Meters

300 Yards

To Fortezza da Basso

PALAZZO DEI CONGRESSI

CONSERVATORIO DI FULIGNO

Piazza della Indipendenza

PALAZZO DEGLI AFFARI

CENACOLO DI FULIGNO

Piazza Adua

VIA VALFONDA

VIA LUIGI ALAMANNI

VIA CENNINI

VIA FIUME

VIA NAZIONALE

VIA FAENZA

VIA GUELFA

VIA SAN ZANOBI

VIA PANICALE

VIA TADDEA

VIA DELL'ARIENTO

MERCATO CENTRALE ①

Piazza del Mercato Centrale

③

②

VIA STURA

BORGO LA NOCE

SANTA MARIA NOVELLA TRAIN STATION

Largo Alinari

PALAZZO DEI CARTELLONI

Piazza della Stazione

VIA DEGLI AVELLI

VIA S. ANTONINO

VIA S. AMARINO

④

Piazza di San Lorenzo

BUS STATION ⑧

MEDICI CHAPELS

SAN LORENZO

Piazza dell'Unità Italiana

MAIN TOURIST INFO ℹ

V. DEI MELARANCIO

VIA DE' CONTI

VIA DE' ZANNETTI

B. SAN LORENZO

VIA DELLA SCALA

VIA DE' CANACCI

BENEDETTI

SANTA MARIA NOVELLA

LAURENTIAN MEDICI LIBRARY

VIA PALAZZUOLO

SANTA MARIA NOVELLA PERFUMERY

VIA PANZANI

VIA DEL GIGLIO

V. DELL'ALLORO

WC

OGNISSANTI

VIA DEL PORCELLANA

VIA DI PAOLINO

LOGGIA DI SAN PAOLO

Piazza di Santa Maria Novella

VIA DELLE BELLE DONNE

VIA DEI BANCHI

VIA DE' CERRETANI

SANTA MARIA MAGGIORE

Piazza di San Giovanni

LOGGIA DI BIGALLO & ℹ

BORGO OGNISSANTI

VIA DEL MORO

VIA DEI FOSSI

VIA DELLA SPADA

TREBBIO

RONDINELLI

ANTINORI

VIA PECORI

SAN GAETANO ⑦

VIA D. VECCHIETTI

BRUNELLESCHI

TOSINGHI

ROMA

LUNGARNO VESPUCCI

VIA DEL SOLE

VIA DE' FEDERIGHI

RUCELLAI PALACE

VIA DELLA VIGNA NUOVA

GIAC.

VIA CORSI

PESCIONI

⑧

ARCH

MEDICI

CALIMALA

Piazza Carlo Goldoni

PALAZZO CORSINI

VIA DEL PARIONE

PARIONCINO

INFERNO

PURGATORIO

STROZZI PALACE

VIA D. STROZZI

V. D. ANSELMI

Piazza della Repubblica

⑮

PONTE ALLA CARRAIA

LUNGARNO CORSINI

SANTA TRINITÀ

SASSETTI

MONALDA

Piazza de' Davanzati

POST

VIA PELLICCERIA

ORSAN-MICHELE

Piazza di Santa Trinita

VIA PORTA ROSSA

DAVANZATI PALACE

MERCATO NUOVO

Piazza Nazaro Sauro

VIA SANTO SPIRITO

Arno River

Piazza de' Frescobaldi

PONTE S. TRINITÀ

BORGO S.S. APOSTOLI

LUNGARNO ACCIAIUOLI

VIA DELLE TERME

BORGO

BOMBARDE

NANETTO

VIA POR S. MARIA

ARMA

⑩

Piazza de' Salt.

⑲

LAMB

S. Stephano

VIA DE' SERRAGLI

MAFFIA

VIA SANTO SPIRITO

OLTRARNO

SANTO SPIRITO

SAN JACOPO

BORGO SAN JACOPO

V. D. RAMAGLI-ANTI

PONTE VECCHIO

To Pitti Palace

Piazza della Passera

Gelateria

SAN MARCO MUSEUM

Piazza di San Marco

UNIVERSITY

VIA VENTISETTE APRILE

VIA ARAZZIERI

VIA SANTA REPARATA

VIA SAN GALLO

CAVOUR

VIA GIORGIO LA PIRA

VIA GUELFA

ACCADEMIA (DAVID)

MUSEUM OF PRECIOUS STONES

LEONARDO MUSEUM

VIA DE'GINORI

VIA

V. D. ALFANI

VIA RICASOLI

16

MEDICI-RICCARDI PALACE

PALAZZO PUCCI

VIA DEI SERVI

ROTUNDA
Piazza Brunelleschi

LEONARDO MUSEUM

VIA DEI PUCCI

VIA BIFFI

VIA MARTELLI

9

VIA M. BUFALINI

HOSPITAL

DUOMO SIGHTS TICKET OFFICE

BAPTISTERY

DUOMO

DUOMO MUSEUM

Piazza di Santa Maria Nuova

Piazza del Duomo

CAMPANILE

17 CANONICA

VIA DELL'OCHE BONIZZI

5 SANTA MARIA DE' RICCI

CALZAIUOLI

STUDIO

OPERA DEL DUOMO STUDIO

VIA DEL CORSO

18

13

14

CERCHI

CONDOTTA

11

12

Piazza della Signoria

LOGGIA

UFFIZI GALLERY

EXIT

VIA DELL'ORIUOLO

MUSEO DI FIRENZE COM' ERA

VIA S. EGIDIO

BORGO PINTI

VIA FIESOLANA

Piazza G. Salvemini

6

VIA PIETRAPIANA

B. D. ALBIZI

POST

VIA DELL'ULIVO

CASA DI DANTE

VIA D. ALIGHIERI

S. MARIA LA BADIA

V. DE' PANDOLFINI

VIA DEL PROCONSOLO

VIA DE' GIRALDI

BARGELLO MUSEUM

VIA DELLA VIGNA VECCHIA

VIA BURELLA

STINCHE PALMIERI

GHIBELLINA

VERDI

VIA DELL'AGNOLO

CASA BUONARROTI

VIA GIA

VERRAZZANO

FICO

V. DE' PEPI

CIMATORI

MAGAZZINI

V. V. TAVO.

Piazza S. Firenze

V. DELL'ANGUILLARA

GONDI

BORGO DE' GRECI

VIA LEONI

CORNO

PALAZZO VECCHIO

WC

VINEGIA

MAGALOTTI

RUSTICI

Piazza Peruzzi

VIA BENTA

Piazza Santa Croce

SANTA CROCE

CASTELLANI

OSTERIA

VIA DE' NERI

20

BRACHE

V. D. BENCI

B. S. CROCE

PAZZI CHAPEL

MOSCA

Piazza Giudici

CASTELLANI

SAPONAI

VAGELLAI

Piazza Mentana

MALENCHINI

LUNG. GEN. DIAZ

CORSO DEI TINTORI

LIBRARY

GALILEO SCIENCE MUSEUM

1 Mercato Centrale Eateries, Perini & Nerbone in the Market
2 Trattoria Mario
3 Pepò
4 Trattoria Gozzi Sergio
5 Enoteca Coquinarius
6 Miso di Riso Vegetaria Bistro
7 Self-Service Rist. Leonardo
8 Paszkowski Café
9 EATaly
10 Rivoire Café
11 Osteria Vini e Vecchi Sapori
12 Frescobaldi Ristorante & Wine Bar
13 Cantinetta dei Verrazzano
14 I Fratellini
15 Caffè La Terrazza

Gelaterie
16 Gelateria Carabè
17 Grom
18 Perchè No! Gelateria
19 Carapina
20 Gelateria de' Neri

The Oltrarno

To Porta San Frediano &

To Santa Maria Novella

Arno

BORGO SAN FREDIANO

VIA DEL LEONE

Piazza del Carmine

BORGO STELLA

Piazza Nazaro Sauro **5**

LUNGARNO GUICCIARDINI

VIA DI SANTO SPIRITO

GEPPI

VIA MAFFIA

VIA DEI SERRAGLI

O L T R A R N O

VIA DE' COVERELLI

BRANCACCI CHAPEL

VIA SANTA MONACA

SANTA MARIA DEL CARMINE

VIA S. AGOSTINO

SANTO SPIRITO

VIA D. S. MARTINO

Piazza di Santo Spirito

MICH. **3**

SDRUCCIOLO DE' PITTI

VIA DEL TEGOLAIO

MAGGIO

4

VIA DELLA CHIESA

VIA DEL CAMPUCCIO

PAL. DE COSIMO RIDOLFI

VIA MAZZETTA

VIA MARSILI

VIA DE'

Giardino Torrigiani

VIA DEI SERRAGLI

VIA DELLE CALDAIE

BORGO

Piazza di San Felice

TICKET OFFICE

Piazzina della Meridiana

VIA ROMANA

Giardino di Analena

To Porta Romana

VIALE DELLA MERIDIANA

L'Isolotto

FONTANA DELL'OCEANO

VIALE DEL CIPRESSI

Restaurants & Other

1. Signorvino
2. Golden View Open Bar
3. Gusta Osteria
4. Trattoria Casalinga
5. Il Santo Bevitore Ristorante & Enoteca Il Santino Gastronomia
6. Trattoria 4 Leoni
7. Olio & Convivium
8. Gelateria della Passera
9. In Tavola Cooking School

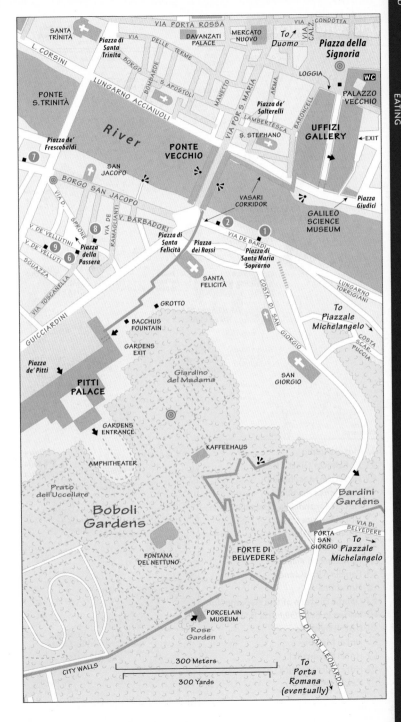

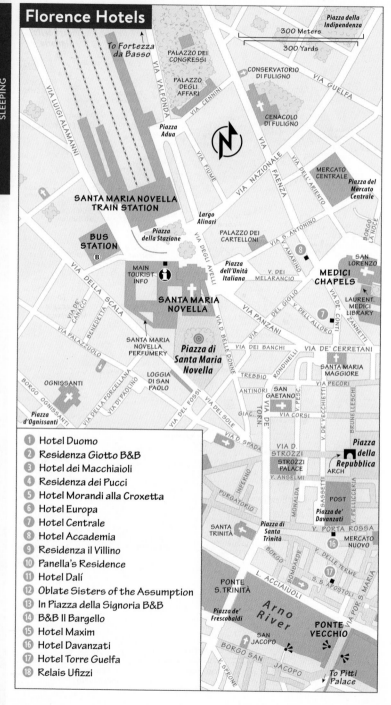

Florence Hotels

1 Hotel Duomo
2 Residenza Giotto B&B
3 Hotel dei Macchiaioli
4 Residenza dei Pucci
5 Hotel Morandi alla Croxetta
6 Hotel Europa
7 Hotel Centrale
8 Hotel Accademia
9 Residenza il Villino
10 Panella's Residence
11 Hotel Dalí
12 Oblate Sisters of the Assumption
13 In Piazza della Signoria B&B
14 B&B Il Bargello
15 Hotel Maxim
16 Hotel Davanzati
17 Hotel Torre Guelfa
18 Relais Ufizzi

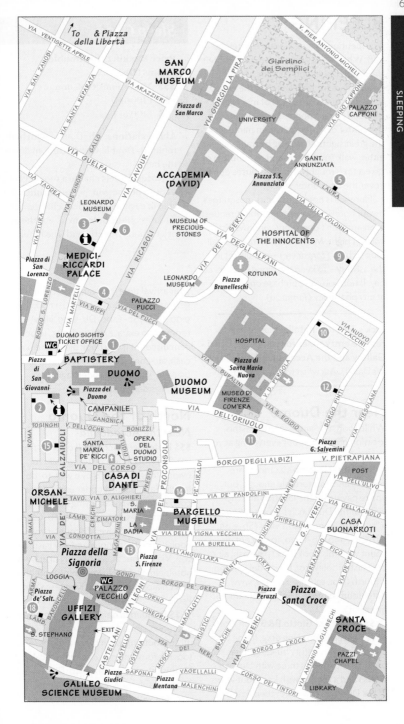

SLEEPING

Competition among Florence hotels is stiff. When things slow down, fancy hotels drop their prices and become a much better value for travelers than the cheap, low-end places. Nearly all of my recommended accommodations are located in the center of Florence, within minutes of the great sights. If arriving by train, you can either walk (usually around 10 minutes) or take a taxi (roughly €6-8), as buses don't cover the city center well.

Florence is notorious for its mosquitoes. If your hotel lacks air-conditioning, request a fan and don't open your windows, especially at night. Many hotels furnish a small plug-in bulb (zanzariere)—usually set in the ashtray—to keep the blood-suckers at bay. If not, you can purchase one cheaply at any pharmacy (farmacia).

Rick's Tip: *Your **hotelier** may be able to reserve entry times for you at the Uffizi Gallery and the Accademia (Michelangelo's David). Ask when you book your room.*

Near the Duomo

While touristy—and expensive—this location puts just about everything at your doorstep.

$$$ Hotel Duomo's 24 rooms are modern and comfortable enough, but you're paying for the location and the views of the Duomo. It's an extra €20 for a "superior" room with a view (Sb-€115, Db-€165-190, Tb-€230, 10 percent discount with this book if you pay cash, air-con, historic elevator, Piazza del Duomo 1, fourth floor, tel. 055-219-922, www. hotelduomofirenze.it, info@hotelduomo firenze.it).

$$ Residenza Giotto B&B is on Florence's upscale shopping drag. In the top floor of a 19th-century building, it has six bright, basic rooms (three with Duomo views) and a terrace with knockout views of the Duomo's tower. Let them know

your arrival time in advance (reception generally open Mon-Sat 9:00-17:00, Sun 9:00-13:00; Sb-€100, Db-€139, view rooms-€10 extra, extra bed-€25, 10 percent discount if you book direct and pay cash, air-con, elevator, Via Roma 6, tel. 055-214-593, www.residenzagiotto.it, info@residenzagiotto.it).

North of the Duomo
Near the Accademia

$$$ Hotel dei Macchiaioli offers 15 fresh, spacious rooms in a restored palazzo owned for generations by a well-to-do family. Eat breakfast under original frescoed ceilings while enjoying modern comforts (Sb-€100, Db-€180, Tb-€240, 10 percent Rick Steves discount if you book directly with hotel and pay cash, air-con, Via Cavour 21, tel. 055-213-154, www. hoteldeimacchiaioli.com, info@hoteldei macchiaioli.com, helpful Francesca and Paolo).

$$ Residenza dei Pucci rents 13 pleasant rooms spread over three floors. The mix of soothing earth tones and aristocratic furniture makes it feel upscale for this price range (Sb-€140, Db-€155, Tb-€175, Qb suite-€243, 10 percent discount with this book if you pay cash, air-con, no elevator, reception open 9:00-20:00, shorter hours off-season— let them know if you'll arrive late, Via dei Pucci 9, tel. 055-281-886, www.residenza deipucci.com, info@residenzadeipucci. com).

$$ Hotel Morandi alla Crocetta, a former convent, envelops you in a 16th-century cocoon. Located on a quiet street with 12 rooms, period furnishings, parquet floors, and original frescoes, it takes you back a few centuries and up a few social classes (Sb-€105, Db-€157, Tb-€187, Qb-€207, big "superior" room-€30 extra, air-con, no elevator, a block off Piazza S.S. Annunziata at Via Laura 50, tel. 055-234-4747, www.hotelmorandi.it, welcome@ hotelmorandi.it).

$$ Hotel Europa, family run since 1970, has an inviting atmosphere, a spacious breakfast room, and 12 rooms, most with views of the Duomo, including one with a terrace (Sb-€89, Db-€150, Tb-€180, Qb-€250, 10 percent discount if you pay cash, mention Rick Steves for best available room, air-con, elevator, Via Cavour 14, tel. 055-239-6715, www.webhotel europa.com, firenze@webhoteleuropa. com).

Near the Medici Chapels

This touristy zone has lots of budget and midrange hotels, stacks of basic trattorias, and easy access to major sights. The mostly pedestrianized Via Faenza is the spine of this neighborhood, with lots of tourist services.

$$$ Hotel Centrale is just a short walk from the Duomo. The 31 large but over-priced rooms are over a businesslike conference center (Db-€237, bigger superior Db-€340, Tb-€295, suites available, 10 percent discount with this book, ask for Rick Steves rate when you reserve, 20 percent discount if booked two months in advance, air-con, elevator, Via dei Conti 3, check in at big front desk on ground floor, tel. 055-215-761, www.hotelcentrale firenze.it, info@hotelcentralefirenze.it).

$$ Hotel Accademia has 21 old-school rooms and a floor plan that defies logic. While it's overpriced and long in the tooth, its location is convenient (small Sb-€70, Db-€145, Tb-€170, 10 percent discount with this book if you book directly with hotel and pay cash, air-con, no elevator, Via Faenza 7, tel. 055-293-451, www. hotelaccademiafirenze.com, info@ hotelaccademiafirenze.com).

East of the Duomo

While convenient to the sights and offering a good value, these places are located mostly along nondescript urban streets, lacking the grit, appeal, or glitz of other neighborhoods.

$$ Residenza il Villino has 10 charming rooms and a picturesque, peaceful little courtyard. Set back from the street, it's a refuge from the bustle of Florence (Sb-€105, small Db-€120, Db-€135, family suite available, book directly with hotel for best prices, ask for discount with this book, air-con, just north of Via degli Alfani at Via della Pergola 53, tel. 055-200-1116, www.ilvillino.it, info@ilvillino.it).

$$ Panella's Residence, once a convent, is today a classy B&B, with five chic, romantic, and ample rooms (Db-€155, bigger "deluxe" Db-€180, extra bed-€40, book direct and mention Rick Steves to get the best rate, discounts for cash and stays of 3 or more nights, air-con, Via della Pergola 42, tel. 055-234-7202, mobile 345-972-1541, www.panellaresidence.com, panella_residence@yahoo.it).

$ Hotel Dalí has 10 cheery rooms in a nice location for a great price. Samanta and Marco run the guesthouse with passion and idealism (S-€40, D-€70, Db-€90, extra bed-€25, request one of the quiet and spacious rooms facing the courtyard when you book, nearby apartments sleep 2-6 people, no breakfast, fans but no air-con, elevator, free parking, 2 blocks behind the Duomo at Via dell'Oriuolo 17 on the second floor, tel. 055-234-0706, www.hoteldali.com, hoteldali@tin.it).

$ Oblate Sisters of the Assumption run an institutional 30-room hotel in a Renaissance building with simple rooms, a dreamy garden, and a quiet, prayerful ambience. Time your arrival and departure to occur during typical business hours (Sb-€50, Db-€90, Tb-€135, Qb-€180, cash only, single beds only, family discounts available, air-con, elevator, Wi-Fi in lobby with suggested donation, 23:30 curfew, €10/day limited parking—request when you book, Borgo Pinti 15, tel. 055-248-0582, sroblateborgopinti@virgilio.it).

South of the Duomo
Between the Duomo and Piazza della Signoria

Buried in the narrow, characteristic lanes in the heart of town, these are the most central of my recommendations (and therefore a little expensive). While this location can be worth the extra cost, nearly every hotel I recommend is conveniently located, given Florence's walkable, traffic-free core.

$$$ In Piazza della Signoria B&B is peaceful, refined, and homey. Fit for a honeymoon, the 10 rooms come with special touches and little extras, and the service is sharp and friendly. The "partial view" rooms require craning your neck to see anything—not worth the extra euros. Guests enjoy socializing at the big, shared breakfast table (viewless Db-€250, partial-view Db-€280, full-view "deluxe" Db-€300, Tb-€280, partial-view Tb-€300, ask for 10 percent discount with this book when you book direct, family apartments, lavish bathrooms, air-con, tiny elevator, Via dei Magazzini 2, tel. 055-239-9546, mobile 348-321-0565, www.inpiazzadellasignoria.com, info@inpiazzadellasignoria.com).

$$ B&B Il Bargello is a home away from home. Hike up three long flights (no elevator) to reach six smart, relaxing rooms. The inviting rooftop terrace has close-up views of Florence's towers (Db-€115, ask for Rick Steves rate when you book directly with hotel and pay cash; fully equipped apartment across the hall sleeps up to six in real beds but you'll share one bathroom: €160/2 people, €15 more per extra person; air-con, 20 yards off Via Proconsolo at Via de' Pandolfini 33 black, tel. 055-215-330, mobile 339-175-3110, www.firenze-bedandbreakfast.it, info@firenze-bedandbreakfast.it).

$$ Hotel Maxim has a prime location

on the main pedestrian drag. While the 26 rooms are straightforward, its narrow, painting-lined halls and cozy lounge have old Florentine charm (Sb-€75, Db-€140, Tb-€160, Qb-€180, book directly with hotel and use promo code "RICK" for 10 percent discount, air-con, elevator, Via de' Calzaiuoli 11, tel. 055-217-474, www.hotel maximfirenze.it, reservation@hotelmaxim firenze.it).

Near Ponte Vecchio

This sleepy zone is handy to several sights and some fine shopping streets, though it lacks a neighborhood feel of its own.

$$$ **Hotel Davanzati** has 25 cheerful rooms with all the comforts. Enjoy drinks and snacks each evening at a candlelit happy hour, plus lots of other extras (Sb-€132, Db-€199, Tb-€259, family rooms available, these rates good with this book though prices soft off-season, 10 percent discount if you pay cash, free loaner laptop in every room, free on-demand videos, air-con, fridges, next to Piazza Davanzati at Via Porta Rossa 5—easy to miss so watch for low-profile sign above the door, tel. 055-286-666, www.hotel davanzati.it, info@hoteldavanzati.it).

$$$ **Hotel Torre Guelfa** has grand public spaces and a medieval tower with a panoramic terrace (72 stairs take you up—and back 720 years). Its 31 rooms vary wildly in size and layout. Room 315, with a private terrace (€310), is worth reserving months in advance (Db-€250, higher prices for bigger rooms, ask for Rick Steves discount, family deals, check website for promotions, air-con, elevator, a couple blocks northwest of Ponte Vecchio, Borgo S.S. Apostoli 8, tel. 055-239-6338, www.hoteltorreguelfa.com, info@hoteltorreguelfa.com, Niccolo and Barbara).

$$$ **Relais Uffizi** is a peaceful little gem with 15 classy rooms tucked away down an alleyway off Piazza della Signoria. The lounge has a huge window overlooking the action in the square below (Sb-€120, Db-€180, Tb-€220, more for deluxe rooms, air-con, elevator; from the square, go down the tiny Chiasso de Baroncelli lane—right of the loggia—then turn right on Via Lambertesca and look for entrance on your right; official address is Chiasso del Buco 16; tel. 055-267-6239, www.relais uffizi.it, info@relaisuffizi.it).

TRANSPORTATION

Getting Around Florence

I organize my sightseeing geographically and do it all on foot. Think of Florence as a Renaissance treadmill—it requires a lot of walking.

By Bus

The city's full-size buses don't cover the old center well (the whole area around the Duomo is off-limits to motorized traffic). Pick up a map of transit routes at the ATAF windows at the train station (TIs do not have them); you'll also find routes online (www.ataf.net). Of the many bus lines, I find these the most helpful for seeing outlying sights:

Bus **#12** goes from the train station to Porta Romana, up to San Miniato Church and Piazzale Michelangelo. Bus #13 makes the return trip down the hill.

The train station and Piazza San Marco are two major hubs near the city center; to get between these two, either walk (about 15 minutes) or take bus #1, #6, #14, or #23.

Minibuses run every 10 minutes from 7:00 to 21:00 (less frequent on Sun), winding through the town center and up and down the river—just €1.20 gets you a 1.5-hour joyride. These buses also connect many major parking lots with the historic center (buy tickets from machines at lots).

Bus **#C1** stops behind Palazzo Vecchio and Piazza Santa Croce, then heads north, passing near the Accademia before ending up at Piazza Libertà.

Bus #C2 twists through the congested old center from the train station, passing near Piazza della Repubblica and Piazza della Signoria to Piazza Beccaria.

Bus #C3 goes up and down the Arno River, with stops near Ponte Vecchio, the Carraia bridge to the Oltrarno (including Pitti Palace), and beyond.

Bus #D goes from the train station to Ponte Vecchio, cruises through the Oltrarno (passing Pitti Palace), and finishes at Ponte San Niccolò.

Buying Bus Tickets: Buy bus tickets at tobacco shops (*tabacchi*), newsstands, or the ATAF ticket windows inside the train station. Validate your ticket in the machine on board (€1.20/90 minutes, €4.70/4 tickets, €5/24 hours, €12/3 days, €18/week, day passes aren't always available in tobacco shops, tel. 800-424-500, www.ataf.net). You can sometimes buy tickets on board, but you'll pay more (€2) and you'll need exact change. City buses are free with the Firenze Card (see page 576).

By Taxi

The minimum cost for a taxi ride is €5 (or €8.30 after 22:00, or €7 on Sun); rides in the center of town should be charged as tariff #1. A taxi ride from the train station to the Duomo costs about €8. Taxi fares and supplements (e.g., €2 extra if you call a cab rather than hail one) are clearly explained on signs in each taxi. Official, regulated cabs have a yellow banner on the door that says *Taxi/Comune di Firenze* with a red fleur-de-lis, and are marked

with official phone numbers (4390 or 4242). Before getting in a cab, mention your destination and ask for an approximate cost (*"Più o meno, quanto costa?"* pew oh MEH-noh, KWAHN-toh KOH-stah). If you can't get a straight answer or the price is outrageous, walk away. It can be hard to find a cab on the street; call 055-4390 or 055-4242 to summon one, or have your hotelier or restaurateur call for you.

Arriving and Departing

Florence is Tuscany's transportation hub, with fine train, bus, and plane connections to virtually anywhere in Italy.

By Train

Florence's main train station is called **Santa Maria Novella** (*Firenze S.M.N.* on schedules and signs). The city also has two suburban train stations: **Firenze Rifredi** and **Firenze Campo di Marte.** Note that some trains don't stop at the main station—before boarding, confirm that you're heading for S.M.N., or you may overshoot the city. (If this happens, don't panic; the other stations are a short taxi ride from the center.)

Rick's Tip: Don't trust "porters" *who want to help carry your bags (they're not official), and politely decline offers of help using the ticket machines by anyone other than uniformed staff.*

To orient yourself to Santa Maria Novella Station, stand with your back to the tracks. Look left to see the green cross of a 24-hour pharmacy (*farmacia*) and the exit to the taxi queue. **Baggage storage** (*deposito bagagli*) is also to the left, halfway down track 16 (daily 6:00-23:00, passport required, maximum 40 pounds). **Fast-food outlets** and a **bank** are also along track 16. Directly ahead of you is the main hall (*salone biglietti*), where you can buy train and bus tickets. **Pay WCs** are to the right, near the head of track 5.

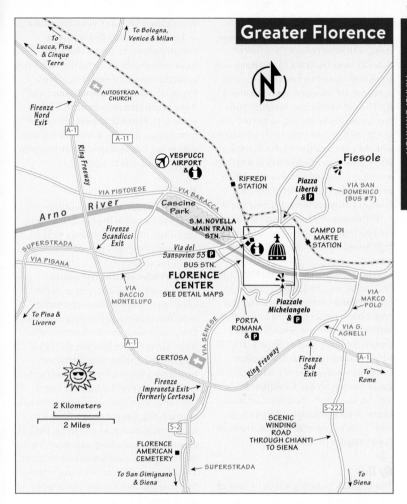

Greater Florence

To reach the **TI,** walk away from the tracks and exit the station; it's straight across the square, 100 yards away, by the stone church.

To buy **ATAF city bus tickets,** stop at windows #8-9 in the main hall—and ask for a transit map while you're there (TIs do not have them).

Getting to the Duomo and City Center: Orienting yourself with your back to the tracks, the Duomo and town center are to your left. Out the doorway to the left, you'll find city buses and the taxi stand. Taxis cost about €6-8 to

the Duomo. To walk into town (10-15 minutes), exit the station straight ahead through the main hall, and head straight across the square outside, toward the Church of Santa Maria Novella (and the TI). On the far side of the square, keep left and head down the main Via dei Panzani, which leads directly to the Duomo.

TRAIN CONNECTIONS

For travel within Italy, don't stand in line at a window in the station. Use the self-service ticket (biglietto) machines that display schedules, issue tickets, and make reservations for rail-pass holders.

There are two train companies: **Trenitalia,** with most connections (toll tel. 892-021, www.trenitalia.it) and **Italo,** with some high-speed routes (no rail passes accepted, tel. 06-0708, www.italotreno.it). The self-service machines for both companies are bright red, so be sure you select the right one (machines are labeled with the company name). For Trenitalia information, use window #18 or #19 (take a number). The Italo information office and Trenitalia Frecciaclub (first-class lounge) are opposite track 5, near the exit.

The departures listed below are operated by Trenitalia; Italo offers additional high-speed connections to major Italian cities.

From Florence by Train to: Pisa (2-3/hour, 45-75 minutes), **Lucca** (2/hour, 1.5 hours), **Siena** (direct trains hourly, 1.5-2 hours; bus is better because Siena's train station is far from the center), **Milan** (hourly, 2 hours), **Venice** (hourly, 2-3 hours, may transfer in Bologna; often crowded—reserve ahead), **Assisi** (8/day direct, 2-3 hours), **Orvieto** (hourly, 2 hours, some with change in Campo di Marte or Rifredi Station), **Rome** (2-3/hour, 1.5 hours, most require seat reservations), **Naples** (hourly, 3 hours).

By Bus

The BusItalia Station is 100 yards west of the train station on Via Santa Caterina da Siena. To get to Florence's city center, exit the station through the main door, and turn left along the busy street toward the brick dome. Downtown Florence is straight ahead and to the right.

BUS CONNECTIONS

Generally it's best to buy bus tickets in the station, as you'll pay 30 percent more if you buy tickets onboard. The bus posts schedules for regional trips, and video monitors show imminent departures. Bus service drops dramatically on Sunday. Bus info: tel. 800-373-760 (Mon-Fri 9:00-

15:00, closed Sat-Sun), www.fsbusitalia.it.

From Florence by Bus to: Siena (roughly 2/hour, 1.25-hour *rapida/via superstrada* buses are faster than the train, avoid the slower *ordinaria* buses, www.sienamobilita.it), **Montepulciano** (1-2/day, 2 hours, change in Bettolle, LFI bus, www.lfi.it), **Florence airport** (2/hour, 30 minutes, pay driver and immediately validate ticket, usually departs from platform 1, first bus departs at 5:30).

By Car

The autostrada has several exits for Florence. Get off at the Nord, Scandicci, Impruneta (formerly Certosa), or Sud exits and follow signs toward—but not into—the *Centro*.

Don't drive into the city center. Instead, park on the outskirts and take a bus, tram, or taxi in. Florence's traffic-reduction system is baffling even to locals. Every car passing into the "limited traffic zone" (*Zona Traffico Limitato,* or ZTL) is photographed; those who don't have a permit get a €100 ticket in the mail (with an "administrative" fee from the rental company). If you get lost and cross the line several times...you get several fines. If you have a reservation at a hotel within the ZTL area—and it has parking—ask in advance if they can get you permission to enter town. The ZTL zone is Florence's historic center (the core plus much of the Oltrarno)—nearly anywhere you'd want to go.

Using **bus-only lanes** (usually marked with yellow stripes) is another expensive mistake that results in a ticket in the mail.

If you're picking up a **rental car** upon departure, don't struggle with driving in the center. Taxi with your luggage to the car-rental office, and head out from there.

The city center is ringed with big, efficient **parking lots** (signposted with a big *P*). Check www.firenzeparcheggi.it for details on parking lots, availability, and prices. From the freeway, follow the signs to *Centro,* then *Stadio,* then *P*.

If arriving from the north, park at **Parcheggio del Parterre,** just beyond Piazza della Libertà. They have 600 spots and never fill up completely (€2/hour, €20/day, €70/week, automated, pay with cash or credit card, open 24 hours daily, tel. 055-500-1994). To get into town, find the taxi stand at the elevator exit, or ride one of the minibuses that connect major parking lots with the city center (see www.ataf.net for routes).

Parcheggio Sansovino, a convenient lot for drivers coming from the south, is on the Oltrarno side of the river, right at a tram stop (€1/hour, €12/day, 24 hours daily, Via Sansovino 53—from A-1 take the Firenze Scandicci exit, tel. 055-363-362, www.scaf.fi.it). Park, then ride four quick stops to Santa Maria Novella Station.

By Plane

Amerigo Vespucci Airport, also called Peretola Airport, is about five miles northwest of the city (open 5:00-23:00, no overnighting allowed, TI, airport code: FLR, airport info tel. 055-306-1830, flight info tel. 055-306-1300—domestic only, www.aeroporto.firenze.it).

Shuttle buses (to the far right as you exit the arrivals hall) connect the airport with Florence's train and bus stations (2/hour, 30 minutes, runs 5:00-23:30, €6—

buy ticket on board and validate immediately). If you're changing to a different intercity bus in Florence (for instance, one bound for Siena), stay on the bus through the first stop (at the train station); it will continue on to the bus station nearby. Allow about €25 and 30 minutes for a taxi.

The airport's **car rental** offices share one big parking lot just a three-minute drive away. Streets around the airport are a dizzying maze, making it tricky to find the place to drop off your car. One option is to drive to the airport, wait for the shuttle bus to show up, then follow that bus to the lot.

By Private Car Service

For small groups with more money than time, hiring a private car service to zip comfortably to nearby towns can be a good value. Consider **Transfer Chauffeur Service** (tel. 338-862-3129, www.transfercs.com, marco.masala@transfercs.com, Marco) or **Prestige Rent** (office near Piazza della Signoria at Via Porta Rossa 6 red, tel. 055-398-6598, mobile 333-842-4047, www.prestigerent.com, usa@prestigerent.com, Saverio). Or you could simply hire a **taxi** after agreeing upon a rate (e.g., €120 from your Florence hotel to your Siena hotel).

The
Cinque Terre

Along a six-mile stretch of the Riviera lies the Cinque Terre (CHINK-weh TAY-reh), gently carving a good life out of difficult terrain. With a traffic-free charm—a happy result of their natural isolation—these five *(cinque)* towns are the rugged alternative to the glitzy resorts nearby. With sun, sea, sand (well, pebbles), and wine, this is pure, unadulterated Italy.

Each addictively photogenic village fills a ravine with a lazy hive of human activity—calloused locals and sunburned travelers enjoying a unique mix of culture and nature. Enjoy swimming, hiking, and evening romance in one of God's great gifts to tourism. While the Cinque Terre is now discovered (and can be crowded midday, when tourist boats and cruise ships drop by), I've never seen happier, more relaxed tourists. Most of the crowds are day-trippers, so make a point to get the most out of those cool, relaxed, and quiet hours early in the day and in the evening.

I cover the five towns in order from south to north—from Riomaggiore to Monterosso. Vernazza is my top choice for a home base, while Monterosso, the most resorty of the five towns, is an excellent runner-up, offering maximum comfort and ease. Avoid visiting in winter, when tall, crashing waves batter the charm out of the Cinque Terre.

THE CINQUE TERRE IN 2 DAYS

This string of five villages dotting the Italian Riviera makes an idyllic escape from the obligatory museums of turnstile Italy. The ideal stay is two full days (or three days to really relax). It's easiest to arrive and depart by train. If you have a car, park it in one of the few lots (then catch a shuttle bus into town).

Within the Cinque Terre, you can connect the towns in three ways: by train, boat, or foot. Trains are cheap, boats are more scenic, and hiking lets you enjoy more pasta. Consider supplementing the often frustratingly late trains with the sometimes more convenient boats.

Study your options, and piece together your best visit, mixing hiking, swimming, trains, boat rides, and a search for the best focaccia.

You could spend one day hiking from town to town (or take a boat or train partway, or as the return trip). For the best light, coolest temperatures, and fewest

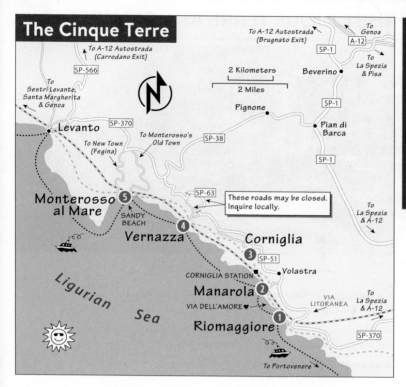

The Cinque Terre

To A-12 Autostrada
(Brugnato Exit)

To Genoa

A-12

SP-1

To La Spezia & Pisa

To A-12 Autostrada
(Carrodano Exit)

SP-566

Beverino

To Sestri Levante, Santa Margherita & Genoa

2 Kilometers

2 Miles

Pignone

SP-1

SP-370

Levanto

To Monterosso's Old Town

SP-38

Pian di Barca

SP-1

To New Town (Fegina)

SP-63

These roads may be closed.
Inquire locally.

To La Spezia & A-12

Monterosso al Mare ⑤

SANDY BEACH

Vernazza ④

Corniglia

③ SP-51

Volastra

Ligurian Sea

CORNIGLIA STATION

Manarola ②

VIA DELL'AMORE ♥

VIA LITORANEA

To La Spezia & A-12

Riomaggiore ①

SP-370

To Portovenere

---

crowds, start your hike early. Cool off at a beach. Spend a second day visiting each town, comparing main streets, beaches, and gelato.

In the evenings, linger at a restaurant, enjoy live music at a low-key club, stroll any of the towns, or take a glass of your favorite beverage out to the breakwater to watch the sun slip into the Mediterranean.

Helpful Hints for the Cinque Terre

Book in Advance: Reserve rooms well in advance for May, June, July, and September, and on weekends and holidays. If you want to reserve long in advance, choose a hotel (Monterosso has the most), because smaller places generally don't take reservations very far ahead. Reserve by email, and if you must cancel, do it as early as possible. More formal places have strict cancellation policies.

Shuttle Buses: Each town has a helpful ATC shuttle bus route that generally runs through town and links the train station, nearest parking lot, and destinations farther up in the hills. Take a cheap joyride (€1.50 one-way, €2.50 from driver, free with Cinque Terre park card). For more info, see page 633. The buses don't connect Cinque Terre towns with each other.

Money: Banks and ATMs are plentiful throughout the region.

Internet Access: All Cinque Terre train stations offer free Wi-Fi with a Cinque Terre park card.

Baggage Storage: You can store bags at La Spezia's train station (€3/12 hours, daily 8:00-22:00), at the gift shop in Vernazza's train station (€1/hour for the first 5 hours, daily 8:00-20:00, closed Nov-March, see page 649), and at the Wash and Dry Lavarapido in Monterosso (€5/day, daily 8:00-19:00, Via Molinelli 17).

THE CINQUE TERRE AT A GLANCE

▲▲**Riomaggiore (Town #1)** The biggest and most workaday of the five villages. See page 636.

▲▲**Manarola (Town #2)** Waterfront village dotted with a picturesque mix of shops, houses, and vineyards. See page 641.

▲▲**Corniglia (Town #3)** Quiet hilltop village known for its cooler temperatures (it's the only one of the five villages not on the coast), few tourists, and tradition of fine wines. See page 647.

▲▲▲**Vernazza (Town #4)** The region's gem, crowned with a ruined castle above and a lively waterfront cradling a natural harbor below. See page 649.

▲▲**Monterosso al Mare (Town #5)** Resorty, flat, and spread out, with a charming old town, a modern new town, and the region's best beaches, swimming, and nightlife. See page 660.

Services: Every train station has a free WC, but it's smart to bring your own toilet paper. Otherwise, pop into a bar or restaurant.

Tours: Arbaspàa, which has an office in Manarola, can arrange wine-tasting at a vineyard, cooking classes (6-person minimum), or a fishing trip with sailors (office closed Tue, Via Discovolo 252/A, tel. 0187-920-783, www.arbaspaa.com).

HIKING IN THE CINQUE TERRE

All five towns are connected by good trails, marked with red-and-white paint, white arrows, and some signs. The region has several numbered trails, but most visitors stick to the main coastal trail that connects the villages—that's trail #2. You'll need a Cinque Terre park card to hike this trail.

Trail Closures: Trails can be closed in bad weather or due to landslides. Usually one or two trails are closed at any given time. Official closures are noted on the national park website (www.parco nazionale5terre.it) and are posted at the park-information desks in each town's train station.

Hiking Conditions: Other than the wide, easy Riomaggiore-Manarola segment, the coastal trail is generally narrow, steep, rocky, and comes with lots of challenging steps. Readers often say the trail was tougher than they expected. The rocks can be slippery in the rain (avoid the steep Monterosso-Vernazza stretch if it's wet). Don't venture up on these rocky cliffs without sun protection or water.

When to Go: The coastal trail can be crowded (and hot) at midday. It's better to hike early or later in the day. After dark, there's no lighting on the trails. Before setting out for an evening hike, find out what time the sun sets, and leave yourself plenty of time to arrive at your destination.

Navigation: Maps aren't necessary for the basic coastal hikes described here. But for more serious hikes in the high country, pick up a good hiking map (about €5, sold everywhere). The *Cinque Terre Walking Guide* (sold locally in an English-language edition for about €15) is worth seeking out.

Give a Hoot: To leave the park cleaner than you found it, bring a plastic bag and pick up trail trash along the way.

Cinque Terre Park Cards

The Cinque Terre—villages and all—is a national park. Each town has a well-staffed park information office, which generally serves as an all-purpose town TI as well (listed throughout this chapter).

Visitors hiking between the towns on coastal trails need to pay a park entrance fee. You have two options: the Cinque Terre Trekking Card or the Cinque Terre Treno Multi-Service Card. Both are valid until midnight on the expiration date and include free Wi-Fi at train stations. Write your name on your card or risk a fine. The configuration and pricing of these cards is often in flux—be aware that the following details may change. Those under 18 or over 70 get a discount, as do families of four or more (see www.parconazionale 5terre.it).

The **Cinque Terre Trekking Card** costs €7.50 for one day of hiking or €14.50 for two days (covers trails and ATC shuttle buses plus a few other extras but does not cover trains; buy at trailheads and at most train stations, no validation required).

The **Cinque Terre Treno Multi-Service Card** covers what the Cinque Terre Trekking Card does, plus local trains from Levanto to La Spezia, which includes the five Cinque Terre towns between them. It's sold at TIs inside train stations, but not at trailheads. To break even with this card, you'd have to hike and take three train trips every day (€12/1 day, €23/2 days, validate card at train station).

The Coastal Trail

If all of the main trails between the towns are open, the entire seven-mile coastal hike (which is very hilly between Corniglia and Monterosso) can be completed in about four hours; allow five for dawdling. Take it slow...smell the cactus flowers, notice the scurrying lizards, listen to birds singing in the olive groves, and enjoy vistas on all sides.

If you're hiking the full five-town route, consider these factors: The trail between Riomaggiore (#1) and Manarola (#2) is easiest (when open). The hike between Manarola and Corniglia (#3) has minor hills (for a much steeper, more scenic alternative, consider detouring higher up, via Volastra). The trail from Corniglia to Vernazza (#4) is demanding, and the path from Vernazza to Monterosso (#5) is the most challenging. Starting in Monterosso allows you to tackle the toughest section (with lots and lots of steep, narrow stairs) while you're fresh—and to enjoy some of the region's most dramatic scenery as you approach Vernazza.

Riomaggiore-Manarola (20 minutes): The popular, easy **Via dell'Amore** (Pathway of Love) was washed out by a landslide; the park hopes to reopen it soon—inquire locally. If it's open, here's how to find the trailhead: Face the front of the train station in Riomaggiore (#1), go up the stairs to the right, following signs for *Via dell'Amore*. The photo-worthy promenade winds along the coast to Manarola (#2). A long tunnel and mega-nets protect hikers from mean-spirited falling rocks. A recommended wine bar, Bar & Vini A Piè de Mà, is located at the Riomaggiore trailhead and offers light meals and awesome views. There's a picnic zone, a water fountain, and shade just above the Manarola station (and a WC at Manarola station). If the trail is closed, you can connect these towns by train or a scenic €4 boat trip.

Manarola-Corniglia (45 minutes): The walk from Manarola (#2) to Corniglia (#3) is a little longer, more rugged, and steeper than the Via dell'Amore. To avoid the last stretch (switchback stairs leading up to the hill-capping town of Corniglia), end your hike at Corniglia's train station and catch the shuttle bus to the town center (2/hour, €1.50, free with Cinque Terre park card, usually timed to meet trains).

Corniglia-Vernazza (1.5 hours): The

The trail views are worth the effort.

scenic hike from Corniglia (#3) to Vernazza (#4)—the wildest and greenest section of the coast—is rewarding but hilly. From the Corniglia station and beach, zigzag up to the town (via the steep stairs, the longer road, or the shuttle bus). The trail leads you through vineyards and lots of fragrant and flowery vegetation. If you need a break before reaching Vernazza, stop by Franco's Ristorante and Bar la Torre, with a strip of shady tables perched high above the town.

Vernazza-Monterosso (1.5 hours): The trail from Vernazza (#4) to Monterosso (#5) is a challenging but scenic up-and-down-a-lot trek. Trails are narrow, steep, and crumbly, with a lot of steps, but easy to follow. The views just out of Vernazza, looking back at the town, are spectacular. From there you'll gradually ascend, passing little waterfalls. As you approach Monterosso, you'll descend steeply—on tall, knee-testing stairs—through vineyards, eventually following a rivulet to the sea. The last stretch into Monterosso is along a pleasant, paved pathway clinging to the cliff. You'll end right at Monterosso's old town beach.

Longer Hikes

While the national park charges admission for the coastal trails, they also maintain a free, far more extensive network of trails higher in the hills. Shuttle buses make the going easier, connecting coastal villages and distant trailheads. Ask for pointers at a TI or park office. Manarola-based **Cinque Terre Trekking** is a good resource (daily 9:00-13:00 & 14:00-20:00, Via Discovolo 136, tel. 0187-920-715).

Manarola-Volastra-Corniglia via the High Road (2.5 hours) leads from Manarola up to the village of Volastra, then north through high-altitude vineyard terraces, and steeply down through a forest to Corniglia (about six miles total). You can shave the two steepest miles off this route by taking the shuttle bus from Manarola up to Volastra (€1.50, free with Cinque Terre park card, schedule at park office, about hourly, 15 minutes). Another good option is hiking between **Monterosso and Levanto** (about 3.5 hours one-way, moderately strenuous, take the train to or from Levanto one-way).

Coastal trails are busiest at midday—hike early or late.

↑To Manarola

♥ Via dell'Amore ♥
Cliffs

PARK OFFICE
KIOSK
TRAIN
STATION

WALK
BEGINS

MURALS

ELEVATOR TO
TOP OF TOWN
(INSIDE PED. TUNNEL)

CINQUE
TERRE INFO

VIA PECUNIA

VIA SIGNORINI

PEDESTRIAN
TUNNEL

VIA SANT'ANTONIO

Ligurian Sea

PUNTA

VIA

B

Piazza
Vignaioli

Cliffs

WC
(UNDER
TUNNEL)

VIA SAN GIACOMO

BOAT DOCK
Harbor

BREAKWATER

BOAT
TICKETS

Restaurants
1. Bar Centrale
2. Trattoria la Grotta &
   Il Grottino Ristorante
3. Bar & Vini A Piè de Mà
4. La Zorza Café
5. Enoteca & Ristorante
   Dau Cila
6. Pizzeria/Focacceria
7. Il Pescato Cucinato
8. Siamo Fritti
9. Alimentari Franca

RIOMAGGIORE
(Town #1)

Riomaggiore is a laid-back, work-aday town that feels more "real" than its touristy neighbors. The main drag through town, while traffic-free, feels more urban than "village," and surrounding the harbor is a fascinating tangle of pastel homes leaning on each other like drunken sailors.

Orientation

Arrival in Riomaggiore: The **train station** is separated from the town center by a steep hill. The easiest way to get into town is to take the pedestrian tunnel that begins by the big mural (and parallels the rail tunnel). You'll exit at the bottom of Via Colombo, the main street. Other options: You can take my self-guided walk into town (see next page); catch the shuttle bus at the bottom of Via Colombo and ride it partway up; or ride the elevator up from the pedestrian tunnel (€1/person, daily 7:00-18:00). The **boat** docks near the base of Via Colombo. **Drivers** can park at one of two pay-and-display lots above town (€3.50/hour, €23/day, best to pay in cash).

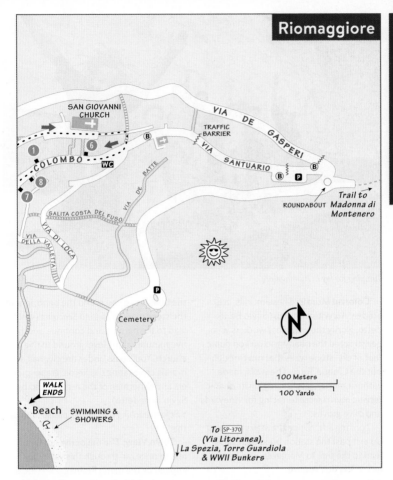

Riomaggiore

Tourist Information: The TI is in the train station at the ticket desk (daily 8:00–20:00, shorter hours off-season, tel. 0187-920-633). If it's crowded, you can buy your hiking pass at the Cinque Terre park info/shop office next door (daily 8:00–20:00, shorter hours off-season, tel. 0187-760-515).

Internet Access: The **park info/ shop office** has four public computers with Internet access upstairs, plus Wi-Fi (€1.50/20 minutes, free with Cinque Terre park card). The recommended **Bar Centrale** and **La Zorza Café** both offer free Wi-Fi with the purchase of a drink.

Services: A WC is near the Co-op grocery on Via Colombo, and another is under the tunnel where the street dead-ends.

◑ Riomaggiore Walk

This partly uphill but easy self-guided loop takes the long way from the station into town. Enjoy some fine views before strolling down the main street to the harbor.

• *Start at the train station. (If you arrive by boat, cross beneath the tracks and take a left, then hike through the tunnel along the tracks to reach the station.) You'll see some…*

Jumping for joy in Riomaggiore

Colorful Murals: These murals, created by Argentinean artist Silvio Benedetto, glorify the nameless workers who constructed the nearly 300 million cubic feet of dry-stone walls that run throughout the Cinque Terre. The walls, made without mortar, give the region its characteristic *muri a secco* terracing for vineyards and olive groves.

Looking left, notice the stairs climbing up just past the station building. These lead to the trail to Manarola, also known as the **Via dell'Amore.**

• *The fastest way into town is to take the pedestrian tunnel (which parallels the tracks from near the murals) straight to the bottom of Via Colombo, just above the marina. But I'd rather take the scenic route, up and over the hill. Facing the mural, turn left, then go right up the wide street just before the station café. Take the stairs leading through the garden on your right to the upper switchback, then, once on high ground, hook back toward the sea. Soon you'll pass the concrete tower marking the top of an elevator near the tunnel entrance, and a bit farther, a fine viewpoint.*

Top o' the Town: Here you're treated to spectacular sea views. Hook left around

the bluff; once you round the bend, ignore the steps marked *Marina Seacoast* (which lead to the harbor) and continue another five minutes along level ground to the church. You'll pass under the city hall, with murals celebrating the heroic grape-pickers and fishermen of the region (also by Silvio Benedetto).

• *Before reaching the church, pause to enjoy the...*

Town View: The major river of this region once ran through this valley, as implied by the name Riomaggiore (local dialect for "river" and "major"). As in the other Cinque Terre towns, the river ravine is now paved over. The romantic arched bridges that once connected the two sides have been replaced by a practical modern road.

The church (established in 1340 and rebuilt in 1870) is dedicated to St. John the Baptist, the patron saint of Genoa, the maritime republic that once dominated the region.

• *Continue straight past the church and along the narrow lane, watching on the right for wide stairs leading down to Riomaggiore's main street...*

Via Colombo: Starting downhill, you'll

pass (on the right, at #62) a good pizzeria/ *focacceria,* facing the Co-op grocery store across the street (at #55). Farther down on the left is the town butcher (*macelleria,* #103). The big covered terrace on the right belongs to Bar Centrale (at #144), the town's most popular hangout.

As you round the bend to the left, notice the old-timey pharmacy just above (on the right). On your left, at #199, peek into the Il Pescato Cucinato shop, where Laura fries up her husband Edoardo's fresh catch; grab a paper cone of deep-fried seafood as a snack. Where the road bends sharply right, notice the bench on your left (just before La Zorza Café)—the hangout for the town's old-timers, who keep a running commentary on the steady flow of people. Straight ahead, you can already see where this street will dead-end. The last shop on the left, Alimentari Franca (at #251), is a well-stocked grocery where you can gather the makings for a picnic.

Where Via Colombo dead-ends, look right to see the tunnel leading back to the station (and the Via dell'Amore to Manarola). Look left to see two sets of stairs. The "up" stairs take you to a park-like square built over the train tracks, which provides the children of the town level land on which to kick their soccer balls. The murals above celebrate the great-grandparents of these very children—the salt-of-the-earth locals who earned a humble living before the age of tourism.

• *The "down" stairs take you to a pay WC and the...*

Marina: This most picturesque corner of Riomaggiore features a cluster of buildings huddling nervously around a postage-stamp square and vest-pocket harbor. Because Riomaggiore lacks the protected harbor of Vernazza, when bad weather is expected, fishermen pull their boats up to the safety of the square. It's a team effort—the signal goes out, and anyone with a boat of their own helps move the whole fleet. Sometimes the fishermen are busy beaching their boats even on a bright, sunny day—an indication that they know something you don't know.

A couple of restaurants—with high prices and memorable seating—look down over the action. Head past them

Riomaggiore's harbor

and up the walkway along the left side of the harbor. Enjoy the views of the town's colorful pastel buildings, with the craggy coastline just beyond. Below you, the breakwater curves out to sea. These rocks are popular with sunbathers by day and romantics at sunset.

For a peek at Riomaggiore's beach, continue around the bluff on this trail toward the Punta di Montenero, the cape that defines the southern end of the Cinque Terre. As you walk you'll pass the rugged boat landing and eventually run into Riomaggiore's beach (*spiaggia*). Ponder how Europeans manage to look relaxed when lounging on football-sized "pebbles."

Experiences

Riomaggiore's rugged **beach** (*spiaggia*) is rocky, but still peaceful and inviting. There's a shower here in the summer, and another closer to town by the boat landing—where many enjoy sunning on and jumping from the rocks.

The town has a **diving center** that rents scuba, snorkeling, and kayaking gear (daily May-Sept 9:00-18:00, open in good weather only—likely weekends only in shoulder season, office down the stairs and under the tracks on Via San Giacomo, tel. 0187-920-011, www.5terrediving.it). Kayak at your own risk. Some readers say that the kayaks tip easily, training is not provided, and lifejackets are not required.

A **hiking trail** rises scenically from Riomaggiore to the 14th-century Madonna di Montenero sanctuary, high above the town (45 minutes). Take the main road inland until you see signs, or ride the shuttle bus 12 minutes from the town center to the sanctuary trail, then walk uphill another 10 minutes. There's a great picnic spot up top.

Eating

Bar Centrale, run by sociable Ivo and Alberto, serves €8-10 pizza, pasta, and popular American fare, with rock music and a fun-loving vibe. During the day, it feels like the village's living room. At night, it offers the liveliest action and best mojitos in town. This popular expat hangout is also a good spot for breakfast (daily 7:30 until late, closed Mon in winter, 30 minutes of free Wi-Fi with drink, Via Colombo 144, tel. 0187-920-208).

Trattoria la Grotta, also in the town center, serves reliable food with a passion for anchovies and mussels in a dramatic, cave-like setting (€11-14 pastas, €11-15 *secondi,* daily 12:00-14:30 & 17:30-22:30, closed Thu in winter, Via Colombo 247, tel. 0187-920-187). The same family runs the upscale **Il Grottino Ristorante** next door (same hours, tel. 0187-920-938).

Bar & Vini A Piè de Mà, at the trailhead of Via dell'Amore, on the Manarola end of town, has piles of charm. A meal or cocktail (€6) on its terrace offers dramatic views and a memory (€8-12 dishes, €4 *panini,* daily 10:00-20:00, June-Sept until 24:00, free Wi-Fi—password on chalkboard, tel. 0187-921-037).

Kayakers flock to Riomaggiore.

The catch of the day

La Zorza Café is a hip, youthful alternative to the other bars in town, with thumping music, a free-style bartender, and a spread of snacks (€6 cocktails, spring-fall daily until late, winter until 21:00, free Wi-Fi with drink, tel. 0187-920-036).

Enoteca & Ristorante Dau Cila (pronounced "dow CHEE-lah") is a cool hideaway in a centuries-old boat shed on the harbor, with extra tables on a rustic deck. It's also cool for cocktails, with a mellow jazz-and-Brazilian-lounge ambience (€9-12 salads and *bruschette* for lunch; €12-19 pastas, €15-18 *secondi;* daily 12:00-24:00, closed Jan-Feb and Mon in March, Via San Giacomo 65, tel. 0187-760-032).

Various eateries along the main drag, which you'll encounter on my self-guided walk, offer good lunches or snacks. At the top of town, the nameless **pizzeria/ focacceria** at #62 is a reliable standby (€3 slices). For deep-fried seafood in a paper cone, try **Il Pescato Cucinato,** where the chalkboard out front explains what's fresh (€5-9, daily 11:20-20:30, Via Colombo 199, mobile 339-262-4815), or **Siamo Fritti,** a few doors away (€5-9, daily 10:00-21:00, Via Colombo 161, mobile 347-826-1729).

For picnic supplies, head to handy **Alimentari Franca,** at the bottom of the main street, conveniently located right by the train-station tunnel and stairs down to the marina (Thu-Tue 8:00-12:45 & 15:30-19:00, closed Wed in winter, Via Colombo 251).

MANAROLA
(Town #2)

Mellow Manarola feels just right. Its hillsides are blanketed with vineyards and it provides the easiest access to the Cinque Terre's remarkable dry-stone terraces. The trail ringing the town's cemetery peninsula provides some of the most accessible and most striking views anywhere.

The town fills a ravine, bookended by its harbor to the west and a hilltop church square to the east. The touristy zone squeezed between the train tracks and the harbor can be congested, but just a few steps uphill, you can breathe again. The higher you go, the less crowded it gets, culminating in the residential zone that clings to the ridge.

Manarola

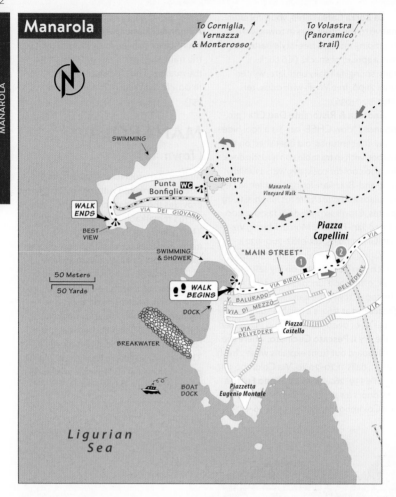

Orientation

Arrival in Manarola: The town is attached to its **train station** by a 200-yard-long tunnel. Walking through the tunnel, you'll reach Manarola's elevated square. To reach the busy harbor, cross the piazza, then go down the other side. To reach the town, hilltop church, and vineyard strolls, turn right. The **boat** docks near the base of the main street and the start of my self-guided walk. **Drivers** can park in one of the two lots just before town (€2/hour), then walk down the road to the church; from there, the street twists down to the main piazza, train-station tunnel, and harbor.

Tourist Information: The TI/national park information office is in the train station (likely daily 7:30-19:30, shorter hours off-season).

Shuttle Bus: The ATC shuttle bus runs from near the post office (halfway up Manarola's main street), stopping first at the parking lots above town, and then going up to Volastra (€1.50 one-way, buy ticket on board for €2.50, free with Cinque Terre park card, about hourly), which hardy hikers can use as the jumping-off

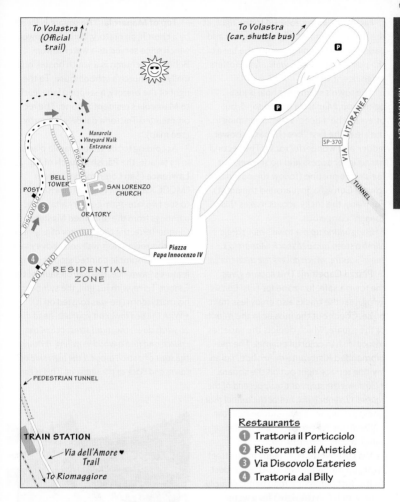

Restaurants
1 Trattoria il Porticciolo
2 Ristorante di Aristide
3 Via Discovolo Eateries
4 Trattoria dal Billy

point for a hike to Corniglia (a higher-altitude alternative to the regular Manarola-Corniglia hike).

Hiking Gear and Tips: Cinque Terre Trekking, near the top of the main street (halfway up to the church), fills its cramped shop with hiking gear (boots, clothes, walking sticks, and more); they also sell hiking maps and offer free advice (daily 9:00-13:00 & 14:00-20:00, shorter hours off-season, Via Discovolo 136, tel. 0187-920-715).

➲ Manarola Walk

From the harbor, this 30-minute, self-guided circular walk shows you the town and surrounding vineyards and ends at a fantastic viewpoint, perfect for a picnic.
• *Start down at the waterfront. Belly up to the wooden banister overlooking the rocky harbor, between the two restaurants.*

The Harbor: Manarola is a picturesque tumble of buildings bunny-hopping down its ravine to the fun-loving waterfront. The breakwater was built just over a decade ago.

Facing the water, look up to the right, at the hillside Punta Bonfiglio cemetery and park. The trail running around the base of the point—where this walk ends—offers magnificent views.

The town's swimming hole is just below you. Manarola has no sand, but offers the best deep-water swimming in the area. The first "beach" has a shower, ladder, and wonderful rocks. The second has tougher access and no shower, but feels more pristine (follow the paved path toward Corniglia, just around the point). For many, the tricky access makes this "beach" dangerous.

• *Hiking inland up the town's main drag, climb a steep ramp to reach Manarola's "new" square, which covers the train tracks.*

Piazza Capellini: This square gives the town a safe, fun zone for kids. Locals living near the tracks also enjoy less train noise. Check out the mosaic in the middle of the square, which depicts the varieties of local fish in colorful enamel. The recommended Ristorante di Aristide has an inviting terrace right out on the square.

• *Go down the stairs at the upper end of the square. On your right, notice the tunnel that leads to Manarola's train station (and the trailhead for the Via dell'Amore to Riomaggiore). But for now, head up...*

Via Discovolo: The sleepy main street twists up through town, lined by modest shops. Just before the road bends sharply right, watch (on the right) for a waterwheel. Mills like this once powered the local olive oil industry. Manarola's stream was covered over by a modern sewage system after World War II. Before then, romantic bridges arched over its ravine. You can peek below the concrete street in several places to see the stream surging below your feet.

Across the street from the waterwheel and a bit farther up, notice the **Cinque Terre Trekking** shop (on your left).

• *Keep switchbacking up until you come to the square at the...*

Top of Manarola: The square is faced by a church, an oratory, and a bell tower, which once served as a watchtower. Behind the church is a youth hostel, originally the church's schoolhouse. To the right of the oratory, a stepped lane leads to Manarola's residential zone. The recommended Trattoria dal Billy is nearby (see map).

According to the white marble plaque in its facade, the **Parish Church of St. Lawrence** (San Lorenzo) dates from "MCCCXXXVIII" (1338). Step inside to see two late-15th-century altarpiece paintings from the unnamed Master of the Cinque Terre, the only painter of any note from this region (left wall and above main altar). The humble painted stone ceiling features Lawrence, the patron saint of the Cinque Terre, with his grill, the symbol of his martyrdom (he was roasted on it).

• *With the bell tower on your left, head about 20 yards down the main street below the church and find a wooden railing. It marks the start of a stroll around the high side of town, and back to the seafront. This is the*

Church of St. Lawrence

beginning of the...

Manarola Vineyard Walk: Don't miss this experience. Follow the wooden railing, enjoying lemon groves and wild red valerian. Along the mostly flat path, you'll get a close-up look at the dry-stone walls and finely crafted vineyards (with dried-heather thatches to protect the grapes from the southwest winds). Smell the rosemary and pick out the remains of an old fort. Notice the S-shape of the main road—once a riverbed. The town's roofs are made of locally quarried slate, rather than tile, and are held down by rocks during windstorms.

Halfway along the lip of the ravine, a path marked *Volastra panoramico (Corniglia)* leads steeply up into the vineyards on the right. This path passes a variety of simple wooden religious scenes, the work of local resident Mario Andreoli. Before his father died, Mario promised him he'd replace the old cross on the family's vineyard—he's been adding figures ever since.

High above, a recent fire burned off the tree cover, revealing ancient terraces that line the terrain. This path also marks the start of the scenic route to Volastra (on the hilltop above), and eventually to Corniglia (see page 647).

• *Continue on the level trail around the base of the hill. Soon the harbor comes into view. Keep looping around the hill for even better views of town. Once you're facing the sea (with the cemetery peninsula below you),*

the trail takes a sharp left and heads down toward the water. When you hit the clifftop fence, the T-intersection gives you a choice: right, to the coastal trail to Corniglia, or left, back to town. Turn left for now. Before descending, watch for the turnoff on the right, detouring into...

The Cemetery: Ever since Napoleon—who was king of Italy in the early 1800s—decreed that cemeteries were health risks, Cinque Terre's burial spots have been located outside the towns. The result: The dearly departed get first-class views. Each cemetery—with evocative yellowed photos and finely carved Carrara marble memorials—is worth a visit.

• *The Manarola cemetery is on...*

Punta Bonfiglio: This point offers commanding views of the entire region. For the best vantage point, take the stairs just below the cemetery (through the green gate), then walk farther out toward the water through a park. Your Manarola finale is the bench at the tip of the point. Pause and take in the view. The easiest way back to town is to take the stairs at the end of the point, which join the main walking path—offering more views on its way back to the harbor.

Eating

These restaurant options are listed from lowest to highest, in terms of quality and elevation.

Touristy restaurants are concentrated in the tight zone between Piazza

Vineyards above Manarola

Manarola's cemetery

Cinque Terre Cuisine

Hanging out at a seaview restaurant while sampling local specialties could become one of your favorite memories.

The staple here is **anchovies** (*acciughe;* ah-CHOO-gay)—ideally served the day they're caught. Even if you've always hated American anchovies, try them fresh here. They can be prepared marinated, butterflied, and deep-fried (sometimes with a delicious garlic/vinegar sauce called *giada*). *Tegame alla vernazzana* is the most typical main course in Vernazza: a casserole-like dish of whole anchovies, potatoes, and tomatoes.

Antipasto here means *antipasti ai frutti di mare* (sometimes called simply *antipasti misti*), a plate of mixed "fruits of the sea." Splitting one of these and a pasta dish can be plenty for two people.

This region is the birthplace of **pesto.** Try it on *trenette* (the long, flat Ligurian noodle ruffled on one side) or *trofie* (short, dense twists made of flour with a bit of potato).

Pansotti are ravioli with ricotta and a mixture of greens, often served with a walnut sauce (*salsa di noci*).

Focaccia, the tasty pillowy bread, also originates here. Locals say the best focaccia is made between the Cinque Terre and Genoa. It comes plain or with onions, sage, or olive bits and is sold in rounds or slices by weight (a portion is about 100 grams, or *un etto*).

The **vino delle Cinque Terre,** while not one of Italy's top wines, flows cheap and easy throughout the region. It's white—great with seafood. **Sciacchetrà** dessert wine is worth the splurge (€4-12 per small glass). Order **torta della nonna** ("grandmother's cake") and dunk chunks of it into your glass.

Capellini and the harbor. While these are mostly interchangeable, the Scorza family works hard at **Trattoria il Porticciolo** (€7-13 pastas, €10-16 *secondi,* Thu-Tue 7:30-23:30, closed Wed, Via Birolli 92, tel. 0187-920-083).

Ristorante di Aristide, right on Piazza Capellini, offers trendy atmosphere and a pleasant outdoor setting (€8-11 pastas, €11-20 *secondi,* €12-18 daily specials). Down the stairs, at the bottom of the main street, is their simpler **café** (€5 omelets, €7 pizzas, sandwiches, salads; Tue-Sun café open 8:00-22:30, restaurant 12:00-22:30, both closed Thu and Jan-Feb, Via Discovolo 290, tel. 0187-920-000).

Via Discovolo, the main street climb-ing up through town from Piazza Capellini to the church, is lined with simpler places, including some grocery stores and a *gelateria.*

Up at the top of town, in the residential zone above the church, **Trattoria dal Billy** offers both good food and impressive views over the valley. With black pasta with seafood and squid ink, mixed seafood starters, and homemade desserts, it's worth the climb. Across the street is an elegant dining room carved into the rock—perfect for a romantic candlelight meal. Dinner reservations are a must (€8-12 pastas, €13-20 *secondi,* generally daily 12:00-15:00 & 18:00-22:00, sometimes closed Thu, Via Aldo Rollandi 122, tel. 0187-920-628, www.trattoriabilly.com).

CORNIGLIA
(Town #3)

According to legend, this tiny, sleepy town's ancient residents produced a wine so famous that vases found at Pompeii touted its virtues. Wine remains Corniglia's lifeblood today.

The only town of the Cinque Terre not on the water, Corniglia (pop. 240) is less visited and feels remote. If you think of the Cinque Terre as the Beatles, Corniglia is Ringo. It has cooler temperatures, a windy overlook on its promontory, and rocky sea access below its train station. The one-time beach has all been washed away. Signs that say *al mare* or *Marina* lead from the town center steeply down to sunning rocks. There are a few restaurants.

Orientation

Arrival in Corniglia: From the **train station,** located deep in a ravine, a footpath zigzags up 385 steps to town (allow at least 15 minutes). Thankfully, the shuttle bus—generally timed to meet arriving trains—connects the station with the hill town's Ciappà square (€1.50 one-way at ticket office, or buy as you board for €2.50, free with Cinque Terre park card, 1-2/hour). **Drivers** can park past Villa Cecio.

Rick's Tip: *To avoid the steep hike to Corniglia and the long descent to the train station,* **use the handy shuttle bus.** *Upon arrival in town (where a schedule is posted at the bus stop), jot down the departure times for the bus and plan your time accordingly.*

Tourist Information: A TI/park information office is at the train station (daily 8:00-20:00, shorter hours off-season).

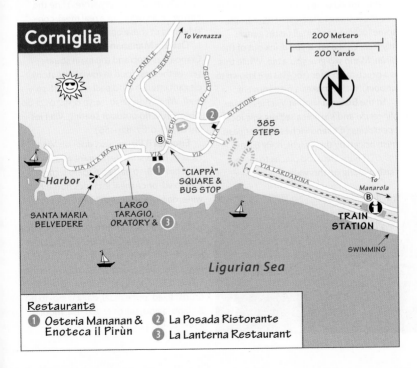

Corniglia

To Vernazza

LOC. CANALE
VIA SIERRA
LOC. CHIOSO
VIA ALLA STAZIONE

200 Meters
200 Yards

N

FIESCHI
B
2
385 STEPS

VIA ALLA MARINA
VIA
1
VIA
"CIAPPÀ" SQUARE & BUS STOP

VIA LARDARINA

To Manarola
B

←Harbor

SANTA MARIA BELVEDERE
LARGO TARAGIO, ORATORY & **3**

TRAIN STATION

SWIMMING

Ligurian Sea

Restaurants
1 Osteria Mananan & Enoteca il Pirùn
2 La Posada Ristorante
3 La Lanterna Restaurant

➡ Corniglia Walk

This self-guided walk might take up to 30 minutes...but only if you let yourself browse and lick a gelato cone.

• *Begin near the bus stop, located at a...*

Town Square: The gateway to this community is Ciappà square, with an ATM, phone booth, old wine press, and bus stop (shuttle buses timed to coordinate with train schedules).

• *Look for the arrow pointing to the centro. Stroll the spine of Corniglia, Via Fieschi. In the fall, the smell of grapes becoming wine wafts from busy cellars. Along this main street, you'll see...*

Corniglia's Enticing Shops: On the right as you enter Via Fieschi, a pair of neighboring, fiercely competitive *gelaterias* jockey for your business. My favorite is **Alberto's Gelateria** (at #74). Before ordering, get a free taste of *miele di Corniglia,* made from local honey.

Farther along, on the left, **Enoteca il Pirùn**—named for an oddly shaped old-fashioned wine pitcher—is located in a cool cantina at Via Fieschi 115. Sample some local wines (small tastes generally free, €3/glass). If you drink out of the *pirùn,* Mario will give you a bib. While this is a practical matter (rookies are known to dribble), it also makes a nice souvenir.

In the **Butiega** shop at Via Fieschi 142, Vincenzo and Veronica sell organic local specialties (€3 sandwiches and *antipasti misti* priced by the weight, daily 8:00-19:30). There are good places to picnic farther along on this walk.

Tiny Corniglia

• *Following Via Fieschi, you'll end up at the...*

Main Square: On Largo Taragio, tables from two bars and a trattoria spill around a WWI memorial and the town's old well. What looks like a church is the Oratory of Santa Caterina. Up the stairs behind the oratory, you'll find a clearing that children use as a soccer field. The stone benches and viewpoint make it a peaceful place for a picnic.

• *From the square, continue up Via Fieschi to the...*

End-of-Town Viewpoint: The Santa Maria Belvedere, named for a church that once stood here, marks the scenic end of Corniglia and makes a super—but sometimes crowded—picnic spot. High to the west (right), the village and sanctuary of San Bernardino straddle a ridge. Below is the tortuous harbor, where locals hoist their boats onto the cruel rocks.

Eating

The typical array of pizzerias, *focaccerias,* and *alimentari* (grocery stores) line the narrow main drag. For a real meal, consider one of these options.

Osteria Mananan—between the Ciappà bus stop and the main square— serves the best food in town in its stony, elegant interior (€10 pastas, €10-16 *secondi,* Wed-Mon 12:30-14:30 & 19:30-22:00, closed Tue, no outdoor seating, Via Fieschi 117, tel. 0187-821-166).

Enoteca il Pirùn, next door on Via Fieschi, has a small restaurant above the wine bar (€8-10 pastas, €10-16 *secondi,* €28 fixed-price meal includes homemade wine, daily 12:00-16:00 & 19:30-23:30, tel. 0187-812-315).

La Posada Ristorante offers dinner in a garden under trees, overlooking the Ligurian Sea. To get here, stroll out of town to the top of the stairs that lead down to the station (€8-10 pastas, €10-16 *secondi,* €18 tourist fixed-price meal, daily 12:00-16:00 & 19:00-23:00, tel. 0187-821-174, mobile 338-232-5734).

La Lanterna, on the main square, is atmospheric, but without particularly charming service (€10-14 pastas, €10-18 *secondi,* daily 12:00-15:00 & 19:30-21:30).

VERNAZZA
(Town #4)

With a ruined castle and a stout stone church, Vernazza is the jewel of the Cinque Terre. Only the occasional noisy train reminds you of the modern world.

Proud of their Vernazzan heritage, local families go back centuries; several generations live together. Fearing the change it would bring, keep-Vernazza-small proponents stopped the construction of a major road into the town and region. Leisure time is devoted to taking part in the *passeggiata*—strolling lazily together up and down the main street. Learn—and live—the phrase *"la vita pigra di Vernazza"* (the lazy life of Vernazza).

The action is at the harbor, where you'll find outdoor restaurants, a bar hanging on the edge of the castle, and a breakwater with a promenade, corralled by a natural amphitheater of terraced hills. In the summer, the beach becomes a soccer field, with teams fielded by bars and restaurants providing late-night entertainment.

Orientation

Arrival in Vernazza: The town's **train station** is only about three train cars long, but the trains are much longer—so most of the cars come to a stop in a long, dark tunnel. Open the door, get out, and walk through the tunnel to the station. From there the main drag flows through town right to the harbor. The **boats** dock at the harborfront square, at the base of main street. **Don't drive to Vernazza.** Roads are in terrible shape and parking is limited. If you're coming from the north, park in Levanto. If arriving from the south, park your car in La Spezia. From either town, hop on the train.

Rick's Tip: *A steep 10-minute hike in either direction from Vernazza gives you a* **classic village photo op.** *For the best light, head toward Corniglia in the morning—best views are just before the ticket booth for the national park—and toward Monterosso in the evening—best views are after the ticket booth.*

Tourist Information: Two information points at the train station face each other across the platform: the gift shop, where you can get answers to basic questions (daily 8:00-20:00, closed in winter), and

Vernazza

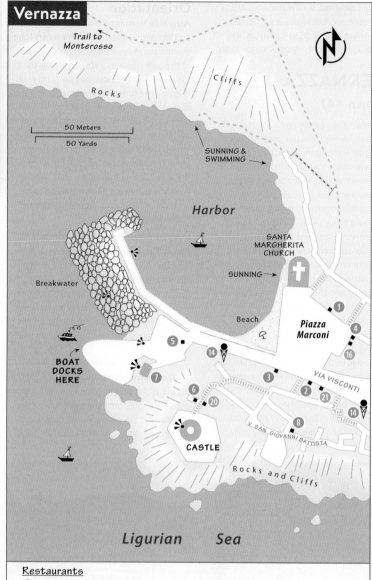

Vernazza

Trail to Monterosso

Cliffs

Rocks

50 Meters
50 Yards

SUNNING & SWIMMING

Harbor

SANTA MARGHERITA CHURCH

SUNNING →

Breakwater

Beach

Piazza Marconi

BOAT DOCKS HERE

VIA VISCONTI

V. SAN GIOVANNI BATTISTA

CASTLE

Rocks and Cliffs

Ligurian   Sea

Restaurants

1. Trattoria del Capitano & Martina Callo Rooms
2. Gianni Franzi Ristorante/Reception
3. Gambero Rosso
4. Ristorante Pizzeria Vulnetia & Nicolina Rooms Reception
5. Pizzeria Baia Saracena
6. Ristorante al Castello
7. Ristorante Belforte
8. Vernazza Wine Experience
9. Trattoria da Sandra
10. Antica Osteria il Baretto
11. Blue Marlin Bar
12. Il Pirata delle Cinque Terre Café

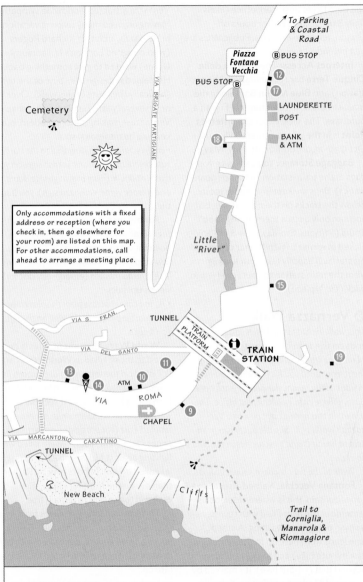

Only accommodations with a fixed address or reception (where you check in, then go elsewhere for your room) are listed on this map. For other accommodations, call ahead to arrange a meeting place.

13 Forno Bakery
14 Gelaterias (3)

Hotels & Rooms
15 Pensione Sorriso
16 Albergo Barbara & Francamaria Reception

17 La Perla delle 5 Terre Rooms, Tonino Basso Rooms & La Rosa dei Venti
18 Camere Fontana Vecchia
19 Giuliano Basso Rooms
20 Monica Lercari Rooms
21 Rosa Vitali Rooms

the train ticket desk/park office (likely daily 8:00-20:00, shorter hours off-season, tel. 0187-812-533). Public WCs are just behind.

Internet Access: The **Il Pirata delle Cinque Terre** bar (behind/above the train station) and **Blue Marlin Bar** (along the main street) both offer free Wi-Fi with a purchase. The slick, expensive **Internet Point** is in the village center (daily June-Oct 9:30-23:00, until 20:00 Nov-May).

Baggage Storage: You can leave your bags at the train-station gift shop (near track 1). Bags are kept in a secure room below the tracks on the main street, but you can only access them during shop hours (€1/hour, €10/day, daily 8:00-20:00, closed in winter). Friendly Francesco and his staff will happily take your luggage from the train station to your hotel—and back (€2-3/piece).

⊙ Vernazza Walk

This walk includes the town squares and ends on the scenic breakwater.

• *From the train station, walk uphill along the stream until you hit the small square in front of the recommended Il Pirata delle Cinque Terre café, near the post office. The stream in this ravine once powered Vernazza's water mill. Shuttle buses run from here to hamlets and sanctuaries in the hills above.*

Walk to the tidy, modern square called...

Fontana Vecchia: Named after a long-gone fountain, this is where older locals remember the river filled with towns-women doing their washing. A steep lane leads from here up to the cemetery (20-minute hike) and to the sanctuary beyond that (1-hour hike). It's marked by an icon of Madonna di Reggio, beloved by the people of Vernazza. Imagine the entire village sadly trudging up here during funerals. (The cemetery is evocative at sunset, when the fading light touches each crypt.)

You may see some construction work going on here. Following the 2011 flood,

Vernazza attracted worldwide sympathy. Having enjoyed many relaxing vacations in Vernazza, architect Richard Rogers (who designed London's Millennium Dome) wanted to give something back. He helped redesign the spine of the town (basically the route of this walk). Over the next several years, his plans will reshape Vernazza—making it more modern, but keeping its traditional soul.

• *Begin your saunter downhill to the harbor. Just before the Pensione Sorriso sign, on your right (at #7, with big brown garage doors and a croce verde Vernazza sign), you'll see the...*

Ambulance Barn: A group of volunteers is always on call for a dash to the hospital, 40 minutes away in La Spezia. A few steps farther down is the town clinic. The *guarda medica* (emergency doctor) sleeps upstairs.

• *At the corner across from the playground, on a marble plaque in the wall on the left, you'll see a...*

World Wars Monument: This is dedicated to those killed in World Wars I and II. Listed on the left are soldiers *morti in combattimento,* who died in World War I; on the right is the WWII section. Some were deported to *Germania;* others—labeled *Part* (for *partigiani,* or partisans, generally communists)—were killed while fighting against Mussolini. After 1943, Hitler called up Italian boys over 15. Rather than die on the front for Hitler, they escaped to the hills to remain free.

The path to Corniglia leaves from here (behind and above the plaque). Behind you is a small square, decorated with big millstones, once used to grind local olives into oil.

From here, Vernazza's tiny river goes underground. Until the 1950s, the river ran openly through the center of town. Old-timers recall the days before the breakwater, when the river cascaded down and the surf sent waves rolling up Vernazza's main drag. (The name "Vernazza" is actually local dialect for "little Venice"—the town once had a string of bridges, evoking those in Venice.)

Corralling this stream under the modern street, and forcing it to take a hard right turn here, contributed to the damage caused by the 2011 flood. After the flood, alpine engineers were imported from Switzerland to redesign the drainage system, so any future floods will be less destructive. They also installed nets above the town to protect it from landslides.

On the left, just past the tracks, you'll see a giant poster with photos of the 2011 flood (*alluvione*) and the shops that it devastated. "The 25th of October" is a day that will live forever in this town's lore.

• *Follow the road downhill to...*

Vernazza's "Commercial Center": Here, you'll pass many locals doing their *vasche* (laps). Next, you'll pass souvenir shops, wine shops, the recommended Blue Marlin Bar, and the tiny stone Chapel of Santa Marta, where Mass is celebrated only on special Sundays. Above and behind the chapel is the Vineria Santa Marta wine bar. Farther down, you'll walk by a *gelateria*, bakery, pharmacy, a grocery, and another *gelateria*. There are plenty of fun and cheap food-to-go options here.

• *On the left, in front of the second gelateria, a stone arch was blasted away by the 2011 flood. Scamper through the hole in the rock to reach Vernazza's shrinking...*

"New Beach": In the flood's aftermath, Vernazza's main drag and harbor were filled with mud and silt. Workers used the debris to fill in even more of this beach,

and for several years Vernazza had a popular beach that felt a world away from the bustle of the main drag. But as time goes on, the erosion from the churning surf is taking it away.

• *Back on the main drag, continue downhill to the...*

Harbor Square (Piazza Marconi) and Breakwater: Vernazza, with the only natural harbor of the Cinque Terre, was established as the sole place boats could pick up the fine local wine. The two-foot-high square stone at the foot of the stairs (on the left) is marked *Sasso del Sego* (stone of tallow). Workers crushed animal flesh and fat in its basin to make tallow, which drained out of the tiny hole below. The tallow was then used to waterproof boats or wine barrels. Stonework is the soul of the region. Take some time to appreciate the impressive stonework of the restaurant interiors facing the harbor.

On the far side (behind the recommended Ristorante Pizzeria Vulnetia), peek into the tiny street with its commotion of arches. Vernazza's most characteristic side streets, called *carugi*, lead up from here. The narrow stairs mark the beginning of the trail that leads up to the quintessential view of Vernazza—and, eventually, on to Monterosso.

Located in front of the harborside church, the tiny piazza—decorated with a river-rock mosaic—is a popular hangout spot. The **church** is unusual for its strange entryway, which faces east (altar side), rather than the more typical western

Vernazza's harbor and breakwater

Sunbathing in Vernazza

orientation. In the 16th century, the townspeople doubled the church in size, causing it to overtake a little piazza that once faced the west facade. From the square, use the "new" entry and climb the steps. Inside, the lighter pillars in the back mark the 16th-century extension. Three historic portable crosses hanging on the walls are replicas of crosses that (locals believe) Vernazza ships once carried on crusades.

• *Finish your town tour seated out on the breakwater. Face the town, and see...*

The Harbor: In a moderate storm, you'd be soaked, as waves routinely crash over the *molo* (breakwater, built in 1972). Waves can rearrange the huge rocks—depositing them onto the piazza and its benches. Freak waves have even washed away tourists. Enjoy the waterfront piazza—carefully.

Vernazza's fishing fleet is down to just a few boats (with the net spools). Vernazzans are still more likely to own a boat than a car, and it's said that you stand a better chance of surviving if you mess with a local man's wife than with his boat. Boats are on buoys, except in winter or when the red storm flag (see the pole at the start of the breakwater) indicates bad seas. At these times, the boats are pulled up onto the square—which is usually reserved for restaurant tables.

The Castle (Castello Doria): On the far right, the castle, which is now a grassy park with great views (and nothing but stones), still guards the town (€1.50 donation, daily 10:00-18:30; from harbor, take stairs by Trattoria Gianni and follow *Ristorante al Castello* signs, tower is a few steps beyond). This was the town's watchtower back in pirate days, and a Nazi lookout in World War II. The castle tower looks new because it was rebuilt after the British bombed it, chasing out the Germans. The squat tower on the water is a great spot for a glass of wine or a meal (from the breakwater, you can follow the rope to Ristorante Belforte and pop inside, past

the actual submarine door; a photo of a major storm showing the entire tower under a wave—not uncommon in the winter—hangs near the bar).

The Town: Before the 12th century, pirates made the coast uninhabitable, so the first Vernazzans lived in the hills above (near the Reggio Sanctuary). The town itself—and its towers, fortified walls, and hillside terracing—are mostly from the 12th through the 15th centuries.

Vernazza has two halves. *Sciuiu* (Vernazzan dialect for "flowery") is the sunny side on the left, and *luvegu* (dank) is the shady side on the right. Houses below the castle were connected by an interior arcade. The square before you is locally famous for some of the area's finest restaurants. The big red central house—on the site where Genoan warships were built in the 12th century—used to be a guardhouse.

In the Middle Ages, there was no beach or square. The water went right up to the buildings, where boats would tie up, Venetian-style. Buildings had a water gate and a front door on the higher inland side. There was no pastel plaster—just fine stonework (traces survive above the Trattoria del Capitano).

Above the Town: The small, round tower above the red guardhouse reminds us of the town's importance in the Middle Ages. Back then, Back then, the enemies of key ally Genoa were Vernazza's enemies. Franco's Ristorante and Bar la

Castle at Vernazza

Torre, just above and beyond the tower, welcomes hikers starting or finishing the Corniglia-Vernazza hike. That tower recalls a time when the entire town was fortified by a stone wall. Vineyards fill the mountainside beyond the town; notice the many terraces.

The Church, School, and City Hall: Vernazza's Ligurian Gothic church, built with black stones quarried from Punta Mesco (the distant point behind you), dates from 1318. The gray stone marks the church's 16th-century expansion. The gray-and-red house above the spire is the elementary school. Older students go to the "big city," La Spezia. The red building to the right of the schoolhouse, a former monastery, is the city hall.

Finally, on the top of the hill is the town cemetery. It's only fair that hardworking Vernazzans—who spend their lives climbing up and down the hillsides—are rewarded with an eternal world-class view.

Experiences

The harbor's sandy cove has sunning rocks and showers by the breakwater. There's also a ladder on the breakwater

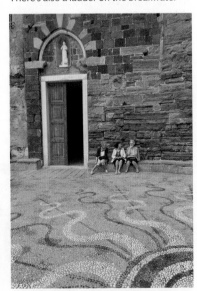
Santa Margherita Church

for deep-water access. The sunbathing lane directly under the church has a shower. Vernazza's **"new beach"** can be accessed through a hole halfway along its main drag.

Save Vernazza began as a post-flood relief organization but has evolved into an advocacy group, emphasizing sustainable tourism. "Voluntourism" activities, scheduled regularly through the high season, include rebuilding terrace walls and harvesting grapes (reservations required, lunch and wine provided, generally 2/week late May-Oct 8:30-13:30, mobile 349-357-3572, www.savevernazza.com, workwithus@savevernazza.com).

Vernazza's skimpy business community is augmented Tuesday mornings (8:00-13:00), when cars and trucks pull into town for a tailgate **market.**

Eating

Vernazza's restaurants are worth the splurge. All take pride in their cooking. Wander around at about 20:00 and compare the ambience, but don't wait too long—many kitchens close at 22:00. To get an outdoor table on summer weekends, reserve ahead. Expect to spend around €10-12 for pastas, €14-21 for *secondi,* and €2-3 for a cover charge.

Harborside restaurants and bars are easygoing. You're welcome to grab a cup of coffee or glass of wine and disappear somewhere on the **breakwater,** returning your glass when you're done.

Rick's Tip: *If you dine in Vernazza but are staying in Monterosso, be sure to* **check train schedules before sitting down to eat,** *as trains run less frequently in the evening (with a nearly 2-hour wait after the 21:30 departure).*

Harborside
Trattoria del Capitano serves a short menu of straightforward local dishes, including €12 *spaghetti allo scoglio*—pasta

entangled with seafood (€8-14 pastas, €14-22 *secondi*, Feb-Nov Wed-Mon from 8:00 for breakfast, 12:00-15:30 & 18:30-22:00, closed Tue except in Aug, closed Dec-Jan, tel. 0187-812-201).

Gianni Franzi is an old standby with well-prepared seafood and reliable, friendly service. While the outdoor seating is basic, the indoor setting is classy (€9-14 pastas, €11-22 *secondi*, check their *menù cucina tipica Vernazza,* Thu-Tue 12:00-15:00 & 19:00-22:00, closed Wed except in Aug, tel. 0187-812-228).

Gambero Rosso is a venerable place with a fine interior and perhaps the best seating on the harbor (€10-16 pastas, €16-25 *secondi*, March-Nov Fri-Wed 12:00-16:30 & 19:00-22:00, closed Thu and Dec-Feb, Piazza Marconi 7, tel. 0187-812-265).

Ristorante Pizzeria Vulnetia has a jovial atmosphere and serves regional specialties and pizzas, making it a good choice for budget and family meals (€6-10 pizzas, €11-13 pastas, €13-18 *secondi*, Tue-Sun 12:00-22:00, closed Mon, Piazza Marconi 29, tel. 0187-821-193, Giuliano and Tullio).

Pizzeria Baia Saracena ("Saracen Bay") is the other budget option on the harbor, with a memorable atmosphere and reasonable prices (€6-10 salads, €7-10 pizzas and pastas, Sat-Thu 10:30-22:00, closed Fri, tel. 0187-812-113, Luca).

By the Castle

Ristorante al Castello is high above town, just below the castle, with commanding views. Reserve one of the dozen romantic cliff-side seaview tables for two. Their "spaghetti on the rocks" (noodles with shellfish) is a family specialty (€15 pastas, €15-20 *secondi*, May-Oct Thu-Tue 12:00-15:00 for lunch, 19:00-22:00 for dinner, closed Wed and Nov-April, tel. 0187-812-296).

Ristorante Belforte serves a blend of traditional and creative cuisine. The off-menu *baccalà pastellato* plate takes fried cod to new heights. Reserve ahead for tables on the view terrace (€14-17 pastas, €22-30 *secondi*, April-Oct Wed-Mon 12:00-16:00 & 19:00-22:00, closed Tue and Nov-March, tel. 0187-812-222, Michela).

Vernazza Wine Experience hides out at the top of town, just under the castle. It's romantic, with mellow music, wines, and the €10 small plates that match them. It's pricey, but the quality is excellent and the view is unforgettable (daily 17:00-21:00, hike from harborfront and turn left before castle, Via S. Giovanni Battista 31, tel. 331-343-3801).

Rick's Tip: *After the restaurants close down, Vernazza is quiet except for a couple of* **nightspots: Blue Marlin Bar** *and* **Il Pirata delle Cinque Terre.** *All Vernazza bars must close by 24:00.*

On or near the Main Street

Several of Vernazza's inland eateries manage to compete without the harbor ambience, but with slightly cheaper prices.

Trattoria da Sandro, on the main

drag, mixes quality cuisine, including award-winning stuffed mussels, with friendly service (€8-13 pastas, €13-18 *secondi,* Wed-Mon 12:00-15:00 & 18:30-22:00, closed Tue, Via Roma 62, tel. 0187-812-223).

Antica Osteria il Baretto is a solid bet for homey, reasonably priced traditional cuisine, including homemade fish ravioli (€9-14 pasta, €10-22 *secondi,* Tue-Sun 12:00-22:00, closed Mon, indoor and outdoor seating in summer, Via Roma 31, tel. 0187-812-381).

Blue Marlin Bar, just below the train station, serves a short, creative menu of more casual dishes. It also serves breakfast and dominates the late-night scene with home-cooked food until 23:00, good drinks, and occasional piano jam sessions (€6-8 pizzas, €9-10 pastas, €10-12 *secondi,* Thu-Tue 7:00-24:00, closed Wed). If you're awaiting a train any time of day, the Blue Marlin's outdoor seating beats the platform.

Il Pirata delle Cinque Terre, behind and above the train station, is popular for breakfast and attracts many travelers for lunch and dinner. Don't come here for the cuisine, but for a memorable evening with the Cannoli twins, who entertain while they serve, and aim their menu squarely at American taste buds (€10-14 pastas, €10 salads, daily 6:30-24:00, Via Gavino).

Other main-street eateries offer a fine range of quick meals. **Forno Bakery** has good focaccia and veggie tarts (at #5). **Pino's grocery store** makes sandwiches to order (generally Mon-Sat 8:00-13:00 & 17:00-19:30, closed Sun).

Gelato

Gelateria Vernazza, near the top of the main street, takes gelato seriously. **Gelateria Amore Mio** (midtown) has great people-watching tables but less exciting gelato. Out on the harbor, **Gelateria Il Porticciolo** is the best, with fresh ingredients and intense flavors.

Sleeping

People recommended here are listed for their communication skills (they speak English, have email, and are reliable with bookings). Anywhere you stay here requires some climbing, but keep in mind that more climbing means better views. Most do not include breakfast. Cash is preferred or required almost everywhere. Night noise can be a problem if you're near the station. Rooms on the harbor come with church bells (but only between 7:00 and 22:00).

Pensions

$$$ Gianni Franzi, a busy restaurant on the harbor square, rents 25 small rooms in three buildings—one funky, two modern—up a hundred tight, winding spiral stairs. The funky ones, which may or may not have private baths, are artfully decorated à la shipwreck, with tiny balconies and grand sea views (*con vista sul mare*). The comfy new (*nuovo*) rooms lack views. Both have modern bathrooms and access to a scenic, cliff-hanging garden. Pick up your keys at the Gianni Franzi restaurant on the harbor square (on Wed, when the restaurant is closed, call ahead to make other arrangements). Check in before 16:00 or call to explain when you're coming (S-€55, D-€110, Db-€130, Tb-€160, view room-€20-30 extra, includes breakfast mid-April-mid-Oct, lower prices at other times, cancellations less than a week in advance charged one night's deposit, closed Jan-Feb, Piazza Marconi 1, tel. 0187-812-228, tel. 0187-821-003, on Wed call mobile 393-9008-155, www. giannifranzi.it, info@giannifranzi.it).

$$$ Pensione Sorriso, the oldest pension in town, rents 13 overpriced, tired rooms above the train station. While the building has charm, it comes with train noise and saggy beds (Sb-€65, D-€70, Db-€110, Db with air-con-€120, T-€90, Tb-€140, breakfast-€10, closed Nov-March, Via Gavino 4, tel. 0187-812-224,

Sleep Code

Price Rankings for Double Rooms (Db)

$$$ Most rooms €100 or more
 $$ €50-100
  $ €50 or less

Abbreviations: Db=Double with bathroom. D=Double with bathroom down the hall

Notes: Hotels charge a room tax of €1.50-6 per person, per night, often payable in cash. Room prices change; verify rates online or by email. For the best prices, book directly with the hotel.

www.pensionesorriso.com, info@pensionesorriso.com).

$$ Albergo Barbara rents nine basic rooms overlooking the harbor square—with small windows and small views—and piles of stairs (D-€60, D with private bath down the hall-€70, Db-€80, big Db with nice harbor view-€120, extra bed-€10, 2-night stay preferred, closed Dec-Feb, reserve online with credit card but pay cash, Piazza Marconi 30, tel. 0187-812-398, mobile 338-793-3261, www.albergo barbara.it, info@albergobarbara.it).

Private Rooms (Affitta Camere)

Private rooms offer the best values in town. Owners may be reluctant to reserve rooms far in advance. Doubles cost €55-120, depending on the view, season, and plumbing—you get what you pay for. Apartments (with kitchens) go for a bit more. Most places accept only cash. Some have killer views, come with lots of stairs, and cost the same as a small, dark place on a back lane over the train tracks. Most owners speak just enough English.

While a few places have all their beds in one building, most have rooms scattered over town. Some have an informal "reception desk" (sometimes at a restaurant or other business) where you can check in. A few places have no reception at all. (On the Vernazza map, I've marked only places that have a fixed address or reception office; if I say "reception," you'll check in there, then continue on to your actual room.) Because this can be confusing, clearly communicate your arrival time (by phone or email) and get instructions on where to meet the owner and pick up the keys. In some cases, they'll meet you at the train station—but only if they know when you're coming.

Some of my favorite places in town are located in the ravine a five-minute, gently uphill stroll behind the train station. While this sleepy zone is less atmospheric and less central, it also has less noise and fewer stairs. The recommended Il Pirata delle Cinque Terre is the neighborhood hub/eatery, and a launderette is next door.

INLAND

Alessandra runs two different sets of rooms in a single elevator-equipped, modern building: bohemian-chic **$$$ La Perla delle 5 Terre** (Db-€100, Tb-€120, 6 clean rooms, no air-con) and colorful **$$$ Tonino Basso** (Db-€120, Tb-€140, 4 rooms, air-con). This is a top choice for modern comfort (contact for both: Via Gavino 34, mobile 339-761-1651, www.toninobasso.com, sassarinialessandra@libero.it).

$$ Camere Fontana Vecchia has eight bright, spacious, quiet rooms overlooking the ravine, across the street from the post office (D-€70, Db-€80, three Db with terrace-€100, Via Gavino 15, tel. 0187-821-130, mobile 333-454-9371, www.cinqueterre camere.com, m.annamaria@libero.it).

$$ Giuliano Basso's four carefully crafted rooms are just above town, straddling a ravine among orange trees. The building is built out of stone by the owner himself—the town's last stone-layer (Db-€80-100, Tb-€120, two rooms have air-con, above train station—take the ramp just before Pensione Sorriso, mobile 333-

341-4792, www.cdh.it/giuliano, giuliano@cdh.it).

$$ La Rosa dei Venti (The Compass Rose) houses three tranquil, airy rooms at the top of town, three floors up from the ravine. One room has a balcony. Call to arrange a meeting time (Db-€80, Tb-€110, Via Gavino 19, tel. 333-762-4679, info@larosadeiventi-vernazza.it).

SCATTERED THROUGH TOWN AND THE HARBORSIDE

La Malà, La Marina Rooms, and Memo Rooms are not located on the map in this chapter; arrange a meeting time and/or ask for directions when you reserve.

$$$ La Malà is Vernazza's jet-setter pad, with four pristine white rooms, hotel-type extras, and a common seaview terrace. It's way up at the top of town, but they'll carry your bags to and from the station (Db-€160, Db suite-€220, includes breakfast at a bar, air-con, mobile 334-287-5718, www.lamala.it, info@lamala.it). They also rent the simpler "Armanda's Room" nearby—a great value, with all the attention and amenities but without the view (Db-€80, includes simple breakfast, air-con).

$$$ La Marina Rooms are run by Christian, who speaks English and meets guests at the station to carry their bags. The beautiful, top-end units are high above the main street. One single works as a tight double, three doubles share a fine oceanview terrace (town view Sb-€60, Db-€110, seaview Db-€150), and two spacious apartments come with fine terraces and views (town-view Db-€120, seaview 2-bedroom apartment with big terrace-€260, mobile 338-476-7472, www.lamarinarooms.com, mapcri@yahoo.it).

$$$ Martina Callo's four simply furnished rooms overlook the square; they're up plenty of steps near the silent-at-night church tower. While the rooms are nothing special, the views are (room #1: Tb-€120 or Qb-€130 with harbor view; room #2: big Qb family room with no view-€120; room #3: Db with grand view terrace-€100; room #4: roomy Db with no

view-€60; air-con, ring bell at Piazza Marconi 26, tel. 0187-812-365, mobile 329-435-5344, www.roomartina.it, roomartina@roomartina.it).

$$ Memo Rooms rents three clean and spacious spaces overlooking the main street, in what feels like a miniature hotel. Enrica will meet you if you call upon arrival (Db-€70, Via Roma 15, mobile 338-285-2385, otherwise tel. 0187-812-360, www.memorooms.com, info@memorooms.com).

$$ Monica Lercari rents several rooms with modern comforts, perched at the top of town (small Db-€80, seaview D-€100, grand seaview terrace D-€120, includes breakfast, air-con, tel. 0187-812-296, mobile 320-025-4515, alcastellovernazza@yahoo.it). Friendly Monica and her husband, Massimo, run the recommended Ristorante al Castello, in the old castle tower overlooking town.

$$ Nicolina Rooms consists of seven units in three different buildings. Two rooms are in the center over the pharmacy, up a few steep steps (Db-€90); another room is on a twisty lane above the harbor (large studio Db with terrace-€200); and four more are in a building beyond the church, with great views (D-€100, Db-€140, two-bedroom suite with harbor view-€180 plus €30/extra person, Wi-Fi and loud church bells in these rooms only). Inquire at Pizzeria Vulnetia on the harbor square (all include breakfast, Piazza Marconi 29, tel. 0187-821-193, mobile 333-842-6879, www.camerenicolina.it, camerenicolina.info@cdh.it).

$$ Rosa Vitali rents two four-person apartments across from the pharmacy overlooking the main street (and beyond the train noise). One has a terrace and fridge (top floor); the other has windows and a full kitchen (Db-€95, Tb-€115, Qb-€130, prices include city tax, cash only, reception just before the tobacco shop near Piazza Marconi at Via Visconti 10, tel. 0187-821-181, mobile 340-267-5009, www.rosacamere.it, rosa.vitali@libero.it).

$$ Francamaria and her husband Andrea rent 10 sharp, comfortable, creative rooms. While their reception desk is on the harbor square (on the ground floor facing the harbor at Piazza Marconi 30—don't confuse it with Albergo Barbara at same address), the rooms they manage are all over town (Db-€95-145 depending on size and view, Qb-€130-160, extra person-€20, cash only, some with air-con, Wi-Fi is spotty, tel. 0187-812-002, mobile 328-711-9728, www.francamaria.com, info@francamaria.com).

MONTEROSSO AL MARE
(Town #5)

Monterosso al Mare is a resort with lots of hotels, rentable beach umbrellas, crowds, and more late-night action than the neighboring towns. Even so, don't expect full-blown Riviera glitz. The small, crooked lanes of the old town cradle Old World charm and locals appreciate quiet, sensitive guests. Strolling the waterfront promenade, you can pick out each of the Cinque Terre towns decorating the coast. After dark, they sparkle.

The only Cinque Terre town built on flat land, Monterosso has two parts: a new town (called Fegina) with a parking lot, train station, and TI; and an old town (Centro Storico). A pedestrian tunnel connects the old with the new, but take a small detour around the point for a nicer walk.

Orientation

Arrival in Monterosso: Trains arrive in the new town. For hotels in the new town, turn right out of the station. For the old town, turn left; it's a scenic, flat 10-minute stroll.

Shuttle buses run along the waterfront between the old town (Piazza Garibaldi, just beyond the tunnel), the train station, and the parking lot at the end of Via Fegina (*Campo Sportivo* stop). The bus saves you a 10-minute schlep with your bags but only runs once an hour (€1.50 one-way, €2.50 on board, free with Cinque Terre park card).

Taxis usually wait outside the train station, but you may have to call (€7 from station to the old town, mobile 335-616-5842, 335-616-5845, or 335-628-0933).

For **drivers,** Monterosso is 30 minutes off the freeway (exit: Carrodano-Levanto); at the fork in the road, follow signs for Fegina to reach the new town (with a huge beachfront guarded lot, €18/24 hours), or for *Monterosso Centro Storico* to get to the old town (Loreto parking garage on Via Roma, same prices). Only locals are allowed to drive between the old and new towns.

Medical Help: English-speaking **Dr. Vitone** charges €50-80 for a simple visit (less for poor students, mobile 338-853-0949, vitonee@yahoo.it).

Tourist Information: The TI Proloco is next to the train station (April-Oct daily 9:00-19:00, closed Nov-March, exit station and go left a few doors, tel. 0187-817-506, www.prolocomonterosso.it). For national park tickets and information, head upstairs within the station to the ticket office near platform 1 (likely daily 8:00-20:00, shorter hours off-season). If you arrive late on a summer day, the old town's Internet café is helpful with tourist information.

Internet Access: The Net, a few steps off the old town's main drag (Via Roma), has high-speed computers and Wi-Fi (under €1/10 minutes). Enzo also happily provides information on the Cinque Terre, and rents rooms (daily 9:30-23:00, off-season until 19:00, Via Vittorio Emanuele 55, tel. 0187-817-288, www.monterossonet.com, info@monterossonet.com).

Baggage Storage: Wash and Dry Lavarapido, two blocks from the station, provides a wonderful €5 bag-check service (€13/load, daily 8:00-19:00, Via Molinelli 17, mobile 339-484-0940).

⊖ Monterosso Walk

This easy, self-guided walk begins at the breakwater. Part 1, focusing on the mostly level town center, takes about 30 minutes; for Part 2, summiting the adjacent hill, allow another hour or so.

PART 1: MONTEROSSO HARBOR AND TOWN CENTER

• Hike out from the dock in the old town and climb five rough steps to the top of the concrete...

Breakwater: If you're visiting by boat, you'll start here anyway. From this point you can survey Monterosso's old town (straight ahead) and new town (stretching to the left, with train station and parking lot).

Looking to the right, you can see all *cinque* of the *terre* from one spot: Vernazza, Corniglia (above the shore), Manarola, and a few buildings of Riomaggiore beyond that.

The partial breakwater (a row of giant rocks in the middle of the harbor) is designed to save the beach from washing away, but sand erosion remains a major problem. While old-timers remember a vast beach, their grandchildren truck in sand each spring to give tourists something to lie on. (The Nazis liked the Cinque Terre, too—find two of their bomb-hardened bunkers, near left and far right.)

The four-star Hotel Porto Roca (pink building high on the hill, on the far right of the harbor) marks the trail to Vernazza. High above, you can see the roads that connect the Cinque Terre with the freeway over the hills.

Two prominent capes define the Cinque Terre. The farther cape is Punta di Montenero (to the right). The closer cape, Punta Mesco (to the left), marks a sea-life sanctuary, home to a rare grass that provides an ideal home for fish eggs. Buoys keep fishing boats away. The cape was once a quarry, providing employment to locals who chipped out the stones used to build the local towns (including the greenish stones making up part of the breakwater below you).

On the far end of the new town, marking the best free beach around, you can

Monterosso al Mare

just see the statue named *Il Gigante* (hard to spot because it blends in with the gray rock). It's 45 feet tall and once held a trident. Made of reinforced concrete, it dates from the early 20th century, when it supported a dance terrace for a *fin de siècle* villa. A violent storm left the giant holding nothing but memories.

• *From the breakwater, walk into the old town. At the top of the beach, notice the openings of two big drains, ready to let flash floods rip through town without destroying things. Walking under the train tracks, venture right into the square and find the statue of a dandy holding what looks like a box cutter.*

Piazza Garibaldi: The statue honors Giuseppe Garibaldi, the dashing firebrand who, in the 1860s, helped unite the people of Italy. Facing Garibaldi, with your back to the sea, you'll see (from right to left) the orange city hall and a big home and recreation center for poor and homeless elderly. You'll also see A Ca' du Sciensa restaurant (with historic town photos inside and upstairs; you're welcome to pop in for a look).

Just under the bell tower (with your back to the sea, it's on your left), a set of covered arcades facing the sea is where the old-timers hang out. The crenellated bell tower marks the church.

• *Go to church (the entrance is on the inland side).*

Church of St. John the Baptist (Chiesa di San Giovanni Battista): Before entering, check out the facade. With white marble from Carrara and green marble from Punta Mesco, this church is typical of the Romanesque style. The marble stripes get narrower the higher they go, creating the illusion of a church that's taller than it really is. Note the delicate stone rose window above the entrance, with 18 slender mullions.

Step inside for more Ligurian Gothic: original marble columns with pointed arches to match. The octagonal baptismal font (in the back of the church) was

carved from Carrara marble in 1359. In the chapel to the right of the high altar, look for the wooden statue of St. Anthony, carved about 1400, which once graced a church that stood atop Punta Mesco. The church itself dates from 1307—see the proud inscription on the left-middle column: "MilleCCCVII." Outside the church, on the side facing the main street, find the high-water mark from an October 1966 flood. Nearly half a century later, the October 2011 flood hit Monterosso. But the church's statues survived, thanks to townspeople who carried them through raging waters to safety.

• *Leaving the church, immediately turn left and go to church again.*

Oratory of the Dead (Oratorio dei Neri): During the Counter-Reformation, the Catholic Church offset the rising influence of the Lutherans by creating brotherhoods of good works. These religious Rotary clubs were called "confraternities." Monterosso had two, nicknamed White and Black. This building is the oratory of the Black group, whose mission—as the macabre interior decor indicates—was to arrange for funerals and take care of widows, orphans, the shipwrecked, and

Church of St. John the Baptist

the souls of those who ignore the request for a €1 donation. It dates from the 16th century; membership has passed from father to son for generations. Notice the fine carved choir stalls (c. 1700) just inside the door, and the haunted-house chandeliers. Look up at the ceiling to find the symbol of the confraternity: a skull-and-crossbones and an hourglass...death awaits us all.

• *On that cheery note, if you're in a lazy mood, you can discreetly split off from our walking tour now to enjoy strolling, shopping, gelato, a day at the beach...or all of the above. If you're up for a hike, continue on to Part 2.*

PART 2: CAPUCHIN CHURCH AND HILLTOP CEMETERY

• *Return to the beach and find the brick steps that lead up to the hill-capping convent (starting between the train tracks and the pedestrian tunnel, and passing in front of Albergo Pasquale). Approaching the bend in the path, watch for the stairs leading steeply and sharply to the right. This lane (Salita dei Cappuccini) is nicknamed Zii di Frati, or...*

Switchbacks of the Friars: Follow the yellow brick road (OK, it's orange...but I couldn't help singing as I skipped skyward). Pause at the terrace above the castle at a statue of St. Francis and a wolf.

Enjoy another opportunity to see all five of the Cinque Terre towns. From here, backtrack 20 yards and continue uphill.

• *When you reach a gate marked Convento e Chiesa Cappuccini, you have arrived at the...*

Church of the Capuchin Friars: The former convent is now manned by a single caretaker. The church's striped Romanesque facade is all fake: not marble, just cheap 18th-century stucco. Go inside and sit in the rear pew. The high altarpiece painting of St. Francis can be rolled up to reveal a statue of Mary behind it. Look at the statue of St. Anthony to the right and smile (you're on convent camera). Wave at the security camera—they're nervous about the precious painting to your left.

This fine painting of the **Crucifixion** is attributed to Anthony van Dyck, the 17th-century Flemish master (though art historians suspect that it was painted by someone in the artist's workshop). Notice the eclipsed sun in the painting, just to the right of the cross. When Jesus died, the earth went dark.

• *Leave and turn left to hike 100 yards uphill to the cemetery that fills the remains of the castle. Look back from the gate and enjoy the view over the town.*

Cemetery in the Ruined Castle: In the Dark Ages, the village huddled within

View from the Capuchin Church

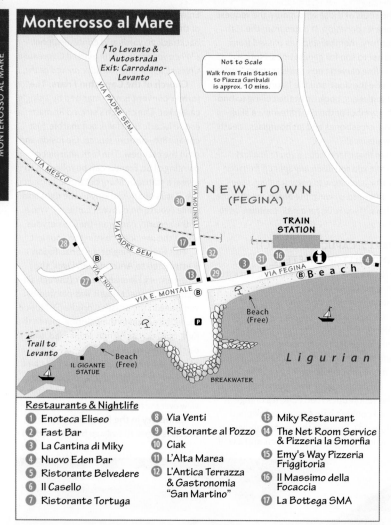

Monterosso al Mare

↑To Levanto &
Autostrada
Exit: Carrodano-
Levanto

Not to Scale

Walk from Train Station
to Piazza Garibaldi
is approx. 10 mins.

VIA PADRE SEM.

VIA MESCO

NEW TOWN
(FEGINA)

VIA MOLINELLI

TRAIN
STATION

VIA PADRE SEM.

VIA 4 NOV.

VIA FEGINA

VIA E. MONTALE

Beach

Beach
(Free)

Trail to
Levanto

Beach
(Free)

IL GIGANTE
STATUE

BREAKWATER

L i g u r i a n

Restaurants & Nightlife

1. Enoteca Eliseo
2. Fast Bar
3. La Cantina di Miky
4. Nuovo Eden Bar
5. Ristorante Belvedere
6. Il Casello
7. Ristorante Tortuga
8. Via Venti
9. Ristorante al Pozzo
10. Ciak
11. L'Alta Marea
12. L'Antica Terrazza & Gastronomia "San Martino"
13. Miky Restaurant
14. The Net Room Service & Pizzeria la Smorfia
15. Emy's Way Pizzeria Friggitoria
16. Il Massimo della Focaccia
17. La Bottega SMA

this castle. You're looking at the oldest part of Monterosso, tucked behind the hill, out of view of 13th-century pirates. Explore the cemetery, keeping in mind that cemeteries are sacred places. *Q.R.P.* is *Qui Riposa in Pace* (a.k.a. R.I.P.). Climb to the summit—the castle's keep, or place of last refuge.

• *From here, your tour is over—any trail leads you back into town.*

Experiences
Beaches

Monterosso's beaches, immediately in front of the train station, are the Cinque Terre's best and most crowded. If you see umbrellas on a beach, it means you'll have to pay a rental fee; otherwise, the sand is free. Figure €20 to rent two chairs and an umbrella for the day. Light lunches are served by beach cafés to sunbathers at their lounge chairs. It's often worth the

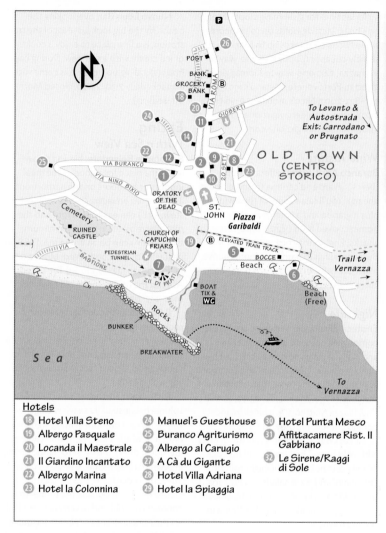

Hotels

18 Hotel Villa Steno
19 Albergo Pasquale
20 Locanda il Maestrale
21 Il Giardino Incantato
22 Albergo Marina
23 Hotel la Colonnina

24 Manuel's Guesthouse
25 Buranco Agriturismo
26 Albergo al Carugio
27 A Cà du Gigante
28 Hotel Villa Adriana
29 Hotel la Spiaggia

30 Hotel Punta Mesco
31 Affittacamere Rist. Il Gabbiano
32 Le Sirene/Raggi di Sole

---

euros to enjoy a private beach. Prices get soft in the afternoon. Don't use your white hotel towels; most hotels will give you beach towels—sometimes for a fee. The local hidden beach, which is free, gravelly, and less crowded, is tucked away under Il Casello restaurant at the east end of town, near the trailhead to Vernazza. Another free beach is at the far-west end, near the Gigante statue.

Samba rents kayaks on the beach (€7/hour for 1-person kayak, €12/hour for 2-person kayak, cheaper for longer rentals, to the right of train station as you exit, mobile 339-681-2265, Domenico). The adjacent **La Pineta** beach also rents stand-up paddleboards (€12/hour, Diego).

Boat Rides

Stefano or **Nico** can take you on a cruise around the Cinque Terre (€100/hour, one hour is enough for a quick spin, two hours includes time for swimming stops). Stefano's boat, *Matilde,* holds up to six people, while Nico's boat takes up to four and is slightly cheaper (about €50 one-way to Vernazza, €80 one-way to Riomaggiore, €300 to Portovenere, Stefano's mobile 333-821-2007, Nico's mobile 339-564-0907, www.matildenavigazione.com, info@matildenavigazione.com).

Wine Tasting

Buranco Agriturismo offers visits to their vineyard and cantina (reserve 2 days ahead). You'll taste some of their wines plus a grappa and a *limoncino,* along with home-cooked food (€20-30/person with snacks, English may be limited, follow Via Buranco uphill to path, 10 minutes above town, tel. 0187-817-677, www.buranco cinqueterre.it).

Nightlife

Enoteca Eliseo, the best wine bar in town, comes with operatic ambience. Eliseo and his wife, Mary, love music as much as they love wine. Eliseo offers an education in grappa, stocking more than a hundred varieties (Wed-Mon 12:00-23:30, closed Tue, Piazza Matteotti 3, a block inland behind church, tel. 0187-817-308).

At **Fast Bar,** Customers mix travel tales with cold beer. The crowd (and the rock 'n' roll) gets noisier as the night rolls on (€5 *panini* and €7-9 salads usually served until midnight, Fri-Wed 9:30-late, closed Thu except in peak season; Via Roma in the old town).

La Cantina di Miky, in the new town just beyond the train station, is a trendy bar-restaurant with an extensive cocktail and grappa menu and occasional live music. Manuel offers a fun "five villages" wine-tasting with local meats and cheeses (€15/person for just wine, €20/person with food). It's the best place in town for top-end Italian beers (Thu-Tue until late, closed Wed, Via Fegina 90, tel. 0187-802-525).

Nuovo Eden Bar, overlooking the beach by the big rock just east of the train station, is a fine place to enjoy a cocktail or ice cream with a sea view. During happy hour (17:00-19:00), cocktails come with a snack (daily 7:30-24:00, closed Mon off-season).

Eating
With a Sea View

Ristorante Belvedere, big and sprawling, is *the* place for a good-value meal indoors or outdoors on the harborfront. Their *anfora belvedere* (mixed seafood stew, €48) can easily feed four and the *misto mare* plate (2-person minimum, €15/person) can be an entire meal (€8-10 pastas, €10-19 *secondi,* Wed-Mon 12:00-14:30 & 18:00-22:00, closed Tue except Aug, on the harbor in the old town, tel. 0187-817-033).

Il Casello, with outdoor tables on a rocky outcrop, is the only place for a fun meal overlooking the old town beach (€9-13 pastas, €14-18 *secondi,* daily April-Oct 12:00-22:00, closed Nov-March, mobile 333-492-7629).

Ristorante Tortuga is a worthwhile splurge because of its seaview elegance, with gorgeous outdoor seating high on a bluff and white-tablecloth-and-candles interior. It offers the most romantic dining in town (€14-19 pastas, €15-20 *secondi,* Tue-Sun 12:00-15:00 & 18:00-22:00, closed Mon, just outside the tunnel that connects the old and new town—or climb up the ramp in front of Albergo Pasquale, tel. 0187-800-065, mobile 333-240-7956).

In the Old Town

Via Venti is a quiet trattoria hidden in an alley deep in the heart of the old town. Imaginative seafood dishes use the day's catch and freshly made pasta. There's nothing pretentious, just good cooking, service, and prices (€13-14 pastas, €16-20 *secondi,* Fri-Wed 12:00-14:30 & 18:30-22:30, closed Thu, Via XX Settembre 32, tel. 0187-818-347).

Ristorante al Pozzo is a local favorite, with one of the best wine lists in town, homemade pasta, and wonderful seafood *antipasti misti* (€10-16 pastas, €15-25 *secondi,* Fri-Wed 12:00-15:00 & 18:30-22:30, closed Thu, Via Roma 24, tel. 0187-817-575).

Ciak is known for its huge, sizzling terra-cotta crock for two crammed with the day's catch. Reservations are smart in summer (€12-14 pastas, €18-20 *secondi,* Thu-Tue 12:00-15:00 & 18:00-22:30, closed Wed, Piazza Don Minzoni 6, tel. 0187-817-014, www.ristoranteciak.net).

L'Alta Marea is buried in the old town two blocks off the beach, and has covered tables out front for people-watching. Try the special fish ravioli or fresh, steamed mussels (€10-13 pastas and pizza, €15-17 *secondi,* 10 percent discount with cash and this book, Thu-Tue 12:00-15:00 & 18:00-22:00, closed Wed, Via Roma 54, tel. 0187-817-170).

Gastronomia "San Martino" is a warm, humble place (with almost no ambience) that serves good, inexpensive dishes on plastic plates (€6 pastas, €10 *secondi,* Tue-Sun 12:00-15:00 & 18:00-22:00, closed Mon, next to recommended L'Antica Terrazza hotel at Vicolo San Martino 2, mobile 346-109-7338).

In the New Town

Miky is my Cinque Terre favorite, with well-dressed locals packed into a classy environment. Their elegantly presented, subtly flavored food celebrates local ingredients and traditions. All their pasta is "pizza pasta"—cooked normally but finished in a bowl that's encased in a thin pizza crust (€13-21 fun-to-share *antipasti,* €17-18 pastas, €18-30 *secondi,* €8 sweets, Wed-Mon 12:00-15:00 & 19:00-23:00, closed Tue, reservations wise in summer, in the new town 100 yards from train station at Via Fegina 104, tel. 0187-817-608, www.ristorantemiky.it).

La Cantina di Miky, a few doors down (toward the station), is more youthful and informal than Miky, but serves Ligurian specialties in Miky's family tradition. Sit downstairs, in the garden, or overlooking the sea. They have creative desserts and large selection of Italian microbrews (€10-13 pastas, €14-18 *secondi,* Thu-Tue 12:00-24:00, closed Wed, Via Fegina 90, tel. 0187-802-525).

Light Meals, Takeout Food, and Breakfast

In the old town, shops and bakeries sell pizza and focaccia for an easy picnic. **Pizzeria la Smorfia** is the local favorite (€6-8 small pizzas, €14-19 large pizzas, Fri-Wed 11:00-24:00, Via Vittorio Emanuele 73, tel. 0187-818-395). Other options are **Il Frantoio** (Fri-Wed 9:00-13:45 & 16:30-19:30, closed Thu, just off Via Roma at Via Gioberti 1) and **Emy's Way Pizzeria Friggitoria,** which also serves up deep-fried seafood to-go (€5-9 pizza, €3-7 *fritti,* daily 11:00-20:00, later in summer, along the skinny street next to the church).

Il Massimo della Focaccia, right at the train station, is a good bet for a €3-4 light meal with a sea view (Thu-Tue 9:00-19:00, closed Wed except June-Aug, Via Fegina 50 at the entry to the station). **La Bottega SMA** is a smart minimart with deli items and sandwiches; pay by weight (daily 8:00-13:00 & 16:30-19:30 except Wed and Sun until 13:00, near Lavarapido at Vittoria Gianni 21).

For breakfast, try **Bar Gio,** near the train station on the waterfront (continental breakfasts). In the old town, look for **Wine & Food** (€10 "American Breakfast," Via Vittorio Emanuele 26) and **Bar Davi** (American option, daily 7:00 until late, may close Wed).

Sleeping

Rooms in Monterosso are a better value than similar rooms in crowded Vernazza. The TI Proloco just outside the train station can give you a list of €70-80 double rooms.

In the Old Town

$$$ **Hotel Villa Steno** features great view balconies, panoramic gardens, and a roof terrace. It's a 15-minute hike (or €8 taxi ride) from the train station to the top of the old town. Ask for a free Cinque Terre info packet and a glass of local wine when you check in (Sb-€120, Db-€190, Tb-€230, Qb-€265, includes breakfast, laundry, parking-€10—reserve in advance, Via Roma 109, tel. 0187-817-028 or 0187-818-336, www.villasteno.com, steno@pasini.com).

$$$ **Albergo Pasquale** is modern and comfortable, with 15 seaview rooms, located just a few steps from the beach, boat dock, tunnel entrance to the new town, and train tracks. While there is some train noise, the soundtrack is mostly a lullaby of waves. It has an elevator and offers easier access than most (same prices and welcome drink as Villa Steno; air-con, laundry service, Via Fegina 8, tel. 0187-817-550 or 0187-817-477, www.hotelpasquale.it, pasquale@pasini.com).

$$$ **Locanda il Maestrale** rents six small, stylish rooms in a sophisticated, peaceful inn. Despite its modern comforts, it retains centuries-old character under frescoed ceilings (small Db-€115, Db-€150, superior Db-€180, prices lower off-season, 10 percent Rick Steves discount if you book directly with hotel and pay cash, air-con, Via Roma 37, tel. 0187-817-013, mobile 338-4530-531, www.locandamaestrale.net, maestrale@monterossonet.com).

$$$ **Il Giardino Incantato** ("The Enchanted Garden") is a charming, comfortable four-room B&B in a tasteful 16th-century Ligurian home in the heart of the old town. Sip their homemade *limoncino* upon check-in and have breakfast under lemon trees in a hidden garden (Db-€150-170, Db suite-€180-200, air-con, free minibar and tea and coffee service, laundry service-€15/load, Via Mazzini 18, tel. 0187-818-315, mobile 333-264-9252, www.ilgiardinoincantato.net, giardino_incantato@libero.it).

$$$ **L'Antica Terrazza** rents four classy rooms right in town. With minimal stairs and a pretty terrace overlooking the pedestrian street, it's a good deal (D-€85, Db-€115, air-con, Vicolo San Martino 1, mobile 380-138-0082 or 347-132-6213, www.anticaterrazza.com, post@antica terrazza.com).

$$$ **Albergo Marina** offers 23 decent rooms, a free buffet featuring local specialties from 14:00 to 17:00 daily, and a garden with lemon trees (Db-€150, Tb-€175, Qb-€200, elevator, air-con, free use of kayak and snorkel equipment, Via Buranco 40, tel. 0187-817-613, www.hotelmarina5terre.com, marina@hotelmarina5terre.com).

$$$ **Hotel la Colonnina** has 21 big rooms, generous if dated public spaces, and leafy terraces. It's buried in the town's sleepy back streets (Db-€158, Tb-€198, Qb-€248, cash only, air-con, fridges, elevator, in the old town a block inland from the main square at Via Zuecca 6, tel. 0187-817-439, www.lacolonninacinqueterre.it, info@lacolonninacinqueterre.it, Cristina).

$$$ **Manuel's Guesthouse,** perched high above the town, is a garden getaway with six big, bright rooms. After climbing the killer stairs from the town center, their killer terrace is hard to leave. Ask them to carry your bags up the hill (Db-€130, big Db with grand-view balcony-€140, cash only, air-con, up about 100 steps behind church—Via San Martino 39, mobile 333-439-0809, www.manuelsguesthouse.com, manuelsguesthouse@libero.it).

$$$ **Buranco Agriturismo,** a 10-minute hike above the old town, has wonderful gardens and views over the vine-covered valley. It's a rare opportunity to stay in a farmhouse but still be able to get to town on foot (2-6 people-€60/person including breakfast, €30/child under 10, air-con, €10 taxi from station, tel. 0187-817-677, mobile 349-434-8046, www.burancocinqueterre.it, info@buranco.it).

$$ **Albergo al Carugio,** simple and

practical, has nine rooms in an apartment-style building at the top of the old town (Db-€85, no breakfast, air-con, Via Roma 100, tel. 0187-817-453, www.alcarugio.it, info@alcarugio.it, Andrea and Simona).

$$ The Net Room Service is run by Enzo, who owns the Internet point in town (and speaks perfect English). He manages a dozen or so apartments—most in the old town and a few in the new town, away from the train noise. Enzo's office functions as your reception (Db-€60-80, Qb-€120-150, prices based on size and view, 2- or 3-night minimum stay, Via Vittorio Emanuele 55, tel. 0187-817-288, mobile 335-778-5085, www.monterossonet.com, info@monterossonet.com).

In the New Town

$$$ A Cà du Gigante is a tiny yet stylish and comfortable refuge with nine rooms about 100 yards from the beach (Db-€160, Db seaview suite-€180, 10 percent discount with 3-night stay and this book, air-con, free parking, Via IV Novembre 11, tel. 0187-817-401, www.ilgigantecinque terre.it, gigante@ilgigantecinqueterre.it).

$$$ Hotel Villa Adriana is a big, contemporary, bright hotel set in a peaceful garden with a pool, free parking, and a no-stress style. They rent 54 rooms—some with terraces and/or sea views (Sb-€95, Db-€175, all with showers, air-con, elevator, free loaner bikes, Via IV Novembre 23, tel. 0187-818-109, www.villaadriana.info, info@villaadriana.info).

$$$ Hotel la Spiaggia is a venerable, old, 19-room place facing the beach. Half of the rooms come with sea views (Db-€170, view Db-€180, extra bed-€30, free parking, cash only, air-con, elevator, Via Lungomare 96, tel. 0187-817-567, www.laspiaggiahotel.com, hotellaspiaggia@libero.it).

$$$ Hotel Punta Mesco is a tidy haven renting 17 quiet, casual rooms. While none have views, 10 rooms have small terraces (Db-€153, Tb-€185, €10 discount with

cash, air-con, parking, Via Molinelli 35, tel. 0187-817-495, www.hotelpuntamesco.it, info@hotelpuntamesco.it).

$$ Affittacamere Ristorante il Gabbiano is a touristy restaurant right on the beach, renting five quiet, air-conditioned rooms upstairs. Three rooms face the sea with small balconies, while two are at the back, facing a garden. The Gabbiano family restaurant serves as your reception (seaview rooms: Db-€110, Tb-€130, Qb-€160; garden-view rooms: Db-€100; cash only, air-con, Via Fegina 84, tel. 0187-817-578, www.affittacamereristoranteil gabbiano.com, affittacamereilgabbiano@live.it).

$ Le Sirene/Raggi di Sole, with nine simple rooms in two humble buildings, is about the cheapest place in town, run from a hole-in-the-wall reception desk a block from the station. Request the Le Sirene building, which doesn't have train noise and is more spacious and airy than Raggi di Sole (Sb-€70, Db-€90, third person-€30, fans, Via Molinelli 10, mobile 331-788-1088, www.sirenerooms.com, sirenerooms@gmail.com).

TRANSPORTATION

Getting Around the Cinque Terre

The five towns are connected by trains, boats, and trails (for hiking, see page 633). Little shuttle buses provide local transport per town.

By Train

By train, the five towns are just a few minutes apart. Along the coast here, trains go in only two directions: *"per* [to] *Genova"* (the Italian spelling of Genoa), northbound; or *"per La Spezia,"* southbound.

Tickets (about €2) are good for 75 minutes in one direction, so you can conceivably use one for a brief stopover. A 40-kilometer ticket (€4) is good for six hours in one direction. Buy tickets at the train station, at the ticket window, Cinque Terre park desk, or from machines on the platform. Validate your ticket before you board by stamping it in the green-and-white machines. Conductors levy stiff fines for riding with a good but unstamped ticket. You can buy several tickets at once and use them as you like, validating as you go.

Rick's Tip: *If you have a* **Eurail Pass,** *don't use up one of your valuable travel days on the cheap Cinque Terre.*

Trains run about hourly in each direction, connecting all five towns. Shops, hotels, and restaurants often post the current schedule, and may also hand out copies. Check the key on the printed schedules carefully: certain departures listed are for only weekdays, only Sundays, etc.

In the **station,** real-time **monitors** are the best, most current source of information. They show the departure times and directions of the next trains (and, if they're late—*in ritardo*). Northbound trains are marked for *Genova, Levanto,* or *Sestri Levante;* southbound trains are marked for *La Spezia* or *Sarzana.* (Most northbound trains that stop at all Cinque Terre towns will list Sestri Levante as the *destinazione.*) To be sure you get on the right train, know your train's number and final destination. **Important:** Any train stopping at Vernazza, Corniglia, or Manarola is going to all the towns. Trains from Monterosso, Riomaggiore, or La Spezia sometimes skip lesser stations, so confirm that the train will stop at the town you need.

Accept the unpredictability of Cinque Terre trains—they're often late. Relax while you wait—buy an ice cream or cup of coffee at a station bar. Scout the platform you need in advance, and then, when the train comes, hop on.

Know your stop. The train stations are small and the trains are long, so (especially in Vernazza) you might have to get

off deep in a tunnel. The door won't open automatically—twist the black handle, or lift up the red one. If a door isn't working, go quickly to the next car to try another.

By Boat

From Easter through October, **daily boat service** connects Monterosso, Vernazza, Manarola, and Riomaggiore hourly through the summer (between 10:00 and 15:00—especially on weekends). In peaceful weather, boats can be more reliable than trains, but if seas are rough, they don't run at all.

Boats depart Monterosso about hourly (10:30-18:00), stopping at the Cinque Terre towns (except at Corniglia) and ending up an hour later in nearby Portovenere. (Portovenere-Monterosso boats run 8:50-18:00.) The ticket price depends on the length of the boat ride (ranging from €4 for a short ride between towns, to €15 for a five-town, one-way ticket with stops; a five-town all-day pass is €20). Round-trip tickets are cheaper than two one-way trips.

Buy **tickets** at stands at each town's harbor (tel. 0187-732-987 and 0187-818-440). Boats are not covered by Cinque Terre park cards. **Schedules** are posted at docks, harbor bars, Cinque Terre park offices, and hotels (www.navigazione golfodeipoeti.it).

Rick's Tip: *In calm weather,* **boats connect the towns about as frequently as the trains,** *though at different times; if you're in a rush, take whichever form of transport is leaving first. In the unpredictable Cinque Terre, a departure now is worth two a little later.*

By Shuttle Bus

ATC shuttle buses (which locals call *pulmino*) connect each town with its closest parking lot and various points in the hills—but do not connect the towns with each other. The one you're most likely to use runs between Corniglia's sea-level train station and its hilltop town center. Most rides cost €1.50 one-way (€2.50 from driver, free with Cinque Terre park card). Ask about tickets and bus schedules at park info offices or TIs, or note the times posted at bus stops. Shuttle service is unreliable; confirm the details carefully. Shuttles may not run from 12:30 to 15:00, when they break for lunch. As you board, tell the driver where you want to go. Departures often coordinate with train arrival times. Some (but not all) departures from Vernazza, Manarola, and Riomaggiore go beyond the parking lots and high into the hills. To soak in the scenery, ride up and hike down, or pay €3 for a 30-45-minute round-trip (€5 on board).

Arriving and Departing
By Train
Most big, fast trains from elsewhere in Italy speed right past the Cinque Terre, though some stop in Monterosso. Unless you're coming from a nearby town, you'll usually have to change trains at least once to reach Vernazza, Corniglia, or Manarola.

Generally, if you're coming from the north, you'll change trains in Sestri Levante or Genoa (specifically, Genoa's Piazza Principe station). If you're coming from the south or east, you'll probably switch trains in La Spezia (change at La Spezia Centrale station—don't make the mistake of getting off at La Spezia Migliarina). Check your full schedule and route options in the train station before you leave (use the kiosks or ask at a ticket window).

TRAIN CONNECTIONS
While a few local trains go to more distant points (Milan or Pisa), it's generally much faster to catch a major train from Monterosso, La Spezia, or Sestri Levante (local train info tel. 0187-817-458, www.trenitalia.com).

From Monterosso by Train to: Venice (5/day, 6 hours, change in Milan), **Milan** (8/day direct, otherwise hourly with change in Genoa, 3-4 hours), **Genoa** (hourly, 1.5 hours), **Pisa** (hourly, 1-2 hours), **Sestri Levante** (hourly, 30 minutes, most trains to Genoa stop here), **La Spezia** (2-3/hour, 15-30 minutes), **Levanto** (2-3/hour, 4 minutes), **Rome** (hourly, 4.5 hours, change in La Spezia).

From La Spezia Centrale by Train to: Rome (8/day direct, more with transfers in Pisa, 3-4.5 hours), **Pisa** (about hourly, 1-1.5 hours), **Florence** (5/day direct, 2.5 hours, otherwise nearly hourly with change in Pisa), **Milan** (about hourly, 3 hours direct or with change in Genoa), **Venice** (about hourly, 5-6 hours, 1-3 changes).

By Taxi
Cinqueterre Taxi covers all five towns, providing transport to the nearest port or airport (mobile 334-776-1946 or 347-652-0837, www.cinqueterretaxi.com).

By Car
The five towns are close together and have good public transportation connections by train and boat. Given the narrow roads and lack of parking, bringing a car to the Cinque Terre is a bad idea. If your plan requires it, however, here are some basic tips: Stay in a hotel that includes parking, or park at **Monterosso** (€18/day), **Riomaggiore** (€23/day), or **Manarola** (€2/hour). They each have parking lots and a shuttle bus to get you into town. Don't drive to **Vernazza**—the roads are in poor condition and a flood blew out its main parking lot.

Parking anywhere on the Cinque Terre is a mess in July and August. If you must find parking, try to arrive between 9:00 and 11:00, when overnight visitors are usually departing. Or you could park your car at a guarded lot or garage in **Levanto** or **La Spezia,** then take the train into the Cinque Terre town of your choice.

Venice

Venice is a world apart. Built on a hundred islands, its exotic-looking palaces are laced together by graceful bridges over sun-speckled canals. Romantics revel in the city's atmosphere of elegant decay, seeing the peeling plaster as a metaphor for beauty in decline. And first-time visitors are often stirred deeply, waking from their ordinary lives to a fantasy world unlike anything they've ever seen.

Those are strong reactions, considering that Venice today, frankly, can also be an overcrowded tourist trap. While there are about 270,000 people in greater Venice (counting the mainland, not counting tourists), the old town has a small-town feel. To see small-town Venice away from the touristic flak, escape the Rialto-San Marco tourist zone and savor the town early and late. At night, when the hordes of day-trippers have gone, another Venice appears. Glide in a gondola through quiet canals. Dance across a floodlit square. Pretend it's Carnevale, don a mask—or just a clean shirt—and become someone else for a night.

VENICE IN 2 DAYS

Venice's greatest sight is the city itself, easily worth two days. It can be Europe's best medieval wander if you make time to stroll and explore.

Day 1: In the morning, take the slow vaporetto #1 from the train station down the Grand Canal to St. Mark's Square. Stop off midway at the Rialto market (Rialto Mercato) to grab an early lunch at the *cicchetti* (appetizer) bars nearby. Resume your ride down the Grand Canal to St. Mark's Square. Spend the afternoon on the square, exploring St. Mark's Basilica, Doge's Palace, Bridge of Sighs, the Correr Museum, and Campanile bell tower (open late in summer).

On any evening: Do a pub crawl for dinner (except on Sun, when most pubs are closed), or dine later at a restaurant. Enjoy a gondola ride (or, the budget version, a moonlit vaporetto, ideally one with open-air front seats). Catch a Vivaldi concert. Hum along with the dueling orchestras on St. Mark's Square, whether you get a drink or just stroll.

Day 2: Spend the morning shopping and exploring as you make your way over the Rialto Bridge to the Frari Church for the art. Head to the Dorsoduro neighborhood for lunch, then devote the afternoon to more art—at the Accademia (Venetian art), Peggy Guggenheim Collection (modern art), and Ca' Rezzonico (18th-century palace).

Too many museums? Go on a photo safari through back streets and canals.

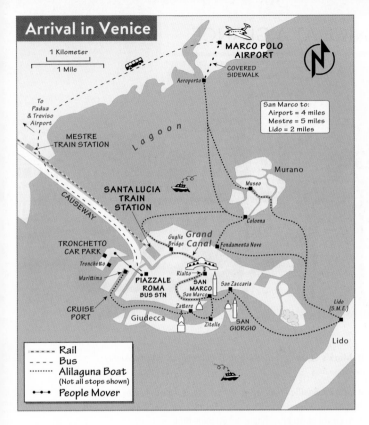

Arrival in Venice

MARCO POLO AIRPORT

1 Kilometer

1 Mile

COVERED SIDEWALK

Aeroporto

To Padua & Treviso Airport

MESTRE TRAIN STATION

La g o o n

San Marco to:
Airport = 4 miles
Mestre = 5 miles
Lido = 2 miles

Murano

Museo

SANTA LUCIA TRAIN STATION

CAUSEWAY

Colonna

Guglie Bridge Grand Canal

Fondamenta Nove

TRONCHETTO CAR PARK

Tronchetto

Marittima

Rialto

SAN MARCO

San Marco

San Zaccaria

PIAZZALE ROMA BUS STN

CRUISE PORT

Giudecca

Zattere

Zitelle

SAN GIORGIO

Lido (S.M.E.)

Lido

----- Rail
- - - Bus
·········· Alilaguna Boat
(Not all stops shown)
•—• People Mover

Or take a short vaporetto trip to the San Giorgio Maggiore island for a sublime view of Venice.

With extra time: Visit the lagoon islands of Murano, Burano, and Torcello. For beach time, it's the Lido (across the lagoon via vaporetto).

Rick's Tip: *Venice is* **crowded with cruise-ship passengers and day-trippers** *daily from 10:00 to about 17:00. Major sights are busiest in the late morning, which makes that a delightful time to explore the back lanes. The sights that have crowd problems get even more packed when it rains.*

ORIENTATION

Venice is shaped like a fish. Its major thoroughfares are canals. The Grand Canal winds through the middle of the fish, starting at the mouth where all the people and food enter, passing under the Rialto Bridge, and ending at St. Mark's Square (Piazza San Marco). Park your 21st-century perspective at the mouth and let Venice swallow you whole.

Venice has six districts *(sestieri)*: **San Marco** (from St. Mark's Square to the Accademia Bridge), **Castello** (the area east of St. Mark's Square), **Dorsoduro** (the "belly" of the fish, on the far side of the Accademia Bridge), **Cannaregio** (between the train station and the Rialto Bridge), **San Polo** (west of the Rialto Bridge), and **Santa Croce** (the "eye" of

VENICE AT A GLANCE

▲▲▲**St. Mark's Square** Venice's grand main square. **Hours:** Always open. See page 694.

▲▲▲**St. Mark's Basilica** Cathedral with mosaics, saint's bones, treasury, museum, and viewpoint of square. **Hours:** Mon-Sat 9:45-17:00, Sun 14:00-17:00 (until 16:00 Nov-Easter). See page 694.

▲▲▲**Doge's Palace** Art-splashed palace of former rulers, with prison accessible through Bridge of Sighs. **Hours:** Daily April-Oct 8:30-19:00, Nov-March 8:30-17:30. See page 701.

▲▲▲**Rialto Bridge** Distinctive bridge spanning the Grand Canal, with a market nearby. **Hours:** Bridge—always open; market—souvenir stalls open daily, produce market closed Sun, fish market closed Sun-Mon. See page 706.

▲▲**Correr Museum** Venetian history and art. **Hours:** Daily April-Oct 10:00-19:00, Nov-March 10:00-17:00. See page 703.

▲▲**Accademia** Venice's top art museum. **Hours:** Mon 8:15-14:00, Tue-Sun 8:15-19:15. See page 704.

▲▲**Peggy Guggenheim Collection** Popular display of 20th-century art. **Hours:** Wed-Mon 10:00-18:00, closed Tue. See page 706.

▲▲**Frari Church** Franciscan church featuring Renaissance masters. **Hours:** Mon-Sat 9:00-18:00, Sun 13:00-18:00. See page 706.

▲▲**Scuola San Rocco** "Tintoretto's Sistine Chapel." **Hours:** Daily 9:30-17:30. See page 707.

▲**Campanile** Dramatic bell tower on St. Mark's Square with elevator to the top. **Hours:** Daily Easter-June and Oct 9:00-19:00, July-Sept 9:00-21:00; Nov-Easter 9:30-15:45. See page 703.

▲**Bridge of Sighs** Famous enclosed bridge, part of Doge's Palace, near St. Mark's Square. **Hours:** Always viewable. See page 706.

▲**La Salute Church** Striking church dedicated to the Virgin Mary. **Hours:** Daily 9:00-12:00 & 15:00-17:30. See page 706.

▲**Ca' Rezzonico** Posh Grand Canal palazzo with 18th-century Venetian art. **Hours:** Wed-Mon 10:00-18:00, Nov-March until 17:00, closed Tue year-round. See page 706.

Nearby Islands

▲▲**Burano** Sleepy island known for lacemaking and lace museum. **Hours:** Museum open Tue-Sun 10:00-18:00, Nov-March until 17:00, closed Mon year-round. See page 710.

▲**San Giorgio Maggiore** Island facing St. Mark's Square, featuring church with Palladio architecture, Tintoretto paintings, and fine views back on Venice. **Hours:** daily 9:00-19:00, Nov-March closes at dusk. See page 704.

▲**Murano** Island famous for glass factories and glassmaking museum. **Hours:** Glass Museum open daily 10:00-18:00, Nov-March until 17:00. See page 709.

▲**Torcello** Near-deserted island with old church, bell tower, and museum. **Hours:** Church—daily March-Oct 10:30-18:00, Nov-Feb 10:00-17:00; museum—closed Mon. See page 710.

▲**Lido** Family-friendly beach. See page 710.

San Michele Cemetery island on the lagoon. **Hours:** Daily 7:30-18:00, Oct-March until 16:30. See page 708.

the fish, across the canal from the train station).

The easiest way to navigate is by landmarks. Many street corners have a sign pointing you to (per) the nearest major landmark, such as San Marco, Accademia, Rialto, Ferrovia (train station), and Piazzale Roma (the bus station). Determine whether your destination is in the direction of a major signposted landmark, then follow the signs through the maze. Obedient visitors stick to the main thoroughfares as directed by these signs...but miss the charm of back-street Venice.

Beyond the city's core lie several other islands, including San Giorgio Maggiore (with great views of Venice), San Michele (old cemetery), Murano (famous for glass), Burano (lacemaking), Torcello (old church), and the skinny Lido (with Venice's beach). The island that matters to drivers is Tronchetto, with the huge parking lot at the entrance to Venice.

Rick's Tip: *It's OK to* **get lost in Venice.** *Remind yourself, "I'm on an island, and I can't get off." When it comes time to find your way, just follow the arrows on building corners or simply ask a local,* **"Dov'è San Marco?"** *("Where is St. Mark's?") Most Venetians speak some English. If they don't, listen politely, watch where their hands point, say "Grazie," and head in that direction. If you're lost, pop into a hotel and ask for their business card—it probably comes with a map and a prominent "You are here."*

Tourist Information

Venice's TIs are understaffed and don't have many free printed materials. Their website, www.turismovenezia.it, can be more helpful than an actual TI office. If you need to check or confirm something, try phoning the TI at 041-529-8711. Other useful websites are www.aguestinvenice.com (sights and events), www.venicefor visitors.com (general travel advice), www.venicelink.com (public and private trans-

portation tickets), and www.museicivici veneziani.it (city-run museums in Venice).

If you must visit a TI, you'll find offices near **St. Mark's Square** (daily 8:30-19:00, in the far-left corner with your back to the basilica), at the **airport** (daily 9:00-20:00), next to the **bus station** (daily 8:30-14:00, inside the huge white parking garage building), and inside the **train station,** along track 1 (daily 8:30-19:00). You'll also find an info and ticket stand in a big white kiosk in front of the station near the vaporetto stop. This kiosk is run by local transport companies and mainly sells transportation and event tickets, but they provide helpful information (daily 9:00-16:00).

Rick's Tip: *Beware of* **travel agencies that masquerade as TIs** *but serve fancy hotels and tour companies. They're in the business of selling things you don't need.*

Maps: Venice demands a good map. Hotels give away freebies, but it's worth investing in a good one (around €5) that shows all the tiny alleys; they're sold at bookstores and newstands. Also consider a mapping **app** for your smartphone. The **City Maps 2Go** app has good maps that are searchable even when you're not online.

Sightseeing Passes

Venice offers an array of passes for sightseeing and transit. For most people, the best choice is the **Museum Pass,** which covers entry into the Doge's Palace, Correr Museum, Ca' Rezzonico (Museum of 18th-Century Venice), and sights on the islands: the Glass Museum on Murano, and the Lace Museum on Burano. At €24, this pass is the best value if you plan to see the Doge's Palace/Correr Museum and even just one of the other covered museums. (Families get a small price break on multiple passes.) Buy it at any of the participating museums or, for €0.50 extra, via links on their websites.

Note that some major sights are not covered on any pass, including the Accademia, Peggy Guggenheim Collection, Scuola San Rocco, and the Campanile, along with the three sights within St. Mark's Basilica that charge admission.

Light sightseers could get by with just an €18 **combo-ticket** that covers both the Doge's Palace and the Correr Museum. To bypass the long line at the palace, buy your combo-ticket at the never-crowded Correr (or online for a €0.50 surcharge).

I'd skip the **Venice Card** (a.k.a. "city pass," covers 11 city-run museums and 16 churches for €40) and the cheaper **San Marco Pack** (covers Doge's Palace and several sights for €26). It's hard to make either of these passes pay off (valid for 7 days, www.veneziaunica.com).

Rolling Venice is a youth pass offering discounts at dozens of sights and shops, but its best deal is for transit. If you're under 30 and want to buy a 72-hour transit pass, it'll cost you just €20—rather than €40 (€4 pass for ages 14-29, sold at TIs and VèneziaUnica shops, www.venezia unica.com).

Tours

🎧 To sightsee on your own, download my **free audio tours** that illuminate some of Venice's top sights (see page 14).

Avventure Bellissime Venice Tours offers several two-hour walks, including a St. Mark's Square tour called the "Original Venice Walking Tour" (€25, includes church entry, most days at 11:00, Sun at 14:00); a 60-minute private boat tour of the Grand Canal (€46, daily at 16:30, eight people maximum); and more. Rick Steves readers get a 10 percent discount on full-priced tours (email them for promo code, then book online, tel. 041-970-499, www. tours-italy.com, info@tours-italy.com).

Debonair guide **Alessandro Schezzini** organizes two-hour Venetian pub tours, including appetizers and wine at three pubs (€35/person, any night on request at 18:00, depart from top of Rialto Bridge,

better to book by email—alessandro@ schezzini.it—than by phone, mobile 335-530-9024, www.schezzini.it).

Artviva Tours offers many intro and themed tours (Grand Canal, Venice Walk, Doge's Palace, Gondola Tour), plus a €80 "Learn to Be a Gondolier" tour. Rick Steves readers get a 10 percent discount (at www. artviva.com/ricksteves, username "rick-steves" and password "reader").

Walks Inside Venice is a dynamic duo of women—and their tour-guide colleagues—enthusiastic about teaching in Venice and outlying destinations (€225/3 hours per group up to 6; €62.50 for a 14:30 Mon-Sat 2.5-hour walking tour; Roberta: mobile 347-253-0560; Sara: mobile 335-522-9714; www.walksinsidevenice.com, info@walksinsidevenice.com).

Tour Leader Venice, a.k.a. Treviso Car Service, offers transfers (e.g., to/from airport) and tours outside of Venice, including the Dolomites (mobile 348-900-0700; www.trevisocarservice.com, tvcarservice@gmail.com).

Helpful Hints

Theft and Safety: The dark, late-night streets of Venice are generally safe. Even so, pickpockets (often well dressed) work the crowded main streets, docks, and *vaporetti*. Your biggest risk is inside St. Mark's Basilica, near the Accademia and Rialto bridges, or on a tightly packed vaporetto.

A handy *polizia* station is on the right side of St. Mark's Square as you face the basilica (at #63, near Caffè Florian). To call the police, dial 113. The Venice TI handles complaints—which must be submitted in writing—about crooks, including gondoliers, restaurants, and hotel rip-offs (fax 041-523-0399, complaint.apt@ turismovenezia.it).

It's illegal for street vendors to sell knockoff handbags, and it's also illegal for you to buy them; both you and the vendor can get big fines.

Medical Help: Venice's **Santi Giovanni**

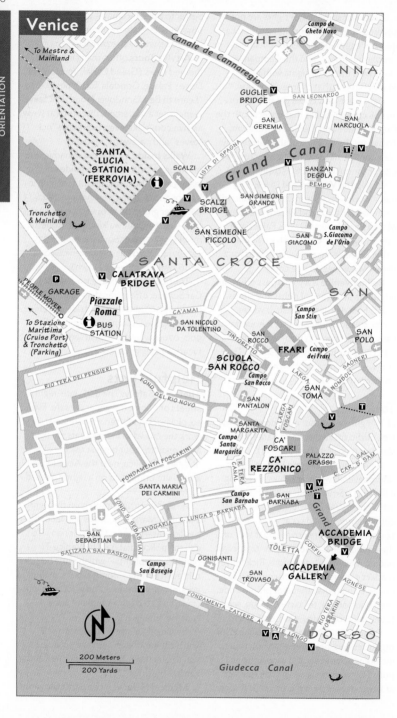

Venice

To Mestre &
Mainland

GHETTO

CANNA

Canale de Cannaregio

GUGLIE
BRIDGE

SAN LEONARDO

SAN
GEREMIA

SAN
MARCUOLA

LISTA DI SPAGNA

SANTA
LUCIA
STATION
(FERROVIA)

SCALZI

Grand Canal

SAN ZAN
DEGOLÀ
BEMBO

To
Tronchetto
& Mainland

SCALZI
BRIDGE

SAN SIMEONE
GRANDE

Campo
S.Giacomo
de l'Orio

SAN SIMEONE
PICCOLO

SAN
GIACOMO

SANTA CROCE

SAN

PEOPLE MOVER

GARAGE

P

CALATRAVA
BRIDGE

CA'AMAI

Campo
San Stin

SAN
POLO

To Stazione
Marittima
(Cruise Port)
& Tronchetto
(Parking)

Piazzale
Roma

BUS
STATION

SAN NICOLO
DA TOLENTINO

TINTORETTO

SAN
ROCCO

FRARI

Campo
dei Frari

SAONERI

RIO TERA DEI PENSIERI

FOND. DEL RIO NOVO

SCUOLA
SAN ROCCO

Campo
San Rocco

C. LARGA
FOSCARI

SAN
TOMA

LARGA

NOMBOLI

SAN
PANTALON

T

SANTA
MARGARITA

Campo
Santa
Margarita

CA'
FOSCARI

CA'
REZZONICO

PALAZZO
GRASSI

C. CAR. S. SAM.

SAL

FONDAMENTA FOSCARINI

R. TERA
CANAL

SANTA MARIA
DEI CARMINI

Campo
San Barnaba

SAN
BARNABA

Grand Canal

ACCADEMIA
BRIDGE

C. LUNGA S. BARNABA

AVOGARIA

SAN
SEBASTIAN

SALIZADA SAN BASEGIO

TOLETTA

CORFU

ACCADEMIA
GALLERY

Campo
San Basegio

OGNISANTI

SAN
TROVASO

AGNESE

RIO TERA
FOSCARINI

FONDAMENTA ZATTERE AL PONTE LONGO

DORSO

N

A

200 Meters

200 Yards

Giudecca Canal

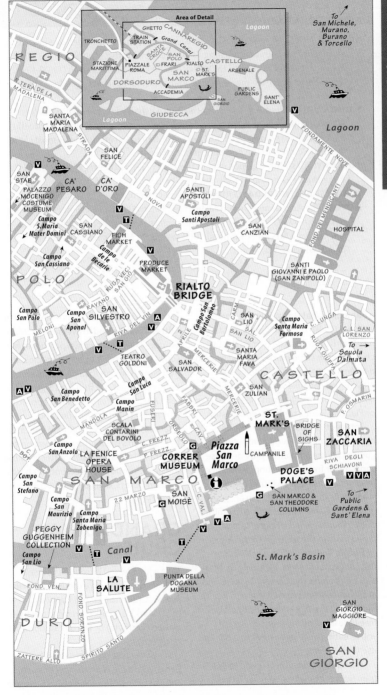

Daily Reminder

SUNDAY: While anyone is welcome to worship, most churches are closed to sightseers on Sunday morning. They reopen in the afternoon: St. Mark's Basilica (14:00-17:00, until 16:00 Nov-Easter) and Frari Church (13:00-18:00). The Rialto open-air market's fish and produce sections are closed, as are most pubs.

MONDAY: All sights are open except the Rialto fish market, Lace Museum (on the island of Burano), and Torcello church museum (on the island of Torcello). The Accademia closes at 14:00. Don't side-trip to Verona today, as most sights there are closed in the morning, if not all day.

TUESDAY: All sights are open except the Peggy Guggenheim Collection and Ca' Rezzonico (Museum of 18th-Century Venice).

WEDNESDAY/THURSDAY/FRIDAY: All sights are open.

NOTES: The Accademia is open earlier (daily at 8:15) and closes later (19:15 Tue-Sun) than most sights in Venice. Some sights close earlier off-season (such as the Correr Museum, Campanile bell tower, St. Mark's Basilica, and Church of San Giorgio Maggiore).

e Paolo hospital (tel. 118) is a 10-minute walk from both the Rialto and San Marco neighborhoods, located behind the big church of the same name on Fondamenta dei Mendicanti (toward Fondamente Nove). You can take vaporetto #4.1 from San Zaccaria, or #5.2 from the train station or Piazzale Roma, to the Ospedale stop.

Internet Access: Almost all hotels have Wi-Fi, many have a computer that guests can use, and most provide these services for free. A few shops with pricey Internet access can be found on back streets (€5/hour, marked with an @ sign).

Water: Carry a water bottle to refill at public fountains fed by pure, safe water piped in from the foothills of the Alps.

Public Toilets: Public pay WCs are near major landmarks, including St. Mark's Square (behind the Correr Museum and at the waterfront park, Giardinetti Reali), Rialto, and the Accademia Bridge. Use free toilets in any museum or any café you're eating in, or get a drink at a bar and use their WC for free.

Travel Agencies: If you need to get train tickets or make seat reservations,

save a trip to the train station and head to **Oltrex Change and Travel** near St. Mark's Square. They charge a €5-per-ticket fee (daily 9:00-13:00 & 14:00-17:30, closed Sun Nov-April; on Riva degli Schiavoni, one bridge past the Bridge of Sighs at Castello 4192, faces San Zaccaria vaporetto stop; tel. 041-476-1926, Luca and Beatrice). Otherwise, **Agenzie 365,** in the train station's main lobby, sells vaporetto and train tickets and has shorter lines than the ticket windows (8 percent surcharge on train tickets, daily 8:00-20:00, tel. 041-275-9412).

GRAND CANAL CRUISE

Take a joyride and introduce yourself to Venice by boat, an experience worth ▲▲▲. Cruise the Grand Canal all the way to St. Mark's Square, starting at the train station (Ferrovia) or the bus station (Piazzale Roma).

If it's your first trip down the Grand Canal, you might want to stow this book and just take it all in—Venice is a barrage on the senses that hardly needs narration. But these notes give the cruise a little meaning and help orient you to this great city.

You can break up the tour by hopping on and off at various sights described in greater depth later in the chapter. Just remember: a single-fare vaporetto ticket is good for just one hour; passes let you hop on and off all day.

I've organized this tour by boat stop. I'll point out both what you can see from the current stop, and what to look forward to as you cruise to the next stop.

Orientation

Length of This Tour: Allow 45 minutes.

Cost: €7 for a one-hour vaporetto ticket, or covered by a transit pass—the best choice if you want to hop on and off.

Getting There: This tour starts at the Ferrovia vaporetto stop (at Santa Lucia train station). It also works if you board upstream from Ferrovia at Piazzale Roma, a five-minute walk over the Calatrava Bridge from the Ferrovia stop.

Catching Your Boat: This tour is designed for **slow boat #1** (which takes about 45 minutes). The **express boat #2** travels the same route, but it skips some stops and takes 25 minutes, making it hard to sightsee. Also, some #2 boats terminate at Rialto; confirm that you're on a boat that goes all the way to San Marco.

Where to Sit: You're more likely to find an empty seat if you catch the vaporetto at Piazzale Roma. Try to snag a seat in the bow—in front of the captain's bridge—for the perfect vantage point for spotting sights left, right, and forward. Not all boats have seats in the bow, but some of the older *vaporetti* do. Otherwise, your options are sitting inside (and viewing the passing sights through windows); standing in the open middle deck; or sitting outside in the back (where you'll miss the wonderful forward views). The left side of the boat has a slight edge, with more sights and the best light late in the day.

Stops to Consider: Some interesting stops are Mercato Rialto (fish market and famous bridge), Ca' Rezzonico (Museum of 18th-Century Venice), Accademia (art museum and the nearby Peggy Guggenheim Collection), and Salute (huge art-filled church).

Audio Tour: 🎧 If you download my free audio tour (see page 14), you won't even have to look at the book.

Grand Canal

Overview

The Grand Canal is Venice's "Main Street." At more than two miles long, nearly 150 feet wide, and nearly 15 feet deep, it's the city's largest canal, lined with its most impressive palaces. It's the remnant of a river that once spilled from the mainland into the Adriatic. The sediment it carried formed barrier islands that cut Venice off from the sea, forming a lagoon.

Venice was built on the marshy islands of the former delta, sitting on wood pilings driven nearly 15 feet into the clay (alder was the preferred wood). About 25 miles of canals drain the city, dumping like streams into the Grand Canal. Technically, Venice has only three canals: Grand, Giudecca, and Cannaregio. The 45 small waterways that dump into the Grand Canal are referred to as rivers (e.g., Rio Novo).

Venice is a city of palaces, dating from the days when the city was the world's richest. The most lavish palaces formed a grand architectural cancan along the Grand Canal. Once frescoed in reds and blues, with black-and-white borders and gold-leaf trim, they made Venice a city of dazzling color. This cruise is the only way to truly appreciate the palaces, approaching them at water level, where their main entrances were located. Today, strict laws prohibit any changes in these buildings. So while landowners gnash their teeth, we can enjoy Europe's best-preserved medieval city—slowly rotting. Many of the grand buildings are now vacant. Others harbor chandeliered elegance above mossy, empty, often flooded ground floors.

❺ Self-Guided Cruise

Start reading the tour when your vaporetto reaches Ferrovia.

❶ *Ferrovia*

The **Santa Lucia train station,** one of the few modern buildings in town, was built in 1954. It's been the gateway into Venice since 1860, when the first station was built. "F.S." stands for "Ferrovie dello Stato," the Italian state railway system.

More than 20,000 people a day commute in from the mainland, making this the busiest part of Venice during rush hour. The **Calatrava Bridge,** just upstream, was built in 2008 to alleviate some of the congestion.

❷ *Riva de Biasio*

Venice's main thoroughfare is busy with all kinds of boats: taxis, police boats, garbage boats, ambulances, construction cranes, and even brown-and-white UPS boats. Somehow they all manage to share the canal in relative peace.

About 25 yards past the Riva de Biasio stop, look left down the broad **Cannaregio Canal** to see what was the **Jewish Ghetto.** The twin, pale-pink, six-story "skyscrapers"—the tallest buildings you'll see at this end of the canal—are reminders of how densely populated the community was.

Ferrovia vaporetto stop

Calatrava Bridge

Founded in 1516 near a copper foundry (a *geto*), this segregated community gave us our word "ghetto."

❸ San Marcuola

At this stop, facing a tiny square just ahead, stands the unfinished Church of San Marcuola, one of only five churches fronting the Grand Canal. Centuries ago, this canal was a commercial drag of expensive real estate in high demand by wealthy merchants. About 20 yards ahead on the right (across the Grand Canal) stands the stately gray **Turkish "Fondaco" Exchange,** one of the oldest houses in Venice. Its horseshoe arches and roofline of triangles are reminders of its Byzantine heritage. Turbaned Turkish traders docked here, unloaded their goods into the warehouse on the bottom story, then went upstairs for a home-style meal and a place to sleep. Venice in the 1500s was cosmopolitan, welcoming every religion and ethnicity—so long as they carried cash. (Today the building contains the city's Museum of Natural History—and Venice's only dinosaur skeleton.)

Just 100 yards ahead on the left, Venice's **Casinò** is housed in the palace where German composer Richard Wagner (*The Ring*) died in 1883. See his distinct, strong-jawed profile in the white plaque on the brick wall. In the 1700s, Venice was Europe's Vegas, with casinos and prostitutes everywhere. *Casinòs* ("little houses" in Venetian dialect) have long provided Italians with a handy escape from daily life. Today, they're run by the state to keep Mafia influence at bay. Notice the fancy front porch, which greets high rollers arriving by taxi or hotel boat.

❹ San Stae

The San Stae Church sports a delightful Baroque facade. Opposite the San Stae stop is a little canal opening. On the second building to the right of that opening, look for the peeling plaster that once made up **frescoes** (you can barely distinguish the scant remains of little angels on the lower floors). Imagine the facades of the Grand Canal at their finest. Most of them would have been covered in frescoes by the best artists of the day. As colorful as the city is today, it's still only a faded, sepia-toned remnant of a long-gone era, a time of lavishly decorated, brilliantly colored palaces.

Just ahead, jutting out on the right, is the ornate white facade of **Ca' Pesaro,** which houses the International Gallery of Modern Art. "*Ca'*" is short for *casa* (house).

In this city of masks, notice how the rich marble facades along the Grand Canal mask what are generally just simple, no-nonsense brick buildings. Most merchants enjoyed showing off. However, being smart businessmen, they only decorated the side of the buildings that would

All kinds of boats ply the canal.

A classic canal view

Grand Canal

Vaporetto Stops

1. Ferrovia
2. Riva de Biasio
3. San Marcuola
4. San Stae
5. Ca' d'Oro
6. Rialto Mercato
7. Rialto
8. San Silvestro
9. Sant'Angelo
10. San Tomà
11. Ca' Rezzonico
12. Accademia
13. Santa Maria del Giglio
14. Salute
15. San Marco
16. San Zaccaria

Map labels:

Canale de Cannaregio

GUGLIE BRIDGE

SAN GEREMIA

To Jewish Ghetto

STRADA

PALAZZO CORRER CONTARINI

SAN MARCUOLA

CASINÒ

PALAZZO GRITTI

PALAZZO VENDRAMIN CALERGI

PALAZZO FLANGINI

Grand Canal

LISTA DI SPAGNA

PALAZZO GIOVANELLI

TURKISH "FONDACO" EXCHANGE

SCALZI

PALAZZO CALBO-CROTTA

PALAZZO MARCELLO

SANTA LUCIA TRAIN STATION (FERROVIA)

PAL. GRITTI

SAN ZAN DEGOLÀ

PALAZZO CA' TRON

SCALZI BRIDGE

PALAZZO DONÀ BALBI

SAN SIMEONE PICCOLO

SANTA CROCE

CALATRAVA BRIDGE

SAN

PIAZZALE ROMA
& PEOPLE MOVER
TO STAZIONE MARITTIMA
& TRONCHETTO

FRARI

PALAZZO CAPPELLO-LAYARD

SAN TOMÀ

PALAZZO BARBARIGO

PALAZZO GIUSTINIANI

PALAZZO BALBI

PALAZZO MOCENIGO

FIRE STATION

CA' FOSCARI

PALAZZO VECCHIA

PALAZZO GIUSTINIAN

PALAZZO MORO LIN

CA' REZZONICO

PALAZZO GRASSI

PALAZZO MALIPIERO-CAPPELLO

PALAZZO LOREDAN

PALAZZO FALIER

PALAZZO CONTARINI DEGLI SCRIGNI

PALAZZO GIUSTINIAN LOLIN

PALAZZO QUERINI

PALAZZO BARBARO

ACCADEMIA BRIDGE & GALLERY

PALAZZO BARBARIGO

FONDAMENTA ZATTERE AL PONTE LONGO

Giudecca Canal

DORSODURO

To Zattere

687

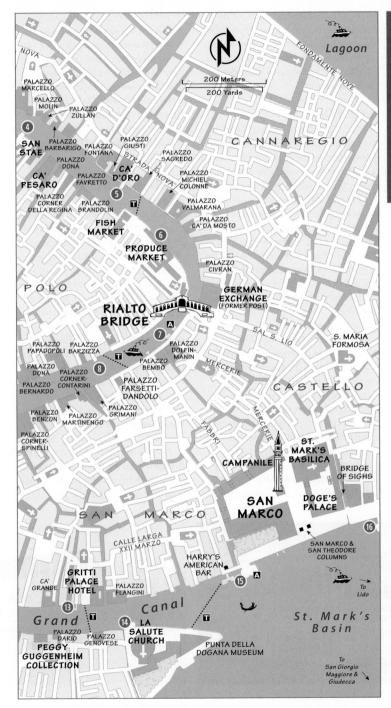

be seen and appreciated. But look back as you pass Ca' Pesaro. It's the only building you'll see with a fine side facade. Ahead, on the left (just before the next stop), is Ca' d'Oro with its glorious triple-decker medieval arcade.

❺ Ca' d'Oro

The lacy **Ca' d'Oro** (House of Gold) is the best example of Venetian Gothic architecture on the canal. Its three stories offer different variations on balcony design, topped with a spiny white roofline. Venetian Gothic mixes traditional Gothic (pointed arches and round medallions stamped with a four-leaf clover) with Byzantine styles (tall, narrow arches atop thin columns), filled in with Islamic frills. Like all the palaces, this was originally painted and gilded to make it even more glorious than it is now. Today the Ca' d'Oro is an art gallery.

Look at the Venetian chorus line of palaces in front of the boat. On the right is the arcade of the covered **fish market,** with the open-air **produce market** just beyond (closed Sun). It bustles in the morning but is quiet the rest of the day. This is a great scene to wander through—even though European Union hygiene standards have made it cleaner but less colorful than it once was.

Find the **traghetto** gondola ferrying shoppers—standing like Washington crossing the Delaware—back and forth.

There are seven *traghetto* crossings along the Grand Canal, each one marked by a classy low-key green-and-black sign. Driving a *traghetto* isn't these gondoliers' normal day jobs. As a public service, all gondoliers are obliged to row the *traghetto* a few days a month. Make a point to use them. At €2 a ride, *traghetti* offer the cheapest gondola rides in Venice (but at this price, don't expect them to sing to you).

❻ Mercato Rialto

Boats stop here (but only between 8:00 and 20:00) to serve the busy market. The long and officious-looking building at this stop is the Venice courthouse. Straight ahead in the distance, rising above the huge post office, is the tip of the Campanile (bell tower), crowned by its golden angel at St. Mark's Square, where this tour will end. The **German Exchange** (100 yards directly ahead, on left side) was the trading center for German metal merchants in the early 1500s (once a post office, it will soon be a shopping center).

You'll cruise by some trendy and beautifully situated wine bars on the right, but look ahead as you round the corner and see the impressive Rialto Bridge come into view.

A major landmark of Venice, the **Rialto Bridge** is lined with shops and tourists. Constructed in 1588, it's the third bridge built on this spot. Until the 1850s, this was

Ca' d'Oro—the house of gold

Mercato Rialto

the only bridge crossing the Grand Canal. With a span of 160 feet and foundations stretching 650 feet on either side, the Rialto was a massive engineering feat in its day. Earlier Rialto Bridges could open to let big ships in, but not this one. When this new bridge was completed, much of the Grand Canal was closed to shipping and became a canal of palaces.

When gondoliers pass under the fat arch of the Rialto Bridge, they take full advantage of its acoustics: *"Volare, oh, oh..."*

❼ Rialto

Rialto, a separate town in the early days of Venice, has always been the commercial district, while San Marco was the religious and governmental center. Today, a winding street called the Mercerie connects the two, providing travelers with human traffic jams and a mesmerizing gauntlet of shopping temptations. This is the only stretch of the historic Grand Canal with landings upon which you can walk. They unloaded the city's basic necessities here: oil, wine, charcoal, iron. Today, the quay is lined with tourist-trap restaurants.

Venice's sleek, black, graceful **gondo-**las are a symbol of the city (for more on gondolas, see page 710). With about 500 gondoliers joyriding amid the churning *vaporetti*, there's a lot of congestion on the Grand Canal. Pay attention—this is where most of the gondola and vaporetto accidents take place. While the Rialto is the highlight of many gondola rides, gondoliers understandably prefer the quieter small canals. Watch your vaporetto driver curse the better-paid gondoliers.

❽ San Silvestro

We now enter a long stretch of important **merchants' palaces,** each with proud and different facades. Because ships couldn't navigate beyond the Rialto Bridge, the biggest palaces—with the major shipping needs—line this last stretch of the navigable Grand Canal.

Palaces like these were multifunctional: ground floor for the warehouse, offices and showrooms upstairs, and the living quarters above the offices on the "noble floors" (with big windows designed to let in maximum light). Servants lived and worked on the top floors (with the smallest windows). For fire-safety reasons, the kitchens were also located on the top

Rialto Bridge

floors. Peek into the noble floors to catch a glimpse of their still-glorious chandeliers of Murano glass.

❾ Sant'Angelo

Notice how many buildings have a foundation of waterproof white stone (*pietra d'Istria*) upon which the bricks sit high and dry. Many canal-level floors are abandoned as the rising water level takes its toll.

The **posts**—historically painted gaily with the equivalent of family coats of arms—don't rot underwater. But the wood at the waterline, where it's exposed to oxygen, does. On the smallest canals, little blue gondola signs indicate that these docks are for gondolas only (no taxis or motor boats).

❿ San Tomà

Fifty yards ahead, on the right side (with twin obelisks on the rooftop) stands **Palazzo Balbi,** the palace of an early-17th-century captain general of the sea. This palace, like so many in the city, flies three flags: Italy (green-white-red), the European Union (blue with ring of stars), and Venice (a lion on a field of red and gold).

Just past the admiral's palace, look immediately to the right, down a side canal. On the right side of that canal, before the bridge, see the traffic light and the **fire station** (the 1930s Mussolini-era building with four arches hiding fireboats parked and ready to go).

Best Views in Venice

- A slow vaporetto ride down the **Grand Canal** on a sunny day—or a misty early morning—is a shutterbug's delight.
- On St. Mark's Square, enjoy views from the soaring **Campanile** or the balcony of St. Mark's Basilica (both require admission).
- The **Rialto** and **Accademia Bridges** provide free, expansive views of the Grand Canal, along with a cooling breeze.
- Get off the main island for a view of the Venetian skyline: Ascend **San Giorgio Maggiore's bell tower,** or venture to **Giudecca Island** to visit the swanky bar of the Molino Stucky Hilton Hotel (free shuttle boat leaves from near the San Zaccaria-M.V.E. vaporetto dock).

The impressive **Ca' Foscari,** with a classic Venetian facade (on the corner, across from the fire station), dominates the bend in the canal. This is the main building of the University of Venice, which has about 25,000 students. Notice the elegant lamp on the corner—needed in the old days to light this intersection.

The grand, heavy, white **Ca' Rezzonico,** just before the stop of the same name,

Navigational posts

Ca' Foscari

houses the Museum of 18th-Century Venice (see page 706). Across the canal is the cleaner and leaner **Palazzo Grassi,** the last major palace built on the canal, erected in the late 1700s. It was purchased by a French tycoon and now displays a contemporary art collection.

⑪ Ca' Rezzonico

Up ahead, the Accademia Bridge leads over the Grand Canal to the **Accademia Gallery** (right side), filled with the best Venetian paintings (see page 704). The bridge was put up in 1934 as a temporary structure. Locals liked it, so it stayed. It was rebuilt in 1984 in the original style.

⑫ Accademia

From here, look through the graceful bridge and way ahead to enjoy a classic view of **La Salute Church,** topped by a crown-shaped dome supported by scrolls. This Church of Saint Mary of Good Health was built to thank God for delivering Venetians from the devastating plague of 1630 (which had killed about a third of the city's population).

The low, white building among greenery (100 yards ahead, on the right, between the Accademia Bridge and the church) is the **Peggy Guggenheim Collection.** The American heiress "retired" here, sprucing up a palace that had been abandoned mid-construction. Peggy willed the city her fine collection of modern art (see page 706).

As you approach the next stop, notice on the right how the line of higgledy-piggledy palaces evokes old-time Venice. Two doors past the Guggenheim, Palazzo Dario has a great set of characteristic **funnel-shaped chimneys.** These forced embers through a loop-the-loop channel until they were dead—required in the days when stone palaces were surrounded by humble, wooden buildings, and a live spark could make a merchant's workforce homeless. Three doors farther is the **Salviati building,** which once served as a

glassworks. Its Art Nouveau mosaic, done in the early 20th century, features Venice as a queen being appreciated by the big shots of society.

⑬ Santa Maria del Giglio

Back on the left stands the fancy **Gritti Palace hotel.** Hemingway and Woody Allen both stayed here (but not together).

Take a deep whiff of Venice. What's all this nonsense about stinky canals? All I smell is my shirt. By the way, how's your captain? Smooth dockings? To get to know him, stand up in the bow and block his view.

⑭ Salute

The huge **La Salute Church** towers overhead as if squirted from a can of Catholic Reddi-wip.

As the Grand Canal opens up into the lagoon, the last building on the right with the golden ball is the 17th-century **Customs House,** which now houses the Punta della Dogana contemporary art museum. Its two bronze Atlases hold a statue of Fortune riding the ball. Arriving ships stopped here to pay their tolls.

La Salute Church

Is Venice Sinking?

Venice has battled rising water levels since the fifth century. Several factors, both natural and artificially-constructed, cause Venice to flood about 100 times a year—usually from October until late winter—a phenomenon called the *acqua alta*.

Venice sits atop sediments deposited at the ancient mouth of the Po River, which are still settling. Early industrial projects, such as offshore piers and the bridge to the mainland, affected the sea floor and tidal cycles, making the city more vulnerable to flooding. Twentieth-century industry pumped massive amounts of groundwater out of the aquifer beneath the lagoon for nearly 50 years before the government stopped the practice in the 1970s. In the last century, Venice has sunk by about nine inches.

Meanwhile, the waters around Venice are rising, especially in winter. The notorious *acqua alta* happens when an unusually high tide combines with strong winds and a storm. When a storm—an area of low pressure—travels over a body of water, it pulls the surface of the water up into a dome. As strong sirocco winds from Africa blow storms north up the Adriatic, they push this high water ahead of the front, causing a surging tide. Add the worldwide sea-level rise that's resulted from climate change, and the high sea gets that much higher.

During the *acqua alta*, the first puddles appear in the center of paved squares, pooling around the limestone grates. These grates cover cisterns that long held Venice's only source of drinking water. Surrounded by the lagoon and beset by constant flooding, this city had no natural source of fresh water. For centuries, residents carried water from the mainland. In the ninth century, they devised a way to collect rainwater by using paved, cleverly sloped squares as catchment systems, with limestone filters covering underground clay tubs. Venice's population grew markedly once citizens were able to access fresh water from these "wells." Several thousand cisterns provided the city with drinking water up until 1886, when an aqueduct was built. Now the wells are capped, and rain drains from squares into the lagoon—or up from it, as the case may be.

In 2003, a consortium of engineering firms began construction on the MOSE Project. Named for the acronym of its Italian name, *Modulo Sperimentale Elettromeccanico,* it's also a nod to Moses and his (albeit temporary) mastery over the sea. Underwater gates are being installed on the floor of the sea at the three inlets where it enters Venice's lagoon. When the seawater rises above a certain level, air will be pumped into the gates, causing them to rise and shut out the Adriatic. Will it work? Time and tides will tell.

⓯ *San Marco*

Up ahead on the left, the green pointed tip of the Campanile marks **St. Mark's Square,** the political and religious center of Venice...and the final destination of this tour. You could get off at the San Marco stop and go straight to St. Mark's Square (and you'll have to if you're on vaporetto #2, which terminates here). But I'm staying on the #1 boat for one more stop, just past St. Mark's Square (it's a quick walk back).

Survey the lagoon. Opposite St. Mark's Square, across the water, the ghostly white church with the pointy bell tower is **San Giorgio Maggiore,** with great views of Venice (see page 704). Next to it is the residential island Giudecca, stretching from close to San Giorgio Maggiore to the Hilton Hotel (good nighttime view, far-right end of island).

Still on board? If you are, as we leave the San Marco stop, prepare for a drive-by view of St. Mark's Square. First comes the bold white facade of the old mint (marked by a tiny cupola, where Venice's golden ducat, the "dollar" of the Venetian Republic, was made) and the library facade. Then come the twin columns, topped by St. Theodore and St. Mark, who've welcomed visitors since the 15th century. Between the columns, catch a glimpse of two giant figures atop the **Clock Tower**—they've been whacking their clappers every hour since 1499. The domes of **St. Mark's Basilica** are soon eclipsed by the lacy facade of the **Doge's Palace.** Next you'll see the **Bridge of Sighs** (leading from the palace to the prison—check out the maximum-security bars), many gondolas with their green breakwater buoys, and then the grand harborside promenade—the **Riva.**

Follow the Riva with your eye, past elegant hotels to the green area in the distance. This is the largest of Venice's few **parks,** which hosts the annual Biennale festival. Much farther in the distance is the **Lido,** the island with Venice's beach. Its sand and casinos are tempting, though its car traffic disrupts the medieval charm of Venice.

The Campanile and Doge's Palace dominate the waterside view of Venice.

⑯ *San Zaccaria*

OK, you're at your last stop. Quick—muscle your way off this boat! (If you don't, you'll eventually end up at the Lido.)

At San Zaccaria, you're right in the thick of the action. A number of other *vaporetti* depart from here (see page 731). Otherwise, it's a short walk back along the Riva to St. Mark's Square. Ahoy!

SIGHTS

Venice's city museums offer youth and senior discounts to Americans and other non-EU citizens. When you see a 🎧 in a listing, it means the sight is covered in a free audio tour (via my Rick Steves Audio Europe app—see page 14).

San Marco District

▲▲▲ ST. MARK'S SQUARE (PIAZZA SAN MARCO)

This grand square is surrounded by splashy, historic buildings and sights: St. Mark's Basilica, Doge's Palace, Campanile bell tower, and Correr Museum. The square is filled with music, lovers, tourists, and pigeons by day. It's your private rendezvous with the Venetian past late at night, when it becomes Europe's most romantic dance floor.

🎧 For a detailed explanation of St. Mark's Square, download my free **audio tour.**

With your back to the church, survey one of Europe's great urban spaces, and the only square in Venice to merit the title "Piazza." Nearly two football fields long, it's surrounded by the offices of the republic. On your right are the "old offices" (16th-century Renaissance). On your left are the "new offices" (17th-century High Renaissance). Napoleon called the piazza "the most beautiful drawing room in Europe," and added to the intimacy by building the final wing, opposite the basilica.

The **Clock Tower** (Torre dell'Orologio), built during the Renaissance in 1496, marks the entry to the main shopping drag, called the Mercerie (or "Marzarie," in Venetian dialect), which connects St. Mark's Square with the Rialto Bridge. From the piazza, you can see the bronze men (Moors) swing their huge clappers at the top of each hour. In the 17th century, one of them knocked an unsuspecting worker off the top and to his death—probably the first-ever killing by a robot. Notice one of the world's first "digital" clocks on the tower facing the square (the time flips every five minutes). You can go inside the Clock Tower with a prebooked guided tour that takes you close to the clock's innards and out to a terrace with good views over the square (€12 combo-ticket includes Correr Museum—where the tour starts—but doesn't cover Doge's Palace; €7 for the tour if you already have a Museum Pass or Correr/Doge's Palace combo-ticket; tours in English Mon-Wed at 10:00 and 11:00, Thu-Sun at 14:00 and 15:00; no kids under age 6). The Clock Tower tour requires reservations: call 848-082-000 or book online at http://torreorologio.visitmuve.it. You can also try dropping by the Correr Museum for same-day reservations.

Rick's Tip: *If you're **bombed by a pigeon**, resist the initial response to wipe it off immediately—it'll just smear into your hair. Wait until it dries, and it should flake off cleanly. But if the poop splatters on your clothes, wipe it off immediately to avoid a stain.*

▲▲▲ ST. MARK'S BASILICA (BASILICA DI SAN MARCO)

Built in the 11th century, this basilica's distinctly Eastern-style architecture underlines Venice's connection with Byzantium (which protected it from the ambition of Charlemagne and his Holy Roman Empire). It's decorated with booty from returning sea captains—a Venetian trophy chest. The interior glows mysteriously

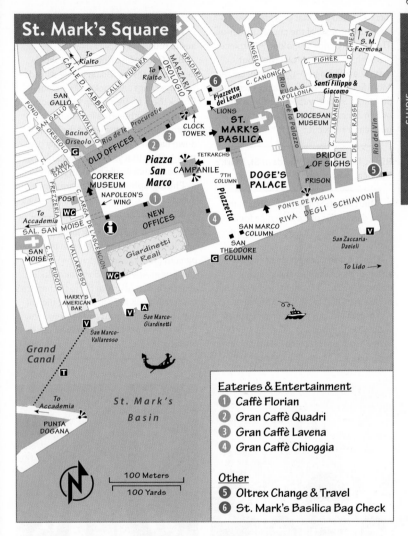

St. Mark's Square

To Rialto

CALLE D. FABBRI

To Rialto

SAN
GALLO

CALLE FIUBERA

C. CAVALETTO

FOND. ORSEOLO

SAN GALLO

Bacino
Orseolo

G

OLD OFFICES

Rio de le Procuratie

MARZARIA OROLOGIO

SPADARIA

C. ANGELO

C. CANONICA

Rio RUGA G.

APOLLONIA

C. FIGHER

Campo
Santi Filippo &
Giacomo

To
S. M.
Formosa

C. D. CHIESA

Piazzetta
dei Leoni

LIONS

CLOCK
TOWER

ST.
MARK'S
BASILICA

DIOCESAN
MUSEUM

de la Palazzo

C. DE LE RASSE

C. D. ALBANESI

Rio del Vin

C. RAMO SALVA

FRENZARIA

POST

CORRER
MUSEUM

NAPOLEON'S
WING

Piazza
San
Marco

TETRARCHS

CAMPANILE

7TH
COLUMN

DOGE'S
PALACE

BRIDGE
OF SIGHS

PRISON

5

To
Accademia

C. LARGA DE L'ASCENSION

WC

SAL. SAN MOISÈ

NEW
OFFICES

i

Piazzetta

PONTE DE PAGLIA

RIVA DEGLI SCHIAVONI

SAN
MOISÈ

C. DEL RIDOTTO

C. VALLARESSO

Giardinetti
Reali

WC

SAN MARCO
COLUMN

SAN
THEODORE
G COLUMN

San Zaccaria-
Danieli

V

To Lido →

HARRY'S
AMERICAN
BAR

V A

San Marco-
Giardinetti

V

San Marco-
Vallaresso

Grand
Canal

T

To
Accademia

PUNTA
DOGANA

St. Mark's
Basin

St. Mark's
Basin

N

100 Meters

100 Yards

Eateries & Entertainment
1 Caffè Florian
2 Gran Caffè Quadri
3 Gran Caffè Lavena
4 Gran Caffè Chioggia

Other
5 Oltrex Change & Travel
6 St. Mark's Basilica Bag Check

with gold mosaics and colored marble. Since about A.D. 830, the saint's bones have been housed on this site.

Cost: Basilica entry is free, but you can pay €2 for an online reservation that lets you skip the line (well worth it).

Three separate exhibits within the church charge admission: the **Treasury** (€3, includes audioguide); **Golden Altarpiece** (€2); and **San Marco Museum** (€5). The San Marco Museum has the

original bronze horses (copies of these overlook the square), a balcony offering a remarkable view over St. Mark's Square, and various works related to the church.

Hours: Church open Mon-Sat 9:45-17:00, Sun 14:00-17:00 (Sun until 16:00 Nov-Easter), interior brilliantly lit daily 11:30-12:30; museum open daily 9:45-16:45, including on Sunday mornings when the church itself is closed; if considering a Sunday visit, note that the museum has two balconies that provide views to some, but not all, of the church's interior. The treasury and the Golden Altarpiece are both open Easter-Oct Mon-Sat 9:45-17:00, Sun 14:00-17:00; Nov-Easter Mon-Sat 9:45-16:00, Sun 14:00-16:00. On St. Mark's Square, vaporetto: San Marco or San Zaccaria, tel. 041-270-8311, www.basilicasanmarco.it.

Rick's Tip: *To* **avoid crowds** *at* **St. Mark's Basilica,** *go early or late.*

Theft Alert: St. Mark's Basilica is the most dangerous place in Venice for pickpocketing—inside, it's always a crowded jostle.

Dress Code: Modest dress (no bare knees or bare shoulders) is strictly enforced for men, women, and even kids. Shorts are OK if they cover the knees.

Tours: Free, hour-long English **tours** (heavy on the mosaics' religious symbolism) are offered many days at 11:00 (meet in atrium, schedule varies, see schedule board just inside entrance).

🎧 Download my free St. Mark's Basilica **audio tour.**

Bag Check: Small purses and shoulder-slung bags are usually allowed inside, but larger bags and backpacks are not. Check them for free for up to one hour at the nearby church called Ateneo San Basso, 30 yards to the left of the basilica, down narrow Calle San Basso (daily 9:30-17:00). Note that you generally can't check small bags that would be allowed inside.

Photography: No photos are allowed inside.

Rick's Tip: *Those* **checking large bags** *usually get to* **skip the line,** *as do their companions (at the guard's discretion). Leave your bag at Ateneo San Basso and pick up your claim tag. Take your tag to the basilica's tourist entrance. Keep to the left of the railing where the line forms and show your tag to the gatekeeper. He'll generally let you in, ahead of the line.*

St. Mark's Basilica

Gold mosaics pave every surface of St. Mark's interior.

St. Mark's Basilica

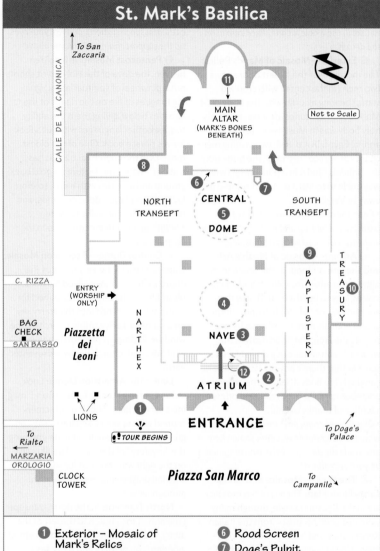

To San Zaccaria

CALLE DE LA CANONICA

11
MAIN ALTAR
(MARK'S BONES BENEATH)

Not to Scale

8

6

7

NORTH TRANSEPT

CENTRAL
5
DOME

SOUTH TRANSEPT

9

C. RIZZA

ENTRY (WORSHIP ONLY)

4

B A P T I S T E R Y

T R E A S U R Y

10

BAG CHECK

Piazzetta dei Leoni

N A R T H E X

NAVE 3

SAN BASSO

12

ATRIUM

2

LIONS

1

To Rialto

ENTRANCE

To Doge's Palace

MARZARIA OROLOGIO

TOUR BEGINS

CLOCK TOWER

Piazza San Marco

To Campanile

1 Exterior – Mosaic of Mark's Relics	**6** Rood Screen
2 Atrium – Mosaic of Noah's Ark & the Great Flood	**7** Doge's Pulpit
	8 Nicopeia Icon
3 Nave – Mosaics & Greek-Cross Floor Plan	**9** Discovery of Mark Mosaic
4 Pentecost Mosaic	**10** Treasury
5 Central Dome – Ascension Mosaic	**11** Golden Altarpiece
	12 Stairs up to Museum

➲ SELF-GUIDED TOUR

• *Start outside in the square, far enough back to take in the whole facade. Then zero in on the details.*

❶ Exterior—Mosaic of Mark's Relics: The mosaic over the far left door shows two men (in the center, with crooked staffs) bearing a coffin with the body of St. Mark. Seven centuries after his death, his holy body was in Muslim-occupied Alexandria, Egypt. In A.D. 828, two visiting merchants of Venice "rescued" the body from the "infidels," hid it in a pork barrel (which was unclean to Muslims), and spirited it away to Venice.

• *Enter the atrium (entrance hall) of the basilica, and look up and to the right into an archway decorated with fine mosaics.*

❷ Atrium—Mosaic of Noah's Ark and the Great Flood: In the scene to the right of the entry door, Noah and sons are sawing logs to build a boat. Below that are three scenes of Noah putting all species of animals into the ark, two by two. Across the arch, the flood drowns the wicked. Noah sends out a dove twice to see whether there's any dry land where he can dock. He finds it, leaves the ark with a gorgeous rainbow overhead, and offers a sacrifice of thanks to God.

• *Climb seven steps, pass through the doorway, and enter the nave. Loiter somewhere just inside the door (crowd permitting) and let your eyes adjust.*

❸ The Nave—Mosaics and Greek-Cross Floor Plan: These golden mosaics are in the Byzantine style, though many were designed by artists from the Italian Renaissance and later. The often-overlooked lower walls are covered with colorful marble slabs, cut to expose the grain, and laid out in geometric patterns. Even the floor is mosaic, with mostly geometrical designs. It rolls like the sea. Venice is sinking and shifting, creating these cresting waves of stone. The church is laid out with four equal arms, topped with domes, radiating from the center to form a Greek cross (+).

• *Find the chandelier near the entrance doorway (in the shape of a Greek cross cathedral space station), and run your eyes up the support chain to the dome above.*

❹ Pentecost Mosaic: In a golden heaven, the dove of the Holy Spirit shoots out a pinwheel of spiritual lasers, igniting tongues of fire on the heads of the 12 apostles below, giving them the ability to speak other languages without a Rick Steves phrase book. One of the oldest mosaics in the church (c. 1125), it has distinct "Byzantine" features: a gold background and apostles with halos, solemn faces, almond eyes, delicate hands, and rumpled robes, all facing forward.

• *Shuffle along with the crowds up to the central dome.*

❺ Central Dome—Ascension Mosaic: Gape upward to the very heart of the church. Christ—having lived his miraculous life and having been crucified for man's sins—ascends into the starry sky on a rainbow. In Byzantine churches, the window-lit dome represented heaven, while the dark church below represented earth.

Under the Ascension Dome: Look around at the church's furniture and imagine a service here. The **❻** rood screen, topped with 14 saints, separates the congregation from the high altar, heightening the "mystery" of the Mass. The **❼** pulpit on the right was reserved for the doge, who led prayers and made important announcements.

North Transept: In the north transept (the arm of the church to the left of the altar), today's Venetians pray to a painted wooden icon of Mary and Baby Jesus known as **❽** Nicopeia, or "Our Lady of Victory" (on the east wall of the north transept, it's a small painting crusted over with a big stone canopy). In its day, this was the ultimate trophy—the actual icon used to protect the Byzantine army in war, looted by the Crusaders.

• *In the south transept (to the right of the main altar), find the dim mosaic high up on*

Ⓐ *The altar and tomb of St. Mark*

Ⓑ *Mosaic showing St. Mark's body being carried into the church*

Ⓒ *Noah's Ark mosaic*

Ⓓ *Central dome and the Ascension mosaic*

the three-windowed wall above the entrance to the treasury.

⑨ Discovery of Mark Mosaic: This mosaic isn't a biblical scene; it depicts the miraculous event that capped the construction of the present church.

It's 1094, the church is nearly complete (see the domes shown in cutaway fashion), and they're all set to re-inter Mark's bones under the new altar. There's just one problem: During the decades of construction, they forgot where they'd stored his body!

So (in the left half of the mosaic), all of Venice gathers inside the church to bow down and pray for help finding the bones. The doge (from the Latin *dux*, meaning leader) leads them. Soon after (the right half), the patriarch (far right) is inspired to look inside a hollow column where he finds the relics. Everyone turns and applauds, including the womenfolk (left

San Marco Museum offers close-up views of mosaics.

side of scene), who stream in from the upper-floor galleries. The relics were soon placed under the altar in a ceremony that inaugurated the current structure.

Additional Sights: The ❿ **Treasury** (Tesoro; ask for the included and informative audioguide when you buy your ticket) and ⓫ **Golden Altarpiece** (Pala d'Oro) give you the easiest way outside of Istanbul or Ravenna to see the glories of the Byzantine Empire. Venetian crusaders looted the Christian city of Constantinople and brought home piles of lavish loot (perhaps the lowest point in Christian history until the advent of TV evangelism). Much of this plunder is stored in the Treasury of San Marco. Most of these treasures were made in about A.D. 500, while Western Europe was stuck in the Dark Ages. Beneath the high altar lies the body of St. Mark ("Marce") and the Golden Altarpiece, made of 250 blue-backed enamels with religious scenes, all set in a gold frame and studded with 15 hefty rubies, 300 emeralds, 1,500 pearls, and assorted sapphires, amethysts, and topaz (c. 1100).

In the ⓬ **San Marco Museum** (Museo di San Marco) upstairs, you can see an up-close mosaic exhibition, a fine view of the church interior, a view of the square from the balcony with bronze horses, and (inside, in their own room) the original horses, which were stolen from Constantinople during the notorious Fourth Crusade. The staircase up to the museum is in the atrium, near the basilica's main entrance, marked by a sign that says *Loggia dei Cavalli, Museo.*

▲▲▲DOGE'S PALACE (PALAZZO DUCALE)

The seat of the Venetian government and home of its ruling duke, or doge, this was the most powerful half-acre in Europe for 400 years. The Doge's Palace was built to show off the power and wealth of the Republic. The doge lived with his family on the first floor up, near the halls of power. From his once-lavish (now sparse) quarters, you'll follow the one-way tour through the public rooms of the top floor, finishing with the Bridge of Sighs and the prison. The place is wallpapered with masterpieces by Veronese and Tintoretto.

Cost and Hours: €18 combo-ticket

Doge's Palace

includes Correr Museum, also covered by Museum Pass—see page 678, daily April-Oct 8:30-19:00, Nov-March 8:30-17:30, last entry one hour before closing, café, photos allowed without flash, next to St. Mark's Basilica, just off St. Mark's Square, vaporetto stops: San Marco or San Zaccaria, tel. 041-271-5911, http://palazzoducale.visitmuve.it.

Rick's Tip: *To* **avoid long lines at the Doge's Palace,** *buy your combo-ticket at the* **Correr Museum** *across the square; then go straight to the Doge's Palace turnstile, skirting along to the right, entering at the "prepaid tickets" entrance. It's also possible to* **buy advance tickets online**—*at least 48 hours in advance—on the museum website (€0.50 fee).*

Tours: The **audioguide** tour is dry but informative (€5, 1.5 hours, need ID for deposit). For a 1.25-hour live **guided tour,** consider the Secret Itineraries Tour, which takes you into palace rooms otherwise not open to the public (€20, includes Doge's Palace admission but not Correr Museum admission; €14 with combo-ticket; three English-language tours each morning). Though the tour skips the palace's main hall, you're welcome to visit the hall afterward on your own. Reserve ahead for this tour in peak season—it can fill up as much as a month in advance. Book online (http://palazzoducale.visitmuve.it, €0.50 fee), or reserve by phone (tel. 848-082-000, from the US dial 011-39-041-4273-0892), or you can try just showing up at the info desk. Avoid the Doge's Hidden Treasures Tour—it reveals little that would be considered a "treasure" and is a waste of €20.

Visiting the Doge's Palace: You'll see the restored facades from the **courtyard.** Notice a grand staircase (with nearly naked Moses and Paul Newman at the top). Even the most powerful visitors climbed this to meet the doge. This was the beginning of an architectural power trip.

In the **Senate Hall,** the 120 senators met, debated, and passed laws. Tintoretto's large **Triumph of Venice** on the ceiling (central painting, best viewed from the top) shows the city in all its glory. Lady Venice is up in heaven with the Greek gods, while barbaric lesser nations swirl up to give her gifts and tribute.

The **Armory**—a dazzling display originally assembled to intimidate potential adversaries—shows remnants of the military might that the empire employed to keep the East-West trade lines open (and the Venetian economy booming).

The giant **Hall of the Grand Council** (175 feet by 80 feet, capacity 2,600) is where the entire nobility met to elect the senate and doge. It took a room this size to contain the grandeur of the Most Serene Republic. Ringing the top of the room are portraits of the first 76 doges (in chronological order). The one at the far end that's blacked out (in the left corner) is the notorious Doge Marin Falier, who opposed the will of the Grand Council in 1355. He was tried for treason, beheaded, and airbrushed from history.

On the wall over the doge's throne is Tintoretto's monsterpiece, **Paradise,** the largest oil painting in the world. Christ and Mary are surrounded by a heavenly host of 500 saints. The painting leaves you feeling that you get to heaven not by being a good Christian, but by being a good Venetian.

Cross the covered **Bridge of Sighs** over

Tintoretto, Triumph of Venice

the canal to the **prisons.** Circle the cells. Notice the carvings made by prisoners—from olden days up until 1930—on some of the stone windowsills of the cells, especially in the far corner of the building.

Cross back over the Bridge of Sighs, pausing to look through the marble-trellised windows at all of the tourists.

More Sights on the Square

▲▲CORRER MUSEUM (MUSEO CORRER)

This uncrowded museum gives you a good, easy-to-manage overview of Venetian history and art. The doge memorabilia, armor, banners, statues (by Canova), and paintings (by the Bellini family and others) re-create the festive days of the Venetian Republic. And it's all accompanied by English descriptions and breathtaking views of St. Mark's Square. The Correr Museum is a quiet refuge—a place to rise above St. Mark's Square when the piazza is too hot, too rainy, or too crowded.

Cost and Hours: €18 combo-ticket also includes the Doge's Palace and the two lesser museums inside the Correr (National Archaeological Museum and the Monumental Rooms of the Marciana National Library); for €12 you can see the Correr Museum and tour the Clock Tower on St. Mark's Square, but this ticket doesn't include the Doge's Palace; daily April-Oct 10:00-19:00, Nov-March 10:00-17:00, last entry one hour before closing; bag check free and mandatory for bags bigger than a large purse, no photos, elegant café; enter at far end of square directly opposite basilica, tel. 041-240-5211, http://correr.visitmuve.it.

▲CAMPANILE (CAMPANILE DI SAN MARCO)

This dramatic bell tower replaced a shorter tower, part of the original fortress that guarded the entry of the Grand Canal. That tower crumbled into a pile of bricks in 1902, a thousand years after it was built. Construction is underway to strengthen the base of the rebuilt tower. Ride the elevator 325 feet to the top for the best view in Venice (especially at sunset). For an ear-shattering experience, be on top when the bells ring. The golden archangel Gabriel at the top always faces into the wind. Beat the crowds and enjoy the crisp morning air at 9:00 or the cool evening breeze at 18:00. Go inside to buy tickets; the kiosk in front just rents €4 audioguides and is operated by a private company.

Rick's Tip: Beat the crowds *at* the Campanile *by going early or going late (it's open until 21:00 July-Sept). Or head to the similar* **San Giorgio Maggiore bell tower** *across the lagoon. The lines are shorter and the view is just as good.*

Cost and Hours: €8, daily Easter-June and Oct 9:00-19:00, July-Sept 9:00-21:00, Nov-Easter 9:30-15:45, may close during thunderstorms, tel. 041-522-4064, www.basilicasanmarco.it.

Canova, Paris

Behind St. Mark's Basilica
▲ BRIDGE OF SIGHS

This much-photographed bridge connects the Doge's Palace with the prison. Supposedly, a condemned man would be led over this bridge on his way to the prison, take one last look at the glory of Venice, and sigh—a notion popularized in the Romantic 19th century. Though overhyped, it's undeniably tingle-worthy—especially after dark, when the crowds have dispersed and it's just you and floodlit Venice.

Getting There: The Bridge of Sighs is around the corner from the Doge's Palace. From the palace, walk toward the waterfront, turn left along the water, and look up the first canal on your left. You can walk across the bridge (from the inside) by visiting the Doge's Palace.

Across the Lagoon from St. Mark's Square
▲ SAN GIORGIO MAGGIORE

This is the dreamy church-topped island you can see from the waterfront by St. Mark's Square. The striking church, designed by Palladio, features art by Tin-

toretto, a bell tower, and good views of Venice.

Cost and Hours: Free entry to church; daily 9:00-19:00, Nov-March closes at dusk. The bell tower costs €6 and is accessible by elevator (runs until 30 minutes before the church closes but is not accessible Sun during services).

Getting There: To reach the island from St. Mark's Square, take the one-stop, three-minute ride on vaporetto #2 from San Zaccaria (single ticket-€4, 6/hour, ticket valid for one hour; direction: Tronchetto).

Dorsoduro District
▲▲ ACCADEMIA (GALLERIA DELL'ACCADEMIA)

Venice's top art museum, packed with highlights of the Venetian Renaissance, features paintings by the Bellini family, Titian, Tintoretto, Veronese, Tiepolo, Giorgione, Canaletto, and Testosterone. It's just over the wooden Accademia Bridge from the San Marco action.

Cost and Hours: €9, free first Sun of the month, Mon 8:15-14:00, Tue-Sun 8:15-19:15, last entry 45 minutes before closing, dull audioguide-€6, no flash photos

Bridge of Sighs

San Giorgio Maggiore

allowed. At Accademia Bridge, vaporetto: Accademia, tel. 041-522-2247, www. gallerieaccademia.org.

Rick's Tip: *Just 360 people are allowed into the* **Accademia** *gallery at one time. It's most crowded on Tuesday mornings and whenever it rains;* **it's least crowded Wednesday, Thursday, and Sunday mornings** *(before about 10:00) and late afternoons (after about 17:00). It's possible to book tickets in advance (€1.50/ticket surcharge; online at www.gallerieaccademia.org or call 041-520-0345), but it's unnecessary if you avoid the busiest times.*

Renovation: A major expansion and renovation has been dragging on for years. Paintings come and go, and the actual locations of the pieces are hard to pin down. Still, the museum contains the best art in Venice. If you don't find a particular piece you'd like to see, check Room 23, which seems to be the holding pen for displaced art.

Visiting the Accademia: The Accademia is the greatest museum anywhere for Venetian Renaissance art and a good overview of painters whose works you'll see all over town. Venetian art is underrated and misunderstood. It's nowhere near as famous today as the work of the Florentine Renaissance, but it's livelier, more colorful, and simply more fun, with historical slices of Venice, ravishing nudes, and very human Madonnas. The Venetian love of luxury shines through in this collection, which starts in the Middle Ages and runs to the 1700s. Look for grand canvases of colorful, spacious settings, peopled with happy locals in extravagant clothes having a great time.

Medieval highlights include elaborate altarpieces and golden-haloed Madonnas, all painted at a time when realism, depth of field, and emotion were considered beside the point. Medieval Venetians, with their close ties to the East, borrowed techniques such as gold-leafing, frontal poses, and "iconic" faces from the religious icons of Byzantium (modern-day Istanbul).

Among early masterpieces of the Renaissance are Mantegna's studly *St. George* and Giorgione's mysterious *Tempest*. As the Renaissance reaches its heights, so do the paintings, such as Titian's magnificent *Presentation of the Virgin*. It's a religious scene, yes, but it's really just an excuse to display secular splendor (Titian was the most famous painter of his day—perhaps even more famous than Michelangelo). Veronese's sumptuous *Feast in the House of Levi* also has an ostensibly religious theme (in the middle, find Jesus eating his final meal)—but it's outdone by the luxury and optimism of Renaissance Venice. Life was a good thing and beauty was to be enjoyed. (Veronese

Veronese, Feast in the House of Levi

was hauled before the Inquisition for painting such a bawdy Last Supper...so he fine-tuned the title.) End your tour with Guardi's and Canaletto's painted "post-cards" of the city—landscapes for visitors who lost their hearts to the romance of Venice.

▲▲PEGGY GUGGENHEIM COLLECTION

The popular museum of far-out art, housed in the American heiress' former retirement palazzo, offers one of Europe's best reviews of the art of the first half of the 20th century. Stroll through styles represented by artists whom Peggy knew personally—Cubism (Picasso, Braque), Surrealism (Dalí, Ernst), Futurism (Boccioni), American Abstract Expressionism (Pollock), and a sprinkling of Klee, Calder, and Chagall.

Cost and Hours: €15, usually includes temporary exhibits, Wed-Mon 10:00-18:00, closed Tue, audioguide-€7, pricey café, 5-minute walk from Accademia Bridge, vaporetto: Accademia or Salute, tel. 041-240-5411, www.guggenheim-venice.it.

▲LA SALUTE CHURCH (SANTA MARIA DELLA SALUTE)

This impressive church with a crown-shaped dome was built and dedicated to the Virgin Mary by grateful survivors of the 1630 plague.

Cost and Hours: Free entry to church, €3 to enter sacristy; daily 9:00-12:00 & 15:00-17:30, 10-minute walk from Accademia Bridge, vaporetto: La Salute, tel. 041-274-3928.

▲CA' REZZONICO (MUSEUM OF 18TH-CENTURY VENICE)

This Grand Canal palazzo offers the most insightful look at the life of Venice's rich and famous in the 1700s. Wander under ceilings by Tiepolo, among furnishings from that most decadent century, enjoying views of the canal and paintings by Guardi, Canaletto, and Longhi.

Cost and Hours: €10, Wed-Mon 10:00-18:00, Nov-March until 17:00, closed Tue year-round, audioguide-€5; ticket office closes one hour before museum does, no flash photos, café, vaporetto: Ca' Rezzonico, tel. 041-241-0100, http://carezzonico.visitmuve.it.

San Polo District
▲▲▲RIALTO BRIDGE

One of the world's most famous bridges, this distinctive and dramatic stone structure crosses the Grand Canal with a single confident span. The arcades along the top of the bridge help reinforce the structure... and offer some enjoyable shopping diversions, as does the **market** surrounding the bridge (produce market closed Sun, fish market closed Sun-Mon).

▲▲FRARI CHURCH (BASILICA DI SANTA MARIA GLORIOSA DEI FRARI)

My favorite art experience in Venice is seeing art in the setting for which it was designed—as it is at the Frari Church. The Franciscan "Church of the Brothers" and the art that decorates it are warmed by the spirit of St. Francis. It features the work of three great Renaissance masters: Donatello, Giovanni Bellini, and Titian—each showing worshippers the glory of God in human terms.

Cost and Hours: €3, Mon-Sat 9:00-18:00, Sun 13:00-18:00, modest dress recommended, no photos, on Campo dei Frari, near San Tomà vaporetto and *traghetto* stops, tel. 041-272-8618, www.basilicadeifrari.it.

Tours: You can rent an **audioguide** for €2, or ∩ download my free Frari Church **audio tour.**

Concerts: The church occasionally hosts small theatrical performances (usually around €15, buy tickets at church, for details see the church's website, www.basilicadeifrari.it).

Visiting the Frari Church: In **Donatello's wood statue of St. John the Baptist** (just to the right of the high altar), the prophet of the desert—dressed in animal skins and nearly starving from his diet of bugs 'n' honey—announces the coming of the Messiah. Donatello was a Florentine working at the dawn of the Renaissance.

Bellini's Madonna and Child with Saints and Angels painting (in the sacristy farther to the right) came later, done by a Venetian in a more Venetian style— soft focus without Donatello's harsh realism. While Renaissance humanism demanded Madonnas and saints that were accessible and human, Bellini places them in a physical setting so beautiful that it creates its own mood of serene holiness. The genius of Bellini, perhaps the greatest Venetian painter, is obvious in the pristine clarity, rich colors (notice Mary's clothing), believable depth, and reassuring calm of this three-paneled altarpiece.

Finally, glowing red and gold like a stained-glass window over the high altar, **Titian's Assumption of the Virgin** sets the tone of exuberant beauty found in the otherwise sparse church. Titian the Venetian—a student of Bellini—painted steadily for 60 years...you'll see a lot of his art. As stunned apostles look up past the swirl of arms and legs, the complex composition of this painting draws you right to the radiant face of the once-dying, now-triumphant Mary as she joins God in heaven.

For many, these three pieces of art make a visit to the Accademia Gallery unnecessary (though they may whet your appetite for more). Before leaving, check out the Neoclassical pyramid-shaped Canova monument flanking the nave just inside the main entrance and (opposite that) the grandiose tomb of Titian. Compare the carved marble *Assumption* behind Titian's tombstone portrait with the painted original above the high altar.

▲▲SCUOLA SAN ROCCO

Sometimes called "Tintoretto's Sistine Chapel," this lavish meeting hall has some 50 large, colorful Tintoretto paintings plastered to the walls and ceilings. The best paintings are upstairs, especially the *Crucifixion* in the smaller room. View the neck-breaking splendor with the mirrors available in the Grand Hall.

Frari Church

Titian, Assumption of the Virgin

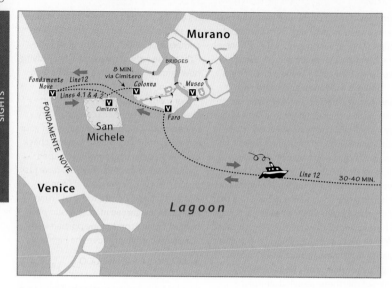

Cost and Hours: €10, includes audioguide, daily 9:30-17:30, no photos, next to the Frari Church, tel. 041-523-4864, www.scuolagrandesanrocco.it.

Venice's Lagoon

The island of Venice sits in a lagoon—a calm section of the Adriatic protected from wind and waves by the natural break-water of the Lido. The Lido is Venice's beach—nice for a break on a sunny day.

Beyond the church-topped island of San Giorgio Maggiore (directly in front of St. Mark's Square), four interesting islands hide out in the lagoon: San Michele, Murano, Burano, and Torcello. These islands make a good, varied, and long day trip.

Getting to the Lagoon: You can travel to any of the islands by vaporetto. Because single vaporetto tickets (€7) expire after one hour, getting a vaporetto pass (€20/24 hours) for a lagoon excursion makes more sense.

For a route that takes you to San Michele, Murano, Burano, and Torcello, start at the **Fondamente Nove** vaporetto stop on the north shore of Venice (the "back" of the fish). Lines #4.1 and #4.2

converge here before heading out to Murano. Catch either one (every 10 minutes); you'll first cross to San Michele (whose stop is called Cimitero) in six minutes, then continue another three minutes to Murano-Colonna. Stroll through Murano, then leave that island from a different stop: Murano-Faro, where you can board vaporetto #12 for the 30-minute trip to Burano. From Burano, head to Torcello on vaporetto #9 (5-minute trip each way). To make a quick return to Venice from Burano, hop vaporetto #12, which returns you to Fondamente Nove (45 minutes).

SAN MICHELE (A.K.A. CIMITERO)

This is the cemetery island—and the final resting place of a few foreign VIPs, from poet Ezra Pound to composer Igor Stravinsky. The stopover is easy, since *vaporetti* come every 10 minutes. If you enjoy wandering through old cemeteries, you'll dig this one—it's full of flowers, trees, and birdsong, and has an intriguing chapel (cemetery open daily 7:30-18:00, Oct-March until 16:30; reception to the left as you enter, free WC to the right, no picnicking).

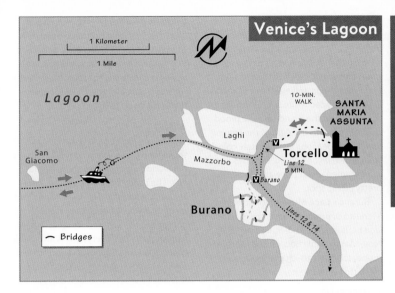

Venice's Lagoon

1 Kilometer

1 Mile

Lagoon

10-MIN. WALK

SANTA MARIA ASSUNTA

Laghi

San Giacomo

Mazzorbo

Torcello
Line 12 5 MIN.

Burano

Burano

Lines 12 & 14

~ Bridges

VENICE SIGHTS

▲MURANO

Murano is famous for its glassmaking. From the Colonna vaporetto stop, skip the glass shops in front of you, walk to the right, and wander up the street along the canal, **Fondamenta dei Vetrai** (Glass-makers' Embankment). The Faro district of Murano, on the other side of the canal, is packed with factories (*fabriche*) and their furnaces (*fornaci*). You'll pass dozens of **glass shops.** Early along this promenade, at #47, is the venerable **Venini** shop, with glass a cut above the rest, and with an interior showing off the ultimate in modern Venetian glass design (Mon-Sat 9:30-18:00, closed Sun).

Murano's **Glass Museum** (Museo Vetrario) traces the history of this delicate art (€8, daily 10:00-18:00, Nov-March until 17:00, tel. 041-739-586, http://museo vetro.visitmuve.it).

Rick's Tip: Venetian glass blowers claim that much of the cheap glass you'll see in Venice is imported from China. **Genuine Venetian glass** *comes with the Murano seal.*

Murano's Fondamenta dei Vetrai

Firing up the glass furnace on Murano

▲▲BURANO

Known for lacemaking, Burano offers a delightful, vibrantly colorful village alternative to big, bustling Venice. The tight **main drag** is packed with tourists and lined with shops, selling lace or Burano's locally produced white wine. Wander to the far side of the island, and the mood shifts. Explore to the right of the leaning tower for a peaceful yet intensely colorful, small-town lagoon world. Benches line a little promenade at the water's edge—a pretty picnic spot.

Burano's **Lace Museum** (Museo del Merletto di Burano) shows the island's lace heritage (€5, Tue-Sun 10:00-18:00, Nov-March until 17:00, closed Mon year-round, tel. 041-730-034, http://museo merletto.visitmuve.it).

▲TORCELLO

This is the birthplace of Venice, where some of the first mainland refugees settled, escaping the barbarian hordes. Today, it's marshy and shrub-covered, the least-developed island (pop. 20). There's little to see except the church (a 10-minute walk from the dock; the oldest in Venice, and still sporting some impressive mosaics), a climbable bell tower, and a modest museum of Roman sculpture and medieval sculpture and manuscripts (€12 combo-ticket covers museum, church, and bell tower; €9 combo-ticket covers church and bell tower; both combo-tickets include audio-guide; museum only—€3; church and bell tower—€5 each; church open daily March-Oct 10:30-18:00, Nov-Feb 10:00-17:00, museum and campanile close 30 minutes earlier and museum closed Mon; museum tel. 041-730-761, church/bell tower tel. 041-730-119).

▲LIDO

Venice's nearest beach is the Lido, across the lagoon on an island connected to the mainland (which means some car traffic). The sandy beach is pleasant, family-friendly, and good for swimming. Rent an umbrella, buy beach gear at the shop, get food at the self-service café, or have a drink at the bar. Everything is affordable and in the same building (vaporetto: Lido S.M.E., walk 10 minutes on Gran Viale S. Maria Elisabetta to beach entry).

EXPERIENCES

Gondola Rides

Riding a gondola is simple, expensive, and one of the great experiences in Europe. Gondoliers hanging out all over town are eager to have you hop in for a ride. It's a rip-off for cynics, but a must for romantics.

The price for a gondola starts at €80 for a 40-minute ride during the day. You can divide the cost—and the romance—among up to six people per boat, but only two get the love seat. Prices jump to €100 after 19:00—when it's most romantic and

Colorful Burano

Burano lace is prized.

A Dying City?

Venice's population (58,000 in the historic city) is half what it was just 30 years ago, and people are leaving at a rate of a thousand a year. Of those who stay, 25 percent are 65 or older.

Sad, yes, but imagine raising a family here: Apartments are small, high up, and expensive. Humidity and occasional flooding make basic maintenance a pain. Home-improvement projects require navigating miles of red tape, and you must follow regulations intended to preserve the historical ambience. Everything is expensive because it has to be shipped in from the mainland. You can easily get glass and tourist trinkets, but it's hard to find groceries or get your shoes fixed. Running basic errands involves lots of walking and stairs—imagine crossing over arched bridges while pushing a child in a stroller and carrying a day's worth of groceries.

With millions of visitors a year (150,000 a day at peak times), on any given day Venetians are likely outnumbered by tourists. Despite government efforts to subsidize rents and build cheap housing, the city is losing its residents. The economy itself is thriving, thanks to tourist dollars and rich foreigners buying second homes. But the culture is dying. Even the most hopeful city planners worry that in a few decades Venice will not be a city at all, but a museum, a cultural theme park, a decaying Disneyland for adults.

relaxing. Adding a singer and an accordionist will cost an additional €120. If you value budget over romance, save money by recruiting fellow travelers to split a gondola. Prices are standard and listed on the gondoliers' association website (go to www.gondolavenezia.it, click on "Using the Gondola," and look under "charterage").

Rick's Tip: *For* **cheap gondola thrills** *during the day, stick to the €2 one-minute ferry ride on a Grand Canal traghetto. At night, vaporetti are nearly empty, and it's a great time to cruise the Grand Canal on slow boat #1.*

Dozens of gondola stations (*servizio gondole*) are set up along canals all over town. Because your gondolier might offer narration or conversation during your ride, talk with several and choose one you like. Review the map and discuss the route; it's a good way to see if you enjoy the gondolier's personality and language skills. Establish the price, route, and duration of the trip before boarding, enjoy your ride, and pay only when you're finished. While prices are pretty firm, you might find them softer during the day. Most gondoliers honor the official prices, but a few might try for some extra euros, particularly by insisting on a tip. (While not required or even expected, if your gondolier does the full 40 minutes and entertains you en route, a 5-10 percent tip is appreciated; if he's surly or rushes through the trip, skip

A gondola station

it.) While gondoliers can be extremely charming, locals say that anyone who falls for one of these Venetian Romeos "has slices of ham over her eyes." Don't be surprised if your gondolier answers mobile-phone calls during the ride (have you ever called your loved one at work?).

If you've hired musicians and want to hear a Venetian song (*un canto Veneziano*), try requesting "*Venezia La Luna e Tu.*" Asking to hear "*O Sole Mio*" (which comes from Naples) is like asking a Chicago lounge singer to sing "Swanee River."

It's worth the extra cost to experience a gondola ride at night. The moon sails past otherwise unseen buildings and silhouettes gaze down from bridges while window glitter spills onto the black water. Put the camera down and make time for you and your partner to enjoy a threesome with Venice.

Festivals

Venice's most famous festival is **Carnevale,** the celebration Americans know as Mardi Gras (usually late Jan to early Feb, www.carnevale.venezia.it). Carnevale, which means "farewell to meat," originated as a wild, two-month-long party leading up to the austerity of Lent. In its heyday—the 1600s and 1700s—you could do pretty much anything with anybody from any social class if you were wearing a mask. These days it's a tamer 18-day celebration, culminating in a huge dance lit with fireworks on St. Mark's Square. Some Venetians don masks and join in the fun; others skip town.

Every year, the city hosts the world-class **Venice Biennale International Art Exhibition,** alternating between art in odd years and architecture in even years. The exhibition spreads over the Arsenale and Giardini park (take vaporetto #1 or #2 to Giardini-Biennale; for details and an events calendar, see www.labiennale.org). The actual exhibition usually runs from June through November, but other loosely connected events—film, dance, theater—are held throughout the year (as early as February) in various venues.

A gondola ride at night is worth the price.

Nightlife

You must experience Venice after dark. The city is quiet at night, as tour groups stay on the mainland and day-trippers return to their beach resorts and cruise ships. Gondolas cost more, but are worth it.

St. Mark's Square

Streetlamp halos, floodlit history, and a ceiling of stars make St. Mark's Square magic at midnight. After dark, **dueling café orchestras** entertain. They feature similar food, prices, and a three- to five-piece combo playing a selection of classical and pop hits. You can hang out for free behind the tables (allowing you to move on easily to the next orchestra when the musicians take a break). Dancing on the square is free—and encouraged.

If you spring for a seat to enjoy a concert, it can be about €13-22 well spent (for a drink and the cover charge for music). It's acceptable to nurse a drink for an hour—you're paying for the music with the cover charge. To save money (but forego proximity to the music), you can sip your coffee at the bar, because the law limits the charge for coffee at a bar.

Caffè Florian (on the right as you face the church) is the most famous Venetian café and was one of the first places in Europe to serve coffee. The outside tables are the main action, but walk inside through the richly decorated rooms where Casanova, Lord Byron, Charles Dickens,

and Woody Allen have all paid too much for a drink (cappuccino €9, €6 cover charge when orchestra is playing, daily 10:00-24:00, shorter hours in winter, www.caffeflorian.com).

Gran Caffè Quadri, opposite the Florian, has equally illustrious clientele, including the writers Stendhal and Dumas, and composer Richard Wagner.

The scene at **Gran Caffè Lavena,** near the Clock Tower, can be great, in spite of its politically incorrect but dazzling chandelier.

Gran Caffè Chioggia, on the Piazzetta facing the Doge's Palace, charges a bit less than the others, and has just one or two musicians, usually a pianist, playing cocktail jazz. The touristy **Bar Americano,** under the Clock Tower, is lively until late (but lacks live music).

Rick's Tip: *You'll hear about the famous* **Harry's American Bar,** *which sells overpriced food and cocktails, but* **it's a tourist trap**...*and the last place Hemingway would drink today. It's cheaper to get a drink at any of the hole-in-the-wall bars just off St. Mark's Square.*

Concerts

Venice is a city of the Baroque era. For about €25, you can take your pick of traditional Vivaldi concerts in churches throughout town. You'll find young, frilly

Carnevale is a masked extravaganza.

The evening café scene on St. Mark's Square

costumed Vivaldis hawking concert tickets on many corners. Most shows start at 20:30 and generally last 1.5 hours. Hotels sell tickets at face-value.

Tickets can usually be bought the same day as the concert, so don't bother with websites that sell tickets with a surcharge. Musicians in wigs and tights offer better spectacle; musicians in black-and-white suits are better performers.

The **Interpreti Veneziani orchestra,** considered the best group in town, generally performs 1.5-hour concerts nightly at 21:00 inside the sumptuous San Vidal Church (€27, church ticket booth open daily 9:30-21:00, north end of Accademia Bridge, tel. 041-277-0561, www.interpreti veneziani.com).

Musica a Palazzo is an evening of opera at a Venetian palace on the Grand Canal. You'll spend about 45 minutes each in three sumptuous rooms as musicians perform (about 2.25 hours total). They generally present three different operas on successive nights. With these surroundings, under Tiepolo frescoes, you'll be glad you dressed up. There are only 70 seats, so book in advance by phone or online (€75, nightly at 20:30, Palazzo Barbarigo Minotto, Fondamenta Duodo o Barbarigo, vaporetto: Santa Maria del Giglio, San Marco 2504, mobile 340-971-7272, www.musicapalazzo.com).

Check at the TI or the TI's website (www.turismovenezia.it) for listings of church concerts as well as other entertainment and events. The free monthly *Un Ospite di Venezia* lists all the latest in English (free at fancy hotels, or check www.aguestinvenice.com).

EATING

While touristy restaurants are the scourge of Venice, my recommended places are popular with locals and respect the tourists who happen by.

First trick: Walk away from triple-language menus. Second trick: Eat fish. Many seafood dishes are the catch-of-the-day. Note that seafood (and steak) may be sold by weight—per 100 grams or *etto*—rather than a set price; be savvy or be surprised. Third trick: Eat later. A place that feels touristy at 19:00 can be filled with locals at 21:00.

Budget Eating: Unique to Venice, *cicchetti* bars specialize in small appetizers that can combine to make a quick, tasty meal (see "The Stand-Up Progressive Venetian Pub-Crawl Dinner" later in this section).

Takeout pizza is one of the cheapest ways to eat in Venice. Small hole-in-the-wall shops in every neighborhood sell takeout pizza—round, by the slice, or by weight. Takeout prices increase dramatically as you near the Rialto and St. Mark's Square.

The Rialto open-air market is great for picnic gatherers (closed Sun), though any respectable grocery (*alimentari*) will do. As for supermarkets, a handy **Co-op** is between St. Mark's and Campo Santa Maria Formosa (daily 8:30-20:00, on the corner of Salizada San Lio and Calle del Mondo Novo at Castello 5817). A **Billa** supermarket is in Dorsoduro (daily 8:30-23:00, vaporetto: San Basilio).

Gelato: It's easy to find in any neigh-

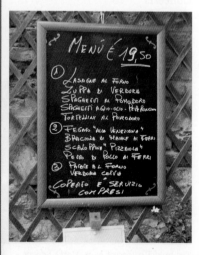

MENÚ € 19,50

① LASAGNE AL FORNO
ZUPPA DI VERDURA
SPAGHETTI AL POMODORO
SPAGHETTI AGLIO-OLIO-PEPERONCINO
TORTELLINI AL POMODORO

② FEGATO "ALLA VENEZIANA"
BRACIOLA DI MAIALE AI FERRI
SCALOPPINA "PIZZAIOLA"
PETTO DI POLLO AI FERRI

③ PATATE AL FORNO
VERDURA COTTA

COPERTO E SERVIZIO
COMPRESI

Venetian Cuisine

Venetian cuisine relies heavily on fish, shellfish, risotto, and polenta.

Antipasti: Popular choices include *antipasto di mare* (a marinated mix of fish and shellfish served chilled) and *sarde in saor* (sardines marinated with onions). *Cicchetti* are Venetian tapas, the finger-food appetizers served in some pubs.

First courses (*primi*): Venice's favorite dish is risotto, a short-grain rice simmered in broth and often flavored with seafood (*risotto nero* is risotto made with squid and its ink; *risotto ai porcini* contains porcini mushrooms). Other first courses are *risi e bisi* (rice and peas), *pasta e fagioli* (pasta and bean soup), and *bigoli in salsa* (fat whole-wheat noodles with anchovy sauce). Pasta is commonly served *alla buzzara* (with a rich seafood-tomato sauce). You'll also see plenty of polenta—boiled cornmeal served soft or cut into firm slabs and grilled.

Second courses (*secondi*): It's mostly *frutti di mare* (seafood). The most common fish are farmed, not wild—such as *branzino* (sea bass), *orata* (sea bream), *salmone* (salmon), and *rombo* (turbot, a flounder-like flatfish). The weirder the animal (eel, octopus, frogfish), the more local it is. *Baccalà* is dried Atlantic salt cod that's rehydrated and often served with polenta. Other choices are calamari, *cozze* (mussels, often steamed in broth), *gamberi* (shrimp), *moleche col pien* (fried soft-shell crabs), *pesce spada*

Pasta with shellfish is a favorite.

(swordfish), *rospo* (frogfish, a small marine fish), *seppia* (cuttlefish, a squid-like creature; can be served in its own ink, often over spaghetti); *sogliola* (sole, served poached or oven-roasted), *vitello di mare* ("sea veal," like swordfish—firm, pink, mild, and grilled), and *vongole* (small clams, often steamed with herbs and wine). *Fritto misto di pesce* is assorted deep-fried seafood (often calamari and prawns). *Zuppa di pesce* is seafood stew.

Cocktails: The most popular *aperitivo* (pre-dinner drink) is *spritz,* which mixes white wine, soda, and ice with either Campari (bitter) or Aperol (sweeter), garnished with an olive or skewer of fruit. Other options include the *bellini* (Prosecco and white-peach puree) and *tiziano* (grape juice and Prosecco). A popular *digestivo* (after-dinner drink) is *sgroppino:* squeezed lemon juice, lemon gelato, and vodka.

borhood. Several cafés on St. Mark's Square have gelato counters in summer, including **Gran Caffè Lavena** (at #134) and **Todaro** (on the corner of the Piazzetta at #5, near the water and across from the Doge's Palace). I like the inventive **Grom** chain, with branches on Campo dei Frari (facing Frari Church) and Campo San Barnaba. **Gelatoteca Suso** serves delectable flavors on the San Marco side of the Rialto Bridge (next to recommended Rosticceria San Bartolomeo, on Calle de la Bissa). **Il Doge** also sells Sicilian-style *granita,* slushy ice with fresh fruit (on bustling Campo Santa Margarita).

Near the Rialto Bridge
North of the Bridge

These restaurants and wine bars are located beyond Campo Santi Apostoli, on or near the Strada Nova, the main drag going from Rialto toward the train station.

At bright and alpine-paneled **Trattoria da Bepi,** chef Loris carries on his mother's passion for good, traditional Venetian cuisine. Ask for seasonal specialties: The seafood appetizer plate and crab dishes are excellent. Enjoy good seating inside or out (€9-13 pastas, €14-20 *secondi,* Fri-Wed 12:00-14:30 & 19:00-22:00, closed Thu, half a block off Campo Santi Apostoli on Salizada Pistor, Cannaregio 4550, tel. 041-528-5031).

More expensive **Vini da Gigio** has a traditional Venetian menu and a classy but unsnooty setting that's a pleasant mix of traditional and contemporary (€14-18 pastas, €22-24 *secondi,* Wed-Sun 12:00-14:30 & 19:00-22:30, closed Mon-Tue, 4 blocks from Ca' d'Oro vaporetto stop on Fondamenta San Felice, behind church on Campo San Felice, Cannaregio 3628a, tel. 041-528-5140).

East of the Rialto Bridge

The next few places hide away in the twisty lanes between the Rialto Bridge and Campo Santa Maria Formosa. Osteria da Alberto is a tad farther north of the others, in Cannaregio.

Rosticceria San Bartolomeo is a cheap self-service diner, with different counters serving up different types of food—pastas, *secondi,* fried goodies, etc. Get it to go, grab a tiny table, or munch at the bar—but skip the pricier upper-floor restaurant. To find it, imagine the statue on Campo San Bartolomeo walking backward 20 yards, turning left, and going under a passageway—now, follow him (€7-9, €2 glasses of wine, prices listed on wall behind counter, no cover and no service

charge, daily 9:00-21:30, San Marco 5424a, tel. 041-522-3569).

Osteria al Portego is a small, friendly neighborhood eatery near Campo San Lio. The *cicchetti* here (€1-3) make a great meal—best enjoyed early, around 18:00—but consider sitting down for dinner from the menu. For a table from 18:00 to 21:00, reserve ahead. From Rosticceria San Bartolomeo (listed earlier), continue over a bridge to Campo San Lio, turn left, and follow Calle Carminati straight 50 yards over another bridge (€14-15 pastas, €15-18 *secondi,* €1 glasses of house wine, daily 11:00-15:00 & 17:30-22:00, on Calle de la Malvasia, Castello 6015, tel. 041-522-9038).

Osteria da Alberto, up near Campo Santa Maria Novo, offers excellent daily specials and a good house wine in a woody and characteristic interior. Reserve ahead and request a table in front (€13-17 seafood dishes, €9-12 pastas, daily 12:00-15:00 & 18:30-22:30; on Calle Larga Giacinto Gallina, midway between Campo Santi Apostoli and Campo San Zanipolo/ Santi Giovanni e Paolo, and next to Ponte de la Panada bridge, Cannaregio 5401; tel. 041-523-8153, www.osteriadaalberto.it).

Rialto Market Area

The market end of the Rialto Bridge is great for menu browsing, bar-hopping, drinks, and snacks, as well as sit-down restaurants. You'll find lots of hardworking hole-in-the-walls catering to locals needing a quick, affordable, tasty bite. It's crowded by day, nearly empty early in the evening, and packed with clubbers later.

My listings below include a stretch of dark and rustic pubs serving *cicchetti* (Venetian tapas), a strip of trendy places fronting the Grand Canal, and several places at the market and nearby. All but the last eatery **(Osteria al Ponte Storto)** are within 200 yards of the market and each other.

Pubs: The 100-yard-long **"Cicchetti Strip,"** which starts two blocks inland

The Stand-Up Progressive Venetian Pub-Crawl Dinner

My favorite Venetian dinner is a pub crawl (*giro d'ombra*)—a tradition unique to Venice, where no cars means easy crawling. (*Giro* means stroll, and *ombra*—slang for a glass of wine—means shade, from the old days when a portable wine bar scooted with the shadow of the Campanile bell tower across St. Mark's Square.)

Venice's residential back streets hide characteristic bars (*bacari*) with countless trays of interesting toothpick munchies (*cicchetti*) and blackboards listing wines served by the glass. The *cicchetti* selection is best early, so start your evening by 18:00. Most bars are closed on Sunday. For a stress-free pub crawl, take a tour with Alessandro Schezzini (see page 679).

Cicchetti bars have a social stand-up zone and cozy tables where you can sit down with your *cicchetti* or order from a simple menu. Food generally costs the same price whether you stand or sit. Crowds sometimes happily spill into the street.

While you can order a plate, Venetians prefer going one-by-one...sipping their wine and trying this...then give me one of those...and so on. Try deep-fried mozzarella cheese, gorgonzola, calamari, artichoke hearts, and anything ugly on a toothpick. *Crostini* (small toasted bread with a topping) are popular, as are marinated seafood, olives, and prosciutto with melon. Meat and fish (*pesce;* PESH-ay) can be expensive; veggies (*verdure*) are cheap, at about €3 for a meal-sized plate. In many places, there's a set price per food item (e.g., €1.50). To get a plate of assorted appetizers for €8, ask for "*Un piatto classico di cicchetti misti da €8*" (oon pee-AH-toh KLAH-see-koh dee cheh-KET-tee MEE-stee dah OH-toh eh-OO-roh). Bread sticks (*grissini*) are free.

Bar-hopping Venetians enjoy an *aperitivo*—a before-dinner drink. Boldly order a Bellini, a *spritz con Aperol,* or a Prosecco, and draw approving looks from the natives. A small glass of house red or white wine (*ombra rosso or ombra bianco*) or a small beer (*birrino*) costs about €1. *Vin bon,* Venetian for fine wine, is €2-6 per little glass. A good last drink is *fragolino,* the local sweet wine—*bianco* or *rosso*. It often comes with a little cookie (*biscotti*) for dipping.

from the Rialto Market (along Sotoportego dei Do Mori and Calle de le Do Spade), is beloved for its conviviality and tasty bar snacks. These four places (listed in the order you'll reach them, if coming from the Rialto Bridge) serve food all day, but the spread is best around noon (generally open daily 12:00-15:00 & 18:00-20:00 or 21:00, but the first two are closed Sun). Look for the list of snacks (€1.50-2) and wine by the glass (€1-2.50) at the bar or on the wall. Bustling one-room **Bar all'Arco** is known for its tiny open-faced sandwiches (San Polo 436, Francesco, Anna, Matteo). **Cantina Do Mori** has been famous with locals (since 1462) and travelers (since 1982) for fine wine and *francobolli*, a selection of 20 tiny, mayo-soaked sandwiches nicknamed "stamps" (San Polo 430). More of a sit-down place, **Osteria ai Storti** is run by Alessandro, who enjoys educating travelers (€10 pastas, €12-15 *secondi*, daily except closed Sun off-season, around the corner from Cantina Do Mori on Calle San Matio, San Polo 819). **Cantina Do Spade** is expertly run by Francesco and is also good for sit-down meals (30 yards down Calle de le Do Spade from Osteria ai Storti at San Polo 860, tel. 041-521-0583).

Canalside Seating: What I call the "Bancogiro Stretch," just past the Rialto Bridge, between Campo San Giacomo and the Grand Canal, has some of Venice's best canalside seating. Unless otherwise noted, all are open daily and serve drinks, *cicchetti,* and somewhat pricey sit-down meals. While you can get a drink anytime, dinner is typically served only after 19:00 or 19:30. During mealtimes, table seating is limited to those ordering full meals. After dinner, this stretch becomes a trendy nightspot. I list them in the order you'll reach them from the Rialto Bridge. **Bar Naranzaria** serves Italian dishes with a few Japanese options (€14 pastas, €17-24 *secondi*). **Caffè Vergnano** is the cheapest (€2 cover charge, €10-13 salads, pizzas, and pastas). Friendly **Osteria al Pescador** serves local specialties (€14-15 *primi,* €17-22 *secondi,* closed Tue off-season). **Bar Ristorante Bancogiro** has romantic dining upstairs, but no canal views (€17-18 pastas, €22-26 *secondi,* nice €17 cheese plate, closed Mon, tel. 041-523-2061, www.osteria bancogiro.it). Modern **Bar Ancòra** has a piano player during busy times (€13 pastas, €18 *secondi, cicchetti* at the bar).

At the Market: **Al Mercà** (literally "At the Market"), a few steps away and off the canal, is a lively little nook with a happy local crowd, welcoming to tourists. Stand at the bar or in the square—there are no tables and no interior (Mon-Sat 10:00-14:30 & 18:00-21:00, closed Sun, on Campo Cesare Battisti, San Polo 213).

Tourist-friendly **Ristorante Vini da Pinto,** facing the fish market, has a large menu and relaxing outdoor seating (fixed-price, three-course seafood meal €17, grander versions €20-25, €9-14 pastas, €14-28 *secondi,* daily 12:00-22:00, Campo de le Becarie, San Polo 367a, tel. 041-522-4599).

Romantic Canalside Settings

If you want a meal with a canal view, it generally comes with lower quality and/or a higher price. But if you're determined to take home a canalside memory, these places can be great.

Near the Rialto Bridge: The "Bancogiro Stretch" offers fine places to enjoy a drink and/or a snack.

You'll also see tourist-trap eateries lining the Grand Canal just south of the Rialto Bridge. These places usually offer lousy food and aggressive "service." If you really want to eat here, ask if there's a minimum charge before you sit down (most places have one). If you order just a simple pizza or pasta and a drink for €15 total, you can savor the ambience without breaking the bank.

In the Dorsoduro Neighborhood: **Bar Foscarini,** next to the Accademia Bridge, offers decent pizzas overlooking the canal with no cover or service charge. **Terrazza del Casin dei Nobili,** overlooking the wide Giudecca Canal, is nice just before sunset. Both are listed under "In Dorsoduro" eateries.

Farther Inland, off Campo San Aponal: Osteria al Ponte Storto, on a quiet canalside corner a block off the main drag, is worth seeking out for its good-value main dishes and peaceful location (€13-18 daily specials, Tue-Sun 12:00-15:00 & 19:00-21:45, closed Mon, down Calle Bianca from San Aponal Church, San Polo 1278, tel. 041-528-2144).

Near St. Mark's Square

At **Ristorante Antica Sacrestia,** the owner greets you personally. This classic sit-down restaurant serves wonderful €14 pizzas, a humdrum €24 *menù del giorno,* and creative fixed-price meals (€35, €55, or €80), designed to overwhelm you with too much food. You can also order à la carte; try the €22 seafood antipasto (€14-18 pastas and pizzas, €22-35 *secondi,* no cover, Tue-Sun 11:30-15:00 & 18:00-23:00, closed Mon, behind San Zaninovo/ Giovanni Novo Church on Calle Corona, Castello 4463, tel. 041-523-0749).

For a quick meal just steps away from St. Mark's Square, try **"Sandwich Row"**— Calle de le Rasse. The lane is lined with places to get a decent sandwich at an affordable price with a place to sit (most places open daily 7:00-24:00, €1 extra to sit; from the Bridge of Sighs, head down the Riva and take the second lane on the left). **Birreria Forst** serves meaty €3 sandwiches with tasty sauce (daily 9:30-22:00, air-con, Castello 4540, tel. 041-523-0557, Romina). Modern **Bar Verde** offers fun people-watching (big €4-5 sandwiches, splittable €9-10 salads, fresh pastries, at the end of Calle de le Rasse facing Campo Santi Filippo e Giacomo, Castello 4526). Church-run **Ristorante alla Basilica,** just one street behind St. Mark's Basilica, serves €14 fixed-price lunches, often amid noisy school groups (Tue-Sun 11:45-15:00, closed Mon, air-con, Calle dei Albanesi, Castello 4255, tel. 041-522-0524, www. allabasilicavenezia.it).

Rick's Tip: *Though* **you can't legally picnic on St. Mark's Square,** *you're allowed to munch your meal at nearby* **Giardinetti Reali,** *the small park along the waterfront, west of the Piazzetta.*

North of St. Mark's Square

For a marginally less touristy scene, walk a few blocks north to inviting Campo Santa Maria Formosa.

Osteria alle Testiere is my top dining splurge in Venice. Its respected chef, Luca, serves up creative, market-fresh seafood, homemade pastas, and fine wine in "Venetian Nouvelle" style. It's tight and homey, with the focus on food and service. This is a good spot to let loose and trust your host. Make reservations for dinner (€22 pastas, €26 *secondi,* €50 for dinner, lunch 12:30-14:30, dinner seatings 19:00 and 21:30, closed Sun-Mon, on Calle del Mondo Novo, just off Campo Santa Maria Formosa, Castello 5801, tel. 041-522-7220, www.osterialletestiere.it).

Osteria al Mascaron dishes up rustic-yet-sumptuous pastas with steamy seafood to salivating foodies. The pastas (€24-36) are meant for two, but it's OK to ask for a single portion. The €16 *antipasto misto* makes a terrific light meal (€16-19 main dishes, Mon-Sat 11:00-15:00 & 17:30-23:00, closed Sun, reservations smart Fri-Sat, Wi-Fi; on Calle Lunga Santa Maria Formosa, a block past Campo Santa Maria Formosa, Castello 5225; tel. 041-522-5995, www.osteriamascaron.it).

In Dorsoduro

All of these recommendations are within a 10-minute walk of the Accademia Bridge and well worth the walk.

Near the Accademia Bridge

Bar Foscarini, next to the Accademia Bridge and Galleria, offers €10-16 pizzas and *panini.* The food is decent and the drinks pricey, but you're paying for the memorable Grand Canal view. It's best for lunch but also serves breakfast (daily 8:00-23:00, until 20:30 Nov-April, on Rio Terà A. Foscarini, Dorsoduro 878c, tel. 041-522-7281, Paolo and Simone).

Al Vecio Marangon, about 100 yards west of the Accademia, glows like a dream come true, tucked away from the frenzy of Venice. This stylish bar serves *cicchetti* and pastas within its tight and picturesque interior or at a line of outdoor tables. Consider the splittable *piatto di cicchetti misti* (€17). Arrive early or be prepared to wait (daily 12:00-23:00, on Calle de la Toletta, Dorsoduro 1210, tel. 041-523-5768).

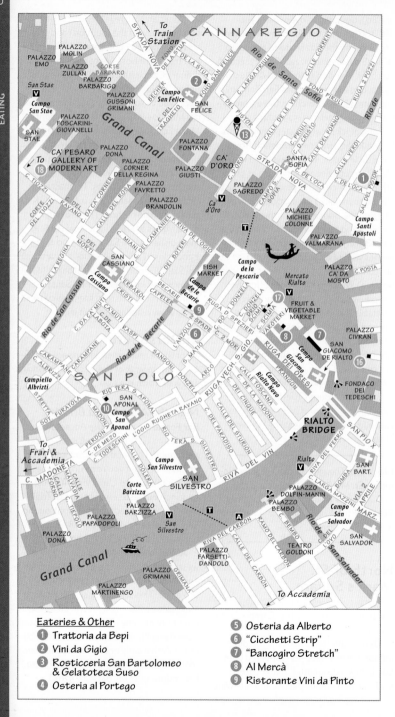

Restaurants & Hotels near the Rialto Bridge

100 Meters
100 Yards

CANNAREGIO

C. VENIER
C. NUOVA
l'Acqua Dolce
C. DEL FORNO
C. DE LA MADONA
To Vaporetto Dock
FONDAMENTE NOVE

C. PROVERBI
PRETI
Campo de la Cason
SANTI APOSTOLI
Rio dei Santi Apostoli
Campo Corner
MAGAZEN
RIO TERA
SALIZADA SAN CANZIAN
SAN GIO. GRIS.
MARCO POLO BOOKSHOP
Rio de San Gio Grisostomo
SAN GRISOSTOMO
ASEO
COIN DEP'T STORE

SAN CANZIAN
C. MAL
Campo San Canzian
Campo Santa Maria Nova
BOLDU
BAGATAN
MIRACOLI
C. WIDMANN
SANTA MARIA DEI MIRACOLI
5
CALLE LARGA GALLINA
C. CASTELI
C. DE LA ERBE
Rio de la Panada
CALLE DE LA TESTA
FONDAMENTA DEI MENDICANTI
Rio dei Mendicanti
HOSPITAL
Campo dei Santi Giovanni e Paolo
F. DANDOLO
COLLEONI STATUE
SANTI GIOVANNI E PAOLO (SAN ZANIPOLO)
SALIZADA S. ZANIPOLO

4
C. SCALETA
FRUTARIOL
C. PIOMBO
Campo Santa Marina
LARGA
Rio del Piombo
MARCELLO
Rio de Santa Marina
C. DEL DOSSO
CASTELLO
15
C. BRESSANA
MADONA
F. FELZI
OSPEDALETO

Campo S. Bartolomeo
WC
3
BISSA
PONTE S. ANTONIO
C. CARMINATI
C. DE
L'AQUILA NERA
C. DEI STAGNERI
C. DE L'AQUILA NERA
Rio de la Fava
SAN LIO
SALIZADA SAN LIO
C. FAVA
DEL PARADISO
VENIERA
FOND. DEI PRETI
Rio d. Pestrin
Campo Santa Maria Formosa
C. LUNGA S. MARIA FORMOSA
ACQUA ALTA BOOKSHOP & PAPIER MACHÉ MASK SHOP
12
C. DEI ORBI

S. SALV.
Campo de la Fava
SANTA MARIA FAVA
POST
MARZ CAPITELLO
S. ZUL.
C. DE ACQUE
RAC. DE MEZO
MARZ
CALLE DE MEZO
To San Marco
R. MALVASIA
C. SAN ANTONIO
MONDO NOVO
11
14
C. DE LE BANDE
SANTA MARIA FORMOSA
Rio de S. M. Formosa
RUGA GIUFFA
C. MEZO
C. DIETRO MAGAZEN
CALLE QUERINI
F. D. REMEDIO
C. DIETRO MAGAZEN
To San Marco

SAN MARCO

---

10 Osteria al Ponte Storto
11 Osteria alle Testiere
12 Osteria al Mascaron
13 Grom Gelateria
14 Co-op Supermarket

Hotels
15 Locanda la Corte
16 Hotel al Ponte Antico
17 Pensione Guerrato
18 To Hotel al Ponte Mocenigo

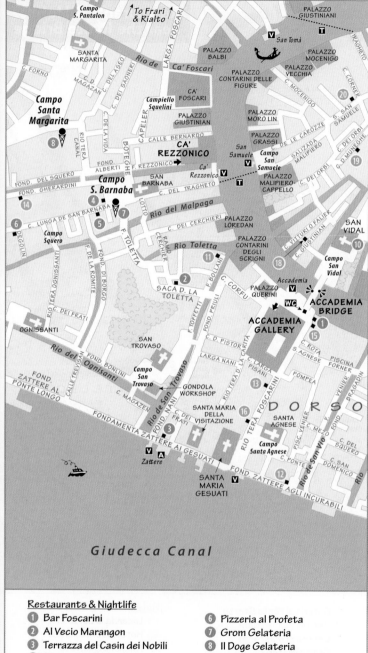

Giudecca Canal

Restaurants & Nightlife

1. Bar Foscarini
2. Al Vecio Marangon
3. Terrazza del Casin dei Nobili
4. Ristoteca Oniga
5. Enoteca e Trattoria la Bitta

6. Pizzeria al Profeta
7. Grom Gelateria
8. Il Doge Gelateria
9. Musica a Palazzo
10. Interpreti Veneziani Concerts

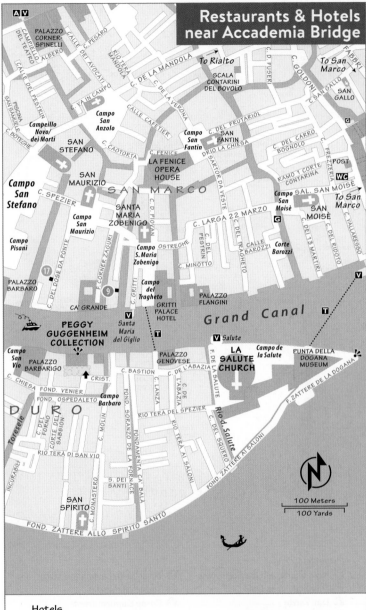

Restaurants & Hotels near Accademia Bridge

Hotels
11 Pensione Accademia
12 Hotel la Calcina
13 Hotel Belle Arti
14 Casa Rezzonico
15 Hotel Galleria
16 Don Orione Religious Guest House
17 Novecento Hotel
18 Foresteria Levi
19 Istituto Ciliota
20 Albergo San Samuele

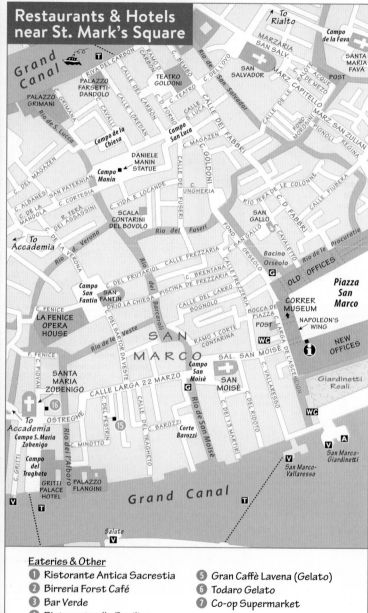

Restaurants & Hotels near St. Mark's Square

Grand Canal

RIVA DEL CARBON

PALAZZO GRIMANI

PALAZZO FARSETTI-DANDOLO

C. GRIMANA

RAMO P. CARBON

C. DEL CARBON

CALLE DEL CARBON

CALLE LOREDAN

CAVALLI

Campo de la Chiesa

C. BEMBO

TEATRO GOLDONI

C. TEATRO

C. FORNO

CALLE S. LUCA

Campo San Luca

Rio del l'Ovo

CALLE DEL SALVADOR

C. DEL SALVADOR

SAN SALVADOR

To Rialto

MARZARIA SAN SALV.

Campo de la Fava

SANTA MARIA FAVÀ

C. LOTE ACQUE

POST

MARZ. CAPITELLO

C. DE LE

CALLE DEI FABBRI

FOND. MOROSINI

MARZ. SAN ZULIAN

PIGNOLI REGINA

C. DEL MAGAZEN

C. MAGAZEN

C. ALBANESI

SAN PATERNIAN

C. DE LA MANDOLA

R. TERA DEI ASSASSINI

C. CORTESIA

C. DE LA VERONA

Campo Manin

DANIELE MANIN STATUE

C. GOLDONI

C. DEI FUSERI

C. VIDA E LOCANDE

C. UNGHERIA

SCALA CONTARINI DEL BOVOLO

Rio del Fuseri

RIO TERA DE LE COLONNE

C. D FABBRI

CALLE FIUBERA

SAN GALLO

To Accademia

RIO D. VERONA

VERONA

Rio d. Verona

Campo San Fantin

SAN FANTIN

C. FENICE

LA FENICE OPERA HOUSE

F. FENICE

C. PIOVAN

SANTA MARIA ZOBENIGO

CALLE FREZZARIA

C. DEL FRUTARIOL

Rio del Barcaroli

C. BRENTANA

PISCINA DE FREZZARIA

DRIO LA CHIESA

CALLE DEL CARRO

CALLE FREZZARIA

BOGNOLO

C. DEL SARTOR DA VESTE

Rio de le Veste

SAN MARCO

RAMO 1 CORTE CONTARINA

SAL. SAN MOISÈ

CALLE LARGA 22 MARZO

OSTREGHE

Rio del l'Alboro

C. DEL PESTRIN

CALLE DEL TRAGHETO

C. MINOTTO

Campo S. Maria Zobenigo

Campo del Traghetto

C. GRITTI

GRITTI PALACE HOTEL

PALAZZO FLANGINI

BOCCA DE PIAZZA

CORRER MUSEUM

POST

NAPOLEON'S WING

WC

Campo San Moisè

SAN MOISÈ

Corte Barozzi

CALLE BAROZZI

Rio de San Moisè

C. DEI 13 MARTIRI

C. DEL RIDOTTO

C. VALLARESSO

SAL. SAN GALLO

FOND. ORSEOLO

Bacino Orseolo

Rio de le Procuratie

OLD OFFICES

Piazza San Marco

NEW OFFICES

Giardinetti Reali

WC

San Marco-Vallaresso

San Marco-Giardinetti

Grand Canal

Salute

To Accademia

C. VALLARESSO

CALLE LARGA DE L'ASCENSION

16

15

Eateries & Other

1. Ristorante Antica Sacrestia
2. Birreria Forst Café
3. Bar Verde
4. Ristorante alla Basilica

5. Gran Caffè Lavena (Gelato)
6. Todaro Gelato
7. Co-op Supermarket

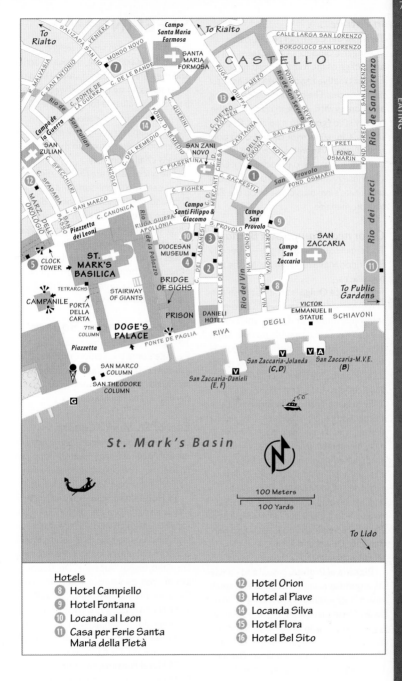

SALIZADA S. LIO
CALLE LARGA SAN LORENZO
BORGOLOCO SAN LORENZO

Campo
Santa Maria
Formosa

To Rialto

CASTELLO

R. MALVASIA
C. SAN ANTONIO
SAN LIO
MONDO NOVO
C. DE LE BANDE

SANTA
MARIA
FORMOSA

RUGA GIUFFA
C. MEZO
FOND. SAN SEVERO
Rio de San Severo
FOND. F. SAN LORENZO
Rio de San Lorenzo

C. PONTE DE
LA GUERRA
Rio de
San Julian

C. QUERINI

C. PIETRO
MAGAZEN

CALLE LARGA S.CASTAGNA
SAL. ZORZI

C. D. PRETI
FOND.
OSMARIN
FOND. GRECI

Campo de
la Guerra

SAN
ZULIAN

FOND. D'REMEDIO

SAN ZANI
NOVO

C. SACRESTIA

San Provolo

FOND. OSMARIN

C. SPECCHIERI
C. DEL REMEDIO
C. PIASENTINA
MERCANTI CHIESA
C. SACRESTIA

San
Provolo

C. SPADARIA
MARZ. DELL'
OROLOGIO
BASSO
S. BASSO
C. CANZOLO
C. FIGHER

Campo
Santi Filippo &
Giacomo

Campo San
Provolo

SAN
ZACCARIA

Rio dei Greci

Piazzetta
dei Leoni

L. SAN MARCO
C. CANONICA
Ruga Giuffa
APOLLONIA
C.D.
Rio de la Palazzo

S. PROVOLO

Campo
San
Zaccaria

CLOCK
TOWER

ST.
MARK'S
BASILICA

DIOCESAN
MUSEUM

C. DEL ALBANESI
CALLE DE LE RASSE

CORTE NUOVA
Rio del Vin

SAN
ZACCARIA

TETRARCHS

STAIRWAY
OF GIANTS

BRIDGE
OF SIGHS

To Public
Gardens

CAMPANILE

PORTA
DELLA
CARTA

PRISON

DANIELI
HOTEL

COL. VIN

VICTOR
EMMANUEL II
STATUE

SCHIAVONI

7TH
COLUMN

DOGE'S
PALACE

PONTE DE PAGLIA

RIVA

DEGLI

Piazzetta

SAN MARCO
COLUMN

SAN THEODORE
COLUMN

San Zaccaria-Jolanda
(C,D)

San Zaccaria-M.V.E.
(B)

San Zaccaria-Danieli
(E, F)

St. Mark's Basin

N

100 Meters

100 Yards

To Lido

Hotels

⑧ Hotel Campiello
⑨ Hotel Fontana
⑩ Locanda al Leon
⑪ Casa per Ferie Santa
   Maria della Pietà

⑫ Hotel Orion
⑬ Hotel al Piave
⑭ Locanda Silva
⑮ Hotel Flora
⑯ Hotel Bel Sito

In Zattere

Terrazza del Casin dei Nobili, overlooking the Giudecca Canal, takes full advantage of the romantic setting sun. Expect creative regional specialties at tolerable prices. The breezy seaside seating also comes with *vaporetti* noise from the nearby stop (good €9-13 pizzas, €14-18 pastas, €16-26 *secondi,* daily 12:00-23:00; from Zattere vaporetto stop, turn left to Dorsoduro 924; tel. 041-520-6895). On Wednesday and Sunday evenings in summer, there's live music nearby on the Zattere promenade.

On or near Campo San Barnaba

This small square is a delight—especially for dinner. Make reservations for the first two places.

Ristoteca Oniga is all about fresh fish and other sea creatures, with a chic-and-shipshape interior and great tables on the square. The accessible menu always includes a vegetarian dish (€12-15 pastas, €18-25 *secondi,* daily 12:00-14:30 & 19:00-22:30, Campo San Barnaba, Dorsoduro 2852, tel. 041-522-4410, www.oniga.it).

Enoteca e Trattoria la Bitta is dark and woody, with a soft-jazz bistro feel, tight seating, and a small back patio. The small daily menu is focused on local ingredients (including rabbit but not fish) and a "slow food" ethic. It serves only dinner, not lunch (€10-11 pastas, €18-27 *secondi,* seatings 19:00 and 21:00, Mon-Sat 18:30-23:00, closed Sun, cash only, just off Campo San Barnaba on Calle Lunga San Barnaba, Dorsoduro 2753a, tel. 041-523-0531).

Pizzeria al Profeta, casual and convivial, is popular for its great pizza and steak, with a large interior and a leafy garden out back (€8-10 pizzas, €11-16 pastas, €15-25 *secondi,* Wed-Mon 12:00-14:30 & 19:00-22:30, closed Tue; from Campo San Barnaba, walk down Calle Lunga San Barnaba; Dorsoduro 2671, tel. 041-523-7466).

SLEEPING

I've listed rooms in several neighborhoods: St. Mark's bustle, the Rialto action, and the quiet Dorsoduro area behind the Accademia. Note that hotel websites are particularly valuable for Venice, because they often include detailed directions that can help you get to your rooms with a minimum of wrong turns in this navigationally challenging city.

The prices listed are for one-night stays in peak season (April-June and Sept-Oct) and assume you're booking directly with the hotel (not through a TI or online hotel-booking engine). Prices can spike during festivals. Almost all places drop prices in July and August, and again from November through March (except during Christmas and Carnevale). A €180 double can cost €80-90 in winter.

Near St. Mark's Square

To get here from the train station or Piazzale Roma bus station, ride the slow vaporetto #1 to San Zaccaria or the fast #2 (which also leaves from Tronchetto parking lot) to San Marco.

East of St. Mark's Square

Located near the Bridge of Sighs, just off the Riva degli Schiavoni waterfront promenade, these places rub drainpipes with Venice's most palatial five-star hotels.

$$ Hotel Campiello, lacy and bright, was once part of a 19th-century convent. Ideally located 50 yards off the waterfront on a tiny square, its 16 rooms offer a comfortable refuge for travelers (Sb-€130, Db-€180, bigger "superior" Db-€200-210, air-con, elevator; just steps from the San Zaccaria vaporetto stop, Castello 4647; tel. 041-520-5764, www.hcampiello.it, campiello@hcampiello.it). They also rent three modern family apartments (the largest sleeps 6 for €380/night).

$$ Hotel Fontana, two bridges behind St. Mark's Square, is a pleasant family-run place with 15 sparse but classic rooms

Sleep Code

Price Rankings for Double Rooms (Db)
$$$ Most rooms €180 or more
$$ €130-180
$ €130 or less

Abbreviations: Db=Double with bathroom. D=Double with bathroom down the hall

    Notes: Hotels charge a room tax of €1.50-6 per person, per night, often payable in cash. Room prices change; verify rates online or by email. For the best prices, book directly with the hotel.

overlooking a lively square. The quieter rooms are on the garden side (Sb-€120, Db-€180, family rooms, 10 percent cash discount, 2 rooms have terraces for €20 extra, air-con, elevator, Wi-Fi in common areas, on Campo San Provolo at Castello 4701, tel. 041-522-0579, www.hotel fontana.it, info@hotelfontana.it).

    $$ Locanda al Leon, which feels like a medieval tower house, is conscientiously run and rents 13 reasonably priced rooms just off Campo Santi Filippo e Giacomo (Db-€170, Db with square view-€190, Tb-€220, Qb-€250; for the best rates, book directly with hotel, pay cash, and show this book; air-con, 2 apartments with kitchens, Campo Santi Filippo e Giacomo, Castello 4270, tel. 041-277-0393, www.hotelalleon.com, leon@hotelalleon.com). Their down-the-street annex, **B&B Marcella,** has three newer, classy, and spacious rooms for the same rates.

    $ Casa per Ferie Santa Maria della Pietà rents 53 beds in 15 rooms just a block off the Riva, with a fabulous lagoon-view roof terrace that rivals more luxurious hotels. It's institutional, with generous public spaces and dorm-style comfort. Shared bathrooms are down the hall (bed in dorm room-€35-50, S-€70-85,

D-€120-135, higher prices are for Fri and Sat, 2-night minimum on weekends in peak season, only twin beds, air-con, 100 yards from San Zaccaria-Pietà vaporetto dock, down Calle de la Pietà from La Pietà Church at Castello 3701, take elevator to third floor, tel. 041-244-3639, www.bed andvenice.it, info@bedandvenice.it).

North of St. Mark's Square

$$ Hotel Orion rents 21 simple, welcoming rooms in the center of the action. Steep stairs (there's no elevator) take you from the touristy street into a peaceful world high above (Db-€130-190, Tb-€160-220, air-con, 2 minutes inland from St. Mark's Square, 10 steps toward St. Mark's from San Zulian Church at Calle Spadaria 700a, tel. 041-522-3053, www. hotelorion.it, info@hotelorion.it).

    $$ Hotel al Piave, with 28 rooms above a bright, tight lobby and breakfast room, is comfortable and cheery in a nice neighborhood (Db-€165, larger "superior" Db-€220, Tb-€220, Qb-€270; family suites-€300 for 4, €330 for 5; lots of narrow stairs, air-con, on Ruga Giuffa at Castello 4838, tel. 041-528-5174, www.hotelal piave.com, info@hotelalpiave.com).

    $$ Locanda Silva is a big, scruffy, but beautifully located hotel with a 1960s feel, renting 23 decent rooms. Some are cheaper, with shared bathrooms (S-€70, Sb-€85, D-€90, D with toilet but shared shower-€100, Db-€150, Tb-€160, Qb-€180, 10 percent off if you stay at least 2 nights, discounts valid only with cash, closed Dec-Jan, air-con, lots of stairs, on Fondamenta del Remedio at Castello 4423, tel. 041-522-7643, www. locandasilva.it, info@locandasilva.it).

Near Campo Santa Maria Formosa

Farther north, the quiet Castello area lies beyond inviting Campo Santa Maria Formosa.

    $$ Locanda la Corte is elegant but not snooty. Its 14 attractive, high-ceilinged rooms border a small, quiet courtyard (standard Db-€150, deluxe Db-€170, suites and family rooms available, air-con, on Calle Bressana at Castello 6317, tel. 041-241-1300, www.locandalacorte.it, info@locandalacorte.it, Marco).

West of St. Mark's Square

These more expensive hotels are solid choices in a more elegant neighborhood.

$$$ Hotel Flora, almost on the Grand Canal, is formal, with uniformed staff and grand public spaces, yet the 40 rooms have a homey warmth. The garden oasis is a sanctuary for weary guests (generally Db-€280, air-con, elevator, family apartment, on Calle Bergamaschi at San Marco 2283a, tel. 041-520-5844, www.hotelflora.it, info@hotelflora.it).

$$$ Hotel Bel Sito offers pleasing Old World character, 34 smallish rooms, generous public spaces, a peaceful courtyard, and a picturesque location—facing a church on a small square between St. Mark's Square and the Accademia (Sb-€110-200, Db-€200-320, "superior" rooms with view cost more, air-con, elevator; near Santa Maria del Giglio vaporetto stop—line #1, on Campo Santa Maria Zobenigo/del Giglio at San Marco 2517, tel. 041-522-3365, www.hotelbelsito venezia.it, info@hotelbelsitovenezia.info).

Near the Rialto Bridge

These places are on opposite sides of the Grand Canal, within a short walk of the Rialto Bridge. Express vaporetto #2 brings you to the Rialto quickly from the train station, the Piazzale Roma bus station, and the parking-lot island of Tronchetto, but you'll need to take the "local" vaporetto #1 to reach the minor stops closer to the last two listings (or take #2 and walk over Rialto Bridge to reach them).

$$$ Hotel al Ponte Antico is exquisite, professional, and small. With nine plush rooms, a velvety royal living/breakfast room, and its own dock for water taxis, it's perfect for a romantic stay. Because its

wonderful terrace overlooks the Grand Canal and Rialto Bridge, its rooms without a canal view may be a better value (Db-€325, "superior" Db-€400, deluxe canal-front Db-€490, air-con, 100 yards from Rialto Bridge at Cannaregio 5768, use Rialto vaporetto stop, tel. 041-241-1944, www.alponteantico.com, info@alponte antico.com).

$$ Pensione Guerrato, right above the colorful Rialto produce market, has 22 spacious, charming rooms in an 800-year-old building. It's simple, airy, and wonderfully characteristic (D-€95, Db-€135, Tb-€155, Qb-€175, Quint/b-€185, air-con; on Calle drio la Scimia at San Polo 240a, take vaporetto #1 to Rialto Mercato stop to save walk over bridge; tel. 041-528-5927, www.pensioneguerrato.it). The Guerrato also rents family apartments in the old center (great for groups of 4-8) for around €60 per person.

$$ Hotel al Ponte Mocenigo is a 10-minute walk northwest of the Rialto Bridge, but it's a great value. This 16th-century Venetian palazzo has a garden terrace and 10 beautifully appointed and tranquil rooms. Take vaporetto #1 to the San Stae stop, head inland along the right side of the church, and take the first left down tiny Calle della Campanile (Sb-€115, Db-€160, "superior" Db-€180, extra bed-€25, air-con, Santa Croce 2063, tel. 041-524-4797, www.alpontemocenigo.com, info@alpontemocenigo.com).

Near the Accademia Bridge

As you step over the Accademia Bridge, touristy Venice is replaced by a sleepy village laced with canals. This quiet area is a 15-minute walk from the Rialto or St. Mark's Square. The fast vaporetto #2 to the Accademia stop is the typical way to get here from the train station, Piazzale Roma bus station, Tronchetto parking lot, or St. Mark's Square (early and late, #2 terminates at the Rialto stop, where you change to #1). For hotels near the Zattere stop, good options are vaporetto #5.1 or the Alilaguna speedboat from the airport.

South of the Accademia Bridge, in Dorsoduro

$$$ **Pensione Accademia** fills the 17th-century Villa Maravege like a Bellini painting, with 27 comfortable, elegant rooms, grand public spaces, and breezy gardens (Sb-€180, standard Db-€300, bigger "superior" Db-€350, Tb-€390, Qb-€430, must pay first night in advance, air-con, no elevator but most rooms on ground floor or one floor up, on Fondamenta Bollani at Dorsoduro 1058, tel. 041-521-0188, www.pensioneaccademia. it, info@pensioneaccademia.it).

$$$ **Hotel la Calcina,** once home to English writer John Ruskin, maintains a 19th-century formality. It comes with three-star comforts in a professional yet intimate package. The peaceful waterside setting faces Giudecca Island (Sb-€165, Sb with view-€190, Db-€280, Db with view-€370, price depends on size, check for discounts online, air-con, no elevator and lots of stairs, rooftop terrace, buffet breakfast outdoors in good weather on platform over lagoon, near Zattere vaporetto stop at south end of Rio de San Vio at Dorsoduro 780, tel. 041-520-6466, www.lacalcina.com, info@lacalcina.com).

$$$ **Hotel Belle Arti** lacks personality but has a grand entry, an inviting garden terrace, and 67 heavily decorated rooms (Sb-€150, Db-€240, Tb-€270, air-con, elevator, 100 yards behind Accademia art museum on Rio Terà A. Foscarini at Dorsoduro 912a, tel. 041-522-6230, www. hotelbellearti.com, info@hotelbellearti. com).

$$ **Casa Rezzonico** is a tranquil getaway with seven inviting rooms, each overlooking the grassy private garden terrace or the canal (Sb-€140, Db-€180, Tb-€210, Qb-€240, air-con, near Ca' Rezzonico vaporetto stop—line #1, a few blocks past Campo San Barnaba on Fondamenta Gherardini at Dorsoduro 2813,

tel. 041-277-0653, www.casarezzonico.it, info@casarezzonico.it).

$$ **Hotel Galleria** has 10 tight, old-fashioned, velvety rooms, most with views of the Grand Canal. Some rooms are quite narrow (S-€95, D-€150, Grand Canal view D-€160, skinny Grand Canal view Db-€180, palatial Grand Canal view Db-€240, breakfast in room, ceiling fans, free mini-bar, 30 yards from Accademia art museum, tel. 041-523-2489, www. hotelgalleria.it, info@hotelgalleria.it).

$$ **Don Orione Religious Guest House** is a big cultural center dedicated to the work of a local man who became a saint in modern times. With 80 rooms filling an old monastery, it feels like a modern retreat center, but is also clean and peaceful. It's a good value supporting a fine cause: Profits go to mission work in the developing world. From the Zattere vaporetto stop, turn right, then turn left. It's just after the church at #909a (Sb-€98, Db-€170, Tb-€220, Qb-€264, groups welcome, air-con, elevator, on Rio Terà A. Foscarini, Dorsoduro 909a, tel. 041-522-4077, www.donorione-venezia.it, info@donorione-venezia.it).

North of the Accademia Bridge

These places are between the Accademia Bridge and St. Mark's Square.

$$$ **Novecento Hotel** rents nine plush rooms on three floors, complemented by a welcoming lounge, a stylish living room, and a small breakfast garden. The decor mingles Art Deco with North African and Turkish accents (Db-€270, bigger "superior" Db/Tb-€290, air-con, lots of stairs, on Calle del Dose, off Campo San Maurizio at San Marco 2683, tel. 041-241-3765, www.novecento.biz, info@novecento.biz).

$$$ **Foresteria Levi,** run by a foundation that promotes research on Venetian music, offers 32 quiet, institutional yet comfortable rooms. The loft quads are a good deal for families. Reserve directly and pay cash to get the best rates (generally around Db-€200, Qb-€250, air-con,

elevator, on Calle Giustinian at San Marco 2893, tel. 041-277-0542, www.foresteria levi.it, info@foresterialevi.it).

$$ Istituto Ciliota is church-owned, efficient, clean, and plainly furnished, with 30 dorm-like rooms and a tranquil garden. With industrial-strength comfort but little character, it's a fine value. During the school year, half the rooms are used by students (Sb–€90, Db–€150, no extra beds possible, cheaper with longer stays, air-con, mini-fridges in each room, elevator, on Calle de le Muneghe just off Campo San Stefano, San Marco 2976, tel. 041-520-4888, www.ciliota.it, info@ ciliota.it).

$$ Albergo San Samuele rents 10 budget rooms in an old *palazzo* near Campo San Stefano. It's in a great locale and the rooms with shared bath are a good deal (S–€80, D–€110, Db–€150, extra bed-€30, no breakfast, fans, on Salizada San Samuele at San Marco 3358, tel. 041-520-5165, www.hotelsansamuele.com, info@hotel sansamuele.com, Judith).

TRANSPORTATION

Getting Around Venice

Narrow pedestrian walkways connect Venice's docks, squares, bridges, and courtyards. To navigate on foot, look for yellow signs on street corners pointing you to (*per*) the nearest major landmark (such as *Per Rialto*). Determine whether your destination is in the direction of a major signposted landmark, then follow the signs through the maze.

Some helpful street terminology: *Campo* means square, a *campiello* is a small square, *calle* (pronounced "KAH-lay" with an "L" sound) means "street," and a *ponte* is a bridge. A *fondamenta* is the embankment along a canal or the lagoon. A *rio terà* is a street that was once a canal and has been filled in. A *sotoportego* is a covered passageway. *Salizzada* literally means a paved area (usually a wide street). The abbreviations S. and S.S.

mean "saint" and "saints," respectively. Don't get hung up on the exact spelling of street and square names, which may sometimes appear in Venetian dialect (which uses *de la, novo,* and *vechio*) and other times in standard Italian (which uses *della, nuovo,* and *vecchio*).

Every building in Venice has a house number. The numbers relate to the district (each with about 6,000 address numbers), not the street. If you need to find a specific address, it helps to know its district, street, house number, and nearby landmarks.

By Vaporetto

These motorized bus-boats run by the public transit system (ACTV) work like city buses except that they never get a flat, the stops are docks, and if you get off between stops, you might drown. You can purchase tickets and passes at docks and from ACTV affiliate VèneziaUnica (ACTV—tel. 041-2424, www.actv.it; VèneziaUnica—www.veneziaunica.com).

TICKETS AND PASSES

Individual Vaporetto Tickets: A single ticket costs €7. Kids age 6 and up pay the same fare as an adult (kids under 6 travel free). Tickets are good for one hour in one direction; you can hop on and off at stops and change boats during that time. Your ticket (a plastic card embedded with a chip) is refillable; put more money on it at the automated kiosks to avoid waiting in line at the ticket window. The fare is reduced to €4 for a few one-stop runs (*corsa semplice*) that are hard to do by foot, including the route from Fondamente Nove to Murano-Colonna, and from San Zaccaria to San Giorgio Maggiore.

Vaporetto Passes: Because a single ticket costs €7, an unlimited-use *vaporetti* pass pays for itself quickly (€20/24 hours, €30/48 hours, €40/72 hours, €60/7-day pass). For example, the 48-hour pass pays for itself after just five rides (for example:

to your hotel on your arrival, on a Grand Canal joyride, into the lagoon and back, and to the train station). Smaller and/or outlying stops, such as Sant'Elena and Biennale, are unstaffed—another good reason to buy a pass. It's fun to be able to hop on and off spontaneously, and avoid long ticket lines. On the other hand, many tourists just walk through Venice and rarely use a boat.

Passes are also valid on some of ACTV's mainland buses, including bus #2 to Mestre (but not the #5 to the airport or the airport buses run by ATVO, a separate company). Passholders get a discounted fare for all ACTV buses that originate or terminate at Marco Polo Airport (€4 one-way, €8 round-trip, must be purchased at the same time as the pass; otherwise, the airport shuttle costs €6 one-way, €11 round-trip).

Travelers between ages 14 and 29 can get a 72-hour pass for €20 if they also buy a **Rolling Venice** discount card for €4 (sold at TIs and VèneziaUnica shops, www.veneziaunica.com).

Buying and Validating Tickets and Passes: Purchase tickets and passes from machines at most stops, from ticket windows at larger stops, or from the VèneziaUnica offices at the train station, bus station, and Tronchetto parking lot.

Before you board, validate your ticket or pass at the small white machine on the dock. If you're unable to purchase a ticket before boarding, seek out the conductor immediately to buy a single ticket (or risk a €52 fine).

IMPORTANT VAPORETTO LINES

For most travelers, only two vaporetto lines matter: line #1 and line #2, which leave every 10 minutes or so and go up and down the Grand Canal, between the "mouth" of the fish at one end and St. Mark's Square at the other. **Line #1** is the slow boat, taking 45 minutes and making every stop along the way. **Line #2** takes 25 minutes, stopping only at Tronchetto (parking lot), Piazzale Roma (bus station),

Ferrovia (train station), Rialto Bridge, San Tomà (Frari Church), San Samuele (opposite Ca' Rezzonico—an easy *traghetto* ride across), Accademia Bridge, and San Marco (west end of St. Mark's Square, end of the line).

Sorting out the different directions of travel can be confusing. Some boats run on circular routes, in one direction only (for example, lines #5.1 and #5.2, plus the non-Murano sections of lines #4.1 and #4.2). Line #2 runs in both directions and is almost, but not quite, a full loop. The #2 boat leaving from the San Marco stop goes in one direction (up the Grand Canal), while from the San Zaccaria stop—just a five-minute walk away—it goes in the opposite direction (around the tail of the "fish"). Make sure you use the correct stop to avoid taking the long way around to your destination.

To clear up any confusion, ask a ticket-seller or conductor on the dock for help. Get a copy of the most current ACTV map and timetable (in English and Italian, theoretically free at ticket booths but usually unavailable—can be downloaded from www.actv.it). System maps are posted at stops, but it's helpful to print out your own copy of the map from the ACTV website before your trip.

BOARDING AND RIDING *VAPORETTI*

Many stops have at least two boarding platforms, and large stops—such as San Marco, San Zaccaria, Rialto, Ferrovia (train station), and Piazzale Roma—have multiple platforms. At these larger stops, electronic boards display which boats are coming next, when, and from which platform they leave; each platform is assigned a letter (clearly marked above the gangway). At smaller stops without electronic displays, signs on each platform show the vaporetto lines that stop there and the direction they are headed. As you board, confirm your destination by looking for an electronic sign on the boat or just asking the conductor.

You may notice some *vaporetti* sporting

Handy Vaporetti *from San Zaccaria, near St. Mark's Square*

Several *vaporetti* leave from the San Zaccaria docks, located 150 yards east of St. Mark's Square. There are four separate San Zaccaria docks spaced about 70 yards apart, with a total of six different berths, lettered A to F: Danieli (E and F), Jolanda (C and D), M.V.E. (B), and Pietà (A). While this may sound confusing, in practice it's simple: Check the big electronic board (next to the Jolanda C/D dock), which indicates the departure time, line number, destination, and berth letter of upcoming *vaporetti*. Once you've figured out which boat you want, go to that letter berth and hop on. They're all within about a five-minute stroll of each other.

- **Line #1** goes up the Grand Canal, making all the stops, including San Marco, Rialto, Ferrovia (train station), and Piazzale Roma (but it does not go as far as Tronchetto). In the other direction, it goes from San Zaccaria to Arsenale and Giardini before ending on the Lido.
- **Line #2** zips over to San Giorgio Maggiore, the island church across from St. Mark's Square (5 minutes, €4 ride). From there, it continues on to stops on the island of Giudecca, the parking lot at Tronchetto, and then down the Grand Canal. Note: You cannot ride the #2 up the Grand Canal (for example, to Rialto or the train station) directly from this stop—you'll need to walk five minutes along the waterfront, past St. Mark's Square, to the San Marco-Giardinetti dock and hop on the #2 there.
- **Line #4.1** goes to San Michele and Murano in 45 minutes.
- **Line #7** is the summertime express boat to Murano (25 minutes).
- The **Molino Stucky shuttle boat** takes even nonguests to the Hilton Hotel, with its popular view bar (free, 20-minute ride, leaves at 0:20 past the hour from near the San Zaccaria-M.V.E. dock).
- **Lines #5.1** and **#5.2** are the *circulare* (cheer-koo-LAH-ray), making a loop around the perimeter of the island, with a stop at the Lido—perfect if you just like riding boats. Line #5.1 goes counterclockwise, and #5.2 goes clockwise.
- The **Alilaguna** shuttle to and from the airport stops here as well.

a *corsa bis* sign, indicating that they're running a shortened or altered route, and that riders may have to hop off partway (e.g., at Rialto) and wait for the next boat. If you see a *corsa bis* sign, before boarding ask the conductor whether the boat is going to your desired destination (e.g., "San Marco?").

By Traghetto
Only four bridges cross the Grand Canal, but *traghetti* (shuttle gondolas) ferry locals and in-the-know tourists across the Grand

Canal at seven handy locations. Just step in, hand the gondolier €2, and enjoy the

ride—standing or sitting. Note that some *traghetti* are seasonal, some stop running as early as 12:30, and all stop by 18:00. *Traghetti* are not covered by any transit pass.

By Water Taxi

Venetian taxis, like speedboat limos, hang out at busy points along the Grand Canal. Prices are regulated: €15 for pickup, then €2 per minute; €5 per person for more than four passengers; and €10 between 22:00 and 6:00. If you have more bags than passengers, the extra ones cost €3 apiece. Despite regulation, prices can be soft; negotiate and settle on the price or rate before stepping in. For travelers with lots of luggage or small groups who can split the cost, taxi boat rides can be a time-saving convenience—and a cool indulgence. For a little more than €100 an hour, you can have a private, unguided taxi-boat tour. You may find more competitive rates if you prebook through the Consorzio Motoscafi water taxi association (tel. 041-522-2303, www. motoscafivenezia.it).

Arriving and Departing

A two-mile-long causeway (with highway and train lines) connects the island to Mestre, the sprawling mainland section of Venice. Don't stop in Mestre unless you're changing trains or parking your car.

Marco Polo Airport

Venice's small, modern airport is on the mainland shore of the lagoon, six miles north of the city (airport code: VCE). There's one sleek terminal, with a TI (daily 9:00-20:00), car-rental agencies, ATMs, a bank, and a few shops and eateries. For flight info, call 041-260-9260, visit www. veniceairport.com, or ask your hotelier.

Treviso Airport is the next-closest airport.

GETTING BETWEEN MARCO POLO AIRPORT AND VENICE

There are several good options (including by boat) to get from the airport to Venice.

Form of Transport	Speed	Cost
Alilaguna boat	Slow	Moderate
Water taxi	Fast	Expensive
Airport bus to Piazzale Roma	Medium	Cheap
Land taxi to Piazzale Roma	Medium	Moderate

An advantage of the Alilaguna boats and water taxis is that you can reach my recommended hotels very simply, with no changes. Both kinds of boats leave from the airport's boat dock, an eight-minute walk from the terminal. Exit the arrivals hall and turn left, following signs along a paved, level, covered sidewalk.

When flying out of Venice, plan to arrive at the airport two hours before your flight, and remember that just getting there can easily take up to two hours. Water transport can be slow, and small Alilaguna boats fill up quickly. In an emergency, hop in a water taxi and get to the airport in 30 minutes.

ALILAGUNA AIRPORT BOATS

These boats make the slow, scenic journey across the lagoon, shuttling passengers between the airport and a number of different stops on the island of Venice (€15, €27 round-trip, €1 surcharge if bought on boat, €1-2 less if bought online, includes 1 suitcase and 1 piece of hand luggage, additional bags–€3 each, roughly 2/hour, 1-1.5-hour trip depending on destination). Alilaguna boats are not part of the ACTV vaporetto system, so they aren't covered by city transit passes. But they do use the same docks and ticket windows as the regular *vaporetti*. You can buy tickets for Alilaguna online at www.venicelink.com.

The two key Alilaguna lines—blue and orange—take about the same amount of time to reach St. Mark's Square. From the airport, the **blue line** (*linea blu*) heads first to Fondamente Nove (on the "back" of Venice's fish, 40 minutes), then loops around the "tail" of the fish to San Zaccaria and San Marco (about 1.5 hours) before continuing on to Zattere and the cruise terminal (almost 2 hours). The **orange line** (*linea arancio*) runs down the Grand Canal, reaching Guglie (45 minutes), Rialto (1 hour), and San Marco (1.5 hours). In high season, the **red line** takes you to St. Mark's in one hour with fewer stops. It circumnavigates Murano and then runs parallel to the blue line, ending at Giudecca Zitelle (hourly, from the airport 9:40-18:40, from Zitelle to the airport 8:10-18:10). For a full schedule, visit the TI, see the website (www.alilaguna.it), call 041-240-1701, ask your hotelier, or scan the schedules posted at the docks.

From the Airport to Venice: You can buy Alilaguna tickets at the airport's TI, the ticket desk in the terminal, and at the ticket booth at the dock. Any ticket seller can tell you which line you need. Boats from the airport run roughly twice an hour (blue line from 6:15, orange line from 8:15, both run until about midnight).

From Venice to the Airport: Ask your hotelier which dock and which line is best. Blue line boats leave Venice as early as 3:50 in the morning for passengers with early flights. Scope out the dock and buy tickets in advance to avoid last-minute stress.

WATER TAXIS

Luxury taxi speedboats zip directly between the airport and the closest dock to your hotel, getting you to within steps of your final destination in about 30 minutes. The official price is €110 for up to four people; add €10 for every extra person (10-passenger limit). You may get a higher quote—politely talk it down. A taxi can be a smart investment for small groups and those with an early departure.

From the airport, arrange your ride at the water-taxi desk or with the boat captains lounging at the dock. From Venice, book your taxi trip the day before you leave. Your hotel will help (since they get a commission), or you can book directly with the Consorzio Motoscafi water taxi association (tel. 041-522-2303, www.motoscafivenezia.it).

AIRPORT SHUTTLE BUSES

Buses between the airport and Venice are fast, frequent, and cheap. They take you across the bridge from the mainland to the island, dropping you at Venice's bus station, at the "mouth" of the fish on a square called Piazzale Roma. From there, you can catch a vaporetto down the Grand Canal—convenient for hotels near the Rialto Bridge and St. Mark's Square.

Two bus companies run between Piazzale Roma and the airport: ACTV and ATVO. ATVO buses go nonstop and take 20 minutes. ACTV buses make a few stops en route and take 30 minutes. ACTV offers a discounted fare if you also buy a vaporetto pass (€4 one-way, €8 round-trip). The service is equally good (either bus: €6 one-way, €11 round-trip, runs about 5:00-24:00, 2/hour, drops to 1/hour early and late, check schedules at www.atvo.it or www.actv.it).

From the Airport to Venice: Both buses leave from just outside the arrivals terminal. Buy tickets from the TI, the ticket desk in the terminal, the kiosk near baggage claim, or ticket machines. ATVO tickets are not valid on ACTV buses and vice versa. Double-check the destination; you want Piazzale Roma. If taking ACTV, you want bus #5.

From Venice to the Airport: At Piazzale Roma, buy your ticket from the ACTV windows (in the building by the bridge) or the ATVO office (at #497g) before heading out to the platforms. The newsstand in the center of the lot also sells tickets.

LAND TAXI OR PRIVATE MINIVAN

It takes about 20 minutes to drive from the airport to Piazzale Roma or the cruise port. A **land taxi** can do the trip for about €40. To reserve a private minivan, contact **Treviso Car Service** (minivan-€55, seats up to 8; car–€50, seats up to 3; mobile 348-900-0700 or 333-411-2840, www.trevisocarservice.com, tvcarservice@gmail.com).

By Train

All trains to "Venice" stop at Venezia Mestre (on the mainland). Most continue on to **Santa Lucia Station** (a.k.a. Venezia S.L.) on the island of Venice itself. If your train happens to terminate at Mestre, you'll need to buy a Mestre-Santa Lucia ticket at a machine for €1.25 and validate it before hopping any nonexpress, regional train (with an R or RV prefix) for the ride across the causeway to Venice (6/hour, 10 minutes).

Santa Lucia train station is right on the Grand Canal, an easy vaporetto ride or fascinating 45-minute walk to St. Mark's Square. In high season, you'll find an info/ticket stand run by transport companies in a white kiosk out front, next to the dock for vaporetto #2. The station has a **TI desk** and **baggage check** (daily 6:00-23:00, no lockers, along track 1). Pay **WCs** are at track 1.

Before heading into town, confirm your departure plan (use the ticket machines or study the *partenze*/departures posters on walls). Minimize your time in the station—the banks of user-friendly ticket machines take euros and credit cards, display schedules, and issue tickets. There are two train companies: **Trenitalia,** with most connections, has green-and-white machines (toll tel. 892-021, www.trenitalia.it); the red machines are for the high-speed **Italo** service (no rail passes accepted, cheaper in advance, tel. 06-0708, www.italotreno.it). **Ticket offices** for both Trenitalia and Italo are in the corner, near track 14. If you need international tickets or live help, head to the ticket windows (Trenitalia open 6:00-21:00; Italo open 8:15-20:10). Or take care of these tasks online or at a downtown travel agency (€5/ticket fee).

Getting from the Train Station to Downtown: Walk straight out of the station to the canal. You'll see vaporetto docks and ticket booths on both sides. The electronic signs show which boats are leaving when and from which platform. The slow boat down the Grand Canal is #1. The fast boat is #2; make sure that "Rialto" is among the destinations listed. If you're staying in the Dorsoduro neighborhood near the Zattere stop, take vaporetto #5.1. A water taxi from the train station to central Venice costs about €60-70 (the taxi dock is straight ahead).

TRAIN CONNECTIONS

Note that the departures listed below are operated by Trenitalia; a competing private rail company called Italo offers additional high-speed connections to major Italian cities including **Bologna, Florence,** and **Rome** but doesn't accept rail passes (visit www.italotreno.it).

From Venice by Train to: Padua (2/hour, 25-50 minutes); **Verona** (2/hour, 1.5-2.5 hours); **Bolzano/Dolomites** (to Bolzano about hourly, 3-3.5 hours, transfer in Verona; catch bus from Bolzano into mountains); **Milan** (2/hour, most direct on high-speed ES trains, 2.5 hours); **Cinque Terre/Monterosso** (5/day, 6 hours, change in Milan); **Florence** (hourly, 2-3 hours, often crowded so make reservations); **Rome** (roughly hourly, 3.5 hours, overnight possible); **Naples** (almost hourly, 5.5-7 hours with changes in Bologna or Rome).

By Car

The freeway dead-ends after crossing the causeway to Venice (drive under the speed limit or you'll get a ticket thanks to the speed cameras). At the end of the road you have two parking choices: garages at Tronchetto or Piazzale Roma.

The **Tronchetto garage** is much bigger, farther out, cheaper, and well-connected by vaporetto (€3-5/hour, €21/24 hours, discounts for longer stays, tel. 041-520-7555, www.veniceparking.it).

Switzerland

Mountainous, efficient Switzerland is one of Europe's most appealing destinations. A tiny country (about twice the size of New Jersey), it's wedged neatly between Germany, Austria, France, and Italy.

Switzerland melds the best of all worlds—and adds a healthy dose of chocolate, cowbells, and cable cars. Fiercely independent and decidedly high-tech, the Swiss (at 8 million strong) stubbornly hold on to their quaint traditions, too. Join cheesemakers in a high valley, try to call the shepherds on an alphorn, and hike through some of the world's most stunning mountain scenery to find the perfect perch for a picnic.

CUISINE SCENE AT A GLANCE

The Swiss eat when we do and enjoy a straightforward, no-nonsense cuisine. Specialties include delicious fondue, a melted cheese dish called raclette, *Rösti* (hash browns), and 100 varieties of cheese.

The exorbitant prices at Swiss restaurants are up to double what you'd pay in neighboring Germany. If you're on a budget, think of restaurants as a luxury for special occasions, and self-service cafeterias and supermarkets as everyday options (covered below).

At **restaurants,** the cheapest main courses start at just under 20 SF—typically starchy dishes topped with meat or cheese (pasta, pizza, and potato dishes) or sausages with kraut or potato salad. Meat courses (served with a starch and vegetable) will run you from 25-45 SF at an average restaurant. Many, but not all, restaurants offer a daily special—a main course for about 20 SF (at least Mon-Fri at lunch, sometimes weekends and evenings, too). High-priced drinks quickly run up the cost of a meal.

Different kinds of restaurants offer different experiences. Hotels often serve fine food. A *Gaststätte* is a simple, less expensive restaurant. A *Weinstübli* (wine bar) or *Bierstübli* (tavern) usually serves food.

Most restaurants tack a menu onto their door for browsers and have an English menu inside. If you're not too hungry, order from the *kleine Hunger* (small hunger) section of the menu. Many restaurants offer half-portions, which is a great relief on your budget (although two people save even more by sharing one full portion).

Tipping: If you buy your food at a counter, don't tip. Service is included at restaurants with table service, but it's customary to round up the bill (no more than 5-10 percent; for a 19-SF meal, pay 20 SF). Give the tip directly to your server. Rather than leaving coins on the table, the Swiss usually pay with paper, saying how much they'd like the bill to be (for example, for an 8.10-SF meal, give a 20-SF bill and say *"Neun Franken"*—"Nine francs"—to get 11 SF change). Rounding up isn't required, though, and no one will come running after you if you don't.

Budget Options: Grocery stores, such as the midrange Migros and Co-op, are the hungry hiker's best budget bet. The larger stores have a great selection of prepared foods and picnic fixings. These include a variety of salads (green, potato, pasta, or meat), hard-boiled eggs, sandwiches, cheese, single portions of cake and ice cream, chocolate bars, and sometimes a hot-meal counter. By law, most supermarkets are required to close on Sunday, with a few exceptions, such as stores in train stations.

Self-service cafeterias have good food at much lower prices than restaurants. You'll find them in bigger cities, usually at downtown branches of Co-op, Migros, and Manor supermarkets. While cafeteria food may not be inventive, it is typical, fresh, and high-quality.

Tempting bakeries sell sandwiches, quiches, and pastries—enough to make a filling meal.

Swiss Alps:
The Berner Oberland

Head into the Alps to hike high above the clouds and the stress of the real world. This is just the place to recharge your touristic batteries and take a vacation from your busy vacation. The crunchy footsteps of happy hikers, the whistle of marmots, the clang of cowbells, and the fluff of down comforters are the dominant sounds.

Your gateway to the rugged Berner Oberland, the mountainous part of the canton of Bern, is the grand old resort town of Interlaken, a transportation hub. Use it as a springboard for alpine thrills.

Head deep into the heart of the Alps by train and cable car, riding to stops just this side of heaven—the villages in the Lauterbrunnen Valley. The cliff-hangers are Gimmelwald, Mürren, and Wengen, while Lauterbrunnen is on the valley floor. Use any of these as a base to explore alpine whitecaps at higher elevations, including the 9,748-foot Schilthorn peak.

What are you waiting for? The sun's coming out and the Alps beckon.

THE SWISS ALPS IN 2 DAYS

If the weather's decent, explore the two areas that tower above either side of the Lauterbrunnen Valley: On one side is the summit of Jungfrau (and beneath it, the tiny settlement of Kleine Scheidegg and touristy Wengen). On the other side is the summit of the Schilthorn, overlooking the villages of petite Gimmelwald and resorty Mürren.

Ideally, spend three nights in the region, with a day exploring each side of the valley. On one day, you could zip up to the Schilthorn in the morning for panoramic views, then tackle a hike or two (on the Schilthorn side) in the afternoon.

On the other day, explore the Jung-

frau side. My favorite hike is the gentle downhill trail from Männlichen to Kleine Scheidegg, facing a panoramic mountain view the entire way. From there, you could take a pricey train up up up to the Jungfraujoch (for the highest viewpoint in the region), or simply train (or hike) down to Wengen (which is connected by train to Lauterbrunnen).

With another day, you could take more hikes, explore all the towns, or even relax.

For a summary of the wildly scenic activities this region has to offer—from cogwheel train rides and sky-high lifts to spectacular hikes and mountain biking—read "Exploring the Alps" on page 768.

Home Bases: Figuring out what you want to do will help you choose the best home base. For accommodations without the expense and headache of mountain lifts, consider the valley-floor village of Lauterbrunnen. But for alpine wonder, stay on a scenic ridge high above the valley. The rustic hamlet of Gimmelwald and the resort town of Mürren are both on the cable-car route to the Schilthorn. Wengen, perched on the opposite side of the valley, has the lift to Männlichen (for the great Männlichen to Kleine Scheidegg hike) and is on the train route to Kleine Scheidegg, departure point for the Jungfraujoch train.

No matter where you stay, good hiking opportunities abound, but keep in mind that higher-altitude trails (such as Männlichen to Kleine Scheidegg) are best from June through October, and can be covered with snow off-season.

Rick's Tip: *In* **bad weather,** *take a low-altitude hike (see recommendations on page 773), hang out at Mürren's Sportzentrum (sauna, steam bath, pool), visit the Lauterbrunnen Valley Folk Museum, or tour the Swiss Open-Air Museum at Ballenberg.*

Weather: Let your plans flex with the weather. The highest-altitude lifts are very expensive, and it only makes sense to splurge if you have a good chance of seeing an alpine panorama (usually clearest early in the morning) instead of fog or clouds. If the weather is good—go! Ask at your hotel or the TI for the latest info or check www.jungfrau.ch or www.schilthorn.ch. Webcams showing live video from the famous (and most expensive-to-reach) peaks play just about wherever you go in the area.

INTERLAKEN

When the 19th-century Romantics redefined mountains as something more than cold and troublesome obstacles, Interlaken became the original alpine resort. Ever since, tourists have flocked to the Alps "because they're there." Interlaken's glory days are over, its elegant old hotels eclipsed by newer, swankier alpine resorts. Today, it's an alpine gateway (rated ▲), with shops filled with chocolate bars, Swiss Army knives, and sunburned backpackers.

Interlaken (pop. 5,500) is a good administrative and shopping center. Take care of business, give the town a quick look...then head for the hills.

Orientation

Interlaken straddles a river that connects two alpine lakes: Lake Brienz and Lake Thun. The older part of town (called Unterseen) is on the right bank of the Aare River and has a cute village square. The newer section (Interlaken proper), with most services and both train stations, is on the river's left bank.

Tourist Information: A small TI operates at the **Interlaken Ost train station** in summer and is convenient if you're arriving there (June-Sept Mon-Fri 8:00-12:00 & 13:30-18:00, Sat 9:00-12:00, closed Sun and Oct-May).

Otherwise, visit the **main TI,** located under the 18-story skyscraper on the main street between the town's two train stations; it's a 10-minute stroll from either (generally Mon-Fri 8:00-18:00, Sat 8:00-16:00, closed Sun except July-Aug 10:00-16:00, off-season closed during weekday lunch hour, Höheweg 37, tel. 033-826-5300, www.interlaken.ch). Pick up the timetable and the hiking guide published by the Jungfraubahn mountain railway (both include a good map of the area);

Rustic Gimmelwald

Towns, Villages, and Resorts

▲▲▲**Gimmelwald** Wonderfully rustic time-warp, cliff-hanging village—and fine home base—overlooking the Lauterbrunnen Valley from the Schilthorn side. See page 755.

▲▲**Mürren** Pleasant resort town near Gimmelwald, midway up the Schilthorn cable-car line; a good high-mountain home base for those who want more amenities than little Gimmelwald offers. See page 761.

▲▲**Kleine Scheidegg** Small resort area with breathtaking views of Eiger, Mönch, and Jungfrau peaks; several hotels and restaurants (see page 767); and train station for pricey ride to the high-altitude Jungfraujoch (see page 770).

▲**Lauterbrunnen** Small town and transit hub in the middle of the Lauterbrunnen Valley. From here, a cable car goes up to Grütschalp (with connections to Mürren and Gimmelwald), a cogwheel train runs up to Wengen and Kleine Scheidegg, and the PostBus goes to Stechelberg (near the Schilthornbahn lift). See page 750.

▲**Interlaken** Big town between Lake Brienz and Lake Thun, at the "entrance" to the Berner Oberland. See page 741.

▲**Wengen** Touristy, cliff-hanging resort town, with lift up to Männlichen for views and hikes; on the train route from Lauterbrunnen to Kleine Scheidegg. See page 767.

Top Lifts and Trains

▲▲▲**Schilthornbahn** Cable car soaring from Stechelberg in the Lauterbrunnen Valley to the 9,748-foot Schilthorn peak, with Piz Gloria revolving restaurant, James Bond exhibit, and stupendous views. Stops at Gimmelwald, Mürren, and Birg along the way. See page 768.

▲▲▲**Jungfraubahn** Train running from Kleine Scheidegg station and through tunnel inside Eiger and Mönch mountainsides to 11,333-foot Jungfraujoch saddle, with observation deck, restaurants, tip-top views, and snow activities. See page 770.

Walks and Hikes

▲▲▲**Männlichen to Kleine Scheidegg** Easy, mostly downhill ridge hike from cable-car station at Männlichen to Kleine Scheidegg, with spectacular views of Eiger and more. See page 776.

▲▲**Cloudy-Day Lauterbrunnen Valley Walk** Pleasant, level, easy walk along valley floor, plus short trail to Staubbach Falls at upper end of town—good bad-weather options. See page 773.

▲▲**North Face Trail** Easy, view-filled hike from the top of Allmendhubel funicular to the villages of Mürren and Gimmelwald, passing farms with food service, mountain huts, and meadows. See page 773.

▲▲**Birg to Gimmelwald via Bryndli** High, scenic, difficult hike from Birg cable-car station below Schilthorn summit down to Gimmelwald. Trail winds past knobby summit of Bryndli, with nonstop views. See page 778.

▲▲**Schynige Platte to First** Demanding ridge walk from Schynige Platte train station to gondola station at First, with fabulous views of Jungfrau-area peaks and Lake Brienz. See page 779.

▲**Allmendhubel to Grütschalp** Fairly easy walk from Allmendhubel down to Grütschalp, with views of the Jungfrau (from Mürren, take the funicular to Allmendhubel, then hike to Grütschalp). See page 776.

More Sightseeing Options

▲▲**Ballenberg** Open-air folk museum near Interlaken, on Lake Brienz. See page 744.

▲**Trümmelbach Falls** Lauterbrunnen Valley's most powerful falls, accessed via elevator ride up into the mountain and dramatic walk through several wet caves. See page 752.

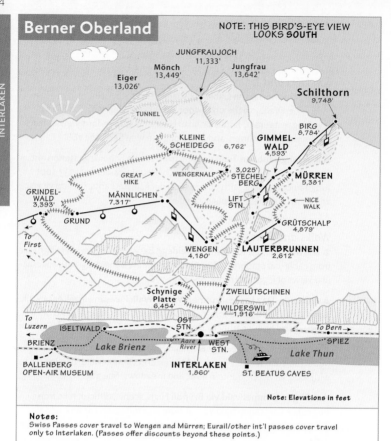

Berner Oberland

NOTE: THIS BIRD'S-EYE VIEW
LOOKS **SOUTH**

JUNGFRAUJOCH
11,333'

Mönch
13,449'

Jungfrau
13,642'

Eiger
13,026'

Schilthorn
9,748'

TUNNEL

BIRG
8,784'

KLEINE
SCHEIDEGG 6,762'

GIMMEL-
WALD
4,593'

GREAT
HIKE

WENGERNALP

3,025'
STECHEL-
BERG

MÜRREN
5,381'

GRINDEL-
WALD
3,393'

MÄNNLICHEN
7,317'

LIFT
STN.

NICE
WALK

GRUND

GRÜTSCHALP
4,879'

To
First

WENGEN
4,180'

LAUTERBRUNNEN
2,612'

Schynige
Platte
6,454'

ZWEILÜTSCHINEN

WILDERSWIL
1,916'

To
Luzern

ISELTWALD.

OST
STN.

To Bern

BRIENZ

Lake Brienz

Aare
River

WEST
STN.

SPIEZ

Lake Thun

BALLENBERG
OPEN-AIR MUSEUM

INTERLAKEN
1,860'

ST. BEATUS CAVES

Note: Elevations in feet

Notes:
Swiss Passes cover travel to Wengen and Mürren; Eurail/other int'l passes cover travel
only to Interlaken. (Passes offer discounts beyond these points.)

and the *Here & Now* monthly entertainment guide. The TI also sells tickets for the Swiss rail system and books adventure sports. If you're planning to visit Kleine Scheidegg resort, the Jungfraujoch, or other destinations served by the Jungfraubahn train, you'll find their ticket counter inside the TI, too.

Rick's Tip: *On **Sundays and holidays,** hotels are open and lifts and trains run, but many stores are closed. At higher altitudes many hotels, restaurants, and shops **close off-season:** from **late April until late May,** and again **from mid-October to early December.***

Sights

▲▲SWISS OPEN-AIR MUSEUM AT BALLENBERG

Near Interlaken, at the far end of Lake Brienz, is this rich collection of more than 100 traditional and historic buildings, brought here from every region of the country. All the houses are carefully furnished and many feature traditional craftspeople at work. The sprawling 50-acre park, laid out roughly as a huge Swiss map (Italian Swiss in the south, Appenzell in the east, and so on), is a natural preserve providing a wonderful setting for this culture-on-a-lazy-Susan look at Switzerland.

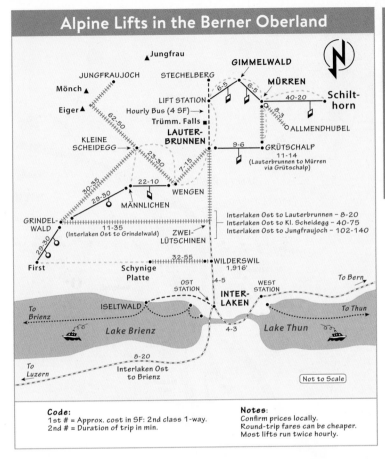

Alpine Lifts in the Berner Oberland

▲ Jungfrau

JUNGFRAUJOCH   STECHELBERG   **GIMMELWALD**

Mönch ▲   **MÜRREN**

LIFT STATION   6-5   6-5   40-20   **Schilt-horn**

Eiger ▲   Hourly Bus (4 SF)→   8-3

62-50   Trümm. Falls ■   **LAUTER-BRUNNEN**   ○ ALLMENDHUBEL

KLEINE   23-30   9-6   GRÜTSCHALP
SCHEIDEGG →   11-14
(Lauterbrunnen to Mürren
via Grütschalp)

30-35   7-15

29-30   22-10   WENGEN

MÄNNLICHEN   Interlaken Ost to Lauterbrunnen – 8-20
Interlaken Ost to Kl. Scheidegg – 40-75
Interlaken Ost to Jungfraujoch – 102-140

GRINDEL-
WALD   11-35   ZWEI-
(Interlaken Ost to Grindelwald)   LÜTSCHINEN

29-30

First   32-55   WILDERSWIL
1,916'

Schynige
Platte   OST   4-5   WEST
STATION   STATION   To Bern →

ISELTWALD   **INTER-LAKEN**

To
Brienz   *Lake Brienz*   4-3   *Lake Thun*   To Thun →

8-20

To
Luzern   Interlaken Ost
to Brienz   Not to Scale

Code:
1st # = Approx. cost in SF: 2nd class 1-way.
2nd # = Duration of trip in min.

Notes:
Confirm prices locally.
Round-trip fares can be cheaper.
Most lifts run twice hourly.

Ballenberg has entrances at either end (east and west, about a mile apart). Pick up a daily craft demonstration schedule at the entry, and buy the 2-SF map/guide so you'll know where you are. There are daily events and demonstrations (near the east entry), hundreds of traditional farm animals (like furry-legged roosters, near the merry-go-round in the center), and a chocolate shop (under the restaurant on the east side). The farmhouse from Uesslingen (#621) has an interesting display of wattle-and-daub (half-timbered) construction, and house #331 has a fun farmers' shop.

An outdoor cafeteria with reasonable prices is inside the west entrance, and fresh bread, sausage, mountain cheese, and other goodies are on sale in several houses. Picnic tables and grills with free firewood are scattered throughout the park.

Outside the park, the little village of **Brienzwiler** (near the east entrance) is practically a museum of its own, with wooden architecture and a lovely pint-size church.

Cost and Hours: 22 SF, covered by Swiss Travel Pass (see page 781); houses open daily mid-April-Oct 10:00-17:00, grounds and restaurants 9:00-18:00; tel. 033-952-1030, www.ballenberg.ch.

Interlaken

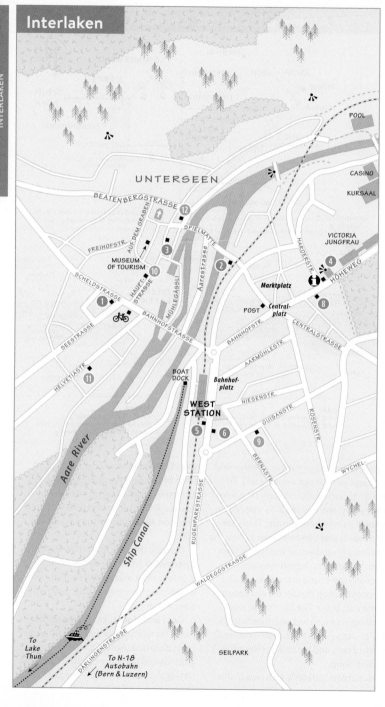

POOL

CASINO

KURSAAL

UNTERSEEN

BEATENBERGSTRASSE

SPIELMATTE

VICTORIA
JUNGFRAU

FREIHOFSTR.

AUF DEM GRABEN

12

3

HARDERSTR.

Höheweg

MUSEUM
OF TOURISM

10

Aarestrasse

2

4

Marktplatz

SCHELDSTRASSE

HAUPT-
STRASSE

MÜHLEGÄSSLI

POST

Central-
platz

8

1

BAHNHOFSTRASSE

CENTRALSTRASSE

SEESTRASSE

BAHNHOFSTR.

AARMÜHLESTR.

HELVETIASTR.

11

BOAT
DOCK

Bahnhof-
platz

NIESENSTR.

GUISANSTR.

ROSENSTR.

WEST
STATION

5

6

9

BERNSTR.

WYCHEL

Aare River

Ship Canal

RÜGENPARKSTRASSE

WALDEGGSTRASSE

SEILPARK

To
Lake
Thun

DÄRLINGENSTRASSE

To N-18
Autobahn
(Bern & Luzern)

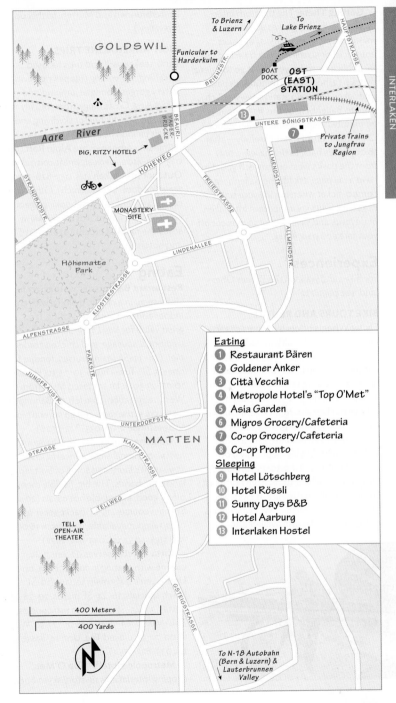

Getting There: The trip from Interlaken to Ballenberg takes about 20 minutes by car (pay parking at either entrance) or 50 minutes by train and bus. By public transport, you'll first go to Brienz by train (2/hour, 15-20 minutes, depart Interlaken Ost train station; www.rail.ch), then to Ballenberg by bus #151 (hourly, 20 minutes, departs Brienz train station). Check bus return times carefully—after 18:00, buses back to Brienz leave only from the park's west entrance. If you don't have a rail pass, ask for the Ballenberg combo-ticket when buying your train ticket: It covers your trip from Interlaken or beyond, and saves about 10 percent off your fare and park entry.

Experiences

For hikes and walks in the Berner Oberland, see page 772.

BIKE TOURS AND RENTAL

Flying Wheels offers bike tours of varying length and difficulty, including a three-hour Interlaken-only tour (99 SF) and a tour of the Lauterbrunnen Valley up to Stechelberg (159 SF, 6 hours) that includes a picnic and Trümmelbach Falls visit. They also rent bikes, including electric bikes (bikes-35 SF/day, electric bikes-50 SF/day, tandem bikes available, includes helmet; May-Sept daily 9:00-20:00, April and Oct 9:30-18:30, closed Nov-March, across street from northeast corner of Höhematte Park at Höheweg 133, tel. 033-557-8838, www.flyingwheels.ch). (Bike rental is also available at

Lauterbrunnen and Mürren, farther up the valley.)

HIGH-ADRENALINE TRIPS

Thrill-seekers will find trips focused on rafting, canyoning (rappelling down watery gorges), bungee jumping, and paragliding. Costs range from roughly 150 SF to 200 SF—higher for skydiving and hot-air balloon rides. Interlaken's two dominant companies are **Alpin Raft** (tel. 033-823-4100, www.alpinraft.com) and **Outdoor Interlaken** (tel. 033-826-7719, www.outdoor-interlaken.ch). Other companies are generally just booking agents for these two outfits. For an overview, study the racks of brochures at most TIs and hotels.

Eating

Restaurant Bären is across the river in Unterseen, in a classic building with cozy indoor and fine outdoor seating. It's a great value for *Rösti,* fondue, raclette, fish, traditional sausage, and chicken cordon bleu (24-34-SF main courses, fondue for one-25 SF; Tue-Thu 16:30-23:30, Fri-Sun 10:00-23:30 or later, closed Mon; from the West train station, turn left on Bahnhofstrasse, cross the river, and go several blocks to Seestrasse 2; tel. 033-822-7526).

Goldener Anker, the local hangout, hosts occasional small concerts. Over its 35 years, it's launched some of Switzerland's top bands. The big, flexible menu offers good, affordable hot meals (20-40-SF main courses, 15-SF backpacker specials, takeout available, daily from 16:00, Marktgasse 57, tel. 033-822-1672).

Città Vecchia serves decent Italian cuisine with seating indoors or out, on Unterseen's leafy main square (19-SF lunch specials, 16-24-SF pizzas, 20-28-SF pastas, 37-45-SF meat and fish courses, Thu-Mon 11:30-13:45 & 18:00-22:30, Wed 18:00-22:30, closed Tue, Untere Gasse 5, tel. 033-822-1754).

Metropole Hotel's "Top O'Met," capping Interlaken's 18-story skyscraper, serves traditional and modern food with awesome views at down-to-earth prices (daily lunch deals, 25-35-SF main courses, 50-SF fondue for two; open daily June-Sept 8:00-23:00, Oct-May 10:00-22:00; hot food served 11:30-14:00 & 18:00-21:00 or 22:00, Höheweg 37, just step into Metropole Hotel and take elevator to top, tel. 033-828-6666).

Asia Garden offers cheap meals by the West train station (14-20-SF main courses including rice, daily 11:00-23:00, take out or eat in, Rugenparkstrasse 4, tel. 033-821-2022).

The **Migros** supermarket is across the street from the West train station (Mon-Thu 8:00-19:00, Fri until 21:00, Sat 8:00-18:00, closed Sun), with a ground-floor cafeteria (13-19-SF main courses, cafeteria also open Sun mid-July-mid-Aug 10:00-17:00, Rugenparkstrasse 1). The **Co-op** supermarket, across the square from the Ost train station, also has a good cafeteria (supermarket hours similar to Migros, cafeteria closes 30-60 minutes before store and opens Sun 9:00-17:00, Untere Bönigstrasse 10). Smaller groceries in both train stations are open daily until 21:00; **Co-op Pronto** is open even later (daily 6:00-22:30, 30 yards west of TI at Höheweg 26).

Sleeping

Towns nestled in the mountains make better, more scenic bases, but in case you need to stay in Interlaken, I've listed decent options.

Rick's Tip: *If you are staying overnight in Interlaken,* **get a local Visitor Card from your hotelier**—*it lets you* **ride buses free** *in town.*

$$$ Hotel Lötschberg has a sun terrace, 24 rooms, four apartments, and lots of thoughtful touches (Db-165-185 SF, big Db-220 SF, closed Nov-mid-April, elevator in main building, free laundry

Sleep Code

Price Rankings for Double Rooms (Db)

$$$ Most rooms 170 SF or more
$$ 100-170 SF
$ 100 SF or less

Abbreviations: Db=Double with bathroom. D=Double with bathroom down the hall.

Notes: Room prices change; verify rates online or by email. For the best prices, book directly with the hotel.

machines, free loaner bikes; lounge with microwave, fridge, and free tea and coffee; 3-minute walk from West train station: turn right from station, after Migros at the circle go left to General-Guisan-Strasse 31; tel. 033-822-2545, www.lotschberg.ch, hotel@lotschberg.ch).

$$$ Hotel Rössli, across the river from the West train station, has standard rooms (Db-180 SF), "economy" rooms with a private bath down the hall (D-163 SF) and "budget" rooms with shared facilities (D-131 SF; reserve on hotel website for best rates, closed Dec-mid-Jan, lots of stairs, comfy lounge, Hauptstrasse 10, tel. 033-822-7816, www.roessli-interlaken.ch, info@roessli-interlaken.ch).

$$ Sunny Days B&B has nine homey rooms in a quiet residential neighborhood (Db-120-168 SF, prices vary with room size and view, 1-night stay-20 SF extra, laundry-18 SF/load, patio; from West train station: exit left and take first bridge to your left, after crossing two bridges turn left on Helvetiastrasse and go 3 blocks to #29; tel. 033-822-8343, mobile 079-672-3037, www.sunnydays.ch, mail@sunnydays.ch).

$$ Hotel Aarburg offers nine plain, peaceful rooms over a restaurant in Unterseen, a 10-minute walk from the

West train station (Db-140-150 SF, 2 doors from launderette at Beatenbergstrasse 1, tel. 033-822-2615, www.hotel-aarburg.ch, hotel-aarburg@quicknet.ch).

$ Interlaken Hostel is right next to the Ost train station in a big, sterile building with 220 beds, including some private singles, doubles, and quads (dorm bed-37-49 SF, Db-129 SF, includes sheets and breakfast, nonmembers pay 6 SF extra, 17.50 SF four-course dinner, bike rental, laundry-10 SF/load, Wi-Fi and pay guest computer, no curfew, check-in 15:00-24:00, Untere Bönigstrasse 3, tel. 033-826-1090, www.youthhostel.ch/interlaken, interlaken@youthhostel.ch).

Transportation
By Train
Interlaken has two train stations: Ost (East) and West. Interlaken Ost is the name you'll see most often on train schedules, and it's the transfer point for narrow-gauge trains to the high mountains (to Lauterbrunnen, Gimmelwald, etc.) and to Luzern. Use this station if you're headed to those destinations or staying at the Interlaken Hostel (next door). Interlaken Ost has free WCs, lockers, ticket counters (daily 6:00-19:30), and a summer-only branch TI.

Interlaken West is closer to downtown shopping and services. All trains from western Switzerland—Bern, the Golden Pass, Basel—stop at Interlaken West, and then continue to Interlaken Ost. Interlaken West has free WCs, lockers (by track 1), and ticket counters (daily 6:40-19:00), but no TI.

It's a pleasant 20-minute walk between the West and Ost train stations, an easy 3-minute trip by train (2-3/hour, 3.60 SF), or a 10-minute trip on any of several local buses (3.60 SF; #21, #102, #103, or #104).

TRAIN CONNECTIONS
Interlaken, Bern, Basel, and Frankfurt are linked by an express train, but for most other destinations you'll change in Bern.

Train info: Toll tel. 0900-300-300 or www.rail.ch.

From Interlaken Ost to: Lauterbrunnen Valley (1-2/hour, 20 minutes), **Bern** (2/hour, 55 minutes, some change in Spiez), **Zürich** (2/hour, 2 hours, most change in Bern), **Zürich Airport** (2/hour, 2.25 hours, change in Bern and sometimes Spiez), **Luzern** (hourly, 1.75 hours), **Zermatt** (1-2/hour, 2.25 hours, change in Spiez and Visp).

By Car
You can drive from Interlaken to Lauterbrunnen and all the way to Stechelberg, but not to Gimmelwald (park at the cable-car station near Stechelberg and ride up on the lift; see page 761) or to Mürren, Wengen, or Kleine Scheidegg (park in Lauterbrunnen and take the cable car to Mürren, or the cogwheel train to Wengen or Kleine Scheidegg).

LAUTERBRUNNEN

Located at (2,612 feet) under sheer cliffs with a signature waterfall, Lauterbrunnen (rated ▲) is the valley's commercial center and transportation hub, making it a fine launch pad for Jungfrau and Schilthorn adventures. Lauterbrunnen is convenient (and good in bad weather), though I prefer sleeping at higher-elevation Mürren, Gimmelwald, or Wengen.

Orientation
In addition to its train station and cable car, the one-street town is just big enough to have all the essential services.

Tourist Information: Stop by the friendly TI to check the weather forecast, find out about guided walks and events, and buy hiking maps or regional train or lift tickets (June-Sept daily 8:30-12:00 & 14:00-18:30; Oct-May Tue-Sat 9:00-12:00 & 13:30-17:00, closed Sun-Mon; on the main street a few houses up from the train station, tel. 033-856-8568, www.mylauterbrunnen.com).

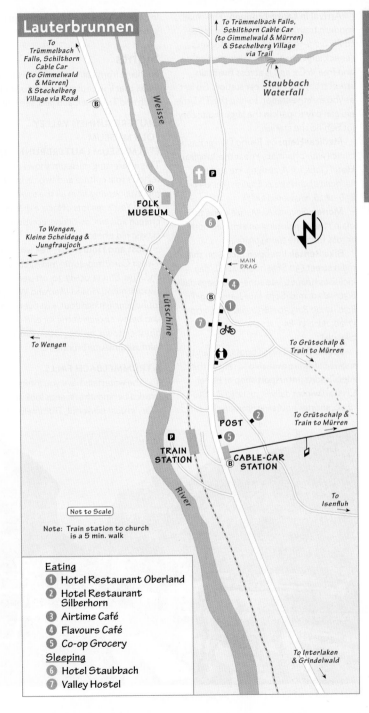

Lauterbrunnen

To Trümmelbach Falls, Schilthorn Cable Car (to Gimmelwald & Mürren) & Stechelberg Village via Road

To Trümmelbach Falls, Schilthorn Cable Car (to Gimmelwald & Mürren) & Stechelberg Village via Trail

Staubbach Waterfall

Weisse

FOLK MUSEUM

To Wengen, Kleine Scheidegg & Jungfraujoch

Lütschine

MAIN DRAG

To Wengen

To Grütschalp & Train to Mürren

To Grütschalp & Train to Mürren

POST

TRAIN STATION

CABLE-CAR STATION

River

To Isenfluh

To Interlaken & Grindelwald

Not to Scale

Note: Train station to church is a 5 min. walk

Eating
1. Hotel Restaurant Oberland
2. Hotel Restaurant Silberhorn
3. Airtime Café
4. Flavours Café
5. Co-op Grocery

Sleeping
6. Hotel Staubbach
7. Valley Hostel

Arrival in Lauterbrunnen: The small, modern train station has a ticket office (daily 6:00-19:30), a few small lockers (check larger bags at the ticket office), and free WCs, and is across the main street from the cable-car station. Go left as you exit the station to find the TI. Drivers can pay to park in the large multistory lot behind the station.

Medical Help: Dr. Bruno Durrer has a clinic (with pharmacy) near the Jungfrau Hotel (look for *Arzt* sign). He and his associate both speak English (tel. 033-856-2626, answered 24/7).

Money: Several ATMs are along the main street, including one immediately across from the train station.

Bike Rental: Imboden Bike is on the main street (30 SF/4 hours, 40 SF/day, includes helmet, late June-mid-Sept daily 8:30-18:30, mid-Sept-late June Mon-Fri 8:30-12:00 & 13:30-18:30, Sat-Sun 9:00-17:00, tel. 033-855-2114, www.imboden-bike.ch).

Sports Gear: Hiking boots, skis, and snowboards are available to rent at the Alpia Sports/Intersport shop at Hotel Crystal (winter daily 8:30-12:30 & 13:30-18:00, shorter hours in summer, closed in May, tel. 033-855-3292, www.alpia sport.ch).

Sights

For hikes from Lauterbrunnen, including walks that link Lauterbrunnen to Staubbach and Trümmelbach falls, see page 773.

LAUTERBRUNNEN VALLEY FOLK MUSEUM (TALMUSEUM LAUTERBRUNNEN)

This interesting museum shows off the region's folk culture and two centuries of mountaineering from all the towns of this valley. You'll see lots of lace, exhibits on cheese and woodworking, cowbells, and classic old photos.

Cost and Hours: 5 SF, free with hotel Visitor Card, mid-June-mid-Oct Tue and Thu-Sun 14:00-17:30, off-season by appointment, closed Mon and Wed year-round, English handout, just over bridge and below church at the far end of Lauterbrunnen town, tel. 033-855-3586, www.talmuseumlauterbrunnen.ch.

▲TRÜMMELBACH FALLS

If all the waterfalls have you intrigued, sneak a behind-the-scenes look at the valley's most powerful, Trümmelbach Falls.

Traditional cow culture thrives in the Berner Oberland.

Ride the elevator up through the mountain, climb up to the upper falls, and then hike down through several caves (wet, with lots of stairs, and claustrophobic for some). You'll see the melt from the Eiger, Mönch, and Jungfrau grinding like God's band saw through the mountain at the rate of up to 5,200 gallons a second. The upper area is the best; if your legs ache, skip the lower falls and ride down on the elevator. A café (with WC) is directly across from the bus stop. The ticket kiosk for the falls is a three-minute walk beyond the café.

Cost and Hours: 11 SF, daily July-Aug 8:30-18:00, early April-June and Sept-Oct 9:00-17:00, closed Nov-early April, opening date varies with ice conditions, tel. 033-855-3232, www.truemmelbach faelle.ch.

Getting There: The falls are about halfway between Lauterbrunnen and the Schilthornbahn cable-car station; from either, it's a short ride on the PostBus or a 45-minute walk. Or combine a visit to Trümmelbach with a walk on the valley floor; see page 773.

STAUBBACH FALLS

The second highest waterfall in Switzerland (nearly 900 feet) is literally in Lauterbrunnen's back yard—just follow the trail past the church toward the sound of rushing water. Its spray looks like falling dust—*Staub*—hence the name. A trail is cut into the cliff to take visitors up "behind" the falls (in winter, it's closed due to the danger of rock slides).

Eating

Hotel Restaurant Oberland serves tasty, good-value meals, including traditional Swiss dishes. Linger on the huge front porch into the evening (16-23-SF pizzas, 20-SF raclette, 23-27-SF main courses, daily 11:30-21:00, tel. 033-855-1241).

Hotel Restaurant Silberhorn, with an elegant dining room, is the local choice for a fancy dinner out. Call to reserve a view table (23-SF lunch specials, 18-35-SF main courses, daily 12:00-14:00 & 18:00-21:00, classy indoor and outdoor seating, above the cable-car station, tel. 033-856-2210).

Airtime Café is like an alpine Starbucks with hot drinks, homemade treats, breakfast, simple lunches, and light early dinners (9.50-SF sandwiches, 6-SF meat pies, daily 9:00-19:00, closed Nov, tel. 033-855-1515).

Flavours is a café without a hint of yodeling or cowbells, serving breakfasts, salads, sandwiches, and ice cream (15-SF lunches, May-Oct daily 9:00-18:30, closed Nov-April, tel. 033-855-3652).

The small but well-stocked **Co-op** supermarket is on the main street across from the station (daily 8:00-19:00, shorter hours and closed Sun off-season).

Sleeping

The prices listed are typical for high summer (July-Aug). Expect lower prices in winter (when many hotels close). Free parking is easy to find.

Lauterbrunnen Valley Folk Museum

Staubbach Falls is in Lauterbrunnen's backyard.

$$$ Hotel Silberhorn is a formal 35-room, three-star hotel, a hundred yards uphill from the train station. Almost every double room comes with a fine view and balcony (Db-179-189 SF, bigger "superior" Db-209-219 SF, price depends on demand and room quality, lots of stairs, dinner-30 SF, tel. 033-856-2210, www.silberhorn.com, info@silberhorn.com).

$$ Hotel Staubbach is one of the oldest hotels in the valley (1890). It has the casual feel of a family-friendly national park lodge, with 33 simple and comfortable rooms. Rooms that face up the valley have incredible views (D-130 SF, Db-160-180 SF, family rooms, price depends on view, closed mid-Nov-March, elevator, 10-minute walk up from station on the left, tel. 033-855-5454, www.staubbach.com, hotel@staubbach.com).

$$ Hotel Oberland is cheerfully located in the center of town, with tidy, bright rooms, most with balconies and views of the Staubbach waterfall or Jungfrau (Db-150-160 SF, family rooms and apartments, some rooms in nearby Crystal annex, popular with my tour groups, 5-minute walk up from station on the right, free parking, tel. 033-855-1241, www.hoteloberland.ch, info@hoteloberland.ch).

$ Valley Hostel is practical and comfortable, offering 92 inexpensive beds for quieter travelers of all ages, including families, with a pleasant garden (dorm bed-28 SF/person, bunk D-66 SF, double-bedded D-76 SF, breakfast extra, kitchen, coin-op laundry, reception open 8:00-12:00 & 16:00-21:00, 5-minute walk up from train station, tel. 033-855-2008, www.valleyhostel.ch, info@valleyhostel.ch).

Rick's Tip: **Hotels in the Berner Oberland** *issue free* **Visitor Cards** *(Gästekarten) that include small discounts on some sights (paid for by your room tax).*

Transportation

The valley-floor towns of Lauterbrunnen and Stechelberg have connections by mountain train, bus, and cable car to the traffic-free villages, peaks, and hikes high above. Prices and trip durations given are one-way and per leg unless otherwise noted.

From Lauterbrunnen

By Train to: Wengen (2/hour, 15 minutes, 6.60 SF), **Kleine Scheidegg** (1-2/hour, 30 minutes, 30 SF), **Jungfraujoch** (1-2/hour, 2 hours, 90 SF, change in Kleine Scheidegg, see details on page 780); **Männlichen** (for hike to Kleine Scheidegg—take train to Wengen and change to cable car), **Interlaken Ost** (1-2/hour, 20 minutes, 7.40 SF).

By Cable Car to: Grütschalp (2-4/hour, 6 minutes), where the train waits to take you to **Mürren** (another 14 minutes); total trip time 20 minutes (total one-way cost 11 SF).

By PostBus to: Schilthornbahn cable-car station, near Stechelberg (buses timed to depart a few minutes after trains arrive in Lauterbrunnen, 15-minute ride, 4.40 SF, covered by Swiss Travel Pass—see page 781).

By Car to: Schilthornbahn cable-car station, near Stechelberg (10-minute drive, pay parking lot).

From Stechelberg / Base of Schilthornbahn Cable Car

By Cable Car to: Gimmelwald (2/hour, 5 minutes, 6.20 SF), on to **Mürren** (2/hour, 10 minutes, 11 SF, change in Gimmelwald), ending up at **Schilthorn** (2/hour, 22 minutes, 102 SF round-trip, change in Gimmelwald, Mürren, and Birg).

GIMMELWALD

Located at 4,593 feet, Gimmelwald's mountain views are dominated by the huge, sheer cliff face called the Schwarzmönch ("Black Monk"). The three peaks above (and behind) it are the Eiger, Mönch, and Jungfrau.

Saved from developers by its "avalanche zone" classification, Gimmelwald (rated ▲▲▲) was once among the poorest places in Switzerland. Its traditional economy was stuck in the hay, and its farmers survived because of visitors, Swiss government subsidies, and working ski lifts in winter. Although Gimmelwald's population dropped in the last century from 300 to about 120 residents, its traditions survive. Tough and proud, local families harvest enough to feed only about 15 cows each. But they'd have it no other way.

For some, there's little to see in this village. Others, like me, enjoy sitting on a bench and learning why they say, "If heaven isn't what it's cracked up to be, send me back to Gimmelwald."

Gimmelwald's farmers raise just enough hay for their cows.

Rick's Tip: Thanks to local schoolteachers Olle and Maria and their son Sven, **Gimmelwald has a helpful website** *(www.gimmelwald.ch) where you can check out photos, get directions for the best hikes, and see all the latest on activities and rooms for rent.*

⊙ Gimmelwald Walk

Gimmelwald, though tiny, with one zigzag street, offers a fine look at a traditional Swiss mountain community.

• *Start this quick self-guided walk at the...*

Cable-Car Station: When the lift came in the 1960s, the village's back end became its front door. As you walk out of the station, pause at the big Infopoint map to orient yourself. Then turn right (uphill).

Gimmelwald is still a farm village. As you start up the street, you'll see a sweet little hut on the right. Set on stilts to keep out mice, the hut was used for storing cheese. The rocks on the rooftop here and throughout the town are not decorative—they keep the shingles on through wild storms. Behind the cheese hut stands the former village schoolhouse, the largest structure in town (in Catholic towns, the biggest building is the church; in Protestant towns, it's the school). Gimmelwald's students now go to school in Lauterbrunnen and the building is used as a chapel when the Protestant pastor makes his monthly visit. The little gray tower-like structure on the roof is the town fire siren. Now turn around: On the other side of the street, next to the little playground, is a bench with a nice view. Just beyond it is the recommended Mountain Hostel and Restaurant.

• *Walk up the lane 50 yards, past the town's Dalí-esque art gallery (who's showing in the phone booth?), to Gimmelwald's...*

"Times Square": The yellow alpine "street sign" shows where you are, the altitude (1,370 meters, or 4,470 feet), how

Cow Culture

Traditional Swiss cow farmers could make more money for much easier work in another profession. In a good year, farmers produce enough cheese to break even—supporting their families on government subsidies of about $5,000 per cow. (Governments here support traditional farming as much for tourism as for cheese.) But these farmers choose to keep tradition alive.

The cows' grazing ground ranges in elevation by as much as 5,000 feet throughout the year. In early summer, farmers strap elaborate ceremonial bells on cows and take them up to high-elevation stables called "alps," where they stay for about 100 days. The farmers hire a team of cheesemakers to work at each alp—mostly hippies, students, and city slickers eager to spend the summer in solitude. Each morning, they get up at 5:00 to milk the cows; take them to pasture; and make the cheese, milking the cows again when they come home in the evening. In the summer, the milk is made into alp cheese (it's too difficult to get it down to the market in liquid form). In the winter, with the cows at lower altitudes, the fresh milk is sold as milk.

Each alp also has a resident herd of pigs. Cheesemaking leftovers (*Molke*, whey) can alter the ecosystem if thrown out—but pigs love the stuff. (The pigs parade up with the cows, but no one notices.) Cheesemakers say bathing in whey improves the complexion…but maybe that's just the altitude talking.

Meanwhile, the farmers, glad to be free of their bovine responsibilities in summer, turn their attention to making hay, storing it above the huts. In the fall, the cows come down from the alps and spend the winter moving from hut to hut, eating the hay the farmers spent the summer preparing for them.

Throughout the year, you'll see farmers moving their herds to various elevations. If snow is in the way, farmers sometimes use cable cars to move their cows.

---

many hours (*Std.*) and minutes it takes to walk to nearby points, and which tracks are serious hiking paths (marked with red and white; further indicated along the way with red and white patches of paint on stones). You're surrounded by buildings that were built as duplexes, divided vertically right down the middle to house two separate families. Look for the Honesty Shop at Pension Gimmelwald, which features local crafts and little edibles for sale (summer only).

Behind the sign, the lettering high up on the post office is a folksy blessing: "Summer brings green, winter brings snow. The sun greets the day, the stars greet the night. This house will protect you from rain, cold, and wind. May God give us his blessings." Small as Gimmelwald is, it still has daily mail service. The postman comes down from Mürren each day (by golf cart in summer, sled in win-

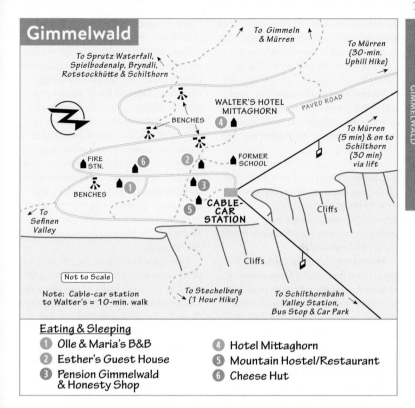

Gimmelwald

To Gimmeln & Mürren

To Mürren (30-min. Uphill Hike)

To Sprutz Waterfall, Spielbodenalp, Bryndli, Rotstockhütte & Schilthorn

WALTER'S HOTEL MITTAGHORN

PAVED ROAD

BENCHES

④

To Mürren (5 min) & on to Schilthorn (30 min) via lift

FIRE STN.   ⑥   ②   FORMER SCHOOL

BENCHES   ①   ③

⑤   CABLE-CAR STATION

Cliffs

To Sefinen Valley

Cliffs

Not to Scale

Note: Cable-car station to Walter's = 10-min. walk

To Stechelberg (1 Hour Hike)

To Schilthornbahn Valley Station, Bus Stop & Car Park

Eating & Sleeping

① Olle & Maria's B&B
② Esther's Guest House
③ Pension Gimmelwald & Honesty Shop
④ Hotel Mittaghorn
⑤ Mountain Hostel/Restaurant
⑥ Cheese Hut

ter) to deliver and pick up mail. The date on this building indicates when it was built or rebuilt (1911). Gimmelwald has a strict building code: For instance, shutters can only be painted certain colors.

• *From this tiny intersection, walk away from the cable-car station and follow the town's...*

Main Street: Walk up the road past the garden-gnome greeting committee on the right. On the left, notice the announcement board: one side for tourist news, the other for local news (such as deals on chain-saw sharpening and upcoming shooting competitions). Cross the street and admire the big barn, dated 1995. At one front corner is a cow-scratcher. Swiss cows have legal rights (for example, in the winter they must be taken out for exercise at least three times a week). This big barn is built in a modern style. Traditionally, barns were small (like those on the hillside

high above) and closer to the hay. But with trucks and paved roads, hay can be moved more easily, and farm businesses need more cows to be viable. Still, even a big, well-run farm hopes just to break even. The industry survives only with government subsidies (see sidebar on page 756). As you wander, you'll also see private

"Main Street" in Gimmelwald

garden patches. Until recently, most locals grew their own vegetables—often enough to provide most of their family's needs.

• Go just beyond the next barn. On your right is a...

Water Fountain/Trough: This is the site of the town's historic water supply—still drinkable. Village kids love to bathe and wage water wars here when the cows aren't drinking from it.

• Detour left down a gravel path (along a wooden fence). First you'll pass the lovingly tended pea-patch gardens of the woman with the best green thumb in the village (on your left). Continue along the path, which ends after 50 yards at another water trough in front of a house called...

Husmättli: This is the oldest building in town, from 1658. (There are more 17th-century buildings on the road that zigzags down from Gimmelwald into the Sefinen Valley.) Study the log-cabin construction. Many old houses were built without nails. The wood was logged up the valley and cut on the water-powered village mill (also in the Sefinen Valley). Gimmelwald heats with wood, and since

the wood needs to age a couple of years to burn well, it's stacked everywhere.

From here (at the water trough in front of Husmättli), look up to find a house with 10 solar panels on the roof—it belongs to teachers Olle and Maria. As part of a green energy policy, a Swiss building code requires that new structures provide 30 percent of their own power. Switzerland is gradually moving away from nuclear power; its last reactor is supposed to close in 2034. The panels you see heat the water that Olle and Maria use for bathing and home heating; they fire up their furnace only from November to February.

• Return to the main paved road and continue onward.

Twenty yards along, on the left, look for the house with the Self Service sign. Open the door and you'll find a refrigerator with local cheese sold on the honor system by the Rubin family. Just outside the door, in the summer months, you may see a bunch of scythes hanging above a sharpening stone. Farmers pound, rather than grind, the blade to get it razor-sharp for efficient mowing on slopes too rocky or steep

Gimmelwald offers a fine look at traditional Swiss mountain life.

for machines or grazing animals. Feel a blade...carefully.

A few steps farther, notice the cute **cheese hut** on the right. This is where the cheese you saw on sale is produced. The hut's front wall is an art gallery with nail shoes used as flower pots. Nail shoes grip the steep, wet fields—this is critical for a farmer's safety, especially when carrying a sharp scythe. Even today, farmers buy metal tacks and fasten them to boots. The hut is full of strong cheese—up to three years old.

Look up. In the summer, a few goats are kept here behind the hut (rather than at a high alp) to provide families with fresh milk (about a half-gallon per day per goat). The farmers fence the goats in so they eat only this difficult-to-harvest grass.

On the left (at the *B&B* sign) is Olle and Maria's home. They ran the local school until it closed in 2010. Now they both commute to teach at schools in other villages.

• *Fifty yards farther along on the right is the house called...*

Alpenrose: This is the old village school building, in use from about 1810 to 1930. Now it's a family home. You might see big ceremonial cowbells hanging under the eaves on the uphill side. These swing from the necks of cows during the procession from town to the high Alps (mid-June) and back down (mid-Sept).

• *At the end of town, pause where a lane branches off to the left, leading into the dramatic...*

Sefinen Valley: At the bottom of this wild valley is a stream that rushes down towards Stechelberg. All the old homes in town are made from wood cut from the left-hand side of this valley (shady side, slow-growing, better timber) and milled on the valley floor.

• *A few steps ahead, the road switches back at the...*

Gimmelwald Fire Station (Feuerwehrmagazin): Peer through the windows in the door at the tractor-like engines. Then walk up around the hairpin bend to the notice board on the side of the building. The *Föhnwacht Reglement* sheet explains rules to keep the village from burning down during the Föhn season, a period of fierce dry winds. During this time, there's a 24-hour fire watch, and even smoking cigarettes outdoors is forbidden. Mürren was devastated by a Föhn-caused fire in the 1920s. Villagers in Gimmelwald—mindful of the quality of their volunteer fire department—are particularly careful. The town hasn't had a terrible fire in its history (a rare feat among alpine villages).

Check out the other posted notices. This year's Swiss Army calendar tells reservists when and where to go (in all four official Swiss languages). Every Swiss male does a 22-week stint in the military, then serves three weeks a year in the reserves until age 34. The *Schiessübungen* poster details the shooting exercises required this year.

• *Unless you're really pooped, continue uphill along the road.*

High Road to Hotel Mittaghorn: The resort town of Mürren hovers in the distance. And high on the left, notice the hay field with terraces. These are from WWII days, when Switzerland, wanting self-sufficiency, required all farmers to grow potatoes. Today, this field is a festival of alpine flowers in season (best at this altitude in May and June).

• *In a couple of minutes, you'll reach a peaceful set of benches, just off the lane on the downhill side, which let you savor the view. Just beyond is the Hotel Mittaghorn and steps downhill, which bring you quickly back to Gimmelwald's "Times Square."*

Eating and Sleeping

Pleasantly stuck in the past, the village has only a few eateries and accommodations—all of them quirky and memorable. Only Pension Gimmelwald and the Mountain Hostel serve meals to the public. Room rates are listed without breakfast (except for the hostel) and include the local tax, which gives you free entry to the public swimming pool in nearby Mürren (the Sportzentrum—see page 762). You'll meet a lot of my readers in this town. This is a disappointment to some; others enjoy the chance to be part of a fun extended family.

$$$ At Olle and Maria's B&B, the Eggimanns rent three rooms—Gimmelwald's most comfortable and expensive—in their alpine-sleek house. Two rooms with shared bath are upstairs, while the "double" with private bath is a ground-level studio apartment with a private entrance (D-130-160 SF, Db with kitchenette-190 SF, optional breakfast-20 SF, 3-night minimum, cash or PayPal only, nonrefundable 50 percent deposit via PayPal required, laundry service-15 SF/ load; from cable car, continue straight for 200 yards along the town's only road, look for *B&B* sign on left; tel. 033-855-3575, www.gimmelwald.ch/ollebnb.htm, oeggimann@bluewin.ch).

$$ Esther's Guest House, overlooking the main intersection, rents seven clean, basic, and comfortable rooms with a two-night minimum. Three rooms have private bathrooms, and all share a generous lounge and kitchen (big D-140 SF, small viewless Db-140 SF, Db-170 SF, family rooms, breakfast-16 SF, sack lunches available, low ceilings, tel. 033-855-5488, www.esthersguesthouse.ch, info@esthersguesthouse.ch). Esther also rents two five-person apartments with kitchenettes next door (3-night minimum).

$$ Pension Gimmelwald is an old farmhouse converted into a family-style inn, with 12 simple shared-bath rooms, a restaurant, and a cozy bar. Aside from the rooms, they have a six-bed dorm (33 SF) that attracts more mature guests than a typical hostel. Its terrace has gorgeous views across the valley (D-110 SF, 10 percent discount for 3 nights for Rick Steves readers if you book direct, breakfast-14 SF, dinner-30 SF, open June-mid-Oct

and late Dec-mid-April, 2-minute walk up from cable-car station, tel. 033-855-1730, www.pensiongimmelwald.com, pensiongimmelwald@gmail.com). Its **restaurant** has a simple menu featuring local produce served in a rustic indoor dining room or on a jaw-dropping view terrace (18-25-SF main dishes, daily 10-SF backpacker special, daily mid-June-Sept and late Dec-mid-April 12:00-15:00 & 18:00-21:00, bar open until 23:00, closed off-season). Small groceries are on sale at its little **Honesty Shop** (closed off-season).

$ Hotel Mittaghorn is a classic, creaky, thin-walled, alpine place with superb views. The hotel has three rooms with private showers and four rooms that share a coin-operated shower (D-90-110 SF, 2-night minimum, cash only, open May-Oct, a 5-minute climb up the path from the village center, tel. 033-855-1658, www.mittaghorn.com, mittaghorn@gmail.com; reserve by e-mail—generally answered April-Oct only). If you'd like dinner, confirm by phone the day before your arrival. If no one's there when you check in, look for a card in the hallway directing you to your room.

$ Mountain Hostel is a beehive of activity: as clean as its guests, cheap, respectable, and friendly. The 50-bed hostel has a self-service kitchen, bar, pool table, and healthy plumbing. It's mostly a college-age crowd; families and older travelers will be more comfortable elsewhere (bunk in dorm room-45 SF, includes sheets and breakfast, show-

ers-1 SF, laundry-5 SF, open mid-April-Oct, from the lift station it's 20 yards up the path to the left, tel. 033-855-1704, www.mountainhostel.com, info@mountainhostel.com). Its **restaurant** comes with mountain-high energy, a youthful spirit, and breathtaking terrace views (simple 17-22-SF main courses, popular 16-19-SF pizzas, mid-April-Oct daily 12:00-21:00, closed rest of year).

Rick's Tip: *Consider packing in a* **picnic meal from Lauterbrunnen or Mürren,** *which have grocery stores and cafés selling sandwiches to go.*

Transportation

To get from Lauterbrunnen to Gimmelwald, you have two options, outlined below. For times and prices, see page 768.

1. Schilthornbahn Cable Car: The faster, easier way—best in bad weather or at the end of a long day with lots of luggage—is by road and then cable car. The cable-car station, near Stechelberg, is a 10-minute drive or 15-minute bus ride from Lauterbrunnen. Drivers can park at a pay lot at the cable-car station; otherwise, ride the PostBus from Lauterbrunnen (buses depart with the arrival of trains in Lauterbrunnen). The cable car whisks you in five thrilling minutes up to Gimmelwald (and continues to Mürren).

The Schilthornbahn cable car is closed for servicing for a week in late April or early May and for a month from early November through early December. If you're here during this time, you'll ride the cargo cable car from the valley floor directly up to Mürren, where a small bus shuttles you down to Gimmelwald.

2. Grütschalp Cable Car and Mürren Train: This is the more scenic route. Catch the cable car from Lauterbrunnen to Grütschalp. As you glide upward, notice the bed of the now-abandoned 100-year-old funicular train track below you. At Grütschalp, a special vintage train will roll you along the incredibly scenic cliffside to Mürren (the total trip takes 20 minutes). From there, either walk to the middle of Mürren and take a left down a moderately steep paved path 30 minutes to Gimmelwald, or walk 10 minutes across Mürren to catch the Schilthornbahn cable car down to Gimmelwald.

MÜRREN

At 5,381 feet, Mürren is pleasant as an alpine resort can be: traffic-free and filled with cafés, prefab-rustic chalets, old-timers with walking sticks, and all the comforts of home without the pretension of more famous resorts. Surrounded by a fortissimo chorus of mountains, the town (rated ▲▲) has endless hiking options (some require the help of a cliffside train, a funicular, or a cable car).

Mürren dates from 1384, but its historic character is hard to spot amid tourist development. Still, it's a peaceful town, with 400 permanent residents. There's not enough business to keep a bank or proper bakery open (bread is baked down in Lauterbrunnen and shipped up). Depending on the time of year, Mürren can be lively (in winter and summer, the population swells to 4,000) or completely dead (spring and fall).

Orientation

Mürren perches high on a ledge 2,000 feet above the Lauterbrunnen Valley. You can walk from one end of town to the other in about 10 minutes.

Tourist Information: Mürren's TI, in the town sports complex, can help you find a room and gives hiking advice (daily June-Oct 8:30-19:00, Dec-April until 20:00; May and Nov 8:00-12:00 & 13:00-17:00; above the village, follow signs to *Sportzentrum,* tel. 033-856-8686, www.mymuerren.ch).

Money: An ATM is at the cable-car station.

Bike Rental: You can rent mountain

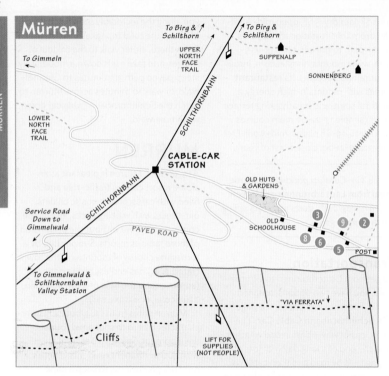

Mürren

To Gimmeln

To Birg & Schilthorn

To Birg & Schilthorn

UPPER NORTH FACE TRAIL

SUPPENALP

SONNENBERG

LOWER NORTH FACE TRAIL

SCHILTHORNBAHN

CABLE-CAR STATION

OLD HUTS & GARDENS

Service Road Down to Gimmelwald

SCHILTHORNBAHN

PAVED ROAD

OLD SCHOOLHOUSE

❸ ❾ ❷

❽ ❻ ❺

POST

To Gimmelwald & Schilthornbahn Valley Station

"VIA FERRATA"

Cliffs

LIFT FOR SUPPLIES (NOT PEOPLE)

bikes at Stäger Sport—ask about return-ing the bike in Lauterbrunnen for an extra fee (30 SF/half-day, 40 SF/day, includes helmet, daily 9:00-12:00 & 13:00-18:00, closed late Oct-mid-May, in middle of town, tel. 033-855-2355, www.staegersport.ch). A bigger bike-rental shop, Imboden Bike, is in Lauterbrunnen.

R & R: The slick **Sportzentrum** (sports center), which houses the TI, offers a world of indoor activities, including a sauna and steam bath. The pool is free with the Visitor Card given out by hotels and hostels (otherwise 12 SF, daily June-Oct 13:00-20:00, Dec-March until 21:00, April-May until 18:00, closed Nov, tel. 033-856-8686, www.sportzentrum-muerren.ch). In season, they offer mini-golf, table tennis, and a fitness room.

❯ Mürren Walk

Mürren has long been a top ski resort, but a walk across town offers a glimpse into a time before ski lifts. This stroll takes you through town on the main drag, from the train station (where you'll arrive if coming from Lauterbrunnen) to the cable-car station, then to the Allmendhubel funic-ular station.

• Start at the...

Train Station: The first trains pulled into Mürren in 1891. (A circa 1911 car is permanently parked at Grütschalp's sta-tion.) A display case inside the station displays an original car from the nar-row-gauge, horse-powered line that rolled fancy visitors from here into town. The current station, built in 1964, comes with impressive engineering for heavy cargo. Look out back, where a small truck can be loaded up, attached to the train, and driven away.

• Wander into town along the main road (take the lower, left fork) for a stroll under the...

Alpin Palace Hotel: This towering

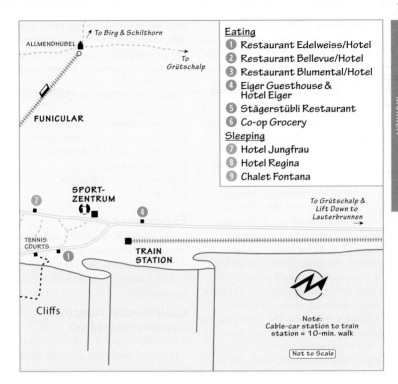

Eating
1 Restaurant Edelweiss/Hotel
2 Restaurant Bellevue/Hotel
3 Restaurant Blumental/Hotel
4 Eiger Guesthouse & Hotel Eiger
5 Stägerstübli Restaurant
6 Co-op Grocery
Sleeping
7 Hotel Jungfrau
8 Hotel Regina
9 Chalet Fontana

ALLMENDHUBEL
To Birg & Schilthorn
To Grütschalp
FUNICULAR
SPORT-ZENTRUM
To Grütschalp & Lift Down to Lauterbrunnen
TENNIS COURTS
TRAIN STATION
Cliffs
Note: Cable-car station to train station = 10-min. walk
Not to Scale

place was the "Grand Palace Hotel" until it burned in 1928. Today it's closed, and no one knows its future. The small wooden platform on the left—looking like a suicide springboard—is the place where snow-removal trucks dump their loads over the cliff in the winter. Look back at the meadow below the station: This is a favorite grazing spot for chamois (the animals,

not the rags). Ahead, at Hotel Edelweiss, step to the far corner of the restaurant terrace for a breathtaking view stretching from the big three (Eiger, Mönch, and Jungfrau) on the left to the lonely cattle farm in the high alp on the right. Then look down.

• Continue toward an empty lot with a grand view.

Viewpoints: There are plans for a big apartment-hotel to be built here, but the project is waiting for investment money. Detour from the main street around the cliff-hanging tennis court. Stop at one of the little romantic shelters built into the far wall. Directly below, at the base of the modern wall, is the start of a 1.5-mile via ferrata, a "trail" with a steel-cable guide that mountaineers use to venture safely along the cliff all the way to Gimmelwald. You can see the Gimmelwald lift station in the distance.

• Return to the main street and continue to...

You'll have many hiking options from Mürren.

"Downtown" Mürren: This main intersection (where the small service road leads down to Gimmelwald) has the only grocery store in town (the Co-op). A bit farther on, the tiny fire barn (labeled *Feuerwehr*) has a list showing the leaders of the volunteer force and their responsibilities. The old barn behind it on the right evokes the time, not so long ago, when the town's barns housed cows. Imagine Mürren with more cows than people, rather than with more visitors than residents.

About 65 feet beyond the fire barn (across the street from the old schoolhouse—Altes Schulhaus), detour right uphill a few steps into the oldest part of town. Explore the windy little lanes, admiring the ancient woodwork on the houses and the cute little pea patches.

• *Back on the main drag, continue to the far end of Mürren, where you come to the...*

Cable-Car Station: The larger cars that dock in the back of the station take hikers and skiers up to the Schilthorn and run down to the valley via Gimmelwald. The smaller cable car out front goes directly (and steeply) to the valley floor. This was the main route down to Stechelberg until 1987, but today it is only for cargo, garbage, and backup passenger service in spring and fall when the newer cars are closed for maintenance.

• *Hiking back into town along the high road, you'll enter...*

Upper Mürren: You'll pass Mürren's two churches, the Allmendhubel funicular station, and the Sportzentrum (with swimming pool and TI).

• *Our walk is finished. Enjoy the town and the views.*

Experiences

During the height of summer and ski season, Mürren offers plenty of activities for those willing to seek them out. In spring and fall, it's quiet. For hikes from Mürren, see page 773.

ALLMENDHUBEL FUNICULAR (ALLMENDHUBELBAHN)

A surprisingly rewarding funicular (built in 1912, renovated in 1999) carries nature lovers from Mürren up to Allmendhubel, a perch offering a Jungfrau view that,

Mürren's cute town center

though much lower, rivals the Schilthorn. At the station, notice the 1920s bobsled. Consider mixing a mountain lift, grand views, and a hike with your meal by eating at the restaurant on Allmendhubel (good chef, open daily until 17:00).

Allmendhubel is good for families. The funicular is fun, a big playground awaits at the top, and the views are great. The hikes are fairly easy and the trails are well-maintained. This is also the departure point for the North Face hike and walks to Grütschalp (see page 773). While at Allmendhubel, consider its flower trail, a 20-minute loop with nice mountain views and (from June to Sept) a chance to see more than 150 different alpine flowers blooming.

Cost and Hours: 8 SF one-way, 13 SF round-trip, half-price with Swiss Travel Pass—see page 781, early June-mid-Oct daily 9:00-17:00, runs every 20 minutes, tel. 033-855-2042 or 033-856-2141, www. schilthorn.ch.

Eating

Except where noted, all of the recommended restaurants and hotels close in spring (anywhere from Easter to early June) and again in fall (sometime between late September and mid-December). Half-board can be a good idea if you're staying in Mürren.

These hotels have **restaurants** open to the public: **Edelweiss** (more formal), **Bellevue** (with elegant alpine-lounge ambience), **Blumental** (with a characteristic cellar—lively when open), and the **Eiger Guesthouse** (a popular sports bar-type hangout with pool tables, games, and Wi-Fi). The latter three are good for a drink after dinner as well.

Stägerstübli, in the town center, is a restaurant in an upscale 1902 tearoom. Sitting on its terrace, you know who's out and about in town (17-22-SF *Rösti*, 20-37-SF meat dishes, big portions, daily 11:30-20:30, closes for a week in early Sept, tel. 033-855-1316).

The **Co-op** is the only grocery store in town, with good picnic fixings and sandwiches (Mon-Fri 8:00-12:00 & 13:45-18:30, Sat until 16:00, closed Sun, closed Tue-Thu afternoons in spring and fall).

Sleeping

$$$ Hotel Eiger, a four-star hotel dramatically and conveniently situated across from the tiny train station, is a good but expensive bet. Family-run for four generations, it offers all the services you'd expect in a big city (plush lounge, indoor swimming pool, and sauna) while maintaining a woody, Old World elegance in its 50 rooms. Family suites, while pricey (390-410 SF), can be a good value for groups of four or five (Db-275-295 SF, view Db-295-345 SF, grand breakfast, discounts for stays of 3 nights or more, email for best deals, half-board with five-course dinner-55 SF/person, elevator, tel. 033-856-5454, www. hoteleiger.com, info@hoteleiger.com).

$$$ At Hotel Edelweiss, it's all about the location—convenient and literally hanging on the cliff with devastating views. It's a big, modern building with 30 basic rooms, some with balconies (small Db-160-190 SF, larger view Db-190-220 SF, 10 percent discount for 2 nights, half-board-35 SF, elevator, piano in lounge, self-serve laundry-10 SF/load, tel. 033-856-5600, www.edelweiss-muerren.ch, info@edelweiss-muerren.ch). Its **restaurant** offers incredible views and good prices, too (17-20-SF pizzas, 18-20-SF *Rösti*, 24-SF fondue, sandwiches; daily main dish 19 SF or 24 SF with soup and dessert, family-friendly, tel. 033-856-5600).

$$$ Hotel Bellevue has a homey lounge, solid woodsy furniture, a great view terrace, and 19 great rooms—most with balconies and views (viewless hillside Db-180 SF, view Db-200-230 SF—150 SF if staying 2 nights or more in early June or Sept-Oct, tel. 033-855-1401, www.muerren.ch/bellevue, bellevue@muerren.ch, Ruth and Othmar Suter). Its

Jägerstübli restaurant has a spectacular view terrace, a sophisticated indoor area, and a cozy, antler-filled hunters' room guaranteed to disgust vegetarians (34-40-SF lamb and game, *Rösti* and bratwurst dishes 20-25 SF, nonmeat dishes available, daily 11:30-14:00 & 18:00-21:00, tel. 033-855-1401).

$$$ Hotel Jungfrau offers 29 modern and comfortable rooms and an apartment for up to six people (Db-150-210 SF, email for best deals, extra bed-80 SF, elevator, laundry service-25 SF, Wi-Fi in common areas, pay Wi-Fi in rooms, close to TI/Sportzentrum, tel. 033-856-6464, www.hoteljungfrau.ch, mail@hoteljungfrau.ch).

$$ Hotel Blumental has 16 older but nicely furnished rooms, plus 6 modern rooms in the chalet out back (Db-150-170 SF, if booking direct and staying 3 nights in Sept-Oct ask for 10 percent Rick Steves discount, half-board-35 SF, tel. 033-855-1826, www.muerren.ch/blumental, blumental@muerren.ch). Its elegant, romantic **restaurant La Grotte** specializes in Swiss cuisine with some international and vegetarian dishes (18-35-SF main courses, 22-25-SF fondue served for one or more, 15-SF pastas, daily from 17:00, tel. 033-855-1826).

$$ Eiger Guesthouse offers 12 good, small, budget rooms across from the train station in a simply furnished, renovated older building. Four of the rooms share two sets of bathroom facilities (D-100-120 SF, Db-130-170 SF, family rooms, ask

for their Rick Steves special—a bunk double with a 2-night minimum at a good price, closed Nov, lots of stairs, game room, view terrace, tel. 033-856-5460, www.eigerguesthouse.com, info@eigerguesthouse.com). Its easygoing, ground-floor pub **restaurant** is a busy local hangout with a mostly Italian menu (15-23-SF pizzas—less for takeout, meal-sized salads, 22-33-SF main courses, inexpensive house wine, Wi-Fi and game room, daily 8:00-23:30, closed Nov, tel. 033-856-5460).

$$ Hotel Regina is a big creaky woodpile with 52 basic rooms (most with shared toilets and showers) near the cable-car station. For solo travelers it's a decent value (S-65 SF, D-105-125 SF, Db-135-155 SF, family rooms, Wi-Fi in common areas, tel. 033-855-4242, www.reginamuerren.ch, info@reginamuerren.ch).

$ Chalet Fontana is a fine budget option, with five crisp, clean, and comfortable rooms (D-90 SF, large D-100 SF, cash only, closed late Oct-April, fridge in common kitchen, Wi-Fi, across street from Stägerstübli restaurant in town center, mobile 078-642-3485, www.chaletfontana.ch, chaletfontana@gmail.com). It also rents a family apartment with kitchen, bathroom, and breakfast (two bedrooms with 3 beds each—check website for pricing).

Transportation

There are two ways to get to Mürren: via the **Grütschalp cable car and train** from Lauterbrunnen (take the cable car from Lauterbrunnen to meet the train at Grütschalp; 20 minutes total) or on the **Schilthornbahn cable car** near Stechelberg (see page 768). The train and cable-car stations (which have lockers and free WCs) are at opposite ends of Mürren. For several weeks in spring and fall, one (but never both) of these routes closes down for maintenance.

OTHER ALPINE RETREATS

Wengen

Wengen is a bigger, fancier Mürren at 4,180 feet on the east side of the valley, with grand hotels, restaurants, shops, and terrific views. This traffic-free resort, rated ▲, is an easy train ride above Lauterbrunnen and halfway up to Kleine Scheidegg and Männlichen. From Wengen, you can catch the Männlichen lift (www.maennlichen.ch) up to the ridge and take the rewarding, gradually downhill Männlichen to Kleine Scheidegg hike (described on page 776).

Orientation

Wengen's **TI** is a two-minute walk from the station: Go up to the main drag, turn left, and you'll see it on the right (Tourist Center Wengen). They have info on hiking and sell trail maps (daily 9:00-18:00, closes for lunch Sat-Sun off-season, tel. 033-856-8585, www.wengen.ch).

Eating and Sleeping

Each of the recommended hotels also has a restaurant. The good-sized **Co-op grocery,** across the square from the train station, is great for picnic fixings (daily 8:00-18:30, closed Sun off-season).

Above the Train Station: $$$ Hotel Berghaus, in a quiet area a five-minute walk from the main street, offers 19 rooms above a fine **restaurant** (Db-194-256 SF, family room, elevator, Wi-Fi on ground floor, open June–Sept and mid-Dec–early April, tel. 033-855-2151, www.berghaus-wengen.ch, info@berghaus-wengen.ch). At the train station, dial #25 on the hotel phone to request a free pickup. To walk to the hotel from the main drag, head up the street across from Hotel Bernerhof, bear right at the fork, go 200 yards more past the church, and it's on the left.

$$$ Romantik Hotel Schönegg, at the top end of Wengen's main road, is a centrally located splurge, with 20 rooms newly remodeled with alpine materials. All rooms have balconies and great views (Db-270-290 SF, cozy family room with fireplace, sauna, half-board-35 SF/person in good **restaurant** with big terrace, tel. 033-855-3422, www.hotel-schoenegg.ch, mail@hotel-schoenegg.ch).

Below the Train Station: $$$ Bären Hotel offers 17 tidy rooms with modern bathrooms. Half-board is included in the rates; the inviting **restaurant** offers garden-fresh Swiss cuisine (17.50-SF lunch specials, Db-220-260 SF, 20 SF/person less without half-board, family rooms, elevator, kids' playroom, table tennis, tel. 033-855-1419, www.baeren-wengen.ch, info@baeren-wengen.ch). From the station, cross the street to the Co-op grocery, turn right and go under the rail bridge, and follow the road down the hill—the hotel will be on your right.

Kleine Scheidegg

At 6,762 feet, this high settlement above the timberline is the closest you can stay to the Jungfraujoch, offering a chance to sleep face-to-face with the Eiger. The last train down to Lauterbrunnen leaves Kleine Scheidegg at 18:30.

Eating and Sleeping

A central place to eat is Restaurant Bahnhof, but Restaurant Grindelwaldblick has better food. If you're hiking down from Männlichen, it's easy to stop at Restaurant Grindelwaldblick on your way.

$$$ Hotel Bellevue des Alpes is a very expensive but potentially worthwhile splurge. This old 60-room alpine hotel lovingly maintains 1930s elegance. The hallway is like a museum lined with old photos (Db-380-550 SF, includes breakfast and sumptuous four-course dinner, four floors and no elevator, no TVs, closed mid-April-mid-June and mid-Sept-mid-Dec, tel. 033-855-1212, www.scheidegg-hotels.ch, welcome@scheidegg-hotels.ch).

$$ Restaurant Bahnhof is handy, in the train-station building (dorm bed-54 SF with breakfast, 74 SF also includes dinner; D-139 SF with breakfast, D-179 SF with breakfast and dinner; open year-round, tel. 033-828-7828, www.bahnhof-scheidegg.ch, info@bahnhof-scheidegg.ch).

$ Restaurant Grindelwaldblick, a 10-minute hike up along the path toward Männlichen and visible from the train station, is charming, romantic, and remote. The **restaurant**, with a great sun terrace and a cozy interior, sells good three-course lunches (20 SF) and 25-SF dinners. It has 90 beds. You can't get wheeled luggage up along the path by yourself, but for 10 SF they'll bring it up for you (dorm bed-43 SF, includes sheets and breakfast, closed Nov and May, tel. 033-855-1374, www.grindelwaldblick.ch, grindelwaldblick@grindelwald.ch).

EXPLORING THE ALPS

Scenic Lifts and Trains

Many people enjoy a high-altitude thrill ride to one of the scenic viewpoints described here (the Schilthornbahn and the Jungfraujoch), but they're quite expensive. You can also enjoy the mountains on foot with the help of more modestly priced lifts (such as the Allmendhubel funicular up from Mürren, and the lift from Wengen to Männlichen; for specifics, see "Hiking," later).

▲▲▲SCHILTHORNBAHN

The Schilthornbahn cable car carries skiers, hikers, and sightseers effortlessly to the nearly 10,000-foot summit of the **Schilthorn,** where the Piz Gloria cable-car station awaits, with its revolving restaurant, shop, and panorama terrace. At the top, you have a spectacular view of the Eiger, Mönch, and Jungfrau mountains on the horizon.

Times and Prices: You can ride to the Schilthorn and back from several points—the cable-car station near Stechelberg on the valley floor (102 SF), cliff-hanging Gimmelwald (92 SF), or the higher Mürren (80 SF). Snare a 25 percent discount for early and late rides (leaving Stechelberg 7:25-8:55 and 15:25-16:25; no late discount in high season) and in spring and fall (roughly May and Oct). If you have a Swiss Travel Pass (free ride from valley to Mürren, 50 percent discount Mürren-Schilthorn) or Eurail pass (25 percent off the whole trip), you might as well go whenever you like, because you can't double up discounts. If you're staying a few days in Mürren or Gimmelwald and planning to go up, the Schilthornbahn's Holiday Pass could make sense (free travel on all routes between Lauterbrunnen and the peak, 120 SF/4 days or 140 SF/6 days, available May-Oct only).

*Rick's Tip: Many expensive **alpine lifts offer discounted tickets** for the first (and sometimes last) trip of the day.*

Lifts go twice hourly, and the ride from Gimmelwald (including two transfers) to the Schilthorn takes 30 minutes. Lifts run all year, except during maintenance closures (a week in April and four weeks in Nov-Dec). Drivers can leave their cars at the pay lot at the valley station near Stechelberg. For more information, including current weather conditions, see www.schilthorn.ch or call 033-826-0007.

Ascending the Schilthorn: As the cable car floats between Gimmelwald and Mürren you'll see fields of wooden tripods, which serve two purposes: They stop avalanches and shelter newly planted trees. Made of wood, they're designed to eventually rot when the tree they protect is strong enough to survive the winter snowpack. From Mürren to Birg, keep an eye on the altitude meter. You can pause at Birg, which has the scary Skyline Walk (cliff-hanging viewing platform with transparent floor), a Thrill Walk (suspension walkway), and a café with a terrace.

At the Top: Head up two escalators to the Skyline View Platform. Outside, information boards identify each peak, and directional signs point hikers toward some seriously steep downhill climbs. Watch paragliders set up, psych up, and take off, flying 45 minutes with the birds to distant Interlaken. Walk along the ridge out back and step onto the Piz Gloria view platform at the end of the fenced area. This is a great place for a photo of the mountain-climber you. Youth hostelers—not realizing that rocks may hide under the snow—scream down the ice fields on plastic-bag sleds from the mountaintop. (There's an English-speaking doctor in Lauterbrunnen—see page 752.)

Back inside, peek in the Souvenir Top Shop or head down the stairs and follow the maze that leads to the Bond World 007 exhibit and cinema. This interactive exhibit, well-signed in English, is worth a few minutes for even non-Bond fans. It takes you behind the scenes of the 1969 James Bond movie, *On Her Majesty's Secret Service,* which used the Schilthorn as one of its major locations (and financed the complex's completion). Step into the role of James Bond and try your hand at flying a helicopter to Piz Gloria or bobsledding down the Alps in the simulators. Don't miss the opportunity to morph your face onto one of several Bond stars

Viewing platform at the top of the Schilthorn

(pictures available in the gift shop for a fee, of course).

At the end of the exhibit, the Bond World 007 cinema shows a 20-minute video of the natural wonders of the area, highlights a few activities—including racing down the famous Inferno ski run, briefly shares the story of the Schilthornbahn lift itself, and shows a substantial clip from *On Her Majesty's Secret Service.* If you haven't had enough Bond yet, peruse the 007 Walk of Fame, where cast and crew members from the film have left their handprints and personal messages (on the ridge to the Piz Gloria view platform).

You can hike down from the Schilthorn, but it's tough. (Hiking *up* from Gimmelwald or Mürren is easier on your knees... if you don't mind a 5,000-foot altitude gain.) For information on **hikes** from lift stations along the Schilthorn cable-car line, see "Hiking," later. My favorite "hike" from the Schilthorn is simply along the ridge out back, to get away from the station and be all alone on top of an Alp.

Summit-High Breakfast: The generous 29.50-SF "007 Breakfast Buffet" is served 8:00-10:30 on the top floor of the Piz Gloria. Save a few francs by adding the breakfast buffet to your lift ticket before heading up. The restaurant also serves salads (5-16 SF), soups (8-11 SF), and main dishes (19-36 SF) all day at prices that don't rise with the altitude.

▲▲▲JUNGFRAUBAHN

The literal high point of any trip to the Swiss Alps is a train ride through the Eiger mountain to the **Jungfraujoch** (the saddle between the Mönch and Jungfrau mountains). At 11,333 feet, it's Europe's highest train station. (If you have a heart or lung condition, check with your doctor before making this ascent.) You can enjoy the Berner Oberland without taking this trip—it's long, slow, expensive, crowded, and cold. But if the weather's good and you have a spare day and spare cash, it's fun to be up on a snowy glacier in midsummer. The views are exhilarating.

Planning Your Trip: Visiting the Jungfraujoch takes most of a day. The trip up from Lauterbrunnen takes a little under two hours each way, with a change of trains halfway at Kleine Scheidegg. If you're coming from Interlaken, Gimmelwald, or Mürren, add another half-hour. You'll want at least 1.5 hours at the top—more if you eat, hike, or sled. Expect outdoor temperatures to be around freezing in summer—so if you plan to go outside, bring a hat and gloves, as well as shoes with good traction, sunglasses, and sunscreen. Even if you stay inside, the train is chilly, and you'll need a jacket. It's smart to buy tickets the day before (they can sell out in peak season). Check the weather forecast at www.jungfrau.ch before committing. If it's cloudy, skip the trip.

Times and Prices: The train runs about twice hourly year-round. Round-trip fares are 204 SF from Interlaken Ost, 184 SF from Lauterbrunnen, 170 SF from Wengen, and 124 SF from Kleine Scheidegg. At peak periods (especially July-Aug), trains

Enjoy a sky-high breakfast.

Ride the Jungfraubahn to Europe's highest train station.

are standing-room only, and you shouldn't expect to get a seat. You can guarantee a seat (above Kleine Scheidegg only) for 5 SF extra when you make your reservation, but only on three departures per day, which limits your choices.

From May to late October, the first, second, and last trips of the day cost 25 percent less (first trips leave Interlaken Ost at 6:35/7:05 and Lauterbrunnen at 7:07/7:37—to get the discount you must leave the top by 13:00; last trip leaves Interlaken Ost at 14:05 and Lauterbrunnen at 14:37, but gives you only an hour at the top). Eurail pass holders get 25 percent off and can't combine discounts, so they should go whenever they want. The same goes for Swiss Travel Pass holders, who travel free as far as Wengen and pay only from there (also 25 percent off). For more information, visit www.jungfrau.ch or call 033-828-7233.

Ascending the Jungfraujoch: The final 50 minutes of the trip—from Kleine Scheidegg—is mostly in a tunnel. On the ascent, the train makes two five-minute stops at two "stations" actually halfway up the notorious North Face of the Eiger. You have time to look out windows and marvel at how people could climb the Eiger—and how the Swiss built this train track more than a hundred years ago. Newer train cars run multilingual videos about the history of the train line.

At the Top: Once you reach the top, breathe deep, take it easy, and move slowly—you're way high up and your body isn't used to such altitudes. Study the map to see your options. The main building has a reasonably priced self-service restaurant with expensive beverages, pricier restaurants with table service, luggage lockers, and touristy shops. A roped-in, snowy lookout plateau affords amazing views both north and south. Slip-slide along the corridors of the ice palace, which has some modest carvings. The "Alpine Sensation" is a cute, cheesy diorama with moving model trains.

You'll walk through a short tunnel to reach the most interesting parts of the complex. Take the elevator up to the Sphinx observation deck at 11,700 feet. (The Jungfrau Panorama is a 360-degree

Jungfraujoch overlooks the longest glacial flow in the Alps.

video that's pleasantly distracting while you wait in line for the elevator.) Here, the views are truly astounding—deep below to the north are Kleine Scheidegg, Gimmelwald, and in the distance, Interlaken; to the south spreads the Aletsch Glacier—Europe's longest, at nearly 11 miles. The Sphinx has a tiny snack stand and a few benches where you can sit to munch a sandwich. There's a scientific measurement station here, and back downstairs by the elevator are some posters with interesting statistics on recent climate warming and the recovery of the ozone layer.

Just outside, a "Snow Fun" zone set up on the Aletsch Glacier offers skiing and snowboarding (35 SF), sledding (15 SF), and a zip line (20 SF—prices include equipment; 45 SF for all three activities, April-Oct only). If properly equipped (you'll want poles and hiking boots), you can hike an hour across the ice to Mönchsjochhütte (a mountain hut with a small restaurant).

You could combine one of the best hikes in the region—from Männlichen to Kleine Scheidegg—with your trip up to the Jungfraujoch (see page 770).

Hiking

This area offers days of hikes. Many are a fun combination of trails, mountain trains, and cable-car rides. The information below can help you decide which hike to tackle, but isn't intended as a turn-by-turn guide. Good hiking maps and more detailed trail descriptions are essential—and available from TIs and hotels. Before setting out on any hike, check locally to be sure you've made the best match between your skills, gear, and trail conditions. Snow can persist on trails even into summer.

Hiking Tips

Before any serious hiking, invest in a **good hiking map** at any TI, and ask about current weather and trail conditions. For easy hikes, it's usually enough to use the 3-D maps in the free brochures (called Wandern/Hiking) published by the Schilthornbahn (for the west side of the valley) and the Jungfraubahn (for the east side); they're available at stations, hotels, and TIs. These overview maps of the mountainsides also make attractive souvenirs.

Don't forget a **water bottle** and some **munchies.** It's wise to carry **sun protection,** an **extra layer of clothing,** and basic **first-aid supplies.** Know when the last lifts run in the afternoon. Trails are well-marked, with yellow signs listing destinations and the estimated time it'll take you to walk there. Once under way, don't mind the fences (although be aware that wires can be solar-powered electric); a hiker has the right of way in Switzerland.

Keep an eye on the **weather.** Locals know the weather report (as much of their income depends on it). Clouds can roll in anytime, but on warm summer days, skies are usually clearest in the morning. All over the region, TV sets are tuned to the local weather station, with real-time views from all the famous peaks. Check **weather reports** and view **live webcams** at www.jungfrau.ch and www.schilthorn.ch. For more detailed weather reports in English, visit www.meteoswiss.admin.ch.

Rick's Tip: **If it rains, don't despair.** *Clouds can roll out just as quickly. With good rain gear and the right choice of trail, you can still enjoy a hike, with surprise views as the clouds break. Some good* **bad-weather hikes** *are the North Face trail, the walk from Mürren/Allmendhubel to Grütschalp, and the Lauterbrunnen Valley walk, including a visit to Trümmelbach Falls.*

Snow can curtail your hiking plans, even in July. Before setting out on any hike, get advice from the TI or a knowledgeable local. The high trails (Männlichen to Kleine Scheidegg, Schynige Platte to First, and anything from Schilthorn or Birg) are typically passable only from June into October.

Easier Hikes

▲▲CLOUDY-DAY LAUTERBRUNNEN VALLEY WALK

Take a pleasant walk on the easy trail along the floor of the Lauterbrunnen Valley. You don't ever need to (and shouldn't) walk along the main road, which parallels the river. A fine, paved, mostly vehicle-free farm lane (great for bikers) goes all the way along the valley on the opposite side of the river from the main road. Small bridges let you cross from the lane to the main road at various points. Near Lauterbrunnen, there's also a path right next to the river.

From Lauterbrunnen: For a smell-the-cows-and-flowers lowland walk—ideal for a cloudy day, weary body, or tight budget—try this three-mile, basically level ramble: Take the PostBus from Lauterbrunnen town to the Schilthornbahn cable-car station, then follow the river back to Staubbach Falls, near the town church (you can reverse the route, but it's

a gradual uphill to Stechelberg; see page 753 for more about Staubbach Falls).

As you amble back toward Lauterbrunnen, you can detour to Trümmelbach Falls (figure 45 minutes from the Schilthornbahn station to the falls, and another 45 minutes to Lauterbrunnen; see page 753). For a shorter walk back, ride the bus only as far as Trümmelbach and start from there.

Along the way between Trümmelbach Falls and Lauterbrunnen, look up to see BASE jumpers—parachutists who leap from cliffs. Also, in this "Valley of Many Waterfalls" (literally—there are 72), you'll see cone-like mounds piled against the sides of the cliffs, formed by centuries of rocks hurled by tumbling rivers.

From Gimmelwald or Mürren: If you're staying in Gimmelwald or Mürren, try this plan: Take the Schilthornbahn lift down to the station near Stechelberg, then walk 1.5 hours along the river to Lauterbrunnen (side-tripping to Trümmelbach Falls after 45 minutes). To return to Gimmelwald or Mürren from Lauterbrunnen, take the cable car up to Grütschalp (10 minutes); then you can either take the train (10 min) or hike (1 hour) to Mürren. From Mürren, it's a downhill walk (30 minutes) to Gimmelwald. (This loop trip can be reversed or started at any point along the way—such as Lauterbrunnen or Mürren.)

▲▲NORTH FACE TRAIL (FROM MÜRREN)

For a pleasant, family-friendly 2.5-hour hike, head out along this four-mile trail, starting at 6,385 feet and finishing at 5,375 feet (some stretches can be challenging if you're not in shape). As with any trail described here, before starting out, get a trail map from the Mürren TI or the cable-car station and confirm the route.

To reach the trail, ride the Allmendhubel funicular up from Mürren (good restaurant at top, see page 762). From there, follow the signed route, which loops counterclockwise around to Mürren.

Trümmelbach Falls

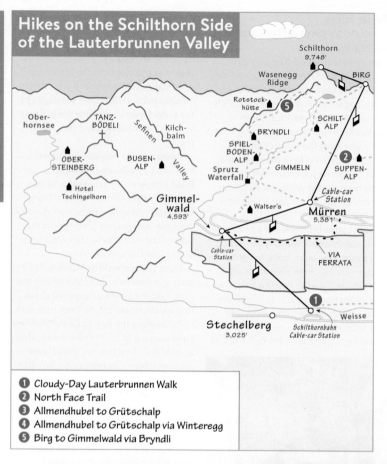

Hikes on the Schilthorn Side of the Lauterbrunnen Valley

Schilthorn
9,748'

Wasenegg Ridge

BIRG

Rotstock-hütte

5

SCHILT-ALP

BRYNDLI

SPIEL-BODEN-ALP

GIMMELN

SUPPEN-ALP

2

Ober-hornsee

TANZ-BÖDELI

Kilch-balm

Sefinen Valley

OBER-STEINBERG

BUSEN-ALP

Sprutz Waterfall

Hotel Tschingelhorn

Gimmel-wald
4,593'

Walter's

Cable-car Station

Mürren
5,381'

Cable-car Station

VIA FERRATA

1

Stechelberg
3,025'

Weisse

Schilthornbahn
Cable-car Station

1. Cloudy-Day Lauterbrunnen Walk
2. North Face Trail
3. Allmendhubel to Grütschalp
4. Allmendhubel to Grütschalp via Winteregg
5. Birg to Gimmelwald via Bryndli

The family-friendly North Face trail takes you past flowery meadows and mountain huts.

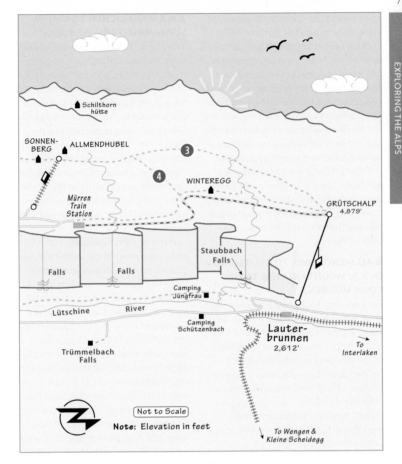

As this trail doesn't technically begin at Allmendhubel, you'll start by following signs to *Sonnenberg*. Then just follow the blue signs. You'll enjoy great views, flowery meadows, mountain huts, and a dozen information boards along the way, describing the fascinating climbing history of the great peaks around you.

Along the trail, you'll pass four farms (technically "alps," as they are only open in the summer) that serve meals and drinks. Sonnenberg was allowed to break the all-wood building code with concrete for protection against avalanches. Suppenalp is quainter. Lean against the house with a salad, soup, or sandwich and enjoy the view. Below Suppenalp, a five-minute walk toward Mürren takes you to a small public park with a zipline and a slide.

Older huts are built into the protected side of rocks and outcroppings, in anticipation of avalanches. Above Suppenalp, Blumental ("Flower Valley") is hopping with marmots. Because hunters are not allowed near lifts, animals have learned that these are safe places to hang out—giving tourists a better chance of spotting them.

The trail leads up and over to a group of huts called Schiltalp (good food, drink, and service, and a romantic farm setting). If the poles under the eaves have bells, the cows are up here. If not, the cows are still at the lower farms. Half the cows in Gimmelwald (about 100) spend their summers here. In July, August, and September, you can watch cheese being made and have a snack or drink. Thirty years ago, each family had its own hut. Labor was cheap and available. Today, it's a communal thing, with several families sharing the expense of a single cow herder. Cow herders are master cheesemakers and have veterinary skills, too.

From Schiltalp, the trail winds gracefully down toward Spielbodenalp. From there, you can finish the North Face trail, continuing down and left through meadows and the hamlet of Gimmeln, then back to Mürren.

▲ALLMENDHUBEL TO GRÜTSCHALP (A.K.A. MOUNTAIN VIEW TRAIL, FROM MÜRREN)

For a not-too-tough two-hour walk with great Jungfrau views, ride the funicular from Mürren to Allmendhubel and walk to Grütschalp (a drop of about 1,500 feet), where you can catch the train back to Mürren or the funicular down to Lauterbrunnen. You'll see this route called the "Mountain View trail" on maps and brochures. An easier version goes from Allmendhubel to Grütschalp via Winteregg and its cheese farm.

For an easy family stroll with grand views, walk from Mürren just above the train tracks either to Winteregg (40 minutes, restaurant, playground, train station) or through even better scenery on to Grütschalp (1 hour, train station).

▲▲▲MÄNNLICHEN TO KLEINE SCHEIDEGG (FROM WENGEN)

This scenic walk is the best of all worlds: both dramatic and relatively easy (2.5 miles, 1-1.5 hours, 900-foot altitude drop to Kleine Scheidegg). It's entertaining all the way, with glorious mountain views. If you missed the plot, it's the Young Maiden (Jungfrau) being protected from the Ogre (Eiger) by the Monk (Mönch). The trail usually opens sometime in June and closes due to snow in October. Ask about conditions and get a map at the lift stations or at TIs; there are also useful webcams at www.maennlichen.ch and www.jungfrau.ch.

If the weather's good, start off bright and early. From the Lauterbrunnen train station, take the little mountain train up to Wengen. Sit on the right side of the train for great valley and waterfall views. In Wengen, buy a picnic at the Co-op grocery across the square from the station (daily 8:00-18:30 in summer), walk across town, and catch the lift to Männlichen, located on top of the ridge high above you (22 SF, half-price with Swiss Travel Pass—see page 781, 3-4/hour, 2-minute trip, runs June-mid-Oct only, first ascent at 8:30, at 8:00 in early July-Aug, tel. 033-855-2933, www.maennlichen.ch). The lift can be open even if the trail is closed; if the weather is questionable, confirm that the Männlichen to Kleine Scheideggtrail is open before ascending. Don't waste time in Wengen if it's sunny—you can linger

Cow bells on a herder's hut

Easy trail between Mürren and Grütschalp

back here after your hike.

Riding the gondola from Wengen to Männlichen, you'll go over the old lift station (inundated by a 1978 avalanche that buried a good part of Wengen—notice there's no development in the "red zone" above the tennis courts). Farms are built with earthen ramps on the uphill side in anticipation of the next slide. The forest of avalanche fences near the top was built after that 1978 avalanche. As you ascend you can also survey Wengen—the bright red roofs mark new vacation condos, mostly English-owned and used only a few weeks a year.

When you get to the station at the top of the Wengen-Männlichen lift, see if they have any free "king for a day" envelopes near the ticket window; these fun souvenirs open up to make a panoramic crown that names the mountains you're seeing.

For a detour that'll give you an easy king- or queen-of-the-day feeling, turn left from the lift station, and hike uphill 10 minutes to the little peak (Männlichen Gipfel, 7,500 feet) topped with a crown-shaped viewpoint.

Then go back to the lift station (which

has a great kids' area) and enjoy the walk—facing spectacular alpine panorama views—to Kleine Scheidegg for a picnic or restaurant lunch. To start the hike, leave the Wengen-Männlichen lift station to the right. Walk past the second Männlichen lift station (this one leads to Grindelwald, the touristy town in the valley to your left). Ahead of you in the distance, left to right, are the north faces of the Eiger, Mönch, and Jungfrau; in the foreground is the Tschuggen peak, and just behind it, the Lauberhorn. This hike takes you around the left (east) side of this ridge. Simply follow the signs for Kleine Scheidegg, and you'll be there in about an hour—a little more for gawkers, picnickers, and photographers. You might have to tiptoe through streams of melted snow—or some small snow banks, even well into the summer—but the path is well-marked, well-maintained, and mostly level all the way to Kleine Scheidegg.

About 35 minutes into the hike, you'll reach a bunch of benches and a shelter with incredible unobstructed views of all three peaks—the perfect picnic spot. Fifteen minutes later, on the left, you'll

Hiking from Männlichen to Kleine Scheidegg: Wow!

see the first sign of civilization: Restaurant Grindelwaldblick (the best lunch stop up here, open daily, closed Nov and May, described on page 768). Hike to the restaurant's fun mountain lookout to survey the Eiger and look down on the Kleine Scheidegg (rated ▲▲ for its spectacular panoramic mountain view). After 10 more minutes, you'll be at the Kleine Scheidegg train station, with plenty of lunch options (including Restaurant Bahnhof, described on page 768).

Optional Add-Ons: From Kleine Scheidegg, you can catch the train up to "the top of Europe" (see Jungfraujoch listing, earlier). Or you can head downhill to Wengen by train or on foot (gorgeous 30-minute hike to the Wengernalp station, a little farther to the Allmend stop; 60 more steep minutes from there into Wengen—not dangerous, but requires a good set of knees). The alpine views might be accompanied by the valley-filling mellow sound of cow bells, alphorns, and distant avalanches. If the weather turns bad or you run out of steam, catch the train at any of the stations along the way. Avoid the boring final descent from Wengen to Lauterbrunnen—it's knee-killing steep; catch the train instead.

Rick's Tip: The Berner Oberland has **great skiing and snowboarding** *in winter. Three ski areas cluster around the Lauterbrunnen Valley:* **Mürren-Schilthorn** *(best for experts),* **Kleine Scheidegg-Männlichen** *(busiest, best variety of runs), and* **Grindelwald-First** *(best for beginners and intermediates, lower elevation means iffier snowpack). For info and prices, see www.jungfrauwinter.ch.*

Difficult Hikes
Several tough trails lead down from the Schilthorn (there's a reason that virtually all visitors take the cable car down). Only a serious, experienced hiker should

consider walking all or part of the way down into Mürren or Gimmelwald. Proper shoes and clothing (weather can change quickly) and good knees are required. Don't attempt to hike down unless the trail is clear of snow. While it's possible to make the steep descent directly from the top of the Schilthorn, I prefer the less strenuous (but still challenging) hike from the intermediate cable-car station at Birg.

▲▲BIRG TO GIMMELWALD VIA BRYNDLI (FROM THE SCHILTHORN)
You can combine this difficult downhill hike from the Birg cable-car station with a visit to the Schilthorn by buying the round-trip excursion early-bird fare (it's cheaper than the Gimmelwald-Schilthorn-Birg ticket). Visit the summit first, then descend via cable car to Birg to hike down.

The most interesting trail from Birg to Gimmelwald is the high one via Grauseeli lake and Wasenegg Ridge to Bryndli, then down to Spielbodenalp and the Sprutz Waterfall. Warning: This trail drops 4,500 feet, is quite steep and slippery in places, and can take four hours. Locals take their kindergartners on this hike, but Americans unused to alpine hikes shouldn't attempt it.

From the Birg lift station, hike toward the Schilthorn, taking your first left down and passing along the left side of the little Grauseeli lake. From the lake, a gravelly trail leads down rough switchbacks (including a stretch where the path

narrows and you can hang onto a guide cable against the cliff face) until it levels out. When you see a rock painted with arrows pointing to Mürren and Rotstock-hütte, follow the path to Rotstockhütte (traditional old farm with light meals and drinks), traversing the cow-grazed mountainside.

The safer, well-signposted approach to Bryndli is to drop down to Rotstockhütte, then climb back up to Bryndli. Thrill-seekers instead follow Wasenegg Ridge. It's more scary than dangerous if you're sure-footed and can handle the 50-foot-long "tightrope-with-handrail" section along an extremely narrow ledge with a thousand-foot drop. This trail gets you to Bryndli with the least altitude drop. A barbed-wire fence leads you to Bryndli's knobby little summit, where you'll enjoy an incredible 360-degree view and a chance to sign your name on the register stored in the little wooden box.

From Bryndli, a steep trail winds directly down toward Gimmelwald and soon hits a bigger, easier trail. The trail bends right (just before the farm/restaurant at Spielbodenalp), leading to Sprutz. Walk under the Sprutz Waterfall, then follow a steep, wooded trail that deposits you in a meadow of flowers at the top side of Gimmelwald.

▲▲SCHYNIGE PLATTE TO FIRST (ABOVE INTERLAKEN)

The best day I've had hiking in the Berner Oberland was when I made this demanding six-hour ridge walk, with Lake Brienz on one side and all that Jungfrau beauty on the other. Start at the Wilderswil train station (just outside Interlaken), and catch the little train up to Schynige Platte (6,560 feet; 32 SF, every 40 minutes, 55 minutes, runs late May-late Oct only). The high point on the trail is Faulhorn (8,790 feet, with a famous mountaintop hotel). From here, hike on to First (7,110 feet), where you ride a small mini-gondola down to Grindelwald (29 SF; runs continuously—until at least 17:00 in summer)

and catch a train back via Zweilutsch-inen to wherever you're staying. The TI at Wilderswil train station produces a great Schynige Platte map/guide narrating the train ride up and describing various hiking options from there.

At the Schynige Platte station, look for a promotional booth run by Lowa, a local manufacturer of top-end hiking boots. They provide free loaners (already broken in) to hikers who'd like to give their boots a try.

Easier Options at Schynige Platte: For a shorter (3-hour) ridge walk, consider the well-signposted Panoramaweg, a loop from Schynige Platte to Daub Peak.

The alpine flower park at the Schynige Platte station offers a delightful stroll through several hundred alpine flowers, including a chance to see edelweiss growing in the wild (free, late May-late Oct daily 8:30-18:00, www.alpengarten.ch).

Mountain Biking

Mountain biking is popular and accepted, as long as you stay on the clearly marked mountain-bike paths. You can rent bikes at **Stäger Sport** in Mürren (see page 761) or **Imboden Bike** in Lauterbrunnen (see page 752). The Lauterbrunnen shop is bigger, has a wider selection of bikes, and is likely to be open when the Mürren one isn't. If you pick up a bike in Mürren, ask if you can drop it at the Lauterbrunnen train station.

As with any activity in the mountains,

get maps and seek advice locally before venturing out. I've outlined some of the most popular bike rides below.

Lauterbrunnen to Interlaken: This is a gentle downhill ride on a peaceful bike path across the river from the road (don't bike on the road itself). You can return to Lauterbrunnen by train (you'll have to buy a regular ticket for the bike). Or rent a bike in Interlaken, take the train to Lauterbrunnen, and ride back.

Lauterbrunnen Valley (between Stechelberg and Lauterbrunnen town): This delightful, easy bike path features plenty of diversions along the way (see "Cloudy-Day Lauterbrunnen Valley Walk" on page 773).

Mürren to Winteregg to Grütschalp and Back: This fairly level route takes you through high country, with awesome mountain views.

Mürren to Winteregg to Lauterbrunnen: This scenic descent, on a service road with loose gravel, takes you to the Lauterbrunnen Valley floor.

Mürren to Gimmelwald: This is a pleasant, downhill road. For a sweat-free return, catch the lift (with your bike) from Gimmelwald back to Mürren.

TRANSPORTATION

Getting Around the Berner Oberland

For more than a century, this region has been the target of nature-worshiping pilgrims. And Swiss engineers and visionaries have made the most exciting alpine perches accessible.

By Lifts and Trains

Part of the fun here—and most of the expense—is riding the many mountain trains and lifts (gondolas and cable cars). To keep expenses down, explore each side of the valley separately, rather than criss-cross repeatedly between them.

Trains connect Interlaken to Wilder-

swil, Lauterbrunnen, Wengen, Kleine Scheidegg, the Jungfraujoch, and also Grindelwald. Lifts connect Wengen to Männlichen; Grindelwald to First; Lauterbrunnen to Grütschalp (where a train connects to Mürren); and the cable-car station near Stechelberg to Gimmelwald, Mürren, and the Schilthorn.

For an overview of your many options, study the "Alpine Lifts in the Berner Oberland" map on page 745 and the "Berner Oberland at a Glance" sidebar on page 742. Lifts generally go at least twice hourly, from about 7:00 until about 20:00 (sneak preview: www.jungfrau.ch or www. schilthorn.ch).

Beyond Interlaken, trains and lifts into the Jungfrau region are 25 percent off with a Eurail pass (doesn't require a flexi-day); with the Swiss Travel Pass, they're covered up to Wengen or Mürren (uphill from there, pass holders get 25-50 percent off). Ask about discounts for early-morning and late-afternoon trips, youths, seniors, families, groups (assemble a party of 10 and you'll save about 25 percent), and those staying awhile. Generally, round-trips are double the one-way cost, though some high-up trains and lifts are 10-20 percent cheaper. It's possible to buy a package covering all of your lifts at once, but then you don't have the flexibility to change with the weather.

POPULAR PASSES

Because of high ticket prices, rail passes are a good deal in Switzerland, often even for just a short trip. However, if you'll be

traveling with a Eurail pass, you won't need to get a separate pass for Switzerland and you can skip over the rest of this section.

For such a little country, Switzerland has a surprising array of train passes and deals. I've listed the most popular ones here. For detailed advice on figuring out the smartest rail pass options for your train trip, visit www.ricksteves.com/rail. Prices listed below are subject to change.

Passes sold in US and in Switzerland: The following passes are sold at any staffed Swiss train station, but can be ordered in advance from home—a good idea if you'll be entering Switzerland by train from a neighboring country and need to have the pass on hand to cover the Swiss portion of your journey.

The **Swiss Travel Pass** is the basic version, covering all trains, boats, and buses, plus admission to most Swiss museums, and offering a half-price discount on most high-mountain trains and lifts. It comes as either a flexipass or a consecutive-day pass (which is generally the better deal: 210 SF/3-day, 251 SF/4-day, 363 SF/8-day; prices are for second class—first class is 50 percent more expensive). Both types of passes cover the cost of transportation for a specified number of days (but do not cover seat or overnight-train reservations).

The **Half-Fare Travel Card** gives you a 50 percent discount on all national and private trains (in either class), postal buses, boats, and many lifts (120 SF for one month). This can save you money if your Swiss travel adds up to more than 240 SF in point-to-point tickets.

Parents getting either a Swiss Travel Pass or one-month Half-Fare Travel Card can request a **Swiss Family Card** for free; this allows kids 6–15 ride to free with a parent as long as they're listed on the card. Kids 6–15 without a Family Card (or not accompanied by a parent) pay half of the full adult pass price; kids under 6 ride for free.

Passes sold only in Switzerland: You can buy the following passes at any staffed Swiss train station, though you won't need either pass if you're planning to buy a Swiss Travel Pass or Half-Fare Travel Card.

A **Junior Card** is a good deal for parents who won't be buying a Swiss Pass. Valid across Switzerland, a Junior Card allows kids under 16 to travel free with at least one parent. The card pays for itself within the first hour of travel on trains and lifts (30 SF/one child, 60 SF/two or more children).

The **Berner Oberland Regional Pass** covers most trains, buses, and lifts in this area (and all the way to Bern and Luzern). It offers a half-price discount on most high-mountain trains and lifts (such as the Mürren-Schilthorn cable car, and the train from Kleine Scheidegg up to the Jungfraujoch). While it could save you money over individual tickets, it's not much cheaper than a Swiss Travel Pass that covers the whole country (4 days-240 SF, 6 days-300 SF, 8 days-340 SF, valid May-Oct, www.regiopass-berneroberland.ch).

By Car

Interlaken, Lauterbrunnen, and Stechelberg are accessible by car. You can't drive to Gimmelwald, Mürren, Wengen, or Kleine Scheidegg, but don't let that stop you from staying up in the mountains: Park the car and zip up on a lift. To catch the lift to Gimmelwald and Mürren (and the Schilthorn), park at the cable-car station near Stechelberg (4 SF/2 hours, 10 SF/day; for more on the cable car, see page 761). To catch the train to Wengen or Kleine Scheidegg, park at the train station in Lauterbrunnen (2.50 SF/2 hours, 11 SF/9-24 hours).

By Bus

A convenient local bus, called the PostBus, connects points along the valley, including a stop at the Schilthornbahn cable-car station (www.postauto.ch).

Germany

Germany (Deutschland) is energetic and organized. The European Union's most populous country and biggest economy, Germany is home to 82 million people—one-third Catholic and one-third Protestant. It's 138,000 square miles (about half the size of Texas) and bordered by nine countries. Germany is young compared with most of its European neighbors ("born" in 1871) but was a founding member of the EU.

Germany offers travelers an intriguing mix: rollicking Munich, the little medieval-walled town of Rothenburg, the sleepy villages lining the mighty Rhine, and the surprising city of Berlin, whose monuments embody the country's past turbulence and modern resurgence.

CUISINE SCENE AT A GLANCE

Germanic food is filling, meaty, and—by European standards—inexpensive. Each region has its specialties, which are often good values. Be adventurous.

Traditional **restaurants** go by many names. At a beer hall (*Brauhaus*) or a beer garden (*Biergarten*), you can get big, basic, stick-to-the-ribs meals and huge liter beers (called *ein Mass* in German, or "*ein* pitcher" in English). Many beer halls have a cafeteria system; the food is usually *selbstdienst* (self-service). Any real beer garden will keep a few tables (those without tablecloths) available for customers who buy only beer and bring their own food.

Gasthaus, Gasthof, and *Gaststube* all loosely describe an informal, inn-type eatery. A *Kneipe* is a bar, and a *Keller* (or *Ratskeller*) is a restaurant or tavern located in a cellar. A *Weinstube* serves wine and usually traditional (that is, meaty) food as well.

Most eateries have menus tacked onto their front doors, with an English menu inside. Many restaurants offer inexpensive €6-9 weekday hot-lunch specials that aren't listed on the regular menu (look for the *Tageskarte* or *Tagesangebot,* or just ask—may be offered at dinner, too). For smaller portions, order from the *kleine Hunger* (small hunger) section of the menu. Vegetarians can opt for big dinner-size salads.

At any restaurant, a *Stammtisch* sign hanging over or on a table means that it's reserved for regulars.

Tipping: If you order your food at a counter, don't tip. At restaurants that have table service, a gratuity is included in your bill, so you don't need to tip further, but it's nice to round up your bill about 10 percent for great service.

Rather than leaving coins behind on the table (considered slightly rude), Germans usually pay directly: When the server comes by with the bill, simply hand over paper money, stating the total you'd like to pay. For example, if paying for a €10 meal with a €20 bill, while handing your money to the server, say "Eleven, please" (or "*Elf, bitte*" if you've got your German numbers down). The server will keep a €1 tip and give you €9 in change.

Lately, some restaurants in well-touristed areas have added a "Tip is not included" line, in English, at the bottom of the bill. This is misleading, as the prices on any menu in Germany *do* include service. I would not tip one cent more at a restaurant that includes this note on the bill.

Budget Options: It's easy to get a meal in Germany for €10 or less. Bakeries sell cheap sandwiches and often have tables. Department-stores usually have self-service cafeterias. A *Schnellimbiss* is a small fast-food takeaway stand that sells bratwurst and other grilled sausage. Some stands and shops sell Turkish-style *Döner Kebab* (gyro-like, pita-wrapped rotisserie meat).

Munich

Munich ("München" in German) is one of Germany's most historic, artistic, and entertaining cities. Until 1871, it was the capital of an independent Bavaria. Its imperial palaces and grand boulevards constantly remind visitors that Munich has long been a political and cultural powerhouse.

Walking through Munich, you'll understand why it is consistently voted one of Germany's most livable cities. It's safe, clean, cultured, built on a human scale, and close to the beauties of nature. Though Munich is a major metropolis, its low-key atmosphere has led Germans to dub it "Millionendorf"—the "village of a million people."

Orient yourself in Munich's old center, with its colorful pedestrian zones. Immerse yourself in the city's art and history—crown jewels, Baroque theater, royal palaces, great paintings, and beautiful parks. Spend time in a frothy beer hall or outdoor *Biergarten,* prying big pretzels from no-nonsense beer maids amidst an oompah atmosphere.

MUNICH IN 3 DAYS

Day 1: Follow the "Munich City Walk" laid out in this chapter, visiting sights along the way. After lunch, tour the Residenz.

On any evening: Try a beer hall one night and a beer garden on another. Stroll through Marienplatz and the core pedestrian streets. Have a dinner picnic at the English Garden.

Day 2: Visit the Dachau Memorial in the morning. Later, if the weather's fine, rent a bike to enjoy the English Garden. Or tour the top art museum, the Alte Pinakothek.

Day 3: Take your pick of these fine sights: Egyptian Museum, Deutsches Museum, Neue Pinakothek, Munich City Museum, and—away from the center—the Nymphenburg Palace and BMW-Welt and Museum.

With extra time: Day-trip options include a day-long bus tour to see "Mad" King Ludwig's famous Neuschwanstein Castle, the inspiration for Disneyland's castle (see "Tours" on following page).

ORIENTATION

The tourist's Munich is circled by a ring road (site of the old town wall) marked by four old gates: Karlstor (near the main train station—the Hauptbahnhof), Sendlinger Tor, Isartor (near the river), and Odeonsplatz (no surviving gate, near the palace). Marienplatz marks the city's center. A great pedestrian-only zone (Kaufingerstrasse and Neuhauser Strasse) cuts this circle in half, running neatly from the Karlstor and the train station through Marienplatz to the Isartor. Orient yourself along this east-west axis. Ninety percent of the sights and hotels I recommend are within a 20-minute walk of Marienplatz and each other.

Tourist Information

Munich has two helpful city-run TIs (www.muenchen.de). One is in front of the **main train station** (Mon-Sat 9:00-20:00, Sun 10:00-18:00, with your back to the tracks, walk through the central hall, step outside, and turn right). The other TI is on Munich's main square, **Marienplatz,** below the glockenspiel (Mon-Fri 9:00-19:00, Sat 9:00-16:00, Sun 10:00-14:00).

Private Munich Ticket offices inside the TIs sell concert and event tickets (www.muenchenticket.de). The free magazine *In München* lists all movies and entertainment in town (in German, organized by date).

At counter #1 in the train station's main *Reisezentrum* (travel center, opposite track 21), the hardworking, eager-to-help **EurAide desk** is a godsend for Eurailers and budget travelers. Paid by the German rail company to help you design your train travels (including day trips), EurAide makes reservations and sells train tickets, *couchettes,* and sleepers for the same price you'd pay at the other counters (open May-Oct Mon-Fri 8:30-20:00, Sat 8:30-14:00, closed Sun; off-season Mon-Fri 10:00-19:00, closed Sat-Sun and Jan-Feb, www.euraide.com). As EurAide helps about 500 visitors per day in the summer, a line can build up; do your homework and have a list of questions ready.

Tours

Munich's two largest tour companies, Radius Tours and Munich Walk, run comparable tours in Munich as well as day trips to Dachau, Neuschwanstein Castle, and other places. Both offer discounts to Rick Steves readers.

Munich Walk uses Marienplatz as its meeting point (tel. 089/2423-1767, www.munichwalktours.de). Consider a walking tour (€12-15, daily year-round, 2-2.5 hours), "Beer and Brewery" tour (€28, May-mid-Sept on Mon, Wed, and Fri-Sat at 18:15, fewer tours off-season, 3.5 hours), Bavarian food-tasting tour with lunch at Viktualienmarkt (€24 includes food), or bike tour (€25, April-Oct Sat-Sun only).

Radius Tours has a convenient office and meeting point in the main train station, in front of track 32 (tel. 089/543-487-7730, www.radiustours.com). Consider a walking tour (€13-15, daily at 10:00, 2-2.5 hours), "Bavarian Beer and Food" tour with samples and a visit to the Beer and Oktoberfest Museum (€30, April-mid-Oct Mon-Sat 18:00, 3.5 hours, reserve well in advance), or a 3.5-hour bike tour (€25, April-mid-Oct daily at 10:00).

Gray Line Tours has hop-on, hop-off city bus tours that leave from in front of the Karstadt department store at Bahnhofplatz, directly across from the train station (buses run 9:40-18:00). Choose the basic, 1-hour "Express Circle," or the more extensive 2.5-hour "Grand Circle," which includes Nymphenburg Palace and BMW-Welt and Museum and is an efficient way to see both. Just show up and pay the driver (€17 Express tour—valid all day, €22 Grand tour—valid 24 hours, daily in season, tel. 089/5490-7560, www.sightseeing-munich.com).

Rick's Tip: *If you're interested in a* **Gray Line bus tour** *of the city or to nearby castles,* **get discounted tickets at EurAide** *(cash only). They also sell* **Munich Walk** *tour tickets.*

While you can do many **day trips from Munich** on your own by train, going as part of an organized group can be convenient. All-day tours to **Neuschwanstein** are offered by **Radius,** using **public transit** (€42, €35 with rail pass, does not include castle admission; daily April-Dec;

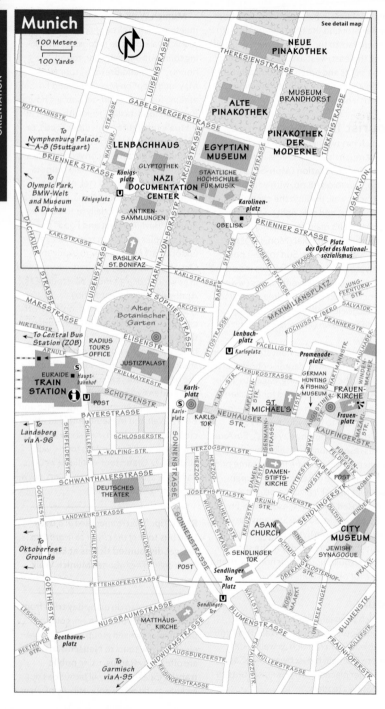

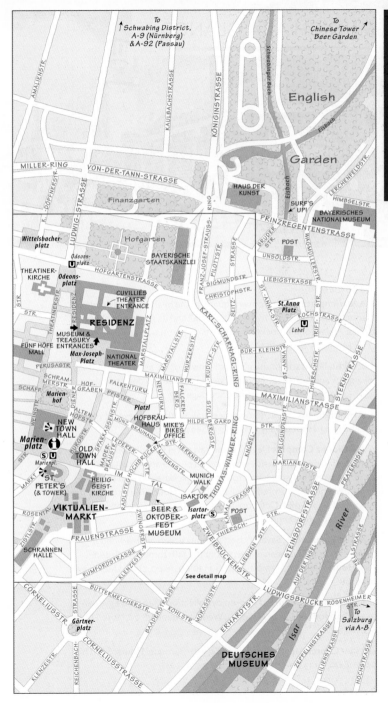

MUNICH AT A GLANCE

In the Center

▲▲**Marienplatz** Munich's main square, at the heart of a lively pedestrian zone, watched over by New Town Hall and its glockenspiel show. **Hours:** Always open; glockenspiel jousts daily at 11:00 and 12:00, plus 17:00 May-Oct. See page 792.

▲▲**Viktualienmarkt** Munich's "small-town" open-air market, perfect for a quick snack or meal. **Hours:** Closed Sun; beer garden open daily 10:00-22:00 (weather permitting). See page 797.

▲▲**Hofbräuhaus** World-famous beer hall, worth a visit even if you're not chugging. **Hours:** Daily 9:00-23:30. See page 805.

▲▲**Residenz Complex** Elegant palace awash in Bavarian opulence. Complex includes the Residenz Museum (private apartments), Residenz Treasury (housing royal crowns and knickknacks), and the impressive, heavily restored Cuvilliés Theater. **Hours:** Museum and treasury—daily April-mid-Oct 9:00-18:00, mid-Oct-March 10:00-17:00; theater keeps shorter hours. See page 808.

▲▲**Alte Pinakothek** Bavaria's best painting gallery, with a wonderful collection of European masters from the 14th through 19th century. **Hours:** Tue 10:00-20:00, Wed-Sun 10:00-18:00, closed Mon. See page 818.

▲▲**Egyptian Museum** Easy-to-enjoy collection of ancient Egyptian treasures. **Hours:** Tue 10:00-20:00, Wed-Sun 10:00-18:00, closed Mon. See page 822.

▲**Asam Church** Small church dripping with Baroque. **Hours:** Sat-Thu 9:00-18:00, Fri 13:00-18:00. See page 801.

▲**Munich City Museum** The city's history in five floors. **Hours:** Tue-Sun 10:00-18:00, closed Mon. See page 816.

▲**Neue Pinakothek** The Alte's twin sister, with paintings from 1800 to 1920. **Hours:** Wed 10:00-20:00, Thu-Mon 10:00-18:00, closed Tue. See page 821.

▲**English Garden** The largest city park on the Continent, packed with locals, tourists, surfers, and nude sunbathers. (On a bike, I'd rate this ▲▲.) **Hours:** Always open. See page 822.

▲**Deutsches Museum** Germany's version of our Smithsonian Institution, with 10 miles of science and technology exhibits. **Hours:** Daily 9:00-17:00. See page 824.

Outside the City Center

▲▲**Nymphenburg Palace Complex** Impressive summer palace, featuring a hunting lodge, coach museum, fine royal porcelain collection, and vast park. **Hours:** Park—daily 6:00-dusk, palace buildings—daily April-mid-Oct 9:00-18:00, mid-Oct-March 10:00-16:00. See page 825.

▲▲**BMW-Welt and Museum** The carmaker's futuristic museum and floating-cloud showroom, highlighting BMW past, present, and future. **Hours:** BMW-Welt building—exhibits daily 9:00-18:00; museum—Tue-Sun 10:00-18:00, closed Mon. See page 830.

▲▲**Dachau Memorial** Notorious Nazi concentration camp, now a powerful museum and memorial. **Hours:** Daily 9:00-17:00. See page 850.

Jan-March tours run Mon, Wed, and Fri-Sun; reserve ahead, www.radiustours.com), and by **Gray Line Tours** via **private bus** (€51, does not include castle admission, daily all year, www.sightseeing-munich.com). Although they're a little more expensive, I prefer the guided private bus tours because you're guaranteed a seat (public transportation in summer is routinely standing-room only).

For organized tours to **Dachau,** see page 850.

Six people splitting the cost can make a **private guide** affordable. I've had great days with **Georg Reichlmayr** (€165/3 hours, tel. 08131/86800, mobile 0170-341-6384, www.muenchen-stadtfuehrung.de, info@muenchen-stadtfuehrung.de) and **Monika Hank** (€120/2 hours, €140/3 hours, tel. 089/311-4819, mobile 0172-547-8123, monika.hank@web.de).

Rick's Tip: *Supposedly* **"free" walking tours are advertised all over town.** *Tipping is expected, and the guides actually have to pay the company for each person who takes the tour—so unless you tip more than they owe the company, they don't make a penny. Expect a sales pitch for the company's other, paid tours.*

Helpful Hints

Museum Tips: Museums closed on Monday include the Alte Pinakothek, Munich City Museum, the BMW Museum, and the Beer and Oktoberfest Museum (also closed Sun). The Neue Pinakothek closes on Tuesday. The art museums are generally open late one night a week.

Taxi: Call 089/21610.

Private Driver: Johann Fayoumi is reliable and speaks English (€70/hour, mobile 0174-183-8473, www.firstclass limousines.de).

Car Rental: Several car-rental agencies are located upstairs at the train station, opposite track 21 (open daily, hours vary).

MUNICH CITY WALK

With its pedestrian-friendly historic core, big, modern Munich feels like an easygoing Bavarian town. On this self-guided walk, rated ▲▲▲, we'll start in the central square, see its famous glockenspiel, stroll through a thriving open-air market, and visit historic churches with lavish Baroque decor. We'll sample chocolates and take a spin through the world's most famous beer hall.

Length of This Tour: It takes two or three hours to walk through a thousand years of Munich's history; allow extra time if you want to take a break to tour the museums (details under "Sights").

🎧 Download my free Munich City Walk audio tour.

⊙ Self-Guided Walk

• *Begin at the heart of the old city, with a stroll through...*

❶ *Marienplatz*

Riding the escalator out of the subway into sunlit Marienplatz (mah-REE-enplatz, "Mary's Square," rated ▲▲) gives you a fine first look at the glory of Munich: great buildings, outdoor cafés, and people bustling and lingering like the birds and breeze with which they share this square.

The square is both old and new: For a thousand years, it's been the center of Munich. It was the town's marketplace and public forum, standing at a crossroads along the Salt Road, which ran between Salzburg and Augsburg.

Lining one entire side of the square is the impressive facade of the **New Town Hall** (Neues Rathaus), with its soaring 280-foot spire. The structure looks medieval, but it was actually built in the late 1800s (1867-1908). The style is "Neo"-Gothic—pointed arches over the doorways and a roofline bristling with prickly spires. The 40 statues look like medieval saints, but they're from around 1900, depicting more recent Bavarian kings and nobles. This medieval-looking style was all the rage in the 19th century as Germans were rediscovering their historical roots and uniting as a modern nation.

The New Town Hall is famous for its **glockenspiel.** A carillon in the tower chimes a tune while colorful figurines come out on the balcony to spin and dance. It happens daily at 11:00 and 12:00 all year (also at 17:00 May-Oct). The *Spiel* of the glockenspiel tells the story of a noble wedding that actually took place on the market square in 1568. You see the wedding procession and the friendly joust of knights on horseback. The duke and his bride watch the action as the groom's family (in Bavarian white and blue) joyfully jousts with the bride's French family (in red and white). Below, the barrel-makers—famous for being the first to dance in the streets after a deadly plague lifted—do their popular jig. Finally, the solitary cock crows.

At the very top of the New Town Hall is a statue of a child with outstretched arms, dressed in monk's garb and holding a book in its left hand. This is the **Münchner Kindl,** the symbol of Munich. The town got its name from the people who

first settled here: the monks *(Mönchen)*. You'll spot this mini monk all over town, on everything from the city's coat of arms to souvenir shot glasses to ad campaigns (often holding not a book, but maybe a beer or a smartphone). The city symbol was originally depicted as a grown man, wearing a gold-lined black cloak and red shoes. By the 19th century, artists were representing him as a young boy, then a gender-neutral child, and, more recently, a young girl. These days, a teenage girl dressed as the *Kindl* kicks off the annual Oktoberfest by leading the opening parade on horseback, and then serves as the mascot throughout the festivities.

For great **views** of the city, you can ride an elevator to the top of the New Town Hall tower (€2.50, May-Sept daily 10:00-19:00; Oct-April Mon-Fri 10:00-17:00, closed Sat-Sun, elevator located under glockenspiel).

The **golden statue** at the top of the column in the center of Marienplatz honors the square's namesake, the Virgin Mary. Sculpted in 1590, it was a rallying point in the religious wars of the Reformation. Back then, Munich was a bastion of southern-German Catholicism against the heresies of Martin Luther to the north.

New Town Hall

Glockenspiel

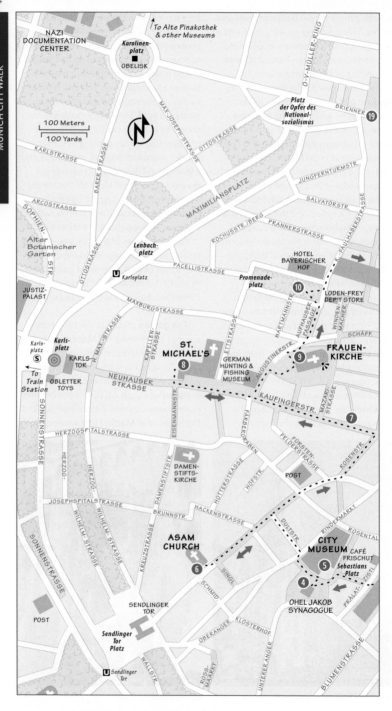

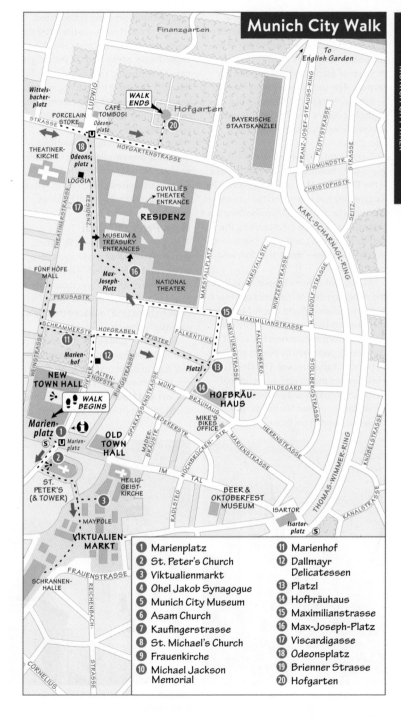

Munich City Walk

1 Marienplatz
2 St. Peter's Church
3 Viktualienmarkt
4 Ohel Jakob Synagogue
5 Munich City Museum
6 Asam Church
7 Kaufingerstrasse
8 St. Michael's Church
9 Frauenkirche
10 Michael Jackson Memorial
11 Marienhof
12 Dallmayr Delicatessen
13 Platzl
14 Hofbräuhaus
15 Maximilianstrasse
16 Max-Joseph-Platz
17 Viscardigasse
18 Odeonsplatz
19 Brienner Strasse
20 Hofgarten

Notice how, at the four corners of the statue, cherubs fight the four great biblical enemies of civilization: the dragon of war, the lion of hunger, the rooster-headed monster of plague and disease, and the serpent. The serpent represents heresy —namely, Protestants. Bavaria is still Catholic country, and Protestants weren't allowed to worship openly here until about 1800.

To the right of the New Town Hall, the gray pointy building with the green spires is the **Old Town Hall** (Altes Rathaus). On its adjoining bell tower, find the city seal. It has the Münchner Kindl (symbolizing the first monks), a castle (representing the first fortifications), and a lion (representing the first ruler—Henry the Lion, who built them).

As you look around, keep in mind that the Allies bombed Marienplatz and much of Munich during World War II. Most of the buildings had to be rebuilt. The Old Town Hall looks newer now because it was completely destroyed by bombs and had to be rebuilt after the war. The New Town Hall survived the bombs, and it served as the US military headquarters after the Americans occupied Munich in 1945.

Before moving on, face the New Town Hall one more time and get oriented. Straight ahead is north. To the left is the pedestrian shopping street called Kaufingerstrasse, which leads to the old gate called Karlstor and the train station. To the right, the street leads to the Isartor gate and the Deutsches Museum. This east-west axis cuts through the historic core of Munich.

• *Turn around to the right to find Rindermarkt, the street leading from the southeast corner of Marienplatz. Head to St. Peter's Church, just beyond the square, with its steeple poking up above a row of buildings.*

❷ St. Peter's Church

The oldest church in town, St. Peter's stands on the hill where Munich's original monks probably settled—perhaps as far back as the ninth century (though the city marks its official birthday as 1158). Today's church (from 1368) replaced the original monastery church.

St. Peter's ("Old Peter" to locals) is part of the soul of the city. There's even a popular song about it that goes, "Munich is not Munich without St. Peter's."

Cost and Hours: Church-free, tower-€2, Mon-Fri 9:00-18:30, Sat-Sun 10:00-

Old Town Hall

Climb the tower of St. Peter's Church for great views.

18:30, off-season until 17:30.

Visiting the Church: On the outside of the church, notice the 16th- and 17th-century tombstones plastered onto the wall. Originally, people were buried in the holy ground around the church. But in the Napoleonic age, the cemeteries were dug up and relocated outside the city walls for hygienic and space reasons. They kept a few tombstones here as a reminder.

Step inside. (If there's a Mass in progress, visitors are welcome, but stay in the back. If there's no Mass, feel free to explore.) Typical of so many Bavarian churches, it's whitewashed and light-filled, with highlights in pastel pinks and blues framed by gold curlicues. The ceiling painting opens up to the heavens, where Peter is crucified upside down.

Some photos (on a pillar near the entrance) show how St. Peter's was badly damaged in World War II—the roof caved in, and the altar was damaged. But the beloved church was rebuilt and restored, thanks to donations—half from the Augustiner brewery, the rest from private donors. The accuracy of the restoration was possible thanks to Nazi catalog photos. For decades after World War II, the bells played a popular tune that stopped before the last note, reminding locals that the church still needed money to rebuild.

Explore further. The nave is lined with bronze statues of the apostles, and the altar shows a statue of St. Peter being adored by four Church fathers. The finely crafted, gray iron fences that line the nave were donated after World War II by the local blacksmiths of the national railway. The precious and fragile sandstone Gothic chapel altar (to the left of the main altar) survived the war only because it was buried in sandbags.

Find the second chapel on the left side. Now there's something you don't see every day: a skeleton in a box. As the red Latin inscription says, this is St. Munditia. In the fourth century, she was beheaded by the Romans for her Christian faith.

Munich has more relics of saints than any city outside Rome. That's because it was the Pope's Catholic bastion against the rising tide of Protestantism in northern Europe during the Reformation. In 1675, St. Munditia's remains were given to Munich by the Pope as thanks for the city's devoted service. It was also a vivid reminder to the faithful that those who die for the cause of the Roman Church go directly to heaven without waiting for Judgment Day.

It's a long climb to the top of the **spire** (306 steps, no elevator)—much of it with two-way traffic on a one-lane staircase—but the view is dynamite. Try to be two flights from the top when the bells ring at the top of the hour. Then, when your friends back home ask you about your trip, you'll say, "What?"

• *Just beyond St. Peter's, join the busy commotion of the…*

❸ *Viktualienmarkt*

The market (rated ▲▲, closed Sun) is a lively world of produce stands and budget eateries. Browse your way through

Viktualienmarkt

The History of Munich

Born from Salt and Beer (1100-1500)
Munich began in the 12th century, when Henry the Lion (Heinrich der Löwe) established a lucrative salt trade near a monastery of "monks"—München. After Henry's death, an ambitious merchant family, the Wittelsbachs, took over. By the 1400s, Munich's market bustled with trade in salt and beer, the twin-domed Frauenkirche drew pilgrims, and the Wittelsbachs made their home in the Residenz. When the various regions of Bavaria united in 1506, Munich became the capital.

Religious Wars, Plagues, Decline (1500-1800)
While Martin Luther and the Protestant Reformation raged in northern Germany, Munich became the Catholic heart of the Counter-Reformation, decorated in the ornate Baroque and Rococo style of its Italian allies. Religious wars and periodic plagues left the city weakened. While the rest of Europe modernized, Munich remained behind the times.

The Golden Age of Kings (1806-1886)
When Napoleon invaded, the Wittelsbach duke surrendered and was rewarded with a grander title: King of Bavaria. Munich boomed. **Maximilian I** (r. 1806-1825), a.k.a. Max Joseph, rebuilt in Neoclassical style—grand columned buildings connected by broad boulevards. **Ludwig I** (r. 1825-1848) turned Munich into a modern railroad hub and budding industrial city. His son **Maximilian II** (r. 1848-1864) continued the modernization program. **Ludwig II** (r. 1864-1886) didn't much like Munich, preferring to build castles in the Bavarian countryside (for his story, see page 826).

the stalls and pavilions, as you make your way to the market's main landmark, the blue-and-white striped maypole. Early in the morning, you can still feel small-town Munich here. Remember, Munich has been a market town since its earliest days as a stop on the salt-trade crossroads. By the 1400s, the market bustled, most likely beneath a traditional maypole, just like you see today.

Besides salt, Munich gained a reputation for beer. By the 15th century, more than 30 breweries pumped out the golden liquid, brewed by monks who were licensed to sell it. They stored their beer in cellars under courtyards kept cool by the shade of bushy chestnut trees—a tradition Munich's breweries still stick to.

The market's centerpiece seems to be its **beer garden** (daily 10:00-22:00, weather permitting). Its picnic tables are filled with hungry and thirsty locals, all in the shade of the traditional chestnut trees. Shoppers pause here for a late-morning snack of *Weisswurst*—white sausage—served with mustard, a pretzel, and a beer. Here, you can order just a half-liter—unlike at other *Biergartens* that only sell by the full liter. As is the tradition at all of the city's beer gardens, some tables (those without tablecloths) are set aside for patrons who bring their own

End of the Wittelsbachs (1886-1918)

When Bavaria became part of the newly united Germany, Berlin overtook Munich as Germany's power center. Then World War I devastated Munich. After the war, mobs of poor, angry Münchners roamed the streets. In 1918, they drove out the last Bavarian king, ending 700 years of Wittelsbach rule.

Nazis and World War II (1918-1945)

In the power vacuum, a fringe group emerged—the Nazi party, headed by Adolf Hitler. Hitler rallied the Nazis in a Munich beer hall, leading a failed coup d'état known as the Beer Hall Putsch (1923). When the Nazis eventually took power in Berlin, they remembered their roots, dubbing Munich "Capital of the Movement." In World War II, nearly half the city was leveled by Allied air raids.

Munich Rebuilds (1945-Present)

After the war, with generous American aid, Münchners rebuilt. Nazi authorities had created a photographic archive of historic sights, which now came in handy. Munich chose to preserve its low-rise, medieval feel, but with a modern infrastructure. For the 1972 Olympic Games, they built a futuristic stadium, a sleek new subway system, and one of Europe's first pedestrian-only zones—Kaufinger-strasse. In 1990, when Germany reunited, Berlin once again became the country's focal point, relegating Munich to a backseat role.

Today's Munich is home to more banks and financial firms than any German city besides Frankfurt. With a population of 1.5 million, Munich is Germany's third-largest city, after Berlin and Hamburg. A center for book publishing, Munich also hosts universities, two TV networks, the electronics giant Siemens, the German branch of Microsoft, and BMW, maker of world-famous cars ("Bayerische Motoren Werke"—Bavarian Motor Works). Safe, clean, cultured, and productive, Munich is a success story.

food; they're welcome here as long as they buy a drink. The Viktualienmarkt is ideal for a light meal (see page 797).

Now make your way to the towering **maypole.** Throughout Bavaria, colorfully ornamented maypoles decorate town squares. Many are painted, like this one, in Bavaria's colors, white and blue. The decorations are festively replaced every year on the first of May. Traditionally, rival communities try to steal each other's maypole. Locals guard their new pole day and night as May Day approaches. Stolen poles are ransomed only with lots of beer for the clever thieves.

The decorations that line each side of the pole explain which merchants are doing business in the market. Munich's maypole gives prominence (on the

The market's maypole

bottom level) to a horse-drawn wagon bringing in beer barrels. And you can't have a kegger without coopers—find the merry barrelmakers, the four cute guys dancing. Today, traditional barrel making is enjoying a comeback as top breweries like to have real wooden kegs.

The bottom of the pole celebrates the world's oldest food law. The German Beer Purity Law (*Reinheitsgebot*) of 1487 actually originated here in Bavaria. It stipulated that beer could consist only of three ingredients: barley, hops, and water. (Later they realized that a fourth ingredient, yeast, is always present in fermentation.) Why was beer so treasured? Back in the Middle Ages, it was considered liquid food.

From the maypole, take in the bustling scene around you. The market was modernized in the 1800s as the city grew. Old buildings were torn down, replaced with stalls and modern market halls. Now, in the 21st century, it's a wonder such a traditional place survives—especially because it sits on the most expensive real estate in town. But locals love their market, so the city protects these old-time shops, charging them only a small percentage of their gross income, enabling them to carry on.

• *At the bottom end of the Viktualienmarkt, spot* **Café Frischhut,** *with its colorful old-time sign hanging out front (at Prälat-Zistl-Strasse 8). This is Munich's favorite place to stop for a fresh* Schmalznudel—*a traditional fried-dough treat (best enjoyed warm with a sprinkling of sugar).*

Across the street, you'll pass the Pschorr beer hall. Continue just past it to a modern glass-and-iron building, the **Schrannenhalle.** *This 1800s grain exchange has been renovated into a high-end mall of deli shops. Chocoholics could detour downstairs here into* **Milka Coco World** *for tasty samples (and a good WC).*

When you're ready to move on, exit the Schrannenhalle midway down on the right-hand side (or if it's closed, walk around the top of the building to Prälat-Zistl-Strasse

and turn left). You'll spill out into Sebastiansplatz, a small square lined with healthy eateries. Continue through Sebastiansplatz and veer left, where you'll see a cube-shaped building, the...

❹ *Ohel Jakob Synagogue*

This modern synagogue anchors a revitalized Jewish quarter. In the 1930s, about 10,000 Jews lived in Munich, and the main synagogue stood near here. Then, in 1938, Hitler demanded that the synagogue be torn down. By the end of World War II, Munich's Jewish community was gone. But thanks to Germany's acceptance of religious refugees from former Soviet states, the Jewish population has now reached its prewar size. The new synagogue was built in 2006. There's also a kindergarten and day school, playground, fine kosher restaurant (at #18), and bookstore. Standing in the middle of the square, notice the low-key but efficient security.

While the synagogue is shut tight to nonworshippers, its architecture is striking from the outside. Lower stones of travertine evoke the Wailing Wall in Jerusalem, while an upper section represents the tent that held important religious wares during the 40 years of wandering through the desert. The synagogue's door features the first 10 letters of the Hebrew alphabet, symbolizing the Ten Commandments.

The cube-shaped **Jewish History Museum** (behind the cube-shaped synagogue) is stark and windowless. The

Ohel Jakob Synagogue

museum's small permanent collection focuses on Munich's Jewish history; good temporary exhibits might justify the entry fee (€6, ticket gets you half-price admission to Munich City Museum, Tue-Sun 10:00-18:00, closed Mon, St.-Jakobs-Platz 16, tel. 089/2339-6096, www.juedisches-museum-muenchen.de).

• *Facing the synagogue, on the same square, is the...*

⑤ Munich City Museum (Münchner Stadtmuseum)

The highs and lows of Munich's history are covered in this surprisingly honest municipal museum (rated ▲). It covers the cultural upheavals of the early 1900s, Munich's role as the birthplace of the Nazis, and the city's renaissance during Germany's postwar "economic miracle." There's scant information posted in English, but an included audioguide can fill in the gaps.

• *You can stop and tour the museum now (see page 816). Otherwise, continue through the synagogue's square, past the fountain, across the street, and one block farther to the pedestrianized Sendlinger Strasse. Down the street 100 yards to the left, the fancy facade (at #62) marks the...*

⑥ Asam Church (Asamkirche)

This tiny church (rated ▲) is a slice of heaven on earth—a gooey, drippy Baroque masterpiece by Bavaria's top two Rococonuts—the Asam brothers. Just 30 feet wide, it was built in 1740 to

Asam Church

fit within this row of homes. Originally, it was a private chapel where these two brother-architects could show off their work (on their own land, next to their home and business headquarters—to the left), but it's now a public place of worship.

Cost and Hours: Free, Sat-Thu 9:00-18:00, Fri 13:00-18:00, tel. 089/2368-7989. The church is small, so visitors are asked not to enter during Mass (held Tue and Thu-Fri 17:00-18:00, Wed 8:30-9:30, and Sun 10:00-11:00).

Visiting the Church: This place of worship served as a promotional brochure to woo clients, and is packed with every architectural trick in the book. Imagine approaching the church not as a worshipper, but as a shopper representing your church's building committee. First stand outside: Hmmm, the look of those foundation stones really packs a punch. And the legs hanging over the portico... nice effect. Those starbursts on the door would be a hit back home, too.

Then step inside: I'll take a set of those over-the-top golden capitals, please. We'd also like to order the gilded garlands draping the church in jubilation, and the twin cupids capping the confessional. And how about some fancy stucco work, too? (Molded-and-painted plaster was clearly an Asam brothers specialty.) Check out the illusion of a dome painted on the flat ceiling—that'll save us lots of money. The yellow glass above the altar has the effect of the thin-sliced alabaster at St. Peter's in Rome, but it's within our budget! And, tapping the "marble" pilasters to determine that they are just painted fakes, we decide to take that, too. Crammed between two buildings, light inside this narrow church is limited, so there's a big, clear window in the back for maximum illumination—we'll order one to cut back on our electricity bill.

On the way out, say good-bye to the gilded grim reaper in the narthex (left side as you're leaving) as he cuts the thread of life—reminding all who visit of our mortality...and, by the way, that shrouds have no pockets.

• Leaving the church, look to your right, noticing the Sendlinger Tor at the end of the street—part of the fortified town wall that circled Munich in the 14th century. Then turn left and walk straight up Sendlinger Strasse. Walk toward the Münchner Kindl, still capping the spire of the New Town Hall in the distance, and then up (pedestrian-only) Rosenstrasse, until you hit Marienplatz and the big, busy...

❼ *Kaufingerstrasse*

This car-free street leads you through a great shopping district, past cheap department stores, carnivals of street entertainers, and good old-fashioned slicers and dicers. As far back as the 12th century, this was the town's main commercial street. Traders from Salzburg and Augsburg would enter the town through the fortified Karlstor. This street led past the Augustiner beer hall (opposite St. Michael's Church to this day), right to the main square and cathedral.

Up until the 1970s, the street was jammed with car traffic. Then, for the 1972 Olympics, it was turned into one of Europe's first pedestrian zones. At first, shopkeepers were afraid that would ruin business. Now it's Munich's living room. Nearly 9,000 shoppers pass through it each hour. Merchants nearby are begging for their streets to become traffic-free, too.

The 1972 Olympics transformed this part of Munich—the whole area around Marienplatz was pedestrianized and the transit system expanded. Since then, Munich has become one of the globe's greenest cities. Skyscrapers have been banished to the suburbs, and the nearby Frauenkirche is still the tallest building in the center.

• Stroll a few blocks away from Marienplatz toward the Karlstor, until you arrive at the big church on the right.

❽ *St. Michael's Church (Michaelskirche)*

This is one of the first great Renaissance buildings north of the Alps. The ornate facade, with its sloped roofline, was inspired by the Gesù Church in Rome—home of the Jesuit order. Jesuits saw themselves as the intellectual defenders of Catholicism. St. Michael's was built in the late 1500s—at the height of the Protestant Reformation—to serve as the northern outpost of the Jesuits. Appropriately, the facade features a statue of Michael fighting a Protestant demon.

Cost and Hours: Church—free, open daily generally 8:00-19:00, stays open later on Sun and summer evenings; crypt—€2, Mon-Fri 9:30-16:30, Sat until 14:30, closed Sun; frequent concerts—check the schedule outside; tel. 089/231-7060.

Visiting the Church: Inside, admire the ornate Baroque interior, topped with a barrel vault, the largest of its day. Stroll up the nave to the ornate pulpit, where Jesuit priests would hammer away at Reformation heresy. The church's acoustics are spectacular, and the choir—famous in

St. Michael's Church

Munich—sounds heavenly singing from the organ loft high in the rear.

The **crypt** (*Fürstengruft*, down the stairs by the altar) contains 40 stark, somewhat forlorn tombs of Bavaria's ruling family, the Wittelsbachs. There's the tomb of Wilhelm V, who built this church, and Maximilian I, who saved Munich from Swedish invaders during the Thirty Years' War. Finally, there's Otto, who went insane and was deposed in 1916, virtually bringing the Wittelsbachs' seven-century reign to an end.

The most ornate tomb holds the illustrious Ludwig II, known for his fairy-tale castle at Neuschwanstein. Ludwig didn't care much for Munich. He escaped to the Bavarian countryside, where he spent his days building castles, listening to music, and dreaming about knights of old. His excesses earned him the nickname "Mad" King Ludwig. But of all the Wittelsbachs, it's his tomb that's decorated with flowers—placed here by romantics still mad about their "mad" king.

• *Our next stop, the Frauenkirche, is a few hundred yards away. Backtrack a couple of blocks up Kaufingerstrasse to the wild boar statue, which marks the* **German Hunting and Fishing Museum.** *This place has outdoorsy regalia, kid-friendly exhibits, and the infamous Wolpertinger—a German "jackalope" created by creative local taxidermists. At the boar statue, turn left on Augustinerstrasse, which leads to Munich's towering, twin-domed cathedral, the...*

❾ *Frauenkirche*

These twin onion domes are the symbol of the city. They're unusual in that most Gothic churches have either pointed steeples or square towers. Some say Crusaders, inspired by the Dome of the Rock in Jerusalem, brought home the idea. Or it may be that, due to money problems, the towers weren't completed until Renaissance times, when domes were popular. Whatever the reason, the Frauenkirche's domes may be the inspiration for the

characteristic domed church spires that mark villages all over Bavaria.

Cost and Hours: Free, open daily generally 7:00-19:00, tel. 089/290-0820.

Rick's Tip: *If the* **Frauenkirche** *towers are closed for renovation during your visit, you can enjoy great* **city views** *from* **New Town Hall** *(elevator) or the towers of* **St. Peter's Church** *(stairs only).*

Visiting the Church: The church was built in just 22 years, from 1466 to 1488. It's made of brick—easy to make locally, and cheaper and faster to build with than stone. Construction was partly funded by the sale of indulgences (which let sinners bypass purgatory on the way to heaven). It's dedicated to the Virgin—Our Lady (*Frau*)—and has been the city's cathedral since 1821.

Step inside, and remember that much of this church was destroyed during World War II. The towers survived, and the rest was rebuilt essentially from scratch.

Near the entrance is a big, black, ornate monument honoring Ludwig IV the Bavarian (1282-1347), who was elected Holy Roman Emperor—a big deal. The

Frauenkirche

Frauenkirche was built a century later with the express purpose of honoring his memory. His monument was originally situated in front at the high altar, right near Christ. Those Wittelsbachs—always trying to be associated with God. This alliance was instilled in people through the prayers they were forced to recite: "Virgin Mary, mother of our duke, please protect us."

Nearby, a relief (over the back pew on the left) honors one of Munich's more recent citizens. Joseph Ratzinger was born in Bavaria in 1927, became archbishop of the Frauenkirche (1977-1982), then moved to the Vatican, where he later served as Pope Benedict XVI (2005-2013).

Now walk slowly up the main aisle, enjoying stained glass right and left. This glass is obviously modern, having replaced the original glass that was shattered in World War II. Ahead is the high altar, under a huge hanging crucifix. Find the throne—the ceremonial seat of the local bishop. From here, look up to the tops of the columns, and notice the tiny painted portraits. They're the craftsmen from five centuries ago who helped build the church.

Now walk behind the altar to the apse, where there are three tall windows. These still have their original 15th-century glass. To survive the bombs of 1944, each pane had to be lovingly removed and stored safely away.

• *Our next stop is at Promenadeplatz, about 400 yards north of here. Facing the altar, take the left side exit and walk straight 50 yards until you see a tiny but well-signed passageway (to the left) called the Aufhauser Passage. Follow it through a modern building, where you'll emerge at a park (surrounded by concrete) called Promenadeplatz. Detour a few steps left into the park, where you'll find a colorful modern memorial.*

⑩ Michael Jackson Memorial

When Michael Jackson was in town, he'd stay at the Hotel Bayerischer Hof, like many VIPs. Fans would gather in the park waiting for him to appear at his window. He'd sometimes oblige (but his infamous baby-dangling incident happened in Berlin, not here). When he died in 2009, devotees created this memorial by taking over a statue of Renaissance composer Orlando di Lasso. They still visit daily, leave a memento, and keep it tidy.

• *Now backtrack and turn left, up Kardinal-Faulhaber-Strasse. The street is lined with former 18th-century mansions that have since become offices and bank buildings. At #11, turn right and enter a modern shopping mall called the **Fünf Höfe Passage.** The place tries to take your basic shopping mall and give it more class. It's divided into five connecting courtyards (the "fünf Höfe"), spruced up with bubbling fountains, exotic plants, and a hanging garden.*

Emerging on a busy pedestrian street, turn right, and head down the street (noticing the Münchner Kindl again high above), to a big green square: Marienhof, with the most aristocratic grocery store in all of Germany.

⑪ Marienhof

This square, tucked behind the New Town Hall, was left as a green island after the wartime bombings. If you find that the square's all dug up, it's because Munich has finally started building an additional subway tunnel here. With virtually the entire underground system converging on nearby Marienplatz, this new tunnel will provide a huge relief to the city's con-

Marienhof

gested subterranean infrastructure.

On the far side of Marienhof is ⓬ **Dallmayr Delicatessen.** When the king called out for dinner, he called Alois Dallmayr. This place became famous for its exotic and luxurious food items: tropical fruits, seafood, chocolates, fine wines, and coffee (there are meat and cheese counters, too). As you enter, read the black plaque with the royal seal by the door: *Königlich Bayerischer Hof-Lieferant* ("Deliverer for the King of Bavaria and his Court"). Catering to royal and aristocratic tastes (and budgets), it's still the choice of Munich's old rich (closed Sun, www.dallmayr.com).

• *Leaving Dallmayr, turn right and then right again to continue along Hofgraben. Walk three blocks gently downhill to Platzl—"small square." (If you get turned around, just ask any local to point you toward the Hofbräuhaus.)*

⓭ *Platzl*

As you stand here—admiring classic facades in the heart of medieval Munich—recall that everything around you was flattened in World War II. Here on Platzl, the reconstruction happened in stages: From 1945 to 1950, they removed 12 million tons of bricks and replaced roofs to make buildings weather-tight. From 1950 to 1972, they redid the exteriors. From 1972 to 2000, they refurbished the interiors. Today, the rebuilt Platzl sports new—but old-looking—facades.

Officials estimate that hundreds of unexploded bombs still lie buried under Munich. As recently as 2012, they found a 550-pound bomb in Schwabing, a neighborhood just north of the old city center. They had to evacuate the neighborhood and detonate the bomb.

Today's Platzl hosts a lively mix of places to eat and drink—pop-culture chains like Starbucks and Hard Rock Café alongside top-end restaurants like the recommended Wirtshaus Ayingers and Schuhbecks (Schuhbecks Eis is a favorite for ice cream; Pfisterstrasse 9-11).

• *At the bottom of the square (#9), you can experience the venerable...*

⓮ *Hofbräuhaus*

The world's most famous beer hall (rated ▲▲) is a trip. Whether or not you slide your lederhosen on its polished benches, it's a great experience just to walk through the place in all its rowdy glory (with its own gift shop).

Before going in, check out the huge arches at the entrance and the crown logo. The original brewery was built here in 1583. As the crown suggests, it was the Wittelsbachs' personal brewery to make the "court brew" *(Hof Brau).* In 1880, the brewery moved out, and this 5,000-seat food-and-beer palace was built in its place. After being bombed in World War II, the Hofbräuhaus was one of the first places to be rebuilt (German priorities).

Now, take a deep breath and go on in. Dive headlong into the sudsy Hofbräu mosh pit. Don't be shy. Everyone's drunk anyway. The atmosphere is thick with the sounds of oompah music, played here every night of the year.

You'll see locals stuffed into lederhosen and dirndls, giant gingerbread cookies that sport romantic messages, and kiosks selling postcards of the German (and apparently beer-drinking) ex-pope. Notice the quirky 1950s-style painted ceiling, with Bavarian colors, grapes, chestnuts, and fun "eat, drink, and be merry" themes. You'll see signs on some tables reading

Hofbräuhaus

Stammtisch, meaning they're reserved for regulars, and their racks of old beer steins made of pottery and pewter. Beer halls like the Hofbräuhaus sell beer only by the liter mug, called a *Mass* (mahs). You can get it light *(helles)* or dark *(dunkles)*. A slogan on the ceiling above the band reads, *Durst ist schlimmer als Heimweh*—"Thirst is worse than homesickness" (daily 9:00-23:30, live oompah music during lunch and dinner; for details on eating here, see page 834).

• *Leaving the Hofbräuhaus, turn right and walk two blocks, then turn left when you reach the street called...*

⑮ Maximilianstrasse

This broad east-west boulevard, lined with grand buildings and exclusive shops, introduces us to Munich's Golden Age of the 1800s. In that period, Bavaria was ruled by three important kings: Max Joseph, Ludwig I, and Ludwig II. They transformed Munich from a cluster of medieval lanes to a modern city of spacious squares, Neoclassical monuments, and wide boulevards. At the east end of this boulevard is the palatial home of the Bavarian parliament.

The street was purposely designed for people and for shopping, not military parades. And to this day, Maximilianstrasse is busy with shoppers browsing Munich's most exclusive shops.

• *Maximilianstrasse leads to a big square—Max-Joseph-Platz.*

⑯ Max-Joseph-Platz

The square is fronted by two big buildings: the National Theater (with its columns) and the Residenz (with its intimidating stone facade).

The **Residenz,** the former "residence" of the royal Wittelsbach family, started as a crude castle (c. 1385). Over the centuries, it evolved into one of Europe's most opulent palaces (see page 808).

The centerpiece of the square is a grand statue of **Maximilian I**—a.k.a. Max

Joseph. In 1806, Max was serving in the long tradition of his Wittelsbach family as the city's duke...until Napoleon invaded and deposed him. But then Napoleon—eager to marry into the aristocracy—agreed to reinstate Max, with one condition: that his daughter marry Napoleon's stepson. Max Joseph agreed, and was quickly crowned not duke but king of Bavaria.

Max Joseph and his heirs ruled as constitutional monarchs. Now a king, Max Joseph was popular; he emancipated Protestants and Jews, revamped the Viktualienmarkt, and graced Munich with grand buildings like the **National Theater.** This Neoclassical building, opened in 1818, celebrated Bavaria's strong culture, deep roots, and legitimacy as a nation; four of Richard Wagner's operas were first performed here. It's now where the Bavarian State Opera and the Bavarian State Orchestra perform. (The Roman numerals MCMLXIII in the frieze mark the year the theater reopened after the WWII bombing restoration—1963.)

• *Leave Max-Joseph-Platz opposite where you entered, walking alongside the Residenz on Residenzstrasse for about 100 yards to the next grand square. But before you get to Odeonsplatz, pause at the first corner on the left and look down Viscardigasse at the gold-cobbled swoosh in the pavement.*

⑰ Viscardigasse

The cobbles in Viscardigasse recall one of Munich's most dramatic moments: It

Max-Joseph-Platz

was 1923, and Munich was in chaos. World War I had left Germany in shambles. Angry mobs roamed the streets. Out of the fury rose a new and frightening movement—Adolf Hitler and the Nazi Party. On November 8, Hitler launched a coup, later known as the Beer Hall Putsch, to try to topple the German government. It started with a fiery speech by Hitler in a beer hall a few blocks from here (which no longer exists). The next day, Hitler and his mob of 3,000 Nazis marched up Residenzstrasse. A block ahead, where Residenzstrasse spills into Odeonsplatz, stood a hundred government police waiting for the Nazi mob. Shots were fired. Hitler was injured, and 16 Nazis were killed, along with four policemen. The coup was put down, and Hitler was sent to a prison outside Munich. During his nine months there, he wrote down his twisted ideas in his book *Mein Kampf.*

Ten years later, when Hitler finally came to power, he made a memorial at Odeonsplatz to honor the "first martyrs of the Third Reich." Germans were required to raise their arms in a *Sieg Heil* salute as they entered the square. The only way to avoid the indignity of saluting Nazism was to turn left down Viscardigasse instead. That stream of shiny cobbles marks the detour taken by those brave dissenters.

• *But now that Hitler's odious memorial is long gone, you can continue to...*

⓲ *Odeonsplatz*

This square links Munich's illustrious past with the Munich of today. It was laid out by the Wittelsbach kings in the 1800s. They incorporated the much older (yellow) church that was already on the square, the Theatinerkirche. This church contains about half of the Wittelsbach tombs. The church's twin towers and 230-foot-high dome are classic Italian Baroque, reflecting Munich's strong Catholic bent in the 1600s.

Nearby, overlooking the square from the south, is an arcaded loggia filled with statues. In the 1800s, the Wittelsbachs commissioned this Hall of Heroes to honor Bavarian generals. It was modeled after the famous Renaissance loggia in Florence. Odeonsplatz was part of the Wittelsbachs' grand vision of modern urban planning.

At the far end of the square, several wide boulevards lead away from here.

Odeonsplatz and Theatinerkirche

First, face west (left) down ⑲ **Brienner Strasse** (watch out for bikes). In the distance, and just out of sight, a black obelisk commemorates the 30,000 Bavarians who marched with Napoleon to Moscow and never returned. Beyond the obelisk is the grand Königsplatz, or "King's Square," with its Neoclassical buildings. Back in the 1930s, Königsplatz was the center of the Nazi party. Remember, Munich was the cradle of Nazism. Today, the Nazi shadow has largely lifted from that square (only two buildings from that era remain) and Königsplatz is home to Munich's cluster of great art museums. A few miles beyond Königsplatz is the Wittelsbachs' impressive summer home, Nymphenburg Palace.

Now turn your attention 90 degrees to the right. The boulevard heading north from Odeonsplatz is Ludwigstrasse. It stretches a full mile, flanked by an impressive line of uniform 60-foot-tall buildings in the Neo-Gothic style. In the far distance is the city's Triumphal Arch, capped with a figure of Bavaria, a goddess riding a lion-drawn chariot. The street is named for the great Wittelsbach builder-king, Ludwig I, who truly made Munich into a grand capital. ("I won't rest," he famously swore, "until Munich looks like Athens.") Ludwigstrasse was used for big parades and processions, as it leads to that Roman-style arch.

Beyond the arch—and beyond what you can see—lie the suburbs of modern Munich, including the city's modern skyscrapers and the famous BMW headquarters. Yes, Munich is a major metropolis, but you'd hardly know it by walking through its pleasant streets and parks.

• *We'll finish our walk in the enjoyable Hofgarten. Its formal gate is to your right as you're facing up Ludwigstrasse. Step through the gate and enter the...*

⑳ *Hofgarten*

This elegant "garden of the royal court" is a delight. Built by the Wittelsbachs as their own private backyard to the Resi-

denz palace, it's now open to everyone. Just inside the gate is an arcade decorated with murals commissioned by Ludwig I in the early 1800s. While faded, they still tell the glorious story of Bavaria from 1155 until 1688. The garden's 400-year-old centerpiece is a Renaissance-style temple with great acoustics. (There's often a musician performing here for tips.) It's decorated with the same shell decor as was popular inside the Residenz.

Take some time to enjoy the garden as the royals did, or for a good antidote to all the beer halls, try the venerable **Café Tambosi,** with its chairs lined up facing the boulevard as if to watch a parade. In the garden beyond the café tables is a gravel *boules* court.

• *This walk is done. Where to go next? You're near the English Garden (just a few blocks away—see the map; people surf under the bridge east of Haus der Kunst), the Residenz complex, and the Odeonsplatz U-Bahn stop for points elsewhere.*

SIGHTS

Most of the top sights in the city center are covered on my self-guided walk. But there's much more to see in this city.

Rick's Tip: *If you're unsure about which of Munich's top two palaces to visit, the* **Residenz** *is more central and has the best interior, while* **Nymphenburg** *has the finest garden and outdoor views.*

▲▲Residenz Complex

For 500 years, this was the palatial "residence" and seat of power of the ruling Wittelsbach family. It began (1385) as a crude castle with a moat around it. The main building was built from 1550 to 1650, and decorated in Rococo style during the 18th century. The final touch was the grand south facade modeled after Florence's Pitti Palace. In March 1944, Allied air raids left the Residenz in shambles, so much of what we see today is reconstructed.

The vast Residenz complex is divided into three sections, each with its own admission ticket: The **Residenz Museum** is a long hike through 90 lavishly decorated rooms. The **Residenz Treasury** shows off the Wittelsbach crown jewels. The **Cuvilliés Theater** is an ornate Rococo opera house. You can see the three sights individually or get a combo-ticket to see them all. I consider the museum and treasury to be the essential Residenz visit, with the Cuvilliés Theater as extra credit.

Rick's Tip: *The Bavarian Palace Department offers a* **14-day ticket** *(called the* **Mehrtagesticket***) that covers admission to Munich's Residenz and Nymphenburg Palace complexes, as well as the Neuschwanstein and Linderhof castles in Bavaria. If you're planning to visit at least three of these sights within a two-week period, the pass will likely pay for itself (€24, €44 family/partner pass, purchase at participating sights or online at www.schloesser.bayern.de).*

Planning Your Time: Start your visit with the Residenz Treasury because it's small and you can easily manage your time there. Then visit the sprawling Residenz Museum, where you can wander until you say "Enough." The Cuvilliés Theater doesn't take long to see and is easy to fit in at the start or end. If you run out of time or energy, you can reenter on the same ticket to visit anything you missed. The entrances on Max-Joseph-Platz and Residenzstrasse both lead to the ticket office, gift shop, and start of the treasury and museum tours.

Cost and Hours: Residenz Museum-€7, Residenz Treasury-€7 (both include audioguides), Cuvilliés Theater-€3.50; €11 combo-ticket covers museum and treasury; €13 version covers all three; treasury and museum open daily April-mid-Oct 9:00-18:00, mid-Oct-March 10:00-17:00; theater open April-mid-Sept Mon-Sat 14:00-18:00, Sun 9:00-18:00; mid-Sept-March Mon-Sat 14:00-17:00, Sun 10:00-17:00; for all three sights, last entry is one hour before closing, tel. 089/290-671, www.residenz-muenchen.de.

The Residenz—the "residence" of Bavaria's rulers

RESIDENZ TREASURY (SCHATZKAMMER)

The treasury shows off a thousand years of Wittelsbach crowns and knickknacks. You'll see the regalia used in Bavaria's coronation ceremonies, valuable liturgical objects and relics, and miscellaneous wonders that dazzled the Wittelsbachs' European relatives. It's the best treasury in Bavaria, with fine 13th- and 14th-century crowns and delicately carved ivory and glass.

◆ Self-Guided Tour: In **Room 1,** the oldest jewels are 200 years older than Munich itself. The gem-studded 11th-century Crown of Kunigunde (on the left) is associated with the saintly Bavarian queen, who was crowned Holy Roman Empress in 1014 in St. Peter's Basilica in Rome. The pearl-studded prayer book of Charles the Bald (Charlemagne's grandson) allowed the book's owner to claim royal roots dating all the way back to that first Holy Roman Emperor crowned in 800. The spiky Crown of an English Queen (c. 1370) is actually England's oldest crown, brought to Munich by an English princess who married a Wittelsbach duke. The lily-shaped Crown of Henry II (c. 1270-1280) dates from Munich's roots, when the town was emerging as a regional capital.

Along the right side of the room are religious objects such as reliquaries and portable altars. The tiny mobile altar allowed a Carolingian king to pack light in 890—and still have a little Mass while on the road. Many of the precious objects in this room were confiscated from the collections of various prince-bishops when their realms came under Bavarian rule in the Napoleonic era (c. 1800).

Room 3: Study the reliquary with St. George killing the dragon—sparkling with more than 2,000 precious stones. Get up close (it's OK to walk around the rope posts)...you can almost hear the dragon hissing. A gold-armored St. George, seated atop a ruby-studded ivory horse, tramples an emerald-green dragon. The golden box below contained the supposed relics of St. George, who was the patron saint of the Wittelsbachs. If you could lift the minuscule visor, you'd see that the carved ivory face of St. George is actually the Wittelsbach Duke Wilhelm V—the great champion of the Catholic Counter-Reformation—slaying the dragon of Protestantism.

Room 4: The incredibly realistic carved ivory crucifixes from 1630 were done by local artist Georg Petel. Look at the flesh of Jesus' wrist pulling around the nails. In the center of the room is the intricate portable altarpiece (1573-74) of Duke Albrecht V, the Wittelsbach ruler who (as we'll see in the Residenz Museum) made a big mark on the Residenz.

Room 5: The freestanding glass case (#245) holds the impressive royal regalia of the 19th-century Wittelsbach kings—the crown, scepter, orb, and sword that were given to the king during the cor-

Crown of Henry II

St. George reliquary

onation ceremony. (The smaller pearl crown was for the queen.) They date from the early 1800s when Bavaria had been conquered by Napoleon. The Wittelsbachs struck a deal that allowed them to stay in power under the elevated title of "king" (not just "duke" or "elector" or "prince-archbishop"). These objects were made in France by the same craftsmen who created Napoleon's crown.

Rooms 6-10: The rest of the treasury has objects that are more beautiful than historic. Admire the dinnerware made of rock crystal (Room 6), stone (Room 7), and gold and enamel (Room 8). Room 9 has a silver-gilt-and-marble replica of Trajan's Column. Finally, explore the "Exotica" of Room 10, including a green Olmec figure, knives from Turkey, and a Chinese rhino-horn bowl with a teeny-tiny Neptune inside.

• *From the micro-detail of the treasury, it's time to visit the expansive Residenz Museum. Cross the hall, exchange your treasury audioguide for the museum audioguide, and enter the...*

RESIDENZ MUSEUM (RESIDENZMUSEUM)

Though called a "museum," what's really on display here are the 90 rooms of the Residenz itself: the palace's spectacular banquet and reception halls, and the Wittelsbachs' lavish private apartments. The rooms are decorated with period (but generally not original) furniture: chandeliers, canopied beds, Louis XIV-style chairs, old clocks, tapestries, and dinnerware of porcelain and silver. It's the best place to glimpse the opulent lifestyle of Bavaria's late, great royal family. (Whatever happened to the Wittelsbachs, the longest continuously ruling family in European history? They're still around, but they're no longer royalty, so most of them have real jobs now—you may well have just passed one on the street.)

❸ **Self-Guided Tour:** The place is big. Follow the museum's prescribed route, using this section to hit the highlights and

supplementing it with the audioguide. Grab a free museum floor plan to help locate room numbers mentioned here. The route can vary because rooms are occasionally closed off.

• *One of the first "rooms" you encounter (it's actually part of an outdoor courtyard) is the...*

❶ **Shell Grotto** (Room 6): This artificial grotto is made of volcanic tuff and covered completely in Bavarian freshwater shells. In its day, it was an exercise in man controlling nature—a celebration of the Renaissance humanism that flourished in the 1550s. Mercury—the pre-Christian god of trade and business—oversees the action. Check out the statue in the courtyard—in the Wittelsbachs' heyday, red wine would have flowed from the mermaid's breasts and dripped from Medusa's severed head.

• *Before moving on, note the door marked OO, leading to handy WCs. Now continue into the next room, the...*

❷ **Antiquarium** (Room 7): This low, arched hall stretches 220 feet end to end. It's the oldest room in the Residenz, built around 1550. The room was, and still is, a festival banquet hall. The ruler presided from the raised dais at the near end (warmed by the fireplace). Two hundred dignitaries can dine here, surrounded by allegories of the goodness of just rule on the ceiling.

The hall is lined with busts of Roman emperors. In the mid-16th century, Europe's royal families (such as the Wittelsbachs) collected and displayed such busts, implying a connection between themselves and the enlightened ancient Roman rulers. There was such huge demand for these classical statues in the courts of Europe that many of the "ancient busts" were fakes cranked out by crooked Romans. Still, a third of the statuary you see here is original.

The small paintings around the room show 120 Bavarian villages as they looked in 1550. Even today, when a Bavarian historian wants a record of how his village once looked, he comes here. Notice the town of Dachau in 1550 (in the archway closest to the entrance door).

• *Keep going through a few more rooms, then up a stairway to the upper floor. Pause in the* **Black Hall** *(Room 13) to admire the head-spinning trompe l'oeil ceiling, which makes the nearly flat roof appear to be a much grander arched vault. From here, the prescribed route winds through a number of rooms surrounding a large courtyard.*

❸ **Upper Floor Apartments** (Rooms 14-45): In this series of rooms we get the first glimpse of the Residenz Museum's forte: chandeliered rooms decorated with ceiling paintings, stucco work, tapestries, parquet floors, and period furniture.

Rooms to the left of the Black Hall are the **Electoral Apartments** (Rooms 22-31), the private apartments of the monarch and his consort.

In the long **All Saints Corridor** (Room 32), you can glance into the adjoining All Saints' Chapel. This early-19th-century chapel, commissioned by Ludwig I, was severely damaged in World War II, didn't reopen until 2003, and is still being refurbished.

From the All Saints Corridor you can reach the **Charlotte Chambers/ Court-Garden Rooms,** a long row of impressive rooms across the courtyard from the Electoral Apartments, first used to house visiting rulers. Some of them later served as the private rooms of Princess Charlotte, Max Joseph's daughter.

• *Your visit eventually reaches a hallway—* ❹ *Room 45—where you have a choice: to the left is the "short" route that heads directly to the stunning Ornate Rooms (described later). But we'll take the "long" route to the right (starting in Room 47) that adds a dozen-plus rooms to your visit.*

❺ **The "Long" Route:** Use your Residenz-issued map to find some of the following highlights. The large **Imperial Hall** is in Room 111; the **Stone Rooms** (104-109) are so-called for their colorful marble—both real and fake. Then come several small rooms, where the centerpiece painting on the ceiling is just blank black, as no copy of the original survived World War II.

The **Reliquary Room** (Room 95) harbors a collection of gruesome Christian relics (bones, skulls, and even several mummified hands) in ornate golden cases.

The Antiquarium, the palace's banquet hall

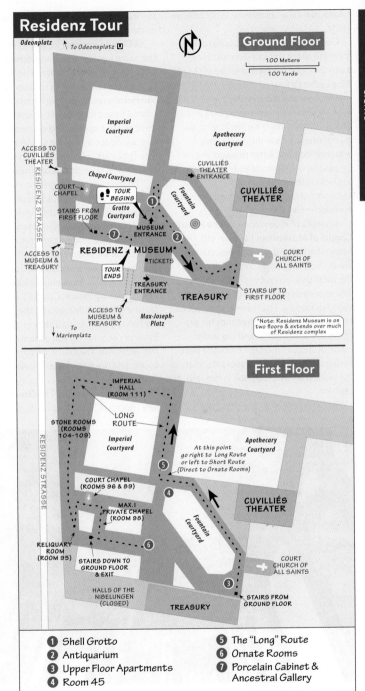

Residenz Tour

Ground Floor

Odeonsplatz

To Odeonsplatz

100 Meters
100 Yards

Imperial
Courtyard

Apothecary
Courtyard

ACCESS TO
CUVILLIÉS
THEATER

CUVILLIÉS
THEATER
ENTRANCE

CUVILLIÉS
THEATER

Chapel Courtyard

COURT
CHAPEL

TOUR
BEGINS

STAIRS FROM
FIRST FLOOR

*Grotto
Courtyard*

Fountain
Courtyard

MUSEUM
ENTRANCE

ACCESS TO
MUSEUM &
TREASURY

RESIDENZ MUSEUM*

TICKETS

COURT
CHURCH OF
ALL SAINTS

TOUR
ENDS

TREASURY
ENTRANCE

ACCESS TO
MUSEUM &
TREASURY

*Max-Joseph-
Platz*

TREASURY

STAIRS UP TO
FIRST FLOOR

To
Marienplatz

*Note: Residenz Museum is on
two floors & extends over much
of Residenz complex

First Floor

IMPERIAL
HALL
(ROOM 111)

STONE ROOMS
(ROOMS
104-109)

LONG
ROUTE

Imperial
Courtyard

At this point
go right to Long Route
or left to Short Route
(Direct to Ornate Rooms)

Apothecary
Courtyard

COURT CHAPEL
(ROOMS 96 & 89)

MAX.I
PRIVATE CHAPEL
(ROOM 98)

CUVILLIÉS
THEATER

RELIQUARY
ROOM
(ROOM 95)

STAIRS DOWN TO
GROUND FLOOR
& EXIT

Fountain
Courtyard

COURT
CHURCH OF
ALL SAINTS

HALLS OF THE
NIBELUNGEN
(CLOSED)

TREASURY

STAIRS FROM
GROUND FLOOR

1 Shell Grotto
2 Antiquarium
3 Upper Floor Apartments
4 Room 45
5 The "Long" Route
6 Ornate Rooms
7 Porcelain Cabinet &
Ancestral Gallery

• *A few more steps brings you to the balcony of the...*

Court Chapel (Rooms 96/89): Dedicated to Mary, this late-Renaissance/early-Baroque gem was the site of "Mad" King Ludwig's funeral after his mysterious murder—or suicide—in 1886. (He's buried in St. Michael's Church, described on page 802.) About 75 years earlier, in 1810, his grandfather and namesake (Ludwig I) was married here. After the wedding ceremony, carriages rolled his guests to a rollicking reception, which turned out to be such a hit that it became an annual tradition—Oktoberfest.

A couple of rooms ahead is the **Private Chapel of Maximilian I** (Room 98). Duke Maximilian I, the dominant Bavarian figure in the Thirty Years' War, built one of the most precious rooms in the palace. The miniature pipe organ (from about 1600) still works. The room is sumptuous, from the gold leaf and the fancy hinges to the miniature dome and the walls made of stucco "marble." Note the post-Renaissance perspective tricks decorating the walls; they were popular in the 17th century.

• *Whichever route you take—long or short—you'll eventually reach a set of rooms known as the...*

6 Ornate Rooms (Rooms 55-62): As the name implies, these are some of the richest rooms in the palace. The Wittelsbachs were always trying to keep up with the Habsburgs, and these ceremonial rooms—used for official business—were designed to impress. The decor and furniture are Rococo—over-the-top Baroque. The family art collection, now in the Alte Pinakothek, once decorated these walls.

The rooms were designed in the 1730s by François de Cuvilliés, a Belgian who first attracted notice as the clever court dwarf for the Bavarian ruler. He was sent to Paris to study art and returned to become the court architect. Besides the Residenz, he designed the Cuvilliés Theater and the Amalienburg lodge at Nymphenburg Palace. Cuvilliés' style, featuring incredibly intricate stucco tracery twisted into unusual shapes, defined Bavarian Rococo. As you glide through this section of the palace, be sure to appreciate the gilded stucco ceilings above you.

Each room is unique. The **Green Gallery** (Room 58)—named for its green silk

Every Residenz room is unique and ornate.

damask wallpaper—was the ballroom. Imagine the parties they had here—aristocrats in powdered wigs, a string quartet playing Baroque tunes, a card game going on, while everyone admired the paintings on the walls or themselves reflected in the mirrors. The **State Bedroom** (Room 60), though furnished with a canopy bed, wasn't an actual bedroom—it was just for show. Rulers invited their subjects to come at morning and evening to stand at the railing and watch their boss ceremonially rise from his slumber to symbolically start and end the working day.

Perhaps the most ornate of these Ornate Rooms is the **Cabinet of Mirrors** (Room 61) and the adjoining **Cabinet of Miniatures** (Room 62) from 1740. In the Cabinet of Mirrors, notice the fun visual effects of the mirrors around you—the corner mirrors make things go on forever. Then peek inside the coral red room (the most royal of colors in Germany) and imagine visiting the duke and having him take you here to ogle miniature copies of the most famous paintings of the day, composed with one-haired brushes.

• *After exploring the Ornate Rooms (and the many, many other elaborate rooms here on the upper floor), find the staircase (near Room 65) that heads back downstairs. On the ground floor, you emerge in the long Ancestral Gallery (Room 4). Before walking down it, detour to the right, into Room 5.*

❼ **Porcelain Cabinet** (Room 5) and **Ancestral Gallery** (Room 4): In the 18th century, the royal family bolstered their status with an in-house porcelain works. See how the mirrors enhance the porcelain vases, creating the effect of infinite pedestals. If this inspires you to acquire some pieces of your own, head to the Nymphenburg Porcelain Store at Odeonsplatz (see page 833).

The Ancestral Gallery (Room 4) was built in the 1740s to display portraits of the Wittelsbachs. All official guests had to pass through here to meet the duke (and his 100 Wittelsbach relatives). The room's symbolism reinforced the Wittelsbachs' claims to being as powerful as the Habsburgs of Vienna.

Midway down the hall, find the family tree labeled (in Latin) "genealogy of an imperial family." The tree is shown being planted by Hercules to boost their royal street cred. Opposite the tree are two notable portraits: Charlemagne, the first Holy Roman Emperor, and to his right, Louis IV (wearing the same crown), the first Wittelsbach H.R.E., crowned in 1328. For the next 500 years, this lineage was used to substantiate the family's claim to power as they competed with the Habsburgs. (After failing to sort out their differences through strategic weddings, the two families eventually went to war.)

Allied bombs took their toll on this hall. The central ceiling painting has been restored, but since there were no photos documenting the other two ceiling paintings, those spots remain empty. Looking carefully at the walls, you can see how each painting was hastily cut from its frame. That's because—though most of Munich's museums were closed during World War II to prevent damage—the Residenz remained open to instill confidence in local people. It wasn't until 1944, when bombs were imminent, that the last-minute order was given to hide the paintings away.

• *Your Residenz Museum tour is over. The doorway at the end of the hall leads back to the museum entrance. If you're visiting the Cuvilliés Theater, from the exit walk straight through the courtyard to Residenzstrasse. Take a right and pass by the two green lions standing guard just ahead. Walk to the far end of the lane until you reach a fountain. Just above a doorway to the left you'll see a nondescript sign that says* Cuvilliés Theater.

CUVILLIÉS THEATER

In 1751, this was Germany's ultimate Rococo theater. Mozart conducted here several times. Designed by the same brilliant architect who designed the Ornate Rooms in the palace, this theater is dazzling enough to send you back to the days of divine monarchs.

It's an intimate, horseshoe-shaped performance venue, seating fewer than 400. The four tiers of box seats were for the four classes of society: city burghers on bottom, royalty next up (in the most elaborate seats), and lesser courtiers in the two highest tiers. The ruler occupied the large royal box directly opposite the stage. "Mad" King Ludwig II occasionally bought out the entire theater to watch performances here by himself.

François Cuvilliés' interior is exquisite. Red, white, and gold hues dominate. Most of the decoration is painted wood, even parts that look like marble. Even the proscenium above the stage—seemingly draped with a red-velvet "curtain"—is actually made of carved wood. Also above the stage is an elaborate Wittelsbach coat of arms. The balconies seem to be supported by statues of the four seasons and are adorned with gold garlands. Cuvilliés achieved the Rococo ideal of giving theater-goers a multimedia experience—uniting the beauty of his creation with the beautiful performance on stage. It's still a working theater.

WWII bombs completely obliterated the old Cuvilliés Theater, which originally stood at a different location a short distance from here. Fortunately, much of the carved wooden interior had been removed from the walls and stored away for safekeeping. After the war, they built this entirely new building near the ruins of the old theater and paneled it with the original decor.

Near the Residenz

▲MUNICH CITY MUSEUM (MÜNCHNER STADTMUSEUM)

The museum's permanent exhibit on Munich's history is interesting, but it's exhaustive, and there's no posted English information. I'd use the following mini tour for an overview, then supplement it with the audioguide and English booklet.

Cost and Hours: €4 includes good audioguide, more for special (skippable) exhibits, Tue-Sun 10:00-18:00, closed Mon, ticket gets you half-price admission to Jewish History Museum, St.-Jakobs-Platz 1, tel. 089/2332-2370, www.muenchner-stadtmuseum.de. The

Cuvilliés Theater

humorous Servus Heimat souvenir shop in the courtyard is worth a stop.

Eating: The museum's recommended Stadt Café is handy for a good meal (see page 837).

Visiting the Museum: Start in the ticketing hall with the wooden model showing Munich today. Find the Frauenkirche, Isar River, New Town Hall, Residenz...and no skyscrapers. The city looks remarkably similar in scale to the model (in the next room) from 1570.

Ground Floor—Medieval: A big gray statue of Henry the Lion introduces us to the city's 12th-century founder. The eight statues of Morris dancers (1480) became a symbol of the vibrant market town (and the tradition continued with the New Town Hall glockenspiel's dancing coopers). On the rest of the ground floor, paintings, armor, and swords capture more medieval ambience.

First Floor—1800s: The "New Munich" was created when the city was expanded beyond the old medieval walls (see the illuminated view of the city from 1761 in the "Canaletto-Blick," opposite the top of the stairs). The city was prosperous, as evidenced by the furniture and paintings on display. In the center of the room, find big paintings ("Effigies") of the century's magnificent kings—Maximilian I, Maximilian II, and Ludwig I.

Second Floor—Munich 1900: As Munich approached its 700th birthday, it was becoming aware of itself as a major capital. The Münchner Kindl logo

was born. It was a city of artists (Wagner operas, Lenbach portraits, Von Stuck soirées), *Jugendstil* furniture, beer, and a cosmopolitan outlook (see the "emperor panorama," the big barrel-shaped 3-D peep show of African/Asian peoples). But after the destruction of World War I, Munich became a hotbed of discontent. The "revue" room shows the city's clash of ideas: communists, capitalists, Nazis, and the anarchic theater of comedian Karl Valentin and early works by playwright Bertolt Brecht. A nearby display gives some background on Munich's role as the birthplace of Nazism (much more thoroughly covered in the museum's National Socialism wing).

From here, you can detour upstairs to the **third floor puppet theater** to see an extensive collection of marionettes, Punch-and-Judy hand puppets, and paper cutouts of this unique Bavarian art form with a long cabaret tradition.

Back on the second floor, finish with a kaleidoscope of images capturing the contemporary Munich scene—rock music, World Cup triumphs, beer gardens, and other things that are..."typically Munich."

National Socialism Wing: This small but worthwhile exhibit of photos and uniforms takes you chronologically through the Nazi years, focused on Munich: the post-WWI struggles, Hitler's 1923 Beer Hall Putsch, his writing of *Mein Kampf*, the mass rallies in Königsplatz and Odeonsplatz, establishment of the Dachau concentration camp, and the destruction rained on Munich in World War II.

Museum Quarter (Kunstareal)

This quarter's cluster of blockbuster museums displays art spanning from 3000 B.C. right up to the present. Of the seven museums in the quarter, we'll focus on the top three: Egyptian Museum, Alte Pinakothek, and Neue Pinakothek. Most people don't come to Munich for the art,

Munich City Museum

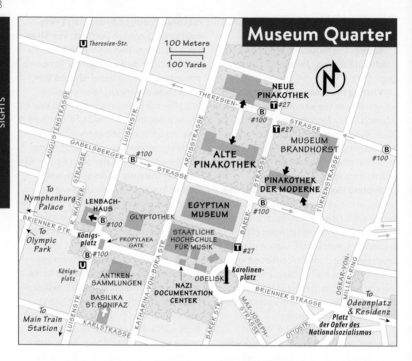

Museum Quarter

but this group makes a case for the city's world-class status.

Getting There: Handy tram #27 whisks you right to the Pinakothek stop from Karlsplatz (between the train station and Marienplatz). You can also take bus #100 from the train station, or walk 10 minutes from the Theresienstrasse or Königsplatz stops on the U-2 line.

▲▲ALTE PINAKOTHEK

Bavaria's best painting gallery (the "Old Art Gallery," pronounced ALL-teh pee-nah-koh-TEHK) shows off a world-class collection of European masterpieces from the 14th to 19th century, starring the two tumultuous centuries (1450-1650) when Europe went from medieval to modern. See paintings from the Italian Renaissance (Raphael, Leonardo, Botticelli, Titian) and the German Renaissance it inspired (Albrecht Dürer). The Reformation of Martin Luther eventually split Europe into two subcultures—Protestants and Catholics—with their two distinct art styles

(exemplified by Rembrandt and Rubens, respectively). Because of a major renovation project, expect some galleries to be closed when you visit.

Cost and Hours: €4 during renovation (otherwise €7), €1 on Sun, open Tue 10:00-20:00, Wed-Sun until 18:00, closed Mon, free and excellent audioguide (€4.50 on Sun), pleasant Café Klenze; U-2: Theresienstrasse, tram #27, or bus #100; Barer Strasse 27, tel. 089/2380-5216, www.pinakothek.de/alte-pinakothek.

➜ **Self-Guided Tour:** All the paintings we'll see are on the upper floor, which is laid out like a barbell. This tour starts at one fat end and works its way through the "handle" to the other end. From the ticket counter, head up the stairway to the left to reach the first rooms.

German Renaissance (Room II): Albrecht Altdorfer's *The Battle of Issus* (*Schlacht bei Issus*) shows a world at war. Masses of soldiers are swept along in the currents and tides of a battle completely

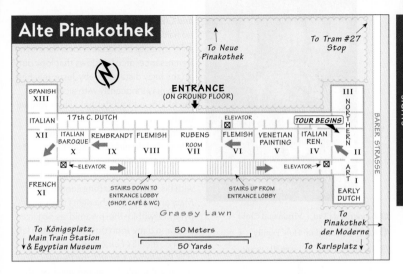

Alte Pinakothek

To Neue Pinakothek

To Tram #27 Stop

ENTRANCE (ON GROUND FLOOR)

SPANISH XIII

ITALIAN XII

17th C. DUTCH

ELEVATOR

TOUR BEGINS

III NORTHERN ART I

BARER STRASSE

ITALIAN BAROQUE X | REMBRANDT IX | FLEMISH VIII | RUBENS ROOM VII | FLEMISH VI | VENETIAN PAINTING V | ITALIAN REN. IV | II

ELEVATOR

ELEVATOR

FRENCH XI

STAIRS DOWN TO ENTRANCE LOBBY (SHOP, CAFÉ & WC)

STAIRS UP FROM ENTRANCE LOBBY

EARLY DUTCH

Grassy Lawn

To Königsplatz, Main Train Station & Egyptian Museum

50 Meters

50 Yards

To Pinakothek der Moderne

To Karlsplatz

beyond their control, their confused motion reflected in the swirling sky. Though the painting depicts Alexander the Great's history-changing victory over the Persians (find the Persian king Darius turning and fleeing), it could as easily have been Germany in the 1520s. Christians were fighting Muslims, peasants battled masters, and Catholics and Protestants were squaring off for a century of conflict. The armies melt into a huge landscape, leaving the impression that

Dürer, Self-Portrait in Fur Coat

the battle goes on forever.

Albrecht Dürer's larger-than-life *Four Apostles (Johannes und Petrus* and *Paulus und Marcus)* are saints of a radical new religion: Martin Luther's Protestantism. Just as Luther challenged Church authority, Dürer—a friend of Luther's—strips these saints of any rich clothes, halos, or trappings of power and gives them down-to-earth human features: receding hairlines, wrinkles, and suspicious eyes. The inscription warns German rulers to follow the Bible rather than Catholic Church leaders. The figure of Mark—a Bible in one hand and a sword in the other—is a fitting symbol of the dangerous times.

Dürer's *Self-Portrait in Fur Coat (Selbstbildnis im Pelzrock)* looks like Jesus Christ but is actually 28-year-old Dürer himself, gazing out, with his right hand solemnly giving a blessing. This is the ultimate image of humanism: the artist as an instrument of God's continued creation.

Italian Renaissance (Room IV): With the Italian Renaissance—the "rebirth" of interest in the art and learning of ancient Greece and Rome—artists captured the realism, three-dimensionality, and symmetry found in classical statues. Twenty-one-year-old Leonardo da Vinci's *Virgin*

A *Leonardo da Vinci*, Virgin and Child

B *Raphael*, Canigiani Holy Family

C *Rubens*, Rubens and Isabella Brant

and Child *(Maria mit dem Kinde)* need no halos—they radiate purity. Mary is a solid pyramid of maternal love, flanked by Renaissance-arch windows that look out on the hazy distance. Baby Jesus reaches out to play innocently with a carnation, the blood-colored symbol of his eventual death.

Raphael's *Canigiani Holy Family (Die hl. Familie aus dem Hause Canigiani)* takes Leonardo's pyramid form and runs with it. Father Joseph forms the peak, with his staff as the strong central axis. Mary and Jesus (on the right) form a pyramid-within-the-pyramid, as do Elizabeth and baby John the Baptist on the left.

In Botticelli's *Lamentation over Christ (Die Beweinung Christi)*, the Renaissance "pyramid" implodes, as the weight of the dead Christ drags everyone down, and the tomb grins darkly behind them.

Venetian Painting (Room V): In Titian's *Christ Crowned with Thorns (Die Dornenkrönung)*, a powerfully built Christ sits, silently enduring torture by prison guards. The painting is by Venice's greatest Renaissance painter, but there's no symmetry, no pyramid form, and the brushwork is intentionally messy and Impressionistic. By the way, this is the first painting we've seen that is done on canvas rather than wood, as artists experimented with vegetable-oil-based paints.

Rubens and Baroque (Room VII): Europe's religious wars split the Continent in two—Protestants in the northern countries, Catholics in the south. (Germany itself was divided, with Bavaria remaining Catholic.) The Baroque style, popular in Catholic countries, featured large canvases, bright colors, lots of flesh, rippling motion, wild emotions, grand themes... and pudgy winged babies, the sure sign of Baroque. This room holds several canvases by the great Flemish painter Peter Paul Rubens.

In Rubens' 300-square-foot *Great Last Judgment (Das Grosse Jüngste Gericht)*, Christ raises the righteous up to heaven (left side) and damns the sinners to hell (on the right). This swirling cycle of nudes was considered risqué and kept under wraps by the very monks who'd commissioned it.

Rubens and Isabella Brant shows the artist with his first wife, both of them the picture of health, wealth, and success. They lean together unconsciously, as people in love will do, with their hands clasped in mutual affection. When his first wife died, 53-year-old Rubens found a replacement—16-year-old Hélène Fourment, shown in an adjacent painting (just to the left) in her wedding dress. You may recognize Hélène's face in other Rubens paintings.

The Rape of the Daughters of Leucippus (*Der Raub der Töchter des Leukippos*) has many of Rubens' most typical elements— fleshy, emotional, rippling motion; bright colors; and a classical subject. The legendary twins Castor and Pollux crash a wedding and steal the brides as their own. The chaos of flailing limbs and rearing horses is all held together in a subtle X-shaped composition. Like the weaving counterpoint in a Baroque fugue, Rubens balances opposites.

Rembrandt and Dutch (Room IX): From Holland, Rembrandt van Rijn's *Six Paintings from the Life of Christ* are a down-to-earth look at supernatural events. The *Adoration* (*Die Anbetung der Hirten*) of Baby Jesus takes place in a 17th-century Dutch barn with ordinary folk as models. The canvases are dark brown, lit by strong light. The Adoration's light source is the Baby Jesus himself— literally the "light of the world." In the *Deposition* (*Kreuzabnahme*), the light bounces off Christ's pale body onto his mother, Mary, who has fainted in the shadows, showing how his death also hurts her. The drama is underplayed, with subdued emotions. In the *Raising of the Cross* (*Kreuzaufrichtung*), a man dressed in blue is looking on—a self-portrait of Rembrandt.

▲NEUE PINAKOTHEK

The Alte Pinakothek's younger sister is an easy-to-like collection located just across the street, showing paintings from 1800 to 1920. Breeze through a smattering of Romantics on your way to the museum's highlight: some world-class Impressionist paintings, and one of Van Gogh's *Sunflowers*.

Cost and Hours: €7, €1 on Sun, open Wed 10:00-20:00, Thu-Mon until 18:00, closed Tue, well-done audioguide is usually free but €4.50 on Sun, classy Café Hunsinger in basement spills into park; U-2: Theresienstrasse, tram #27, or bus #100; Barer Strasse 29, but enter on Theresienstrasse, tel. 089/2380-5195, www.pinakothek.de/neue-pinakothek.

Visiting the Museum: Pick up the audioguide and floor plan, and follow their prescribed route. Along the way, be sure to hit these highlights.

Rooms 1-3: In Room 1, Jacques-Louis David's curly-haired *Comtesse de Sorcy* shows the French noblewoman dressed in the ancient-Greek-style fashions popular during the Revolution. Room 3 features English painters—Turner's stormy seascapes and Gainsborough's contemplative *Mrs. Thomas Hibbert*. Nearby, you'll see other less-famous works by other major European artists.

Rooms 4-18: These rooms—the bulk of the museum—feature colorful, pretty, realistic (and mostly forgettable) paintings

Stieler, King Ludwig I in Coronation Robes (*detail*)

by German Romantics. In the remarkable *King Ludwig I in Coronation Robes* (Room 8), the young playboy king is both regal and rakish. (You can learn more on the king, the artist, and their Gallery of Beauties at Nymphenburg Palace; see page 828.) Caspar David Friedrich (Room 9) is Germany's best-known chronicler of the awe-inspiring power of nature (though these small canvases aren't his best). Carl Spitzweg's tiny *The Poor Poet* (Room 12) is often reproduced. Room 13 has huge (hard-to-miss) canvases: *The Destruction of Jerusalem by Titus* and the nationalist-themed *Thusnelda Led in Germanicus' Triumph*, showing a German noblewoman and her son, captured by the Romans, being paraded before the emperor.

Rooms 19-22: In these rooms, you'll find classic examples of all the Impressionist and Post-Impressionist masters: Degas' snapshots of women at work, Monet's sunny landscapes and water lilies, Manet's bourgeois Realism, Cézanne's still lifes, and Gauguin's languid Tahitian ladies. Van Gogh's *Sunflowers* is one of 11 such canvases he did.

In the final rooms, see works by Gustav Klimt and Munich's answer to Klimt, Franz von Stuck.

▲▲EGYPTIAN MUSEUM (STAATLICHES MUSEUM ÄGYPTISCHER KUNST)

To enjoy this museum, you don't need a strong interest in ancient Egypt (but you may have one by the time you leave). This new space was custom-made to evoke the feeling of being deep in an ancient tomb, from the wide staircase outside that descends to the narrow entry, to the twisty interior rooms that grow narrower and more catacomb-like as you progress. The museum's clever design creates a low-stress visit—just follow the one-way route marked by brass arrows in the floor.

Cost and Hours: €12, €6 on Sun, open Tue 10:00-20:00, Wed-Sun until 18:00, closed Mon; U-2 or U-8 to Königsplatz, tram #27 to Karolinenplatz, or bus #100 to Pinakothek stop; 10-minute walk from main train station, Gabelsbergerstrasse 35, tel. 089/2892-7630, www.smaek.de.

Near the River

▲ENGLISH GARDEN (ENGLISCHER GARTEN)

Munich's "Central Park," the largest urban park on the Continent, was laid out in 1789 by an American, Benjamin Thompson (who left New England when the American Revolution broke out). More than 100,000 locals commune with nature here on sunny summer days. The park stretches three miles from the center, past the university and the trendy Schwabing quarter. For the best quick visit, take bus #100 or tram #18 to the Nationalmuseum/Haus der Kunst stop. Under the bridge, you may see surfers. Follow the path, to the right of the surfing spot, downstream until you reach the big lawn. The Chinese Tower beer garden is just beyond the tree-covered hill to the right. Follow the oompah music and walk to the hilltop temple, with a postcard view of the city on your way. Afterward, instead of

Chinese Tower beer garden

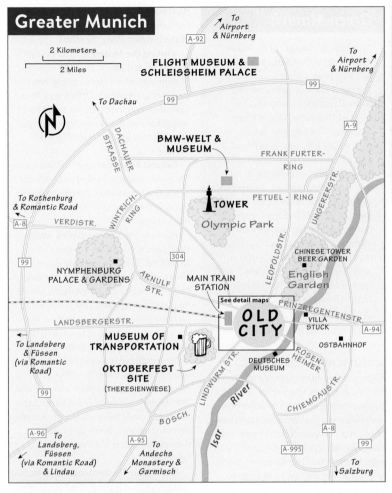

Greater Munich

2 Kilometers

2 Miles

To Airport & Nürnberg

A-92

To Airport & Nürnberg

FLIGHT MUSEUM & SCHLEISSHEIM PALACE

99

To Dachau

99

A-9

BMW-WELT & MUSEUM

FRANK FURTER-RING

PETUEL - RING

TOWER

Olympic Park

To Rothenburg & Romantic Road

A-8

VERDISTR.

DACHAUER STRASSE

WINTRICH-RING

99

NYMPHENBURG PALACE & GARDENS

304

ARNULF STR.

MAIN TRAIN STATION

LEOPOLDSTR.

UNGERERSTR.

CHINESE TOWER BEER GARDEN

English Garden

See detail maps

OLD CITY

PRINZREGENTENSTR.

VILLA STUCK

A-94

LANDSBERGERSTR.

To Landsberg & Füssen (via Romantic Road)

MUSEUM OF TRANSPORTATION

OKTOBERFEST SITE (THERESIENWIESE)

LINDWURM STR.

DEUTSCHES MUSEUM

ROSEN-HEIMER

OSTBAHNHOF

CHIEMGAUSTR.

BOSCH.

Isar River

A-96 To Landsberg, Füssen (via Romantic Road) & Lindau

A-95 To Andechs Monastery & Garmisch

A-8

99

A-995

To Salzburg

English Garden

retracing your steps, you can walk (or take bus #54 a couple of stops) to the Giselastrasse U-Bahn station and return to town on the U-3 or U-6.

A rewarding respite from the city, the park is especially fun—and worth ▲▲—on a bike under the summer sun and on warm evenings (to rent some wheels, see page 848). Caution: While local law requires sun worshippers to wear clothes on the tram, the park is sprinkled with buck-naked sunbathers—quite a shock to prudish Americans (they're the ones riding their bikes into the river and trees).

Green Munich

Although the capital of a conservative part of Germany, Munich has long been a liberal stronghold. For nearly two decades, the city council has been controlled by a Social Democrat/Green Party coalition. The city policies are pedestrian-friendly—you'll find much of the town center closed to normal traffic, with plenty of bike lanes and green spaces. As you talk softly and hear birds rather than motors, it's easy to forget you're in the center of a big city. On summer Mondays, the peace and quiet make way for "blade Monday"—when streets in the center are closed to cars and as many as 30,000 inline skaters swarm around town in a giant rolling party.

▲DEUTSCHES MUSEUM

Enjoy wandering through rooms of historic airplanes, spaceships, mining, the harnessing of wind and water power, hydraulics, musical instruments, printing, chemistry, computers, astronomy, and nanotechnology...it's the Louvre of technical know-how. The museum is dated, and not all the displays have English descriptions—but major renovations are under way. About a third of the collection will likely be closed during your visit, but with 11 acres of floor space and 10 miles of exhibits, even those on roller skates will still need to be selective. Use my mini tour to get oriented, then study the floor plan and choose which departments interest you.

Cost and Hours: €11, daily 9:00-17:00, worthwhile €7 English guidebook, tel. 089/21791, www.deutsches-museum.de.

Getting There: Take tram #16 to the Deutsches Museum stop. Alternatively, take the S-Bahn or tram #18 to Isartor, then walk 300 yards over the river, following signs. (The entrance is near the far end of the building along the river.)

Visiting the Museum: After buying your ticket, ask about the day's schedule of demonstrations (for example, electric power or glass-blowing). Pick up a floor plan, then continue past the ticket taker, straight ahead, into a vast high-ceilinged room (Room 10) dominated by a tall-masted ship.

Ground Floor: Get oriented and locate the handy elevator behind you—it's one of the few elevators in this labyrinthine building that goes to all six floors. Now, let's explore.

Room 10's exhibit on **marine navigation** is anchored by the 60-foot sailing ship *Maria*. Take the staircase down, where you can look inside her cut-away hull and imagine life below decks. Before heading back upstairs, find the bisected U1 submarine (on the wall farthest from the entrance)—the first German *U-Boot* (undersea boat), dating from 1906.

Now make your way to several new technology exhibits—DNA and nano-technology. Children will enjoy the "Kinderreich" (downstairs in Room 24) and the exciting twice-daily high-voltage demonstrations (Room 9) showing the noisy creation of a five-foot bolt of lightning.

First Floor: The **aeronautics** collection occupies virtually the entire floor (Room 33). You'll see early attempts at flight—gliders, hot-air balloons, and a model of the airship pioneered by Germany's Count Zeppelin. The highlight is a Wright Brothers double-decker airplane from 1909—six years after their famous first flight, when they began to manufacture multiple copies of their prototype. By World War I, airplanes were becoming a formidable force. The Fokker tri-plane was made famous by Germany's war ace the Red Baron (Manfred von Richthofen, whose exploits, I've heard, prompted enemies to drop the f-bomb). The exhibit continues into WWII-era Junkers and Messer-schmitts and postwar passenger planes.

Second Floor: Gathered together near the main elevator, you'll find a replica of prehistoric **cave paintings** (Room 39) and daily **glass-blowing** demonstrations (Room 40).

Third Floor: The third floor traces the **history of measurement,** including time (from a 16th-century sundial and an 18th-century clock to a scary Black Forest wall clock complete with grim reaper), weights, and geodesy (surveying and mapping). In the computer section (Rooms 52-53), you go from the ancient abacus to a 1956 Univac computer—as big as a room, with a million components, costing a million dollars, and with less computing power than your smartphone.

Floors 4-6: If you have trouble finding your way to these floors, there's always that main elevator. The focus here is on **astronomy.** A light-show exhibit (Room 62) traces the evolution of the universe. The recently renovated planetarium (Room 63) requires a €2 extra ticket (purchase at the info desk beforehand)—but the lecture is in German. Finally, you emerge on the museum rooftop—the "sundial garden" (Room 64)—with great views. On a clear day, you can see the Alps.

▲▲Nymphenburg Palace Complex

For 200 years, this oasis of palaces and gardens just outside Munich was the Wittelsbach rulers' summer vacation home, a getaway from the sniping politics of court life in the city. Their kids could play, picnic, ride horses, and frolic in the ponds and gardens, while the adults played cards, listened to music, and sipped coffee on the veranda. It was at Nymphenburg that a 7-year-old Mozart gave a widely heralded concert, 60-year-old Ludwig I courted the femme fatale Lola Montez, and "Mad" King Ludwig II (Ludwig I's grandson) was born and baptized.

Today, Nymphenburg Palace and the surrounding one-square-mile park are a great place for a royal stroll or discreet picnic. Indoors, you can tour the Bavarian royal family's summer quarters and visit the Royal Stables Museum (carriages, sleighs, and porcelain). If you have time, check out playful extras, such as a hunting lodge (Amalienburg), bathhouse (Badenburg), pagoda (Pagodenburg), and fake ruins (Magdalenenklause). The complex also houses a humble natural history museum and Baroque chapel. Allow at least three hours (including travel time) to see the palace complex at a leisurely pace.

Cost and Hours: Palace-€6; combo-ticket-€11.50 (€8.50 off-season) covers the palace, Royal Stables Museum, and outlying sights open in summer. All of these sights are open daily April-mid-Oct 9:00-18:00, mid-Oct-March 10:00-16:00—except for Amalienburg and the other small palaces in the park, which are closed mid-Oct-March. The park is open daily 6:00-dusk and free to enter. Tel. 089/179-080, www.schloss-nymphenburg.de.

Getting There: The palace is three miles northwest of central Munich. Take tram #17 (direction: Amalienburgstrasse) from the north side of the train station (or catch it at Karlsplatz). In 15 minutes you reach the Schloss Nymphenburg stop. From the bridge by the tram stop, you'll see the palace—a 10-minute walk away. The palace is a pleasant 30-minute bike ride from the main train station (either follow Arnulfstrasse all the way to Nymphenburg, or turn up Landshuter Allee—at Donersburgerbrücke—then follow Nymphenburger Strasse until you hit the canal that stretches to the palace). Biking in the palace grounds is not permitted.

Eating: A café serves lunches in the former palm house, behind and to the right of the palace (open year-round). More eating options are near the tram stop.

NYMPHENBURG PALACE

In 1662, after 10 years of trying, the Bavarian ruler Ferdinand Maria and his wife, Henriette Adelaide of Savoy, finally had a son, Max Emanuel. In gratitude for a male heir, Ferdinand gave this land to his Italian wife, who proceeded to build an Italian-style Baroque palace. Their son expanded the palace to today's size. (Today's Wittelsbachs, who still refer to themselves as "princes" or "dukes," live in one wing of the palace.)

The palace interior, while interesting, is much less extensive than Munich's Residenz—you can visit only 16 rooms. The place is stingy on free information; you'll need the serviceable audioguide if you'd like more info than what I've provided below.

⊘ **Self-Guided Tour:** Your visit starts in the **Great Hall** (a.k.a. **Stone Hall**). As the central room of the palace, this light and airy space was the dining hall, site of big Wittelsbach family festivals. One of the grandest and best-preserved Rococo rooms in Bavaria (from about 1758), it sports elaborate stucco work and a ceiling fresco by Johann Baptist Zimmermann (of Wieskirche fame).

Zimmerman's fresco opens a sunroof to the heavens, where Greek gods cavort. In the sunny center, Apollo drives his chariot to bring the dawn, while bearded Zeus (astride an eagle) and peacock-carrying Juno look on. The rainbow symbolizes the peace brought by the enlightened Wittelsbachs. Around the borders of the painting, notice the fun optical illusions: For example, a painted dog holds a stucco bird in its mouth. The painting's natural setting and joie de vivre reflect the pastoral pleasures enjoyed here at the Wittelsbachs' summer home. At one end of the fresco (away from the windows) lounges a lovely maiden with flowers in her hair: it's Flora, the eponymous nymph who inspired this "nymph's castle"—Nymphenburg.

From here, two wings stretch to the left and right. They're mirror images of one another: antechamber, audience chamber, bedchamber, and private living quarters. Guests would arrive here in the Great Hall for an awe-inspiring first impression, then make their way through a series of (also-impressive) waiting rooms for their date with the Wittelsbach nobility.

Nymphenburg Palace

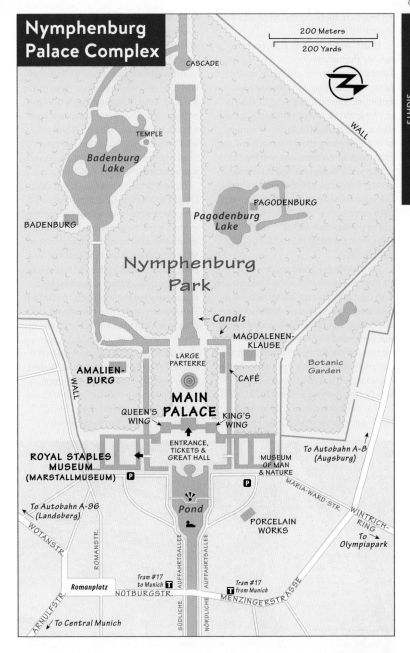

Nymphenburg
Palace Complex

200 Meters

200 Yards

CASCADE

TEMPLE

Badenburg
Lake

PAGODENBURG

Pagodenburg
Lake

BADENBURG

WALL

Nymphenburg
Park

← Canals

MAGDALENEN-
KLAUSE

LARGE
PARTERRE

AMALIEN-
BURG

WALL

CAFÉ

Botanic
Garden

MAIN
PALACE

QUEEN'S
WING

KING'S
WING

ENTRANCE,
TICKETS &
GREAT HALL

ROYAL STABLES
MUSEUM
(MARSTALLMUSEUM)

P

MUSEUM
OF MAN
& NATURE

To Autobahn A-8
(Augsburg)

P

MARIA-WARD-STR.

To Autobahn A-96
(Landsberg)

Pond

PORCELAIN
WORKS

WINTRICH-
RING

To
Olympiapark

WOTANSTR.

ROMANSTR.

AUFFAHRTSALLEE

SÜDLICHE

Romanplatz

Tram #17
to Munich

NOTBURGSTR.

AUFFAHRTSALLEE

NÖRDLICHE

Tram #17
from Munich

MENZINGERSTRASSE

ARNULFSTR.

← To Central Munich

• *The tour continues to the left (as you look out the big windows).*

North Wing (Rooms 2-9): Breeze quickly through this less interesting wing, filled with tapestries and Wittelsbach portraits (including curly-haired Max Emanuel, who built this wing). Pause in the long corridor lined with paintings of various Wittelsbach palaces. The ones of Nymphenburg show the place around 1720, back when there was nothing but countryside between it and downtown (and gondolas plied the canals). Imagine the logistics when the royal family—with their entourage of 200—decided to move out to the summer palace.

• *Return to the Great Hall and enter the other wing.*

South Wing (Rooms 10-20): Pass through the gold-and-white Room 10 and turn right into the red-walled Audience Chamber. The room calls up the exuber-ant time of Nymphenburg's founding cou-ple, Ferdinand and Henriette. A portrait on the wall shows them posing together in their rich courtly dress. Another painting depicts them in a Greek myth: Henri-ette (as the moon-goddess Diana) leads little Max Emanuel by the hand, while Ferdinand (as her mortal lover Endymion)

receives the gift of a sword. The ceiling painting (of the earth goddess Cybele) and the inlaid table also date from the time of Nymphenburg's first family.

After admiring the Queen's Bedroom and Chinese lacquer cabinet, head down the long hall to **King Ludwig I's Gallery of Beauties.** The room is decorated top to bottom with portraits of 36 beautiful women (all of them painted by Joseph Stieler between 1827 and 1850). Ludwig I was a consummate girl-watcher.

Ludwig prided himself on his ability to appreciate beauty regardless of social rank. He enjoyed picking out the prettiest women from the general public and, with one of the most effective pickup lines of all time, inviting them to the palace for a portrait. Who could refuse? The portraits were on public display in the Residenz, and catapulted their subjects to stardom. The women range from commoners to princesses, but notice that they share one physical trait—Ludwig obviously preferred brunettes. The portraits are done in the modest and slightly sentimental Bieder-meier style popular in central Europe, as opposed to the more flamboyant Roman-ticism (so beloved of Ludwig's "mad" grandson) also thriving at that time.

The Great Hall has remained unchanged since 1758.

Most of these portraits have rich stories behind them, none more than the portrait of Lola Montez, the king's most notorious mistress. The portrait shows her the year she met Ludwig (she was 29, he was 60), wearing the black-lace mantilla and red flowers of a Spanish dancer. (And where in the "gallery of beauties" is the portrait of Ludwig's wife, Queen Therese? She's not here...you'll have to duck into the elegant, green Queen's Study to see her portrait.)

Pass through the blue Audience Room (with elaborate curtain rods and mahogany furniture in the French-inspired Empire style) and into the (other) **Queen's Bedroom.** The room has much the same furniture it had on August 25, 1845, when Princess Marie gave birth to the future King Ludwig II. Little Ludwig (see his bust, next to brother Otto's) was greatly inspired by Nymphenburg—riding horses in summer, taking sleigh rides in winter, reading poetry at Amalienburg. The love of nature and solitude he absorbed at Nymphenburg eventually led Ludwig to abandon Munich for his castles in the remote Bavarian countryside. By the way, note the mirror in this bedroom. Royal births were carefully witnessed, and the mirror allowed for a better view. While

Ludwig's birth was well-documented, his death was shrouded in mystery.

PALACE GROUNDS

The wooded grounds extend far back beyond the formal gardens and are popular with joggers and walkers (biking is not allowed). Find a bench for a low-profile picnic. The park is laced with canals and small lakes, where court guests once rode on Venetian-style gondolas.

ROYAL STABLES MUSEUM (MARSTALLMUSEUM)

These former stables (to the left of the main palace as you approach the complex) are full of gilded coaches that will make you think of Cinderella's journey to the king's ball. Upstairs, a porcelain exhibit shows off some of the famous Nymphenburg finery. If you don't want to visit the main palace, you can buy a €4.50 ticket just for this museum (no audioguide available).

Visiting the Museum: Wandering through the collection, you can trace the evolution of **300 years of coaches—** getting lighter and with better suspension as they were harnessed to faster horses. In the big entrance hall is a golden carriage drawn by eight fake white horses. In 1742, it carried Karl Albrecht Wittelsbach to Frankfurt to be crowned Holy Roman Emperor. As emperor, he got eight horses—kings got only six. The event is depicted in a frieze on the museum wall; Karl's carriage is #159.

Other objects bear witness to the good times of the relaxed Nymphenburg lifestyle. You'll see the sleigh of Max Emanuel, decorated with a carved Hercules. The carousel (not always on display) was for the royal kids.

Next up are things owned by Ludwig II—several sleighs, golden carriages, and (in the glass cases) harnesses. Ludwig's over-the-top coaches were Baroque. But this was 1870. The coaches, like the king, were in the wrong century.

Head upstairs to a collection of

Stieler, Lola Montez *(detail)*

Nymphenburg porcelain. Historically, royal families such as the Wittelsbachs liked to have their own porcelain factories to make fit-for-a-king plates, vases, and so on. The Nymphenburg Palace porcelain works is still in operation (their factory store on Odeonsplatz is happy to see you). Find the large room with copies of 17th-century Old Masters' paintings from the Wittelsbach art collection (now at the Alte Pinakothek). Ludwig I had these paintings copied onto porcelain for safekeeping into the distant future. Take a close look—they're exquisite.

AMALIENBURG

Three hundred yards from Nymphenburg Palace, hiding in the park (head into the sculpted garden and veer to the left, following signs), you'll find a fine little Rococo hunting lodge, which takes just a few minutes to tour. In 1734, Elector Karl Albrecht had it built for his wife, Maria Amalia. Amalienburg was designed by François de Cuvilliés (of Residenz fame) and decorated by Johann Baptist Zimmermann. It's the most worthwhile of the four small "extra" palaces buried in the park that are included on the combo-ticket. The others are the Pagodenburg, a Chinese-inspired pavilion; Badenburg, an opulent bathing house and banquet hall; and the Magdalenenklause, a mini palace that looks like a ruin from the outside but has an elaborate altar and woody apartments inside.

Visiting Amalienburg: As you approach, circle to the front and notice the facade. Above the pink-and-white grand entryway, Diana, goddess of the chase, is surrounded by themes of the hunt and flanked by busts of satyrs. The queen would shoot from the perch atop the roof. Behind a wall in the garden, dogs would scare nonflying pheasants. When they jumped up in the air above the wall, the sporting queen—as if shooting skeet—would pick the birds off.

Tourists now enter this tiny getaway through the back door. Doghouses under gun cupboards fill the first room. In the fine yellow-and-silver bedroom, the bed is flanked by portraits of Karl Albrecht and Maria Amalia—decked out in hunting attire. She liked her dogs. The door under the portrait leads to stairs to the rooftop pheasant-shooting perch.

The mini Hall of Mirrors is a blue-and-silver commotion of Rococo nymphs designed by Cuvilliés. In the next room, paintings depict court festivities, formal hunting parties, and no-contest kills (where the animal is put at an impossible disadvantage—like shooting fish in a barrel). Finally, the kitchen is decorated with Chinese-style drawings on Dutch tile.

Outside the Center
▲▲ BMW-WELT AND MUSEUM
At the headquarters of BMW ("beh-em-VEH" to Germans), Beamer dreamers can visit two space-age buildings to learn more about this brand's storied heritage.

Royal Stables Museum

Amalienburg

The renowned *Autos* and *Motorräder* are beautifully displayed (perhaps even fetishized), but visitors who aren't car enthusiasts might find them less impressive. This vast complex—built on the site of Munich's first airstrip and home to the BMW factory since 1920—has four components: the headquarters (in the building nicknamed "the Four Cylinders"—not open to the public), the factory (tourable with advance reservations), the showroom (called BMW-Welt—"BMW World"), and the BMW Museum.

Cost and Hours: Museum—€10, Tue-Sun 10:00-18:00, closed Mon; BMW-Welt showroom—free, daily 9:00-18:00, tel. 089/125-016-001, www.bmw-welt. com/en.

Tours: English tours are offered of both the museum (€13, 1.5 hours, call ahead for times) and BMW-Welt (€7, daily at 14:00, 80 minutes). Factory tours must be booked at least two months in advance (€8, 2.5 hours, Mon-Fri only, ages 7 and up, book by calling 089/125-016-001, more info at www.bmw-werk-muenchen.de; ask at the BMW-Welt building about cancellations—open spots are released to the public 15 minutes before each tour).

Getting There: It's easy: Ride the U-3 to Olympia-Zentrum; the stop faces the BMW-Welt entry. To reach the museum, walk through BMW-Welt and over the swoopy bridge. This area also makes for a pleasant destination by bike, and is easily reached, and well-signed, from the English Garden.

Visiting the BMW-Welt: The futuristic, bowl-shaped **BMW Museum** encloses a world of floating walkways linking exhibits highlighting BMW motorcycle and car design and technology through the years. The museum traces the Bavarian Motor Works' history since 1917, when the company began making airplane engines. Motorcycles came next, followed by the first BMW sedan in 1929. You'll see how design was celebrated here from the start. Exhibits showcase motorsports, roadsters, and luxury cars. Stand on an *E* for English to hear the chief designer talk about his favorite cars in the "treasury." And the 1956 BMW 507 is enough to rev almost anyone's engine.

The futuristic BMW-Welt is a one-of-a-kind auto showroom.

The **BMW-Welt** building itself—a cloud-shaped, glass-and-steel architectural masterpiece—is reason enough to visit. It's free and filled with exhibits designed to enthuse car lovers so they'll find a way to afford a Beamer. While the adjacent museum reviews the BMW past, BMW-Welt shows you the present and gives you a breathtaking look at the future. This is where customers come to pick up their new Beamers (stand on the sky bridge to watch in envy), and where hopeful customers-to-be come to nurture their automotive dreams.

EXPERIENCES

Oktoberfest

A carnival of beer, pretzels, and wurst that draws visitors from all over the globe, Oktoberfest lasts just over two weeks, starting on the third Saturday in September and usually ending on the first Sunday in October (www.oktoberfest.de). It's held at the Theresienwiese fairground south of the main train station, in a meadow known as the "Wies'n" (VEE-zen), where eight

huge tents can each seat several thousand beer drinkers. The festivities kick off with an opening parade, followed by a two-week frenzy of drinking, dancing, music, and food. A million gallons of beer later, they roast the last ox.

If you'll be here during the festivities, reserve a room early. During the fair, the city functions even better than normal, but is admittedly more expensive and crowded. It's a good time to sightsee, even if beer-hall rowdiness isn't your cup of tea.

The enormous beer tents are often full, especially on weekends—if possible, avoid going on a Friday or Saturday night. For some cultural background, hire a local guide (see page 792) or go with a group (Radius Tours, for example, offers a €110 tour that includes two beers, half a chicken, and guaranteed seating, Sun-Fri at 10:00, no tours on Sat, reserve ahead, www.radiustours.com; Size Matters Beer Tour runs one for €120, includes breakfast, lunch, four beers, and reserved seating, www.sizemattersbeertour.de).

In the city center, the humble **Beer and Oktoberfest Museum** (Bier- und Oktoberfestmuseum), offers exhibits

and artifacts on the origins of the celebration and the centuries-old quest for the perfect beer (apparently achieved in Munich). The oldest house in the city center, the museum's home is noteworthy in itself (€4, Tue-Sat 13:00-18:00, closed Sun-Mon, between the Isartor and Viktualienmarkt at Sterneckerstrasse 2, tel. 089/2423-1607, www.bier-und-oktoberfestmuseum.de).

Rick's Tip: *The Theresienwiese fairground also hosts a* **Spring Festival** *(Frühlings-festival, two weeks in late April-early May, www.fruehlingsfest-muenchen.de), and* **Tollwood,** *an artsy, multicultural event held twice a year—once in summer (late June-July) and in winter (alternative Christmas market, late Nov-Dec, www.tollwood.de).*

Shopping

The most glamorous shopping area is around Marienplatz. It's fun to window shop, even if you have no plans to buy.

The upscale **Ludwig Beck** department store, with six floors of designer clothing, has been a local institution since 1861 (Mon-Sat 9:30-20:00, closed Sun, Marienplatz).

The third floor of department store **Loden-Frey Verkaufshaus** is dedicated to classic Bavarian wear (*Trachten*) for men and women (Mon-Sat 10:00-20:00, closed Sun, a block west of Marienplatz at Maffeistrasse 7, tel. 089/210-390, www.loden-frey.com).

The **Nymphenburg Porcelain Store** carries contemporary and classic dinnerware and figurines (Mon-Sat 10:00-18:00, closed Sun, Odeonsplatz 1, tel. 089/282-428, www.nymphenburg.com).

The **Hugendubel bookstore** on Karlsplatz has some English offerings (Mon-Sat 10:00-20:00, closed Sun, Karlsplatz 12, tel. 089-3075-7575, www.hugendubel.de).

Nightlife

Here are a few nightlife alternatives to the beer hall scene. Ballet and opera fans can check the schedule at the **Bayerisch Staatsoper,** centrally located next door to the Residenz. Book at least two months ahead—seats range from €13 to pricey (Max-Joseph-Platz 2, tel. 089/2185-1920, www.bayerische.staatsoper.de). The **Hotel Bayerischer-hof's** posh nightclub hosts major jazz acts plus pop/soul/disco (Promenadeplatz 2, tel. 089/212-0994, www.bayerischerhof.de). For Broadway-style musicals (most in German), try the **Deutsches Theatre,** located near the train station (Schwan-thalerstrasse 13, tel. 089/5523-4444, www.deutsches-theater.de).

EATING

Munich's cuisine is traditionally seasoned with beer. In beer halls, beer gardens, or at the Viktualienmarkt, try the most typical meal in town: *Weisswurst* (white-colored veal sausage—peel off the skin before eating, often available only until noon) with *süsser Senf* (sweet mustard), a salty *Brezel* (pretzel), and *Weissbier* ("white" wheat beer). Another traditional favorite is *Obatzda* (a.k.a. *Obatzter*), a mix of soft cheeses, butter, paprika, and often garlic or onions that's spread on bread. *Brotzeit,* literally "bread time," gets you a wooden platter of cold cuts,

cheese, and pickles and is a good option for a light dinner.

Beer Halls and Gardens

For those in search of the boisterous, clichéd image of the beer hall, nothing beats the Hofbräuhaus (the only beer hall in town where you'll find oompah music). Locals prefer the innumerable beer gardens. On a warm day, when you're looking for the authentic outdoor beer-garden experience, your best options are the Augustiner (near the train station), the small beer garden at the Viktualienmarkt (near Marienplatz), or the sea of tables in the English Garden.

Rick's Tip: *By law,* **any place serving beer** *must admit the public (whether or not they're customers) to* **use the bathrooms.**

Near Marienplatz

The **Hofbräuhaus** (HOAF-broy-howz) is the world's most famous beer hall. While it's grotesquely touristy, it's a Munich must. Drop by anytime for a large or light meal or just for a drink. Choose from four

zones: the rowdy main hall on the ground floor, a quieter courtyard under the stars, a dainty restaurant with mellow music one floor up, or the giant festival hall under a big barrel vault on the top floor. They sell beer by the *Mass* (one-liter mug, €8)—and they claim to sell 10,000 of these liters every day. Live oompah music plays at lunch and dinner (daily 9:00-23:30, 5-minute walk from Marienplatz at Platzl 9, tel. 089/2901-3610, www.hofbraeuhaus. de).

Wirtshaus Ayingers, just across the street from the Hofbräuhaus, is less chaotic. It serves quality Bavarian food—especially the schnitzels—and beer from Aying, a village south of Munich. There's lively outside seating on the cobbles facing the tourist chaos or a simple woody interior (€14-18 main courses, daily 11:00-24:00, Platzl 1a, tel. 089/2370-3666, www. ayingers.de).

Andechser am Dom, at the rear of the twin-domed Frauenkirche on a breezy square, is a local staple serving Andechs beer and great food to appreciative regulars. Münchners favor the dark beer (ask for *dunkles*), but I love the light (*helles*). The *Gourmetteller* is a great sampler of

Munich's Beer Scene

In Munich's beer halls (*Brauhäuser*) and beer gardens (*Biergartens*), meals are inexpensive, white radishes are salted and cut in delicate spirals, and surly beer maids pull mustard packets from their cleavage. Beer is truly a people's drink—and the best is in Munich. The big question among connoisseurs is "Which brew today?"

Huge liter beers (*ein Mass* or "*ein* pitcher") cost about €8. You can order your beer *helles* (light), *dunkles* (dark), or ask for a *Weiss* or *Weizen* ("white" or wheat-based beer—cloudy and sweet) or a *Radler* (half lemon soda, half beer).

Beer-hall food is usually *selbstdienst* (self-service)—a sign may say *Bitte bedienen Sie sich selbst* (please serve yourself). If two prices are listed, *Schank* is for self-service, while *Bedienung* is for table service. At a large *Biergarten,* assemble your dream feast by visiting various counters, marked by type of food (*Bier* or *Bierschänke* for beer, *Bratwürste* for sausages, *Brotzeiten* for lighter fare served cold, and so on). Look for these specialties:

Fleischpfanzerl (or *Fleischklösse* or *Frikadellen*): Meatballs

Grosse Brez'n: Gigantic pretzel

Hendl (or *Brathähnchen*): Roasted chicken

Radi: Radish thinly spiral-cut and salted

Schweinrollbraten: Pork belly

Schweinshax'n (or *Hax'n*): Pork knuckle

Spareribs: Spareribs

Steckerlfisch: A whole fish (usually mackerel) herbed and grilled on a stick

their specialties, but you can't go wrong with *Rostbratwurst* with kraut (€8-20 main courses, daily 10:00-24:00, Weinstrasse 7a, reserve during peak times, tel. 089/2429-2920, www.andechser-am-dom.de).

Nürnberger Bratwurst Glöckl am Dom, around the corner from Andechser am Dom, offers a more traditional, fiercely Bavarian evening. Dine outside under the trees or in the dark, medieval interior. Enjoy the tasty little *Nürnberger* sausages with kraut (€10-20 main courses, daily 10:00-24:00, Frauenplatz 9, tel. 089/291-9450, www.bratwurst-gloeckl.de).

Altes Hackerhaus serves its traditional Bavarian fare with a slightly fancier feel in one of the oldest buildings in town. It offers a small courtyard and a fun forest of characteristic nooks. This place is greatly appreciated for its Hacker-Pschorr beer (€8-10 wurst dishes, €9-25 main courses,

daily 10:30-24:00, Sendlinger Strasse 14, tel. 089/260-5026, www.hackerhaus.de).

Munich's **Ratskeller** fills the City Hall's vast cellar and also has some tables in the courtyard with 360-degree views. While it's hectic and touristy, locals still enjoy the timeless atmosphere (€14-24 main courses, daily 10:00-24:00, Marienplatz 8, tel. 089/219-9890, www.ratskeller.com).

Der Pschorr, an upscale beer hall occupying a former slaughterhouse, has a terrace overlooking the Viktualienmarkt and serves what many consider Munich's finest beer. With organic "slow food" and chilled glasses, this place mixes modern with classic dishes. The sound of the hammer tapping wooden kegs every few minutes lets patrons know their beer is good and fresh (€15-25 main courses, daily 10:00-24:00, Viktualienmarkt 15, at end of Schrannenhalle, tel. 089/442-383-940, www.der-pschorr.de).

The small **beer garden** at the center of the Viktualienmarkt has just about the best budget eating in town; it's just steps from Marienplatz. There's table service wherever you see a tablecloth; to picnic, choose a table without one—but you must buy a drink from the counter (daily 10:00-22:00). Countless stalls surround the beer garden and sell wurst, sandwiches, and produce.

Rick's Tip: *Most beer gardens have a €1 deposit (Pfand) for their big glass steins. When you're finished drinking, take the mug and your deposit token (Pfandmarke) to the return man (Pfandrückgabe) for your refund. If you buy a bottled beer, pour it into the glass before you check out; otherwise you'll pay two deposits (one for the glass, the other for the bottle).*

Spatenhaus has served elegant food in a woody setting since 1896—maybe it's not even right to call its almost refined restaurant a "beer hall." You can also eat outside, on the square facing the opera and palace. It's pricey, but you won't find better Bavarian cuisine. The upstairs restaurant is a more formal dining room—reservations are advised (€15-30 main courses, daily 9:30-24:00, on Max-Joseph-Platz opposite opera, Residenzstrasse 12, tel. 089/290-7050, www.spatenhaus.de).

Near the Train Station

Augustiner Beer Garden, a true under-the-leaves beer garden packed with Münchners, is a delight. In fact, most Münchners consider Augustiner the best beer garden in town—which may be why it has 5,000 seats. There's no music, it's away from the tourist hordes, and it serves up great beer, good traditional food, huge portions, reasonable prices, and perfect conviviality. The outdoor self-service ambience is best, making this place ideal on a nice summer evening (figure €15 for a main course and a drink). Parents

with kids can sit at tables adjoining a sizable playground. There's also indoor and outdoor seating at a more expensive restaurant with table service (daily 11:00-24:00, Arnulfstrasse 52, 3 looooong blocks from station going away from the center—or take tram #16/#17 one stop to Hopfenstrasse, tel. 089/594-393, www.augustinerkeller.de).

Park Café is a nice hideaway, tucked inside the Alter Botanischer Garden, just north of the train station. When it's hot, the prime spot is the beer garden out back, where you can also order Bavarian food from self-service counters or classy cocktails and cuisine from an international menu (€9-20 main courses). The indoor section is modern and cozy and features DJs or live music in the late evening (daily 10:00-24:00, beer garden opens at 11:30, Sophienstrasse 7, tel. 089/5161-7980, www.parkcafe089.de).

In the English Garden

For outdoor ambience and a cheap meal, spend an evening at **Chinese Tower beer garden** (*Chinesischer Turm Biergarten*). You're welcome to B.Y.O. food and grab one of the 6,000 seats, or buy from the food stalls. This is a fine opportunity to try a *Steckerlfisch*, sold at a separate kiosk (daily, long hours in good weather, usually live music, playground, tel. 089/383-8730, www.chinaturm.de; take tram #18 from main train station or Sendlinger Tor to Tivolistrasse, or U-3 or U-6 to Giselastrasse and then bus #54 or #154 two stops).

Restaurants

Man does not live by beer alone. Well, maybe some do. But here are some alternatives for the rest of us.

On and near Marienplatz

Glockenspiel Café is good for a coffee or a meal with a bird's-eye view down on the Marienplatz action—I'd come for the view more than the food (€12-24 main courses, Mon-Sat 9:00-24:00, Sun 10:00-19:00, ride elevator from Rosenstrasse entrance, opposite glockenspiel at Marienplatz 28, tel. 089/264-256).

Blatt Salate is a self-serve salad bar on a side street between the Frauenkirche and the New Town Hall; it's a great little hideaway for a healthy, quick lunch (€12-14 vegetarian and meat salads and soups, Mon-Fri 11:00-21:30, Sat until 18:00, closed Sun, Schäfflerstrasse 7, tel. 089/2102-0281).

Around the Viktualienmarkt

Restaurant Opatija, in the Viktualienmarkt passage a few steps from Marienplatz, is homey and efficient, with an eclectic mix of Italian, Balkan, and German favorites. Choose between the comfortable indoor section and the outdoor seating in a quiet courtyard. It's family-friendly, and they do takeout (good €7-8 pizzas, €8-13 main courses, daily 11:30-21:30, enter the passage at Viktualienmarkt 6 or Rindermarkt 2, tel. 089/2323-1995).

Die Münchner Suppenküche ("Munich Soup Kitchen"), a self-service soup joint at the Viktualienmarkt, is fine for a small, cozy sit-down lunch at picnic tables under a closed-in awning. The maroon chalkboard lists the soups of the day—I go for the goulash or the carrot soup (€4-6 soup meals, Mon-Sat 10:00-18:00, closed Sun, near corner of Reichenbachstrasse and Frauenstrasse, tel. 089/260-9599).

Stadt Café is a lively café serving healthy fare with an inventive mix of Italian, German, vegetarian, salads, and a big selection of cakes by the slice. This no-frills restaurant draws newspaper readers, stroller moms, and locals meeting for a drink. Dine in the quiet cobbled courtyard, inside, or outside facing the new synagogue (daily specials for €7-12, daily 10:00-24:00, in same building as Munich City Museum, St.-Jakobs-Platz 1, tel. 089/266-949).

Prinz Myshkin Vegetarian Restaurant is an upscale vegetarian eatery in the old center. The seasonal menu is clever and appetizing, the arched ceilings are cool, and the outside seating is on a quiet street. They also have vegetarian sushi, pastas, Indian dishes, and their own baker, so they're proud of their sweets (€14-20 main courses, daily 11:00-23:00, Hackenstrasse 2, tel. 089/265-596).

Sebastiansplatz is a long, pedestrianized square between the Viktualienmarkt and the synagogue, lined with bistros handy for a quick lunch. All serve €10 main courses on the busy cobbled square or inside—just survey the scene and choose. The **Schrannenhalle,** the former grain exchange overlooking the square, is busy with creative, modern eateries and gourmet delis (Mon-Sat 10:00-20:00, closed Sun).

Near Odeonsplatz

Café Tambosi has an Italian-influenced menu, Viennese elegance inside, and a relaxing garden setting out back (€9-20 main courses, daily 8:00-24:00, Odeonsplatz 18, tel. 089/298-322).

Café Luitpold is where Munich's high society comes to sip its coffee and nibble on exquisite cakes. The café is proudly home to the original *Luitpoldtorte*—sponge cake with layers of marzipan and buttercream, covered in dark chocolate (Tue-Sat 8:00-23:00, Sun-Mon 9:00-19:00, Brienner Strasse 11, tel. 089/242-8750).

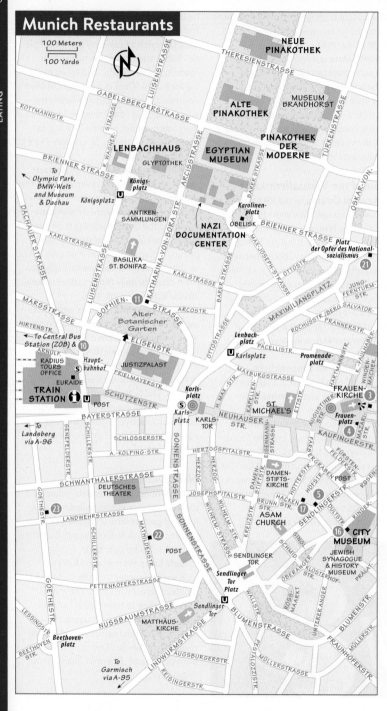

Munich Restaurants

100 Meters
100 Yards

NEUE PINAKOTHEK

THERESIENSTRASSE

MUSEUM BRANDHORST

ALTE PINAKOTHEK

LENBACHHAUS

GLYPTOTHEK

EGYPTIAN MUSEUM

PINAKOTHEK DER MODERNE

To Olympic Park, BMW-Welt and Museum & Dachau

Königs-platz

Königsplatz

Karolinen-platz

OBELISK

Platz der Opfer des National-sozialismus

ANTIKEN-SAMMLUNGEN

NAZI DOCUMENTATION CENTER

BRIENNER STRASSE

BASILIKA ST. BONIFAZ

KARLSTRASSE

KARLSTRASSE

21

MAXIMILIANSPLATZ

11

Alter Botanischer Garten

Lenbach-platz

Karlsplatz

Promenade-platz

To Central Bus Station (ZOB) & 10

JUSTIZPALAST

FRAUEN-KIRCHE 3

Haupt-bahnhof

RADIUS TOURS OFFICE

EURAIDE

TRAIN STATION

Karls-platz

Karls-platz

KARLS-TOR

ST. MICHAEL'S

Frauen-platz

4

KAUFINGERSTR.

POST

To Landsberg via A-96

NEUHAUSER-STR.

DEUTSCHES THEATER

DAMEN-STIFTS-KIRCHE

5

17

ASAM CHURCH

16

CITY MUSEUM

23

22

POST

SENDLINGER TOR

JEWISH SYNAGOGUE & HISTORY MUSEUM

Sendlinger Tor Platz

Sendlinger Tor

MATTHÄUS-KIRCHE

Beethoven-platz

To Garmisch via A-95

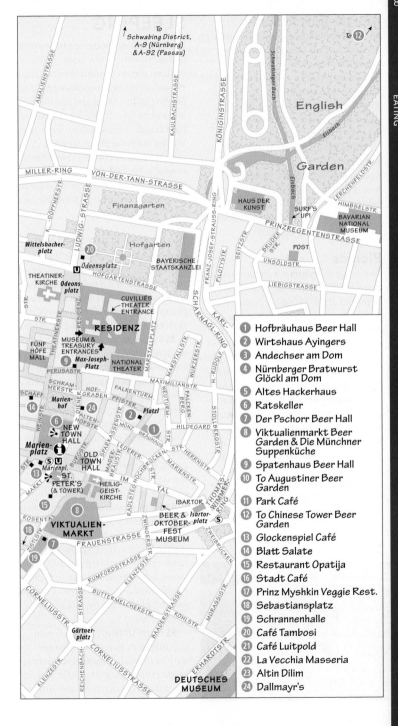

1. Hofbräuhaus Beer Hall
2. Wirtshaus Ayingers
3. Andechser am Dom
4. Nürnberger Bratwurst Glöckl am Dom
5. Altes Hackerhaus
6. Ratskeller
7. Der Pschorr Beer Hall
8. Viktualienmarkt Beer Garden & Die Münchner Suppenküche
9. Spatenhaus Beer Hall
10. To Augustiner Beer Garden
11. Park Café
12. To Chinese Tower Beer Garden
13. Glockenspiel Café
14. Blatt Salate
15. Restaurant Opatija
16. Stadt Café
17. Prinz Myshkin Veggie Rest.
18. Sebastiansplatz
19. Schrannenhalle
20. Café Tambosi
21. Café Luitpold
22. La Vecchia Masseria
23. Altin Dilim
24. Dallmayr's

Near the Train Station

La Vecchia Masseria, between Sendlinger Tor and the train station hotels, serves Italian food inside amid cozy Tuscan farmhouse decor, or outside in a beautiful flowery courtyard (€6-8 pizza or pasta, €14-16 main courses, daily 11:30-23:30, reservations smart, Mathildenstrasse 3, tel. 089/550-9090).

Altin Dilim, a cafeteria-style Turkish restaurant, is a standout among the many hole-in-the-wall Middle Eastern places near the station. A handy pictorial menu helps you order (€5 *Döner Kebab*, €8-13 main courses, daily 10:00-24:00, Goethes-trasse 17, tel. 089/9734-0869).

Picnics

The crown in **Dallmayr's** emblem reflects that even the royal family assembled its picnics at this historic delicatessen. Assemble a royal (pricey) spread to munch in the nearby Hofgarten or visit the classy cafés that serve light meals on the ground and first floors (Mon-Sat 9:30-19:00, closed Sun, behind New Town Hall, Dienerstrasse 13-15, tel. 089/213-5110).

The **supermarkets** that hide in the basements of department stores are on the upscale side, such as the **Galeria Kaufhof** stores at Marienplatz and Karl-splatz, and the **Karstadt** across from the train station. Cheaper options include the **REWE** in the basement at Fünf Höfe (entrance is in Viscardihof) or the **Lidl** at Schwantaler Strasse 31, near the train-station hotels. They're generally open daily (until 20:00) except closed on Sunday.

SLEEPING

I've listed accommodations in two neigh-borhoods: within a few blocks of the cen-tral train station (Hauptbahnhof), and in the old center, between Marienplatz and Sendlinger Tor. Although I give the approx-imate price for a double room, hotels also have singles (which can be double rooms offered at a lower price), triples, and sometimes quads (which I term "family rooms" in listings). During major conven-tions and events, prices can increase 20 to 300 percent (worst at Oktoberfest; reserve well in advance).

Near the Train Station

Good-value hotels cluster in the multi-cultural area immediately south of the station. Some find it colorful; for others it feels seedy after dark (with erotic cinemas and men loitering in the shadows). It's sketchy only for those in search of trouble.

$$$ Marc München—polished, modern, and with 80 newly renovated rooms—is a good option if you need more luxury than the other listings here. It's just a half-block from the station on a rela-tively tame street, and has a nice lobby and classy breakfast spread. The cheaper "superior king" rooms are the best value (Db-€147-221, ask about Rick Steves dis-count, pay parking, air-con, Senefelder-strasse 12, tel. 089/559-820, www.hotel-marc.de, info@hotel-marc.de).

$$ Hotel Monaco is a delightful hide-away, tucked inside the fifth floor of a giant, nondescript building two blocks from the station (D-€75, Db-€79-99, family rooms, breakfast-€9, cash pre-ferred, Schillerstrasse 9, entrance on Adolf-Kolping-Strasse, tel. 089/545-9940, www.hotel-monaco.de, info@hotel-monaco.de).

$$ Hotel Uhland is a stately man-sion that rents 29 rooms with mod-ern bathrooms in a genteel, residential neighborhood a slightly longer walk from the station (toward the Theresienwiese

Oktoberfest grounds). It's been in the Hauzenberger and Reim families for 60 years (small Db-€95, big Db-€105-118, family rooms, limited free parking, Uhlandstrasse 1, tel. 089/543-350, www.hotel-uhland.de, info@hotel-uhland.de). From the station, take bus #58 (direction: Silberhornstrasse) to Georg-Hirth-Platz, or walk 15 minutes: Out the station's south exit, cross Bayerstrasse, take Paul-Heyse-Strasse three blocks to Georg-Hirth-Platz, then take a soft right on Uhlandstrasse.

$$ Hotel Belle Blue, three blocks from the station, has 30 rooms and is a great value if you are looking for modern furnishings and air-conditioning (Db-€96, Schillerstrasse 21, tel. 089/550-6260, www.hotel-belleblue.de, info@hotel-belleblue.com, Irmgard). Their two apartments are perfect for families (7-night minimum in summer).

$$ Hotel Bristol is efficient, with 57 business-like rooms. It's located across the street from the Sendlinger Tor U-Bahn station (Db-€97, breakfast-€9.50, air-con in lobby, pay parking, Pettenkoferstrasse 2, tel. 089/5434-8880, www.bristol-munich.de, info@bristol-munich.de).

$$ Hotel Deutsches Theater, filled with brass and marble, has 27 three-star rooms. The back rooms face the courtyard of a neighboring theater, so there can be some noise (Db-€90-100, family rooms, pricier suites, breakfast-€9, Landwehrstrasse 18, tel. 089/545-8525, www.hoteldeutschestheater.de, info@hoteldeutschestheater.de).

$$ Hotel Europäischer Hof, across the street from the station, is a huge, impersonal hotel with 150 decent rooms. During cool weather, when you can keep the windows shut, the street-facing rooms are an acceptable option. Courtyard-facing rooms are quieter—and more expensive, except for a few cheap rooms with shared bath (streetside Db-€100; courtyard D with head-to-toe twin beds-€60; ask about Rick Steves discount, pay parking, Bayerstrasse 31, tel. 089/551-510, www.

Sleep Code

Price Rankings for Double Rooms (Db)
$$$ Most rooms €130 or more
$$ €90-130
$ €90 or less

Abbreviations: Db=Double with bathroom. D=Double with bathroom down the hall.

Notes: Room prices change; verify rates online or by email. For the best prices, book direct with the hotel.

heh.de, info@heh.de).

$ Hotel Royal is one of the best values in the neighborhood (as long as you can look past the strip joints flanking the entry). While institutional, it's clean and plenty comfortable. Most important, it's energetically run by Pasha and Christiane. Each of its 40 rooms is fresh and bright (Db-€74-94, family rooms, comfort rooms on quiet side cost €10 extra—worth it in summer when you'll want the window open, ask about Rick Steves discount, Schillerstrasse 11a, tel. 089/5998-8160, www.hotel-royal.de, info@hotel-royal.de).

$ Litty's Hotel is a basic hotel offering 37 small rooms with little personality (D-€72-€78, Db-€88, Wi-Fi at reception reaches lower floors, near Schillerstrasse at Landwehrstrasse 32c, tel. 089/5434-4211, www.littyshotel.de, info@littyshotel.de).

$ The CVJM (YMCA), open to all ages, rents 85 beds in clean, slightly worn rooms with sinks in the rooms and showers and toilets down the hall. Doubles are head-to-head; triples are like doubles with a bunk over one of the beds (D-€64; only €10/night more per person during Oktoberfest—reserve 6-12 months ahead; includes linens and breakfast

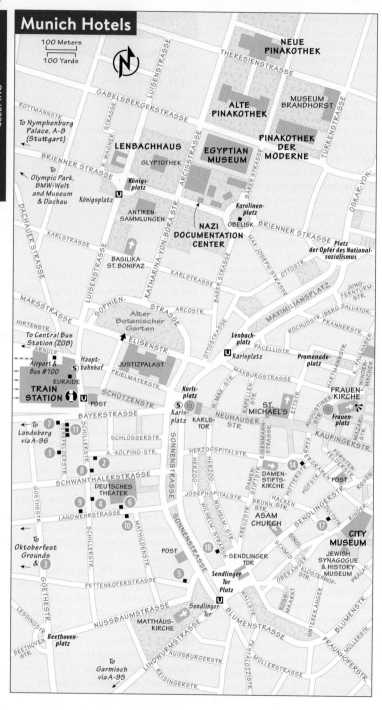

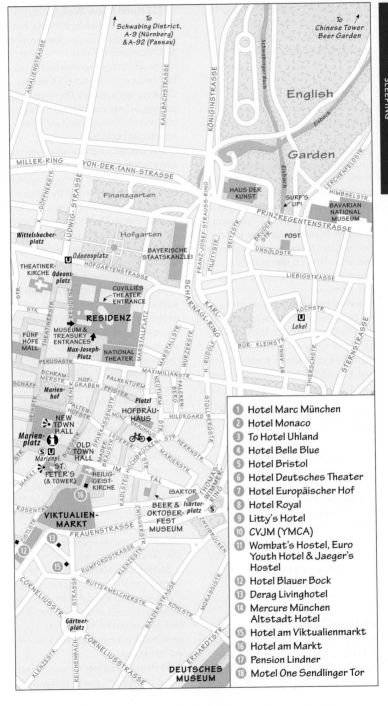

1. Hotel Marc München
2. Hotel Monaco
3. To Hotel Uhland
4. Hotel Belle Blue
5. Hotel Bristol
6. Hotel Deutsches Theater
7. Hotel Europäischer Hof
8. Hotel Royal
9. Litty's Hotel
10. CVJM (YMCA)
11. Wombat's Hostel, Euro Youth Hotel & Jaeger's Hostel
12. Hotel Blauer Bock
13. Derag Livinghotel
14. Mercure München Altstadt Hotel
15. Hotel am Viktualienmarkt
16. Hotel am Markt
17. Pension Lindner
18. Motel One Sendlinger Tor

but no lockers; cheap Wi-Fi by reception, Landwehrstrasse 13, tel. 089/552-1410, www.cvjm-muenchen.org/hotel/jugendhotel, hotel@cvjm-muenchen.org).

"Hostel Row"

All three of the following hostels on Senefelderstrasse are casual and well-run, with friendly management, and all cater to the needs of young beer-drinking backpackers enjoying Munich on a shoestring. With 900 cheap dorm beds, this is a spirited street. There's no curfew, and each place has a lively bar that rages until the wee hours. All have 24-hour receptions, Wi-Fi, laundry facilities, lockers, and included linens. None has a kitchen, but each offers a buffet breakfast. Sleep cheap in big dorms, or spend more for a 2- to 4-bed room.

$ Wombat's Hostel, perhaps the most hip and colorful, rents cheap doubles and dorm beds with lockers. The dorms are fresh and modern, and there's a relaxing and peaceful winter garden (dorm bed-€23-32, Db-€84, Senefelderstrasse 1, tel. 089/5998-9180, www.wombats.eu, office@wombats-munich.de).

$ Euro Youth Hotel fills a rare pre-WWII building (dorm bed-€22-33, D-€70-85, includes breakfast for private rooms, Senefelderstrasse 5, tel. 089/5990-8811, www.euro-youth-hotel.de, info@euro-youth-hotel.de).

$ Jaeger's Hostel, with 300 cheap beds, has fun and efficiency—plus the only air-conditioning on the street. This seems to be the quietest hostel of the group (dorm bed-€19-32, hotel-quality Db-€79-84, Senefelderstrasse 3, tel. 089/555-281, www.jaegershostel.de, office@jaegershostel.de).

In the Old Center

A few good deals remain in the area south of Marienplatz, going toward the Sendlinger Tor. This neighborhood is more genteel and is convenient for sightseeing.

$$$ Hotel Blauer Bock, formerly a dormitory for Benedictine monks, has been on the same corner near the Munich City Museum since 1841. Its 70 remodeled rooms are classy, if spartan for the price, but the location is great (D-€70-100, Db-€135-165, premium Db-€190-220, pay parking, Sebastiansplatz 9, tel. 089/231-780, www.hotelblauerbock.de, info@hotelblauerbock.de).

$$$ Derag Livinghotel's 83 sleek, tech-savvy rooms are located right off the Viktualienmarkt. Half the rooms are less modern and have kitchenette suites. If you can nab a double room for less than €180, it's a good deal (Db-€165-250 though official rates much higher, breakfast-€19.50, air-con, pay parking, Frauenstrasse 4, tel. 089/885-6560, www.deraghotels.de, vitualienmarkt@derag.de).

$$$ Mercure München Altstadt Hotel is reliable, with all the modern comforts in its 75 business-class rooms, and is located on a quiet street close to the Marienplatz action. A few newer but less expensive rooms are available on the first floor (Db-€186, air-con, block south of the pedestrian zone at Hotterstrasse 4, tel. 089/232-590, www.mercure-muenchen-altstadt.de, h3709@accor.com).

$$$ At **Hotel am Viktualienmarkt,** everything about this 27-room hotel is small but well-designed, including the elevator and three good-value, tiny single rooms. It's on a small side street a couple of blocks from the Viktualienmarkt (Db-€135, family rooms, Utzschneiderstrasse 14, tel. 089/231-1090, www.hotel-am-viktualienmarkt.de, reservierung@hotel-am-viktualienmarkt.de).

$$ Hotel am Markt, right next to the Viktualienmarkt, has 32 decent rooms; it's a better deal if you skip the expensive breakfast (Db-€112-124, breakfast-€12, Heiliggeiststrasse 6, tel. 089/225-014, www.hotel-am-markt.eu, service@hotel-am-markt.eu).

$$ Pension Lindner is clean and quiet, with nine pleasant, pastel-bouquet rooms off a bare stairway. Frau Sinzinger offers a warm welcome and good buffet breakfasts, but she rarely has room for last-minute bookings (D-€75, Db-€100, cash discount on doubles and triples, Dultstrasse 1, tel. 089/263-413, www.pension-lindner.com, info@pension-lindner.com, Marion Sinzinger).

$$ Motel One Sendlinger Tor is a busy, inexpensive, 241-room chain hotel with rushed-but-pleasant staff in a fine location around the corner from the Sendlinger Tor tram and U-Bahn stop. The stylish, modern rooms are fairly tight but are a good value—and sell out a few weeks in advance. Streetside rooms on upper floors have great views. When booking on their website, make sure to choose the Sendlinger Tor location—they have six other hotels in Munich (Db-€94, breakfast-€9.50, air-con, pay parking, Herzog-Wilhelm-Strasse 28, tel. 089/5177-7250, www.motel-one.com, muenchen-sendlingertor@motel-one.com).

TRANSPORTATION

Getting Around Munich

Much of Munich is walkable. But given that the city is laced by many trams, buses, and subways, it's worth learning the system and considering getting a day pass. Public transit also makes it super-easy to access sights outside the historic core, such as Dachau or Nymphenburg Palace. Cabbies are honest and professional, but taxis are expensive (about €12 between the Hauptbahnhof and Marienplatz) and generally unnecessary.

By Subway, Tram, and Bus

Subways are called U-Bahns and S-Bahns. (S-Bahns are actually commuter railways that run underground through the city and are covered by rail passes—but it's smarter to save your limited number of pass days for long-distance trips.) These transit lines are numbered (for example, S-3 or U-5). The U-Bahn lines mainly run north-south, while the S-Bahn lines are generally east-west. For more info, visit the transit customer-service center underground at the main train station or Marienplatz (closed Sun), call 0800-344-226-600 (Mon-Fri only), or visit www.mvv-muenchen.de.

TICKETS

The entire transit system (subway/bus/tram) works on the same tickets. There are four concentric zones—white, green, yellow, and orange. Almost everything described in this chapter is within the white/inner zone, except for Dachau (green zone) and the airport (orange zone).

Transit tickets are sold at booths in the subway and at ticket machines with the MVV logo. Machines take coins and €5-50 bills; newer ones take PIN-enabled credit cards, too. Start the transaction by choosing "English," then press "Transit Association-MVV," which displays the array of tickets and passes available.

A one-zone **regular ticket** (Einzelfahrkarte, €2.70) is good for three hours in one direction, including changes and stops. For short rides (four stops max, only two of which can be on the subway lines), buy the **short-stretch ticket** (Kurzstrecke, €1.40). The **all-day pass** (Single-Tageskarte, €6.20) for the white/inner zone is a great deal for a single traveler.

All-day small-group passes (Partner-Tageskarte) are an even better deal—they cover all public transportation for up to five adults (two kids count as one adult, so two adults and six kids can travel with this ticket). A Partner-Tageskarte for the white/inner zone costs €11.70 (the €14.80 **XXL** version includes Dachau; the €22.30 **Gesamtnetz** version includes the airport). These partner tickets are a real steal—the only catch is that you've got to stay together.

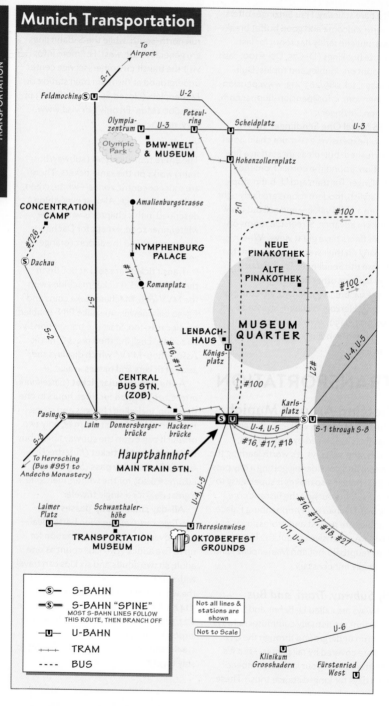

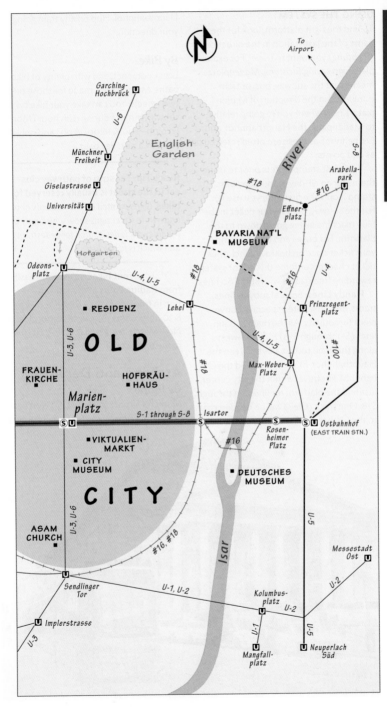

Garching-Hochbrück **U** U-6

English Garden

To Airport

River

S-8

Arabella-park **U** #16

Münchner Freiheit **U**

Giselastrasse **U**

Universität **U**

#18

Effner-platz

#18

BAVARIA NAT'L MUSEUM

Hofgarten

Odeons-platz **U**

U-4, U-5

#16

U-4

Prinzregent-platz **U**

■ RESIDENZ

O L D

#18

Lehel **U**

U-3, U-6

FRAUEN-KIRCHE ■

HOFBRÄU-HAUS ■

U-4, U-5

#100

Marien-platz

#18

Max-Weber-Platz **U**

S-1 through S-8 Isartor

S **U**   **S**   **S** **U** Ostbahnhof (EAST TRAIN STN.)

■ VIKTUALIEN-MARKT

Rosen-heimer Platz

■ CITY MUSEUM

#16

C I T Y

■ DEUTSCHES MUSEUM

U-3, U-6

ASAM CHURCH ■

#16, #18

Isar

U-5

Messestadt Ost **U**

Sendlinger Tor **U**

U-1, U-2

Kolumbus-platz **U**

U-2

U Implerstrasse

U-2

U-3

U-1

U-5

U Neuperlach Süd

Mangfall-platz

USING THE SYSTEM

To find the right platform, look for the name of the last station in the direction (*Richtung*) you want to travel. For example, a sign saying *Richtung: Marienplatz* means that the subway, bus, or tram is traveling in the direction of Marienplatz. Know where you're going relative to Marienplatz, the Hauptbahnhof, and Ostbahnhof, as these are often referred to as end points.

You must stamp tickets prior to using them (for an all-day or multiday pass, stamp it only the first time you use it). For the subway, punch your ticket in the blue machine *before* going down to the platform. For buses and trams, stamp your ticket once on board. Plainclothes ticket checkers enforce this honor system, rewarding freeloaders with stiff €60 fines.

Handy Lines: Several subway lines, trams, and buses are especially convenient for tourists. All the main S-Bahn lines (S-1 through S-8) run east-west along the main tourist axis between the Hauptbahnhof, Marienplatz, and the Ostbahnhof. For travel within the city center, just find the platform for lines S-1 through S-8. One track (*Gleis*) will be headed east to the Ostbahnhof, the other west to the Hauptbahnhof. Hop on any train going your direction.

By Bike

Level, compact, and with plenty of bike paths, Munich feels made for those on two wheels. You can take your bike on the subway, but not during rush hour (Mon-Fri 6:00-9:00 & 16:00-18:00) and only if you buy a bike day pass.

Rick's Tip: *The* **strip of pathway closest to the street is usually reserved for bikes.** *Signs painted on the sidewalk or blue-and-white street signs show which part of the sidewalk is designated for pedestrians and which is for cyclists.*

You can **rent bikes** quickly and easily from **Radius Tours** in the train station in front of track 32 (daily April-Oct 8:30-19:00, May-Aug until 20:00; closed Nov-March, tel. 089/543-487-7730, www.radiustours.com).

Arriving and Departing
By Plane

Munich's airport (code: MUC) is an easy 40-minute ride on the S-1 or S-8 **subway**

(every 20 minutes from 4:00 in the morning until almost 2:00 in the morning). The S-8 is a bit quicker and easier; the S-1 line has two branches and some trains split—if you ride the S-1 to the airport, be certain your train is going to the *Flughafen* (airport). The Munich *Gesamtnetz* day pass ("Airport-City-Day-Ticket") is worth getting if you'll be making even one more public transport trip that day. The trip is free with a validated and dated rail pass.

The **Lufthansa airport bus** links the airport with the main train station (€10.50, €17 round-trip, 3/hour, 45 minutes, buses depart train station 5:15-19:55, buy tickets on bus; from inside the station, exit near track 26 and look for yellow *Airport Bus* signs; www.airportbus-muenchen.de). Avoid taking a **taxi** from the airport—it's a long, expensive drive (roughly €65). Airport info: tel. 089/97500, www.munich-airport.de.

By Train

For quick help at the main train station (München Hauptbahnhof), stop by the service counter in front of track 18. For better English and more patience, drop by the EurAide desk at counter #1 in the *Reisezentrum* (see page 787). Train info: toll tel. 0180-699-6633, www.bahn.com.

You'll find a city-run **TI** (out front of station and to the right) and **lockers** (opposite track 26). Up the stairs opposite track 21 are **car-rental agencies** (over-looking track 22).

Subway lines, trams, and buses connect the station to the rest of the city (though some of my recommended hotels are within walking distance of the station). If you get lost in the underground maze of subway corridors while you're trying to get to the train station, follow the signs for *DB* (Deutsche Bahn) to surface successfully. Watch out for the hallways with blue ticket-stamping machines in the middle—these lead to the subway, where you could be fined if nabbed without a validated ticket.

From Munich by Train to: Füssen (hourly, 2 hours), **Oberammergau** (nearly hourly, 2 hours, change in Murnau), **Salzburg,** Austria (2/hour, 1.5 hours on fast trains, 2 hours on slower trains eligible for Bayern-Ticket), **Cologne** (2/hour, 4.5 hours, some with 1 change), **Würzburg** (1-2/hour, 2 hours), **Rothenburg** (hourly, 2.5-4 hours, 2-3 changes), **Frankfurt** (hourly, 3.5 hours), **Dresden** (every 2 hours, 6 hours, change in Leipzig or Nürnberg), **Hamburg** (hourly direct, 6.5 hours), **Berlin** (1-2/hour, 6.5 hours).

By Bus

Munich's central bus station (ZOB) is by the Hackerbrücke S-Bahn station (from the train station, it's one S-Bahn stop; www.muenchen-zob.de). The Romantic Road bus leaves from here (see page 882).

NEAR MUNICH

DACHAU MEMORIAL

Established in 1933, Dachau was the first Nazi concentration camp. In its 12 dismal years of operation, more than 200,000 prisoners from across Europe were incarcerated here—and at least 41,500 died, many of them murdered. The memorial on the grounds today, rated ▲▲, is an effective voice from our modern but grisly past, pleading "Never again."

Planning Your Time: Allow about five hours, giving you at least 2.5 hours at the camp, and including round-trip travel from central Munich.

Cost and Hours: Free, daily 9:00-17:00. Note that the museum discourages parents from bringing children under age 12.

Getting There on Your Own: The camp is a 45-minute trip from downtown Munich. The **Munich XXL day pass** covers the entire journey, both ways (€8.30/person, €14.80/partner ticket for up to 5 adults).

Take the S-2 (direction: Petershausen) from any of the central S-Bahn stops in Munich to Dachau (3/hour, 20-minute trip from Hauptbahnhof). Then, at Dachau station, go down the stairs and follow the crowds out to the bus platforms; find the one marked *KZ-Gedenkstätte-Concentration Camp Memorial Sight*. Here, catch bus #726 and ride it seven minutes to the KZ-Gedenkstätte stop (3/hour). Before you leave this bus stop, be sure to note the return times back to the station.

Drivers follow Dachauer Strasse from downtown Munich to Dachau-Ost, then follow *KZ-Gedenkstätte* signs.

Getting There by Guided Tour: Two companies offer good-value tours to Dachau from Munich for about the same price (€24, includes public transportation, €2 Rick Steves discount). It's smart to reserve the day before, especially for morning tours. Choose between **Radius** (April-mid-Oct daily at 9:15 and 12:15, mid-Oct-March daily at 10:00, tel. 089/543-487-7730, www.radiustours.

Dachau today

com) and **Munich Walk** (April-Oct daily at 10:15 and 13:15, Nov-March daily at 10:15, tel. 089/2423-1767, www.munichwalktours.de).

Visitors Center: The visitors center, outside the camp wall, lacks exhibits, but has a bookstore with English-language books on Holocaust themes, a small cafeteria, and a WC (more WCs inside the camp).

At the center's information desk, you can rent an audioguide or sign up for a tour. The €3.50 **audioguide** covers the grounds and museum in 1.5 hours. **Guided walks** in English start from the visitors center (€3, daily at 11:00 and 13:00, 2.5 hours, limited to 30 people, so show up early—especially in summer, tel. 08131/669-970, www.kz-gedenkstaette-dachau.de).

➔ Self-Guided Tour

You enter the camp, like the prisoners did, through the infamous **iron gate** that held the taunting slogan *Arbeit macht*

frei ("Work makes you free"). Inside are these key stops: the museum, the bunker behind the museum, the restored barracks, and a pensive walk across the huge but now-empty camp to the memorials and crematorium at the far end.

Museum: Before touring the rooms, check show times for the museum's powerful 22-minute documentary film, a sobering, graphic, and sometimes grisly account of the rise of Hitler and the atrocities committed at the camp (usually shown 5 times/day in English). The

Iron gate with "Work makes you free" slogan

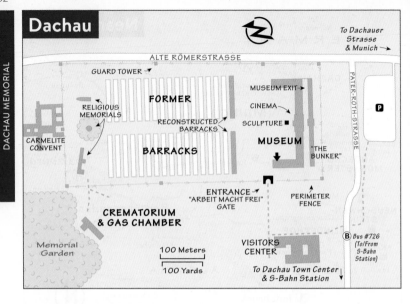

Dachau

To Dachauer Strasse & Munich →

ALTE RÖMERSTRASSE

GUARD TOWER ↗

FORMER

MUSEUM EXIT →

CINEMA

RELIGIOUS MEMORIALS

RECONSTRUCTED BARRACKS

SCULPTURE ■

MUSEUM

CARMELITE CONVENT

BARRACKS

"THE BUNKER"

PATER-ROTH-STRASSE

P

ENTRANCE ↗
"ARBEIT MACHT FREI" GATE

PERIMETER FENCE

CREMATORIUM & GAS CHAMBER

Memorial Garden

100 Meters

100 Yards

VISITORS CENTER

Ⓑ Bus #726 (To/From S-Bahn Station)

To Dachau Town Center & S-Bahn Station ↓

museum is organized chronologically, everything is thoughtfully described in English, and computer touch-screens let you watch early newsreels.

Rooms 1-2 cover the founding of the camp and give an overview of the Nazi camp system. Some were concentration camps, like Dachau, and others were extermination camps, built with the express purpose of executing people on a mass scale. Photos and posters chronicle the rise of Hitler in the 1920s.

Rooms 3-7 are devoted to the early years of the camp. Besides political activists, prisoners included homosexuals,

The Bunker (camp prison)

Jehovah's Witnesses, Roma, and Jews. The camp was run by the SS (Schutz-staffel), the organization charged with Germany's internal security. Dachau was a strictly regimented work camp: a wake-up call at 4:00, an 11-hour workday, roll call at 5:15 and 19:00, lights out at 21:00. The labor was hard, whether quarrying or hauling loads or constructing the very buildings you see today. The rations were meager, rule-breakers were punished severely, and all manner of torture took place here.

Rooms 8-15 document the war years and their immediate aftermath. After Germany invaded Poland on September 1, 1939, conditions at Dachau deteriorated. The original camp had been designed to hold just under 3,000 inmates. In 1937 and 1938, the camp was expanded, with barracks intended to hold 6,000 prisoners. During the war, the prisoner population swelled, and the Nazis found other purposes for the camp. It was less a concentration camp for German dissidents and more a dumping ground for foreigners and POWs. It was used as a special prison for 2,000 Catholic priests. From Dachau, Jewish prisoners were sent east to the gas chambers. Inmates were put to use as slave labor for the German war machine—many were shipped to nearby camps to make armaments. Prisoners were used as human guinea pigs for war-related medical experiments of human tolerance for air pressure, hypothermia, and biological agents like malaria.

As the Allies closed in on both fronts, Dachau was bursting with more than 30,000 prisoners jammed into its 34 barracks. Disease broke out, and food ran short in the winter of 1944-1945. With coal for the crematorium running low, the corpses of those who died were buried in mass graves outside the camp site. The Allies arrived on April 29. After 12 years of existence, Dachau was finally liberated.

Bunker: This was a cellblock for prominent "special prisoners," such as failed Hitler assassins, German religious leaders, and politicians who challenged Nazism. Exhibits profile the inmates and the SS guards who worked at Dachau, and allow you to listen to some inmates' testimonies. Cell #2 was the interrogation room. Cell #9 was a "standing cell"—inmates were tortured here by being forced to stay on their feet for days at a time.

Barracks: Take a look inside to get an idea of what sleeping and living conditions were like in the terribly overcrowded camp. When the camp was at its fullest, there was only about one square yard of living space per inmate.

Religious Remembrance Sights: At the far end of the camp, in space that once housed the camp vegetable garden, there are now several places of meditation and worship (Jewish to your right, Catholic straight ahead, and Protestant to your left). Beyond them, just outside the camp, is a Carmelite convent. In the garden near the crematoria is a Russian Orthodox shrine.

Camp Crematoria: These facilities were used to dispose of the bodies of prisoners. The larger concrete crematorium was built to replace the smaller wooden one. One of its rooms is a gas chamber, which worked on the same principles as the much larger one at Auschwitz, and was originally disguised as a shower room (the fittings are gone now). It was never put to use at Dachau for mass murder, but some historians suspect that a few people were killed in it experimentally. The memorial garden that now surrounds the crematoria is the main place of remembrance at Dachau.

Memorials throughout Dachau remind visitors: Never Again.

Rothenburg
and the
Romantic Road

The Romantic Road through Bavaria's medieval heart-land is strewn with picturesque villages, farmhouses, onion-domed churches, Baroque palaces, and walled cities. The route, which runs from Würzburg to Füssen, is the most scenic way to connect Frankfurt with Munich. No trains run along the full length of the Romantic Road, but Rothenburg (ROH-tehn-burg), the most interesting town along the way, is easy to reach by rail. Drivers can either zero in on Rothenburg or take some extra time to meander from town to town on the way. For nondrivers, a tour bus travels the Romantic Road once daily in each direction.

Countless travelers have searched for the elusive "untouristy Rothenburg." There are many contenders (such as Michelstadt, Miltenberg, Bamberg, Bad Windsheim, and Dinkelsbühl), but none holds a candle to the king of medieval German cuteness. Even with crowds, overpriced souvenirs—and, yes, even the over-promoted, dry *Schneeballen* pastries—Rothenburg is the best. Save time and mileage and be satisfied with the winner.

ROTHENBURG AND THE ROMANTIC ROAD IN 2 DAYS

I'd spend one full day in Rothenburg this way: Start with my self-guided town walk, including a visit to St. Jakob's Church (for the carved altarpiece) and the Imperial City Museum (historic artifacts). Spend the afternoon visiting the Medieval Crime and Punishment Museum and taking my "Schmiedgasse-Spitalgasse Shopping Stroll," followed by a walk on the wall (from Spitaltor to Klingentor).

Cap your day with the entertaining Night Watchman's Tour at 20:00. Locals love *"Die blaue Stunde"* (the blue hour)—

the time just before dark when city lamps and the sky hold hands. Be sure to be out enjoying the magic of the city at this time.

Other evening options include beer-garden fun (at Gasthof Rödertor) if the weather's good, or the English Conversation Club (at Altfränkische Wein-stube am Klosterhof) if it's Wednesday.

With extra time in Rothenburg, spread out your sightseeing and add the Old Town Historic Walk (offered by the TI), the Town Hall Tower climb, and the German Christmas Museum.

If you're driving, take in the top Romantic Road highlights en route, devoting a half-day to the sights on your way to Rothenburg and another half-day after leaving it.

ROTHENBURG OB DER TAUBER

In the Middle Ages, when Berlin and Munich were just wide spots on the road, Rothenburg ob der Tauber was a "free imperial city" beholden only to the Holy Roman Emperor. From 1150 to 1400, because of its strategic location on trade routes and the abundant resources of its surrounding farmlands, Rothenburg thrived, with a whopping population of 6,000. But the Thirty Years' War and a plague that followed did the town in. With no money to fix up its antiquated buildings, Rothenburg languished. Today, it's the country's best-preserved medieval walled town, enjoying tremendous popularity without losing its charm.

Rick's Tip: *Germany has several towns named Rothenburg.* **Make sure you're going to Rothenburg ob der Tauber** *(not "ob der" any other river). People really do sometimes drive or ride the train to the wrong Rothenburg by accident.*

Two-thirds of the 2,000 people who live within Rothenburg's walls are employed to serve tourists. Rothenburg is at its best in spring and fall, crowded in summer (but still fun), and dead in winter except for December (when its Christmas Market bustles).

While roughly 2 million people visit each year, most come only on day trips. Rothenburg is yours after dark, when the groups vacate and the town's floodlit cobbles seem made for romance.

Orientation

Think of the town map as a human head. Its nose—the castle garden—sticks out to the left, and the skinny lower part forms a neck, with the youth hostel and a recommended hotel being the Adam's apple. The town is a delight on foot. No sights or hotels are more than a 15-minute walk from the train station or each other.

Rick's Tip: *A* **fun pictorial town map,** *which also helpfully indicates some walking paths in the countryside beyond the town walls, is available for free with this book at the* **Friese shop** *(see page 876).*

Most of the buildings you'll see were in place by 1400. The city was born around

Picturesque Rothenburg ob der Tauber

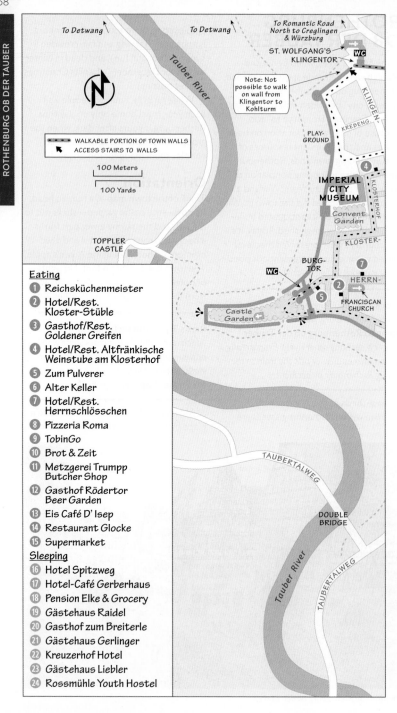

To Detwang

To Detwang

To Romantic Road
North to Creglingen
& Würzburg

ST. WOLFGANG'S
KLINGENTOR

WC

Tauber River

KLINGEN-

KREDENG-

Note: Not
possible to walk
on wall from
Klingentor to
Kohlturm

PLAY-
GROUND

KLOSTERHOF

IMPERIAL
CITY
MUSEUM

Convent
Garden

WALKABLE PORTION OF TOWN WALLS
ACCESS STAIRS TO WALLS

100 Meters

100 Yards

KLOSTER-

TOPPLER
CASTLE

BURG-
TOR

WC

HERRN-

Castle
Garden

FRANCISCAN
CHURCH

TAUBERTALWEG

DOUBLE
BRIDGE

Tauber River

TAUBERTALWEG

Eating

1. Reichsküchenmeister
2. Hotel/Rest. Kloster-Stüble
3. Gasthof/Rest. Goldener Greifen
4. Hotel/Rest. Altfränkische Weinstube am Klosterhof
5. Zum Pulverer
6. Alter Keller
7. Hotel/Rest. Herrnschlösschen
8. Pizzeria Roma
9. TobinGo
10. Brot & Zeit
11. Metzgerei Trumpp Butcher Shop
12. Gasthof Rödertor Beer Garden
13. Eis Café D'Isep
14. Restaurant Glocke
15. Supermarket

Sleeping

16. Hotel Spitzweg
17. Hotel-Café Gerberhaus
18. Pension Elke & Grocery
19. Gästehaus Raidel
20. Gasthof zum Breiterle
21. Gästehaus Gerlinger
22. Kreuzerhof Hotel
23. Gästehaus Liebler
24. Rossmühle Youth Hostel

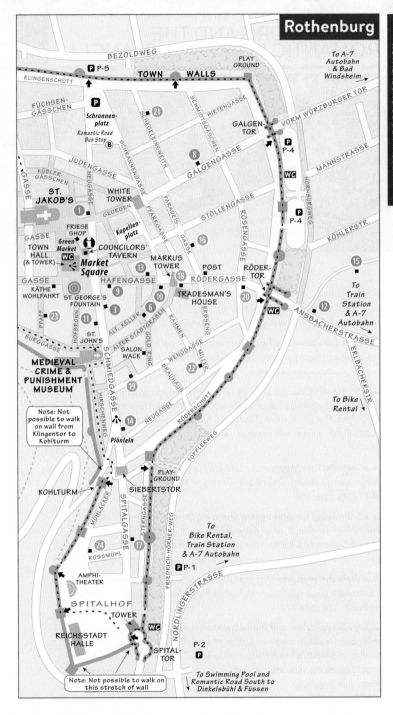

Rothenburg

BEZOLDWEG

P-5

TOWN WALLS

PLAY GROUND

KLINGENSCHÜTT

To A-7 Autobahn & Bad Windsheim

FÜCHSEN-GÄSSCHEN

21

VORM WÜRZBURGER TOR

Schrannen-platz
Romantic Road Bus Stop
B

SCHEGELENSWEIH

HIRTENGASSE

GALGEN-TOR

P-4

MANNSTRASSE

JUDENGASSE

SCHRANNENGASSE

GALGENGASSE

8

WC

HORNBURGWEG

KÜBLER-GÄSSCHEN

HEUGASSE

WHITE TOWER

Georgen.

PARADEIS

PFARRGASSE

STOLLENGASSE

ROSENGASSE

P-4

ST. JAKOB'S

1

KÖHLERSTR.

GASSE

FRIESE SHOP
Green Market
TOWN HALL (& TOWER)
WC
Market Square

Kapellen-platz

16

POST

RÖDER-TOR

15

COUNCILORS' TAVERN

MARKUS TOWER

18

RÖDERGASSE

To Train Station & A-7 Autobahn

GASSE

13

HAFENGASSE

20

12

KÄTHE WOHLFAHRT

ST. GEORGE'S FOUNTAIN

9

10

TRADESMAN'S HOUSE

WC

ANSBACHERSTRASSE

23

11

ST. JOHN'S

3

6

ALT. KELLER

GOLD RING

RAIMEN

ERBSENG

ERLBACHERSTR.

PFAFF.

HOFBRONN

BURGGASSE

ALTER STADTGRABEN

BRÄUHAUS

WENGGASSE

MILLER.

22

To Bike Rental

MEDIEVAL CRIME & PUNISHMENT MUSEUM

SALON WACK

19

SCHMIEDGASSE

HIRSCHENWEG

NEUGASSE

RÖDERSCHÜTT

TOPPLERWEG

Note: Not possible to walk on wall from Klingentor to Kohlturm

14

Plönlein

PLAY-GROUND

KOHLTURM

SIEBERTSTOR

MÜHLACKER

SPITALGASSE

STERNGASSE

FRIEDRICH-HÖRNER-WEG

To Bike Rental, Train Station & A-7 Autobahn

P-1

24

ROSSMÜHL.

17

AMPHI-THEATER

SPITALHOF

TOWER

WC

NORDLINGERSTRASSE

P-2

REICHSSTADT HALLE

SPITAL-TOR

To Swimming Pool and Romantic Road South to Dinkelsbühl & Füssen

Note: Not possible to walk on this stretch of wall

ROTHENBURG AND THE ROMANTIC ROAD AT A GLANCE

Rothenburg

▲▲▲**Rothenburg Town Walk** A self-guided loop, starting and ending on Market Square, covering the town's top sights. See page 864.

▲▲**Night Watchman's Tour** Germany's best hour of medieval wonder, led by an amusing, medieval-garbed guide. **Hours:** Mid-March-Dec nightly at 20:00. See page 862.

▲▲**St. Jakob's Church** Home to Tilman Riemenschneider's breath-taking, wood-carved Altar of the Holy Blood. **Hours:** Daily April-Oct 9:00-17:15, Dec 10:00-16:45, Nov and Christmas-March 10:00-12:00 & 14:00-16:00, on Sun wait to enter until services end at 10:45. See page 866.

▲▲**Imperial City Museum** An artifact-filled sweep through Rothenburg's history. **Hours:** Daily April-Oct 9:30-17:30, Nov-March 13:00-16:00. See page 869.

▲▲**Schmiedgasse-Spitalgasse Shopping Stroll** A fun look at crafts and family-run shops, on a (mostly) picturesque street running between Market Square and the town's most impressive tower, Spitaltor. See page 871.

▲▲**Walk the Wall** A strollable wall encircling the town, providing great views and a good orientation to Rothenburg. **Hours:** Always open and walkable. See page 873.

▲▲**Medieval Crime and Punishment Museum** Specializing in everything connected to medieval justice, this exhibit is a cut above the tacky torture museums around Europe. **Hours:** Daily April 11:00-17:00, May-Oct 10:00-18:00, Nov and Jan-Feb 14:00-16:00, Dec and March 13:00-16:00. See page 874.

▲**Old Town Historic Walk** Covers the serious side of Rothenburg's history and the town's architecture. **Hours:** Easter-Oct and Dec daily at 14:00. See page 862.

▲**Historical Town Hall Vaults** An insightful look at Rothenburg during the Catholics-vs.-Protestants Thirty Years' War. **Hours:** Daily May-Oct 9:30-17:30, shorter hours off-season, closed Jan-Feb. See page 866.

▲**Town Hall Tower** Rothenburg's tallest perch, with a commanding view. **Hours:** Daily in season 9:00-12:30 & 13:00-17:00. See page 874.

▲**German Christmas Museum** Tells the interesting history of Christmas decorations. **Hours:** April-Dec daily 10:00-17:30, shorter and irregular hours Jan-March. See page 875.

Along the Romantic Road

▲▲**Wieskirche** Lovely Baroque-Rococo church set in a meadow. **Hours:** Daily April-Oct 8:00-20:00, Nov-March 8:00-17:00; interior closed to sightseers during services: Sun 8:00-13:00; Tue, Wed, and Sat 10:00-12:00; and Fri 17:00-20:00. See page 883.

▲**Nördlingen** Workaday town with one of the best walls in Germany and a crater left by an ancient meteor. See page 883.

▲**Dinkelsbühl** A town like Rothenburg's little sister, cute enough to merit a short stop. See page 884.

▲**Creglingen's Herrgottskirche** Church featuring Riemenschneider's greatest carved altarpiece. See page 885.

▲**Weikersheim** Picturesque town with an impressive palace, Baroque gardens, and a quaint town square. See page 885.

its long-gone castle fortress—built in 1142, destroyed in 1356—which was located where the castle garden is now. You can see the shadow of the first town wall, which defines the oldest part of Rothenburg, in its contemporary street plan. Two gates from this wall still survive: the Markus Tower and the White Tower. The richest and biggest houses were in this central part. The commoners built higgledy-piggledy houses farther from the center, but still inside the present walls.

Although Rothenburg is technically in Bavaria, the region around the town strongly identifies itself as "Franken," one of Germany's many medieval dukedoms ("Franconia" in English).

Tourist Information: The TI is on Market Square (May-Oct and Dec Mon-Fri 9:00-18:00, Sat-Sun 10:00-17:00; off-season Mon-Fri 9:00-17:00, Sat 10:00-13:00, closed Sun; Marktplatz 2, tel. 09861/404-800, www.tourismus.rothenburg.de, run by Jörg Christöphler). The free city map comes with a walking guide, and the *Events* booklet covers the basics in English. The TI has one free public computer with Internet access (15-minute maximum).

Bike Rental: Rad & Tat rents bikes for €14 for a 24-hour day (otherwise €10/6 hours, also has electric bikes; Mon-Fri 9:00-18:00, Sat until 13:00, closed Sun; Bensenstrasse 17, tel. 09861/87984, www.mietraeder.de). To reach it, leave the old town heading toward the train station, take a right on Erlbacher Strasse, cross the tracks, and look across the street from the Lidl supermarket.

Taxi: For a taxi, call 09861/2000 or 09861/7227.

Tours

▲▲NIGHT WATCHMAN'S TOUR

This tour is flat-out the most entertaining hour of medieval wonder anywhere in Germany. The Night Watchman (a.k.a. Hans-Georg Baumgartner) jokes like a medieval John Cleese as he lights his lamp and takes tourists on his rounds, telling slice-of-gritty-life tales of medieval Rothenburg. This is the best evening activity in town (€8, teens-€5, free for kids 12 and under, mid-March-Dec nightly at 20:00, in English, meet at Market Square, www.nightwatchman.de).

▲OLD TOWN HISTORIC WALK

The TI offers 1.5-hour guided walking tours in English. Just show up and pay the guide directly—there's always room. Take this tour for the serious side of Rothenburg's history, and to make sense of the town's architecture; you won't get as much of that on the fun—and completely different—Night Watchman's Tour. It would be a shame not to take advantage of this informative tour just because you took the other (€7, Easter-Oct and Dec daily at 14:00, no English tours off-season, departs from Market Square).

PRIVATE GUIDES

A local historian can really bring the ramparts alive. Reserve a guide by emailing the TI (€75/1.5 hours, €95/2 hours, info@rothenburg.de, more info at www.tourismus.rothenburg.de—look under "Tourism Service," then "Guided Tours"). I've had good experiences with **Martin Kamphans,** who also works as a potter (tel. 09861/7941, www.stadtfuehrungen-rothenburg.de, post@stadtfuehrungen-rothenburg.de), and **Daniel Weber** (mobile 0795-8311, www.toot-tours.com, mail@toot-tours.com).

Rothenburg's Night Watchman

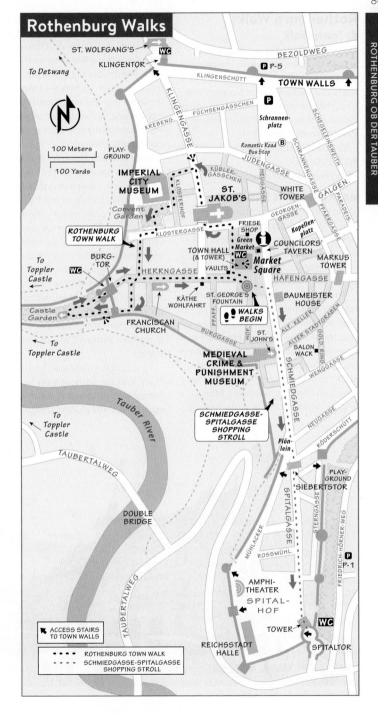

Rothenburg Walks

ST. WOLFGANG'S
WC
KLINGENTOR
To Detwang
BEZOLDWEG
P P-5
KLINGENSCHÜTT
TOWN WALLS
P
Schrannen-platz
Romantic Road Bus Stop **B**
KREBENG.
KLINGENGASSE
FÜCHSENGÄSSCHEN
SCHRANNENGASSE
SCHEGELEINSWETH
GALGEN.
PARADIES
PFARRGASSE

N

100 Meters
100 Yards

PLAY-GROUND
IMPERIAL CITY MUSEUM
KÜBLER-GÄSSCHEN
KLOSTERHOF
ST. JAKOB'S
JUDENGASSE
HEUGASSE
GEORGEN-GASSE
WHITE TOWER

Convent Garden
ROTHENBURG TOWN WALK
KLOSTERGASSE
FRIESE SHOP
Green Market
WC
Kapellen-platz
COUNCILORS' TAVERN
MARKUS TOWER

To Toppler Castle
WC
BURG-TOR
HERRNGASSE
TOWN HALL (& TOWER)
VAULTS
Market Square
HAFENGASSE
BAUMEISTER HOUSE

Castle Garden
KÄTHE WOHLFAHRT
ST. GEORGE'S FOUNTAIN
WALKS BEGIN
ALT. KELLER
ALTER STADTGRABEN
GÖD RING
SALON WACK
WENGGASSE

To Toppler Castle
FRANCISCAN CHURCH
PFAFF.
BURGGASSE
HOF
ST. JOHN'S
NEUGASSE
RÖDERSCHÜTT

Tauber River
MEDIEVAL CRIME & PUNISHMENT MUSEUM
SCHMIEDGASSE

SCHMIEDGASSE-SPITALGASSE SHOPPING STROLL
Plön-lein

To Toppler Castle
TAUBERTALWEG
SIEBERTSTOR
PLAY-GROUND
SPITALGASSE
STERNGASSE
FRIEDRICH-HÖRNER-WEG
P P-1

DOUBLE BRIDGE
MÜHLACKER
ROSSMÜHL.

TAUBERTALWEG
AMPHI-THEATER
SPITAL-HOF

ACCESS STAIRS TO TOWN WALLS
- - - - ROTHENBURG TOWN WALK
- - - - SCHMIEDGASSE-SPITALGASSE SHOPPING STROLL

REICHSSTADT HALLE
TOWER
WC
SPITALTOR

Rothenburg Walks
⊙ *Town Walk*

This self-guided loop, worth ▲▲▲, weaves the town's top sights together, takes about an hour without stops, and starts and ends on Market Square. (This is roughly the same route followed by city guides on their daily Old Town Historic Walk, described earlier.)

🎧 Download my free Rothenburg Town Walk audio tour.

• *Start the walk on Market Square.*

MARKET SQUARE SPIN-TOUR

Stand in front of the fountain at the bottom of Market Square (watch for occasional cars) and spin 360 degrees clockwise, starting with the Town Hall tower. Now do it again, this time more slowly to take in some details:

Town Hall and Tower: Rothenburg's tallest spire is the Town Hall tower (Rathausturm). At 200 feet, it stands atop the old Town Hall, a white, Gothic, 13th-century building. Notice the tourists enjoying the best view in town from the black top of the tower (see page 874 for details on climbing the tower). After a fire in 1501 burned down part of the original building, a new Town Hall was built alongside what survived of the old one (fronting the square). This half of the rebuilt complex is in the Renaissance style from 1570. The double eagles you see decorating many buildings here are a repeated reminder that this was a "free imperial city" belonging directly to the (Habsburg) Holy Roman Emperor, a designation that came with benefits.

Meistertrunk Show: At the top of Market Square stands the proud Councilors' Tavern (clock tower from 1466). In its day, the city council—the rich guys who ran the town government—drank here. Today, it's the **TI** and the focus of most tourists' attention when the little doors on either side of the clock flip open and the wooden figures (from 1910) do their thing. Be on Market Square at the top of any hour (between 10:00 and 22:00) for the ritual gathering of the tourists to see the less-than-breathtaking re-enactment of the Meistertrunk ("Master Draught") story:

In 1631, in the middle of the Thirty Years' War, the Catholic army took this Protestant town and was about to do its rape, pillage, and plunder thing. As was

Rothenburg's Town Hall and Tower

the etiquette, the mayor had to give the conquering general a welcoming drink. The general enjoyed a huge tankard of local wine. Feeling really good, he told the mayor, "Hey, if you can drink this entire three-liter tankard of wine in one gulp, I'll spare your town." The mayor amazed everyone by drinking the entire thing, and Rothenburg was saved. (While this is a nice story, it was dreamed up in the late 1800s for a theatrical play designed—effectively—to promote a romantic image of the town. In actuality, if Rothenburg was spared, it had likely bribed its way out of the jam.) The city was occupied and ransacked several times in the Thirty Years' War, and it never recovered—which is why it's such a well-preserved time capsule today.

For the best show, don't watch the clock; watch the open-mouthed tourists gasp as the old windows flip open. At the late shows, the square flickers with camera flashes.

Bottom of Market Square: As this was the most-prestigious address in town, it's ringed by big homes with big carriage gates. One of the finest is just downhill from the bottom end of the square—the **Baumeister** ("master builder") **Haus,** where the man who designed and built the Town Hall lived. It features a famous Renaissance facade with statues of the seven virtues and the seven vices. The statues are copies; the originals are in the Imperial City Museum (described later on this walk).

Behind you, take in the big 17th-century **St. George's fountain.** Its long metal gutters could slide to deposit the water into villagers' buckets. It's part of Rothenburg's ingenious water system: Built on a rock, the town had one real source above the town, which was plumbed to serve a series of fountains; water flowed from high to low through Rothenburg. Its many fountains had practical functions beyond providing drinking water—some were stocked with fish on market days

and during times of siege, and their water was useful for fighting fire. Because of its plentiful water supply—and its policy of requiring relatively wide lanes as fire breaks—the town never burned entirely, as so many neighboring villages did.

Two fine half-timbered buildings behind the fountain show the old-time lofts with warehouse doors and pulleys on top for hoisting. All over town, lofts like these were filled with grain. A year's supply was required by the city so they could survive any siege. The building behind the fountain is an art gallery showing off work by members of the local artists' association. To the right is Marien Apotheke, an old-time pharmacy mixing old and new in typical Rothenburg style.

The broad street running under the Town Hall tower is **Herrngasse.** The town originated with its castle fortress (built in 1142 but now long gone; a lovely garden now fills that space). Herrngasse connected the castle to Market Square. The last leg of this circular walking tour will take you from the castle garden up Herrngasse and back here.

For now, walk a few steps down Herrngasse and stop by the arch under the Town Hall tower (between the new and old town halls). On the wall to the left of the gate are the town's measuring rods—a reminder that medieval Germany was made of 300 independent little countries, many with their own weights and measures. Merchants and shoppers knew that these were the local standards: the

Herrngasse

rod (4.3 yards), the *Schuh* ("shoe," roughly a foot), and the *Ell* (from elbow to fingertip—four inches longer than mine...climb up and try it). The protruding cornerstone you're standing on is one of many all over town—originally to protect buildings from careening horse carts. In German, going recklessly fast is called "scratching the cornerstone."

• *Careen around that stone and under the arch to find the...*

▲HISTORICAL TOWN HALL VAULTS (HISTORIENGEWÖLBE)

The vaults house an eclectic and grade-schoolish little museum that gives a waxy but interesting look at Rothenburg during the Catholics-vs.-Protestants Thirty Years' War. Popping in here can help prep your imagination to filter out the tourists and picture ye olde Rothenburg along the rest of this walk. With helpful English descriptions, it offers a look at "the fateful year 1631," a replica of the mythical Meistertrunk tankard, an alchemist's workshop, and a dungeon complete with three dank cells and some torture lore.

Cost and Hours: €3, daily May-Oct 9:30-17:30, shorter hours off-season, closed Jan-Feb, tel. 09861/86751.

• *Leaving the museum, turn left (past a venerable and much-sketched-and-photographed door) and find a posted copy of a centuries-old map showing the territory of Rothenburg.*

MAP OF ROTHENBURG CITY TERRITORY

In 1537 Rothenburg actually ruled a little country—one of about 300 petty dukedoms like this that made up what is today's Germany. The territory spanned a 12-by-12-mile area (about 400 square kilometers), encompassing 180 villages—a good example of the fragmentation of feudal Germany. While not to scale (Rothenburg is actually less than a mile wide), the map is fun to study. In the 1380s, Mayor Toppler purchased much

of this territory. In 1562, the city sold off some of its land to neighboring dukes, which gave it the money for all the fine Renaissance buildings that embellish the town to this day.

• *Continue through the courtyard and into a square called...*

GREEN MARKET (GRÜNER MARKT)

Once a produce market, this parking lot fills with Christmas stands during December. Notice the clay-tile roofs. These "beaver tail" tiles became standard after thatched roofs were outlawed to prevent fires. Today, all of the town's roofs are made of these. The little fences stop heaps of snow from falling off the roof and onto people below. A free public WC is on your left, and the recommended Friese gift shop is on your right.

• *Continue straight ahead to St. Jakob's Church. Study the exterior first, then pay to go inside.*

▲▲ST. JAKOB'S CHURCH (ST. JAKOBSKIRCHE)

Rothenburg's main church is home to Tilman Riemenschneider's exquisitely rendered, wood-carved *Altar of the Holy Blood.*

Cost and Hours: €2.50, daily April-Oct 9:00-17:15, Dec 10:00-16:45, Nov and Christmas-March 10:00-12:00 & 14:00-16:00, on Sun wait to enter until services end at 10:45.

Tours and Information: A free, helpful English info sheet is available. Concerts

Map of Old Rothenburg

and a tour schedule are posted on the door. Guided tours in English run on Sat at 15:30 (April-Oct) for no extra charge. The worthwhile audioguide (€2, 45 minutes) lets you tailor your education, offering a dual commentary—historical and theological—for a handful of important stops in the church.

Visiting the Church: Start by viewing the exterior of the church. Next, enter the church, where you'll see the main nave first, then climb above the pipe organ (in the back) to finish with the famous carved altar.

Exterior: Outside the church, under the little roof at the base of the tower, you'll see 14th-century statues (mostly original) showing Jesus praying at Gethsemane, a common feature of Gothic churches. The sculptor is anonymous—in the Gothic age (pre-Albrecht Dürer), artists were just nameless craftspeople working only for the glory of God. Five yards to the left (on the wall), notice the nub of a sandstone statue—a rare original, looking pretty bad after 500 years of weather and, more recently, pollution. Most original statues are now in the city museum. The better-preserved statues you see on the church are copies.

Before entering, notice how the church was extended to the west and actually built over the street. The newer chapel was built to accommodate pilgrims and to contain the sumptuous Riemenschneider carved altarpiece.

If it's your wedding day, take the first

entrance—marked by a very fertile Eve and, around the corner, Adam showing off an impressive six-pack. Otherwise, head toward the church's second (down-hill) door. Before going inside, notice the modern statue at the base of the stairs. This is **St. James** (a.k.a. Sankt Jakob in German, Santiago in Spanish, and Saint-Jacques in French). You can tell this important saint by his big, floppy hat, his walking stick, the gourd on his hip (used by pilgrims to carry water), and—most importantly—the scallop shell in his hand. St. James' remains are entombed in the grand cathedral of Santiago de Compostela, in the northwestern corner of Spain. The medieval pilgrimage route called the Camino de Santiago (recently back in vogue) passed through here on its way to that distant corner of Europe. Pilgrims would wear the scallop shell as a symbol of their destination (where that type of marine life was abundant). To this day, the word for "scallop" in many languages carries the name of this saint: *Jakobsmuschel* in German, *coquille Saint-Jacques* in French, and so on.

Inside the Church: Built in the 14th century, this church has been Lutheran since 1544. The interior was "purified" by Romantics in the 19th century—cleaned of everything Baroque or not original and refitted in the Neo-Gothic style. (For example, the baptismal font in the middle of the choir and the pulpit above the second pew *look* Gothic, but are actually Neo-Gothic.) The stained-glass windows behind the altar, which are most colorful in the morning light, are originals from the 1330s. Admiring this church, consider what it says about the priorities of a town of just a few thousand people who decided to use their collective wealth to build such a place. The size of a church is a good indication of the town's wealth when it was built. Medallions and portraits of Rothenburg's leading families and church leaders line the walls above the choir in the front of the church.

St. Jakob's Church

The **main altar,** from 1466, is by Friedrich Herlin. Below Christ are statues of six saints—including St. James (a.k.a. Jakob), with the telltale shell on his floppy hat. Study the painted panels—ever see Peter with spectacles (below the carved saints)? Go around the back of the altarpiece to look at the doors. In the upper left, you'll see a painting of Rothenburg's Market Square in the 15th century, looking much like it does today, with the exception of the full-Gothic Town Hall (as it was before the big fire of 1501). Notice Christ's face on the white "veil of Veronica" (center of back side, bottom edge). It follows you as you walk from side to side—this must have given the faithful the religious heebie-jeebies four centuries ago.

The **Tabernacle of the Holy Eucharist** (just left of the main altar—on your right as you walk back around) is a century older. It stored the wine and bread used for Holy Communion. Before the Reformation, this was a Roman Catholic church, which meant that the bread and wine were considered to be the actual body and blood of Jesus (and therefore needed a worthy repository). Notice the unusual Trinity: The Father and Son are bridged by a dove, which represents the Holy Spirit. Stepping back, you can see that Jesus is standing on a skull—clearly "overcoming death."

Now, as pilgrims did centuries ago, climb the stairs at the back of the church that lead up behind the pipe organ to a loft-like chapel. Here you'll find the artistic highlight of Rothenburg and perhaps the most wonderful wood carving in all of Germany: the glorious 500-year-old, 35-foot-high **Altar of the Holy Blood.** Tilman Riemenschneider, the Michelangelo of German woodcarvers, carved this from 1499 to 1504 (at the same time Michelangelo was working on his own masterpieces). The altarpiece was designed to hold a rock-crystal capsule—set in the cross you see high above—that contains a precious scrap of tablecloth stained in the shape of a cross by a drop of communion wine.

The altar is a realistic commotion, showing that Riemenschneider—a High Gothic artist—was ahead of his time. Below, in the scene of the Last Supper, Jesus gives Judas a piece of bread, marking him as the traitor, while John lays his head on Christ's lap. Judas, with his big bag of cash, could be removed from the scene (illustrated by photos on the wall nearby), as was the tradition for the four days leading up to Easter.

Everything is portrayed exactly as described in the Bible. In the relief panel on the left, Jesus enters the walled city of Jerusalem. Notice the exacting attention to detail—down to the nails on the horseshoe. In the relief panel on the right, Jesus prays in the Garden of Gethsemane.

Before continuing on, take a moment to simply linger over the lovingly executed details: the curly locks of the apostles' hair and beards, and the folds of their garments; the delicate vines intertwining above their heads; Jesus' expression, at once tender and accusing.

• After leaving the church, walk around the corner to the right and under the chapel (built over the road). Go two blocks down Klingengasse and stop at the corner of the street called Klosterhof. Looking farther ahead of you down Klingengasse, you see the...

Altar of the Holy Blood

KLINGENTOR

This cliff tower was Rothenburg's water reservoir. From 1595 until 1910, a 900-liter (240-gallon) copper tank high in the tower provided clean spring water—pumped up by river power—to the privileged. To the right of the Klingentor is a good stretch of wall rampart to walk. To the left, the wall is low and simple, lacking a rampart because it guards only a cliff.

Now find the shell decorating a building on the street corner next to you. That's once again the symbol of St. James, indicating that this building is associated with the church.

• *Turn left down Klosterhof, passing the shell and, on your right, the colorful, recommended Altfränkische Weinstube am Klosterhof pub. As you approach the next stop, notice the lazy Susan embedded in the wall (to the right of the museum door), which allowed cloistered nuns to give food to the poor without being seen.*

▲▲IMPERIAL CITY MUSEUM (REICHSSTADT-MUSEUM)

You'll get a vivid and artifact-filled sweep through Rothenburg's history at this excellent museum, housed in a former Dominican convent.

Cost and Hours: €4.50, €3 more to take photos (not worth it for most), daily April-Oct 9:30-17:30, Nov-March 13:00-16:00, pick up English info sheet at entrance, additional English descriptions posted, Klosterhof 5, tel. 09861/939-043, www.reichsstadtmuseum.rothenburg.de.

Visiting the Museum: As you follow the *Rundgang/Tour* signs to the left, watch for the following highlights:

Immediately inside the entry, a glass case shows off the 1616 Prince Elector's colorful glass tankard (which inspired the famous legend of the Meistertrunk, created in 1881 to drive tourism) and a set of golden Rothenburg coins. Down the hall, find a modern city model and trace the city's growth, its walls expanding like rings on a big tree. Around the corner (before going upstairs), you'll see medieval and Renaissance sculptures, including original sandstone statues from St. Jakob's Church and original statues that once decorated the Baumeister Haus near Market Square. Upstairs in the nuns' dormitory are craftsmen's signs that once hung outside shops (see if you can guess the craft before reading the museum's label), ornate locks, tools for various professions, and a valuable collection of armor and weapons. You'll then see old furniture and the Baroque statues that decorated the organ loft in St. Jakob's Church from 1669 until the 19th century, when they were cleared out to achieve "Gothic purity." Take time to enjoy the several rooms and shop fronts outfitted as they would have been centuries ago.

The painting gallery is lined with Romantic paintings of Rothenburg, which served as the first tourist promotion, and give visitors today a chance to envision the city as it appeared in centuries past. Look for the large, gloomy work by Englishman Arthur Wasse (labeled *"Es spukt"*)—does that door look familiar?

Back downstairs, circle around the cloister to see a 14th-century convent kitchen (*Klosterküche*) with a working model of the lazy Susan (give it a swing) and a massive chimney (step inside and look up); an exhibit of Jewish culture in Rothenburg through the ages (*Judaika*); and the grand finale (in the *Konventsaal*), the *Rothenburger Passion*. This 12-panel series of paintings showing scenes leading

Imperial City Museum

up to Christ's Crucifixion—originally intended for the town's Franciscan church (which we'll pass later)—dates from 1492.

• *Leaving the museum, go around to the right and into the Convent Garden (when locked at night, continue straight to the T-intersection and turn right).*

CONVENT GARDEN

This spot is a peaceful place to work on your tan...or mix a poisoned potion. Monks and nuns—who were responsible for concocting herbal cures in the olden days, finding disinfectants, and coming up with ways to disguise the taste of rotten food—often tended herb gardens. Smell (but don't pick) the *Pfefferminze* (peppermint), *Heidewacholder* (juniper/gin), *Rosmarin* (rosemary), *Lavandel* (lavender), and the tallest plant, *Hopfen* (hops...monks were the great medieval brewers). Don't smell the plants that are poisonous (potency indicated by the number of crosses, like stars indicating spiciness on a restaurant menu). Appreciate the setting, taking in the fine architecture and expansive garden—all within the city walls, where land was at such a premium. It's a reminder of the power of the pre-Reformation Church.

• *Exit opposite from where you entered, angling left through the nuns' garden, leaving via an arch along the far wall. Then turn right and go downhill to the...*

TOWN WALL

This part of the wall takes advantage of the natural fortification provided by the cliff (view through bars, look to far right), and is therefore much shorter than the ramparts.

• *Angle left along the wall. Cross the big street (Herrngasse, with the Burgtor tower on your right—which we'll enter from outside momentarily) and continue downhill on Burggasse until you hit the town wall. Turn right, go through a small tower gate, and park yourself at the town's finest viewpoint.*

CASTLE GARDEN VIEWPOINT

From here, enjoy a fine view of fortified Rothenburg. You're looking at the Spitaltor end of town (with the most interesting gate and the former hospital). After this walk, you can continue with my "Schmiedgasse-Spitalgasse Shopping Stroll," which leads from Market Square down to this end of town, and then enter the city walls and walk the ramparts 180 degrees to the Klingentor tower (which we saw earlier on our walk, in the distance just after St. Jakob's Church). The droopy-eyed building at the far end of town (today's youth hostel) was the horse mill—which provided grinding power when the water mill in the valley below was not working (during drought or siege). Stretching below you is the fine parklike land around the Tauber River, nicknamed the "Tauber Riviera."

• *Now explore deeper into the park.*

CASTLE GARDEN (BURGGARTEN) AND THE BURGTOR GATE

The park before you was a castle fortress until it was destroyed in the 14th century.

Convent Garden

Burgtor Gate

The chapel (50 yards straight into the park, on the left) is the only surviving bit of the original castle. In front of the chapel is a memorial to local Jews killed in a 1298 slaughter. A few steps beyond that is a flowery trellis that provides a fine picnic spot. If you walk all the way out to the garden's far end, you'll find another great viewpoint (well past the tourists, and considered by local teenagers the best place to make out).

When you're ready to leave the park, approach the Burgtor, the ornate fortified gate flanked by twin stubby towers, and imagine being locked out in the year 1400. (There's a WC on the left.) The tall tower behind the gate was accessed by a wooden drawbridge—see the chain slits above the inner gate, and between them the "pitch" mask with holes designed to allow defenders to pour boiling Nutella on attackers. High above is the town coat of arms: a red (*roten*) castle (*Burg*).

Go through the gate and study the big wooden door with the tiny "eye of the needle" door cut into it. If trying to enter town after curfew, you could bribe the guard to let you through this door, which was small enough to keep out any fully armed attackers. Note also the square-shaped hole on the right and imagine the massive timber that once barricaded the gate.

• *Now, climb up the big street, Herrngasse, as you return to your starting point.*

HERRNGASSE

Many towns have a Herrngasse, where the richest patricians and merchants (the *Herren*) lived. Predictably, it's your best chance to see the town's finest old mansions. Strolling back to Market Square, you'll pass, on the right, the **Franciscan Church** (from 1285—the oldest in town). Across the street, the mint-green house at #18 is the biggest patrician house on this main drag. The front door was big enough to allow a carriage to drive through it; a human-sized door cut into it was used by those on foot. The family,

which has lived here for three centuries, has disconnected the four tempting old-time doorbells. The gift shop at #11 (on the right) offers a chance to poke into one of these big landowners' homes and appreciate their structure: living quarters in front above carriage-size doors, courtyard out back functioning as a garage, stables, warehouse, servants' quarters, and a private well.

Farther up, also on the right, is Hotel Eisenhut, Rothenburg's fanciest hotel and worth a peek inside. Finally, passing the Käthe Wohlfahrt Christmas headquarters/shop (described under "Shopping," later) you'll be back at Market Square, where you started this walk.

• *From here, you can continue walking by following my "Schmiedgasse-Spitalgasse Shopping Stroll," next. This stroll ends at the city gate called Spitalor, a good access point for a walk on the town walls.*

◑ Schmiedgasse-Spitalgasse Shopping Stroll

After doing the town walk and visiting the town's three essential interior sights (Imperial City Museum, Medieval Crime and Punishment Museum, and St. Jakob's Church), your next priority might be Rothenburg's shops and its town wall.

I'd propose this fun walk, worth ▲▲, which goes from Market Square in a straight line south (past the best selection of characteristic family-run shops) to the city's most impressive fortification (Spitaltor). From Spitaltor you can access the town wall and walk the ramparts 180 degrees around the city to the Klingentor tower.

Standing on Market Square, with your back to the TI, you'll see a street sloping downward toward the south end of town. That's where you're headed. This street changes names as you walk, from **Obere Schmiedgasse** (upper blacksmith street) to **Spitalgasse** (hospital street), and runs directly to the **Spitaltor** tower and gate.

As you stroll down this delightful lane,

feel welcome to pop in and explore any shop along this cultural and historical scavenger hunt. I've provided the street number and "left" or "right" to indicate the side of the street.

Start on Market Square. The facade of the fine Renaissance **Baumeister Haus** at #3 (left) celebrates a secular (rather than religious) morality, with statues representing the seven virtues and the seven vices. Which ones do you recognize?

At #5 (left) **Gasthof Goldener Greifen** was once the home of the illustrious Mayor Toppler (d. 1408). By the looks of its door (right of the main entrance), the mayor must have had an impressive wine cellar. Note the fine hanging sign of a gilded griffin. Business signs in a mostly illiterate medieval world needed to be easy for all to read. The entire street is ornamented with fun signs like this one. Nearby, a pretzel marks the bakery, and the crossed swords advertise the weapon maker.

Shops on both sides of the street at #7 display examples of *Schneeballen* gone wild. These "snowballs," once a humble way to bake extra flour into a simple treat, are now iced and dolled up a million ways. Long ago, locals used a fork to pierce the middle, but today's tourists eat them like an apple. Watch them crumble.

Waffenkammer, at #9 (left), is "the weapons chamber," where Johannes Wittmann works hard to make a wonderland in which young-at-heart tourists can shop for (and try out) medieval weapons, armor, and clothing. Fun photo ops abound, especially downstairs—where you can try on a set of chain mail and pose with a knight in shining armor.

At #18 (right), **Metzgerei Trumpp,** a top-end butcher, is a carnivores' heaven. Check out the endless wurst offerings in the window—a reminder that in the unrefrigerated Middle Ages meat needed to be smoked or salted.

At the next corner, with **Burggasse,** find the Catholic St. John's Church.

The Medieval Crime and Punishment Museum (just down the lane to the right) marks the site of Rothenburg's first town wall. Below the church (on the right) is an old fountain. Behind and below that find a cute little doggie park complete with a doggie WC.

The **Jutta Korn** shop, on the right at #4, showcases the work of an artisan who has designed jewelry here for 30 years. At #6 (right), **Leyk** sells "lighthouses" made in town, many modeled after local buildings. The **Kleiderey,** an offbeat clothing store at #7 (left), is run by Tina, the Night Watchman's wife. The clothing is inspired by their Southeast Asian travels.

At #13 (left), look opposite to find a narrow lane **(Ander Eich)** that leads to a little viewpoint in the town wall, overlooking the "Tauber Riviera."

Continuing along, at #17 (left), the **Lebe Gesund Vegetarian** shop is all about healthy living. This charming little place seems designed to offer forgiveness to those who loved the butcher's shop but are ready to repent.

The **Käthe Wohlfahrt** shop at #19 (left) is just another of the KW shops around town, all selling German clichés with gusto. Also on the left, at #21, the **An Ra** Shop is where Annett Rafoth designs and sells her flowery clothes. You can pop in to see the actual work in the back. (There's more of An Ra across the street at #26.)

At **Kunsthandlung Leyrer** (on the left,

at #23), Peter Leyrer would love to show you his etchings (if he hasn't retired). He is one of the last artisans using Albrecht Dürer's copper-plate technique to print his art. After he retires, his 3,500 copper plates from all over Germany will go to a museum. Peter and his wife print the black-and-white etchings and then apply watercolor.

At #29 (left), **Glocke Weinladen am Plönlein** is an inviting shop of wine glasses and related accessories. The **Gasthof Glocke,** next door, with its wine-barrel-sized cellar door just waiting for some action, is a respected restaurant and home to the town's last vintner—a wonderful place to try local wines, as they serve flights of five tiny glasses.

The next corner, on the right, is dubbed **Plönlein** and is famously picturesque. If this scene brings you back to your childhood, that's because Rothenburg was the inspiration for the village in the 1940 Disney animated film *Pinocchio*.

Walk a few more yards and look far up the lane **(Neugasse)** to the left. You'll see some cute pastel buildings with uniform windows and rooflines—clues that the buildings were rebuilt after WWII bombings hit that part of town. Straight ahead, the **Siebertstor Tower** marks the next layer of expansion to the town wall. Continue through the tower. The former tannery is now a pub featuring **Landwehr Bräu,** the local brew.

Farther along, at #14 (right), **Antiq & Trödel,** which smells like an antique shop should, is fun to browse through.

Still farther down, on the left, at #25, **Hotel-Café Gerberhaus** is a fine stop for a coffee and cake, with a delicate dining room and a peaceful courtyard hiding out back under the town wall.

The remaining few (boring) blocks take you to **Spitaltor,** the tall tower with a gate marking the end of town, and a good place to begin a ramparts ramble (going counterclockwise), if you're up for it.

Walk through the gate (taking note of the stairs to the right—that's where you could begin your wall walk—described next). Standing outside the wall, ponder this sight as if approaching the city 400 years ago. The wealth of a city was shown by its walls and towers. (Stone was costly—in fact, the German saying for "filthy rich" is "stone rich.") Circle around to the right. Look up at the formidable tower. The guardhouse atop it, one of several in the wall, was manned continuously during medieval times. Above the entry gate, notice the emblem: Angels bless the double eagle of the Holy Roman Emperor, which blesses the town, symbolized by the two red towers.

⊙ Walk the Wall

Just longer than a mile and a half around, providing superb views and a fine orientation, this walk, worth ▲▲, can be done by those under six feet tall in less than an hour. The hike requires no special sense of balance. Much of the walk is covered and is a great option in the rain. Photographers will stay very busy, especially before breakfast or at sunset when the lighting is best and the crowds are gone. You can enter or exit the ramparts at nearly every tower.

While the ramparts circle the city, some stretches aren't walkable per se: Along much of the western side of town, you can't walk atop the wall, but you can walk right alongside it and peek over or through it for great views outward from street

The city ramparts

level. Refer to the map on page 859 to see which portions of the walls are walkable.

If you want to make a full town circuit, Spitaltor—at the south end of town, with the best fortifications—makes a good starting place. From here, it's a counter-clockwise walk along the eastern and northern ramparts. After exiting at Klingentor, you can still follow the wall for a bit, but you'll have to cut inland, away from the wall, when you hit the Imperial City Museum, and again near the Medieval Crime and Punishment Museum. At the Kohlturm tower, back at the southern end of town, you can climb the stairs and walk atop the remaining short stretch of wall to the Spitalhof quarter, where you'll need to exit again. Spitaltor, where you started, is just a *Schneeball*'s toss away.

The TI has installed a helpful series of English-language plaques at about 20 stops along the route. The names you see along the way belong to people who donated money to rebuild the wall after World War II, and those who've more recently donated €1,000 per meter for the maintenance of Rothenburg's heritage.

Sights

Note that a number of sights (including St. Jakob's Church and the Imperial City Museum) have already been covered on the Rothenburg Town Walk.

On and Near Market Square
▲TOWN HALL TOWER
From Market Square you can see tourists on the crow's nest capping the Town Hall's tower. For a commanding view from the town's tallest perch, climb the steps of the tower. It's a rigorous but interesting 214-step climb that gets narrow and steep near the top—watch your head.

Cost and Hours: €2, pay at top, daily in season 9:00-12:30 & 13:00-17:00, enter from the grand steps overlooking Market Square.

▲▲MEDIEVAL CRIME AND PUNISHMENT MUSEUM (MITTELALTERLICHES KRIMINALMUSEUM)
Specializing in everything connected to medieval criminal justice, this exhibit (well-described in English) is a cut above all the tacky and popular torture museums around Europe. In addition to ogling spiked chairs, thumbscrews, and shame masks—nearly everything on display here is an actual medieval artifact—you'll learn about medieval police and criminal law. The museum is more eclectic than its name, and includes exhibits on general history, superstition, biblical art, and so on.

Cost and Hours: €5, daily April 11:00-17:00, May-Oct 10:00-18:00, Nov and Jan-Feb 14:00-16:00, Dec and March 13:00-16:00, last entry 45 minutes before closing, fun cards and posters, Burggasse 3-5, tel. 09861/5359, www.kriminalmuseum.rothenburg.de.

Visiting the Museum: It's a one-way route. Just follow the yellow arrows and you'll see it all. Keep an eye out for several well-done interactive media stations that provide extra background on the museum's highlights.

From the entrance, head downstairs to the **cellar** to see some enhanced-interrogation devices. Torture was common in the Middle Ages—not to punish, but to extract a confession (medieval "justice" required a confession). Just the sight of these tools was often enough to make an innocent man confess. You'll see the rack, "stretching ladder," thumb

screws, spiked leg screws, and other items that would make Dick Cheney proud. Medieval torturers also employed a waterboarding-like technique—but here, the special ingredient was holy water.

Upstairs, on the **first and second floors,** the walls are lined with various legal documents of the age, while the dusty glass cases show off law-enforcement tools—many of them quite creative. Shame was a big tool back then; wrongdoers would be creatively shamed before their neighbors. The town could publicly humiliate those who ran afoul of the law by tying them to a pillory in the main square and covering their faces in an iron mask of shame. The mask's fanciful decorations indicated the crime: Chicken feathers meant promiscuity, horns indicated that a man's wife slept around (i.e., cuckold), and a snout suggested that the person had acted piggishly. A gossip might wear a mask with giant ears (heard everything), eyeglasses (saw everything), and a giant, wagging tongue (couldn't keep her mouth shut). The infamous "iron maiden" started out as more of a "shame barrel"; the internal spikes were added to play up popular lore when it went on display for 18th-century tourists. For more serious offenses, criminals were branded—so that even if they left town, they'd take that shame with them for the rest of their lives. When all else failed, those in charge could always turn to the executioner's sword.

To safely capture potential witches, lawmen used a device resembling a metal collar—with spikes pointing in—that was easy to get into, but nearly impossible to get out of. A neck violin—like a portable version of a stock—kept the accused under control. (The double neck violin could be used to lock together a quarrelsome couple to force them to work things out.) The chastity belts were used to ensure a wife's loyalty (giving her traveling husband peace of mind) and/or to protect women from attack at a time when rape was far more commonplace. The exit routes you through a courtyard garden to a **last building** with temporary exhibits (included in your admission and often interesting) and a café. (If you must buy a *Schneeball*, consider doing it here—where they are small, inexpensive, and fairly edible—and help support the museum.)

▲**GERMAN CHRISTMAS MUSEUM (DEUTSCHES WEIHNACHTSMUSEUM)**
This excellent museum, in a Disney-esque space upstairs in the giant Käthe Wohlfahrt Christmas Village shop, tells the history of Christmas decorations. There's a unique and thoughtfully described collection of tree stands, mini-trees sent in boxes to WWI soldiers at the front, early Advent calendars, old-time Christmas cards, Christmas pyramids, and a look at the evolution of Father Christmas, as well as tree decorations through the ages—including the Nazi era and when you were a kid. The museum is not just a ploy to get shoppers to spend more money, but a serious collection managed by professional curator Felicitas Höptner.

Cost and Hours: €4 most of the year, open April-Dec daily 10:00-17:30, shorter and irregular hours Jan-March, Herrngasse 1, tel. 09861/409-365, www.christmasmuseum.com.

Experiences
Shopping
Be warned...Rothenburg is one of Germany's best shopping towns. Do it here and be done with it. Lovely prints, carvings, wine glasses, Christmas-tree ornaments, and beer steins are popular. Rödergasse is the old town's everyday shopping street. Also try my Shopping Stroll on page 871. There's also a modern shopping center across the street from the train station.

KÄTHE WOHLFAHRT CHRISTMAS HEADQUARTERS
Rothenburg is the headquarters of the **Käthe Wohlfahrt** Christmas trinkets empire, which has spread across the half-timbered reaches of Europe. Rothen-

burg has six or eight Wohlfahrts (all stores open Mon-Sat 9:00-18:30, May-Dec also most Sun 10:00-18:00). Tourists flock to the two biggest, just below Market Square. Start with the **Christmas Village** (Weihnachtsdorf) at Herrngasse 1. This Christmas wonderland is filled with enough twinkling lights (196,000—mostly LEDs) to require a special electrical hookup. You're greeted by instant Christmas mood music (best appreciated on a hot day in July) and tourists hungrily filling little woven shopping baskets with goodies to hang on their trees. Let the spinning, flocked tree whisk you in, and pause at the wall of Steiff stuffed animals, jerking uncontrollably and mesmerizing kids. Then head downstairs to find the vast and sprawling "made in Germany" section, surrounding a slowly spinning 15-foot tree decorated with a thousand glass balls. (Items handmade in Germany are the most expensive.) They often offer a discount on all official KW products to my readers—ask. The fascinating **Christmas Museum** upstairs is described earlier, under "Sights." The smaller shop (across the street at Herrngasse 2) specializes in finely crafted wooden ornaments. Käthe opened her first storefront here in Rothenburg in 1977. The company is now run by her son Harald, who lives in town.

Rick's Tip: *To* **mail your goodies home,** *you can get handy yellow €2.50 boxes at the old town* **post office** *(Mon-Tue and Thu-Fri 9:00-13:00 & 14:00-17:30, Wed 9:00-13:00, Sat 9:00-12:00, closed Sun, inside photo shop at Rödergasse 11). The main post office is in the shopping center across from the train station.*

FRIESE SHOP

Cuckoo with friendliness, trinkets, and reasonably priced souvenirs, the Friese shop has been open for more than 50 years. Shoppers with this book receive tremendous service: a 10 percent discount and a free pictorial map (normally €1.50). Anneliese Friese, who runs the place with her son Bernie and granddaughter Dolores (a.k.a. "Mousy"), charges only her cost for shipping and lets tired travelers leave their bags in her back room for free (Mon-Sat 9:00-18:00, Sun 10:00-18:00, 20 steps off Market Square at Grüner Markt 8—around the corner from TI and across from free public WC, tel. 09861/7166).

Festivals

For one weekend each spring (during Pentecost), *Biergartens* spill out into the street and Rothenburgers dress up in medieval costumes to celebrate Mayor Nusch's **Meistertrunk** victory (www.meistertrunk. de). The **Reichsstadt festival** every September celebrates Rothenburg's history, and the town's **Weindorf festival** celebrates its wine (mid-Aug). For more info, check the TI website: www.tourismus. rothenburg.de.

In winter, Rothenburg is quiet except for its **Christmas Market** in December, when the entire town cranks up the medieval cuteness with concerts and costumes, shops with schnapps, stalls filling squares, hot spiced wine, giddy nutcrackers, and mobs of ear-muffed Germans. Try to avoid Saturdays and Sundays, when big-city day-trippers really clog the grog.

Eating

My recommendations are all within a five-minute walk of Market Square. While all survive on tourism, many still feel like local hangouts. Your choices are typical German or ethnic. You'll see regional Franconian (*fränkische*) specialties advertised, such as the German ravioli called *Maultaschen* and Franconian bratwurst (similar to other brats, but more coarsely ground, with less fat, and liberally seasoned with marjoram). Many restaurants take a midafternoon break, stop serving lunch at 14:00, and end dinner service as early as 20:00.

Traditional German Restaurants

Reichsküchenmeister's interior is like any big-hotel restaurant's, but on a balmy evening, its pleasant, tree-shaded terrace overlooking St. Jakob's Church and reliably good dishes are hard to beat (€10-25 main courses, €7-10 *Flammkuchen*— southern German flatbread, steaks, vegetarian options, daily 11:30-21:30, Kirchplatz 8, tel. 09861/9700).

Hotel Restaurant Kloster-Stüble, on a small street off Herrngasse near the castle garden, is a classy place for delicious traditional cuisine, including homemade *Maultaschen*. Choose from their shaded terrace, sleek and modern dining room, or woody and traditional dining room (€10-20 main courses, Thu-Mon 18:00-21:00, Sat-Sun also 11:00-14:00, closed Tue-Wed, Heringsbronnengasse 5, tel. 09861/938-890).

Gasthof Goldener Greifen, in a historic building with a peaceful garden out back, is just off the main square. The Klingler family serves quality Franconian food at a good price...and with a smile. The ambience is practical rather than posh (€8-17 main courses, €12-15 three-course daily specials, affordable kids' meals, daily 11:30-21:00 except closed Sun in winter, Obere Schmiedgasse 5, tel. 09861/2281).

Rick's Tip: *For a rare chance to* **meet the locals,** *bring your favorite slang and tongue-twisters to the* **English Conversation Club** *at* **Altfränkische Weinstube am Klosterhof.** *Hermann the German and his sidekick Wolfgang are regulars. A big table is reserved from 18:30 on Wednesday evenings. Consider arriving early for dinner, or after 21:00, when the beer starts to sink in and everyone speaks that second language more easily.*

Altfränkische Weinstube am Klosterhof, classically candlelit in a 600-year-old building, seems designed for gnomes to celebrate their anniversaries with gourmet pub grub. It's a clear favorite with locals for an atmospheric drink or late meal. When every other place is asleep, you're likely to find good food, drink, and energy here (€7-15 main courses, hot food served Wed-Mon 18:00-21:30, closed Tue, off Klingengasse at Klosterhof 7, tel. 09861/6404).

Zum Pulverer ("The Powderer") is a

traditional wine bar just inside the Burg-tor gate that serves a menu of affordable regional fare, sometimes with modern flourishes. The interior is a cozy wood-hewn place that oozes history, with chairs carved in the shape of past senators of Rothenburg (€6-14 dishes, Wed-Fri and Mon 17:00-22:00, Sat-Sun 12:00-22:00, closed Tue, Herrengasse 31, tel. 09861/976-182, Bastian).

Alter Keller is a modest, tour-ist-friendly restaurant with a charac-teristic interior and outdoor tables on a peaceful square just a couple blocks off Market Square. The menu has German classics at reasonable prices (€8-14 main dishes, Wed-Sun 11:30-15:00 & 17:30-21:00, closed Mon-Tue, Alter Keller 8, tel. 09861/2268, Markus and Miriam).

A Non-Franconian Splurge

Hotel Restaurant Herrnschlösschen is the local favorite fare, with a small menu of international and seasonal dishes. There's always a serious vegetarian option and a €50 fixed-price meal with matching wine. Sit in the classy dining hall or in the shaded Baroque garden out back. Reser-vations are a must (€20-30 main dishes, Herrngasse 20, tel. 09861/873-890, www.hotel-rothenburg.de).

Breaks from Pork and Potatoes

Pizzeria Roma is the local favorite for pizza and pastas, with good Italian wine. The Magrini family moved here from Tuscany in 1970 and they've been serving pasta ever since (Thu-Tue 11:30-23:00, closed Wed and mid-Aug-mid-Sept, Galgengasse 19, tel. 09861/4540).

TobinGo, just off Market Square, serves cheap and tasty Turkish food to eat in or take away. Their *Döner Kebabs* must be the best €3.70 hot meal in Rothen-burg. For about €1 more, try a less-bready *Dürüm Döner*—same ingredients but in a warm tortilla (daily 10:00-22:00, Hafen-gasse 2).

Sandwiches and Snacks

Brot & Zeit (a pun on *Brotzeit*, "bread time," the German term for snacking), conveniently located a block off Market Square, is like a German bakery dressed up as a Starbucks. Just inside the pic-turesque Markus Tower gate, they sell takeaway coffee, inexpensive sandwiches, and a few hot dishes (Mon-Sat 6:00-18:30, Sun 7:30-18:00, Hafengasse 24, tel. 09861/936-8701).

While any bakery in town can sell you a sandwich for a couple of euros, I like to pop into **Metzgerei Trumpp,** a high-quality butcher shop serving up cheap and tasty sausages on a bun with kraut to go (Mon-Fri 7:30-18:00, Sat until 16:00, usually closed Sun, a block off Market Square at Schmiedgasse 18).

A small **grocery store** is in the center of town (Mon-Fri 7:30-19:00, Sat-Sun until 18:00 except closed Sun off-season, Rödergasse 6). Larger supermarkets are outside the wall: Exit the town through the Rödertor, turn left through the cobbled gate, and cross the parking lot to reach the **Edeka supermarket** (Mon-Fri 8:00-20:00, Sat until 18:00, closed Sun); or head to the even bigger **Kaufland** across from the train station (Mon-Sat 7:00-20:00, closed Sun).

Beer Garden (Biergarten)

Gasthof Rödertor, just outside the wall through the Rödertor, runs a popular backyard *Biergarten,* where a rowdy crowd enjoys classic fare, pizza, and good beer. Their passion is potatoes (May-Sept daily 17:30-23:00 in good weather, table service only—no ordering at counter, Ansbacher Strasse 7, look for wooden gate, tel. 09861/2022). The *Biergarten* is open only in balmy weather, but their indoor restau-rant, with a more extensive menu, is open year-round and also offers a good value (€8-13 main courses, Tue-Sun 11:30-14:00 & 17:30-21:30, closed Mon).

Dessert

Eis Café D'Isep has been making gelato in Rothenburg since 1960, using family recipes that span four generations. Their sidewalk tables are great for lazy people-watching (daily 10:00-22:00, closed early Oct-mid-Feb, one block off Market Square at Hafengasse 17, run by Paolo and Paola D'Isep and son Enrico).

Rothenburg's **bakeries** (*Bäckereien*) offer succulent pastries, pies, and cakes... but skip the bad-tasting *Rothenburger Schneeballen* promoted all over town: bland pie crusts crumpled into a ball and dusted with powdered sugar or frosted with sticky-sweet glop. Instead of wasting your appetite on a *Schneeball*, enjoy a curvy *Mandelhörnchen* (almond crescent cookie), a triangular *Nussecke* ("nut corner"), a round *Florentiner* cookie, a couple of fresh *Krapfen* (like jelly doughnuts), or a soft, warm German pretzel. But if the curiosity is too much to bear, try a fresh, handmade *Schneeball* from a smaller bakery (*frisch* is fresh; *handgemacht* is handmade), and avoid the slick places on the busy tourist avenues.

Wine-Drinking in the Old Center

Restaurant Glocke, a wine bar with a full menu, is run by Rothenburg's oldest and only surviving winemakers, the Thürauf family. The very extensive wine list is in German only because the friendly staff wants to explain your options in person. Their special €5 wine flight lets you sample five Franconian white wines; other flights of reds and dessert wines are offered as well (€8-18 main courses, Mon-Sat 11:00-23:00, food until 22:00, closed Sun, Plönlein 1, tel. 09861/958-990).

Sleeping

Rothenburg is crowded with visitors, but most are day-trippers. Except for the rare Saturday night and during festivals (see page 876), finding a room is easy. If you want to splurge, you'll snare the best value by paying extra for the biggest and best rooms at the hotels I recommend. In the off-season (Nov and Jan-March), hoteliers may be willing to discount.

Train travelers save steps by staying in the Rödertor area (east end of town). Hotels and guesthouses will sometimes pick up tired heavy-packers at the station. If you're driving, call ahead to get directions and parking tips. Save some energy to climb the stairs: No hotels listed here have elevators.

Keep your key when out late. As Rothenburg's hotels are small and mostly family-run, they often lock up early (at about 22:00) and take one day a week off, so you'll need to let yourself in at those times.

In the Old Town

$$$ Hotel Herrnschlösschen prides itself on being the smallest (8 rooms) and most exclusive hotel in Rothenburg. If you're looking for a splurge, this is your best bet. This 1,000-year-old building has a beautiful Baroque garden and every amenity you'd ever want (including a sauna), but you'll pay for them (deluxe Db-€210, pricier suites, see website for seasonal discounts, Wi-Fi, Herrngasse 20, tel. 09861/873890, www.herrnschloesschen. de, info@herrnschloesschen.de).

$$$ Hotel Kloster-Stüble, deep in the old town near the castle garden, is one of my classiest listings. Twenty-one rooms, each with its own special touches, fill two medieval buildings, connected by a modern atrium (traditional Db-€88-108, bigger and modern Db-€140-150, suites and family rooms, kids 5 and under free, just off Herrngasse at Heringsbronnengasse 5, tel. 09861/938-890, www.klosterstueble. de, hotel@klosterstueble.de).

Sleep Code

Price Rankings for Double Rooms (Db)

$$$ Most rooms €85 or more
$$ €60-85
$ €60 or less

Abbreviations: Db=Double with bathroom. D=Double with bathroom down the hall.

Notes: Room prices change; verify rates online or by email. For the best prices, book direct with the hotel.

$$$ **Hotel Spitzweg** is a rustic yet elegant 1536 mansion with 10 big rooms, open beams, antique furniture, and new bathrooms. It's run by gentle Herr Hocher, whom I suspect is the former Wizard of Oz—now retired and in a very good mood (Db-€90-100, family rooms and an apartment, nonsmoking, inviting old-fashioned breakfast room, free parking, Wi-Fi at son-in-law's nearby hotel, Paradeisgasse 2, tel. 09861/94290, www.hotel-spitzweg.de, info@hotel-spitzweg.de).

$$$ **Gasthof Goldener Greifen** is a traditional, 600-year-old place with 14 spacious rooms and all the comforts. It's run by a helpful family that also runs a good restaurant, serving meals in the back garden or dining room (small Db-€75, big Db-€85-104, family rooms, 10 percent less for 3-night stays, nonsmoking, full-service laundry-€8, free loaner bikes for guests, free and easy parking, half a block downhill from Market Square at Obere Schmiedgasse 5, tel. 09861/2281, www.gasthof-greifen-rothenburg.de, info@gasthof-greifen-rothenburg.de).

$$$ **Hotel Gerberhaus** has 20 bright and airy rooms that mix modern amenities with half-timbered elegance. Enjoy the pleasant garden in back and the delightful breakfast buffet (Db-€89-130, family rooms and an apartment, €10 off second and subsequent nights and a *Schneeball* if you book direct and pay cash, nonsmoking, 4 rooms have canopied 4-poster *Himmel* beds, laundry-€10, limited free parking, close to P-1 parking lot, Spitalgasse 25, tel. 09861/94900, www.gerberhaus.rothenburg.de, gerberhaus@t-online.de).

$$ **Hotel Altfränkische Weinstube am Klosterhof** is *the* place for well-heeled bohemians, with seven cozy rooms above the locals' favorite pub. The 600-year-old building has an upscale *Lord of the Rings* atmosphere, with open-beam ceilings, some canopied four-poster beds, and modern plumbing (Db-€69, bigger Db-€82, Db suite-€118, off Klingengasse at Klosterhof 7, tel. 09861/6404, www.altfraenkische.de, altfraenkische-weinstube@web.de).

$$ **Pension Elke** rents 12 comfy rooms above a family grocery store (D-€57, Db-€65-69, cash only, request Rick Steves discount with this book if you stay at least 2 nights; reception in grocery store until 19:00, otherwise go around back and ring bell at top of stairs; near Markus Tower at Rödergasse 6, tel. 09861/2331, www.pension-elke-rothenburg.de, info@pension-elke-rothenburg.de).

$$ **Gästehaus Raidel** rents eight rooms in a 500-year-old house with charming, ramshackle ambience. The beds and furniture are handmade by Norry Raidel himself. He also plays in a Dixieland band, has invented a fascinating hybrid saxophone/trombone called the Norryphone... and loves to jam (Db-€69, family rooms, cash only, pleasant terrace, Wenggasse 3, tel. 09861/3115, Norry asks you to use the reservations form at www.romanticroad.com/raidel).

$$ **Gasthof zum Breiterle** offers 19 comfortable rooms with wooden accents above their restaurant near the Rödertor. Because it sits on a busy street, light sleepers may want to request a room not facing Wenggasse (Db-€78-88, apartment available, reception in restau-

rant, pay parking, Rödergasse 30, tel. 09861/6730, www.breiterle.de, info@breiterle.de).

$$ Gästehaus Gerlinger, a fine value, has five comfortable rooms in a pretty 16th-century house with a small terrace for guests (Db-€62, an apartment, cash only, nonsmoking, easy parking, Schlegeleinsweth 10, tel. 09861/87979, mobile 0171-690-0752, www.pension-gerlinger. de, info@pension-gerlinger.de).

$$ Kreuzerhof Hotel offers 11 decent rooms surrounding a courtyard on a quiet side street near the Rödertor (Db-€75-79, large Db-€92, family deals and rooms—including one for six people, nonsmoking, laundry-€7, parking in courtyard-€4/day, Millergasse 2-6, tel. 09861/3424, www.kreuzerhof.eu, info@kreuzerhof.eu).

$ Gästehaus Liebler rents two large, modern, ground-floor rooms with kitchenettes—great for real privacy close to the action. On the top floor is an attractive two-bedroom apartment (Db-€50, cash only, Rick Steves discount for 2 or more nights with this book, no breakfast but café nearby, nonsmoking, laundry-€5, behind Christmas shop at Pfäffleinsgässchen 10, tel. 09861/709-215, www.gaestehaus-liebler.de, info@gaestehaus-liebler.de).

$ Rossmühle Youth Hostel rents 186 beds in two institutional yet charming buildings. Reception is in the huge building with droopy dormer windows—formerly a horse-powered mill. While most beds are in dorms, there are also 11 doubles (dorm bed-€25, bunk-bed Db-€61; guests over 26 pay €3.50 extra unless traveling with a family, nonmembers pay €4 extra, includes breakfast and sheets, dinner-€7, self-serve laundry with soap-€5, close to P-1 parking lot, entrance on Rossmühlgasse, tel. 09861/94160, www.rothenburg.jugendherberge.de, rothenburg@jugendherberge.de).

Transportation
Arriving and Departing
BY TRAIN

Arriving in Rothenburg: It's a 10-minute walk from the station to Rothenburg's Market Square (following the brown *Altstadt* signs, exit left from station, walk a block down Bahnhofstrasse, turn right on Ansbacher Strasse, and head straight into the Middle Ages). Taxis wait at the station (€6 to any hotel). Day-trippers can leave luggage in station lockers on the platform. Free WCs are behind the Speedy snack bar on track 1.

The station has a touch-screen terminal for fare and schedule information and ticket sales. If you need extra help, visit the combined ticket office/travel agency in the station building (€1-3 surcharge for most tickets, €0.50 charge for questions without ticket purchase, Mon-Fri 10:00-18:00, Sat 9:00-13:00, closed Sun, tel. 09861/7711, train info toll tel. 0180-699-6633, www.bahn.com).

Getting to/from Rothenburg via Steinach: If you take the train to or from Rothenburg, you'll transfer at Steinach. A tiny branch train line shuttles back and forth hourly between the two towns (14 minutes, generally departs Steinach at :35 and Rothenburg at :06). Train connections in Steinach are usually quick and efficient (trains to/from Rothenburg generally use track 5; use the conveyor belts to haul your bags smartly up and down the stairs). Steinach's station is unstaffed but has touch-screen ticket machines (though any ticket to or from Rothenburg will automatically include your transfer).

Note that the last train from Steinach to Rothenburg departs at about 22:30. But all is not lost if you arrive in Steinach after the last train: There's a subsidized taxi service to Rothenburg (cheaper for the government than running an almost-empty train). To use this handy service, called AST *(Anrufsammeltaxi)*, make an appointment with a participating taxi service (call 09861/2000 or 09861/7227) at least an hour in advance (2 hours ahead is better), and they'll drive you from Steinach to Rothenburg for the cheap train fare (€4.60/person) rather than the regular €30 taxi fare.

From Rothenburg (via Steinach) by Train to: Würzburg (hourly, 70 minutes), **Nürnberg** (hourly, 1.5 hours, change in Ansbach), **Munich** (hourly, 2.5-4 hours, 2-3 changes), **Füssen** (hourly, 5 hours, often with changes in Treuchtlingen and Augsburg), **Frankfurt** (hourly, 2.5-3 hours, change in Würzburg), **Frankfurt Airport** (hourly, 3-3.5 hours, change in Würzburg), **Berlin** (hourly, 5.5 hours, 3 changes).

BY CAR

Driving and parking rules in Rothenburg change constantly—ask your hotelier for advice. In general, you're allowed to drive into the old town to get to your hotel. Otherwise, driving within the old walled center is discouraged. Some hotels offer private parking (either free or pay). To keep things simple, park in one of the lots—numbered P-1 through P-5—that line the outside of the town walls (€5/day, buy ticket from *Parkscheinautomat* machines and display, 5- to 10-minute walk to Market Square).

Driving from Frankfurt Airport: Even a jet-lagged zombie can handle the three-hour autobahn drive from the airport to Rothenburg. It's a 75-mile straight shot to Würzburg on the A-3 autobahn; just follow the blue autobahn signs toward *Würzburg*. Then turn south on A-7 and take the *Rothenburg o.d.T.* exit (#108).

NEAR ROTHENBURG

THE ROMANTIC ROAD

Along the Romantic Road, half-timbered towns are ringed by walls and towers, while flowers spill over the windowsills of the well-kept houses. Glockenspiels dance from town halls. Many travelers bypass these small towns by fast train or autobahn. But consider an extra day or two to take in the slow pace of life. I've included an overview of key sights on the route.

By Car

Wander through quaint hills and rolling villages along the scenic 220-mile driving route called the Romantic Road (*Romantische Strasse*, www.romantischestrasse. de). Stop wherever the cows look friendly or a town fountain beckons. If your goal is to meander and explore, don't use GPS—get a good map and follow the brown *Romantische Strasse* signs along two-lane roads. If you use GPS, you'll usually be routed to the nearest fast highway or autobahn, which isn't romantic at all.

If you're driving south of Rothenburg (whether heading toward it or leaving it), you could stop at the Wieskirche and the towns of Nördlingen and Dinkelsbühl.

If you're driving north of Rothenburg, good stops are Creglingen and Weikersheim.

By Bus

The Romantic Road bus runs daily from mid-April to late October. Every day, one bus goes north to south (Frankfurt to Munich to Füssen), and another goes south to north (Füssen to Munich to Frankfurt). You can begin or end your journey at any of the stops—including Rothenburg—along the way. Check the full timetable and prices at www.romantischestrasse.de.

South of Rothenburg

If you're driving from Füssen to Rothenburg, you'll encounter these three sights in this order:

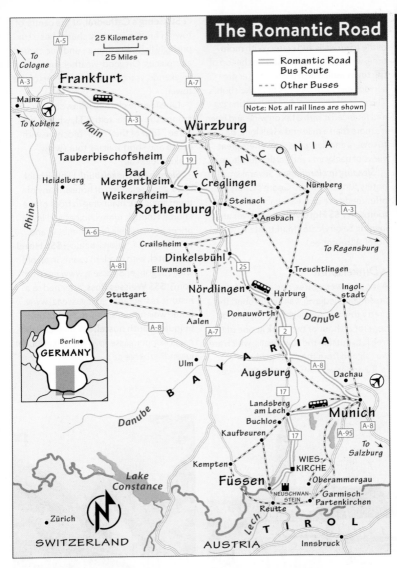

The Romantic Road

25 Kilometers
25 Miles

=== Romantic Road
    Bus Route
--- Other Buses

Note: Not all rail lines are shown

To Cologne

Frankfurt
Mainz
To Koblenz

A-5
A-3
A-3
A-7

Würzburg

Main
Rhine

Tauberbischofsheim
Bad Mergentheim
Weikersheim
Rothenburg

Heidelberg

Creglingen
Steinach
Ansbach

Nürnberg

A-3
To Regensburg

A-6

Crailsheim

Dinkelsbühl
Ellwangen

A-81

25

Treuchtlingen

Stuttgart

Nördlingen
Harburg

Ingol-stadt

Aalen

Donauwörth
Danube

A-8
A-7
2

B A V A R I A

Ulm
Augsburg

A-8
Dachau

17

Berlin
GERMANY

Landsberg am Lech
Buchloe

Munich

Danube

Kaufbeuren

17

A-95
A-8
To Salzburg

Kempten

WIES-KIRCHE

Lake Constance

Füssen

NEUSCHWAN-STEIN

Oberammergau
Garmisch-Partenkirchen

Zürich

Reutte

T I R O L

SWITZERLAND

AUSTRIA

Innsbruck

Lech

N

▲▲ Wieskirche

Germany's most glorious Baroque-Rococo church is beautifully restored and set in a sweet meadow.

▲ Nördlingen

Nördlingen is a real workaday town that has one of the best medieval walls in Germany, not to mention a surprising geo-logic history. For centuries, Nördlingen's residents puzzled over the local terrain, a flattish plain called the Ries, which rises to a low circular ridge that surrounds the town in the distance. In the 1960s, geol-ogists figured out that Nördlingen lies in the middle of an impact crater blasted out 15 million years ago by a meteor.

Head into the center of town by zeroing in on the tower of **St. Georg's Church.** Climb the church tower for sweeping views of the town walls and crater. With more time, walk all the way around on the top of the **town wall,** which is even better preserved than Rothenburg's or Dinkelsbühl's. The town started building the wall in 1327 and financed it with a tax on wine and beer; it's more than a mile and a half long, has 16 towers and five gates, and offers great views of backyards and garden furniture.

Sleeping in Nördlingen: Several small hotels surrounding St. Georg's Church offer mediocre but reasonably priced rooms. Try **$$ Hotel Altreuter,** over an inviting bakery/café (Marktplatz 11, www. hotel-altreuter.de).

▲ Dinkelsbühl

A moat, towers, gates, and a beautifully preserved medieval wall all surround this pretty town. It's a delight to simply stroll here for an hour or two. Park at one of the free lots outside the town walls, which are well signed from the main road.

To orient yourself, head for the tower of **St. Georg's Cathedral,** at the center of town. This 15th-century church has a surprisingly light, airy interior and fine carved altarpieces. On good-weather summer weekends, you can climb to the top of the tower.

Outside the church, follow signs around the corner to the **TI,** which offers a free "Tour of the Town" brochure with a map and short walking tour (www. dinkelsbuehl.de).

Sleeping in Dinkelsbühl: Dinkelsbühl has a good selection of hotels, many of them lining the main drag in front of the church (though more choices and lower prices are available in Rothenburg and Nördlingen). Options include: **$$$ Hezelhof Hotel,** with modern rooms in an old shell (Segringer Strasse 7, www.hezelhof. com); **$$$ Weisses Ross,** attached to a historic restaurant (Steingasse 12, www. hotel-weisses-ross.de); and the town's unique **$ youth hostel,** in a medieval granary (Koppengasse 10, www.dinkelsbuehl. jugendherberge.de).

St. Georg's Church dominates Nördlingen.

Dinkelsbühl

North of Rothenburg
Creglingen

While Creglingen itself isn't worth much fuss, two quick and rewarding sights sit across the road from each other a mile south of town.

The peaceful 14th-century **Herr-gottskirche Church,** worth ▲, is graced with Tilman Riemenschneider's greatest carved altarpiece, completed sometime between 1505 and 1510. The church's other colorful altars are also worth a peek (open daily in summer, afternoons only and closed Mon off-season, www.herrgottskirche.de).

The **Fingerhut Museum,** showing off thimbles (literally, "finger hats"), is far more interesting than it sounds. You'll step from case to case to squint at the collection, which numbers about 4,000 (but still fits in a single room) and comes from all over the world; some pieces are centuries old. Owner Thorvald Greif got a head start from his father, who owned a thimble factory (closed Mon and Jan-Feb, www.fingerhutmuseum.de).

▲Weikersheim

This picturesquely set town, nestled between hills, has a charming little main square offering easy access to a fine park and an impressive palace.

Weikersheim's **palace** (Schloss Weikersheim), across a moat-turned-park from the main square, was built in the late 16th century as the Renaissance country estate of a local count. With its bucolic location and glowing sandstone texture, it gives off a *Downton Abbey* vibe. It's viewable only by a guided tour in German; skip the tour and instead focus on exploring the palace's fine Baroque **gardens** (small entry fee, English audioguide www.schloss-weikersheim.de).

If you have time after your garden visit, Weikersheim's pleasant **town square** and cobbled old town are worth exploring. The **city park** (Stadtpark) makes a nice, free picnic spot, and from it you can peer over the hedge into the palace gardens.

The palace at Weikersheim has fine gardens.

Rhine Valley

The Rhine Valley is storybook Germany, a world of robber-baron castles and fairy-tale legends. Cruise through the most turret-studded stretch of the romantic Rhine, listening for the song of the treacherous Loreley. Get hands-on thrills exploring the Rhineland's greatest castle, Rheinfels. Connoisseurs will also enjoy the fine interior of Marksburg Castle near Koblenz. Farther afield is Burg Eltz (a remarkable castle on the Mosel) and Cologne (with its incredible cathedral).

Spend your nights in a castle-crowned Rhine village, either delightful Bacharach or practical St. Goar. They're 10 miles apart, connected by milk-run trains, riverboats, and a riverside bike path. Bacharach is a more interesting town, but St. Goar has the famous Rheinfels Castle.

Marvel at the Rhine's ever-changing parade. Ever since Roman times, when this was the empire's northern boundary, the Rhine has been one of the world's busiest shipping rivers. Traveling along the river today, you'll see a steady flow of barges with 1,000- to 2,000-ton loads. Cars, buses, and trains rush along highways and tracks lining both banks, making it easy to get around.

If possible, visit the Rhine between April and October, when it's at its touristic best. In winter, some sights close, along with some hotels and restaurants, and only one riverboat runs.

THE RHINE VALLEY IN 1 OR 2 DAYS

With one day and two nights, stay in Bacharach. Cruise the best and most scenic stretch of the river (the hour from Bacharach to St. Goar), and tour Rheinfels Castle. Enjoy dinner in Bacharach, and maybe a wine tasting, too.

For a busier day, take a longer cruise, following all or part of my Rhine Blitz Tour. For example, you could cruise from Bacharach to Braubach (to tour Marksburg Castle), before returning by train to Bacharach.

With a second day, visit Burg Eltz on the Mosel as a day trip. Or bike or hike along the Rhine. This is a fun place to relax and explore.

If you're traveling by **car,** park it at your hotel, cruise the Rhine, and visit Burg Eltz on the Mosel on your drive in or out.

If a Rhine festival coincides with your

RHINE VALLEY AT A GLANCE

On the Rhine

▲▲▲**Rhine Blitz Tour** One of Europe's great joys—touring the Rhine River by boat, train, bike, or car. See page 890.

▲▲▲**Rheinfels Castle** The best opportunity to explore a ruined castle on the river. **Hours:** Mid-March-Oct daily 9:00-18:00, Nov-mid-March possibly Sat-Sun only 11:00-17:00 (call ahead). See page 910.

▲▲**Marksburg Castle in Braubach** The best-preserved medieval castle on the Rhine. **Hours:** Daily April-Oct 10:00-17:00, Nov-March 11:00-16:00. See page 918.

Near the Rhine Valley

▲▲▲**Burg Eltz, on the Mosel** My favorite castle in Europe, set deep in a forest, with a rare furnished interior—take the required guided tour. **Hours:** April-Oct daily from 9:30, last tour departs at 17:30, closed Nov-March. See page 921.

Rhine Overview

Düsseldorf•

Rhine

Cologne•

← UNROMANTIC
RHINE

•Aachen

Bonn•

Berlin•
GERMANY

Remagen•

**BEST OF
THE RHINE**
See detail map

N

BELG.

BURG
ELTZ

• Koblenz

Frankfurt

Cochem•

**St.
Goar•**

Wies-
baden

Main R.

Beilstein •

Oberwesel •

Bingen•

Bacharach

Mainz ✈ Frankfurt

Mosel R.

LUX.

✈
Hahn

Neckar R.

Lux.
City ✈

•Trier

• Heidelberg

GERMANY

FRANCE

50 Kilometers

50 Miles

---

visit, book your room well in advance; study ahead.

Rick's Tip: *Rhine Valley* **guesthouses and hotels often have similar names.** *When reserving, double-check that you're contacting the one in your planned destination.*

RHINE BLITZ TOUR

One of Europe's top thrills is traveling along the Rhine River, enjoying this tour, worth ▲▲▲. For short distances, cruising is best because it's slower. A cruise going upstream (heading south, toward Bingen) takes longer than the same cruise going

downstream (north, toward Koblenz). If you want to draw out a short cruise, go upstream (for instance, from St. Goar to Bacharach).

To cover long distances (e.g., Koblenz to Bingen), consider the train. Or take the boat one way and the train back. See page 909 for specifics on traveling the Rhine.

◐ Self-Guided Tour

This easy tour (you can cut in anywhere) skips most of the syrupy myths filling normal Rhine guides. Follow along on a boat, train, bike, or car. By train, sit on the left (river) side going south from Koblenz; most of the castles listed are viewed from this side.

Castles of the Rhine

Many of the castles of the Rhine were "robber-baron" castles, put there by petty rulers (there were 300 independent little countries in medieval Germany) to levy tolls on passing river traffic. A robber baron would put his castle on, or even in, the river. Then, often with the help of chains and a tower on the opposite bank, he'd stop each ship and get his toll. There were 10 customs stops in the 60-mile stretch between Mainz and Koblenz alone.

Some castles were built to control and protect settlements, and others were the residences of kings. As times changed, so did the lifestyles of the rich and feudal. Many castles were abandoned for more comfortable mansions in the towns.

Most Rhine castles date from the 11th, 12th, and 13th centuries. When the pope successfully asserted his power over the German emperor in 1076, local princes ran wild over the rule of their emperor. The castles saw military action in the 1300s and 1400s, as emperors began reasserting their control over Germany's kingdoms.

The castles were also involved in the Reformation wars, in which Europe's Catholic and Protestant dynasties used a fragmented Germany as their battleground. The Thirty Years' War (1618-1648) devastated Germany. The outcome: Each ruler got the freedom to decide if his people would be Catholic or Protestant, and one-third of Germans died. (Production of Gummi Bears ceased entirely.)

The French—who feared a strong Germany and felt the Rhine was the logical border between them and Germany—destroyed most of the castles as a preventive measure (Louis XIV in the 1680s, the Revolutionary army in the 1790s, and Napoleon in 1806). Many were rebuilt in the Neo-Gothic style in the Romantic Age—the late 1800s—and today are enjoyed as restaurants, hotels, hostels, and museums.

We're tackling 36 miles (58 km) of the 820-mile-long (1,320-km) Rhine. This tour starts at **Koblenz** and heads upstream to **Bingen.** If you're going the other direction, it still works. Just hold the book upside-down. With limited time, cruise just the best stretch: from St. Goar to Bacharach.

This tour is synched with the large black-and-white kilometer markers you'll see along the riverbank. I erected these years ago to make this tour easier to follow. They tell the distance from the Rhine Falls, where the Rhine leaves Switzerland and becomes navigable. Today, river-barge pilots also use these markers to navigate.

🎧 Download my free Best of the Rhine audio tour—it works in either direction.

Little Bacharach's dock and boat ramp

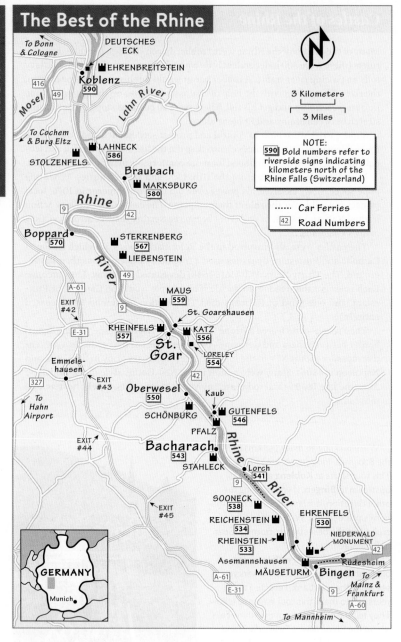

The Best of the Rhine

To Bonn & Cologne

DEUTSCHES ECK

EHRENBREITSTEIN

Koblenz **590**

Mosel

416 49

Lahn River

To Cochem & Burg Eltz

LAHNECK **586**

STOLZENFELS

Braubach

MARKSBURG **580**

Rhine

42

9

Boppard **570**

STERRENBERG **567**

LIEBENSTEIN

River

49

A-61

EXIT #42

E-31

9

MAUS **559**

St. Goarshausen

RHEINFELS **557**

KATZ **556**

St. Goar

LORELEY **554**

Emmels-hausen

EXIT #43

327

To Hahn Airport

Oberwesel **550**

Kaub

SCHÖNBURG

GUTENFELS **546**

PFALZ

42

EXIT #44

Bacharach **543**

STAHLECK

Lorch **541**

9

EXIT #45

SOONECK **538**

REICHENSTEIN **534**

EHRENFELS **530**

RHEINSTEIN **533**

NIEDERWALD MONUMENT

Assmannshausen

MÄUSETURM

Rüdesheim

Bingen

42

A-61

E-31

GERMANY

Munich

9

To Mainz & Frankfurt

A-60

To Mannheim

NOTE:
590 Bold numbers refer to riverside signs indicating kilometers north of the Rhine Falls (Switzerland)

.... Car Ferries
42 Road Numbers

3 Kilometers

3 Miles

From Koblenz to St. Goar

Km 590—Koblenz: This Rhine blitz starts with historic Rhine fanfare, at Koblenz. Koblenz isn't terribly attractive (after being hit hard in World War II), but its place at the historic Deutsches Eck ("German Corner")—the tip of land where the Mosel River joins the Rhine—gives it a certain patriotic charm. A cable car links the Deutsches Eck with the yellow Ehrenbreitstein Fortress across the river.

Km 586—Lahneck Castle: Above the modern autobahn bridge over the Lahn River, this castle (*Burg*) was built in 1240 to defend local silver mines. The castle was ruined by the French in 1688 and rebuilt in the 1850s in Neo-Gothic style.

Km 580—Marksburg Castle: This castle stands bold and white—restored to look like most Rhine castles once did, with their slate stonework covered with stucco to look as if made from a richer stone. You'll spot Marksburg with the three modern chimneys behind it, just before the town of Spay. This is the best-looking of all the Rhine castles and the only surviving medieval castle on the Rhine. Because of its commanding position, it was never attacked in the Middle Ages (though it was captured by the US Army in March of 1945). It's now open as a museum (see page 918 for details).

Km 570—Boppard: Once a Roman town, Boppard has some impressive remains of fourth-century walls. Look for the Roman towers and the substantial chunk of Roman wall near the train station, just above the main square.

If you visit Boppard, head to the fascinating Church of St. Severus below the main square. Find the carved Romanesque crazies at the doorway. Inside, to the right of the entrance, you'll see Christian symbols from Roman times. Also notice the painted arches and vaults (originally, most Romanesque churches were painted this way). Down by the river, look for the high-water (*Hochwasser*) marks on the arches from various flood years. (You'll find these flood marks throughout the Rhine Valley.)

Km 567—Sterrenberg Castle and Liebenstein Castle: These are known as the "Hostile Brothers" castles, across from Bad Salzig. Take the wall between the castles (actually designed to improve the defenses of both castles), add two greedy and jealous brothers and a fair maiden, and create your own legend. Burg Liebenstein is now a fun, friendly, and affordable family-run hotel (Db-€140-150, 9 rooms, suites and family rooms, easy parking, tel. 06773/308, www.castle-liebenstein.com, info@burg-liebenstein.de).

Km 559—Maus Castle: The Maus (mouse) got its name because the next castle was owned by the Katzenelnbogen family. (*Katz* means "cat.") In the 1300s, it was considered a state-of-the-art fortification...until 1806, when Napoleon had it blown up with then-state-of-the-art explosives. It was rebuilt true to its original plans in about 1900. Today, Burg Maus is open for concerts, weddings, and guided

Boppard

Maus Castle

tours in German (weekends only, reservations required, 20-minute walk up, tel. 06771/91011, www.burg-maus.de).

St. Goar to Bacharach: The Best of the Rhine

Km 557—St. Goar and Rheinfels Castle: The pleasant town of St. Goar was named for a sixth-century hometown monk. It originated in Celtic times as a place where sailors would stop, catch their breath, send home a postcard, and give thanks after surviving the seductive and treacherous Loreley crossing. St. Goar is worth a stop to explore its mighty Rheinfels Castle. (For more on St. Goar, see page 909; for a self-guided castle tour, see page 912.)

Km 556—Katz Castle: Burg Katz (Katzenelnbogen) faces St. Goar from across the river. Together, Burg Katz (built in 1371) and Rheinfels Castle had a clear view up and down the river, effectively controlling traffic (there was absolutely no duty-free shopping on the medieval Rhine). Katz got Napoleoned in 1806 and rebuilt in about 1900.

About Km 555: A statue of the Loreley, the beautiful-but-deadly nymph (see next listing for legend), combs her hair at the end of a long spit—built to give barges protection from vicious ice floes that until recent years raged down the river in the winter. The actual Loreley, a cliff (marked by the flags), is just ahead.

Km 554—The Loreley: Steep a big slate rock in centuries of legend and it becomes a tourist attraction—the ultimate Rhinestone. The Loreley (flags on top, name painted near shoreline), rising 450 feet over the narrowest and deepest point of the Rhine, has long been important. It was a holy site in pre-Roman days. The fine echoes here—thought to be ghostly voices—fertilized legend-tellers' imaginations.

Because of the reefs just upstream (at km 552), many ships never made it to St. Goar. Sailors (after days on the river) blamed their misfortune on a *wunderbares Fräulein*, whose long, blond hair almost covered her body. Heinrich Heine's *Song of Loreley* (the CliffsNotes version is on local postcards) tells the story of a count sending his men to kill or capture this siren after she distracted his horny son, who forgot to watch where he was sailing and drowned. When the soldiers cornered the nymph in her cave, she called her father (Father Rhine) for help. Huge waves, the likes of which you'll never see today, rose from the river and carried Loreley to safety. And she has never been seen since.

But alas, when the moon shines brightly and the tour buses are parked, a

The scenic rock cliffs of the Rhine

The Rhine River Trade

Watch the river barges along the Rhine. There's a constant parade of action, and each boat is different. The flag of the boat's home country flies in the stern (Dutch—horizontal red, white, and blue; Belgian—vertical black, yellow, and red; Swiss—white cross on a red field; German—horizontal black, red, and yellow; French—vertical red, white, and blue).

Barge workers have their own subculture. Many own their own ships. The captain lives in the stern, with his family. The family car is often parked on the stern. Workers live in the bow.

Logically, imports (Japanese cars, coal, and oil) go upstream, and exports (German cars, chemicals, and pharmaceuticals) go downstream. A clever captain manages to ship goods in each direction. Recently, giant Dutch container ships (which transport five times the cargo) have been driving many of the traditional barges out of business, presenting the German economy with another challenge.

Going downstream, tugs can push a floating train of up to five barges at once, but upstream, as the slope gets steeper (and the stream gradient gets higher), they can push only one at a time. Before modern shipping, horses dragged boats upstream (the faint remains of towpaths survive at points along the river). From 1873 to 1900, workers laid a chain from Bonn to Bingen, and boats with cogwheels and steam engines hoisted themselves upstream. Today, 265 million tons travel each year along the 530 miles from Basel on the German-Swiss border to the Dutch city of Rotterdam on the Atlantic.

Riverside navigational aids are vital. Boats pass on the right unless they clearly signal otherwise with a large blue sign. Since ships heading downstream can't stop or maneuver as freely, boats heading upstream are expected to do the tricky maneuvering. Cameras monitor traffic and relay warnings of oncoming ships by posting large triangular signals before narrow and troublesome bends in the river. There may be two or three triangles per signpost, depending upon how many "sectors," or segments, of the river are covered. The lowest triangle indicates the nearest stretch of river. Each triangle tells whether there's a ship in that sector. When the bottom side of a triangle is lit, that sector is empty. When the left side is lit, an oncoming ship is in that sector.

The **Signal and River Pilots Museum** (Wahrschauer- und Lotsenmuseum), located at the signal triangles at the upstream edge of St. Goar, explains how barges are safer, cleaner, and more fuel-efficient than trains or trucks (free, May-Sept, Wed and Sat 14:00-17:00, outdoor exhibits always open).

---

soft, playful Rhine whine can still be heard from the Loreley. As you pass, listen carefully ("Sailors...sailors...over my bounding mane").

Km 552—The Seven Maidens: Killer reefs, marked by red-and-green buoys, are called the "Seven Maidens." OK, one more goofy legend: The prince of Schön-

burg Castle (*über* Oberwesel—described next) had seven spoiled daughters who always dumped men because of their shortcomings. Fed up, he invited seven of his knights to the castle and demanded that his daughters each choose one to marry. But they complained that each man had too big a nose, was too fat, too stupid, and so on. The rude and teasing girls escaped into a riverboat. Just downstream, God turned them into the seven rocks that form this reef. While this story probably isn't entirely true, there was a lesson in it for medieval children: Don't be hard-hearted.

Km 550—Oberwesel: The town of Oberwesel, topped by the commanding Schönburg Castle (now a hotel), boasts some of the best medieval wall and tower remains on the Rhine.

Notice how many of the train tunnels along here have entrances designed like medieval turrets—they were actually built in the Romantic 19th century. OK, back to the riverside.

Km 546—Gutenfels Castle and Pfalz Castle, the Classic Rhine View: Burg Gutenfels (now a privately owned hotel) and the shipshape Pfalz Castle (built in the river in the 1300s) worked very effectively to tax medieval river traffic. The town of Kaub grew rich as Pfalz raised its chains when boats came, and lowered them only when the merchants had paid their duty. Those who didn't pay spent time touring its prison, on a raft at the bottom of its well. In 1504, a pope called for the destruction of Pfalz, but the locals withstood a six-week siege, and the castle still stands. Notice the overhanging outhouse (tiny white room between two wooden ones). Pfalz (also known as Pfalzgrafenstein) is tourable but bare and

dull, accessible by ferry from Kaub (€3 entry, April-Oct Tue-Sun 10:00-18:00, closed Mon; closes at 17:00 off-season including March, Nov and Jan-Feb Sat-Sun only, closed Dec, mobile 0172-262-2800, www.burg-pfalzgrafenstein.de).

In Kaub, on the riverfront directly below the castles, a green statue (near the waving flags) honors the German general Gebhard von Blücher. He was Napoleon's

Pfalz Castle (left) and Gutenfels Castle (on hillside)

Stahleck Castle

nemesis. In 1813, as Napoleon fought his way back to Paris after his disastrous Russian campaign, he stopped at Mainz—hoping to fend off the Germans and Russians pursuing him by controlling that strategic bridge. Blücher tricked Napoleon. By building the first major pontoon bridge of its kind here at the Pfalz Castle, he crossed the Rhine and outflanked the French. Two years later, Blücher and Wellington teamed up to defeat Napoleon once and for all at Waterloo.

Immediately opposite Kaub (where the ferry lands, marked by blue roadside flags) is a gaping hole in the mountainside. This marks the last working slate mine on the Rhine.

Km 544—"The Raft Busters": Just before Bacharach, at the top of the island, buoys mark a gang of rocks notorious for busting up rafts. The Black Forest, upstream from here, was once poor, and wood was its best export. Black Foresters would ride log booms down the Rhine to the Ruhr (where their timber fortified coal-mine shafts) or to Holland (where logs were sold to shipbuilders). If they could navigate the sweeping bend just before Bacharach and then survive these "raft busters," they'd come home reckless and horny—the German folkloric equivalent of American cowboys after payday.

Km 543—Bacharach and Stahleck Castle: The town of Bacharach is a great stop (described on page 900). Some of the Rhine's best wine is from this town, whose name likely derives from "altar to Bacchus." Local vintners brag that the medieval Pope Pius II ordered Bacharach wine by the cartload. Perched above the town, the 13th-century Burg Stahleck is now a hostel.

From Bacharach to Bingen

Km 541—Lorch: This stub of a castle is barely visible from the road. Check out the hillside vineyards. Rhine wine is particularly good because the local slate absorbs the heat of the sun and stays warm all night, resulting in sweeter grapes. Wine from the steep side of the Rhine gorge—where grapes are harder to grow and harvest—is tastier and more expensive. Vineyards once blanketed four times as much of the valley as they do today, but modern economics have driven most of them out of business. The vineyards that do survive require government subsidies.

Notice the small car ferry, one of several along the bridgeless stretch between Mainz and Koblenz.

Km 538—Sooneck Castle: Built in the 11th century, this castle was twice destroyed by people sick and tired of robber barons.

Km 534—Reichenstein Castle and **Km 533—Rheinstein Castle:** Both are privately owned, tourable, and connected by a pleasant trail.

Km 530—Ehrenfels Castle: Opposite Bingerbrück and the Bingen station, you'll see the ghostly Ehrenfels Castle, which was clobbered by the Swedes in 1636 and by the French in 1689. Since it had no view of the river traffic to the north, the owner built the cute little *Mäuseturm* (mouse

Sooneck Castle

tower) on an island (the yellow tower you'll see near the train station today). Rebuilt in the 1800s in Neo-Gothic style, it's now used as a Rhine navigation signal station.

Km 528—Niederwald Monument: Across from the Bingen station on a hilltop is the 120-foot-high Niederwald monument, a memorial built with 32 tons of bronze in 1877 to commemorate "the re-establishment of the German Empire." A lift takes tourists to this statue from the famous and extremely touristy wine town of Rüdesheim.

From here, the romantic Rhine becomes the industrial Rhine, and our tour is over.

Getting Around the Rhine

The Rhine flows from Switzerland north to the Netherlands, but the scenic stretch from Mainz to Koblenz hoards all the touristic charm. Studded with the crenellated cream of Germany's castles, it bustles with boats, trains, and highway traffic. Have fun exploring with a mix of big steamers, tiny ferries (*Fähre*), trains, and bikes.

By Boat

While you can do the whole Mainz-Koblenz trip by boat (5.5 hours downstream, 8.5 hours up), I'd focus on the most scenic hour—from St. Goar to Bacharach. Sit on the boat's top deck with your handy Rhine map-guide (or the

kilometer-keyed tour in this chapter) and enjoy the parade of castles, towns, boats, and vineyards.

Two boat companies take travelers along this stretch of the Rhine. Boats run daily in both directions from early April through October, with only one boat running off-season.

Most travelers sail on the bigger, more expensive, and romantic **Köln-Düsseldorfer (K-D) Line** (recommended Bacharach-St. Goar trip: €12.80 one-way, €15.40 round-trip, bikes-€2.80/day, €2 extra if paying with credit card; discounts: up to 30 percent if over 60, 20 percent if you present a connecting train ticket or rail pass; tel. 06741/1634 in St. Goar, tel. 06743/1322 in Bacharach, www.k-d.com).

Complete, up-to-date schedules are posted at any Rhineland station, hotel, TI, and www.k-d.com. Confirm times at your hotel the night before. Purchase tickets at the dock up to five minutes before departure. The boat is never full. Romantics will enjoy the old-time paddle-wheeler *Goethe,* which sails each direction once a day (noted on schedule, confirm time locally).

The smaller **Bingen-Rüdesheimer Line** is slightly cheaper than the K-D, doesn't offer any rail pass deals, and makes three trips in each direction daily from early April through October (buy tickets at ticket booth or on boat, ticket booth only open just before boat departs, 30 percent discount if over 60; departs Bacharach at 10:10, 12:00, and 15:00; departs St. Goar at 11:00, 14:10, and 16:10; tel. 06721/14140, www.bingen-ruedesheimer.de).

By Car

Drivers have these options: 1) skip the boat; 2) take a round-trip cruise from St. Goar or Bacharach; 3) draw pretzels and let the loser drive, prepare the picnic, and meet the boat; 4) rent a bike, bring it on the boat, and bike back; or 5) take the boat one-way and return to your car by

Ehrenfels Castle, with its little "mouse tower" on the river

K-D Line Rhine Cruise Schedule

Boats run from early April through October (usually 5/day, but 3-4/day in early April and most of Oct). From November through March, one boat runs daily for groups, but you can tag along if they know you're coming—call the boat directly (tel. 0172/1360-335) or the main office in Cologne (tel. 0221/2088-318) to confirm. Check www.k-d.com for the latest complete schedule; only a few stops are shown below.

Koblenz	Boppard	St. Goar	Bacharach
—	9:00	10:20	11:30
9:00*	11:00*	12:20*	13:30*
—	13:00	14:20	15:30
—	14:00	15:20	16:30
14:00	16:00	17:20	18:30
13:10	11:50	10:55	10:15
—	12:50	11:55	11:15
—	13:50	12:55	12:15
18:10	16:50	15:55	15:15
20:10*	18:50*	17:55*	17:15*

These sailings are on the 1913 paddle-wheeler Goethe.

train. When exploring by car, don't hesitate to pop onto one of the many little ferries that shuttle across the river.

By Ferry (Across the Rhine)

As there are no bridges between Koblenz and Mainz, you'll see car-and-passenger ferries (usually family-run for generations) about every three miles. Some of the most useful routes are Bingen-Rüdesheim, Lorch-Niederheimbach, Engelsburg-Kaub, and St. Goar-St. Goarshausen (times vary; St. Goar-St. Goarshausen ferry departs each side every 15-20 minutes daily until 24:00, less frequently on Sun; one-way fares: adult-€1.70, car and driver-€4, pay on boat; www.faehre-loreley.de). For a fun little jaunt, take a quick round-trip (by car or bike) with some time to explore the other side.

By Bike

You can bike on either side of the Rhine, but for a designated bike path, stay on the west side, where a 35-mile path runs between Koblenz and Bingen. The six-mile stretch between St. Goar and Bacharach is smooth and scenic, but it's mostly along the highway. The bit from Bacharach south to Bingen hugs the riverside and is car-free. Either way, biking is a great way to explore the valley (though headwinds can slow you down). Many hotels provide free or cheap bikes to guests; some also rent to the public (including Hotel Hillen in Bacharach and Hotel an der Fähre in St. Goar).

Consider biking one-way and taking the bike back on the riverboat, or designing a circular trip using the fun and frequent shuttle ferries. A good target might be Kaub (where a tiny boat shuttles sightseers to the better-from-a-distance castle on the island).

By Train

Hourly milk-run trains hit every town along the Rhine (Bacharach-St. Goar in both directions about :20 after the hour, 10 minutes; Mainz-Bacharach, 40 minutes; Mainz-Koblenz, 1 hour). Tiny stations are not staffed—buy tickets at machines. Though generally user-friendly, the ticket machines are not all created equal. Some claim to only take exact change; others may not accept US credit cards. When buying a ticket, select "English" and follow the instructions carefully. For example, the ticket machine may give you the choice of validating your ticket for that day or a day in the near future—but only for some destinations (when you're not given this option, your ticket will automatically be validated for the day of purchase).

The **Rheinland-Pfalz-Ticket** day pass covers travel on milk-run trains to many destinations in this chapter, including Koblenz. It can save heaps of money, particularly on longer day trips or if there's more than one in your party (1 person-€24, up to 4 additional people-€4/ each, buy from station ticket-machines, good after 9:00 Mon-Fri and all day Sat-Sun, valid on trains labeled *RB*, *RE*, and *MRB*). For a day trip from Bacharach to Burg Eltz (normally €32 round-trip), even one person saves with a Rheinland-Pfalz-Ticket, and a group of five adults saves €120—look for travel partners at breakfast.

BACHARACH

Once prosperous from the wine and wood trade, charming Bacharach (BAHKH-ah-rahkh, with a guttural *kh* sound) is now just a pleasant half-timbered village of 2,000 people working hard to keep its tourists happy. Businesses that have been "in the family" for eons are dealing with succession challenges, as the allure of big-city jobs and a more cosmopolitan life lure away the town's younger generation. But Bacharach retains its time-capsule quaintness.

Orientation

Bacharach cuddles, long and narrow, along the Rhine. The village is easily strollable—you can walk from one end of town to the other along its main drag, Oberstrasse, in about 10 minutes. Bacha-

Riesling wine grapes blanket the Rhine's hillsides.

rach widens at its stream, where more houses trickle up its small valley (along Blücherstrasse) away from the Rhine. The hillsides above town are occupied by vineyards, scant remains of the former town walls, and a castle-turned-youth hostel.

Tourist Information: The TI, on the main street a block-and-a-half from the train station, will store bags for day-trippers (April-Oct Mon-Fri 9:00-17:00, Sat-Sun 10:00-15:00; Nov-March Mon-Fri 9:00-13:00, closed Sat-Sun; from train station, exit right and walk down main street with castle high on your left, TI will be on your right at Oberstrasse 10; tel. 06743/919-303, www.bacharach.de or www.rhein-nahe-touristik.de). They also book 1.5-hour tours in English (€70/group).

Bike Rental: While many hotels loan bikes to guests, the only real bike-rental business in the town center is run by Erich at **Hotel Hillen** (€12/day, daily 9:00-19:00, Langstrasse 18, tel. 06743/1287).

Parking: It's simple to park along the highway next to the train tracks or, better, in the big inexpensive lot by the boat dock (pay with coins at *Parkscheinautomat* and put ticket on dashboard, free overnight).

Private Guides: Thomas Gundlach happily gives 1.5-hour town walks to individuals or small groups for €35 (as well as 4- to 10-hour hiking tours for the more ambitious). He can also drive up to three people around the region in his car (€80/6 hours, mobile 0179-353-6004, thomas_gundlach@gmx.de). **Birgit Wessels** is also good (€45/1.5-hour walk, tel. 06743/937-514, wessels.birgit@t-online.de).

❷ Bacharach Town Walk

• *Start at the Köln-Düsseldorfer ferry dock (next to a fine picnic park).*

Riverfront: View the town from the parking lot—a modern landfill. The Rhine used to lap against Bacharach's town wall, just over the present-day highway. Every few years, the river floods, covering the highway with several feet of water. Flat land like this is rare in the Rhine Valley, where towns are often shaped like the letter "T," stretching thin along the riverfront and up a crease in the hills beyond.

Reefs farther upstream forced boats to

Classic and quaint Bacharach

unload upriver and reload here. Consequently, in the Middle Ages, Bacharach was the biggest wine-trading town on the Rhine. A riverfront crane hoisted huge kegs of prestigious "Bacharach" wine (which, in practice, was from anywhere in the region). Today, the economy is based on tourism.

Look above town. The **castle** on the hill is now a youth hostel. Two of the town's original 16 towers are visible from here (up to 5 if you look really hard). The bluff on the right, with the yellow flag, is the **Heinrich Heine Viewpoint** (the end-point of a popular hike). Old-timers remember when, rather than the flag marking the town as a World Heritage site, a swastika sculpture 30 feet wide and tall stood there. Realizing that it could be an enticing target for Allied planes in the last months of the war, locals tore it down even before Hitler fell.

Nearby, a stele in the park describes the Bingen to Koblenz stretch of the Rhine gorge.

• *Before entering the town, walk upstream through the...*

Riverside Park: New elements of the park are designed to bring people to the riverside and combat flooding. The park was originally laid out in 1910 in the English style: Notice how the trees were planted to frame fine town views, highlighting the most picturesque bits of architecture. The dark, sad-looking monument—its "eternal" flame long snuffed out—is a **war memorial.** The German psyche is permanently scarred by war memories. Today, many Germans would rather avoid monuments like this, which revisit the dark periods before Germany became a nation of pacifists. Take a close look at the monument. Each panel honors sons of Bacharach who died for the Kaiser: in 1864 against Denmark, in 1866 against Austria, in 1870 against France, in 1914 during World War I. The military Maltese cross—flanked by classic German helmets—has a "W" at its center, for Kaiser

Wilhelm. Review the family names on the opposite side of the monument: You may later recognize them on today's restaurants and hotels.

• *Look (but don't go now) upstream from here to see the...*

Trailer Park and Campground: In Germany, trailer vacationers and campers are two distinct subcultures. Folks who travel in motorhomes, like many retirees in the US, are a nomadic bunch, cruising around the countryside and paying a few euros a night to park. Campers, on the other hand, tend to set up camp in one place—complete with comfortable lounge chairs and TVs—and stay put for weeks, even months. They often come back to the same spot year after year, treating it like their own private estate. These camping devotees have made a science out of relaxing. Tourists are welcome to pop in for a drink or meal at the Sonnenstrand campground's terrace café (daily 13:00-21:00; it's a 10-minute walk).

High-water marks indicate the heights reached by floodwaters.

• Continue to where the park meets the play-ground, and then cross the highway to the fortified riverside wall of the Catholic church, decorated with...

High-Water Marks: These recall various floods. Before the 1910 reclamation project, the river extended out to here, and boats would use the rings in this wall to tie up.

• From the church, go under the 1858 train tracks (and past more high-water marks) and hook right past the yellow floodwater yardstick and up the stairs onto the town wall. Atop the wall, turn left and walk under the long arcade. After 30 yards, on your left, notice a...

Well: Rebuilt as it appeared in the 17th century, this is one of seven such wells that brought water to the towns-folk until 1900. Each neighborhood's well also provided a social gathering place and the communal laundry. Walk 50 yards past the well along the wall to an alcove in the medieval tower with a view of the

A facsimile of a 17th-century well

war memorial in the park. You're under the crane tower *(Kranenturm)*. After barrels of wine were moved overland from Bingen past dangerous stretches of river, the precious cargo could be lowered by cranes from here into ships to continue more safely down the river. The Rhine has long been a major shipping route through Germany. In modern times, it's a bottleneck in Germany's train system. The train company gives hotels and residents along the tracks money for soundproof windows (hotels along here routinely have quadruple-pane windows...and earplugs on the nightstand).

• Continue walking along the town wall. Pass the recommended Rhein Hotel just before the...

Markt Tower: This marks one of the town's 15 original 14th-century gates and is a reminder that in that century there was a big wine market here.

• Descend the stairs, pass another well, and follow Marktstrasse away from the river toward the town center, the two-tone church, and the town's...

Main Intersection: From here, Bacha-rach's main street (Oberstrasse) goes right to the half-timbered red-and-white Altes Haus (which we'll visit later) and left 400 yards to the train station. Spin around to enjoy the higgledy-piggledy building styles. The town has a case of the doldrums: The younger generation is moving to the big cities and many long-established family businesses have no one to take over for their aging owners. Bacha-rach's only pub recently closed. In the winter the town is particularly dead.

• To the left (south) of the church, a golden horn hangs over the old...

Posthof: Throughout Europe, the postal horn is the symbol of the postal service. In olden days, when the postman blew this, traffic stopped and the mail sped through. This post station dates from 1724, when stagecoaches ran from Cologne to Frankfurt and would change horses here, Pony Express-style. As you enter, notice the cornerstones at the Posthof entrance, protecting the venerable building from reckless carriage wheels. Inside the old oak doors (on the left) is the actual door to the post office that served Bacharach for 200 years. Find the mark on the wall labeled *Rheinhöhe 3/1-4/2 1850*. This recalls a historic flood caused by an ice jam at the Loreley just downstream. Notice also the fascist eagle in the alcove on the right (from 1936; a swastika once filled its center).

Step into the courtyard—once a carriage house and inn that accommodated Bacharach's first VIP visitors, and now home to the recommended Posthof Bacharach restaurant, with a fine view of the church and a ruined chapel above.

Two hundred years ago, Bacharach's main drag was the only road along the Rhine. Napoleon widened it to fit his cannon wagons. The steps alongside the church lead to the castle.

• *Return to the church, passing the recommended Italian ice-cream café (Eis Café Italia), where friendly Mimo serves his special invention: Riesling wine-flavored gelato.*

Protestant Church: Inside the church (daily May-Sept 10:00-18:00, April and Oct until 17:00, closed Nov-March, English info on a stand near door), you'll find Grotesque capitals, brightly painted in medieval style, and a mix of round Romanesque and pointed Gothic arches. The church was fancier before the Reformation wars, when it (and the region) was Catholic. Bacharach lies on the religious border of Germany and, like the country as a whole, is split between Catholics and Protestants. To the left of the altar, some medieval (pre-Reformation) frescoes survive where an older Romanesque arch was cut by a pointed Gothic one.

If you're considering bombing the town, take note: A blue-and-white plaque just outside the church's door warns that, according to the Hague Convention, this historic building shouldn't be targeted in times of war.

• *Continue down Oberstrasse to the...*

Altes Haus: Dating from 1368, this is the oldest house in town. Notice the 14th-century building style—the first floor is made of stone, while upper floors are half-timbered (in the ornate style common in the Rhine Valley). Some of its windows still look medieval, with small, flattened circles as panes (small because that's all that the glass-blowing technology of the time would allow), pieced together with molten lead (like medieval stained glass in churches). Frau Weber welcomes visitors to enjoy the fascinating ground floor of the recommended Altes Haus restaurant, with its evocative old photos and etchings (consider eating here later).

• *Keep going down Oberstrasse to the...*

Old Mint (Münze): The old mint is marked by a crude coin in its sign. As a practicality, any great trading town needed coinage, and since 1356, Bacharach minted theirs here. Across from the mint, the recommended **Bastian** family's wine garden is a lively place after dark. Above you in the vineyards stands a lonely white-and-red tower—your final destination.

• *At the next street, look right and see the mint tower, painted in the medieval style, and then turn left. Wander 30 yards up Rosenstrasse to the well. Notice the sundial and the wall painting of 1632 Bacharach with its walls intact. Study the fine slate roof over the well: The town's roof tiles were quarried and split right here in the Rhineland.*

Continue another 30 yards up Rosenstrasse to find the tiny-stepped lane behind the well up into the vineyard and to the...

Tall Tower: The slate steps lead to a small path through the vineyard that deposits you at a viewpoint atop the stubby remains of the medieval wall and a tower. The town's towers jutted out from the wall and had only three sides, with the "open" side facing the town. Towers were covered with stucco to make them look more impressive, as if they were made of a finer white stone. If this tower's open, hike up to climb the stairs for the best view. (The top floor has been closed to give nesting falcons some privacy.)

Romantic Rhine View: A grand medieval town spreads before you. For 300 years (1300-1600), Bacharach was big (population 4,000), rich, and politically powerful.

From this perch, you can see the chapel ruins and six surviving **city towers.** Visually trace the wall to the castle. The castle was actually the capital of Germany for a couple of years in the 1200s. When Holy Roman Emperor Frederick Barbarossa went away to fight the Crusades, he left his brother (who lived here) in charge of his vast realm. Bacharach was home to one of the seven electors who voted for the Holy Roman Emperor in 1275. To protect their own power, these prince electors did their best to choose the weakest guy on the ballot. The elector from Bacharach helped select a two-bit prince named Rudolf von Habsburg (from a no-name castle in Switzerland). However, the underestimated Rudolf brutally silenced the robber barons along the Rhine and established the mightiest dynasty in European history. His family line, the Habsburgs, ruled much of Central and Eastern Europe from Vienna until 1918.

Plagues, fires, and the Thirty Years' War (1618-1648) finally did in Bacharach. The town has slumbered for several centuries. Today, the castle houses commoners—40,000 overnights annually by youth hostelers.

In the mid-19th century, painters such as J. M. W. Turner and writers such as Victor Hugo were charmed by the

Altes Haus is the oldest dwelling (1368) in Bacharach.

Rhineland's romantic mix of past glory, present poverty, and rich legend. They put this part of the Rhine on the old Grand Tour map as the "Romantic Rhine." Victor Hugo pondered the ruined 15th-century chapel that you see under the castle. In his 1842 travel book, *Excursions Along the Banks of the Rhine,* he wrote, "No doors, no roof or windows, a magnificent skeleton puts its silhouette against the sky. Above it, the ivy-covered castle ruins provide a fitting crown. This is Bacharach, land of fairy tales, covered with legends and sagas." If you're enjoying the Romantic Rhine, thank Victor Hugo and company.

• Our walk is done. To get back into town, just retrace your steps. Or, to extend this walk, take the level path away from the river that leads along the once-mighty wall up the valley to the next tower, the...

Wood Market Tower: Timber was gathered here in Bacharach and lashed together into vast log booms known as "Holland rafts" (as big as a soccer field) that were floated downstream. Two weeks later the lumber would reach Amsterdam, where it was in high demand as foundation posts for buildings and for the great Dutch shipbuilders. Notice the four stones above the arch on the uphill side of the tower—these guided the gate as it was hoisted up and down.

• From here, cross the street and go downhill into the parking lot. Pass the recommended Pension im Malerwinkel on your right, being careful not to damage the old arch with your head. Follow the creek past a delightful little series of half-timbered homes and cheery gardens known as "Painters' Corner" (Malerwinkel). Resist looking into some pervert's peep show (on the right) and continue downhill back to the village center.

Experiences
Wine Tasting
Bacharach is proud of its wine. Two places in town offer an inexpensive tasting alongside light plates of food.

Bastian's Weingut zum Grüner Baum is rowdy and rustic. Groups of 2-6 people pay €22.50 for a wine carousel of 15 glasses—14 different white wines and 1 lonely red—and a basket of bread. Spin the lazy Susan, share a common cup, and discuss the taste. The Bastian family insists: "After each wine, you must talk to each other." Along with their characteristic interior, they have two nice terraces (daily 12:00-22:00, closed in winter, just past Altes Haus, tel. 06743/1208).

Weingut Karl Heidrich is a fun wine shop and *Stube* in the town center, where Markus and daughters Magdalena and Katharina share their family's centuries-old wine tradition. They offer a variety of carousels with six wines, English descriptions, and bread (€12)—ideal for the more sophisticated wine taster—plus light meals and a €10.50 meat-and-cheese plate (Thu-Tue 11:00-22:00, closed Wed and Nov-mid-April, will ship to US, Oberstrasse 16, tel. 06743/93060).

Rick's Tip: *Bacharach goes to bed early, so if you're looking for* **nightlife,** *head to one of the* **wine-tasting places** *or* **Restaurant Zeus,** *which has long hours and outdoor seating that adds a spark to the town center after dark (daily 17:30-24:00, Koblenzer Strasse 11, tel. 06743/909-7171). The hilltop youth hostel,* **Jugendherberge Stahleck,** *serves cheap wine with priceless views until late in summer.*

Shopping
The **Jost** German gift store, across the main square from the church, carries most everything a souvenir shopper could want—from beer steins to cuckoo clocks—and can ship purchases to the US (March-Oct Mon-Fri 9:00-18:00, Sat-Sun 10:00-18:00, shorter hours in winter, closed Jan-Feb; Blücherstrasse 4, tel. 06743/909-7214). They offer discounts to my readers with a €10 minimum purchase: 10 percent with cash, 5 percent with credit card.

Eating

Restaurants

Bacharach has no shortage of reasonably priced, atmospheric restaurants offering fine indoor and outdoor dining.

The Rhein Hotel's **Stüber Restaurant** is Bacharach's best top-end choice. Andreas Stüber, his family's sixth-generation chef, creates regional plates prepared with a slow-food ethic. The menu changes with the season and is served at river- and track-side seating or indoors with a spacious wood-and-white-tablecloth elegance. Their Posten Riesling is well worth the splurge (€18-25 main courses, €35 fixed-price meals, always good vegetarian and vegan options, daily 17:00-21:15 plus Sat-Sun 11:30-14:15, closed mid-Dec-Feb, call to reserve on weekends or for an outdoor table, facing the K-D boat dock below town center, Langstrasse 50, tel. 06743/1243).

Altes Haus serves classic German dishes within Bacharach's most romantic atmosphere—inside the oldest building in town. Find the cozy little dining room with photos of the opera singer who sang about Bacharach, adding to its fame (€10-20 main courses, Thu-Tue 12:00-15:00 & 18:00-21:30, longer hours on weekends, closed Wed and Dec-Easter, dead center by the Protestant church, tel. 06743/1209).

Casual Options

The **Posthof Bacharach** restaurant and café has nice outdoor seating and a medieval feel, with a view of the ruined chapel above (€8-12 main courses, daily Easter-Oct 12:00-21:00, closed Nov-Easter, Oberstrasse 45-49, tel. 06743/947-1830).

Kleines Brauhaus Rheinterrasse is a funky, family-friendly microbrewery serving meals, fresh-baked bread, and homemade beer under a 1958 circus carousel that overlooks the town and river (Tue-Sun 13:00-22:00, closed Mon, at the downstream end of town, Koblenzer Strasse 14, tel. 06743/919-179).

Bacharacher Pizza and Kebap Haus, on the main drag in the town center, is the town favorite for €4-6 Döner Kebabs, cheap pizzas, and salads (daily 10:00-22:00, Oberstrasse 43, tel. 06743/3127).

Eis Café Italia, on the main street, is known for its refreshing, Riesling-flavored gelato (daily April-mid-Oct 13:00-19:00, closed mid-Oct-March, Oberstrasse 48).

Pick up **picnic supplies** at **Nahkauf,** a basic grocery store (Mon-Fri 8:00-12:00 & 14:00-18:00, Sat 8:30-12:30, closed Sun, Koblenzer Strasse 2). For a gourmet picnic, call the **Rhein Hotel** to reserve a "picnic bag" complete with wine, cheese, small dishes, and a hiking map (€13/person, arrange a day in advance, tel. 06743/1243).

Sleeping

None of the hotels listed here have elevators. The only listings with parking are Pension im Malerwinkel, Pension Winzerhaus, and the youth hostel. At the others, drive in to unload your bags and then park in the public lot. If you'll arrive after 20:00, let your hotel know in advance (none have 24-hour reception desks).

$$$ Rhein Hotel, overlooking the river with 14 spacious and comfortable rooms, is classy, well-run, and decorated with modern flair. Since it's right on the train tracks, its river- and train-side rooms come with quadruple-paned windows and air-conditioning (Db-€96, family rooms, cheaper for longer stays and off-season, free loaner bikes, directly inland from the K-D boat dock at Langstrasse 50, tel. 06743/1243, www.rhein-hotel-bacharach. de, info@rhein-hotel-bacharach.de). Their Stüber Restaurant is considered the best in town.

$$ Hotel zur Post, clean and quiet, is conveniently located right in the town center with no train noise. Its 12 rooms are a good value, offering more solid comfort than old-fashioned character (Db-€71-76, family rooms, Oberstrasse 38, tel. 06743/1277, www.hotel-zur-post-bacharach.de, h.zurpost@t-online.de).

Sleep Code

Price Rankings for Double Rooms (Db)

$$$ Most rooms €90 or more
$$ €60-90
$ €60 or less

Abbreviations: Db=Double with bathroom. D=Double with bathroom down the hall.

Notes: Room prices change; verify rates online or by email. For the best prices, book direct with the hotel.

$$ Hotel Kranenturm, offering castle ambience without the climb, combines hotel comfort with delightful *Privatzimmer* funkiness right downtown. This 16-room hotel is part of the medieval town wall. The rooms in the tower have the best views. While just 15 feet from the train tracks, a combination of medieval sturdiness, triple-paned windows, and included earplugs makes the riverside rooms sleepable (Db-€70, Db in tower room with views-€82, family rooms, cheaper for 3-night stay, cash preferred, €2 extra with credit card, showers can be temperamental, good breakfast, Langstrasse 30, tel. 06743/1308, www.kranenturm.com, hotel-kranenturm@t-online.de).

$$ Pension im Malerwinkel sits like a grand gingerbread house that straddles the town wall in a quiet little neighborhood. The quiet place has 20 rooms, a picturesque garden, views of the vineyards, and easy parking—all a short stroll from the town center (Db-€69, cheaper for 2- to 3-day stays, family rooms, cash only, no train noise, bike rental-€6/day, parking; from Oberstrasse, turn left at the church, walkers can follow the path to the left just before the town gate but drivers must pass through the gate to find the hotel parking lot, Blücherstrasse 41;

tel. 06743/1239, www.im-malerwinkel.de, pension@im-malerwinkel.de).

$ Hotel Hillen, a block south of Hotel Kranenturm, has the train noise and the same ultra-thick windows. It offers five spacious rooms and good hospitality (D with shower-€50, Db-€60, family rooms, 10 percent discount for stays of 2 nights or longer, cash only, closed mid-Nov-Easter, Langstrasse 18, tel. 06743/1287, hotel-hillen@web.de).

$ Pension Winzerhaus has 10 rooms just outside the town walls, directly under the vineyards. The rooms are simple, clean, and modern, and parking is a breeze (Db-€55, family rooms, prices do not include €0.50/person per day tourist tax, cash only, laundry service for fee, free loaner bikes for guests, Blücherstrasse 60, tel. 06743/1294, www.pension-winzerhaus.de, winzerhaus@gmx.de).

$ Irmgard Orth B&B rents three bright rooms, two of which share a bathroom on the hall. Charming Irmgard speaks almost no English, but is exuberant and serves homemade honey with breakfast (D-€40, Db-€42, cash only, Spurgasse 2, tel. 06743/1553—speak slowly, orth.irmgard@gmail.com).

$ Jugendherberge Stahleck hostel is in the 12th-century castle on the hilltop—350 steps above Bacharach—with a royal Rhine view. Open to travelers of any age, this is a gem with 168 beds and a private modern shower and WC in most rooms. The hostel offers hearty all-you-can-eat buffet dinners (18:00-19:30 nightly), and in summer, its pub serves cheap local wine and snacks all day until late. From the train station, it's a €10 taxi ride to the hostel—call 06743/1653 (dorm beds-€21.50, Db-€54, nonmembers pay extra, includes breakfast and sheets, laundry-€6; reception open 7:30-20:00, call if arriving later and check in at bar until 21:30; curfew at 22:00, tel. 06743/1266, www.diejugendherbergen.de, bacharach@diejugendherbergen.de). If driving, don't go in the driveway; park on the street and walk 200 yards.

Transportation
Arriving and Departing
BY TRAIN

Milk-run trains stop at Rhine towns each hour starting as early as 6:00, connecting at Mainz and Koblenz to trains farther afield. Trains between St. Goar and Bacharach depart at about :20 after the hour in each direction (€3.60, buy tickets from the machine in the unstaffed stations, carry cash since some machines won't accept US credit cards).

The durations listed below are calculated from Bacharach; for St. Goar, the difference is only 10 minutes. From Bacharach (or St. Goar), to go anywhere distant, you'll need to change trains in Koblenz for points north, or in Mainz for points south. Milk-run connections to these towns depart hourly, at about :20 past the hour for northbound trains, and at about :30 past the hour for southbound trains. Train info: toll tel. 0180-699-6633, www.bahn.com.

From Bacharach by Train to: St. Goar (hourly, 10 minutes), **Moselkern** near Burg Eltz (hourly, 1.5 hours, change in Koblenz), **Cologne** (hourly, 1.5-2 hours with change in Koblenz, 2.5 hours direct), **Frankfurt Airport** (hourly, 1 hour, change in Mainz or Bingen), **Frankfurt** (hourly, 1.5 hours, change in Mainz or Bingen), **Rothenburg ob der Tauber** (every 2 hours, 4.5 hours, 3-4 changes), **Munich** (hourly, 5 hours, 2 changes), **Berlin** (hourly, 7 hours, 1-3 changes).

BY CAR

Bacharach and St. Goar are near Frankfurt and its airport, just an hour's drive away. Some travelers find that the Rhine Valley, with its small towns, makes a pleasant first (or last) stop in Germany.

If you're following my two-week itinerary, and you're driving north from Rothenburg to Bacharach, allow 3 hours, or figure on a 3.5-hour drive if you route your trip through Creglingen and Weikersheim (to visit Romantic Road sights mentioned on page 219). When leaving the Rhine, you could drive to Cologne or Frankfurt, drop off the car, and take the train to Berlin (or elsewhere).

ST. GOAR

St. Goar (sahnkt gwahr) is a classic Rhine tourist town. Its hulk of a castle overlooks a half-timbered shopping street and leafy riverside park, busy with sightseeing ships and contented strollers. Rheinfels Castle, once the mightiest on the river, is the single best Rhineland ruin to explore. While the town of St. Goar itself is less interesting than Bacharach, be sure to explore beyond the shops: Thoughtful little placards (in English) offer facts about each street, lane, and square. St. Goar also makes a good base for hiking or biking the region. A tiny car ferry will shuttle you back and forth across the busy Rhine from here.

Orientation

St. Goar is dominated by its mighty castle, Rheinfels. The village—basically a wide spot in the road at the foot of Rheinfels' hill—isn't much more than a few hotels and restaurants. From the riverboat docks, the main drag—a dull pedestrian mall without history—cuts through town before ending at the road up to the castle.

Tourist Information: The helpful TI, which books rooms and stores bags for free, is on the pedestrian street, three blocks from the K-D boat dock and train station (May-Sept Mon-Fri 9:00-18:00, Sat 10:00-13:00, closed Sun; shorter hours and closed Sat-Sun in off-season; from train station, go downhill around church and turn left, Heerstrasse 86, tel. 06741/383, www.st-goar.de).

Bike Rental: Hotel an der Fähre rents bikes for a fair price, but you need to call ahead to reserve (€10/day, pickup after 10:00, Heerstrasse 47, tel. 06741/980-577).

Parking: A free lot is at the downstream (north) end of town, by the harbor. For on-street parking by the K-D boat dock and recommended hotels, get a ticket from the machine (*Parkscheinautomat*) and put it on the dashboard (€4/day, daily 9:00-18:00, coins only, free overnight). Make sure you press the button for a day ticket.

Sights

▲▲▲RHEINFELS CASTLE (BURG RHEINFELS)

Sitting like a dead pit bull above St. Goar, this once mightiest of Rhine castles rumbles with ghosts from its hard-fought past. This hollow but interesting shell offers your single best hands-on ruined-castle experience on the river. As impressive and evocative as it is, it's but a shadow of its former self.

Cost and Hours: €5, family card–€10, mid-March-Oct daily 9:00-18:00, Nov-mid-March possibly Sat-Sun only 11:00-17:00 (call ahead), last entry one hour before closing—weather permitting.

Information: The free castle map is helpful, but the €0.50 English booklet is of no real value, except to real history buffs. If it's damp, be careful of slippery stones. Tel. 06741/7753; in winter, tel. 06741/383, www.st-goar.de.

Services: A handy WC is immediately across from the ticket booth (check out the guillotine urinals—stand back when you pull to flush).

Rick's Tip: *To explore **the castle tunnels at Rheinfels, bring a flashlight**—or buy one at the ticket office. For real medieval atmosphere, they also sell candles with matches.*

Getting to the Castle: A **taxi** up from town costs €5 (tel. 06741/7011). Or take the kitschy "tschu-tschu" **tourist train** (€3 one-way, €4 round-trip, 8 minutes to the top, hours vary but generally April-Oct daily 9:30-16:30, departs from town at :15 and :45, from castle at :00 and :30, some narration, mobile 0171-445-1525). The train usually waits between the train station and the K-D dock, or at the Catholic Church just past the top end of the pedestrian street. **Parking** at the castle costs €1/hour (cash only).

To **hike** up to the castle, you can simply follow the main road up through the railroad underpass at the top end of the pedestrian street. But it's more fun to take the nature trail: Start at the St. Goar train station. Take the underpass under the tracks at the north end of the station, climb the steep stairs uphill, turn right (following *Burg Rheinfels* signs), and keep straight along the path just above the

St. Goar on the Rhine

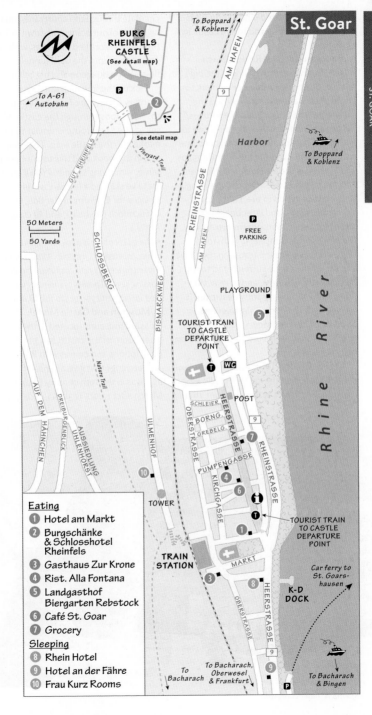

St. Goar

To Boppard & Koblenz

BURG RHEINFELS CASTLE
(See detail map)

To A-61 Autobahn

See detail map

Harbor

To Boppard & Koblenz

GUT RHEINFELS

Vineyard Trail

SCHLOSSBERG

RHEINSTRASSE

AM HAFEN

FREE PARKING

50 Meters
50 Yards

BISMARCKWEG

Nature Trail

PLAYGROUND

TOURIST TRAIN TO CASTLE DEPARTURE POINT

WC

Rhine River

AUF DEM HÄHNCHEN

DREIBURGENBLICK

AUSSIEDLUNG UHLENHORST

ULMENHOF

SCHLEIER
OBERSTRASSE
BORNG
GREBELG
HEERSTRASSE
POST

PUMPENGASSE

KIRCHGASSE

TOWER

TRAIN STATION

MARKT

OBERSTRASSE

HEERSTRASSE

RHEINSTRASSE

TOURIST TRAIN TO CASTLE DEPARTURE POINT

Car ferry to St. Goarshausen

K-D DOCK

To Bacharach
To Bacharach, Oberwesel & Frankfurt
To Bacharach & Bingen

Eating
1. Hotel am Markt
2. Burgschänke & Schlosshotel Rheinfels
3. Gasthaus Zur Krone
4. Rist. Alla Fontana
5. Landgasthof Biergarten Rebstock
6. Café St. Goar
7. Grocery

Sleeping
8. Rhein Hotel
9. Hotel an der Fähre
10. Frau Kurz Rooms

old city wall. Small red-and-white signs show the way, taking you to the castle in 15 minutes.

Background: Burg Rheinfels *was* huge—for five centuries, it was the biggest castle on the Rhine. Built in 1245 to guard a toll station, it soon earned the nickname "the unconquerable fortress." In the 1400s, the castle was thickened to withstand cannon fire. Rheinfels became a thriving cultural center and, in the 1520s, was visited by the artist Albrecht Dürer and the religious reformer Ulrich Zwingli. It saw lots of action in the Thirty Years' War (1618-1648), and later became the strongest and most modern fortress in the Holy Roman Empire. It withstood a siege of 28,000 French troops in 1692. But eventually the castle surrendered to the French without a fight, and in 1797, the French Revolutionary army destroyed it. For years, the ruined castle was used as a source of building stone, and today—while still mighty—it's only a small fraction of its original size.

⊙ Self-Guided Tour: Rather than wander aimlessly, visit the castle by following this tour. We'll start at the museum, then circulate through the courtyards, up to the highest lookout point, and down around through the fortified ramparts, with an option to go into the dark tunnels. We'll finish in the dungeon and big cellar.

Pick up the free map and use its commentary to navigate from red signpost to red signpost through the castle. My self-guided tour route is similar to the one marked on the castle map. That map, the one in this book, and this tour all use the same numbering system. (You'll notice that I've skipped a few stops—just walk on by signs for ❷ *Darmstädter Bau,* ❺ *Stables,* ⓫ *Fuchsloch* (foxhole), and ⓭ *Gunsmiths' Tower.*)

• *The ticket office is under the castle's clock tower, labeled* ❶ Uhrturm. *Walk through the entranceway and continue straight, passing several points of interest (which we'll visit later), until you get to the* ❸ *museum.*

Museum and Castle Model: The pleasant museum, located in the only finished room of the castle, has good English descriptions and comes with Romantic Age etchings that give a sense of the place as it was in the 19th century (daily mid-March-Oct 10:00-12:30 & 13:00-17:30;

Rheinfels' inner courtyard

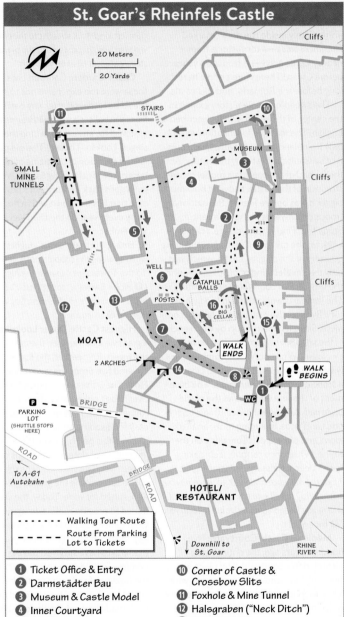

St. Goar's Rheinfels Castle

20 Meters
20 Yards

Cliffs

STAIRS

SMALL
MINE
TUNNELS

MUSEUM

Cliffs

Cliffs

WELL

CATAPULT
BALLS

POSTS

BIG
CELLAR

MOAT

2 ARCHES

WALK
ENDS

WALK
BEGINS

WC

BRIDGE

PARKING
LOT
(SHUTTLE STOPS
HERE)

ROAD

To A-61
Autobahn

BRIDGE

ROAD

HOTEL/
RESTAURANT

Downhill to
St. Goar

RHINE
RIVER

· · · · · · Walking Tour Route

— — — Route From Parking
Lot to Tickets

1 Ticket Office & Entry
2 Darmstädter Bau
3 Museum & Castle Model
4 Inner Courtyard
5 Stables
6 Well
7 High Battery
8 Clock Tower Lookout
9 Stairs to Battlements

10 Corner of Castle &
Crossbow Slits
11 Foxhole & Mine Tunnel
12 Halsgraben ("Neck Ditch")
13 Gunsmiths' Tower
14 Dungeon
15 Slaughterhouse
16 Big Cellar

closed Nov-mid-March).

The seven-foot-tall carved stone immediately inside the door (marked *Flammensäule*)—a tombstone from a nearby Celtic grave—is from 400 years before Christ. There were people here long before the Romans...and this castle.

The sweeping castle history exhibit in the center of the room is well-described in English. The massive fortification was the only Rhineland castle to withstand Louis XIV's assault during the 17th century. At the far end of the room is a model reconstruction of the castle, showing how much bigger it was before French Revolutionary troops destroyed it in the 18th century. Study this. Find where you are. (Hint: Look for the tall tower.) This was the living quarters of the original castle, which was only the smallest ring of buildings around the tiny central courtyard (13th century). The ramparts were added in the 14th century. By 1650, the fortress was largely complete. Since its destruction by the French in the late 18th century, it's had no military value. While no WWII bombs were wasted on this ruin, it served St. Goar as a stone quarry for generations. The basement of the museum shows the castle pharmacy and an exhibit of Rhine-region odds and ends, including tools, an 1830 loom, and photos of icebreaking on the Rhine. While once routine, icebreaking hasn't been necessary here since 1963.

• *Exit the museum and walk 30 yards directly out, slightly uphill into the castle courtyard, where you'll see a sign for the inner courtyard (❹ Innenhof).*

Medieval Castle Courtyard: Five hundred years ago, the entire castle encircled this courtyard. The place was self-sufficient and ready for a siege, with a bakery, pharmacy, herb garden, brewery, well (top of yard), and livestock. During peacetime, 300 to 600 people lived here; during a siege, there would be as many as 4,000. The walls were plastered and painted white. Bits of the original 13th-century plaster survive.

• *Continue through the courtyard under the Erste Schildmauer (first shield wall) sign, turn left, and walk straight to the two old wooden upright posts. Find the pyramid of stone catapult balls on your left.*

Castle Garden: Catapult balls like these were too expensive not to recycle—they'd be retrieved after any battle. Across from the balls is a well (❻ *Brunnen*)—essential for any castle during the age of sieges. Look in. Thirsty? The old posts are for the ceremonial baptizing of new members of the local trading league. While this guild goes back centuries, it's now a social club that fills this court with a huge wine party every year on the third weekend of September.

• *Climb uphill to the castle's highest point by walking along the cobbled path (look for the To the Tower sign) up past the high battery (❼ Hohe Batterie) to the castle's best viewpoint—up where the German flag waves (signed ❽ Uhrturm).*

Highest Castle Tower Lookout: Enjoy a great view of the river, the castle, and the forest. Remember, the fortress once covered five times the land it does today. Notice how the other castles (across the river) don't poke above the top of the Rhine canyon. That would make them easy for invading armies to see.

From this perch, survey the Rhine Valley, cut out of slate over millions of years by the river. The slate absorbs the heat of the sun, making the grapes grown here well-suited for wine. Today, the slate is mined to provide roofing. Imagine St. Goar himself settling here 1,500 years ago, establishing a place where sailors—thankful to have survived the dangerous Loreley—would stop and pray. Imagine the frozen river of years past, when the ice would break up and boats would huddle in man-made harbors like the one below for protection. Consider the history of trade on this busy river—from the days when castles levied tolls on ships, to the days when boats would be hauled upstream with the help of riverside towpaths, to the

21st century when 300 ships a day move their cargo past St. Goar. And imagine this castle before the French destroyed it... when it was the mightiest structure on the river, filled with people and inspiring awe among all who passed.

• *Return to the catapult balls, walk down-hill and through the tunnel, and veer left through the arch marked* ❾ *zu den Wehr-gängen ("to the Battlements"). Pause here, just before the stairs, to look up and see the original 13th-century core of the castle. Now go down two flights of stairs. Turn left and step into the dark, covered passageway. From here, we'll begin a rectangular walk, taking us completely around (counterclockwise) the perimeter of the castle.*

Covered Defense Galleries with "Minutemen" Holes: Soldiers—the castle's "minutemen"—had a short commute: defensive positions on the outside, home in the holes below on the left. Even though these living quarters were padded with straw, life was unpleasant.

• *Continue straight through the dark gallery, up the stairs, and to the corner of the castle, where you'll see a red signpost with the number* ❿. *Stand with your back to the corner of the wall.*

Corner of Castle: Gape up. That's the original castle tower. A three-story, half-timbered building originally rose beyond the tower's stone fortification. The two stone tongues near the top, just around the corner (to the right), supported the toilet. (Insert your own joke here.) Turn around and face the wall. The three crossbow slits were once steeper. The bigger hole on the riverside was for hot pitch.

• *Continue out along the back side of the castle. At the corner, turn left.*

Thoop...You're Dead: Look ahead at the smartly placed crossbow slit. While you're lying there, notice the stonework. The little round holes were for the scaffolds they used as they built up, which indicate that this stonework is original. Notice also the fine stonework on the

chutes. More boiling pitch...now you're toast, too.

• *Pick yourself up and keep going along the castle perimeter. Pass under the first of three arches and pause at the gray railing to enjoy the view. Look up the valley and uphill where the sprawling fort stretched (as far as the tiny farm on the ridge, a half-mile away). Below, just outside the wall, is land where invaders would gather. The mine tunnels are under there, waiting to blow up any attackers.*

Now continue under two more arches, jog left, go down five steps and into an open field, and walk toward the wooden bridge. The "old" wooden bridge is actually modern.

Dark Tunnel Detour: For a short detour through a castle tunnel—possible only if you have a light—turn your back to the main castle (with the modern bridge to your left) and face the stone dry-moat labeled ⓬ *Halsgraben "Neck Ditch."* (You'll exit in a few minutes at the high railing above the red #12 sign.) Go 20 yards down the path to the right, and enter the tunnel at the bottom of the wall, following the red *Hoher Minengang* sign. At the end of the short, big tunnel, take two steps up and walk eight level steps, turn left, and follow the long uphill ramp (this is where

it's pitch-black, and adults will need to watch their heads). At the end, a spiral staircase takes you up to the high-railing opening you saw earlier, and then back to the courtyard.

• *When ready to leave this courtyard, angle left (under the* zum Verlies/Dungeon *sign, before the bridge) through two arches and through the rough entry to the* **⓮** Verlies *(dungeon) on the left.*

Dungeon: This is one of six dungeons. You just walked through an entrance prisoners only dreamed of 400 years ago. They came and went through the little square hole in the ceiling. The holes in the walls supported timbers that thoughtfully gave as many as 15 residents something to sit on to keep them out of the filthy slop that gathered on the floor. Twice a day, they were given bread and water. Some prisoners actually survived longer than two years in here. While the town could torture and execute, the castle had permission only to imprison criminals in these dungeons. Consider this: According to town records, the two men who spent the most time down here—2.5 years each— died within three weeks of regaining their freedom. Perhaps after a diet of bread and water, feasting on meat and wine was simply too much.

• *Continue through the next arch, under the white arrow, then turn left and walk 30 yards to the* **⓯** Schlachthaus.

Slaughterhouse: Any proper castle was prepared to survive a six-month siege. With 4,000 people, that's a lot of provisions. The cattle that lived within the walls were slaughtered in this room. The castle's mortar was congealed here (by packing all the organic waste from the kitchen into kegs and sealing it). Notice the drainage gutters. "Running water" came through from drains built into the walls (to keep the mortar dry and therefore strong...and less smelly).

• *Back outside, climb the modern stairs to the left (look for the* Zum Ausgang *sign). A skinny, dark passage leads you into the...*

Big Cellar: This **⓰** *Grosser Keller* was a big pantry. When the castle was smaller, this was the original moat—you can see the rough lower parts of the wall. The original floor was 13 feet deeper. The drawbridge rested upon the stone nubs on the left. When the castle expanded, the moat became this cellar. Halfway up the walls on the entrance side of the room, square holes mark spots where timbers made a storage loft, perhaps filled with grain. In the back, an arch leads to the wine cellar (sometimes blocked off) where finer wine was kept. Part of a soldier's pay was wine... table wine. This wine was kept in a single 180,000-liter stone barrel (that's 47,550 gallons), which generally lasted about 18 months.

The count owned the surrounding farmland. Farmers got to keep 20 percent of their production. Later, in more liberal feudal times, the nobility let them keep 40 percent. Today, the German government leaves the workers with 60 percent...and provides a few more services.

• *You're free. Climb out, turn right, and leave. For coffee on a terrace with a great view, visit Schlosshotel Rheinfels, opposite the entrance.*

Shopping

The Montag family runs two shops (one specializes in steins and the other in cuckoo clocks), both at the base of the castle hill road. The stein shop under **Hotel Montag** has Rhine guides and fine steins. The other shop, kitty-corner from the stein shop, boasts "the largest free-hanging cuckoo clock in the world" (both open daily 8:30-18:00, shorter hours Nov-April). They'll ship your souvenirs home—or give you a VAT form to claim your tax refund at the airport if you're carrying your items with you. A couple of other souvenir shops are across from the K-D boat dock.

Eating

Hotel am Markt serves tasty traditional meals with plenty of game and fish at fair prices, with good atmosphere and service. Specialties include marinated roast beef and homemade cheesecake. Choose cozy indoor seating, or dine outside with a river and castle view (€9-15 main courses, daily 8:00-21:00, closed Nov-Feb, Markt 1, tel. 06741/1689).

Burgschänke offers the only reasonably priced lunches up at Rheinfels Castle. It's easy to miss on the ground floor of Schlosshotel Rheinfels (the hotel across from the castle ticket office—enter through the souvenir shop). Its fabulous outdoor terrace has a Rhine view (€8-10 pastas and *Flammkuchen*, €17-19 regional dishes, Sun-Thu 11:00-19:00, Fri-Sat until 21:30, tel. 06741/802-806).

Schlosshotel Rheinfels' dining room is your Rhine splurge, with an incredible indoor view terrace in an elegant, dressy setting. Call to reserve or arrive early if you're coming for breakfast or want a window table (€16 buffet breakfast, €19-28 main courses, also offers multicourse fixed-price meals, daily 7:00-11:00, 12:00-14:00 & 18:30-21:00, tel. 06741/8020).

Gasthaus Zur Krone, off the main drag, is the local choice for traditional German food. It's cozy and offers some outdoor seating, but no river view (€7-16 main courses, Thu-Tue 11:00-14:30 & 18:00-21:00, closed Wed, next to train station and church at Oberstrasse 38, tel. 06741/1515).

Ristorante Alla Fontana, tucked away on a back lane, serves the best Italian food in town at great prices in a lovely dining room or on a leafy patio (€6-9 pizzas and pasta, Tue-Sun 11:30-14:00 & 17:30-22:00, closed Mon, reservations smart, Pumpengasse 5, tel. 06741/96117).

Landgasthof Biergarten Rebstock is hidden on the far end of town on the banks of the Rhine. They serve schnitzel, beer, and wine. A nice playground nearby keeps the kids busy (April-Oct long hours daily—weather permitting, Am Hafen 1, tel. 06741/980-0337).

Café St. Goar is the perfect spot for a quick lunch or the German tradition of coffee and *kuchen*. Grab something for a picnic or enjoy the seating on the pedestrian-only street out front (Mon-Sat 7:00-18:00, Sun 10:00-18:00, Heerstrasse 95, tel. 06741/1635).

You can also buy picnic fixings on the pedestrian street at the tiny **St. Goarer Stadtladen** grocery store (Tue-Fri 8:00-18:00, Sat 8:00-13:00, closed Sun-Mon, Heerstrasse 106). The benches at St. Goar's waterfront park are great for a scenic picnic.

Sleeping

$$ Hotel am Markt features 17 rustic rooms in the main building (think antlers with a pastel flair), plus 10 classier rooms right next door, and a good restaurant. It's a decent value with all the modern comforts, just a stone's throw from the boat dock and train station (standard Db-€65, bigger Db with view-€80, closed Nov-Feb, pay parking, Markt 1, tel. 06741/1689, www.hotelammarkt1.de, hotel.am.markt@t-online.de).

$$$ Rhein Hotel, two doors down from Hotel am Markt, has 10 quality rooms—most with views and balconies—in a spacious building (Db-€90, larger Db-€100, family rooms, higher prices on Fri-Sat nights, laundry service for fee, closed mid-Nov-Feb, Heerstrasse 71, tel. 06741/981-240, www.rheinhotel-st-goar.de, info@rheinhotel-st-goar.de).

$ Hotel an der Fähre is a simple place on the busy road at the end of town, immediately across from the ferry dock. It rents 12 cheap but decent rooms (D-€45, Db-€55-€60, cash only, street noise but double-glazed windows, closed Nov-Feb, Heerstrasse 47, tel. 06741/980-577, www.hotel-stgoar.de, hotel_anderfaehre@web.de).

$ Frau Kurz offers St. Goar's best B&B, renting three delightful rooms (sharing 2.5 bathrooms) with bathrobes, a breakfast terrace with castle views, a garden, and homemade marmalade (D–€56, 2-night minimum, D–€52 with stay of 4 nights or more, cash only, free and easy parking, no Internet access, bike rental for guests, Ulmenhof 11, tel. 06741/459, www.gaestehaus-kurz.de, fewo-kurz@kabelmail.de). It's a steep five-minute hike from the train station: Exit left from the station, take an immediate left under the tracks, and go partway up the zigzag stairs, turning right through an archway onto Ulmenhof; #11 is just past the tower.

MARKSBURG CASTLE IN BRAUBACH

Medieval invaders decided to give Marksburg a miss thanks to its formidable defenses, leaving it the best-preserved castle on the Rhine today. Worth ▲▲, it can be visited only with a guide on a 50-minute tour. In summer, tours in English normally run daily at 13:00 and 16:00. Otherwise, you can join a German tour (3/hour in summer, hourly in winter) that's almost as good—there are no explanations in English in the castle itself, but your ticket includes an English hand-out. It's an awesome castle, and between the handout and my commentary below, you'll feel fully informed, so don't worry about being on time for the English tours.

Cost and Hours: €6, family card–€15, daily April-Oct 10:00-17:00, Nov-March 11:00-16:00, last tour departs one hour before closing, tel. 02627/206, www.marksburg.de.

Getting There: Marksburg caps a hill above the village of Braubach, on the east bank of the Rhine. By **train**, it's a 10-minute trip from Koblenz to Braubach (1-2/hour); from Bacharach or St. Goar, it takes 1.5-2 hours, depending on the length of the layover in Koblenz. The train is quicker than the **boat** (downstream from Bacharach to Braubach-2 hours, upstream return-3.5 hours). Consider taking the downstream boat to Braubach, and the train back. If traveling with luggage, store it in the convenient lockers in the underground passage at the Koblenz train station (Braubach has no enclosed station—just platforms—and no lockers). If you're coming by **car** from Bacharach or St. Goar, take the car ferry at St. Goar across the Rhine, and drive north to Braubach (parking lot at castle).

If you reach Braubach by train, **walk** into the old town (follow *Altstadt* signs—

Marksburg Castle was built originally as a fortress, not a royal residence.

coming out of tunnel from train platforms, it's to your right); then follow the *Zur Burg* signs to the path up to the castle. Allow 20-30 minutes for the climb up. Scarce **taxis** charge at least €10 from the train platforms to the castle. A green **tourist train** circles up to the castle, but there's no fixed schedule, so don't count on it (Easter-mid-Oct Tue-Sun, no trains Mon or off-season, leaves from Barbarastrasse, tel. 06773/587, www.ruckes-reisen.de).

🔿 **Self-Guided Tour:** Start inside the castle's **first gate.** The dramatic castles lining the Rhine are generally Romantic rebuilds, but Marksburg is the real McCoy—nearly all original construction. It's littered with bits of its medieval past, like the big stone ball that was swung on a rope to be used as a battering ram. Ahead, notice how the inner gate—originally tall enough for knights on horseback to gallop through—was made smaller, and therefore safer from enemies on horseback. Climb the Knights' Stairway, carved out of slate, and pass under the murder hole—handy for pouring boiling pitch on invaders. (Germans still say someone with bad luck "has pitch on his head.")

Coats of Arms: Colorful coats of arms line the wall just inside the gate. These are from the noble families who have owned the castle since 1283. In that year, financial troubles drove the first family to sell to the powerful and wealthy Katzenelnbogen family (who made the castle into what you see today). When Napoleon took this region in 1803, an Austrian family who sided with the French got the keys. When Prussia took the region in 1866, control passed to a friend of the Prussians who had a passion for medieval things—typical of this Romantic period. Then it was sold to the German Castles Association in 1900. Its offices are in the main palace at the top of the stairs.

Romanesque Palace: White outlines mark where the larger original windows were located, before they were replaced by easier-to-defend smaller ones. On the far right, a bit of the original plaster survives. Slate, which is vulnerable to the elements, needs to be covered—in this case, by plaster. Because this is a protected historic building, restorers can use only the traditional plaster methods...but no one knows how to make plaster that works as well as these 800-year-old surviving bits.

Cannons: The oldest cannon here—from 1500—was back-loaded. This was advantageous because many cartridges could be pre-loaded. But since the seal was leaky, it wasn't very powerful. The bigger, more modern cannons—from 1640—were one piece and therefore airtight, but had to be front-loaded. They could easily hit targets across the river from here. Stone balls were rough, so they let the explosive force leak out. The best cannonballs were stones covered in smooth lead—airtight and therefore more powerful and more accurate.

Gothic Garden: Walking along an outer wall, you'll see 160 plants from the Middle Ages—used for cooking, medicine, and witchcraft. *Schierling* (hemlock, in the first corner) is the same poison that killed Socrates.

Inland Rampart: This most vulnerable part of the castle had a triangular construction to better deflect attacks. Notice the factory in the valley. In the 14th century, this was a lead, copper, and silver mine. Today's factory—Europe's largest car-battery recycling plant—uses the old mine shafts as vents (see the three modern smokestacks).

Wine Cellar: Since Roman times, wine has been the traditional Rhineland drink. Because castle water was impure, wine—less alcoholic than today's beer—was the way knights got their fluids. The pitchers on the wall were their daily allotment. The bellows were part of the barrel's filtering system. Stairs lead to the...

Gothic Hall: This hall is set up as a kitchen, with an oven designed to roast an ox whole. The arms holding the pots have notches to control the heat. To this day, when Germans want someone to hurry up, they say, "give it one tooth more." Medieval windows were made of thin sheets of translucent alabaster or animal skins. A nearby wall is peeled away to show the wattle-and-daub construction (sticks, straw, clay, mud, then plaster) of a castle's inner walls. The iron plate to the left of the next door enabled servants to stoke the heater without being seen by the noble family.

Bedroom: This was the only heated room in the castle. The canopy kept in heat and kept out critters. In medieval times, it was impolite for a lady to argue with her lord in public. She would wait for him in bed to give him what Germans still call "a curtain lecture." The deep window seat caught maximum light for needlework and reading. Women would sit here and chat (or "spin a yarn") while working the spinning wheel.

Hall of the Knights: This was the dining hall. The long table is an unattached plank. After each course, servants could replace it with another pre-set plank. Even today, when a meal is over and Germans are ready for the action to begin, they say, "Let's lift up the table." The action back then consisted of traveling minstrels who sang and told of news gleaned from their travels.

Notice the outhouse—made of wood—hanging over thin air. When not in use, its door was locked from the outside (the castle side) to prevent any invaders from entering this weak point in the castle's defenses.

Chapel: This chapel is still painted in Gothic style with the castle's namesake, St. Mark, and his lion. Even the chapel was designed with defense in mind. The small doorway kept out heavily armed attackers. The staircase spirals clockwise, favoring the sword-wielding defender (assuming he was right-handed).

Linen Room: About the year 1800, the castle—with diminished military value—housed disabled soldiers. They'd earn extra money working raw flax into linen.

Two Thousand Years of Armor: Follow the evolution of armor since Celtic times. Because helmets covered the entire head, soldiers identified themselves as friendly by tipping their visor up with their right hand. This evolved into the military salute that is still used around the world today. Armor and the close-range weapons along the back were made obsolete by the invention of the rifle. Armor was replaced with breastplates—pointed (like the castle itself) to deflect enemy fire. This design was used as late as the start of World War I. A medieval lady's armor hangs over the door. While popular fiction has men locking up their women before heading off to battle, chastity belts were actually used by women as protection against rape when traveling.

The Keep: This served as an observation tower, a dungeon (with a 22-square-foot cell in the bottom), and a place of last refuge. When all was nearly lost, the defenders would bundle into the keep and burn the wooden bridge, hoping to outwait their enemies.

Horse Stable: The stable shows off bits of medieval crime and punishment. Cheaters were attached to stones or pillories. Shame masks punished gossip-mongers. A mask with a heavy ball had its victim crawling around with his nose in the mud. The handcuffs with a neck hole were for the transport of prisoners. The pictures on the wall show various medieval capital punishments. Many times, the accused was simply taken into a torture dungeon to see all these tools, and, guilty or not, confessions spilled out of him. On that cheery note, your tour is over.

While you're in the region, consider a stop at Burg Eltz (a beautiful castle on the Mosel River). If you're using public transit, Burg Eltz can make a fine day trip from the Rhine.

BURG ELTZ

My favorite castle in all of Europe—worth ▲▲▲—lurks in a mysterious forest. It's been left intact for 700 years and is decorated and furnished throughout much as it was 500 years ago. Thanks to smart diplomacy, clever marriages, and lots of luck, Burg Eltz (pronounced "boorg elts") was never destroyed. It even survived one five-year siege. It's been in the Eltz family for 850 years.

Getting There

The castle is a pleasant 1.5-hour **walk** from the nearest train station, in the little village of Moselkern—the walk is not only easy, it's the most fun and scenic way to visit the castle.

Hiking to the Castle from Moselkern: You can hike between the Moselkern train station and Burg Eltz in 70 minutes at a steady clip, but allow an extra 20 minutes or so to enjoy the scenery (see map on page 922). The elevation gain is less than 400 feet. (You can reach Moselkern via train from towns on the Rhine—including Bacharach and Cologne—with a change at Koblenz.)

To find the **path up to the castle,** turn right from the Moselkern station along Oberstrasse and continue to the village church. Just past the church, as the street ends, turn right through the underpass. You'll follow the Elzbach stream all the way up to the castle. Just before a stone bridge crosses the stream, take either the footpath or the bridge—they join up again later.

When the road ends at the parking lot of Hotel Ringelsteiner Mühle, stay to the right of the hotel and continue upstream along the easy-to-follow trail—from here, it's another 45 minutes through the forest to the castle.

By Bus from Treis-Karden: From May through October on Saturdays and Sundays only, bus #330 runs to Burg Eltz from the railway station in the town of Treis-Karden (4/day, 30 minutes; confirm times with bus operator at tel. 02671/8976 or at www.vrminfo.de).

By Taxi: You can taxi to the castle from the nearby towns of **Moselkern** (€28 one-way, taxi tel. 02672/1407) or **Karden** (€30 one-way, taxi tel. 02672/1407). If you're planning to taxi from Moselkern, call ahead and ask the taxi to meet your train at Moselkern station. Consider taxiing up to Burg Eltz and then enjoying the hike downhill back to the train station in Moselkern.

By Car: Cars (and taxis) park in a lot near, but not quite at, Burg Eltz. From the lot, hike 15 minutes downhill to the castle or wait (10 minutes at most) for the red castle shuttle bus.

Drive/Hike Combo: If you're traveling by car but would enjoy walking part of the path up to the castle, drive to Moselkern, follow the *Burg Eltz* signs up the Elz Valley, park at Hotel Ringelsteiner Mühle (buy ticket from machine), and hike about 45 minutes up the trail to the castle.

Orientation

Cost and Hours: €9 castle entry includes required 45-minute guided tour and treasury, April-Oct daily from 9:30, last tour departs at 17:30, closed Nov-March, tel. 02672/950-500, www.burg-eltz.de.

Eating at Burg Eltz: The **castle café** serves lunch, with soups and bratwurst-and-fries cuisine (April-Oct daily, cash only).

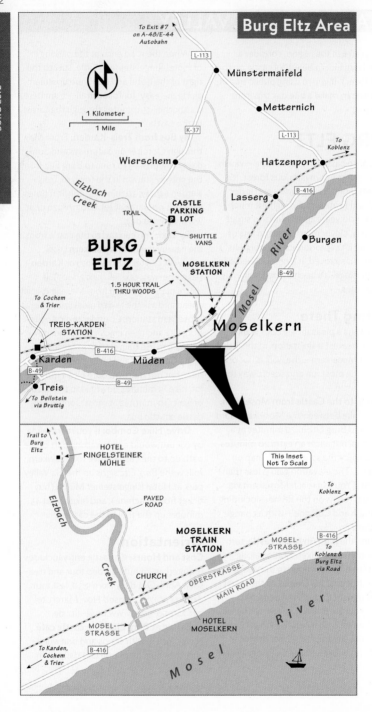

Visiting the Castle

The first record of a *Burg* (castle) on the Elz is from 1157. (Elz is the name of a stream that runs past the castle through a deep valley before emptying into the Mosel.) By about 1490, the castle looked like it does today, with the homes of three big landlord families gathered around a tiny courtyard within one formidable fortification. Today, the excellent tour winds you through two of those homes, while the third is still the residence of the castellan (the man who maintains the castle). This is where members of the Eltz family stay when they're not at one of their other feudal holdings. The elderly countess of Eltz—whose family goes back 33 generations here (you'll see a photo of her family)—enjoys flowers. Each week for 40 years, she's had grand arrangements adorn the public castle rooms.

It was a comfortable castle for its day: 80 rooms made cozy by 40 fireplaces and wall-hanging tapestries. Many of its 20 toilets were automatically flushed by a rain drain. The delightful **chapel** is on a lower floor. Even though "no one should live above God," this chapel's placement was acceptable because it filled a bay window, which flooded the delicate Gothic space with light. The three families met—working out common problems as if sharing a condo complex—in the large "conference room." A carved jester and a rose look down on the big table, reminding those who gathered that they were free to discuss anything ("fool's freedom"—jesters could say anything to the king), but nothing discussed could leave the room (the "rose of silence"). In the **bedroom,** have fun with the suggestive decor: the jousting relief carved into the canopy, and the fertile and phallic figures hiding in the lusty green wall paintings.

Near the exit, the **treasury** fills the four higgledy-piggledy floors of a cellar with the precious, eccentric, and historic mementos of this family that once helped elect the Holy Roman Emperor.

Burg Eltz

Berlin

Over the last two decades, Berlin has been a construction zone. Standing on ripped-up tracks and under a canopy of cranes, visitors have witnessed the rebirth of a great European capital: lively, fun-loving, and captivating.

Berlin is still largely defined by its tumultuous 20th century. The city was Hitler's capital during World War II, and in the postwar years, it became the front line of the Cold War between Soviet-style communism and American-style capitalism. The East-West division was set in stone in 1961 with the Berlin Wall, which would stand for 28 years. In 1990, after the Wall fell, the two Germanys—and the two Berlins—officially became one.

Urban planners seized on the city's reunification and the return of the national government to make Berlin a great capital once again. Today, the old "East Berlin" is where you feel the vibrant pulse of the city, while the old "West Berlin" feels like a chic, classy suburb.

But even as the city busily builds itself into the 21st century, Berlin acknowledges and remembers its past. Thought-provoking memorials confront Germany's difficult history. Lacing these sights into your sightseeing intensifies your understanding of the city. As you walk over what was the Wall and through the well-patched Brandenburg Gate, it's clear that history is not contained in books; it's an evolving story in which we play a part.

BERLIN IN 3 DAYS

Day 1: Begin your day getting oriented to this huge city. For a quick and relaxing once-over-lightly tour, jump on one of the many hop-on, hop-off buses (such as BEX Sightseeing Berlin) that make orientation loops through the city.

Then take Part 1 of my self-guided "Best of Berlin Walk," starting at the Reichstag (reservations required to climb its dome), going through the Brandenburg Gate, and down the boulevard, Unter den Linden. Visit the charming Gendarmenmarkt square. Then tour the German History Museum.

On any evening: Any of these neighborhoods (all near each other) are worth exploring: Hackescher Markt, Oranienburger Strasse, and Prenzlauer Berg. Take in live music or cabaret. Linger at a beer garden, or stroll the banks of the Spree River. Or even continue your sightseeing—a number of sights stay open late, including the Reichstag and its view dome.

Day 2: Start your morning at Bebelplatz with Part 2 of my "Best of Berlin Walk." Along the walk, visit any museum that interests you on Museum Island or nearby: Pergamon, Neues, or the DDR.

In the afternoon, catch a boat tour (or pedal a rented bike) along the parklike banks of the Spree River from Museum Island to the Chancellery. Explore the Hackescher Markt's shops and museums (and stay into the evening).

Day 3: Tour the sights of the Third Reich and Cold War: the Topography of Terror exhibit and Museum of the Wall at Checkpoint Charlie. The Jewish Museum Berlin is also nearby.

In the afternoon, visit the Gemäldegalerie art museum.

Head to Prenzlauer Berg to visit the Berlin Wall Memorial, then stay for the café and nightlife scene.

ORIENTATION

Berlin is huge, with 3.4 million people. The city is spread out and its sights numerous, so you'll need to be well-organized to experience it all. The tourist's Berlin can be broken into several digestible chunks:

Near the landmark **Brandenburg Gate,** you'll find the Reichstag building, Pariser Platz, and memorials to Hitler's victims.

From the Brandenburg Gate, the famous **Unter den Linden boulevard** runs eastward, passing the German History Museum and Museum Island (Pergamon Museum, Neues Museum, and Berlin Cathedral) on the way to Alexanderplatz (TV Tower).

South of Unter den Linden are the delightful Gendarmenmarkt square, noteworthy Nazi sites (including the Topography of Terror), good Wall-related sights (Museum of the Wall at Checkpoint Charlie), and the Jewish Museum.

Across the Spree River are the neighborhoods of Hackescher Markt, Oranienburger Strasse, and Prenzlauer Berg (lively restaurant/nightlife zone). The Berlin Wall Memorial is at the west edge of Prenzlauer Berg.

The Brandenburg Gate—historic and grand

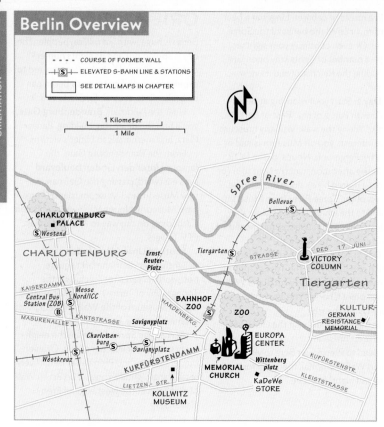

Berlin Overview

- - - - COURSE OF FORMER WALL
—+Ⓢ+— ELEVATED S-BAHN LINE & STATIONS
☐ SEE DETAIL MAPS IN CHAPTER

1 Kilometer
1 Mile

Spree River

Bellevue Ⓢ

CHARLOTTENBURG
■ PALACE
Ⓢ *Westend*

CHARLOTTENBURG

Ernst-
Reuter-
Platz

Tiergarten Ⓢ

STRASSE

DES 17 JUNI

VICTORY
COLUMN

Tiergarten

KAISERDAMM
Central Bus
Station (ZOB) Ⓢ
Ⓑ
Messe
Nord/ICC

KULTUR-
GERMAN
RESISTANCE■
MEMORIAL

MASURENALLEE
KANTSTRASSE

BAHNHOF
ZOO

ZOO

HARDENBERG

Savignyplatz

Charlotten-
burg Ⓢ
Savignyplatz

Ⓢ
Westkreuz

KURFÜRSTENDAMM

EUROPA
CENTER

*Wittenberg
platz*

KURFÜRSTENSTR.

KLEISTSTRASSE

MEMORIAL
CHURCH

KaDeWe
STORE

LIETZEN- STR.

KOLLWITZ
MUSEUM

*Rick's Tip: What Americans called **"East Germany"** was technically the German Democratic Republic—the Deutsche Demokratische Republik, or **DDR** (pronounced day-day-AIR). You'll still see those initials around what was once East Germany. The name for what was **"West Germany"**—the Federal Republic of Germany (Bundesrepublik Deutschland, or **BRD**)—is now the name shared by all of Germany.*

Central Berlin is dominated by the giant **Tiergarten park,** with its angel-topped Victory Column. South of the park are Potsdamer Platz (the Times Square of Berlin, and a transportation hub) and the Kulturforum museum complex, whose highlight is the **Gemäldegalerie,** a treasure chest of European painting. To the north is the huge Hauptbahnhof (the city's main train station).

Western Berlin has the feel of a chic, classy suburb. It focuses on the **Bahnhof Zoo train station** (often marked "Zoologischer Garten" on transit maps) and the grand **Kurfürstendamm boulevard,** nicknamed "Ku'damm" (transportation hub and shopping). Even though the east side of the city is all the rage, big-name stores (like KaDeWe) and restaurants keep the west side buzzing.

Tourist Information

With any luck, you won't have to use Berlin's **TIs.** Appropriately called "infostores," they are unlikely to have the information you need (tel. 030/250-025, www.

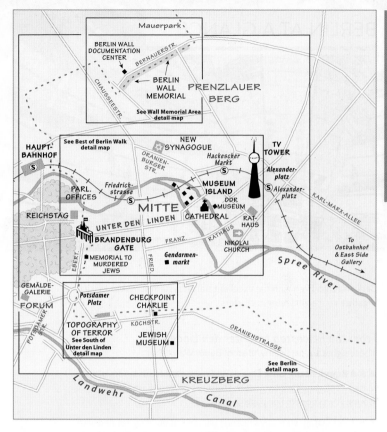

visitberlin.de). You'll find them at the **Hauptbahnhof** train station (daily 8:00-22:00, by main entrance on Europaplatz), at the **Brandenburg Gate** (daily 9:30-19:00, until 18:00 Nov-March), and at the **TV Tower** (daily 10:00-18:00, until 16:00 Nov-March, Panoramastrasse 1a).

Sightseeing Passes

The three-day, €24 **Museum Pass Berlin** is a great value and pays for itself in a hurry. It gets you into more than 50 museums, including the national museums and most of the recommended biggies (though not the German History Museum), on three consecutive days. Sights covered by the pass include the Museum Island museums (including Neues and Pergamon), Gemäldegalerie,

and the Jewish Museum Berlin. Buy it at the TI or any participating museum. The pass generally lets you skip the line and go directly into the museum.

The €18 **Museum Island Pass** (Bereichskarte Museumsinsel) covers all the venues on Museum Island and is a fine value—but for just €6 more, the three-day Museum Pass Berlin gives you triple the days and many more entries.

TIs sell the **WelcomeCard,** a transportation pass that includes discounts for many sights; it's a good value if you'll be using public transit frequently (see page 984).

Helpful Hints

Addresses: Many Berlin streets are numbered with odd and even numbers on

BERLIN AT A GLANCE

Berlin is huge. Even with the excellent transit system, it makes sense to organize your sightseeing in clusters.

From the Reichstag to Unter den Linden

These sights are part of my "Best of Berlin Walk," Part 1.

▲▲▲**Brandenburg Gate** One of Berlin's most famous landmarks, a massive columned gateway, at the former border of East and West. **Hours:** Always open. See page 939.

▲▲▲**Reichstag** Germany's historic parliament building, topped with a striking modern dome you can climb (reservations required). **Hours:** Daily 8:00-24:00, last entry at 22:00. See page 950.

▲▲**Memorial to the Murdered Jews of Europe** Holocaust memorial with almost 3,000 symbolic pillars, plus an exhibition about Hitler's Jewish victims. **Hours:** Memorial always open; information center open Tue-Sun 10:00-20:00, Oct-March until 19:00, closed Mon. See page 940.

▲▲**Unter den Linden** Leafy boulevard through the heart of former East Berlin, lined with some of the city's top sights. **Hours:** Always open. See page 942.

Museum Island and Nearby

You'll stop at Museum Island on my "Best of Berlin Walk," Part 2.

▲▲▲**Pergamon Museum** World-class museum of classical antiquities on Museum Island, partially closed through 2019 (including its famous Pergamon Altar). **Hours:** Daily 10:00-18:00, Thu until 20:00. See page 954.

▲▲▲**German History Museum** The ultimate swing through Germany's tumultuous story, located just west of Museum Island. **Hours:** Daily 10:00-18:00. See page 957.

▲▲**Neues Museum** Egyptian antiquities collection on Museum Island and proud home of the exquisite 3,000-year-old bust of Queen Nefertiti. **Hours:** Daily 10:00-18:00, Thu until 20:00. See page 955.

▲▲**DDR Museum** Quirky collection of communist-era artifacts, located just east of Museum Island. **Hours:** Daily 10:00-20:00, Sat until 22:00. See page 958.

South of Unter den Linden

▲▲**Gendarmenmarkt** Inviting square bounded by twin churches (one with a fine German history exhibit), a chocolate shop, and a concert hall. **Hours:** Always open. See page 958.

▲▲**Topography of Terror** Chilling exhibit documenting the Nazi perpetrators, built on the site of the former Gestapo/SS headquarters. **Hours:** Daily 10:00-20:00. See page 959.

▲▲**Museum of the Wall at Checkpoint Charlie** Kitschy but moving museum with stories of brave Cold War escapes, near the former site of the famous East-West border checkpoint; the surrounding street scene is almost as interesting. **Hours:** Daily 9:00-22:00. See page 961.

▲▲**Jewish Museum Berlin** Engaging, accessible museum celebrating Jewish culture, in a highly conceptual building. **Hours:** Daily 10:00-20:00, Mon until 22:00. See page 963.

Kulturforum Complex

▲▲**Gemäldegalerie** Germany's top collection of 13th- through 18th-century European paintings, featuring Holbein, Dürer, Cranach, Van der Weyden, Rubens, Hals, Rembrandt, Vermeer, Velázquez, and Raphael, located off Tiergarten park. **Hours:** Tue-Fri 10:00-18:00, Thu until 20:00, Sat-Sun 11:00-18:00, closed Mon. See page 965.

Across the Spree River

▲▲▲**Prenzlauer Berg** Lively, colorful neighborhood with hip cafés, restaurants, boutiques, and street life. **Hours:** Always open. See page 969.

▲▲▲**Berlin Wall Memorial** A "docu-center" with videos and displays, several outdoor exhibits, and the lone surviving stretch of an intact Wall section. **Hours:** Visitor Center Tue-Sun 10:00-18:00, closed Mon; outdoor areas accessible 24 hours daily. See page 970.

▲**New Synagogue** Largest prewar synagogue in Berlin. **Hours:** April-Oct Mon-Fri 10:00-18:00, Sun until 19:00; Nov-March exhibit only Sun-Thu 10:00-18:00, Fri until 15:00; closed Sat year-round. See page 969.

City Bus #100 Tour

For a cheap alternative to a hop-on, hop-off bus tour, you could follow this self-guided tour via **City Bus #100** instead. Running from the Bahnhof Zoo train station in western Berlin to Alexanderplatz in eastern Berlin, City Bus #100 laces together the major sights. A basic, single bus ticket is good for two hours of travel in one direction and buses leave every few minutes, so hopping on and off works great (see page 984 for ticketing details).

Here's a quick review of what you'll see: Leaving from Bahnhof Zoo, spot the bombed-out hulk of the **Kaiser Wilhelm Memorial Church,** with its jagged spire and postwar sister church. Then, on the left, the elephant gates mark the entrance to the much-loved **Berlin Zoo.** After a left turn, you cross the canal and pass Berlin's **embassy row.**

The bus then enters the vast 400-acre **Tiergarten** city park, once a royal hunting ground and now packed with cycling paths, joggers, and—on hot days—nude sunbathers. Straight ahead, the **Victory Column** (with the gilded angel) towers above. A block beyond the Victory Column (on the left) is the 18th-century late-Rococo **Bellevue Palace,** the residence of the federal president (if the flag's out, he's in).

Driving along the Spree River (on the left), you'll see several striking **national government** buildings. A metal Henry Moore sculpture entitled *Butterfly* floats in front of the slope-roofed House of World Cultures. Through the trees on the left is the **Chancellery**—Germany's "White House." The big open space is the **Platz der Republik,** where the Victory Column (which you passed earlier) stood until Hitler moved it. The Hauptbahnhof (Berlin's vast main train station, marked by its tall tower with the *DB* sign) is across the field between the Chancellery and the **Reichstag** (Germany's parliament—the old building with the new dome).

Hop off at the next stop (Reichstag/Bundestag) if you'd like to follow my "Best of Berlin Walk." But if you stay on the bus, you'll zip by the next string of sights, in this order:

Unter den Linden, the main east-west thoroughfare, stretches from the **Brandenburg Gate** through Berlin's historic core to the TV Tower in the distance. You'll pass the **Russian Embassy** and the Aeroflot airline office (right). Crossing **Friedrichstrasse,** look right for a Fifth Avenue-style conga line of big, glitzy department stores. Later, on the left, are the **German History Museum, Museum Island,** and the **Berlin Cathedral;** across from these (on the right) is the construction site of the **Humboldt-Forum Berliner Schloss** (with the Humboldt Box visitors center). You'll rumble to a final stop at the transit hub of **Alexanderplatz.**

the same side of the street, often with no connection to the other side (for example, Ku'damm #212 can be across the street from #14). To save steps, check the white street signs on curb corners; many list the street numbers covered on that side of the block.

City Overview: If you don't ascend the Reichstag's dome, try **Panoramapunkt,** which offers a speedy elevator and sky-scraping rooftop views (€6.50, €10.50 for VIP line-skipping ticket, daily 10:00-20:00, until 18:00 in winter, in red-brick building on Potsdamer Platz, S-Bahn and U-Bahn: Potsdamer Platz, tel. 030/2593-7080, www.panoramapunkt.de).

Rick's Tip: *There are still enough idiots on the street to keep the* **con men with their shell games** *in business. Don't be foolish enough to engage with any gambling on the street.*

Medical Help: The US Embassy has a list of local English-speaking doctors (tel. 030/83050, http://germany.usembassy. gov).

Tours
▲▲▲HOP-ON, HOP-OFF BUSES
Several companies offer a circuit of the city with unlimited hop-on, hop-off privileges all day for about €20 (about 15 stops at the city's major tourist spots—Museum Island, Brandenburg Gate, and so on). Go with a live guide rather than the recorded spiel (buses generally run April-Oct daily 10:00-18:00, departures every 10 minutes, last bus leaves all stops at around 16:00, 2-hour loop; Nov-March 2/hour and last departure at 15:00). Try BEX Sightseeing Berlin (www.berlinerstadtrundfahrten.de) or look for brochures in your hotel lobby or at the TI.

▲▲▲WALKING TOURS
Berlin's complex history can be challenging to appreciate on your own, so walking tours are worthwhile. Germany has no regulations controlling who can give city

tours, so guides can be hit-or-miss. To land a great guide, use one of the companies I recommend. They all run tours daily. Most in-city tours cost about €12-15 and last about 3 to 4 hours.

Brewer's Berlin Tours specializes in in-depth walks that can flex with your interests. Their Best of Berlin introductory tour, billed at 6 hours, can last for 8; they also do a shorter 3.5-hour tour (free, tip expected). All tours depart from Bandy Brooks ice-cream shop at the Friedrichstrasse S-Bahn station (mobile 0177-388-1537, www.brewersberlintours.com).

Insider Tour runs the full gamut of itineraries, including pub crawls and a day trip to Dresden. Their tours meet at the McDonald's across from the Bahnhof Zoo train station, and at the AM to PM Bar at the Hackescher Markt S-Bahn station (tel. 030/692-3149, www.insidertour.com).

Original Berlin Walks gives a good overview in four hours (daily year-round). They also offer a Third Reich walking tour and other themes. Tours depart from opposite the Hackescher Markt S-Bahn station (tour info: tel. 030/301-9194, www. berlinwalks.de).

Rick's Tip: *Supposedly* **"free" tours are advertised all over town.** *English-speaking students deliver a memorized script and expect to be tipped (€5 minimum per person is encouraged). While the guides can be highly entertaining, when it comes to walking tours, you get what you pay for.*

PRIVATE GUIDES

Guides charge roughly the same for private tours (€50-60/hour or €200-300/day, confirm when booking). Consider **Nick Jackson,** an archaeologist and historian who makes museums come to life (mobile 0171-537-8768, www.jacksonsberlintours.com), or **Bernhard Schlegelmilch,** an enthusiastic historian who grew up behind the Wall (mobile 0176-6422-9119, www.steubentoursberlin.com).

BOAT TOURS

Several boat companies offer relaxing one-hour trips up and down the Spree River. Boats leave from various docks that cluster near the bridge at the Berlin Cathedral (just off Unter den Linden). For better views, choose a two-story boat with open-deck seating. I enjoy the Historical Sightseeing Cruise from **Stern und Kreisschiffahrt** (€14, mid-March-Nov daily 10:00-19:00, leaves from Nikolaiviertel Dock—cross bridge from Berlin Cathedral toward Alexanderplatz and look right, tel. 030/536-3600, www.sternundkreis.de). Confirm that the boat you choose comes with English commentary.

BEST OF BERLIN WALK

This two-mile self-guided walk, worth ▲▲▲, starts in front of the Reichstag, takes you under the Brandenburg Gate and down Unter den Linden, and finishes on Alexanderplatz. If you have just one day in Berlin, or want a good orientation to the city, simply follow this walk (allowing 2-3 hours at a brisk pace, not counting museum visits). By the end, you'll have seen the core of Berlin and its most important sights.

If you have more time and want to use this walk as a spine for your sightseeing, entering sights and museums as you go, consider doing Part 1 and Part 2 on different days. Part 1 goes from the Reichstag and takes you partway down Unter den Linden, with stops at the Brandenburg Gate, Memorial to the Murdered Jews of Europe, and Friedrichstrasse, the glitzy shopping street. Part 2 continues down Unter den Linden, from Bebelplatz to Alexanderplatz, and features Museum Island and the Spree River, Berlin Cathedral, and iconic TV Tower.

🎧 Download my free Best of Berlin Walk audio tour, which narrates the route.

❷ Self-Guided Walk
Part 1: From the Reichstag to Unter den Linden

During the Cold War, the Reichstag stood just inside the West Berlin side of the Wall. Even though it's been more than 25 years since the Wall came down, you may still feel a slight tingle down your spine as you walk across the former death strip, through the once *verboten* Brandenburg Gate, and into the former communist east.

• *Start your walk directly in front of the Reichstag building, at the big, grassy park called...*

❶ PLATZ DER REPUBLIK

Stand about 100 yards in front of the grand Reichstag building and spin left to survey your surroundings. At the **Reichstag U-Bahn stop** is a big federal building overlooking the Spree River. The huge **main train station** (Hauptbahnhof) is in the distance (see the tower marked *DB*, for Deutsche Bahn—the German rail company). Farther left is the mammoth white concrete-and-glass **Chancellery,** nicknamed the "washing machine" by Berliners for its hygienic, spin-cycle appearance. It's the office of Germany's most powerful person, the chancellor (currently Angela Merkel). To remind the chancellor whom he or she works for, Germany's Reichstag (housing the parliament) is about six feet taller than the Chancellery.

Beyond the Chancellery is the Spree

River. When kings ruled Prussia, government buildings crowded right up to its banks. But today, the riverscape is a people-friendly zone (we'll see it later on this walk).

• *Dominating the Platz der Republik is a giant domed building, the...*

❷ REICHSTAG

The parliament building—the heart of German democracy and worth ▲▲▲— has a short but complicated and emotional history. When it was inaugurated in the 1890s, the last emperor, Kaiser Wilhelm II, disdainfully called it the "chatting home for monkeys" *(Reichsaffenhaus)*. It was placed outside the city's old walls—far from the center of real power, the imperial palace. But it was from the Reichstag that the German Republic was proclaimed in 1918. Look above the door, surrounded by stone patches from WWII bomb damage, to see the motto and promise: *Dem Deutschen Volke* ("To the German People").

In 1933, this symbol of democracy nearly burned down. The Nazis—whose influence on the German political scene was on the rise—blamed a communist plot. A Dutch communist, Marinus van der Lubbe, was eventually convicted and guillotined for the crime. Others believed that Hitler himself planned the fire, using it as a handy excuse to frame the communists and grab power.

The Reichstag was hardly used from 1933 to 1999. Despite the fact that the building had lost its symbolic value, Stalin ordered his troops to take the Reichstag from the Nazis no later than May 1, 1945 (the date of the workers' May Day parade in Moscow). More than 1,500 Nazi soldiers made their last stand here—extending World War II by two days. On April 30, after fierce fighting on its rooftop, the Reichstag fell to the Red Army.

For the building's 101st birthday in 1995, the artist-partners Christo and Jeanne-Claude wrapped the entire thing in silvery gold cloth. It was then wrapped again—in scaffolding—and rebuilt by British architect Lord Norman Foster into the new

The Reichstag is the symbolic heart of German democracy.

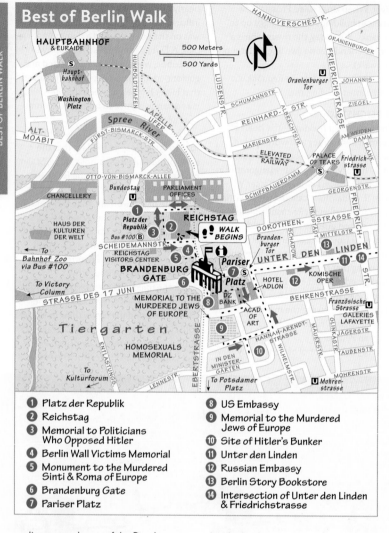

Best of Berlin Walk

1. Platz der Republik
2. Reichstag
3. Memorial to Politicians Who Opposed Hitler
4. Berlin Wall Victims Memorial
5. Monument to the Murdered Sinti & Roma of Europe
6. Brandenburg Gate
7. Pariser Platz
8. US Embassy
9. Memorial to the Murdered Jews of Europe
10. Site of Hitler's Bunker
11. Unter den Linden
12. Russian Embassy
13. Berlin Story Bookstore
14. Intersection of Unter den Linden & Friedrichstrasse

parliamentary home of the Bundestag (Germany's lower house, similar to the US House of Representatives). In 1999, the German parliament convened here for the first time in 66 years. To many Germans, the proud resurrection of the Reichstag symbolizes the end of a terrible chapter in their country's history.

The **glass cupola** rises 155 feet above the ground. Its two sloped ramps spiral 755 feet to the top for a grand view.

Inside the dome, a cone of 360 mirrors reflects natural light into the legislative chamber below. Illuminated from inside after dark, this gives Berlin a memorable nightlight. The environmentally friendly cone—with an opening at the top—also helps with air circulation, expelling stale air from the legislative chamber (no joke) and pulling in fresh, cool air.

Visitors with advance reservations can climb the spiral ramp up into the cupola. If

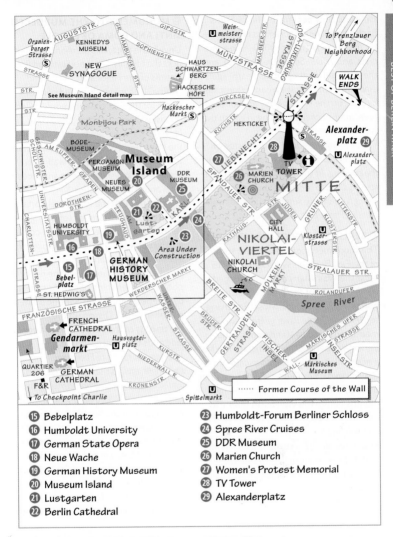

15 Bebelplatz
16 Humboldt University
17 German State Opera
18 Neue Wache
19 German History Museum
20 Museum Island
21 Lustgarten
22 Berlin Cathedral
23 Humboldt-Forum Berliner Schloss
24 Spree River Cruises
25 DDR Museum
26 Marien Church
27 Women's Protest Memorial
28 TV Tower
29 Alexanderplatz

you haven't booked a slot, cross the street to the white booth to check available entry times (for details on making reservations and visiting the interior, including a self-guided dome tour, see page 950).
• *Face the Reichstag and walk to the right. Near the road in front of the building, enmeshed in all the security apparatus and crowds, is a memorial of slate stones embedded vertically in the ground.*

❸ MEMORIAL TO POLITICIANS WHO OPPOSED HITLER

This row of slabs, which looks like a fancy slate bicycle rack, is a memorial to the 96 members of the Reichstag who were persecuted and murdered because their politics didn't agree with Chancellor Hitler's. They were part of the Weimar Republic, the weak and ill-fated attempt at post-WWI democracy in Germany. These were the people who could have stopped

Hitler...so they became his first victims. Each slate slab memorializes one man— his name, party (mostly KPD—Communists, and SPD—Social Democrats), and the date and location of his death—generally in a concentration camp (indicated by "*KZ*" on the slabs). They are honored here, in front of the building in which they worked.

• *Walk along the side of the Reichstag, on busy Scheidemannstrasse, toward the rear of the building. At the intersection with Ebertstrasse, cross to the right (toward the park). Along a railing is a small memorial of white crosses. This is the...*

❹ BERLIN WALL VICTIMS MEMORIAL

This monument commemorates some of the East Berliners who died trying to cross the Wall. Many of them perished within months of the Wall's construction on August 13, 1961. Most died trying to swim the Spree River to freedom. This monument used to stand right on the Berlin Wall behind the Reichstag. The last person killed while trying to escape was 20-year-old Chris Gueffroy, who was shot through the heart in no-man's land nine months before the Wall fell in 1989. (To read more about the Wall, see the sidebar on page 962.)

• *Continue along Ebertstrasse for a few more steps before turning right on a peaceful leafy lane. Within a short distance, on your right, is the...*

❺ MONUMENT TO THE MURDERED SINTI AND ROMA OF EUROPE

Unveiled in 2012, this memorial remembers the roughly 500,000 Sinti and Roma victims of the Holocaust. "Sinti" and "Roma" (the main tribes and correct terms for those more commonly called "Gypsies") were as persecuted by the Nazis as were the Jews. And they lost the same percentage of their population to Hitler. The opaque glass wall, with a timeline in English and German, traces the Nazi abuse and atrocities.

Enter through the rusty steel portal. On the other side is a circular reflecting pool surrounded by stone slabs, some containing the names of the death camps where hundreds of thousands of Sinti and Roma perished. In the water along the rim of the pool is the wrenching poem "Auschwitz," by composer and writer Santino Spinelli, an Italian Roma. Dissonant music evoking the tragedy of the Sinti and Roma genocide adds to the atmosphere.

• *Retrace your steps to Ebertstrasse and continue right, toward the busy intersection dominated by the imposing Brandenburg Gate.*

Take this chance to get oriented. Behind you, as you face the Brandenburg Gate, is **Tiergarten park,** *its center marked by the landmark Victory Column. Now face the gate: It stands at one end of Unter den Linden, the Champs-Elysées of Berlin. In the distance, the red-and-white spire of the TV Tower marks the end of this walk.*

As you cross the street toward the gate,

Memorial to Politicans Who Opposed Hitler

Berlin Wall Victims Memorial

notice the double row of cobblestones beneath your feet—it goes about 25 miles around the city, marking where the Wall used to stand. Now walk under the gate that, for a sad generation, was part of a wall that divided this city.

❻ BRANDENBURG GATE

The historic Brandenburg Gate, rated ▲▲▲, is the last survivor of 14 gates in Berlin's old city wall. This one, dating from 1791, was the grandest and led to the neighboring city of Brandenburg. The gate was the symbol of Prussian Berlin—and later the symbol of a divided Berlin. It's crowned by a majestic four-horse chariot, with the Goddess of Peace at the reins. Napoleon took this statue to the Louvre in Paris in 1806. After the Prussians defeated Napoleon and got it back (1813), she was renamed the Goddess of Victory.

The gate sat unused, part of a sad circle dance called the Berlin Wall, for more than 25 years. Now postcards all over town show the ecstatic day—November 9, 1989—when the world rejoiced at the sight of happy Berliners jamming the gate like flowers on a parade float. Pause a minute and think about struggles for freedom—past and present. There's actually a special room built into the gate for this purpose (see the sidebar). A TI is also within the gate. Around the gate, information boards show how this area changed throughout the 20th century.

The gate sits on a major boulevard running east to west through Berlin. The

The Brandenburg Gate, Arch of Peace

More than 200 years ago, the Brandenburg Gate was designed as an arch of peace, crowned by the Goddess of Peace and showing Mars sheathing his sword. The Nazis misused it as a gate of triumph and aggression. Today a Room of Silence, built into the gate, is dedicated to the peaceful message of the original Brandenburg Gate. As you consider the history of Berlin in this silent and empty room, you may be inspired to read the prayer of the United Nations:

"Oh Lord, our planet Earth is only a small star in space. It is our duty to transform it into a planet whose creatures are no longer tormented by war, hunger, and fear, no longer senselessly divided by race, color, and ideology. Give us courage and strength to begin this task today so that our children and our children's children shall one day carry the name of man with pride."

western segment, called Strasse des 17 Juni (named for a workers' uprising against the DDR government on June 17, 1953), stretches for four miles from the Brandenburg Gate, through the Tiergarten, past the Victory Column, to the Olympic Stadium. But we'll follow this city axis in the opposite direction—east, along Unter den Linden into the core of old imperial Berlin, and past the site where the palace of the Hohenzollern family, rulers of Prussia and then Germany, once stood. The royal palace is a phantom sight, long gone, but its occupants were responsible for just about all you'll see.

• *Pass through the gate and stand in the middle of...*

Brandenburg Gate

❼ PARISER PLATZ

"Parisian Square," so named after the Prussians who defeated Napoleon in 1813, was once filled with important government buildings—all bombed to smithereens in World War II. For decades, it was an unrecognizable, deserted no-man's-land—cut off from the rest of the city by the Wall. Banks, hotels, and embassies have now reclaimed their original places on the square—with a few additions, including a palace of coffee, Starbucks. The winners of World War II enjoy this prime real estate: The American, French, British, and Russian embassies are all on or near this square.

As you face the gate, to your right is the French Embassy, and to your left is the ❽ **US Embassy,** which reopened in its historic pre-WWII location in 2008. For safety's sake, Uncle Sam wanted more of a security zone around the building, but the Germans wanted to keep Pariser Platz a welcoming people zone. The compromise: Extra security was built into the structure. Easy-on-the-eyes barriers keep potential car bombs at a distance, and the front door is on the side farthest from the Brandenburg Gate.

Turn your back to the gate. On the right, jutting into the square, is the ritzy **Hotel Adlon,** long called home by visiting stars and VIPs. In its heyday, it hosted such notables as Charlie Chaplin, Albert Einstein, and Greta Garbo. It was the setting for Garbo's most famous line, "I vant to be alone," uttered in the film *Grand Hotel.* Damaged by the Russians just after World War II, the original hotel was closed when the Wall went up in 1961 and later demolished. Today's grand Adlon was rebuilt in 1997. It was here that Michael Jackson shocked millions by dangling his infant son over a balcony railing.

• *Between the hotel and the US Embassy are two buildings worth a quick visit: the DZ Bank building and the Academy of Arts. We'll enter both.*

DZ Bank Building: This building's architect, Frank Gehry, is famous for Bilbao's Guggenheim Museum, Prague's Dancing House, Seattle's Experience Music Project, Chicago's Pritzker Pavilion, and Los Angeles' Walt Disney Concert Hall. Gehry fans might be surprised at the bank building's low profile. Structures on Pariser Platz are designed so as not to draw attention away from the Brandenburg Gate. But to get your fix of wild and colorful Gehry, step into the lobby. Built as an office complex and conference center, its undulating interior is like a big, slithery fish. Gehry explained, "The form of the fish is the best example of movement. I try to capture this movement in my buildings."

• *Leaving the DZ Bank, turn right and head into the next building, the...*

Academy of Arts (Akademie der Künste): Inside the glassy arcade, just past the café, is the office where Albert Speer, Hitler's architect, planned the rebuilding of postwar Berlin into "Welthauptstadt Germania"—the grandiose "world capital" of Nazi Europe. Pass through the glass door to see Speer's favorite statue, *Prometheus Bound* (c. 1900). This is the kind of art that turned Hitler on: a strong, soldierly, vital man, enduring hardship for a greater cause. Anticipating the bombing of Berlin, Speer had the statue bricked up in the basement here, where it lay undiscovered until 1995.

• *Exit the building out the back. Across the street, to the right, stretches the vast...*

❾ MEMORIAL TO THE MURDERED JEWS OF EUROPE

Completed in 2005, this Holocaust memorial, rated ▲▲, consists of 2,711 gravestone-like pillars. Designed by Jewish-American architect Peter Eisenman, it was Germany's first formal, government-sponsored Holocaust memorial. Using the word "murdered" in the title was intentional and a big deal. Germany, as a nation, was officially admitting to a crime.

Cost and Hours: The memorial is free and always open. The information center is open Tue-Sun 10:00-20:00, Oct-March until 19:00, closed Mon year-round; last entry 45 minutes before closing, S-Bahn: Brandenburger Tor or Potsdamer Platz, tel. 030/2639-4336, www.stiftung-denkmal.de. A €4 audioguide augments the experience.

Visiting the Memorial: The pillars, made of hollow concrete, stand in a gently sunken area, which can be entered from any side. The number of pillars isn't symbolic of anything; it's simply how many fit on the provided land. The pillars are all about the same size, but of differing heights.

Once you enter the memorial, notice that people seem to appear and disappear between the columns, and that no matter where you are, the exit always seems to be up. The memorial is lit and guarded at night.

The monument was criticized for focusing on just one of the groups targeted by the Nazis, but the German government has now erected memorials to other victims—such as the Roma/Sinti memorial we just visited, and a memorial to the regime's homosexual victims, also nearby. It's also been criticized because there's nothing intrinsically Jewish about it. Some were struck that there's no central gathering point or place for a ceremony. Like death, you enter it alone.

There is no one intended interpretation. Is it a symbolic cemetery, or an intentionally disorienting labyrinth? It's up to the visitor to derive the meaning, while pondering this horrible chapter in human history.

Memorial Information Center: The pondering takes place under the sky. For the learning, go under the field of concrete pillars to the state-of-the-art information center. Inside, excellent and thought-provoking installations study the Nazi system of extermination and personalize the plight of victims; there's also space for silent reflection. Exhibits trace the historical context of the Nazi and WWII era, present case studies of how the Holocaust affected 15 Jewish families from around Europe, and document

Memorial to the Murdered Jews of Europe

the different places of genocide. You'll also find exhibits about other Holocaust monuments and memorials, a searchable database of victims, and a video archive of interviews with survivors.

• *Wander through the gray pillars, but eventually emerge on the corner with the Information Center. Cross Hannah-Arendt-Strasse and go a half-block farther. Walk alongside the unpaved parking lot on the left to the info plaque over the...*

⑩ SITE OF HITLER'S BUNKER

You're standing atop the buried remains of the *Führerbunker*. In early 1945, as Allied armies advanced on Berlin, and Nazi Germany lay in ruins, Hitler and his staff retreated to a bunker complex behind the former Reich Chancellery. He stayed there for two months. It was here, as the Soviet army tightened its noose on the capital, that Hitler and Eva Braun, his wife of less than 48 hours, committed suicide on April 30, 1945. A week later, the war in Europe was over. The info board presents a detailed cutaway illustrating the bunker complex plus a timeline tracing its history and ultimate fate (the roof was removed and the bunker filled with dirt, then covered over).

• *From here, you can visit the important but stark Memorial to the Homosexuals Persecuted Under the National Socialist Regime, or you can continue the walk. To do either, first head back to Hannah-Arendt-Strasse.*

*It's a detour to see the **memorial**: go left one block at Hannah-Arendt-Strasse, cross the street, and head down a path into Tiergarten park. There, look for a large, dark gray concrete box. Through a small window you can watch a film loop of same-sex couples kissing—a reminder that life and love are precious.*

*To rejoin the **walk**, turn right on Hannah-Arendt-Strasse, go one block, then head left up Wilhelmstrasse. Because Wilhelmstrasse was a main street of the German government during World War II, it was obliterated by bombs, and all its buildings are new today.*

Imagining Hitler in the 21st Century

Germans tread lightly on their past. It took 65 years for the German History Museum to organize its first exhibit on the life of Hitler. No version of *Mein Kampf*, Hitler's political manifesto, was allowed printed in Germany until 2016, when the publication of a new version (annotated by historians) was greeted with controversy. It's a balancing act, and Germans are still in the process of figuring out how to confront their painful history.

Many visitors to Berlin are curious about Hitler sites, but not much survives from that dark period. The bunker where Hitler killed himself lies hidden underneath a parking lot, marked only by a small information board. The best way to learn about Hitler sites is to take a walking tour focused on the Third Reich (see page 933) or to visit the Topography of Terror (see page 959).

Back on Unter den Linden, head to the median, in front of Hotel Adlon, and take a long look down...

⑪ UNTER DEN LINDEN

In the good old days, this street, rated ▲▲, was one of Europe's grand boulevards. In the 15th century, it was a carriageway leading from the palace to the

Unter den Linden

hunting grounds (today's big Tiergarten). In the 17th century, Hohenzollern princes and princesses moved in and built their palaces here so they could be near the Prussian king. It is divided, roughly at Friedrichstrasse, into a business section, which stretches toward the Brandenburg Gate, and a cultural section, which spreads out toward Alexanderplatz. Frederick the Great wanted to have culture, mainly the opera and the university, closer to his palace and to keep business (read: banks) farther away, near the city walls.

Named centuries ago for its many linden trees, this was the most elegant street of Prussian Berlin before Hitler's time, and the main drag of East Berlin after his reign. Hitler replaced the venerable trees—many 250 years old—with Nazi flags. Popular discontent drove him to replant the trees. Later, Unter den Linden deteriorated into a depressing Cold War cul-de-sac, but it has long since regained its strolling café ambience.

• *In front of Hotel Adlon is the Brandenburger Tor S-Bahn station. Cover a bit of Unter den Linden underground by climbing down its steps and walking along the platform.*

Ghost Subway Station: The Brandenburger Tor S-Bahn station is one of Berlin's former ghost subway stations. It's a time warp, looking much as it did when built in 1936, with dreary old green tiles and original signage. During the Cold War, most underground train tunnels were simply sealed at the border between East and West Berlin. But a few Western lines looped through the East and then back into the West. To make hard Western cash, the Eastern government rented the use of these tracks to the West. For 28 years, as Western trains passed through otherwise blocked-off stations, passengers saw only East German guards and lots of cobwebs. Within days of the fall of the Wall, these stations reopened (one woman who'd left her purse behind in 1961 got a call from the lost-and-found office—it was still there).

• *Walk along the track and exit on the other side, to the right. You'll pop out at the Russian Embassy's front yard.*

⓬ **Russian Embassy:** This was the first big postwar building project in East Berlin. It's in the powerful, simplified Neoclassical style that Stalin liked. While not as important now as it was a few years ago, it's as immense as ever. It flies the Russian white, blue, and red. Find the hammer-and-sickle motif decorating the window frames—a reminder of the days when Russia was the USSR.

• *At the next intersection (Glinkastrasse), cross to the other side of Unter den Linden. At #40 is the...*

⓭ **Berlin Story Bookstore:** Berlin Story is two shops side by side (on the left it's mainly Cold War souvenirs; on the right, the bookstore). The bookshop has just about the best range anywhere of English-language titles on Berlin.

• *A few steps farther down is the...*

⓮ **Intersection of Unter den Linden and Friedrichstrasse:** This is perhaps the most central crossroads in Berlin. And for several years more, it will be a mess as Berlin builds a new connection in its already extensive subway system. All over Berlin, you'll see big, colorful **water pipes** running aboveground. Wherever there are large construction projects, streets are laced with these drainage pipes. Berlin's high water table means that any new basement comes with lots of pumping out.

Brandenburger Tor ghost subway station

Looking at the jaunty DDR-style pedestrian "walk/don't walk" signals at this intersection is a reminder that a little of the old East survives. All along Unter den Linden (and throughout much of the former East Berlin), you'll see the perky red and green men—called **Ampelmännchen.** They were recently threatened with replacement by ordinary signs, but, after a 10-year court battle, the wildly popular DDR signals were kept after all (note the Ampelmann souvenir store across the street).

Before continuing down Unter den Linden, look farther down **Friedrichstrasse.** Before the war, this zone was the heart of Berlin. In the 1920s, Berlin was famous for its anything-goes love of life. This was the cabaret drag, a springboard to stardom for young and vampy entertainers like Marlene Dietrich. Now Friedrichstrasse is lined with department stores and big-time hotels. Consider detouring to the megastore **Galeries Lafayette** (closed Sun); check out the vertical garden on its front wall, have lunch in its basement food court, or, if the weather's nice, pick up some classy munchies here for a picnic. The short walk here provides some of Berlin's most jarring old-versus-new architectural contrasts—be sure to look up as you stroll.

• *We've reached the end of Part 1 of this walk. This is a good place to take a break, if you wish. The charming Gendarmenmarkt, with shops and eateries, is just a couple of blocks away (see page 958). Or, if you continue south down Friedrichstrasse, you'll wind up at Checkpoint Charlie in about 10 minutes (see page 961).*

But if you'd rather tackle Part 2 of this walk now, head down Unter den Linden a few more blocks, past the large equestrian statue of Frederick the Great, then turn right into Bebelplatz.

Part 2: From Bebelplatz to Alexanderplatz

• *Starting at Bebelplatz, head to the center of the square, and find the glass window in the*

Frederick the Great

Berlin was a humble, marshy burg until prince electors from the Hohenzollern dynasty made it their capital in the mid-15th century. Gradually their territory spread and strengthened, becoming the powerful Kingdom of Prussia, which dominated the northern Germanic world—both militarily and culturally.

The only Hohenzollern ruler worth remembering is **Frederick the Great** (1712-1786). This enlightened despot was both a ruthless military tactician and a culture lover. "Old Fritz," as he was called, played the flute, spoke six languages, and counted Voltaire among his friends. Practical and cosmopolitan, Frederick cleverly invited to Prussia Protestants who were being persecuted—including French Huguenots and Dutch traders. Prussia became the beneficiary of these groups' substantial wealth and know-how. Frederick left Berlin a far more modern and enlightened place than he found it. Thanks largely to him, Prussia was well-positioned to become a magnet of sorts for the German unification movement in the 19th century. When Germany first unified, in 1871, Berlin was its natural capital.

pavement. We'll begin with some history and a spin tour.

⑮ BEBELPLATZ

For centuries, up until the early 1700s, Prussia had been likened to a modern-day Sparta—it was all about its military. Voltaire famously said, "Whereas some states have an army, the Prussian army has a state." But Frederick the Great—who ruled from 1740 to 1786—established Prussia not just as a military power, but also as a cultural and intellectual heavyweight. This square was the center of the cultural capital that Frederick envisioned. His grand palace was just down the street.

Imagine that it's 1760. Pan around the square to see Frederick's contributions to Prussian culture. Everything is draped with Greek-inspired Prussian pomp. Sure, Prussia was a militaristic power. But Frederick also built an "Athens on the Spree"—an enlightened and cultured society.

To visually survey the square, start with the university across the street and spin counterclockwise:

⓰ Humboldt University, across Unter den Linden, is one of Europe's greatest. Marx and Lenin (not the brothers or the sisters) studied here, as did the Grimms (both brothers) and more than two dozen Nobel Prize winners. Einstein, who was Jewish, taught here until taking a spot at Princeton in 1932 (smart guy).

Turn 90 degrees to the left to face the former **state library** (labeled *Juristische Fakultät*). Bombed in World War II, the library was rebuilt by the East German government in the original style only because Vladimir Lenin studied law here during much of his exile from Russia. (On the ground floor is Tim's Espressobar, a great little café with light food, student prices, and garden seating.)

The round, Catholic **St. Hedwig's Church,** nicknamed the "upside-down teacup," is a statement of religious and cultural tolerance. The pragmatic Frederick the Great wanted to encourage the integration of Catholic Silesians after his empire annexed their region in 1742, and so the first Catholic church since the Reformation was built in Berlin and dedicated to St. Hedwig, the patron saint of Silesia. Like all Catholic churches in Berlin, St. Hedwig's is not on the street, but stuck in a kind of back lot—indicating inferiority to Protestant churches.

The **⓱ German State Opera** (Staatsoper) was bombed in 1941, rebuilt in 1943, and bombed again in 1945. It's currently undergoing an extensive renovation.

Now look down through the glass you're standing on: The room of empty bookshelves is a memorial repudiating a notorious Nazi **book burning** on this square. In 1933, staff and students from the university threw 20,000 newly forbidden books (authored by Einstein, Hemingway, Freud, and T. S. Eliot, among others) into a huge bonfire on the orders of the Nazi propaganda minister, Joseph

A plaque and memorial on Bebelplatz mark the site of a Nazi book burning.

Goebbels. Hitler chose this square to thoroughly squash the ideals of culture and enlightenment that characterized the Prussian heritage of Frederick the Great. Instead, he was establishing a new age of intolerance, where Germanness was correct and diversity was evil.

A plaque nearby reminds us of the prophetic quote by the German poet Heinrich Heine. In 1820, he wrote, "Where they burn books, in the end they will also burn people." A century later, his books were among those that went up in flames on this spot.

This monument reminds us of that chilling event in 1933, while also inspiring vigilance against the anti-intellectual scaremongers of today, who would burn the thoughts of people they fear to defend their culture from diversity.

• Cross Unter den Linden to the university side and head toward the Greek-temple-like building set in the small chestnut-tree-filled park. This is the…

⑱ NEW GUARDHOUSE

The emperor's former guardhouse (Neue Wache) now holds the nation's main memorial to all "victims of war and tyranny." Look inside, where a replica of the Käthe Kollwitz statue, *Mother with Her Dead Son*, is enshrined in silence. It marks the tombs of Germany's unknown soldier and an unknown concentration camp victim. Read the powerful statement (left of entrance). The memorial, open to the sky,

Memorial at the New Guardhouse

incorporates the elements—sunshine, rain, snow—falling on this modern-day pietà.

• Next to the Neue Wache is Berlin's pink yet formidable Zeughaus (arsenal). Dating from 1695, it's considered the oldest building on the boulevard, and now houses the excellent ⑲ *German History Museum*—well worth a visit, and described in detail on page 957.

Continue across a bridge to reach ⑳ *Museum Island (Museumsinsel), whose imposing Neoclassical buildings house some of Berlin's most impressive museums (including the Pergamon Museum); for details, see page 954.*

For now, we'll check out a few other landmarks on the island. First is the big, inviting park called the…

㉑ LUSTGARTEN

For 300 years, Museum Island's big central square has flip-flopped between being a military parade ground and a people-friendly park, depending upon the political tenor of the time. During the revolutions of 1848, the Kaiser's troops dispersed a protesting crowd that had assembled here, sending demonstrators onto footpaths. Karl Marx later commented, "It is impossible to have a revolution in a country where people stay off the grass."

Hitler enjoyed giving speeches from the top of the museum steps overlooking this square. In fact, he had the square landscaped to fit his symmetrical tastes and propaganda needs.

In 1999, the Lustgarten was made into a park (read the history posted in the corner opposite the church). On a sunny day, it's packed with people relaxing and is one of Berlin's most enjoyable public spaces.

• The huge church next to the park is the…

㉒ BERLIN CATHEDRAL

The century-old Berlin Cathedral (Berliner Dom) wears its bombastic Wilhelmian architecture as a Protestant assertion of strength. It seems to proclaim, "A mighty fortress is our God." The years of Kaiser Wilhelm's rule, from 1888 to 1918, were a busy age of building. Germany had recently been united (1871), and the emperor wanted to give his capital stature and legitimacy. Wilhelm's buildings are over-the-top statements: Neoclassical, Neo-Baroque, and Neo-Renaissance, with stucco and gold-tiled mosaics. This Protestant cathedral is as ornate as if it were Catholic. With the emperor's lead, this sumptuous style came into vogue, and anyone who wanted to be associated with the royal class built this way. (The other big example of Wilhelmian architecture in Berlin is the Reichstag, which we saw earlier.) The church is most impressive from the outside (and there's no way to even peek inside without a pricey ticket).

Inside, the great reformers (Luther, Calvin, and company) stand around the brilliantly restored dome like stern saints guarding their theology. Frederick I (Frederick the Great's gramps) rests in an ornate tomb (right transept, near entrance to dome). The 270-step climb to the outdoor dome gallery is tough but offers pleasant, breezy views of the city at the finish line. The crypt downstairs is not worth a look.

Cost and Hours: €7 includes access to dome gallery, audioguide-€3, Mon-Sat 9:00-20:00, Sun 12:00-20:00, until 19:00 Oct-March, www.berliner-dom.de.

• *Kitty-corner across the main street from the Berlin Cathedral is a huge construction site, known as the...*

㉓ HUMBOLDT-FORUM BERLINER SCHLOSS

For centuries, this was the site of the Baroque palace of the Hohenzollern dynasty of Brandenburg and Prussia. Much of that palace actually survived World War II but was replaced by the communists with a blocky, Soviet-style "Palace" of the Republic—East Berlin's parliament building/entertainment complex and a showy symbol of the communist days. The landmark building fell into disrepair after reunification, and by 2009 had been dismantled.

After much debate about how to use this prime real estate, the German parliament decided to construct the Humboldt-Forum Berliner Schloss, a huge public venue filled with museums, shops, galleries, and concert halls behind a facade constructed in imitation of the

The elegant Berlin Cathedral (flanked by the DDR-era TV Tower)

original Hohenzollern palace. With a €600 million price tag, many Berliners consider the reconstruction plan a complete waste of money. The latest news is that it should be finished by 2019.

In the meantime, the temporary, bright blue **Humboldt-Box** provides info and a viewing platform from which to survey the construction (until it gets in the way and also has to be demolished). Consider popping in for a look at the beautiful model, on the first floor up, showing this area as it was in 1900 (free, daily 10:00-19:00).

• Head to the bridge just beyond the Berlin Cathedral, with views of the riverbank. Consider...

STROLLING AND CRUISING THE SPREE RIVER

This river was once a symbol of division—the East German regime put nets underwater to stymie those desperate enough for freedom to swim to the West. With the reunification of Berlin, however, the Spree River has become people-friendly and welcoming. A parklike trail leads from the Berlin Cathedral to the Hauptbahnhof, with impromptu "beachside" beer gardens with imported sand, BBQs in pocket parks, and lots of locals walking their dogs, taking a lazy bike ride, or jogging.

You may notice "don't drop anchor" signs. There are still unexploded WWII bombs in Berlin, and many are in this river. Every month, several bombs are found at construction sites. Their triggers were set for the hard ground of Scottish testing grounds, and because Berlin sits upon soft soil, an estimated one of every ten bombs didn't explode.

The recommended ㉔ **Spree River cruises** depart from the riverbank near the bridge by the Berlin Cathedral (for details, see page 934). Across the river from the cathedral is the interesting ㉕ **DDR Museum** (see page 958).

• Leaving the bridge, continue walking straight toward the TV Tower, down the big boulevard, which here changes its name to...

KARL-LIEBKNECHT-STRASSE

The first big building on the left after the bridge is the **Radisson Blu Hotel** and shopping center, with a huge aquarium in the center. The elevator goes right through the middle of a deep-sea world. (You can see it from the unforgettable Radisson hotel lobby—tuck in your shirt and walk past the guards with the confidence of a guest who's sleeping there.) Here in the center of the old communist capital, it seems that capitalism has settled in with a spirited vengeance.

In the park immediately across the street (a big jaywalk from the Radisson) are grandfatherly statues of **Marx** and **Engels** (nicknamed the "old pensioners"). Surrounding them are stainless-steel monoliths with evocative photos illustrating the struggles of the workers of the world.

Farther along, where Karl-Liebknecht-Strasse intersects with Spandauer Strasse, look right to see the red-brick **City Hall**. It was built after the revolutions of 1848 and was arguably the first democratic building in the city.

Continue toward ㉖ **Marien Church** (from 1270), with its spire mirroring the TV Tower. Inside, an artist's rendering helps you follow the interesting but faded old "Dance of Death" mural that wraps around the narthex inside the door.

• Immediately across the street from the church, detour a half-block down little Rosenstrasse to find a beautiful memorial set in a park.

Spree River sightseeing boats

㉗ Women's Protest Memorial: This sculpture is a reminder of a successful and courageous protest against Nazi policies. In 1943, when "privileged Jews" (men married to Gentile women) were arrested, their wives demonstrated en masse on this street, where the men were being held in a Jewish community building. They actually won the freedom of their spouses.

• *Back on Karl-Liebknecht-Strasse, look up at the 1,200-foot-tall...*

㉘ TV Tower (Fernsehturm): Built (with Swedish know-how) in 1969 for the 20th anniversary of the communist government, the tower was meant to show the power of the atheistic state at a time when DDR leaders were having the crosses removed from church domes and spires. But when the sun hit the tower—the greatest spire in East Berlin—a huge cross was reflected on the mirrored ball. Cynics called it "God's Revenge." East Berliners dubbed the tower the "Tele-Asparagus." They joked that if it fell over, they'd have an elevator to the West.

The tower has a fine view from halfway up, offering a handy city orientation and an interesting look at the flat, red-roofed sprawl of Berlin—including a peek inside the city's many courtyards (€13 timed-entry tickets, daily until 24:00). Consider a kitschy trip to the observation deck for the view and lunch in its revolving restaurant (mediocre food, reservations smart for dinner, tel. 030/242-3333, www. tv-turm.de).

• *Walk four more minutes down the boulevard past the TV Tower and toward the big railway overpass. Just before the bridge, on the left, is the half-price ticket booth called* **Hekticket**—*stop in to see what's on (for details, see page 973).*

Walk under the train bridge and continue for a long half-block (passing the Galeria Kaufhof mall). Turn right onto a broad pedestrian street, and go through the low tunnel into the big square where blue U-Bahn station signs mark...

㉙ ALEXANDERPLATZ

This square was the commercial pride and joy of East Berlin. The Kaufhof department store was the ultimate shopping mecca for Easterners. It, along with the two big surviving 1920s "functionalist" buildings, defined the square. Alexanderplatz is still a landmark, with a major U-Bahn/S-Bahn station. The once-futuristic, now-retro "World Time Clock," installed in 1969, is a nostalgic favorite and remains a popular meeting point.

Stop in the square for a coffee and to people-watch. You may see the dueling human hot-dog hawkers, who wear ingenious harnesses that let them cook and sell tasty, cheap German sausages on the fly. While the square can get a little rough at night, it's generally a great scene.

• *Our orientation stroll is finished. From here, you can hike back to catch the riverboat tour, visit Museum Island or the German History Museum, or take in the sights south of Unter den Linden.*

The TV Tower punctuates the skyline.

SIGHTS

The Reichstag and Nearby

Many of Berlin's top sights and landmarks are in this area, and are described in detail in the self-guided walk above, including the **Brandenburg Gate** (page 939), the **Memorial to the Murdered Jews of Europe** (page 940), and **Unter den Linden** (page 942).

▲▲▲REICHSTAG

Germany's historic parliament building—completed in 1894, burned in 1933, sad and lonely in a no-man's land throughout the Cold War, and finally rebuilt and topped with a glittering glass cupola in 1999—is a symbol of a proudly reunited nation. It's fascinating to climb up the twin ramps that spiral through its dome. Getting in requires a reservation. For more on the building's exterior and its history, see page 934 of the "Best of Berlin Walk."

Cost and Hours: Free, but reservations required—see below, daily 8:00-24:00, last entry at 22:00, no big luggage allowed, Platz der Republik 1; S- or U-Bahn: Friedrichstrasse, Brandenburger Tor, or Bundestag; tel. 030/2273-2152, www.bundestag.de.

Reservations: To visit the dome, you'll need to **reserve online;** spots often book up several days in advance. Go to www.bundestag.de, and from the "Visit the Bundestag" menu, select "Online registration" (be sure to have the names and birthdates of everyone in your party). You must print and bring your reservation with you.

If you're in Berlin without a reservation, try dropping by the tiny visitors center on the Tiergarten side of Scheidemannstrasse, across from Platz der Republik, to see if any tickets are available (open daily 8:00-20:00, until 18:00 Nov-March; go early to avoid lines; you must book no less than 2 hours and no more than 2 days out; your whole party must be present and ID is required).

Another option for visiting the dome, though pricey, is to make lunch or dinner reservations for the rooftop restaurant, Käfer Dachgarten (daily 9:00-16:30 & 18:30-24:00, last access at 22:00, reserve well in advance at tel. 030/2262-9933 or www.feinkost-kaefer.de/berlin).

Getting In: Report a few minutes before your appointed time to the temporary-looking entrance facility in front of the Reichstag, and be ready to show ID and your reservation printout.

Tours: The free **audioguide** (available after you exit the elevator at the base of the dome) explains the building and narrates the view as you wind up the spiral ramp to the top of the dome; the commentary starts automatically as you step onto the bottom of the ramp.

⊙ Self-Guided Tour: The open, airy lobby towers 100 feet high, with 65-foot-tall colors of the German flag. See-through glass doors show the **central legislative chamber.** The message: There will be no secrets in this government. Look inside. Spreading his wings behind the podium is a stylized German eagle, the *Bundestagsadler* (a.k.a. the "fat hen"), representing the Bundestag (each branch of government has its own symbolic eagle). Notice the doors marked *Ja* (Yes), *Nein* (No), and *Enthalten* (Abstain)...an homage to the Bundestag's traditional "sheep jump" way of counting votes by exiting the chamber through the corresponding door (for critical votes, however, all 631 members vote with electronic cards).

The Reichstag's original facade

Ride the elevator to the base of the glass **dome.** Pick up the free audioguide and take some time to study the photos and read the circle of captions (around the base of the central funnel) for an excellent exhibit telling the Reichstag story. Then study the surrounding architecture: a broken collage of new on old, torn between antiquity and modernity, like Germany's history. Notice the dome's giant and unobtrusive sunscreen that moves as necessary with the sun. Peer down through the skylight to look over the shoulders of the elected representatives at work. For Germans, the best view from here is down—keeping a close eye on their government.

Start at the ramp nearest the elevator and wind up to the top of the **double ramp.** Take a 360-degree survey of the city as you hike: The big park is the **Tiergarten,** the "green lungs of Berlin." Beyond that is the **Teufelsberg** ("Devil's Hill"). Built of rubble from the destroyed city in the late 1940s, it was famous during the Cold War as a powerful ear of the West—notice the telecommunications tower on top.

Find the **Victory Column** (Siegessäule), glimmering in the middle of the park. Hitler moved it in the 1930s from in front of the Reichstag to its present position in the Tiergarten as part of his grandiose vision for postwar Berlin. Next, scenes of the new Berlin spiral into view— **Potsdamer Platz,** marked by the conical glass tower that houses Sony's European headquarters. Continue circling left, and find the green chariot atop the **Brandenburg Gate.** Just to its left is the curving fish-like roof of the **DZ Bank** building, designed by the unconventional American architect Frank Gehry. The **Memorial to the Murdered Jews of Europe** stretches south of the Brandenburg Gate. Next, you'll see **former East Berlin** and the city's next huge construction zone, with a forest of 300-foot-tall skyscrapers in the works. Notice the **TV Tower,** the **Berlin** Cathedral's massive dome, and the golden dome of the **New Synagogue.**

Follow the train tracks in the distance to the left toward Berlin's huge main train station, the **Hauptbahnhof.** Complete your spin-tour with the blocky, postmodern **Chancellery,** the federal government's headquarters. Continue spiraling up. You'll come across all the same sights again, twice, from a higher vantage point.

Inside the Reichstag's glass dome

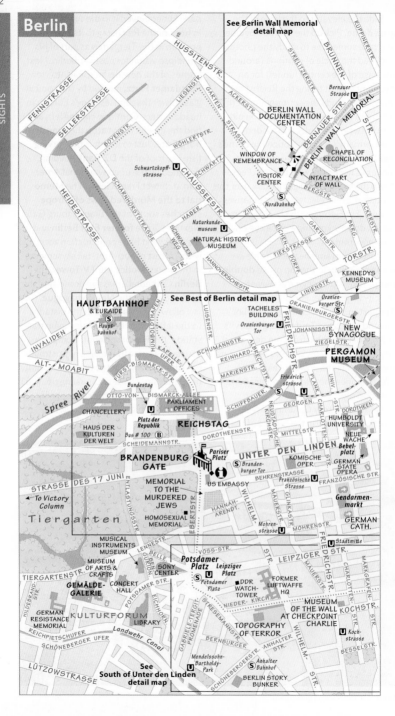

Berlin

See Berlin Wall Memorial detail map

HUSSITENSTR.

FENNSTRASSE

SELLERSTRASSE

HEIDESTRASSE

SCHARNHORSTSTRASSE

BOYENSTR.

LIESENSTR.

GARTEN STRASSE

ACKERSTR.

WÖHLERTSTR.

SCHWARTZ

Schwartzkopff-strasse

CHAUSSEESTR.

BERLIN WALL DOCUMENTATION CENTER

WINDOW OF REMEMBRANCE

VISITOR CENTER

Bernauer Strasse

BERLIN WALL MEMORIAL

CHAPEL OF RECONCILIATION

INTACT PART OF WALL

BERGSTR.

Nordbahnhof

BRUNNEN-STR.

RUPPINERSTR.

STRELITZERSTR.

BERG STR.

ACKERSTR.

HABER-

SCHWARZER WEG

ZINN-STR.

Naturkunde-museum

NATURAL HISTORY MUSEUM

EICHEN-DORFF

TIEKSTRASSE

GARTENSTR.

TORSTR.

HANNOVERSCHESTR.

KENNEDYS MUSEUM

HAUPTBAHNHOF & EURAIDE

Haupt-bahnhof

See Best of Berlin detail map

LINIENSTR.

TACHELES BUILDING

Oranienburger Str.

ORANIENBURGERSTR.

Oranienburger Tor

FRIEDRICHSTR.

JOHANNISSTR.

ZIEGELSTR.

NEW SYNAGOGUE

PERGAMON MUSEUM

INVALIDEN

ALT- MOABIT

Spree River

HUMBOLDTHAFEN

KAPELLE-UFER

FÜRST-BISMARCK-STR.

Bundestag

OTTO-VON- BISMARCK-ALLEE

CHANCELLERY

HAUS DER KULTUREN DER WELT

Platz der Republik

Bus # 100 B

SCHEIDEMANNSTR.

LUISENSTR.

SCHUMANNSTR.

REINHARDTSTR.

MARIENSTR.

ALBRECHTSTR.

PARLIAMENT OFFICES

REICHSTAG

DOROTHEENSTR.

SCHIFFBAUER

NEUSTÄDTISCHE KIRCHSTR.

GEORGEN

Friedrich-strasse

PLANK CHARLOTTEN STR.

UNIV.

DOROTHEEN STR.

HUMBOLDT UNIVERSITY

NEUE WACHE

MITTELSTR.

UNTER DEN LINDEN

Bebel-platz

STRASSE DES 17 JUNI

← To Victory Column

Tiergarten

ENTLASTUNGSSTR.

BRANDENBURG GATE

Pariser Platz

Brandenburger Tor

US EMBASSY

MEMORIAL TO THE MURDERED JEWS

HOMOSEXUAL MEMORIAL

EBERTSTR.

HANNAH-ARENDT-

BEHRENSTRASSE

Französische Strasse

WILHELM-

MAUERSTR.

Mohren-strasse

KOMISCHE OPER

GERMAN STATE OPERA

FRANZÖSISCHE STR.

Gendarmen-markt

GERMAN CATH.

MOHRENSTR.

FRIEDRICHSTR.

Stadtmitte

MUSICAL INSTRUMENTS MUSEUM

MUSEUM OF ARTS & CRAFTS

SONY CENTER

Concert Hall

LENNÉSTR.

BELLE

GURION

TIERGARTENSTR.

GEMÄLDE-GALERIE

GERMAN RESISTANCE MEMORIAL

KULTURFORUM

HILDEBRAND-STR.

REICHPIETSCHUFER

POTSDAMER STR.

EICHHORN

LIBRARY

Landwehr Canal

SCHÖNEBERGER UFER

LÜTZOWSTRASSE

See South of Unter den Linden detail map

VOSS-STR.

Potsdamer Platz

Leipziger Platz

Potsdamer Platz

DDR WATCH-TOWER

FORMER LUFTWAFFE HQ

LEIPZIGER STR.

MARGRAFEN-STR.

CHARLOTTEN-STR.

MAUERSTR.

GABRIELE-TERGIT PROMENADE

STRESEMANNSTR.

NIEDER- KIRCH

TOPOGRAPHY OF TERROR

BERNBURGER

WILHELM-

ANHALTER STR.

MUSEUM OF THE WALL AT CHECKPOINT CHARLIE

KOCHSTR.

Koch-strasse

BESSELSTR.

Mendelssohn-Bartholdy-Park

SCHÖNEBERGER STR.

Anhalter Bahnhof

BERLIN STORY BUNKER

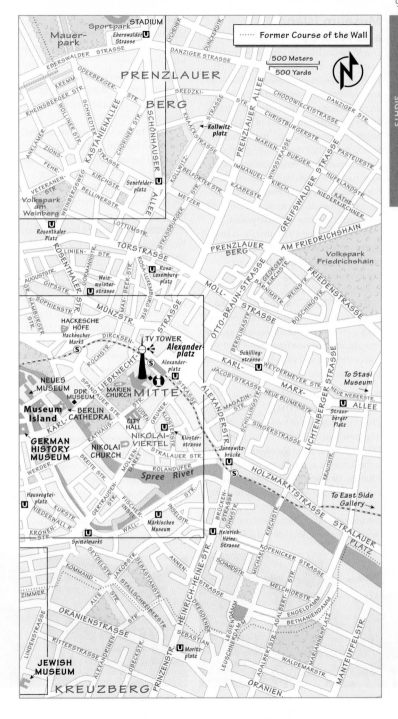

.... Former Course of the Wall

500 Meters
500 Yards

Museum Island and Nearby

The Museum Island complex began taking shape in the 1840s under King Friedrich Wilhelm IV, who envisioned the island as an oasis of culture and learning. A formidable renovation now under way is transforming the island into one of the grandest museum zones in Europe. In the meantime, pardon their dust. I highlight the top two museums: Pergamon and Neues. Also, two recommended museums flank the island: the German History Museum across the river to the west, and the DDR Museum across the river to the east.

Note that three Museum Island landmarks—the **Lustgarten, Berlin Cathedral,** and the **Humboldt-Box**—are described earlier, in my "Best of Berlin Walk"; see page 934.

Getting There: The nearest S-Bahn station to Museum Island is Hackescher Markt, about a 10-minute walk away. From Prenzlauer Berg, ride tram #M-1 to the end of the line, and you're right at the Pergamon Museum.

▲▲▲PERGAMON MUSEUM (PERGAMONMUSEUM)

The star attraction of this world-class museum, part of Berlin's Collection of Classical Antiquities (Antikensammlung), is the fantastic and gigantic Pergamon Altar...but it—and all Hellenistic artworks in the collection—are off-limits to visitors until 2019, as the museum undergoes a major renovation. But there's much more to see here, including the Babylonian Ishtar Gate (slathered with glazed blue tiles from the sixth century B.C.) and ancient Mesopotamian, Roman, and early Islamic treasures.

Cost and Hours: €12, special exhibits extra, daily 10:00-18:00, until 20:00 on Thu, tel. 030/266-424-242, www.smb.museum.

When to Go: Mornings are busiest, and you're likely to find long lines any time of day on Saturday or Sunday. The least-crowded time is Thursday evening.

Crowd-Beating Tips: Avoid lines for the Pergamon by purchasing a timed ticket online, or book a free timed-entry reservation if you have a Museum Pass Berlin or a Museum Island Pass (www.smb.museum).

Visting the Museum: Make ample use of the superb audioguide (included with admission).

From the entry hall, head up the stairs and all the way back to 575 B.C., to the Fertile Crescent—Mesopotamia (today's Iraq). The Assyrian ruler Nebuchadnezzar II, who amassed a vast empire and enormous wealth, wanted to build a suitably impressive processional entryway to his capital city, Babylon, to honor the goddess Ishtar. His creation, the blue **Ishtar Gate,** inspired awe and obedience in anyone who came to his city. This is a reconstruction, using some original components. The gate itself is embellished with two animals: a bull and a mythical dragon-like combination of lion, cobra, eagle, and scorpion. The long hall leading to the main gate—designed for a huge processional

Ishtar Gate

Market Gate of Miletus

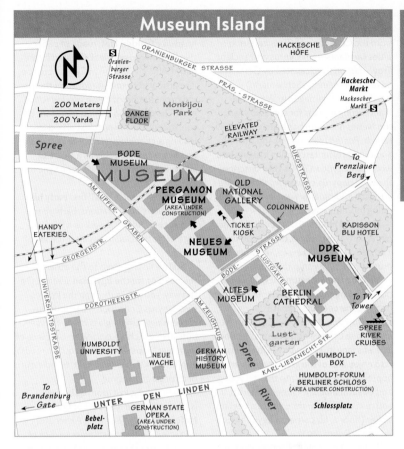

Museum Island

Oranienburger Strasse

ORANIENBURGER STRASSE

HACKESCHE HÖFE

PRÄS.-STRASSE

Hackescher Markt

Hackescher Markt

200 Meters
200 Yards

Monbijou Park

DANCE FLOOR

ELEVATED RAILWAY

Spree

BODE MUSEUM

AM KUPFER-GRABEN

MUSEUM

PERGAMON MUSEUM (AREA UNDER CONSTRUCTION)

OLD NATIONAL GALLERY

COLONNADE

BURGSTRASSE

To Prenzlauer Berg

HANDY EATERIES

GEORGENSTR.

TICKET KIOSK

NEUES MUSEUM

AM LUSTGARTEN

BODE-STRASSE

RADISSON BLU HOTEL

DDR MUSEUM

UNIVERSITÄTSSTRASSE

DOROTHEENSTR.

AM ZEUGHAUS

ALTES MUSEUM

BERLIN CATHEDRAL

ISLAND

To TV Tower

SPREE RIVER CRUISES

HUMBOLDT UNIVERSITY

NEUE WACHE

GERMAN HISTORY MUSEUM

Spree River

Lust-garten

KARL-LIEBKNECHT-STR.

HUMBOLDT-BOX

HUMBOLDT-FORUM BERLINER SCHLOSS (AREA UNDER CONSTRUCTION)

To Brandenburg Gate

UNTER DEN LINDEN

GERMAN STATE OPERA (AREA UNDER CONSTRUCTION)

Bebel-platz

Schlossplatz

of deities to celebrate the new year—is decorated with a chain of blue and yellow glazed tiles with 120 strolling lions (representing the goddess Ishtar). To get the big picture, find the model of the original site in the center of the hall.

Pass through the gate, and flash-forward 700 years to the ancient Roman city of Miletus. Dominating this room is the 95-foot-wide, 55-foot-high **Market Gate of Miletus,** an ancient Anatolian city destroyed by an earthquake centuries ago and now painstakingly reconstructed here in Berlin. The exquisite mosaic floor from a Roman villa in Miletus has two parts: In the square panel, the musician Orpheus strokes his lyre to charm the animals; in

stark contrast, in the nearby rectangular mosaic (from an adjacent room), hunters pursue wild animals.

These main exhibits are surrounded by smaller galleries. Upstairs is the **Museum of Islamic Art.** It contains fine carpets, tile work, the Aleppo Room (with ornately painted wooden walls from an early 17th-century home in today's Syria), and the Mshatta Facade (walls and towers from one of the early eighth-century Umayyad "desert castles," from today's Jordan).

▲▲NEUES (NEW) MUSEUM

Oddly, Museum Island's so-called "new" museum features the oldest stuff around. There are three collections here: the Egyptian Collection (with the famous bust of Queen Nefertiti), the Museum of Pre-history and Early History, and some items from the Collection of Classical Antiquities (artifacts from Cyprus and ancient Troy—famously excavated by German adventurer Heinrich Schliemann).

After being damaged in World War II and sitting in ruins for some 40 years, the Neues Museum has been gorgeously rebuilt. Posted information and the fine audioguide offer fascinating insights into workaday Egyptian life as they describe the vivid papyrus collection, slice-of-life artifacts, and dreamy wax portraits decorating mummy cases.

Cost and Hours: €12, special exhibits extra, daily 10:00-18:00, until 20:00 on Thu, tel. 030/266-424-242, www.neues-museum.de, www.smb.museum.

Visiting the Museum: Pick up a floor plan showing the suggested route, then head up the central staircase.

The top draw here is the Egyptian art—clearly one of the world's best collections. But let's face it: The main reason to visit is to enjoy one of the great thrills in art appreciation—gazing into the still young and beautiful face of Queen Nefertiti. If you're in a pinch for time, make a beeline to her (floor 2, far corner of Egyptian Collection in Room 210).

To tour the whole collection, start at the top (floor 3), which is where you'll find the **prehistory section.** The entire floor is filled with Stone Age, Ice Age, and Bronze Age items. You'll see early human remains, tools, spearheads, and pottery.

The most interesting item on this floor (in corner Room 305) is the tall, cone-head-like **Golden Hat,** made of paper-thin hammered gold leaf. Created by an early Celtic civilization in Central Europe, it's particularly exquisite for something so old (from the Bronze Age, around 1000 B.C.). The circles on the hat represent the sun, moon, and other celestial bodies—leading archaeologists to believe that this headwear could double as a calendar, showing how the sun and moon sync up every 19 years.

Down on floor 2, you'll find **early history** exhibits on migrations, barbarians, and ancient Rome, as well as a fascinating look at the Dark Ages after the fall of Rome.

Still on floor 2, cross to the other side of the building for the **Egyptian** section. On the way, you'll pass through the impressive Papyrus Collection—a large room of seemingly empty glass cases. Press a button to watch a 3,000-year-old piece of primitive "paper" (made of aquatic reeds), imprinted with primitive text, trundle out of its protective home.

Then, finally, in a room all her own, is the 3,000-year-old bust of **Queen Nefertiti** (the wife of King Akhenaton, c. 1340 B.C.)—the most famous piece of Egyptian art in Europe. (She's had it with the paparazzi—photos of her are strictly *verboten.*) Called "Berlin's most beautiful woman," Nefertiti has all the right beauty marks: long neck, symmetrical face, and the perfect amount of makeup. And yet,

Neues Museum

Queen Nefertiti

she's not completely idealized. Notice the fine wrinkles that show she's human (though these only enhance her beauty). Like a movie star discreetly sipping a glass of wine at a sidewalk café, Nefertiti seems somehow more dignified in person. The bust never left its studio, but served as a master model for all other portraits of the queen. (That's probably why the left eye was never inlaid.) Stare at her long enough, and you may get the sensation that she's winking at you. Hey, beautiful!

▲▲▲ GERMAN HISTORY MUSEUM (DEUTSCHES HISTORISCHES MUSEUM)

This fantastic museum, which sits across the river west of Museum Island, is a two-part affair: the pink former Prussian arsenal building and the I. M. Pei-designed annex. The main building (fronting Unter den Linden) houses the permanent collection, offering the best look at German history under one roof, anywhere. The modern annex features good temporary exhibits surrounded by the work of a great contemporary architect. This thoughtfully presented museum—with more than 8,000 artifacts telling not just the story of Berlin, but of all Germany—is clearly the top history museum in town. If you need a break during your visit, there's a restful café with terrace seating in season.

Cost and Hours: €8, excellent €3 audioguide, daily 10:00-18:00, Unter den Linden 2, tel. 030/2030-4751, www.dhm.de.

Getting In: If the ticket-buying line is long at the main entrance, try circling around the back to the Pei annex (to reach it, head down the street to the left of the museum—called Hinter dem Giesshaus), where entry lines are usually shorter (but audioguides for the permanent exhibit are available only at the main desk).

Visiting the Museum: The permanent collection packs two huge rectangular floors of the old arsenal building with historical objects, photographs, and models. From the lobby, head upstairs to the **first floor** and work your way chronologically down. This floor traces German history from A.D. 500 to 1918, with exhibits on early cultures, the Middle Ages, Reformation, Thirty Years' War, German Empire, and World War I. You'll see lots of models of higgledy-piggledy medieval towns and castles, tapestries, suits of armor, busts of great Germans, a Turkish tent from the Ottoman siege of Vienna (1683), flags from German unification in 1871 (the first time "Germany" existed as a nation), exhibits on everyday life in the tenements of the Industrial Revolution, and much more.

History marches on through the 20th century on the **ground floor,** including the Weimar Republic, Nazism, World War II, Allied occupation, and a divided Germany. Propaganda posters trumpet Germany's would-be post-WWI savior, Adolf Hitler. Look for the model of the impossibly huge, 950-foot-high, 180,000-capacity domed hall Hitler wanted to erect in

Exhibits at the German History Museum are comprehensive and thought-provoking.

the heart of Berlin, which he planned to re-envision as Welthauptstadt Germania, the "world capital" of his far-reaching Third Reich. Another model shows the nauseating reality of Hitler's grandiosity: a crematorium at Auschwitz-Birkenau concentration camp in occupied Poland. The exhibit wraps up with chunks of the Berlin Wall, reunification, and a quick look at Germany today.

For architecture buffs, the big attraction is the **Pei annex** behind the history museum, which complements the permanent collection with temporary exhibits. From the old building, cross through the courtyard (with the Pei glass canopy overhead) to reach the annex. A striking glassed-in spiral staircase unites four floors with surprising views and lots of light. It's here that you'll experience why Pei—famous for his glass pyramid at Paris' Louvre—is called the "perfector of classical modernism," "master of light," and a magician at uniting historical buildings with new ones.

▲▲DDR MUSEUM

The exhibits offer an interesting look at life in the former East Germany without the negative spin most museums give. It's well-stocked with kitschy everyday items from the communist period, plus photos, video clips, and concise English explanations. The exhibits are interactive—you're encouraged to pick up and handle anything that isn't behind glass. The reconstructed communist-era home lets you tour the kitchen, living room, and bedrooms. You'll crawl through a Trabant car (East German's answer to the West's popular VW Beetle) and pick up some DDR-era black humor ("East Germany had 39 newspapers, four radio stations, two TV channels...and one opinion").

Cost and Hours: €7, daily 10:00-20:00, Sat until 22:00, just across the Spree from Museum Island at Karl-Liebknecht-Strasse 1, tel. 030/847-123-731, www.ddr-museum.de.

South of Unter den Linden
▲▲GENDARMENMARKT

This delightful, historic square is bounded by twin churches, a tasty chocolate shop, and the Berlin Symphony's concert hall. In summer, it hosts a few outdoor cafés, Biergartens, and sometimes concerts. Wonderfully symmetrical, the square is considered by Berliners to be the finest in town (U6: Französische Strasse; U2 or U6: Stadtmitte; for nearby eateries, see page 975).

The name of the square, which is part French and part German (after the *Gens d'Armes*, Frederick the Great's royal guard, who were headquartered here), reminds us that in the 17th century, a fifth of all Berliners were French émigrés—Protestant Huguenots fleeing Catholic France. Back then, Frederick the Great's tolerant Prussia was a magnet for the persecuted (and their money). These émigrés vitalized Berlin with new ideas, practical knowledge, and their deep pockets.

The church on the south end of the square (left of the concert hall) is the **German Cathedral** (Deutscher Dom). This cathedral was bombed flat in the war and rebuilt only in the 1980s. It houses the thought-provoking "Milestones, Setbacks, Sidetracks" (*Wege, Irrwege, Umwege*) exhibit, which traces the history of the German parliamentary system—worth ▲. While light on actual historical artifacts, the well-done exhibit takes you quickly from the revolutionary days of 1848 to the

Gendarmenmarkt

South of Unter den Linden

1920s, and then more deeply through the tumultuous 20th century (free, Tue-Sun 10:00-19:00, Oct-April until 18:00, closed Mon year-round).

The **French Cathedral** (Französischer Dom), at the north end of the square, offers a viewpoint from the dome up top (€3, daily 10:00-18:00, until 17:30 in Nov-March, 244 steps, enter through door facing square, tel. 030/203-060, www. franzoesischer-dom.de).

Fun fact: Neither church is a true cathedral, as they never contained a bishop's throne; their German titles of *Dom* (cathedral) are actually a mistranslation from the French word *dôme* (cupola).

Fassbender & Rausch, on the corner near the German Cathedral, claims to be Europe's biggest chocolate store. After 150 years of chocolate-making, this family-owned business proudly displays its sweet delights—250 different kinds— on a 55-foot-long buffet. The window

displays feature giant chocolate models of Berlin landmarks—Reichstag, Brandenburg Gate, a chunk of the Wall, and so on. If all this isn't enough to entice you, I have three words: erupting chocolate volcano. Upstairs is an elegant hot-chocolate café with fine views (Mon-Sat 10:00-20:00, Sun from 11:00, corner of Mohrenstrasse at Charlottenstrasse 60, tel. 030/757-882-440).

▲▲TOPOGRAPHY OF TERROR (TOPOGRAPHIE DES TERRORS)

This patch of land was once the nerve center for the Gestapo and the SS, the most despicable elements of the Nazi government. It's chilling to see just how seamlessly and bureaucratically the Nazi institutions and state structures merged to become a well-oiled terror machine. There are few actual artifacts here; it's mostly written explanations and photos, like reading a good textbook standing up. And, while you could read this story anywhere, to take this in atop the Gestapo headquarters is a powerful experience. The exhibits, sited indoors and out, are dense, but WWII historians (even armchair ones) will find it fascinating.

Cost and Hours: Free, includes audioguide for outdoor exhibit, daily 10:00-20:00, outdoor exhibit closes at dusk and in winter, Niederkirchnerstrasse 8, U-Bahn: Potsdamer Platz or Kochstrasse, S-Bahn: Anhalter Bahnhof or Potsdamer Platz, tel. 030/254-5090, www. topographie.de.

Background: This location marks what was once the most feared address in Berlin: the headquarters of the Reich Main Security Office (*Reichssicherheitshauptamt*). These offices served as the engine room of the Nazi dictatorship, as well as the command center of the SS (*Schutzstaffel*, whose members began as Hitler's personal bodyguards), the Gestapo (*Geheime Staatspolizei*, secret state police), and the SD (*Sicherheitsdienst*, the Nazi intelligence agency). This trio (and others) were ultimately consolidated under Heinrich Himmler to become a state-within-a-state, with talons in every corner of German society.

It was from these headquarters that the Nazis administered concentration camps, firmed up plans for their genocide of Jews, and organized the domestic surveillance of anyone opposed to the regime. The building was also equipped with dungeons, where the Gestapo detained and tortured thousands of prisoners.

Visiting the Museum: Start your visit inside, with the extensive **Topography of Terror** exhibit, which walks you through the evolution of Hitler's regime: the Nazi takeover; institutions of terror (Himmler's "SS State"); terror, persecution, and extermination; atrocities in Nazi-occupied countries; and the war's end and postwar. Some images here are indelible, such as photos of SS soldiers stationed at Auschwitz gleefully yukking it up on a retreat in the countryside (as their helpless prisoners were being gassed and burned a few miles away). The exhibit profiles specific members of the various reprehensible SS branches, as well as the groups they targeted: Jews; Roma and Sinti (Gypsies); the unemployed or homeless; homosexuals; and the physically and mentally ill (considered "useless eaters" who consumed resources without contributing work).

Some exhibits at the Topography of Terror are incorporated into a surviving stretch of the Berlin Wall.

Outside, you'll find the exhibit **Berlin 1933-1945: Between Propaganda and Terror** (ask at the information desk inside for the accompanying audioguide). The chronological survey begins with the post-WWI Weimar Republic and continues through the ragged days just after World War II. One display explains how Nazis invented holidays (or injected new Aryan meaning into existing ones) as a means of winning over the public. Other exhibits cover the "Aryanization" of Jewish businesses (they were simply taken over by the state and handed over to new Aryan owners); Hitler's plans for converting Berlin into a gigantic "Welthauptstadt (World Capital) Germania"; and the postwar Berlin Airlift, which brought provisions to some 2.2 million West Berliners whose supply lines were cut off by East Berlin.

Surviving stretches of the Wall are rare in downtown Berlin, but you'll find an **original fragment** of it here (also visible from Niederkirchnerstrasse).

▲CHECKPOINT CHARLIE

This famous Cold War checkpoint was not named for a person, but for its checkpoint number—as in Alpha (#1, at the East-West German border, 100 miles west of here), Bravo (#2, as you enter Berlin proper), and Charlie (#3, the best known because most foreigners passed through here). While the actual checkpoint has long since been dismantled, its former location is home to a fine museum and a mock-up of the original border crossing. The area has become a Cold War freak

show and—as if celebrating the final victory of crass capitalism—is one of Berlin's worst tourist traps. A McDonald's stands defiantly overlooking the former haunt of East German border guards. (For a more sober and intellectually redeeming look at the Wall's history, head for the Berlin Wall Memorial at Bernauer Strasse, described on page 970.)

The rebuilt **guard station** now hosts two actors playing American guards who pose for photos. Notice the larger-than-life **posters** of a young American soldier facing east and a young Soviet soldier facing west. (Look carefully at the "Soviet" soldier. He was photographed in 1999, a decade after there were Soviet soldiers stationed here. He's a Dutch model. His uniform is a nonsensical pile of pins and ribbons with a Russian flag on his shoulder.)

A few yards away (on Zimmerstrasse), a **glass panel** describes the former checkpoint. From there, another double row of **cobbles** in Zimmerstrasse shows the former path of the Wall. A **photo exhibit** stretches up and down Zimmerstrasse, telling the story of the Wall.

Warning: Here and in other places, hustlers charge an exorbitant €10 for a full set of Cold War-era stamps in your passport. Don't be tempted. Technically, this invalidates your passport—which has caused some tourists big problems.

Cost and Hours: Free and always open, Friedrichstrasse 43, near the intersection with Zimmerstrasse, U-Bahn: Kochstrasse or Stadtmitte.

▲▲MUSEUM OF THE WALL AT CHECKPOINT CHARLIE (MAUERMUSEUM HAUS AM CHECKPOINT CHARLIE)

While the famous border checkpoint between the American and Soviet sectors is long gone, its memory is preserved by one of Europe's most cluttered museums. During the Cold War, the House at Checkpoint Charlie stood defiantly—within spitting distance of the border

Checkpoint Charlie

The Berlin Wall (and Its Fall)

The East German government erected the 96-mile-long Wall almost overnight in 1961. It was intended to stop the outward flow of people from the communist East to the capitalist West: Three million souls had leaked out between 1949 and 1961.

The Wall (*Mauer*) was actually two walls, with a no-man's-land in-between. During the 28 years it stood, there were 5,043 documented successful escapes (565 of these were East German guards). At least 138 people died or were killed at the Wall while trying to escape.

As a tangible symbol for the Cold War, the Berlin Wall got a lot of attention from politicians. Two of the 20th century's most repeated presidential quotes were uttered within earshot of the Wall. In 1963, President John F. Kennedy professed American solidarity with the struggling people of Berlin: "*Ich bin ein Berliner.*" In 1987, with the winds of change already blowing westward from Moscow, President Ronald Reagan issued an ultimatum to his Soviet counterpart: "Mr. Gorbachev, tear down this wall."

The actual fall of the Wall had less to do with presidential proclamations than with the obvious failings of the Soviet system, a general thawing in Moscow, the brave civil disobedience of ordinary citizens behind the Wall—and a bureaucratic snafu.

By November 1989, change was in the air. Hungary had already opened its borders to the West that summer, making it impossible for East German authorities to keep people in. Anti-regime protests swept nearby Leipzig, attracting hundreds of thousands of supporters. A rally in East Berlin's Alexanderplatz on November 4—with a half-million protesters chanting, "*Wir wollen raus!*" (We want out!)—persuaded the East German politburo to begin gradually relaxing travel restrictions.

The DDR intended to crack the door to the West, but an unknowing spokesman inadvertently threw it wide open. In back-room meetings early on November 9, officials decided they would allow a few more Easterners to cross into the West. The politburo members then left town for a long weekend. The announcement of the decision was left to Günter Schabowski, who knew only what was on a piece of paper handed to him moments before a routine press conference. At 18:54, Schabowski read the statement on live TV, with little emotion: "exit via border crossings...possible for every citizen." Reporters, unable to believe what they were hearing, prodded him about when the borders would open. Schabowski shrugged and offered his best guess: "*Ab sofort, unverzüglich.*" ("Immediately, without delay.")

Schabowski's words spread like wildfire. East Berliners showed up at Wall checkpoints, demanding that border guards let them pass. Finally, around 23:30, a border guard at the Bornholmer Strasse crossing decided to open the gates. Easterners flooded into the West, embracing their long-separated cousins, unable to believe their good fortune. Once open, the Wall could never be closed again. After that wild night, Berlin faced a fitful transition to reunification. Two cities—and countries—became one at a staggering pace.

guards—showing off all the clever escapes over, under, and through the Wall. Today, while the drama is over and hunks of the Wall stand like trophies at its door, the museum survives as a living artifact of the Cold War days. The yellowed descriptions, which have scarcely changed since that time, tinge the museum with nostalgia. It's dusty, disorganized, and overpriced, with lots of reading involved, but all that just adds to this museum's borderline-kitschy charm. If you're pressed for time, visit after dinner, when most other museums are closed.

Cost and Hours: €12.50, €3.50 audioguide, daily 9:00-22:00, U6 to Kochstrasse or U2 to Stadtmitte, Friedrichstrasse 43, tel. 030/253-7250, www.mauermuseum.de.

Visiting the Museum: Exhibits narrate a gripping history of the Wall, with a focus on the many ingenious **escape attempts** (the early years—with a cruder wall—saw more escapes). You'll see the actual items used to smuggle would-be escapees: a VW bug whose trunk hid a man, two side-by-side suitcases into which a woman

Museum of the Wall at Checkpoint Charlie

squeezed, a makeshift zip line for crossing over the border, a hot-air balloon in which two families floated to safety, an inflatable boat that puttered across the dangerous Baltic Sea, primitive homemade aircraft, two surfboards hollowed out to create just enough space for a refugee, and more. One chilling exhibit lists some 43,000 people who died in "Internal Affairs" internment camps during the transition to communism (1945-1950). Profiles personalize various escapees and their helpers, including John P. Ireland, an American who posed as an eccentric antiques collector so he could transport 10 refugees to safety in his modified Cadillac.

▲▲JEWISH MUSEUM BERLIN (JÜDISCHES MUSEUM BERLIN)

This museum surveys the rich and complicated history of Jews in Germany. The highly conceptual building is a sight in itself, and the museum inside is excellent, particularly if you take advantage of the informative and engaging audioguide. Rather than just reading dry texts, you'll feel this museum as fresh and alive—an exuberant celebration of the Jewish experience that's accessible to all.

Cost and Hours: €8, recommended €3 audioguide, daily 10:00-20:00, Mon until 22:00, last entry one hour before closing, closed on Jewish holidays, Lindenstrasse 9, tel. 030/2599-3300, www.jmberlin.de.

Getting There: Take the U-Bahn to Hallesches Tor, find the exit marked *Jüdisches Museum*, exit straight ahead, then turn right on Franz-Klühs-Strasse. The museum is a five-minute walk ahead on your left.

Eating: The museum's restaurant, Café Schmus, offers good meals in a pleasant setting.

Visiting the Museum: Designed by American architect Daniel Libeskind (the master planner for the redeveloped World Trade Center in New York), the zinc-walled building has a zigzag shape pierced by voids symbolic of the irreplaceable cultural loss caused by the Holocaust.

Enter the 18th-century Baroque building next door, then go through an underground tunnel to reach the museum interior.

Before you reach the exhibit, your visit starts with three **memorial spaces.** Follow the Axis of Exile to a disorienting slanted garden with 49 pillars (evocative of the Memorial to the Murdered Jews of Europe, across town). Next, the Axis of Holocaust, lined with artifacts from Jews imprisoned and murdered by the Nazis, leads to an eerily empty tower shut off from the outside world. The Axis of Continuity takes you to stairs and the main exhibit. A detour partway up the long stairway leads to the Memory Void, a compelling space of "fallen leaves": heavy metal faces that you walk on, making unhuman noises with each step.

Finish climbing the stairs to the top of the museum, and stroll chronologically through the 2,000-year **story of Judaism** in Germany. The exhibit, on two floors, is engaging, with lots of actual artifacts. Interactive bits (you can, for example, spell your name in Hebrew, or write a prayer and hang it from a tree) make it lively for kids.

The top floor focuses on everyday life in **Ashkenaz** (medieval German-Jewish lands). On the middle floor, exhibits detail the rising tide of anti-Semitism in Germany through the 19th century—at a time when many Jews were so secularized that they celebrated Christmas right along with Hanukkah. The exhibit segues into the **dark days** of Hitler—the collapse of the relatively tolerant Weimar Republic, the rise of the Nazis, and the horrific night of November 9, 1938, when, throughout Germany, hateful mobs destroyed Jewish-owned businesses, homes, synagogues, and even entire villages—called "Crystal Night" (Kristallnacht) for the broken glass that glittered in the streets.

The display brings us to the present day, with the question: How do you keep going after six million of your people have been murdered? You'll see how German society reacted to the two largest Nazi trials, complete with historical film clips of the perpetrators. In the last segment, devoted to Jewish life today, German Jews describe their experiences growing up in the postwar years.

The Jewish Museum's fractured façade suggests the dislocation of the Holocaust.

Kulturforum Complex

The Kulturforum, off the southeast corner of Tiergarten park, hosts Berlin's concert hall and several sprawling museums, but only the Gemäldegalerie is a must for art lovers.

▲▲GEMÄLDEGALERIE

Literally the "Painting Gallery," the Gemäldegalerie is Germany's top collection of medieval and Renaissance European paintings (more than 1,400 canvases). They're beautifully displayed in a building that's a work of art in itself. If you're short on time or stamina, start in the North Wing galleries holding Northern European masterworks by Cranach, Dürer, Van Eyck, Brueghel, Rubens, Van Dyck, Hals, and Vermeer (to name just a few). You'll also encounter an impressive stash of Rembrandts. The South Wing is saved for the Italians—Giotto, Botticelli, Titian, Raphael, and Caravaggio.

Cost and Hours: €10, Tue-Fri 10:00-18:00, Thu until 20:00, Sat-Sun 11:00-18:00, closed Mon, audioguide included with entry, great salad bar in cafeteria upstairs, Matthäikirchplatz 4, tel. 030/266-424-242, www.smb.museum.

Getting There: Ride the S-Bahn or U-Bahn to Potsdamer Platz, then walk along Potsdamer Platz.

⊘ Self-Guided Tour: I'll point out a few highlights, focusing on Northern European artists (German, Dutch, and Flemish), with a few Spaniards and Italians thrown in. To go beyond my selections, make ample use of the excellent audioguide.

The collection spreads out on one vast floor surrounding a central hall. Inner rooms have Roman numerals (I, II, III), while adjacent outer rooms are numbered (1, 2, 3).

Rooms I-III/1-4 kick things off with early German paintings (13th-16th century). In Room 1, look for the 1532 portrait of wealthy Hanseatic cloth merchant Georg Gisze by **Hans Holbein the Younger** (1497-1543). Gisze's name appears on several of the notes stuck to the wall behind him. And, typical of detail-rich Northern European art, the canvas is bursting with highly symbolic tidbits. Items scattered on the tabletop and on the shelves behind the merchant represent his lofty status and aspects of his life story. In the vase, the carnation represents his recent engagement, and the herbs symbolize his virtue. And yet, the celebratory flowers have already begun to fade and the scales behind him are unbalanced, reminders of the fleetingness of happiness and wealth.

In Room 2 are fine portraits by the remarkably talented **Albrecht Dürer** (1471-1528), who traveled to Italy during the burgeoning days of the early Renaissance and melded the artistic harmony and classical grandeur he discovered there with a Northern European attention to detail. In his *Portrait of Hieronymus Holzschuher* (1526), Dürer skillfully captured the personality of a friend from Nürnberg, right down to the sly twinkle in his sidelong glance. Technically, the portrait is perfection: Look closely and see each individual hair of the man's beard and fur coat, and even the reflection of the studio's windows in his eyes. Also notice

Holbein the Younger, The Merchant Georg Gisze

Dürer's little pyramid-shaped, D-inside-A signature. Signing one's work was a revolutionary assertion of Dürer's renown at a time when German artists were considered anonymous craftsmen.

Lucas Cranach the Elder (1472-1553), whose works are in Room III, was a court painter for the prince electors of Saxony and a close friend of Martin Luther (and his unofficial portraitist). But *The Fountain of Youth* (1546) is a far cry from Cranach's solemn portrayals of the reformer. Old women helped to the fountain (on the left) emerge as young ladies on the right. Newly nubile, the women go into a tent to dress up, snog with noblemen in the bushes (right foreground), dance merrily beneath the trees, and dine grandly beneath a landscape of phallic mountains and towers. This work is flanked by Cranach's Venus nudes. I sense a pattern here.

Dutch painters (Rooms IV-VI/4-7) were early adopters of oil paint (as opposed to older egg tempera)—its relative ease of handling allowed them to brush the fine details for which they became famous. **Rogier van der Weyden** (Room IV) was a virtuoso of the new medium. In *Portrait of a Woman* (c. 1400-1464), the subject wears a typical winged bonnet, addressing the viewer directly with her fetching blue eyes. In the same room is a remarkable, rare trio of three-panel altarpieces by Van der Weyden: The Marienaltar shows the life of the Virgin Mary; the Johannesaltar narrates the life of John the Baptist—his birth, baptizing Christ (with God and the Holy Spirit hovering overhead), and his gruesome death by decapitation; and the Middelburger Altar tells the story of the Nativity. Savor the fine details in each panel of these altarpieces.

Flash forward a few hundred years to the 17th century and Flemish (Belgian) painting (Rooms VII-VIII/9-10), and it's apparent how much the Protestant Reformation—and resulting Counter-Reformation—changed the tenor of Northern European art. In works by **Peter Paul Rubens** (1577-1640)—including *Jesus Giving Peter the Keys to Heaven*—calm, carefully studied, detail-oriented seriousness gives way to an exuberant Baroque trumpeting of the greatness of the Catholic Church. In the Counter-Reformation world, the Catholic Church had serious competition for the hearts and minds of its congregants. Exciting art like this became a way to keep people in the pews. In the next rooms (VIII and 9) are more Rubens, including the mythological *Perseus Freeing Andromeda* and *The Martyrdom of St. Sebastian by Arrows* (loosely based on a more famous rendition by Andrea Mantegna).

Dutch painting from the 17th century (Rooms IX-XI/10-19) is dominated by the convivial portraits by **Frans Hals** (c. 1582-1666). His 1620 portrait of Catharina Hooft (far corner, Room 13) presents a startlingly self-possessed baby (the newest member of a wealthy merchant family) dressed with all the finery of a queen, adorned with lace and jewels, and clutching a golden rattle. The smiling nurse supporting the tyke offers her a piece of fruit, whose blush of red perfectly matches the nanny's apple-fresh cheeks.

But the ultimate Dutch master is **Rembrandt van Rijn** (1606-1669), whose powers of perception and invention propelled him to fame in his lifetime. Displayed here are several storytelling scenes (Room 16), mostly from classical mythology or biblical stories, all employing Rembrandt's trademark chiaroscuro technique (with a strong contrast between light and dark). In *The Rape of Persephone,* Pluto grabs Persephone from his chariot and races toward the underworld, while other goddesses cling to her robe, trying to save her. In the nearby *Samson and Delilah* (1628), Delilah cradles Samson's head in her lap while silently signaling to a goon to shear Samson's hair, the secret to his strength. A self-portrait (Room X) of a 28-year-old

Rembrandt wearing a beret is paired with the come-hither 1637 *Portrait of Hendrickje Stoffels* (the two were romantically linked). *Samson Threatens His Father-in-Law* (1635) captures the moment just after the mighty Samson (with his flowing hair, elegant robes, and shaking fist) has been told by his wife's father to take a hike. I wouldn't want to cross this guy.

Although **Johannes Vermeer** (1632–1675) is today just as admired as Rembrandt, he was little known in his day, probably because he painted relatively few works for a small circle of Delft collectors. Vermeer was a master at conveying a complicated story through a deceptively simple scene with a few poignant details—whether it's a woman reading a letter at a window, a milkmaid pouring milk from a pitcher into a bowl, or (as in *The Glass of Wine*, Room 18) a young man offering a drink to a young lady. The young man had been playing her some music on his lute (which now sits, discarded, on a chair) and is hoping to seal the deal with some alcohol. The woman is finishing one glass of wine, and her would-be suitor stands ready—almost *too* ready—to pour her another. Vermeer has perfectly captured the exact moment of "Will she or won't she?"

Shift south to Italian, French, and Spanish painting of the 17th and 18th centuries (Rooms XII-XIV/23-28). Venetian cityscapes by Canaletto (who also painted Dresden) and lots of bombastic Baroque art hang in Room XII. Room XIII features big-name Spanish artists Murillo, Zurbarán, and the great **Diego Velázquez** (1599-1660). He gave the best of his talents to his portraits, capturing warts-and-all likenesses that are effortlessly real. His 1630 *Portrait of a Lady* conveys the subject's subtle, sly Mona Lisa smile. Her figure and face (against a dull gray background) are filtered through a pleasant natural light.

From here, the collection itself takes a step backwards—into Italian paintings

Ⓐ *Van der Weyden,* Portrait of a Woman

Ⓑ *Rubens,* Jesus Giving Peter the Keys to Heaven

Ⓒ *Rembrandt,* Self-Portrait with a Velvet Beret

Ⓓ *Vermeer,* The Glass of Wine

of the 13th-16th century (Rooms XV-XVIII/29-41). This section includes some lesser-known works by great Italian Renaissance painters, including Raphael (Rooms XVII and 29, with five different Madonnas, among them the *Terranuova Madonna,* in a round frame) and Sandro Botticelli (Room XVIII).

Across the Spree River

Several interesting, lively neighborhoods lie in a cluster across the river, just north of Museum Island (and easily accessed by the island's bridges and public transit): Hackescher Markt (with fun shops and fine little museums), Oranienburger Strasse (New Synagogue, eateries, and nightlife), and Prenzlauer Berg (Berlin Wall Memorial, eateries, accommodations, and more nightlife).

As you wander through the neighborhoods, you might notice small brass plaques in the sidewalk called *Stolpersteine,* marking the former homes of Jewish and other WWII victims of the Nazis.

Hackescher Markt

On a sunny day, a stroll (or tram ride) through this bursting-with-life area can be as engaging as any museum in town. Located in front of the S-Bahn station of the same name, this is a great people scene day and night. The brick trestle supporting the train track is a classic example of the city's Brandenburg Neo-Gothic brickwork. Most of the brick archways are now filled with hip shops. Within 100 yards of the S-Bahn station, you'll find Turkish and Bavarian restaurants, walking-tour and pub-crawl departure points, and tram #M1 to Prenzlauer Berg. Also nearby are two great examples of Berlin's traditional courtyards *(Höfe)*—one trendy and modern, the other retro-cool, with two fascinating museums.

HACKESCHE HÖFE

A block from the Hackescher Markt S-Bahn station (at Rosenthaler Strasse 40) is a series of eight courtyards bunny-hopping through a wonderfully restored 1907 *Jugendstil* (German Art Nouveau) building. Berlin's apartments are organized like this—courtyard after courtyard leading off the main road. This complex is full of artsy designer shops, popular restaurants, theaters, and cinemas. Courtyard #5 is particularly charming, with a children's park, and an Ampelmann store (see page 973). This courtyard system is a wonderful example of how to make huge city blocks livable. Two decades after the Cold War, this area has reached the final evolution of East Berlin's urban restoration: total gentrification. These courtyards also offer a useful lesson for visitors: Much of Berlin's charm hides off the street front.

HAUS SCHWARZENBERG

Next door (at Rosenthaler Strasse 39), this courtyard has a totally different feel. Owned by an artists' collective, it comes with a bar, cinema, open-air art space, and the basement-level "Dead Chickens" gallery (with far-out hydro-powered art). And within this amazing little zone you'll find two inspirational museums. The **Museum of Otto Weidt's Workshop for the Blind** (Museum Blindenwerkstatt Otto Weidt) vividly tells the amazing story of a Berliner heroically protecting blind and deaf Jews during World War II (free, daily 10:00-20:00). Otto Weidt employed them to produce brooms and brushes, and because that was useful for the Nazi war machine, he managed to

New Synagogue

finagle a special status for his workers. You can see the actual brushmaking factory with pedal-powered machines still lined up. The **Silent Heroes Memorial Center** (Gedenkstätte Stille Helden) is a well-presented exhibit celebrating the quietly courageous individuals who resisted the persecution of the Jews from 1933 to 1945 (free, daily 10:00-20:00).

Oranienburger Strasse

Oranienburger Strasse, a few blocks west of Hackescher Markt, is anchored by an important and somber sight, the New Synagogue. But the rest of this zone (roughly between the synagogue and Torstrasse) is colorful and quirky—especially after dark. The streets behind Grosse Hamburger Strasse flicker with atmospheric cafés, *Kneipen* (pubs), and art galleries.

▲NEW SYNAGOGUE (NEUE SYNAGOGUE)

A shiny gilded dome marks the New Synagogue, now a museum and cultural center. Consecrated in 1866, this was once the biggest and finest synagogue in Germany, with seating for 3,200 worshippers and a sumptuous Moorish-style interior modeled after the Alhambra in Granada, Spain. It was desecrated by Nazis on Crystal Night (Kristallnacht) in 1938, bombed in 1943, and partially rebuilt in 1990. Only the dome and facade have been restored—a window overlooks the vacant field marking what used to be the synagogue. On its facade, a small plaque—added by East Berlin Jews in 1966—reads "Never forget" *(Vergesst es nie)*. Inside, past tight security, the small but moving permanent exhibit called Open Ye the Gates describes the Berlin Jewish community through the centuries. Skip the dome climb for an extra fee; the views are ho-hum.

Cost and Hours: April-Oct Mon-Fri 10:00-18:00, Sun until 19:00; Nov-March exhibit only Sun-Thu 10:00-18:00, Fri until 15:00; closed Sat year-round; audio-guide-€3, Oranienburger Strasse 28/30, enter through the low-profile door in the modern building just right of the domed synagogue facade, S-Bahn: Oranienburger Strasse, www.cjudaicum.de.

Prenzlauer Berg and Nearby
▲▲▲PRENZLAUER BERG

This is one of Berlin's most colorful neighborhoods. The heart of this area, with a dense array of hip cafés, restaurants, boutiques, and street life, is roughly between Helmholtzplatz and Kollwitzplatz and along Kastanienallee (U2: Senefelderplatz and Eberswalder Strasse; or take the S-Bahn to Hackescher Markt and catch tram #M1 north).

"Prenzl'berg," as Berliners call it, was largely untouched during World War II, but its buildings slowly rotted away under the communists. Then, after the Wall fell, it was overrun first with artists and anarchists, then with laid-back hipsters, energetic young families, and clever entrepreneurs who breathed life back into its classic old apartment blocks, deserted factories, and long-forgotten breweries.

Years of rent control kept things affordable for its bohemian residents. But now landlords are free to charge what the market will bear, and the vibe is changing. This is ground zero for Berlin's baby boom: Tattooed and pierced young moms and dads, who've joined the modern rat race without giving up their alternative flair, push their youngsters in designer strollers

Relaxing in Prenzlauer Berg

past trendy boutiques and restaurants.

Aside from the **Berlin Wall Memorial** at its western edge (see next) and the **Mauerpark** (Wall Park, once part of the Wall's death strip, today a Prenzlauer Berg green space), the area has few real sights—it's just a lively, laid-back neighborhood ignoring its wonderful late-19th-century architecture high overhead.

▲▲▲BERLIN WALL MEMORIAL (GEDENKSTÄTTE BERLINER MAUER)

While tourists flock to Checkpoint Charlie, this memorial is Berlin's most substantial attraction relating to its gone-but-not-forgotten Wall. Exhibits line up along several blocks of Bernauer Strasse, stretching northeast from the Nordbahnhof S-Bahn station. You can enter two different museums plus various open-air exhibits and memorials, see several fragments of the Wall, and peer from an observation tower down into a preserved, complete stretch of the Wall system (as it was during the Cold War). To brush up on the basics before your visit, read the sidebar on page 962.

The Berlin Wall, which was erected virtually overnight in 1961, ran right along Bernauer Strasse. People were suddenly separated from their neighbors across the street. This stretch was particularly notorious because existing apartment buildings were incorporated into the structure of the Wall itself. Film footage and photographs from the era show Berliners worriedly watching workmen seal off these buildings from the West, brick by brick. Some people attempted to leap to freedom from upper-story windows, with mixed results. One of the unfortunate ones was Ida Siekmann, who fell to her death from her third-floor apartment on August 22, 1961, and is considered the first casualty of the Berlin Wall.

Cost and Hours: Free; Visitor Center and Documentation Center open Tue-Sun 10:00-18:00, closed Mon, outdoor areas accessible 24 hours daily, memorial chapel closes at 17:00; Bernauer Strasse 111, tel. 030/4679-86666, www.berliner-mauer-gedenkstaette.de.

Getting There: Take the S-Bahn (line S-1, S-2, or S-25—all handy from Potsdamer Platz, Brandenburger Tor, Friedrichstrasse, Oranienburger Strasse, or Hackescher Markt) to the Nordbahnhof. Exit by following signs for *Bernauer Strasse*.

Fragments of the Berlin Wall in the memorial area

Berlin Wall Memorial Area

Berlin Wall Memorial
······ **Former Course of the Wall**

500 Meters
500 Yards

STADIUM

STAGE

Mauer-park Sportpark

FLEA MARKET (SUN.)

EBERSWALDER STR.

Eberswalder Strasse

DANZIGER

PRENZLAUER BERG

Bernauer Strasse

KREMM.

ODERBERGER STR.

SREDZKISTR.

KNACK

SCHWEDTER

BERLIN WALL DOCUMENTATION CENTER

CHAPEL OF RECONCILIATION

WINDOW OF REMEMBRANCE

VISITOR CENTER

INTACT PART OF WALL

Kollwitz-platz

Jewish Cem.

ANKLAMER

ZIONS-

FEHR.

KIRCHSTR.

Senefelder-platz

BERGSTR.

VETERANEN-STR.

BELLINERSTR.

Nordbahnhof

Volkspark am Weinberg

ZEHDENICKER

LOTTUMSTR.

INVALIDEN-STR.

Rosenthaler Platz

○ **Self-Guided Tour:** Here's an overview of the route you'll take. From the Nordbahnhof station (which has some interesting Wall history in itself), head to the Visitor Center to get your bearings, then explore the assorted Wall fragments and other sights in the park across the street. Work your way up Bernauer Strasse to the Documentation Center, Wall System, memorial chapel, and remaining signposts (look for the escape-tunnel paths marked in the grass), until you reach the Bernauer Strasse U-Bahn station (or continue beyond the U-Bahn stop to see all the outdoor exhibits, which stretch up to the Mauerpark).

Nordbahnhof: This S-Bahn station was one of the "ghost stations" of Cold War Berlin. It was built in 1926, closed in 1961, and opened again in 1989. As it was a dogleg of the East mostly surrounded by the West, Western subway trains had permission to use the underground tracks to zip through this station (without stop-

ping, of course) en route between stops in the West. East German border guards, who were stationed here to ensure that nobody got on or off those trains, were locked into their surveillance rooms to prevent them from escaping. (But one subway employee and his family used the tunnels to walk to the West and freedom.)

Follow signs down a long yellow hall to the Bernauer Strasse exit. Climbing the stairs up to the street, ponder that the doorway at the top (marked by the *Sperrmauer 1961-1989* plaque) was a bricked-off no-man's-land until 1989. Stepping outside, you'll see a park full of outdoor exhibits (directly across the street) and the Visitor Center (in a low rust-colored building kitty-corner across the street).

Visitor Center (Bezucherzentrum): This small complex has a helpful information desk, and two good movies that provide context for a visit (they run in English at :30 after the hour, about 30 minutes for the whole spiel): *The Berlin Wall* offers a great 15-minute overview of its history. That's followed by *Walled In!,* an animated 12-minute film illustrating the Wall as it functioned here at Bernauer Strasse. Before leaving, pick up the helpful brochures explaining the outdoor exhibits.

Wall Fragments and Other Sights: Across the street from the Visitor Center is a long stretch of Wall. The park behind it is scattered with a few more Wall chunks as well as monuments and memorials honoring its victims. To get your bearings, find the small model of the entire area when the Wall still stood (just across the street from the Nordbahnhof). The rusty "Window of Remembrance" monument honors slain would-be escapees. Before it was the no-man's-land between the walls, this area was the parish graveyard for a nearby church; ironically, DDR officials had to move a thousand graves from here to create a "death strip."

Berlin Wall Documentation Center (Dokumentationszentrum Berliner Mauer): The center's excellent **exhibit** is geared to a new generation of Berliners who can hardly imagine their hometown split so brutally in two. The ground floor details the logistics of the city's division and its effects on Berliners. Have a seat and listen to the riveting personal accounts of escapees—and of the border guards armed with machine guns and tasked with stopping them. The next floor up gives the historical and political context behind the Wall's construction and eventual destruction. Photos let you track the progression of changes at this exact site from 1965 to 1990.

Leaving the exhibit, climb the open-air staircase to an observation deck that gives you a bird's-eye view of the last remaining stretch of the complete Wall system— guard tower, barbed wire, and all.

Stretch of Intact Wall System: This is the last surviving intact bit of the complete Wall system (with both sides of its Wall—capped by the round pipe that made it tougher for escapees to get a grip—and its no-man's-land death strip). The guard tower came from a different part of the Wall; it was actually purchased on that great capitalist invention, eBay (somewhere, Stalin spins in his grave). View it from the observation deck, then visit it from ground level, where wall panels explain each part of the system. Plaques along the sidewalk mark the locations of escapes or deaths.

Chapel of Reconciliation (Kapelle der Versöhnung): Just beyond the Wall section (to the left), this chapel marks the spot of the late-19th-century Church of Reconciliation, which survived WWII bombs—but not the communists. Notice the larger footprint of the original church in the field around the chapel. When the Wall was built, the church wound up right in the middle of the death strip. It was torn down in 1985, supposedly because it got in the way of the border guards' sight lines. Inside the church, the carved wooden altarpiece was saved from the original structure. The chapel

Intact part of the Wall

Chapel of Reconciliation

hosts daily prayer services for the victims of the Wall.

Outdoor Exhibits: The memorial also includes a string of open-air exhibits along Bernauer Strasse that stretch all the way from the Nordbahnhof to the intersection with Schwedter Strasse and Oderberger Strasse, near the Mauerpark, at the heart of Prenzlauer Berg. Video and audio clips, photos, and huge photographic murals let you in on more stories of the Wall—many of which took place right where you're standing.

EXPERIENCES

Shopping

Berlin Story, a big, cluttered, fun bookshop, has a knowledgeable staff and the best selection anywhere in town of English-language books and helpful magazines on Berlin (Mon-Sat 10:00-19:00, Sun 10:00-18:00, Unter den Linden 40, tel. 030/2045-3842).

If you're taken with the city's unofficial mascot, the Ampelmännchen (traffic-light man), you'll find a world of souvenirs slathered with his iconic red and green image at **Ampelmann Shops** (several locations, including along Unter den Linden at #35, near Gendarmenmarkt at Markgrafenstrasse 37, near Museum Island inside the DomAquarée mall, and in the Hackesche Höfe).

Fun and funky **designer shops** fill the **Hackesche Höfe** and are easy to find throughout Prenzlauer Berg, particularly along Kastanienallee and Oderberger Strasse.

Flea markets abound on weekends; virtually every neighborhood hosts one on a regular basis. The most central is along **Am Kupfergraben,** just across the canal from the Pergamon Museum, with lots of books, music, and art (Sat-Sun 10:00-17:00). One of the biggest is right next to the **Tiergarten park** on Strasse des 17 Juni, with great antiques, more than 200 stalls, and fun fast-food stands (Sat-Sun 6:00-16:00, S-Bahn: Tiergarten). The rummage market in Prenzlauer Berg's **Mauerpark** comes with lots of inventive snack stalls—and on Sunday afternoons, **karaoke** (Sat-Sun 7:00-17:00, U-Bahn: Eberswalder Strasse).

On the opposite end of the price spectrum are the swanky shopping centers clustered around **Gendarmenmarkt.** Find the corner of Jägerstrasse and Friedrichstrasse and wander through the **Quartier 206** department store. The adjacent, middlebrow Quartier 205 has more affordable prices.

In western Berlin, it's fun to browse through **Kaufhaus des Westens** (everyone calls it **KaDeWe**), one of Europe's fanciest department stores, with a good selection of souvenirs...and just about anything else you can think of. The top floor holds the Winter Garden Buffet view **cafeteria.** A **deli/food department** is on the sixth floor, along with a **ticket office** that sells music and theater tickets for all events (18 percent fee but access to all tickets; daily 10:00-20:00, Fri until 21:00, closed Sun, S-Bahn: Zoologischer Garten or U-Bahn: Wittenbergplatz, www. kadewe.de).

Nightlife

Berlin is a happening place for nightlife—whether it's clubs, pubs, jazz, cabaret, concerts, or even sightseeing.

Berlin Programm lists a nonstop parade of events (www.berlinprogramm. de); *Exberliner Magazine* doesn't have as much hard information, but is colorfully written in English (sold at kiosks, www. exberliner.com).

Hekticket, Berlin's ticket clearinghouse, offers tickets in advance and **same-day half-price tickets.** Drop by or call after 14:00 to see what's on the push list for this evening (Mon-Fri 12:00-18:00, closed Sat-Sun, half-price sales start at 14:00, near Alexanderplatz at Karl-Liebknecht-Strasse 13, tel. 030/230-9930, www.hekticket.de). **KaDeWe** also sells tickets for events (see last listing in "Shopping").

Rick's Tip: *Stretch your sightseeing day into the night. These museums are open late every day:* Reichstag *(last entry at 22:00),* Museum of the Wall at Checkpoint Charlie *(until 22:00),* Topography of Terror *(until 20:00), and* Jewish Museum Berlin *(Tue-Sun until 20:00, 22:00 on Mon). The* Museum Island*'s museums are open until 20:00 on Thursdays. Outdoor monuments such as the* Berlin Wall Memorial *and the* Memorial to the Murdered Jews of Europe *are safe and well-lit late into the night, even though their visitor centers close earlier.*

Jazz

B-Flat Acoustic Music and Jazz Club, in the heart of eastern Berlin, has live music nightly—and shares a courtyard with a tranquil tea house (shows vary from free to €10-13 cover, open Sun-Thu from 20:00 with shows starting at 21:00, Fri-Sat from 21:00 with shows at 22:00, a block

from Rosenthaler Platz U-Bahn stop at Rosenthaler Strasse 13, tel. 030/283-3123, www.b-flat-berlin.de).

Rock and Roll

Berlin has a vibrant rock and pop scene, with popular venues at the Spandau Citadel, Olympic Stadium, and the outdoor Waldbühne ("Forest Stage"). Check out what's playing on posters in the U-Bahn, on the *Zitty* website (www.zitty.de), or at any ticket agency.

Cabaret

Bar Jeder Vernunft offers modern-day cabaret in western Berlin. This variety show—under a classic old tent perched atop the modern parking lot of the Berliner Festspiele theater—is a hit with German speakers, and can be fun for those who don't speak the language (as some of the music shows are in a sort of *Deutsch*-English hybrid). Some Americans even perform here periodically. Shows change regularly (about €22-30, performances generally Tue-Sat at 20:00, Sun at 19:00, seating can be cramped, south of Ku'damm at Schaperstrasse 24, U3 or U9:

Festivals keep Berlin lively year-round.

Spichernstrasse, tel. 030/883-1582, www. bar-jeder-vernunft.de).

Nightclubs and Pubs

Oranienburger Strasse is a trendy scene, with bars and restaurants spilling out onto sidewalks filled with people strolling. Nearby, the hip **Prenzlauer Berg** neighborhood is packed with everything from smoky pubs to small art bars and dance clubs (best scene is around Helmholtzplatz, U2: Eberswalder Strasse).

EATING

Near Unter den Linden

Georgenstrasse, a block behind the Pergamon Museum and under the S-Bahn tracks, is lined with fun eateries filling the arcade of the train trestle. **Deponie3** is a reliable Berlin *Kneipe* (bar) usually filled with students from nearby Humboldt University. Garden seating in the back is nice if you don't mind the noise of the S-Bahn directly above you. The interior is a cozy, wooden wonderland. They serve basic salads, traditional Berlin dishes, and hearty daily specials (daily from 10:00, under S-Bahn arch #187 at Georgenstrasse 5, tel. 030/2016-5740).

Käse König am Alex has been serving traditional sauerkraut-type dishes since 1933. It's fast, the photo menu makes ordering fun, and prices are great (daily, Panoramastrasse 1 under the TV Tower, tel. 030/8561-5220). Nearby, **Brauhaus Mitte** is a fun, DDR-era beer hall that makes its own beer and offers a menu of Berliner specialties and Bavarian dishes (daily 11:00-24:00, across from the TV Tower at Karl-Liebknecht-Strasse 13, tel. 030/3087-8989).

Near Gendarmenmarkt

The twin churches of Gendarmenmarkt are surrounded by upscale restaurants serving lunch and dinner to local professionals. If in need of a quick-yet-classy

lunch, stroll around the square and along Charlottenstrasse. For a quick bite, head to the cheap *Currywurst* stand behind the German Cathedral.

Lutter & Wegner Restaurant is wellknown for its Austrian cuisine (schnitzel and sauerbraten), with fun sidewalk seating or a dark and elegant interior (€9-18 starters, €16-24 main dishes, daily 11:00-24:00, Charlottenstrasse 56, tel. 030/202-9540).

Augustiner am Gendarmenmarkt, next door to Lutter & Wegner, has a classic beer-hall atmosphere, offers good beer and Bavarian cuisine (€6-12 light meals, €10-20 bigger meals, daily 10:00-24:00, Charlottenstrasse 55, tel. 030/2045-4020).

Galeries Lafayette Food Circus is a festival of eateries in the basement of the landmark department store. You'll find a good deli and prepared-food stands (most options €10-15, cheaper €5-10 sandwiches and savory crêpes, Mon-Sat 10:00-20:00, closed Sun, Friedrichstrasse 76-78, U-Bahn: Französische Strasse, tel. 030/209-480).

Hackescher Markt and Nearby

Weihenstephaner Bavarian Restaurant serves upmarket traditional cuisine for around €10-15 a plate and excellent beer in the atmospheric cellar, the inner courtyard, and on the streetside terrace (daily 11:00-23:00, Neue Promenade 5 at Hackescher Markt, tel. 030/8471-0760).

Restaurants on Oranienburger Strasse, a few blocks west of Hackescher Markt, come with happy hours and lots of cocktails. **Aufsturz,** a lively pub, serves pub grub and a huge selection of beer and whisky to a young crowd (Oranienburger Strasse 67). **Amrit Lounge** serves Indian food outdoors with an umbrella-drink Caribbean ambience (€10-14 meals, long hours daily, Oranienburger Strasse 45). Next door is **QBA,** a fun Cuban bar and restaurant.

Schwarzwaldstuben, between Oranienburger Strasse and Rosenthaler Platz, is a Black Forest-themed pub—which explains the antlers and cuckoo clocks. It's friendly, with good service, food, and prices. If they're full, you can eat at the long bar or at one of the sidewalk tables (€7-16 meals, daily 9:00-23:00, Tucholskystrasse 48, tel. 030/2809-8084).

Gipsy Restaurant serves good, reasonably priced German and Italian dishes in a bohemian-chic atmosphere (daily 12:30-23:00, at Clärchens Ballhaus, Auguststrasse 24, tel. 030/282-9295).

Near Rosenthaler Platz

Surrounding the U8: Rosenthaler Platz station, a short stroll or tram ride from the Hackescher Markt S-Bahn station, and an easy walk from the Oranienburger Strasse action, this busy neighborhood has several enticing options.

My Smart Break is a great spot to pick up a freshly made deli sandwich, hummus plate, salad, or other healthy snack. Linger in the interior, grab one of the sidewalk tables, or get it to go (€5-8 sandwiches, daily 8:00-23:00, Rosenthaler Strasse 67, tel. 030/2390-0303).

Transit is a stylish Thai/Indonesian/pan-Asian restaurant with a creative menu of €3 small plates and €8 big plates. Two people can make a filling meal out of three or four dishes (daily 11:00-24:00, cash only, Rosenthaler Strasse 68, tel. 030/2478-1645).

Restaurant Simon dishes up tasty Italian and German specialties—enjoy them in the restaurant's simple yet atmospheric interior, or opt for parkside seating across the street (€8-15 main dishes, Mon-Sat 17:00-23:00, closed Sun, cash only, Auguststrasse 53, at intersection with Kleine Auguststrasse, tel. 030/2789-0300).

In Prenzlauer Berg

The area surrounding the elevated Eberswalder Strasse U-Bahn station is the

Berliner Street Fare

In Berlin, it's easy to eat cheap, with a glut of *Imbiss* snack stands, bakeries (for sandwiches), and falafel/kebab counters. Train stations have grocery stores, as well as bright and modern fruit-and-sandwich bars.

Sausage stands are everywhere. Most specialize in **Currywurst,** a grilled pork sausage smothered with curry sauce. It was created in Berlin after World War II, when a cook got her hands on some curry and Worcestershire sauce from British troops stationed here. *Currywurst* comes either **mit Darm** (with casing) or **ohne Darm** (without casing). **Berliner Art**—"Berlin-style"—means that the sausage is boiled *ohne Darm*, then grilled. Either way, the grilled sausage is then chopped into small pieces or cut in half and topped with sauce. While some places simply use ketchup and sprinkle on some curry powder, real *Currywurst* joints use tomato paste, Worcestershire sauce, and curry. With your wurst comes either a toothpick or small wooden fork; you'll usually get a plate of fries as well.

Other good street foods to consider are **Döner Kebab** (Turkish-style skewered meat slow-roasted and served in a sandwich) and **Frikadelle** (like a hamburger patty; often called **Bulette** in Berlin).

Two companies, Grillwalker and Grillrunner, outfit their cooks in clever harnesses that let them grill and sell hot dogs from under an umbrella. For something quick, cheap, and tasty, find one of these portable human hot-dog stands.

epicenter of Prenzlauer Berg. It's worth the 10- to 15-minute walk from most of my recommended hotels.

Prater Biergarten offers both a rustic indoor restaurant and Berlin's oldest beer garden (with a family-friendly playground), each proudly offering its own microbrew. In the beer garden, step up to the counter and order (daily in good weather 12:00-24:00). The restaurant serves serious *Biergarten* cuisine and good salads (€10-20 plates, Mon-Sat 18:00-24:00, Sun from 12:00, cash only, Kastanienallee 7, tel. 030/448-5688).

Zum Schusterjungen Speisegaststätte ("The Cobbler's Apprentice") is a classic eatery that retains its circa-1986 DDR decor. Famous for its filling €9-13 meals (including schnitzel and Berlin classics such as pork knuckle), it has a strong local following (daily 12:00-24:00, corner of Lychener Strasse and Danziger Strasse 9, tel. 030/442-7654).

La Bodeguita del Medio Cuban Bar Restaurant is pure fun, with an ambience that makes you want to dance. The main dishes are big enough to split and you can even puff a Cuban cigar at the sidewalk tables. Come early to eat or late to drink (€4-10 tapas, Cuban ribs and salad, Tue-Sun 18:00-24:00, closed Mon, cash only, a block from U2: Eberswalder Strasse at Lychener Strasse 6, tel. 030/4050-0601).

Konnopke's Imbiss has been cooking up the city's best *Currywurst* for more than 70 years. Located beneath the U2 viaduct, the stand was demolished in 2010 during roadwork. Berliners rioted, and Konnopke's was rebuilt in a slick glass-and-steel hut. Don't confuse this with the nearby Currystation—look for the real Konnopke's (Mon-Fri 9:00-20:00, Sat from 11:30, closed Sun; Kastanienallee dead-ends at the elevated train tracks, and under them you'll find Konnopke's at Schönhauser Allee 44A, tel. 030/442-7765).

Restaurant Die Schule is a modern, no-frills place to sample traditional German dishes tapas-style (good indoor and outdoor seating, daily 11:00-22:00, Kastanienallee 82, tel. 030/780-089-550).

Funky pubs and nightspots fill the area around Helmholtzplatz (and elsewhere in Prenzlauer Berg). Oderberger Strasse is a fun zone to explore. For dessert, **Kauf Dich Glücklich** serves an enticing array of sweet Belgian waffles and ice cream in a candy-sprinkled, bohemian lounge (Mon-Fri 11:00-24:00, Sat-Sun from 10:00, indoor and outdoor seating—or get your dessert to go, Oderberger Strasse 44, tel. 030/4862-3292).

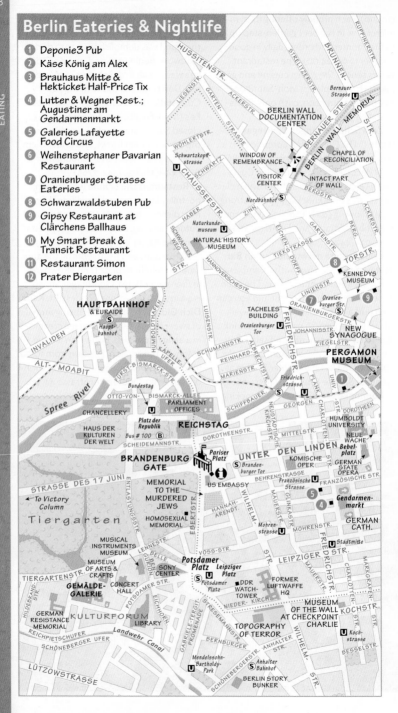

Berlin Eateries & Nightlife

1. Deponie3 Pub
2. Käse König am Alex
3. Brauhaus Mitte & Hekticket Half-Price Tix
4. Lutter & Wegner Rest.; Augustiner am Gendarmenmarkt
5. Galeries Lafayette Food Circus
6. Weihenstephaner Bavarian Restaurant
7. Oranienburger Strasse Eateries
8. Schwarzwaldstuben Pub
9. Gipsy Restaurant at Clärchens Ballhaus
10. My Smart Break & Transit Restaurant
11. Restaurant Simon
12. Prater Biergarten

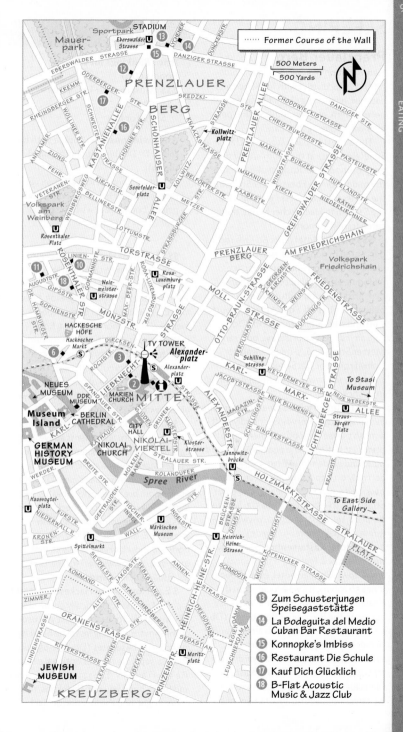

...... Former Course of the Wall

500 Meters
500 Yards

Mauerpark

Sportpark **STADIUM**

Eberswalder Strasse

LYCHENER STR.

DUNCKERSTR.

DANZIGER STRASSE

PRENZLAUER

EBERSWALDER STRASSE

KREMMENER STR.

ODERBERGER STR.

BERG

RHEINSBERGER STR.

SCHWEDTER STR.

WOLLINER STR.

KASTANIENALLEE

CHORINER STR.

SCHÖNHAUSER ALLEE

SREDZKI-STRASSE

KNAACKSTRASSE

PRENZLAUER ALLEE

CHODOWIECKISTRASSE

DANZIGER STR.

CHRISTBURGER STRASSE

Kollwitzplatz

MARIEN-STRASSE

WINSSTRASSE

WINSTRASSE

PASTEURSTR.

IMMANUEL-KIRCH

GREIFSWALDER STRASSE

HUFELANDSTR.

NIEDERKIRCHNER

KÄTHE-

ANKLAMER STR.

ZIONS-

FEHR-

VETERANEN-STR.

WEINBERGSWEG

BELLINERSTR.

KIRCHSTR.

KOLLWITZ-STR.

BELFORTER STR.

RAABESTR.

METZER

STRASSBURGER STR.

ROSA-LUXEMBURG-STR.

Volkspark am Weinberg

Rosenthaler Platz

ROSENTHALER STR.

LINIENSTR.

GORMANNSTR.

Weinmeisterstrasse

MAX-BEER-STR.

Senefelderplatz

Kollwitzplatz

PRENZLAUER BERG

AM FRIEDRICHSHAIN

Volkspark Friedrichshain

TORSTRASSE

MOLL-

Rosa-Luxemburgplatz

OTTO-BRAUN-STRASSE

GEORGEN-KIRCHSTR.

BÄRNIMSTR.

WEINS-STR.

BÜSCHINGSTR.

FRIEDENSTRASSE

AUGUSTSTR.

GIPSSTR.

GR. HAMBURGER

SOPHIENSTR.

HACKESCHE HÖFE

MÜNZSTR.

DIRCKSEN-

Hackescher Markt

ROCHSTR.

LIEBKNECHT-

SPANDAUER STR.

TV TOWER

Alexanderplatz

Alexanderplatz

KARL-

SCHILLING-strasse

WEYDEMEYER STR.

LICHTENBERGER STRASSE

NEUES MUSEUM

DDR MUSEUM

MARIEN CHURCH

MITTE

KARL-MARX-

JACOBYSTRASSE NEUE BLUMENSTR.

MAGAZIN-STR.

SCHILLINGSTR.

SINGERSTRASSE

To Stasi Museum

NEUE WEBERSTR.

Strausberger Platz

ALLEE

Museum Island

KARL-

BERLIN CATHEDRAL

STUDEN

GRUNER-

KLOSTER-STR.

ALEXANDERSTR.

GERMAN HISTORY MUSEUM

CITY HALL

NIKOLAI CHURCH

RATHAUS-

MOLKEN-MARKT

NIKOLAI-VIERTEL

Klosterstrasse

Jannowitzbrücke

STRALAUER STR.

WERDER-

BREITE STR.

ROLANDUFER

Spree River

HOLZMARKTSTRASSE

To East Side Gallery →

Hausvogteiplatz

GEETRAUDEN-

INSEL-STR.

BRÜCKEN-

KIRCHSTR.

MICHAELKIRCHSTRASSE

KÖPENICKER STRASSE

STRALAUER PLATZ

KURSTR.

NIEDERWALL-

WALL-

Märkisches Museum

FISCHER-INSEL

KRAUTSTR.

KRONEN-STR.

Spittelmarkt

SEYDEL STR.

JAKOBSTR.

SEBASTIANSTR.

ANNEN-

Heinrich-Heine-Strasse

SCHMIDSTR.

DRESDENER

KOMMAND-

ALTE STR.

STALLSCHREIBERSTR.

HEINRICH-HEINE-STR.

SEBASTIAN-

LEGIENDAMM

LEUSCHNERDAMM

ZIMMER-

JEWISH MUSEUM

ORANIENSTRASSE

RITTERSTRASSE

LINDENSTRASSE

ALEXANDRINEN-

LÖBECKSTR.

PRINZEN-STR.

Moritzplatz

KREUZBERG

13 Zum Schusterjungen Speisegaststätte

14 La Bodeguita del Medio Cuban Bar Restaurant

15 Konnopke's Imbiss

16 Restaurant Die Schule

17 Kauf Dich Glücklich

18 B-Flat Acoustic Music & Jazz Club

SLEEPING

Prenzlauer Berg

Gentrification has enlivened this colorful and gritty district with fun shops and eateries, happening nightlife—and great hotels. Think of the graffiti as some people's way of saying they care.

The closest U-Bahn stops are U2: Senefelderplatz at the south end of the neighborhood, U8: Rosenthaler Platz in the middle, or U2: Eberswalder Strasse at the north end. Or, for less walking, take the S-Bahn to Hackescher Markt, then catch tram #M1 north.

$$$ Myer's Hotel rents 60 lush rooms decorated in rich colors with classy furnishings. The gorgeous public spaces, including an art-filled patio and garden, host frequent cultural events. This peaceful hub is off a quiet garden courtyard and tree-lined street (Db-€108-235, air-con, elevator, sauna, bike rental, Metzer Strasse 26, 5-minute walk to Kollwitzplatz or U2: Senefelderplatz, tel. 030/440-140, www.myershotel.de, info@myershotel.de).

$$$ Hotel Jurine is a pleasant 53-room business-style hotel whose friendly staff aims to please. In good weather, enjoy the breakfast buffet on the peaceful backyard patio and garden (Db-€130-160, air-con only on upper floor, elevator, garage parking if you reserve ahead, Schwedter Strasse 15, 10-minute walk to U2: Senefelderplatz, tel. 030/443-2990, www.hotel-jurine.de, mail@hotel-jurine.de).

$$$ Hotel Kastanienhof, which offers helpful service, feels like a traditional small-town German hotel, even though it has 50 rooms. It's well-located on the Kastanienallee #M1 tram line, with easy access to the Prenzlauer Berg bustle (Db-€100-180, some rooms with air-con and/or balcony—request when you book, breakfast-€9, pay parking, 20 yards from #M1 Zionskirche tram stop at Kastanienallee 65, tel. 030/443-050, www.kastanienhof.biz, info@kastanienhof.biz).

$$ The Circus Hotel, with 60 colorful rooms, is fun, comfortable, and an excellent value. It overlooks a noisy intersection, so ask for a back room (Db-€95-€105, breakfast-€9, elevator, loaner iPads in rooms, mellow ground-floor restaurant, Rosenthaler Strasse 1, directly at U8: Rosenthaler Platz, tel. 030/2000-3939, www.circus-berlin.de, info@circus-berlin.de). The Circus also offers a range of spacious, modern **apartments** both within the hotel and two blocks away on Choriner Strasse.

$ Karlito Apartmenthaus has 12 comfortable, modern apartments above a hip café on a tranquil side street near Hackescher Markt. All the sleek, Ikea-esque units have miniature balconies (Db-€80-95, in-room breakfast-€10, elevator, bike rental, Linienstrasse 60—check in at Café Lois around the corner on Gormannstrasse, U8: Rosenthaler Platz, or 350 yards from S-Bahn: Hackescher Markt, mobile 0179-704-9041, www.karlito-apartments.de, info@karlito-apartments.de).

$ EasyHotel Berlin Hackescher Markt is part of an unapologetically cheap chain where you pay for exactly what you use—nothing more, nothing less. The hotel has inexpensive base rates (Db-€35-65), then charges separate fees for optional extras like Wi-Fi and TV. The 125 rooms are small and basic, but if you skip the extras, the price is right, and the location at Hackescher Markt is wonderful (elevator, request quieter back room, Rosenthaler Strasse 69, tel. 030/4000-6550, www. easyhotel.com).

$$$ **Hotel Augustinenhof** is on a side street near all the Oranienburger Strasse action. It's a clean hotel with 66 spacious rooms, nice woody floors, and some of the most comfortable beds in Berlin. Rooms in front overlook the courtyard of the old Imperial Post Office, rooms in back are quieter, and some rooms have older, thin windows (Db-€100-150, elevator, Auguststrasse 82, 50 yards from S-Bahn: Oranienburger Strasse, tel. 030/3088-6710, www.hotel-augustinenhof.de, augustinenhof@albrechtshof-hotels.de).

Farther East, in Friedrichshain

$ **Michelberger Hotel,** in the heart of gritty but gentrifying Friedrichshain, is so self-consciously hip that it'd be just too much...if it weren't for its helpful, friendly staff. Its 113 bright rooms are reasonably priced, and its common spaces—a bar/lounge and a breezy courtyard restaurant—are genuinely welcoming (Db-€80-90, bigger "loft" doubles and suites available, breakfast extra, elevator, bike rental; from atop Warschauer Strasse S-Bahn station turn left to cross the bridge—it's across from the U-Bahn station and #M10 tram stop at Warschauer Strasse 39; tel. 030/2977-8590, www.michelbergerhotel. com, reservations@michelbergerhotel. com).

$ **Ostel** is a fun, retro-1970s apartment building that re-creates the DDR lifestyle and interior design. All the furniture and room decorations have been meticulously collected and restored to their former socialist glory—only the psychedelic wallpaper is a replica (Db-€59, also 4-person apartments; no breakfast but supermarket next door, 24-hour reception, Wi-Fi in lobby, bike rental, free parking, free use of the community barbeque, right behind Ostbahnhof station on the cor-

ner of Strasse der Pariser Kommune at Wriezener Karree 5, tel. 030/2576-8660, www.ostel.eu, contact@ostel.eu).

Hotelesque Hostels

$$ **Meininger** is a budget-hotel chain with several locations in Berlin. With sleek, nicely decorated rooms, these can be a great value, even for nonhostelers. They have three particularly appealing branches: in Prenzlauer Berg (Schönhauser Allee 19 on Senefelderplatz), at Oranienburger Strasse 67 (next to the Aufsturz pub), and near the Hauptbahnhof, at Ella-Traebe-Strasse 9 (dorm bed-€20-40, Db-€70-120, all locations: breakfast extra, elevator, 24-hour reception, guest kitchen, bike rental, pay parking, tel. 030/666-36100, www.meininger-hostels. com, welcome@meininger-hostels.com).

$ **The Circus Hostel** is a brightly colored, well-run place with 230 beds, a trendy lounge, and a bar downstairs. It has typical hostel dorms as well as some private rooms; for a few big steps up in comfort, see the listing for the Circus Hotel (dorm bed-€23-31, Db-€85, also apartments, breakfast extra, no curfew, elevator, guest iPads, bike rental, Weinbergsweg 1A, U8: Rosenthaler Platz, tel. 030/2000-3939, www.circus-berlin.de, info@circus-berlin.de).

$ **EastSeven Hostel** rents the best cheap beds in Prenzlauer Berg. It's sleek and modern, with all the hostel services and more: 60 beds, inviting lounge, guest kitchen, lockers, quiet backyard terrace, and bike rental. Children are welcome. Easygoing people of any age are comfortable here (dorm bed-€15-25, D-€54-60, breakfast extra, laundry, no curfew, 100 yards from U2: Senefelderplatz at Schwedter Strasse 7, tel. 030/9362-2240, www.eastseven.de, info@eastseven.de).

$ **Hotel Transit Loft,** actually more of a hostel, is located in a refurbished factory. Its 81 stark, high-ceilinged rooms and wide-open lobby have an industrial touch. The reception is open 24 hours, with a bar

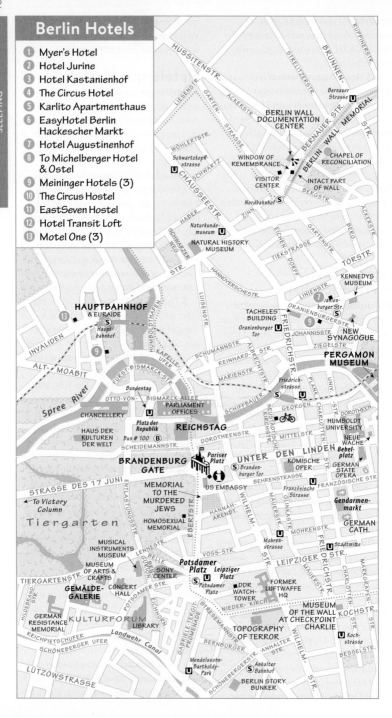

Berlin Hotels

1. Myer's Hotel
2. Hotel Jurine
3. Hotel Kastanienhof
4. The Circus Hotel
5. Karlito Apartmenthaus
6. EasyHotel Berlin Hackescher Markt
7. Hotel Augustinenhof
8. To Michelberger Hotel & Ostel
9. Meininger Hotels (3)
10. The Circus Hostel
11. EastSeven Hostel
12. Hotel Transit Loft
13. Motel One (3)

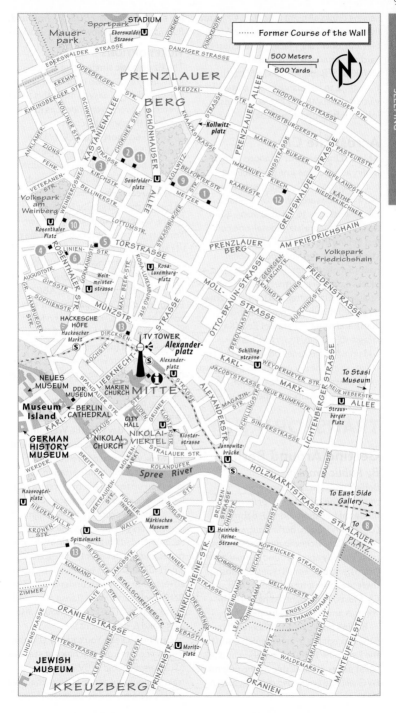

serving drinks all night long (Db-€73, family rooms, includes sheets and breakfast, elevator, down alley facing inner courtyard at Immanuelkirchstrasse 14A; U2/U5/U8 or S-Bahn: Alexanderplatz, then tram #M4 to Hufelandstrasse and walk 50 yards; tel. 030/4849-3773, www.transit-loft.de, loft@hotel-transit.de).

Across the City

$ Motel One has eight locations across Berlin; all have the same posh-feeling-but-small rooms. The four most convenient locations are right on Alexanderplatz (Dircksenstrasse 36, tel. 030/2005-4080, berlin-alexanderplatz@motel-one.com); just behind the Hauptbahnhof (Invalidenstrasse 54, tel. 030/3641-0050, berlin-hauptbahnhof@motel-one.com); a few blocks east of Gendarmenmarkt (Leipziger Strasse 50, U2: Spittelmarkt, tel. 030/2014-3630, berlin-spittelmarkt@motel-one.com); and near the Bahnhof Zoo (Kantstrasse 10, tel. 030/3151-7360, berlin-kudamm@motel-one.com). They tend to charge the same prices (Db-€84, breakfast extra, air-con, guest iPads, elevator, limited pay parking, www.motel-one.com).

TRANSPORTATION

Getting Around Berlin
By Public Transit

Berlin's consolidated transit system uses the same ticket for its many modes of transportation: U-Bahn (*Untergrund-Bahn*, Berlin's subway), S-Bahn (*Stadtschnellbahn*, or "fast urban train," mostly aboveground), *Strassenbahn* (tram), and bus. For all types of transit, there are three lettered zones (A, B, and C). Most of your sightseeing will be in zones A and B (the city proper).

Berlin's public transit is operated by BVG (except the S-Bahn, which is run by the Deutsche Bahn). Timetables and the latest prices are available on the helpful BVG website (www.bvg.de). Get and use the excellent *Discover Berlin by Train and Bus* map-guide at subway ticket windows.

TICKET OPTIONS

The €2.70 **basic single** ticket (*Einzelfahrschein*) covers two hours of travel in one direction. It's easy to make this ticket stretch to cover several rides...as long as they're in the same direction.

The €1.60 **short-ride** ticket (*Kurzstrecke Fahrschein*) covers a single ride of up to six bus/tram stops or three subway stations (one transfer allowed on subway). You can save on short-ride tickets by buying them in groups of four.

The €9 **four-trip** ticket (*4-Fahrten-Karte*) is the same as four basic single tickets at a small discount.

The **day pass** (*Tageskarte*) is good until 3:00 the morning after you buy it (€6.90 for zones AB, €7.40 for zones ABC). For longer stays, consider a seven-day pass (*Sieben-Tage-Karte*; €29.50 for zones AB, €36.50 for zones ABC), or the WelcomeCard (described below). The *Kleingruppenkarte* lets groups of up to five travel all day (€16.90 for zones AB, €17.40 for zones ABC).

If you plan to cover a lot of ground using public transportation during a two- or three-day visit, the **Welcome-Card** is usually the best deal (available at TIs; www.visitberlin.de/welcomecard). It covers all public transportation and gives you up to 50 percent discounts on lots of minor and a few major museums (including Checkpoint Charlie), sightseeing tours (including 25 percent off the recommended Original Berlin Walks), and music and theater events. It's especially smart for families, as each adult card also covers up to three kids under age 15. The Berlin-only card covers transit zones AB (€19.50/48 hours, €27.50/72 hours, also 4-, 5-, and 6-day options).

Buying Tickets: You can buy U-Bahn/S-Bahn tickets from machines at stations. (They are also sold at BVG pavilions at train stations and at the TI, from machines on board trams, and on buses from drivers, who'll give change.) *Erwachsener* means "adult"—anyone age 14 or older.

Boarding Transit: As you board the bus or tram, or enter the subway, punch your ticket in a clock machine to validate it (or risk a €60 fine; stamp passes only the first time you ride).

By Taxi

Cabs are easy to flag down, and taxi stands are common. A typical ride within town costs €8-10, and a crosstown trip will run about €15. If possible, use cash—paying with a credit card comes with a hefty surcharge (about €4, regardless of the fare).

Money-Saving Taxi Tip: For any ride of less than two kilometers (about a mile), take advantage of the *Kurzstrecke* (short-stretch) rate. To get this rate, it's important that you flag the cab down on the street—not at or even near a taxi stand. You must ask for the *Kurzstrecke* rate as soon as you hop in: Confidently say *"Kurzstrecke, bitte"* (KOORTS-shtreh-keh, BIT-teh), and your driver will grumble and flip the meter to a fixed €4 rate (for a ride that would otherwise cost €7).

By Bike

Flat Berlin is a bike-friendly city, but be careful—Berlin's motorists don't brake for bicyclists (and bicyclists don't brake for pedestrians).

Take a Bike—near the Friedrichstrasse S-Bahn station—is owned by a lovely Dutch-German couple who know a lot about bikes and have a huge inventory (3-gear bikes: €12.50/day, more for better bikes, includes helmets, daily 9:30-19:00, Neustädtische Kirchstrasse 8, tel. 030/2065-4730, www.takeabike.de).

ARRIVING AND DEPARTING

By Train

Berlin's grandest train station is Berlin Hauptbahnhof (a.k.a. "der Bahnhof",

abbreviated Hbf). All long-distance trains arrive here.

Services: On the main floor, you'll find the **TI** and a Deutsche Bahn information center/ticket office; up one level are a 24-hour **pharmacy** and **lockers** (directly under track 14).

Rick's Tip: *EurAide is an American-run information desk with answers to your questions about train travel around Europe. It's located at counter 12 inside the Deutsche Bahn information center on the Hauptbahnhof's first upper level. This is a good place to make fast-train and* **couchette** *reservations (closed Jan-Feb and Sat-Sun year-round; www.euraide.com).*

Getting into Town: Taxis and buses wait outside the station, but the S-Bahn is probably the best means of connecting to your destination within Berlin. It's simple: All S-Bahn trains are on tracks 15 and 16 at the top of the station. All trains on track 15 go east, stopping at Friedrichstrasse, Hackescher Markt (with connections to Prenzlauer Berg), Alexanderplatz, and Ostbahnhof.

To reach hotels in the Prenzlauer Berg neighborhood, it's fastest to take any train on track 15 two stops to Hackescher Markt, exit to Spandauer Strasse, go left, and cross the tracks to the tram stop. Here you'll catch tram #M1 north (direction: Schillerstrasse).

From Berlin by Train to: Frankfurt (hourly, 4 hours), **Bacharach** (hourly, 7 hours, 1-3 changes), **Würzburg** (hourly, 4 hours, 1 change), **Rothenburg** (hourly, 5.5 hours, 3 changes), **Munich** (1-2/hour, 6.5 hours, night train possible).

By Plane

You'll likely use **Tegel Airport,** which is four miles from the center (airport code: TXL). **Bus** #TXL goes between the airport, the Hauptbahnhof (stops by Washingtonplatz entrance), and Alexanderplatz. A **taxi** costs about €30 to Alexanderplatz.

The Netherlands

The Netherlands—sometimes referred to by its nickname, "Holland"—is one of Europe's most densely populated, wealthiest, and best-organized countries. Occupying a delta near the mouth of three large rivers, the Netherlands ("low lands") has battled the sea for centuries, reclaiming low-lying land and converting it into fertile farmland.

The Netherlands has 16.8 million people: 80 percent are Dutch, and half have no religious affiliation. Despite its small size (16,000 square miles—about twice the size of New Jersey), the Netherlands boasts the planet's 23rd-largest economy. It also has one of Europe's lowest unemployment rates, relying heavily on foreign trade through its port at Rotterdam, Europe's largest.

Amsterdam, laced with grand canals and criss-crossed by bikes, has the powerhouse sights, while the nearby town of Haarlem is wonderfully *gezellig*—this much-prized Dutch virtue means having an atmosphere of relaxed coziness.

Treat yourself to new taste experiences in the Netherlands: Try pickled herring at an outdoor stand, enjoy a sweet "syrup waffle" (*stroopwafel*), and sip an old *jenever* with a new friend. It's *gezellig*.

CUISINE SCENE AT A GLANCE

Traditional Dutch food is basic and hearty, with lots of bread, soup, fish, and meat. Lunch and dinner are served at typical American times (roughly 12:00-14:00 and 18:00-21:00). For the Dutch, dinner is the biggest meal of the day, consisting of meat or seafood with boiled potatoes, cooked vegetables, and a salad. Popular drinks are light, pilsner-type beer and gin (*jenever*).

The tastiest "Dutch" cuisine comes from the former colony of Indonesia. Seek out an *Indisch* restaurant to experience a *rijsttafel* ("rice table"). The spread usually includes many dishes, ranging from small sides to entrée-sized plates (some are spicy) and a big bowl of rice. A *rijsttafel* can be split (when restaurants allow it) and still fill two hungry tourists. Vegetarian versions are always available. For a smaller version, order *nasi rames* (several portions on one plate). Or try *bami goreng* (stir-fried noodles) or *nasi goreng* (fried rice), served with *rijsttafel* items.

A *café* or *eetcafé* serves simple fare in a generally comfortable but no-nonsense setting.

Pancake restaurants serve sweet and savory pancakes (*pannenkoeken*) all day. Dutch pancakes are halfway between a fluffy American-style pancake and a thin French crêpe.

Bruin cafés ("brown cafés") are named for their nicotine-stained walls, though smoking was banned indoors in 2008. They serve drinks and Dutch food in a dimly lit bar-like setting.

A *salon de thé* serves tea, coffee, sandwiches, and pastries. In contrast, a "coffeeshop" is the code word for an establishment where marijuana is sold and consumed, though most offer drinks and munchies, too.

Tipping: At restaurants, tipping is not necessary (15 percent service is usually included in the menu price), but a tip of about 5-10 percent is a nice reward for good service. In bars, rounding up to the next euro ("keep the change") is appropriate if you get table service, rather than ordering at the bar.

Budget Options: Take-out places serve fast food and sandwiches (*broodjes*). Small stands sell *friets* (french fries, served with mayonnaise), pickled herring, falafels (fried chickpea balls in pita bread), *shoarmas* (lamb in pita bread), or *döner kebabs* (a Turkish version of a *shoarma*). And it's easy to forage for picnic fare at delis and groceries.

Amsterdam

In Amsterdam, you'll enjoy good living, cozy cafés, street-corner jazz, great art, stately history, and a spirit of live and let live. The city still looks much like it did in the 1600s—the Dutch Golden Age—when it was the cradle of capitalism. Wealthy, democratic burghers built a wonderland of canals lined with trees and townhouses topped with fancy gables. Immigrants, outcasts, and political rebels were drawn here by its open-minded atmosphere, while painters such as young Rembrandt captured that atmosphere on canvas.

For centuries, the city has advocated tolerance for things other places try to forbid. Its international sea-trading port has always attracted sailors and businessmen, so it was profitable to allow them to have a little fun. In the 1960s, Amsterdam became a magnet for Europe's hippies. Since then, it's become a world capital of alternative lifestyles. This bold experiment in freedom may box your Puritan ears. Prostitution is allowed in the Red Light District, while "smartshops" sell psychedelic drugs, and marijuana is openly sold and smoked in "coffeeshops."

Take in all of the city's charms, then pause to watch the clouds blow past its stately old gables—and see the Golden Age reflected in its quiet canals.

AMSTERDAM IN 2 DAYS

Day 1: In the morning, follow my self-guided Amsterdam City Walk, leading from the train station to Leidseplein, via the Amsterdam Museum (which you could tour now), and the flower market. Stop for lunch along the walk.

From Leidseplein, take a one-hour canal boat tour (unless you'd rather save it for an evening activity).

Later in the day, tour the Anne Frank House. Reserve online (or waste an hour or two standing in line).

On any evening: Have an Indonesian *rijsttafel* dinner, wander through Vondelpark (rent a bike?), or stroll the eye-opening Red Light District (but not after 22:30). Visit late-night sights: The Van Gogh Museum is open late most Fridays and some Saturdays (until 22:00), and the Anne Frank Museum is open until 21:00 or 22:00 on many nights. Nurse a drink at a traditional "brown" café or take a canal boat ride. Get high at a coffeeshop if you want; it's legal!

Day 2: Visit these top museums—

Amsterdam Neighborhoods

NORTH AMSTERDAM

EYE FILM INSTITUTE

IJ Channel

WEST AMSTERDAM

CENTRAL STATION

CRUISE TERMINAL

Damrak

SEX

JORDAAN

Dam Square

RED LIGHT DISTRICT

NORTHEAST AMSTERDAM

ANNE FRANK HOUSE

Singel

Singelgracht

CENTRAL AMSTERDAM

MARITIME MUSEUM

Rokin

MINT TOWER

WATERLOO- PLEIN

JEWISH QUARTER

LEIDSE- PLEIN

Heren-gracht

Keizers- gracht

REMBRANDT- PLEIN

SOUTHEAST AMSTERDAM

ARTIS ZOO

Prinsen- gracht

SOUTHERN CANAL BELT

Amstel

Singelgracht

Vondelpark

VAN GOGH MUSEUM

RIJKSMUSEUM

River

N

SOUTHWEST AMSTERDAM

500 Meters

500 Yards

Rijksmuseum and Van Gogh—next to each other on Museumplein (it's smart to reserve both museums online in advance). To minimize crowds (which are heaviest at midday), start with the Van Gogh Museum when it opens at 9:00. Visit the Rijksmuseum after lunch (crowds begin to subside after 14:00). In between visiting these two major museums, have lunch (cafés are at the museums and nearby), hang out at lively Museumplein, tour the Stedelijk (modern art), or visit Vondelpark.

With extra time: You could easily spend another day or two in Amsterdam, visiting anything else that appeals: the Dutch Resistance Museum, Amstelkring, Hermitage Amsterdam, Netherlands Maritime Museum, or the street markets (Albert Cuyp and Waterlooplein, closed

Sun). And you can day-trip to the cozy town of Haarlem (see page 1049).

ORIENTATION

Amsterdam's **Central Station** (Amsterdam Centraal), on the north edge of the city, is your starting point, with the TI, bike rental, and trams branching out to all points. The street called **Damrak** is the main north-south axis, connecting Central Station with **Dam Square** (people-watching and hangout center). From this main street, the city spreads out like a fan, with 90 islands, hundreds of bridges, and a series of concentric canals—named **Singel** (the original moat), **Herengracht** (Gentleman's Canal), **Keizersgracht** (Emperor's Canal), and **Prinsengracht** (Prince's Canal)—that were laid out in

▲▲▲**Rijksmuseum** Best collection anywhere of the Dutch Masters—Rembrandt, Hals, Vermeer, and Steen—in a spectacular building. **Hours:** Daily 9:00-17:00. See page 1013.

▲▲▲**Van Gogh Museum** More than 200 paintings by the angst-ridden artist. **Hours:** Daily 9:00-18:00, Fri until 22:00 March-Oct, Sat until 22:00 July-Aug and Oct. See page 1018.

▲▲▲**Anne Frank House** Young Anne's hideaway during the Nazi occupation. **Hours:** April-Oct daily 9:00-22:00; Nov-March daily 9:00-19:00, Sat until 21:00. See page 1023.

▲▲**Stedelijk Museum** The Netherlands' top modern-art museum, recently and extensively renovated. **Hours:** Daily 10:00-18:00, Fri until 22:00. See page 1021.

▲▲**Vondelpark** City park and concert venue. **Hours:** Always open. See page 1022.

▲▲**Amsterdam Museum** History museum tracing city's growth from fishing village to trading capital to today, plus some Rembrandts and a playable carillon. **Hours:** Daily 10:00-17:00. See page 1026.

▲▲**Amstelkring Museum** Catholic church hidden in the attic of a 17th-century merchant's house. **Hours:** Mon-Sat 10:00-17:00, Sun and holidays 13:00-17:00. See page 1026.

▲▲**Netherlands Maritime Museum** Rich seafaring story of the Netherlands, told with vivid artifacts. **Hours:** Daily 9:00-17:00. See page 1028.

▲▲**Hermitage Amsterdam** Russia's Tsarist treasures, on loan from St. Petersburg. **Hours:** Daily 10:00-17:00. See page 1028.

▲▲**Dutch Resistance Museum** History of the Dutch struggle against the Nazis. **Hours:** Tue-Fri 10:00-17:00, Sat-Mon 11:00-17:00. See page 1029.

▲**Museumplein** Square with art museums, street musicians, and green space. **Hours:** Always open. See page 1022.

▲**Leidseplein** Lively square with cafés and street musicians. **Hours:** Always open, best on sunny afternoons. See page 1022.

▲**Red Light District** Women of the world's oldest profession on the job. **Hours:** Best from noon into the early evening; avoid late at night. See page 1027.

▲**Hash, Marijuana, and Hemp Museum** All the dope, from history and science to memorabilia. **Hours:** Daily 10:00-23:00. See page 1027.

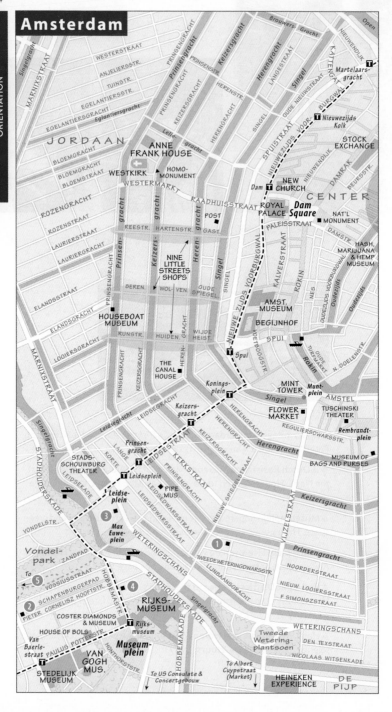

Amsterdam

SINGELGRACHT

MARNIXSTRAAT

WESTERSTRAAT

ANJELIERSSTR.

TUINSTR.

EGELANTIERSSTR.

EGELANTIERSGRACHT

Eglantiersgracht

JORDAAN

BLOEMGRACHT

BLOEMGRACHT

BLOEMSTRAAT

ROZENGRACHT

ROZENSTRAAT

LAURIERSTRAAT

LAURIERGRACHT

ELANDSSTRAAT

ELANDSGRACHT

LOOIERSGRACHT

MARNIXSTRAAT

PRINSENGRACHT

KEIZERSGRACHT

Lelie-gracht

ANNE FRANK HOUSE

WESTKIRK

HOMO-MONUMENT

WESTERMARKT

RAADHUISSTRAAT

POST

GAST.

REESTR. HARTENSTR.

NINE LITTLE STREETS SHOPS

BEREN.   WOL- VEN.

OUDE SPIEGEL

HOUSEBOAT MUSEUM

RUNSTR.   HUIDEN-   WIJDE HEIST.

THE CANAL HOUSE

Koningsplein

Keizersgracht

Prinsengracht

STADS-SCHOUWBURG THEATER

LEIDSEGRACHT

LEIDSEKADE

LANGE LEIDSEDWARSSTRAAT

KORTE

Leidseplein

Leidse-plein

PIPE MUS.

PRINSENGRACHT

KERKSTRAAT

LEIDSESTRAAT

HERENGRACHT

KEIZERSGRACHT

Prinsen-gracht

Keizers-gracht

Heren-gracht

Singel

Singel

MINT TOWER Muntplein

Singel

FLOWER MARKET

REGULIERSDWARSSTR.

TUSCHINSKI THEATER

Rembrandt-plein

MUSEUM OF BAGS AND PURSES

Keizersgracht

Prinsengracht

NOORDERSTRAAT

NIEUW. LOOIERSSTRAAT

F. SIMONSZSTRAAT

VIJZELSTRAAT

3

Max Euweplein

STADHOUDERSKADE

VONDELSTR.

Vondel-park

ZANDPAD

To 5

VOSSIUSSTRAAT

SCHAPENBURGERPAD

2

PIETER CORNELISZ HOOFTSTR.

HOBBEMASTR.

4

WETERINGSCHANS

WETERINGSCHANS

LIJNBAANSGRACHT

TWEEDE WETERINGDWARSSTR.

1

STADHOUDERSKADE

RIJKS-MUSEUM

Singelgracht

HOBBEMAKADE

Tweede Wetering-plantsoen

DEN TEXSTRAAT

NICOLAAS WITSENKADE

DE PIJP

COSTER DIAMONDS & MUSEUM

HOUSE OF BOLS

Van Baerle-straat

PAULUS POTTERSTR.

Rijks-museum

Museum-plein

VAN GOGH MUS.

STEDELIJK MUSEUM

HONTHORSTSTR.

To US Consulate & Concertgebouw

To Albert Cuypstraat (Market)

HEINEKEN EXPERIENCE

SINGELGRACHT

PRINSENGRACHT

KEIZERSGRACHT

PRINSENGRACHT

KEIZERSGRACHT

HERENGRACHT

PRINSENGRACHT

KEIZERSGRACHT

HERENGRACHT

SINGEL

PRINSENGRACHT

KEIZERSGRACHT

HERENGRACHT

PRINSENGRACHT

KEIZERSGRACHT

HERENGRACHT

PRINSENGRACHT

Brouwers- gracht

Open

NIEUWENDIJK

Martelaars-gracht

KATTENGT.

SINGEL

Nieuwezijds Kolk

STOCK EXCHANGE

SPUISTRAAT NIEUWEZIJDS VOOR- NIEUWSTRAAT

OUDE NIEUWSTRAAT

BURGWAL

NIEUWENDIJK

NIEUWEZIJDS VOORBURGWAL

DAMRAK

BEURSSTR.

Dam

NEW CHURCH

CENTER

Dam Square

ROYAL PALACE

PALEISSTRAAT

NAT'L MONUMENT

DAMSTR.

HASH, MARIJUANA & HEMP MUSEUM

KALVERSTRAAT

ROKIN

NES

OUDEZIJDS VOORBURGWAL

OUDEZIJDS

AMST. MUSEUM

BEGIJNHOF

SPUI

Spui

Rokin

N. DOELENSTR.

AMSTEL

Singel

HERENGRACHT

NIEUWE SPIEGELSTRAAT

VOETBOOGSTR.

NIEUWE ZIJDS VOORBURGWAL

OUDE TURFMARKT

AMSTEL

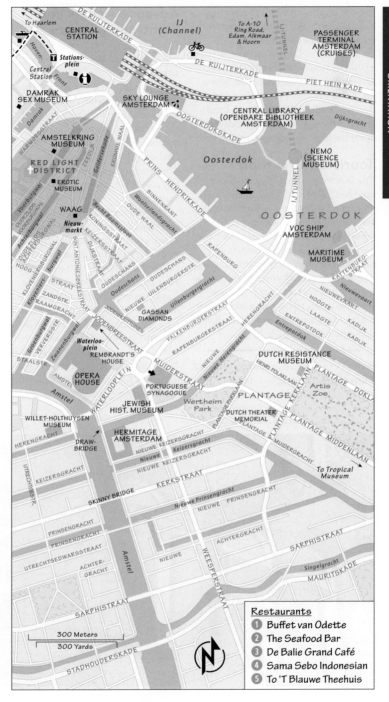

To Haarlem
DE RUIJTERKADE
CENTRAL
STATION
IJ
(Channel)
To A-10
Ring Road,
Edam, Alkmaar
& Hoorn
IJTUNNEL
PASSENGER
TERMINAL
AMSTERDAM
(CRUISES)

Stations-plein
Central
Station
Front
DE RUIJTERKADE
PIET HEIN KADE

DAMRAK
SEX MUSEUM
Damrak
SKY LOUNGE
AMSTERDAM
CENTRAL LIBRARY
(OPENBARE BIBLIOTHEEK
AMSTERDAM)
Dijksgracht

AMSTELKRING
MUSEUM
RED LIGHT
DISTRICT
EROTIC
MUSEUM
WARMOESSTRAAT
Oosterdok
NEMO
(SCIENCE
MUSEUM)
IJTUNNEL

WAAG
Nieuw-markt
Voorburgwal
OUDEZIJDS VOORBURGWAL
ACHTERBURGWAL
OUDEZIJDS
Achterburgwal
HOOG-
KLOVENIERSBURGWAL
Recht Boomssloot
KONINGSSTRAAT
KEIZERSSTRAAT
DIJKSTRAAT
SINT ANTONIESBREESTRAAT
BINNENKANT
Waalseilandsgracht
OUDE WAAL
ZEEDIJK
GELDERSEKADE
KROMME WAAL
PRINS HENDRIKKADE

OOSTERDOK

VOC SHIP
AMSTERDAM
MARITIME
MUSEUM

OOSTERDOKSKADE

KATTEN-BURGERSTRAAT
Nieuwevaart
RAPENBURG

ZANDSTR.
RAAMGRACHT
STRAAT
Groenburgwal
VERVERSSTR.
OUDESCHANS
OUDESCHANS
NIEUWE UILENBURGERSTR.
Oudeschans
JODENBREESTRAAT
JODENHOUTTUINEN
GASSAN
DIAMONDS
Uilenburgergracht
VALKENBURGERSTRAAT
HERENGRACHT
NIEUWEVAART
HOOGTE
LAAGTE
KADIJK
KADIJK
ENTREPOTDOK
Entrepotdok

STAALSTR.
AMSTEL
Waterloo-plein
Zwanenburgwal
REMBRANDT'S
HOUSE
OPERA
HOUSE
WATERLOOPLEIN
MUIDERSTRAAT
PORTUGUESE
SYNAGOGUE
RAPENBURGERSTRAAT
NIEUWE Herengracht
NIEUWE
DUTCH RESISTANCE
MUSEUM
HENRI POLAKLAAN
PLANTAGE DOKLA
PLANTAGE KERKLAAN

WILLET-HOLTHUYSEN
MUSEUM
DRAW-BRIDGE
HERENGRACHT
KEIZERSGRACHT
JEWISH
HIST. MUSEUM
HERMITAGE
AMSTERDAM
Wertheim
Park
PLANTAGE PARKLAAN
DUTCH THEATER
MEMORIAL
PLANTAGE MUIDERGRACHT
PLANTAGE
Artis
Zoo
PLANTAGE MIDDENLAAN

NIEUWE KEIZERSGRACHT
Nieuwe Keizersgracht
NIEUWE KEIZERSGRACHT
To Tropical
Museum

SKINNY BRIDGE
KERKSTRAAT
KERKSTRAAT
Nieuwe Prinsengracht
NIEUWE PRINSENGRACHT

PRINSENGRACHT
PRINSENGRACHT
UTRECHTSEDWARSSTRAAT
ACHTER-GRACHT
UTRECHTSESTR.
Amstel
NIEUWE
WEESPERSTRAAT
ACHTERGRACHT
SARPHISTRAAT
Singelgracht
MAURITSKADE

SARPHISTRAAT
STADHOUDERSKADE

300 Meters
300 Yards

N

Restaurants

1. Buffet van Odette
2. The Seafood Bar
3. De Balie Grand Café
4. Sama Sebo Indonesian
5. To 'T Blauwe Theehuis

the 17th century, Holland's Golden Age. Amsterdam's major sights are all within walking distance of Dam Square.

To the east of Damrak is the oldest part of the city (today's **Red Light District**), and to the west is the newer part, where you'll find the Anne Frank House and the peaceful **Jordaan** neighborhood. Museums and the bustling square, **Leidseplein,** are at the southern edge of the city center.

Tourist Information

The Dutch name for a TI is "VVV," pronounced "fay fay fay." Amsterdam's main **TI,** located across the street from Central Station, is centrally located, but it's crowded and inefficient, and the free maps are poor quality (Mon-Sat 9:00-17:00, Sun 10:00-16:00, www.iamsterdam.com). The TI sells a good city map (€2.50), walking-tour brochures (€3), skip-the-line museum tickets (though it's easier buying these online), and the *Time Out Amsterdam* entertainment guide (€3).

Rick's Tip: *Inside Central Station, the* **GWK Currency Exchange** *offices (though not officially TIs) can answer basic tourist questions, with shorter lines (daily 9:00-22:00).*

Advance Tickets and Sightseeing Passes

Avoid long ticket lines (common from late March-Oct) by buying **advance tickets** online for the **Rijksmuseum, Van Gogh Museum,** and **Anne Frank House** through each museum's website. Print out your ticket and bring it to the ticket-holder's line for a quick entry. You can also buy advance tickets at TIs (though lines there can be long). Advance reservations for the Anne Frank House can sell out quickly; buy your ticket as soon as you're sure of your itinerary.

The **Museumkaart** (€60) sightseeing pass pays for itself if you visit six museums. Even if you don't plan on that many museums, the ability to skip lines might still be worth the price. But you can't bypass the line at the Anne Frank House (to avoid waiting, you must make an online reservation, even if you have a Museumkaart). At the Van Gogh Museum, you'll need to queue up, though at a much shorter line than ticket-buyers. The Museumkaart is sold at participating museums. For a full list of included sights, see www.amsterdam.info/museums/museumkaart.

Daily Reminder

The biggest Amsterdam sights—the Rijksmuseum, the Van Gogh Museum, and the Anne Frank House—are open daily year-round (the Anne Frank House daily until 22:00 April-Oct).

SUNDAY: The Amstelkring Museum is open only in the afternoon (13:00-17:00). Flea markets and some stores are closed.

MONDAY: All recommended sights are open. Some stores are closed in the morning.

TUESDAY/WEDNESDAY/THURSDAY: All recommended sights are open.

FRIDAY: The Van Gogh Museum is open until 22:00 during peak season (March-Oct). The Stedelijk Museum is open until 22:00.

SATURDAY: The Van Gogh Museum is open until 22:00 during select months (July-Aug and Oct).

NOTE: If you day-trip to Haarlem, keep in mind that its market days are Saturday and Monday, though its museums are closed on Monday.

The **I amsterdam Card** includes a canal boat ride and a transportation pass. It covers the Van Gogh Museum and more, but not the Rijksmuseum or Anne Frank House (€47/24 hours, €57/48 hours, www.iamsterdam.com). Another pass you'll see advertised, the **Holland Pass**, is not worth it.

Rick's Tip: *For a brief visit,* **skip all the sightseeing passes and buy advance tickets online** *instead.*

Tours
▲▲CANAL BOAT TOURS
Boats leave continually from several docks around town for a relaxing, if uninspiring, one-hour introduction to the city, with recorded headphone commentary. Select a tour based on your proximity to its starting point:

Rederij P. Kooij is cheapest (€10, 3/hour in summer 10:00-22:00, 2/hour in winter 10:00-17:00, at corner of Spui and Rokin streets, about 10 minutes from Dam Square, tel. 020/623-3810, www.rederijkooij.nl).

Blue Boat Company's boats depart from near Leidseplein (€15; every half-hour April-Sept 10:00-18:00, hourly Oct-March 10:00-17:00; 1.25 hours, Stadhouderskade 30, tel. 020/679-1370, www.blueboat.nl).

Holland International offers a variety of tours from the docks opposite Central Station (€15.50, 1-hour "100 Highlights" tour with recorded narration, daily 4/hour 9:00-18:00, 2/hour 18:00-22:00; Prins Hendrikkade 33a, tel. 020/217-0500, www.hir.nl).

Rick's Tip: *Boats leave only when full, so* **jump on a full boat to avoid waiting at the dock.**

WALKING TOURS
New Europe Tours uses native, English-speaking students to give irreverent and entertaining three-hour walks. While these are "free tours," the guides rely on tips. While most guides lack a deep understanding of Dutch culture, they're high-energy, with enthusiasm for the contemporary pot-and-prostitution scene (free but tips expected, daily at 11:15 and 14:15, www.neweuropetours.eu). New

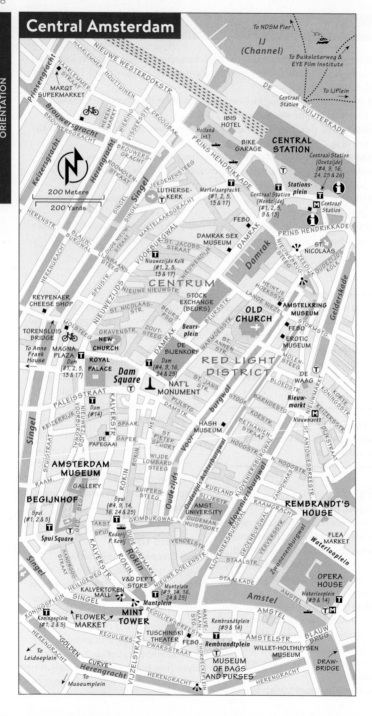

Central Amsterdam

IJ (Channel)

To NDSM Pier

To Buiksloterweg &
EYE Film Institute

To IJPlein

Centraal Station

RUIJTERKADE

NDSM Pier

HAARLEMMERSTRAAT

NIEUWE WESTERDOKSTR.

HAARLEMMER HOUTTUINEN

MARQT SUPERMARKET

Prinsengracht

Brouwersgracht

BROUWERSGRACHT

HEREN-MARKT

WIERINGERSTR.

VISSERSSTR.

DROOGBAK

Holland Int'l

IBIS HOTEL

BIKE GARAGE

PRINS HENDRIKKADE

CENTRAL STATION

Centraal Station (Oostzijde)
(#4, 9, 16, 24, 25 & 26)

Stationsplein

Centraal Station (Westzijde)
(#1, 2, 5, 9 & 13)

Centraal Station

Keizersgracht

Herengracht

Singel

Singel

200 Meters
200 Yards

HERENSTR.

HERENGRACHT

BLAUW-BURGWAL

LIJNBAANS-STEEG

SPUISTRAAT

L.OUDE NIEUW-STRAAT

SINGEL

MARTELAARSGRACHT

JEROENENSTEEG

LUTHERSE-KERK

Martelaargracht
(#1, 2, 5, 13 & 17)

Nieuwezijds Kolk
(#1, 2, 5, 13 & 17)

FEBO

DAMRAK SEX MUSEUM

DAMRAK

PRINS HENDRIKKADE

NIEUWEBRUG-STEEG

OUDEZIJDS KOLK

ST. NICOLAAS

REYPENAER CHEESE SHOP

ROMEIN-STRAAT

ST. JACOBS-STRAAT

NIEUWENDIJK

NIEUWEZIJDS VOORBURGWAL

CENTRUM

NIEUWE NIEUWSTR.

STOCK EXCHANGE (BEURS)

BEURSPSG.

BEURSPLEIN

OLD CHURCH

HEINTJE HOEKSTG.

LANGE NIEZEL

WARMOESSTRAAT

AMSTELKRING MUSEUM

GELDERSKADE

STORMSTG.

FEBO

EROTIC MUSEUM

TORENSLUIS BRIDGE

To Anne Frank House

MOLSTEEG

GRAVENSTR.

ST. NICOLAAS-STR.

ZOUTSTEEG

DAMRAK

ROKIN

NEW CHURCH

ROYAL PALACE

MAGNA PLAZA

Dam
(#1, 2, 5, 13 & 17)

DE BIJENKORF

Dam
(#4, 9, 16, 24 & 25)

Dam Square

NAT'L MONUMENT

RED LIGHT DISTRICT

DE WAAG

MOLENSTEEG

KORTE KONINGSSTR.

Nieuwmarkt

Nieuwmarkt

PALEISSTRAAT

KALVERSTR.

Dam
(#14)

SPAARPOTSTEEG

NES

ST. PIETER SPOORT

PIJLSTG.

DAMSTR.

ST. JANS STR.

VOORBURGWAL

STOOF

BARNDESTG.

KOESTR.

BETHANIEN-STRAAT

HOOGSTRAAT

ST. ANTHONIESBREESTR.

Singel

KEIZERSRIJK

VOORBURGWAL

DE PAPEGAAI

GAPER.

ROKIN

HASH MUSEUM

WIJDE LOMBARD-STEEG

OUDEZIJDS

OUDEZIJDS ACHTERBURGWAL

RUSLAND

KLOVENIERSBURGWAL

RAAMGRACHT

ZANDDWARSSTR.

N. HOOGSTR.

REMBRANDT'S HOUSE

AMSTERDAM MUSEUM

GALLERY

BEGIJNHOF

Spui
(#1, 2 & 5)

Spui
(#4, 9, 14, 16, 24 & 25)

Spui Square

KUIPERS-STEEG

GRIMBURGWAL

SLIJKSTR.

AMST. UNIVERSITY

OUDEMAN-HUISPOORT

GROENBURGWAL

VERVERSTR.

FLEA MARKET

Waterlooplein

GED. BEGIJNENSLOOT

RAAM.

TAKSTR.

KALVERSTR.

Rederij P. Kooij

Spui

OUDE TURFMARKT

ROKIN

VENDELSTR.

NIEUWE DOELENSTR.

STAALSTR.

STAALKADE

Zwanenburgwal

OPERA HOUSE

Waterlooplein
(#9 & 14)

Amstel

Singel

HANDBOOGSTR.

HEILIGEWEG

V&D DEP'T STORE

Muntplein
(#9, 14, 16, 24 & 25)

Muntplein

AMSTEL

BLAUW BRUG

DRAW-BRIDGE

KONINGSPLEIN

Koningsplein
(#1, 2 & 5)

KALVERTOREN MALL

SINGEL

MINT TOWER

FLOWER MARKET

REGULIERSBREE-STR.

Rembrandtplein
(#9 & 14)

HALVE MAAN STG.

"GOLDEN CURVE"

To Leidseplein

To Museumplein

Herengracht

REGULIERSDWARSSTRAAT

VIJZELSTRAAT

TUSCHINSKI THEATER

FEBO

Rembrandtplein

AMSTELSTR.

WILLET-HOLTHUYSEN MUSEUM

MUSEUM OF BAGS AND PURSES

THORBECKEPLEIN

Herengracht

Herengracht

Prinsengracht

Europe also offers paid tours (Red Light District—€12, daily at 19:00; coffeeshop scene—€12, daily at 15:00; Amsterdam by bike—€18.50, includes bike, daily at 12:00). Its walking tours leave from the National Monument on Dam Square; its bike tour leaves from Central Station.

Frank Sanders' **Adam's Apple Tours** offers a two-hour, English-only look at the history and development of Amsterdam, starting at Central Station and ending at Dam Square (€25; May-Sept daily at 10:00, 12:30, and 15:00 based on demand; call 020/616-7867 to confirm times and book, www.adamsapple.nl).

Private Guide Albert Walet personalizes tours, focusing on history, architecture, and water management (€70/2 hours, €120/4 hours, up to 4 people, on foot or by bike, mobile 06-2069-7882, abwalet@yahoo.com).

BIKE TOURS

Yellow Bike Guided Tours offers tours of either two hours (€21, daily at 10:30) or three hours (€25, daily at 13:30), which both include a 20-minute break. They also offer a four-hour, 15-mile tour of the countryside (€31.50, lunch extra, includes

45-minute break, April-Oct daily at 10:30). All tours leave from Nieuwezijds Kolk 29, three blocks from Central Station (reservations smart, tel. 020/620-6940, www.yellowbike.nl).

Joy Ride Bike Tours pedal through the pastoral polder land in 4.5 hours. Helmets, rain gear, and saddlebags are provided free. Book tours in advance; tours meet behind the Rijksmuseum next to the Cobra Café (€30, April-Sept Thu-Mon, meet at 10:15 and depart precisely at 10:30, no tours Tue-Wed, groups limited to 15 people and no kids under 13 years, mobile 06-4361-1798, www.joyridetours.nl). They also offer private tours tailored to your interests.

Helpful Hints

Theft Alert: Tourists are easy targets for petty thieves—especially in the train station, on trams, in and near crowded museums, at places of drunkenness, and at the many hostels. Wear your money belt.

Street Smarts: Beware of silent transportation—trams, electric mopeds, and bicycles—when walking around town. Don't walk on tram tracks or pink/maroon bicycle paths. Before you step off any sidewalk, do a double- or triple-check in both directions to make sure all's clear.

Cash Only: Dutch merchants, who hate paying fees, often refuse credit cards. Expect to pay cash in unexpected places, including grocery stores, cafés, budget hotels, train-station machines and windows, and at some museums.

Maps: Given the city's maze of streets and canals, you should get a good city map (€2.50 at Central Station TI). The free tourist maps can be confusing, except for *Amsterdam Museums: Guide to 44 Museums* (includes tram info and stops, ask for it at the big museums, such as the Van Gogh).

AMSTERDAM CITY WALK

This walk stretches from one end of the old center to the other, tasting all that Amsterdam has to offer along the way: hidden churches, surprising shops, thriving happy-hour hangouts, and eight centuries of history.

Length of This Tour: Allow three hours; this walk is best during the day, when churches and sights are open. Allow extra time if you want to take a break to tour them (details under "Sights").

🎧 Download my free Amsterdam City Walk audio tour.

❸ Self-Guided Walk

This walk starts at the Central Station and ends at Leidseplein, near the Rijksmuseum. The train station and art museum—designed by the same architect—stand like bookends holding the old town together. You'll walk about three miles, heading down Damrak to Dam Square, continuing south down Kalverstraat to the Mint Tower (Munttoren), then wafting through the flower market

(Bloemenmarkt), before continuing south to Leidseplein. Along the way, you can find public toilets (generally €0.50) at fast-food places, near the entrance to the Amsterdam Museum, and in the Kalvertoren mall.

The route basically follows the central tramline, so to zip from any spot to anywhere else, simply hop on tram #1, #2, or #5. Trams #2 and #5 continue to the Rijksmuseum and Van Gogh Museum.

❶ Central Station

The fine Central Station sits on reclaimed land at what was once the harbor mouth. With red brick and prickly spires, it's the first of several Neo-Gothic buildings built in the late 1800s, during Amsterdam's economic revival. One of the towers has a clock dial. The other's dial is a weather vane, with a hand twitching as the wind gusts in each direction—N, Z, O, and W.

Get oriented: *nord, zuid, ost,* and *vest.* Facing the station, you're facing north. Farther north, on the other side of the station, is the IJ (pronounced "eye"), the body of water that gives Amsterdam access to the open sea.

The Neo-Gothic central train station borders the old town.

Turn around 180 degrees and, with your back to the station, face the city, looking south. Amsterdam spreads out before you like a fan, in a series of concentric canals. Ahead of you stretches the street called Damrak, which leads to Dam Square a half-mile away. That's where we're heading.

To the left of Damrak is the city's old (*oude*) town. More recently, that historic neighborhood has become the Red Light District. The big church towering above the old part of town is St. Nicholas Church, built in the 1880s, when Catholics—after about three centuries of oppression—were finally free to worship in public.

To the right of Damrak is the new (*nieuwe*) part of town, where you'll find the Anne Frank House and the Jordaan neighborhood.

The train station is the city's transportation hub. Across the street is the city's main TI, marked by the *VVV* sign.

• *With your back to Central Station, walk south into the city, to the head of Damrak. When you reach the head of Damrak, keep going south, straight along the right side of the street, following the crowds on...*

❷ Damrak

This street was once a riverbed. It's where the Amstel River flowed north into the IJ, which led to a vast inlet of the North Sea called the Zuiderzee. This unique geography turned Amsterdam into a center of trade, with boats sailing up the Amstel

into the interior of Europe, or out to the North Sea, to the rest of the world.

As you stroll along Damrak, look left. The old brick buildings lining the marina aren't historic, but the scene captures a bit of Golden Age Amsterdam. In the 1600s, this was the harbor and those buildings warehoused exotic goods from all over the world. You'll also notice touristy shops selling every Dutch cliché: wooden shoes, tulips, Heineken fridge magnets, and windmill-shaped saltshakers.

At the **Damrak Sex Museum** at Damrak 18, you'll find the city's most notorious commodity on display. As a port town catering to sailors and businessmen away from home, Amsterdam has always accommodated the sex trade.

Continue up Damrak (noting the **canal boats** on your right) for more touristy delectables. You'll pass places selling the popular local fast food: french fries, called **Vlaamse friets** (Flemish fries) here, since they were invented in the Low Countries. The stand at Damrak 41 is a favorite. In cosmopolitan Amsterdam, international cuisine is almost like going local. Indonesian restaurants are especially popular, since that was a former Dutch colony.

We're walking along what was once the Amstel River. Today, the Amstel is channeled into canals and its former mouth is covered by the Central Station. But Amsterdam still remains Europe's fourth-busiest seaport, with more than 100,000 ships a year docking on its outskirts.

• *The long brick building with the square clock tower, along the left side of Damrak, is the...*

❸ Stock Exchange (*Beurs van Berlage*)

This symbol of Amsterdam's long tradition as a trading town was built with nine million bricks on a foundation of pilings—some 5,000 tree trunks hammered vertically into the soil. Opening in 1903, the

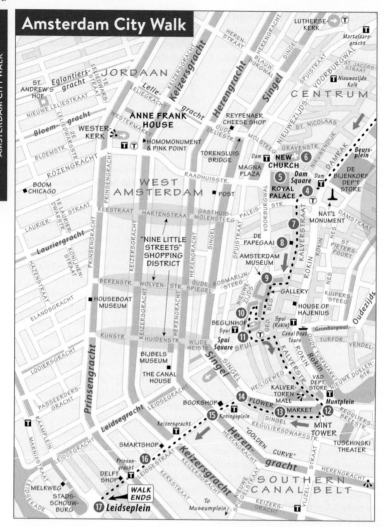

Amsterdam City Walk

Beurs was one of the world's first modernist buildings. Emphasizing function over looks, it helped set the architectural tone for the 20th century.

Continuing along Damrak, make your way to the end of the long building. Amsterdammers have gathered in this neighborhood to trade since medieval times. Back then, "trading stock" meant buying and selling any kind of goods that could be loaded and unloaded onto a

Stock Exchange

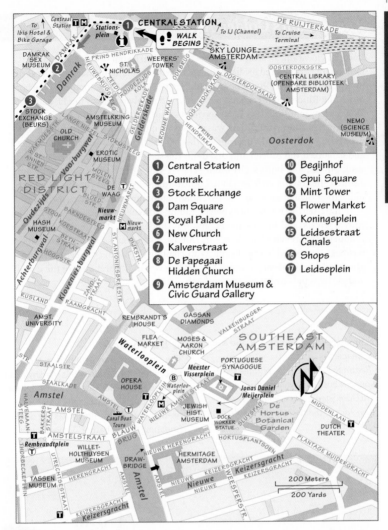

❶ Central Station	❿ Begijnhof
❷ Damrak	⓫ Spui Square
❸ Stock Exchange	⓬ Mint Tower
❹ Dam Square	⓭ Flower Market
❺ Royal Palace	⓮ Koningsplein
❻ New Church	⓯ Leidsestraat Canals
❼ Kalverstraat	⓰ Shops
❽ De Papegaai Hidden Church	⓱ Leidseplein
❾ Amsterdam Museum & Civic Guard Gallery	

boat—goats, chickens, or kegs of beer. Over time, they began exchanging slips of paper, or "futures," rather than actual goods. Traders needed moneychangers, who needed bankers, who made money by lending money. By the 1600s, Amsterdam had become one of the world's first great capitalist cities, loaning money to kings, dukes, and bishops.

When you reach the end of the building, detour left into the square called **Beursplein.** In 1984, the Beurs building was turned into a cultural center, and the stock exchange moved next door to the Euronext complex. See the stock price readout board. How's your Heineken stock doing? Green means it's up; red means it's down.

Before leaving Beursplein, drop into **Café Beurs** and take in its minimalist 1930s interior. The optimistic art heralds a new age of worker-empowering

Amsterdam's Golden Age

Location, location, location! Visualize the physical layout of this man-made city: built on trees, protected by dikes, and laced with canals in the marshy delta at the mouth of the Amstel River. Boats could arrive here from Germany by riverboat down the Rhine, from England across the Channel and down the IJ, and from Denmark by entering the Zuiderzee inlet of the North Sea.

As early as 1300, Amsterdam was already an international trade center of German beer, locally caught herring, cloth, bacon, salt, and wine. Having dammed and canalized the Amstel and diked out the sea tides, the Dutch drained land, sunk pilings, and built a city from scratch. Once the region's leading bishop granted the town a charter (1300), Amsterdammers could set up law courts, judge their own matters, and be essentially autonomous. The town thrived.

In 1602, hardy Dutch sailors began trading with the Far East, bringing Europe spices, jewels, and luxury goods...and the Golden Age. The Dutch East India Company (abbreviated as "VOC" in Dutch), a state-subsidized import/export business, combined nautical skills with capitalist investing to become the first great multinational corporation. Amsterdam was the "warehouse of the world" and perhaps the wealthiest city on earth.

technology, social democracy, and a hope for peace.

• *Return to Damrak, and continue south along the busy boulevard until it opens into Dam Square. Make your way—carefully—across the street to the cobblestone pavement.*

❹ Dam Square

The city got its start right here in about 1250, when fishermen in this marshy delta built a *damme*, blocking the Amstel River, and creating a small village called "Amstel-damme." To the north was the *damrak* (meaning "outer harbor"), a waterway

Dam Square is the historic heart of Amsterdam.

that eventually led to the sea. That's the street we just walked. To the south was the *rokin* (roh-KEEN, "inner harbor"), for river traffic. Nowadays, the Rokin is also a main street. With access to the sea, the fishermen were soon trading with German riverboats traveling downstream and with seafaring boats from Stockholm, Hamburg, and London. Land trade routes converged here as well and a customs house stood in this spot. Dam Square was the center of it all.

Today, Dam Square is still the center of Dutch life. The Royal Palace and major department stores face the square. Mimes, jugglers, and human statues mingle with locals and tourists.

Circling the Square: Pan the square clockwise to take in the sights, starting with the Royal Palace—the large domed building on the west side. To its right stands the New Church (Nieuwe Kerk), located on the pedestrian-only shopping street called Nieuwendijk, which runs parallel to Damrak and stretches all the way to Central Station. Panning past Damrak, see the proud old De Bijenkorf ("The Beehive") department store. The cafeteria on its top floor is great for a light meal with a view (see page 1033).

Farther right, Grand Hotel Krasnapol-sky has a lovely circa-1900 Winter Garden. The white obelisk is the National Monument. A few blocks behind the hotel is the edge of the Red Light District. To the right of the hotel stretches the street called the Nes, lined with edgy live-theater venues. Panning farther right, find Rokin street—Damrak's southern counterpart, continuing past the square. Next, to the right of the touristy Madame Tussauds, is Kalverstraat, a busy pedestrian-only shoppers mall (look for *Rabobank* sign).

❺ Royal Palace (Koninklijk Huis)

Despite the name, this is really the former City Hall—and Amsterdam is one of the cradles of modern democracy. In medieval times, this was where the city council and mayor met. Amsterdam was a self-governing community, proud of its independence and thumbing its nose at royalty. In about 1650, the old medieval town hall was replaced with this one. Its style recalls the democratic Greeks. The triangular pediment features sea creatures cavorting with Neptune—appropriate imagery for sea-trading Amsterdam. The small balcony (just above the entry doors) is where city leaders have long appeared for major speeches, pronouncements,

The Royal Palace got its start as Amsterdam's City Hall.

executions, and (these days) for newly-married royalty to blow kisses to the crowds.

Today, the palace remains one of the four official residences of King Willem-Alexander and is usually open to visitors.
• *A few paces away, to the right as you're facing the Royal Palace, is the...*

❻ New Church (Nieuwe Kerk)

Though called the "New" Church, this building is actually 600 years old—a mere 100 years newer than the "Old" Church in the Red Light District. The sundial above the entrance once served as the city's official timepiece.

While it's pricey to enter the church (which offers little besides the temporary exhibits), cheapskates can see much of it for free. Enter through the "Museum-shop" door (to the left of the main church entrance) and climb the stairs to a balcony with a small free museum and views of the nave.

The church's bare, spacious interior (occupied by a new art exhibit every three months) is different from the Baroque churches throughout Europe. In 1566, Protestant extremists throughout Holland marched into Catholic churches (including this one), lopped off the heads of holy statues, stripped gold angels from the walls, and shattered stained-glass windows in a wave of vandalism.

This iconoclasm (icon-breaking) of 1566 started an 80-year war against Spain and the Habsburgs, leading to Dutch independence in 1648. Catholic churches like this one were converted to the new dominant religion, Calvinist Protestantism (today's Dutch Reformed Church). From then on, Dutch churches downplayed the "graven images" and "idols" of ornate religious art.

At the far left end of the church is an organ from 1655, still played for midday concerts. Opposite the entrance, a stained-glass window shows Count William IV giving the city its "XXX" coat of arms. The window over the entrance portrays the inauguration of Queen Wilhelmina, the steadfast center of the Dutch Resistance during World War II. Once used by the monks, the choir

New Church

WWII obelisk-memorial on Dam Square

became a mausoleum for a Dutch admiral after the Reformation.

This church is where many of the Netherlands' monarchs are married, and all are inaugurated. While on the viewing balcony, imagine the church in action in April of 2013, when King Willem-Alexander—Wilhelmina's great-grandson—was paraded through this church to the golden choir screen. There may be a video of this.

Leave the shop via the main church entrance. On your way out, look up to see stained-glass windows showing Dutch royals from 1579 to 1898.

Back outside, look at the tall, **white obelisk** in the middle of Dam Square. It was built in 1956 as a WWII memorial. The Nazis occupied Holland from 1940 to 1945; in those years, they deported 100,000 Jewish Amsterdammers, driving many—including young Anne Frank and her family—into hiding. Near the end of the war, the "Hunger Winter" of 1944-1945 killed thousands and forced many to survive on little more than tulip bulbs. This national monument both remembers the suffering of that grim time and offers hope for peace.

• *From Dam Square, head south (at the Rabobank sign) on...*

❼ *Kalverstraat*

Kalverstraat (strictly pedestrian-only—even bikers need to dismount and walk) has been a shopping street for centuries, but today it's notorious for a noisy string of chain stores. For a better shopping

Kalverstraat

experience, try the adjacent De Negen Straatjes ("The Nine Little Streets"), about four blocks west of Kalverstraat, where 200 or so elegant shops and cafés mingle along tranquil canals.

• *About 100 yards along, keep a sharp eye out for the next sight (it's fairly easy to miss): On the right, just before and across from the McDonald's, at #58. Now pop into...*

❽ *De Papegaai Hidden Church (Petrus en Paulus Kerk)*

This Catholic church—with a simple white interior, carved wood, and Stations of the Cross paintings (try reading the Dutch captions)—is an oasis of peace amid crass 21st-century commercialism. While it's not a hidden church, it keeps a low profile. That's because it dates from an era when Catholics in Amsterdam were forced to worship in secret.

In the 1500s, Protestants were fighting Catholics all over Europe. As a center for trade, Amsterdam has long made an effort to put business above ideological differences, doing business with all parties. But by 1578 the division had become too wide, and Protestant extremists took political control of the city. They expelled Catholic leaders and outlawed the religion. Catholic churches were stripped of their lavish decoration and converted into Dutch Reformed churches.

For the next two centuries, Amsterdam's Catholics were driven underground. While technically illegal, Catholicism was tolerated (as marijuana is now). Catholics could worship so long as they practiced in humble, unadvertised places, like this church. The church gets its nickname from a parrot (*papegaai*) carved over the entrance of the house that formerly stood on this site. A stuffed parrot hangs in the nave to remember that original *papegaai*.

Today, the church asks visitors for "15 minutes for God" (so says the sign: *een kwartier voor God*)—an indication of how religion has long been a marginal part of secular Amsterdam.

• *Return to Kalverstraat and continue south for about 100 yards. At #92, where Kalverstraat crosses Wijde Kapel Steeg, look to the right at an archway that leads to the entrance and courtyard of the Amsterdam Museum.*

❾ Amsterdam Museum and Civic Guard Gallery

Pause at the entrance to the museum complex to view the archway. On the slumping arch is Amsterdam's coat of arms—a red shield with three Xs and a crown. The X-shaped crosses represent the crucifixion of St. Andrew, the patron saint of fishermen. They also represent the three virtues of heroism, determination, and mercy—symbolism that was declared by the queen after the Dutch experience in World War II. (Before that, they likely symbolized the three great medieval threats: fire, flood, and plague.) The crown dates from 1489, when Maximilian I—a Habsburg emperor—also ruled the Low Countries. He paid off a big loan with help from Amsterdam's city bankers and, as thanks for the cash, let the city use his trademark, the Habsburg crown, on its shield.

Check out the relief above the door, dated 1581. It shows boys around a dove, asking for charity, reminding all who pass that this building was once an orphanage.

Inside, a pleasant café has a shaded courtyard and old lockers for the orphans' uniforms. This exhibit helps you imagine life in the orphanage through the centu-

ries. (There's also a pay toilet.)

The courtyard leads to the **Amsterdam Museum** (described on page 1026). Next to the museum's entrance is a free, glassed-in passageway lined with paintings. If it's closed, you'll need to backtrack to Kalverstraat to continue our walk (continue south, then turn right on Begijnensteeg, then look for the gate leading to the Begijnhof). Otherwise, step into the **Civic Guard Gallery** (Schuttersgalerij).

This hall features group portraits of Amsterdam's citizens, from the Golden Age to modern times. Giant statues of Goliath and a knee-high David (from 1650) watch over the whole thing. Civic Guard paintings from the 1600s established a tradition of group portraits that continues today. The portraits show the men gathered with their Civic Guard militia units. These men defended Holland, but the Civic Guards were also fraternal organizations of businessmen—the Rotary Clubs of the 17th century. Their weapons—pikes and muskets—are mostly symbolic. Modern portraits show today's city leaders posing playfully as Golden Age bigwigs.

Don't miss the colorful patchwork carpet. Each patch represents a country where Dutch immigrants originated—celebrating today's multicultural reality.

• *The gallery offers a shortcut to our next stop, a hidden, peaceful courtyard. To get there, exit out the far end of the Civic Guards Gallery. Once in the light of day, continue ahead one block farther south and find the humble gate on the right, which leads to the...*

❿ Begijnhof

As you enter, keep in mind that this spot isn't just a tourist attraction; it's also a place where people live. Be considerate: Don't photograph the residents or their homes. Be quiet and stick to the area near the churches.

This tranquil courtyard has sheltered women since 1346. It was for centuries the

Dove relief at the Amsterdam Museum

home of a community of Beguines—pious women who removed themselves from the world at large to dedicate their lives to God. When it was first established, it literally was a "woman's island"—a circle of houses facing a peaceful courtyard, surrounded by water.

Begin your visit at the **statue** of one of these charitable sisters, just beyond the church. The Beguines' ranks swelled during the Crusades, when many men took off, never to return, leaving society with an abundance of single women. Later, women widowed by the hazards of overseas trade lived out their days as Beguines. Poor and rich women alike turned their backs on materialism to live in Christian poverty. Though obedient to a mother superior, the members of the lay order of Beguines were not nuns. The Beguines spent their days in prayer and busy with daily tasks—spinning wool, making lace, teaching, and caring for the sick.

Turn your attention to the brick-faced **English Reformed church** (Engelse Kerk). The church was built in 1420 to serve the Beguines. But in 1578, Catholicism was outlawed, and the Dutch Reformed Church took over many Catholic monasteries. Still, the Begijnhof survived; in 1607, this church became Anglican, serving as a refuge for English traders and religious separatists fleeing persecution in England. Strict Protestants such as the Pilgrims found sanctuary in tolerant Amsterdam and worshiped in this church. They later moved to Leiden, where they lived for a

decade before sailing to religious freedom in America. If the church is open, step inside and head to the far end, toward the stained-glass window. It shows the Pilgrims praying before boarding the Mayflower. Along the right-hand wall is an old pew they may have sat on. On the altar is a 1763 Bible.

Back outside, find the **Catholic church,** which faces the English Reformed Church. Step through the low-profile doorway and pick up an English brochure near the entry. This church served Amsterdam's oppressed 17th-century Catholics, who refused to worship as Protestants. It's decorated lovingly, if on the cheap (tap softly on a "marble" column). Amsterdam's Catholics must have eagerly awaited the day when they were legally allowed to say Mass (that day finally came in the 19th century).

Step back outside. The last Beguine died in 1971, but this Begijnhof still thrives, providing subsidized housing to about 100 single women (mostly Catholic seniors).

The statue of the Beguine faces a black **wooden house,** at #34. It's the city's oldest structure, dating from 1528. The whole city once consisted of wooden houses like this. They were eventually replaced with brick houses to minimize the fire danger.

A few steps to the left of the house, find a display of colorful, carved gable stones. These once adorned housefronts and served as street numbers.

• *Near the wooden house and gables, a little corridor leads back into the modern world. Head up a few steps to emerge into lively...*

⓫ Spui Square

Lined with cafés and bars, this square is a popular spot for nightlife and afternoon people-watching. Its name, Spui (spow, rhymes with "now" and means "spew"), recalls the days when water was moved over dikes to keep the place dry.

Head two blocks to the left, crossing busy Kalverstraat, to the bustling street called **Rokin.** A small black statue of

Begijnhof courtyard

Queen Wilhelmina (1880-1962) shows her riding sidesaddle. Remember that she was the iron-willed inspiration for the Dutch Resistance against the Nazis.

Canal cruises depart from the Rondvaart Kooij dock across the water, in the yellow canal house (see "Canal Boat Tours" on page 997).

Turn left on the Rokin and walk up 50 yards to the **House of Hajenius** (at Rokin 92). This temple of cigars is a "paradise for the connoisseur" with "175 years of tradition and good taste." Enter this sumptuous Art Deco building and step back into 1910. Don't be shy—it's as much a free museum as a store for paying customers. The brown-capped canisters (under the wall of pipes, to the right) are for smelling fine pipe tobacco. Sniff three, and appreciate the differences between them. The personal humidifiers (read the explanation) allow locals (famous local names are on the cupboard doors) to call in an order and have their cigars waiting for them at the right humidity. Above the street entry, check out the humidifier pipes pumping moisture into the room. Upstairs in the back is a small, free museum.

From Hajenius, backtrack to Kalverstraat and continue south. You'll pass department stores. **Vroom & Dreesman** has basic supplies (nothing fancy) and a handy, cheap, and cheery La Place Cafeteria (see page 1033). The **Kalvertoren** complex, across Kalverstraat from V&D, is a modern mall. Enter and go inside to ride a slanting glass elevator to the top-floor

café, where a €3 coffee comes with a nice view (generally daily 10:00-18:00).

• *At the center of the square stands the…*

⑫ *Mint Tower (Munttoren)*

This tower marked the limit of the medieval walled city and served as one of its original gates. In the Middle Ages, the city walls were girdled by the Singel canal. Until about 1500, the area beyond here was nothing but marshy fields and a few farms on reclaimed land. The Mint Tower's steeple was added in the year 1620, as you can see written below the clock face. Today, the tower is a favorite of marijuana enthusiasts, who take photos of the clock and its 1620 sign at exactly 4:20 p.m.—the traditional time to quit work and fire one up. (On the 24-hour clock, 4:20 p.m. is 16:20...Du-u-u-ude!)

Before moving on, look left (at about 10 o'clock) down Reguliersbreestraat. Midway down the block, the twin green domes mark the Art Deco **Tuschinski Theater.** Way at the end of the long block (where you see trees) is **Rembrandtplein,** another major center for nightlife (and it also has a fun life-size sculpture group of Rembrandt's *Night Watch*).

• *Continue past the Mint Tower, first walking a few yards south along busy Vijzelstraat (keep an eye out for trams). Then turn right and walk west along the south bank of the Singel canal. The canal is lined with the greenhouse shops of the…*

⑬ *Flower Market (Bloemenmarkt)*

The stands along this busy block sell cut flowers, plants, bulbs, seeds, and garden supplies. Browse your way along while heading for the end of the block. The Netherlands is the largest flower exporter in Europe and a major flower power worldwide. If you're looking for a souvenir, note that certain seeds are marked as OK to bring back through customs into the US (the marijuana starter-kit-in-a-can is probably...not).

Mint Tower

Amsterdam's Canals

Amsterdam's canals are as pretty as they are practical. The city was founded in a marshy river delta, so its citizens needed to keep the water at bay. They built a dike, near where Central Station stands today, to keep out the sea-tide surge. Then they dammed the Amstel River. The excess water was channeled into canals, creating pockets of dry land to build on. Windmills harnessed wind power to pump the excess water into the canals. The canals also added to the transportation infrastructure merchants needed to move their goods.

Today, the city has about 100 canals, most about 10 feet deep. They're crossed by some 1,200 bridges, fringed with 100,000 trees, and bedecked with 2,500 houseboats. A system of locks (back near the Central Station) controls the flow. The locks are opened periodically to flush out the system.

The word *gracht* (pronounced, roughly, "hroht," with guttural flair) can refer to a canal itself, or to the ensemble of a canal and the lanes that border it on each side. A *straat* is a street without a canal, though a few paved-over canals, such as Elandsgracht, have kept their old name.

Canals radiate out from the Central Station. Four matter in your city navigating: **Singel** (the innermost, originally the fortified medieval town's defensive moat); **Herengracht** (named for the aristocrats, or *heren,* who built the Dutch East India Company and lived in mansions along here); **Keizersgracht** (named for the Holy Roman Emperor and also lined with fine mansions); and **Prinsengracht** (the liveliest of the canals, lined with old warehouses and smaller homes).

Memorize this sentence to help you remember the order of the canals: A Single Hairy Kaiser's Prince really knows his canals.

• *The Flower Market ends at the next bridge, where you'll see a square named...*

⓮ *Koningsplein*

This pleasant square, with a popular outdoor *heringhandel* (herring shop), is a great place to choke down a raw herring—a fish with a special place in every

Flower Market

Dutch heart. Herring was the commodity that first put Amsterdam on the trading map. It's also what Dutch sailors ate for protein on long voyages. In season, you'll see the sign—*Hollandse nieuwe*—alerting locals that the herring are "new" (fresh), caught during the May-June season. They eat it chopped up with onions and pickles, using the Dutch-flag toothpick as a utensil.

• *From Koningsplein, turn left, heading straight south to Leidseplein along Leidestraat.*

⓯ *Leidsestraat Canals* and ⓰ *Shops*

At first, the street is just labeled *Koningsplein*. Walk to the first of several grand canals, Herengracht. Looking left down Herengracht, you'll see the **"Golden**

Curve" of the canal. It's lined with town-houses sporting especially nice gables. Amsterdam has many different types of gables—bell-shaped, step-shaped, etc. This stretch is known for its "cornice" gables (straight across), which topped the facades of rich merchants—the *heren*.

After the bridge, Koningsplein becomes Leidsestraat, crowded with shoppers, tourists, bicycles, and trams (stay alert and don't walk on the tram tracks). As the street narrows, trams wait their turn to share a single track.

Cross over the next canal (Keizers-gracht), then find the little **Smartshop**, on the right at Kaisersgracht 508. While "smartshops" like this one are all as above-board as any other in the city, they sell drugs—some of them strong, most of them illegal back home, and not all of them harmless. Because these products are found in nature, the Dutch govern-ment considers them legal. Check out the window displays or go in to browse.

Where Leidsestraat crosses Prinsen-gracht, over the bridge on the right (at Prinsengracht 440), you'll find **The Royal Delft Shop.** This place sells good exam-ples of the glazed ceramics known as Delftware, famous for its distinctive blue-and-white design. Dutch traders learned the technique from the Chinese of the Ming dynasty. The doodads with arms branching off a trunk are popular "flower pagodas," vases for displaying tulips.

• *Looking left, half a block down Prinsen-gracht, you can see the home of the* **Pipe Museum** *(at #488). Unless you're detouring to visit the museum, continue down Leidse-straat and follow it to the big, busy square, called...*

⑰ *Leidseplein*

This is Amsterdam's liveliest square: filled with outdoor tables under trees; ringed with cafés, theaters, and nightclubs; bustling with diners, trams, mimes, and fire-eaters. Locals and tourists come here day and night to sip a coffee or beer in the warmth of the sun or the glow of lantern light.

Do a 360-degree spin: Leidseplein's south side is bordered by the huge Apple Store. Nearby is the city's main theater, the **Stadsschouwburg.** Its company dates to the 17th century and the present build-ing is from 1890. Do its red brick and fan-ciful turrets look familiar? This building,

Leidseplein bustles with action day and night.

the Central Station, and the Rijksmuseum were built by the same architect, Pierre Cuypers, during the city's late 19th-century revival.

Look to the right, down a lane behind the big theater. There you find the **Melkweg** ("Milky Way") nightclub. In the 1970s, this place was almost mythical—an entertainment complex entirely devoted to the young generation and their desires. Even today it offers an edgy array of new acts—step into the lobby or check out posters nearby to see what's on.

Continue panning. The neighborhood beyond Burger King is Amsterdam's **"Restaurant Row,"** featuring countless Thai, Brazilian, Indian, Italian, Indonesian—and even a few Dutch—eateries. Next, on the east end of Leidseplein, is the **Bulldog Café and Coffeeshop,** the flagship of several coffeeshops in town with the Bulldog name. (Note the sign above the door: It once housed the police bureau.) A small green-and-white decal on the window indicates that it's a city-licensed "coffeeshop," where marijuana is sold and smoked legally.

• Our walk is over. But those with more energy could get out their maps and make their way to Vondelpark or the Rijksmuseum (one stop away on tram #2 or #5). To return to Central Station (or to nearly anyplace along this walk), catch tram #1, #2, or #5 from Leidseplein.

Bulldog Café and Coffeeshop

SIGHTS

Most museums require baggage check—usually free (often in coin-op lockers where you get your coin back).

Southwest Amsterdam

▲▲▲ RIJKSMUSEUM

At Amsterdam's Rijksmuseum ("Rijks" rhymes with "bikes"), Holland's Golden Age shines with the best collection anywhere of the Dutch Masters—from Vermeer's quiet domestic scenes and Steen's raucous family meals, to Hals' snapshot portraits and Rembrandt's moody brilliance.

The 17th century saw the Netherlands at the pinnacle of its power. The Dutch had won their independence from Spain, trade and shipping boomed, wealth poured in, the people were understandably proud, and the arts flourished. This era was later dubbed the Dutch Golden Age. With no church bigwigs or royalty around to commission big canvases in the Protestant Dutch Republic, artists had to find different patrons—and they discovered the upper-middle-class businessmen who fueled Holland's capitalist economy. Artists painted their portraits and decorated their homes with pretty still lifes and unpreachy, slice-of-life art.

This delightful museum—recently much improved after a long renovation—offers one of the most exciting and enjoyable art experiences in Europe. As if in homage to Dutch art and history, the Rijksmuseum lets you linger over a vast array of objects and paintings, appreciating the beauty of everyday things.

Cost and Hours: €17.50, not covered by I amsterdam Card, daily 9:00-17:00, last entry 30 minutes before closing, audioguide-€5, cafés on site, tram #2 or #5 from Central Station to Rijksmuseum stop, info tel. 020/674-7047 or switchboard tel. 020/674-7000, www.rijksmuseum.nl. The entrance is off the passageway that tunnels right through the center of the building.

Avoiding Lines and Crowds: You can skip the ticket-buying line by getting your ticket in advance at www.rijksmuseum.nl; you can print out your ticket or save your ticket barcode to your phone or tablet. Many hotels also sell tickets. The ticket is good any time (no entry time specified). A Museumkaart also lets you skip the line.

The museum is most crowded on weekends and holidays, and there's always a peak midday crush around noon. Avoid crowds by coming on Monday or Tuesday, and plan your visit for either first thing in the morning or later in the day (it's least crowded after 15:00).

◉ **Self-Guided Tour:** After showing your ticket (and perhaps renting a videoguide), follow the crowds up the stairway to the top (second) floor, where you emerge into the **Great Hall.** With its stained-glass windows, vaulted ceiling, and murals of Golden Age explorers, it feels like a cathedral to Holland's middle-class merchants. Gaze down the long adjoining hall to the far end, with the "altarpiece" of this cathedral—Rem-

brandt's *Night Watch.* Now, follow the flow of the crowds toward it, into the **Gallery of Honor.** This grand space was purpose-built to hold the Greatest Hits of the Golden Age, by the era's biggest rock stars: Frans Hals, Vermeer, Jan Steen, and Rembrandt.

In the first alcove to the left is the work of **Frans Hals** (c. 1582-1666). Hals was the premier Golden Age portrait painter. Merchants hired him the way we'd hire a wedding photographer. With a few quick strokes, Hals captured not only the features, but also the personality. In *A Militiaman Holding a Berkemeyer* (a.k.a. *The Merry Drinker,* c. 1628-1630), you're greeted by a jovial man in a black hat, capturing the earthy, exuberant spirit of the Dutch Golden Age. Notice the details— the happy red face of the man offering us a *berkemeyer* drinking glass, the sparkle in his eyes, the lacy collar, and the decorative belt buckle. Rather than posing his subject, making him stand for hours saying "cheese," Hals tried to catch him at a candid moment. He often painted common people, fishermen, and barflies, such as

The Rijksmuseum's collections pay homage to Dutch art and history.

this one. He had to work quickly to capture the serendipity of the moment. Hals used a stop-action technique, freezing the man in mid-gesture, with the rough brushwork creating a blur that suggests the man is still moving.

A little farther on is the work of **Johannes Vermeer** (1632-1675). He is the master of tranquility and stillness, creating a clear and silent pool that is a world in itself. Most of his canvases show interiors of Dutch homes, where Dutch women engage in everyday activities, lit by a side window. The Rijksmuseum has the best collection of Vermeers in the world—four of them. (There are only some 34 in captivity.) But each is a small jewel worth lingering over.

Vermeer's *The Milkmaid* (c. 1660) brings out the beauty in mundane things. The subject is ordinary—a kitchen maid—but you could look for hours at the tiny details and rich color tones. These are everyday objects, but they glow in a diffused light: the crunchy crust, the hanging basket, even the rusty nail in the wall with its tiny shadow. In paintings such as *Woman Reading a Letter* (c. 1663), Vermeer's placid scenes often have an air of mystery. The woman is reading a letter. From whom? A lover? A father on a two-year business trip to Indonesia? Not even taking time to sit down, she reads intently, with parted lips and a bowed head. It must be important. (She looks pregnant, adding to the mystery, but that may be the cut of her clothes.) Again, Vermeer has framed a moment of daily life. But within this small world are hints of a wider, wilder world— the light coming from the left is obviously from a large window, giving us a whiff of the life going on outside. The map hangs prominently, reminding us of travel, and perhaps of where the letter is from.

In an alcove nearby is the work of **Jan Steen** (c. 1625-1679, pronounced "yahn stain"). The Norman Rockwell of his day, he painted humorous scenes from the lives of the lower classes. As a tavern

Ⓐ *Hals,* The Merry Drinker
Ⓑ *Vermeer,* The Milkmaid
Ⓒ *Steen,* The Merry Family

owner, he observed society firsthand. Find the painting *Adolf and Catharina Croeser* (a.k.a. *The Burgomaster of Delft and His Daughter*, 1655). Steen's well-dressed burgher sits on his front porch, when a poor woman and child approach to beg, putting him squarely between the horns of a moral dilemma. On the one hand, we see his rich home, well-dressed daughter, and a vase of flowers—a symbol that his money came from morally suspect capitalism. On the other hand, there are his poor fellow citizens and the church steeple, reminding him of his Christian duty. In *The Merry Family* (1668), the family is eating, drinking, and singing like there's no tomorrow. The broken eggshells and scattered cookware symbolize waste and extravagance. The neglected proverb tacked to the fireplace reminds us that children will follow in the footsteps of their parents. Dutch Golden Age families were notoriously lenient with their kids. Even today, the Dutch describe a rowdy family as a "Jan Steen household."

As you get closer to *The Night Watch*, you'll see other works by **Rembrandt van Rijn** (1606-1669), the greatest of all Dutch painters. Whereas most painters specialized in one field—portraits, landscapes, still lifes—Rembrandt excelled in them all. The son of a Leiden miller who owned a waterwheel on the Rhine ("van Rijn"), Rembrandt took Amsterdam by storm with his famous painting *The Anatomy Lesson of Dr. Nicolaes Tulp* (1632, currently in The Hague's Mauritshuis Royal Picture Gallery). The commissions poured in for official portraits, and he was soon wealthy and married. But Holland's war with England (1652-1654) devastated the art market, and Rembrandt's free-spending ways forced him to declare bankruptcy (1656)—the ultimate humiliation in success-oriented Amsterdam. The commissions came more slowly. The money ran out. His mother died. He had to auction off his paintings and furniture to pay debts. He moved out of his fine house to a cheaper place on Rozengracht. His bitter

Rembrandt, The Night Watch

losses added a new wisdom to his work. In his last years, his greatest works were his self-portraits, showing a tired, wrinkled man stoically enduring life's misfortunes. His death effectively marked the end of the Dutch Golden Age.

Start with *Isaac and Rebecca* (a.k.a. *The Jewish Bride*, c. 1665-1669). The man gently draws the woman toward him. She's comfortable enough with him to sink into thought, and she reaches up unconsciously to return the gentle touch. They're young but wizened. This uncommissioned portrait (its subjects remain unknown) is a truly human look at the relationship between two people in love.

At the far end of the Gallery of Honor is the museum's star masterpiece—*The Night Watch* (a.k.a. *The Militia Company of Captain Frans Banninck Cocq*, 1642). This is Rembrandt's most famous—though not necessarily greatest—painting. Created in 1642, when he was 36, it was one of his most important commissions: a group portrait of a company of Amsterdam's Civic Guards to hang in their meeting hall. It's an action shot. With flags waving and drums beating, the guardsmen (who, by the 1640s, were just an honorary militia of rich bigwigs) spill onto the street from under an arch in the back. These guards-

men on the move epitomize the proud, independent, upwardly mobile Dutch.

Why is *The Night Watch* so famous? Compare it with other, less famous group portraits nearby, where every face is visible and everyone is well-lit, flat, and flash-bulb-perfect. By contrast, Rembrandt rousted the Civic Guards off their fat duffs. By adding movement and depth to an otherwise static scene, he took posers and turned them into warriors. He turned a simple portrait into great art.

Now backtrack a few steps to the Gallery of Honor's last alcove to find Rembrandt's *Self-Portrait as the Apostle Paul* (1661). Rembrandt's many self-portraits show us the evolution of a great painter's style, as well as the progress of a genius's life. For Rembrandt, the two were intertwined. In this somber, late self-portrait, the man is 55 but he looks 70. With a lined forehead, a bulbous nose, and messy hair, he peers out from under several coats of glazing, holding old, wrinkled pages. His look is...skeptical? Weary? Resigned to life's misfortunes? Or amused?

This man has seen it all—success, love, money, fatherhood, loss, poverty, death. He took these experiences and wove them into his art. Rembrandt died poor and misunderstood, but he remained his own man to the end.

The Rest of the Rijks: Most visitors are here to see the Golden Age art, but the museum has much, much more. The Rijks is dedicated to detailing Dutch history from 1200 until 2000, with upward of 8,000 works on display. There's everything from an airplane (third floor, in the 20th-century exhibit) to women's fashion and Delftware (lower level). The Asian Art Pavilion shows off 365 objects from Indonesia—a former Dutch colony—as well as items from India, Japan, Korea, and China. (The bronze Dancing Shiva, in Room 1 of the pavilion, is considered one of the best in the world.)

Rembrandt, Self-Portrait

Museumplein

Max Euweplein

To Leidseplein

Blue Boat Company

ZANDPAD

Vondelpark

HOBBEMASTR.

VOSSIUSSTRAAT

Lijnbaansgracht

WETERINGSCHANS

ZIESENISKADE

Singelgracht

Spiegelgracht (#7 & 10)

STADHOUDERSKADE

SAMA SEBO INDONESIAN

P.C. HOOFTSTRAAT

RIJKSMUSEUM

JAN LUIJKENSTR.

Rijksmuseum (#2 & 5)

ASIAN PAVILION

To Heineken Experience

100 Meters

100 Yards

HONTHORSTSTRAAT

COSTER DIAMONDS & MUSEUM

PHILIPS WING

CAFÉ

HOUSE OF BOLS

VAN DE VELDESTRAAT

CAFÉ & RESTAURANT

Van Baerlestraat (#2 & 5)

PAULUS POTTERSTRAAT

PAULUS POTTERSTRAAT

AMSTERDAM SCULPTURE

Pond

HOBBEMASTRAAT

WC

COBRA CAFÉ

Museumplein

Boerenwetering

RUYSDAELKADE

VAN GOGH MUSEUM

VAN BAERLESTRAAT

STEDELIJK MUSEUM

JOHANNES VERMEERSTRAAT

HONTHORST-STRAAT

Museumplein

MUSEUMPLEIN

VAN BAERLESTRAAT

ALBERT HEIJN GROCERY

TENIERS-STR.

JOHANNES VERMEERSTRAAT

To Heineken Experience

HOBBEMAKADE

RUYSDAELKADE

Museumplein (#3, 5, 12)

US CONSULATE

VAN MIEREVELD STRAAT

JOHANNES VERMEERSTRAAT

PIETER DE HOOCHSTRAAT

To Albert Cuypstraat Street Market

CONCERT-GEBOUW

Museumplein (#16 & 24)

GABRIEL METSUSTR.

▲▲▲VAN GOGH MUSEUM

The Van Gogh Museum (we say "van GO," the Dutch say "van hock") is a cultural high even for those not into art. Located near the Rijksmuseum, the museum houses the 200 paintings owned by Vincent's younger brother, Theo. It's a user-friendly stroll through the work and life of one enigmatic man. If you like brightly colored landscapes in the Impressionist style, you'll like this museum. If you enjoy finding deeper meaning in works of art, you'll love it. The mix of Van Gogh's

Van Gogh Museum

creative genius, his tumultuous life, and the traveler's determination to connect to it makes this museum as much a walk with Vincent as with his art.

Cost and Hours: €17, more for special exhibits, free for those under 18, covered by Museumkaart and I amsterdam Card, daily 9:00-18:00, Fri until 22:00 March-Oct, Sat until 22:00 July-Aug and Oct, café on site, tram #2 or #5 from Central Station to Rijksmuseum or Van Baerlestraat stop, tel. 020/570-5200, www.vangoghmuseum.nl.

Avoiding Lines and Crowds: Skip the wait in the ticket-buying line by purchasing advance tickets online (www.vangoghmuseum.nl) or at the TI. Museumkaart holders and I amsterdam Card holders queue up at a shorter line than ticket buyers.

Mid-mornings are most crowded. Consider visiting on a Friday or Saturday evening, when crowds are sparse. Sometimes on Friday evenings, there are musicians or a DJ and a wine bar in the lobby.

Getting In: At the museum, get in the correct queue: 1) timed-entry ticket-holders; 2) other free entries, like the Museeumkaart or I amsterdam Card—they'll direct you to the ticket window to get a free paper ticket; or 3) the ticket-buyers' line. Ask a helpful guard if you're unsure of which queue is for yueue.

❸ **Self-Guided Tour:** The collection is laid out roughly chronologically, through the changes in Vincent van Gogh's life and styles. But you'll need to be flexible—the paintings are spread over three floors, and every few months there's a different array of paintings from the museum's large collection.

Starting on level 0, you're introduced to the artist with self-portraits. Level 1 has his early paintings, level 2 focuses on the man and his contemporaries, and level 3 displays his final works.

The paintings span five periods of Van Gogh's life: the Netherlands, Paris, Arles, St-Rémy, and Auvers-sur-Oise. I've described specific paintings that give a snapshot of a particular period of his life. But, as you tour, don't bother so much about finding those exact paintings. Read the story of Van Gogh's life, and watch his style unfold.

You could see Vincent van Gogh's canvases as a series of suicide notes—or as the record of a life full of beauty...perhaps too full of beauty. He attacked life with a passion, experiencing highs and lows more intensely than the average person. The beauty of the world overwhelmed him; its ugliness struck him as only another dimension of beauty. He tried to absorb the full spectrum of experience, good and bad, and channel it onto a canvas. The frustration of this overwhelming task drove him to madness.

On level 1, work clockwise around the floor and follow the stages of Vincent's life, from roughly 1883 to 1889. Start with his stark, dark early work in **the Netherlands (1880-1885).** These dark, gray canvases show us the hard, plain existence of the people and town of Nuenen, in the rural southern Netherlands. The style is crude—Van Gogh couldn't draw well and would never become a great technician. The paint is laid on thick, as though painted with Nuenen mud. The main subject is almost always dead center, with little or no background, so there's a claustrophobic feeling. We are unable to see anything but the immediate surroundings. For example, *The Potato Eaters* (1885) is set in a dark, cramped room lit by a dim

Van Gogh, **The Potato Eaters**

lamp, where poor workers help themselves to a steaming plate of potatoes. They've earned it. Their hands are gnarly, their faces kind. Vincent deliberately wanted the canvas to be potato-colored.

Vincent then moved from rural, religious, poor Holland to the City of Light, **Paris (March 1886-Feb 1888).** The sun begins to break through, lighting up everything he paints. His canvases are more colorful and the landscapes more spacious, with plenty of open sky, giving a feeling of exhilaration after the closed, dark world of Nuenen.

In the cafés and bars of Paris' bohemian Montmartre district, Vincent met the revolutionary Impressionists. At first, Vincent copied from the Impressionist masters. He painted garden scenes like Claude Monet, café snapshots like Edgar Degas, "block prints" like the Japanese masters, and self-portraits like...nobody else.

In his *Self-Portrait as a Painter* (1887-1888), the budding young artist proudly displays his new palette full of bright new colors, trying his hand at the Impressionist technique of building a scene using dabs of different-colored paint. In *Red Cabbages and Onions* (1887), Vincent quickly developed his own style: thicker paint; broad, swirling brushstrokes; and brighter, clashing colors that make even inanimate objects seem to pulsate with life.

Despite his new sociability, Vincent never quite fit in with his Impressionist friends. He wanted peace and quiet, a place where he could throw himself into his work completely. So he headed for a town in the sunny south of France—**Arles (Feb 1888-May 1889).** After the dreary Paris winter, the colors of springtime overwhelmed him. The blossoming trees inspired him to paint canvas after canvas, drenched in sunlight. One fine example is *The Yellow House* (a.k.a. *The Street*, 1888). Vincent rented this house with the green shutters. (He ate at the pink café next door.) Look at that blue sky! He painted in a frenzy, working feverishly to try and take it all in. His unique style evolved beyond Impressionism—thicker paint, stronger outlines, brighter colors (often applied right from the paint tube), and swirling brushwork that makes inanimate objects pulse and vibrate with life.

Vincent invited his friend Paul Gauguin to join him, envisioning a sort of artists' colony in Arles. He spent months preparing a room upstairs for Gauguin's arrival. He painted *Sunflowers* (1889) to brighten up the place. Vincent saw sunflowers as his signature subject, and he painted a half-dozen versions of them, each a study in intense yellow. He said he wanted the colors to shine "like stained glass."

Gauguin arrived. At first, he and Vincent got along great. But then things went sour. They clashed over art, life, and their prickly personalities. On Christmas Eve 1888, Vincent went ballistic. Enraged during an alcohol-fueled argument, he pulled out a razor and waved it in

Van Gogh, Red Cabbages and Onions

Van Gogh, The Yellow House

Gauguin's face. Gauguin took the hint and quickly left town. Vincent was horrified at himself. In a fit of remorse and madness, he mutilated his own ear and presented it to a prostitute.

The people of Arles realized they had a madman on their hands. A doctor diagnosed "acute mania with hallucinations," and the local vicar talked Vincent into admitting himself to a mental hospital.

On level 2, you may see displays about Van Gogh's contemporaries— his brother Theo and Gauguin—as well as more Van Gogh paintings. The visit concludes on level 3, with Vincent's final paintings.

In **St-Rémy (May 1889-1890)**, in the mental hospital, Vincent continued to paint whenever he was well enough. We see a change from bright, happy landscapes to more introspective subjects. The colors are less bright and more surreal, the brushwork even more furious. The strong outlines of figures are twisted and tortured, such as in *The Garden of Saint Paul's Hospital* (a.k.a. *Leaf Fall,* 1889). A solitary figure (Vincent?) winds along a narrow, snaky path as the wind blows leaves on him. The colors are surreal— blue, green, and red tree trunks with heavy black outlines. A road runs away from us, heading nowhere.

Vincent moved north to **Auvers-sur-Oise (May-July 1890),** a small town near Paris where he could stay under a doctor friend's supervision. *Wheat Field with Crows* (1890) is one of the last paintings Vincent finished. We can try to search the wreckage of his life for the black box explaining what happened, but there's not much there. His life was sad and tragic, but the record he left is one not of sadness, but of beauty—intense beauty.

The windblown wheat field is a nest of restless energy. Scenes like this must have overwhelmed Vincent with their incredible beauty—too much, too fast, with no release. The sky is stormy and dark blue, almost nighttime, barely lit by two suns boiling through the deep ocean of blue. The road starts nowhere, leads nowhere, disappearing into the burning wheat field. Above all of this swirling beauty fly the crows, the dark ghosts that had hovered over his life since Nuenen.

On July 27, 1890, Vincent left his room, walked out to a nearby field, and put a bullet through his chest. He stumbled back to his room, where he died two days later, with Theo by his side.

▲▲STEDELIJK MUSEUM

The Netherlands' top modern-art museum is filled with a fun, far-out, and refreshing collection that includes post-1945 experimental and conceptual art as well as works by Picasso, Chagall, Cézanne, Kandinsky, and Mondrian. The Stedelijk (STAYD-eh-lik), like the Rijksmuseum, also boasts a newly

Van Gogh, Wheat Field with Crows

spiffed-up building, which now flaunts an architecturally daring entry facing Museumplein (near the Van Gogh Museum).

Before entering, notice the architecture of the modern section (aptly nicknamed "the bathtub") abutting the original older building. Once inside, pick up the current map and envision the museum's four main sections: the permanent collection 1850-1950 (ground floor, right half), design (ground floor, left half), permanent collection 1950-2000 (first floor), and the various temporary exhibits (scattered about, usually some on each floor). Each room comes with thoughtful English descriptions. (And if you're into marijuana, I can't think of a better space than the Stedelijk in which to enjoy its effects.)

Cost and Hours: €15, daily 10:00-18:00, Fri until 22:00, top-notch gift shop, café on site, Paulus Potterstraat 13, tram #2 or #5 from Central Station to Van Baerlestraat, tel. 020/573-2911, www.stedelijk.nl. The fine €5 audioguide covers both the permanent and temporary exhibits.

▲MUSEUMPLEIN

Bordered by the Rijks, Van Gogh, and Stedelijk museums, this park-like square is interesting even to art haters. Amsterdam's best acoustics are found underneath the Rijksmuseum, where street musicians perform everything from chamber music to Mongolian throat singing. Mimes, human statues, and crafts booths dot the square. Skateboarders careen across a concrete tube, while locals enjoy

a park bench or a coffee at the Cobra Café. And the climbable "I amsterdam" letters wait for visitors taking selfies.

▲▲VONDELPARK

This huge, lively city park is popular with the Dutch—families, romantic couples, strolling seniors, and hipsters sharing blankets and beers. It's a favored venue for free summer concerts. On a sunny afternoon, it's a hedonistic scene that seems to say, "Parents...relax." The park's 'T Blauwe Theehuis ("The Blue Tea House") is a delightful spot to take in the scene (see page 1035).

Southern Canal Belt

▲LEIDSEPLEIN

Brimming with cafés, this people-watching mecca is an impromptu stage for street artists, accordionists, jugglers, and unicyclists. It's bustling on sunny afternoons. After dark, it's a vibrant tourists' nightclub center. For more on this square, see page 1012.

REMBRANDTPLEIN

One of the city's premier nightlife spots is the leafy Rembrandtplein (and the adjoining Thorbeckeplein). Rembrandt's statue stands here, along with a group of life-size statues giving us *The Night Watch* in 3-D—step into the ensemble for a photo-op. Several late-night dance clubs keep the area lively into the wee hours. Utrechtsestraat is lined with upscale shops and restaurants. Nearby Reguliers-

Modern art fills the Stedelijk Museum.

Vondelpark

dwarsstraat (a street one block south of Rembrandtplein) is a center for gay and lesbian nightclubs.

West Amsterdam

▲▲▲ANNE FRANK HOUSE

A pilgrimage for many, this house offers a fascinating look at the hideaway of young Anne during the Nazi occupation of the Netherlands. Anne, her parents, an older sister, and four others spent a little more than two years in a "Secret Annex" behind her father's business. While in hiding, 13-year-old Anne kept a diary chronicling her extraordinary experience. The thoughtfully designed exhibit offers thorough coverage of the Frank family, the diary, the stories of others who hid, and the Holocaust. Though the eight Jews were eventually discovered, and all but Anne's father died in concentration camps, their story has an uplifting twist—the diary of Anne Frank, an affirmation of the human spirit that cannot be crushed.

Cost and Hours: €9 on site or €9.50 online, April-Oct daily 9:00-22:00; Nov-March daily 9:00-19:00, Sat until 21:00; last entry 30 minutes before closing. Open on most holidays, but closed for Yom Kippur.

Avoiding Lines: Expect heavy crowds from opening to closing during summer months, and during midday hours off-season. To skip the lines, book a timed-entry ticket online as soon as you're sure of your itinerary (€9.50, available up to about two months in advance, www.annefrank.org). Between 9:00 and 15:30, you can only enter the museum with a timed-entry online ticket; there are no onsite ticket sales during that time. After 15:30, you can either enter with an online ticket reservation (recommended), or buy a ticket on site (but expect long ticket-buying lines during summer months). Ticket-buying lines and crowds decrease after 18:00.

With your online ticket in hand, you can bypass the line and ring the buzzer at the low-profile door marked Entrance: Reservations and Online Tickets.

Museumkaart holders (who get in free) can pay €0.50 to reserve an entry time online. If you haven't purchased your Museumkaart yet, you can buy one right there as you enter.

❯ **Self-Guided Tour:** We'll walk through the rooms where Anne Frank, her parents, her sister, another family (Mr. and Mrs. Van Pels and teenage son, Peter) and a single man (Mr. Pfeffer) hid for 25 months in the Secret Annex, its entrance concealed by a bookcase. Begin in the **first-floor offices** where Otto Frank ran a successful business called Opekta, selling spices and pectin for making jelly. Photos and displays (typewriters, balance sheets) show the business life of Otto and his colleagues. During the Nazi occupation, while the Frank family hid in the back of the building, these brave people kept Otto's business running, secretly bringing supplies to the Franks. Upstairs in the

Rembrandtplein

Anne Frank House

Anne Frank House: Secret Annex

2nd FLOOR

FRONT HOUSE

SWINGING BOOKCASE

LANDING

BOOKCASE ENTRANCE

STAIRS (UP)

DOORS

BED

OTTO, EDITH & MARGOT'S ROOM

BED

BED

ANNE'S ROOM

SOFA

BATH-ROOM

Not to Scale

BACK COURTYARD

3rd FLOOR

FRONT HOUSE

FLAT ROOF

STAIRS (DOWN)

BED

MURPHY BED

PETER'S ROOM

STAIRS (UP)

DRESSER

TABLE

LIVING ROOM
(ALSO KITCHEN, DINING ROOM & BEDROOM FOR HERMANN & AUGUSTE)

BACK COURTYARD

Note: Furniture shown is approximately where it was during the Secret Annex years.

second-floor warehouse, two models show the two floors where the eight people hid, living in a tiny apartment smaller than 1,000 square feet.

In July of 1942, the Frank family went into hiding, joined later by the other four. Otto handed over the keys to the business to his "Aryan" colleagues, sent a final postcard to relatives, gave the family cat to a neighbor, spread rumors that they were fleeing to Switzerland, and prepared his family to "dive under" (*onderduik,* as it was called).

The secret bookcase

At the back of the second floor warehouse is the clever hidden passageway into the Secret Annex. Though not exactly a secret (since it's hard to hide an entire building), the annex was a typical backhouse *(achterhuis)*, a common feature in Amsterdam buildings, and the Nazis had no reason to suspect anything on the premises of the legitimate Opekta business.

Pass through the bookcase entrance into **Otto, Edith, and Margot's Room.** The room is tiny, even without the furniture. Imagine yourself and two fellow tourists confined here for two years. Pencil lines on the wall track Margot's and Anne's heights, marking the point at which these growing lives were cut short.

Next is **Anne Frank's Room,** which she had to share with Mr. Pfeffer. Pan the small room clockwise to see some of the young girl's idols in photos and clippings she pasted there herself: American actor Robert Stack, the future Queen Elizabeth II as a child, matinee idol Rudy Vallee, figure-skating actress Sonja Henie, and, on the other wall, actress Greta Garbo, actor Ray Milland, Renaissance man Leonardo da Vinci, and actress Ginger Rogers.

Out the window (which had to be blacked out) is the back courtyard, which had a chestnut tree and a few buildings. These things, along with the Westerkerk bell chiming every 15 minutes, represented the borders of Anne's "outside world."

Ascend the steep staircase—silently—to the **Common Living Room.** This was also the kitchen (note the remains of the stove and sink) and dining room. Otto Frank was well off, and early on, the annex was well-stocked with food. Later, as war and German restrictions plunged Holland into poverty and famine, they survived on canned foods and dried kidney beans. At night, the living room became a sleeping quarters for the Van Pels.

The next space is **Peter van Pels' Room.** Initially, Anne was cool toward Peter, but after two years together, a courtship developed, and their flirtation culminated in a kiss. The **staircase** (no visitor access) leads up to where they stored their food. Anne loved to steal away here for a bit of privacy. At night they'd open a hatch to let in fresh air. From here we leave the Secret Annex, passing displays as we return to the Opekta storeroom and offices in the front house.

On August 4, 1944, a German policeman accompanied by three Dutch Nazis pulled up in a car, politely entered the Opekta office, and went straight to the bookcase entrance. No one knows who tipped them off. Eventually the Franks were sent to Auschwitz, a Nazi extermination camp in Poland (see the transport list, which includes "Anneliese Frank" and their 3-inch-by-5-inch registration cards). On the platform at Auschwitz, they were forcibly separated and sent to different camps. Anne and Margot were sent to Bergen-Belsen. Both died of typhus in March 1945, only weeks before the camp was liberated. The other Secret Annex residents—except Otto—were gassed or died of disease.

The Rest of the Museum: The Otto Frank Room has a 1967 video of Anne's father talking about how the diaries were discovered in the annex. Downstairs you can see Anne's three diaries, which were published after the war. Other displays tell the story of those who helped the Franks, those who survived, and the Anne Frank legacy.

The Anne Frank Foundation is concerned that we learn from Europe's Nazi nightmare. It was Otto Frank's dream that visitors come away from the Anne Frank House with an indelible impression—and a better ability to apply these lessons to our contemporary challenges. He wrote: "The task that Anne entrusted to me continually gives me new strength to strive for reconciliation and for human rights all over the world."

Central Amsterdam, near Dam Square

▲▲AMSTERDAM MUSEUM

Housed in a 500-year-old former orphanage, this creative museum traces the city's growth from fishing village to world trade center to hippie haven. The key is to not get lost somewhere in the 17th century as you navigate the meandering maze of rooms. The museum tries hard to make the city's history engaging and fun (almost too hard—it dropped "history" from its name for fear of putting people off). But the story of Amsterdam is indeed engaging and fun, and this is the only museum in town designed to tell it.

Start with the easy-to-follow "DNA" section, which hits the historic highlights from 1000 to 2000. The city was built atop pilings in marshy soil (the museum stands only four feet above sea level). By 1500, they'd built a ring of canals and established the sea trade. The Golden Age (1600s) is illustrated by fine paintings of citizens, including Rembrandt's portrait of his wife Saskia. The 1800s brought modernization and new technologies, like the bicycle. After the gloom of World War II, Amsterdam emerged to become the "Capital of Freedom." The museum's free pedestrian corridor—lined with old-time group portraits—is a powerful teaser.

Cost and Hours: €12.50, daily 10:00-17:00, includes audioguide, pleasant café on site, Kalverstraat 92, tel. 020/523-1822, www.ahm.nl. This museum is a fine place to buy the Museumkaart (for details, see page 996).

Red Light District

▲▲AMSTELKRING MUSEUM

Although Amsterdam has long been known for its tolerant attitudes, 16th-century politics forced Dutch Catholics to worship discreetly. At this museum near Central Station, you'll find a fascinating, hidden Catholic church filling the attic of three 17th-century merchants' houses.

For two centuries (1578-1795), Catholicism in Amsterdam was illegal but tolerated (like pot in the 1970s). When hardline Protestants took power in 1578, Catholic churches were vandalized and shut down, priests and monks were rounded up and kicked out of town, and Catholic kids were razzed on their way to school. The city's Catholics were forbidden to worship openly, so they gathered secretly to say Mass in homes and offices. In 1663, a wealthy merchant built

Amsterdam Museum

Amstelkring Museum

Our Lord in the Attic (Ons' Lieve Heer op Solder), one of a handful of places in Amsterdam that served as a secret parish church until Catholics were once again allowed to worship in public. This unique church—embedded within a townhouse in the middle of the Red Light District—comes with a bonus: a rare glimpse inside a historic Amsterdam home straight out of a Vermeer painting. Don't miss the silver collection and other exhibits of daily life from 300 years ago.

Cost and Hours: €10, includes audioguide, Mon-Sat 10:00-17:00, Sun and holidays 13:00-17:00, café on site, Oudezijds Voorburgwal 40, tel. 020/624-6604, www.opsolder.nl.

▲RED LIGHT DISTRICT

Ladies of the night tease and tempt here, as they have for centuries, in several hundred display-case windows around Oudezijds Achterburgwal and Oudezijds Voorburgwal, surrounding the Old Church (Oude Kerk). This neighborhood is best visited from noon into the early evening—but drunks and druggies make the streets uncomfortable late at night (after about 22:30).

The neighborhood, one of Amsterdam's oldest, has hosted prostitutes since 1200. Prostitution is entirely legal here. The prostitutes are generally entrepreneurs, running their own businesses, filling out tax returns, and even paying union dues. Popular prostitutes net about €500 a day (charging €30-50 per customer for what's called "S&F" in its abbreviated, printable form).

MARIJUANA SIGHTS

Three related establishments cluster together along a canal in the Red Light District. The **Hash, Marijuana, and Hemp Museum,** worth ▲, is the most worthwhile of the three; it shares a ticket with the less substantial **Hemp Gallery.** Right nearby is **Cannabis College,** a free nonprofit center that's "dedicated to ending the global war against the cannabis plant through public education."

Cost and Hours: Museum and gallery-€9, daily 10:00-23:00, Oudezijds Achterburgwal 148, tel. 020/624-8926, www.hashmuseum.com. College entry free, daily 11:00-19:00, Oudezijds Achterburgwal 124, tel. 020/423-4420, www.cannabiscollege.com.

Red Light District

Northeast Amsterdam

▲▲NETHERLANDS MARITIME MUSEUM (NEDERLANDS SCHEEPVAARTMUSEUM)

This huge, kid-friendly collection of model ships, maps, and sea-battle paintings fills the 300-year-old Dutch Navy Arsenal (cleverly located a little ways from the city center, as this was where they stored the gunpowder). The "Paintings" rooms illustrate how ships changed from sail to steam, and how painting styles changed from realistic battle scenes to Romantic seascapes to Impressionism and Cubism.

The "Navigational Instruments" section has quadrants (a wedge-shaped tool you could line up with the horizon and the stars to determine your location), compasses, and plumb lines. In "Ornamentation," admire the busty gals that adorned the prows of ships, and learn of their symbolic meaning for superstitious sailors.

Downstairs on the first floor, see "Yacht Models" through the ages, from early warships to today's luxury vessels. The section on "Atlases" (i.e., maps) shows how human consciousness expanded as knowledge of the earth grew. The west wing is more kid-oriented and less meaty, with an exhibit on whales and a friendly look at the Golden Age.

The finale is a chance to explore below the decks of an old tall-masted ship, a replica of the *Amsterdam*, an 18th-century cargo ship.

Cost and Hours: €15 covers both museum and ship, both open daily 9:00-17:00, bus #22 or #48 from Central Station to Kattenburgerplein 1, tel. 020/523-2222, www.scheepvaartmuseum.nl.

Southeast Amsterdam

To reach the following sights from the train station, take tram #9 or #14. All of these sights are close to one another and can easily be connected into an interesting walk—or, better yet, a bike ride. Several of the sights in southeast Amsterdam cluster near the large square, Waterlooplein, dominated by the modern opera house.

▲▲HERMITAGE AMSTERDAM

The famous Hermitage Museum in St. Petersburg, Russia, loans art to Amsterdam for a series of rotating, and often exquisitely beautiful, special exhibits in the Amstelhof, a 17th-century former nursing home that takes up a whole city block along the Amstel River.

Why is there Russian-owned art in Amsterdam? The Hermitage collection in St. Petersburg is so vast that they can only show about 5 percent of it at any one time. Therefore, the Hermitage is establishing satellite collections around the world. The one here in Amsterdam is the biggest.

Cost and Hours: Generally €15, but price varies with exhibit, daily 10:00-17:00, come later in the day to avoid crowds, audioguide-€4, mandatory free bag check, café, Nieuwe Herengracht 14, tram

Netherlands Maritime Museum

Dutch Resistance Museum

#9 from the train station, recorded info tel. 020/530-7488, www.hermitage.nl.

▲▲DUTCH RESISTANCE MUSEUM (VERZETSMUSEUM)

This is an impressive look at how the Dutch resisted (or collaborated with) their Nazi occupiers from 1940 to 1945. See propaganda movie clips, study forged ID cards under a magnifying glass, and read about ingenious and courageous efforts to hide local Jews and undermine the Nazi regime. The museum presents the Dutch people's struggle with a timeless moral dilemma: Is it better to collaborate with a wicked system to effect small-scale change—or to resist outright, even if your efforts are doomed to fail? You'll learn why some parts of Dutch society opted for the former, and others for the latter.

Cost and Hours: €10 includes audioguide, Tue-Fri 10:00-17:00, Sat-Mon 11:00-17:00, English descriptions, no flash photos, mandatory and free bag check, tram #9 from station or #14 from Dam Square, Plantage Kerklaan 61, tel. 020/620-2535, www.verzetsmuseum.org.

EXPERIENCES

Smoking

For tourists from lands where you can do hard time for lighting up, the open use of marijuana (a.k.a cannibas) here can feel disturbing, liberating...or maybe just sane. Several decades after being legalized in the Netherlands, marijuana causes about as much excitement here as a bottle of beer. Throughout Amsterdam, you'll see **"coffeeshops"**—cafés selling marijuana, with display cases showing various joints or baggies for sale.

Rules and Regulations: The retail sale of marijuana is strictly regulated, and proceeds are taxed. The minimum age for purchase is 18, and coffeeshops can sell up to five grams of marijuana per person per day. It's also illegal for these shops (or anyone) to advertise marijuana. In fact, in many places, the prospective customer has to take the initiative, and ask to see the menu. In some coffeeshops, you actually have to push and hold down a button to see an illuminated menu—the contents of which look like the inventory of a drug bust.

Shops sell marijuana and hashish both in pre-rolled joints and in baggies. Joints are generally sold individually (€3-5, depending on the strain you choose), though some places sell small packs of three or four joints. Baggies generally contain a gram and go for €8-15. The better pot, though costlier, can actually be a better value, as it takes less to get high—and it's a better high. But if you want to take it easy, cheaper is milder.

Each coffeeshop is allowed to keep an inventory of about a pound of pot in stock: The tax authorities don't want to see more than this on the books at the end of each accounting cycle, and a shop can lose its license if it exceeds this amount. A popular shop—whose supply must be replenished five or six times a day—has to put up with the hassle of constant small deliveries. A shop can sell a ton of pot with no legal problems, as long as it maintains that tiny stock and refills it as needed. The reason? Authorities want shops to stay small and not become export bases.

Smoking Tips

The Dutch are accustomed to mixing tobacco with marijuana—but any place that caters to Americans will have joints without tobacco; you have to ask specifically for a "pure" joint. Shops have loaner bongs and inhalers, and dispense rolling papers like toothpicks. While it's good style to ask first, as long as you're a paying customer (e.g., you buy a cup of coffee), you can generally pop into any coffeeshop and light up, even if you didn't buy your pot there.

Tourists who haven't smoked pot since their college days are famous for overindulging in Amsterdam. Coffeeshop baristas nickname tourists about to pass out "Whitey"—the color their faces turn before they hit the floor. They warn Americans (who aren't used to the strength of the local stuff) to try a lighter leaf. If you overdo it, the key is to eat or drink something sweet to avoid getting sick. Cola is a good fast fix, and coffeeshop staff keep sugar tablets handy. They also recommend trying to walk it off.

Never buy pot on the street in Amsterdam. Well-established coffeeshops are considered much safer; coffeeshop owners have an interest in keeping their trade safe and healthy. They're also patient in explaining the varieties available.

Coffeeshops

Most of downtown Amsterdam's coffeeshops feel grungy and foreboding to American travelers who aren't part of the youth-hostel crowd. The neighborhood places are much more inviting to people without piercings and tattoos. I've listed a few places with a more pub-like ambience for Americans wanting to go local. For locations, see the map on page 1036.

Paradox is the most *gezellig* (cozy) coffeeshop I found—a mellow, graceful place. The managers, Ludo and Wiljan, and their staff are happy to walk you through all your options. This is a rare coffeeshop that serves light meals (single tobacco-free joints-€3, daily 10:00-20:00, loaner bongs, games, Wi-Fi, two blocks from Anne Frank House at Eerste Bloemdwarsstraat 2, tel. 020/623-5639).

The Grey Area—a hole-in-the-wall with three tiny tables—is a perennial winner of Amsterdam's Cannabis Cup awards. It's a welcoming place appreciated both by local aficionados and—judging by the autographed photos on the wall—many famous Americans (say hi to Willie Nelson). You're welcome to just nurse a bottomless cup of coffee (daily 12:00-20:00, they close relatively early out of consideration for their neighbors, between Dam Square and Anne Frank House at Oude Leliestraat 2, tel. 020/420-4301).

Siberië Coffeeshop is a short walk from Central Station, but a friendly, cozy canalside ambience. It's like a mellow Starbucks that hosts occasional astrology readings (daily 11:00-23:00, Fri-Sat until 24:00, Wi-Fi for customers, helpful staff, English menu, Brouwersgracht 11, tel. 020/623-5909).

The Bulldog Café is the touristy chain of coffeeshops. These establishments are youthful and welcoming, with reliable selections, comfortable for green tourists who want to hang out. The flagship branch, in a former police station right on Leidseplein, is handy, offering alcohol upstairs, pot downstairs, and fun outdoor seating on a heated patio (daily 10:00-24:00, later on weekends, Leidseplein 17, tel. 020/625-6278). Their original café still

At a marijuana coffeeshop

sits on the canal near the Old Church in the Red Light District.

"Brown" Cafés

The *bruin* cafés (brown cafés) exemplify the intimate quality that the Dutch hold dear. Like a British pub, these convivial hangouts are the neighborhood's living room. The name comes from the hard-wood decor and nicotine-stained walls. Although smoking was banned several years ago—making these places more inviting to nonsmokers—the pigmentation persists.

In the North Jordaan: **Café 't Pape-neiland** is a classic brown café with Delft tiles, an evocative old stove, and a perch overlooking a canal (drinks but almost no food—€3.50-cheese or liverwurst sandwiches, €4.30-apple pie, daily 10:00-24:00, at northwest end of Prinsengracht at #2, tel. 020/624-1989).

Buried Deep in the Jordaan: **Café 't Smalle** is charming, with three zones: canalside (literally on a barge in the canal), inside around the bar, and a quaint back room up some steep stairs (€3-4 Belgian beers on tap, interesting wines by the glass, simple meals 11:00-17:30, at Egelantiersgracht 12—where it hits Prinsengracht, tel. 020/623-9617).

Between Central Station and the Jordaan: **Proeflokaal Arendsnest** rotates 30 Belgian beers daily "on tap/on draft" (daily 14:00-24:00, Herengracht 90, tel. 020/421-2057). **Café De II Prinsen,** dating from 1910, feels more local. It has a few outdoor tables facing a pretty canal and a lively shopping street (Dutch beers on tap, daily 12:00-24:00, Prinsenstraat 27, tel. 020/428-4488).

Near Rokin: For **Café 't Gasthuys,** see the listing on page 1032.

On Spui Square: **Café Hoppe** is as quintessentially brown as can be, with a good selection of traditional drinks and gins, a packed interior, and fun stools outside (Mon-Thu 14:00-24:00, Fri-Sun 12:00-24:00, Spui 18, tel. 020/420-4420).

Nightlife

On summer evenings, people flock to the main squares for drinks at outdoor tables.

Leidseplein is the liveliest, surrounded by theaters, restaurants, and nightclubs. The slightly quieter Rembrandtplein (with adjoining Thorbeckeplein and nearby Reguliersdwarsstraat) is the center of gay nightlife.

Spui features a full city block of bars. Nieuwmarkt, on the east edge of the Red Light District, is rough, but the least touristy.

The Red Light District (particularly Oudezijds Achterburgwal) is less sleazy in the early evening, and carnival-like as the neon lights come on and the streets fill with tour groups. It starts to feel scuzzy after about 22:30.

The TI's website, www.iamsterdam.com, has good English listings for upcoming events. Newsstands sell *Time Out Amsterdam* and Dutch newspapers (Thu editions generally list events).

Shopping

Amsterdam brings out the browser in anyone. For information, pick up the TI's *Shopping in Amsterdam* brochure.

Street markets, open six days a week (generally 9:30-17:00, closed Sun), include the huge **Albert Cuyp** market (in the De Pijp District near the Rijksmuseum), the **Flower Market** (on the Singel canal near the Mint Tower), and the **Waterlooplein** flea market.

Most shops in the center are open

10:00-18:00 (later on Thu—typically until 20:00 or 21:00); many shopkeepers take Sundays and Monday mornings off.

Handy chain stores include **Hema** (at Kalverstraat 212, in Kalvertoren mall, and at Central Station) and **Vroom & Dreesmann** (V&D, Kalverstraat 203). The high-end **De Bijenkorf** department store, high above Dam Square, sparkles with name brands; the fifth floor is a ritzy self-service cafeteria with a rooftop terrace.

The fun **gift shops at the major art museums**—Rijks and Van Gogh—sell postcards, prints (and tubes to protect them), totes, cups, scarves, and many clever items.

The Nine Little Streets (De Negen Straatjes), between Dam Square and the Jordaan (see map on page 1002), are home to diverse shops and trendy cafés. Walking west from the Amsterdam Museum/Spui Square or south from the Anne Frank House puts you in the thick of things. For a preview, see www.theninestreets.com.

EATING

Amsterdam's restaurant scene has something for every taste. The touristy food scene thrives around Leidseplein, including "Restaurant Row" on Leidsedwarsstraat. The area around Spui Square and that end of Spuistraat is trendy, though not as noisy. For fewer crowds, better food and service, and more charm, head a few blocks west, into the Jordaan district, which has a more authentically Dutch "Restaurant Row" (on Tweede Egelantierssdwarsstraat). For a local take on restaurants, check out www.dutchgrub.com.

Many of my listings are lunch-only (usually termed "café" rather than "restaurant"), good for a handy bite, while many restaurants serve only dinner. Before trekking across town for a meal, check the hours.

Central Amsterdam

You'll likely have lunch at some point in the city's core, but you'll find a better range of choices in the Jordaan area.

On and near Spui

Restaurant Kantjil en de Tijger is lively, modern, and full of happy, youthful eaters who know good value. The food is Indonesian. *Rijsttafels* (traditional "rice tables" with about a dozen small courses) range from €25 to €33 per person. Three can share a meal by getting a *rijsttafel* for two plus a soup or light dish (daily 12:00-23:00, reservations smart, mostly indoor with some outdoor seating, Spuistraat 291, tel. 020/620-0994, www.kantjil.nl).

Restaurant d'Vijff Vlieghen is a museum of a restaurant with an interior right out of a Rembrandt painting. This romantic splurge offers Dutch, French, and international cuisine (€23-27 main courses, €36 three-course dinner, nightly 18:00-22:00, Spuistraat 294, tel. 020/530-4060).

Singel 404, across the Singel canal from Spui and near the Nine Little Streets, is a popular café serving €4-7 sandwiches on bread, bagels, and flatbread (daily 10:30-19:00, food served until 18:00, Singel 404, tel. 020/428-0154).

Café 't Gasthuys, a brown café, offers canalside seating, a long bar, a secluded back room, and sometimes slow service (€6-10 lunch plates, €11-15 main courses, daily 12:00-16:30 & 17:30-22:00, Grimburgwal 7—from Rondvaart Kooij boat dock, head down Langebrugsteeg, and it's one block down on the left, tel. 020/624-8230).

Near Rokin and the Mint Tower

De Jaren Café ("The Years") is a chic yet inviting local favorite. Upstairs is a minimalist restaurant with a canal-view deck. Downstairs is a modern café, great for light lunches or coffee (daily 9:30-24:00, a long block up from Muntplein at Nieuwe Doelenstraat 20, tel. 020/625-5771).

La Place Cafeteria, on the ground floor of the Vroom & Dreesmann (V&D) department store, is a multistory, self-service eatery with a small outdoor terrace upstairs (€5 pizza and sandwiches, Sun-Mon 11:00-19:00, Tue-Wed 10:00-19:30, Thu-Sat 10:00-21:00, at the end of Kalverstraat near Mint Tower, tel. 020/622-0171). The bakery on the ground floor sells fast, healthful takeout food.

Marks and Spencer, up the street from V&D, has an enticing mini-grocery on the ground floor (€4-6 meals, Mon 10:00-20:00, Tue-Sat 9:00-20:00, Thu until 21:00, Sun 11:00-20:00, Kalverstraat 226).

Near Dam Square

Eateries along Damrak are touristy, overpriced, and dreary. But if you need a meal in this area, here are good options.

The Kitchen Cafeteria at De Bijenkorf fills the top floor of a swanky department store with tasty self-service options. It's modern and spacious, with a great outdoor terrace (daily 10:00-19:30, Thu-Fri until 20:30, Dam 1, tel. 088-245-9080).

The narrow, quiet street called Nes, running south from Dam Square and paralleling Rokin one block to the east, is fun to browse. It's home to several small restaurants, including Van Kerkwijk, an unpretentious eatery with a loyal following. There's no written menu—your server describes the fresh, reasonably priced international dishes. They don't take reservations; expect a line (€6 lunches, €8 lunch salads, €11-20 main courses at dinner, daily 11:00-23:00, Nes 41, tel. 020/620-3316).

West Amsterdam, in the Jordaan District

Nearly all of these places are within a few scenic blocks of the Anne Frank House.

The Jordaan's trendiest street, Tweede (2nd) Egelantierssdwarsstraat (sometimes spelled Anjeliersdwarsstraat), is an exuberant scene, with high-energy eateries spilling out into sidewalk seating. One option is the classic Café Sonneveld, which serves basic €10-20 meals, but has great tables facing the street.

La Perla has a wood-fired oven, sidewalk tables on a lively intersection, and a

formal dining room across the street (€12-14 pizzas, daily 12:00-24:00, locations face each other at #14 and #53—take your pick, tel. 020/624-8828).

Eerste (1st) Egelantierssdwarsstraat, one block parallel to "Restaurant Row," has a few more choices; the block before Westerstraat has Indian, tapas, and more. **Kinnaree Thai Restaurant,** features delicious, freshly prepared Thai cuisine (€15 dishes, daily 17:30-22:00, at #14). **Los Pilones,** next door, serves authentic Mexican food (€18 meals, at #6).

Café Restaurant de Reiger is famous for its French-Dutch cuisine, fresh ingredients, ribs, and delightful bistro ambience. They take no reservations—come early and wait at the bar (€10 starters, €20 main courses, Tue-Sun 17:00-24:00, closed Mon, Nieuwe Leliestraat 34, tel. 020/624-7426).

Between Dam Square and the Jordaan

The Pancake Bakery is a backpacker favorite with a creative menu of both savory and dessert pancakes. The scene feels like a bar, with a quieter zone upstairs (€7-15, daily 9:00-21:30, American breakfasts until noon, two blocks north of the Anne Frank House at Prinsengracht 191, tel. 020/625-1333).

Two cafés with outdoor tables face the atmospheric, canal-spanning **"Big Head Square"** (with the landmark statue of a massive noggin honoring Multatuli, a Dutch writer who criticized Dutch colonial abuses). **Café Villa Zeezicht** has all the romance of an Old World café, famous *appeltaarts,* and great people-watching (€10-15, daily 9:00-21:30, Torensteeg 7, tel. 020/626-7433). Across the street, **Café van Zuylen** is bigger, feels more upscale, and has more scenic outdoor tables (open long hours daily, Torensteeg 4, tel. 020/639-1055).

Southern Canal Belt

Stroll colorful Lange Leidsedwarsstraat, the "Restaurant Row" off Leidseplein, but don't expect intimacy or good value. Nearby, busy Leidsestraat offers plenty of budget choices, between Prinsengracht and Herengracht. To escape the crowds, wander a few blocks away from the hubbub to one of these options:

Buffet van Odette serves Mediterranean and Italian cuisine with lots of farm-fresh, seasonal vegetables. A few tables outside face a picturesque canal (€10-15 lunch plates, €12 buffet salad at lunch, dinner-€8-14 starters and €15-19 main courses, always vegetarian option and fish, Wed-Mon 10:00-21:00, closed Tue, Prinsengracht 598, tel. 020/423-6034).

De Balie Grand Café is a venerable eatery in a former prison complex—now also home to galleries and concert venues. They serve salads, sandwiches, and simple plates, and your bill helps support culture and progressive thinking (€8 starters, €18 main dishes, open daily for lunch and dinner, great local beers, free Wi-Fi, Kleine-Gartmanplantsoen 10, tel. 020/553-5130).

Southwest Amsterdam

The area surrounding the museum quarter is upscale, with swanky boulevards. While a few eateries are within a few steps of the museums, my less-touristy picks are generally within a 10-minute walk and have better food and service. They're fine for a lunch or dinner combined with visiting museums, the Albert Cuyp market, or Vondelpark.

The Seafood Bar—modern, slick, and popular—features fresh, sustainable dishes with a Burgundian flair. Reserve ahead during mealtimes (€8-12 sandwiches, €13-18 fish-and-chips, €15-23 main courses and oysters, daily 12:00-22:00, Van Baerlestraat 5, between the Rijksmuseum and Vondelpark, tel. 020/670-8355, www.theseafoodbar.nl).

Sama Sebo Indonesian Restaurant
is a local favorite for *rijsttafel*. I prefer the
energy in the casual "bodega" to the more
formal restaurant—and only the bodega
serves the smaller €18 lunch plate for dinner (Mon-Sat 12:00-15:00 & 17:00-22:00,
closed Sun, reservations smart for dinner,
P.C. Hooftstraat 27, between the Rijksmuseum and Vondelpark, tel. 020/662-81460,
www.samasebo.nl).

The **De Pijp** neighborhood—southeast of the Rijksmuseum—is best known
for its thriving Albert Cuyp market. And
although the market stalls are typically
wrapped up by about 17:00, restaurants stay busy late into the evening.
Restaurant Bazar offers a memorable,
budget-eating experience, with mod
belly-dance music and cheap Middle
Eastern and North African cuisine (€8.50
daily plate, delicious €13 couscous, €16
main dishes, daily 11:00 until late, Albert
Cuypstraat 182, tel. 020/675-0544, http://
bazaramsterdam.nl).

'T Blauwe Theehuis ("The Blue Tea
House") is a venerable meeting point
where all generations gather for drinks and
light meals. The setting, deep in Vondelpark, is like a Monet painting. Sandwiches
are served at tables outside, inside, and on
the rooftop from 11:00 to 16:00, drinks and
apple pie are served all day, and pot smoking—while discreet—is as natural here as
falling leaves (daily 9:00-22:00 in summer,
Vondelpark 5, tel. 020/662-0254).

Cheap and Fast Eats
Grab a meal to go, then find a bench on
a neighborhood square or along a canal.
Sandwiches are cheap at snack bars, delis,
and *broodjes* shops. Ethnic restaurants
serve inexpensive, splittable carryout
meals. To stock up on picnic items, you'll
find mini-markets all around town.

Marqt is an elegant picnicker's dream.
Note that it accepts only credit cards, but
your magnetic-strip card will work fine
(daily 9:00-21:00). You'll find locations in
the Nine Little Streets district (along Keizersgracht, at Wolvenstraat 34), several
blocks from Vondelpark and Leidseplein
(Overtoom 21), south of Rembrandtplein
(Utrechtsestraat 17), and in the emerging
Haarlemmerdijk zone, west of the train
station (Haarlemmerstraat 165).

Albert Heijn grocery stores are
cheaper (daily 8:00-22:00). Central locations are near Dam Square behind the
Royal Palace (Nieuwezijds Voorburgwal
226); near the Mint Tower (Koningsplein
4); on Leidsestraat (at Koningsplein, on
the corner of Leidsestraat and Singel);
and inside Central Station (at the far end
of the passage under the tracks). None of
their stores accepts US credit cards: Bring
cash, and don't get in the checkout lines
marked *PIN alleen*.

Febo, an automated Dutch fried-
food institution, is like a walk-in vending
machine. Branches are north of Leidseplein (Leidsestraat 94), at Damrak 6,
in the Red Light District (facing the Old
Church across the canal, at Oudezijds
Voorburgwal 33), and near Rembrandtplein (Reguliersbreestraat 38).

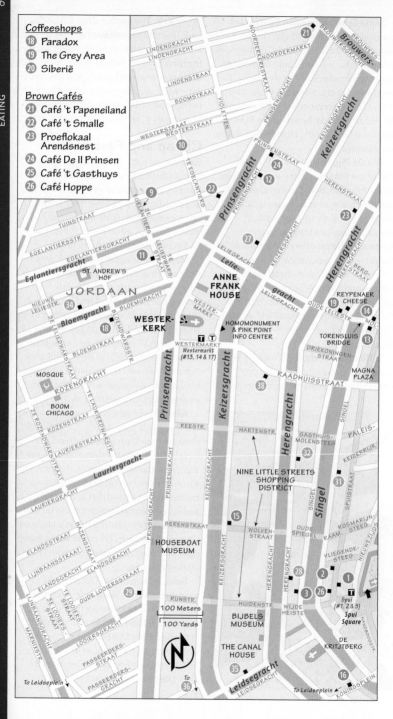

Coffeeshops
- ⑱ Paradox
- ⑲ The Grey Area
- ⑳ Siberië

Brown Cafés
- ㉑ Café 't Papeneiland
- ㉒ Café 't Smalle
- ㉓ Proeflokaal Arendsnest
- ㉔ Café De Il Prinsen
- ㉕ Café 't Gasthuys
- ㉖ Café Hoppe

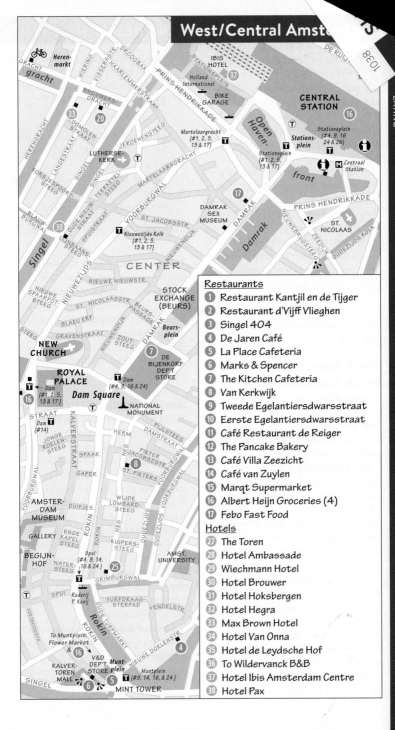

SLEEPING

Amsterdam is a tough city for budget accommodations, and any hotel room under €140 (or B&B room under €100) will have rough edges. Still, you can sleep well and safely in a great location for €100 per double. (To sleep cheaper, stay in nearby Haarlem—covered near the end of this chapter—and commute to Amsterdam.)

Amsterdam is jammed during tulip season (late March-mid-May), conventions, festivals, and on summer weekends. During peak season, some hoteliers won't take weekend bookings for those staying fewer than two or three nights.

Canalside rooms can come with great views—and early-morning construction-crew noise. If you're a light sleeper, ask for a quiet room in the back. Smoking is illegal in hotel rooms. Canal houses have steep stairs with narrow treads; few have elevators.

West Amsterdam
Stately Canalside Hotels

Oozing elegance and class, this area is fairly quiet at night. These hotels, a half-mile apart, both face historic canals. They come with lovely lobbies and rooms from another century.

$$$ **The Toren** is a chandeliered, historic mansion with a peaceful garden for guests out back. It's romantic, classy, and friendly, with 38 rooms on a quiet street two blocks northeast of the Anne Frank House. To get the best prices, check their website for the "daily rate," book direct, and in the "remarks" field, ask for the 10 percent Rick Steves cash discount (Db-€200, deluxe Db-€250, prices bump way up during conferences and decrease in winter, breakfast buffet-€14, air-con, elevator, guest computer, Wi-Fi, Keizersgracht 164, tel. 020/622-6033, www.thetoren.nl, info@thetoren.nl).

$$$ **Hotel Ambassade** laces together 59 rooms in a maze of connected houses.

The public areas are palatial, with antique furnishings and modern art (Db-€280, pricier canal-view doubles and suites, ask for Rick Steves discount when booking, see website for specials, breakfast-€17.50, air-con, elevator, guest computer, Wi-Fi, Herengracht 341, tel. 020/555-0222, www.ambassade-hotel.nl, info@ambassade-hotel.nl).

Simpler Canalside Hotels

These places have basic rooms—some downright spare—and most do without an elevator or other extras—but offer a decent night's sleep in a lovely area.

$$$ **Wiechmann Hotel** has 37 pricey rooms that are sparse but spacious, while the cozy public areas are full of charm (Db-€155-175, family rooms, check online for best price, 15 percent cheaper for 3 or more nights if booking through their website, some canal views, back rooms are quiet, guest computer, Wi-Fi, nicely located at Prinsengracht 328, tel. 020/626-3321, www.hotelwiechmann.nl, info@hotelwiechmann.nl).

$$ **Hotel Brouwer**—woody and old-time homey—has a tranquil yet central location on the Singel canal. Renting eight rooms with canal views, it's so popular that it's often booked three or four months in advance (Db-€128, cash only,

small elevator, guest computer, Wi-Fi, located between Central Station and Dam Square, near Lijnbaanssteeg at Singel 83, tel. 020/624-6358, www.hotelbrouwer.nl, akita@hotelbrouwer.nl).

$$ Hotel Hoksbergen is well-run and welcoming, with 14 rooms in a peaceful canalside setting (Db-€105, apartments-€165-198, fans, Wi-Fi, Singel 301, tel. 020/626-6043, www.hotelhoksbergen. com, info@hotelhoksbergen.nl).

$$ Hotel Hegra is cozy, with nine rooms filling a 17th-century merchant's house (Db-€80-€160, breakfast-€6.50, some rooms with canal view, pay guest computer, Wi-Fi, bike rentals, north of Wolvenstraat at Herengracht 269, tel. 020/623-7877, www.hotelhegra.nl, info@ hotelhegra.nl).

$$ Max Brown Hotel, the flagship of a boutique chain, has a trendy, urban design. Located in a quiet neighborhood near Central Station, it offers 25 modern rooms; rooms with canal views are pricier and breezier (Db-€125-185, rates vary wildly with demand, check online and book directly with hotel for best price, free coffee, continental breakfast, tangled floor plan connecting three canalside buildings, Wi-Fi, Herengracht 13, tel. 020/522-2345, www.maxbrownhotels. com, hello@maxbrownamsterdam.com).

$$ Hotel Van Onna has 41 simple, industrial-strength rooms—some with canal views—in a leafy location. Top-floor attic rooms are snug hideaways (Db-€80-130, family rooms, price depends on season, 5 percent more with credit card, cot-like beds are sufficient, no phones or TVs, guest computer, Wi-Fi, in the Jordaan at Bloemgracht 104, tel. 020/626-5801, www. hotelvanonna.nl, info@hotelvanonna.nl).

B&Bs and Private-Room Rentals

B&Bs offer a chance to feel like a local, while paying less than you would at a hotel.

$$ Maes B&B (pronounced "mahss") and **Heren B&B** offer a total of nine

comfy rooms and nine thoughtfully appointed apartments in two buildings within a three-minute walk of each other. Located where the restaurant-lined Herenstraat meets the picturesque Herengracht and Singel canals, the B&Bs are handy to the train station and Jordaan area (B&B rooms: Db-€125; apartments: Db-€155; guest computer, Wi-Fi, if street noise bothers you ask for room in back, Maes at Herenstraat 26, Heren at Singel 95, tel. 020/427-5165, www.bedandbreakfastamsterdam.com, maesinfo@xs4all.nl).

$$ Herengracht 21 B&B has two stylish, intimate rooms in a canal house filled with art (2-floor Db-€125, canal-view Db-€135, air-con, Wi-Fi, Herengracht 21, tel. 020/625-6305, mobile 06-2812-0962, www.herengracht21.nl, loes@ herengracht21.nl).

$$ With Truelove Guesthouse, you'll feel like you're staying at a friend's house. A tiny antique store on Prinsenstraat doubles as the reception desk for this room-rental service, which offers 15 rooms and apartments in houses in the northern end of the Jordaan. The stylish apartments come with kitchens and pull-out beds (Db-€105-125, Db apartment-€115-180, prices soft in off-season and midweek, 10 percent more with credit card, 2-night minimum on weekends, no breakfast, pick up keys in store at Prinsenstraat 4, store tel. 020/320-2500, mobile 06-2480-5672, www.cosyandwarm-amsterdam.com, trueloveantiek@zonnet.nl).

$ Frederic Rent-a-Bike & Guestrooms, with a bike-rental shop as the reception, is a collection of private rooms on a gorgeous canal just outside the Jordaan, a five-minute walk from Central Station. The 100 beds range from dumpy €75 doubles to spacious, elegant apartments. Some places are ideal for families and groups. All are displayed on the website (from €46/person; these places require a 2-night minimum, occasionally more, phone bookings preferred, book with credit card but pay with cash, no breakfast, Brouwersgracht 78, tel. 020/624-5509, www.frederic.nl, info@frederic.nl, Frederic, Marjolijn, and their son Marne). The excellent bike shop is open daily 9:00-17:30 (€15/24 hours). Readers who rent an apartment get a 50 percent discount on 24-hour bike rentals.

Charming B&Bs in Southern Canal Belt

Within walking distance of the major museums, and steps off the tram line, this neighborhood offers a perfect mix of charm and location.

These canalside mom-and-pop places are within a five-minute walk of rowdy Leidseplein, but generally are in quiet and typically Dutch settings.

$$ Hotel de Leydsche Hof, a hidden gem located on a canal, doesn't charge extra for its views. Its four large rooms are a symphony in white, but be prepared for lots of stairs (Db-€130-150, cash only, 2-night minimum, guest computer, Wi-Fi, Leidsegracht 14, tel. 020/638-2327, mobile 06-3099-2744, www.freewebs.com/leydschehof, loespiller@planet.nl).

$$ Wildervanck B&B offers two tasteful rooms in a 17th-century canal house (big Db on first floor-€140, Db with twin beds on ground floor-€125, 2-night minimum, breakfast in their pleasant dining room, Wi-Fi, west of Leidsestraat at Keizersgracht 498, tel. 020/623-3846, www.wildervanck.com, info@wildervanck.com).

Central Amsterdam

$$$ Hotel Ibis Amsterdam Centre, located next door to Central Station, is modern and efficient. Its 363 rooms offer comfort, good value, and not a hint of charm. When business is slow, usually in mid-summer, they occasionally rent rooms to same-day drop-ins for around €110 (Db-€141-160 Nov-Aug, Db-€200 Sept-Oct, breakfast-€16, check website for deals, book long in advance—especially for Sept-Oct, air-con, elevators, pay guest computer, Wi-Fi; facing Central Station, go left toward the multistory bicycle garage to Stationsplein 49; tel. 020/721-9172, www.ibishotel.com, h1556@accor.com).

$ Hotel Pax is an inexpensive, well-worn hotel on convenient but noisy Raadhuisstraat. It's like a European dorm room, with 11 large, plain, but airy rooms, and several flights of steep steps (D-€65, Db-€85, prices drop dramatically in winter, no breakfast, five rooms share two showers and two toilets but all have in-room sinks, Wi-Fi, Raadhuisstraat 37, tel. 020/624-9735, hotelpax@telfort.nl).

Southwest Amsterdam, near Vondelpark and Museumplein

These options cluster around Vondelpark in a safe neighborhood. They're reasonable values a short walk from the action. Unless noted, the places below have elevators. Many are in a pleasant nook between rollicking Leidseplein and the park, and most are a 5- to 15-minute walk to the Rijks and Van Gogh museums. They are easily connected with Central Station by trams #2 or #5.

$$$ Hotel Piet Hein offers 81 sleek yet comfortable rooms as well as a swanky lounge and a peaceful garden, all on a quiet street (Db-€145-160, extra-posh Db-€180-250, specials on website, breakfast-€9.50, air-con in some rooms, guest computer, Wi-Fi, Vossiusstraat 51, tel. 020/662-7205, www.hotelpiethein.nl, info@hotelpiethein.nl).

$$$ Hotel Fita has 20 bright rooms 100 yards from the Van Gogh Museum and an even shorter hop from the tram stop. The style is modern yet rustic, with nice extras, including espresso machines in every room (Db-€149-179 depending on size, air-con on upper floors, guest computer, Wi-Fi, free laundry service, Jan Luijkenstraat 37, tel. 020/679-0976, www.fita.nl, info@fita.nl).

$$ Hotel Alexander is a modern 34-room hotel on a quiet street. Some rooms overlook the garden patio (Db-€135, prices soft in winter—call or check their website for best deal, breakfast-€10, guest computer, Wi-Fi, tel. 020/589-4020, Vondelstraat 44, www.hotelalexander.nl, info@hotelalexander.nl).

$ Stayokay Vondelpark (IYHF), with 536 beds in 130 rooms, is a top hostel for the under-25 set—but over-25s will feel comfortable here too (€24-42/bed in 4- to 20-bed dorms, D-€68-115—most with bunk beds, higher prices are for March-Oct, members save €2.50, price depends on demand—cheapest when booked in advance, family rooms, lots of school groups, lockers, laundry, pay guest computer, Wi-Fi, bike rental, right on Vondelpark at Zandpad 5, tel. 020/589-8996, www.stayokay.com, vondelpark@stayokay.com).

TRANSPORTATION

Getting Around Amsterdam

Amsterdam is big, and you'll find the trams handy. The longest walk a tourist would make is an hour from Central Station to the Rijksmuseum. When you're on foot, be vigilant for silent but potentially painful bikes, trams, and crotch-high bollards.

By Tram, Bus, and Metro

Amsterdam's public-transit system includes trams, buses, and an underground metro. Of these, trams are most useful for most tourists.

Paper Tickets: Within Amsterdam, a single transit ticket (called a single-use or disposable OV-chipkaart) costs €2.80 and is good for one hour on the tram, bus, and metro, including transfers. Passes good for unlimited transportation are available for 24 hours (€7.50), 48 hours (€12), 72 hours (€16.50), and 96 hours

(€21). Given how expensive single tickets are, consider buying a pass before you buy that first ticket.

The easiest way to buy a ticket or pass is to simply board a tram or bus and pay the conductor (whose station is usually at the rear of the tram; no extra fee). Tickets and passes are also available at metro-station vending machines (which take cash but not US credit cards unless they have a chip), at GVB public-transit offices, and at TIs.

The entire country's public-transit network operates on a system with a multiple-use OV-Chipkaart. However, this system works best for locals and isn't practical for short-time visitors (it requires a nonrefundable €7.50 deposit plus a €2.50 fee to cash out, and can only be reloaded at train stations).

Information: For more on riding public transit, visit the helpful GVB public-transit information office in front of Central Station (Mon-Fri 7:00-21:00, Sat-Sun 10:00-18:00). Its free, multilingual *Public Transport Amsterdam Tourist Guide* includes a transit map and explains ticket options and tram connections to all the sights. Everything is also explained in English on their helpful website at www.gvb.nl.

Riding the Trams: Board the tram at any entrance not marked with a red/white "do not enter" sticker. If you need a ticket or pass, pay the conductor (in a booth at the back); if there's no conductor, pay

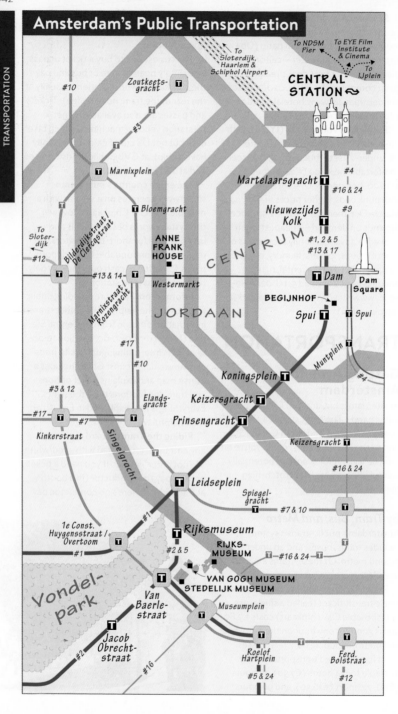

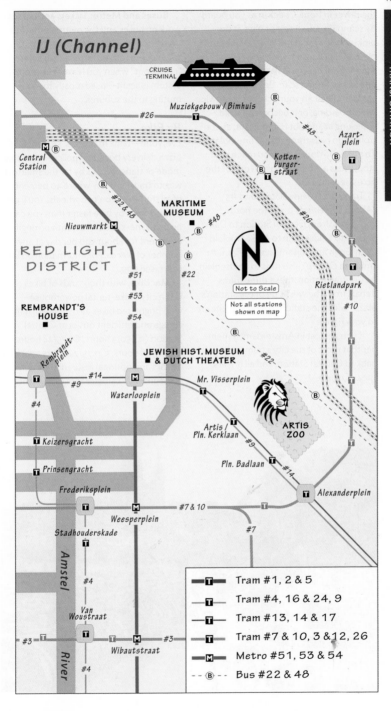

IJ (Channel)

CRUISE TERMINAL

#26 Muziekgebouw / Bimhuis

#48 Azart-plein

Kotten-burger-straat

M B Central Station

#22 & 48

Nieuwmarkt M

MARITIME MUSEUM #48

RED LIGHT DISTRICT

#26 Rietlandpark

#51

#53

#54

#22

#10

Not to Scale

Not all stations shown on map

REMBRANDT'S HOUSE

Rembrandt-plein

JEWISH HIST. MUSEUM & DUTCH THEATER

#22

#14

#9 Waterlooplein

#4

Mr. Visserplein

ARTIS ZOO

Artis / Pln. Kerklaan

Keizersgracht

#9

Prinsengracht

Pln. Badlaan

Frederiksplein

#14 Alexanderplein

#7 & 10

Weesperplein

#7

Stadhouderskade

Amstel

#4

Van Woustraat

#3 #3

Wibautstraat

River

#4

T	Tram #1, 2 & 5
T	Tram #4, 16 & 24, 9
T	Tram #13, 14 & 17
T	Tram #7 & 10, 3 & 12, 26
M	Metro #51, 53 & 54
B	Bus #22 & 48

the driver in front. Check in as you board by scanning your ticket or pass at the pink-and-gray scanner, and "check out" by scanning it again when you get off. The scanner will beep and flash a green light after a successful scan. Be careful not to accidentally scan your ticket or pass twice while boarding, or it becomes invalid. Checking in and out is important, as controllers do pass through and fine violators. To open the door when you reach your stop, press a green button on one of the poles near an exit.

Trams #2 (Nieuw Sloten) and #5 (A'veen Binnenhof) travel the north-south axis, from Central Station to Dam Square to Leidseplein to Museumplein (Van Gogh and Rijksmuseum). Tram #1 (marked Osdorp) also runs to Leidseplein. At Central Station, these three trams depart from the west side of the station's plaza (with the station behind you, they're to your right).

If you get lost in Amsterdam, remember that most of the city's trams take you back to Central Station, and all drivers speak English.

Buses and Metro: Tickets and passes work on buses and the metro as they do on the trams—scan your ticket or pass to "check in" as you enter and again to "check out" when you leave. The metro system is scant—used mostly for commuting to the suburbs.

By Bike

Everyone—bank managers, students, pizza delivery boys, and police—uses this mode of transport. It's by far the smartest way to travel in a city where 40 percent of all traffic rolls on two wheels. You'll get around town by bike faster than you can by taxi. One-speed bikes, with brrringing bells, rent for about €10 per day at any number of places. For information on bike tours, see 999.

MacBike, with thousands of bikes, is the city's bike-rental powerhouse—with bright-red bikes all over town. It has a huge and efficient outlet at Central Station (€7.50/3 hours, €9.75/24 hours, €15.75/48 hours, €21.75/72 hours, more for 3 gears and optional insurance, 25 percent discount with I amsterdam Card; either

leave €50 deposit plus a copy of your passport, or leave a credit-card imprint; free helmets, daily 9:00-17:45; at east end of station—on the left as you're leaving; tel. 020/620-0985, www.macbike.nl). They have two smaller satellite stations at Leidseplein (Weteringschans 2) and Waterlooplein (Nieuwe Uilenburgerstraat 116). Return your bike to the station where you rented it. MacBike sells several pamphlets outlining bike tours with a variety of themes in and around Amsterdam for €1-2.

Lock Your Bike: Bike thieves are bold and brazen in Amsterdam. Bikes come with two locks and stern instructions to use both. The wimpy ones go through the spokes, whereas the industrial-strength chains are meant to be wrapped around the actual body of the bike and through the front wheel, and connected to something stronger than any human. (The steel bike-hitching racks sticking up all around town are called "staples.") Follow your rental agency's locking directions diligently. If you're sloppy, it's an expensive mistake and one that any "included" theft insurance won't cover.

Biking Tips: As the Dutch believe in fashion over safety, no one here wears a helmet. They do, however, ride cautiously, and so should you: Use arm signals, follow the bike-only traffic signals, stay in the obvious and omnipresent bike lanes, and yield to traffic on the right. Fear oncoming trams and tram tracks. Carefully cross tram tracks at a perpendicular angle to avoid catching your tire in the rut. Warning: Police ticket cyclists just as they do drivers. Obey all traffic signals, and walk your bike through pedestrian zones. Fines for biking through pedestrian zones are reportedly €30-50. Leave texting-while-biking to the locals. A handy bicycle route-planner can be found at www.routecraft.com (select "bikeplanner," then click the British flag for English).

By Boat

While the city is great on foot, bike, or tram, you can also get around Amsterdam by boat. **Rederij Lovers** boats shuttle tourists on a variety of routes covering different combinations of the city's top sights. Their Museum Line, for example, costs €18 and stops near the Hermitage, Rijksmuseum/Van Gogh Museum, and Central Station (at least every 45 minutes, 6 stops, 2 hours, tel. 020/530-1090, www.lovers.nl). Most routes come with recorded narration and run daily 10:00-17:30. On the boats and at sales booths in front of Central Station, you can get free brochures listing museum hours and admission prices.

The similar **Canal Bus** is actually a hop-on, hop-off boat, offering 16 stops on three different boat routes (€24/24-hour pass, discounts when booking online, departures daily 9:45-18:30, until 20:45 on Fri-Sun April-Oct, leaves near Central Station and Rederij Lovers dock, tel. 020/217-0500, www.canal.nl).

For do-it-yourself canal tours and lots of exercise, Canal Bus also rents "canal bikes" (a.k.a. paddleboats) at several locations: near the Anne Frank House, near the Rijksmuseum, near Leidseplein, and where Leidsestraat meets Keizersgracht (€8/1 hour, €11/1.5 hours, €14/2 hours, prices are per person, daily July-Aug 10:00-22:00, Sept-June 10:00-18:00).

By Taxi

For short rides, Amsterdam is a bad town for taxis. Given the good tram system and ease of biking, I use taxis less in Amsterdam than in any other city in Europe. The city's taxis have a high drop charge (about €7) for the first two kilometers (e.g., from Central Station to the Mint Tower), after which it's €2.12 per kilometer. Wave one down, find a rare taxi stand, or call (tel. 020/777-7777). All taxis are required to have meters. You'll also see **bike taxis,** particularly near Dam Square and Leidseplein. Negotiate a rate for the trip before you board (no meter), and they'll wheel you wherever you want to go (estimate €1/3 minutes, no surcharge for baggage or extra weight, sample fare from Leidseplein to Anne Frank House: about €6).

Arriving and Departing
By Train

Amsterdam is the country's hub, but all major cities are linked by speedy trains that come and go every 15 minutes or so. Dutch rail schedules are online at www. ns.nl (domestic) and www.nshispeed.nl (international).

The portal connecting Amsterdam to the world is its aptly named Central Station (Amsterdam Centraal).

Trains arrive on a level above the station. Go down the stairs or the escalator (at the "A" end of the platform). As you descend from the platforms, follow signs to *Centrum* to reach the city center.

The station is fully equipped. Help-ful GWK Travelex counters are in both the east and west corridors (currency exchange, hotel reservations, phone cards, and basic tourist information, daily 9:00-22:00, tel. 020/624-6682). Luggage lockers are in the east corridor, under the "B" end of the platforms (€5-7/24 hours, depending on size of bag, always open, can fill up on busy summer weekends). The station has plenty of shops, eateries, and "to go" supermarkets. Platform 2 (at train level) is lined with eateries, including the tall, venerable, 1920s-style First Class Grand Café.

Train Info, Tickets, and Rail Passes: The station's train-information center can require a long wait. You can save lots of time by getting international train tickets and information at the airport upon arrival (wonderful service), at a travel agency, or at a small-town station (such as Haarlem). In Amsterdam's Central Station, international train-ticket offices are near the *Centrum* exits. If you need domestic train tickets, buy these on the day you'll travel; you can't purchase them in advance.

If you need to buy train tickets at the station, remember that credit cards without an electronic chip won't work in the machines or with a live agent. (Sometimes even credit cards with a chip may not work.) Get ample cash for your tickets (ATMs nearby) before lining up at the ticket window. If you want to use cash at the ticket machines, be prepared—they only take coins.

If you have a rail pass, it's quicker to validate it when you arrive at Schiphol Airport than in Amsterdam's Central Station, but keep in mind that you may not want to start using your rail pass the same day; you could buy an inexpensive point-to-point ticket into Amsterdam, and save your flexi-days for a longer journey.

Getting Downtown: To get from the train station to your hotel, you can walk, take a tram, hop on a rental bike, or catch a taxi.

Exiting the station, you're in the heart of the city. Straight ahead is Damrak street, leading to Dam Square (a 10-minute walk away). To your left are the TI, the GVB public-transit information office (see page 1041), and the MacBike bike-rental shop in the station building (see page 1044).

To the right of the station are taxis—pricey, but can be worth it when dealing with baggage, jet lag, and trying to find your hotel (see page 1046 for taxi info).

Trams are easy. Trams #1, #2, and #5 all start here (in front of the station) and follow the same route through the center of town with stops within easy walking distance of most of my recommended hotels. Simply hop on, buy your ticket as you board, and you're on your way. For more on the transit system, see page 1041.

TRAIN CONNECTIONS
From Amsterdam Central Station to:
Schiphol Airport (4-6/hour, 15 minutes, €5, have coins handy to buy from a machine to avoid lines), **Haarlem** (8/hour, 20 minutes), **London** (6/day, 4 hours, Eurostar discounted with rail pass, www.eurostar.com), **Bacharach/St. Goar** (roughly every 2 hours, 4.5-6 hours), **Frankfurt** (every 2 hours, 4 hours direct), **Berlin** (5/day, 6.25 hours), **Munich** (roughly hourly, 7.5-8.75 hours, 1-2 transfers; one direct night train, 10.5 hours), **Paris** (nearly hourly, 3.25 hours direct on fast Thalys train or 4.75 hours with change to Thalys train in Brussels, www.thalys.com).

Thalys has a monopoly on direct trains between Amsterdam and Paris. For passholders, Thalys trains can be a hassle (since you have to prebook your seat reservation, which can sell out quite early), but can save time. When booking Thalys trains, even rail-pass holders need to buy a seat reservation.

By Bus
If you don't have a rail pass, the cheapest way to get to **Paris** is by Eurolines bus (about 6/day, 8 hours, about €46 one-way, €70-86 round-trip; price depends on demand—nonrefundable, advance-purchase one-way tickets as cheap as €17 and round-trip as cheap as €28, check online for deals, Julianaplein 5, Amstel Station, five stops by metro from Central Station, tel. 020/560-8788, www.eurolines.com).

By Plane
Schiphol Airport is located about 10 miles southwest of Amsterdam's city center. Like most of Holland, it is user-friendly and below sea level. With an appealing array of shops, eateries, and other time-killing opportunities, Schiphol (SKIP-pol) is a fine place to arrive, depart, or change planes. A truly international airport, Schiphol has done away with Dutch—signs are in English only.

Information: Schiphol flight information can give you flight times and your airline's contact info (airport code: AMS, toll tel. 0900-0141, from other countries dial +31-20-794-0800, www.schiphol.nl).

Orientation: Though Schiphol officially has four terminals, it's just one big building. You could walk it end to end in about 20 minutes (but allow some time to pass through security checkpoints between certain terminals). All terminals have ATMs, banks, shops, bars, and free Wi-Fi. An inviting shopping and eating zone called Holland Boulevard runs between Terminals 2 and 3.

Arrival at Schiphol: Baggage-claim areas for all terminals empty into the same

arrival zone, called Schiphol Plaza. Here you'll find a busy **TI** (daily 7:00-22:00, near Terminal 2), a train station, and bus stops for getting into the city.

Services: The ABN/AMRO **banks** around the airport offer fair exchange rates. **Service Point,** in Schiphol Plaza at the end of the shopping mall near Terminal 4, is a useful all-purpose service counter that sells SIM cards, has an ATM, and ships packages. Convenient **luggage lockers** are at various points around the airport—allowing you to leave your bag here on a lengthy layover (both short- and long-term lockers, credit card only; biggest bank of lockers near the train station at Schiphol Plaza). To get train information, buy a ticket, or validate your rail pass, take advantage of the "**Train Tickets and Services**" counter (Schiphol Plaza ground level, just past Burger King). They have an easy info desk and generally short lines—so transactions here tend to be much quicker than at Amsterdam's Central Station ticket desks. While you're here, consider validating your rail pass, booking future international train tickets, making seat reservations for later in your trip, or handling any other time-consuming tasks.

GETTING FROM THE AIRPORT TO AMSTERDAM

To get between Schiphol and downtown Amsterdam, you have several options:

By Train: This is your fastest and cheapest option. Direct trains to Amsterdam's Central Station run frequently from Schiphol Plaza (4-6/hour, 15 minutes, €5). Buy tickets at the windows—expect to pay cash unless your credit card has a chip (there are ATMs nearby)—or ticket

machines, which accept coins and credit cards with a chip (start by pressing "I want to go to Amsterdam Centraal"). Schiphol's train station also serves other destinations. When traveling *from* Amsterdam Central to Schiphol, trains generally leave every 15 minutes from track 14a.

By Shuttle Bus: The Connexxion shuttle bus departs from lane A7 in front of the airport and takes you directly to most hotels. There are three different routes, including one to the Westerkerk (near some of my recommended hotels). Ask the attendant which one works best for you (2/hour, 20 minutes, €17 one-way, €27 round-trip, some routes may cost a couple euros more). For trips from Amsterdam to Schiphol, reserve at least two hours ahead (tel. 088-339-4741, www.airporthotelshuttle.nl).

By Public Bus: Bus #197 (departing from lane B9 in front of the airport) is handy for those going to the Leidseplein district (€5, buy ticket from driver).

By Taxi: Allow about €60-70 to downtown Amsterdam. But many hotels have cabs offering a fixed-price airport deal for €45; ask your hotelier for details.

GETTING FROM THE AIRPORT TO HAARLEM

The big red #300 **bus** is direct, stopping at Haarlem's train station and near the Grote Markt/Market Square (4-10/hour, 40 minutes, €4—buy ticket from driver, departs from lane B6 in front of airport). The **train** is just as quick, but you'll have to transfer at the Amsterdam-Sloterdijk station (6/hour, 30-40 minutes, €5.80). Figure about €30-40 to Haarlem by **taxi.**

NEAR AMSTERDAM

HAARLEM

Cute and cozy, yet authentic and handy to the airport, Haarlem gives you small-town warmth overnight, with easy access (20 minutes by train) to Amsterdam during the day. The town gave America's Harlem its name back when New York was New Amsterdam, a Dutch colony.

For centuries Haarlem has been a market town, buzzing with shoppers. Enjoy the market on Monday (clothing) or Saturday (general), when the town's atmospheric main square (Grote Markt) bustles like a Brueghel painting, with cheese, fish, flowers, and families.

Orientation

Getting There: Direct trains run frequently from Amsterdam Central Station (8/hour, 20 minutes). From Schiphol Airport, take a direct bus (4-10/hour, 40 minutes), a train (6/hour, 30-40 minutes, one transfer) or a taxi; see Schiphol connections earlier for details (page 1046).

Arrival in Haarlem: If you arrive at the train station, you'll see that two parallel streets flank the station (Kruisweg and Jansweg). Head up either street, and you'll reach the town square and church within 10 minutes. **Buses** from Schiphol Airport stop both in the center (Centrum/Verwulft stop, a short walk from Grote Markt) and at the train station.

If you arrive by **car**, park in one of the central garages: at the train station or near the Frans Hals Museum. If you take a **taxi**, the drop charge of €7.50 gets you a little over a mile.

Tourist Information: Haarlem's TI (VVV), in the Town Hall building on Grote Markt, is friendlier, more helpful, and less crowded than Amsterdam's, and can give you advice on Amsterdam (April-Sept Mon-Sat 9:30-17:30, Sun 12:00-16:00; Oct-March Mon 13:00-17:30, Tue-Sat 9:30-17:30, closed Sun; tel. 023/531-7325, www.haarlem.nl, info@vvvhaarlem.nl).

Private Guide: Consider hiring **Walter Schelfhout,** a bearded repository of

Haarlem has a small-town feel.

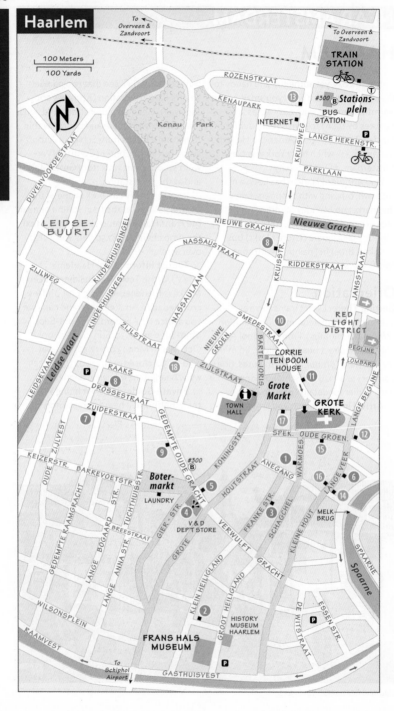

Haarlem

To Overveen & Zandvoort

To Overveen & Zandvoort

TRAIN STATION

100 Meters
100 Yards

ROZENSTRAAT

KENAUPARK

13

#300 **Stations-plein**
BUS STATION

INTERNET

LANGE HERENSTR.

KRUISWEG

PARKLAAN

Kenau Park

LEIDSE-BUURT

DUIVENVOORDESTRAAT

ZIJLWEG

KINDERHUISSINGEL

KINDERHUISVEST

NIEUWE GRACHT

Nieuwe Gracht

NASSAUSTRAAT

8

KRUISSTR.

RIDDERSTRAAT

JANSSTRAAT

ZIJLSTRAAT

NASSAULAAN

SMEDESTRAAT

BARTELJORIS

10

CORRIE TEN BOOM HOUSE

RED LIGHT DISTRICT

BEGIJNE

LOMBARD

LEIDSEVAART

Leidse Vaart

ZIJLSTRAAT

NIEUWE GROEN

18

11

Grote Markt

GROTE KERK

LANGE BEGIJNE

RAAKS

8

DROSSESTRAAT

7

ZUIDERSTRAAT

TOWN HALL

17

SPEK.

OUDE GROEN

12

KEIZERSTR.

OUDE STR.

ZIJLVEST

BARREVOETSTR.

9

#300 **B**

Boter-markt

KONINGSTR.

HOUTSTRAAT

ANEGANG

1

WARMOES

15

16

LANGE VEER

6

GEDEMPTE OUDE GRACHT

GIER-STR.

5

LAUNDRY

4

V & D DEP'T STORE

FRANKE STR.

SCHAGCHEL

3

VERWULFT

KLEINE HOUT

14

MELK-BRUG

SPAARNE

Spaarne

GEDEMPTE RAAMGRACHT

LANGE BOGAARD STR.

TUCHTHUISSTR.

BREESTRAAT

LANGE ANNA STR.

GROTE

KLEIN HEILIGLAND

GROOT HEILIGLAND

VERWULFT GRACHT

DE WITSTRAAT

ESSEN STR.

WILSONSPLEIN

2

HISTORY MUSEUM HAARLEM

FRANS HALS MUSEUM

RAAMVEST

To Schiphol Airport

GASTHUISVEST

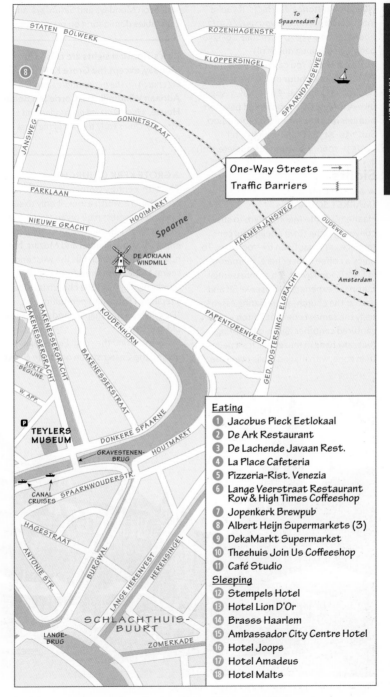

STATEN BOLWERK

ROZENHAGENSTR.

To Spaarnedam

KLOPPERSINGEL

SPAARNDAMSEWEG

⑧

JANSWEG

GONNETSTRAAT

One-Way Streets →

Traffic Barriers

PARKLAAN

NIEUWE GRACHT

HOOIMARKT

Spaarne

HARMENJANSWEG

OUDEWEG

DE ADRIAAN WINDMILL

To Amsterdam

PAPENTORENVEST

GED. OOSTERSING-ELGRACHT

KOUDENHORN

BAKENESSERGRACHT

BAKENESSERGRACHT

KORTE BEGIJNE

BAKENESSERSTRAAT

W. APP

TEYLERS MUSEUM

DONKERE SPAARNE

HOUTMARKT

GRAVESTENEN-BRUG

CANAL CRUISES

SPAARNWOUDERSTR.

HAGESTRAAT

ANTONIE STR.

BURGWAL

LANGE HERENVEST

HERENSINGEL

SCHLACHTHUIS-BUURT

LANGE-BRUG

ZOMERKADE

Eating

① Jacobus Pieck Eetlokaal
② De Ark Restaurant
③ De Lachende Javaan Rest.
④ La Place Cafeteria
⑤ Pizzeria-Rist. Venezia
⑥ Lange Veerstraat Restaurant Row & High Times Coffeeshop
⑦ Jopenkerk Brewpub
⑧ Albert Heijn Supermarkets (3)
⑨ DekaMarkt Supermarket
⑩ Theehuis Join Us Coffeeshop
⑪ Café Studio

Sleeping

⑫ Stempels Hotel
⑬ Hotel Lion D'Or
⑭ Brass Haarlem
⑮ Ambassador City Centre Hotel
⑯ Hotel Joops
⑰ Hotel Amadeus
⑱ Hotel Malts

Haarlem's historical fun facts. If you're into beer lore, Walter's your guy (€91/2 hours, tel. 023/535-5715, mobile 06-1258-9299, schelfhout@dutch.nl).

Bike Rental: You can rent bikes from **Pieters Fietsverhuur** inside the train station (fixed-gear bike-€6.50/day, 3-speed bike-€10/day, €50 deposit and passport number required, Mon-Sat 6:00-24:00, Sun 7:30-24:00, Stationsplein 1, tel. 023/531-7066, www.rijwielshoppieters.nl).

Sights

▲▲GROTE MARKT (MARKET SQUARE)

Haarlem's Grote Markt, where 10 streets converge, is the town's delightful centerpiece...as it has been for 700 years. To enjoy a coffee or beer here, simmering in Dutch good living, is a quintessential European experience. Observe. Sit and gaze at the church, appreciating essentially the same scene that Dutch artists captured centuries ago in oil paintings that now hang in museums. It's a pedestrian zone, with market stalls filling the square on Mondays and Saturdays, and café tables dominating on other days.

Rick's Tip: *Most* **sights are closed on Monday, except the Grote Kerk** *(the big church on the main square)* **and De Adriaan Windmill.** *The* **Corrie ten Boom House,** *which is closed on Sunday and Monday, closes early the rest of the week (15:00).*

▲GROTE KERK (CHURCH)

This 15th-century Gothic church (now Protestant) is worth a look, if only to see Holland's greatest pipe organ (from 1738, 100 feet high). Its more than 5,000 pipes impressed both Handel and Mozart. Note how the organ, which fills the west end, seems to steal the show from the altar. Quirky highlights of the church include a replica of Foucault's pendulum, the "Dog-Whipper's Chapel," and a 400-year-old cannonball.

To enter, find the small *Entrée* sign behind the Coster statue on Grote Markt.

Haarlem's main square is perfect for people-watching.

Cost and Hours: €2.50, Mon-Sat 10:00-17:00, closed Sun to tourists, tel. 023/553-2040, www.bavo.nl.

Concerts: Consider attending—even just part of—a **concert** to hear the Oz-like pipe organ (regular free concerts Tue at 20:15 mid-May–mid-Oct, additional concerts Thu at 16:00 July-Aug; bring a sweater—the church isn't heated).

Rick's Tip: *The local favorite for* **ice cream** *is* **Gelateria Bartoli,** *on the south side of the church (daily March-Sept 10:00-22:00, Oct-Dec 12:00-17:30 in good weather, closed Jan-Feb).*

▲▲FRANS HALS MUSEUM

Haarlem is the hometown of Frans Hals, the foremost Dutch portrait painter of the 17th-century Golden Age. This refreshing museum, once an almshouse for old men back in 1610, displays many of Hals' greatest paintings, crafted in his nearly Impressionistic style. You'll see group portraits and paintings of old-time Haarlem.

Cost and Hours: €12.50, sometimes more with special exhibits, includes audioguide, Tue-Sat 11:00-17:00, Sun 12:00-17:00, closed Mon, Groot Heiligland 62, tel. 023/511-5775, www. franshalsmuseum.nl.

▲CORRIE TEN BOOM HOUSE

Haarlem was home to Corrie ten Boom, popularized by her inspirational 1971 book, *The Hiding Place,* followed in 1975 by a movie of the same name. Both tell about the Ten Boom family's experience protecting Jews from the Nazis. Corrie ten Boom gives the other half of the Anne Frank story—the point of view of those who risked their lives to hide Dutch Jews during the Nazi occupation (1940-1945).

The Ten Boom House can be toured only with a guide; check the sign on the door for the next start time. The gentle, loving one-hour tours in English come with a little evangelizing that some may find objectionable.

Ⓐ *Grote Kerk nave*
Ⓑ *Pew decoration, Grote Kerk*
Ⓒ *Frans Hals Museum*
Ⓓ *Corrie Ten Boom House*

Cost and Hours: Free, but donations accepted; April-Oct Tue-Sat first tour at 10:00, last tour at 15:00; Nov-March Tue-Sat first tour at 11:00, last tour around 15:00; closed Sun-Mon year-round; 50 yards north of Grote Markt at Barteljoris-straat 19; the clock-shop people get all wound up if you go inside—wait in the little side street at the door, where tour times are posted; tel. 023/531-0823, www.corrietenboom.com.

▲DE ADRIAAN WINDMILL

Haarlem's old-time windmill, located just a 10-minute walk from the train station, welcomes visitors with a short video, a little museum, and fine town views.

Cost and Hours: €3.50; March-Nov Mon and Wed-Fri 13:00-17:00, Sat-Sun 10:30-17:00, closed Tue; Dec-Feb Fri-Mon 13:00-16:30, closed Tue-Thu; Papentorenvest 1, tel. 023/545-0259, www.molenadriaan.nl.

CANAL CRUISE

Making a scenic 50-minute loop through and around Haarlem with a live guide who speaks Dutch and sometimes English,

Post Verkade Cruise's little trips are more relaxing than informative (€11; April-Oct daily departures at the top of the hour 12:00-16:00; Nov-March same hours Wed-Sun, reservations required; also evening cruises, across canal from Teylers Museum at Spaarne 11a, tel. 023/535-7723, www.postverkadecruises.nl). **Haarlem Canal Tours** runs similar but longer tours, and uses an open boat. You'll find them farther down Spaarne, across from #17 (€13.50, online reservations smart, 70-75 minutes, leaves every 1.5 hours daily 10:00-19:00, may not run in bad weather and off-season, www.haarlemcanaltours.com).

▲RED LIGHT DISTRICT

This little Red Light District is as precious as a Barbie doll (2 blocks northeast of Grote Markt, off Lange Begijnestraat, no senior or student discounts). Don't miss the mall on Begijnesteeg marked by the red neon sign reading *'t Steegje* ("free"). Just beyond that, the nearby 't Poortje ("office park") costs €6 to enter. Jog to the right to pop into the much more invit-

Canal cruises are a relaxing way to see Haarlem's historic architecture.

ing "Red Lantern" (window-shopping welcome, at Korte Begijnestraat 27). As you wander through this area, remember that although prostitution has been legal here since the 1980s, people here don't condone it; they just find it practical not to criminalize it, but instead to regulate the practice and keep it as safe as possible.

NEAR HAARLEM: ZANDVOORT

For a quick and easy look at the windy coastline, visit nearby Zandvoort, a pretty, manicured resort town. Its sandy beach is lined with cafés, rentable chairs, and a pedestrian promenade. South of the main beach, sunbathers work on all-over tans.

Tourist Information: The helpful TI is on Bakkerstraat 2 (Mon-Fri 9:00-17:00, Sat 10:00-17:00, Sun 11:00-16:00, tel. 023/571-7947, www.vvvzandvoort.nl).

Getting There: It's easy to reach by train, and the station is just around the corner from the beach (4/hour from Haarlem in summer, 10 minutes; 2/hour, 30 minutes from Amsterdam). By bike, it's a breezy 45-minute ride from Haarlem, heading west and following road signs for *Bloemendaal,* then *Zandvoort.*

Smoking

Haarlem is a laid-back place for observing the Dutch approach to recreational marijuana. These easygoing coffeeshops are inviting and particularly friendly to American visitors.

The tiny **Theehuis Join Us**, which feels like a hippie teahouse, was Haarlem's first coffeeshop (c. 1984). Along with a global selection of pot, it has 50 varieties of tea (daily 13:00-22:00, Fri-Sat until 24:00, a block off Grote Markt at Smedestraat 25).

High Times, with a living-room ambience and loaner bongs, offers smokers 12 varieties (Mon-Fri 8:00-23:00, Sat from 9:00, Sun from 11:00, free Internet access for customers, Lange Veerstraat 47, www. coffeeshophightimes.nl).

Nightlife

Grote Markt is lined with trendy bars that seem made for nursing a drink. **Café Studio** is the hot spot (at Grote Markt 25). I'd also duck into the dark interior of **In Den Uiver** (near the Grote Kerk entry at Riviervischmarkt 13). The colorful street called Lange Veerstraat (behind the Grote Kerk) is bordered with lively spots. The square called Boter Grote Markt is more convivial and local—try the nearby **Jopenkerk** brewpub (see listing in "Eating," below).

If you want a more high-powered scene, Amsterdam is just 20 minutes away by train.

Eating

Jacobus Pieck Eetlokaal is popular for its fine-value "global cuisine" good salads, peaceful garden courtyard, and sidewalk tables (Tue-Sat 11:00-16:00 & 17:00-22:00, closed Sun-Mon, cash only, Warmoesstraat 18, behind church, tel. 023/532-6144).

Haarlem's Red Light District

The beach at Zandvoort

De Ark Restaurant, a neighborhood bar, has nothing fancy—just good Dutch and French cuisine at fair prices (€15-18 plates, €19 three-course meal, always veggie options, daily 17:00-22:00, Nieuw Heiligland 3, around corner from Frans Hals Museum, tel. 023/531-1078).

De Lachende Javaan is a long-established Indonesian place serving a memorable *rijsttafel* (€23-28, Tue-Sun 17:00-22:00, closed Mon, Frankestraat 27, tel. 023/532-8792).

La Place, a snazzy chain cafeteria, dishes up fresh, healthy budget food at the Vroom & Dreesmann department store. Sit on the top floor or the roof garden with Haarlem's best view. They offer similar food in the ground-floor café (Mon 12:00-19:00, Tue-Sat 10:00-19:00, Thu until 21:00, Sun 12:00-18:00, Grote Houtstraat 70, on corner of Gedempte Oude Gracht, tel. 023/515-8700).

Pizzeria-Ristorante Venezia is *the* place to go for pizza or pasta (€8-14 choices, daily 13:00-23:00, facing V&D department store at Verwulft 7, tel. 023/531-7753).

Stroll delightful **Lange Veerstraat** behind the church to survey a fun range of restaurants including these favorites:

Visrestaurant Barend, serving traditional seafood (€7-10 starters, €16-20 main courses, Wed-Sun 17:30-21:00, Fri-Sat until 22:00, closed Mon-Tue, Lange Veerstraat 15, tel. 023/532-8694); **Mr. and Mrs. Food and Wine,** with small plates and thoughtful wine pairings (Tue-Sat 17:00-22:00, closed Sun-Mon, Lange Veerstraat 4, tel. 023/531-5935); and **La Plume Restaurant** steakhouse (€20-25 meals, daily 17:00-23:00, *satay* and ribs are favorites, Lange Veerstraat 1, tel. 023/531-3202, www.la-plume.nl).

Jopenkerk brewery is a beer lover's mecca that serves both pub grub and more elegant fare (€8-10 in the pub, €15-23 main dishes in the restaurant, daily 10:00-24:00, Gedempte Voldersgracht 2, tel. 023/533-4114).

Supermarkets: Albert Heijn has three convenient locations; all are cash only. One is in the train station (Mon-Fri 6:30-21:00, Sat 10:00-21:00, Sun 9:00-21:00); another is at Kruisstraat 10 (Mon-Sat 8:00-22:00, Sun 12:00-18:00); and their largest store is near the river and recommended Jopenkerk pub at Drossestraat 11 (Mon-Sat 7:00-22:00, Sun 12:00-18:00). The **DekaMarkt** is a few blocks west of Grote Markt (Mon-Sat 8:00-20:00, Thu-Fri until 21:00, Sun 12:00-18:00, Gedempte Oudegracht 54, near V&D department store).

Sleeping

The helpful Haarlem TI can nearly always find you a €32 bed in a private home, and their website (www.haarlem.nl) has a booking system with good last-minute deals on hotels (€5.50/person fee, two-night minimum; you may get a better price by booking directly with accommodations). To avoid excessive street noise, forgo views for a room in the back. Hotels and the TI have a useful parking brochure.

$$$ Stempels Hotel, modern yet elegant, is located in a renovated 300-year-old building (standard Db-€112-150, pricier rooms and suites, breakfast-€12.50, guest computer, Wi-Fi, elevator, Klokhuisplein 9, tel. 023/512-3910, www.stempelsinhaarlem.nl, info@stempelsinhaarlem.nl).

$$$ Hotel Lion D'Or, across from the train station, is a classy 34-room business hotel with professional comforts and posh decor (Db-€135-150, Fri-Sat Db-€110-125, check website for special deals, 8 percent Rick Steves discount with 2-night stay if you book directly with hotel, air-con, elevator, guest computer, Wi-Fi, Kruisweg 34, tel. 023/532-1750, www.hotelliondor.nl, reservations@hotelliondor.nl).

$$$ Brasss Haarlem rents upscale suites; each cushy room has an open-floor plan with a see-through bathroom (standard Db-€100-150, deluxe Db-€175-195, in-room espresso machine, air-con,

Sleep Code

Price Rankings for Double Rooms (Db)

$$$ Most rooms €95 or more
$$ €60-95
$ €60 or less

Abbreviations: Db=Double with bathroom. D=Double with bathroom down the hall.

Notes: Room prices change; verify rates online or by email. For the best prices, book directly with the hotel.

Wi-Fi, Korte Veerstraat 40, tel. 023/542-7804, www.brassshaarlem.nl, info@brassshaarlem.nl).

$$$ Ambassador City Centre Hotel, with 46 comfortable rooms in a big plain hotel, is located just behind the Grote Kerk (Db-€100, often less off-season, breakfast buffet-€13.50, guest computer, Wi-Fi, Oude Groenmarkt 20, tel. 023/512-5300, www.acc-hotel.nl, info@acc-hotel.

nl). They also run **$$ Hotel Joops,** with 32 rooms, a block away (rooms are €10 cheaper; studios and apartments with kitchenettes for 2-4 people-€110-140 depending on season and number of people).

$$ Hotel Amadeus is charming and has 15 small, bright, and basic rooms, with views of the square in front and quieter rooms in back (Db-€85, check website for special deals, 6 percent Rick Steves discount when booking online with discount code RS1516, Wi-Fi, Grote Markt 10—from square it's a steep climb to lounge, check-in at ground-floor restaurant where there's an elevator accessible during open hours, tel. 023/532-4530, www.amadeus-hotel.com, info@amadeus-hotel.com).

$$ Hotel Malts rents 14 modern, fresh rooms in a central location for a good price (standard Db-€95, big Db with sleeper sofa-€105, check website for best prices, honor bar, no elevator, Wi-Fi, Zijlstraat 58, tel. 023/551-2385, www.maltshotel.nl, info@maltshotel.nl).

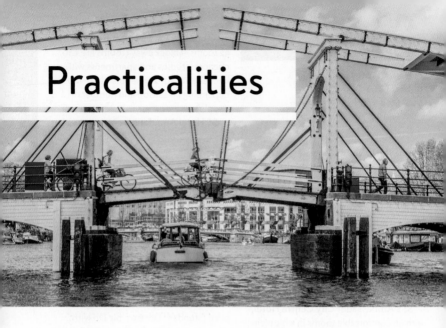

Practicalities

HELP!

Emergency and Medical Help

In any of the countries covered in this book, **dial 112** in an emergency to summon an ambulance or police. You can also ask at your hotel for help—they'll know the nearest medical and emergency services. If you get a minor ailment, do as the locals do and go to a pharmacist for advice.

Theft or Loss

To replace a passport, you'll need to go in person to an embassy (listed next). If your credit and debit cards disappear, cancel and replace them. If your things are lost or stolen, file a police report, either on the spot or within a day or two; you'll need it to submit an insurance claim for lost or stolen rail passes or travel gear, and it can help with replacing your passport or credit and debit cards. For more information, see Ricksteves.com/help.

Damage Control for Lost Cards

If you lose your credit, debit, or ATM card, you can stop people from using your card by reporting the loss immediately to your card company. Visa's and MasterCard's websites list European toll-free numbers by country. If you report your loss within two days, you typically won't be responsible for any unauthorized transactions on your account, although many banks charge a liability fee of $50. You can generally receive a temporary replacement card within two or three business days in Europe.

US Embassies and Consulates

ENGLAND

In London: Tel. 020/7499-9000 (all services), no walk-in passport services, 24 Grosvenor Square, Tube: Bond Street, http://london.usembassy.gov

FRANCE

In Paris: Tel. 01 43 12 22 22, 2 Avenue Gabriel, Mo: Concorde, france.usembassy.gov

Avoiding Theft

Pickpockets are common in crowded, touristy places, but fortunately, violent crime is rare. Thieves don't want to hurt you; they just want your money and gadgets.

My recommendations: Stay alert and wear a money belt (tucked under your clothes) to keep your cash, debit card, credit card, and passport secure; carry only the money you need for the day in your front pocket.

Treat any disturbance (e.g., a stranger bumps into you, spills something on you, or tries to get your attention for an odd reason) as a smoke screen for theft. Be on guard waiting in line at sights, at train stations, and while boarding and leaving crowded buses and subways. Thieves target tourists overloaded with bags or distracted with smartphones.

When paying for something, be aware of how much cash you're handing over (state the denomination of the bill when paying a cabbie) and count your change. For tips on using cash machines smartly, read "Security Tips" under "Cash" on page 1060.

There's no need to be scared; just be smart and prepared.

GERMANY

In Berlin: Tel. 030/83050, Pariser Platz 2; Consular services—tel. 030/8305-1200—answered Mon-Thu 14:00-16:00 only, appointments Mon-Fri 8:30-12:00, closed Sat-Sun and last Thu of month, Clayallee 170; http://germany.usembassy.gov

ITALY

In Rome: 24-hour emergency tel. 06-46741, nonemergency tel. 06-4674-2420, Via Vittorio Veneto 121, http://italy. usembassy.gov

In Florence: Tel. 055-266-951, Lungarno Vespucci 38, http://florence. usconsulate.gov

NETHERLANDS

In Amsterdam: Tel. 020/575-5309, after-hours emergency tel. 070/310-2209, Museumplein 19, http://amsterdam. usconsulate.gov. Online appointments are mandatory for all public services.

SPAIN

In Madrid: Tel. 915-872-200, Calle Serrano 75, http://madrid.usembassy.gov

In Barcelona: Tel. 932-802-227, after-hours emergency tel. 915-872-200, Paseo Reina Elisenda de Montcada 23, http:// barcelona.usconsulate.gov

SWITZERLAND

In Bern: Tel. 031-357-7011, after-hours tel. 031-357-7777, Sulgeneckstrasse 19, services by appointment only Mon-Fri 9:00-11:30, closed Sat-Sun, http://bern. usembassy.gov

MONEY

This section offers advice on how to pay for purchases on your trip (including getting cash from ATMs and paying with plastic), plus tipping.

What to Bring

Bring both a credit card and a debit card. You'll use the debit card at cash machines (ATMs) to withdraw local cash for most purchases, and the credit card to pay for larger items. Some travelers carry a third card, as a backup, in case one gets demagnetized by a rogue machine.

For an emergency stash, bring $200 in hard cash in $20 bills. If you need to exchange the bills, go to a bank; avoid using currency-exchange booths because of their lousy rates and/or outrageous (and often hard-to-spot) fees. For France, where it's hard to change dollars, consider bringing some euros in reserve.

Cash

Cash is just as desirable in Europe as it is at home. Small businesses (mom-and-pop cafés, shops, etc.) prefer that you pay your bills with cash. Some vendors will charge you extra for using a credit card, some won't accept foreign credit cards, and some won't take any credit cards at all. Cash is the best—and sometimes only—way to pay for cheap food, bus fare, taxis, and local guides.

Throughout Europe, ATMs are the standard way for travelers to get cash. They work just like they do at home. To withdraw money from an ATM, you'll need a debit card, plus a four-digit PIN code. Although you can use a credit card to withdraw cash at an ATM, this comes with high bank fees and only makes sense in an emergency.

Security Tips: Shield the keypad when entering your PIN code. When possible, use ATMs located outside banks—a thief is less likely to target a cash machine near surveillance cameras, and if you have trouble with the transaction, you can go inside for help.

Don't use an ATM if anything on the front of the machine looks loose or damaged (a sign that someone may have attached a "skimming" device to capture account information). If a cash machine eats your card, check for a thin plastic insert with a tongue hanging out; thieves use these devices to extract cards.

Stay away from "independent" ATMs such as Travelex, Euronet, YourCash, Cardpoint, and Cashzone, which charge huge commissions and have terrible exchange rates, and may try to trick users into accepting "dynamic currency conversion" (described at the end of "Credit and Debit Cards," next).

If you want to monitor your accounts online during your trip to detect any unauthorized transactions, be sure to use a secure connection.

Exchange Rates

1 euro (€1) = about $1.10. To convert prices in euros to dollars, add 10 percent: €20 is about $22.

1 British pound (£1) = about $1.50. To convert prices in pounds to dollars, add 50 percent. £20 = about $30.

1 Swiss franc (1 SF) = about $1.10. To convert prices in Swiss francs to dollars, add 10 percent.

Check Oanda.com for the latest exchange rates.

Credit and Debit Cards

For purchases, Visa and MasterCard are more commonly accepted than American Express. Just like at home, credit or debit cards work easily at larger hotels, restaurants, and shops. I typically use my debit card to withdraw cash to pay for most purchases.

I use my credit card sparingly: to book hotel reservations, to buy advance tickets for events or sights, to cover major expenses (such as car rentals or plane tickets), to buy train tickets at the ticket counter, and to pay for things online or near the end of my trip (to avoid another visit to the ATM). While you could instead use a debit card for these purchases, a credit card offers a greater degree of fraud protection.

Ask Your Credit- or Debit-Card Company: Before your trip, contact the company that issued your debit or credit cards.

Confirm that your **card will work overseas,** and alert them that you'll be using it in Europe; otherwise, they may deny transactions if they perceive unusual spending patterns.

Ask for the specifics on transaction **fees.** When you use your credit or debit card, you'll typically be charged additional "international transaction" fees of up to 3 percent. If your card's fees seem high, consider getting a different card just for your trip: Capital One (Capitalone.com) and most credit unions have low-to-no international fees.

Verify your daily ATM **withdrawal limit,** and if necessary, ask your bank to adjust it. I prefer a high limit that allows me to take out more cash at each ATM stop and save on bank fees; some travelers prefer to set a lower limit in case their card is stolen. Note that foreign banks also set maximum withdrawal amounts for their ATMs.

Get your bank's emergency **phone number** in the US (but not its 800 number, which isn't accessible from overseas) to call collect if you have a problem.

Ask for your credit card's **PIN** in case you need to make an emergency cash withdrawal or encounter Europe's chip-and-PIN system; the bank won't divulge a PIN over the phone, so allow time for it to be mailed.

Magnetic-Stripe versus Chip-and-PIN Credit Cards: Europeans use chip-and-PIN credit cards that are embedded with an electronic security chip and require a four-digit PIN. Your American-style card (with just the old-fashioned magnetic stripe) will work fine in most places. But it probably won't work at unattended payment machines, such as those at train and subway stations, toll plazas, parking garages, bike-rental kiosks, and gas pumps. If you have problems, try entering your card's PIN, look for a machine that takes cash, or find a clerk who can process the transaction manually.

Major US banks are beginning to offer credit cards with chips. Many of these are not true chip-and-PIN cards, but instead are "chip-and-signature" cards, for which your signature verifies your identity. These cards should work for live transactions and at some payment machines, but won't work for offline transactions such as at unattended gas pumps. If you're concerned, ask if your bank offers a true

chip-and-PIN card. Andrews Federal Credit Union (AndrewsFCU.org) and the State Department Federal Credit Union (SDFCU.org) offer these cards and are open to all US residents.

No matter what kind of card you have, it pays to carry euros; remember, you can always use an ATM to withdraw cash with your magnetic-stripe debit card.

Dynamic Currency Conversion: If merchants or hoteliers offer to convert your purchase price into dollars (called dynamic currency conversion, or DCC), refuse this "service." You'll pay even more in fees for the expensive convenience of seeing your transaction in dollars. Similarly, if an ATM offers to "lock in" or "guarantee" your conversion rate, choose "proceed without conversion" and opt for the local currency (euros, pounds, or Swiss francs) over dollars.

Tipping

Tipping in Europe isn't as automatic and generous as it is in the US. For special service, tips are appreciated, but not expected. As in the US, the right amount depends on your resources and the circumstances, but some general guidelines apply.

Restaurants: You don't need to tip if you order your food at a counter. At restaurants, check the menu to see if service is included; if it isn't, generally a tip of 5-10 percent is normal. France is the exception, where tipping isn't necessary.

Taxis: Round up your fare a bit (for instance, if your fare is €13, pay €14). If the cabbie hauls your bags and zips you to the airport to help you catch your flight, you might want to toss in a little more. But if you feel like you're being driven in circles or otherwise ripped off, skip the tip.

Services: In general, if someone in the service industry does a super job for you, a small tip of a euro or two is appropriate...but not required. If you're not sure whether (or how much) to tip for a service, ask a local for advice.

SLEEPING

I've described my recommended accommodations using a Sleep Code (see sidebar). The prices I list are for one-night stays in peak season, and assume you're booking directly with the hotel, not through a hotel-booking website or TI. Booking services extract a commission from the hotel, which logically closes the door on special deals. Book direct. For tips on making reservations, see next page.

If you're on a budget, it's smart to email several hotels to ask for their best price. Comparison-shop and make your choice. In general, prices can soften if you do any of the following: offer to pay cash, stay at least three nights, or mention this book.

Types of Accommodations
Hotels

In this book, the price for a double room in a hotel ranges from €60 (very basic) to €200-plus (maximum plumbing and the works). You'll pay more for accommodations in bigger cities. While I favor family-run hotels, I also recommend some chain hotels if they're a good value.

If you arrive at your hotel in the morning, your room probably won't be ready. Check your bag safely at the hotel and dive right into sightseeing.

Hoteliers can be a great help and source of advice. Most know their city well, and can assist you with everything from public transit and airport con-

Sleep Code

Price Rankings

To help you sort easily through my listings, I've divided the accommodations into three categories based on the highest price for a basic double room with bath during peak season:

$$$ Higher Priced
$$ Moderately Priced
$ Lower Priced

Prices change without notice; verify the hotel's current rates online or by email. For the best prices, always book directly with the hotel.

Abbreviations

Prices listed in this book are per room, not per person. When a price range is given for a room (such as €100-150), it means the price fluctuates with the season, day of week, size of room, or length of stay; expect to pay the upper end for peak-season stays.

S = Single, **D** = Double/Twin, **T** = Triple, **Q** = Quad, **b** = bathroom

According to this code, a couple staying at a "Db-€140" hotel would pay €140 per night for a double room with a private bathroom. Most hotels also offer single rooms (which can be double rooms they charge less for) and triples (which can be an extra bed added to a double). Some offer larger rooms for four or more people (I call these "family rooms" in the listings).

Unless otherwise noted, hotel staff speak basic English, credit cards are accepted, and hotels have Wi-Fi and/or a guest computer.

Some cities require hoteliers to charge a **tourist tax** (about €1-5/person, per night, often payable only in cash).

Making Hotel Reservations

Reserve your rooms several weeks or even months in advance—or as soon as you've pinned down your travel dates.

Requesting a Reservation: It's easiest to book your room through the hotel's website. (For the best rates, always use the hotel's official site.) If there's no reservation form, or for complicated requests, send an email (see below for a sample request). Most recommended hotels take reservations in English.

The hotelier wants to know:

- the size of your party and type of rooms you need
- your arrival and departure dates, written European-style: day/month/year; also include the total number of nights
- special requests (such as private bathroom vs. down the hall, cheapest room, twin beds vs. double bed, quiet room)
- applicable discounts (such as a Rick Steves reader discount, cash discount, or promotional rate)

Confirming a Reservation: Most places will request a credit-card number to hold your room. If they don't have a secure online reservation form—look for the https—you can email it (I do), but it's safer to share that confidential info via a phone call or fax.

Canceling a Reservation: If you must cancel, it's courteous—and smart—to do so with as much notice as possible, especially for smaller family-run places. Cancellation policies can be strict; read the fine print or ask about these before you book. Many discount deals require prepayment, with no refunds for cancellations.

Reconfirming a Reservation: Always call or email to reconfirm your room reservation a few days in advance. For pensions or small hotels, I call again on my day of arrival to tell my host what time I expect to get there (especially important if arriving late—after 17:00).

From: rick@ricksteves.com
Sent: Today
To: info@hotelcentral.com
Subject: Reservation request for 19-22 July

Dear Hotel Central,
I would like to reserve a room for 2 people for 3 nights, arriving 19 July and departing 22 July. If possible, I would like a quiet room with a double bed and private bathroom inside the room.

Please let me know if you have a room available and the price.

Thank you!
Rick Steves

nections to finding a good restaurant, the nearest launderette, or a late-night pharmacy.

Even at the best places, mechanical breakdowns occur: Sinks leak, hot water turns cold, toilets may gurgle or smell, the Wi-Fi goes out, or the air-conditioning dies when you need it most. Report your concerns clearly and calmly at the front desk. For more complicated issues, don't expect instant results.

To guard against theft in your room, keep valuables out of sight. Some rooms come with a safe, and other hotels have safes at the front desk. I've never bothered using one.

While it's customary to pay for your room upon departure, it can be a good idea to settle your bill the day before, when you're not in a hurry and while the manager's in. That way you'll have time to discuss and address any points of contention.

Above all, keep a positive attitude. Remember, you're on vacation. If your hotel is a disappointment, spend more time out enjoying the city you came to see.

Hostels

A hostel provides cheap dorm beds and sometimes has a few double rooms and family rooms. Travelers of any age are welcome. Most hostels offer kitchen facilities, guest computers, Wi-Fi, and a self-service laundry.

There are two kinds of hostels: **Independent hostels** tend to be easygoing, colorful, and informal (no membership required); try Hostelworld.com, Hostelz. com, or Hostels.com. **Official hostels** are part of Hostelling International (HI), share an online booking site (Hihostels. com), and typically require that you either have a membership card or pay extra per night.

Other Accommodation Options

Renting an apartment can be a fun and cost-effective way to go local. Websites such as Booking.com, Airbnb, VRBO, and FlipKey let you browse properties and correspond directly with European property owners or managers. Airbnb and Roomorama also list rooms in private homes. Beds range from air-mattress-in-living-room basic to plush-B&B-suite posh. If you want a place to sleep that's free, try Couchsurfing.com.

STAYING CONNECTED

Staying connected in Europe gets easier and cheaper every year. The simplest solution is to bring your own device—mobile phone, tablet, or laptop—and use it just as you would at home (following the tips below, such as connecting to free Wi-Fi whenever possible). Or you can travel without a mobile device, using European landlines and computers to connect. These options are described below, and you'll find more specifics at Ricksteves.com/phoning.

Using Your Mobile Device in Europe

Roaming with your mobile device in Europe doesn't have to be expensive. These budget tips and options will keep your costs in check.

Use free Wi-Fi whenever possible. Unless you have an unlimited-data plan, you're best off saving most online tasks for Wi-Fi.

Many cafés—including Starbucks and McDonald's—have free hotspots for customers; look for signs offering it and ask for the Wi-Fi password when you buy something. You'll often find Wi-Fi at TIs, city squares, major museums, public-transit hubs, airports, and aboard trains and buses.

Sign up for an international plan. Most providers offer a global calling plan that cuts the per-minute cost of phone calls and texts, and a flat-fee data plan.

Tips on Internet Security

Using the Internet while traveling brings added security risks, whether you're getting online with your own device or at a public terminal using a shared network.

First, make sure that your device is running the latest version of its operating system and security software. Next, ensure that your device is password- or passcode-protected so thieves can't access your information if your device is stolen. For extra security, set passwords on apps that access key info (such as email or Facebook).

On the road, use only legitimate Wi-Fi hotspots. Ask the hotel or café staff for the specific name of their Wi-Fi network, and make sure you log on to that exact one. Hackers sometimes create a bogus hotspot with a similar or vague name (such as "Hotel Europa Free Wi-Fi"). The best Wi-Fi networks require that you enter a password.

Be especially cautious when checking your online banking, credit-card statements, or other personal-finance accounts. Internet security experts advise against accessing these sites while traveling. Even if you're using your own mobile device at a password-protected hotspot, any hacker who's logged on to the same network may be able see what you're doing. If you do need to log on to a banking website, use a hard-wired connection (such as an Ethernet cable in your hotel room) or a cellular network, which is safer than Wi-Fi.

Never share your credit-card number (or any other sensitive information) online unless you know that the site is secure. A secure site displays a little padlock icon, and the URL begins with *https* (instead of the usual *http*).

Your normal plan may already include international coverage (T-Mobile's does).

Before your trip, call your provider or check online to confirm that your phone will work in Europe, and research your provider's international rates. Activate the plan a day or two before you leave, then remember to cancel it when your trip's over.

Minimize the use of your cellular network. When you can't find Wi-Fi, you can use your cellular network to connect to the Internet, text, or make voice calls. When you're done, avoid further charges by manually switching off "data roaming" or "cellular data" (in your device's Settings menu). Another way to make sure you're not accidentally using data roaming is to put your device in "airplane" or "flight" mode (which also disables phone calls

and texts), and then turn on Wi-Fi as needed.

Don't use your cellular network for bandwidth-gobbling tasks, such as Skyping, downloading apps, and watching YouTube: Save these for when you're on Wi-Fi. Using a navigation app such as Google Maps over a cellular network can take lots of data, so do this sparingly or use it offline.

Limit automatic updates. By default, your device constantly checks for a data connection and updates apps. It's smart to disable these features so your apps will only update when you're on Wi-Fi, and to change your device's email settings from "auto-retrieve" to "manual" (or from "push" to "fetch").

It's also a good idea to keep track of your data usage. On your device's menu,

Phoning Cheat Sheet

Here are instructions for dialing, along with an example of how to call one of my recommended hotels in Paris (tel. 01-45-51-63-02).

Calling from the US to Europe: Dial 011 (US access code), country code (33 for France), and phone number.* To call the recommended hotel in Paris, I dial 011-33-1-45-51-63-02. Please see note about time zones below.

Calling from Europe to the US: Dial 00 (Europe access code), country code (1 for US), area code, and phone number. To call my office in Edmonds, Washington, I dial 00-1-425-771-8303.

Calling country to country within Europe: Dial 00, country code, and phone number.* To call the Paris hotel from England, I dial 00-33-1-45-51-63-02.

Calling within a European country: Dial the entire phone number, including the initial zero (if there is one). To call the Paris hotel from Nice, I dial 01-45-51-63-02 (France doesn't use area codes).

Calling with a mobile phone: The "+" sign on your mobile phone automatically selects the access code you need (for a "+" sign, press and hold "0").* To call the Paris hotel from the US or Europe, I dial +33-01-45-51-63-02.

For more dialing help, see Howtocallabroad.com.

*If the European phone number starts with zero, drop it when calling from another country (except Italian numbers, which retain the zero).

Country	Country Code	Country	Country Code
Austria	43	Hungary	36
Belgium	32	Ireland/N Ireland	353/44
Croatia	385	Italy	39
Czech Republic	420	Netherlands	31
Denmark	45	Norway	47
England	44	Portugal	351
France	33	Scotland	44
Germany	49	Spain	34
Greece	30	Switzerland	41

Time Zones: When calling from the US to Europe, keep Europe's time zones in mind, especially if you're trying to hit business hours. The countries covered in this book are six/nine hours ahead of the East/West Coasts of the US, except for England. England, which is one hour earlier than most of continental Europe, is five/eight hours ahead of the East/West Coasts of the US. For an online converter, see Timeanddate.com/worldclock.

look for "cellular data usage" or "mobile data" and reset the counter at the start of your trip.

Use calling/messaging apps for cheaper calls and texts. Certain calling and messaging services let you make voice/video calls and send texts for free or cheap. With an app installed on your phone, tablet, or laptop, you can log on to a Wi-Fi network and contact friends or family members who use the same service.

With apps like Google+ Hangouts, Whats App, Viber, Facebook Messenger, and iMessage, you can **text** for free. Skype, Viber, FaceTime, and Google+ Hangouts let you make free **voice and video calls**. With some of these services (if you buy credit in advance), you can call any mobile phone or landline worldwide for just pennies per minute.

Public Phones and Computers

It's possible to travel in Europe without a mobile device. You can check email or browse websites using public computers and Internet cafés, and make calls from your hotel room and/or public phones.

If you use your **hotel room** phone, you'll generally be charged a fee for local and even "toll-free" calls, as well as long-distance or international calls—ask at the front desk for rates before you dial.

Since you're never charged for receiving calls, it's fine to have someone from the US call you in your room. Ask the staff if your room has a direct telephone number.

If the fees are low, hotel phones can be used inexpensively for calls made with cheap international phone cards (sold at post offices, newsstands, street kiosks, tobacco shops, and train stations). You'll either get a prepaid card with a toll-free number and a scratch-to-reveal PIN code, or a code printed on a receipt.

You'll see **public pay phones** in a few post offices and train stations. The phones generally come with multilingual instructions, and most work with insertable phone cards (sold at post offices, newsstands, etc.). With the exception of Great Britain, each European country has its own insertable phone card that works only in its country. Avoid using an international phone card at German pay phones—a surcharge for their use effectively eliminates any savings.

Public computers are easy to find. Many hotels have one in their lobby for guests to use; otherwise you can find them at Internet cafés and public libraries.

TRANSPORTATION

This section covers the basics on trains, buses, rental cars, and flights.

Trains

Considering the efficiency of Europe's trains (and buses), you'd never need to use a car.

You can buy point-to-point tickets (either in advance or as you travel) or buy a railpass.

High-speed, long-distance, international, and overnight trains are more likely to require **reservations.** If so, you automatically get reservations when you buy point-to-point tickets, but if you're using a rail pass, you'll need to make any required reservations yourself. You can reserve the more critical journeys from home (through Ricksteves.com/rail); otherwise you can make them all at one time at any staffed station in Europe.

To check **train schedules** online, see Bahn.com (Germany's excellent Europe-wide timetable).

Tickets

Point-to-point tickets are just that: tickets bought individually to get you from Point A to Point B.

First Class vs. Second Class: First-class tickets usually cost 50 percent more than second-class tickets. First-class cars

Point-to-Point Train Tickets: Cost & Time

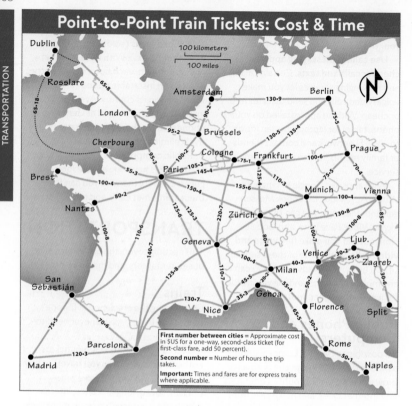

First number between cities = Approximate cost in $US for a one-way, second-class ticket (for first-class fare, add 50 percent).

Second number = Number of hours the trip takes.

Important: Times and fares are for express trains where applicable.

are more spacious and less crowded than second class, but riding in second class gets you there at the same time, and with the same scenery.

Discount Fares: If you reserve a ticket on a fast train in advance and are comfortable committing to particular departure times, you can usually enjoy substantial savings over full-fare tickets. Discounted fares go on sale several months in advance and remain available until one day before departure—unless all the cheap seats sell out early (which often happens). Rules vary per country.

Savings on Slow Trains: You can save money on point-to-point tickets if you're willing to limit yourself to regional trains.

Buying Tickets: You can buy tickets directly at a **train station** at the counter or from machines, but since not all machines take American credit cards, you may need

to go to the counter. If lines are long at the station, it can be quicker to buy tickets from a **travel agency** in town (at a small fee, but less of a language barrier). Or you can buy tickets **online** in advance from the train company's website (Eurostar. com for the Chunnel linking England and France, Sncf.com for France, Bahn.com for Germany, Trenitalia.com for Italy, Ns.nl for the Netherlands, Sbb.ch for Switzerland, and hard-to-use Renfe.com for Spain).

If you must board a train without a ticket, find the **conductor** before he finds you (or he'll fine you) and ask to buy a ticket (you'll pay extra for this service).

Rail Passes

A rail pass covers train travel in one or more countries for a certain number of days (either a continuous span of days or a number of days spread over a wider window of time). Depending on how many trips you take, passes can offer a savings over regular point-to-point tickets.

For a multi-country trip, a Eurail pass generally offers the best deal. For instance, the **Select Pass** covers travel in two, three, or four adjacent countries (e.g., Italy, Switzerland, France, and Germany). The **Global Pass** covers most of Europe (but not Great Britain). These passes are available in a **saverpass** version, which gives a 15 percent discount for two or more companions traveling together. Passes covering three or more countries require adults (age 26 and over) to pay for first class. Youths under 26 travel cheaper in first or second class. But note that up to two kids under 12 can travel free with each adult.

For detailed advice on figuring out the smartest rail pass options for your train trip, visit Ricksteves.com/rail. Most rail passes have to be purchased outside of Europe.

Long-Distance Buses

While buses don't offer as extensive a network as trains, they do cover the most popular cities for travelers, quite often with direct connections. Bus tickets are sold on the spot (on board and/or at kiosks at some bus terminals), but because the cheapest fares often sell out, it's best to book online as soon as you're sure of your plans (at a minimum, book a few days ahead to nab the best prices).

Renting a Car

Research car rentals before you go. It's cheapest to arrange most car rentals from the US. Consider several companies to compare rates. Most of the major US rental agencies (including Avis, Budget, Enterprise, Hertz, and Thrifty) have offices throughout Europe. The two major Europe-based agencies are Europcar and Sixt, and consolidators include Auto Europe/Kemwel (Autoeurope.com—or the often cheaper Autoeurope.eu) and Europe by Car (Europebycar.com).

Always read the fine print carefully for add-on charges—such as one-way drop-off fees, airport surcharges, or mandatory insurance policies—that aren't included in the "total price."

For the best deal, rent by the week with unlimited mileage. I normally rent the smallest, least-expensive model with a stick shift (generally cheaper than an automatic). If you need an automatic, request one in advance; be aware that these cars are usually larger models.

Figure on paying roughly $250 for a one-week rental. Allow extra for supplemental insurance, fuel, tolls, and parking. For trips of three weeks or more, leasing can save you money on insurance and taxes (see next page).

If you want to rent a car for only a couple of days to explore a region, you could work directly with a local rental company, reserving in advance by email or phone.

Picking Up Your Car: Compare pickup costs (downtown can be less expensive than the airport) and explore drop-off options. Always check the hours of the location you choose: Many rental offices close from midday Saturday until Monday morning and, in smaller towns, at lunchtime.

When you pick up the car, check it thoroughly. Rental agencies in Europe are very strict when it comes to charging for even minor damage, so make sure any damage is noted on your rental agreement. Before driving off, find out how your car's gearshift, lights, turn signals, wipers, radio, and fuel cap function, and know what kind of fuel the car takes (diesel vs. unleaded). When you return the car, make sure the agent verifies its condition with you. Some drivers take pictures of the returned vehicle as proof of its condition.

Car Insurance Options

When you rent a car, you are liable for a very high deductible, sometimes equal to the entire value of the car. Limit your financial risk with one of these three options:

• Buy Collision Damage Waiver (CDW) coverage with a low or zero deductible from the car-rental company.

• Get coverage through your credit card, which is free if your card automatically includes zero-deductible coverage. But in case of damage, it can be time-consuming to resolve the charges with your credit-card company. Before you decide on this option, quiz your credit-card company about how it works.

• Get collision insurance as part of a larger travel-insurance policy. If you're already purchasing a policy for your trip, adding collision coverage can be economical. Travel Guard is one of the companies that offers this add-on.

For **more on car-rental insurance**, see Ricksteves.com/cdw.

Leasing

For trips of three weeks or more, consider leasing, which automatically includes zero-deductible collision and theft insurance. Leasing provides you a new car with unlimited mileage and a 24-hour emergency assistance program. You can lease for as little as 21 days to as long as 5.5 months. Cars can most easily be picked up and returned in France, but you can pick up or drop off in neighboring countries for a fee. Car leases must be arranged from the US. One of many companies offering affordable leasing is Europe by Car (Europebycar.com/lease).

Driving

Be aware of typical European road rules; for example, some countries require headlights to be turned on at all times, and nearly all forbid talking on a mobile phone without a hands-free headset. Seat belts are mandatory for all, and two beers under those belts are enough to land you in jail. You're required to use low-beam headlights if it's overcast, raining, or snow-

ing. In Europe, you're not allowed to turn right on a red light, unless a sign or signal specifically authorizes it, and on expressways it's illegal to pass drivers on the right.

Be warned that driving is restricted in many Italian city centers. If you drive in an area marked *Zona Traffico Limitato* (ZTL, often shown above a red circle), your license plate can be photographed and a hefty (€100-plus) fine mailed to your home without you ever being stopped by a cop.

You'll pay to use tollways in Italy, France, and Spain, and will need to buy a toll sticker if you enter Switzerland.

At self-service gas pumps and automated parking garages, your US credit and debit cards might not work. Carry cash to fuel your trip.

If you have questions about road rules, ask your car-rental company or check the US State Department website (Travel.State.gov, search for your country in the "Learn about your destination" box, then click on "Travel & Transportation").

Flights

The best comparison search engine for both international and intra-European flights is Kayak.com. For inexpensive flights within Europe, try Skyscanner.com.

Flying to Europe: Start looking for international flights at least four to six months before your trip, especially for peak-season travel. Off-season tickets can usually be purchased a month or so in advance. Depending on your itinerary, it can be efficient to fly into one city and out of another.

Flying within Europe: If you're considering a train ride that's more than five hours long, a flight may save you both time and money. When comparing your options, factor in the time it takes to get to the airport and how early you'll need to arrive to check in.

These days you can fly within Europe on major airlines affordably for around $100 a flight. If you're using a budget

Resources from Rick Steves

Begin Your Trip at Ricksteves.com

My mobile-friendly **website** is *the* place to explore Europe. You'll find thousands of fun articles, videos, photos, and radio interviews; a wealth of money-saving tips for planning your dream trip; my travel talks and blog; and guidebook updates (Ricksteves.com/update).

Our **Travel Forum** is an immense collection of message boards, where our travel-savvy community answers questions and shares personal travel experiences—and our well-traveled staff chimes in when they can help.

Our **online Travel Store** offers bags and accessories designed to help you travel smarter and lighter. These include my popular bags (which I live out of four months a year), money belts, totes, toiletries kits, adapters, guidebooks, planning maps, and more.

Choosing the right **rail pass** for your trip can drive you nutty. Our website will help you find the perfect fit for your itinerary and your budget: We offer easy, one-stop shopping for rail passes, seat reservations, and point-to-point tickets.

Guidebooks, Video, Audio Europe, and Tours

Books: *Rick Steves Best of Europe* is just one of many books in my series on European travel, which includes country and city guidebooks, Snapshot guides (excerpted chapters from my country guides), Pocket Guides (full-color little books on big cities), and my budget-travel skills handbook, *Rick Steves Europe Through the Back Door*. My phrase books are practical and budget-oriented. A more complete list of my titles appears near the end of this book.

Video: My public television series, *Rick Steves' Europe,* covers Europe from top to bottom with over 100 half-hour episodes. To watch full episodes online for free, see Ricksteves.com/tv. Or to raise your travel I.Q. with video versions of our popular classes (including my talks on travel skills, packing smart, most European countries, and European art), see Ricksteves.com/travel-talks.

Audio: My weekly public radio show, *Travel with Rick Steves,* features interviews with travel experts from around the world. A complete archive is available at Ricksteves.com/radio, and much of this audio content is available for free, along with my audio tours of Europe's top sights, through my **Rick Steves Audio Europe** app (see page 14).

Tours: Want to travel with greater efficiency and less stress? We organize tours with more than three dozen itineraries reaching the best destinations in this book...and beyond. You'll enjoy great guides and a fun but small group of travel partners. For all the details, and to get our tour catalog and a free Rick Steves Tour Experience DVD, visit Ricksteves.com or call us at 425/608-4217.

carrier, be aware of the potential drawbacks and restrictions: nonrefundable and nonchangeable tickets, minimal or nonexistent customer service, pricey and time-consuming treks to secondary airports, and stingy baggage allowances with steep overage fees. If you're traveling with lots of luggage, a cheap flight can quickly become a bad deal. To avoid unpleasant surprises, read the small print before you book.

Flying to the US and Canada: Because security is extra tight for flights to the US, be sure to give yourself plenty of time at the airport. It's also important to charge your electronic devices before you board because security checks may require you to turn them on (see TSA.gov for the latest rules).

CONVERSIONS

Numbers and Stumblers

- Europeans write a few of their numbers differently than we do: 1 = 1, 4 = 4, 7 = 7.
- In Europe, dates appear as day/month/year; Christmas is 25/12.
- Commas are decimal points and decimals are commas. A dollar and a half is $1,50. One thousand is 1.000.
- When counting with fingers, start with your thumb. If you hold up your first finger to request one item, you'll probably get two.
- What Americans call the second floor of a building is the first floor in Europe.
- On escalators and moving sidewalks, Europeans keep the left "lane" open for passing. Keep to the right.

Clothing and Shoe Sizes

Shoppers can use these US-to-European comparisons as general guidelines, but note that no conversion is perfect.

Women: For clothing or shoe sizes, add 30 (US shirt size 10 = European size 40; US shoe size 8 = European size 38-39).

Men: For shirts, multiply by 2 and add about 8 (US size 15 = European size 38). For jackets and suits, add 10. For shoes, add 32-34.

Children: For clothing, subtract 1-2 sizes for small children and subtract 4 for juniors. For shoes up to size 13, add 16-18, and for sizes 1 and up, add 30-32.

Metric Conversions

A **kilogram** equals 1,000 grams and about 2.2 pounds. One hundred **grams** (a common unit of sale at markets) is about a quarter-pound.

One **liter** is about a quart, or almost four to a gallon.

A **kilometer** is six-tenths of a mile. To convert kilometers to miles, cut the kilometers in half and add back 10 percent of the original (120 km: 60 + 12 = 72 miles). One **meter** is 39 inches.

Using the **Celsius** scale, 0°C equals 32°F. To roughly convert Celsius to Fahrenheit, double the number and add 30. For weather, 28°C is 82°F—perfect. For health, 37°C is just right. At a launderette, 30°C is cold, 40°C is warm (default setting), and 60°C is hot.

Packing Checklist

Clothing

- ❑ 5 shirts: long- & short-sleeve
- ❑ 2 pairs pants or skirt
- ❑ 1 pair shorts or capris
- ❑ 5 pairs underwear & socks
- ❑ 1 pair walking shoes
- ❑ Sweater or fleece top
- ❑ Rainproof jacket with hood
- ❑ Tie or scarf
- ❑ Swimsuit
- ❑ Sleepwear

Money

- ❑ Debit card
- ❑ Credit card(s)
- ❑ Hard cash ($20 bills)
- ❑ Money belt or neck wallet

Documents & Travel Info

- ❑ Passport
- ❑ Airline reservations
- ❑ Rail pass/train reservations
- ❑ Car-rental voucher
- ❑ Driver's license
- ❑ Student ID, hostel card, etc.
- ❑ Photocopies of all the above
- ❑ Hotel confirmations
- ❑ Insurance details
- ❑ Guidebooks & maps
- ❑ Notepad & pen
- ❑ Journal

Toiletries Kit

- ❑ Toiletries
- ❑ Medicines & vitamins
- ❑ First-aid kit
- ❑ Glasses/contacts/sunglasses
  (with prescriptions)
- ❑ Earplugs
- ❑ Packet of tissues (for WC)

Miscellaneous

- ❑ Daypack
- ❑ Sealable plastic baggies
- ❑ Laundry soap
- ❑ Clothesline
- ❑ Sewing kit
- ❑ Travel alarm/watch

Electronics

- ❑ Smartphone or mobile phone
- ❑ Camera & related gear
- ❑ Tablet/ereader/media player
- ❑ Laptop & flash drive
- ❑ Earbuds or headphones
- ❑ Chargers
- ❑ Plug adapters

Optional Extras

- ❑ Flipflops or slippers
- ❑ Mini-umbrella or poncho
- ❑ Travel hairdryer
- ❑ Belt
- ❑ Hat (for sun or cold)
- ❑ Picnic supplies
- ❑ Water bottle
- ❑ Fold-up tote bag
- ❑ Small flashlight
- ❑ Small binoculars
- ❑ Small towel or washcloth
- ❑ Inflatable pillow
- ❑ Tiny lock
- ❑ Address list (to mail postcards)
- ❑ Postcards/photos from home
- ❑ Extra passport photos
- ❑ Good book

French Survival Phrases

When using the phonetics, try to nasalize the n̲ sound.

English	French	Pronunciation
Good day.	Bonjour.	bohn̲-zhoor
Mrs. / Mr.	Madame / Monsieur	mah-dahm / muhs-yur
Do you speak English?	Parlez-vous anglais?	par-lay-voo ahn̲-glay
Yes. / No.	Oui. / Non.	wee / nohn̲
I understand.	Je comprends.	zhuh kohn̲-prahn̲
I don't understand.	Je ne comprends pas.	zhuh nuh kohn̲-prahn̲ pah
Please.	S'il vous plaît.	see voo play
Thank you.	Merci.	mehr-see
I'm sorry.	Désolé.	day-zoh-lay
Excuse me.	Pardon.	par-dohn̲
(No) problem.	(Pas de) problème.	(pah duh) proh-blehm
It's good.	C'est bon.	say bohn̲
Goodbye.	Au revoir.	oh vwahr
one / two	un / deux	uhn̲ / duh
three / four	trois / quatre	twah / kah-truh
five / six	cinq / six	san̲k / sees
seven / eight	sept / huit	seht / weet
nine / ten	neuf / dix	nuhf / dees
How much is it?	Combien?	kohn̲-bee-an̲
Write it?	Ecrivez?	ay-kree-vay
Is it free?	C'est gratuit?	say grah-twee
Included?	Inclus?	an̲-klew
Where can I buy / find...?	Où puis-je acheter / trouver...?	oo pwee-zhuh ah-shuh-tay / troo-vay
I'd like / We'd like...	Je voudrais / Nous voudrions...	zhuh voo-dray / noo voo-dree-ohn̲
...a room.	...une chambre.	ewn shahn̲-bruh
...a ticket to _____.	...un billet pour _____.	uhn̲ bee-yay poor _____
Is it possible?	C'est possible?	say poh-see-bluh
Where is...?	Où est...?	oo ay
...the train station	...la gare	lah gar
...the bus station	...la gare routière	lah gar root-yehr
...tourist information	...l'office du tourisme	loh-fees dew too-reez-muh
Where are the toilets?	Où sont les toilettes?	oo sohn̲ lay twah-leht
men	hommes	ohm
women	dames	dahm
left / right	à gauche / à droite	ah gohsh / ah dwaht
straight	tout droit	too dwah
When does this open / close?	Ça ouvre / ferme à quelle heure?	sah oo-vruh / fehrm ah kehl ur
At what time?	À quelle heure?	ah kehl ur
Just a moment.	Un moment.	uhn̲ moh-mahn̲
now / soon / later	maintenant / bientôt / plus tard	man̲-tuh-nahn̲ / bee-an̲-toh / plew tar
today / tomorrow	aujourd'hui / demain	oh-zhoor-dwee / duh-man̲

For more user-friendly French phrases, check out *Rick Steves' French Phrase Book and Dictionary* or *Rick Steves' French, Italian & German Phrase Book*.

In a French Restaurant

English	French	Pronunciation
I'd like / We'd like...	Je voudrais / Nous voudrions...	zhuh voo-dray / noo voo-dree-ohn
...to reserve...	...réserver...	ray-zehr-vay
...a table for one / two.	...une table pour un / deux.	ewn tah-bluh poor uhn / duh
Is this seat free?	C'est libre?	say lee-bruh
The menu (in English), please.	La carte (en anglais), s'il vous plaît.	lah kart (ahn ahn-glay) see voo play
service (not) included	service (non) compris	sehr-vees (nohn) kohn-pree
to go	à emporter	ah ahn-por-tay
with / without	avec / sans	ah-vehk / sahn
and / or	et / ou	ay / oo
special of the day	plat du jour	plah dew zhoor
specialty of the house	spécialité de la maison	spay-see-ah-lee-tay duh lah may-zohn
appetizers	hors d'oeuvre	or duh-vruh
first course (soup, salad)	entrée	ahn-tray
main course (meat, fish)	plat principal	plah pran-see-pahl
bread	pain	pan
cheese	fromage	froh-mahzh
sandwich	sandwich	sahnd-weech
soup	soupe	soop
salad	salade	sah-lahd
meat	viande	vee-ahnd
chicken	poulet	poo-lay
fish	poisson	pwah-sohn
seafood	fruits de mer	frwee duh mehr
fruit	fruit	frwee
vegetables	légumes	lay-gewm
dessert	dessert	day-sehr
mineral water	eau minérale	oh mee-nay-rahl
tap water	l'eau du robinet	loh dew roh-bee-nay
milk	lait	lay
(orange) juice	jus (d'orange)	zhew (doh-rahnzh)
coffee / tea	café / thé	kah-fay / tay
wine	vin	van
red / white	rouge / blanc	roozh / blahn
glass / bottle	verre / bouteille	vehr / boo-tay
beer	bière	bee-ehr
Cheers!	Santé!	sahn-tay
More. / Another.	Plus. / Un autre.	plew / uhn oh-truh
The same.	La même chose.	lah mehm shohz
The bill, please.	L'addition, s'il vous plaît.	lah-dee-see-ohn see voo play
Do you accept credit cards?	Vous prenez les cartes?	voo pruh-nay lay kart
tip	pourboire	poor-bwahr
Delicious!	Délicieux!	day-lee-see-uh

Spanish Survival Phrases

Spanish has a guttural sound similar to the J in Baja California. In the phonetics, the symbol for this clearing-your-throat sound is the italicized *h*.

English	Spanish	Pronunciation
Good day.	*Buenos días.*	**bway**-nohs **dee**-ahs
Do you speak English?	*¿Habla Usted inglés?*	**ah**-blah oo-**stehd** een-**glays**
Yes. / No.	*Sí. / No.*	see / noh
I (don't) understand.	*(No) comprendo.*	(noh) kohm-**prehn**-doh
Please.	*Por favor.*	por fah-**bor**
Thank you.	*Gracias.*	**grah**-thee-ahs
I'm sorry.	*Lo siento.*	loh see-**ehn**-toh
Excuse me.	*Perdóneme.*	pehr-**doh**-nay-may
(No) problem.	*(No) problema.*	(noh) proh-**blay**-mah
Good.	*Bueno.*	**bway**-noh
Goodbye.	*Adiós.*	ah-dee-**ohs**
one / two	*uno / dos*	**oo**-noh / dohs
three / four	*tres / cuatro*	trays / **kwah**-troh
five / six	*cinco / seis*	**theen**-koh / says
seven / eight	*siete / ocho*	see-**eh**-tay / **oh**-choh
nine / ten	*nueve / diez*	**nway**-bay / dee-**ayth**
How much is it?	*¿Cuánto cuesta?*	**kwahn**-toh **kway**-stah
Write it?	*¿Me lo escribe?*	may loh ay-**skree**-bay
Is it free?	*¿Es gratis?*	ays **grah**-tees
Is it included?	*¿Está incluido?*	ay-**stah** een-kloo-**ee**-doh
Where can I buy / find...?	*¿Dónde puedo comprar / encontrar...?*	**dohn**-day **pway**-doh kohm-**prar** / ayn-kohn-**trar**
I'd like / We'd like...	*Quiero / Queremos...*	kee-**ehr**-oh / kehr-**ay**-mohs
...a room.	*...una habitación.*	**oo**-nah ah-bee-tah-thee-**ohn**
...a ticket to ____.	*...un billete para ____.*	oon bee-**yeh**-tay **pah**-rah ____
Is it possible?	*¿Es posible?*	ays poh-**see**-blay
Where is...?	*¿Dónde está...?*	**dohn**-day ay-**stah**
...the train station	*...la estación de trenes*	lah ay-stah-thee-**ohn** day **tray**-nays
...the bus station	*...la estación de autobuses*	lah ay-stah-thee-**ohn** day ow-toh-**boo**-says
...the tourist information office	*...la oficina de turismo*	lah oh-fee-**thee**-nah day too-**rees**-moh
Where are the toilets?	*¿Dónde están los servicios?*	**dohn**-day ay-**stahn** lohs sehr-**bee**-thee-ohs
men	*hombres, caballeros*	**ohm**-brays, kah-bah-**yay**-rohs
women	*mujeres, damas*	moo-**heh**-rays, **dah**-mahs
left / right	*izquierda / derecha*	eeth-kee-**ehr**-dah / day-**ray**-chah
straight	*derecho*	day-**ray**-choh
When do you open / close?	*¿A qué hora abren / cierran?*	ah kay **oh**-rah **ah**-brehn / thee-**ay**-rahn
At what time?	*¿A qué hora?*	ah kay **oh**-rah
Just a moment.	*Un momento.*	oon moh-**mehn**-toh
now / soon / later	*ahora / pronto / más tarde*	ah-**oh**-rah / **prohn**-toh / mahs **tar**-day
today / tomorrow	*hoy / mañana*	oy / mahn-**yah**-nah

In a Spanish Restaurant

English	Spanish	Pronunciation
I'd like / We'd like...	Quiero / Queremos...	kee-**ehr**-oh / kehr-**ay**-mohs
...to reserve...	...reservar...	ray-sehr-**bar**
...a table for one / two.	...una mesa para uno / dos.	**oo**-nah **may**-sah **pah**-rah **oo**-noh / dohs
Non-smoking.	No fumador.	noh foo-mah-**dohr**
Is this table free?	¿Está esta mesa libre?	ay-**stah ay**-stah **may**-sah lee-bray
The menu (in English), please.	La carta (en inglés), por favor.	lah **kar**-tah (ayn een-**glays**) por fah-**bor**
service (not) included	servicio (no) incluido	sehr-**bee**-thee-oh (noh) een-kloo-**ee**-doh
cover charge	precio de entrada	**pray**-thee-oh day ayn-**trah**-dah
to go	para llevar	**pah**-rah yay-**bar**
with / without	con / sin	kohn / seen
and / or	y / o	ee / oh
menu (of the day)	menú (del día)	may-**noo** (dayl **dee**-ah)
specialty of the house	especialidad de la casa	ay-spay-thee-ah-lee-**dahd** day lah **kah**-sah
tourist menu	menú turístico	meh-**noo** too-**ree**-stee-koh
combination plate	plato combinado	**plah**-toh kohm-bee-**nah**-doh
appetizers	tapas	**tah**-pahs
bread	pan	pahn
cheese	queso	**kay**-soh
sandwich	bocadillo	boh-kah-**dee**-yoh
soup	sopa	**soh**-pah
salad	ensalada	ayn-sah-**lah**-dah
meat	carne	**kar**-nay
poultry	aves	**ah**-bays
fish	pescado	pay-**skah**-doh
seafood	marisco	mah-**ree**-skoh
fruit	fruta	**froo**-tah
vegetables	verduras	behr-**doo**-rahs
dessert	postres	**poh**-strays
tap water	agua del grifo	**ah**-gwah dayl **gree**-foh
mineral water	agua mineral	**ah**-gwah mee-nay-**rahl**
milk	leche	**lay**-chay
(orange) juice	zumo (de naranja)	**thoo**-moh (day nah-**rahn**-hah)
coffee	café	kah-**feh**
tea	té	tay
wine	vino	**bee**-noh
red / white	tinto / blanco	**teen**-toh / **blahn**-koh
glass / bottle	vaso / botella	**bah**-soh / boh-**tay**-yah
beer	cerveza	thehr-**bay**-thah
Cheers!	¡Salud!	sah-**lood**
More. / Another.	Más. / Otro.	mahs / **oh**-troh
The same.	El mismo.	ehl **mees**-moh
The bill, please.	La cuenta, por favor.	lah **kwayn**-tah por fah-**bor**
tip	propina	proh-**pee**-nah
Delicious!	¡Delicioso!	day-lee-thee-**oh**-soh

Italian Survival Phrases

English	Italian	Pronunciation
Good day.	*Buon giorno.*	bwohn **jor**-noh
Do you speak English?	*Parla inglese?*	**par**-lah een-**gleh**-zay
Yes. / No.	*Si. / No.*	see / noh
I (don't) understand.	*(Non) capisco.*	(nohn) kah-**pees**-koh
Please.	*Per favore.*	pehr fah-**voh**-ray
Thank you.	*Grazie.*	**graht**-see-ay
You're welcome.	*Prego.*	**preh**-go
I'm sorry.	*Mi dispiace.*	mee dee-spee-**ah**-chay
Excuse me.	*Mi scusi.*	mee **skoo**-zee
(No) problem.	*(Non) c'è un problema.*	(nohn) cheh oon proh-**bleh**-mah
Good.	*Va bene.*	vah **beh**-nay
Goodbye.	*Arrivederci.*	ah-ree-veh-**dehr**-chee
one / two	*uno / due*	**oo**-noh / **doo**-ay
three / four	*tre / quattro*	tray / **kwah**-troh
five / six	*cinque / sei*	**cheeng**-kway / **seh**-ee
seven / eight	*sette / otto*	**seh**-tay / **oh**-toh
nine / ten	*nove / dieci*	**noh**-vay / dee-**ay**-chee
How much is it?	*Quanto costa?*	**kwahn**-toh **koh**-stah
Write it?	*Me lo scrive?*	may loh **skree**-vay
Is it free?	*È gratis?*	eh **grah**-tees
Is it included?	*È incluso?*	eh een-**kloo**-zoh
Where can I buy / find...?	*Dove posso comprare / trovare...?*	**doh**-vay **poh**-soh kohm-**prah**-ray / troh-**vah**-ray
I'd like / We'd like...	*Vorrei / Vorremmo...*	voh-**reh**-ee / voh-**reh**-moh
...a room.	*...una camera.*	**oo**-nah **kah**-meh-rah
...a ticket to _____.	*...un biglietto per _____.*	oon beel-**yeh**-toh pehr _____
Is it possible?	*È possibile?*	eh poh-**see**-bee-lay
Where is...?	*Dov'è...?*	doh-**veh**
...the train station	*...la stazione*	lah staht-see-**oh**-nay
...the bus station	*...la stazione degli autobus*	lah staht-see-**oh**-nay **dehl**-yee ow-toh-boos
...tourist information	*...informazioni per turisti*	een-for-maht-see-**oh**-nee pehr too-**ree**-stee
...the toilet	*...la toilette*	lah twah-**leh**-tay
men	*uomini / signori*	**woh**-mee-nee / seen-**yoh**-ree
women	*donne / signore*	**doh**-nay / seen-**yoh**-ray
left / right	*sinistra / destra*	see-**nee**-strah / **deh**-strah
straight	*sempre dritto*	**sehm**-pray **dree**-toh
What time does this open / close?	*A che ora apre / chiude?*	ah kay **oh**-rah ah-**pray** / kee-**oo**-day
At what time?	*A che ora?*	ah kay **oh**-rah
Just a moment.	*Un momento.*	oon moh-**mehn**-toh
now / soon / later	*adesso / presto / tardi*	ah-**deh**-soh / **preh**-stoh / **tar**-dee
today / tomorrow	*oggi / domani*	**oh**-jee / doh-**mah**-nee

In an Italian Restaurant

English	Italian	Pronunciation
I'd like...	Vorrei...	voh-**reh**-ee
We'd like...	Vorremmo...	vor-**reh**-moh
...to reserve...	...prenotare...	preh-noh-**tah**-ray
...a table for one / two.	...un tavolo per uno / due.	oon **tah**-voh-loh pehr **oo**-noh / **doo**-ay
Is this seat free?	È libero questo posto?	eh **lee**-beh-roh **kweh**-stoh **poh**-stoh
The menu (in English), please.	Il menù (in inglese), per favore.	eel meh-**noo** (een een-**gleh**-zay) pehr fah-**voh**-ray
service (not) included	servizio (non) incluso	sehr-**veet**-see-oh (nohn) een-**kloo**-zoh
cover charge	pane e coperto	**pah**-nay ay koh-**pehr**-toh
to go	da portar via	dah **por**-tar **vee**-ah
with / without	con / senza	kohn / **sehnt**-sah
and / or	e / o	ay / oh
menu (of the day)	menù (del giorno)	meh-**noo** (dehl **jor**-noh)
specialty of the house	specialità della casa	speh-chah-lee-**tah deh**-lah **kah**-zah
first course (pasta, soup)	primo piatto	**pree**-moh pee-**ah**-toh
main course (meat, fish)	secondo piatto	seh-**kohn**-doh pee-**ah**-toh
side dishes	contorni	kohn-**tor**-nee
bread	pane	**pah**-nay
cheese	formaggio	for-**mah**-joh
sandwich	panino	pah-**nee**-noh
soup	zuppa	**tsoo**-pah
salad	insalata	een-sah-**lah**-tah
meat	carne	**kar**-nay
chicken	pollo	**poh**-loh
fish	pesce	**peh**-shay
seafood	frutti di mare	**froo**-tee dee **mah**-ray
fruit / vegetables	frutta / legumi	**froo**-tah / lay-**goo**-mee
dessert	dolce	**dohl**-chay
tap water	acqua del rubinetto	**ah**-kwah dehl roo-bee-**neh**-toh
mineral water	acqua minerale	**ah**-kwah mee-neh-**rah**-lay
milk	latte	**lah**-tay
(orange) juice	succo (d'arancia)	**soo**-koh (dah-**rahn**-chah)
coffee / tea	caffè / tè	kah-**feh** / teh
wine	vino	**vee**-noh
red / white	rosso / bianco	**roh**-soh / bee-**ahn**-koh
glass / bottle	bicchiere / bottiglia	bee-kee-**eh**-ray / boh-**teel**-yah
beer	birra	**bee**-rah
Cheers!	Cin cin!	cheen cheen
More. / Another.	Di più. / Un altro.	dee pew / oon **ahl**-troh
The same.	Lo stesso.	loh **steh**-soh
The bill, please.	Il conto, per favore.	eel **kohn**-toh pehr fah-**voh**-ray
Do you accept credit cards?	Accettate carte di credito?	ah-cheh-**tah**-tay **kar**-tay dee **kreh**-dee-toh
tip	mancia	**mahn**-chah
Delicious!	Delizioso!	day-leet-see-**oh**-zoh

For more user-friendly Italian phrases, check out *Rick Steves' Italian Phrase Book & Dictionary* or *Rick Steves' French, Italian, and German Phrase Book*.

German Survival Phrases

When using the phonetics, pronounce ī like the long i in "light." Bolded syllables are stressed.

English	German	Pronunciation
Good day.	Guten Tag.	**goo**-tehn tahg
Do you speak English?	Sprechen Sie Englisch?	**shprehkh**-ehn zee **ehgn**-lish
Yes. / No.	Ja. / Nein.	yah / nīn
I (don't) understand.	Ich verstehe (nicht).	ikh fehr-**shtay**-heh (nikht)
Please.	Bitte.	**bit**-teh
Thank you.	Danke.	**dahng**-keh
I'm sorry.	Es tut mir leid.	ehs toot meer līt
Excuse me.	Entschuldigung.	ehnt-**shool**-dig-oong
(No) problem.	(Kein) Problem.	(kīn) proh-**blaym**
(Very) good.	(Sehr) gut.	(zehr) goot
Goodbye.	Auf Wiedersehen.	owf **vee**-der-zayn
one / two	eins / zwei	īns / tsvī
three / four	drei / vier	drī / feer
five / six	fünf / sechs	fewnf / zehkhs
seven / eight	sieben / acht	**zee**-behn / ahkht
nine / ten	neun / zehn	noyn / tsayn
How much is it?	Wieviel kostet das?	**vee**-feel **kohs**-teht dahs
Write it?	Schreiben?	**shrī**-behn
Is it free?	Ist es umsonst?	ist ehs oom-**zohnst**
Included?	Inklusive?	in-kloo-**zee**-veh
Where can I buy / find...?	Wo kann ich kaufen / finden...?	voh kahn ikh **kow**-fehn / **fin**-dehn
I'd like / We'd like...	Ich hätte gern / Wir hätten gern...	ikh **heh**-teh gehrn / veer **heh**-tehn gehrn
...a room.	...ein Zimmer.	īn **tsim**-mer
...a ticket to ____.	...eine Fahrkarte nach ____	**ī**-neh **far**-kar-teh nahkh
Is it possible?	Ist es möglich?	ist ehs **mur**-glikh
Where is...?	Wo ist...?	voh ist
...the train station	...der Bahnhof	dehr **bahn**-hohf
...the bus station	...der Busbahnhof	dehr **boos**-bahn-hohf
...the tourist information office	...das Touristen-informations-büro	dahs too-**ris**-tehn-in-for-maht-see-**ohns**-**bew**-roh
...the toilet	...die Toilette	dee toh-**leh**-teh
men	Herren	**hehr**-rehn
women	Damen	**dah**-mehn
left / right	links / rechts	links / rehkhts
straight	geradeaus	geh-**rah**-deh-**ows**
What time does this open / close?	Um wieviel Uhr wird hier geöffnet / geschlossen?	oom **vee**-feel oor veerd heer geh-**urf**-neht / geh-**shloh**-sehn
At what time?	Um wieviel Uhr?	oom **vee**-feel oor
Just a moment.	Moment.	moh-**mehnt**
now / soon / later	jetzt / bald / später	yehtst / bahld / **shpay**-ter
today / tomorrow	heute / morgen	**hoy**-teh / **mor**-gehn

In a German Restaurant

English	German	Pronunciation
I'd like / We'd like...	Ich hätte gern / Wir hätten gern...	ikh **heh**-teh gehrn / veer **heh**-tehn gehrn
...a reservation for...	...eine Reservierung für...	**ī**-neh reh-zer-**feer**-oong fewr
...a table for one / two.	...einen Tisch für eine Person / zwei Personen.	**ī**-nehn tish fewr **ī**-neh pehr-zohn / tsvī pehr-**zoh**-nehn
Nonsmoking.	Nichtraucher.	**nikht**-rowkh-er
Is this seat free?	Ist hier frei?	ist heer frī
Menu (in English), please.	Speisekarte (auf Englisch), bitte.	**shpī**-zeh-kar-teh (owf **ehng**-lish) **bit**-teh
service (not) included	Trinkgeld (nicht) inklusive	**trink**-gehlt (nikht) in-kloo-**zee**-veh
cover charge	Eintritt	**īn**-trit
to go	zum Mitnehmen	tsoom **mit**-nay-mehn
with / without	mit / ohne	mit / **oh**-neh
and / or	und / oder	oont / **oh**-der
menu (of the day)	(Tages-) Karte	(**tah**-gehs-) **kar**-teh
set meal for tourists	Touristenmenü	too-**ris**-tehn-meh-**new**
specialty of the house	Spezialität des Hauses	shpayt-see-ah-lee-**tayt** dehs **how**-zehs
appetizers	Vorspeise	**for**-shpī-zeh
bread / cheese	Brot / Käse	broht / **kay**-zeh
sandwich	Sandwich	**zahnd**-vich
soup	Suppe	**zup**-peh
salad	Salat	zah-**laht**
meat	Fleisch	flīsh
poultry	Geflügel	geh-**flew**-gehl
fish	Fisch	fish
seafood	Meeresfrüchte	**meh**-rehs-**frewkh**-teh
fruit	Obst	ohpst
vegetables	Gemüse	geh-**mew**-zeh
dessert	Nachspeise	**nahkh**-shpī-zeh
mineral water	Mineralwasser	min-eh-**rahl**-vah-ser
tap water	Leitungswasser	**lī**-toongs-vah-ser
milk	Milch	milkh
(orange) juice	(Orangen-) Saft	(oh-**rahn**-zhehn-) zahft
coffee / tea	Kaffee / Tee	kah-**fay** / tay
wine	Wein	vīn
red / white	rot / weiß	roht / vīs
glass / bottle	Glas / Flasche	glahs / **flah**-sheh
beer	Bier	beer
Cheers!	Prost!	prohst
More. / Another.	Mehr. / Noch eins.	mehr / nohkh īns
The same.	Das gleiche.	dahs **glīkh**-eh
Bill, please.	Rechnung, bitte.	**rehkh**-noong **bit**-teh
tip	Trinkgeld	**trink**-gehlt
Delicious!	Lecker!	**lehk**-er

For more user-friendly German phrases, check out *Rick Steves' German Phrase Book and Dictionary* or *Rick Steves' French, Italian & German Phrase Book.*

Dutch Survival Phrases

Most people speak English, but if you learn the pleasantries and key phrases, you'll connect better with the locals. To pronounce the guttural Dutch "g" (indicated in phonetics by h), make a clear-your-throat sound, similar to the "ch" in the Scottish word "loch."

English	Dutch	Pronunciation
Hello.	Hallo.	**hah**-loh
Good day.	Dag.	dah
Good morning.	Goedemorgen.	**hoo**-deh-mor-hehn
Good afternoon.	Goedemiddag.	**hoo**-deh-mid-dah
Good evening.	Goedenavond.	**hoo**-dehn-ah-fohnd
Do you speak English?	Spreekt u Engels?	shpraykt oo **eng**-ehls
Yes. / No.	Ja. / Nee.	yah / nay
I (don't) understand.	Ik begrijp (het niet).	ik beh-**hripe** (heht neet)
Please. (can also mean "You're welcome")	Alstublieft.	**ahl**-stoo-bleeft
Thank you.	Dank u wel.	dahnk oo vehl
I'm sorry.	Het spijt me.	heht spite meh
Excuse me.	Pardon.	**par**-dohn
(No) problem.	(Geen) probleem.	(hayn) **proh**-blaym
Good.	Goede.	**hoo**-deh
Goodbye.	Tot ziens.	toht zeens
one / two	een / twee	ayn / t'vay
three / four	drie / vier	dree / feer
five / six	vijf / zes	fife / zehs
seven / eight	zeven / acht	**zay**-fehn / aht
nine / ten	negen / tien	**nay**-hehn / teen
What does it cost?	Wat kost het?	vaht kohst heht
Is it free?	Is het vrij?	is heht fry
Is it included?	Is het inclusief?	is heht in-**kloo**-seev
Can you please help me?	Kunt u alstublieft helpen?	koont oo **ahl**-stoo-bleeft **hehl**-pehn
Where can I buy / find...?	Waar kan ik kopen / vinden...?	var kahn ik **koh**-pehn / **fin**-dehn
I'd like / We'd like...	Ik wil graag / Wij willen graag...	ik vil hrah / vy **vil**-lehn hrah
...a room.	...een kamer.	ayn **kah**-mer
...a train / bus ticket to _____	...een trein / bus kaartje naar _____	ayn trayn / boos **kart**-yeh nar
...to rent a bike.	...een fiets huren.	ayn feets **hoo**-rehn
Where is...?	Waar is...?	var is
...the train / bus station	...het trein / bus station	heht trayn / boos **staht**-see-ohn
...the tourist info office	...de VVV	deh fay fay fay
...the toilet	...het toilet	heht **twah**-leht
men / women	mannen / vrouwen	**mah**-nehn / **frow**-ehn
left / right	links / rechts	links / rehts
straight ahead	rechtdoor	**reht**-dor
What time does it open / close?	Hoe laat gaat het open / dicht?	hoo laht haht heht **oh**-pehn / diht
now / soon / later	nu / straks / later	noo / strahks / **lah**-ter
today / tomorrow	vandaag / morgen	**fahn**-dah / **mor**-hehn

In a Dutch Restaurant

The all-purpose Dutch word *alstublieft* (ahl-stoo-bleeft) means "please," but it can also mean "here you are" (when the server hands you something), "thanks" (when taking payment from you), or "you're welcome" (when handing you change). Here are other words that might come in handy at restaurants:

English	Dutch	Pronunciation
I'd like / We'd like...	*Ik will graag / Wij willen graag...*	ik vil *hrah* / vy **vil**-lehn *hrah*
...a table for one / two.	*...een tafel voor een / twee.*	ayn **tah**-fehl for ayn / t'vay
...to reserve a table.	*...een tafel reserveren.*	ayn **tah**-fehl ray-zehr-feh-rehn
...the menu (in English).	*...het menu (in het Engels).*	heht meh-**noo** (in heht **eng**-ehls)
Is this table free?	*Is deze tafel vrij?*	is **day**-zeh **tah**-fehl fry
to go	*om mee te nemen*	ohm may teh **nay**-mehn
with / without	*met / zonder*	meht / **zohn**-der
and / or	*en / of*	ehn / of
special of the day	*dagschotel*	**dahs**-hoh-tehl
specialty of the house	*huisspecialiteit*	**hows**-shpeh-shah-lee-tite
breakfast	*ontbijt*	**ohnt**-bite
lunch	*middagmaal*	**mid**-dah-mahl
dinner	*avondmaal*	**ah**-fohnd-mahl
appetizers	*hapjes*	**hahp**-yehs
main courses	*hoofdgerechten*	**hohfd**-heh-reh-tehn
side dishes	*bijgerechten*	**bye**-heh-reh-tehn
bread / cheese	*brood / kaas*	brohd / kahs
sandwich	*sandwich*	**sand**-vich
soup / salad	*soep / sla*	soop / slah
meat / chicken / fish	*vlees / kip / vis*	flays / kip / fis
fruit / vegetables	*vrucht / groenten*	fruht / **hroon**-tehn
dessert / pastries	*gebak*	heh-**bahk**
I am vegetarian.	*Ik ben vegetarisch.*	ik behn vay-heh-**tah**-rish
mineral water / tap water	*mineraalwater / kraanwater*	min-eh-rahl-**vah**-ter / **krahn**-vah-ter
milk / (orange) juice	*melk / (sinaasappel) sap*	mehlk / **see**-nahs-ah-pehl (sahp)
coffee / tea	*koffie / thee*	**koh**-fee / tay
wine / beer	*wijn / bier*	vine / beer
red / white	*rode / witte*	**roh**-deh / **vit**-teh
glass / bottle	*glas / fles*	hlahs / flehs
Cheers!	*Proost!*	prohst
More. / Another.	*Meer. / Nog een.*	mayr / noh ayn
The same.	*Het zelfde.*	heht **zehlf**-deh
The bill, please.	*De rekening, alstublieft.*	deh **ray**-keh-neeng **ahl**-stoo-bleeft
Do you accept credit cards?	*Accepteert u kredietkaarten?*	**ahk**-shehp-tayrt oo kray-deet-**kar**-tehn
Is service included?	*Is bediening inbegrepen?*	is beh-**dee**-neeng in-beh-**hray**-pehn
tip	*fooi*	foy
Tasty.	*Lekker.*	**leh**-ker
Enjoy!	*Smakelijk!*	**smah**-keh-like

INDEX

INDEX

MAP INDEX

Start your trip at

Our website enhances this book and turns

Explore Europe

At ricksteves.com you can browse through thousands of articles, videos, photos and radio interviews, plus find a wealth of money-saving travel tips for planning your dream trip. And with our mobile-friendly website, you can easily access all this great travel information anywhere you go.

TV Shows

Preview the places you'll visit by watching entire half-hour episodes of Rick Steves' Europe (choose from all 100 shows) on-demand, for free.

r-icksteves.com

your travel dreams into affordable reality

Radio Interviews

Enjoy ready access to Rick's vast library of radio interviews covering travel tips and cultural insights that relate specifically to your Europe travel plans.

Travel Forums

Learn, ask, share! Our online community of savvy travelers is a great resource for first-time travelers to Europe, as well as seasoned pros. You'll find forums on each country, plus travel tips and restaurant/hotel reviews. You can even ask one of our well-traveled staff to chime in with an opinion.

Travel News

Subscribe to our free Travel News e-newsletter, and get monthly updates from Rick on what's happening in Europe.

Audio Europe™

Rick's Free Travel App

Get your FREE Rick Steves Audio Europe™ app to enjoy...

- Dozens of self-guided tours of Europe's top museums, sights and historic walks
- Hundreds of tracks filled with cultural insights and sightseeing tips from Rick's radio interviews
- All organized into handy geographic playlists
- For Apple and Android

With Rick whispering in your ear, Europe gets even better.

Find out more at ricksteves.com

Pack Light and Right

Gear up for your next adventure at ricksteves.com

Light Luggage

Pack light and right with Rick Steves' affordable, custom-designed rolling carry-on bags, backpacks, day packs and shoulder bags.

Accessories

From packing cubes to moneybelts and beyond, Rick has personally selected the travel goodies that will help your trip go smoother.

Shop at ricksteves.com

Save time and energy

This guidebook is your independent-travel toolkit. But for all it delivers, it's still up to you to devote the time and energy it takes to manage the preparation and logistics that are essential for a happy trip. If that's a hassle, there's a solution.

Rick Steves Tours

A Rick Steves tour takes you to Europe's most

great tours, too!

with minimum stress

interesting places with great guides and small groups of 28 or less. We follow Rick's favorite itineraries, ride in comfy buses, stay in family-run hotels, and bring you intimately close to the Europe you've traveled so far to see. Most importantly, we take away the logistical headaches so you can focus on the fun.

Join the fun

This year we'll take 25,000 free-spirited travelers— nearly half of them repeat customers—along with us on four dozen different itineraries, from Ireland to Italy to Istanbul. Is a Rick Steves tour the right fit for your travel dreams? Find out at ricksteves.com, where you can also get Rick's latest tour catalog and free Tour Experience DVD.

Europe is best experienced with happy travel partners. We hope you can join us.

See our itineraries at ricksteves.com

Rick Steves

BEST OF GUIDES

Best of France
Best of Germany
Best of Ireland
Best of Italy
Best of Spain

EUROPE GUIDES

Best of Europe
Eastern Europe
Europe Through the Back Door
Mediterranean Cruise Ports
Northern European Cruise Ports

COUNTRY GUIDES

Croatia & Slovenia
England
France
Germany
Great Britain
Ireland
Italy
Portugal
Scandinavia
Scotland
Spain
Switzerland

CITY & REGIONAL GUIDES

Amsterdam & the Netherlands
Belgium: Bruges, Brussels, Antwerp & Ghent
Barcelona
Budapest
Florence & Tuscany
Greece: Athens & the Peloponnese
Istanbul
London
Paris
Prague & the Czech Republic
Provence & the French Riviera
Rome
Venice
Vienna, Salzburg & Tirol

SNAPSHOT GUIDES

Basque Country: Spain & France
Berlin
Copenhagen & the Best of Denmark
Dublin
Dubrovnik
Edinburgh
Hill Towns of Central Italy
Italy's Cinque Terre
Krakow, Warsaw & Gdansk
Lisbon

Maximize your travel skills with a good guidebook.

Loire Valley
Madrid & Toledo
Milan & the Italian Lakes District
Naples & the Amalfi Coast
Northern Ireland
Norway
Sevilla, Granada & Southern Spain
St. Petersburg, Helsinki & Tallinn
Stockholm

POCKET GUIDES

Amsterdam
Athens
Barcelona
Florence
London
Munich & Salzburg
Paris
Prague
Rome
Venice
Vienna

TRAVEL CULTURE

Europe 101
European Christmas
European Easter
Postcards from Europe
Travel as a Political Act

RICK STEVES' EUROPE DVDs

12 New Shows 2015–2016
Austria & the Alps

The Complete Collection 2000-2016
Eastern Europe
England & Wales
European Christmas
European Travel Skills & Specials
France
Germany, BeNeLux & More
Greece, Turkey & Portugal
The Holy Land: Israelis & Palestinians Today
Iran
Ireland & Scotland
Italy's Cities
Italy's Countryside
Scandinavia
Spain
Travel Extras

PHRASE BOOKS & DICTIONARIES

French
French, Italian & German
German
Italian
Portuguese
Spanish

PLANNING MAPS

Britain, Ireland & London
Europe
France & Paris
Germany, Austria & Switzerland
Ireland
Italy
Spain & Portugal

RickSteves.com @RickSteves

Rick Steves books are available at bookstores
and through online booksellers.

PHOTO CREDITS

Avalon Travel
An imprint of Perseus Books
A Hachette Book Group company
1700 Fourth Street
Berkeley, CA 94710

Printed in China by RR Donnelley, Shenzhen

First printing January 2017

ISBN 978-1-63121-177-5
ISSN 1096-7702

For the latest on Rick's talks, guidebooks, Europe tours, public radio show, free audio tours, and
public television series, contact Rick Steves' Europe, 130 Fourth Avenue North, Edmonds, WA
98020, 425/771-8303, www.ricksteves.com, rick@ricksteves.com.

RICK STEVES' EUROPE
Special Publications Manager: Risa Laib
Managing Editor: Jennifer Madison Davis
Project Editor: Suzanne Kotz
Editorial & Production Assistant: Jessica Shaw
Graphic Content Director: Sandra Hundacker
Maps & Graphics: David C. Hoerlein, Mary Rostad

AVALON TRAVEL
Editorial Director: Kevin McLain
Senior Editor and Series Manager: Madhu Prasher
Editor: Jamie Andrade
Associate Editor: Sierra Machado
Copy Editor: Naomi Adler Dancis
Proofreader: Kelly Lydick
Indexer: Stephen Callahan
Interior Design & Layout: McGuire Barber Design
Cover Design: Kimberly Glyder Design
Maps & Graphics: Kat Bennett

COVER PHOTOS
Front Cover Photos: Top, left: phone booth and Big Ben, London, England © Piksel | Dreams-
time.com; middle: Berner Oberland in Switzerland © Naturepixel | Dreamstime.com; right: The
Eiffel Tower in Paris, France © satina/123rf.com. Bottom: Vernazza, Cinque Terre, Italy © Martin
Molcan | Dreamstime.com
Back Cover Photos: Left: the Burg Eltz castle on Germany's Mosel River © Rick Steves
Middle: canal in Amsterdam, Netherlands © Dennis Van De Water | Dreamstime.com
Right: (take from the top middle Sagrada Familia image on the front cover of Best of Spain)

Want More Europe?

Maximize the experience with Rick Steves as your guide

Guidebooks
Dozens of European city and country guidebooks

Phrase Books
French, Italian, German, Spanish and more

Rick's TV Shows
100 episodes from public television's *Rick Steves' Europe*

Free! Rick's Audio Europe™ App
Get free audio tours for the big sights in Paris, Venice, Florence, Rome, and more

Small Group Tours
More than 40 itineraries from Oslo to Istanbul

For all the details, visit ricksteves.com